Lecture Notes in Computer Science 5366

Commenced Publication in 1973
Founding and Former Series Editors:
Gerhard Goos, Juris Hartmanis, and Jan van Leeuwen

Maria Garcia de la Banda   Enrico Pontelli (Eds.)

Logic Programming

24th International Conference, ICLP 2008
Udine, Italy, December 9-13 2008
Proceedings

 Springer

Volume Editors

Maria Garcia de la Banda
Monash University
Clayton School of Information Technology
Clayton, VIC 3800, Australia
E-mail: Maria.GarciadelaBanda@infotech.monash.edu.au

Enrico Pontelli
New Mexico State University
Department of Computer Science
Las Cruces, NM 88003, USA
E-mail: epontell@cs.nmsu.edu

Library of Congress Control Number: 2008940424

CR Subject Classification (1998): D.1.6, I.2.3, D.3, F.3, F.4

LNCS Sublibrary: SL 2 – Programming and Software Engineering

ISSN	0302-9743
ISBN-10	3-540-89981-2 Springer Berlin Heidelberg New York
ISBN-13	978-3-540-89981-5 Springer Berlin Heidelberg New York

springer.com

© Springer-Verlag Berlin Heidelberg 2008
Printed in Germany

Typesetting: Camera-ready by author, data conversion by Scientific Publishing Services, Chennai, India
Printed on acid-free paper   SPIN: 12581351   06/3180   5 4 3 2 1 0

Preface

This volume contains the proceedings of the 24th International Conference on Logic Programming (ICLP 2008). The conference took place in Udine, Italy during December 9–13, 2008. The conference focuses on the foundations, developments, and applications in the area of logic programming. The ICLP series of conferences is aimed at providing a technical forum for presenting and disseminating innovative research results in the field of logic programming. The conference features technical presentations, tutorials, invited speakers, and a number of co-located events, including:

- The First Workshop on Answer Set Programming and Other Computing Paradigms (ASPOCP 2008)
- The Annual Meeting of the ISO/IEC JTC1/SC22/WG17 working group on the standardization of Prolog
- The Third International Workshop on Applications of Logic Programming to (Semantic) Web and Web Services (ALPSWS'08)
- The 18th Workshop on Logic-based Methods in Programming Environments (WLPE 2008)
- The 8th Colloquium on Implementation of Constraint Logic Programming Systems (CICLOPS 2008)
- The 15th RCRA Workshop on Experimental Evaluation of Algorithms for Solving Problems with Combinatorial Explosion

ICLP 2008 also featured two special events. The first was the 4th ICLP Doctoral Student Consortium, an event specifically organized to encourage participation and interaction between doctoral students working in the area of logic programming. The second event was a special session celebrating 20 years of Stable Model Semantics. The session featured two guests of honor – Michael Gelfond and Vladimir Lifschitz, original creators of the Stable Model Semantics – two invited speakers (David Pearce and Nicola Leone) and six position presentations (by Chitta Baral, Marc Denecker, Thomas Eiter, Victor W. Marek, Ilkka Niemelä, and Torsten Schaub).

The ICLP program included four tutorials—Carla Piazza and Alberto Policriti (Systems Biology), Tom Schrijvers (Constraint Handling Rules), Peter O'Hearn (Separation Logic), and Angelo Montanari (Temporal Logics). The program also included two invited presentations, by Vítor Santos Costa (Life of a Logic Programming System) and by Pedro Domingos. An additional highlight of the program was a session aimed at uniting and inspiring the Prolog community, organized by Tom Schrijvers and Bart Demoen.

The technical program was composed of 37 full papers and 26 short papers. The acceptance rate was 3.16 for full papers (117 submissions) and 2.31 for short papers (60 submissions). The submissions originated from 31 countries

(Australia, Austria, Belgium, Brazil, Canada, Chile, China, Denmark, Estonia, Finland, France, Germany, Greece, Hungary, Indonesia, Ireland, Israel, Italy, Japan, South Korea, The Netherlands, Poland, Portugal, Singapore, Spain, Sweden, Switzerland, UK, Ukraine, USA, and Vietnam).

As in previous years, the Program Committee selected the best paper and the best student paper. The Best Paper Award went to Michael Fink for his paper "Equivalences in Answer-Set Programming by Countermodels in the Logic of Here-and-There," while the Best Student Paper Award went to Shay B. Cohen, Robert J. Simmons, and Noah A. Smith for their paper "Dynamic Programming Algorithms as Products of Weighted Logic Programs."

ICLP 2008 was organized by the Association for Logic Programming (ALP), in collaboration with the Organizing Committees of the co-located events, the Dipartimento di Matematica e Informatica of the Università degli Studi di Udine, the Department of Computer Science at New Mexico State University, and the Clayton School of IT at Monash University. The event received generous sponsorships from the Association for Logic Programming, New Mexico State University, the National Science Foundation, National ICT Australia, the Università degli Studi di Udine, the Gruppo Nazionale per il Calcolo Scientifico, the Swedish Institute of Computer Science, Agemont, MIUR Project FIRB RBNE03B8KK, Kodak, and the municipality of Udine. The organization would also like to acknowledge the support of the Gruppo Ricercatori e Utenti di Logic Programming (GULP).

Many people contributed to the success of the conference, to whom we would like to extend our sincere gratitude. The General Chair, Agostino Dovier, established an outstanding Organizing Committee and worked hard to ensure a successful event, providing leadership in all aspects of the organization process. The members of the Program Committee provided invaluable help in the process of selecting papers and developing the conference program. The numerous referees invested countless hours in reading submissions and providing professional reviews. Andrea Formisano and Mirosław Truszczyński organized a fantastic special session to celebrate the 20 Years of Stable Model Semantics. Son Cao Tran (the Workshop Chair) and Tom Schrijvers and David S. Warren (Doctoral Consortium Chairs), and Bart Demoen (Prolog Programming Contest Chair) contributed to the addition of exciting and well-organized events to the program. The organization benefited from the hard work of Marcello Balduccini and Alessandro Dal Palú (Publicity Chairs), Raffaele Cipriano (Web Master), and the local organizing team: Alberto Casagrande, Elisabetta De Maria, Luca Di Gaspero, and Carla Piazza.

Last but not least, we wish to extend our heartfelt thanks to all the authors who submitted their excellent research contributions to the conference.

December 2008   Maria Garcia de la Banda
                                                                           Enrico Pontelli

Organization

ICLP 2008 was organized by the Association for Logic Programming, in collaboration with the Dipartimento di Matematica e Informatica (Università degli Studi di Udine), the Department of Computer Science (New Mexico State University), and the Clayton School of IT (Monash University).

Organizing Committee

General Chair	Agostino Dovier (Università di Udine)
Program Co-chairs	Maria Garcia de la Banda (Monash University)
	Enrico Pontelli (New Mexico State University)
Workshop Chair	Tran Cao Son (New Mexico State University)
Doctoral Consortium	Tom Schrijvers (K.U.Leuven)
	David S. Warren (SUNY Stony Brook)
20 Years of Stable Models	Andrea Formisano (Università di Perugia)
	Mirosław Truszczyński (University of Kentucky)
Programming Competition	Bart Demoen (K.U.Leuven)
Publicity	Marcello Balduccini (Kodak Research Labs)
	Alessandro Dal Palù (Università di Parma)
Web Master	Raffaele Cipriano (Università di Udine)
Local Organization	Alberto Casagrande (Università di Udine)
	Elisabetta De Maria (Università di Udine)
	Luca Di Gaspero (Università di Udine)
	Carla Piazza (Università di Udine)

Program Committee

Salvador Abreu	Universidade de Évora, Portugal
Sergio Antoy	Portland State University, USA
Pedro Barahona	Universidade Nova de Lisboa, Portugal
Chitta Baral	Arizona State University, USA
Gerhard Brewka	University of Leipzig, Germany
Manuel Carro	Universidad Politecnica de Madrid, Spain
Michael Codish	Ben-Gurion University of the Negev, Israel
Alessandro Dal Palù	Università di Parma, Italy
Bart Demoen	K.U.Leuven, Belgium
Agostino Dovier	Università di Udine, Italy
John Gallagher	Roskilde University, Denmark
Michael Gelfond	Texas Tech University, USA
Carmen Gervet	Boston University, USA
Gopal Gupta	University of Texas at Dallas, USA

Manuel V. Hermenegildo	Universidad Politecnica de Madrid, Spain
Andy King	University of Kent, UK
Michael Maher	National ICT, Australia
Juan José Moreno-Navarro	Universidad Politecnica de Madrid, Spain
Alberto Pettorossi	Università di Roma Tor Vergata, Italy
Brigitte Pientka	McGill University, Canada
Gianfranco Rossi	Università di Parma, Italy
Fariba Sadri	Imperial College, UK
Vítor Santos Costa	Universidade do Porto, Portugal
Tran Cao Son	New Mexico State University, USA
Paolo Torroni	Università di Bologna, Italy
Frank D. Valencia	École Polytechnique de Paris, France
Mark Wallace	Monash University, Australia

Referees

José Alferes	Marco Correia	Andrea Formisano
Edward M. Alférez Salinas	Stefania Costantini	Lars-Ake Fredlund
	Jim Cunningham	Hans Fugal
María Alpuente	Olivier Danvy	Emilio J. Gallego-Arias
Jesús Aranda	Fabien De Marchi	Alejandro Javier Garcia
Francisco Azevedo	Danny De Schreye	Marco Gavanelli
Matteo Baldoni	Marc Denecker	Martin Gebser
Marcello Balduccini	Enrico Denti	Samir Genaim
Mutsunori Banbara	Nachum Dershowitz	Laura Giordano
Ajay Bansal	Luca Di Gaspero	Matthew Giuca
Federico Bergenti	Alessandra Di Pierro	Hai-Feng Guo
Piero Bonatti	Daniel Diaz	Vineet Gupta
Lucas Bordeaux	Carmel Domshlak	Michael Hanus
Luca Bortolussi	Gregory J. Duck	James Harland
Martin Brain	Inês Dutra	Olivier Hermant
Bernd Brassel	Thomas Eiter	Ángel Herranz
Annamaria Bria	Michael Elhadad	Christopher Hogger
Krysia Broda	Islam Elkabani	Jacob Howe
William E. Byrd	Esra Erdem	Giovambattista Ianni
Pedro Cabalar	Wolfgang Faber	Dragan Ivanovic
Rui Camacho	Claudia Faggian	Matt Jadud
Amadeo Casas	Moreno Falaschi	Tomi Janhunen
Martine Ceberio	Claudio Fernandes	Gerda Janssens
Federico Chesani	Maribel Fernandez	Jesús Almendros
Pablo Chico de Guzmán	Paolo Ferraris	Srividya Kona
Sandeep Chintabathina	Michel Ferreira	George Katsirelos
Henning Christiansen	Fabio Fioravanti	Vladik Kreinovich
Raffaele Cipriano	Sebastian Fischer	Herbert Kuchen
Marco Comini	Nuno Fonseca	Michael Leuschel

Vladimir Lifschitz
James Lipton
Francesca
   Alessandra Lisi
Chongbing Liu
Francisco López-Fraguas
Lunjin Lu
Gergerly Lukacsy
Toni Mancini
Maarten Mariën
Julio Mariño
Guillem Marpons
Viviana Mascardi
Peter McBrien
Paola Mello
Yunsong Meng
Fred Mesnard
Laurent Michel
Richard Min
Angelo Montanari
Ricardo Morales
José Morales
Jorge Navas
Pascal Nicolas
Vitor Nogueira
Peter Novak
Carlos Olarte
Eugenio Omodeo
David Pearce
Vasco Pedro
Olivier Perriquet
Jean-Marc Petit
Tu Phan

Giulio Piancastelli
Carla Piazza
Inna Pivkina
Axel Polleres
António Porto
Maurizio Proietti
Gabriele Puppis
Iván Pérez
Frank Raiser
C.R. Ramakrishnan
Francesco Ricca
Fabrizio Riguzzi
Nikos Rizopoulos
Ricardo Rocha
Riccardo Rosati
Salvatore Ruggieri
Emad Saad
Kostis Sagonas
Diptikalyan Saha
Chiaki Sakama
Pedro Salgueiro
Vítor Santos Costa
Andrew Santosa
Francesco Scarcello
Peter Schachte
Torsten Schaub
Peter Schneider-Kamp
Tom Schrijvers
Hirohisa Seki
Valerio Senni
Christian Servin
Fernando Silva
Axel Simon

Jon Sneyers
Sebastian Spiegler
Fausto Spoto
Peter J. Stuckey
Martin Sulzmann
Terrance Swift
Péter Szeredi
Paul Tarau
Arianna Tocchio
Yana Todorova
Hans Tompits
Irena Trajkovska
Mirosław Truszczyński
Hudson Turner
Christian Urban
Peter Van Weert
Vasco T. Vasconcelos
Joost Vennekens
Andrew Verden
Dirk Vermeir
Toby Walsh
Kewen Wang
David S. Warren
Richard Watson
Gregory Wheeler
Jan Wielemaker
Herbert Wiklicky
Sebastian Will
Stefan Woltran
Yan Zhang
Yuanlin Zhang
Neng-Fa Zhou
Zsolt Zombori

Table of Contents

Invited Position Presentations

Best Paper Awardees

Regular Papers

Applications I

Algorithms, Systems, and Implementations I

Semantics and Foundations I

Analysis and Transformations

Semantics and Foundations II

Semantics and Foundations III

Applications II

CHRs and Extensions

Semantics and Foundations IV

Algorithms, Systems, and Implementations II

Short Papers

Semantics and Foundations

Implementations and Systems

Answer Set Programming and Extensions

Constraints, Optimizations, and Applications

Applications

Analysis, Transformations, and Implementations

Doctoral Consortium Presentations

The Life of a Logic Programming System

Vítor Santos Costa

DCC-FCUP & CRACS
University of Porto, Portugal
vsc@dcc.fc.up.pt

1 Introduction

Logic Programming and the Prolog language have a major role in Computing. Prolog, and its derived languages, have been widely used in a impressive variety of application domains. Thus, a bit of the history of Logic Programming reflects in the history of systems such as Dec-10 Prolog [32], M-Prolog [15], C-Prolog [19], Quintus Prolog [20], SICStus Prolog [6], BIM-Prolog [17], ECLiPSe [1], BinProlog [30], SWI-Prolog [34], CIAO [14], and B-Prolog [35], to mention but a few. I briefly present the evolution of one such system, YAP, and present a personal perspective on the challenges ahead for YAP (and for Logic Programming).

2 A Little Bit of History

The early eighties saw great advancements in Prolog and logic programming. One of the most exciting developments was David H. D. Warren's new abstract interpreter (eventually called the Warren Abstract Machine or WAM [33]) which become the foundation of Quintus Prolog [20]. Quintus motivated many Prolog systems, including YAP which was started by Luis Damas and colleagues in 1984 at the University of Porto. At the time, Luis Damas had just returned from the University of Edinburgh, where he had completed his PhD on type systems. He was also interested in logic programming and, while at Edinburgh, had designed one of the first Prolog interpreters, written in the IMP programming language for the EMAS operating system (which would become the basis for the famous C-Prolog interpreter [19]). Together with Miguel Filgueiras, who also had experience in Prolog implementation [12], he started work on a new Prolog interpreter with special backtracking that was soon abandoned as it proved too inefficient. Lus Damas then went on with the development of another one based on the WAM. The goal was to design a compact, very fast system emulator, written in assembly. To do so, Luis Damas wrote the a compiler in C and an emulator in 68000 assembly code. I joined this effort in 1985.

Arguably, one of the strengths of YAP derives from Luis Damas' experience in Edinburgh: the internal data-types were well defined from the start and always facilitated development. YAP adopted many of the contributions originally proposed for the WAM: it used a depth-first design to visit terms, and it was one the first Prologs to do indexing on sub-terms [24]. YAP also provided a very fast

M. Garcia de la Banda and E. Pontelli (Eds.): ICLP 2008, LNCS 5366, pp. 1–6, 2008.

development environment, due to its fast compiler. The combination of compilation and execution speed attracted a strong user community, mainly in Artificial Intelligence (Moniz Pereira's group supported the first YAP port, to the VAX architecture). A major user was the European Union Eurotra project [2] for which YAP developed *sparse functors*: one of the first attempts at using named fields of structures in Prolog. A version of YAP that supports sparse functors was still in use in Denmark just a few years ago.

The second chapter in YAP's history started on the mid nineties. Activity in YAP had slowed down. One problem was that the system had become very complex, mainly due to the need to support several different computer architectures in assembly (at the time: 68k, VAX, MIPS, SPARC, HP-RISC, Intel). Unfortunately, a first attempt at using a C interpreter resulted in a much slower system than with the assembly emulator. On the other hand, the user community was not only alive but growing, as Rui Camacho had taken YAP to the Turing Institute Machine Learning (ILP) Group, where it was eventually adopted by ILP systems such as P-Progol, later Aleph [29], and IndLog [5]. Second, researchers such as me and Fernando Silva, had returned to Porto and were interested in Parallel Logic Programming. While SICStus Prolog would have been an ideal platform, it was a closed source system (later, an early version of SICStus Prolog was used for Ciao Prolog [14]). YAP therefore became a vehicle of research first in parallelism [13] and later in tabling [22]. A new, fast C-based emulator was written toward this purpose [25] and brought YAP back to the rank of the fastest Prolog systems [11].

Interest in YAP grew during the late nineties, leading to the third chapter in YAP's story. Feedback from the user community had shown that fundamental issues with YAP's usability were not being properly addressed. As hardware scaled up and users had more data to process, it became clear that there was a scalability problem: Prolog programs perform well for small applications, but often just die or perform unbearably slowly as application size grows. Effort has therefore been done to rethink the basics, step by step. The first step was rewriting the garbage collection [7]. But the main developments so far have been in indexing: it had become clear to the author that the WAM's approach to indexing simply does not work for the kind of data one is expected to process today. Just-In-Time indexing [26] tries to address the problem with the least effort possible, the Prolog way!

3   Challenges

Prolog is a well-known language. It is widely used, and it is a remarkably powerful tool. The core of Prolog has been very stable throughout the years, both in terms of language design and in terms of implementation. Yet, there have been several developments, many within the Logic Programming community, and many more outside. Addressing these developments and the needs of a world very different from when Prolog was created, presents both difficulties and opportunities. Some (though not all) questions from a personal perspective are as follows:

1. Hardware evolved from a VAX 11/750 or an Apple-II with a 6502 at 1MHz with 48KB of memory to a 2-core CPU running at 2.5GHz with 4GB of memory. Thus, we can now fit in main memory databases that are 5 of 6 orders of magnitude larger than when Prolog was invented, and run them in our 4 orders of magnitude faster CPU. Can we afford to rely on the old WAM design even today?
2. Programming Languages have changed: we now have object-oriented languages, functional languages, scripting languages, domain-specific languages. What can Prolog learn from these languages?
3. Logic Programming has changed: there has been tremendous progress (personal favorites are the work on tabling and the impressive progress in negation). How best to feed that progress back to a system such as YAP?
4. The WWW: Prolog and logic programming have not been able to take a place in the foundations of the Web. Should they?
5. Knowledge Representation: Prolog inherits from First Order Logic. The last few years have made it clear that quite often one wants to integrate a logic representation with uncertain data. Is it doable? How best to do so?

Compiler Implementation Technology. Implementation Technology in Prolog needs to be rethought. On the low level, Just-In-Time technology is a natural match to Prolog and it has shown to work well, but we have just scratched the surface [28]. Progress in compilers, such as GCC, may make compilation affordable again. At a higher level, more program rewriting at compilation-time should be done. Determinacy detection is well known [9] and should be available. Simple techniques, such as query reordering, can change program performance hugely for database queries. They should be easily available.

A step further: code expansion for recursive procedures is less of a problem, so why not rethink old ideas such as Krall's VAM [16], and Beer's uninitialised variables [3,31]? Moreover, years of experience with CIAO should provide a good basis for rethinking global analysis [4].

Last, but not least, Prolog implementation is not just about pure Horn clauses. We need to rethink global structures and side-effects. In the author's opinion, this will be critical for the success of parallel Prolog. We also need to provide better tools to help users improving performance.

Language Technology. At this point in time, there is no dominant language nor framework. But, arguably, some lessons can be taken:

- *Libraries and Data-Structures*: languages need to provide useful, reusable code;
- *Interfacing*: it should be easy to communicate with other languages, and especially with domain languages, such as SQL for databases, and R for statistics.
- *Typing*: it is not clear whether static typing is needed, but it is clear that it is useful, and that it is popular in the research community.

A personal belief is that progress in this area requires collaboration between different Prolog systems, namely so that it will be easy to reuse libraries and code. YAP and SWI-Prolog are working together in this direction.

Logic Programming Technology. Experience has shown that it is hard to move results from Logic Programming research to Prolog systems. One illustrative example is XSB Prolog [23]: on the one hand, the XSB system has been a vehicle for progress in logic programming, supporting the tabling of definite and normal programs. On the other hand, progress in XSB has not been widely adopted. After more 10 years, even tabling of definite programs is not widely available in other Prolog systems.

The main reason for that is complexity: it is just very hard to implement some of the novel ideas proposed in logic programming. Old work suggests that logic programming itself may help in this direction [8]. Making it easy to change and control Prolog execution in a flexible way is a fundamental challenge for Prolog.

The WWW. It has become very important to be able to reason and manipulate data in the web. Surprisingly, one can see relatively little contribution from the Logic Programming Community. It is unclear why this is so, as Prolog should have a major role to play, at least in the semantic web. Query answering of decidable description logics such as subsets of OWL can be performed with tabled logic programs [18]. Initial results offer hope that YapTab is competitive with specialised systems.

Uncertainty. The last few years have seen much interest in what is often called Statistical Relational Learning (SRL). Several languages designed for this purpose build directly upon Prolog. PRISM [27] is one of the most popular examples: progress in PRISM has stimulated progress in the underlying Prolog system, B-Prolog. Problog [10] is an exciting recent development, and supporting Problog has already lead to progress in YAP.

If SRL languages that rely on Prolog are a challenge to Prolog, SRL languages that *do not* rely on Prolog are also a very interesting, if different, challenge. Markov Logic Networks (MLNs) [21] are a good example: they use bottom-inference and incremental query evaluation. The future will tell how much Prolog and Logic Programming can contribute to and benefit from from these systems.

4   Conclusions

I presented a personal perspective on the history, and challenges of Logic Programming, based on personal experience both as an implementor, and as an user. There are a number of challenges to Prolog. In fact, one would like to make "Prolog" faster, more attractive to the CS Community and, above all, more useful. To do so, much work has to be done, and change has to occur. I believe this is clearly seen by the community.

I would like to thank all the YAP collaborators and users that make this project possible and worthwhile. They are to many to mention here, but I would like to remember in this talk Ricardo Lopes, whose contribution was so unfortunately cut short. We will always remember you!

References

1. Aggoun, A., Chan, D., Dufresne, P., Falvey, E., Grant, H., Herold, A., Macartney, G., Meier, M., Miller, D., Mudambi, S., Perez, B., van Rossum, E., Schimpf, J., Tsahageas, P.A., de Villeneuve, D.H.: ECLiPSe 3.5 User Manual. ECRC (December 1995)

2. Arnold, D.J., Krauwer, S., Rosner, M., des Tombe, L., Varile, G.B.: The $< c, a >, t$ framework in eurotra: a theoretically committed notation for mt. In: Proceedings of the 11th conference on Computational linguistics, Morristown, NJ, USA, pp. 297–303. Association for Computational Linguistics (1986)

3. Beer, J.: Concepts, Design, and Performance Analysis of a Parallel Prolog Machine. LNCS, vol. 404. Springer, Heidelberg (1989)

4. Bueno, F., Banda, M.G.d.l., Hermenegildo, M.V.: Effectiveness of Abstract Interpretation in Automatic Parallelization: A Case Study in Logic Programming. In: ACM TOPLAS (1998)

5. Camacho, R.: Learning stage transition rules with Indlog. In: Proceedings of the 4th International Workshop on Inductive Logic Programming GMD-Studien, Gesellschaft für Mathematik und Datenverarbeitung MBH, vol. 237, pp. 273–290 (1994)

6. Carlsson, M., Widen, J.: SICStus Prolog User's Manual. Technical report, Swedish Institute of Computer Science, SICS Research Report R88007B (1988)

7. Castro, L.F., Santos Costa, V.: Understanding Memory Management in Prolog Systems. In: Codognet, P. (ed.) ICLP 2001. LNCS, vol. 2237, pp. 11–26. Springer, Heidelberg (2001)

8. Chen, W., Warren, D.S.: Query evaluation under the well-founded semantics. In: Proc. of 12th PODS, pp. 168–179 (1993)

9. Dawson, S., Ramakrishnan, C.R., Ramakrishnan, I.V., Sagonas, K.F., Skiena, S., Swift, T., Warren, D.S.: Unification factoring for efficient execution of logic programs. In: POPL 1995, pp. 247–258. ACM Press, New York (1995)

10. De Raedt, L., Kimmig, A., Toivonen, H.: ProbLog: A probabilistic Prolog and its application in link discovery. In: Veloso, M. (ed.) IJCAI, pp. 2462–2467 (2007)

11. Demoen, B., Nguyen, P.-L.: So Many WAM Variations, So Little Time. In: Palamidessi, C., Moniz Pereira, L., Lloyd, J.W., Dahl, V., Furbach, U., Kerber, M., Lau, K.-K., Sagiv, Y., Stuckey, P.J. (eds.) CL 2000. LNCS, vol. 1861, pp. 1240–1254. Springer, Heidelberg (2000)

12. Filgueiras, M.: A prolog interpreter working with infinite terms. In: Implementations of Prolog, Campbell, pp. 250–258 (1984)

13. Gupta, G., Pontelli, E., Ali, K., Carlsson, M., Hermenegildo, M.: Parallel Execution of Prolog Programs: A Survey. ACM Transactions on Programming Languages and Systems 23(4), 1–131 (2001)

14. Hermenegildo, M.V., Bueno, F., Carro, M., López, P., Morales, J.F., Puebla, G.: An overview of the ciao multiparadigm language and program development environment and its design philosophy. In: Degano, P., De Nicola, R., Meseguer, J. (eds.) Concurrency, Graphs and Models. LNCS, vol. 5065, pp. 209–237. Springer, Heidelberg (2008)

15. Koves, P., Szeredi, P.: Getting the Most Out of Structure-Sharing. SZKI. In: Collection of Papers on Logic Programming (November 1993)
16. Krall, A.: The vienna abstract machine. The Journal of Logic Programming 1-3 (October 1996)
17. Mariën, A.: Improving the Compilation of Prolog in the Framework of the Warren Abstract Machine. PhD thesis, Katholiek Universiteit Leuven (September 1993)
18. Motik, B., Sattler, U., Studer, R.: Query answering for owl-dl with rules. In: McIlraith, S.A., Plexousakis, D., van Harmelen, F. (eds.) ISWC 2004. LNCS, vol. 3298, pp. 549–563. Springer, Heidelberg (2004)
19. Pereira, F.: C-Prolog 1.5 User Manual. SRI International, Menlo Park (1987)
20. Quintus Prolog User's Guide and Reference Manual—Version 6 (April 1986)
21. Richardson, M., Domingos, P.: Markov logic networks. Machine Learning 62, 107–136 (2006)
22. Rocha, R., Silva, F., Costa, V.S.: On Applying Or-Parallelism and Tabling to Logic Programs. Theory and Practice of Logic Programming Systems 5(1-2), 161–205 (2005)
23. Sagonas, K.F., Swift, T., Warren, D.S., Freire, J., Rao, P.: The XSB programmer's manual. Technical report, State University of New York at Stony Brook (1997), http://xsb.sourceforge.net/
24. Santos Costa, V.: Implementação de Prolog. Provas de aptidão pedagógica e capacidade científica, Universidade do Porto (December 1988)
25. Santos Costa, V.: Optimising bytecode emulation for prolog. In: Nadathur, G. (ed.) PPDP 1999. LNCS, vol. 1702, pp. 261–267. Springer, Heidelberg (1999)
26. Santos Costa, V., Sagonas, K., Lopes, R.: Demand-driven indexing of prolog clauses. In: Dahl, V., Niemelä, I. (eds.) ICLP 2007. LNCS, vol. 4670, pp. 305–409. Springer, Heidelberg (2007)
27. Sato, T., Kameya, Y.: Parameter learning of logic programs for symbolic-statistical modeling. Journal of Artificial Intelligence Research 15, 391–454 (2001)
28. Silva, A.F.d., Santos Costa, V.: Design, implementation, and evaluation of an dynamic compilation framework for the yap system. In: Dahl, V., Niemelä, I. (eds.) ICLP 2007. LNCS, vol. 4670, Springer, Heidelberg (2007)
29. Srinivasan, A.: The Aleph Manual (2001)
30. Tarau, P.: BinProlog 4.00 User Guide. Technical Report 95-1, Département d'Informatique, Université de Moncton (February 1995), http://clement.info.umoncton.ca
31. van Roy, P.: Aquarius Prolog. IEEE Computer (1992)
32. Warren, D.H.D.: Applied Logic—Its Use and Implementation as a Programming Tool. PhD thesis, Edinburgh University, Available as Technical Note 290, SRI International (1977)
33. Warren, D.H.D.: An Abstract Prolog Instruction Set. Technical Note 309, SRI International (1983)
34. Wielemaker, J.: SWI-Prolog 5.1: Reference Manual. SWI, University of Amsterdam, Roetersstraat 15, 1018 WB Amsterdam, The Netherlands (1997-2003)
35. Zhou, N.-F., Takagi, T., Kazuo, U.: A Matching Tree Oriented Abstract Machine for Prolog. In: Warren, D.H.D., Szeredi, P. (eds.) Proceedings of the Seventh International Conference on Logic Programming, pp. 158–173. MIT Press, Cambridge (1990)

Uniting the Prolog Community

Tom Schrijvers* and Bart Demoen

Department of Computer Science, K.U.Leuven, Belgium

In his article *A Wake-Up Call for the Logic Programming Community*, published in the December 2007 issue of the ALP Newsletter, the first author raised concerns about the viability of the Prolog programming language in the near future. The article had a pessimistic undertone, but expressed the hope that the current evolution can be reversed by uniting the Prolog community. Now, almost a year later, it is time for more optimistic news and we are happy that the ALP —through the ICLP 2008 program chairs—has given us the opportunity to re-iterate the arguments, present the recent positive developments and involve the whole community.

The concerns raised in the ALP Newsletter have been known for years, but it takes repeated raising of voices to make the community more aware of the issues: one big problem is that the Prolog community has been too fragmented. This is true at several levels: at the system side one notes that there are too many incompatible Prolog systems around, their structure and libraries are different, their implementation technology is very diverse, and their aims are difficult to reconcile (research or industrial deployment). In short: unity lacks, there is too little community feeling. Instead, competition rules, and it is no healthy competition.

At the user base we see a wide range, from enthusiastic beginning Prolog programmers who need basic books and tutorials, students who are forced to learn Prolog for their courses, and professionals making money because they master the most intricate aspects of Prolog programming. Despite some thriving system specific user mailing lists, there is a lack of community feeling. The silence on `comp.lang.prolog` is a witness for that.

And there is the ISO problem: while the expectations were high that a standard would increase the acceptance of Prolog in wider circles, and that it would become effectively more easy to run the same Prolog program under several engines, the reality is different. Despite many (also recent) efforts, the ISO committee seems unable to make substantial progress on the core standard, let alone to impose the modules standard.

As for applications ... each system's maintainer has a few private success stories, but who remembers *The Prolog 1000 Database*? Don't we want it back?

Some of these issues can be solved only by (re-)uniting the community at all levels, for others more drastic actions are needed. But let us describe what has happened already, and why this rekindles our faith in a prosperous future for Prolog.

---

* Tom Schrijvers is a post-doctoral researcher of the Fund for Scientific Research - Flanders.

M. Garcia de la Banda and E. Pontelli (Eds.): ICLP 2008, LNCS 5366, pp. 7–8, 2008.

About a year ago, Jan Wielemaker and Vitor Santos Costa - the main drives behind SWI-Prolog and Yap - started talking concretely about letting their systems evolve towards each other. One important issue was the library structure and its contents. Jan and Vitor had been *stealing* each other's code already, but more was needed. Since then, real progress on the libraries has been made, and how this was achieved gradually is reported on in the event at ICLP 2008. Quite importantly is here also that the operator import/(re-)export facilities were synchronized. Other issues are being talked about and will be resolved, sometimes on a per-need basis: both systems support threads and it would be nice if they adhered to a common standard. Maybe ISO could play a role here, but it should be quick! Both systems have a different C-interface: Yap already can emulate the SWI-Prolog C-interface, but more commonality is the plan. The module system is another hot potato: neither of the systems is inclined to implement ISO part II on Modules, but the current differences between them hinder other common functionality related to libraries and term expansion. SWI-Prolog has (once more) plans to incorporate tabling. And very recently, the first (big) steps were set towards a common (optional) type system (see somewhere else in these proceedings).

The importance of this collaboration is less in what has been achieved until now, than in the fact that it shows the will and commitment to defragment the Prolog systems landscape, and to unite two popular systems. Such collaboration enhances the enthusiasm of implementors, contributors and users alike. From now on, a library contributed to Yap, is useful to the user community of two Prolog systems, not one. From now on, the application written for SWI-Prolog will run on Yap, and while developing it might have been easier in the former, running it might be faster in the latter: the application writer really benefits from the larger compatibility.

Sure, we are being carried away a bit here, but that is the result of being involved in joining forces: optimism!

The ALP Newsletter article mentioned earlier set a challenge to the Prolog systems. The challenge was for two Prolog systems to team up and start collaborating on mutual compatibility and shared libraries. That challenge has been met: the two cooperating systems present themselves at ICLP 2008.

The other challenge is to the Prolog community as a whole: let's work together on a more collaborative Prolog programming environment and actively support the effort. There are many ways to do so: by conducting research on these systems and citing them, by contributing library code and improving documentation, by teaching our students to use these systems and giving them assignments for writing libraries and tools. And very importantly, more Prolog systems must enter the collaboration: they are very welcome! That is the way to make our community grow, to attract new people and raise business interest.

Acknowledgements. The first author is grateful for all the positive feedback from the community on his ALP Newsletter article.

Constraint Handling Rules
A Tutorial for (Prolog) Programmers

Tom Schrijvers*

Department of Computer Science, K.U.Leuven, Belgium

Abstract. Constraint Handling Rules (CHR) [2,5] is a high-level programming language based on multi-headed, committed-choice, guarded multiset rewrite rules. Originally designed in 1991 by Frühwirth for the particular purpose of adding user-defined constraint solvers to a host-language, CHR has matured over the last decade to a powerful and elegant general-purpose language with a wide spectrum of application domains.

Different semantics have been proposed for the language, based on various logics (first-order logic, linear logic, . . .). These logics, in combination with rewriting techniques, have been used to study program properties such as soundness and completeness, confluence, termination, . . . While that line of work treats CHR as a calculus, this tutorial teaches CHR as a proper programming language.

As a programming language, CHR seems simple enough: The programmer specifies a number of rewrite rules, and the CHR engine applies these rules exhaustively to an initial (multi-)set of constraints. Yet, this simplicity hides great power: e.g., the power to quickly prototype new constraint solvers, the power to implement Prolog's co-routining predicates `freeze/2` and `when/2` in a single CHR rule each, and the power to subsume Guarded Horn Clauses while still not exploiting CHR's full potential. Moreover, CHR is the only declarative language known in which every algorithm can be implemented with optimal space and time complexity [4].

Unfortunately, few Prolog programmers are aware of the CHR language or that it is available in their Prolog system. These programmers are unable to tap into CHR's power, so they have to go to great length to accomplish even simple tasks. Or they simply give up. This tutorial shows how to use CHR for solving their problems quickly and elegantly. Simple examples teach interactively how to write and reason about CHR programs, and what problems one can solve effectively with CHR.

This tutorial starts with ground CHR, the three types of rules, and the refined semantics [1] which is based on the notion of the active constraint and its occurrences. Other topics covered are triggering of rules, the propagation history, the use of data structures and the host language, declarations and impure features, and the common pitfalls of CHR.

This tutorial intends to make the attendants aware of CHR's strengths as a programming language, and teaches them when and how to apply

---

* Tom Schrijvers is a post-doctoral researcher of the Fund for Scientific Research - Flanders.

M. Garcia de la Banda and E. Pontelli (Eds.): ICLP 2008, LNCS 5366, pp. 9–10, 2008.

CHR for small to medium sized problems. The full set of tutorial slides is available at `http://www.cs.kuleuven.be/~dtai/projects/CHR/`.

About the Speaker. Tom Schrijvers is a post-doctoral researcher at the K.U.Leuven in Belgium, who has defended his Ph.D. thesis on *Analyses, Optimizations and Extensions of Constraint Handling Rules* in 2005 [3]. His CHR implementation, the K.U.Leuven CHR system, is the most advanced in its kind and is in wide-spread use in many Prolog systems. Tom uses CHR on a daily basis, for implementing his compiler, for supporting his type checking and test generation research, or simply for gaining an edge in the Prolog Programming Contest.

References

1. Duck, G.J., Stuckey, P.J., García de la Banda, M., Holzbaur, C.: The refined operational semantics of Constraint Handling Rules. In: Demoen, B., Lifschitz, V. (eds.) ICLP 2004. LNCS, vol. 3132, pp. 90–104. Springer, Heidelberg (2004)
2. Frühwirth, T.: Theory and practice of Constraint Handling Rules. J. Logic Programming, Special Issue on Constraint Logic Programming 37(1-3), 95–138 (1998)
3. Schrijvers, T.: Analyses, optimizations and extensions of Constraint Handling Rules. PhD thesis, K.U. Leuven, Belgium (June 2005)
4. Sneyers, J., Schrijvers, T., Demoen, B.: The computational power and complexity of Constraint Handling Rules. In: ACM TOPLAS (accepted, 2008)
5. Sneyers, J., Van Weert, P., Schrijvers, T., De Koninck, L.: As time goes by: Constraint Handling Rules – A survey of CHR research between 1998 and 2007. Journal of Theory and Practice of Logic Programming (submitted, 2008)

Back to Interval Temporal Logics

(Extended Abstract)

Angelo Montanari

Department of Mathematics and Computer Science,
University of Udine, Udine, Italy
angelo.montanari@dimi.uniud.it

Interval-based temporal reasoning naturally arises in a variety of fields, including artificial intelligence (temporal knowledge representation, systems for temporal planning and maintenance, qualitative reasoning, theories of events), theoretical computer science (specification and design of hardware components, concurrent real-time processes), temporal databases (event modeling, temporal aggregation), and computational linguistics (analysis of progressive tenses, semantics and processing of natural languages) [10].

Despite the relevance of interval-based temporal reasoning, however, interval temporal logics are far less studied and popular than point-based ones for their higher conceptual and computational complexity. The main reason is probably that undecidability is a common feature of most systems of propositional interval logics, including Halpern and Shoham's Modal Logic of Time Intervals HS [11], Venema's CDT logic [15], Moszkowski's Propositional Interval Temporal Logic PITL [13], and this does not come as a surprise, since formulas of these logics translate to binary relations over the underlying ordering and the validity and satisfiability problems translate into dyadic second-order logic.

The case of HS is paradigmatic. Such a twenty years old logic can be viewed as the logic Allen's relations [1] since its operators allow one to express each one of the thirteen basic temporal relations that may hold between any pair of intervals (on a linear ordering). In [11], Halpern and Shoham show that HS is undecidable under very weak assumptions on the class of interval structures over which it is interpreted. They prove that validity in HS over the classes of all linear models, all discrete linear models, and all dense linear models is undecidable. They also prove that validity in HS over any of the orderings of the natural numbers, integers, or reals is even not recursively axiomatizable.

For a long time, results of this nature have discouraged attempts for practical applications and further research on interval temporal logics. The search for a way out was basically confined to the identification of severe syntactic and/or semantic restrictions to impose to the logic to obtain decidable fragments. As an example, in [13] Moszkowski shows that PITL decidability can be recovered by constraining atomic propositions to be point-wise and defining truth at an interval as truth at its initial point (locality) . However, in all these cases interval temporal logics are actually reducible to point-based ones, thus loosing their peculiarities.

M. Garcia de la Banda and E. Pontelli (Eds.): ICLP 2008, LNCS 5366, pp. 11–13, 2008.

A renewed interest for interval temporal logics has been recently stimulated by the discovery of expressive decidable fragments of HS. Propositional interval logics of temporal neighborhood as well as propositional interval logics of the subinterval relation are meaningful fragments of HS, that allow one to express fairly natural relations between intervals, which turn out to be decidable when interpreted over various classes of interval temporal structures.

The aim of this tutorial is to provide an overview of problems, techniques, and results in the area of interval temporal logics, with a special emphasis on (un)decidability results and tableau-based decision procedures.

We shall start with a short introduction to the variety of interval logics that can be obtained by making different choices for the set of modal operators, and the interval relations associated with them, and the class of ordered structures in which they are interpreted [10]. Then, we shall focus our attention on expressiveness issues [5,14]. First, we shall briefly discuss the relationships between interval-based and point-based temporal logics. Then, we shall recall some basic expressive completeness results for interval temporal logics. Finally, we shall summarize what is known about the classification of the fragments of HS with respect to their expressiveness (bisimulation games between interval structures come into play here), which is far from being complete. Next, we shall survey known positive and negative results about decidability of interval temporal logics, briefly presenting the main techniques so far exploited in both directions (reductions from tiling problems are extensively used in the undecidability proofs) [11,12,13,15]. In particular, we shall describe the work that has been done to identify the boundaries between decidability and undecidability of HS fragments [6,7]. The last (and most detailed) part of the tutorial will be devoted to the presentation of tableau-based decision procedures for neighborhood logics and logics of the subinterval relation [2,3,4,8,9]. We shall start with an intuitive account of the reasons why operators of interval temporal logics are in many respects more difficult to deal with than those of point-based ones. Then, we shall describe the distinctive features of various tableau systems for such logics and we shall describe their behavior on some simple examples.

We shall conclude the tutorial by outlining some open issues belonging to the research agenda for interval temporal logics. Even though propositional interval temporal logics have recently been studied more actively, they are still rather under-explored in several respects: a complete analysis of expressiveness is still lacking, the exploration of the possibility of extending language and semantics of (qualitative) interval temporal logics with explicit reference to lengths of intervals has been just started, significant results can be expected from the search for new decidable fragments of HS and the work on the design and development of efficient decision procedures, devising (efficient) model-checking algorithms for interval temporal logics is a completely unexplored research direction, applications of interval temporal logic tools in various domains, including bioinformatics, planning systems, and temporal databases, look very promising.

References

1. Allen, J.F.: Maintaining knowledge about temporal intervals. Communications of the ACM 26(11), 832–843 (1983)
2. Bresolin, D., Goranko, V., Montanari, A., Sala, P.: Tableau-based decision procedure for the logic of proper subinterval structures over dense orderings. In: Areces, C., Demri, S. (eds.) Proc. of the 5th Int. Workshop on Methods for Modalities (M4M), pp. 335–351 (2007)
3. Bresolin, D., Goranko, V., Montanari, A., Sala, P.: Tableau Systems for Logics of Subinterval Structures over Dense Orderings. In: Olivetti, N. (ed.) TABLEAUX 2007. LNCS, vol. 4548, pp. 73–89. Springer, Heidelberg (2007)
4. Bresolin, D., Goranko, V., Montanari, A., Sala, P.: Tableau-based decision procedures for the logics of subinterval structures over dense orderings. Journal of Logic and Computation (to appear, 2008)
5. Bresolin, D., Goranko, V., Montanari, A., Sciavicco, G.: On Decidability and Expressiveness of Propositional Interval Neighborhood Logics. In: Artemov, S.N., Nerode, A. (eds.) LFCS 2007. LNCS, vol. 4514, pp. 84–99. Springer, Heidelberg (2007)
6. Bresolin, D., Goranko, V., Montanari, A., Sciavicco, G.: Propositional interval neighborhood logics: Expressiveness, decidability, and undecidable extensions. Annals of Pure and Applied Logic (to appear, 2008)
7. Bresolin, D., Della Monica, D., Goranko, V., Montanari, A., Sciavicco, G.: Decidable and undecidable fragments of halpern and shoham's interval temporal logic: Towards a complete classification. In: Cervesato, I., Veith, H., Voronkov, A. (eds.) LPAR 2008. LNCS, vol. 5330, pp. 590–604. Springer, Heidelberg (2008)
8. Bresolin, D., Montanari, A., Sala, P.: An optimal tableau-based decision algorithm for Propositional Neighborhood Logic. In: Thomas, W., Weil, P. (eds.) STACS 2007. LNCS, vol. 4393, pp. 549–560. Springer, Heidelberg (2007)
9. Bresolin, D., Montanari, A., Sciavicco, G.: An optimal decision procedure for Right Propositional Neighborhood Logic. Journal of Automated Reasoning 38(1-3), 173–199 (2007)
10. Goranko, V., Montanari, A., Sciavicco, G.: A road map of interval temporal logics and duration calculi. Journal of Applied Non-Classical Logics 14(1-2), 9–54 (2004)
11. Halpern, J.Y., Shoham, Y.: A propositional modal logic of time intervals. Journal of the ACM 38(4), 935–962 (1991)
12. Hodkinson, I., Montanari, A., Sciavicco, G.: Non-finite axiomatizability and undecidbility of interval temporal logics with C, D, and T. In: Kaminski, M., Martini, S. (eds.) Proc. of the 17th Annual Conference of the EACSL (CSL). LNCS, vol. 5213, pp. 308–322. Springer, Heidelberg (2008)
13. Moszkowski, B.: Reasoning about digital circuits. Tech. rep. stan-cs-83-970, Dept. of Computer Science, Stanford University, Stanford, CA (1983)
14. Venema, Y.: Expressiveness and completeness of an interval tense logic. Notre Dame Journal of Formal Logic 31(4), 529–547 (1990)
15. Venema, Y.: A modal logic for chopping intervals. Journal of Logic and Computation 1(4), 453–476 (1991)

Systems Biology: Models and Logics*

C. Piazza[1] and A. Policriti[1,2]

[1] Dept. of Math. and Computer Science, University of Udine, Udine, Italy
[2] Institute of Applied Genomics, Udine, Italy
{piazza,policriti}@dimi.uniud.it

Abstract. The field of systems biology focuses on creating a finely detailed picture of biological mechanisms. Recently, the need has arisen for more and more sophisticated and mathematically well founded computational tools, capable of analyzing those models that are and will be at the core of Systems Biology. The challenge consists in faithfully implementing such computational models in software packages exploiting the potential trade-offs among usability, accuracy, and scalability when dealing with large amounts of data. The aim of this presentation is that of introducing some emerging problems and proposed solutions in this context.

In particular, after an introductory first part, in the second part we will focus on the use of Hybrid Systems in Systems Biology. Hybrid systems are dynamical systems presenting both discrete and continuous evolution, originally proposed to study embedded systems, where a discrete control acts on a continuously changing environment. The presence of both discrete and continuous dynamics makes this formalism appealing also for modeling biological systems. However, the situation in this case is subtler, basically because there is no "natural" separation of discrete and continuous components. It comes as no surprise, therefore, that Hybrid Systems have been used in Systems Biology in rather various ways. Some approaches, like the description of biological switches, concentrate on the use of model-checking routines. Other applications, like the switching between continuous and discrete/stochastic simulation, focus on the exploitation of the interplay between discreteness and continuity in order to reduce the computational burden of numerical simulation, yet maintaining an acceptable precision. We will survey some of the main uses of Hybrid Automata in Systems Biology, through a series of cases studies that we deem interesting and paradigmatic, discussing both actual and foreseeable, logical and implementation issues.

---

* This work is partially supported by PRIN "BISCA" 2006011235 and FIRB "LIBI" RBLA039M7M.

Separation Logic Tutorial

Peter O'Hearn[*]

Queen Mary, Univ. of London

Separation logic is an extension of Hoare's logic for reasoning about programs that manipulate pointers. It is based on the *separating conjunction* $P * Q$, which asserts that P and Q hold for separate portions of computer memory.

This tutorial on separation logic has three parts.

1. *Basics.* Concentrating on highlights from the early work [1,2,3,4].
2. *Model Theory.* The model theory of separation logic evolved from the general resource models of bunched logic [5,6,7], and includes an account of program dynamics in terms of their interaction with resource [8,9].
3. *Proof Theory.* I will describe those aspects of the proof theory, particularly new entailment questions (frame and anti-frame inference [10,11]), which are important for applications in mechanized program verification.

1 Basics

The Separating Conjunction. I introduce the separating conjunction by example. Consider the following memory structure.

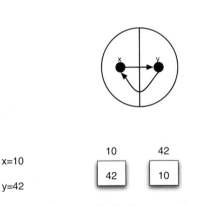

We read the formula at the top of this figure as "*x* points to *y*, *and separately* *y* points to *x*". Going down the middle of the diagram is a line which represents a heap partitioning: a separating conjunction asks for a partitioning that divides memory into parts satisfying its two conjuncts.

At the bottom of the figure we have given an example of a concrete memory description that corresponds to the diagram. There, x and y have values 10 and

[*] I gratefully acknowledge the support of an EPSRC Advanced Fellowship and a Royal Society Wolfson Research Merit Award.

M. Garcia de la Banda and E. Pontelli (Eds.): ICLP 2008, LNCS 5366, pp. 15–21, 2008.

42 (in the "environment", or "register bank"), and 10 and 42 are themselves locations with the indicated contents (in the "heap", or even "RAM"). It should be clear how the picture corresponds to the concrete structure. It is simplest to think in terms of the picture semantics of separation logic, but if confusion arises as to what diagrams mean you can always drop down to the RAM level.

The indicated separating conjunction above is true of the pictured memory because the parts satisfy the conjuncts. That is, the components

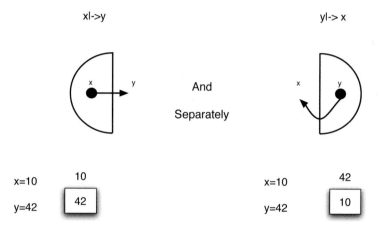

are separate sub-states that satisfy the relevant conjuncts.

It can be confusing to see a diagram like the one on the left where "x points to y and yet to nowhere". This is disambiguated in the RAM description below the diagram. In the more concrete description x and y denote values (10 and 42), x's value is an allocated memory address which contains y's value, but y's value is not allocated. Notice also that, in comparison to the first diagram, the separating conjunction splits the heap/RAM, but it does *not* split the association of variables to values: heap cells, but not variable associations, are deleted from the original situation to obtain the sub-states.

When reasoning about programs that manipulate data structures, one normally wants to use inductively-defined predicates that describe such structures. Here is a definition for a predicate that describes binary trees:

$$\text{tree}(E) \iff if \ E = \text{nil} \ then \ \text{emp}$$
$$else \ \exists x, y. \ (E \mapsto l: x, r: y) \ * \ \text{tree}(x) \ * \ \text{tree}(y)$$

In this definition we have used a record notation $(E \mapsto l: x, r: y)$ for a "points-to predicate" that describes a single[1] record E that contains x in its l field and y in its r field. nil can be taken to be any non-addressible number[2]. The separating conjunction between this assertion and the two recursive instances of tree ensures that there are no cycles, and the separating conjunction between the two subtrees ensures that we have a tree and not a dag. The emp predicate in the base case

---

[1] It denotes a *singleton heap* , a heaplet wth only one cell.

[2] You can map these notions to the RAM model, or just imagine a record model.

of the inductive definition describes the empty heap (or portion of heap). A consequence of this is that when tree(E) holds there are no extra cells, not in the tree, in a state satisfying the predicate. This is a key specification pattern often employed in separation logic proofs: we use assertions that describe only as much state as is needed, and nothing else.

At this point you might think that I have described an exotic-looking formalism for writing assertions about heaps and you might wonder: why bother? In fact, the mere ability to describe heaps is not at all important in and of itself, and in this separation logic adds nothing significant to traditional predicate logic. It is only when we consider the interaction between assertions and operations for mutating memory that the point of the formalism begins to come out.

In-place Reasoning. I am going to try something that might seem eccentric: I am going to give you a program proof, without telling you the inference rules it uses. I am hoping that you will find the reasoning steps I show to be intuitively understandable, prior to becoming embroiled in too many formalities. Whether I succeed in my aim is, of course, for you to judge.

Consider the following procedure for disposing the elements in a tree.

```
procedure DispTree(p)
local i, j;
if  p≠nil then
     i = p→l ; j:= p→r; DispTree(i); DispTree(j); free(p)
```

This is the expected procedure that walks a tree, recursively disposing left and right subtrees and then the root pointer. It uses a representation of tree nodes with left, right and data fields, and the empty tree is represented by nil.

The specification of DispTree is just

$$\{\mathsf{tree}(p)\} \; \mathtt{DispTree}(p) \; \{\mathsf{emp}\}$$

which says that if you have a tree at the beginning then you end up with the empty heap at the end. The crucial part of the proof, in the if branch, is:

$$\{p\mapsto[l\colon x, r\colon y] * \mathsf{tree}(x) * \mathsf{tree}(y)\}$$
$$i := p\to l; \; j := p\to r;$$
$$\{p\mapsto[l\colon i, r\colon j] * \mathsf{tree}(i) * \mathsf{tree}(j)\}$$
$$\mathtt{DispTree}(i);$$
$$\{p\mapsto[l\colon i, r\colon j] * \mathsf{tree}(j)\}$$
$$\mathtt{DispTree}(j);$$
$$\{p\mapsto[l\colon i, r\colon j]\}$$
$$\mathtt{free} \; p$$
$$\{\mathsf{emp}\}$$

After we enter the conditional statement we know that $p\neq$nil, so that (according to the inductive definition) p points to left and right subtrees occupying separate storage. Then the roots of the two subtrees are loaded into i and j. The first recursive call operates in-place on the left subtree, removing it, the second call removes the right subtree, and the final instruction frees the root pointer p. This verification uses the procedure specification as a recursive assumption.

I am leading to a more general suggestion: try thinking about reasoning in separation logic as if you are an interpreter. The formulae are like states, *symbolic* states. Execute the procedure forwards, updating formulae in the usual way you do when thinking about in-place update of memory. In-place reasoning works not only for disposal, but for heap mutation and allocation as well [1,2].

One thing at work in the "proof" above is a rule

$$\frac{\{P\}\ C\ \{Q\}}{\{R*P\}\ C\ \{R*Q\}}\ \text{Frame Rule}$$

that lets us tack on additional assertions "for free", as it were. For instance, in the second recursive call the frame axiom R selected is $p \mapsto [l: i, r: j]$ and $\{P\} C \{Q\}$ is a substitution instance of the procedure spec: this captures that the recursive call does not alter the root pointer. Generally, the frame rule that lets us use "small specifications" that only talk about the cells that a program touches [3].

Perspective. The essential points that I have tried to illustrate are the following.

(i) The separating conjunction fits together with inductive definitions in a way that supports natural descriptions of mutable data structures [1].

(ii) Axiomatizations of pointer operations support *in-place reasoning*, where a portion of a formula is updated in place when passing from precondition to postcondition, mirroring the operational locality of heap update [1,2].

(iii) Frame axioms, which state what does not change, can be avoided when writing specifications [2,3].

These points together enable specifications and proofs for pointer programs that are dramatically simpler than was possible previously, in many (not all) cases approaching the simplicity associated with proofs of pure functional programs.

2   Model Theory and Proof Theory

Above I have concentrated on the basics of separation logic, emphasizing that to "think like an interpreter" is a good approximation to program proving. The model-theoretic underpinnings of this point of view rest on a number of theorems about the semantics of imperative programs, and their interaction with the semantics of Hoare triples [8,9].

The most significant developments in proof theory have stemmed from an inference procedure of Berdine and Calcagno in their work on the Smallfoot tool [12]. Special versions of their inference rules have been used to enable loop-invariant discovery in abstract interpreters [13,14], which have been extended to ever-more-expressive abstract domains (e.g., [15,16,17,18,19]).

A pivotal development has been identification of the notion of *frame inference*, which gives a way to find the "leftover" portions of heap needed to automatically apply the frame rule in program proofs. Technically, this is done by solving an extension to the usual entailment question

$$A \vdash B * \text{?frame}$$

where the task is, given A and B, to find a formula ?frame which makes the entailment valid. This extended entailment capability is used at procedure call sites, where A is an assertion at the call site and B a precondition from a procedure's specification. Frame inference was first solved by Berdine and Calcagno by using information from failed proofs of the standard entailment question $A \vdash B$ (related ideas were developed in [20]). It is used in several automatic verification and analysis tools based on separation logic [21,16,22,23,24].

More recently, there has been work on an, in a sense, inverse problem

$$A * \text{?anti-frame} \vdash B$$

where the task is to find a description of the missing or needed portion of heap ?anti-frame that makes the entailment valid. This is a separation-logic cousin of the classic abductive inference question. It has been used in [11] to synthesize preconditions of procedures, by attempting to infer descriptions of just the portions of heap that they need to run without producing a memory fault. The joint abduction/frame inference question, termed "bi-abduction" in [11], forms the basis of a compositional program analysis, where Hoare triples for a procedure are generated without knowing the procedure's calling context.

I have concentrated on the basics of separation logic, on its semantics, and on proof theory as it is relevant to automatic proof tools and abstract interpreters. There have been significant developments in several other directions.

- Iterative proof, where the semantics of the logic is embedded in a higher-order logic (e.g., [25,26,27]).
- Web data structures, using non-symmetric separation (context with hole)[28].
- Object-oriented programing, where the logic is used to address longstanding aliasing problems (e.g., [29,24]).
- Concurrency, where the logic is used to control sharing of memory between concurrent threads (starting with [30,31]).

Space prevents more comprehensive references here: The reader may consult the page www.dcs.qmul.ac.uk/~ohearn/localreasoning.html for further pointers.

References

1. Reynolds, J.C.: Intuitionistic reasoning about shared mutable data structure. In: Millennial Perspectives in Computer Science. Proceedings of the 1999 Oxford–Microsoft Symposium in Honour of Sir Tony Hoare, Palgrave, pp. 303–321 (2000)
2. Isthiaq, S., O'Hearn, P.W.: BI as an assertion language for mutable data structures. In: 28th POPL, pp. 36–49 (2001)
3. O'Hearn, P., Reynolds, J., Yang, H.: Local reasoning about programs that alter data structures. In: Fribourg, L. (ed.) CSL 2001 and EACSL 2001. LNCS, vol. 2142, pp. 1–19. Springer, Heidelberg (2001)
4. Reynolds, J.C.: Separation logic: A logic for shared mutable data structures. In: 17th LICS, pp. 55–74 (2002)
5. O'Hearn, P.W., Pym, D.J.: The logic of bunched implications. Bulletin of Symbolic Logic 5(2), 215–244 (1999)

6. Pym, D.J.: The Semantics and Proof Theory of the Logic of Bunched Implications. Applied Logic Series. Kluwer Academic Publishers, Dordrecht (2002)

7. Pym, D., O'Hearn, P., Yang, H.: Possible worlds and resources: the semantics of BI. Theoretical Computer Science 315(1), 257–305 (2004)

8. Yang, H., O'Hearn, P.: A semantic basis for local reasoning. In: Nielsen, M., Engberg, U. (eds.) FOSSACS 2002. LNCS, vol. 2303, pp. 402–416. Springer, Heidelberg (2002)

9. Calcagno, C., O'Hearn, P., Yang, H.: Local action and abstract separation logic. In: 22nd LICS, pp. 366–378 (2007)

10. Berdine, J., Calcagno, C., O'Hearn, P.W.: Symbolic execution with separation logic. In: Yi, K. (ed.) APLAS 2005. LNCS, vol. 3780. Springer, Heidelberg (2005)

11. Calcagno, C., Distefano, D., O'Hearn, P., Yang, H.: Compositional shape analysis. Imperial College DOC Tech. Report 2008/12

12. Berdine, J., Calcagno, C., O'Hearn, P.W.: Smallfoot: Automatic modular assertion checking with separation logic. In: 4th FMCO, pp. 115–137 (2006)

13. Distefano, D., O'Hearn, P., Yang, H.: A local shape analysis based on separation logic. In: Hermanns, H., Palsberg, J. (eds.) TACAS 2006. LNCS, vol. 3920, pp. 287–302. Springer, Heidelberg (2006)

14. Magill, S., Nanevski, A., Clarke, E., Lee, P.: Inferring invariants in Separation Logic for imperative list-processing programs. In: 3rd SPACE Workshop (2006)

15. Berdine, J., Cook, B., Distefano, D., O'Hearn, P.: Automatic termination proofs for programs with shape-shifting heaps. In: Ball, T., Jones, R.B. (eds.) CAV 2006. LNCS, vol. 4144, pp. 386–400. Springer, Heidelberg (2006)

16. Gotsman, A., Berdine, J., Cook, B., Sagiv, M.: Thread-modular shape analysis. In: PLDI 2007 (2007)

17. Guo, B., Vachharajani, N., August, D.: Shape analysis with inductive recursion synthesis. In: PLDI (2007)

18. Berdine, J., Calcagno, C., Cook, B., Distefano, D., O'Hearn, P., Wies, T., Yang, H.: Shape analysis of composite data structures. In: Damm, W., Hermanns, H. (eds.) CAV 2007. LNCS, vol. 4590. Springer, Heidelberg (2007)

19. Magill, S., Tsai, M.-S., Lee, P., Tsay, Y.-K.: THOR: A tool for reasoning about shape and arithmetic. In: Gupta, A., Malik, S. (eds.) CAV 2008. LNCS, vol. 5123. Springer, Heidelberg (2008)

20. Rinetzky, N., Bauer, J., Reps, T., Sagiv, M., Wilhelm, R.: A semantics for procedure local heaps and its abstractions. In: 32nd POPL, pp. 296–309 (2005)

21. Gotsman, A., Berdine, J., Cook, B.: Interprocedural shape analysis with separated heap abstractions. In: Yi, K. (ed.) SAS 2006. LNCS, vol. 4134, pp. 240–260. Springer, Heidelberg (2006)

22. Nguyen, H.H., Chin, W.-N.: Enhancing program verification with lemmas. In: Gupta, A., Malik, S. (eds.) CAV 2008. LNCS, vol. 5123. Springer, Heidelberg (2008)

23. Yang, H., Lee, O., Berdine, J., Calcagno, C., Cook, B., Distefano, D., O'Hearn, P.: Scalable shape analysis for systems code. In: Gupta, A., Malik, S. (eds.) CAV 2008. LNCS, vol. 5123. Springer, Heidelberg (2008)

24. Distefano, D., Parkinson, M.: jStar: Towards Practical Verification for Java. In: OOPSLA (2008)

25. Marti, N., Affeldt, R., Yonezawa, A.: Verification of the heap manager of an operating system using separation logic. In: 3rd SPACE Workshop (2006)

26. Tuch, H., Klein, G., Norrish, M.: Types, bytes, and separation logic. In: 34th POPL, pp. 97–108 (2007)

27. Myreen, M.O., Gordon, M.J.C.: Hoare logic for realistically modelled machine code. In: Grumberg, O., Huth, M. (eds.) TACAS 2007. LNCS, vol. 4424. Springer, Heidelberg (2007)
28. Gardner, P., Smith, G., Wheelhouse, M., Zarfaty, U.: Local Hoare reasoning about DOM. In: 27th PODS, pp. 261–270 (2008)
29. Parkinson, M., Bierman, G.: Separation logic and abstraction. In: 32nd POPL, pp. 59–70 (2005)
30. O'Hearn, P.W.: Resources, concurrency and local reasoning. Theoretical Computer Science (Reynolds Festschrift) 375(1-3), 271–307 (2007)
31. Brookes, S.D.: A semantics of concurrent separation logic. Theoretical Computer Science (Reynolds Festschrift) 375(1-3), 227–270 (2007)

Authorization and Obligation Policies in Dynamic Systems

Michael Gelfond[1] and Jorge Lobo[2]

[1] Texas Tech University
mgelfond@cs.ttu.edu
[2] IBM T. J. Watson Research Center
jlobo@us.ibm.com

Abstract. The paper defines a language for specifying authorization and obligation policies of an intelligent agent acting in a changing environment and presents several ASP based algorithms for checking compliance of an event with a policy specified in this language. The language allows representation of defeasible policies and is based on theory of action and change.

1 Introduction

The goal of this paper is to provide a simple language for specifying authorization and obligation policies of an intelligent agent acting in a changing environment. We refer to a pair consisting of an agent and its environment as a *dynamic system*. We limit our attention to dynamic systems which can be reasonably well represented by transition diagrams whose nodes correspond to possible physical states of the environment and arcs are labeled by actions. A transition $\langle \sigma, a, \sigma' \rangle$ belongs to such a transition diagram $\mathcal{T}$ iff σ' may be a state resulting from the execution of action a in state σ. If action a is deterministic and executable in σ then there exists exactly one such σ'. The system's diagram $\mathcal{T}$ contains all physically possible trajectories of the system. By an agent's *policy* we mean a description, $\mathcal{P}$, of a subset of trajectories of $\mathcal{T}$ deemed to be preferable by the system's designer. We often refer to such trajectories as *compliant* with $\mathcal{P}$.

We start with describing *authorization policy* of an agent $\mathcal{A}$ of a dynamic system $\langle \mathcal{A}, \mathcal{T} \rangle$ – a set of conditions under which an agent's action is or is not permitted. Note that the agent's use of the authorization policy can differ from application to application. Some authorization policies can be strict – no unauthorized action can be performed by an agent. In other cases an autonomous agent can opt for performing an unauthorized action. In this case the agent may be forced to pay a penalty, be commended for the initiative or loose his job for insubordination. In all these cases though it is important to be able to determine when an action is authorized and when it is not. Of course the agent can do this only on the basis of his general knowledge of the world, the system's current state, and its own abilities, and goals. The algorithms for checking compliance of agent's actions to his policies can be used by the agent for deciding what actions to perform as well as by an outside observers evaluating the agent's behaviour. Similar observations are true

M. Garcia de la Banda and E. Pontelli (Eds.): ICLP 2008, LNCS 5366, pp. 22–36, 2008.

for *obligation policy* – a set of conditions defining the actions the agent is obligated to perform or to abstain from performing in a given state.

In section 2 we describe the syntax and semantics of a language $\mathcal{APL}$ for specifying authorization policies of dynamic systems. We also discuss several methods for checking compliance of authorization policies using the methods of *Answer Set Programming* [1]. Section 3 expands $\mathcal{APL}$ with obligation policies.

2   Authorization Policy

In this section we define the syntax and semantics of the language $\mathcal{APL}$ for describing authorization policies in a dynamic system $\langle \mathcal{A}, \mathcal{T} \rangle$, and describe how checking compliance of actions and trajectories of the system can be reduced to computing answer sets of logic programs under the answer set semantics [2]. As expected, particular reductions will depend on the knowledge available to the reasoner checking the compliance. One of our main goals is simplicity of the language and a high level of elaboration tolerance of its policies. This of course should be balanced by the expressiveness of the language and the ability to check compliance in a reasonable amount of time.

2.1   Syntax

Let us consider a dynamic system described by an agent, $\mathcal{A}$, and a transition diagram $\mathcal{T}$ over some fixed signature Σ with sorts:

- *fluent* – functions whose values can change as a result of actions;
- *action* – by actions we mean *elementary actions*;
- *domain dependent sorts* representing elements of a particular domain.

We use (possibly indexed) letters f and e to denote elements of first two sorts. Possibly indexed letter a denotes *compound actions* – sets of (simultaneously executed) elementary actions. The corresponding capital letters denote variables ranging over the corresponding sorts. The set of elementary actions will be divided into the set of *agent's actions* and the set of *exogenous actions*. The former are actions executed by the agent $\mathcal{A}$ of the dynamic system. The latter are actions performed by other agents viewed as part of $\mathcal{A}$'s environment or by nature. Expressions of the form $f = y$ where f is a fluent and y is a possible value of f will be called *fluent atom*. Expressions of the form $e = true$ and $e = false$ will be referred to as *action atoms*. A Σ-*atom* is a fluent or action atom of Σ. Σ-atoms $l = true$ and $l = false$ will be often written as l and $\neg l$ respectively.

Recall that a *state* of $\mathcal{T}$ consists of an assignment of values to all the fluents of Σ. If $\langle \sigma, a, \sigma' \rangle$ is a transition of $\mathcal{T}$ then the pair $\langle \sigma, a \rangle$ will often be referred to as an *event*.

Now we are ready to define the language $\mathcal{APL}(\Sigma)$ for specifying authorization policy of an agent whose environment is described by $\mathcal{T}$.

The signature of $\mathcal{APL}(\Sigma)$ is obtained from Σ by adding a new predicate symbol $permitted(e)$, a collection of terms, $d_1, \ldots, d_n$ used to denote default authorization rules of $\mathcal{APL}(\Sigma)$, and the relation $prefer(d_1, d_2)$.

Definition 1. *[Authorization Policy]*
Authorization policy statements are expressions of the form

$$permitted(e) \text{ if } cond \tag{1}$$

$$\neg permitted(e) \text{ if } cond \tag{2}$$

$$d : \text{normally } permitted(e) \text{ if } cond \tag{3}$$

$$d : \text{normally } \neg permitted(a) \text{ if } cond \tag{4}$$

$$prefer(d_1, d_2) \tag{5}$$

where by *cond* we mean a collection of atoms of $\mathcal{APL}(\Sigma)$ not containing atoms formed by *prefer*.[1] (The last restriction is not necessary but it slightly simplifies the presentation). If *cond* is empty we simply omit "if *cond*" from the sentence. The first two statements will be referred to as *strict* policies. The next two will be called *defeasible*. Names of defeasible authorization statements are optional and can be omitted. By *authorization policy* we mean a collection of authorization policy statements.

Example 1. [Mission Command]
Consider the following (imaginary) policy requirements for mission authorization and command [3] :

1. A military officer is not allowed to command a mission he authorized.
2. A colonel is allowed to command a mission he authorized.
3. A military observer can never authorize a mission.

To express this policy we must have some information about transition system $\mathcal{T}_m$ which serves as a mathematical model of our domain. We assume that the signature, Σ_m of $\mathcal{T}_m$, contains two domain dependent sorts, *mission* and *commander*. Possibly indexed variables M and C range over missions and commanders respectively; Σ_m also contains

actions: $authorize(C, M)$ and $assume\_command(C, M)$;
fluents: $authorized(C, M)$, $commands(C, M)$, $colonel(C)$, and $observer(C)$.

Since the first two authorization policy statements of our example are contradictory we naturally assume them to be defeasible. The first policy statement will be expressed as[2]
$d_1(C, M) \quad : \quad \text{normally } \neg permitted(assume\_command(C, M)) \text{ if } authorized (C, M)$
The second statement will be expressed as

$d_2(C, M) : \text{normally } permitted(assume\_command(C, M)) \text{ if } colonel(C)$

---

[1] The full version of the language will include dynamic preferences, i.e. statements of the form $prefer(d_1, d_2)$ if *cond*. Conceptually the extension is not difficult but require a little more space.

[2] Note that the names of defaults contain the default variables.

Since the second defeasible policy is more specific we assume that it is preferred over the first one and, accordingly, add the sentence

$$prefer(d_2(C, M), d_1(C, M))$$

The last policy statement seems to be strict and will be represented by

$$\neg permitted(authorize(C, M)) \text{ if } observer(C)$$

We will denote the resulting policy by $\mathcal{P}_m$.

2.2 Semantics

The semantics of an authorization policy $\mathcal{P}$ will determine a mapping $\mathcal{P}(\sigma)$ from states of $\mathcal{T}$ into *permissions* – sets of statements of the form $permitted(e)$, and *denials* – sets of statements of the form $\neg permitted(e)$.

To give the intuitively correct definition of $\mathcal{P}(\sigma)$ we should be able to refer to valid consequences of defaults expressed by defeasible rules of our authorization policy. This can be done by interpreting policies, states and events in terms of logic programs under the answer set semantics – a non-monotonic logical formalism well suited for reasoning with defaults. To this end we first translate authorisation statements of $\mathcal{APL}$ into their *logic programming counterparts*. The translation, lp, is defined as follows:

- $lp(f = y) =_{def} val(f, y)$;
- $lp(permitted(e)) =_{def} permitted(e)$.
- $lp(\neg permitted(e)) =_{def} \neg permitted(e)$.
- If S is a set of atoms then $lp(S) =_{def} \{lp(at) : at \in S\}$.
- lp of a strict policy statement, SPS, of $\mathcal{P}$ is obtained from SPS by simply replacing "if" by the "$\leftarrow$".
- A defeasible policy statement, DPS, is translated by lp into a standard Answer Set Prolog default rule:
  $permitted(e) \leftarrow lp(cond),$
  $\qquad\qquad not\ ab(d),$
  $\qquad\qquad not\ \neg permitted(e).$
  or
  $\neg permitted(e) \leftarrow lp(cond),$
  $\qquad\qquad not\ ab(d),$
  $\qquad\qquad not\ permitted(e).$
- The preference between two defeasible policies, d_1 and d_2 is translated by lp into
  $ab(d_2) \leftarrow lp(cond_1)$
  where $cond_1$ is the condition of d_1.

Finally

Definition 2. *[Logic programming counterparts of policies and events]*

$$lp(\mathcal{P}) =_{def} \{lp(st) : \ st \ \in \mathcal{P}\}$$
$$lp(\mathcal{P}, \sigma) =_{def} lp(\mathcal{P}) \cup lp(\sigma)$$

These programs will be used to define important properties of authorization policies as well as their semantics:

Definition 3. *[Consistency of Authorization Policy]*
An authorization policy $\mathcal{P}$ for $\langle \mathcal{A}, \mathcal{T} \rangle$ is called *consistent* if for every state σ of $\mathcal{T}$ logic program $lp(\mathcal{P}, \sigma)$ is consistent, i.e. has an answer set.

Definition 4. *[$\mathcal{P}(\sigma)$ for authorization]*
Let $\mathcal{P}$ be a consistent authorization policy for $\langle \mathcal{A}, \mathcal{T} \rangle$. Then

- $permitted(e) \in \mathcal{P}(\sigma)$ iff a logic program $lp(\mathcal{P}, \sigma)$ entails $permitted(e)$[3].
- $\neg permitted(e) \in \mathcal{P}(\sigma)$ iff a logic program $lp(\mathcal{P}, \sigma)$ entails $\neg permitted(e)$.

Definition 5. *[Policy Compliance]*

- An event $\langle \sigma, a \rangle$ is *strongly compliant* with authorization policy $\mathcal{P}$ if for every $e \in a$ we have that $permitted(e) \in \mathcal{P}(\sigma)$.
- An event $\langle \sigma, a \rangle$ is *weakly compliant* with $\mathcal{P}$ if for every $e \in a$ we have that $\neg permitted(e) \notin \mathcal{P}(\sigma)$.
- An event $\langle \sigma, a \rangle$ is *not compliant* with $\mathcal{P}$ if for some $e \in a$ we have that $\neg permitted(e) \in \mathcal{P}(\sigma)$.
- A path $\langle \sigma_0, a_0, \sigma_1, ..., \sigma_{n-1}, a_{n-1}, \sigma_n \rangle$ of $\mathcal{T}$ is said to be *strongly (weakly) compliant* with $\mathcal{P}$ if for every $0 \leq i < n$ the event $\langle \sigma_i, a_i \rangle$ is strongly (weakly) compliant with $\mathcal{P}$.

Notice that $lp(\mathcal{P}, \sigma)$ may have answer sets S_1 and S_2 such that $permitted(e) \in S_1$ and $permitted(e) \notin S_2$. According to our definition $permitted(e)$ is not a consequence of $\mathcal{P}$, i.e. ambiguity is treated as a complete absence of knowledge. In some cases (probably most of the time) the system designer may want to avoid ambiguity and to limit himself to policies satisfying the following condition:

Definition 6. *[Categoricity]*
An authorization policy $\mathcal{P}$ for $\langle \mathcal{A}, \mathcal{T} \rangle$ is called *categorical* if for every state σ of $\mathcal{T}$ logic program $lp(\mathcal{P}, \sigma)$ as categorical, i.e. has exactly one answer set.

To illustrate these definitions let us go back to Example 1.

Example 2. [Mission Command Revisited]
Let us populate the domain of Example 1 with a mission, m_1 and a commander c_1. One can use standard answer set programming techniques to easily prove that for any state σ and action e executable in σ the program $lp(\mathcal{P}_m, \sigma)$ is consistent (and categorical). Hence policy $\mathcal{P}_m$ is consistent and unambiguous.

Now let us consider an event $\langle \sigma_0, e_0 \rangle$ where

$\sigma_0 = \{colonel(c_1), authorized(c_1, m_1), \neg commands(c_1, m_1), \neg observer(c_1)\}$
   and

$e_0 = assume\_command(c_1, m_1)$.

The answer set of $lp(\mathcal{P}_m, \sigma_0)$ contains $permitted(e_0)$ and hence the event is strongly compliant with $\mathcal{P}_m$. Similarly one can check that an event $\langle \sigma_1, e_0 \rangle$ where

---

[3] A logic program Π entails literal l ($\Pi \models l$) if l belongs to every answer set of Π.

$$\sigma_1 = \{\neg colonel(c_1), authorized(c_1, m_1), \neg commands(c_1, m_1), \neg observer(c_1)\}$$

is not compliant with $\mathcal{P}_m$. Finally consider a policy $\mathcal{P}'_m$ obtained from $\mathcal{P}_m$ by removing its first authorization rule. Again one can easily check that the event $\langle \sigma_1, e_0 \rangle$ is weakly (but not strongly) compliant with $\mathcal{P}'_m$.

2.3   Checking Compliance

In this section we discuss the ways to automatically check compliance of an agent's behaviour with consistent authorization policy $\mathcal{P}$ of $\langle \mathcal{A}, \mathcal{T} \rangle$. The algorithms will obviously depend on the type of input information and the goals of the checker. Let us start with the simplest possible scenario:

Scenario 1: an agent, acting in an environment $\mathcal{T}$, has *complete knowledge about his current state, σ, and contemplates the execution of action e.*

The following proposition, which follows immediately from the definition of compliance and properties of ASP logic programs, reduces the task to checking consistency of logic programs.

Proposition 1. *[Checking compliance of a completely known event]*

- Event $\langle \sigma, e \rangle$ is strongly compliant with consistent policy $\mathcal{P}$ of $\mathcal{T}$ iff a logic program

$$lp(\mathcal{P}, \sigma) \cup \{\leftarrow permitted(e)\}$$

  is inconsistent.
- Event $\langle \sigma, e \rangle$ is weakly compliant with $\mathcal{P}$ iff a logic program

$$lp(\mathcal{P}, \sigma) \cup \{\leftarrow \neg permitted(e)\}$$

  is consistent.
- Event $\langle \sigma, e \rangle$ is not compliant with policy $\mathcal{P}$ iff a logic program

$$lp(\mathcal{P}, \sigma) \cup \{\leftarrow \neg permitted(e)\}$$

  is inconsistent.

Now let us look at the slight generalization of this scenario.

Scenario 2: Suppose that the *agent's knowledge about the current state is limited to the values of some (but not necessarily all) fluents.*

Let us denote the collection of such fluent atoms by s, and assume that $\delta(s)$ consists of all states of the system containing s. If an event $\langle \sigma, e \rangle$ is strongly (weakly) compliant with the agent's policy for every $\sigma \in \sigma(s)$ then the execution of e is obviously authorized (not prohibited); if for every $\sigma \in \sigma(s)$ the event $\langle \sigma, e \rangle$ is not permitted the agent will be wise not to perform e. Otherwise the agent does not have enough information to determine compliance of the event. But how our reasoner can check which of the above conditions (if any) are satisfied? It is obvious that to be able to do that he needs sufficient knowledge about $\delta(s)$.

The precise logical form of this knowledge depends on the way we choose to describe our transition system $\mathcal{T}$. For the purposes of this paper we assume that such description is given by an action theory, A, in an action language $\mathcal{AL}$ [4] Such action theories provide a concise and convenient way of describing a large class of discrete dynamic systems. In particular we will need *static causal laws* (often referred to as *state constraints*) of $\mathcal{AL}$ – statements of the form

$$f = y \text{ if } P \tag{6}$$

where P is a collection of atoms of signature Σ of $\mathcal{T}$. We say that a (partial) assignment of values to fluents of Σ *satisfies* (6) if it contains $f = y$ or does not contain P. A *state* of a transition system defined by action theory A is a complete assignment of values to fluents which satisfies all the static causal laws of A. Partial assignment satisfying these laws is called a *simple knowledge state* of an agent with action theory A.

To compute $\sigma(s)$ we expand the translation lp of our policy statements into logic programs to the laws of the form (6): function lp will map (6) into

$$val(f, y) \leftarrow lp(P).$$

(The translation follows [5].) Let D be the collection of all statements of the form

$$val(f, y_1) \text{ or } \ldots \text{ or } val(f, y_k)$$

where f is a fluent, $\{y_1, \ldots, y_k\}$ is the set of all its possible values, and let SL be the set of all static causal laws from the action theory A describing $\mathcal{T}$. The following proposition reduces computing of $\delta(s)$ to finding answer sets of logic programs.

Proposition 2. *[States compatible with partial knowledge state s]*
Let s be a simple knowledge state of an agent with action theory A. Then $\sigma \in \delta(s)$ iff $lp(\sigma)$ is an answer set of $lp(s) \cup D \cup lp(SL)$.

The following proposition provides the means for checking authorization status of action e given a simple knowledge state s of an agent whose transition diagram is given by an action theory A.

Proposition 3. *[Checking compliance given simple knowledge state]*
For any consistent authorization policy $\mathcal{P}$

- Event $\langle \sigma, e \rangle$ is strongly compliant with $\mathcal{P}$ for every $\sigma \in \delta(s)$ iff program $lp(\mathcal{P}, s) \cup D \cup lp(SL) \cup \{\leftarrow permitted(e)\}$ is inconsistent.
- If $\mathcal{P}$ is categorical then an event $\langle \sigma, e \rangle$ is weakly compliant with $\mathcal{P}$ for every $\sigma \in \delta(s)$ iff program $lp(\mathcal{P}, s) \cup D \cup lp(SL) \cup \{\leftarrow not \, \neg permitted(e)\}$ is inconsistent.
- Event $\langle \sigma, e \rangle$ is not compliant with $\mathcal{P}$ for every $\sigma \in \delta(s)$ iff program $lp(\mathcal{P}, s) \cup D \cup lp(SL) \cup \{\leftarrow \neg permitted(e)\}$ is inconsistent.

- If $\mathcal{P}$ is categorical then an event $\langle \sigma, e \rangle$ is not compliant with $\mathcal{P}$ for some $\sigma \in \delta(s)$ iff program $lp(\mathcal{P}, s) \cup D \cup lp(SL) \cup \{\leftarrow \text{ not } \neg permitted(e)\}$ is consistent.

Scenario 3: In many cases however the agent's knowledge base contains neither current physical nor current simple knowledge state of the system. Instead, as in the agent architecture from [6], it may maintain history, H_n, of the system's activity – *the complete or partial description of the initial state σ_0 together with a collection of actions $e_0, \ldots, e_{n-1}$ performed in the domain up to the current time-step n*[4]. We discuss how, given this information, the agent can check if he is permitted to execute a particular action e. First we will reify steps of history and define a new function, $lp(\mathcal{P}, I)$, obtained by adding step I as an additional (last) parameter to predicates from the definition of function lp. For instance,

$$lp(f = y, I) =_{def} val(f, y, I),$$

$$lp(e, I) =_{def} occurs(e, I),$$

etc. Similarly, for any history $H_n = \langle s, [e_0, \ldots, e_{n-1}] \rangle$

$$lp(\mathcal{P}, H_n) =_{def} lp(\mathcal{P}, I) \cup lp(s, 0) \cup lp(e_0, 0) \cup \ldots \cup lp(e_{i-1}, I - 1).$$

By D_0 we denote the collection of all statements of the form

$$val(f, y_1, 0) \text{ or } \ldots \text{ or } val(f, y_k, 0)$$

where f is a fluent and $\{y_1, \ldots, y_k\}$ is the set of all its possible values.

Finally, let $Check_1(H_n)$ and $Check_2(H_n)$ be pairs of rules

$$\neg strongly\_compliant \leftarrow occurs(E, I), \text{ not } permitted(E, I)$$

$$\leftarrow \text{ not } \neg strongly\_compliant$$

and

$$\neg weakly\_compliant \leftarrow occurs(E, I), \neg permitted(E, I)$$

$$\leftarrow \text{ not } \neg weakly\_compliant$$

respectively. Let us recall that a trajectory $\sigma_0, e_0, \ldots, e_{n-1}, \sigma_n$ of $\mathcal{T}$ is called a *model* of history $H_n = \langle s, [e_0, \ldots, e_{n-1}] \rangle$ if $s \subseteq \sigma_0$ [1]. Intuitively such models are possible past compatible with the agent's knowledge. Policy compliance of an agent with history H_n can be checked using the following proposition.

Proposition 4. *[Checking compliance given system's history]]*
For any categorical authorization policy $\mathcal{P}$ and history H_n of the system

- Every model of H_n is strongly compliant with $\mathcal{P}$ iff a program $lp(\mathcal{P}, H_n) \cup D \cup lp(A) \cup Check_1$ is inconsistent.
- Every model of H_n is weakly compliant with $\mathcal{P}$ iff a program $lp(\mathcal{P}, H_n) \cup D \cup lp(A) \cup Check_2$ is inconsistent.

---

[4] In addition history can contain observations of values of particular fluents at any step $0 \leq i \leq n$.

3   Obligation Policy

Now we are ready to consider obligation policies. As before we assume a fixed dynamic system described by an agent, $\mathcal{A}$, and a transition diagram $\mathcal{T}$ over signature Σ, and define syntax and semantics of the policy language, $\mathcal{AOPL}(\Sigma)$, allowing specification of authorization and obligation policies.

3.1   Syntax

The signature of the new language, $\mathcal{AOPL}(\Sigma)$, is obtained from the signature of $\mathcal{APL}(\Sigma)$ by adding a new predicate symbol $obl(E)$ where E is an elementary action of $\mathcal{A}$ or negation of such an action. Intuitively if $obl(e)$ is true in a state σ of a dynamic system $\langle \mathcal{A}, \mathcal{T} \rangle$ then agent $\mathcal{A}$ has an obligation of executing e in this state; if instead $obl(\neg e)$ holds in σ then $\mathcal{A}$ is obligated to refrain from executing this action.

Definition 7. *[Obligation Policy]*
Obligation policy statements of $\mathcal{AOPL}(\Sigma)$ are expressions of the form

$$obl(happening) \text{ if } cond \tag{7}$$

$$\neg obl(happening) \text{ if } cond \tag{8}$$

$$d : \text{normally } obl(happening) \text{ if } cond \tag{9}$$

$$d : \text{normally } \neg obl(happening) \text{ if } cond \tag{10}$$

$$prefer(d_1, d_2) \tag{11}$$

where *happening* stands for an elementary action of $\mathcal{A}$ or its negation and *cond* is a collection of atoms of $\mathcal{AOPL}(\Sigma)$ not containing atoms formed by *prefer*. The form of obligation rules is very similar to that of authorization rules. Syntactically permissions are replaced by obligations and actions by *happenings* – actions or their negations.

Example 3. [Student's Responsibilities]

Let us consider the following sentence from the list of student's responsibilities "Students are expected not to miss classes, to do their homework independently and to submit it on time". To represent this information we start with introducing sorts, *student, class, meeting* and *assignment* of the corresponding signature Σ. Students could be represented by names or social security numbers and classes by the corresponding course numbers (e.g. *cs4101*). Meetings and assignments will be represented by records $m(class, pos\_int)$ and $a(class, pos\_int)$. For instance, $m(cs4101, 3)$ refers to the third meeting of the class *cs4101* while $a(cs4101, 5)$ refers to the fifth assignment given to students of this class. Signature Σ will also contain fluents

$enrolled(student, class)$,
$due\_date(meeting, assignment)$.

For instance Mary may be enrolled in $cs4101$ ($enrolled(Mary, cs4101)$) and the due date for the third assignment in this class may be the seventh class meeting, $due\_date(m(cs4101, 7), a(cs4101, 3)))$.

We will also need the following actions

$attend(student, meeting)$,
$submit(student, assignment, meeting)$,
$accept\_unauthorized\_help(student)$.

Now we need to think about our understanding of the obligation policy rules from our example. Are they strict or defeasible? The informal specification does not say and hence the decision is left to us. One can easily imagine the situation when the first rule can be canceled for some particular student and/or meeting by the introduction of some exceptional circumstances. A person can be released from the first obligation because of illness, family emergencies, etc. Instead of putting these exceptions in the condition of the first rule we adopt a more elaboration tolerant approach and view the rule as defeasible. This leads us to the following formal rule:

$d_1(S, C, N)$: normally $obl(attend(S, m(C, N)))$ if $enrolled(S, C)$.

In the properly extended signature an exception to this default can be represented as follows

$\neg obl(attend(S, M))$ if $family\_emergency(S, M)$.

where $family\_emergency(S, M)$ holds if student S has family emergency at the time of meeting M. Similarly for other exceptions. The second rule basically tells the students not to cheat. Since cheating is never justified we make this a strict obligation policy rule.

$obl(\neg accept\_unauthorized\_help(S))$.

The knowledge base we are building may be extended by possible exceptions to the third rule. Hence we make it defeasible: Normally a student S should submit its assignment N_1 for class C at the N_2'th meeting of class C if S is enrolled in C and N_2 is the deadline for the assignment.

$d_2(S, C, N_1, N_2)$: normally $obl(submit(S, a(C, N_1), m(C, N_2))$ if
$\qquad\qquad\qquad enrolled(S, C)$,
$\qquad\qquad\qquad due\_date(m(C, N_2), a(C, N_1)))$.

As expected preference between defeasible obligation policies will be used when policies lead to contradictory obligations. For instance a religious obligation of abstaining from work during important religious holidays can contradict the obligation of attending classes. Some schools allow such holidays to be a sufficient excuse for not attending classes, while others do not. In a simplified form the new obligation can be expressed as

$d_3(S, M)$: normally $obl(\neg attend(S, M))$ if $religious\_holiday(M)$.

where $religious\_holiday(M)$ holds if some important religious holiday occurs at the same day as the meeting M. If the designer of our knowledge base believes that religious obligations overrule secular once he can expand the base by

$$prefer(d_3(S, m(C, N)), d_1(S, C, N)).$$

The opposite preference can be given by a more secularly minded designer. Of course if no preference is given the user of the base may have two different contradictory obligations. Such a policy however will be ambiguous and will allow the user freedom to decide if one or both obligations should be ignored and accept the corresponding rewards and punishments. As with authorization policies the designer should attempt to avoid ambiguity and limit himself to categorical policies.

3.2   Semantics

To define the semantics of $\mathcal{AOPL}(\Sigma)$ we expand the function $\mathcal{P}(\sigma)$ from the definition of the semantics of authorization policy of $\mathcal{APL}(\Sigma)$. In addition to permissions and denials the function will now return *obligations* the agent of a dynamic system has in a state σ. As expected this can be done by expanding logical counterpart lp defined above by mapping statements of the form (7) and (8) to logic programming rules

$$obl(h) \leftarrow lp(cond)$$

$$\neg obl(h) \leftarrow lp(cond).$$

Statements (9) and (10) will be mapped into rules

$$obl(h) \leftarrow lp(cond).$$
$$\qquad not\ ab(d),$$
$$\qquad not\ \neg obl(h).$$

$$\neg obl(h) \leftarrow lp(cond).$$
$$\qquad not\ ab(d),$$
$$\qquad not\ obl(h).$$

The notions of consistency and categoricity of a policy of a new language remains unchanged. The function $\mathcal{P}(\sigma)$ is expanded as follows

Definition 8. *[$\mathcal{P}(\sigma)$ for obligations]*
Let $\mathcal{P}$ be a consistent policy for $\langle \mathcal{A}, \mathcal{T} \rangle$. Then $obl(h) \in \mathcal{P}(\sigma)$ iff a logic program $lp(\mathcal{P}, \sigma)$ entails $obl(h)$.

Let $\mathcal{P}_a$ be a policy obtained from $\mathcal{P}$ by dropping its obligation rules; $\mathcal{P}_o$ is obtained from $\mathcal{P}$ by dropping its authorization rules. Obviously $\mathcal{P} = \mathcal{P}_a \cup \mathcal{P}_o$. We say that $\mathcal{P}_a$ is an authorization policy *induced* by $\mathcal{P}$. Similarly for $\mathcal{P}_o$.

Definition 9. *[Policy compliance]*
An event $\langle \sigma, a \rangle$ is *compliant* with obligation policy $\mathcal{P}$ if

1. For every $obl(e) \in \mathcal{P}(\sigma)$ we have that $e \in a$, and
2. For every $obl(\neg e) \in \mathcal{P}(\sigma)$ we have that $e \notin a$.

An event $\langle \sigma, a \rangle$ is *strongly (weakly) compliant* with arbitrary policy $\mathcal{P}$ from $\mathcal{AOPL}(\Sigma)$ if it is strongly (weakly) compliant with the authorization policy induced by $\mathcal{P}$ and with the obligation policy induced by $\mathcal{P}$.

Compliance of events with respect to an obligation policy can be checked by ASP methods similar to those used in Section 2.3. Space limitations preclude discussing the corresponding details.

4   Related Work

To illustrate the relationship between our work and more traditional methods for representing and reasoning with policies let us consider Role-based Access Control (RBAC) – a method used in computer system security for restricting system access to authorized users. The signature of a typical policy of RBAC contains object constants for users (called subjects), their roles (e.g. job functions or titles), operations (e.g. read or write) and resources (e.g. files or disk or databases) to which these operations can be applied. There are relations $plays\_role(S, R)$ – a user S plays a role R, $has\_permission(R, O, D)$ – every user playing a role R has the permission to apply operation O to resource D, and $R_1 \leq R_2$ - R_1 inherits permissions from R_2. There is also an action $execute(S, O, D)$ – user S executes operation O on resource D. States of the system should satisfy a constraint

$$has\_permission(R_1, P) \ \ \text{if} \ \ has\_permission(R_2, P),$$
$$R_1 \leq R_2.$$

A typical permission policy has the form:

$$permitted(execute(S, O, D)) \ \ \text{if} \ \ plays\_role(S, R),$$
$$has\_permission(R, O, D).$$

Hence the RBAC approach seems to be a very narrow special case of the methodology for specifying and reasoning about policies suggested in this paper. Note that S can get access to the system (and therefore change its state) only if he is granted permission to do so. Normally the user will not be able to record his actions in the system's log. This will be done by an administrator with his own set of policies not expressible in the language of RBAC. Our method allows natural specification and reasoning with combined, administrative and access control policies. Authorization policies are typically defined as inputs to access control systems. Most access control system more or less follow the operational model behind the XML access control language XACML [7]: given the current state of a system there is a (some times partial) function encoding the policy that maps the state and an operation on the system into a decision as to whether the operation is permitted. Most formal modeling work and analysis of policies make the simplified assumption that policies depend on a subset of the state that does not change over time or if it changes the changes are only made by an administrator of the access control system and they are ignored. For example a system implementing Access Control Lists (ACL) fixes a list of subjects for each operation or a set of operations and if the subject requesting permission to execute the operation is in the list the operation is permitted.[5] Only administrators are allowed to make changes to the ACL. In RBAC only administrators can define new roles and assign permissions to roles. More sophisticated associations can be made between subjects and permissions if one can express the associations as predicates over the state. This is what is expressed operationally with a function in the definition of XACML policies. Still these predicates are on parts of the state that don't change over time (i.e., they change only by administrative changes of the system). There is a large body of work in policy analysis and policy modeling but mostly in these static situations. Barker [8] uses stratified logic programs to describe RBAC-like systems. In a series of papers Jojadia and his co-authors [9,10,11,12] developed the Flexible Authorization Framework (FAF) using stratified logic programs. FAF is a very sophisticated extension of RBAC that incorporates positive and negative authorizations as well as methods to express different conflict resolution *policies*, all in the context of access control to relational databases. They handle some state dynamics but it is limited to their database system model. Stoller et al. [13] use planning techniques to characterize the complexity and solve problems over administrative operations in RBAC systems. Kolovski et al. [14] use description logic to formalize and analyze XACML policies including administrative policies. Halpern and Weissman use a subset of first order logic to specified policies (without the system) and do analysis [15].

The closest to our work are the models presented in [16] and [17]. [16] is mostly concerned with obligations. The authors, as we do, present a model for obligations and authorizations that incorporates the model of a system where the policies are supposed to be enforced. Although the authors claim that minimal changes will accommodate a more general model, obligations are expressed as a condition to obtain authorization to access to a resource. In our case obligations are separate from authorizations and we can represent mutual dependencies between obligations and authorizations. Their model is agnostic to how system transitions and policies are represented. Systems are considered to be a set of state traces (sequences) and obligations abstract functions constraining that set. We have shown in the paper that by choosing an action theory described in an $\mathcal{A}$-like language, we can check system properties using ASP logic programs. Theirs is a theoretical framework to define obligations, ours is more a specification framework where we would like to facilitate the definition of policies and check system properties. Craven et al.[17] also model authorizations, obligations and the system together. They use the event calculus [18] for system description and ASP logic programs to represent the policies. Their main goal is to prove properties of the policies, not of the systems. They use abductive constraint logic programming as proof framework [19]. Finally, [20] provides a model of non-monotonic authorization based on a paraconsistent variant of extended logic programs ASP semantics. Despite multiple differences this can be viewed as a precursor of our work. One fundamental difference between all the work referenced above (except

---

[5] This is call a white list. There is a complementary implementation (black list) in which only subjects not in the list are permitted to execute the operation.

that in [20]) and ours is the presence of defeasible policies. Policies are assumed to be strict limiting the modeling of complex scenarios.

5   Conclusion

We presented a simple and general language, $\mathcal{AOPL}(\Sigma)$, for specifying authorization and obligation policies of an intelligent agent acting in a changing environment and presented several ASP based algorithms for checking compliance of an event with a policy specified in this language. The language has the following distinctive features:

- Our approach allows to represent and reason about both, static and dynamic domains.
- The ability to represent defeasible policies improves elaboration tolerance of the policies and flexibility of the agent's behavior.
- Policy specifications and algorithms can be naturally incorporated into various software systems including agents with high degree of autonomy, access control and other security system, etc. They can be used by an agent for finding authorized sequences of actions to achieve their goals and to fulfill their obligations, as well as by systems monitoring such a compliance.
- The compliance checking methods are based on theory of action and change and on answer set programming. This allows the use of general reasoning techniques and systems (answer set solvers) and simplifies the correctness proofs of the corresponding algorithms.

in the full version of this paper we will test the expressibility of our language on the wide variety of policies and refine and expand the ASP based methods for checking event compliance and other policy related reasoning tasks.

Acknowledgments. We would like to thank Vladimir Lifschitz for drawing our attention to work by T. Woo and S. Lam.

References

1. Baral, C.: Knowledge Representation, Reasoning and Declarative Problem Solving. Cambridge University Press, Cambridge (2003)
2. Gelfond, M., Lifschitz, V.: The stable model semantics for logic programming. In: Proceedings of ICLP 1988, pp. 1070–1080 (1988)
3. Bandara, A., Calo, S., Lobo, J., Lupu, E., Russo, A., Sloman, M.: Toward a formal characterization of policy specification and analysis. In: Electronic Proceedings of the Annual Conference of ITA, ACITA (2007)
4. Baral, C., Gelfond, M.: Reasoning agents in dynamic domains. In: Minker, J. (ed.) Logic-Based Artificial Intelligence, pp. 257–279. Kluwer Academic, Dordrecht (2000)
5. Turner, H.: Representing actions in logic programs and default theories: A situation calculus approach. J. Log. Program. 31(1-3), 245–298 (1997)

6. Balduccini, M., Gelfond, M.: The aaa architecture: An overview. In: AAAI Spring Symposium 2008 on Architectures for Intelligent Theory-Based Agents, AITA 2008 (2008)
7. OASIS Standard: extensible access control markup language (XACML) v2.0 (2005)
8. Barker, S.: Security policy specification in logic. In: Proc. of Int. Conf. on Artificial Intelligence, pp. 143–148 (June 2000)
9. Jajodia, S., Samarati, P., Subrahmanian, V., Bertino, E.: A unified framework for enforcing multiple access control policies. In: Proc. of the ACM Int. SIGMOD Conf. on Management of Data (May 1997)
10. Jajodia, S., Samarati, P., Subrahmanian, V.: A logical language for expressing authorizations. In: Proc. of the IEEE Symposium on Security and Privacy, p. 31 (1997)
11. Jajodia, S., Samarati, P., Sapino, M.L., Subrahmanian, V.S.: Flexible support for multiple access control policies. ACM Trans. Database Syst. 26(2), 214–260 (2001)
12. Chen, S., Wijesekera, D., Jajodia, S.: Incorporating dynamic constraints in the flexible authorization framework. In: Samarati, P., Ryan, P.Y.A., Gollmann, D., Molva, R. (eds.) ESORICS 2004. LNCS, vol. 3193, pp. 1–16. Springer, Heidelberg (2004)
13. Stoller, S.D., Yang, P., Ramakrishnan, C.R., Gofman, M.I.: Efficient policy analysis for administrative role based access control. In: ACM Conference on Computer and Communications Security, pp. 445–455 (2007)
14. Kolovski, V., Hendler, J.A., Parsia, B.: Analyzing web access control policies. In: WWW, pp. 677–686 (2007)
15. Halpern, J.Y., Weissman, V.: Using first-order logic to reason about policies. In: Proc. of 16th IEEE Computer Security Foundations Workshop, pp. 251–265 (2003)
16. Dougherty, D.J., Fisler, K., Krishnamurthi, S.: Obligations and their interaction with programs. In: Biskup, J., López, J. (eds.) ESORICS 2007. LNCS, vol. 4734, pp. 375–389. Springer, Heidelberg (2007)
17. Craven, R., Lobo, J., Lupu, E., Ma, J., Russo, A., Sloman, M., Bandara, A.: A formal framework for policy analysis. Technical Report, Department of Computing, Imperial College, London (2008)
18. Kowalski, R., Sergot, M.: A logic-based calculus of events. New Generation Computing 4, 67–95 (1986)
19. Kakas, A.C., Michael, A., Mourlas, C.: ACLP: Abductive constraint logic programming. J. Log. Program. 44(1-3), 129–177 (2000)
20. Woo, T.Y.C., Lam, S.S.: Authorizations in distributed systems: A new approach. Journal of Computer Security 2(2-3), 107–136 (1993)

Twelve Definitions of a Stable Model

Vladimir Lifschitz

Department of Computer Sciences, University of Texas at Austin, USA
vl@cs.utexas.edu

Abstract. This is a review of some of the definitions of the concept of a stable model that have been proposed in the literature. These definitions are equivalent to each other, at least when applied to traditional Prolog-style programs, but there are reasons why each of them is valuable and interesting. A new characterization of stable models can suggest an alternative picture of the intuitive meaning of logic programs; or it can lead to new algorithms for generating stable models; or it can work better than others when we turn to generalizations of the traditional syntax that are important from the perspective of answer set programming; or it can be more convenient for use in proofs; or it can be interesting simply because it demonstrates a relationship between seemingly unrelated ideas.

1 Introduction

This is a review of some of the definitions, or characterizations, of the concept of a stable model that have been proposed in the literature. These definitions are equivalent to each other when applied to "traditional rules"—with an atom in the head and a list of atoms, some possibly preceded with the negation as failure symbol, in the body:

$$A_0 \leftarrow A_1, \ldots, A_m, not\ A_{m+1}, not\ A_n. \tag{1}$$

But there are reasons why each of them is valuable and interesting. A new characterization of stable models can suggest an alternative picture of the intuitive meaning of logic programs; or it can lead to new algorithms for generating stable models; or it can work better when we turn to generalizations of the traditional syntax that are important from the perspective of answer set programming (ASP); or it can be more convenient for use in proofs, such as proofs of correctness of ASP programs; or, quite simply, it can intellectually excite us by demonstrating a relationship between seemingly unrelated ideas.

We concentrate here primarily on programs consisting of finitely many rules of type (1), although generalizations of this syntactic form are mentioned several times in the second half of the paper. Some work on the stable model semantics (for instance, [13], [18], [33], [2]) is not discussed here simply because it is about extending, rather than modifying, the definitions proposed earlier; this kind of work does not tell us much new about stable models of traditional programs.

The paper begins with comments on the relevant work that had preceded the invention of stable models—on the semantics of logic programming (Section 2) and on formal nomonotonic reasoning (Section 3). Early contributions

M. Garcia de la Banda and E. Pontelli (Eds.): ICLP 2008, LNCS 5366, pp. 37–51, 2008.

that can be seen as characterizations of the class of stable models in terms of nonmonotonic logic are discussed in Section 4. Then we review the definition of stable models in terms of reducts (Section 5) and turn to its characterizations in terms of unfounded sets and loop formulas (Section 6). After that, we talk about three definitions of a stable model that use translations into classical logic (Sections 7 and 8) and about the relation between stable models and equilibrium logic (Section 9).

In recent years, two interesting modifications of the definition of the reduct were introduced (Section 10). And we learned that a simple change in the definition of circumscription can give a characterization of stable models (Section 11).

2   Minimal Models, Completion, and Stratified Programs

2.1   Minimal Models vs. Completion

According to [41], a logic program without negation represents the least (and so, the only minimal) Herbrand model of the corresponding set of Horn clauses. On the other hand, according to [4], a logic program represents a certain set of first-order formulas, called the program's completion.

These two ideas are closely related to each other, but not equivalent. Take, for instance, the program

$$p(a, b). \\ p(X, Y) \leftarrow p(Y, X). \tag{2}$$

The minimal Herbrand model

$$\{p(a, b), p(b, a)\}$$

of this program satisfies the program's completion

$$\forall XY (p(X, Y) \leftrightarrow ((X = a \wedge Y = b) \vee p(Y, X))) \wedge a \neq b.$$

But there also other Herbrand interpretations satisfying the program's completion—for instance, one that makes p identically true.

Another example of this kind, important for applications of logic programming, is given by the recursive definition of transitive closure:

$$q(X, Y) \leftarrow p(X, Y). \\ q(X, Z) \leftarrow q(X, Y), q(Y, Z). \tag{3}$$

The completion of the union of this program with a definition of p has, in many cases, unintended models, in which q is weaker than the transitive closure of p that we want to define.

Should we say then that Herbrand minimal models provide a better semantics for logic programming than program completion? Yes and no. The concept of completion has a fundamental advantage: it is applicable to programs with negation. Such a program, viewed as a set of clauses, usually has several minimal Herbrand models, and some of them may not satisfy the program's completion. Such "bad" models reflect neither the intended meaning of the program nor the behavior of Prolog. For instance, the program

$$p(a). \quad p(b). \quad q(a).$$
$$r(X) \leftarrow p(X), not \ q(X). \tag{4}$$

has two minimal Herbrand models:

$$\{p(a), p(b), q(a), r(b)\} \tag{5}$$

("good") and

$$\{p(a), p(b), q(a), q(b)\} \tag{6}$$

("bad"). The completion of (4)

$$\forall X (p(X) \leftrightarrow (X = a \lor X = b)) \land \forall X (q(X) \leftrightarrow X = a)$$
$$\land \forall X (r(X) \leftrightarrow (p(X) \land \neg q(X))) \land a \neq b$$

characterizes the good model.

2.2   The Challenge

In the 1980s, the main challenge in the study of the semantics of logic programming was to invent a semantics that

- in application to a program without negation, such as (2), describes the minimal Herbrand model,
- in the presence of negation, as in example (4), selects a "good" minimal model satisfying the program's completion.

Such a semantics was proposed in two papers presented at the 1986 Workshop on Foundations of Deductive Databases and Logic Programming [1], [44]. That approach was not without defects, however. First, it is limited to programs in which recursion and negation "don't mix." Such programs are called stratified. Unfortunately, some useful Prolog programs do not satisfy this condition. For instance, we can say that a position in a two-person game is winning if there exists a move from it to a non-winning position (cf. [40]). This rule is not stratified: it recursively defines winning in terms of non-winning. A really good semantics should be applicable to rules like this.

Second, the definition of the semantics of stratified programs is somewhat complicated. It is based on the concept of the iterated least fixpoint of a program, and to prove the soundness of this definition one needs to show that this fixpoint doesn't depend on the choice of a stratification. A really good semantics should be a little easier to define.

The stable model semantics, as well as the well-founded semantics [42,43], can be seen as an attempt to generalize and simplify the iterated fixpoint semantics of stratified programs.

3   Nonmonotonic Reasoning

Many events in the history of research on stable models can be only understood if we think of it as part of a broader research effort—the investigation of nonmonotonic reasoning. Three theories of nonmonotonic reasoning are particularly relevant.

3.1   Circumscription

Circumscription [28,28,29] is a syntactic transformation that turns a first-order sentence F into the conjunction of F with another formula, which expresses a minimality condition (the exact form of that condition depends on the "circumscription policy"). This additional conjunctive term involves second-order quantifiers.

Circumscription generalizes the concept of a minimal model from [41]. The iterated fixpoint semantics of stratified programs can be characterized in terms of circumscription also [20]. On the other hand, circumscription is similar to program completion in the sense that both are syntactic transformations that make a formula stronger. The relationship between circumscription and program completion was investigated in [37].

3.2   Default Logic

A default theory in the sense of [36] is characterized by a set W of "axioms"—first-order sentences, and a set D of "defaults"—expressions of the form

$$\frac{F \ : \ \mathsf{M}\,G_1, \ldots, \mathsf{M}\,G_n}{H}, \tag{7}$$

where $F, G_1, \ldots, G_n, H$ are first-order formulas. The letter M, according to Reiter, is to be read as "it is consistent to assume." Intuitively, default (7) is similar to the inference rule allowing us to derive the conclusion H from the premise F, except that the applicability of this rule is limited by the justifications $G_1, \ldots, G_n$; deriving H is allowed only if each of the justifications can be "consistently assumed."

This informal description of the meaning of a default is circular: to decide which formulas can be derived using one of the defaults from D we need to know whether the justifications of that default are consistent with the formulas that can be derived from W using the inference rules of classical logic and the defaults from D—including the default that we are trying to understand! But Reiter was able to turn his intuition about M into a precise semantics. His theory of defaults tells us under what conditions a set E of sentences is an "extension" for the default theory with axioms W and defaults D.

In Section 4 we will see that one of the earliest incarnations of the stable model semantics was based on treating rules as defaults in the sense of Reiter.

3.3   Autoepistemic Logic

According to [32], autoepistemic logic "is intended to model the beliefs of an agent reflecting upon his own beliefs." The definition of propositional autoepistemic logic builds on the ideas of [30] and [31].

Formulas of this logic are constructed from atoms using propositional connectives and the modal operator L ("is believed"). Its semantics specifies, for any set A of formulas ("axioms"), which sets of formulas are considered "stable expansions" of A. Intuitively, Moore explains, the stable expansions of A are "the possible sets of beliefs that a rational agent might hold, given A as his premises."

In Section 4 we will see that one of the earliest incarnations of the stable model semantics was based on treating rules as autoepistemic axioms in the sense of Moore. The term "stable model" is historically related to "stable expansions" of autoepistemic logic.

3.4   Relations between Nonmonotonic Formalisms

The intuitions underlying circumscription, default logic, and autoepistemic logic are different from each other, but related. For instance, circumscribing (that is, minimizing the extent of) a predicate p is somewhat similar to adopting the default

$$\frac{\text{true} \; : \; \mathsf{M} \, \neg p(X)}{\neg p(X)}$$

(if it is consistent to assume that X does not have the property p, conclude that it doesn't). On the other hand, Moore observes that "a formula is consistent if its negation is not believed"; accordingly, Reiter's M is somewhat similar to the combination $\neg\mathsf{L}\neg$ in autoepistemic logic, and default (7), in propositional case, is somewhat similar to the autoepistemic formula

$$F \wedge \neg\mathsf{L}\neg G_1 \wedge \cdots \wedge \neg\mathsf{L}\neg G_n \to H.$$

However, the task of finding precise and general relationships between these three formalisms turned out to be difficult. Discussing technical work on that topic is beyond the scope of this paper.

4   Definitions A and B, in Terms of Translations into Nonmonotonic Logic

The idea of [14] is to think of the expression *not A* in a logic program as synonymous with the autoepistemic formula $\neg\mathsf{L}A$ ("A is not believed"). Since autoepistemic logic is propositional, the program needs to be grounded before this transformation is applied. After grounding, each rule (1) is rewritten as a formula:

$$A_1 \wedge \cdots \wedge A_m \wedge \neg A_{m+1} \wedge \cdots \wedge \neg A_n \to A_0, \tag{8}$$

and then L inserted after each negation. For instance, to explain the meaning of program (4), we take the result of its grounding

$$\begin{aligned}
&p(a). \quad p(b). \quad q(a). \\
&r(a) \leftarrow p(a), not\; q(a). \\
&r(b) \leftarrow p(b), not\; q(b).
\end{aligned} \tag{9}$$

and turn it into a collection of formulas:

$$p(a), \quad p(b), \quad q(a),$$
$$p(a) \wedge \neg \mathsf{L}\, q(a) \rightarrow r(a),$$
$$p(b) \wedge \neg \mathsf{L}\, q(b) \rightarrow r(b).$$

The autoepistemic theory with these axioms has a unique stable expansion, and the atoms from that stable expansion form the intended model (5) of the program.

This epistemic interpretation of logic programs—what we will call *Definition A*—is more general than the iterated fixpoint semantics, and it is much simpler. One other feature of Definition A that makes it attractive is the simplicity of the underlying intuition: negation as failure expresses the absence of belief.

The "default logic semantics" proposed in [3] is translational as well; it interprets logic programs as default theories. The head A_0 of a rule (1) turns into the conclusion of the default, the conjunction $A_1 \wedge \cdots \wedge A_m$ of the positive members of the body becomes the premise, and each negative member *not* A_i turns into the justification $\mathsf{M}\neg A_i$ ("it is consistent to assume $\neg A_i$"). For instance, the last rule of program (4) corresponds to the default

$$\frac{p(X) \;:\; \mathsf{M}\,\neg q(X)}{r(X)}. \tag{10}$$

There is no need for grounding, because defaults are allowed to contain variables. This difference between the two translations is not essential though, because Reiter's semantics of defaults treats a default with variables as the set of its ground instances. Grounding is simply "hidden" in the semantics of default logic.

This *Definition B* of the stable model semantics stresses an analogy between rules in logic programming and inference rules in logic. Like Definition A, it has an epistemic flavor, because of the relationship between the "consistency operator" M in defaults and the autoepistemic "belief operator" L (Section 3.4).

The equivalence between these two approaches to semantics of traditional programs follows from the fact that each of them is equivalent to Definition C of a stable model reviewed in the next section. This was established in [12] for the autoepistemic semantics and in [26] for the default logic approach.

5   Definition C, in Terms of the Reduct

Definitions A and B are easy to understand—assuming that one is familiar with formal nonmonotonic reasoning. Can we make these definitions direct and avoid explicit references to autoepistemic logic and default logic?

This question has led to the most widely used definition of the stable model semantics, *Definition C* [12]. The *reduct* of a program Π relative to a set M of atoms is obtained from Π by grounding followed by

(i) dropping each rule (1) containing a term *not* A_i with $A_i \in M$, and
(ii) dropping the negative parts *not* $A_{m+1}, \ldots,$ *not* A_n from the bodies of the remaining rules.

We say that M is a *stable model* of Π if the minimal model of (the set of clauses corresponding to the rules of) the reduct of Π with respect to X equals X. For instance, the reduct of program (4) relative to (5) is

$$p(a). \quad p(b). \quad q(a).$$
$$r(b) \leftarrow p(b). \tag{11}$$

The minimal model of this program is the set (5) that we started with; consequently, that set is a stable model of (4).

Definition C was independently invented in [10].

6   Definitions D and E, in Terms of Unfounded Sets and Loop Formulas

According to [39], stable models can be characterized in terms of the concept of an unfounded set, which was introduced in [42] as part of the definition of the well-founded semantics. Namely, a set M of atoms is a stable model of a (grounded) program Π iff

(i) M satisfies Π,[1] and
(ii) no nonempty subset of M is unfounded for Π with respect to M.[2]

According to [17], this *Definition D* can be refined using the concept of a *loop*, introduced many years later by [23]. If we require, in condition (i), that M satisfy the *completion* of the program, rather than the program itself, then it will be possible to relax condition (ii) and require only that no *loop* contained in M be unfounded; there will be no need then to refer to arbitrary nonempty subsets in that condition.

In [23] loops are used in a different way. They associated with every loop X of Π a certain propositional formula, called the *loop formula* for X. According to their *Definition E*, M is a stable model of Π iff M satisfies the completion of Π conjoined with the loop formulas for all loops of Π.

The invention of loop formulas has led to the creation of systems for generating stable models that use SAT solvers for search ("SAT-based answer set programming"). Several systems of this kind performed well in a recent ASP system competition [11].

---

[1] That is, M satisfies the propositional formulas (8) corresponding to the rules of Π.
[2] To be precise, unfoundedness is defined with respect to a partial interpretation, not a set of atoms. But we are only interested here in the special case when the partial interpretation is complete, and assume that complete interpretations are represented by sets of atoms in the usual way.

7   Definition F, in Terms of Circumscription

We saw in Section 4 that a logic program can be viewed as shorthand for an autoepistemic theory or a default theory. The characterization of stable models described in [25, Section 3.4.1] relates logic programs to the third nonmonotonic formalism reviewed above, circumscription. Like Definitions A and B, it is based on a translation, but the output of that translation is not simply a circumscription formula; it involves also some additional conjunctive terms.

The first step of that translation consists in replacing the occurrences of each predicate symbol p in the negative parts $\neg A_{m+1} \wedge \cdots \wedge \neg A_n$ of the formulas (8) corresponding to the rules of the program with a new symbol p' and forming the conjunction of the universal closures of the resulting formulas. The sentence obtained in this way is denoted by $C(\Pi)$. For instance, if Π is (4) then $C(\Pi)$ is

$$p(a) \wedge p(b) \wedge q(a) \wedge \forall X (p(X) \wedge \neg q'(X) \rightarrow r(X)).$$

The translation of Π is a conjunction of two sentences: the circumscription of the old (non-primed) predicates in $C(\Pi)$ and the formulas asserting, for each of the new predicates, that it is equivalent to the corresponding old predicate. For instance, the translation of (4) is

$$\text{CIRC}[C(\Pi)] \wedge \forall X (q'(X) \leftrightarrow q(X)); \tag{12}$$

the circumscription operator CIRC is understood here as the minimization of the extents of p, q, r.

The stable models of Π can be characterized as the Herbrand interpretations satisfying the translation of Π, with the new (primed) predicates removed from them ("forgotten").

An interesting feature of this *Definition F* is that, unlike Definitions A–E, it does not involve grounding. We can ask what non-Herbrand models of the translation of a logic program look like. Can it be convenient in some cases to represent possible states of affairs by such "non-Herbrand stable models" of a logic program? A non-Herbrand model may include an object that is different from the values of all ground terms, or there may be several ground terms having the same value in it; can this be sometimes useful?

We will return to the relationship between stable models and circumscription in Section 11.

8   Definitions G and H, in Terms of Tightening and the Situation Calculus

We will talk now about two characterizations of stable models that are based, like Definition F, on translations into classical logic that use auxiliary predicates.

For a class of logic programs called tight, stable models are identical to Herbrand models of the program's completion [6]. (Programs (2) and (3), used above to illustrate peculiarities of the completion semantics, are not tight.) *Definition G*

[45] is based on a process of "tightening" that makes an arbitrary traditional program tight. This process uses two auxiliary symbols: the object constant 0 and the unary function constant s ("successor"). Besides, the tightened program uses auxiliary predicates with an additional numeric argument. Intuitively, $p(X, N)$ expresses that there exists a sequence of N "applications" of rules of the program that "establishes" $p(X)$. The stable models of a program are described then as Herbrand models of the completion of the result of its tightening, with the auxiliary symbols "forgotten."

We will not reproduce here the definition of tightening, but here is an example: the result of tightening program (4) is

$$p(a, s(N)). \quad p(b, s(N)). \quad q(a, s(N)).$$
$$r(X, s(N)) \leftarrow p(X, N), not\ q(X).$$
$$p(X) \leftarrow p(X, N).$$
$$q(X) \leftarrow q(X, N).$$
$$r(X) \leftarrow r(X, N).$$

Rules in line 1 tell us that $p(a)$ can be established in any number of steps that is greater than 0; similarly for $p(b)$ and $q(a)$. According to line 2, $r(X)$ can be established in $N + 1$ steps if $p(X)$ can be established in N steps and $q(X)$ cannot be established at all (note that an occurrence of a predicate does not get an additional numeric argument if it is negated). Finally, an atom holds if it can be established by some number N of rule applications.

Definition H [21] treats a rule in a logic program as an abbreviated description of the effect of an action—the action of "applying" that rule—in the situation calculus.[3] For instance, if the action corresponding to the last rule of (4) is denoted by $lastrule(X)$ then that rule can be viewed as shorthand for the situation calculus formula

$$p(X, S) \wedge \neg \exists S(q(X, S)) \to r(X, do(lastrule(X), S))$$

(if $p(X)$ holds in situation S and $q(X)$ does not hold in any situation then $r(X)$ holds after executing action $lastrule(X)$ in situation S).

In this approach to stable models, the situation calculus function *do* plays the same role as adding 1 to N in Wallace's theory. Instead of program completion, Lin and Reiter use the process of turning effect axioms into successor state axioms, which is standard in applications of the situation calculus.

9   Definition I, in Terms of Equilibrium Logic

The logic of here-and-there, going back to the early days of modern logic [15], is a modification of classical propositional logic in which propositional interpretations in the usual sense—assignments, or sets of atoms—are replaced by pairs (X, Y)

---

[3] See [38] for a detailed description of the situation calculus [27] as developed by the Toronto school.

of sets of atoms such that $X \subseteq Y$. (We think of X as the set of atoms that are true "here", and Y as the set of the atoms that are true "there.") The semantics of this logic defines when (X, Y) *satisfies* a formula F.

In [35], the logic of here-and-there was used as a starting point for defining a nonmonotonic logic closely related to stable models. According to that paper, a pair (Y, Y) is an *equilibrium model* of a propositional formula F if F is satisfied in the logic of here-and-there by (Y, Y) but is not satisfied by (X, Y) for any proper subset X of Y. A set M of atoms is a stable model of a program Π iff (M, M) is an equilibrium model of the set of propositional formulas (8) corresponding to the grounded rules of Π.

This *Definition I* is important for two reasons. First, it suggests a way to extend the concept of a stable model from traditional rules—formulas of form (1)—to arbitrary propositional formulas: we can say that M is a stable model of a propositional formula F if (M, M) is an equilibrium model of F. This is valuable from the perspective of answer set programming, because many "nonstandard" constructs commonly used in ASP programs, such as choice rules and weight constraints, can be viewed as abbreviations for propositional formulas [7]. Second, Definition I is a key to the theorem about the relationship between the concept of strong equivalence and the logic of here-and-there [19].

10   Definitions J and K, in Terms of Modified Reducts

In [5] the definition of the reduct reproduced in Section 5 is modified by including the positive members of the body, along with negative members, in the description of step (i), and by removing step (ii) altogeher. In other words, in the modified process of constructing the reduct relative to M we delete from the program all rules (1) containing in their bodies a term A_i such that $A_i \notin M$ or a term *not* A_i such that $A_i \in M$; the other rules of the program remain unchanged. For instance, the modified reduct of program (4) relative to (5) is

$$p(a). \quad p(b). \quad q(a).$$
$$r(b) \leftarrow p(b), not\ q(b).$$

Unlike the reduct (11), this modified reduct contains negation as failure in the last rule. Generally, unlike the reduct in the sense of Section 5, the modified reduct of a program has several minimal models.

According to *Definition J*, M is a stable model of Π iff M is a minimal model of the modified reduct of Π relative to M.

In [9] the definition of the reduct is modified in a different way. The reduct of a program Π in the sense of [9] is obtained from the formulas (8) corresponding to the grounding rules of Π by replacing every maximal subformula of F that is not satisfied by M with "false". For instance, the formulas corresponding to the grounded rules (9) of (4) are the formulas

$$p(a), \quad p(b), \quad q(a),$$
$$\text{false} \to \text{false},$$
$$p(b) \wedge \neg \text{false} \to r(b).$$

Definition K: M is a stable model of Π iff M is a minimal model of the reduct of Π in the sense of [9] relative to M.

Definitions J and K are valuable because, like definition I, they can be extended to some nontraditional programs. The former was introduced, in fact, in connection with the problem of extending the stable model semantics to programs with aggregates. The latter provides a satisfactory solution to the problem of aggregates as well. Furthermore, it can be applied in a straightforward way to arbitrary propositional formulas, and this generalization of the stable model semantics turned out to be equivalent to the generalization based on equilibrium logic that was mentioned at the end of Section 9.

11   Definition L, in Terms of Modified Circumscription

In [8] a modification of circumscription is defined that is called the *stable model operator*, SM. According to their *Definition L*, an Herbrand interpretation M is a stable model of Π iff M satisfies $\mathrm{SM}[F]$ for the conjunction F of the universal closures of the formulas (8) corresponding to the rules of Π.

Syntactically, the difference between SM and circumscription is really minor. If F contains neither implications nor negations then $\mathrm{SM}[F]$ does not differ from $\mathrm{CIRC}[F]$ at all. If F has "one level of implications" and no negations (as, for instance, when F corresponds to a set of traditional rules without negation, such as (2) and (3)), $\mathrm{SM}[F]$ is equivalent to $\mathrm{CIRC}[F]$. But SM becomes essentially different from CIRC as soon as we allow negation in the bodies of rules.

The difference between $\mathrm{SM}[F]$ and the formulas used in Definition F is that the former does not involve auxiliary predicates and consequently does not require additional conjunctive terms relating auxiliary predicates to the predicates occurring in the program.

Definition L combines the main attractive feature of Definitions F, G, and H—no need for grounding—with the main attractive feature of Definitions I and K—applicability to formulas of arbitrarily complex logical form. In [16] this fact is used to give a semantics for an ASP language with choice rules and aggregates without any references to grounding.

Among the other definitions of a stable model discussed in this paper, Definition I, based on equilibrium logic, is the closest relative of Definition L. Indeed, in [34] the semantics of equilibrium logic is expressed by quantified Boolean formulas, and we can say that Definition L eliminated the need to ground the program using the fact that the approach of that paper can be easily extended from propositional formulas to first-order formulas.

A characterization of stable models that involves grounding but is otherwise similar to Definition L is given in [24]. It has emerged from research on the nonmonotonic logic of knowledge and justified assumptions [22].

12   Conclusion

Research on stable models has brought us many pleasant surprises.

At the time when the theory of iterated fixpoints of stratified programs was the best available approach to semantics of logic programming, it was difficult to expect that an alternative as general and as simple as Definition C would be found. And prior to the invention of Definition K, who could think that Definition C can be extended to choice rules, aggregates and more without paying any price in terms of the simplicity of the process of constructing the reduct?

A close relationship between stable models and a nonclassical logic that had been invented decades before the emergence of logic programming was a big surprise. The possibility of defining stable models by twisting the definition of circumscription just a little was a surprise too.

There was a time when the completion semantics, the well-founded semantics, and the stable model semantics—and a few others—were seen as rivals; every person interested in the semantics of negation in logic programming would tell you then which one was his favorite. Surprisingly, these bitter rivals turned out to be so closely related to each other on a technical level that they eventually became good friends. One cannot study the algorithms used today for generating stable models without learning first about completion and unfounded sets.

And maybe the biggest surprise of all was that an attempt to clarify some semantic issues related to negation in Prolog was destined to be enriched by computational ideas coming from research on the design of SAT solvers and to give rise to a new knowledge representation paradigm, answer set programming.

Acknowledgements

Many thanks to Michael Gelfond, Joohyung Lee, Nicola Leone, Yuliya Lierler, Fangzhen Lin, Victor Marek, and Mirek Truszczyński for comments on a draft of this note. I am also grateful to Mirek and to Andrea Formisano for the invitation to contribute a paper to the special session on stable models planned as part of ICLP'08. This work was partially supported by the National Science Foundation under Grant IIS-0712113.

References

1. Apt, K., Blair, H., Walker, A.: Towards a theory of declarative knowledge. In: Minker, J. (ed.) Foundations of Deductive Databases and Logic Programming, pp. 89–148. Morgan Kaufmann, San Mateo (1988)
2. Balduccini, M., Gelfond, M.: Logic programs with consistency-restoring rules. In: Working Notes of the AAAI Spring Symposium on Logical Formalizations of Commonsense Reasoning (2003),
   http://www.krlab.cs.ttu.edu/papers/download/bg03.pdf
3. Bidoit, N., Froidevaux, C.: Minimalism subsumes default logic and circumscription in stratified logic programming. In: Proc. LICS 1987, pp. 89–97 (1987)
4. Clark, K.: Negation as failure. In: Gallaire, H., Minker, J. (eds.) Logic and Data Bases, pp. 293–322. Plenum Press, New York (1978)

5. Faber, W., Leone, N., Pfeifer, G.: Recursive aggregates in disjunctive logic programs: Semantics and complexity. In: Alferes, J.J., Leite, J. (eds.) JELIA 2004. LNCS, vol. 3229. Springer, Heidelberg (2004)

6. Fages, F.: A fixpoint semantics for general logic programs compared with the well-supported and stable model semantics. New Generation Computing 9, 425–443 (1991)

7. Ferraris, P., Lifschitz, V.: Weight constraints as nested expressions. Theory and Practice of Logic Programming 5, 45–74 (2005)

8. Ferraris, P., Lee, J., Lifschitz, V.: A new perspective on stable models. In: Proceedings of International Joint Conference on Artificial Intelligence (IJCAI), pp. 372–379 (2007)

9. Ferraris, P.: Answer sets for propositional theories. In: Baral, C., Greco, G., Leone, N., Terracina, G. (eds.) LPNMR 2005. LNCS, vol. 3662, pp. 119–131. Springer, Heidelberg (2005)

10. Fine, K.: The justification of negation as failure. In: Proceedings of the Eighth International Congress of Logic, Methodology and Philosophy of Science, pp. 263–301. North Holland, Amsterdam (1989)

11. Gebser, M., Liu, L., Namasivayam, G., Neumann, A., Schaub, T., Truszczyński, M.: The first answer set programming system competition. In: Baral, C., Brewka, G., Schlipf, J. (eds.) LPNMR 2007. LNCS, vol. 4483, pp. 3–17. Springer, Heidelberg (2007)

12. Gelfond, M., Lifschitz, V.: The stable model semantics for logic programming. In: Kowalski, R., Bowen, K. (eds.) Proceedings of International Logic Programming Conference and Symposium, pp. 1070–1080. MIT Press, Cambridge (1988)

13. Gelfond, M., Lifschitz, V.: Logic programs with classical negation. In: Warren, D., Szeredi, P. (eds.) Proceedings of International Conference on Logic Programming (ICLP), pp. 579–597 (1990)

14. Gelfond, M.: On stratified autoepistemic theories. In: Proceedings of National Conference on Artificial Intelligence (AAAI), pp. 207–211 (1987)

15. Heyting, A.: Die formalen Regeln der intuitionistischen Logik. In: Sitzungsberichte der Preussischen Akademie der Wissenschaften. Physikalisch-mathematische Klasse, pp. 42–56 (1930)

16. Lee, J., Lifschitz, V., Palla, R.: A reductive semantics for counting and choice in answer set programming. In: Proceedings of the AAAI Conference on Artificial Intelligence (AAAI), pp. 472–479 (2008)

17. Lee, J.: A model-theoretic counterpart of loop formulas. In: Proceedings of International Joint Conference on Artificial Intelligence (IJCAI), pp. 503–508 (2005)

18. Lifschitz, V., Tang, L.R., Turner, H.: Nested expressions in logic programs. Annals of Mathematics and Artificial Intelligence 25, 369–389 (1999)

19. Lifschitz, V., Pearce, D., Valverde, A.: Strongly equivalent logic programs. ACM Transactions on Computational Logic 2, 526–541 (2001)

20. Lifschitz, V.: On the declarative semantics of logic programs with negation. In: Minker, J. (ed.) Foundations of Deductive Databases and Logic Programming, pp. 177–192. Morgan Kaufmann, San Mateo (1988)

21. Lin, F., Reiter, R.: Rules as actions: A situation calculus semantics for logic programs. Journal of Logic Programming 31, 299–330 (1997)

22. Lin, F., Zhao, Y.: ASSAT: Computing answer sets of a logic program by SAT solvers. In: Proceedings of National Conference on Artificial Intelligence (AAAI), pp. 112–117 (2002)

23. Lin, F., Zhao, Y.: ASSAT: Computing answer sets of a logic program by SAT solvers. Artificial Intelligence 157, 115–137 (2004),
    http://www.cs.ust.hk/faculty/flin/papers/assat-aij-revised.pdf
24. Lin, F., Zhou, Y.: From answer set logic programming to circumscription via logic of GK. In: Proceedings of International Joint Conference on Artificial Intelligence, IJCAI (2007)
25. Lin, F.: A Study of Nonmonotonic Reasoning. PhD thesis, Stanford University (1991)
26. Marek, V., Truszczyński, M.: Stable semantics for logic programs and default theories. In: Proc. North American Conf. on Logic Programming, pp. 243–256 (1989)
27. McCarthy, J., Hayes, P.: Some philosophical problems from the standpoint of artificial intelligence. In: Meltzer, B., Michie, D. (eds.) Machine Intelligence, vol. 4, pp. 463–502. Edinburgh University Press, Edinburgh (1969)
28. McCarthy, J.: Circumscription—a form of non-monotonic reasoning. Artificial Intelligence 13, 27–39, 171–172 (1980)
29. McCarthy, J.: Applications of circumscription to formalizing common sense knowledge. Artificial Intelligence 26(3), 89–116 (1986)
30. McDermott, D., Doyle, J.: Nonmonotonic logic I. Artificial Intelligence 13, 41–72 (1980)
31. McDermott, D.: Nonmonotonic logic II: Nonmonotonic modal theories. Journal of ACM 29(1), 33–57 (1982)
32. Moore, R.: Semantical considerations on nonmonotonic logic. Artificial Intelligence 25(1), 75–94 (1985)
33. Niemelä, I., Simons, P.: Extending the Smodels system with cardinality and weight constraints. In: Minker, J. (ed.) Logic-Based Artificial Intelligence, pp. 491–521. Kluwer, Dordrecht (2000)
34. Pearce, D., Tompits, H., Woltran, S.: Encodings for equilibrium logic and logic programs with nested expressions. In: Brazdil, P.B., Jorge, A.M. (eds.) EPIA 2001. LNCS, vol. 2258, pp. 306–320. Springer, Heidelberg (2001)
35. Pearce, D.: A new logical characterization of stable models and answer sets. In: Dix, J., Pereira, L., Przymusinski, T. (eds.) NMELP 1996. LNCS (LNAI), vol. 1216, pp. 57–70. Springer, Heidelberg (1997)
36. Reiter, R.: A logic for default reasoning. Artificial Intelligence 13, 81–132 (1980)
37. Reiter, R.: Circumscription implies predicate completion (sometimes). In: Proceedings of International Joint Conference on Artificial Intelligence (IJCAI), pp. 418–420 (1982)
38. Reiter, R.: Knowledge in Action: Logical Foundations for Specifying and Implementing Dynamical Systems. MIT Press, Cambridge (2001)
39. Saccá, D., Zaniolo, C.: Stable models and non-determinism in logic programs with negation. In: Proceedings of ACM Symposium on Principles of Database Systems (PODS), pp. 205–217 (1990)
40. van Emden, M., Clark, K.: The logic of two-person games. In: Micro-PROLOG: Programming in Logic, pp. 320–340. Prentice-Hall, Englewood Cliffs (1984)
41. van Emden, M., Kowalski, R.: The semantics of predicate logic as a programming language. Journal of ACM 23(4), 733–742 (1976)
42. Van Gelder, A., Ross, K.A., Schlipf, J.S.: Unfounded sets and well-founded semantics for general logic programs. In: Proceedings of the Seventh ACM SIGACT-SIGMOD-SIGART Symposium on Principles of Database Systems, Austin, Texas, March 21-23, 1988, pp. 221–230. ACM Press, New York (1988)

43. Van Gelder, A., Ross, K., Schlipf, J.: The well-founded semantics for general logic programs. Journal of ACM 38(3), 620–650 (1991)
44. Van Gelder, A.: Negation as failure using tight derivations for general logic programs. In: Minker, J. (ed.) Foundations of Deductive Databases and Logic Programming, pp. 149–176. Morgan Kaufmann, San Mateo (1988)
45. Wallace, M.: Tight, consistent and computable completions for unrestricted logic programs. Journal of Logic Programming 15, 243–273 (1993)

Sixty Years of Stable Models

David Pearce

Universidad Rey Juan Carlos, Madrid, Spain

Overview

Twenty years ago Michael Gelfond and Vladimir Lifschitz published their celebrated paper on the stable model semantics of logic programs. Today, having built on and enlarged those key ideas of twenty years ago, answer set programming (ASP) has emerged as a flourishing paradigm of declarative programming, rich in theoretical advances and maturing applications. This is one aspect of the legacy of stable models, and a very important one. Another aspect, equally important, but somewhat farther from the limelight today, resides in the ability of stable models to provide us with a valuable method of reasoning - to give it a name let us call it *stable reasoning*. In the full version of this essay I examine some of the foundational concepts underlying the approach of stable models. I try to answer the question: "What is a stable model?" by searching for a purely logical grasp of the stability concept. In so doing, I shall discuss some concepts and results in logic from around 60 years ago. In particular, I look at questions such as:

- How does a notion of stability presented in a work on intuitionistic mathematics in 1947 relate to the Gelfond-Lifschitz concept of 1988?
- How does the notion of constructible falsity published in 1949 help to explain certain properties of negation arising in the language of ASP?
- Why is a seminal paper by McKinsey and Tarski, published in 1948, important for understanding the relations between answer sets and epistemic logic?

Relating stable models and answer sets to logical concepts and results from the 1940s and even earlier sets the stage for a second line of discussion. I shall consider different techniques for studying the mathematical foundations of stable reasoning and ASP. One of these is based on classical, propositional and predicate logic. Its main advantage is its familiarity, its wealth of results and its suitability for rapid prototyping. Its drawback is that it lies, in a sense that can be made precise, one level removed from the action. We first have to translate, manipulate and modify, before we obtain relevant representations in classical logic that we could have obtained in simpler fashion using a non-classical logic. The second approach is based directly on a well-known non-classical logic. I use it to make some recommendations not only how stable reasoning and the foundations of ASP can best be grasped and further studied, but also on some specific topics for future research.

M. Garcia de la Banda and E. Pontelli (Eds.): ICLP 2008, LNCS 5366, p. 52, 2008.

The DLV Project: A Tour from Theory and Research to Applications and Market*

Nicola Leone and Wolfgang Faber

Department of Mathematics, University of Calabria, 87036 Rende (CS), Italy
{leone,faber}@mat.unical.it

Abstract. DLV is one of the most succesful and widely used ASP systems. It is based on stable model semantics, and supports a powerful language extending Disjunctive Logic Programming with many expressive constructs, including aggregates, strong and weak constraints, functions, lists, and sets. In this paper, we describe the long tour from basic research on languages and semantics, studies on algorithms and complexity, design and implementation of prototypes, up to the realization of a powerful and efficient system, which won the last ASP competition, is employed in industrial applications, and is even ready for marketing and commercial distribution. We report on the experience we got in more than twelve years of work in the DLV project, focusing on most recent developments, industrial applications, trends, and market perspectives.

1 Introduction

Disjunctive Logic Programming [1] under the stable model semantics [2,3] (DLP, ASP)[1] is a powerful formalism for Knowledge Representation and Reasoning. Disjunctive logic programs are logic programs where disjunction is allowed in the heads of the rules and negation may occur in the bodies of the rules. Disjunctive logic programs under stable model semantics are very expressive: they allow us to express, in a precise mathematical sense, *every* property of finite structures over a function-free first-order structure that is decidable in nondeterministic polynomial time with an oracle in NP [4]. The high knowledge modeling power of DLP has implied a renewed interest in this formalism in the recent years, due to the need for representing and manipulating complex knowledge, arising in Artificial Intelligence and in other emerging areas, like Knowledge Management and Information Integration.

In this paper, we overview the DLV project, which has been active for more than twelve years, and has led to the development of the DLV system – the state-of-the-art implementation of disjunctive logic programming. DLV is widely used by researchers all over the world, and it is competitive, also from the viewpoint of efficiency, with the most advanced ASP systems. Indeed, at the First Answer Set Programming System Competition [5][2], DLV won in the Disjunctive Logic Programming category. And

---

* Supported by M.I.U.R. within projects "Potenziamento e Applicazioni della Programmazione Logica Disgiuntiva" and "Sistemi basati sulla logica per la rappresentazione di conoscenza: estensioni e tecniche di ottimizzazione."

[1] ASP stands for Answer Set Programming, with answer-set being an alternative name for stable-model, which is more frequently used than the latter today.

[2] See also http://asparagus.cs.uni-potsdam.de/contest/

M. Garcia de la Banda and E. Pontelli (Eds.): ICLP 2008, LNCS 5366, pp. 53–68, 2008.
© Springer-Verlag Berlin Heidelberg 2008

DLV finished first also in the general category MGS (Modeling, Grounding, Solving — also called royal competition, which is open to all ASP systems). Importantly, DLV is profitably employed in many real-word applications, and has stimulated quite some interest also in industry (see Section 7). The key reasons for the success of DLV can be summarized as follows:

Advanced knowledge modeling capabilities. DLV provides support for declarative problem solving in several respects:

- High expressiveness of its knowledge representation language, extending disjunctive logic programming with many expressive constructs, including aggregates, weak constraints, functions, lists, and sets. These constructs not only increase the expressiveness of the language; but they also improve its knowledge modeling power, enhancing the usability in real-world contexts.
- Full declarativeness: ordering of rules and subgoals is immaterial, the computation is sound and complete, and its termination is always guaranteed.
- A number of front-ends for dealing with specific AI applications [6,7,8,9], information extraction [10], Ontology Representation and Reasoning [11,12].

Solid Implementation. Much effort has been spent on sophisticated algorithms and techniques for improving the performance, including

- Database optimization techniques: indexing, join ordering methods [13], Magic Sets [14,15].
- Search optimization techniques: heuristics [16,17,18], backjumping techniques [19,20], pruning operators [21].

DLV is able to solve complex problems and can deal with data-intensive applications by evaluating the program in mass-memory on a language subset [22,23].

Interoperability. A number of powerful mechanisms have been implemented to allow DLV to interact with external systems:

- Interoperability with Semantic Web reasoners: DLVHEX [24].
- Interoperability with relational DBMSs: ODBC interface [25,22].
- Calling external (C++) functions from DLV programs: DLVEX [26].
- Calling DLV from Java programs: Java Wrapper [27].

In the following, we report on the long tour which has led to the DLV system implementation, focusing on most recent developments, industrial applications, trends, and market perspectives.

2   Ancestry

Probably the earliest relevant roots of DLV are to be found in the 1950ies, when McCarthy proposed the use of *logical formulas* as a basis for a knowledge representation language [28,29]. It was soon realized, however, that classical logic is not always adequate to model commonsense reasoning [30]. As an alternative, it has been suggested to represent commonsense reasoning using logical languages with non-monotonic consequence relations, which allow new knowledge to invalidate some of the previous conclusions. This observation has led to the development and investigation of new logical formalisms, nonmonotonic logics, on which nonmonotonic logic programming has been based.

In the 1980ies, Minker proposed Disjunctive Logic Programming (DLP) [1], which allows for disjunctions instead of just atoms in rule heads, yielding (in general) a more expressive language. Early methods for implementations have been proposed already in the book by Lobo, Minker, and Rajasekar [31]. In the early 1990ies nonmonotonic and disjunctive logic programming have been succesfully merged in the semantic proposals by Gelfond and Lifschitz [3] and Przymusinski [32], called Stable Model Semantics, and yielding what is today known as Answer Set Programming (ASP),[3] Stable Logic Programming, ASP-Prolog, or simply Disjunctive Logic Programming (DLP).

After a few early attempts on implementing DLP [33,34,35], the foundation of what would become the DLV system was laid in the seminal works [36] and [37]. These articles essentially contain an abstract description of the basic DLV algorithm.

3 Implementing the Core System

The core system of DLV works on a set of disjunctive rules, i.e., clauses of the form

$$a_1 \text{ v } \cdots \text{ v } a_n \text{ :- } b_1, \cdots, b_k, \text{not } b_{k+1}, \cdots, \text{not } b_m$$

where atoms $a_1, \ldots, a_n, b_1, \ldots, b_m$ may contain variables and each of n, k, m may be 0. If $n = 0$, then the clause is referred to as an integrity constraint, as the empty head acts like falsity. If $n = 1$ and $k = m = 0$, the rule is referred to as a fact, and for facts :- is usually omitted. The intuitive reading of such a rule is "If all $b_1, \ldots, b_k$ are true and none of $b_{k+1}, \ldots, b_m$ is true, then at least one atom in $a_1, \ldots, a_n$ must be true." Additionally, there is a stability criterion [2,3], which also implies minimality of truth.

Disjunctive logic programming is strictly more expressive that disjunction-free logic programming, it can represent some problems which cannot be encoded in OR-free programs, and cannot be translated even to SAT in polynomial time. We next show an example of a problem, called *strategic companies*, where disjunction is strictly needed.

Example 1. Suppose there is a collection $C = \{c_1, \ldots, c_m\}$ of companies c_i owned by a holding, a set $G = \{g_1, \ldots, g_n\}$ of goods, and for each c_i we have a set $G_i \subseteq G$ of goods produced by c_i and a set $O_i \subseteq C$ of companies controlling (owning) c_i. O_i is referred to as the *controlling set* of c_i. This control can be thought of as a majority in shares; companies not in C, which we do not model here, might have shares in companies as well. Note that, in general, a company might have more than one controlling set. Let the holding produce all goods in G, i.e. $G = \bigcup_{c_i \in C} G_i$.

A subset of the companies $C' \subseteq C$ is a *production-preserving* set if the following conditions hold: (1) The companies in C' produce all goods in G, i.e., $\bigcup_{c_i \in C'} G_i = G$.

---

[3] Stable Models are also called Answer Sets, and we will often use the latter name which is more frequently used today.

(2) The companies in C' are closed under the controlling relation, i.e. if $O_i \subseteq C'$ for some $i = 1, \ldots, m$ then $c_i \in C'$ must hold.

A subset-minimal set C', which is *production-preserving*, is called a *strategic set*. A company $c_i \in C$ is called *strategic*, if it belongs to some strategic set of C.

In the following, we adopt the setting from [38] where each product is produced by at most two companies (for each $g \in G \,|\{c_i \mid g \in G_i\}| \leq 2$) and each company is jointly controlled by at most three other companies, i.e. $|O_i| \leq 3$ for $i = 1, \ldots, m$ (in this case, the problem is still Σ_2^P-hard). For a given instance of STRATCOMP, the program will contain the following facts:

- $company(c)$ for each $c \in C$,
- $prod\_by(g, c_j, c_k)$, if $\{c_i \mid g \in G_i\} = \{c_j, c_k\}$, where c_j and c_k may possibly coincide,
- $contr\_by(c_i, c_k, c_m, c_n)$, if $c_i \in C$ and $O_i = \{c_k, c_m, c_n\}$, where c_k, c_m, and c_n are not necessarily distinct.

Given this instance representation, the problem itself can be represented by the following two rules:

$$s1 : strat(Y) \vee strat(Z) :- prod\_by(X, Y, Z).$$
$$s2 : strat(W) :- contr\_by(W, X, Y, Z), strat(X), strat(Y), strat(Z)$$

Here $strat(X)$ means that company X is a strategic company.

DLV today can solve instances with thousands of companies in reasonable time.

The main tasks for computing a DLP program in a (by now) typical architecture are eliminating variables by instantiation (*grounding*), creating candidate answer sets (*generation*), and finally checking their stability (*checking*). It is worthwhile noting that, due to the higher expressiveness of DLP, the (stability) *checking* is a co-NP-complete task for disjunctive programs, while it is polynomially doable for OR-free programs.

In November 1996 the DLV project started in Vienna, its goal being the production of a performant system for computing answer sets of disjunctive logic programs. A working system was produced fairly quickly, and the first description of the system was presented at LPNMR 1997 [39]. The basic architecture of the system as presented in that paper stands until today more or less unchanged. The paper also introduced the grounding module, which proved to be a strong component of the system. Along with the basic model generator, it also described the model checker (a key module which is not needed for dealing with nondisjunctive programs) and various forms of dependency graphs.

The following major publication about the system was at KR 1998 [40], in which the newly created front-ends (brave and cautious reasoning, various forms of diagnostic reasoning, and a subset of the then-unpublished SQL-3 (later SQL98) language (see also Section 4), which allows for recursion in SQL. Another main focus of this work were the benchmarks. DLV was compared to two of the most competitive systems of the era, Smodels [41] (as yet without Lparse) and DeReS [42], and found to be competitive.

The computational core modules of DLV continued to be improved. A major step was the move to a more goal-oriented computation, by introducing a new truthvalue or atom class named "must-be-true" [43] together with a suitable heuristic. These features proved to boost the system's performance on many benchmarks. In fact, work on tuning the heuristics has been continued ever since, giving rise to a number of significant improvements [16,44,45]. Other enhancements of the model generator were the comparison of various pruning operators [46,21] employed during model construction, which also yields considerable performance gains on certain kinds of problem.

Also DLV's model checker has been improved by introducing a new, lightweight technique which permits the use of a SAT solver to decide model stability [47]. It has been shown that the introduction of this technique significantly improves performance on the hardest (Σ_2^P-complete) problems that DLV can handle in a uniform way.

The grounding module is a very important part of DLV, as on the one hand it solves a difficult problem and on the other hand it should output a program that is as small as possible, as the efficiency of all subsequent computations will in general depend on this size. Thus, grounding optimizations are very important and often have a profound impact on the overall system performance, cf. [48,13,20,17]. The enhancement of grounding by "porting" optimization techniques from relational databases to DLP, has been one of the most effective improvements of DLV for real-world applications.

4   Language Extensions and Their Optimization

Early on, extensions of the basic language were a main focus of DLV. The first of these was the introduction of support for brave and cautious query answering, first described in [49]. In nonmonotonic reasoning, these are the two major modes for answering queries. In DLV, a program with a query is transformed into a program the structure and meaning of which depends on the reasoning mode. Answer sets are then computed for the transformed program: For brave reasoning, each answer set supports the truth of the query, while for cautious reasoning, an answer set is a witness for the falsity of the query.

Example 2. In order to check whether a company c is strategic in Example 1, one can write a query $strat(c)$?. Brave reasoning on this query decides whether c is strategic, while cautious reasoning decides whether c is contained in each strategic set.

For query evaluation, an adaption of the Magic Sets method to (fragments of) the DLV language has been introduced as an optimization [15,14]. The basic idea is to make the process more query oriented, and consider only a fragment of the program which is sufficient to answer the query. In addition, if constants are present in the query, this optimization attempts to minimize also the rule instantiations to those that are necessary to answer the query correctly.

The introduction of weak constraints [50,51] was the next major language extension. A weak constraint is a construct of the form

$$:\sim b_1, \cdots, b_k, \text{not } b_{k+1}, \cdots, \text{not } b_m.[w : l]$$

where for $m \geq k \geq 0$, $b_1, \ldots, b_m$ are atoms, while w (the *weight*) and l (the *level*) are positive integer constants or variables occuring in $b_1, \ldots, b_m$. For convenience, w

and/or l might be omitted and are set to 1 in this case. The idea is that weak constraints should preferably be satisfied, with the weight and level specifying a penalty in case a weak constraint is not satisfied. Basically, for each answer set we can associate a vector of weights, which are the sum of weights of unsatisfied weak constraints of a specific level. Optimal answer sets are then selected by first choosing those answer sets having the least weight for the highest level, among these those having the least weight for the next highest level and so on (that is, the optimum of a lexicographical ordering).

Example 3. For instance, if one wants to avoid scenarios in which company c is contained in a strategic set (and thus be bound to sold), we may add a weak constraint

$$:\sim strat(c). \ [1:1]$$

in this way, if strategic sets exist which do not contain c, then only those will be computed. However, this is a preference criterion: if there exists no one missing c, then the other answer sets will be anyway computed.

Having weak constraints actually increases the expressiveness of the language and incurred some fairly crucial modifications of the core system. For instance, the model generator potentially is activated twice in the presence of weak constraints: Once for determining the optimal value of answer sets and a second time for enumerating the optimal answer sets.

Especially with the advent of data-intensive applications, it became clear that some interface to databases is necessary, as extracting data from a database and putting it into a temporary text file is not a very practical option. After initial trials with proprietary interfaces, eventually an ODBC interface has been provided, which abstracts from the actual database used, and allows for both importing input data from and exporting answer set data to an external database.

A major language extension was the introduction of aggregates [52]. Aggregate atoms consist of an aggregation function (currently one of cardinality, sum, product, maximum, minimum), which is evaluated over a multiset of terms, which are determined by the truthvalues of standard (non-aggregate) atoms. The syntax is

$$L \prec_1 \mathbf{F}\{ Vars : Conj \} \prec_2 U$$

where $\mathbf{F}$ is a function #count, #min, #max, #sum, #times, $\prec_1, \prec_2 \in \{=, <, \leq, >, \geq\}$, and L and U, the guards, are integers or variables.

Intuitively, a symbolic set $\{X, Y : a(X, Y), \text{not } p(Y)\}$ stands for the set of pairs (X, Y) making the conjunction $a(X, Y), \text{not } p(Y)$ true, i.e., $S = \{(X, Y) \mid \exists Y \text{ such that } a(X, Y) \land \text{not } p(Y) \text{ is true}\}$. When evaluating an aggregate function over it, the projection on the first elements of the pairs is considered, which yields a multiset in general. The value yielded by the function application is compared against the guards in order to determine the truth value of the aggregate. DLV comes with full support for non-recursive aggregates, as described in [52]. To this end, specialized data structures were introduced, and the model generation algorithm was significantly enhanced in order to deal with aggregates.

In presence of recursion through aggregates, special care is needed for defining the semantics of aggregates.

Example 4. Consider $a(1) \text{ :- } \#\text{count}\{X{:}a(X)\} < 1.$
we see that in this example $a(1)$ can be true only if $a(1)$ is false. Therefore, any answer set containing $a(1)$ should not include $a(1)$, and any answer set not containing $a(1)$ should include $a(1)$, which are both infeasible conditions and therefore no answer should exist for this program.

However, looking at $a(1) \text{ :- } \#\text{count}\{X{:}a(X)\} > 0.$
intuitively, $a(1)$ can become true only if $a(1)$ is true, which would thus be a self-support for $a(1)$. One would expect that in any answer set $a(1)$ is false.

In a way, the first program behaves just like $a(1) \text{ :- not } a(1).$ while the second one is like $a(1) \text{ :- } a(1).$ Thus, "easy" approaches treating aggregate atoms like negative atoms are bound to give incorrect results on programs such as the second.

In [53,54] a semantics has been presented, which deals with these issues in a simple, but effective way. Later, in [55,56], characterizations of this semantics using an adapted version of unfounded sets has been presented, which paved the way for a reasonable implementation for recursive aggregates. Currently, a special version of DLV exists, which supports an ample class of programs with recursive aggregates under this semantics. This will eventually be integrated in the main distribution of DLV.

The latest extension of DLV language is the addition of functions, lists, and sets, along with a rich library of built-in functions for their manipulation [57]. This is a very relevant extension, which lifts up the expressive power of the language allowing to encode any computable function. Even if the integration in the main distribution of DLV is under development, this extension is already spread and succesfully used in many universities and research institutes.[4]

5   Frontends, Backends and Research-Applications

DLV has been succesfully integrated as a computational engine in systems which use it as an oracle, usually acting as frontends and/or backends to DLV. Also the implementation of brave and cautious query answering described in Section 4 can be viewed as such a frontend, but since it seamlessly integrates into the language we have described it as a language extension.

The first major frontend was the diagnosis frontend [6], which is now integrated into the DLV distribution. It supports various modes of abductive- and consistency-based diagnosis by transforming the input into a DLV program and extracting the diagnoses of the answer sets. Later, also diagnosis with penalization [9] has been studied and implemented using DLV.

The second frontend which became included in the DLV distribution supported object programs which can be linked via inheritance constructs, as described in [58]. Also this could be viewed as a language extension by considering programs not in any object as belonging to a special, isolated object. Also in this case the input is transformed into a standard DLV program and the resulting answer sets are cleaned of the intermediate symbols introduced by the translation.

---

[4] We refrain from providing further details, since the paper describing the extension of DLV with functions is reported in this book.

The last major frontend to be included into the DLV distribution was the support for finding plans for domains formulated in the action language $\mathcal{K}$ [59,7,60]. In this case, the interaction with DLV is somewhat more complex, and also the extraction of plans from answer sets is slightly more involved than in the frontends discussed so far.

There are several other systems which wrap around DLV; a few of these can also use other ASP systems in place of DLV.

There are actually two such systems for ASP with preferences, where the preferences are expressed between rules. The system plp [61] transforms these programs into a standard ASP program and extracts the preferred answer sets from the answer sets of the transformed program. A different approach has been presented in [62], which uses a metainterpretation technique. In this context, this means that the propositional atoms of the preference programs become terms in the transformed program, where the extensional database defines the program structure and an intensional fixed part characterizes the semantics.

The system nlp is an implementation for computing answer sets for programs with nested expressions, which relax the structural requirements for connectors occurring in rules [63]. Also here the program with nested expressions is transformed, introducing several intermediate predicates on the way, which are finally filtered from the output.

The system A-POL provides a solver for programs with partial order constructs by transforming them to standard DLV programs [64].

A major endeavor and interdisciplinary success has been the coupling between Answer Set Programming and Description Logic. System NLP-DL [65,66] uses DLV on its ASP side. It turned out that for certain tasks DLV can perform much better than Description Logic systems in this sort of coupling.

DLV has also been used inside a system for strong equivalence testing and associated program simplification [67]. Also in this case, it is used as a backend for deciding whether some rule is redundant or can be simplified.

Two systems have been devised which work on action descriptions in the language $\mathcal{K}$ and on plans, one for monitoring plan execution (KMonitor) [68], and another one which diagnoses plan execution failures (KDiagnose) [69]. Another system implements query answering on action descriptions (AD-Query) [70]. All of these systems use DLV for solving various computational tasks arising during their execution.

Recently, a system for Answer Set Optimization [71] has been presented, which handles programs with preferences expressed among atoms (rather than rules as for plp described earlier). In this case, DLV is used for producing candidate answer sets, which are then tested for optimality by other software.

Finally, we mention spock, a system for debugging ASP programs [72,73], which may be configured to use DLV as its computational core.

6   Spin-Off Projects

Several projects have spun off DLV over the time. A fairly early one was the DLV Java wrapper, described in [27]. Since industrial applications (cf. Section 7) are frequently developed in a Java environment, some means had to be found to interact with DLV from Java. The DLV Java wrapper project provides interfaces, which are in some way inspired by ODBC or JDBC. They allow for creating DLV programs, passing them to DLV, invoking DLV and getting back and analyzing the answer sets produced. This software has been succesfully applied in industrial settings described in Section 7.

DLVT [74] is a project which enhances DLV by so-called templates. These templates can be viewed as abstractions for programs, which can then be used by instantiating them for a particular setting. The semantics for these constructs is defined by expanding the respective templates, and allows for modular programming in DLV.

Again experiences with industrial applications motivated the creation of DLVEX [26]. The main observation was that it is often necessary to delegate certain computational tasks in programs to functions evaluated outside of DLV's proper language. This requirement arises because ASP is not well-suited for certain tasks such as string-handling, various numeric computations and similar features. Moreover it allows for easy language extensions, the idea being to define a suitable semantics for a generic extension, the semantics for a particular extension then being automatically provided by the generic definition. It can also be seen as an easy means for providing new data types and associated operations. Several libraries have already been provided for DLVEX, including numeric operations, string handling, manipulation of biological data, and more. It is planned that these features will be merged into standard DLV in the near future.

A system which is similar in spirit is dlvhex [24], which also allows for external calls. However, while DLVEX is situated at the grounding level, in dlvhex these external predicates may be evaluated at an arbitrary stage of the computation. For instance, the truthvalue of an atom may be determined by the answer that a Description Logic reasoner provides for a query, where the state of the Description Logic reasoner itself may be determined by the truthvalue of atoms occurring in the dlvhex program. This project has received a lot of attention by the Semantic Web community.

A spin-off of DLV which seems very attractive for real-world applications, where large amount of data are to be dealt with, is DLV^{DB}. The basic idea undelying DLV^{DB} [23,22] is to create a close interaction between DLV and databases, delegating some computational tasks to the database engine. The motivation is that if some data is obtained from a database anyway, it might be more efficient to reason on it directly where it resides; this becomes particularly important if the data size does not fit main memory (which is a typical case in real world applications). Moreover, if input data is spread over different databases, DLV^{DB} provides suitable constructs to reason on them transparently. Finally, as many database engines give the possibility to attach stored function calls to queries, DLV^{DB} allows for attaching such function calls to declarative programs, allowing for solving procedural sub-tasks directly on the database.

Essentially forming a language extension, a system for supporting parametric connectives [75] in the language of DLV has been implemented, which should eventually be integrated into regular DLV. Parametric connectives allow for dynamically creating disjunctions and conjunctions during grounding. This is especially useful if one does not know in advance which or how many options there will be in a particular instance of a program. For instance, for the well-known 3-colorability problem it is known in advance that there are exactly three colors available, and one can exploit this knowledge for writing a concise program that includes a disjunction involving the three colors. When one is interested in n-colorability instead, one cannot write a similar disjunction, as it depends on the problem instance how many colors will be available. With parametric disjunctions, this can be done as the disjunction will be dynamically created based on the extension of some predicate. The following program encodes n-colorability by means of parametric disjunction:

$$\bigvee \{col(X, C) : color(C)\} \; :\!- \; vertex(X)$$
$$:\!- \; col(X, C), col(Y, C), edge(X, Y), X \neq Y$$

A project for improving runtimes of basic DLV is to endow the model generator with a reason calculus and backjumping [19]. These techniques are quite well-known in SAT solving, and in this project those methods have been considerably adapted to suit the ASP world, and the DLV system in particular. It has been shown that these techniques are beneficial with respect to runtime, and they will eventually be included in mainline DLV.

Based on the reason calculus discussed above, another side project has been established that defines VSIDS-like heuristics for ASP, and DLV in particular [76]. This kind of heuristics tries to look back on the computation and guide choices based on previous experiences. Standard DLV does the opposite, it looks ahead by performing a tentative computational step and analyzing the output. Eventually it is planned to integrate also this kind of heuristics into DLV.

A recent effort to improve the scalability of DLV has been the parallelization of DLV's grounding module [77]. The original implementation was sequential, but conceptually the grounding procedure has potential for parallel processing. The implementation is done having a multiprocessor machine with shared memory in mind.

7 Industry-Level Applications and Commerce

Unlike many other ASP systems, DLV has a history of applications on the industrial level. An important application area, in which DLV has been succesfully applied, is Information Integration. The European Commission funded a project on Information Integration, which produced a sophisticated and efficient data integration system, called INFOMIX, which uses DLV at its computational core [78]. The powerful mechanisms for database interoperability, together with magic sets [15,14] and other database optimization techniques [13,79], which are implemented in DLV, make DLV very well-suited for handling information integration tasks. And DLV (in INFOMIX) was succesfully employed in an advanced real-life application, in which data from various legacy databases and web sources must be integrated for the information system of the University of Rome "La Sapienza".

The DLV system has been experimented also with an application for Census Data Repair [80], in which errors in census data are identified and eventually repaired. This application includes a formalization of error models and hypothetical reasoning on possible repairs. DLV has been employed at CERN, the European Laboratory for Particle Physics, for an advanced deductive database application that involves complex knowledge manipulation on large-sized databases. The Polish company Rodan Systems S.A. has exploited DLV in a tool for the detection of price manipulations and unauthorized use of confidential information, which is used by the Polish Securities and Exchange

Commission. In the area of self-healing Web Services[5] the most recent extension of DLV with function symbols is succesfully exploited for implementing the computation of minimum cardinality diagnoses [81]. Function symbols are employed to replace existential quantification, which is needed to model the existence of values in case the semantics of Web Services is unknown, e.g., because of faulty behaviors.

Thanks to the high expressivity of the language and to its solid implementation DLV has been attractive for many other similar applications. However, the most valuable applications from a commercial viewpoint are those in the area of Knowledge Management, which have been realized by the company EXEURA s.r.l., with the support of the DLVSYSTEM s.r.l. (see below).

The experience gained in these real-world settings confirmed plans to promote DLV also commercially. To this end, the key people involved in DLV founded the company DLVSYSTEM s.r.l. in September 2005. This company is located in Calabria, Italy, and its main goal is to license DLV to interested partners in industry as well as to provide consultancy and support for its use in an industrial context.

The main licensee so far has been EXEURA, a spin-off company of the University of Calabria having a branch also in Chicago, which extensively uses DLV in its Knowledge Management (KM) products. Three main industrial prototypes of Exeura, currently in production, are strongly based on DLV: OntoDLV, Olex, and HiLeX.

OntoDLV is a system for ontology specification and reasoning [82,11]. The system supports a powerful ontology representation language, called OntoDLP, extending Disjunctive Logic Programming with all the main ontology features including classes, inheritance, relations, and axioms. OntoDLP is strongly typed, and includes also complex type constructors, like lists and sets. Importantly, OntoDLV supports powerful rule-based reasoning on ontologies, by incorporating the DLV system. The semantic peculiarities of DLP, like the Closed World Assumption (CWA) and the Unique Name Assumption (UNA), allow to overcome some limits of OWL, making OntoDLV very suitable for Enterprise Ontologies. It is worth noting that OntoDLV supports a powerful interoperability mechanism with OWL, allowing the user to retrieve information from OWL ontologies, and build rule-based reasoning on top of OWL ontologies. Moreover, through the exploitation of DLV^{DB}, OntoDLV is able to deal also with data-intensive applications, by working in mass-memory when main memory is not sufficient. The system is already used in a number of real-world applications including agent-based systems, information extraction, and text classification.

HiLeX [10] supports a semantic-aware approach to information extraction from unstructured data (i.e., documents in several formats, e.g., html, txt, doc, pdf, etc). In HiLeX information extraction is "Ontology driven", and exploits a domain description expressed through an OntoDLP ontology. A pre-processing phase transforms the input document in a set of logical facts, extraction patterns are rewritten into logical rules, and the whole process of information extraction amounts to answer set computation, which is carried out by the DLV system. The HiLex system has been succesfully applied for the extraction of clinical data (stored in flat text format in Italian language) from an Electronic Medical Record (EMR), and for the extraction of data from balance sheets.

---

[5] http://wsdiamond.di.unito.it

Olex is a rule-based system for text classification [83,84]. Roughly, given an ontology of the domain, Olex assigns each input document to the classes of the ontology which are relevant for it (by recognizing and analyzing the concepts treated in the document). For instance, Olex can automatically classify ANSA news according with their contents (Sport, Economy, Politics, etc.). Olex classifiers are learned automatically in a "training phase", and expressed by DLP rules. The document classification process amounts to answer set computation, which is performed by the DLV system. Olex has been succesfully applied in a number of real world applications in various industries including health-care, tourism, and insurance.

Exeura is currently concentrating its efforts on the implementation of a data-mining suite, where DLV will be employed for reasoning on top of the results of data mining.

References

1. Minker, J.: On Indefinite Data Bases and the Closed World Assumption. In: Loveland, D.W. (ed.) CADE 1982. LNCS, vol. 138, pp. 292–308. Springer, Heidelberg (1982)
2. Gelfond, M., Lifschitz, V.: The Stable Model Semantics for Logic Programming. In: ICLP/SLP 1988, pp. 1070–1080. MIT Press, Cambridge (1988)
3. Gelfond, M., Lifschitz, V.: Classical Negation in Logic Programs and Disjunctive Databases. NGC 9, 365–385 (1991)
4. Eiter, T., Gottlob, G., Mannila, H.: Disjunctive Datalog. ACM TODS 22(3), 364–418 (1997)
5. Gebser, M., Liu, L., Namasivayam, G., Neumann, A., Schaub, T., Truszczyński, M.: The first answer set programming system competition. In: Baral, C., Brewka, G., Schlipf, J. (eds.) LPNMR 2007. LNCS, vol. 4483, pp. 3–17. Springer, Heidelberg (2007)
6. Eiter, T., Faber, W., Leone, N., Pfeifer, G.: The Diagnosis Frontend of the dlv System. AI Communications 12(1-2), 99–111 (1999)
7. Eiter, T., Faber, W., Leone, N., Pfeifer, G., Polleres, A.: A Logic Programming Approach to Knowledge-State Planning, II: the DLV$^{\mathcal{K}}$ System. AI 144(1-2), 157–211 (2003)
8. Eiter, T., Faber, W., Leone, N., Pfeifer, G., Polleres, A.: Answer Set Planning under Action Costs. In: Flesca, S., Greco, S., Leone, N., Ianni, G. (eds.) JELIA 2002. LNCS, vol. 2424, pp. 186–197. Springer, Heidelberg (2002)
9. Perri, S., Scarcello, F., Leone, N.: Abductive Logic Programs with Penalization: Semantics, Complexity and Implementation. TPLP 5(1-2), 123–159 (2005)
10. Ruffolo, M., Manna, M., Gallucci, L., Leone, N., Saccà, D.: A Logic-Based Tool for Semantic Information Extraction. In: Fisher, M., van der Hoek, W., Konev, B., Lisitsa, A. (eds.) JELIA 2006. LNCS, vol. 4160, pp. 506–510. Springer, Heidelberg (2006)
11. Ricca, F., Leone, N.: Disjunctive Logic Programming with types and objects: The DLV^{+} System. Journal of Applied Logics 5(3), 545–573 (2007)
12. Ricca, F., Leone, N., De Bonis, V., Dell'Armi, T., Galizia, S., Grasso, G.: A DLP System with Object-Oriented Features. In: Baral, C., Greco, G., Leone, N., Terracina, G. (eds.) LPNMR 2005. LNCS, vol. 3662, pp. 432–436. Springer, Heidelberg (2005)
13. Leone, N., Perri, S., Scarcello, F.: Improving ASP Instantiators by Join-Ordering Methods. In: Eiter, T., Faber, W., Truszczyński, M. (eds.) LPNMR 2001. LNCS, vol. 2173, pp. 280–294. Springer, Heidelberg (2001)
14. Faber, W., Greco, G., Leone, N.: Magic Sets and their Application to Data Integration. JCSS 73(4), 584–609 (2007)
15. Cumbo, C., Faber, W., Greco, G.: Enhancing the magic-set method for disjunctive datalog programs. In: Demoen, B., Lifschitz, V. (eds.) ICLP 2004. LNCS, vol. 3132. Springer, Heidelberg (2004)

16. Faber, W., Leone, N., Pfeifer, G.: Experimenting with Heuristics for Answer Set Programming. In: IJCAI 2001, pp. 635–640 (2001)
17. Perri, S., Scarcello, F., Catalano, G., Leone, N.: Enhancing DLV instantiator by backjumping techniques. AMAI 51(2-4), 195–228 (2007)
18. Faber, W., Leone, N., Ricca, F.: Heuristics for Hard ASP Programs. In: IJCAI 2005, pp. 1562–1563 (2005)
19. Ricca, F., Faber, W., Leone, N.: A Backjumping Technique for Disjunctive Logic Programming. AI Communications 19(2), 155–172 (2006)
20. Leone, N., Perri, S., Scarcello, F.: BackJumping Techniques for Rules Instantiation in the DLV System. In: NMR 2004, pp. 258–266 (2004)
21. Calimeri, F., Faber, W., Leone, N., Pfeifer, G.: Pruning Operators for Disjunctive Logic Programming Systems. Fundamenta Informaticae 71(2-3), 183–214 (2006)
22. Terracina, G., Leone, N., Lio, V., Panetta, C.: Experimenting with recursive queries in database and logic programming systems. TPLP 8, 129–165 (2008)
23. Terracina, G., De Francesco, E., Panetta, C., Leone, N.: Enhancing a DLP system for advanced database applications. In: Calvanese, D., Lausen, G. (eds.) RR 2008. LNCS, vol. 5341, pp. 119–134. Springer, Heidelberg (2008)
24. Eiter, T., Ianni, G., Schindlauer, R., Tompits, H.: A Uniform Integration of Higher-Order Reasoning and External Evaluations in Answer Set Programming. In: IJCAI 2005, Edinburgh, UK, pp. 90–96 (2005)
25. Leone, N., Lio, V., Terracina, G.: DLV^{DB}: Adding Efficient Data Management Features to ASP. In: Lifschitz, V., Niemelä, I. (eds.) LPNMR 2004. LNCS, vol. 2923, pp. 341–345. Springer, Heidelberg (2003)
26. Calimeri, F., Cozza, S., Ianni, G.: External sources of knowledge and value invention in logic programming. AMAI 50(3-4), 333–361 (2007)
27. Ricca, F.: The DLV Java Wrapper. In: ASP 2003, Messina, Italy, pp. 305–316 (2003), http://CEUR-WS.org/Vol-78/
28. McCarthy, J.: Programs with Common Sense. In: Proceedings of the Teddington Conference on the Mechanization of Thought Processes, pp. 75–91. Her Majesty's Stationery Office (1959)
29. McCarthy, J., Hayes, P.J.: Some Philosophical Problems from the Standpoint of Artificial Intelligence. In: Machine Intelligence 4, pp. 463–502. Edinburgh University Press (1969) reprinted in [85]
30. Minsky, M.: A Framework for Representing Knowledge. In: The Psychology of Computer Vision, pp. 211–277. McGraw-Hill, New York (1975)
31. Lobo, J., Minker, J., Rajasekar, A.: Foundations of Disjunctive Logic Programming. The MIT Press, Cambridge (1992)
32. Przymusinski, T.C.: Stable Semantics for Disjunctive Programs. NGC 9, 401–424 (1991)
33. Subrahmanian, V., Nau, D., Vago, C.: WFS + Branch and Bound = Stable Models. IEEE TKDE 7(3), 362–377 (1995)
34. Seipel, D., Thöne, H.: DisLog – A System for Reasoning in Disjunctive Deductive Databases. In: DAISD 1994, Universitat Politecnica de Catalunya (UPC), pp. 325–343 (1994)
35. Pfeifer, G.: Disjunctive Datalog — An Implementation by Resolution. Master's thesis, TU Wien, Wien, Österreich (1996); Supported by Eiter, T.
36. Leone, N., Rullo, P., Scarcello, F.: Declarative and Fixpoint Characterizations of Disjunctive Stable Models. In: ILPS 1995, Portland, Oregon, pp. 399–413. MIT Press, Cambridge (1995)
37. Leone, N., Rullo, P., Scarcello, F.: Disjunctive Stable Models: Unfounded Sets, Fixpoint Semantics and Computation. Information and Computation 135(2), 69–112 (1997)
38. Cadoli, M., Eiter, T., Gottlob, G.: Default Logic as a Query Language. IEEE TKDE 9(3), 448–463 (1997)

39. Eiter, T., Leone, N., Mateis, C., Pfeifer, G., Scarcello, F.: A Deductive System for Non-monotonic Reasoning. In: Fuhrbach, U., Dix, J., Nerode, A. (eds.) LPNMR 1997. LNCS, vol. 1265, pp. 363–374. Springer, Heidelberg (1997)

40. Eiter, T., Leone, N., Mateis, C., Pfeifer, G., Scarcello, F.: The KR System dlv: Progress Report, Comparisons and Benchmarks. In: KR 1998, pp. 406–417 (1998)

41. Niemelä, I., Simons, P.: Efficient Implementation of the Well-founded and Stable Model Semantics. In: ICLP 1996, Bonn, Germany, pp. 289–303. MIT Press, Cambridge (1996)

42. Cholewiński, P., Marek, V.W., Truszczyński, M.: Default Reasoning System DeReS. In: KR 1996, Cambridge, Massachusetts, USA, pp. 518–528 (1996)

43. Faber, W., Leone, N., Pfeifer, G.: Pushing Goal Derivation in DLP Computations. In: Gelfond, M., Leone, N., Pfeifer, G. (eds.) LPNMR 1999. LNCS, vol. 1730, pp. 177–191. Springer, Heidelberg (1999)

44. Faber, W., Leone, N., Pfeifer, G.: Optimizing the Computation of Heuristics for Answer Set Programming Systems. In: Eiter, T., Faber, W., Truszczyński, M. (eds.) LPNMR 2001. LNCS, vol. 2173, pp. 288–301. Springer, Heidelberg (2001)

45. Faber, W., Leone, N., Ricca, F.: Solving Hard Problems for the Second Level of the Polynomial Hierarchy: Heuristics and Benchmarks. Intelligenza Artificiale 2(3), 21–28 (2005)

46. Calimeri, F., Faber, W., Leone, N., Pfeifer, G.: Pruning Operators for Answer Set Programming Systems. In: NMR 2002, pp. 200–209 (2002)

47. Koch, C., Leone, N., Pfeifer, G.: Enhancing Disjunctive Logic Programming Systems by SAT Checkers. AI 15(1-2), 177–212 (2003)

48. Faber, W., Leone, N., Mateis, C., Pfeifer, G.: Using Database Optimization Techniques for Nonmonotonic Reasoning. In: DDLP 1999, pp. 135–139. Prolog Association of Japan (1999)

49. Eiter, T., Leone, N., Mateis, C., Pfeifer, G., Scarcello, F.: Progress Report on the Disjunctive Deductive Database System dlv. In: Andreasen, T., Christiansen, H., Larsen, H.L. (eds.) FQAS 1998. LNCS, vol. 1495, pp. 148–163. Springer, Heidelberg (1998)

50. Buccafurri, F., Leone, N., Rullo, P.: Enhancing Disjunctive Datalog by Constraints. IEEE TKDE 12(5), 845–860 (2000)

51. Faber, W.: Disjunctive Datalog with Strong and Weak Constraints: Representational and Computational Issues. Master's thesis, TU Wien (1998)

52. Faber, W., Pfeifer, G., Leone, N., Dell'Armi, T., Ielpa, G.: Design and implementation of aggregate functions in the dlv system. TPLP (accepted for publication, 2008)

53. Faber, W., Leone, N., Pfeifer, G.: Recursive aggregates in disjunctive logic programs: Semantics and complexity. In: Alferes, J.J., Leite, J. (eds.) JELIA 2004. LNCS, vol. 3229, pp. 200–212. Springer, Heidelberg (2004)

54. Faber, W., Leone, N., Pfeifer, G.: Semantics and complexity of recursive aggregates in answer set programming. AI (accepted for publication, 2008)

55. Calimeri, F., Faber, W., Leone, N., Perri, S.: Declarative and Computational Properties of Logic Programs with Aggregates. In: IJCAI 2005, pp. 406–411 (2005)

56. Faber, W.: Unfounded Sets for Disjunctive Logic Programs with Arbitrary Aggregates. In: Baral, C., Greco, G., Leone, N., Terracina, G. (eds.) LPNMR 2005. LNCS, vol. 3662, pp. 40–52. Springer, Heidelberg (2005)

57. Calimeri, F., Cozza, S., Ianni, G., Leone, N.: Computable Functions in ASP: Theory and Implementation. In: de la Banda, M.G., Pontelli, E. (eds.) ICLP 2008. LNCS, vol. 5366, pp. 407–424. Springer, Heidelberg (2008)

58. Buccafurri, F., Faber, W., Leone, N.: Disjunctive Logic Programs with Inheritance. TPLP 2(3) (2002)

59. Eiter, T., Faber, W., Leone, N., Pfeifer, G., Polleres, A.: A Logic Programming Approach to Knowledge-State Planning: Semantics and Complexity. ACM TOCL 5(2), 206–263 (2004)

60. Eiter, T., Faber, W., Leone, N., Pfeifer, G., Polleres, A.: Answer Set Planning under Action Costs. JAIR 19, 25–71 (2003)

61. Delgrande, J.P., Schaub, T., Tompits, H.: A Framework for Compiling Preferences in Logic Programs. TPLP 3(2), 129–187 (2003)
62. Eiter, T., Faber, W., Leone, N., Pfeifer, G.: Computing Preferred and Weakly Preferred Answer Sets by Meta-Interpretation in Answer Set Programming. In: AAAI 2001 Spring Symposium on ASP, California, USA, pp. 45–52. AAAI Press, Menlo Park (2001)
63. Pearce, D., Sarsakov, V., Schaub, T., Tompits, H., Woltran, S.: A Polynomial Translation of Logic Programs with Nested Expressions into Disjunctive Logic Programs: Preliminary Report. In: NMR 2002 (2002)
64. Osorio, M., Corona, E.: The A-Pol system. In: Answer Set Programming (2003)
65. Eiter, T., Lukasiewicz, T., Schindlauer, R., Tompits, H.: Combining Answer Set Programming with Description Logics for the Semantic Web. In: KR 2004, Whistler, Canada, pp. 141–151 (2004); Extended Report RR-1843-03-13, Institut für Informationssysteme, TU Wien (2003)
66. Eiter, T., Ianni, G., Schindlauer, R., Tompits, H.: Nonmonotonic description logic programs: Implementation and experiments. In: Baader, F., Voronkov, A. (eds.) LPAR 2004. LNCS, vol. 3452, pp. 511–527. Springer, Heidelberg (2005)
67. Eiter, T., Traxler, P., Woltran, S.: An Implementation for Recognizing Rule Replacements in Non-ground Answer-Set Programs. In: Fisher, M., van der Hoek, W., Konev, B., Lisitsa, A. (eds.) JELIA 2006. LNCS, vol. 4160, pp. 477–480. Springer, Heidelberg (2006)
68. Eiter, T., Fink, M., Senko, J.: KMonitor - A Tool for Monitoring Plan Execution in Action Theories. In: Baral, C., Greco, G., Leone, N., Terracina, G. (eds.) LPNMR 2005. LNCS, vol. 3662, pp. 416–421. Springer, Heidelberg (2005)
69. Eiter, T., Erdem, E., Faber, W., Senko, J.: A Logic-Based Approach to Finding Explanations for Discrepancies in Optimistic Plan Execution. Fundamenta Informaticae 79(1-2), 25–69 (2007)
70. Eiter, T., Fink, M., Senko, J.: A Tool for Answering Queries on Action Descriptions. In: Fisher, M., van der Hoek, W., Konev, B., Lisitsa, A. (eds.) JELIA 2006. LNCS, vol. 4160, pp. 473–476. Springer, Heidelberg (2006)
71. Caroprese, L., Trubitsyna, I., Zumpano, E.: Implementing prioritized reasoning in logic programming. In: ICEIS 2007, pp. 94–100 (2007)
72. Brain, M., Gebser, M., Pührer, J., Schaub, T., Tompits, H., Woltran, S.: Debugging asp programs by means of asp. In: Baral, C., Brewka, G., Schlipf, J. (eds.) LPNMR 2007. LNCS, vol. 4483, pp. 31–43. Springer, Heidelberg (2007)
73. Gebser, M., Pührer, J., Schaub, T., Tompits, H.: A Meta-Programming Technique for Debugging Answer-Set Programs. In: AAAI 2008, pp. 448–453. AAAI Press, Menlo Park (2008)
74. Calimeri, F., Ianni, G., Ielpa, G., Pietramala, A., Santoro, M.C.: A system with template answer set programs. In: Alferes, J.J., Leite, J. (eds.) JELIA 2004. LNCS, vol. 3229, pp. 693–697. Springer, Heidelberg (2004)
75. Perri, S., Leone, N.: Parametric connectives in disjunctive logic programming. AI Communications 17(2), 63–74 (2004)
76. Maratea, M., Ricca, F., Faber, W., Leone, N.: Look-back techniques and heuristics in dlv: Implementation, evaluation and comparison to qbf solvers. Journal of Algorithms in Cognition, Informatics and Logics 63(1-3), 70–89 (2008)
77. Calimeri, F., Perri, S., Ricca, F.: Experimenting with Parallelism for the Instantiation of ASP Programs. Journal of Algorithms in Cognition, Informatics and Logics 63(1-3), 34–54 (2008)
78. Leone, N., Gottlob, G., Rosati, R., Eiter, T., Faber, W., Fink, M., Greco, G., Ianni, G., Kałka, E., Lembo, D., Lenzerini, M., Lio, V., Nowicki, B., Ruzzi, M., Staniszkis, W., Terracina, G.: The INFOMIX System for Advanced Integration of Incomplete and Inconsistent Data. In: SIGMOD 2005, Baltimore, Maryland, USA, pp. 915–917. ACM Press, New York (2005)

79. Calimeri, F., Citrigno, M., Cumbo, C., Faber, W., Leone, N., Perri, S., Pfeifer, G.: New dlv features for data integration. In: Alferes, J.J., Leite, J. (eds.) JELIA 2004. LNCS, vol. 3229, pp. 698–701. Springer, Heidelberg (2004)
80. Franconi, E., Palma, A.L., Leone, N., Perri, S., Scarcello, F.: Census Data Repair: a Challenging Application of Disjunctive Logic Programming. In: Nieuwenhuis, R., Voronkov, A. (eds.) LPAR 2001. LNCS, vol. 2250, pp. 561–578. Springer, Heidelberg (2001)
81. Friedrich, G., Ivanchenko, V.: Diagnosis from first principles for workflow executions. Tech. Rep., `http://proserver3-iwas.uni-klu.ac.at/download_area/Technical-Reports/technical_report_2008_02.pdf`
82. Ricca, F., Gallucci, L., Schindlauer, R., Dell'Armi, T., Grasso, G., Leone, N.: OntoDLV: an ASP-based System for Enterprise Ontologies. Journal of Logic and Computation (Forthcoming)
83. Cumbo, C., Iiritano, S., Rullo, P.: Reasoning-Based Knowledge Extraction for Text Classification. In: Proceedings of Discovery Science, 7th International Conference, Padova, Italy, pp. 380–387 (2004)
84. Curia, R., Ettorre, M., Gallucci, L., Iiritano, S., Rullo, P.: Textual Document Pre-Processing and Feature Extraction in OLEX. In: Proceedings of Data Mining 2005, Skiathos, Greece (2005)
85. McCarthy, J.: Formalization of Common Sense, papers by John McCarthy edited by V. Lifschitz, Ablex (1990)

Using Answer Set Programming for Knowledge Representation and Reasoning: Future Directions

Chitta Baral

Department of Computer Science and Engineering
Arizona State University
Tempe, AZ 85287-8809

Since the proposal of the stable model semantics [1] of logic programs there has been a lot of developments that make answer set programs a suitable language for various kinds of knowledge representation. The building blocks that make answer set programming a suitable knowledge representation language include theoretical results, implementation and applications. The book [2] compiles most of the results that were available until 2002. Since then many additional results have been developed. However, many challenges and issues need to be further addressed before knowledge based intelligent systems become more prevalent.

One of the first challenge is to explore the extension of answer set programming so that it can model additional knowledge representation concepts in a natural way. Such concepts include representation of probabilistic information and representation and reasoning beyond the Herbrand Universe. Closely related to that is to explore ways to develop answer set programming systems that are not bogged down by grounding and can deal with numbers as easily as constraint logic programming systems do.

Secondly, to develop large knowledge bases (answer set programs) additional software engineering tools need to be developed. In particular, theory and systems that allow for modular development and verification of knowledge bases is needed. In addition, similar to libraries in other programming languages, we need to develop a knowledge library or knowledge repository so that knowledge base development need not start from scratch, and knowledge engineers have a easy way to reuse already developed knowledge modules.

Even with all the above developments, knowledge acquisition is a big challenge and we need to explore ways to automatically translate knowledge already expressed in other formats to answer set programs. In particular, large bodies of knowledge are currently expressed in natural language. Thus we need to explore how such knowledge can be translated to answer set program modules.

The above are some of the challenges and issues that would tremendously contribute to the wide spread development and usage of knowledge based intelligent systems. Some progress have been made in all of the above directions and we will discuss them.

M. Garcia de la Banda and E. Pontelli (Eds.): ICLP 2008, LNCS 5366, pp. 69–70, 2008.

References

1. Gelfond, M., Lifschitz, V.: The stable model semantics for logic programming. In: ICLP/SLP, pp. 1070–1080. The MIT Press, Cambridge (1988)
2. Baral, C.: Knowledge Representation, Reasoning and Declarative Problem Solving. Cambridge University Press, Cambridge (2003)

Building a Knowledge Base System for an Integration of Logic Programming and Classical Logic

Marc Denecker and Joost Vennekens

Department Computer Science, Katholieke Universiteit Leuven
Celestijnenlaan 200A, B-3001 Heverlee, Belgium
{marc.denecker,joost.vennekens}@cs.kuleuven.be

Abstract. This paper presents a Knowledge Base project for FO(ID), an extension of classical logic with inductive definitions. This logic is a natural integration of classical logic and logic programming based on the view of a logic program as a definition. We discuss the relationship between inductive definitions and common sense reasoning and the strong similarities and striking differences with ASP and Abductive LP. We report on inference systems that combine state-of-the-art techniques of SAT and ASP. Experiments show that FO(ID) model expansion systems are competitive with the best ASP-solvers.

1   Introduction

Logic Programming (LP) with stable model semantics is commonly regarded as an effective KR system when used according to the ASP computational paradigm. Our position is that all the attractive features of the semantics and the ASP approach notwithstanding, there are alternative approaches that are better suited to address KR challenges, without compromising on computational adequacy. Our approach aims at a fundamental goal in the field of Knowledge Representation and Reasoning (KRR): to develop a Knowledge Base System (KBS), a system storing (declarative) domain knowledge and able to solve a range of tasks and problems in that domain, by applying various forms of inference on its knowledge base. As an example, imagine a KBS storing a specification of course scheduling at a university, and able to solve or support tasks of generating schedules at the start of the year, but also of verifying correctness of hand-made or revised schedules, of updating or revising the current schedule under additional or changed requirements, etc., all using the same KB.

The difference between the KBS paradigm and *declarative programming frameworks* such LP, ASP or Constraint Logic Programming (CLP), lies in the reuse of the KB for solving *different* problems and tasks requiring *different* forms of inference: deduction, model checking, model generation, update and revision, abduction, learning, etc. Thus, a KB does not encode a solution for a specific problem, nor is it a *declarative program* with an operational semantics induced by one specific form of inference. The KB is "only" a formal representation of declarative properties of the domain. This imposes a strong requirement on the KB language: its expressions should be interpretable as (informal) propositions about the domain, and this interpretation, its *informal semantics*, should be as clear, precise and objective as possible. First order logic (FO) is a language that satisfies this requirement by excellence. For example, if $H/1$, $M/1$ and

M. Garcia de la Banda and E. Pontelli (Eds.): ICLP 2008, LNCS 5366, pp. 71–76, 2008.

$F/1$ represent humans, men and women, then the sentence $\forall x(H(x) \supset M(x) \vee F(x))$ expresses the property that *humans are men or (inclusive or) women*. Our project uses an extension of FO with a concept whose informal meaning is understood with great precision throughout mathematics: the notion of an *inductive definition*. As we will argue, the resulting logic FO(ID) can be viewed as an integration of FO and LP.

Building a KBS is a compound research goal consisting of many subgoals which are challenging in their own right: development of KB languages and methodologies, building different sorts of inference systems, etc. Even when working on one of these subgoals, there are two reasons to keep the KBS paradigm in the back of our mind. The first is that the KBS paradigm focusses our research by putting constraints on the languages and systems to be developed. For example, the KBS paradigm induces us to work with truly declarative KR languages; it also induces us study what knowledge is required to solve practical tasks and what forms of inference are needed for this. The second reason is that recent trends in computational logic suggest that building a useful KBS may not be as impossible as many believe now.

A fundamental constraint in building a KBS is the trade-off between expressivity of its KB language and efficiency of its inference engines. On the one hand, we need rich, expressive languages to specify in sufficient detail the background knowledge needed to solve real-world problems. On the other hand, expressive KB languages lead to computationally complex inference problems, which may be intractable or even undecidable. E.g., given FO's undecidability, there is no hope to use theorem proving for reliable problem solving in a full FO knowledge base. This consideration has led, e.g., the description logic area (DL) to build deductive knowledge bases for severely restricted versions of FO. The price is that in such languages, it is often hard or even impossible to specify the background knowledge required to solve many practical tasks.

The way out of this apparent deadlock, and the main hope for building practical applications using KBSs with more expressive KB languages, lies in the use of "cheaper" forms of inference, such as finite model checking, finite or bounded model generation or expansion, or approximate reasoning. In this respect, it is exciting to see recent trends in areas such as ASP, SAT and DL, that show that many real-world problems can indeed be solved by such forms of inference. ASP plays a prominent role in this evolution. It is based on the observation that deduction is often the *wrong* form of inference; what we often want as a solution for a task is (part of) a finite structure/interpretation satisfying a domain theory. In LP, the ASP paradigm was preceded by a somewhat similarly flavored paradigm based on abduction [1]. As stated in [2], the idea of finite model generation as a computational paradigm can also be applied for other languages than ASP. Indeed, some of the successful applications of SAT-systems, e.g., in planning, are by generating finite models as solutions to problems [3]. Other successful applications of SAT (e.g., in verification) are for problems of computing entailment or satisfiability of a domain theory in the context of a finite or bounded universe [4]. Another promising computational paradigm is approximate reasoning, which was developed and used recently for expressive description logics [5]. By integrating these forms of inference, a KBS system might be built that is able to solve a useful class of practical problems.

The next sections recall the main ideas underlying FO(ID), its role for KR and its relation to LP and ASP, and discuss the inference tools under development for this logic.

2   The KB-language FO(ID)

In ASP, an answer set program is a sort of default theory [6]. From in the early days of LP, an alternative -but implicit- view was of a logic program as a definition; e.g., in completion semantics [7], or in datalog where intentional predicates are defined in terms of extensional ones. Many prototypical logic programs (e.g., member, append, transitive closure, etc.) are undeniably inductive (i.e., recursive) definitions. Also, the syntactical correspondence between LP and the way inductive definitions are often phrased in mathematics is more than striking. E.g.:

Definition 1. *The satisfaction relation $\models$ of propositional logic is defined by induction on the structure of formulas:*

- *$I \models P$ if P is an atom and $P \in I$.*
- *$I \models \varphi \wedge \psi$ if $I \models \varphi$ and $I \models \phi$.*
- *$I \models \neg\varphi$ if $I \not\models \varphi$ (i.e., it is not the case that $I \models \varphi$).*

This non-monotone inductive definition consists mainly of a set of informal rules, the third one with negation in the body. But the correspondence with logic programs goes beyond the syntactical level. Such an inductive definition defines a relation by describing how to construct it. The defined relation consists of *all and only* the tuples produced by a rule during this construction process. Thus, such inductive definitions consist of a set of informal rules augmented with a precise, natural, informal form of Closed World Assumption (CWA).

An inductive definition is a precise, well-understood informal language construct of mathematicians which makes this concept amenable for logical formalization. A natural, modular syntax for representing such inductive definitions is as a set of rules

$$\forall \overline{x}(A \leftarrow \varphi)$$

where A is an atom of a defined predicate, $\leftarrow$ is called the definitional implication (to be distinguished from material implication) and φ a FO formula which may contain (classical) negation. Such a rule set aims to define the defined predicates in the head in terms of the other, called *open* symbols. In [8,9], the thesis was argued that the parameterized form of well-founded semantics (WFS) defined in [10] formalizes all common forms of inductive definitions in mathematics. This parameterized WFS constructs a unique, possibly three-valued interpretation for the defined predicates in terms of any given interpretation of the open symbols of the definition.

The above formal construct has historical roots in LP. The syntax and the parameterized WFS were presented first in [10], not as formal construct to represent definitions but as an extended datalog program. A logic program corresponds to a definition defining all its predicates. Given that inductive definitions include CWA, this view matches with the standard view of a logic program as a collection of clauses under CWA. An abductive logic program [1] corresponds to a definition whose open predicates are the abducible ones. A definition with open predicates might be viewed as a collection of clauses with a parameterized form of CWA, where the open symbols of the definition are unconstrained and the CWA of inductive definitions derives the defined predicates from the interpretation of the open symbols.

Our KB language FO(ID) is obtained by integrating such definitions in FO. Our motivation for this is that, on the one hand, we believe that FO and its connectives and quantifiers ($\land, \neg, \forall, \dots$) are indispensable for KR. Extrapolating [11], we believe that any expressive KB language will have a sizable overlap with FO. (E.g., ASP constraints are a form of FO formulas in disguise.) On the other hand, expressing inductive definitions such as reachability and transitive closure is a well-known weakness of FO. Hence, it makes perfect sense to extend FO with inductive definitions. Formally, an FO(ID) theory is a set of FO axioms and definitions[1]. A model of such a theory is a (2-valued) structure satisfying all FO axioms and being a well-founded model of all definitions. Conceptually, FO(ID) can be seen as an expressive description logic using definitions for the TBox and FO for the ABox. It is also strongly related to fixpoint extensions of FO [12].

FO(ID) is a conceptually clean (read "non-hybrid") integration of FO and LP, and combines the strengths of both. In particular, inductive definitions are a precise natural non-monotonic construct from mathematics but they are also very useful for representing *common sense knowledge*. We already mentioned the relation to CWA. It follows that the methodologies for representing defaults and exceptions developed for LP under WFS, work also using FO(ID) definitions. As shown in [13], there is a straightforward modular mapping from logic programs under stable semantics into a sublogic of FO(ID). This means that methodologies for KR using this formalism can be emulated in FO(ID). Likewise for the KR methodologies of ALP: an abductive logic framework consisting of an abductive program and a set of FO constraints, can be viewed as an FO(ID) theory with one definition.

Inductive definitions include CWA but seem strongly related to another concept of common sense knowledge, namely causality. Recall that a definition defines a relation by describing how to construct it. Thus, such definitions implicitly describe a sort of mathematical construction processes which show strong similarity with causal ramification processes. In [14], we defined a logic for modeling non-deterministic probabilistic causality by extending definitions with causal rules with probabilities and disjunction in the head.

We thus argue that FO(ID)'s definition construct not only compensates for FO's weakness on expressing inductive definitions but also for FO's weakness on expressing common sense knowledge. Hence, FO(ID) might provide a solid theoretical underpinning for the recent attempts to integrate monotone and non-monotone logic, in particular the family of hybrid logics that combine logic programming with description logics [15].

3   Reasoning in FO(ID)

Several forms of inference for FO(ID) are under development. Most progress has been obtained for finite *model expansion* (MX). Model expansion is a sort of finite model generation in which the goal is to compute (finite) models M of an input theory T that expand a finite input structure I interpreting an subvocabulary σ (i.e., $M \models T$ and

---

[1] In [9], an FO(ID) theory is defined more generally, as a set of a boolean combinations of FO formulas and definitions.

$M|_\sigma = I$). Thus, the input structure I fixes a finite domain and is useful to store data which are available in many MX-problems. In [16], MX was proposed as an alternative declarative programming paradigm that generalizes finite Herbrand model generation and offers some practical and theoretical advantages. Every MX problem in FO is an NP search problem; the same holds for every logic for which finite model checking is polynomial in the size of the domain. Inversely, MX in FO *captures NP*: for any NP class $\mathcal{C}$ of finite σ-structures, there exists an FO theory $T_\mathcal{C}$ such that σ-structure $I \in \mathcal{C}$ iff I can be expanded to a model of $T_\mathcal{C}$.

Several model generation or expansion systems are available for languages based on FO, such as aspps [13] and MXG [17]. Our group has developed the IDP system[2], an MX solver for a rich extension of full FO, including an order-sorted type system, inductive definitions, partial functions, arithmetic, existential quantifiers with numerical bounds and aggregates such as cardinality, minimum, maximum and sum. Though in principle none of these extensions increase the class of problems that can be solved using MX in FO [16], they do often considerably simplify the modeling task and increase the class of problems that can be solved in practice. For instance, *reachability* in the context of a finite domain can be expressed in FO, but not in a natural manner. On the other hand, it can easily be expressed by an inductive definition, and a solver able to natively handle such definitions is more efficient than a SAT solver on FO encodings of reachability.

To illustrate language and system, assume that company A wishes to take control over company B, by spending at most a fixed amount of say 100M buying shares in other companies. This is expressed in the following theory, together with the recursive definition of $Controls(a, b)$ and a definition for $Shares(a, b, s)$ expressing that, after the purchases, a has s shares in b:

$$Controls(A, B)$$
$$Sum(\{c | \exists s(Buy(A, b, s) \land c = s \times Cost(b))\}) \leq 100$$
$$\left\{ \forall a\, b\, (Controls(a, b) \leftarrow 50 < Sum(\{s | \begin{matrix} (z = a \lor Controls(a, z)) \land \\ Shares(z, b, s) \end{matrix} \})) \right\}$$
$$\left\{ \forall a\, b\, s\, (Shares(a, b, s) \leftarrow s = Sum(\{s' | \begin{matrix} Buy(a, b, s') \lor \\ IShares(a, b, s') \end{matrix} \})) \right\}$$

Note that it may be cheaper for A to buy shares in third companies than directly in B. IDP can solve this problem as an MX problem using an input structure specifying the initial shareholders in $IShares$ and the cost of the shares in the function $Cost$.

The IDP system consists of a grounder that uses approximate reasoning to reduce grounding size and a propositional solver built on top of the minisat solver. In a series of experiments[2], we compared IDP to a number of other MX and ASP systems over a range of different problems. More concretely, we considered (Lparse+)Clasp, DLV, MXG, aspps and IDP. The IDP system had the best performance on at least three aggregated measures: number of solved instances, number of instances solved in less than 10 seconds, and total time.

---
[2] A description of the IDP system and details of the experiments can be obtained via
http://www.cs.kuleuven.be/$\sim$dtai/krr/LaSh.html

4   Conclusion

We believe that the best strategy to consolidate LP's contributions to KR and to certify LP's long term future as a KR language, is to show what it contributes to classical logic and to integrate it with the latter. This is what FO(ID) achieves. We stressed the strong relation between inductive definitions and concepts of common sense reasoning such as CWA and causality. Thus, the "logic programs", i.e., the definitions, in FO(ID) compensate for FO's weakness on representing inductive definitions and common sense knowledge. The feasibility of using this logic for problem solving is demonstrated by the model expansion system IDP. This system supports a rich extension of FO(ID) and, by integrating state-of-the-art technologies from SAT and ASP, it is competitive with the best ASP systems.

References

1. Kakas, A.C., Kowalski, R., Toni, F.: Abductive logic programming. Journal of Logic and Computation 2(6), 719–770 (1992)
2. Marek, V.W., Truszczyński, M.: Stable models and an alternative logic programming paradigm. In: Apt, K.R., Marek, V.W., Truszczyński, M., Warren, D.S. (eds.) The Logic Programming Paradigm: a 25-Year Perspective, pp. 375–398. Springer, Heidelberg (1999)
3. Kautz, H., Selman, B.: Pushing the envelope: Planning, propositional logic, and stochastic search. In: AAAI 1996 (1996)
4. Prasad, M., Biere, A., Gupta, A.: A survey of recent advances in sat-based formal verification. Intl. Journal on Software Tools for Technology Transfer (STTT) 7(2) (2005)
5. Stuckenschmidt, H.: Partial matching using approximate subsumption. In: AAAI 2007 (2007)
6. Gelfond, M., Lifschitz, V.: The stable model semantics for logic programming. In: International Joint Conference and Symposium on Logic Programming (JICSLP 1988), pp. 1070–1080. MIT Press, Cambridge (1988)
7. Clark, K.L.: Negation as failure. In: Gallaire, H., Minker, J. (eds.) Logic and Databases, pp. 293–322. Plenum Press (1978)
8. Denecker, M., Bruynooghe, M., Marek, V.: Logic programming revisited: Logic programs as inductive definitions. ACM Transactions on Computational Logic 2(4), 623–654 (2001)
9. Denecker, M., Ternovska, E.: A logic of non-monotone inductive definitions. Transactions On Computational Logic (TOCL) 9(2) (2008)
10. Van Gelder, A.: The alternating fixpoint of logic programs with negation. Journal of Computer and System Sciences 47(1), 185–221 (1993)
11. Moore, R.: The role of logic in knowledge representation and commonsense reasoning. In: AAAI 1982, pp. 428–433 (1982)
12. Libkin, L.: Elements of Finite Model Theory. Springer, Heidelberg (2004)
13. East, D., Truszczyński, M.: Predicate-calculus-based logics for modeling and solving search problems. ACM Trans. Comput. Log. 7(1), 38–83 (2006)
14. Vennekens, J., Denecker, M., Bruynooghe, M.: Representing causal information about a probabilistic process. In: Fisher, M., van der Hoek, W., Konev, B., Lisitsa, A. (eds.) JELIA 2006. LNCS, vol. 4160, pp. 452–464. Springer, Heidelberg (2006)
15. Eiter, T., Lukasiewicz, T., Schindlauer, R., Tompits, H.: Combining answer set programming with description logics for the semantic web. In: KR 2004 (2004)
16. Mitchell, D.G., Ternovska, E.: A framework for representing and solving NP search problems. In: AAAI 2005, pp. 430–435 (2005)
17. Mitchell, D., Ternovska, E., Hach, F., Mohebali, R.: Model expansion as a framework for modelling and solving search problems. Technical Report TR2006-24, Simon Fraser University (2006)

SMS and ASP: Hype or TST?*

Thomas Eiter

Institute of Information Systems, TU Vienna
`eiter@kr.tuwien.ac.at`

Abstract. Twenty years of stable model semantics (SMS) and almost ten years of Answer Set Programming (ASP) are a good reason for a moment of reflection on these important concepts. This position paper gives a personal account of their history, aspects of ASP, and emphasizes the role of theory and practice in this area.

1 Introduction

It is now 20 years since Michael Gelfond and Valdimir Lifschitz proposed in their famous paper [1] the stable model semantics (SMS) for logic programs with arbitrary use of negation in rule bodies, which at that time and in the years following was just one of many proposals to give a meaning to such programs. A few years later, they extended in [2] the semantics to programs with a second kind of negation (called "strong negation" or sometimes "classical negation") and with disjunction in the rule heads, and introduced the term "answer sets" for the models of these programs, which consist of sets of ground literals rather than of ground atoms, as customary in logic programming.

The impact of these papers was enormous, and perhaps nobody would have guessed that two decades later, the seminal paper [1] is one of the most cited documents in Computer Science (as of February 26, 2008, according to citeseerx[1] it ranks #29, while [2] ranks #158), and among the very top papers in Artificial Intelligence. In fact, these papers were foundational for the current standard semantics of non-monotonic (disjunctive) logic programs that adopts a *multiple models view*. Furthermore, these papers laid the foundations for the *Answer Set Programming (ASP)* paradigm, which exploits logic programs and answer sets as a declarative means to problem solving. The paradigm, whose name was coined by Lifschitz [3] and which was suggested also by others (e.g. [4,5]), is a booming stream in knowledge representation and reasoning to date; without ASP, there would perhaps be less fuss about SMS and no celebration at this conference.

A moment of reflection about the history of SMS, its current status and possible future is appropriate, which will done from various perspectives in this session. I share here some of my personal views and observations; the SMS and ASP era largely overlaps with my academic career and strongly influenced it.

---

* Work supported by Austrian Science Fund (FWF) grants P18019, P20840 & P20841.

[1] `http://citeseerx.ist.psu.edu/stats/articles`

M. Garcia de la Banda and E. Pontelli (Eds.): ICLP 2008, LNCS 5366, pp. 77–82, 2008.

2   Questions about ASP

There are quite a few questions that people have asked me when talking about this subject outside the community. Some of these questions are interesting, I think, to position ASP better in the landscape of research and development, to sharpen its aims, and perhaps to clarify possible misunderstandings; the reply to these questions here is not canonical, just my personal opinion.

- *Is ASP a hype?* For ASP being a hype, the interest in it is (still) far too little compared to other subjects that may be considered as hypes in retro-perspective, such as object-oriented databases systems (OODB) in the 1980/90s. It depends on when to consider something as a hype; e.g., whether there is tremendous (perhaps hysteric) interest, and whether disappearance as in the case of OODBs plays a role. ASP has emerged on a steadily (and not rapidly) growing pace, reaching different fields and applications. It is more previous lack of awareness of the concept that may raise the impression of a hype. Partly this may be attributed to comparably little propaganda, but there are also other factors.

- *Is ASP a better Prolog?* This question is natural, given the close relationship between ASP and Prolog; furthermore, ASP is sometimes is also called *Answer Set Prolog (A-Prolog)* [6]. ASP is *not* a better Prolog; while similar, it is just different and has different aims. Prolog is a powerful tool that was laid out as a general problem programming language. Mastered by its user, it is a sword in the hands of a samurai, but without training difficult to handle. ASP instead is not conceived for such generality and aims at specific problems that may occur in more complex problems; also, the more liberal use of syntax in ASP compared to Prolog, which governs search to reach high efficiency, would make it difficult to reach comparable efficiency in a full-fledged setting and range of applications.

- *Is ASP a hammer for all nails?* Naturally, enthusiasm and blind conviction can drive one to apply a tool to whatever problem is coming up, be it feasible or not. This is not to be mixed with vital curiosity, which may also lead to failures as feasibility in practice is sometimes hard to predict. As evident from the reply to the previous question, ASP is clearly not a hammer for all nails. Its deployment to certain application areas (e.g., data integration or workflow management) was initiated from there, recognizing the usefulness of the tool.

- *What is the killer application of ASP?* As to date, there is no "killer application" of ASP like the Semantic Web is for Description Logics. The question is, however, whether a killer application is really needed to justify an approach. ASP has a number of fruitful uses in a range of applications, that allow to build advanced systems and solve problems (better) than before; it is attractive (similar as Prolog) for prototyping, as an executable specification language, when the knowledge engineering may be still in flux, with a repertoire of language constructs provided by the various ASP engines. Like for AI in general, silent use of "ASP inside" may be more rewarding than a killer application.

There are many more questions, e.g., why to use ASP and not SAT solving or CSP; what are specific benefits of ASP etc., which others will address here.

3 SMS and ASP: A Historical Account

To some extent, the history of SMS and ASP mirrors history of AI in a microcosm, and can be divided into periods of ups and downs with respect to attention and emotional affectedness: enthusiasm, depression close to disappearance, renewed interest, and flourishing. Theory and practice played important roles, being Siamese twins that are tied together, such that the one can on the longer run not survive without the other. In particular, foundational studies of complexity and computation played an important role as driver of research to cast the theory of SMS into implemented systems, which where the key to ASP. In turn, such systems and applications tackled with them raised a number of theoretical issues and challenging problems for research, be it efficient algorithms and methods for program evaluation, which necessarily also involved a better understanding of semantic properties; extensions of the core language to accommodate needs in practice, be it "syntactic sugar" that can be compiled away, or real increase in expressiveness; or be it programming methodology.

Enthusiasm. In the 1980's, there was reviving enthusiasm about AI, triggered by the success of expert systems. Common-sense reasoning, which is inherently non-monotonic, had been identified as an important capability, and formalisms like Reiter's Default Logic, McCarthy's Circumscription, or McDermott & Doyle's Nonmonotonic Logics, followed by Moore's Autoepistemic Logic, had been devised; ambitious projects like *CYC* or the *5th Generation project* were launched.

The issue of defining semantics to program with non-monotonic "negation as failure" turned out to be highly nontrivial and, in fact, raised a "war of semantics" between rival proposals that started in the late 1980es and kept the field of nonmonotonic logic programming busy for many years. Answer set semantics can be viewed, as shown in [2] already, as a fragment of Reiter's Default Logic, and by this resemblance might seem less innovative. The crucial point, however, is that this fragment is "handy" for expressing knowledge with rules. Furthermore, [2] avoided problems of Default Logic with logical disjunction, giving it a meaning that can be seen as provability from a model and generalizes Minker's minimal model semantics. Another important aspect is that there are numerous characterizations of stable models resp. answer sets, in diverse settings and underlying intuitions, which provides evidence for robustness of the concept.

Depression. After initial enthusiasm, the interest in SMS and answer sets started to decrease close to the mid 1990s. While the theory had been advanced and the basic characteristics of the SMS and answer sets had been outlined, comprising both semantical and computational properties, there were some aspects that made the prospects for future development unclear:

- On the semantical side, the war of semantics was still waging, and real world applications or implementations were not in sight.
- On the computational side, SMS was shown to have tremendous expressivity, far beyond recursive enumerability, that made implementations unrealistic. Already in the propositional case, the semantics is NP-complete (in terms of consistency checking), and more expensive depending on the constructs available (e.g., NP^{NP}-complete for disjunction). These complexity results were noticed, but their relevance for implementation not fully recognized in the beginning.
- The interest in non-monotonic reasoning declined in general, as hopes and early expectations could not be fulfilled.

At this time, research on SMS and answer sets was endangered to become, in the terminology of David Harel, *TST* (*Theory for the Sake of Theory*) research, disconnected to practical relevance.[2] Fortunately, it did not take this turn.

The advent of systems. Based on SMS theory and guided by computational complexity results, first systems were then developed from the mid 1990s on, for normal and disjunctive logic programs, with Smodels (TU Helsinki) [7] and DLV (TU Vienna/ Univ. Calabria) [8] being those on which perhaps most efforts have been spent over the years.[3] However, initial systems were rather slow, mirroring the worst case complexity of the problems.[4] Serious research efforts and innovation were made in order to speed them up significantly, and the systems progressed continuously over the years.

With the advent of systems, it was also realized that SMS engines could serve as a host for problem solving and other formalisms; e.g., the DLV project application back in 1995, which actually targeted a deductive database system, sketched applications in model-based diagnosis which then led to DLV's diagnosis front end. The successive formulation of the ASP idea around 1999, which borrows from the earlier idea of SAT solving, seems then a natural consequence (witnessed by the fact that it was proposed by several people independently).

Flourishing. Once the idea of ASP had been articulated, it immediately found broader interest, and dedicated meetings were initiated. The first Workshop on Answer Set Programming, organized by Alessandro Provetti and Tran Cao Son, took place 2001 in Stanford within the AAAI Spring Symposium series, and was a big success. Since then this workshop has been held biannually, and ASP has become a major stream of work not only in Non-monotonic Reasoning, but also in

---

[2] In his invited talk at PODS'94, Harel gave a taxonomy of work in theory, in which the unhealthiest category is TST. He deplored that TST may receive high recognition by self-adulation, while good theory motivated from practice is disregarded. In fact, most of the talk he complained about the poor initial reception of his—nowadays widely used—state charts approach, reading from unfavorable review reports.

[3] The earlier DeReS system (Univ. Kentucky) targeted default logic, facing all the problems of the richer formalism.

[4] I still remember Gerald Pfeifer, one of the chief DLV developers, crying after runs of the first DLV prototype: 'This will never work, reasonable performance is an illusion!'

Logic Programming (as witnessed by this ICLP edition). The great interest also led to a EU project in the Working Group on Answer Set Programming (WASP), which was a concerted effort to further the paradigm, creating the backbone for the research network of the ASP community in the European sector.

The increasing interest in ASP has led to advances in various aspects: more and improved ASP solvers, employing new algorithms and techniques; language extensions and enhancements; and a growing range of applications in the last years. This involved a great deal of theoretical work (to mention here, as examples, algorithms to compute answer sets using SAT solvers, or aggregates in programs), and in fact theory and application have been in close and fruitful interplay. To date, ASP is more lively than ever and the threat of TST seems far. However, it still has not unleashed its full potential, and more efforts are needed to consolidate ASP into a long term success.

4   Conclusion

There are some lessons that we can learn from the evolution of SMS and ASP:

- Theory and application are two legs on which any area in the computing sciences has to stand upon, and in fact in need of each other. Without applications (of whatever sort), research is endangered to end in TST, isolated in its own world doomed to perish sooner or later. Fortunately, SMS escaped this threat.
- Implementations and systems, as draft and imperfect they may be, are vital to push research forward. An experimental testbed to work with is very valuable, and helps generating new ideas and research problems. Thus, it should not take too long until such systems are around. As for SMS, it took almost too long.
- Along with systems, applications are an important driver of research and a source of new challenging theoretical problems.
- In turn, a solid theory and understanding of computational properties is needed in order to build effective implementations. Some ASP systems are highly sophisticated and aim to solve problem instances, depending on preliminary analysis, with appropriate algorithms and resources. Respective knowledge about problem complexity played, e.g., a major role in the design of the DLV system.
- Needs or opportunities may be emerging, as they are not always foreseeable from the beginning. After all, stable models were not conceived for an ASP paradigm but rather as a stepping stone to query-answering from non-monotonic logic programs; the idea to use them for ASP was more a byproduct.

SMS and ASP flourish to date, and one may have great expectations about their future. However, deploying ASP on an industrial scale needs further efforts, and new generations of ASP solvers must be developed. Connected with this are many research challenges: ASP with function symbols, program equivalence and optimization, incremental model building, modularity, non-ground processing, programming methodology, embedded ASP, and software tools are avenues for exciting research on theory and applications, for sure for another 20 years.

References

1. Gelfond, M., Lifschitz, V.: The stable model semantics for logic programming. In: Proc. 5h Int'l Conf. & Symp. on Logic Progr., pp. 1070–1080. MIT Press, Cambridge (1988)
2. Gelfond, M., Lifschitz, V.: Classical negation in logic programs and disjunctive databases. New Generation Computing 9, 365–385 (1991)
3. Lifschitz, V.: Action languages, answer sets and planning. In: The Logic Programming Paradigm – A 25-Year Perspective, pp. 357–373. Springer, Heidelberg (1999)
4. Marek, V.W., Truszczyński, M.: Stable models and an alternative logic programming paradigm. In: The Logic Programming Paradigm, pp. 375–398. Springer, Heidelberg (1999)
5. Niemelä, I.: Logic programming with stable model semantics as a constraint programming paradigm. Ann. Math. Artif. Intell. 25, 241–273 (1999)
6. Gelfond, M.: Representing knowledge in A-Prolog. In: Kakas, A.C., Sadri, F. (eds.) Computational Logic: Logic Programming and Beyond. LNCS, vol. 2408, pp. 413–451. Springer, Heidelberg (2002)
7. Niemelä, I., Simons, P.: Smodels–An implementation of the stable model and well-founded semantics for normal logic programs. In: Fuhrbach, U., Dix, J., Nerode, A. (eds.) LPNMR 1997. LNCS (LNAI), vol. 1265, pp. 420–429. Springer, Heidelberg (1997)
8. Eiter, T., Leone, N., Mateis, C., Pfeifer, G., Scarcello, F.: A deductive system for non-monotonic reasoning. In: Fuhrbach, U., Dix, J., Nerode, A. (eds.) LPNMR 1997. LNCS (LNAI), vol. 1265, pp. 364–375. Springer, Heidelberg (1997)

Quo Vadis Answer Set Programming?

Past, Present, and Future

V.W. Marek

Department of Computer Science
University of Kentucky
Lexington, KY 40506-0046, USA

Abstract. We discuss the development, current state and the future of Answer Set Programming, making predictions that are not necessarily accurate.

1 How Did It Happen, or Prehistory

In early 1984, less than a year after I joined CSD, University of Kentucky, my former student, late Witold Lipski suggested that I look at nonmonotonic logic. It will be *next big thing*, he wrote and suggested reading papers by Raymond Reiter. I went a step further and went to the first Nonmonotonic Logic Workshop in Mohonk, NY. That workshop was, in fact, co-organized by Reiter. Fate had it - the organizers made me share the room with Vladimir Lifschitz who immediately straightened up my wrong ideas on nonmonotonic logic. I knew that change of semantics from all models to a subclass may result in a nonmonotonic consequence operation; this phenomenon was observed by professional logicians earlier. But what I did not know was that the idea was to formalize (fragments of) commonsense reasoning.

That same year another fortunate event of my scientific life occurred – Mirek Truszczynski joined our department. Two years later we understood what autoepistemic logic was really about and what the algorithms for manipulation of modal formulas in autoepistemic context were. In 1987 Michael Gelfond visited us in Lexington and talked about the use of autoepistemic logic to provide semantics for negation in logic programming [2]; the goal that at that time appeared elusive. Then, in 1988 we got the seminal paper of Gelfond and Lifschitz [3]. I presented it at our Logic and AI seminar. Very quickly we understood that the technique was closely related to that of Reiter (via appropriate fixpoint construct). Putting it all together, Mirek and I realized that the complexity of basic problems related to stable semantics can be established. It all came together quickly.

We looked at the implementation of stable semantics almost immediately, although we did not know what this can do for us. Eric and Elisabeth Freeman were our students at the time and they implemented a very simple stable semantics solver (no bells and whistles). While I cannot find the written report of that work (but there was one), my recollection is that it could handle programs with 30 variables at most. Mirek and I then moved to a more ambitious project called DeReS (Default Reasoning System). Today forgotten, it was an implementation of Reiter's logic and thus stable semantics as well. Two Ph.D. students, Paweł Cholewiński and Artur Mikitiuk worked with Mirek and me

M. Garcia de la Banda and E. Pontelli (Eds.): ICLP 2008, LNCS 5366, pp. 83–87, 2008.

on that project. By 1993, the area was mature enough so Mirek and I could publish a monograph of the results so far [10].

It was Ilkka Niemelä who, like Mirek and I, came to stable semantics through autoepistemic logic. He made a breakthrough in the implementation of stable semantics with his *smodels*. What was very important in that research and implementation was the first grounder, *lparse*, built in collaboration with Patrik Simons. Another important system, dlv was started in Vienna and continued in Vienna and Calabria. This one was a solver for the disjunctive logic programming; a powerful extension of stable semantics.

In 1991, Anil Nerode, V.S. Subrahmanian and I started the conference series called *Logic Programming and Nonmonotonic Reasoning*, alternating every other year with Nonmonotonic Logic Workshop. This action created a community which exists today.

In 1998 Mirek and I, and independently Ilkka realized that stable model semantics can be used *efficiently and user-friendly* for solving NP-search problems. By pure coincidence that same year Krzysztof Apt wanted to have a workshop for 25 years of logic programming (and an accompanying volume) and we, in Lexington, had a venue: the beautiful Pleasant Hill, a place where a (now extinct) religious group of Shakers built its paradise on earth. Mirek and I presented the idea there. A catchy name was needed and was provided by Vladimir.

2   What Do We Have Now

When we met at Stanford in 2001 for the first ASP workshop, the name was there and the issue was how better and faster ASP solvers could be built. Bart Selman was asked for an invited presentation and he talked about the progress with SAT solvers, a technology which in the past number of years made a tremendous leap forward based on several theoretical advances, better data structures and more careful implementations. The class of problems solved by SLP solvers and SAT solvers is exactly the same. But SAT solvers were significantly faster (not uniformly, but on average). Not only systems such as *sato* and *grasp* but truly lightning-speed systems like *chaff* were showing the way forward. Both *smodels* and dlv used improvements that were suggested by the SAT community, but not everything that the SAT community used was directly applicable. A new idea was needed and the next big thing in ASP was the appearance of ASSAT, the system built by Fangzhen Lin and Yuting Zhao. Its novel idea was based on a careful studies of reasons why some supported models are not stable. In the hindsight, one could see that it was all about the cycles in the call graph (and since Apt, Blair and Walker, and then later work by Stefania Costantini and Alessandro Provetti we knew that there was a connection). But the issue was that while the completion of the program can easily be reduced to a propositional theory without significant increase in the size of the resulting theory, adding the clauses "killing" the cycles increases the size of the corresponding theory exponentially. Fortunately, it turned out that this can be done piecemeal, maybe killing *some* cycles (this was called by Lin and Zhao *adding loop formulas*) was enough. There are, unfortunately exponentially many loop formulas (as explained in [7]), but not all of them have to be there to find stable model.

I am sure that there are various ways ASSAT and other systems based on the idea of loop formulas can be viewed. For me ASSAT and *cmodels* are examples of the approach that has been successful in many other areas, namely so-called *Satisfiability modulo theories* (SMT) where a back-end SAT engine is used as a generator and enumerator for *candidate assignment*. In this approach (very successful in a variety of applications in electronic design automation [14], but also in other areas, for instance Lintao Zhang and Ilya Mironov SAT attack on hash function collisions), a propositional theory generating some assignments is used to assist the programmer in systematic search for solution. The domain specific engine (in this case checker that tests if the assignment indeed a stable model) is used as a front-end. Thus, SAT is used as a back-end enumerator, and (possibly optimized) checker is used as the front-end, neatly tying ASP to SAT.

May be it is just a sign of times, but a new thing in this period was the appearance of ASP competition and a benchmarking environment *Asparagus*. It looks like it is no longer possible to talk about solving without actually solving it.

The pioneering work of Niemelä resulted in extending ASP to the context where constructs such as cardinality constraints and weight constraints can be used within the programs. This extended significantly the conciseness of knowledge representation with ASP and should result in better usability of the ASP in practice. We need new types of constraints that can be added to stable semantics to facilitate the tasks of programmers.

3   Where to from Here

There is, as of now, very little commercial development of ASP. The system closest to the use as a non-academic, "for-profit" software is, clearly, `dlv` (of course I may not be aware of all that is available). There are several reasons for this situation. In my mind, the most important issue is the lack of easy explanation of stable semantics to a "programmer from the street". While the Computer Engineering students can (and even often are) taught about SAT, I suspect that it would be quite difficult to explain to a *general audience* the semantics of logic programs. I tried this in the past, and failed (below Ph.D. students' level, of course). There are many equivalent descriptions of stable semantics (viz. recent text by Lifschitz [5]), but we should somehow make it explainable on undergraduate, or beginning graduate level. It is even more difficult to explain disjunctive logic programming (or am I just inept?). This, in my mind, is the most important stumbling block for applicability of ASP in electronic design automation, the area driving progress in SAT. This is an important issue: once the *initial investment* in understanding stable semantics is made, the advantages of stable semantics are obvious. To give one example (due to Mirek) implementing Cannibals and Missionaries puzzle in ASP is easy; doing it directly with SAT is unpleasant. That is knowledge representation with ASP is much easier, and we should take advantage of this phenomenon.

The question of software engineering for ASP still needs answers and tools. There were meetings and papers, but we still are far away from production-level environments, or even understanding what are those problems that software engineering is supposed to handle in this area.

Another problem is the working with databases. The `dlv` system is a nice exception; for a number of years now they paid attention to the issues of getting data from and to databases. It is not difficult, and in principle ASP systems can even simulate SQL, but, of course this should not be done, database systems do this better.

Yet another issue is the availability of data types. I do not mean only the basic issues such as availability of string manipulation (important with database applications) but it is possible to define type systems over user defined types (as done within extensional database). As long as reasonable limitations are imposed (for instance length of available lists is specified) this can be done. To the best of my knowledge such constructs were not studied in the ASP context. But may be I am a pessimist here. Adding XML constructs (as suggested by Thomas Eiter in his work on Semantic Web) may do the same thing.

In recent years there was a lot of work on various forms of equivalence of programs. This clearly has a software engineering flavor (like *does my subroutine always do the same thing as your subroutine*). In my mind, however strong equivalence is something else. Namely, it attempts to find a *correct* logic for stable logic semantics (and more generally, disjunctive logic programming). The connections of logics such as intuitionistic logic and programs were observed early. The most amazing thing of strong equivalence is the use of the maximal intermediate logic HT (Gödel-Smetanich logic)[6]. It is surprising that this logic appears in the context of software engineering of ASP. Whether it really will take us somewhere beyond theoretical progress – remains to be seen.

As we progress with the theory of ASP we need a better bounds on both the number of answer sets and on the bounds on time needed to find first solution [9].

The work of Niemelä on constraints [13] were followed by many (myself and Jeff Remmel included). But we still do not have a definitive account of the treatment of constraints in ASP. It is, in fact quite important, as (in my view) successful implementation of those constraints resulted in the increased interest in some of these constraints in SAT (of course 0-1 Integer Programming is another candidate for the source of this influence).

Generally, since the very beginning (and this is the legacy of Logic Programming), the importance of Knowledge Representation with ASP was of primary interest to all of us. This is different from the attitude of the sister community, SAT, where these issues were not so prominent (although, of course SAT planning is, primarily an issue in knowledge representation). Several extensive articles and even a book [4,1] were devoted to this issue in ASP. This all needs to be seen in the major context mentioned at the beginning; the problems with explaining of ASP to the wider community of potential users, especially in electronic design automation. It is not enough to use ASP (say for model checking, [15]), the issue is to convince others to use it. For that reason, for instance dlv offers a front-end which uses the solver as a back-end engine.

Time for conclusions. As is clear from my presentation, I believe that a simpler, clearer, less technical descriptions of ASP must be found. Being by nature an optimist, I believe that they will be found. The elegance of knowledge representation with ASP will then open the possibility of a wider use of ASP. I also believe that one way or another we are bound to get closer with SAT community. Signs of this phenomenon are already seen. So, I do not know how the celebrations of the 40th anniversary of stable semantics of logic programs will look like. But I am sure there will be a lot to celebrate.

References

1. Baral, C.: Knowledge Representation, Reasoning and Declarative Problem Solving. Cambridge University Press, Cambridge (2003)
2. Gelfond, M.: On stratified autoepistemic theories. In: Proceedings of AAAI 1987, pp. 207–211 (1987)
3. Gelfond, M., Lifschitz, V.: The stable model semantics for logic programming. In: Proceedings of the International Joint Conference and Symposium on Logic Programming, pp. 1070–1080. MIT Press, Cambridge (1988)
4. Gelfond, M., Leone, N.: Logic Programming and Knowledge Representation – A-Prolog perspective. Artificial Intelligence 138, 3–38 (2002)
5. Lifschitz, V.: Twelve Definitions of a Stable model. This volume
6. Lifschitz, V., Pearce, D., Valverde, A.: Strongly equivalent logic programs. ACM Transactions on Computational Logic 2, 526–541 (2001)
7. Lifschitz, V., Razborov, A.: Why are there so many loop formulas? ACM Transactions on Computational Logic 7, 261–268 (2006)
8. Lin, F., Zhao, Y.: ASSAT: Computing answer sets of a logic program by SAT solvers. Artificial Intelligence Journal 157, 115–137 (2004)
9. Lonc, Z., Truszczyński, M.: Computing minimal models, stable models and answer sets. Theory and Practice of Logic Programming 6, 395–449 (2006)
10. Marek, V.W., Truszczyński, M.: Nonmonotonic Logic, Context-Dependent Reasoning. Springer, Berlin (1993)
11. Marek, V., Truszczyński, M.: Stable Models and an Alternative Logic Programming Paradigm. In: The Logic Programming Paradigm. Series Artificial Intelligence, pp. 375–398. Springer, Heidelberg (1999)
12. Niemelä, I.: Logic programs with stable model semantics as a constraint programming paradigm. Annals of Mathematics and Artificial Intelligence 25, 241–273 (1999)
13. Niemelä, I., Simons, P., Soininen, T.: Stable Model Semantics of Weight Constraint Rules. In: Gelfond, M., Leone, N., Pfeifer, G. (eds.) LPNMR 1999. LNCS, vol. 1730, pp. 317–331. Springer, Heidelberg (1999)
14. Nieuwenhuis, R., Oliveras, A., Tinelli, C.: Abstract DPLL and Abstract DPLL Modulo Theories. In: Baader, F., Voronkov, A. (eds.) LPAR 2004. LNCS, vol. 3452, pp. 36–50. Springer, Heidelberg (2005)
15. Tang, C., Ternovska, E.: Model Checking Abstract State Machines with Answer Set Programming. Fundamenta Informaticae 77, 105–141 (2007)

Answer Set Programming without Unstratified Negation

Ilkka Niemelä

Helsinki University of Technology (TKK)
Department of Information and Computer Science
Ilkka.Niemela@tkk.fi

Abstract. The paper argues that for answer set programming purposes it is not necessary to use unstratified negation but it is more appropriate to employ a basic language based on simple choice constructs, integrity constraints, and stratified negation. This offers a framework that enables natural problem encodings and smooth extensions, for instance, with constraints and aggregates.

1 Introduction

The stable model semantics [1] was introduced originally to provide a declarative account of negation as failure in normal logic programs used in logic programming systems such as Prolog. In particular, the challenge was to capture the problematic case of recursion through negation, i.e., *unstratified negation.*

In the mid 1990s systems capable of computing stable models for tens of thousands of (ground) rules were emerging [2,3]. Then it was realized that logic programs with stable models could be used in a novel way to solve challenging search problems [4,5,6]. The name *answer set programming* (ASP) was coined to this new paradigm where the idea is to see rules as constraints characterizing a set of (stable) models. Now a given search problem can be solved by encoding the problem as a set of rules such that the stable models of the rules correspond to the solutions of the original problem. Hence, a solution to a given problem can be found by giving the logic program encoding as input to an ASP solver which computes a stable model of the encoding and then a solution of the original problem can be extracted from the computed stable model.

ASP has its origins in the stable model semantics of normal programs. Naturally this class of programs has provided the basic logic program language for ASP and it has been the starting point for extensions including disjunctions and aggregates which increase expressivity and often also complexity. In particular, unstratified negation is an essential part of ASP based on normal programs because without recursion through negation a normal program has at most one stable model and, hence, is not possible to capture potential solutions to a given problem as alternative stable models. For example, to encode a choice whether to include an atom a in a stable model or not we need to introduce a new atom, say $\bar{a}$, and employ unstratified negation as in the two rules:

$$a \leftarrow \text{not } \bar{a} \qquad \bar{a} \leftarrow \text{not } a.$$

M. Garcia de la Banda and E. Pontelli (Eds.): ICLP 2008, LNCS 5366, pp. 88–92, 2008.

Such encodings using negation through recursion are very challenging to understand and develop. To overcome the problem, normal programs were extended, for example, by disjunctions [7] and various choice constructs [8,9].

The paper reconsiders the role of normal programs allowing unstratified negation as the basic language for ASP. It argues that for ASP purposes it is not necessary to use unstratified negation but it is more suitable to employ a basic language based on simple choice constructs, integrity constraints, and stratified negation. This offers a framework where recursive definitions are allowed, problem encoding can be done in a very direct way using a generate and test approach, and unstratified negation is easy to capture if needed. Moreover, the approach provides a basic language which is straightforward to extend with different kinds of constraints and aggregates without changing the underlying ideas in the semantics and where primitives such as disjunction [7] that increase expressivity (and complexity) can be added.

2   SCI Programs

We put forward a class of logic programs which we call **SCI** programs (for Stratified negation, Choice constructs, and Integrity constraints) where programs consist of normal rules of the form (1), choice rules of the form (2) and integrity constraints of the form (3)

$$a \leftarrow b_1, \ldots, b_m, \text{not } c_1, \ldots, \text{not } c_n \qquad (1)$$
$$\{a_1, \ldots, a_l\} \leftarrow b_1, \ldots, b_m, \text{not } c_1, \ldots, \text{not } c_n \qquad (2)$$
$$\leftarrow b_1, \ldots, b_m, \text{not } c_1, \ldots, \text{not } c_n \qquad (3)$$

where a_i, b_j, c_k are all atoms. As usual the positive literals $b_1, \ldots, b_m$ and negative literals not $c_1, \ldots,$ not c_n are called the body of the rule and a ($\{a_1, \ldots, a_l\}$) is the head for a normal (choice) rule and for integrity constraints the head is empty. For a **SCI** program P we denote by $\text{NR}(P)$, $\text{CR}(P)$, and $\text{IC}(P)$ the sets of normal rules, choice rules and $\text{IC}(P)$ integrity constraints, respectively.

In **SCI** programs unstratified negation is not allowed and programs are required to be stratified in the usual sense [10]: for each program there should exist a mapping S from the predicate symbols in the program to natural numbers such that for each rule and each predicate symbol p appearing in the head (i) $S(p) \geq S(q)$ holds for every predicate symbol q appearing in the positive body literals and (ii) $S(p) > S(q)$ holds for every predicate symbol q appearing in the negative body literals of the rule.

3   Semantics of SCI Programs

Choice and integrity rules can be seen as special cases of the cardinality constraints in [11] and, hence, the stable model semantics for **SCI** programs can be defined using a Gelfond-Lifschitz type of a reduct generalized to choice rules as done in [11] (or more generally for abstract constraint atoms in [12]) .

However, here we propose a slightly different method of defining the semantics which coincides with the approach explained above for **SCI** programs but provides a more direct path to extending the language as will be discussed below. We outline the method in the ground case, i.e., for programs without variables. Generalizing it to programs with variables can be done in the usual way by Herbrand instantiation.

Models of a program are sets of atoms and a positive (negative) literal a (not a) is satisfied in a model S if $a \in S$ ($a \notin S$). A normal rule of the form (1) is satisfied by a model S if the head is satisfied whenever all the body literals are satisfied. A choice rule is satisfied in any model and an integrity constraint is satisfied if at least one of the body literals is not. A model S satisfies a set of rules P if it satisfies all the rules (denoted by $S \models P$).

Given a set S of atoms (a candidate model) the **SCI**-reduct P^S of P w.r.t. S is the set of rules including all normal rules $NR(P)$ in P and a rule

$$a_l \leftarrow b_1, \ldots, b_m, \text{not } c_1, \ldots, \text{not } c_n$$

for each choice rule of the form (2) in $CR(P)$ with $a_l \in S$. Notice that P^S is a normal stratified program without integrity constraints and it has a unique canonical model which can be defined iteratively bottom up layer by layer in the stratification, for details see [10]. For a normal stratified program P we denote the unique stratified model by $StM(P)$[1].

Definition 1. *For a **SCI** program P, a set of atoms S is a stable model of P iff $S \models IC(P)$ and $S = StM(P^S)$.*

Example 1. Consider the program P

$$c \leftarrow a \qquad b \leftarrow \text{not } a \qquad \{a\} \leftarrow \text{not } d \qquad \leftarrow \text{not } a$$

Now $S_1 = \{a, c\}$ is a stable model of P because it satisfies the only integrity constraint (last rule) in P and it is the stratified model of the reduct P^{S_1} consisting of the first two rules and the rule $a \leftarrow \text{not } d$. However, $S_2 = \{b\}$ is not a stable model because it does not satisfy the integrity constraint and $S_3 = \{a, b, c\}$ is not a stable model because it is not the stratified model of the reduct P^{S_3}. In fact, S_1 is the only stable model of P.

Example 2. The choice rules enable very natural encodings without using unstratified negation. We illustrate this with an encoding of the Hamiltonian circuit problem for directed graphs, i.e., the problem of finding a path in a graph visiting each node exactly once and returning to the starting node. We assume that the graph is given using a set of facts of the form $edge(v, u)$, $vtx(v)$ specifying the edges and vertices and a fact $start(w)$ for some arbitrary starting vertex for the circuit. In the encoding below the circuit is represented by the predicate $hc(\cdot, \cdot)$. The first rule introduces for each edge a choice whether to include the edge in

---

[1] Note that for a stratified normal program P the unique model coincides with the stable model and the well-founded model of P.

the circuit or not and the two other rules on the left require that a vertex can have at most one immediate successor and predecessor in the circuit. The rules on the right state that each vertex needs to be reachable through the circuit from the starting node of the circuit.

$$\{hc(V,U)\} \leftarrow edge(V,U) \qquad\qquad r(V) \leftarrow hc(S,V), start(S)$$
$$\leftarrow hc(V,U), hc(V,W), U \neq W \qquad r(V) \leftarrow r(U), hc(U,V)$$
$$\leftarrow hc(U,V), hc(W,V), U \neq W \qquad \leftarrow not\ r(V)$$

4   Capturing Unstratified Negation

In **SCI** programs unstratified negation is not allowed and an interesting question is whether it can be captured with a suitable translation in terms choices, integrity constraints and stratified negation. In fact, this is possible because a literal not p with (unstratified) negation can be seen as a new atom $\bar{p}$ for which a choice needs to be made whether to include $\bar{p}$ in the model such that a model cannot contain both p and $\bar{p}$ but one of them needs to be included.

Hence, a normal program P can be translated to a **SCI** program tr(P) where all unstratified negations (or in fact all negative literals) in P can be eliminated as follows. For each atom p in P, we introduce a new atom $\bar{p}$ and add the following three rules in the translation:

$$\{\bar{p}\} \leftarrow \qquad\qquad \leftarrow p, \bar{p} \qquad\qquad \leftarrow not\ p, not\ \bar{p}$$

Then each negative literal not p in the rules can be replaced $\bar{p}$.

It can be shown that given a normal program P (i) if S is a stable model of P, then $S \cup \{\bar{p} \mid p \in \mathrm{At(P)} - S,\}$ is a stable model of the **SCI** program tr(P) and (ii) if S is a stable model of tr(P), then $S \cap \mathrm{At(P)}$ is a stable model of P, where $\mathrm{At(P)}$ is the set of atoms in P.

5   Extending SCI Programs

One of the advantages of the approach is that it is very straightforward and unproblematic to extend the framework with new kinds of constraints and aggregates. The idea is to require that these extensions can appear only in bodies of rules and only in a stratified way, i.e., predicates used in a constraint or aggregate need to be defined on an earlier stratum. Then it is straightforward to the generalize the stratified model to handle novel kinds of constraints, see for instance [13].

Notice that a rule with a constraint in the head can be directly represented with a choice rule and an integrity constraint. For example, a rule such as

$$odd(a_1, ..., a_l) \leftarrow b, not\ c$$

stating that an odd number of atoms $a_1, ..., a_l$ should be selected if b, not c hold, can be encoded using two rules:

$$\{a_1, ..., a_l\} \leftarrow b, not\ c \qquad\qquad \leftarrow not\ odd(a_1, ..., a_l), b, not\ c.$$

There are some cases where positive recursion through a constraint has clear semantics and is usable in practical applications, for example, in the case of monotone constraints. For such cases it is straightforward to relax the notion of stratification to allow positive recursion through such constraints and to extend the semantics to handle this case [12].

Acknowledgments. The financial support of the Academy of Finland (project 122399) is gratefully acknowledged.

References

1. Gelfond, M., Lifschitz, V.: The stable model semantics for logic programming. In: Proceedings of the 5th International Conference on Logic Programming, pp. 1070–1080. The MIT Press, Cambridge (1988)
2. Niemelä, I., Simons, P.: Efficient implementation of the well-founded and stable model semantics. In: Proceedings of the Joint International Conference and Symposium on Logic Programming, pp. 289–303. The MIT Press, Cambridge (1996)
3. Eiter, T., Leone, N., Mateis, C., Pfeifer, G., Scarcello, F.: The KR system dlv: Progress report, comparisons and benchmarks. In: Proceedings of the 6th International Conference on Principles of Knowledge Representation and Reasoning, pp. 406–417. Morgan Kaufmann Publishers, San Francisco (1998)
4. Niemelä, I.: Logic programs with stable model semantics as a constraint programming paradigm. In: Proceedings of the Workshop on Computational Aspects of Nonmonotonic Reasoning (1998); Extended version appeared in Annals of Mathematics and Artificial Intelligence 25(3,4), 241–273 (1999)
5. Marek, W., Truszczyński, M.: Stable models and an alternative logic programming paradigm. In: The Logic Programming Paradigm: a 25-Year Perspective, pp. 375–398. Springer, Heidelberg (1999)
6. Lifschitz, V.: Answer set planning. In: Proceedings of the 16th International Conference on Logic Programming, pp. 25–37. The MIT Press, Cambridge (1999)
7. Gelfond, M., Lifschitz, V.: Classical negation in logic programs and disjunctive databases. New Generation Computing 9, 365–385 (1991)
8. Soininen, T., Niemelä, I.: Developing a declarative rule language for applications in product configuration. In: Gupta, G. (ed.) PADL 1999. LNCS, vol. 1551, pp. 305–319. Springer, Heidelberg (1999)
9. Niemelä, I., Simons, P., Soininen, T.: Stable model semantics of weight constraint rules. In: Proceedings of the 5th International Conference on Logic Programming and Nonmonotonic Reasoning, pp. 317–331. Springer, Heidelberg (1999)
10. Apt, K., Blair, H., Walker, A.: Towards a theory of declarative knowledge. In: Minker, J. (ed.) Foundations of Deductive Databases and Logic Programming, pp. 89–148. Morgan Kaufmann Publishers, San Francisco (1988)
11. Simons, P., Niemelä, I., Soininen, T.: Extending and implementing the stable model semantics. Artificial Intelligence 138(1-2), 181–234 (2002)
12. Marek, V., Niemelä, I., Truszczyński, M.: Programs with monotone abstract constraint atoms. Theory and Practice of Logic Programming 8(2), 167–199 (2008)
13. Kemp, D.B., Stuckey, P.J.: Semantics of logic programs with aggregates. In: Proceedings of the 1991 International Symposium on Logic Programming, pp. 387–401. MIT Press, Cambridge (1991)

Here's the Beef: Answer Set Programming!

Torsten Schaub[*]

Universität Potsdam, Institut für Informatik, August-Bebel-Str. 89,
D-14482 Potsdam
torsten@cs.uni-potsdam.de

At the occasion of the Third International Conference on Principles of Knowledge Representation and Reasoning [1] in 1992, Ray Reiter delivered an invited talk entitled *"Twelve Years of Nonmonotonic Reasoning Research: Where (and What) Is the beef?"*,[1,2] reflecting the state and future of the research area of Nonmonotonic Reasoning (NMR;[2]). Ray Reiter describes it in [3] as a "flourishing subculture" making many outside researchers "wonder what on earth this stuff is good for." Although he seemed to be rather optimistic about the future of NMR, he nonetheless saw its major contribution on the theoretical side, providing "important insights about, and solutions to, many outstanding problems, not only in AI but in computer science in general." Among them, he lists "Logic Programming implementations of nonmonotonic reasoning".

Although the link between Michael Gelfond and Vladimir Lifschitz' Stable Model Semantics for Logic Programming [4] and NMR formalisms like Ray Reiter's Default Logic [5] were discovered soon after the proposal of Stable Model Semantics,[3] it still took some years until the first such implementation was conceived, namely, the *smodels* system [8,9]. The emergence of such a highly efficient and robust system has boosted the combination of Logic Programming and NMR and finally led to a novel declarative programming paradigm, referred to as Answer Set Programming (ASP;[10,11,12,13,14]). Since its inception, ASP has been regarded as the computational embodiment of Nonmonotonic Reasoning and a primary candidate for an effective tool for Knowledge Representation and Reasoning. After all, it seems nowadays hard to dispute that ASP brought new life to Logic Programming and NMR research and has become a major driving force for these two fields, helping dispel gloomy prophecies of their impending demise.

Meanwhile, the prospect of ASP has been demonstrated in numerous application scenarios, including bio-informatics [15,16], configuration [17], database integration [18], diagnosis [19], hardware design [20], insurance industry [21], model checking [22], phylogenesis [23,24], planing [12], security protocols [25], etc.[4] A highlight among these applications is arguably the usage of ASP for the high-level control of the space shuttle [26,27]. The increasing popularity of ASP is for one thing due to the

---

[*] Affiliated with Simon Fraser University, Canada, and Griffith University, Australia.

[1] By then twelve years after the publication of the Special Issue of the Artificial Intelligence Journal on Nonmonotonic Reasoning.

[2] See also http://en.wikipedia.org/wiki/Where's_the_beef

[3] Logic Programming under Stable Model Semantics turned out to be a special case of Default Logic, with stable models corresponding to default extensions [6,7].

[4] See also http://www.kr.tuwien.ac.at/research/projects/WASP/report.html

M. Garcia de la Banda and E. Pontelli (Eds.): ICLP 2008, LNCS 5366, pp. 93–98, 2008.
© Springer-Verlag Berlin Heidelberg 2008

availability of efficient off-the-shelf ASP systems [28,29,30,31,32] and for another due to its rich modeling language, jointly allowing for an easy yet efficient handling of knowledge-intensive applications. Essentially all ASP systems that have been developed so far contain two major components. The first of them, a *grounder*, grounds an input program, that is, produces its compact propositional equivalent, often by appeal to advanced database techniques. The input language goes well beyond that of Prolog, offering among others, integrity constraints, classical negation, disjunction, and various types of aggregates. The second component, a *solver*, accepts the ground program and actually computes its answer sets (which amount to the stable models of the original program). Modern ASP solvers rely on advanced Boolean constraint solving techniques, stemming from the area of Satisfiability Checking and allowing for tackling application problems encompassing millions of variables. All in all, ASP has become an efficient and expressive declarative problem solving paradigm, particularly well-suited for knowledge-intensive applications.

Taking up Ray Reiter's challenge after sixteen years, *my* obvious answer is that Answer Set Programming is the *beef* of twenty-eight years of NMR research! Although twenty-eight years appear to be quite a while, successful neighboring areas such as Description Logics (DLs) and Satisfiability Checking (SAT) look back onto similar histories, taking major references in their field, like [33] and [34,35], respectively. Nonetheless both areas have prospered in recent years due to their success in industrially relevant application areas. SAT is the key technology underlying Bounded Model Checking [36] and DLs have become standard ontology languages for the Semantic Web [37]. Although different factors have abetted these success stories, in the end, their breakthrough was marked by their establishment as salient technologies in their respective application areas. What can ASP learn from this? First of all, we should keep building upon strong formal foundations, just as SAT and DLs do. However, ASP should gear its research vision towards application scenarios in order to make ASP technology more efficient, more robust, more versatile, and in the end ready for real applications. This orientation is such a fruitful approach, being full of interesting and often fundamental research questions.

Second, we have to foster the dissemination of ASP in order to increase its perception. Apart from promoting ASP in our academic and industrial environment, teaching ASP is an important means to enhance the common awareness of it. This does not necessarily mean to teach full-fledged ASP courses, which is difficult in view of many encrusted curricula, but rather to incorporate ASP in AI-related classes as a tool for illustrating typical reasoning patterns in Knowledge Representation and Reasoning, like closed-world reasoning, abduction, planning, etc. And after all, to put it in Ray Reiter's words, it's the ASP community's duty to show "what on earth this stuff is good for."

ASP has staked its claim in being an attractive approach to declarative problem solving in combing an expressive modelling language with efficient solving technology. But how does it scale? In fact, this is not only a matter of performance but also of applicability and usability. Here is my personal view.

Performance. Modern ASP solvers are based on advanced Boolean constraint technology and exhibit a similar performance as advanced SAT solvers [38]. Unlike SAT, however, ASP offers a uniform modelling language admitting variables. In fact, grounding non-propositional logical specifications constitutes a major bottle-neck in both ASP and SAT.[5] While this problem is addressed in SAT anew for each application, ASP centralizes this task in its grounders. The more surprising it is that there is so little work devoted to grounding within the ASP community (cf. [39,40,41,42]). This is a central yet neglected research topic. Apart from in-creasing research efforts in grounding, another major research theme is the devel-opment of program optimizers. That is, systems that transform highly declarative logic programs into equivalent ones, for which the overall solving time is signifi-cantly shorter than for the original program. In view of the vast literature on pro-gram equivalence in ASP (cf. [43,44,45,46,47]) the field appears to be well farmed for this endeavor.

Usability. At first, many people are impressed by the ease of modelling in ASP. How-ever, once they attack the first more complex problem and draft their first buggy encoding, they become often lost in the flat of declarativity. The solving process is completely transparent. No handle is available for finding out why the wrong or no solution is obtained. Also, when performance matters, it is still an art to come up with an efficient encoding, and often the result trades off declarativity. What is needed are dedicated tools, techniques, and methodologies to facilitate the de-velopment of answer set programs. In a nutshell, we need Software Engineering capacities that are adept enough to match ASP's high level of declarativity. First work on this can be found in [48,49,50,51] but much more work is needed.

Applicability. Many practical applications of ASP motivate extensions or combina-tions with other problem-solving paradigms. Looking at SAT's breakthrough in planning and model checking [52,36], it is interesting to observe that both involved dealing with an increasing bound on the solution size. Meanwhile dedicated SAT solvers allow for addressing this issue [53,54]. Also, a whole sub-area of SAT, known as SAT modulo theories, deals with the integration of other problem-solving paradigms. So far, ASP is making only modest steps in similar directions. For in-stance, a first approach to incremental ASP solving is described in [55] and the combination of ASP and Constraint Processing is explored in [56,57,58]. More cross-fertilization with neighboring fields is needed to tackle real applications.

Last but not least, we have to foster the exchange within the ASP community as well as to neighboring fields like Constraint Processing and SAT and moreover re-enforce the link to ASP's parental research areas, Logic Programming and NMR. We need to improve the inter-operability of our systems and tools through specifying interfaces and fixing some standards. We need common benchmark and problem reposi-tories and encourage comprehensive system competitions going beyond specific declar-ative solving paradigms. Otherwise, I am afraid that we will never turn our beef into a steak!

Acknowledgements. I would like to thank Gerd Brewka, Martin Gebser, Mirosław Truszczyński, and Stefan Woltran for fruitful comments on an earlier draft.

---

[5] Interestingly, in SAT, recourse to first-order theorem proving seems not an option because of the high performance of Boolean constraint technology.

References

1. Nebel, B., Rich, C., Swartout, W. (eds.): Proceedings of the Third International Conference on Principles of Knowledge Representation and Reasoning (KR 1992). Morgan Kaufmann, San Francisco (1992)
2. Ginsberg, M. (ed.): Readings in Nonmonotonic Reasoning. Morgan Kaufmann, San Francisco (1987)
3. Reiter, R.: Twelve years of nonmonotonic reasoning research: Where (and what) is the beef? In: [1], p. 789
4. Gelfond, M., Lifschitz, V.: The stable model semantics for logic programming. In: Kowalski, R., Bowen, K. (eds.) Proceedings of the Fifth International Conference and Symposium of Logic Programming (ICLP 1988), pp. 1070–1080. The MIT Press, Cambridge (1988)
5. Reiter, R.: A logic for default reasoning. Artificial Intelligence 13(1-2), 81–132 (1980)
6. Marek, V., Truszczyński, M.: Stable semantics for logic programs and default theories. In: Lusk, E., Overbeek, R. (eds.) Proceedings of the North American Conference on Logic Programing, pp. 243–256. The MIT Press, Cambridge (1989)
7. Bidoit, N., Froidevaux, C.: General logical databases and programs: Default logic semantics and stratification. Information and Computation 91(1), 15–54 (1991)
8. Niemelä, I., Simons, P.: Evaluating an algorithm for default reasoning. In: Working Notes of the IJCAI 1995 Workshop on Applications and Implementations of Nonmonotonic Reasoning Systems, pp. 66–72 (1995)
9. http://www.tcs.hut.fi/Software/smodels
10. Niemelä, I.: Logic programs with stable model semantics as a constraint programming paradigm. Annals of Mathematics and Artificial Intelligence 25(3-4), 241–273 (1999)
11. Marek, V., Truszczyński, M.: Stable models and an alternative logic programming paradigm. In: Apt, K., Marek, W., Truszczyński, M., Warren, D. (eds.) The Logic Programming Paradigm: a 25-Year Perspective, pp. 375–398. Springer, Heidelberg (1999)
12. Lifschitz, V.: Answer set programming and plan generation. Artificial Intelligence 138(1-2), 39–54 (2002)
13. Gelfond, M., Leone, N.: Logic programming and knowledge representation — the A-Prolog perspective. Artificial Intelligence 138(1-2), 3–38 (2002)
14. Baral, C.: Knowledge Representation, Reasoning and Declarative Problem Solving. Cambridge University Press, Cambridge (2003)
15. Tran, N., Baral, C.: Reasoning about triggered actions in AnsProlog and its application to molecular interactions in cells. In: Dubois, D., Welty, C., Williams, M. (eds.) Proceedings of the Ninth International Conference on Principles of Knowledge Representation and Reasoning (KR 2004), pp. 554–564. AAAI Press, Menlo Park (2004)
16. Dworschak, S., Grell, S., Nikiforova, V., Schaub, T., Selbig, J.: Modeling biological networks by action languages via answer set programming. Constraints 13(1-2), 21–65 (2008)
17. Soininen, T., Niemelä, I.: Developing a declarative rule language for applications in product configuration. In: Gupta, G. (ed.) PADL 1999. LNCS, vol. 1551, pp. 305–319. Springer, Heidelberg (1999)
18. Leone, N., Greco, G., Ianni, G., Lio, V., Terracina, G., Eiter, T., Faber, W., Fink, M., Gottlob, G., Rosati, R., Lembo, D., Lenzerini, M., Ruzzi, M., Kalka, E., Nowicki, B., Staniszkis, W.: The INFOMIX system for advanced integration of incomplete and inconsistent data. In: Özcan, F. (ed.) Proceedings of the ACM SIGMOD International Conference on Management of Data (SIGMOD 2005), pp. 915–917. ACM Press, New York (2005)
19. Eiter, T., Faber, W., Leone, N., Pfeifer, G.: The diagnosis frontend of the dlv system. AI Communications 12(1-2), 99–111 (1999)
20. Erdem, E., Wong, M.: Rectilinear Steiner tree construction using answer set programming. In: [59], pp. 386–399

21. Beierle, C., Dusso, O., Kern-Isberner, G.: Using answer set programming for a decision support system. In: Baral, C., Greco, G., Leone, N., Terracina, G. (eds.) LPNMR 2005. LNCS, vol. 3662, pp. 374–378. Springer, Heidelberg (2005)
22. Heljanko, K., Niemelä, I.: Bounded LTL model checking with stable models. Theory and Practice of Logic Programming 3(4-5), 519–550 (2003)
23. Kavanagh, J., Mitchell, D., Ternovska, E., Manuch, J., Zhao, X., Gupta, A.: Constructing Camin-Sokal phylogenies via answer set programming. In: Hermann, M., Voronkov, A. (eds.) LPAR 2006. LNCS, vol. 4246, pp. 452–466. Springer, Heidelberg (2006)
24. Brooks, D., Erdem, E., Erdogan, S., Minett, J., Ringe, D.: Inferring phylogenetic trees using answer set programming. Journal of Automated Reasoning 39(4), 471–511 (2007)
25. Aiello, L., Massacci, F.: Verifying security protocols as planning in logic programming. ACM Transactions on Computational Logic 2(4), 542–580 (2001)
26. Nogueira, M., Balduccini, M., Gelfond, M., Watson, R., Barry, M.: An A-prolog decision support system for the space shuttle. In: Ramakrishnan, I. (ed.) PADL 2001. LNCS, vol. 1990, pp. 169–183. Springer, Heidelberg (2001)
27. Balduccini, M., Gelfond, M.: Model-based reasoning for complex flight systems. In: Proceedings of the Fifth AIAA Conference on Aviation, Technology, Integration, and Operations (ATIO 2005) (2005)
28. Simons, P., Niemelä, I., Soininen, T.: Extending and implementing the stable model semantics. Artificial Intelligence 138(1-2), 181–234 (2002)
29. Leone, N., Pfeifer, G., Faber, W., Eiter, T., Gottlob, G., Perri, S., Scarcello, F.: The DLV system for knowledge representation and reasoning. ACM Transactions on Computational Logic 7(3), 499–562 (2006)
30. Lin, F., Zhao, Y.: ASSAT: computing answer sets of a logic program by SAT solvers. Artificial Intelligence 157(1-2), 115–137 (2004)
31. Giunchiglia, E., Lierler, Y., Maratea, M.: Answer set programming based on propositional satisfiability. Journal of Automated Reasoning 36(4), 345–377 (2006)
32. Gebser, M., Kaufmann, B., Neumann, A., Schaub, T.: Conflict-driven answer set solving. In: Veloso, M. (ed.) Proceedings of the Twentieth International Joint Conference on Artificial Intelligence (IJCAI 2007), pp. 386–392. AAAI Press/The MIT Press (2007)
33. Brachman, R., Schmolze, J.: An overview of the KL-ONE knowledge representation system. Cognitive Science 9(2), 189–192 (1985)
34. Davis, M., Putnam, H.: A computing procedure for quantification theory. Journal of the ACM 7, 201–215 (1960)
35. Davis, M., Logemann, G., Loveland, D.: A machine program for theorem-proving. Communications of the ACM 5, 394–397 (1962)
36. Clarke, E., Biere, A., Raimi, R., Zhu, Y.: Bounded model checking using satisfiability solving. Formal Methods in System Design 19(1), 7–34 (2001)
37. Baader, F., Horrocks, I., Sattler, U.: Description logics as ontology languages for the semantic web. In: Hutter, D., Stephan, W. (eds.) Mechanizing Mathematical Reasoning, pp. 228–248. Springer, Heidelberg (2005)
38. Gomes, C., Kautz, H., Sabharwal, A., Selman, B.: Satisfiability solvers. In: Lifschitz, V., van Hermelen, F., Porter, B. (eds.) Handbook of Knowledge Representation. Elsevier, Amsterdam (2008)
39. Syrjänen, T.: Omega-restricted logic programs. In: Eiter, T., Faber, W., Truszczyński, M. (eds.) LPNMR 2001. LNCS, vol. 2173, pp. 267–279. Springer, Heidelberg (2001)
40. Syrjänen, T.: Cardinality constraint programs. In: Alferes, J., Leite, J. (eds.) JELIA 2004. LNCS, vol. 3229, pp. 187–199. Springer, Heidelberg (2004)
41. Leone, N., Perri, S., Scarcello, F.: Backjumping techniques for rules instantiation in the DLV system. In: Delgrande, J., Schaub, T. (eds.) Proceedings of the Tenth International Workshop on Nonmonotonic Reasoning (NMR 2004), pp. 258–266 (2004)

42. Gebser, M., Schaub, T., Thiele, S.: GrinGo: A new grounder for answer set programming. In: [60], pp. 266–271

43. Lifschitz, V., Pearce, D., Valverde, A.: Strongly equivalent logic programs. ACM Transactions on Computational Logic 2(4), 526–541 (2001)

44. Turner, H.: Strong equivalence made easy: nested expressions and weight constraints. Theory and Practice of Logic Programming 3(4-5), 609–622 (2003)

45. Eiter, T., Fink, M.: Uniform equivalence of logic programs under the stable model semantics. In: Palamidessi, C. (ed.) ICLP 2003. LNCS, vol. 2916, pp. 224–238. Springer, Heidelberg (2003)

46. Eiter, T., Fink, M., Tompits, H., Woltran, S.: Simplifying logic programs under uniform and strong equivalence. In: Lifschitz, V., Niemelä, I. (eds.) LPNMR 2004. LNCS, vol. 2923, pp. 87–99. Springer, Heidelberg (2003)

47. Oikarinen, E., Janhunen, T.: Modular equivalence for normal logic programs. In: Brewka, G., Coradeschi, S., Perini, A., Traverso, P. (eds.) Proceedings of the Seventeenth European Conference on Artificial Intelligence (ECAI 2006), pp. 412–416. IOS Press, Amsterdam (2006)

48. Brain, M., de Vos, M.: Debugging logic programs under the answer set semantics. In: de Vos, M., Provetti, A. (eds.) Proceedings of the Third International Workshop on Answer Set Programming (ASP 2005). CEUR Workshop Proceedings (CEUR-WS.org), pp. 141–152 (2005)

49. Syrjänen, T.: Debugging inconsistent answer set programs. In: Dix, J., Hunter, A. (eds.) Proceedings of the Eleventh International Workshop on Nonmonotonic Reasoning (NMR 2006), Clausthal University of Technology, Institute for Informatics, pp. 77–83 (2006)

50. Pontelli, E., Son, T.: Justifications for logic programs under answer set semantics. In: Etalle, S., Truszczyński, M. (eds.) ICLP 2006. LNCS, vol. 4079. Springer, Heidelberg (2006)

51. Brain, M., Gebser, M., Pührer, J., Schaub, T., Tompits, H., Woltran, S.: Debugging ASP programs by means of ASP. In: [60], pp. 31–43

52. Kautz, H., Selman, B.: Planning as satisfiability. In: Neumann, B. (ed.) Proceedings of the Tenth European Conference on Artificial Intelligence (ECAI 1992), pp. 359–363. Wiley, Chichester (1992)

53. Eén, N., Sörensson, N.: Temporal induction by incremental SAT solving. Electronic Notes in Theoretical Computer Science 89(4) (2003)

54. Claessen, K., Sörensson, N.: New techniques that improve MACE-style finite model finding. In: Baumgartner, P., Fermüller, C. (eds.) Proceedings of the Workshop on Model Computation — Principles, Algorithms, Applications (2003)

55. Gebser, M., Kaminski, R., Kaufmann, B., Ostrowski, M., Schaub, T., Thiele, S.: Engineering an incremental ASP solver. In: Dovier, A., Garcia de la Banda, M., Pontelli, E. (eds.) Proceedings of the Twenty-fourth International Conference on Logic Programming (ICLP 2008) (to appear, 2008)

56. Elkabani, I., Pontelli, E., Son, T.: Smodels with CLP and its applications: A simple and effective approach to aggregates in ASP. In: [59], pp. 73–89

57. Baselice, S., Bonatti, P., Gelfond, M.: Towards an integration of answer set and constraint solving. In: Gabbrielli, M., Gupta, G. (eds.) ICLP 2005. LNCS, vol. 3668, pp. 52–66. Springer, Heidelberg (2005)

58. Mellarkod, V., Gelfond, M.: Integrating answer set reasoning with constraint solving techniques. In: Garrigue, J., Hermenegildo, M. (eds.) Proceedings of the Ninth International Symposium of Functional and Logic Programming, pp. 15–31. Springer, Heidelberg (2008)

59. Demoen, B., Lifschitz, V. (eds.): ICLP 2004. LNCS, vol. 3132. Springer, Heidelberg (2004)

60. Baral, C., Brewka, G., Schlipf, J. (eds.): LPNMR 2007. LNCS, vol. 4483. Springer, Heidelberg (2007)

Equivalences in Answer-Set Programming by Countermodels in the Logic of Here-and-There

Michael Fink

Institut für Informationssysteme, Technische Universität Wien,
Favoritenstraße 9-11, A-1040 Vienna, Austria
fink@kr.tuwien.ac.at

Abstract. In Answer-Set Programming different notions of equivalence, such as the prominent notions of strong and uniform equivalence, have been studied and characterized by various selections of models in the logic of Here-and-There (HT). For uniform equivalence however, correct characterizations in terms of HT-models can only be obtained for finite theories, respectively programs. In this paper, we show that a selection of countermodels in HT captures uniform equivalence also for infinite theories. This result is turned into coherent characterizations of the different notions of equivalence by countermodels, as well as by a mixture of HT-models and countermodels (so-called equivalence interpretations), which are lifted to first-order theories under a very general semantics given in terms of a quantified version of HT. We show that countermodels exhibit expedient properties like a simplified treatment of extended signatures, and provide further results for non-ground logic programs. In particular, uniform equivalence coincides under open and ordinary answer-set semantics, and for finite non-ground programs under these semantics, also the usual characterization of uniform equivalence in terms of maximal and total HT-models of the grounding is correct, even for infinite domains, when corresponding ground programs are infinite.

Keywords: answer-set programming, uniform equivalence, knowledge representation, program optimization.

1 Introduction

Logic programming under the answer-set semantics, called Answer-Set Programming (ASP), is a fundamental paradigm for nonmonotonic knowledge representation [1]. It is distinguished by a purely declarative semantics and efficient solvers [2,3,4,5]. Initially providing a semantics for rules with default negation in the body, the answer-set semantics [6] has been continually extended in terms of expressiveness, and recently the formalism has been lifted to a general answer-set semantics for first-order theories [7].

In a different line of research, the restriction to Herbrand domains for programs with variables, i.e., non-ground programs, has been relaxed in order to cope with open domains [8]. The open answer-set semantics has been further generalized by dropping the unique names assumption [9] for application settings where it does not apply, for instance, when combining ontologies with nonmontonic rules [10].

As for a logical characterization of the answer-set semantics, the logic of Here-and-There (HT), a nonclassical logic extending intuitionistic logic, served as a basis.

M. Garcia de la Banda and E. Pontelli (Eds.): ICLP 2008, LNCS 5366, pp. 99–113, 2008.

Equilibrium Logic selects certain minimal HT-models for characterizing the answer-set semantics for propositional theories and programs. It has recently been extended to Quantified Equilibrium Logic (QEL) for first-order theories on the basis of a quantified version of Here-and-There (QHT) [11]. Equilibrium Logic serves as a viable formalism for the study of semantic comparisons of theories and programs, like different notions of equivalence [12,13,14,15,16]. The practical relevance of this research originates in program optimization tasks that rely on modifications that preserve certain properties [17,18,19].

In this paper, we contribute by tackling an open problem concerning uniform equivalence of propositional theories and programs. Intuitively, two propositional logic programs are uniformly equivalent if the have the same answer sets under the addition of an arbitrary set of atoms to both programs. As has been shown in [20], so-called UE-models, a selection of HT-models based on a maximality criterion, do not characterize uniform equivalence for infinite propositional programs. Moreover, uniform equivalence of infinite programs cannot be captured by any selection of HT-models [20], as this is the case, e.g., for strong equivalence.

While the problem might seem esoteric at a first glance, since infinite propositional programs are rarely dealt with in practice, it is relevant when turning to the non-ground setting, respectively first-order theories, where infinite domains, such as the natural numbers, are encountered in many application domains.

The main contributions can be summarized as follows:

- We show that uniform equivalence of possibly infinite propositional theories, and thus programs, can be characterized by certain countermodels in HT. However, HT is not 'dual' (wrt. the characterization of countermodels) in the following sense: The countermodels of a theory Γ cannot be characterized by the models of a theory Γ'. Therefore, we also study *equivalence interpretations*, a mixture of models and countermodels of a theory, that can be characterized by a transformation of the theory if it is finite. We characterize classical equivalence, answer-set equivalence, strong equivalence, and uniform equivalence by appropriate selections of countermodels and equivalence interpretations.
- We lift these results to first-order theories by means of QHT, essentially introducing uniform equivalence for first-order theories under the most general form of answer-set semantics currently considered. We prove that, compared to QHT-models, countermodels alow for a simplified treatment of extended signatures.
- Finally, we show that the notion generalizes uniform equivalence for logic programs, and prove that it coincides for open and ordinary answer-set semantics. For finite non-ground programs under both ordinary and open answer-set semantics, we establish that uniform equivalence can be handled by the usual characterization in terms of HT-models of the grounding also for infinite domains.

Our results provide an elegant, uniform model-theoretic characterization of the different notions of equivalence considered in ASP. They generalize to first-order theories without finiteness restrictions, and are relevant for practical ASP systems that handle finite non-ground programs over infinite domains. For the sake of presentation, the technical content is split into two parts, discussing the propositional case first (Sections 2 and 3), and addressing first order theories and nonground programs in Sections 4 and 5.

2 Preliminaries

We start with the propositional setting and briefly summarize the necessary background. Corresponding first-order formalisms will be introduced when discussing first-order theories, respectively non-ground logic programs.

2.1 Propositional Here-and-There

In the propositional case we consider formulas of a propositional signature $\mathcal{L}$, i.e., a set of propositional constants, and the connectives $\wedge$, $\vee$, $\rightarrow$, and $\perp$ for conjunction, disjunction, implication, and falsity, respectively. Furthermore we make use of the following abbreviations: $\phi \equiv \psi$ for $(\phi \rightarrow \psi) \wedge (\psi \rightarrow \phi)$; $\neg\phi$ for $\phi \rightarrow \perp$; and $\top$ for $\perp \rightarrow \perp$. A formula is said to be *factual*[1] if it is built using $\wedge$, $\vee$, $\perp$, and $\neg$ (i.e., implications of the form $\phi \rightarrow \perp$), only. A theory Γ is factual if every formula of Γ has this property.

The logic of here-and-there is an intermediate logic between intuitionistic logic and classical logic. Like intuitionistic logic it can be semantically characterized by Kripke models, in particular using just two worlds, namely "*here*" and "*there*" (assuming that the *here* world is ordered before the *there* world). Accordingly, interpretations (HT-interpretations) are pairs (X, Y) of sets of atoms from $\mathcal{L}$, such that $X \subseteq Y$. An HT-interpretation is *total* if $X = Y$. The intuition is that atoms in X (the *here* part) are considered to be true, atoms not in Y (the *there* part) are considered to be false, while the remaining atoms (from $Y \setminus X$) are undefined.

We denote classical satisfaction of a formula ϕ by an interpretation X, i.e., a set of atoms, as $X \models \phi$, whereas satisfaction in the logic of here-and-there (an HT-model), symbolically $(X, Y) \models \phi$, is defined recursively:

1. $(X, Y) \models a$ if $a \in X$, for any atom a,
2. $(X, Y) \not\models \perp$,
3. $(X, Y) \models \phi \wedge \psi$ if $(X, Y) \models \phi$ and $(X, Y) \models \psi$,
4. $(X, Y) \models \phi \vee \psi$ if $(X, Y) \models \phi$ or $(X, Y) \models \psi$,
5. $(X, Y) \models \phi \rightarrow \psi$ if (i) $(X, Y) \not\models \phi$ or $(X, Y) \models \psi$, and (ii) $Y \models \phi \rightarrow \psi$[2].

An HT-interpretation (X, Y) satisfies a theory Γ, iff it satisfies all formulas $\phi \in \Gamma$. For an axiomatic proof system see, e.g., [13].

A total HT-interpretation (Y, Y) is called an *equilibrium model* of a theory Γ, iff $(Y, Y) \models \Gamma$ and for all HT-interpretations (X, Y), such that $X \subset Y$, it holds that $(X, Y) \not\models \Gamma$. An interpretation Y is an *answer set* of Γ iff (Y, Y) is an equilibrium model of Γ.

We will make use of the following simple properties: if $(X, Y) \models \Gamma$ then $(Y, Y) \models \Gamma$; and $(X, Y) \models \neg\phi$ iff $Y \models \neg\phi$; as well as of the following lemma.

Lemma 1 (Lemma 5 in [21]). *Let ϕ be a factual propositional formula. If $(X, Y) \models \phi$ and $X \subseteq X' \subseteq Y$, then $(X', Y) \models \phi$.*

---

[1] When uniform equivalence of theories is considered, then factual theories can be considered instead of facts—hence the terminology—see also the discussion at the end of this section.

[2] That is, Y satisfies $\phi \rightarrow \psi$ classically.

2.2 Propositional Logic Programming

A (*disjunctive*) rule r is of the form

$$a_1 \vee \cdots \vee a_k \vee \neg a_{k+1} \vee \cdots \vee \neg a_l \leftarrow b_1, \ldots, b_m, \neg b_{m+1}, \ldots, \neg b_n, \qquad (1)$$

where $a_1, \ldots, a_l, b_1, \ldots, b_n$ are atoms of a propositional signature $\mathcal{L}$, such that $l \geq k \geq 0$, $n \geq m \geq 0$, and $l + n > 0$. We refer to "$\neg$" as *default negation*. The *head* of r is the set $H(r) = \{a_1, \ldots, a_k, \neg a_{k+1}, \ldots, \neg a_l\}$, and the *body* of r is denoted by $B(r) = \{b_1, \ldots, b_m, \neg b_{m+1}, \ldots, \neg b_n\}$. Furthermore, we define the sets $H^+(r) = \{a_1, \ldots, a_k\}$, $H^-(r) = \{a_{k+1}, \ldots, a_l\}$, $B^+(r) = \{b_1, \ldots, b_m\}$, and eventually $B^-(r) = \{b_{m+1}, \ldots, b_n\}$. A *program* Π (over $\mathcal{L}$) is a set of rules (over $\mathcal{L}$).

An interpretation I, i.e., a set of atoms, satisfies a rule r, symbolically $I \models r$, iff $I \cap H^+(r) \neq \emptyset$ or $H^-(r) \not\subseteq I$ if $B^+(r) \subseteq I$ and $B^-(r) \cap I = \emptyset$. Adapted from [6], the *reduct* of a program Π with respect to an interpretation I, symbolically Π^I, is given by the set of rules

$$a_1 \vee \cdots \vee a_k \leftarrow b_1, \ldots, b_m,$$

obtained from rules in Π, such that $H^-(r) \subseteq I$ and $B^-(r) \cap I = \emptyset$.

An interpretation I is called an *answer set* of Π iff $I \models \Pi^I$ and it is subset minimal among the interpretations of $\mathcal{L}$ with this property.

2.3 Notions of Equivalence

For any two theories, respectively programs, and a potential extension by Γ, we consider the following notions of equivalence which have been shown to be the only forms of equivalence obtained by varying the logical form of extensions in the propositional case in [21].

Definition 1. *Two theories Γ_1, Γ_2 over $\mathcal{L}$ are called*

- classically equivalent, $\Gamma_1 \equiv_c \Gamma_2$, *if they have the same classical models;*
- answer-set equivalent, $\Gamma_1 \equiv_a \Gamma_2$, *if they have the same answer sets, i.e., equilibrium models;*
- strongly equivalent, $\Gamma_1 \equiv_s \Gamma_2$, *if, for any theory Γ over $\mathcal{L}' \supseteq \mathcal{L}$, $\Gamma_1 \cup \Gamma$ and $\Gamma_2 \cup \Gamma$ are answer-set equivalent;*
- uniformly equivalent, $\Gamma_1 \equiv_u \Gamma_2$, *if, for any factual theory Γ over $\mathcal{L}' \supseteq \mathcal{L}$, $\Gamma_1 \cup \Gamma$ and $\Gamma_2 \cup \Gamma$ are answer-set equivalent.*

Emanating from a logic programming setting, uniform equivalence is usually understood wrt. sets of *facts* (i.e., atoms). Obviously, uniform equivalence wrt. factual theories implies uniform equivalence wrt. sets of facts. The converse direction has been shown as well for general propositional theories in [21](cf. Theorem 2). Therefore, in general there is no difference whether uniform equivalence is considered wrt. sets of facts or factual theories. The latter may be regarded as facts, i.e., rules with an empty body, of so-called nested logic program rules. One might also consider sets of disjunctions of atomic formulas and their negations (i.e., clauses), accounting for facts according to the definition of program rules in this paper. Note that clauses constitute factual formulas and the classical transformation of clauses into implications is not valid under answer set semantics (respectively in HT).

3   Equivalence of Propositional Theories by HT-Countermodels

Uniform equivalence is usually characterized by so-called UE-models, i.e., total and maximal non-total HT-models, which fail to capture uniform equivalence for infinite propositional theories.

Example 1 ([20]). Let Γ_1 and Γ_2 over $\mathcal{L} = \{a_i \mid i \geq 1\}$ be the following propositional theories

$$\Gamma_1 = \{a_i \mid i \geq 1\}, \text{ and } \Gamma_2 = \{\neg a_i \to a_i, \ a_{i+1} \to a_i \mid i \geq 1\}.$$

Both, Γ_1 and Γ_2, have the single total HT-model $(\mathcal{L}, \mathcal{L})$. Furthermore, Γ_1 has no non-total HT-model $(X, \mathcal{L})$, i.e, such that $X \subset \mathcal{L}$, while Γ_2 has the non-total HT-models $(X_i, \mathcal{L})$, where $X_i = \{a_1, \ldots, a_i\}$ for $i \geq 0$. Both theories have the same total and maximal non-total (namely none) HT-models. But they are not uniformly equivalent as witnessed by the fact that $(\mathcal{L}, \mathcal{L})$ is an equilibrium model of Γ_1 but not of Γ_2.   □

The reason for this failure is the inability of the concept of maximality to capture differences exhibited by an infinite number of HT-models.

3.1   HT-Countermodels

The above problem can be avoided by taking HT-countermodels that satisfy a closure condition instead of the maximality criterion.

Definition 2. *An HT-interpretation* (X, Y) *is an* HT-countermodel *of a theory* Γ *if* $(X, Y) \not\models \Gamma$. *The set of HT-countermodels of a theory* Γ *is denoted by* $C_s(\Gamma)$.

Intuitively, an HT-interpretation fails to be an HT-model of a theory Γ when the theory is not satisfied at one of the worlds (*here* or *there*). Note that satisfaction at the *there* world amounts to classical satisfaction of the theory by Y. A simple consequence is that if $Y \not\models \Gamma$, then (X, Y) is an HT countermodel of Γ for any $X \subseteq Y$. At the *here* world, classical satisfaction is a sufficient condition but not necessary. For logic programs, satisfaction at the *here* world is precisely captured by the reduct of the program Π wrt. the interpretation at the *there* world, i.e., if $X \models \Pi^Y$.

Definition 3. *A total HT-interpretation* (Y, Y) *is*

- total-open *in a set* S *of HT-interpretations if* $(Y, Y) \in S$ *and* $(X, Y) \notin S$ *for every* $X \subset Y$.
- total-closed *in a set* S *of HT-interpretations if* $(X, Y) \in S$ *for every* $X \subseteq Y$.

We say that an HT-interpretation (X, Y) *is* there-closed *in a set* S *of HT-interpretations if* $(X', Y) \in S$ *for every* $X \subseteq X' \subset Y$.

A set S of HT-interpretations is total-closed, respectively total-open, if every total HT-interpretation $(Y, Y) \in S$ is total-closed in S, respectively total-open in S. By the remarks on the satisfaction at the *there* world above, it is obvious that every total HT-countermodel of a theory is also total-closed in $C_s(\Gamma)$. Consequently, $C_s(\Gamma)$ is a total-closed set for any theory Γ. By the same argument, if (X, Y) is an HT-countermodel such that $X \subset Y$ and $Y \not\models \Gamma$, then (X, Y) is there-closed in $C_s(\Gamma)$. The more relevant cases concerning the characterization of equivalence are HT-countermodels (X, Y) such that $Y \models \Gamma$.

Example 2. Consider the theory Γ_1 in Example 1 and a non-total HT-interpretation $(X, \mathcal{L})$. Since $(X, \mathcal{L})$ is non-total, $X \subset \mathcal{L}$ holds, and therefore $(X, \mathcal{L}) \not\models a_i$, for some $a_i \in \mathcal{L}$. Thus, we have identified a HT-countermodel of Γ_1. Moreover the same argument holds for any non-total HT-interpretation of the from $(X', \mathcal{L})$ (in particular such that $X \subseteq X' \subset Y$). Therefore, $(X, \mathcal{L})$ is there-closed in $C_s(\Gamma_1)$.

The intuition that, essentially, there-closed countermodels can be used instead of maximal non-total HT-models for characterizing uniform equivalence draws from the following observation. If (X, Y) is a maximal non-total HT-model, then every (X', Y), such that $X \subset X' \subset Y$, is a there-closed HT-countermodel. However, there-closed HT-countermodels are not sensitive to the problems that infinite chains cause for maximality.

Given a theory Γ, let $C_u(\Gamma)$ denote the set of there-closed HT-interpretations in $C_s(\Gamma)$.

Theorem 1. *Two propositional theories Γ_1, Γ_2 are uniformly equivalent iff they have the same sets of there-closed HT-countermodels, in symbols $\Gamma_1 \equiv_u \Gamma_2$ iff $C_u(\Gamma_1) = C_u(\Gamma_2)$.*

Proof. For the only-if direction, assume that two theories, Γ_1 and Γ_2, are uniformly equivalent. Then they are classically equivalent, i.e., they coincide on total HT-models, and therefore also on total HT-countermodels. Moreover, since every theory has a total-closed set of countermodels [22], we conclude that Γ_1 and Γ_2 coincide on all HT-models (X, Y) such that (Y, Y) is a (common) total HT-countermodel. Note that all these models are there-closed.

To prove our claim, it remains to show that Γ_1 and Γ_2 coincide on there-closed HT-countermodels (X, Y) such that (Y, Y) is an HT-model of both theories. Consider such a there-closed HT-countermodel of Γ_1. Then, (Y, Y) is a total HT-model of $\Gamma_1 \cup X$ and no $X' \subset Y$ exists such that $(X', Y) \models \Gamma_1 \cup X$, either because it is an HT-countermodel of Γ_1 (in case $X \subseteq X' \subset Y$) or of X (in case $X' \subset X$). Thus, Y is an answer set of $\Gamma_1 \cup X$ and, by hypothesis since X is factual, it is also an answer set of $\Gamma_2 \cup X$. The latter implies for all $X \subseteq X' \subset Y$ that $(X', Y) \not\models \Gamma_2 \cup X$. All these HT-interpretations are HT-models of X. Therefore we conclude that they all are HT-countermodels of Γ_2 and hence (X, Y) is a there-closed HT-countermodel of Γ_2. Again by symmetric arguments, we establish the same for any there-closed HT countermodel (X, Y) of Γ_2 such that (Y, Y) is a common total HT-model. This proves that Γ_1 and Γ_2 have the same sets of there-closed HT countermodels.

For the if direction, assume that two theories, Γ_1 and Γ_2, have the same sets of there-closed HT-countermodels. This implies that they have the same total HT-countermodels (since these are total-closed and thus there-closed) and hence the same total HT-models. Consider any factual theory Γ' such that Y is an answer set of $\Gamma_1 \cup \Gamma'$. We show that Y is an answer set of $\Gamma_2 \cup \Gamma'$ as well. Clearly, $(Y, Y) \models \Gamma_1 \cup \Gamma'$ implies $(Y, Y) \models \Gamma'$ and therefore $(Y, Y) \models \Gamma_2 \cup \Gamma'$. Consider any $X \subset Y$. Since Y is an answer set of $\Gamma_1 \cup \Gamma'$, it holds that $(X, Y) \not\models \Gamma_1 \cup \Gamma'$. We show that $(X, Y) \not\models \Gamma_2 \cup \Gamma'$. If $(X, Y) \not\models \Gamma'$ this is trivial, and in particular the case if $(X, Y) \models \Gamma_1$. So let us consider the case where $(X, Y) \not\models \Gamma_1$ and $(X, Y) \models \Gamma'$. By Lemma 1 we conclude from the latter that, for any $X \subseteq X' \subset Y$, $(X', Y) \models \Gamma'$. Therefore, $(X', Y) \not\models \Gamma_1$, as well. This implies that (X, Y) is a there-closed HT-countermodel of Γ_1. By hypothesis, (X, Y) is a there-closed HT-countermodel of Γ_2, i.e., $(X, Y) \not\models \Gamma_2$. Consequently, $(X, Y) \not\models \Gamma_2 \cup \Gamma'$. Since this argument applies to any $X \subset Y$, (Y, Y) is an equilibrium model of $\Gamma_2 \cup \Gamma'$, i.e., Y is an answer set of $\Gamma_2 \cup \Gamma'$. The same argument with Γ_1 and Γ_2 interchanged, proves that Y is an answer set of $\Gamma_1 \cup \Gamma'$ if it is an answer set of $\Gamma_2 \cup \Gamma'$. Therefore, the answer sets of $\Gamma_1 \cup \Gamma'$ and $\Gamma_2 \cup \Gamma'$ coincide for any factual theory Γ', i.e., Γ_1 and Γ_2 are uniformly equivalent. $\qquad\square$

Example 3. Reconsider the theories in Example 1. Every non-total HT-interpretation $(X, \mathcal{L})$ is an HT-countermodel of Γ_1, and thus, each of them is there-closed. On the other hand, none of these HT-interpretations is an HT countermodel of Γ_2. Therefore, Γ_1 and Γ_2 are not uniformly equivalent. $\qquad\square$

Countermodels have the drawback however, that they cannot be characterized directly in HT itself, i.e., as the HT-models of a 'dual' theory. The usage of "dual" here is non-standard compared to its application to particular calculi or consequence relations, but it likewise conveys the idea of a dual concept. In this sense HT therefore is non-dual:

Proposition 1. *Given a theory Γ, in general there is no theory Γ' such that (X, Y) is an HT-countermodel of Γ iff it is a HT-model of Γ', for any HT-interpretation (X, Y).*

3.2   Characterizing Equivalence by means of Equivalence Interpretations

The characterization of countermodels by a theory in HT essentially fails due to total HT-countermodels. However, total HT-countermodels of a theory are not necessary for characterizing equivalence, in the sense that they can be replaced by total HT-models of the theory for this purpose.

Definition 4. *An HT-countermodel (X, Y) of a theory Γ is called a* here-countermodel *of Γ if $Y \models \Gamma$.*

Definition 5. *An HT-interpretation is an* equivalence interpretation *of a theory Γ if it is a total HT-model of Γ or a here-countermodel of Γ. The set of equivalence interpretations of a theory Γ is denoted by $E_s(\Gamma)$.*

Theorem 2. *Two theories Γ_1 and Γ_2 coincide on their HT-countermodels iff they have the same equivalence interpretations, symbolically $C_s(\Gamma_1) = C_s(\Gamma_2)$ iff $E_s(\Gamma_1) = E_s(\Gamma_2)$.*

As a consequence of this result, and the usual relationships on HT-models, we can characterize equivalences of propositional theories also by selections of equivalence interpretations, i.e., a mixture of non-total HT countermodels and total HT-models, such that the characterizations, in particular for uniform equivalence, are also correct for infinite theories.

Given a theory Γ, let $C_c(\Gamma)$, resp. $E_c(\Gamma)$, denote the restriction to total HT-interpretations in $C_s(\Gamma)$, resp. in $E_s(\Gamma)$. $C_a(\Gamma)$ is the set of there-closed HT-interpretations of the form $(\emptyset, Y)$ in $C_s(\Gamma)$ such that $(Y, Y) \notin C_s(\Gamma)$, and $E_a(\Gamma)$ is the set of total-open HT-interpretations in $E_s(\Gamma)$ (i.e., equilibrium models). Finally, $E_u(\Gamma)$ denotes the set of there-closed HT-interpretations in $E_s(\Gamma)$.

Corollary 1. *Given two propositional theories Γ_1 and Γ_2, the following propositions are equivalent for $e \in \{c, a, s, u\}$:*

$$(1)\ \Gamma_1 \equiv_e \Gamma_2; \quad (2)\ C_e(\Gamma_1) = C_e(\Gamma_2); \quad (3)\ E_e(\Gamma_1) = E_e(\Gamma_2).$$

Example 4. In our running example, $C_u(\Gamma_1) \neq C_u(\Gamma_2)$, as well as $E_u(\Gamma_1) \neq E_u(\Gamma_2)$, by the remarks on non-total HT-interpretations in Example 3.   □

Since equivalence interpretations do not encompass total HT-countermodels, we attempt a direct characterization in HT.

Proposition 2. *Let M be an HT-interpretation over $\mathcal{L}$. Then, $M \in E_s(\Gamma)$ for a theory Γ iff $M \models \Gamma_\phi$ for some $\phi \in \Gamma$, where $\Gamma_\phi = \{\neg\neg\psi \mid \psi \in \Gamma\} \cup \{\phi \to (\neg\neg a \to a) \mid a \in \mathcal{L}\}$.*

For infinite propositional theories, we thus end up with a characterization of equivalence interpretations as the union of the HT-models of an infinite number of (infinite) theories. At least for finite theories, however, a characterization in terms of a (finite) theory is obtained (even for a potentially extended infinite signature).

If $\mathcal{L}' \supset \mathcal{L}$ and $M = (X, Y)$ is an HT-interpretation over $\mathcal{L}'$, then $M|_{\mathcal{L}}$ denotes the restriction of M to $\mathcal{L}$: $M|_{\mathcal{L}} = (X|_{\mathcal{L}}, Y|_{\mathcal{L}})$. The restriction is *totality preserving*, if $X \subset Y$ implies $X|_{\mathcal{L}} \subset Y|_{\mathcal{L}}$.

Proposition 3. *Let Γ be a theory over $\mathcal{L}$, let $\mathcal{L}' \supset \mathcal{L}$, and let M an HT-interpretation over $\mathcal{L}'$ such that $M|_{\mathcal{L}}$ is totality preserving. Then, $M \in C_s(\Gamma)$ implies $M|_{\mathcal{L}} \in C_s(\Gamma)$.*

Theorem 3. *Let Γ be a finite theory over $\mathcal{L}$, and let M be an HT-interpretation. Then, $M \in E_s(\Gamma)$ iff $M|_{\mathcal{L}} \models \bigvee_{\phi \in \Gamma} \bigwedge_{\psi \in \Gamma_\phi} \psi$, and $M|_{\mathcal{L}}$ is totality preserving.*

4   Generalization to First-Order Theories

Since the characterizations, in particular of uniform equivalence, presented in the previous section capture also infinite theories, they pave the way for generalizing this notion of equivalence to non-ground settings without any finiteness restrictions. In this section we study first-order theories.

As first-order theories we consider sets of sentences (closed formulas) of a first-order signature $\mathcal{L} = \langle \mathcal{F}, \mathcal{P} \rangle$ in the sense of classical first-order logic. Hence, $\mathcal{F}$ and $\mathcal{P}$ are pairwise disjoint sets of function symbols and predicate symbols with an associated arity, respectively. Elements of $\mathcal{F}$ with arity 0 are called object constants. A 0-ary predicate symbol is a propositional constant. Formulas are constructed as usual and variable-free formulas or theories are called *ground*. A sentence is said to be *factual* if it is built using connectives $\wedge$, $\vee$, and $\neg$ (i.e., implications of the form $\phi \to \bot$), only. A theory Γ is factual if every sentence of Γ has this property. The abbreviations introduced for propositional formulas carry over: $\phi \equiv \psi$ for $(\phi \to \psi) \wedge (\psi \to \phi)$; $\neg\phi$ for $\phi \to \bot$; and $\top$ for $\bot \to \bot$.

4.1 Static Quantified Logic of Here-and-There

Semantically we refer to the static quantified version of here-and-there with decidable equality as captured axiomatically by the system $\mathbf{QHT}^s_=$ [13]. It is characterized by Kripke models of two worlds with a common universe (hence static) that interpret function symbols in the same way.

More formally, consider a first-order interpretation I of a first-order signature $\mathcal{L}$ on a universe $\mathcal{U}$. We denote by $\mathcal{L}^I$ the extension of $\mathcal{L}$ obtained by adding pairwise distinct names c_ε as object constants for the objects in the universe, i.e., for each $\varepsilon \in \mathcal{U}$. We write $\mathcal{C}_\mathcal{U}$ for the set $\{c_\varepsilon \mid \varepsilon \in \mathcal{U}\}$ and identify I with its extension to $\mathcal{L}^I$ given by $I(c_\varepsilon) = \varepsilon$. Furthermore, let t^I denote the value assigned by I to a ground term t (of signature $\mathcal{L}^I$), and let $\mathcal{L}_\mathcal{F}$ denote the restriction of $\mathcal{L}$ to function symbols (thus including object constants). By $\mathcal{B}_{\mathcal{P},\mathcal{C}_\mathcal{U}}$ we denote the set of atomic formulas built using predicates from $\mathcal{P}$ and constants $\mathcal{C}_\mathcal{U}$.

We represent a first-order interpretation I of $\mathcal{L}$ on $\mathcal{U}$ as a pair $\langle I|_{\mathcal{L}_\mathcal{F}}, I|_{\mathcal{C}_\mathcal{U}}\rangle,$[3] where $I|_{\mathcal{L}_\mathcal{F}}$ is the restriction of I on function symbols, and $I|_{\mathcal{C}_\mathcal{U}}$ is the set of atomic formulas from $\mathcal{B}_{\mathcal{P},\mathcal{C}_\mathcal{U}}$ which are satisfied in I. Correspondingly, classical satisfaction of a sentence ϕ by a first-order interpretation $\langle I|_{\mathcal{L}_\mathcal{F}}, I|_{\mathcal{C}_\mathcal{U}}\rangle$ is denoted by $\langle I|_{\mathcal{L}_\mathcal{F}}, I|_{\mathcal{C}_\mathcal{U}}\rangle \models \phi$. We also define a subset relation for first-order interpretations I_1, I_2 of $\mathcal{L}$ on $\mathcal{U}$ (ie., over the same domain) by $I_1 \subseteq I_2$ if $I_1|_{\mathcal{C}_\mathcal{U}} \subseteq I_2|_{\mathcal{C}_\mathcal{U}}$.[4]

A QHT-interpretation of $\mathcal{L}$ is a triple $\langle I, J, K\rangle$, such that (i) I is an interpretation of $\mathcal{L}_\mathcal{F}$ on $\mathcal{U}$, and (ii) $J \subseteq K \subseteq \mathcal{B}_{\mathcal{P},\mathcal{C}_\mathcal{U}}$.

The satisfaction of a sentence ϕ of signature $\mathcal{L}^I$ by a QHT-interpretation $M = \langle I, J, K\rangle$ (a QHT-model) is defined as:

1. $M \models p(t_1, \ldots, t_n)$ if $p(c_{t_1^I}, \ldots, c_{t_n^I}) \in J$;
2. $M \models t_1 = t_2$ if $t_1^I = t_2^I$;
3. $M \not\models \bot$;
4. $M \models \phi \wedge \psi$ if $M \models \phi$ and $M \models \psi$,
5. $M \models \phi \vee \psi$, if $M \models \phi$ or $M \models \psi$,
6. $M \models \phi \rightarrow \psi$ if (i) $M \not\models \phi$ or $M \models \psi$, and (ii) $\langle I, K\rangle \models \phi \rightarrow \psi$[5];
7. $M \models \forall x \phi(x)$ if $M \models \phi(c_\varepsilon)$ for all $\varepsilon \in \mathcal{U}$;
8. $M \models \exists x \phi(x)$ if $M \models \phi(c_\varepsilon)$ for some $\varepsilon \in \mathcal{U}$;.

A QHT-interpretation $M = \langle I, J, K\rangle$ is called a *QHT-countermodel* of a theory Γ iff $M \not\models \Gamma$; it is called *total* if $J = K$. A total QHT-interpretation $M = \langle I, K, K\rangle$ is called a *quantified equilibrium model* (*QEL-model*) of a theory Γ, iff $M \models \Gamma$ and $M' \not\models \Gamma$, for all QHT-interpretations $M' = \langle I, J, K\rangle$ such that $J \subset K$. A first-order interpretation $\langle I, K\rangle$ is an *answer set* of Γ iff $M = \langle I, K, K\rangle$ is a QEL-model of a theory Γ.

In analogy to the propositional case, we will use the following simple properties.

Lemma 2. *If* $\langle I, J, K\rangle \models \phi$ *then* $\langle I, K, K\rangle \models \phi$.

Lemma 3. $\langle I, J, K\rangle \models \neg\phi$ *iff* $\langle I, K\rangle \models \neg\phi$.

---

[3] We use angle brackets to distinguish from HT-interpretations.

[4] Note that one could additionally require that $I_1|_{\mathcal{L}_\mathcal{F}} = I_2|_{\mathcal{L}_\mathcal{F}}$, which is not necessary for our purpose, however.

[5] That is, $\langle I, K\rangle$ satisfies $\phi \rightarrow \psi$ classically.

4.2   Characterizing Equivalence by QHT-countermodels

We aim at generalizing uniform equivalence for first-order theories, in its most liberal form, which means wrt. factual theories. For this purpose, we first lift Lemma 1.

Lemma 4. *Let ϕ be a factual sentence. If $\langle I, J, K \rangle \models \phi$ and $J \subseteq J' \subseteq K$, then $\langle I, J', K \rangle \models \phi$.*

The different notions of closure naturally extend to (sets of) QHT-interpretations. In particular, a total QHT-interpretation $M = \langle I, K, K \rangle$ is called *total-open* in a set S of QHT-interpretations, if $M \in S$ and $\langle I, J, K \rangle \notin S$ for every $J \subset K$. It is called *total-closed* if $\langle I, J, K \rangle \in S$ for every $J \subset K$. A QHT-interpretation $\langle I, J, K \rangle$ is *there-closed* in a set S of QHT-interpretations if $\langle I, J', K \rangle \in S$ for every $J \subseteq J' \subset K$.

The first main result lifts the characterization of uniform equivalence for theories by HT-countermodels to the first-order case.

Theorem 4. *Two first-order theories are uniformly equivalent iff they have the same sets of there-closed QHT-countermodels.*

We next turn to an alternative characterization by a mixture of QHT-models and QHT-countermodels as in the propositional case. A QHT-countermodel $\langle I, J, K \rangle$ of a theory Γ is called QHT here-countermodel of Γ if $\langle I, K \rangle \models \Gamma$. A QHT-interpretation $\langle I, J, K \rangle$ is an QHT equivalence-interpretation of a theory Γ, if it is a total QHT-model of Γ or a QHT here-countermodel of Γ. In slight abuse of notation, we reuse the notation S_e, $S \in \{C, E\}$ and $e \in \{c, a, s, u\}$, for respective sets of QHT-interpretations, and arrive at the following formal result:

Theorem 5. *Two theories coincide on their QHT-countermodels iff they have the same QHT equivalence-interpretations, in symbols $C_s(\Gamma_1) = C_s(\Gamma_2)$ iff $E_s(\Gamma_1) = E_s(\Gamma_2)$.*

As a consequence of these two main results, we obtain an elegant, unified formal characterization of the different notions of equivalence for first-order theories under generalized answer-set semantics.

Corollary 2. *Given two first-order theories Γ_1 and Γ_2, the following propositions are equivalent for $e \in \{c, a, s, u\}$: $\Gamma_1 \equiv_e \Gamma_2$; $C_e(\Gamma_1) = C_e(\Gamma_2)$; $E_e(\Gamma_1) = E_e(\Gamma_2)$.*

Moreover, QHT-countermodels allow for a simplified treatment of extended signatures, which is not the case for QHT-models. For QHT-models it is known that $M \models \Gamma$ implies $M|_{\mathcal{L}} \models \Gamma$ (cf. e.g., Prop. 3 in [10]), hence $M|_{\mathcal{L}} \not\models \Gamma$ implies $M \not\models \Gamma$, i.e., $M|_{\mathcal{L}} \in C_s(\Gamma)$ implies $M \in C_s(\Gamma)$. The converse direction holds for totality preserving restrictions.

Proposition 4. *Let M be a QHT-interpretation over $\mathcal{L}$ on $\mathcal{U}$. Then, $M \in E_s(\Gamma)$ for a theory Γ iff $M \models \Gamma_\phi(M)$ for some $\phi \in \Gamma$, where $\Gamma_\phi(M) = \{\neg\neg\psi \mid \psi \in \Gamma\} \cup \{\phi \to (\neg\neg a \to a) \mid a \in \mathcal{B}_{\mathcal{P}, \mathcal{C}_\mathcal{U}}\}$.*

Theorem 6. *Let Γ be a theory over $\mathcal{L}$, let $\mathcal{L}' \supset \mathcal{L}$, and let M an HT-interpretation over $\mathcal{L}'$ such that $M|_{\mathcal{L}}$ is totality preserving. Then, $M \in C_s(\Gamma)$ implies $M|_{\mathcal{L}} \in C_s(\Gamma)$.*

Proof. Let $M = \langle I', J', K' \rangle$, $M|_{\mathcal{L}} = \langle I, J, K \rangle$, and assume $M \not\models \Gamma$. First, suppose $\langle I', K', K' \rangle \not\models \Gamma$, i.e., there exists a sentence $\phi \in \Gamma$, such that $\langle I', K', K' \rangle \not\models \phi$. We show that $\langle I, K, K \rangle \not\models \phi$ by induction on the formula structure of ϕ.

Let us denote $\langle I, K, K \rangle$ by N and $\langle I', K', K' \rangle$ by N'. For the base case, consider an atomic sentence ϕ. If ϕ is of the form $p(t_1, \ldots, t_n)$, then $p(c_{t_1^I}, \ldots, c_{t_n^I}) \notin K$ because $N' \not\models \phi$. By the fact that $K \subseteq K'$ we conclude that $p(c_{t_1^I}, \ldots, c_{t_n^I}) \notin K$ and hence $N \not\models \phi$. If ϕ is of the form $t_1 = t_2$ then $N' \not\models \phi$ implies $t_1^I \neq t_2^I$, and thus $N \not\models \phi$. If ϕ is $\bot$ then $N' \not\models \phi$ and $N \not\models \phi$. This proves the claim for atomic formulas.

For the induction step, assume that $N' \not\models \phi$ implies $N \not\models \phi$, for any sentence of depth $n - 1$, and let ϕ be a sentence of depth n. We show that $M|_{\mathcal{L}} \models \phi$ implies $M \models \phi$. Suppose ϕ is the conjunction or disjunction of two sentences ϕ_1 and ϕ_2. Then ϕ_1 and ϕ_2 are sentences of depth $n - 1$. Hence, $N' \not\models \phi_1$ implies $N \not\models \phi_1$, and the same for ϕ_2. Therefore, if N' is a QHT-countermodel of one or both of the sentences then so is N, which implies $N' \not\models \phi$ implies $N \not\models \phi$ if ϕ is the conjunction or disjunction of two sentences. As for implication, let ϕ be of the form $\phi_1 \rightarrow \phi_2$. In this case, $N' \not\models \phi$ implies $N' \models \phi_1$ and $N' \not\models \phi_2$. Therefore, $N \models \phi_1$ by the usual sub-model property for QHT-models, and $N \not\models \phi_2$ by assumption. Hence, $N \not\models \phi$. Eventually, consider a quantified sentence ϕ, i.e., ϕ is of the form $\forall x \phi_1(x)$ or $\exists x \phi_1(x)$. In this case, $N' \not\models \phi$ implies $N' \not\models \phi_1(c_\varepsilon)$ for some, respectively all, $\varepsilon \in \mathcal{U}$. Since each of the sentences $\phi_1(c_\varepsilon)$ is of depth $n - 1$, the same is true for N by assumption. It follows that $N' \not\models \phi$ implies $N \not\models \phi$ also for quantified sentences ϕ of depth n, and therefore, for any sentence ϕ of depth n. This concludes the inductive argument and proves the claim for total QHT-countermodels.

Moreover, because QHT-countermodels are total-closed, this proves the claim for any QHT-countermodel $M = \langle I', J', K' \rangle$, such that $\langle I', K', K' \rangle \not\models \Gamma$.

We continue with the case that $\langle I', K', K' \rangle \models \Gamma$. Then $J' \subset K'$ holds, which means that M is a QHT equivalence-interpretation of Γ. Therefore, $M \not\models \phi$ for some $\phi \in \Gamma$. Additionally, $M \models \neg\neg\psi$ for all $\psi \in \Gamma$ (recall that $\langle I', K', K' \rangle \models \Gamma$, thus $\langle I', K' \rangle \models \Gamma$). By construction this implies $M \models \Gamma_\phi(M|_{\mathcal{L}})$. Therefore, $M|_{\mathcal{L}} \models \Gamma_\phi(M|_{\mathcal{L}})$, i.e., $M|_{\mathcal{L}}$ is a QHT equivalence-interpretation of Γ. Since the restriction is totality preserving, $M|_{\mathcal{L}}$ is non-total. This proves $M|_{\mathcal{L}} \not\models \Gamma$. $\qquad\square$

Since QHT equivalence-interpretations consist of non-total QHT-countermodels and total QHT-models, the result carries over to QHT equivalence-interpretations. However, QHT-models do not satisfy such an extended property:

Example 5. Consider the theory $\Gamma = \{q(X) \rightarrow p(X)\}$ over $\mathcal{L} = \langle \{c_1\}, \{p, q\} \rangle$, and let $\mathcal{L}' = \langle \{c_1, c_2\}, \{p, q\} \rangle$. Then, $M = \langle id, \{p(c_1)\}, \{p(c_1), q(c_1)\} \rangle$ is a QHT-model of Γ over $\mathcal{L}$ on $\mathcal{U} = \{c_1, c_2\}$. However, $M' = \langle id, \{p(c_1), q(c_2)\}, \{p(c_1), p(c_2), q(c_1), q(c_2)\} \rangle$ is not a QHT-model of Γ on $\mathcal{U}$, although $M'|_{\mathcal{L}} = M$ is totality preserving.

Moreover, it is indeed necessary that the reduction is totality preserving. For instance, $M = \langle id, \{p(c_1), q(c_2)\}, \{p(c_1), p(c_2), q(c_2)\} \rangle$ is a non-total QHT-countermodel, but $M|_{\mathcal{L}} = \langle id, \{p(c_1)\}, \{p(c_1)\} \rangle$ is a QHT-model of Γ. $\qquad\square$

5 Non-ground Logic Programs

In this section we apply the characterizations obtained for first-order theories to non-ground logic programs under various extended semantics—compared to the traditional semantics in terms of Herbrand interpretations. For a proper treatment of these issues, further background is required and introduced (succinctly, but at sufficient detail) below.

In non-ground logic programming, we restrict to a function-free first-order signature $\mathcal{L} = \langle \mathcal{F}, \mathcal{P} \rangle$ (i.e., $\mathcal{F}$ contains object constants only) without equality. A *program* Π (over $\mathcal{L}$) is a set of rules (over $\mathcal{L}$) of the form (1). A rule r is *safe* if each variable occurring in $H(r) \cup B^-(r)$ also occurs in $B^+(r)$; a rule r is *ground*, if all atoms occurring in it are ground. A program is safe, respectively ground, if all of its rules enjoy this property.

Given Π over $\mathcal{L}$ and a universe $\mathcal{U}$, let $\mathcal{L}^{\mathcal{U}}$ be the extension of $\mathcal{L}$ as before. The *grounding of* Π wrt. $\mathcal{U}$ and an interpretation $I|_{\mathcal{L}_{\mathcal{F}}}$ of $\mathcal{L}_{\mathcal{F}}$ on $\mathcal{U}$ is defined as the set $grd_{\mathcal{U}}(\Pi, I|_{\mathcal{L}_{\mathcal{F}}})$ of ground rules obtained from $r \in \Pi$ by (i) replacing any constant c in r by c_{ε} such that $I|_{\mathcal{L}_{\mathcal{F}}}(c) = \varepsilon$, and (ii) all possible substitutions of elements in $\mathcal{C}_{\mathcal{U}}$ for the variables in r.

Adapted from [6], the *reduct* of a program Π with respect to a first-order interpretation $I = \langle I|_{\mathcal{L}_{\mathcal{F}}}, I|_{\mathcal{C}_{\mathcal{U}}} \rangle$ on universe $\mathcal{U}$, in symbols $grd_{\mathcal{U}}(\Pi, I|_{\mathcal{L}_{\mathcal{F}}})^I$, is given by the set of rules

$$a_1 \vee \cdots \vee a_k \;\leftarrow\; b_1, \ldots, b_m,$$

obtained from rules in $grd_{\mathcal{U}}(\Pi, I|_{\mathcal{L}_{\mathcal{F}}})$ of the form (1), such that $I \models a_i$ for all $k < i \le l$ and $I \not\models b_j$ for all $m < j \le n$.

A first-order interpretation I satisfies a rule r, $I \models r$, iff $I \models \Gamma_r$, where $\Gamma_r = \forall \boldsymbol{x}(\beta_r \to \alpha_r)$, $\boldsymbol{x}$ are the free variables in r, α_r is the disjunction of $H(r)$, and β_r is the conjunction of $B(r)$. It satisfies a program Π, symbolically $I \models \Pi$, iff it satisfies every $r \in \Pi$, i.e., if $I \models \Gamma_{\Pi}$, where $\Gamma_{\Pi} = \bigcup_{r \in \Pi} \Gamma_r$.

A first-order interpretation I is called a *generalized answer set* of Π iff it satisfies $grd_{\mathcal{U}}(\Pi, I|_{\mathcal{L}_{\mathcal{F}}})^I$ and it is subset minimal among the interpretations of $\mathcal{L}$ on $\mathcal{U}$ with this property.

Traditionally, only *Herbrand interpretations* are considered as the answer sets of a logic program. The set of all (object) constants occurring in Π is called the *Herbrand universe* of Π, symbolically $\mathcal{H}$. If no constant appears in Π, then $\mathcal{H} = \{c\}$, for an arbitrary constant c. A Herbrand interpretation is any interpretation I of $\mathcal{L}_{\mathcal{H}} = \langle \mathcal{H}, \mathcal{P} \rangle$ on $\mathcal{H}$ interpreting object constants by identity, id, i.e., $I(c) = id(c) = c$ for all $c \in \mathcal{H}$. A Herbrand interpretation I is an *ordinary answer set* of Π iff it is subset minimal among the interpretations of $\mathcal{L}_{\mathcal{H}}$ on $\mathcal{H}$ satisfying $grd_{\mathcal{H}}(\Pi, id)^I$.

Furthermore, an *extended Herbrand interpretation* is an interpretation of $\mathcal{L}$ on $U \supseteq \mathcal{F}$ interpreting object constants by identity. An extended Herbrand interpretation I is an *open answer set* [8] of Π iff it is subset minimal among the interpretations of $\mathcal{L}$ on $\mathcal{U}$ satisfying $grd_{\mathcal{U}}(\Pi, id)^I$.

Note that since we consider programs without equality, we semantically resort to the logic $\mathbf{QHT^s}$, which results from $\mathbf{QHT^s_=}$ by dropping the axioms for equality. Concerning Kripke models, however, in slight abuse of notation, we reuse QHT-models as defined for the general case. A QHT-interpretation $M = \langle I, J, K \rangle$ is called an (extended) QHT Herbrand interpretation, if $\langle I, K \rangle$ is an (extended) Herbrand interpretation. Given a program Π, $\langle I, K \rangle$ is a generalized answer set of Π iff $\langle I, K, K \rangle$ is a QEL-model of Γ_{Π}, and $\langle I, K \rangle$ is an open, respectively ordinary, answer set of Π iff $\langle I, K, K \rangle$ is an extended Herbrand, respectively Herbrand, QEL-model of Γ_{Π}. Notice that the static interpretation of constants introduced by Item (i) of the grounding process is essential for this correspondences in terms of **QHT^s**. In slight abuse of notation, we further on identify Π and Γ_Π.

As already mentioned for propositional programs, uniform equivalence is usually understood wrt. sets of *ground facts* (i.e., ground atoms). Obviously, uniform equivalence wrt. factual theories implies uniform equivalence wrt. ground atoms. We show the converse direction (lifting Theorem 2 in [21]).

Proposition 5. *Given two programs Π_1, Π_2, then $\Pi_1 \equiv_u \Pi_2$ iff $(\Pi_1 \cup A) \equiv_a (\Pi_2 \cup A)$, for any set of ground atoms A.*

Thus, there is no difference whether we consider uniform equivalence wrt. sets of ground facts or factual theories. Since one can also consider sets of clauses, i.e. disjunctions of atomic formulas and their negations, which is a more suitable representation of facts according to the definition of program rules in this paper, we adopt the following terminology. A rule r is called a *fact* if $B(r) = \emptyset$, and a *factual program* is a set of facts. Then, by our result $\Pi_1 \equiv_u \Pi_2$ holds for programs Π_1, Π_2 iff $(\Pi_1 \cup \Pi) \equiv_a (\Pi_2 \cup \Pi)$, for any factual program Π.

5.1   Uniform Equivalence under Herbrand Interpretations

The results in the previous section generalize the notion of uniform equivalence to programs under generalized open answer-set semantics and provide alternative characterizations for other notions of equivalence. They apply to programs under open answer-set semantics and ordinary answer-set semantics, when QHT-interpretations are restricted to extended Herbrand interpretations and Herbrand interpretations, respectively. For programs Π_1 and Π_2 and $e \in \{c, a, s, u\}$, we use $\Pi_1 \equiv_e^{\mathcal{E}} \Pi_2$ and $\Pi_1 \equiv_e^{\mathcal{H}} \Pi_2$ to denote (classical, answer-set, strong, or uniform) equivalence under open answer-set semantics and ordinary answer-set semantics, respectively.

Corollary 3. *Given two programs Π_1 and Π_2, it holds that*

- *$\Pi_1 \equiv_e^{\mathcal{E}} \Pi_2$, $C_e^{\mathcal{E}}(\Pi_1) = C_e^{\mathcal{E}}(\Pi_2)$, and $E_e^{\mathcal{E}}(\Pi_1) = E_e^{\mathcal{E}}(\Pi_2)$ are equivalent; and*
- *$\Pi_1 \equiv_e^{\mathcal{H}} \Pi_2$, $C_e^{\mathcal{H}}(\Pi_1) = C_e^{\mathcal{H}}(\Pi_2)$, and $E_e^{\mathcal{H}}(\Pi_1) = E_e^{\mathcal{H}}(\Pi_2)$ are equivalent;*

where $e \in \{c, a, s, u\}$, and superscript $\mathcal{H}$ $(\mathcal{E})$ denotes the restriction to (extended) Herbrand interpretations.

For safe programs the notions of open answer set and ordinary answer set coincide [10]. Note that a fact is safe if it is ground. We obtain that uniform equivalence coincides under the two semantics even for programs that are not safe. Intuitively, the potential addition of arbitrary facts accounts for the difference in the semantics since it requires to consider larger domains than the Herbrand universe.

Theorem 7. *Let Π_1, Π_2 be programs over $\mathcal{L}$. Then, $\Pi_1 \equiv_u^{\mathcal{E}} \Pi_2$ iff $\Pi_1 \equiv_u^{\mathcal{H}} \Pi_2$.*

Finally, we turn to the practically relevant setting of finite, possibly unsafe, programs under Herbrand interpretations, i.e., ordinary (and open) answer-set semantics. For finite programs, uniform equivalence can be characterized by HT-models of the grounding, also for infinite domains. In other words, the problems of "infinite chains" as in Example 1 cannot be generated by the process of grounding.

Theorem 8. *Let Π_1, Π_2 be finite programs over $\mathcal{L}$. Then, $\Pi_1 \equiv_u^{\mathcal{H}} \Pi_2$ iff Π_1 and Π_2 have the same (i) total and (ii) maximal, non-total extended Herbrand QHT-models.*

6   Conclusion

Countermodels in equilibrium logic have recently been used in [22] to show that propositional disjunctive logic programs with negation in the head are strongly equivalent to propositional theories, and in [23] to generate a minimal logic program for a given propositional theory.

By means of Quantified Equilibrium Logic, in [13], the notion of strong equivalence has been extended to first-order theories with equality, under the generalized notion of answer set we have adopted. QEL has also been shown to capture open answer-sets [8] and generalized open answer-sets [9], and is a promising framework to study hybrid knowledge bases providing a unified semantics, since it encompasses classical logic as well as disjunctive logic programs under the answer-set semantics [10].

Our results complete the picture by making uniform equivalence, which so far has only been dealt with for finite programs under ordinary answer-set semantics, amenable to these generalized settings without any finiteness restrictions, in particular on the domain. Thus, we arrived at a uniform model-theoretic characterization of the notions of equivalence studied in ASP. We have also shown that for finite programs, i.e., those programs solvers are able to deal with, infinite domains do not cause the problems observed for infinite propositional programs, when dealing with uniform equivalence in terms of HT-models of the grounding.

The combination of ontologies and nonmonotonic rules is an important issue in knowledge representation and reasoning for the Semantic Web. Therefore, the study of optimizations and correspondences under an appropriate semantics, such as the generalizations of answer-set semantics characterized by QEL, constitute an interesting topic for further research of relevance in this application domain. Like for Datalog, uniform equivalence may serve investigations on query equivalence and query containment in these hybrid settings. The simplified treatment of extended signatures for countermodels and equivalence interpretations is expected to be of avail, in particular for the study of relativized notions of equivalence and correspondence [24].

On the foundational level, our results raise the interesting question whether extensions of intuitionistic logics that allow for a direct characterization of countermodels, would provide a more suitable formal apparatus for the study of (at least uniform) equivalence in ASP.

Acknowledgements. I am grateful for suggestions by the anonymous reviewers to improve presentation. This work was partially supported by the Austrian Science Fund (FWF) under grants P18019 and P20841.

References

1. Baral, C.: Knowledge Representation, Reasoning and Declarative Problem Solving. Cambridge University Press, Cambridge (2003)
2. Leone, N., Pfeifer, G., Faber, W., Eiter, T., Gottlob, G., Perri, S., Scarcello, F.: The DLV system for knowledge representation and reasoning. ACM TOCL 7(3), 499–562 (2006)

3. Janhunen, T., Niemelä, I.: GnT - A solver for disjunctive logic programs. In: Lifschitz, V., Niemelä, I. (eds.) LPNMR 2004. LNCS, vol. 2923, pp. 331–335. Springer, Heidelberg (2003)
4. Lin, F., Zhao, Y.: ASSAT: Computing answer sets of a logic program by SAT solvers. Artif. Intell. 157(1-2), 115–137 (2004)
5. Gebser, M., Kaufmann, B., Neumann, A., Schaub, T.: clasp: A conflict-driven answer set solver. In: Baral, C., Brewka, G., Schlipf, J. (eds.) LPNMR 2007. LNCS, vol. 4483, pp. 260–265. Springer, Heidelberg (2007)
6. Gelfond, M., Lifschitz, V.: Classical Negation in Logic Programs and Disjunctive Databases. New Generation Computing 9, 365–385 (1991)
7. Ferraris, P., Lee, J., Lifschitz, V.: A new perspective on stable models. In: Veloso, M.M. (ed.) IJCAI 2007, pp. 372–379 (2007)
8. Heymans, S., Nieuwenborgh, D.V., Vermeir, D.: Open answer set programming for the semantic web. J. Applied Logic 5(1), 144–169 (2007)
9. Heymans, S., de Bruijn, J., Predoiu, L., Feier, C., Nieuwenborgh, D.V.: Guarded hybrid knowledge bases. CoRR abs/0711.2155 (2008) (to appear in TPLP)
10. de Bruijn, J., Pearce, D., Polleres, A., Valverde, A.: Quantified equilibrium logic and hybrid rules. In: Marchiori, M., Pan, J.Z., de Sainte Marie, C. (eds.) RR 2007. LNCS, vol. 4524, pp. 58–72. Springer, Heidelberg (2007)
11. Pearce, D., Valverde, A.: Quantified equilibrium logic an the first order logic of here-and-there. Technical Report MA-06-02, Univ. Rey Juan Carlos (2006)
12. Eiter, T., Fink, M., Tompits, H., Woltran, S.: Strong and Uniform Equivalence in Answer-Set Programming: Characterizations and Complexity Results for the Non-Ground Case. In: Veloso, M.M., Kambhampati, S. (eds.) AAAI 2005, pp. 695–700. AAAI Press, Menlo Park (2005)
13. Lifschitz, V., Pearce, D., Valverde, A.: A characterization of strong equivalence for logic programs with variables. In: Baral, C., Brewka, G., Schlipf, J. (eds.) LPNMR 2007. LNCS, vol. 4483, pp. 188–200. Springer, Heidelberg (2007)
14. Woltran, S.: A common view on strong, uniform, and other notions of equivalence in answer-set programming. TPLP 8(2), 217–234 (2008)
15. Faber, W., Konczak, K.: Strong order equivalence. AMAI 47(1-2), 43–78 (2006)
16. Inoue, K., Sakama, C.: Equivalence of logic programs under updates. In: Alferes, J.J., Leite, J. (eds.) JELIA 2004. LNCS, vol. 3229, pp. 174–186. Springer, Heidelberg (2004)
17. Eiter, T., Fink, M., Tompits, H., Traxler, P., Woltran, S.: Replacements in non-ground answer-set programming. In: Doherty, P., Mylopoulos, J., Welty, C.A. (eds.) KR 2006, pp. 340–351. AAAI Press, Menlo Park (2006)
18. Lin, F., Chen, Y.: Discovering classes of strongly equivalent logic programs. JAIR 28, 431–451 (2007)
19. Janhunen, T., Oikarinen, E., Tompits, H., Woltran, S.: Modularity aspects of disjunctive stable models. In: Baral, C., Brewka, G., Schlipf, J. (eds.) LPNMR 2007. LNCS, vol. 4483, pp. 175–187. Springer, Heidelberg (2007)
20. Eiter, T., Fink, M., Woltran, S.: Semantical characterizations and complexity of equivalences in answer set programming. ACM TOCL 8(3) (2007)
21. Pearce, D., Valverde, A.: Uniform equivalence for equilibrium logic and logic programs. In: Lifschitz, V., Niemelä, I. (eds.) LPNMR 2004. LNCS, vol. 2923, pp. 194–206. Springer, Heidelberg (2003)
22. Cabalar, P., Ferraris, P.: Propositional theories are strongly equivalent to logic programs. TPLP 7(6), 745–759 (2007)
23. Cabalar, P., Pearce, D., Valverde, A.: Minimal logic programs. In: Dahl, V., Niemelä, I. (eds.) ICLP 2007. LNCS, vol. 4670, pp. 104–118. Springer, Heidelberg (2007)
24. Oetsch, J., Tompits, H., Woltran, S.: Facts do not cease to exist because they are ignored: Relativised uniform equivalence with answer-set projection. In: AAAI, pp. 458–464. AAAI Press, Menlo Park (2007)

Dynamic Programming Algorithms as Products of Weighted Logic Programs

Shay B. Cohen, Robert J. Simmons, and Noah A. Smith

School of Computer Science
Carnegie Mellon University
{scohen,rjsimmon,nasmith}@cs.cmu.edu

Abstract. Weighted logic programming, a generalization of bottom-up logic programming, is a successful framework for specifying dynamic programming algorithms. In this setting, proofs correspond to the algorithm's output space, such as a path through a graph or a grammatical derivation, and are given a weighted score, often interpreted as a probability, that depends on the score of the base axioms used in the proof. The desired output is a function over all possible proofs, such as a sum of scores or an optimal score. We describe the PRODUCT transformation, which can merge two weighted logic programs into a new one. The resulting program optimizes a product of proof scores from the original programs, constituting a scoring function known in machine learning as a "product of experts." Through the addition of intuitive constraining side conditions, we show that several important dynamic programming algorithms can be derived by applying PRODUCT to weighted logic programs corresponding to *simpler* weighted logic programs.

1   Introduction

Weighted logic programming has found a number of applications in fields such as natural language processing, machine learning, and computational biology as a technique for declaratively specifying dynamic programming algorithms. Weighted logic programming is a generalization of bottom-up logic programming, with the numerical scores for proofs often interpreted as probabilities, implying that the weighted logic program implements *probabilistic* reasoning.

We describe a program transformation, PRODUCT, that is of special interest in weighted logic programming. PRODUCT transforms two weighted logic programs into a new one that implements probabilistic inference under an unnormalized probability distribution built as a product of the input programs' distributions, known in machine learning as a "product of experts." While this property has been exploited in a variety of ways in applications, there has not, to our knowledge, been a formal analysis or generalization in terms of the weighted logic programming representation.

The contribution of this paper is a general, intuitive, formal setting for dynamic programming algorithms that process two or more conceptually distinct structured inputs. Indeed, we show that many important dynamic programming algorithms can be derived using simpler "factor" programs and the PRODUCT transformation.

M. Garcia de la Banda and E. Pontelli (Eds.): ICLP 2008, LNCS 5366, pp. 114–129, 2008.
© Springer-Verlag Berlin Heidelberg 2008

$$\text{reachable}(\mathsf{Q}) :\text{- initial}(\mathsf{Q}). \tag{1}$$

$$\text{reachable}(\mathsf{Q}) :\text{- reachable}(\mathsf{P}), \text{edge}(\mathsf{P}, \mathsf{Q}). \tag{2}$$

Fig. 1. A simple bottom-up logic program for graph reachability

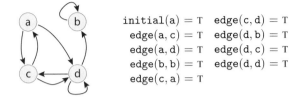

$$\text{initial}(a) = \text{T} \quad \text{edge}(c, d) = \text{T}$$
$$\text{edge}(a, c) = \text{T} \quad \text{edge}(d, b) = \text{T}$$
$$\text{edge}(a, d) = \text{T} \quad \text{edge}(d, c) = \text{T}$$
$$\text{edge}(b, b) = \text{T} \quad \text{edge}(d, d) = \text{T}$$
$$\text{edge}(c, a) = \text{T}$$

Fig. 2. A directed graph and the corresponding initial database

The paper is organized as follows. In §2 we give an overview of weighted logic programming. In §3 we describe products of experts, a concept from machine learning that motivates our framework. In §4 we describe our framework and its connection to product of experts. In §5 we give derivations of several well-known algorithms using our framework.

2 Weighted Logic Programming

To motivate weighted logic programming, we begin with a logic program for single-source connectivity on a directed graph, shown in Fig. 1. In the usual bottom-up interpretation of this program, an initial database would describe the edge relation and one (or more) roots as axioms of the form initial(a) for some a, and repeated forward inference would be applied on the two rules above to find the least database closed under those rules. However, in traditional logic programming this program can *only* be understood as a program calculating connectivity over a graph. Solving a different but structurally similar problem, such as a single-source shortest path, requires a rather different program to be written, and most solutions that have been presented require some form of non-deterministic committed choice [1,2].

Traditional logic programming is interpreted over Boolean values. A proof is a tree of valid inferences, and a valid proof is one where all of the leaves of the proof tree are axioms which are known to be true, and a true atomic proposition is one that has at least one valid proof. In weighted logic programming we generalize this notion to axioms, proofs, and atomic propositions "having values" rather than just "being true/valid." A Boolean logic program takes the value of a proof to be the *conjunction* of the value of its axioms (so the proof has value "true" as long as all the propositions at the leaves are true-valued axioms), and takes the value of a proposition to be the *disjunction* of the values of its proofs (so an atomic proposition has value "true" if it has one true-valued proof). The single-source connectivity program would describe the graph in Fig. 2 by assigning T as the value of all the existing edges and the proposition initial(a).

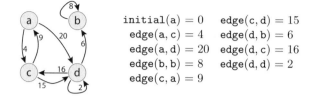

initial(a) = 0   edge(c, d) = 15
edge(a, c) = 4   edge(d, b) = 6
edge(a, d) = 20   edge(d, c) = 16
edge(b, b) = 8   edge(d, d) = 2
edge(c, a) = 9

Fig. 3. A cost graph and the corresponding initial database

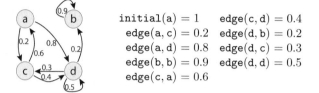

initial(a) = 1   edge(c, d) = 0.4
edge(a, c) = 0.2   edge(d, b) = 0.2
edge(a, d) = 0.8   edge(d, c) = 0.3
edge(b, b) = 0.9   edge(d, d) = 0.5
edge(c, a) = 0.6

Fig. 4. A probabilistic graph and the corresponding initial database. With stopping probabilities made explicit, this would encode a Markov model.

2.1 Non-boolean Programs

With Weighted logic programming, the axioms and propositions can be understood as having non-Boolean values. In Fig. 3, axioms of the form edge(X, Y) are given a value corresponding to the cost along the edge in the graph, and the axiom initial(a) is given the value 0. If we take the value or "score" of a proof to be the the *sum* of the values of its axioms, and then take the value of a proposition to be the *minimum* score over all possible proofs, then the program from Fig. 1 describes *single-source shortest path*. We replace the operators :- (disjunction) and , (conjunction) with min = and +, respectively, and interpret the program over the non-negative numbers. With a specific execution strategy, the result is Dijkstra's single-source shortest path algorithm.

Whereas Fig. 3 describes a cost graph, in Fig. 4 weights on edges are to be interpreted as *probabilities*, so that the graph can be seen as a Markov model or probabilistic finite-state network over which random walks are well-defined.[1] If we replace :- (disjunction) and , (conjunction) with max = and ×, then the value of reachable(X) for any X is the probability of the most likely path from a to X. For instance, reachable(a) ends up with the value 1, and reachable(b) ends up with value 0.16, corresponding to the path from a → d → b, whose weight is initial(a) × edge(a, d) × edge(d, b).

If we keep the initial database from Fig. 4 but change our operators from max = and × to += and ×, the result is a program for *summing* over the probabilities of all distinct paths that start in a and lead to X, for each vertex X. This quantity is known as the "path sum" [3]. The path sum for b, for instance, is 10—this is not a probability, but rather a sum of probabilities of many paths, some of which are prefixes of each other.

---

[1] For each vertex, the out-going edges' weights must be non-negative and sum to a value less than or equal to one. Remaining probability mass is assumed to go to a "stopping" event, as happens with probability 0.1 in vertex b in Fig. 4.

$$\texttt{reachable(Q)} \oplus= \texttt{initial(Q)}. \tag{3}$$

$$\texttt{reachable(Q)} \oplus= \texttt{reachable(P)} \otimes \texttt{edge(P, Q)}. \tag{4}$$

Fig. 5. The logic program from Fig. 1, rewritten to emphasize that it is generalized to an arbitrary semiring

These three related weighted logic programs are useful generalizations of the reachability logic program. Fig. 5 gives a generic representation of all four algorithms in the Dyna language [4]. The key difference among them is the *semiring* in which we interpret the weights.[2] Reachability uses the Boolean semiring $\langle \{\text{T}, \text{F}\}, \vee, \wedge, \text{F}, \text{T} \rangle$, single-source shortest path uses $\langle \mathbb{R}_{\geq 0} \cup \{\infty\}, \min, +, \infty, 0 \rangle$, the most-probable path variant uses $\langle [0, 1], \max, \times, 0, 1 \rangle$, and the probabilistic path-sum variant uses $\langle \mathbb{R}_{\geq 0} \cup \{\infty\}, +, \times, 0, 1 \rangle$. The formalism we describe here requires semirings that are closed under finite products and infinite sums—in our running example, this corresponds to the idea that there may be infinite paths through a graph, all with finite length.

Weighted logic programming arose in the computational linguistics community [5] after it was argued by Shieber, Schabes, and Pereira [6] and Sikkel [7] that many parsing algorithms for non-deterministic grammars could be represented as deductive logic programs, and McAllester [8] showed that this representation facilitates reasoning about asymptotic complexity. Other developments include a connection between weighted logic programs and hypergraphs [9], optimal A^* search for maximizing programs [10], semiring-general agenda-based implementations [11], improved k-best algorithms [12], and program transformations to improve efficiency [13].

2.2 Formal Definition

A weighted logic program is a set of "Horn equations" [13] describing a set of declarative, usually recursive equations over an abstract semiring:

$$\texttt{consequent}(\mathbf{U}) \oplus= \texttt{antecedent}_1(\mathbf{W_1}) \otimes \ldots \otimes \texttt{antecedent}_n(\mathbf{W_n}).$$

Here $\mathbf{U}$ and the $\mathbf{W_i}$ are sequences of variables $X_1, \ldots, X_k$. If $\mathbf{U} \subseteq \bigcup_{i=1}^{n} \mathbf{W}_i$ for every rule, then the program is *range-restricted* or *fully grounded*.

A weighted logic program is specified on an arbitrary semiring, and can be interpreted in any semiring $\langle \mathbb{K}, \oplus, \otimes, \mathbf{0}, \mathbf{1} \rangle$, as previously described.

Typically the proof and value of a *specific* theorem are desired. We assume that this theorem is called goal and takes zero arguments. A computationally uninteresting but perfectly intuitive way to present a weighted logic program is

$$\texttt{goal} \oplus= \texttt{axiom}_1(\mathbf{W_1}) \otimes \ldots \otimes \texttt{axiom}_n(\mathbf{W_n}).$$

The value of the proposition/theorem goal is a semiring-sum over all of its proofs, starting from the axioms, where the value of any single proof is the semiring-product of

---

[2] An algebraic semiring consists of five elements $\langle \mathbb{K}, \oplus, \otimes, \mathbf{0}, \mathbf{1} \rangle$, where $\mathbb{K}$ is a domain closed under $\oplus$ and $\otimes$, $\oplus$ is a binary, associative, commutative operator, $\otimes$ is a binary, associative operator that distributes over $\oplus$, $\mathbf{0} \in \mathbb{K}$ is the $\oplus$-identity, and $\mathbf{1} \in \mathbb{K}$ is the $\otimes$-identity.

the axioms involved. This is effectively encoded using the inference rules as a sum of products of sums of products of ... sums of products, exploiting distributivity and shared substructure for efficiency. Dynamic programming algorithms, useful for problems with a large degree of shared substructure, are often encoded as weighted logic programs.

In many practical applications, as in our reachability example in Section 2.1, values are interpreted as probabilities to be maximized or summed or costs to be minimized.

3   Products of Experts

In machine learning, probability models learned from example data are often used to make predictions. For example, to predict the value of a random variable Y (ranging over values denoted y in a domain denoted $\mathcal{Y}$; here, $\mathcal{Y}$ corresponds to the set of proofs) given that random variable X has an observed value $x \in \mathcal{X}$ (here, $\mathcal{X}$ ranges over initial databases, i.e., sets of axioms), the Bayes decision rule predicts:

$$\hat{y} = \operatorname*{argmax}_{y \in \mathcal{Y}} p(Y = y \mid X = x) = \operatorname*{argmax}_{y \in \mathcal{Y}} \frac{p(Y = y, X = x)}{p(X = x)} \qquad (5)$$

In other words, the prediction $\hat{y}$ should be the element of $\mathcal{Y}$ that maximizes $p(Y = y \mid X = x)$, the likelihood of the event $Y = y$ given that the event $X = x$ has happened. By the definition of conditional probability, this quantity is equivalent to the ratio of the *joint* probability that $X = x \wedge Y = y$ to the *marginal* probability that $X = x$. Dynamic programming algorithms are available for solving many of these maximization problems, such as when Y ranges over paths through a graph or grammar derivations.

Of recent interest are probability models p that take a *factored form*, for example:

$$p(X = x, Y = y) \propto p_1(X = x, Y = y) \times \ldots \times p_n(X = x, Y = y) \qquad (6)$$

where $\propto$ signifies "proportional to" and suppresses the means by which the probability distribution is re-normalized to sum to one. This kind of model is called a *product of experts* [14]. Intuitively, the probability of an event under p can only be large if "all the experts concur," i.e. if the probability is large under each of the p_i. Any single expert can make an event arbitrarily unlikely (even impossible) by giving it very low probability.

The attraction of such probability distributions is that they modularize complex systems [15,16]. They can also offer computational advantages when solving Eq. 5 [17]. Further, the expert factors can often be trained (i.e., estimated from data) separately, speeding up expensive but powerful machine learning methods [18,19].

This idea is still useful even when not dealing with probabilities. Suppose each expert p_i is a function $\mathcal{X} \times \mathcal{Y} \rightarrow \{0, 1\}$ that returns 1 if and only if the arguments x and y satisfy some constraints; it implements a relation. Then the "product" relation is just the intersection of all pairs $\langle x, y \rangle$ for which all the expert factors' relations hold.

To the best of our knowledge, there has been no attempt to formalize the following intuitive idea about products of experts: algorithms for summing and maximizing mutually-constrained pairs of product-proof values should resemble the individual algorithms for each of the two separate proofs' values. Our formalization is intended to aid in algorithm

$$\text{reachable}_1(Q_1) \oplus= \text{initial}_1(Q_1). \tag{7}$$

$$\text{reachable}_1(Q_1) \oplus= \text{reachable}_1(P_1) \otimes \text{edge}_1(P_1, Q_1). \tag{8}$$

$$\text{reachable}_2(Q_2) \oplus= \text{initial}_2(Q_2). \tag{9}$$

$$\text{reachable}_2(Q_2) \oplus= \text{reachable}_2(P_2) \otimes \text{edge}_2(P_2, Q_2). \tag{10}$$

Fig. 6. Two identical "experts" for generalized graph reachability, duplicates of the program in Fig. 5

$$\text{reachable}_{1 \circ 2}(Q_1, Q_2) \oplus= \text{initial}_1(Q_1) \otimes \text{initial}_2(Q_2). \tag{11}$$

$$\text{reachable}_{1 \circ 2}(Q_1, Q_2) \oplus= \text{reachable}_2(P_2) \otimes \text{edge}_2(P_2, Q_2) \otimes \text{initial}_1(Q_1). \tag{12}$$

$$\text{reachable}_{1 \circ 2}(Q_1, Q_2) \oplus= \text{reachable}_1(P_1) \otimes \text{edge}_1(P_1, Q_1) \otimes \text{initial}_2(Q_2). \tag{13}$$

$$\text{reachable}_{1 \circ 2}(Q_1, Q_2) \oplus= \text{reachable}_{1 \circ 2}(P_1, P_2) \otimes \text{edge}_1(P_1, Q_1) \otimes \text{edge}_2(P_2, Q_2). \tag{14}$$

Fig. 7. Four rules that, in addition to the rules in Fig. 6, define the product of experts of reachable_1 and reachable_2

development as new kinds of random variables are coupled, with a key practical advantage: the expert factors are known because they fundamentally *underlie* the main algorithm. Indeed, we call our algorithms "products" because they are derived from "factors."

4   Products of Weighted Logic Programs

In this section, we will motivate products of weighted logic programs in the context of the running example of generalized graph reachability. We will then define the PROD-UCT transformation precisely and describe the process of specifying new algorithms as constrained versions of product programs.

Fig. 6 defines two "experts," copies of the graph reachability program from Fig. 5. We are interested in a new predicate $\text{reachable}_{1 \circ 2}(Q_1, Q_2)$, which for any particular X and Y should be equal to the product of $\text{reachable}_1(X)$ and $\text{reachable}_2(Y)$. We could define the predicate by adding the following rule to the program in Fig. 6:

$$\text{reachable}_{1 \circ 2}(Q_1, Q_2) \oplus= \text{reachable}_1(Q_1) \otimes \text{reachable}_2(Q_2).$$

This program is a bit simplistic, however; it merely describes calculating the "experts" independently and then combining them at the end. The key to the PRODUCT transformation is that the predicate of $\text{reachable}_{1 \circ 2}$ can alternatively be calculated by adding the following four rules to Fig. 6:

$$\text{reachable}_{1 \circ 2}(Q_1, Q_2) \oplus= \text{initial}_1(Q_1) \otimes \text{initial}_2(Q_2).$$
$$\text{reachable}_{1 \circ 2}(Q_1, Q_2) \oplus= \text{initial}_1(Q_1) \otimes \text{reachable}_2(P_2) \otimes \text{edge}_2(P_2, Q_2).$$
$$\text{reachable}_{1 \circ 2}(Q_1, Q_2) \oplus= \text{reachable}_1(P_1) \otimes \text{edge}_1(P_1, Q_1) \otimes \text{initial}_2(Q_2).$$
$$\text{reachable}_{1 \circ 2}(Q_1, Q_2) \oplus= \text{reachable}_1(P_1) \otimes \text{edge}_1(P_1, Q_1) \otimes$$
$$\text{reachable}_2(P_2) \otimes \text{edge}_2(P_2, Q_2).$$

Then, because $\text{reachable}_{1 \circ 2}(Q_1, Q_2)$ was defined above to be the product of $\text{reachable}_1(Q_1)$ and $\text{reachable}_2(Q_2)$, it should be clear that the last rule can be rewritten to obtain the factored program in Fig. 7. This program computes over pairs of paths in two graphs.

4.1   The PRODUCT Transformation

The PRODUCT program transformation is shown in Fig. 8. For each desired product of experts, where one "expert," the predicate p, is defined by n rules and the other expert q by m rules, the transformation defines the product of experts for p∘q with $n \times m$ new rules, the cross product of inference rules from the first and second experts. The value of a coupled proposition p∘q in $\mathcal{P}'$ will be equal to the semiring product of p's value and q's value in $\mathcal{P}$ (or, equivalently, in $\mathcal{P}'$).

Input: A logic program $\mathcal{P}$ and a set $\mathcal{S}$ of pairs of predicates (p, q).
Output: A program $\mathcal{P}'$ that extends $\mathcal{P}$, additionally computing the product predicate p∘q for
　　　　every pair $(p, q) \in \mathcal{S}$ in the input.
　1: $\mathcal{P}' \leftarrow \mathcal{P}$
　2: **for all** pairs (p, q) in $\mathcal{S}$ **do**
　3:　　**for all** rules in $\mathcal{P}$, of the form $p(\mathbf{W}) \oplus= A_1 \otimes \ldots \otimes A_n$ **do**
　4:　　　　**for all** rules in $\mathcal{P}$, of the form $q(\mathbf{X}) \oplus= B_1 \otimes \ldots \otimes B_m$ **do**
　5:　　　　　　**let** $r \leftarrow [p{\circ}q(\mathbf{W}, \mathbf{X}) \oplus= A_1 \otimes \ldots \otimes A_n \otimes B_1 \otimes \ldots \otimes B_m]$
　6:　　　　　　**for all** pairs of antecedents in r $(s(\mathbf{Y}), t(\mathbf{Z}))$ such that $(s, t) \in \mathcal{S}$ **do**
　7:　　　　　　　　remove the antecedents $s(\mathbf{Y})$ and $t(\mathbf{Z})$ from r
　8:　　　　　　　　insert the antecedent $s{\circ}t(\mathbf{Y}, \mathbf{Z})$ to r
　9:　　　　　　**end for**
10:　　　　　　add r to $\mathcal{P}'$
11:　　　　**end for**
12:　　**end for**
13: **end for**
14: **return** $\mathcal{P}'$

Fig. 8. This figure describes PRODUCT, a non-deterministic program transformation that adds new rules to WLP $\mathcal{P}$ that compute the product of experts of predicates from the original program. We implicitly rename variables to avoid conflicts between rules.

Note that lines 6–8 are non-deterministic under certain circumstances, because if the antecedent of the combined program is $a(X) \otimes a(Y) \otimes b(Z)$ and the algorithm is computing the product of a and b, then the resulting antecedent could be either $a{\circ}b(X, Z) \otimes a(Y)$ or $a{\circ}b(Y, Z) \otimes a(X)$. Our procedure arbitrarily selects one of the possibilities.

4.2   Constraining the Product of Experts

Any program $\mathcal{P}'$ that comes out after applying PRODUCT on $\mathcal{P}$ computes the product of experts of p and q (where $(p, q) \in \mathcal{S}$). More specifically, any ground instances of $p(\mathbf{X})$ and $q(\mathbf{Y})$ have the same value in $\mathcal{P}$ and $\mathcal{P}'$, and the value of $p{\circ}q(\mathbf{X}, \mathbf{Y})$ in $\mathcal{P}'$ is $p(\mathbf{X}) \otimes q(\mathbf{Y})$.[3] However, the same program could have been implemented more straightforwardly by merely introducing a new inference rule for the goal.

---

[3] The full proof can be found in [20].

$$\text{reachable}_{1 \circ 2}(Q_1, Q_2) \oplus= \text{initial}_1(Q_1) \otimes \text{initial}_2(Q_2). \tag{15}$$

$$\text{reachable}_{1 \circ 2}(Q_1, Q_2) \oplus= \text{reachable}_{1 \circ 2}(P_1, P_2) \otimes \text{edge}_1(P_1, Q_1) \otimes \text{edge}_2(P_2, Q_2). \tag{16}$$

Fig. 9. By removing all but these two rules from the product of experts in Fig. 7, we require both paths to have the same number of steps

$$\text{reachable}_{1 \circ 2}(Q) \oplus= \text{initial}_1(Q) \otimes \text{initial}_2(Q). \tag{17}$$

$$\text{reachable}_{1 \circ 2}(Q) \oplus= \text{reachable}_{1 \circ 2}(P) \otimes \text{edge}_1(P, Q) \otimes \text{edge}_2(P, Q). \tag{18}$$

Fig. 10. By further constraining the program in Fig. 9 to require that the $Q_1 = Q_2$ at all points, we require both paths to be identical

Yet, the output of the **PRODUCT** transformation is a starting point for describing dynamic programming algorithms that do two similar actions—traversing a graph, scanning a string, parsing a sentence—at the same time and in a coordinated fashion. Exactly what "coordinated fashion" means depends on the problem, and answering that question determines how the problem is constrained.

If we return to the running example of generalized graph reachability, the program as written has eight rules, four from Fig. 6 and four from Fig. 7. Two examples of constrained product programs are given in Fig. 9 and Fig. 10. In the first example in Fig. 9, the only change is that all but two rules have been removed from the program in Fig. 7. Whereas in the original product program $\text{reachable}_{1 \circ 2}(Q_1, Q_2)$ corresponded to the product of the weight of the "best" path from the initial state or states of graph 1 to Q_1 and the weight of the "best" path from the initial state or states of graph 2 to Q_2, the new program computes the best paths from the two origins to the two destinations with the additional requirement that the paths be the *same length*—the rules that were deleted allowed for the possibility of a prefix on one path or the other.

If our intent is for the two paths to not only have the same length but to visit vertices in the same sequence, then we can further constrain the program to only define $\text{reachable}_{1 \circ 2}(Q_1, Q_2)$ where $Q_1 = Q_2$, at which point it might as well be written $\text{reachable}_{1 \circ 2}(Q)$. This is what is done in Fig. 10.

The choice of paired predicates $\mathcal{S}$ is important for the final WLP which **PRODUCT** returns and it also limits the way we can add constraints to derive a new WLP. Automatically deriving $\mathcal{S}$ from data in a machine learning setting is an open question for future research. When **PRODUCT** is applied on two copies of the same WLP (concatenated together to a single program), a natural schema for selecting paired predicates arises, in which we pair a predicate from one program with the same predicate from the other program. This natural pairing leads to the derivation of several useful, known algorithms, to which we turn in Section 5.

5   Examples

In this section, we describe three classes of algorithms that can be understood as constrained products of simpler weighted logic programs.

$$\text{dist}(P) \oplus= \text{start}(P). \tag{19}$$

$$\text{dist}(P) \oplus= \text{dist}(P) \otimes \text{staycost}. \tag{20}$$

$$\text{dist}(P+1) \oplus= \text{dist}(P) \otimes \text{s}(C,P). \tag{21}$$

Fig. 11. A program for scanning over a string

$$\text{dist}_{1\circ2}(P_1, P_2) \oplus= \text{start}_1(P_1) \otimes \text{start}_2(P_2). \tag{22}$$

$$\text{dist}_{1\circ2}(P_1, P_2+1) \oplus= \text{start}_1(P_1) \otimes \text{dist}_2(P_2) \otimes \text{s}(C_2, P_2). \tag{23}$$

$$\text{dist}_{1\circ2}(P_1+1, P_2) \oplus= \text{dist}_1(P_1) \otimes \text{s}(C_1, P_1) \otimes \text{start}_2(P_2). \tag{24}$$

$$\text{dist}_{1\circ2}(P_1, P_2+1) \oplus= \text{dist}_{1\circ2}(P_1, P_2) \otimes \text{s}_2(C_2, P_2) \otimes \text{staycost}_1. \tag{25}$$

$$\text{dist}_{1\circ2}(P_1+1, P_2) \oplus= \text{dist}_{1\circ2}(P_1, P_2) \otimes \text{s}_1(C_1, P_1) \otimes \text{staycost}_2. \tag{26}$$

$$\text{dist}_{1\circ2}(P_1+1, P_2+1) \oplus= \text{dist}_{1\circ2}(P_1, P_2) \otimes \text{s}_2(C_1, P_1) \otimes \text{s}_2(C_2, P_2) \boxed{\text{if } C_1 = C_2.} \tag{27}$$

Fig. 12. Edit distance derived from the **PRODUCT** transformation on two copies of Fig. 11, with a side condition (boxed)

5.1 Edit Distance

Edit distances [21] are important measures of the difference between two strings, and they underlie many algorithms in computational biology and computational linguistics. The DNA fragment "ACTAGCACTTAG" can be encoded as a set of axioms $\text{s}(a, 1)$, $\text{s}(c, 2)$, $\text{s}(t, 3)$, ..., $\text{s}(g, 12)$, and we can describe a specification of the dynamic program for edit distance by using the product of a trivial "cursor" program that scans over a string, described in Fig. 11.

We generally interpret Fig. 11 over the the "cost minimization" semiring, replacing $\oplus=$ with $\min=$ and $\otimes$ with $+$. The value of all the axioms of the form $\text{start}(P)$ (giving the starting position) or $\text{s}(C, P)$ (indicating the position of a character) is 0, but the value of staycost is some finite, nonzero value representing the penalty if the cursor stays in one place. Note that under this semiring interpretation, the rule (20) will never be used; the value of staycost only becomes relevant when the **PRODUCT** of the scanning program with itself is determined.

The output of **PRODUCT** on two copies of the scanning program is shown in Fig. 12, though three rules are removed.[4] One important change is made to clause 27, the addition of the *side condition* $C_1 = C_2$, which requires that when both P_1 and P_2 advance, the character at position P_1 in string 1 and the character at position P_2 in string two must be identical. This captures the essential requirement of the edit distance calculation: changing a symbol in one string to an identical symbol in the other string incurs no "edit" and no cost. It is worth noting that the clause 27 could have equivalently been written by unifying C_1 with C_2:

$$\text{dist}_{1\circ2}(P_1+1, P_2+1) \oplus= \text{dist}_{1\circ2}(P_1, P_2) \otimes \text{s}_2(C, P_1) \otimes \text{s}_2(C, P_2).$$

---

[4] The three removed rules are the two different combinations of clause 19 and clause 20 in Fig. 11, as well as the combination of clause 20 with itself. These three rules are redundant if we are computing in the minimum-cost semiring.

The first and last clauses in the edit distance program (22 and 27) are the essential ones; the other five clauses essentially describe extensions to edit distance that can be added, turned off, or modified to obtain different edit distances. Clause 23 allows a penalty-free prefix to be added to the second string, for instance matching string 1, "BOVIK" against string 2, "HARRY BOVIK," and clause 24 allows a penalty-free prefix to be deleted from to the first string. Clause 25 describes that insertions can be made with cost $\mathtt{staycost}_1$, for instance in matching string one "H. BOVIK" against "H. Q. BOVIK", and clause 26 describes deletions from the first string to reach the second.

5.2 Finite-State Algorithms

Specifications of weighted finite-state automata (WFSAs) and transducers (WFSTs) are superficially similar to the reachability problem of Sec. 1, but with edge relations ($\mathtt{edge}(P, Q)$) augmented by symbols (WFSAs: $\mathtt{arc}(P, Q, A)$) or pairs of input-output symbols (WFSTs: $\mathtt{arc}(P, Q, A, B)$). Weighted finite-state machines are widely used in speech and language processing [22].

Weighted Finite State Automata. Fig. 13 describes an algorithm for recognizing paths in a weighted finite state automaton. (With the appropriate semirings, it finds the most probable path or the path-sum.) If the PRODUCT of that algorithm with itself is taken, we can follow similar steps in Sec. 4.2 and add a constraint to clause 33 that requires the two paths' symbols to be identical, we get the recognizer for the *(weighted) intersection* of the two WFSAs (itself a WFSA). Weighted intersection generalizes intersection, and can be used, for example, to determine whether a specific string (itself an FSA) is in the regular language of the FSA and, in the probabilistic case, its associated probability.

Weighted Finite-State Transducers. Suppose we take the PRODUCT transformation of the WFST recognition algorithm (not shown, but similar to Fig. 13 but using $\mathtt{arc}(P, Q, A, B)$ as arc axioms) with itself and constrain the result by removing all but the three interesting rules (as before) and requiring that B_1 (the "output" along the first edge) always be equal to A_2 (the "input" along the second edge). The result is shown

$$\mathtt{goal} \oplus= \mathtt{path}(Q) \otimes \mathtt{final}(Q). \tag{28}$$

$$\mathtt{path}(Q) \oplus= \mathtt{initial}(Q). \tag{29}$$

$$\mathtt{path}(Q) \oplus= \mathtt{path}(P) \otimes \mathtt{arc}(P, Q, A). \tag{30}$$

Fig. 13. The weighted logic program describing (weighted) recognition in a probabilistic finite state automaton

$$\mathtt{goal}_{1 \circ 2} \oplus= \mathtt{path}_{1 \circ 2}(Q_1, Q_1) \otimes \mathtt{final}_1(Q_2) \otimes \mathtt{final}_2(Q_2). \tag{31}$$

$$\mathtt{path}_{1 \circ 2}(Q_1, Q_2) \oplus= \mathtt{initial}_1(Q_1) \otimes \mathtt{initial}_2(Q_2). \tag{32}$$

$$\mathtt{path}_{1 \circ 2}(Q_1, Q_2) \oplus= \mathtt{path}_{1 \circ 2}(P_1, P_2) \otimes \mathtt{arc}_1(P_1, Q_1, A_1) \otimes \mathtt{arc}_2(P_2, Q_2, A_2) \boxed{\text{if } A_1 = A_2.} \tag{33}$$

Fig. 14. The weighted logic program describing (weighted) recognition by an intersection of two finite state automata, derived from Fig. 13 in the manner of Fig. 9

$$\text{goal}_{1 \circ 2} \oplus= \text{path}_{1 \circ 2}(Q_1, Q_1) \otimes \text{final}_1(Q_2) \otimes \text{final}_2(Q_2). \tag{34}$$

$$\text{path}_{1 \circ 2}(Q_1, Q_2) \oplus= \text{initial}_1(Q_1) \otimes \text{initial}_2(Q_2). \tag{35}$$

$$\text{path}_{1 \circ 2}(Q_1, Q_2) \oplus= \text{path}_{1 \circ 2}(P_1, P_2) \otimes \text{arc}_1(P_1, Q_1, A_1, B_1) \otimes \text{arc}_2(P_2, Q_2, A_2, B_2) \boxed{\text{ if } B_1 = A_2.}$$

Fig. 15. The weighted logic program describing a composition of two finite state transducers, derived from Fig. 13 in the manner of Fig. 9 and Fig. 14

in Fig. 15; this is the recognition algorithm for the WFST resulting from *composition* of two WFSTs. Composition permits small, understandable components to be cascaded and optionally compiled, forming complex but efficient models over strings.

5.3   Context-Free Parsing

Parsing natural languages is a difficult, central problem in computational linguistics [23]. Consider the sentence "Shay saw Robert with binoculars." One analysis (the most likely in the real world) is that Shay had the binoculars and saw Robert through them. Another is that *Robert* had the binoculars, and Shay saw the binocular-endowed Robert. Fig. 16 shows syntactic parses into noun phrases (**NP**), verb phrases (**VP**), etc., corresponding to these two meanings. It also shows part of a context-free grammar describing English sentences in Chomsky normal form [24],[5] and an encoding of the grammar and string using axioms. A proof corresponds to a CF derivation of the string.

In [6], the authors show that parsing with CFGs (and other grammars) can be formalized as a logic program, and in [5] this framework is extended to the weighted case. If weights are interpreted as probabilities, then these two semiring interpretations can either find the "weight" of the parse with maximum weight or the total weight of all parse trees (a measure of the "total grammaticality" of a sentence). In this section, we give the specification of the weighted CKY algorithm [25], which is a dynamic programming algorithm for parsing using a context-free grammar in Chomsky normal form. The CKY algorithm is shown in Fig. 17. We show that fundamental algorithms for weighted (probabilistic) parsing can be derived as constrained **PRODUCT**s of CKY.

The unconstrained **PRODUCT** of CKY with itself (Fig. 18) is not inherently interesting. It is worth noting, however, that clause 43 there was a choice as to how to merge the c_1 and c_2 possibilities. The choice would not have existed if, instead of the presentation of CKY in Fig. 17, a common *binarized* variant of the algorithm, which introduces a new predicate in order to have at most two antecedents per Horn equation, had been fed to **PRODUCT**. The choice that we made in pairing was consistent with the choice that is forced in the binarized CKY program.

Product of Grammars. Fig. 19 describes a more interesting constrained version of Fig. 18. In particular, in all cases the constraints $I_1 = I_2$, $J_1 = J_2$, $K_1 = K_2$, $N_1 = N_2$ are added, so that instead of writing $c_{1 \circ 2}(X_1, I_1, J_1, X_2, I_2, J_2)$ we just write $c_{1 \circ 2}(X_1, X_2, I, J)$. This program simultaneously parses two different sentences using two different grammars, but

---

[5] Chomsky normal form (CNF) means that the rules in the grammar are either binary with two nonterminals or unary with a terminal. We do not allow ϵ rules, which in general are allowed in CNF grammars.

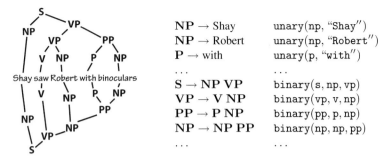

Fig. 16. An ambiguous sentence that can be parsed two ways in English (left), some of the Chomsky normal form rules for English grammar (center), and the corresponding axioms (right). There would also need to be five axioms of the form string("Shay", 1), string("saw", 2), etc.

$$\text{goal} \oplus= \text{start}(S) \otimes \text{length}(N) \otimes c(S, 0, N). \tag{36}$$

$$c(X, I-1, I) \oplus= \text{unary}(X, W) \otimes \text{string}(W, I). \tag{37}$$

$$c(X, I, K) \oplus= \text{binary}(X, Y, Z) \otimes c(Y, I, J) \otimes c(Z, J, K). \tag{38}$$

Fig. 17. CKY: a weighted logic program implementing weighted CKY for algorithms involving weighted context free grammars in Chomsky normal form. Strictly speaking, CKY refers to a naïve bottom-up evaluation strategy for this program.

$$\text{goal}_{1o2} \oplus= \text{length}_1(N_1) \otimes \text{length}_2(N_2) \otimes \tag{39}$$
$$\text{start}_1(S_1) \otimes \text{start}_2(S_2) \otimes c_{1o2}(S_1, 0, N_1, S_2, 0, N_2).$$

$$c_{1o2}(X_1, I_1 - 1, I_1, X_2, I_2 - 1, I_2) \oplus= \text{unary}_1(X_1, W_1) \otimes \text{string}_1(W_1, I_1) \otimes \tag{40}$$
$$\text{unary}_2(X_2, W_2) \otimes \text{string}_2(W_2, I_2).$$

$$c_{1o2}(X_1, I_1 - 1, I_1, X_2, I_2, K_2) \oplus= \text{unary}_1(X_1, W_1) \otimes \text{string}_1(W_1, I_1) \otimes \tag{41}$$
$$\text{binary}_2(X_2, Y_2, Z_2) \otimes c_2(Y_2, I_2, J_2) \otimes c_2(Z_2, J_2, K_2).$$

$$c_{1o2}(X_1, I_1, K_1, X_2, I_2 - 1, I_2) \oplus= \text{unary}_2(X_2, W_1) \otimes \text{string}_2(W_2, I_2) \otimes \tag{42}$$
$$\text{binary}_1(X_1, Y_1, Z_1) \otimes c_1(Y_1, I_1, J_1) \otimes c_1(Z_1, J_1, K_1).$$

$$c_{1o2}(X_1, I_1, K_1, X_2, I_2, K_2) \oplus= \text{binary}_1(X_1, Y_1, Z_1) \otimes \text{binary}_2(X_2, Y_2, Z_2) \otimes \tag{43}$$
$$c_{1o2}(Y_1, I_1, J_1, Y_2, I_2, J_2) \otimes c_{1o2}(Z_1, J_1, K_1, Z_2, K_2, J_2).$$

Fig. 18. The full output of the PRODUCT transformation on two copies of CKY in Fig. 17

both parses must have the same *structure*. This constraint, then, can be compared to the constraints placed on the product of two graph-reachability programs to ensure that both paths have the same length.

Lexicalized CFG Parsing. An interesting variant of the previous rule involves *lexicalized grammars*, which are motivated in Fig. 20. Instead of describing a grammar using nonterminals denoting phrases (e.g., NP and VP), we can define a (context-free) *dependency grammar* [26] that encodes the syntax of a sentence in terms of parent-child relationships between words. In the case of the example of Fig. 20, the arrows below

$$\text{goal}_{1o2} \mathrel{\oplus}= \text{length}(N) \otimes \text{start}_1(S_1) \otimes \text{start}_2(S_2) \otimes c_{1o2}(S_1, S_2, 0, N). \tag{44}$$

$$c_{1o2}(X_1, X_2, I-1, I) \mathrel{\oplus}= \text{unary}_1(X_1, W_1) \otimes \text{string}_1(W_1, I) \otimes \tag{45}$$
$$\text{unary}_2(X_2, W_2) \otimes \text{string}_2(W_2, I).$$

$$c_{1o2}(X_1, X_2, I, K) \mathrel{\oplus}= \text{binary}_1(X_1, Y_1, Z_1) \otimes \text{binary}_2(X_2, Y_2, Z_2) \otimes \tag{46}$$
$$c_{1o2}(Y_1, Y_2, I, J) \otimes c_{1o2}(Z_1, Z_2, J, K).$$

Fig. 19. The program in Fig. 18 constrained to require parsing two different sentences with the same parse tree

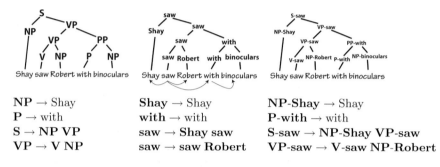

Fig. 20. On the left, the grammar previously shown. In the middle, a context-free *dependency grammar*, whose derivations can be seen as parse trees (above) or a set of dependencies (below). On the right, a lexicalized grammar. Sample rules are given for each grammar.

$$\text{goal}_{1o2} \mathrel{\oplus}= \text{length}(N) \otimes \text{start}_1(S_1) \otimes \text{start}_2(S_2) \otimes c_{1o2}(S_1, S_2, 0, N). \tag{47}$$

$$c_{1o2}(X_1, X_2, I-1, I) \mathrel{\oplus}= \text{unary}_1(X_1, W_1) \otimes \text{unary}_2(X_2, W_2) \otimes \text{string}(W, I). \tag{48}$$

$$c_{1o2}(X_1, X_2, I, K) \mathrel{\oplus}= \text{binary}_1(X_1, Y_1, Z_1) \otimes \text{binary}_2(X_2, Y_2, Z_2) \otimes \tag{49}$$
$$c_{1o2}(Y_1, Y_2, I, J) \otimes c_{1o2}(Z_1, Z_2, J, K).$$

Fig. 21. Constraining Fig. 18 to simultaneously parse the *same* sentence with two grammars

the sentence in the middle establish "saw" as the root of the sentence; the word "saw" has three children (arguments and modifiers), one of which is the word "with," which in turn has the child "binoculars."

The simplest approach to describing a dependency grammar is to define it as a Chomsky normal form grammar where the nonterminal set is equivalent to the set of terminal symbols (so that the terminal "with" corresponds to a unique nonterminal **with**, and so on) and where all rules have the form $\mathbf{P} \to \mathbf{P}\,\mathbf{C}$, $\mathbf{P} \to \mathbf{C}\,\mathbf{P}$, and $\mathbf{W} \to w$ (where $\mathbf{X}$ is the nonterminal version of terminal x).

Fig. 21 describes a further constrained program that, instead of parsing two unique strings in two different grammars with the same structure, parses a single string in two different grammars with the same structure. This new grammar recognizes a string if and only if both of the original grammars recognize it with isomorphic trees—a kind of "derivation intersection." (This is not to be confused with intersections of context-free *languages*, which are not in general context-free languages [24].)

If we encode the regular grammar in the $\texttt{unary}_1$ and $\texttt{binary}_1$ relations and encode a dependency grammar in the $\texttt{unary}_2$ and $\texttt{binary}_2$ relations, then the product is a *lexicalized grammar*, like the third example from Fig. 20. In particular, it describes a lexicalized context-free grammar with a product of experts probability model [15], because the weight given to the production $\mathbf{A\text{-}X} \rightarrow \mathbf{B\text{-}X}\ \mathbf{C\text{-}Y}$, for instance, is the semiring-product of the weight given to the production $\mathbf{A} \rightarrow \mathbf{B}\ \mathbf{C}$ and the weight given to the dependency based production $\mathbf{X} \rightarrow \mathbf{X}\ \mathbf{Y}$. If, instead of the axioms of the form $\texttt{binary}_1(X_1, Y_1, Z_1)$ and $\texttt{binary}_2(X_2, Y_2, Z_2)$ there were axioms of the form $\texttt{binary}_{1 \circ 2}(X_1, X_2, Y_1, Y_2, Z_1, Z_2)$ and clause 46 was changed accordingly, then the result would be a general lexicalized CKY [27].

Synchronous Parsing. Another extension to context-free parsing, *synchronous* parsing, can be derived using **PRODUCT** from two instances of CKY. Here two strings are parsed, each in a different alphabet with a different grammar (e.g., a French sentence and its English translation). A synchronous derivation consists of two trees and a correspondence between their nodes; different degrees of isomorphism may be imposed (e.g., in natural language, reordering is common, but dependencies tend to be mirrored through word-level translation). Constraining the **PRODUCT** of CKY with itself with side conditions to impose a one-to-one correspondence of nonterminals leads to a weighted logic program for a formalism known as inversion transduction grammar [28]. Constraining the **PRODUCT** of a more general CKY that includes empty unary rules "$\mathbf{X} \rightarrow \epsilon$" and leaving rules that pair $\texttt{unary}$ with $\texttt{binary}$ antecedents removes the requirement that the sentences have the same length. In addition, the **PRODUCT** of the lexicalized CKY with itself leads to WLPs for more complex parsers like those described in [29] and [30] for more expressive formalisms.[6]

6 Conclusion

We have described a general framework for dynamic programming algorithms whose solutions correspond to proof values in two mutually constrained weighted logic programs. Our framework includes a program transformation, **PRODUCT**, which combines the two weighted logic programs that compute over two structures into a single weighted logic program for a joint proof. Appropriate constraints, encoded intuitively as variable unifications or side conditions in the WLP, are then added manually. The framework naturally captures many existing algorithms.

Acknowledgments

The authors acknowledge helpful comments from three anonymous ICLP reviewers, Jason Eisner, Frank Pfenning, David Smith, and Sylvia Rebholz. This research was supported by an NSF graduate fellowship to the second author and NSF grant IIS-0713265 and an IBM faculty award to the third author.

---

[6] To derive the general synchronous parser described in [28] we have to perform another step of axiom generalization, described in [20]. In the current form, the axioms are factored as well.

References

1. Greco, S., Zaniolo, C.: Greedy algorithms in Datalog. Theory Pract. Log. Program 1(4), 381–407 (2001)
2. Ganzinger, H., McAllester, D.A.: Logical algorithms. In: Stuckey, P.J. (ed.) ICLP 2002. LNCS, vol. 2401, pp. 209–223. Springer, Heidelberg (2002)
3. Tarjan, R.E.: A unified approach to path problems. Journal of the ACM 28(3), 577–593 (1981)
4. Eisner, J., Goldlust, E., Smith, N.A.: Dyna: A declarative language for implementing dynamic programs. In: Proc. of ACL (companion volume) (2004)
5. Goodman, J.: Semiring parsing. Computational Linguistics 25(4), 573–605 (1999)
6. Shieber, S.M., Schabes, Y., Pereira, F.C.N.: Principles and implementation of deductive parsing. Journal of Logic Programming 24(1–2), 3–36 (1995)
7. Sikkel, K.: Parsing Schemata: A Framework for Specification and Analysis of Parsing Algorithms. Springer-Verlag New York, Inc., Secaucus, NJ, USA (1997)
8. McAllester, D.A.: On the complexity analysis of static analyses. In: Cortesi, A., Filé, G. (eds.) SAS 1999. LNCS, vol. 1694, pp. 312–329. Springer, Heidelberg (1999)
9. Klein, D., Manning, C.D.: Parsing and hypergraphs. New developments in parsing technology, 351–372 (2004)
10. Felzenszwalb, P.F., McAllester, D.: The generalized A^* architecture. Journal of Artificial Intelligence Research 29, 153–190 (2007)
11. Eisner, J., Goldlust, E., Smith, N.A.: Compiling comp ling: practical weighted dynamic programming and the dyna language. In: HLT 2005: Proceedings of the conference on Human Language Technology and Empirical Methods in Natural Language Processing, Morristown, NJ, USA, pp. 281–290. Association for Computational Linguistics (2005)
12. Huang, L., Chiang, D.: Better k-best parsing. In: Proceedings of the Ninth International Workshop on Parsing Technologies (IWPT 2005), Vancouver, Canada (2005)
13. Eisner, J., Blatz, J.: Program transformations for optimization of parsing algorithms and other weighted logic programs. In: Wintner, S. (ed.) Proceedings of FG 2006: The 11th Conference on Formal Grammar, pp. 45–85. CSLI Publications (2007)
14. Hinton, G.E.: Training products of experts by minimizing contrastive divergence. Neural Comput. 14(8), 1771–1800 (2002)
15. Klein, D., Manning, C.D.: Fast exact inference with a factored model for natural language parsing. In: Advances in Neural Information Processing Systems, pp. 3–10. MIT Press, Cambridge (2002)
16. Liang, P., Klein, D., Jordan, M.: Agreement-based learning. In: Platt, J., Koller, D., Singer, Y., Roweis, S. (eds.) Advances in Neural Information Processing Systems, vol. 20, pp. 913–920. MIT Press, Cambridge (2008)
17. Chiang, D.: Hierarchical phrase-based translation. Comput. Linguist. 33(2), 201–228 (2007)
18. Cohen, S.B., Smith, N.A.: Joint morphological and syntactic disambiguation. In: Proceedings of EMNLP-CoNLL 2007, pp. 208–217 (2007)
19. Sutton, C., McCallum, A.: Piecewise training for undirected models. In: Proceedings of the 21th Annual Conference on Uncertainty in Artificial Intelligence (UAI 2005), Arlington, Virginia, p. 568. AUAI Press (2005)
20. Cohen, S.B., Simmons, R.J., Smith, N.A.: Products of weighted logic programs. Technical Report CMU-LTI-08-009, Carnegie Mellon University (2008)
21. Levenshtein, V.: Binary codes capable of correcting spurious insertions and deletions of ones. Problems of Information Transmission 1, 8–17 (1965)
22. Mohri, M.: Finite-state transducers in language and speech processing. Comput. Linguist. 23(2), 269–311 (1997)

23. Manning, C., Schütze, H.: Foundations of Statistical Natural Language Processing. MIT Press, Cambridge (1999)
24. Hopcroft, J.E., Ullman, J.D.: Introduction to Automata Theory, Languages, and Computation. Addison-Wesley, Reading (1979)
25. Cocke, J., Schwartz, J.T.: Programming languages and their compilers: Preliminary notes. Technical report, Courant Institute of Mathematical Sciences, New York University (1970)
26. Gaifman, H.: Dependency systems and phrase-structure systems. Information and Control 8 (1965)
27. Eisner, J., Satta, G.: Efficient parsing for bilexical context-free grammars and head automaton grammars. In: Proceedings of the 37th annual meeting of the Association for Computational Linguistics on Computational Linguistics, Morristown, NJ, USA, pp. 457–464. Association for Computational Linguistics (1999)
28. Wu, D.: Stochastic inversion transduction grammars and bilingual parsing of parallel corpora. Computational Linguistics 23(3), 377–404 (1997)
29. Melamed, I.D.: Multitext grammars and synchronous parsers. In: NAACL 2003: Proceedings of the 2003 Conference of the North American Chapter of the Association for Computational Linguistics on Human Language Technology, Morristown, NJ, USA, pp. 79–86. Association for Computational Linguistics (2003)
30. Zhang, H., Gildea, D.: Stochastic lexicalized inversion transduction grammar for alignment. In: ACL 2005: Proceedings of the 43rd Annual Meeting on Association for Computational Linguistics, Morristown, NJ, USA, pp. 475–482. Association for Computational Linguistics (2005)

Detecting Inconsistencies in Large Biological Networks with Answer Set Programming*

Martin Gebser[1], Torsten Schaub[1], Sven Thiele[1], Björn Usadel[2], and Philippe Veber[1]

[1] University of Potsdam, Institute for Informatics, August-Bebel-Str. 89, D-14482 Potsdam
[2] Max Planck Institute of Molecular Plant Physiology, Am Mühlenberg 1, D-14476 Potsdam

Abstract. We introduce an approach to detecting inconsistencies in large biological networks by using Answer Set Programming. To this end, we build upon a recently proposed notion of consistency between biochemical/genetic reactions and high-throughput profiles of cell activity. We then present an approach based on Answer Set Programming to check the consistency of large-scale data sets. Moreover, we extend this methodology to provide explanations for inconsistencies in the data by determining minimal representations of conflicts. In practice, this can be used to identify unreliable data or to indicate missing reactions.

1 Introduction

Molecular biology has seen a technological revolution with the establishment of high-throughput methods in the last years. These methods allow for gathering multiple orders of magnitude more data than was procurable before. Furthermore, there is an increasing number of biological repositories on the web, such as KEGG, AraCyc, EcoCyc, RegulonDB, and others, incorporating thousands of biochemical reactions and genetic regulations. For combining huge amounts of experimental data with the knowledge gathered in these repositories, one needs appropriate and powerful knowledge representation tools that allow for modeling complex biological systems and their behavior.

In this paper, we deal with the analysis of high-throughput measurements in molecular biology, like microarray data or metabolic profiles [1]. Up to now, it is still a common practice to use expression profiles merely for detecting over- or under-expressed genes under specific conditions, leaving the task of making biological sense out of tens of gene identifiers to human experts. However, many efforts have also been made these years to make a better use of high-throughput data, in particular, by integrating them into large-scale models of transcriptional regulation or metabolic processes [2,3].

One possible approach consists in investigating the compatibility between the experimental measurements and the knowledge available in reaction databases. This can be done by using formal frameworks, for instance, those developed in [4] and [5]. A crucial feature of this methodology is its ability to cope with qualitative knowledge (for instance, reactions lacking kinetic details) and noisy data. In this work, we rely on the so-called *Sign Consistency Model* (SCM) due to Siegel et al. [4]. SCM imposes

---

* A preliminary version of this paper was presented at the Workshop on Constraint Based Methods for Bioinformatics (WCB'08).

M. Garcia de la Banda and E. Pontelli (Eds.): ICLP 2008, LNCS 5366, pp. 130–144, 2008.

constraints between experimental measurements and a graph representation of cellular interactions, called an *influence graph* [6].

Building on SCM, we develop declarative techniques based on *Answer Set Programming* (ASP) [7,8,9] to detect and explain inconsistencies in large data sets. This approach has several advantages. First, it allows us to formulate biological problems in a declarative way, thus easing the communication with biological experts. Second, although we do not detail it here, the rich modeling language facilitates integrating different knowledge representation and reasoning techniques, like abduction, planning, explanation, prediction, etc., in a uniform and transparent way. And finally, modern ASP solvers are based on advanced Boolean constraint solving technology and thus provide us with highly efficient inference engines. Apart from modeling the aforementioned biological problems in ASP, our major concern lies with the scalability of the approach. To this end, we do not only illustrate our application domain on an example but, moreover, design an artificial yet biologically meaningful benchmark suite indicating that an ASP-based approach scales well on the considered class of applications.

To begin with, we introduce SCM in Section 2. Section 3 briefly describes ASP, providing the syntax and semantics used in our application. In Section 4, we develop an ASP formulation of checking the consistency between experimental profiles and influence graphs. We further extend this approach in Section 5 to identifying minimal representations of conflicts if the experimental data is inconsistent with an influence graph. Section 6 is dedicated to an empirical evaluation of our approach along with an exemplary case study illustrating our application domain. Section 7 concludes this paper with a brief discussion and an outlook on future work.

2   Influence Graphs and Sign Consistency Constraints

Influence graphs [6] are a common representation for a wide range of dynamical systems. In the field of genetic networks, they have been investigated for various classes of systems, ranging from ordinary differential equations [10] to synchronous [11] and asynchronous [12] Boolean networks. Influence graphs have also been introduced in the field of qualitative reasoning [13] to describe physical systems where a detailed quantitative description is not available. This has also been the main motivation for using influence graphs for knowledge representation in the context of biological systems.

An *influence graph* is a directed graph whose vertices are the input and state variables of a system and whose edges express the effects of variables on each other. An edge $j \rightarrow i$ means that the variation of j in time influences the level of i. Every edge $j \rightarrow i$ of an influence graph is labeled with a sign, either + or −, denoted by $\sigma(j, i)$, where + (−) indicates that j tends to increase (decrease) i. An example influence graph is given in Figure 1; it represents a simplified model for the operon lactose in *E. coli*.

In SCM, *experimental profiles* are supposed to come from steady state shift experiments where, initially, the system is at steady state, then perturbed using control parameters, and eventually, it settles into another steady state. It is assumed that the data measures the differences between the initial and the final state. Thus, for genes, proteins, or metabolites, we know whether the concentration has increased or decreased, while quantitative values are unavailable, unessential, or unreliable. By $\mu(i)$, we denote

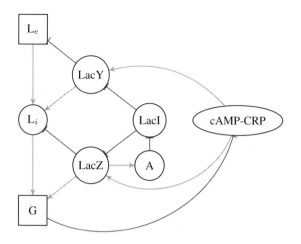

Fig. 1. Simplified model of operon lactose in *E. coli*, represented as an influence graph. The vertices represent either genes, metabolites, or proteins, while the edges indicate the regulations among them. Green edges with an arrow stand for positive regulations (activations), while red edges with a tee head stand for negative regulations (inhibitions). Vertices G and L$_e$ are considered to be inputs of the system, that is, their signs are not constrained via their incoming edges.

the sign, again either + or −, of the variation of a species i between the initial and the final condition. One can easily enhance this setting by also considering null (or more precisely, non-significant) variations, by exploiting the concept of sign algebra [13].

Given an influence graph (as a representation of cellular interactions) and a labeling of its vertices with signs (as a representation of experimental profiles), we now describe the constraints that relate both. Informally, for every non-input vertex i, the observed variation $\mu(i)$ should be explained by the influence of at least one predecessor j of i in the influence graph. Thereby, the *influence* of j on i is given by the sign $\mu(j)\sigma(j,i) \in \{+,-\}$, where the multiplication of signs is derived from that of numbers. Sign consistency constraints can then be formalized as follows.

Definition 1 (Sign Consistency Constraints). *Let* (V,E,σ) *be an influence graph, where* V *is the set of vertices,* E *the set of edges, and* $\sigma : E \rightarrow \{+,-\}$ *a labeling of the edges. Furthermore, let* $\mu : V \rightarrow \{+,-\}$ *be a vertex labeling.*

Then, for every non-input vertex $i \in V$, *the sign* $\mu(i)$ *of* i *is consistent, if there is some edge* $j \rightarrow i$ *in* E *such that* $\mu(i) = \mu(j)\sigma(j,i)$.

The notion of (sign) consistency is extended to whole influence graphs in the natural way, requiring the sign of each non-input vertex to be consistent. In practice, influence graphs and experimental profiles are likely to be partial. Thus, we say that a partial labeling of the vertices is consistent with a partially labeled influence graph, if there is some consistent extension of vertex and edge labelings to all vertices and edges.

Table 1 shows four different vertex labelings for the influence graph given in Figure 1. Total labeling μ_1 is consistent with the influence graph: the variation of each vertex (except for input vertex L$_e$) can be explained by the effect of one of its regulators.

Table 1. Some vertex labelings (reflecting measurements of two steady states) for the influence graph depicted in Figure 1; unobserved values are indicated by a question mark '?'

Species	L_e	L_i	G	LacY	LacZ	LacI	A	cAMP-CRP
μ_1	−	−	−	−	−	+	−	+
μ_2	+	+	−	+	−	+	−	−
μ_3	+	?	−	?	?	+	?	?
μ_4	?	?	?	−	+	?	?	+

For instance, in μ_1, LacY receives a positive influences from cAMP-CRP as well as a negative influence from LacI, the latter accounting for the decrease of LacY. The second labeling, μ_2, is not consistent: this time LacY receives only negative influences from cAMP-CRP and LacI, and its increase cannot be explained. Furthermore, partial vertex labeling μ_3 is consistent with the influence graph in Figure 1, as setting the signs of L_i, LacY, LacZ, A, and cAMP-CRP to +, −, −, −, and +, respectively, extends μ_3 to a consistent total labeling. In contrast, μ_4 cannot be extended consistently.

3   Answer Set Programming

This section provides a brief introduction to ASP (see [9] for details), a declarative paradigm for knowledge representation and reasoning, offering a rich modeling language [14,15] along with highly efficient inference engines based on Boolean constraint solving technology [16,17,18,19]. The basic idea of ASP is to encode a problem as a logic program such that its answer sets represent solutions to the original problem.

In view of our application, we take advantage of the elevated expressiveness of disjunctive programs, being able to capture problems at the second level of the polynomial hierarchy [20,21]. A *disjunctive logic program* over an alphabet $\mathcal{A}$ is a finite set of *rules* of the form

$$a_1; \ldots; a_l \leftarrow b_{l+1}, \ldots, b_m, not\ c_{m+1}, \ldots, not\ c_n\ , \qquad (1)$$

where a_i, b_j, c_k are *atoms* for $0 < i \leq l < j \leq m < k \leq n$. A *literal* is an atom a or its (default) negation *not* a. A rule r as in (1) is called a *fact*, if $l = n = 1$, and an *integrity constraint*, if $l = 0$. Let $head(r) = \{a_1, \ldots, a_l\}$ be the *head* of r and $body(r) = \{b_{l+1}, \ldots, b_m, not\ c_{m+1}, \ldots, not\ c_n\}$ be the *body* of r. Given a set L of literals, let $L^+ = \{a \in \mathcal{A} \mid a \in L\}$ and $L^- = \{a \in \mathcal{A} \mid not\ a \in L\}$.

An interpretation is represented by the set of atoms that are true in it. A *model* of a program P is an interpretation in which all rules in P are true according to the standard definition of truth in propositional logic (while treating rules and default negation as implications and classical negation, respectively). Note that the (empty) head of an integrity constraint is false wrt every interpretation, while the empty body is true wrt every interpretation. Answer sets of P are particular models of P satisfying an additional stability criterion. Roughly, a set X of atoms is an answer set, if for every rule of form (1), X contains a minimum of atoms among $a_1, \ldots, a_l$ whenever $b_{l+1}, \ldots, b_m$ belong to X and no $c_{m+1}, \ldots, c_n$ belongs to X. However, note that the disjunction in heads of rules, in general, is not exclusive. Formally, an *answer set* X of a program P is a $\subseteq$-minimal model of

$$\{head(r) \leftarrow body(r)^+ \mid r \in P, body(r)^- \cap X = \emptyset\} \, .$$

For example, program $\{a; b \leftarrow. \ c; d \leftarrow a, \ not \ b \leftarrow b.\}$ has answer sets $\{a, c\}$ and $\{a, d\}$.

Although answer sets are usually defined on ground (i.e., variable-free) programs, the rich modeling language of ASP allows for non-ground problem encodings, where schematic rules stand for their ground instantiations. Grounders, like *gringo* [22] and *lparse* [15], are capable of combining a problem encoding and an instance (typically a set of ground facts) into an equivalent ground program, processed by some ASP solver. We follow this methodology and provide encodings for the problems considered below.

4   Checking Consistency

We now come to the first main question addressed in this paper, namely, how to check whether an experimental profile is consistent with a given influence graph. Note that, if the profile provides us with a sign for each vertex of the influence graph, the task can be accomplished simply by checking whether each non-input vertex receives at least one influence matching its variation. However, as soon as the experimental profile has missing values (which is very likely in practice), the problem becomes NP-hard [23]. In fact, a Boolean satisfiability problem over clauses $\{C_1, \ldots, C_m\}$ and variables $\{x_1, \ldots, x_n\}$ can be reduced as follows: introduce unlabeled input vertices $x_1, \ldots, x_n$, non-input vertices $C_1, \ldots, C_m$ labeled +, and edges $x_j \rightarrow C_i$ labeled + (−) if x_j occurs positively (negatively) in C_i. It is not hard to check that the labeling of $C_1, \ldots, C_m$ by + is consistent with the obtained influence graph iff $\{C_1, \ldots, C_m\}$ is satisfiable.

We next provide a logic program such that each of its answer sets matches a consistent extension of vertex and edge labelings. Our encodings as well as instances are available at [24]. For clarity, we here present them in a simplified manner and omit some convenient but unessential encoding optimizations. Our program is composed of three parts, described in the following subsections.

4.1   Problem Instance

An influence graph as well as an experimental profile are given by ground facts. For each species i, we introduce a fact $vertex(i)$, and for each edge $j \rightarrow i$, a fact $edge(j, i)$. If $s \in \{+, -\}$ is known to be the variation of a species i or the sign of an edge $j \rightarrow i$, it is expressed by a fact $observedV(i, s)$ or $observedE(j, i, s)$, respectively. Finally, a vertex i is declared to be input via a fact $input(i)$.

For example, negative regulation LacI $\rightarrow$ LacY in the influence graph shown in Figure 1 and observation + for LacI (as with μ_3 in Table 1) give rise to the following facts:

$$\begin{aligned}
&vertex(\text{LacI}). \\
&vertex(\text{LacY}). \\
&edge(\text{LacI}, \text{LacY}). \hspace{3cm} (2)\\
&observedV(\text{LacI}, +). \\
&observedE(\text{LacI}, \text{LacY}, -).
\end{aligned}$$

Note that the absence of a fact of form *observedV*(LacY, *s*) means that the variation of LacY is unobserved (as with μ_3). In (2), we use LacI and LacY as names for constants associated with the species in Figure 1, but not as first-order variables. Similarly, for uniformity of notations, + and − are written in (2) for constants identifying signs.

4.2   Generating Solution Candidates

As mentioned above, our goal is to check whether an experimental profile is consistent with an influence graph. If so, it is witnessed by total labelings of the vertices and edges, which are generated via the following rules:

$$labelV(V, +); labelV(V, -) \leftarrow vertex(V).$$
$$labelE(U, V, +); labelE(U, V, -) \leftarrow edge(U, V). \tag{3}$$

Moreover, the following rules ensure that known labels are respected by total labelings:

$$labelV(V, S) \leftarrow observedV(V, S).$$
$$labelE(U, V, S) \leftarrow observedE(U, V, S). \tag{4}$$

Note that the stability criterion for answer sets demands that a known label derived via rules in (4) is also derived via rules in (3), thus, excluding the opposite label. In fact, the disjunctive rules used in this section could actually be replaced with non-disjunctive rules via "shifting" [25], given that our first encoding results in a so-called *head-cycle-free* (HCF) [26] ground program. However, the disjunctive rules in (3) will be reused in Section 5 where they cannot be compiled away. Also note that HCF programs, for which deciding answer set existence stays in NP, are recognized as such by disjunctive ASP solvers [19,27,28]. Hence, the purely syntactic use of disjunction is not harmful.

The following ground rules are obtained by combining the schematic rules in (3) and (4) with the facts in (2):

$$labelV(\text{LacI}, +); labelV(\text{LacI}, -) \leftarrow vertex(\text{LacI}).$$
$$labelV(\text{LacY}, +); labelV(\text{LacY}, -) \leftarrow vertex(\text{LacY}).$$
$$labelE(\text{LacI}, \text{LacY}, +); labelE(\text{LacI}, \text{LacY}, -) \leftarrow edge(\text{LacI}, \text{LacY}). \tag{5}$$
$$labelV(\text{LacI}, +) \leftarrow observedV(\text{LacI}, +).$$
$$labelE(\text{LacI}, \text{LacY}, -) \leftarrow observedE(\text{LacI}, \text{LacY}, -).$$

One can check that the program consisting of the facts in (2) and the rules in (5) admits two answer sets, the first one including *labelV*(LacY, +) and the second one including *labelV*(LacY, −). On the remaining atoms, both answer sets coincide by containing the atoms in (2) along with *labelV*(LacI, +) and *labelE*(LacI, LacY, −).

4.3   Testing Solution Candidates

We now check whether generated total labelings satisfy the sign consistency constraints stated in Definition 1, requiring an influence of sign *s* for each non-input vertex *i* with variation *s*. We thus define *receive*(*i*, *s*) to indicate that *i* receives an influence of sign *s*:

$$receive(V, +) \leftarrow labelE(U, V, S), labelV(U, S).$$
$$receive(V, -) \leftarrow labelE(U, V, S), labelV(U, T), S \neq T. \tag{6}$$

Inconsistent labelings, where a non-input vertex does not receive any influence matching its variation, are then ruled out by integrity constraints of the following form:

$$\leftarrow labelV(V, S), not\ receive(V, S), not\ input(V). \tag{7}$$

Note that the schematic rules in (6) and (7) are given in the input language of grounder *gringo* [22], available at [29]. This allows us to omit an explicit listing of some (domain) predicates in the bodies of rules, which would be necessary when using *lparse* [15]. At [24], we provide encodings both for *gringo* and also more verbose ones for *lparse*.

Starting from the answer sets described in the previous subsection, the included atoms *labelE*(LacI, LacY, −) and *labelV*(LacI, +) allow us to derive *receive*(LacY, −) via a ground instance of the second rule in (6), while *receive*(LacY, +) is underivable. After adding *receive*(LacY, −), the solution candidate containing *labelV*(LacY, −) satisfies the ground instances of the integrity constraint in (7) obtained by substituting LacY for V. Assuming LacI to be an input, as it can be declared via fact *input*(LacI), we thus obtain an answer set containing *labelV*(LacY, −), expressing a decrease of LacY. In contrast, since *receive*(LacY, +) is underivable, the solution candidate containing *labelV*(LacY, +) violates the following ground instance of (7):

$$\leftarrow labelV(\text{LacY}, +), not\ receive(\text{LacY}, +), not\ input(\text{LacY}).$$

That is, the solution candidate with *labelV*(LacY, +) does not pass the consistency test.

5   Identifying Minimal Inconsistent Cores

In view of the usually large amount of data, it is crucial to provide concise explanations, whenever an experimental profile is inconsistent with an influence graph (i.e., if the logic program given in the previous section has no answer set). To this end, we adopt a strategy that was successfully applied on real biological data [30]. The basic idea is to isolate minimal subgraphs of an influence graph such that the vertices and edges cannot be labeled consistently. This task is closely related to extracting Minimal Unsatisfiable Cores (MUCs) [31] in the context of Boolean satisfiability (SAT) [16]. In allusion, we call a minimal subgraph of an influence graph whose vertices and edges cannot be labeled consistently a *Minimal Inconsistent Core* (MIC). Note that identifying a MUC is D^P-complete [31,32], which is why we use disjunctive programs to encode MICs.

For illustration, consider the influence graph and the MIC shown in Figure 2. One can check that the observed simultaneous increase of **B** and **D** is not consistent with the influence graph, but the reason for this might not be apparent at first glance. However, once the depicted MIC is extracted, we immediately see that the increase of **B** implies an increase of **A**, so that the observed increase of **D** cannot be explained.

We next provide an encoding for identifying MICs, where a problem instance, that is, an influence graph along with an experimental profile, is represented by facts as specified in Section 4.1. The encoding then consists of three parts: the first generating MIC candidates, the second asserting inconsistency, and the third verifying minimality. The generating part comprises the rules in (3) and (4), and in addition, it includes:

$$active(V); inactive(V) \leftarrow vertex(V), not\ input(V). \tag{8}$$

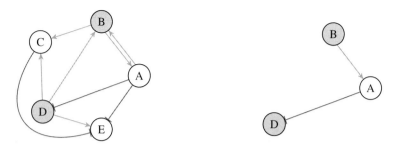

Fig. 2. A partially labeled influence graph and a contained MIC

This additional rule permits guessing non-input vertices to be marked as active. The subgraph of the influence graph consisting of the active vertices, their regulators, and the connecting edges forms a MIC candidate, tested via the two encoding parts below.

5.1   Testing for Inconsistency

By adapting a methodology used in [21], the following subprogram makes sure that the active vertices belong to a subgraph that cannot be labeled consistently, while all possible labelings of the residual vertices and edges are (implicitly) taken into account:[1]

$$opposite(U,V) \leftarrow labelE(U,V,-), labelV(U,S), labelV(V,S).$$
$$opposite(U,V) \leftarrow labelE(U,V,+), labelV(U,S), labelV(V,T), S \neq T.$$
$$bottom \leftarrow active(V), opposite(U,V) : edge(U,V).$$
$$\leftarrow not\ bottom.$$
$$labelV(V,+) \leftarrow bottom, vertex(V).$$
$$labelV(V,-) \leftarrow bottom, vertex(V).$$
$$labelE(U,V,+) \leftarrow bottom, edge(U,V).$$
$$labelE(U,V,-) \leftarrow bottom, edge(U,V).$$

In this (part of the) encoding, $opposite(U,V)$ indicates that the influence of regulator U on V is opposite to the variation of V. If all regulators of an active vertex V have such an opposite influence, the sign consistency constraint for V is violated, in which case atom $bottom$ along with all labels for vertices and edges are derived. Note that the stability criterion for an answer set X imposes that $bottom$ and all labels belong to X only if the active vertices cannot be labeled consistently. Finally, integrity constraint $\leftarrow not\ bottom$ necessitates the inclusion of $bottom$ in any answer set, thus, stipulating an inevitable sign consistency constraint violation for some active vertex.

Reconsidering our example in Figure 2, the ground instances of (8) permit guessing $active(\mathbf{A})$ and $active(\mathbf{D})$. When labeling $\mathbf{A}$ with $+$ (or assuming $labelV(\mathbf{A},+)$ to be true), we derive $opposite(\mathbf{A},\mathbf{D})$ and $bottom$, producing in turn all labels for vertices and edges. Furthermore, setting the sign of $\mathbf{A}$ to $-$ (or $labelV(\mathbf{A},-)$ to true) makes us derive

---

[1] In the language of *gringo* (and *lparse* [15]), the expression $opposite(U,V) : edge(U,V)$ used below refers to the conjunction of all ground atoms $opposite(j,i)$ for which $edge(j,i)$ holds.

opposite(**B**, **A**), which again gives *bottom* and all labels for vertices and edges. We have thus verified that the sign consistency constraints for **A** and **D** cannot be jointly satisfied, given the observed increases of **B** and **D**. That is, active vertices **A** and **D** are sufficient to explain the inconsistency between the observations and the influence graph.

5.2 Testing for Minimality

It remains to be verified whether the sign consistency constraints for all active vertices are necessary to identify an inherent inconsistency. This test is based on the idea that, excluding any active vertex, the sign consistency constraints for the other active vertices should be satisfied by appropriate labelings. This can be implemented as follows:

$$labelV'(W, V, +); labelV'(W, V, -) \leftarrow active(W), vertex(V).$$
$$labelE'(W, U, V, +); labelE'(W, U, V, -) \leftarrow active(W), edge(U, V).$$
$$labelV'(W, V, S) \leftarrow active(W), observedV(V, S).$$
$$labelE'(W, U, V, S) \leftarrow active(W), observedE(U, V, S).$$
$$receive'(W, V, +) \leftarrow labelE'(W, U, V, S), labelV'(W, U, S).$$
$$receive'(W, V, -) \leftarrow labelE'(W, U, V, S), labelV'(W, U, T), S \neq T.$$
$$\leftarrow labelV'(W, V, S), active(V), V \neq W, not\ receive'(W, V, S).$$

This subprogram is similar to the consistency check encoded via the rules in (3), (4), (6), and (7). However, sign consistency constraints are only checked for active vertices, and they must be satisfiable for all but an arbitrary active vertex W. As W ranges over all (non-input) vertices of an influence graph, each active vertex is taken into consideration.

For the influence graph in Figure 2, it is easy to see that the sign consistency constraint for **A** is satisfied by setting the sign of **A** to +, expressed by atom *labelV'*(**D**, **A**, +) in the ground rules obtained from the above encoding. In turn, the sign consistency constraint for **D** is satisfied by setting the sign of **A** to –. This is reflected by atom *labelV'*(**A**, **A**, –), allowing us to derive *receive'*(**A**, **D**, +), so that the ground instance of the above integrity constraint containing *labelV'*(**A**, **D**, +) is satisfied.

6 Empirical Evaluation and Application

For assessing the scalability of our approach, we start by conceiving a parameterizable set of artificial yet biologically meaningful benchmarks. After that, we present a typical application stemming from real biological data, illustrating the exertion in practice.

6.1 Checking Consistency

We first evaluate the efficiency of our approach on randomly generated instances, aiming at structures similar to those found in biological applications. Instances are composed of an influence graph, a complete labeling of its edges, and a partial labeling of its vertices. Our random generator takes three parameters: (i) the number α of vertices in the influence graph, (ii) the average degree β of the graph, and (iii) the proportion γ

Table 2. Run-times for consistency checking with *claspD*, *cmodels*, *dlv*, and *gnt*

α	claspD Berkmin	claspD VMTF	claspD VSIDS	cmodels	dlv	gnt
500	0.14	0.11	0.11	0.16	0.46	0.71
1000	0.41	0.25	0.25	0.35	1.92	3.34
1500	0.79	0.38	0.38	0.53	4.35	7.50
2000	1.33	0.51	0.51	0.71	8.15	13.23
2500	2.10	0.66	0.66	0.89	13.51	21.88
3000	3.03	0.80	0.79	1.07	20.37	31.77
3500	3.22	0.93	0.92	1.15	21.54	34.39
4000	4.35	1.06	1.06	1.36	30.06	46.14

of observed variations for vertices. To generate an instance, we compute a random graph with α vertices (the value of α varying from 500 to 4000) under the model by Erdős-Rényi [33]. Each pair of vertices has equal probability to be connected via an edge, whose label is chosen independently with probability 0.5 for both signs. We fix the average degree β to 2.5, which is considered to be a typical value for biological networks [34]. Finally, $\lfloor \gamma \alpha \rfloor$ vertices are chosen with uniform probability and assigned a label with probability 0.5 for both signs. For each number α of vertices, we generated 50 instances using five different values for γ, viz., 0.01, 0.02, 0.033, 0.05, and 0.1. All instances can be found at [24].

We used *gringo* [22,29] (version 2.0.0) for combining the generated instances and the encoding given in Section 4 into equivalent ground logic programs. For deciding consistency by computing an answer set (if it exists), we ran disjunctive ASP solvers *claspD* [19] (version 1.1) with "Berkmin", "VMTF", and "VSIDS" heuristics, *cmodels* [17,27] (version 3.75) using *zchaff* [35], *dlv* [28] (build BEN/Oct 11), and *gnt* [36] (version 2.1). All runs were performed on a Linux machine equipped with an AMD Opteron 2 GHz processor and a memory limit set to 2GB RAM.

Table 2 shows the average run-times over 50 instances per number α of vertices in seconds, including grounding times of *gringo* and solving times. We checked that grounding times of *gringo* increase linearly with the number α of vertices, and they do not vary significantly over γ. For all solvers, run-times also increase linearly in α.[2] In fact, for fixed α values, we found two clusters of instances: consistent ones where total labelings were easy to compute and inconsistent ones where inconsistency was detected from preassigned labels only. This tells us that the influence graphs generated as described above are usually (too) easy to label consistently, and inconsistency only happens if it is explicitly introduced via fixed labels. However, such constellations are not unlikely in practice (cf. Section 6.3), and isolating MICs from them, as done in the next subsection, turned out to be hard for most solvers. Finally, greater values for γ led to an increased proportion of inconsistent instances, without making them much harder.

---

[2] Longer run-times of *claspD* with "Berkmin" in comparison to the other heuristics are due to a more expensive computation of heuristic values in the absence of conflict information. Furthermore, the time needed for performing "Lookahead" slows down *dlv* as well as *gnt*.

Table 3. Run-times for grounding with *gringo* and solving with *claspD*

α	*gringo*	*claspD Berkmin*	*claspD VMTF*	*claspD VSIDS*
50	0.24	1.16 (0)	0.65 (0)	0.97 (0)
75	0.55	39.11 (1)	1.65 (0)	3.99 (0)
100	0.87	41.98 (1)	3.40 (0)	4.80 (0)
125	1.37	15.47 (0)	47.56 (1)	10.73 (0)
150	2.02	54.13 (0)	48.05 (0)	15.89 (0)
175	2.77	30.98 (0)	116.37 (2)	23.07 (0)
200	3.82	42.81 (0)	52.28 (1)	24.03 (0)
225	4.94	99.64 (1)	30.71 (0)	41.17 (0)
250	5.98	194.29 (3)	228.42 (5)	110.90 (1)
275	7.62	178.28 (2)	193.03 (4)	51.11 (0)
300	9.45	241.81 (2)	307.15 (7)	124.31 (0)

6.2 Identifying Minimal Inconsistent Cores

We now investigate the problem of finding a MIC within the same setting as in the previous subsection. Because of the elevated size of ground instantiations and problem difficulty, we varied the number α of vertices from 50 to 300, thus, using considerably smaller influence graphs than before. We again use *gringo* for grounding, now taking the encoding given in Section 5. As regards solving, we restrict our attention to *claspD* because all three of the other solvers showed drastic performance declines.

Table 3 shows average run-times over 50 instances per number α of vertices in seconds for grounding with *gringo* and solving with *claspD* using "Berkmin","VMTF", and "VSIDS" heuristics. Timeouts, indicated in parentheses, are taken as maximum time of 1800 seconds. We observe a quadratic increase in grounding times of *gringo*, which is in line with the fact that ground instantiations for our MIC encoding grow quadratically with the size of influence graphs. In fact, the schematic rules in Section 5.2 give rise to α copies of an influence graph. Considering solving times spent by *claspD* for finding one MIC (if it exists), we observe that they are relatively stable, in the sense that they are tightly correlated to grounding times. This regularity again confirms that, though it is random, the applied generation pattern tends to produce rather uniform influence graphs. Finally, we observed that unsatisfiable instances, i.e., consistent instances without any MIC, were easier to solve than the ones admitting answer sets. We conjecture that this is because consistent total labelings provide a disproof of inconsistency as encoded in Section 5.1.

As our experimental results demonstrate, computing a MIC is computationally harder than just checking consistency. This is not surprising because the related problem of identifying a MUC is D^P-complete [31,32]. With our declarative technique, we spot the quadratic space blow-up incurred by the MIC encoding in Section 5 as a bottleneck. It is an interesting open question whether more economical encodings can be found.

6.3 Biological Case Study

In the following, we present the results of applying our approach to real-world data of genetic regulations in yeast. We tested the gene-regulatory network of yeast provided

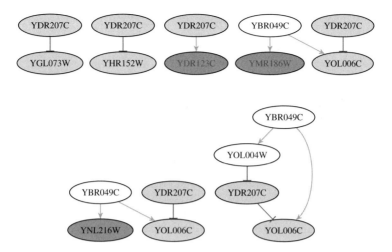

Fig. 3. Some exemplary MICs obtained by comparing the regulatory network in [37] with a genetic profile from [38]

in [37] against genetic profile data of SNF2 knock-outs [38] from the Saccharomyces Genome Database. The regulatory network of yeast contains 909 genetic or biochemical regulations, all of which have been established experimentally, among 491 genes.

Comparing the yeast regulatory network with the genetic profile of SNF2, we found the data to be inconsistent with the network, which was easily detected using the approach from Section 4. Applying our diagnosis technique from Section 5, we obtained a total of 19 MICs. While computing the first MIC took only about 2.5 seconds using *gringo* and *claspD*, the computation of all MICs was considerably harder, taking 3 minutes and 38 seconds with *claspD* using "VMTF" embedded into a wrapper script that excludes already computed MICs via integrity constraints. In fact, the minimality encoding in Section 5.2 admits multiple answer sets corresponding to the same MIC because the variations of vertices not connected to the MIC can be chosen freely, thus producing copies of the same solution. Even though the encodings available at [24] already address this redundancy, they do not yet establish a one-to-one correspondence between MICs and answer sets since the determined consistent labelings of the subgraphs of a MIC are not necessarily unique. For achieving one-to-one correspondence, this redundancy must also be eliminated, which is a subject to future work.

Six of the computed MICs are exemplarily shown in Figure 3. While the first three of them are pretty obvious, we also identified more complex topologies. However, our example demonstrates that the MICs obtained in practice are still small enough to be understood easily. For finding suitable corrections to the inconsistencies, it is often even more helpful to display the connections between several overlapping MICs. Observe that all six MICs in Figure 3 are related to gene YDR207C, and in Figure 4, we show the subgraph of the yeast regulatory network obtained by connecting them. In this representation, one can see that the observed increase of YDR207C is not compatible with the variation of any of its four targets, but the variation of YDR207C itself can be explained by its direct and indirect regulators. This suggests to first check the correctness

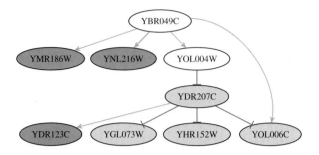

Fig. 4. Subgraph obtained by connecting the six MICs given in Figure 3

of the observation that YDR207C has increased, and depending on the result, to consider additional regulations that might be missing in the yeast regulatory network. In fact, potential uses of our diagnosis technique applied to real-world data include identifying unreliable data and missing reactions in a systematic and more targeted way.

7   Discussion

We have provided an approach based on ASP to investigate the consistency between experimental profiles and influence graphs. In case of inconsistency, the concept of a MIC can be exploited for identifying concise explanations, pointing to unreliable data or missing reactions. The problem of finding MICs is closely related to the extraction of MUCs in the context of SAT. From a knowledge representation point of view, however, we argue for our ASP-based technique, as it allows for an elegant declarative way to describe problems in terms of a uniform encoding and specific instances.

By now, a variety of efficient ASP tools are available, both for grounding and for solving logic programs. Our empirical assessment of them (on random as well as real data) has in principle demonstrated the scalability of the approach. As elegance and flexibility in problem modeling are major advantages of ASP, our investigation might make it attractive also for related biological questions, beyond the ones addressed in this paper. For instance, natural extensions of the presented techniques allow for accomplishing prediction and repair. In the future, it will also be interesting to explore how far the performance of ASP tools can be tuned by varying and optimizing the given encodings, e.g., in order to compute all MICs more effectively. In turn, challenging applications like the one presented here might contribute to the further improvement of ASP tools, as they might be geared towards efficiency in such application domains.

Acknowledgments. Philippe Veber was supported by a grant from DAAD. This work was partially funded by the GoFORSYS project (http://www.goforsys.org/; Grant 0313924). The authors would like to thank Roland Kaminski for fruitful comments on our encoding and Carito Guziolowski for providing the data on yeast.

References

1. Joyce, A., Palsson, B.: The model organism as a system: Integrating 'omics' data sets. Nature Reviews Molecular Cell Biology 7(3), 198–210 (2006)
2. Klamt, S., Stelling, J.: Stoichiometric and constraint-based modelling. In: System Modeling in Cellular Biology: From Concepts to Nuts and Bolts, pp. 73–96. MIT Press, Cambridge (2006)
3. Friedman, N., Linial, M., Nachman, I., Pe'er, D.: Using Bayesian networks to analyze expression data. Journal of Computational Biology 7(3-4), 601–620 (2000)
4. Siegel, A., Radulescu, O., Le Borgne, M., Veber, P., Ouy, J., Lagarrigue, S.: Qualitative analysis of the relation between DNA microarray data and behavioral models of regulation networks. Biosystems 84(2), 153–174 (2006)
5. Gutierrez-Rios, R., Rosenblueth, D., Loza, J., Huerta, A., Glasner, J., Blattner, F., Collado-Vides, J.: Regulatory network of Escherichia coli: Consistency between literature knowledge and microarray profiles. Genome Research 13(11), 2435–2443 (2003)
6. Soulé, C.: Graphic requirements for multistationarity. Complexus 1(3), 123–133 (2003)
7. Marek, V., Truszczyński, M.: Stable models and an alternative logic programming paradigm. In: The Logic Programming Paradigm: a 25-Year Perspective, pp. 375–398. Springer, Heidelberg (1999)
8. Niemelä, I.: Logic programs with stable model semantics as a constraint programming paradigm. Annals of Mathematics and Artificial Intelligence 25(3-4), 241–273 (1999)
9. Baral, C.: Knowledge Representation, Reasoning and Declarative Problem Solving. Cambridge University Press, Cambridge (2003)
10. Soulé, C.: Mathematical approaches to differentiation and gene regulation. Comptes Rendus Biologies 329, 13–20 (2006)
11. Remy, É., Ruet, P., Thieffry, D.: Graphic requirements for multistability and attractive cycles in a Boolean dynamical framework. Advances in Applied Mathematics (to appear, 2008)
12. Richard, A., Comet, J.: Necessary conditions for multistationarity in discrete dynamical systems. Discrete Applied Mathematics 155(18), 2403–2413 (2007)
13. Kuipers, B.: Qualitative reasoning: Modeling and simulation with incomplete knowledge. MIT Press, Cambridge (1994)
14. Simons, P., Niemelä, I., Soininen, T.: Extending and implementing the stable model semantics. Artificial Intelligence 138(1-2), 181–234 (2002)
15. Syrjänen, T.: Lparse 1.0 user's manual,
    http://www.tcs.hut.fi/Software/smodels/lparse.ps.gz
16. Mitchell, D.: A SAT solver primer. Bulletin of the European Association for Theoretical Computer Science 85, 112–133 (2005)
17. Giunchiglia, E., Lierler, Y., Maratea, M.: Answer set programming based on propositional satisfiability. Journal of Automated Reasoning 36(4), 345–377 (2006)
18. Gebser, M., Kaufmann, B., Neumann, A., Schaub, T.: clasp: A conflict-driven answer set solver. In: Baral, C., Brewka, G., Schlipf, J. (eds.) LPNMR 2007. LNCS, vol. 4483, pp. 260–265. Springer, Heidelberg (2007)
19. Drescher, C., Gebser, M., Grote, T., Kaufmann, B., König, A., Ostrowski, M., Schaub, T.: Conflict-driven disjunctive answer set solving. In: Proceedings of the Eleventh International Conference on Principles of Knowledge Representation and Reasoning (KR 2008), pp. 422–432. AAAI Press, Menlo Park (2008)
20. Garey, M., Johnson, D.: Computers and Intractability: A Guide to the Theory of NP-Completeness. W. Freeman and Co., New York (1979)
21. Eiter, T., Gottlob, G.: On the computational cost of disjunctive logic programming: Propositional case. Annals of Mathematics and Artificial Intelligence 15(3-4), 289–323 (1995)

22. Gebser, M., Schaub, T., Thiele, S.: GrinGo: A new grounder for answer set programming. In: Baral, C., Brewka, G., Schlipf, J. (eds.) LPNMR 2007. LNCS, vol. 4483, pp. 266–271. Springer, Heidelberg (2007)

23. Veber, P., Le Borgne, M., Siegel, A., Lagarrigue, S., Radulescu, O.: Complex qualitative models in biology: A new approach. Complexus 2(3-4), 140–151 (2004)

24. http://www.cs.uni-potsdam.de/wv/bioasp

25. Gelfond, M., Lifschitz, V., Przymusinska, H., Truszczyński, M.: Disjunctive defaults. In: Proceedings of the Second International Conference on Principles of Knowledge Representation and Reasoning (KR 1991)., pp. 230–237. Morgan Kaufmann, San Francisco (1991)

26. Ben-Eliyahu, R., Dechter, R.: Propositional semantics for disjunctive logic programs. Annals of Mathematics and Artificial Intelligence 12(1-2), 53–87 (1994)

27. Lierler, Y.: cmodels – SAT-based disjunctive answer set solver. In: Baral, C., Greco, G., Leone, N., Terracina, G. (eds.) LPNMR 2005. LNCS, vol. 3662, pp. 447–451. Springer, Heidelberg (2005)

28. Leone, N., Pfeifer, G., Faber, W., Eiter, T., Gottlob, G., Perri, S., Scarcello, F.: The DLV system for knowledge representation and reasoning. ACM Transactions on Computational Logic 7(3), 499–562 (2006)

29. http://sourceforge.net/projects/potassco

30. Guziolowski, C., Veber, P., Le Borgne, M., Radulescu, O., Siegel, A.: Checking consistency between expression data and large scale regulatory networks: A case study. Journal of Biological Physics and Chemistry 7(2), 37–43 (2007)

31. Dershowitz, N., Hanna, Z., Nadel, A.: A scalable algorithm for minimal unsatisfiable core extraction. In: Biere, A., Gomes, C.P. (eds.) SAT 2006. LNCS, vol. 4121, pp. 36–41. Springer, Heidelberg (2006)

32. Papadimitriou, C., Yannakakis, M.: The complexity of facets (and some facets of complexity). In: Proceedings of the Fourteenth Annual ACM Symposium on Theory of Computing (STOC 1982), pp. 255–260. ACM Press, New York (1982)

33. Erdős, P., Rényi, A.: On random graphs. Publicationes Mathematicae 6, 290–297 (1959)

34. Jeong, H., Tombor, B., Albert, R., Oltvai, Z., Barabási, A.: The large-scale organization of metabolic networks. Nature 407, 651–654 (2000)

35. http://www.princeton.edu/~chaff/zchaff.html

36. Janhunen, T., Niemelä, I., Seipel, D., Simons, P., You, J.: Unfolding partiality and disjunctions in stable model semantics. ACM Transactions on Computational Logic 7(1), 1–37 (2006)

37. Guelzim, N., Bottani, S., Bourgine, P., Képès, F.: Topological and causal structure of the yeast transcriptional regulatory network. Nature Genetics 31, 60–63 (2002)

38. Sudarsanam, P., Iyer, V., Brown, P., Winston, F.: Whole-genome expression analysis of snf/swi mutants of Saccharomyces cerevisiae. Proceedings of the National Academy of Sciences of the United States of America 97(7), 3364–3369 (2000)

A Logic Programming Approach to Home Monitoring for Risk Prevention in Assisted Living

Alessandra Mileo[1], Davide Merico[2], and Roberto Bisiani[2]

[1] QUA_SI Research Center, NOMADIS Research Lab., Università degli Studi di Milano-Bicocca, viale dell'Innovazione 110, I–20125 Milano
[2] Dipartimento di Informatica, Sistemistica e Comunicazione, Università degli Studi di Milano-Bicocca, viale Sarca 336/14, I–20126 Milano

Abstract. Monitoring a patient in his home environment is necessary to ensure continuity of care in home settings, but this activity must not be too much invasive and a burden for clinicians. For this reason we prototyped a system called SINDI (Secure and INDependent lIving), focused on i) collecting a limited amount of data about the person and the environment through Wireless Sensor Networks (WSN), and ii) reasoning about these data both to contextualize them and to support clinicians in understanding patients' well being as well as in predicting possible evolutions of their health. Our hierarchical logic-based model of health combines data from different sources, sensor data, tests results, commonsense knowledge and patient's clinical profile at the lower level, and correlation rules between aspects of health (*items*) across upper levels. The logical formalization and the reasoning process are based on Answer Set Programming. The expressive power of this logic programming paradigm allows efficient reasoning to support prevention, while declarativity simplifies rules specification by clinicians and allows automatic encoding of knowledge. This paper describes how these issues have been targeted in the application scenario of the SINDI system.

1 Background and Motivations

In the last twenty years there has been a significant increase of the average age of the population in most western countries and the number of senior citizens has been and will be constantly growing. Living independently in their own homes is a key factor for these people in order to improve their quality-of-life and to reduce the costs for the community. For this reason there has been a strong development of computer technology applied to specific fields of medical sciences for the delivery of clinical care outside of hospitals. For example, Telemedicine and Clinical Decision Support Systems have been used to collect and transmit complex clinical data and to implement diagnosis at-a-distance. We have designed a system, called SINDI (Secure and INDependent lIving), that complements these techniques by taking into account the health evolution of patients over long periods of time and the contextual setting, so as to identify what is best for the patient in his specific context [1].

M. Garcia de la Banda and E. Pontelli (Eds.): ICLP 2008, LNCS 5366, pp. 145–159, 2008.
© Springer-Verlag Berlin Heidelberg 2008

We address those elderly that are clinically stable although they might be affected by chronic diseases and physical decline (more than 90% of the population over 65 has more than one chronic desease). Since their health condition does not require constant monitoring of complex biomedical parameters, these patients do not need, and are less tolerant of, invasive sensors.

Many user-centered systems that analyse user's behavior and detect emergencies have been developed. They often cater to the identification of predefined patterns of behavior rather than to the assessment of health in general, and they are mainly based on statistical analysis of data, thus needing substantial training to be adapted to a particular patient.

We use monitoring to support prevention, causal diagnosis and emergency detection in the same framework and provide a global representation and reasoning model for general health assessment, combining medical knowledge, patient's clinical profile and context evaluation through sensor data.

In particular, we want to address the fact that clinicians need to be supported in i) understanding patients' physical, mental and social settings as they evolve, ii) predicting what could follow with respect to particular changes in one or more aspects of the patients' general health and iii) identifying correlated aspects that may be the cause for a negative change in the patient's general health.

The first aspect is related to the contextualization of worsenings of the general health status of the patient at hand, not only with respect to similar clinical cases, but giving more importance to aspects that turn out to be important for that specific patient. The second aspect refers to prediction, i.e. the identification of items which might be indicators of a negative event; this would allow to act *before* major symptoms and to plan appropriate short- and long-term interventions, thus reducing risks. The third aspect is more similar to diagnosis, but it is a *local* process rather than a case-based one, in that it takes into account patient's clinical and environmental settings when causal correlations are identified.

The need of making the system user-centered and medically sound lead us to include some medical knowledge in the reasoning phase. In this way it is possible to trace general habits and their correlation with the patient's well-being according to the evaluation methods of clinical practice.

To perform these reasoning tasks and encode the relative knowledge into a common model, we believe Answer Set Programming (ASP) constitutes a powerful declarative framework for knowledge representation and reasoning because:

1. the effectiveness of the implementation makes it possible to express deductions, default reasoning, constraints, choices and qualitative preferences;
2. declarativity allows the automatic encoding of medical knowledge, thus making the system easily extensible and medically sound;
3. the use of contextual information and the way new knowledge can be taken into account, makes it possible to deal with incomplete information and enhance context-awareness.

In our framework, dynamic data about the person and the environment are unobtrusively captured and aggregated by the Wireless Sensors Network (WSN).

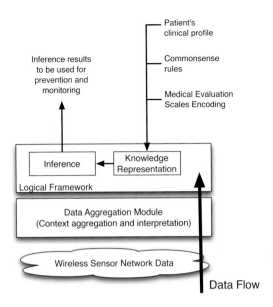

Fig. 1. Data flow

At higher level, these data are combined and interpreted by an inference engine to help caregivers detect patients' physical, mental and social status as it evolves.

Figure 1 shows a very high-level overview of the architecture of our system and the correlation between its components.

This variety of information makes it possible to both automatically adapt the results of the reasoning process when new information is available and deal with user and context-specific constraints.

Medical soundness and context-awareness improve the reliability of the system because the combination of different sources of information (sensors, medical knowledge, clinical profile, user defined constraints) that change over time make the system more reliable (i.e. much better able to disambiguate situations, thus reducing false positives) and adaptive (e.g. easily extended on the face of new available information).

We did not consider the introduction of robots for assisted living as in other approaches [2] because, besides their high costs of set up and maintenance, their presence is rather intrusive and the help they can provide is marginal.

We implemented communication facilities based on a set-top box that handles TV programming, communication with the outside world and an agenda through the TV remote control, since it is a widely accessible tool. Real-time emergency detection has also been considered in the implementation of the system.

Section 2 describes the design and implementation of the Wireless Sensor Networks supporting SINDI's intelligence. We then introduce the logical framework and describe the Hierarchical Knowledge Representation model in Section 3, while details about the implementation of the model are presented in Section 4.

Section 5 contains preliminary evaluations, while considerations about future developments of SINDI are given in Section 6.

2   Home Monitoring: Context Aggregation and Interpretation

Wireless Sensor Networks (WSNs) [3] consist of nodes that are capable of interacting with the environment by sensing and controlling physical parameters; the nodes use packet radio communication to exchange data. These networks are typically used to collect data for long periods of time without assistance. Specific scenarios for WSNs include habitat monitoring, industrial control, embedded sensing, medical data collection, building automation, fire detection, traffic monitoring, etc.

In the last few years, many interesting systems were developed in the area of WSNs for assisted living and healthcare [4,5]. Similarly to these systems, the WSN of SINDI monitors environmental and physiological data of individuals in their residences. In order to fulfill the requirements of SINDI's monitoring, we had to address some specific aspects of WSNs such as (i) hierarchical organization and topology control, enabling more reliable localization and data routing, as well as lower power consumption, (ii) dynamic network configuration providing enough flexibility to deal with heterogeneous sensors and (iv) data aggregation to avoid redundant messages.

The SINDI Wireless Sensor Network (SINDI-WSN) is composed by (i) a reference node in every zone (typically a room), always active and connected to household power, used for network coordination but also with sensing capabilities (ii) battery-powered nodes used for sensing the environment data or capture particular events and (iii) a wearable monitoring device called Inertial MeasUrement Device (IMUD), (iv) a master processor. The wearable monitoring device is used for the user's localization and movement detection. The master processor is the coordinator node of the network. It is the gateway of the network and it has storage, processing power and main memory capabilities in the ballpark of an average PC.

The network is organized hierarchically, as follows. The environment in which the user lives is divided into zones and every zone is controlled by one base node. Moreover, every zone can be divided into several sensing areas where one or more environment nodes operate. The master processor manages the entire network applying topology-control mechanisms and routing algorithms.

The configuration of the environment nodes can be easily managed and single activities turned on or off by a base node for its zone or by the master processor node for the whole network. The presence of an always active base node in every zone simplifies data routing because the environmental nodes are guaranteed to always find a listening node. Therefore, they can simply send a message with the proper sensor data and quickly enter in sleep-mode without wasting precious energy. Data aggregation is another crucial feature since it remarkably reduces the traffic in the network and eliminates redundant data [6]. Semantic aggregations have been investigated in several papers among, e.g. [7] and [8]. In our system, data aggregation is supported by the possibility of defining simple aggregation rules at zone level in order to avoid redundant messages to be sent over the network, e.g. when nobody is detected in a zone (or in particular areas), data from the nodes in that particular zone can be aggregated. A middleware environment that provides dynamic topology-control, hierarchical routing [9], localization, data aggregation, and communication services has been designed and developed in order to carry the data captured by SINDI-WSN and to feed the reasoning system.

We now give some formal notions about the logical framework of SINDI, and then concentrate on the Health Care Knowledge Representation and Reasoning model.

3   The Logic-Based Model of Health

3.1   Preliminary Notions

In order to allow the system to perform reasoning tasks, data collected by the WSN and knowledge about the home healthcare domain must be represented in a formal way. The declarative logical framework we use is that of Answer Set Programming (ASP), based on the *stable model* semantics for Logic Programs proposed by Gelfond and Lifschitz [10]. Thanks to its expressiveness and to the availability of efficient implementations [11,12], ASP started to play a relevant role in decision problem solving and it has been widely used in planning, diagnosis and, more generally, Knowledge Representation and Reasoning [13].

We want to recall some basic definitions. In ASP a given problem is represented by a logic program whose results are given in terms of *answer sets*.

An *answer set* for a logic program is a minimal (in the sense of set-inclusion) set of literals satisfying the logic rules included in the program.

A rule r is an expression of the form

$$r: \ L_0 \ \leftarrow \ L_1, \ldots, \ L_m, \ not \ L_{m+1}, \ldots, \ not \ L_n \ . \tag{1}$$

where L_i $(i = 0..n)$ are literals, *not* is a logical connective called *negation as failure* and $n \geq m \geq 0$. We define $L_0 = head(r)$ as the *head* of rule r, and $body(r) = L_1, \ldots, L_m, \ not \ L_{m+1}, \ldots, \ not \ L_n$ as the *body* of r. Rules r with $head(r) = \emptyset$ are called *integrity constraints*, while if $body(r) = \emptyset$, we refer to r as *a fact*. Rules with variables (upper case names) are taken as a shorthand for the sets of all their ground instantiations.

3.2   Hierarchical Model of Health Care: Knowledge Representation

A careful analysis of health care in home settings suggested us that health-related items can be classified into three levels which hierarchically influence each other: Functionality level, Activities of Daily Living (ADL) level and Risk Assessment level. Significant aspects of health assessment at each level (referred to as *items*) have been identified according to the medical practice in health assessment of the elderly [14] and encoded in our declarative framework in form of logic facts.

Table 1. Logical encoding of patient's profile: static description and dynamic evaluation

Static Predicates	Description	Dynamic Predicates	Description
test(Name,Value)	test results	lev(L,I)	association items-level
drug(Name)	list of drugs	obs(I,V_i,T)	evaluation of an item
pathol(Name)	list of pathologies	obsind(Ind,V_i,T)	evaluation of an indicator
profile(X,Name,V)	X={drug,pathol}	link(I,Ind)	association item-indicator
	V={yes,no}	range(Ind,V_i)	range of values
		ord(Ind, V_i,Num)	order of values

A lower layer (State level) contains aggregated context data as well as static and dynamic evaluations of significant aspects of patient's clinical settings (referred to as *indicators*).

Predicates used for static description and dynamic evaluation are listed in table 1, where I represents an item, L is a level, V_i are values, Ind represents indicators, Num is an ordinal[1] for V and T is a timestamp.

At higher level, each indicator can be associated with one or more items. Items are thus characterized by an initial evaluation (predicate *obs()* in table 1), and a set of indicators used for differential evaluation (predicate *obsind()* in table 1).

Every time the inference process is run, the system compares the values of indicators from the previous inference with the actual values to detect worsenings in health status through differential evaluations. Results of differential evaluations make it possible to detect indicators subjected to worsenings and to identify critical items: the higher is the number of worsenings associated with an item, the more the item is critical.

Logic rules used to detect worsenings by differential evaluation are detailed in section 4.

The reasoning process takes also into account medical knowledge about causal correlations between items and combines it with results of differential evaluations to show how the patient's health can evolve in terms of functional disability (Functionality level), dependencies in performing daily activities (ADL level) and risks assessment (Risk Assessment level).

In the following subsections we give details about items at each level and indicators (at the state level) associated to them. Our choice has been guided by geriatric practitioners we are collaborating with to set the real testing phase of SINDI. Details about causal correlations and reasoning are presented in section 4.

State Level. Static aspects of the clinical profile include results of specific tests, pathologies and drug intake, while dynamic aspects are represented by indicators. Context-dependent information considered at this level includes:

1. personal details: biomedical parameters such as temperature and weight;
2. environmental properties: average light value, humidity, temperature, presence of stairs or carpets in a given room or area of interest;

---

[1] Higher numbers correspond to worse health evaluation for the item.

3. basic activities: movement activity can be easily captured by the wearable sensor, and we consider it as characterized by *motion* (walking, standing still), *position* (sit, lay, stand) and *orientation* (straight, turning);
4. localization: how the patient moves from one room/area to another;
5. interaction with objects: we consider two kinds of binary interaction according to sensors associated with the specific object, i.e. *pressure* (chair and bed objects) and *switch* (doors, windows and devices); interaction modes can be easily extended by adding appropriate declarative descriptions.

The encoding of context-related data in form of logic predicates is used by the logic component of the aggregation middleware to infer values of those indicators that are not directly available from aggregated sensors data.

Example 1. As an example, consider the indicator *quality of sleep*. To understand the quality of sleep it is necessary to reason about the night activity, thus this indicator is evaluated by applying a set of logic rules that take into account contextual information (i.e. localization, state of bed object, movement, etc.) and some auxiliary predicates (start/end of night time, restless night, insomnia, etc.). A simplified version of the ASP code to infer quality of sleep follows:[2]

```
nighstart(T) :- is_in(bedroom,bed,T),
                wearable_device(off,T).
nightend(T0) :- exitbed(T0), wearable_device(on,T),
                nightime(T1), not exitbed(T2),
                T1<T0<T, T0<T2<T.
break(T) :- nightime(T1), nightend(T2), exitbed(T),
            T1<T<T2.
exitbed(T) :- bed(mobile,T1), bed(empty,T),
              not bed(mobile,T2), T1<T2<T.
```

Functionality Level. The system considers the following functional disabilities:

1. *balance* and *gait*, initially evaluated through the appropriate part of the Tinetti-POMA [15] medical scale; indicators are represented by aspects of the scale that can be easily captured and evaluated through the wearable sensor, i.e. standing, sitting, turning and walking;
2. *nutrition*, initially evaluated by means of the Mini Nutritional Assessment [16] test; the indicator is the Body Mass Index (BMI), stored every hour;
3. *vision*, initially evaluated through specific tests; indicators are the level of light during the day and at the sunset (artificial light may indicate a problem), evaluated and stored every hour;
4. *mental and cognitive capabilities*, evaluated by means of the Mini Mental [17] and Clock Drawing [18] tests; indicators are represented by i) a computer aided questionnaire and counting ability, evaluated and stored once a week, and ii) the quality of sleep, daily evaluated and stored;

---

[2] Note that symbol ":-" in the encoding corresponds to "←" in logic ASP rules.

5. *insomnia*, initially evaluated by means of a questionnaire; the indicator is again the quality of sleep;
6. *emotional stability*, initially evaluated by means of the GDS test [19]; the indicator is a computer-aided version of the GDS test.

ADL Level. At this level we consider the Activities of Daily Living (ADL) as evaluated in the Katz scale [20], in particular:

1. transfer (mobility) has the same indicators as balance and gait;
2. dressing has the same indicators as balance and visual functionalities;
3. feeding has the same indicators as nutrition functionality;
4. toileting has no indicators in the current version.

We want to point out that reasoning at this level is not aimed at activity recognition as in other approaches to monitoring [21]. We rather concentrate on possible inter-dependencies that may arise in performing ADL, according to correlations with items at other levels, because this is crucial for prevention.

Risk Assessment Level. The risks we consider in the SINDI system are represented by the potentially most dangerous situation for elderly people at home, namely:

1. *risk of falls*, initially evaluated according to the Tinetti POMA scale; it has the same indicators as balance and gait functionalities;
2. *risk of depression*, initially evaluated according to the GDS scale [19]; the indicators are nutrition, balance, gait and sleep functionalities;
3. *frailty*, initially evaluated through a combination of GDS test, Mini Mentale test and Katz evaluation; the indicators are the same as those of nutrition, balance, gait, vision and emotional functionalities plus some additional ones like walk speed, age, number of pathologies, number of drugs and number of activities in which the patient needs help;
4. *risk of dependency*, evaluated according to the Katz index; it has as indicator the number of ADL's that cannot be easily performed;
5. *malnutrition*, evaluated by means of the Mini Nutritional Assessment test with BMI as indicator;
6. *isolation*: the indicators are the number of visitors and the time spent out of the house.

4   The Reasoning Capabilities

In our system we describe a home healthcare scenario by a declarative representation of the domain at different levels. Inference is also performed at each level by separate logic programs to detect i) functional disabilities, every hour, ii) dependencies in performing Activities of Daily Living, every day and iii) risk assessment, every day.

In order to deal with emergencies, SINDI can be configured to detect some triggers. Such triggers can either generate a direct action (e.g. emergency call) or rely on the reasoning system. As an example, temperature over $45\,°C$ is set as a trigger for an emergency call, while an opening window needs to be contextualized using specific rules, to check whether it is an intrusion.

Besides domain knowledge encoded as illustrated in the previous section, two further aspects are necessary for the reasoning process: *differential evaluations* and *correlation rules*. Differential evaluation of an item I at level L through the indicators Ind_i is possible by comparing the value V_i^0 of each associated indicator at the beginning of the previous inference (time $T = 0$) and the (eventually aggregated) value V_i^1 of the same indicator at the temporal interval being evaluated (time $T = 1$). For some indicators such as standing and sitting, several evaluations may be available for the time interval (hour or day) considered in the inference process. Given that a single value has to be provided for each indicator in a given interval, the data extraction module taking data from the database and passing them to the ASP engine is in charge of computing the most frequent value for that interval. This choice is the result of a discussion with geriatrics experts and can be motivated by the fact that the slow trend of physical and cognitive decline of the elderly makes evaluations uniform in a short period of time such as an hour or a day, and isolated values that are far from te most frequent one can be due to occasional awkward movements rather than to a disability. The logic rules to detect worsenings look like those in equation 2.

$$
\begin{aligned}
worse(L, I, Ind_i) \leftarrow\ & obsind(Ind_i, V_i^0, 0), obsind(Ind, V_i^1, 1), \\
& link(I, Ind_i), lev(L, I), \\
& ord(Ind_i, V_i^1, N_1), ord(Ind_i, V_i^0, N), N < N_1.
\end{aligned}
\tag{2}
$$

Although differential evaluations can also indicate improvements, we only consider worsenings, as they are much more relevant with respect to risk prevention. The reasoning system can easily be extended to consider also health improvements and use them to evaluate response to medical treatments.

Do not forget that a negative differential evaluation can also be obtained via specific tests periodically submitted to the patient (every three or six month when no critical situations are identified). In this case, the new observation $obs(L, I, V, T + 1)$ is compared with the last complete observation available $obs(L, I, V, T)$.

Correlation rules concern dependencies among a cause (I_1) and an effect (I). Different dependencies are allowed in our model:

1. negative/positive influence of an item I on another item I_1;
2. directly proportional influence of an item I on another item I_1;
3. inversely proportional influence of an item I on another item I_1;

Each of these correlations can be *strict* or *possible*. In the first release of the system we concentrated on strict and possible negative influence, since they are more relevant for our purposes. All other dependencies can be easily introduced and encoded in the system, and we are considering this in the implementation of the following prototype of SINDI.

Correlation rules can be specified by clinicians and are automatically mapped into ASP to express negative/possibly-negative influence of an item I_k on another item I_j, respectively encoded by predicate $r\_neg(I_j, I_k)$ and $poss\_r\_neg(I_j, I_k)$ respectively.

Consider the structure of items and correlation rules as an oriented graph stratified into levels.

Each item I_j at a level L, $I_j(L)$, can be connected to another item $I_k(L')$ in two different ways:

1. an oriented arc from $I_j(L)$ to $I_k(L')$: if $I_j(L)$ gets worse, this has a negative influence on $I_k(L')$;
2. an oriented dotted arc from $I_j(L)$ to $I_k(L')$: if $I_j(L)$ gets worse, this *may* have a negative influence on $I_k(L')$.

In addition, the layered structure is used to avoid possibly infinite propagation of dependencies when the reasoning process investigates the search space.

As already mentioned, the inference process considers items of each level separately. No matter which level is being evaluated, the system first characterizes every item in the graph as being either *stable* (none of the indicators got worse for that item) or *unstable* (one or more indicators got worse for that item in the interval being evaluated), represented respectively by predicates $n\_stable(L, I)$ and $stable(L, I)$, that are inferred by applying default rules in equations 3.

$$
\begin{aligned}
n\_stable(L, I) &\leftarrow worse(L, I, Ind), lev(L, I) \ . \\
stable(L, I) &\leftarrow not\ n\_stable(L, I), lev(L, I) \ .
\end{aligned}
\tag{3}
$$

This distinction is crucial to determine the behaviour of the system when it reasons about each $I_j(L)$ at the specific level L:

a) if $I_j(L)$ is *stable*, the system performs the following reasoning task:
  - it predicts the amount of risk for $I_j(L)$ to get unstable, as follows:
    * it investigates the direct connections determined by correlations rules, to identify items $I_k(L')$ that may influence $I_k(L)$;
    * it check each $I_k(L')$ to see whether it is unstable and, in this case, guess that $I_j(L)$ could be at risk in the near future due to its correlation to $I_k(L')$;
b) if $I_j(L)$ is *unstable*, the system performs three different reasoning tasks:
  - it identifies possible negative effects of the worsening of $I_j(L)$ on other items $I_k(L')$ according to correlation rules, represented by oriented arcs from $I_j(L)$ to $I_k(L')$; [3]
  - it performs *local* diagnosis, detecting causes of the worsening of $I_j(L)$ among the directly correlated items that have been marked as unstable;

---

[3] Propagation of negative effects is not considered since the layered structure of the graph allows to identify them simply by investigating results of the inference for $I_k(L')$ when items at level L' are evaluated.

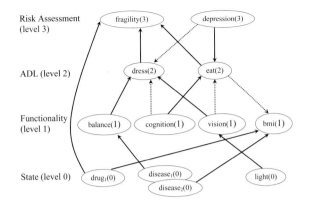

Fig. 2. Graph of correlations for example 2

- it contextualizes the worsening of $I_j(L)$ providing values of all correlated items (both stable and unstable ones); in order to select items that are more likely related to $I_j(L)$, the search goes either up in the hierarchy of levels, or down to lower levels in a monotonic way.

To conclude this section, we present a simple example of how the reasoning system can support clinicians in understanding the evolution of health state of the patients monitored.

Example 2. Consider the graph in figure 2. Suppose that the reasoning system is investigating ADL's (level 2) and no item is unstable at this level. Suppose also that when evaluating indicators the system identifies *visual* functionality as unstable. Results of the inference process with respect to prediction indicates that ADLs *dress* and *eat* are both at risk due to the *visual* functionality, but in one case (for the *eat* ADL) the risk is only possible.

Suppose now that, in the same setting, appropriate tests show that ADL *eat* is unstable (i.e. there is an increasing level of dependency in performing *eat*) and the *visual* functionality is still unstable due to light indicators. The inference process returns the following results, summarized in table 2:

1. *prediction*: risk of fragility and nutrition functionality have to be monitored carefully since they may get worse due to *eat* dependency;
2. *local diagnosis*: dependency for *eat* may be due to a functional disability in vision;
3. *contextualization*: upwards in the hierarchical model, risk of depression is identified as being correlated to ADL *eat*, while downwards we have cognition and vision; vision is in turn correlated to the analysis of lights level indicators; values of all these items are provided to clinicians through appropriate interfaces, helping contextualization of the worsening of ADL *eat*.

In a more complex schema of dependencies, multiple paths can make reasoning a hard task. For this reason we keep the graph structure hierarchical: each level

Table 2. Results of reasoning tasks for example 2: ADL analysis

Item's stability	Prediction	Local diagnosis	Contextualization
stable(adl,dress)	risky(risk,frag,adl,eat)	p_cause(adl,eat,func,vis)	ctx(adl,eat,risk,depr)
n_stable(adl,eat)	risky(func,bmi,adl,eat)		ctx(adl,eat,func,cog)
n_stable(func,vis)			ctx(adl,eat,func,vis)
			ctx(adl,eat,state,light)

is considered separately with respects to items of all other levels. The expressive power of ASP can also helps because it makes it possible to deal with complex graphs maintaining the computational complexity rather low.

5   Preliminary Evaluation

The SINDI system has been designed to preserve some properties that turn out to be crucial in the assisted living context.

To preserve unobtrusiveness, we decided not to use cameras: dynamic data about the person and the environment are captured by the WSN. The user-friendly interaction with SINDI is based on a TV screen, controlled by a device that is similar to a TV remote. Modularity and computational efficiency stem from the declarative nature of ASP and the availability of efficient solvers, while the use of off-the-shelf components in SINDI considerably reduces overall costs.

In the preliminary evaluation we did several tests on the WSN and on the inference engine. As for the WSN, the localization algorithm recognizes the correct area 90% of the time without further filtering techniques, and movement recognition is correct 95% of the time. With respect to the inference engine, we evaluated ASP programs by using *Lparse* as grounder and the *Clasp* solver [12] that supports constraints, choice rules and weight rules [22] and can solve complex reasoning tasks very efficiently due to the heuristics used, combining ASP expressivity with boolean constraint solving. In the testing phase of SINDI, we used Clasp both to generate the backlog (a few months of data) and to test the global performance of the system.

Time of execution on some selected instances are summarized in table 3, where time is expressed in seconds. The worst cases have been observed for instances where the number of correlations was more than 6 times the number of items. This can be due to the high number of bidirectional correlations among items, derived by the random generation of instances. According to geriatric practitioners, similar cases are not common in real settings and, except for those instances, the reasoning process scales well.

Context aggregation and interpretation at the state level remains the harder task. In evaluating indicators, delegating part of the aggregation process to the WSN nodes lowered the computational time up to 60% for instances of medium complexity (i.e. for a person that is active from 30 to 40 per cent of the time in a day). This of course does not include situations in which emergencies arise, since they are detected almost immediately by triggering events.

Table 3. ASP reasoning performance

Number of Items	State Level		Number of Correlations	Upper Levels
	WSN + ASP	ASP only		
20	140.05	205.07	30/70/130	0.69/1.01/2.03
30	169.71	481.22	120	1.03
50	201.32	589.03	200	1.37
70	241.11	603.16	250	1.68

6   Conclusions and Future Work

Our SINDI assistive monitoring system combines new WSN technologies and efficient reasoning techniques to allow constant monitoring and health assessment of people in a context-aware setting.

The context-dependent reasoning process is based on differential evaluations and dependencies between health-related items. The combination of different sources of information (sensors, medical knowledge, clinical profile, user defined constraints) that change over time makes the system more reliable (i.e. much better able to disambiguate situations, thus reducing false positives) and adaptive (e.g. easily extended on the face of new available information). Domain knowledge is encoded into the ASP logical framework, thus enhancing unobtrusiveness, modularity, declarativity and efficiency. The declarative approach makes it easier for clinicians to specify dependencies in a general way and allows automatic logical encoding.

Despite the potential of the SINDI system in supporting prevention in a home healthcare scenario, there are still a few issues to be investigated. One of them is related to the outputs (in terms of evaluation of risky situations) provided by the system. One of the interesting aspects of using ASP semantics in this context is that all possible correlations among factors of different levels are considered equally important and valid. There are efficient techniques to enforce priorities and ordering relations among solutions of an ASP program [23,24], and it would be interesting to investigate how to apply these techniques in the healthcare scenario. The graphical representation of dependencies and the results of the reasoning tasks suggest that automatic methods can be applied to the analysis of the history of inferences. We want to investigate these issues to include them in the next release of the system.

Preliminary tests showed that SINDI could be a powerful and efficient tool for clinicians to support prevention and to help understanding health evolution, as well as for patients and their relatives for a better quality of life. Nonetheless, we are aware of the fact that more detailed and extensive experimental results are needed to evaluate the effectiveness of this approach in real contexts, and to provide significant empirical data. All these aspects will be concretely taken into account in the next few months in the context of a real deployment of SINDI in a geriatrics hospital.

References

1. Tonelli, M.R.: The limits of evidence-based medicine. Respir Care 46(12), 1435–1440 (2001)
2. Cesta, A., Pecora, F.: The robocare project: Intelligent systems for elder care. In: AAAI Fall Symposium on Caring Machines: AI in Elder Care, Washington, DC, USA (2005)
3. Akyildiz, I.F., Weilian, S., Sankarasubramaniam, Y., Cayirci, E.E.: A survey on sensor networks. IEEE Communications Magazine 40(8), 102–114 (2002)
4. Malan, D., Fulford-Jones, T., Wesh, M., Moulton, S.: Codeblue: An ad hoc sensor network infrastructure for emergency medical care. In: MobySys Workshop on Applications of Mobile Embedded Systems, Boston, Massachusetts, USA, pp. 12–14 (2004)
5. Wood, A., Virone, G., Doan, T., Cao, Q., Selavo, L., Wu, Y., Fang, L., He, Z., Lin, S., Stankovic, J.: Alarm-net: Wireless sensor networks for assisted-living and residential monitoring. Technical Report CS-2006-11, Dep. of Computer Science, University of Virginia (2006)
6. Krishnamachari, B., Estrin, D., Wicker, S.B.: The impact of data aggregation in wireless sensor networks. In: 22nd International Conference on Distributed Computing Systems, Washington, DC, USA, pp. 575–578. IEEE Computer Society, Los Alamitos (2002)
7. Whitehouse, K., Zhao, F., Liu, J.: Semantic streams: A framework for composable semantic interpretation of sensor data. In: Römer, K., Karl, H., Mattern, F. (eds.) EWSN 2006. LNCS, vol. 3868, pp. 5–20. Springer, Heidelberg (2006)
8. Liu, J., Zhao, F.: Towards semantic services for sensor-rich information systems. In: 2nd International Conference on Broadband Networks, pp. 44–51 (2005)
9. Heinzelman, W., Chandrakasan, A., Balakrishnan, H.: Energy-efficient communication protocol for wireless sensor networks. In: International Conference on System Sciences, Washington, DC, USA, p. 8020. IEEE Computer Society, Los Alamitos (2000)
10. Gelfond, M., Lifschitz, V.: The stable model semantics for logic programming. In: International Conference on Logic Programming, Seattle, Washington, pp. 1070–1080 (1988)
11. Leone, N., Pfeifer, G., Faber, W., Eiter, T., Gottlob, G., Perri, S., Scarcello, F.: The dlv system for knowledge representation and reasoning. ACM Trans. Comput. Log. 7(3), 499–562 (2006)
12. Gebser, M., Kaufmann, B., Neumann, A., Schaub, T.: clasp: A conflict-driven answer set solver. In: Ninth International Conference on Logic Programming and Nonmonotonic Reasoning, pp. 260–265. Springer, Heidelberg (2007)
13. Baral, C., Gelfond, M.: Logic programming and knowledge representation-the a-prolog perspective. Artif. Intell. 138(1-2), 3–38 (2002)
14. Fleming, K.C., Evans, J.M., Weber, D.C., Chutka, D.S.: Practical functional assessment of elderly persons: A primary-care approach. Mayo Clinic Proceedings 70(9), 890–910 (1995)
15. Tinetti, M., Williams, T., Mayewski, P.: Fall risk index for elderly patients based on number of chronic disabilities. American Journal of Medicine 80, 429–434 (2002)
16. Guigoz, Y., Vellas, B., Garry, P.: Mini nutritional assessment: A practical assessment tool for grading the nutritional state of elderly patients. Facts and Research in Gerontology 2, 15–59 (1994)

17. Folstein, M.F., Folstein, S.E., McHugh, P.R.: "mini-mental state". A practical method for grading the cognitive state of patients for the clinician. Psychiatric Research 12(3), 189–198 (1975)
18. Yamamoto, S., Mogi, N., Umegaki, H., Suzuki, Y., Ando, F., Shimokata, H., Iguchi, A.: The clock drawing test as a valid screening method for mild cognitive impairment. Dementia and Geriatric Cognitive Disordorders 18, 172–179 (2004)
19. Yesavage, J., Brink, T., Rose, T., Lum, O., Huang, V., Adey, M., Leirer, V.: Development and validation of a geriatric depression screening scale: A preliminary report. Journal of Psychiatric Research 17(1), 37–49 (1982–1983)
20. Katz, S., Downs, H., Cash, H., Grotz, R.: Progress in development of the index of adl. Gerontologist 10(1), 20–30 (1970)
21. Pollack, M.E.: Intelligent technology for an aging population: The use of ai to assist elders with cognitive impairment. AI Magazine 26(2), 9–24 (2005)
22. Niemelä, I., Simons, P.: Extending the smodels system with cardinality and weight constraints. In: Logic-based artificial intelligence, Norwell, MA, USA, pp. 491–521. Kluwer Academic Publishers, Dordrecht (2001)
23. Brewka, G.: Logic programming with ordered disjunction. In: Eighteenth national conference on Artificial intelligence, Menlo Park, CA, USA, pp. 100–105. American Association for Artificial Intelligence (2002)
24. Brewka, G., Niemelä, I., Syrjänen, T.: Implementing ordered disjunction using answer set solvers for normal programs. In: Logics in Artificial Intelligence - Journées Européennes sur la Logique en Intelligence Artificielle, Cosenza, Italy, pp. 444–455. Springer, Heidelberg (2002)

Automatic Composition of Melodic and Harmonic Music by Answer Set Programming

Georg Boenn[1], Martin Brain[2], Marina De Vos[2], and John ffitch[2]

[1] Cardiff School of Creative & Cultural Industries
University of Glamorgan
Pontypridd, CF37 1DL, UK
gboenn@glam.ac.uk
[2] Department of Computer Science
University of Bath
Bath, BA2 7AY, UK
{mjb,mdv,jpff}@cs.bath.ac.uk

Abstract. The composition of most styles of music is governed by rules. The natural statement of these rules is declarative ("The highest and lowest notes in a piece must be separated by a consonant interval") and non deterministic ("The base note of a key can be followed by any note in the key"). We show that by approaching the automation and analysis of composition as a knowledge representation task and formalising these rules in a suitable logical language, powerful and expressive intelligent composition tools can easily be built. This paper describes the use of answer set programming to construct an automated system that can compose both melodic and harmonic music, diagnose errors in human compositions and serve as a computer-aided composition tool. The use of a fully declarative language and an "off-the-shelf" reasoning engine allows the creation of tools which are significantly simpler, smaller and more flexible than those produced by existing approaches. It also combines harmonic and melodic composition in a single framework, which is a new feature in the growing area of algorithmic composition.

1 Introduction

Music, although it seeks to communicate via emotions, is almost always governed by complex and rigorous rules which provide the base from which artistic expression can be attempted. In the case of musical composition, in most styles there are rules which describe the progression of a melody, both at the local level (the choice of the next note) and at the global level (the overall structure). Other rules describe the harmony, which arises from the relationship between the melodic line and the supporting instruments.

These rules were developed to guide and support human composers working in the style of their choice, but we wish to demonstrate here that by using knowledge representation techniques, we can create a computer system that can reason about and apply compositional rules. Such a system will provide a simple and flexible way of composing music automatically, but, provided that the representation technology used is sufficiently flexible to allow changes at the level of the rules themselves, it will also help the human composer to understand, explore and extend the rules he is working with.

M. Garcia de la Banda and E. Pontelli (Eds.): ICLP 2008, LNCS 5366, pp. 160–174, 2008.

This paper describes ANTON, an automatic composition system based on an implementation of one set of compositional rules, those governing tonal Western music, using Answer Set Programming (ASP). The paper provides an overview of the musical context and the particular problems of algorithmic composition on both melodic and harmonic forms. This is followed by a description of the ASP that we use, before giving more details of our innovative system, its design, performance and outputs. We conclude with directions for future work in both music research and the development of our system.

2 Music

Creating melodies, that is sequences of pitched sounds, is not as easy as it looks. We have cultural preferences for certain sequences of notes and preferences dictated by the biology of how we hear. This may be viewed as an artistic (and hence not scientific) issue, but most of us would be quick to challenge the musicality of a composition created purely by random whim. Students are taught rules of thumb to ensure that their works do not run counter to cultural norms and also fit the algorithmically definable rules of pleasing harmony when sounds are played together.

"Western tonal" simply refers to what most people in the West think of as "classical music", the congenial Bach through Brahms music which feels comfortable to the modern western ear because of its adherence to familiar rules. Students of composition in conservatoires are taught to write this sort of music as basic training. They learn to write melodies and to harmonise given melodies in a number of sub-versions. If we concentrate on early music then the scheme often called "Palestrina Rules" is an obvious example for the basis of this work. Similarly, harmonising Bach chorales is a common student exercise, and has been the subject of many computational investigations using a variety of methods.

In this paper, we take the somewhat arid technical rules and embed them within a modern computational system, which enables us to contemplate many original ways of exploiting the fact that they are simultaneously available; the rules themselves can be explored, extended and refined, or student exercises can be evaluated to ensure that they are indeed "valid". We will be able to complete partial systems, such as producing a melody consonant with a given harmony structure, as well as, more adventurously, to create new melodies.

We have used the teaching at one conservatoire in Köln to provide the basic rules, which were then refined in line with the general style taught. The point about generating melodies is that the "tune" must be capable of being accompanied by one or more other lines of notes, to create a harmonious whole. The requirement for the tune to be capable of harmonisation is a constraint that turns a simple sequence (a *monody*) to a *melody*.

Our experience with this work is to realise how many acceptable melodies can be created with only a few rules, and as we add rules, how much better the musical results are. This concept is developed further in Section 5.

In this particular style of music complete pieces are not usually created in one go. Composers create a number of sections of melody, harmonising them as needed, and possibly in different ways, and then structuring the piece around these basic sections. Composing between 4 bars and 16 bars is not only an appropriate task, it is actually what the human would do, creating component form which the whole is constructed. So although the system described here may be limited in its melodic scope, it has the potential to become a useful tool across a range of sub-styles.

3   Automatic Composition

A common problem in musical composition can be summarised in the question "where is the next note coming from?". For many composers over the years the answer has been to use some process to generate notes. It is clear that in many pieces from the Baroque period that simple note sequences are being elaborated in a fashion we would now call algorithmic. For this reason we can say that algorithmic composition is a subject that has been around for a very long time. It is usual to credit Mozart's Musikalisches Würfelspiel (Musical Dice Game) [1] as the oldest classical algorithmic composition, although there is some doubt if the game form is really his. In essence the creator provides a selection of short sections, which are then assembled according to a few rules and the roll of a set of dice to form a Minuet[1]. Two dice are used to choose the 16 minuet measures from a set of 176, and another die selects the 16 trio measures[2], this time from 96 possible. This gives a total number of 1.3×10^{29} possible pieces. This system however, while using some rules, relies on the coherence of the individual measures. It remains a fun activity, and recently web pages have appeared that allow users to create their own original(ish) "Mozart" compositions.

More recent algorithmic composition systems have concentrated on the generation of monody[3], either from a mathematical sequence, chaotic processes, or Markov chains, trained by consideration of acceptable other works. Frequently the systems rely on a human to select which monodies should be admitted, based on judgement rather than rules. Great works have been created this way, in the hands of great talents. Major descriptions of mathematical note generators can be found for example in *Formalized Music* [2]. Probably the best known of the Markov chain approach is Cope's significant corpus of Mozart pastiche [3].

In another variation on this approach, the accompanist, either knowing the chord structure and style in advance, or using machine-listening techniques, infers a style of accompaniment. The former of these approaches can be found in commercial products, and the latter has been used by some jazz performers to great effect.

A more recent trend is to cast the problem as one of constraint satisfaction. For example PWConstraints is an extension for IRCAM's Patchwork, a Common-Lisp-based graphical programming system for composition. It uses a custom constraint solver employing backtracking over finite integer domains. OMSituation and OMClouds are similar and were more recently developed for Patchwork's successor OpenMusic. A detailed evaluation of them can be found in [4], where the author gives an example of a 1st-species counterpoint (two voices, note against note) after [5] developed with

---

[1] A dance form in triple time, *i.e.* with 3 beats in each measure.
[2] A Trio is a short contrasting section played before the minuet is repeated.
[3] A monody is a single solo line, in opposition to homophony and polyphony.

Strasheela, a constraint system for music built on the multi-paradigm language Oz. Our musical rules however implement the melody and counterpoint rules described by [6], which we find give better musical results.

One can distinguish between *improvisation* systems and *composition* systems. In the former the note selection progresses through time, without detailed knowledge of what is to come. In practice this is informed either by knowing the chord progression or similar musical structures [7], or using some machine listening. In this paper we are concerned with *composition*, so the process takes place out of time, and we can make decisions in any order.

It should also be noted that these algorithmic systems compose pieces of this music of this style in either a melodic or a harmonic fashion, and are frequently associated with computer-based synthesis. We consider these two sub-problems separately.

3.1 Melodic Composition

In melodic generation a common approach is the use of some kind of probabilistic finite state automaton or an equivalent scheme, which is either designed by hand (some based on chaotic oscillators or some other stream of numbers) or built via some kind of learning process. Various Markov models are commonly used, but there have been applications of n-grams, genetic algorithms and neural nets. What these methods have in common is that there is no guarantee that melodic fragments generated have acceptable harmonic derivations. Our approach, described below is fundamentally different in this respect, as our rules cover both aspects simultaneously.

In contrast to earlier methods, which rely on learning, and which are capable of giving only local temporal structure, a common criticism of algorithmic melody [8], we do not rely on learning and hence we can aspire to a more global whole melody approach. In addition we are no longer subject to the limitations of the kind of process which, because it only works in time in one direction, is hard to use in a partially automated fashion; for example operations like "fill in the 4 notes between these sections" is not a problem for us.

We are also trying to move beyond experiments with random note generation, which we have all tried and abandoned because the results are too lacking in structure. Predictably, the alternative of removing the non-determinism at the design stage (or replacing with a probabilistic choice) runs the risk of 'sounding predictable'! There have been examples of good or acceptable melodies created like this, but the restriction inherent in the process means it probably works best in the hands of geniuses.

3.2 Harmonic Composition

A common usage of algorithmic composition is to add harmonic lines to a melody; that is notes played at the same time as the melody that are in general consonant and pleasing. This is exemplified in the harmonisation of 4-part chorales, and has been the subject of a number of essays in rule-based or Markov-chain systems. Perhaps a pinnacle of this work is [9] who used early expert system technology to harmonise in the style of Bach, and was very successful. Subsequently there have been many other systems, with a range of technologies. There is a review included in [10].

Clearly harmonisation is a good match to constraint programming based systems, there being accepted rules[4]. It also has a history from musical education.

But these systems all start with a melody for which at least one valid harmonisation exists, and the program attempts to find one, which is clearly soluble. This differs significantly from our system, as we generate the melody and harmonisation together, the requirement for harmonisation affecting the melody.

4   Answer Set Programming

Due to space constraints, only a brief overview of answer set semantics and Answer Set Programming (ASP) is given here. The interested reader is referred to [11] for a more in-depth coverage of the definitions and ideas presented in this section.

The *answer set semantics* is a model based semantics for normal logic programs. Following the notation of [11], we refer to the language over which answer set semantics is defined as *AnsProlog*. Programs in *AnsProlog* are sets of rules of the form:

$$a \leftarrow b, \text{not } c.$$

where a, b and c are atoms. Intuitively, this means "if b is known and c is not known, then a is known". The set of conditions of a rule (on the right hand side of the arrow) are known as the *body*, written as $B(r)$, and the atom that is the consequence of the rule is referenced as the *head* of the rule, written $H(r)$. The body is split further in two sets of atoms, $B^+(r)$ and $B^-(r)$ depending on whether the atom appears positively or negatively. Rules are satisfied with respect to a set of atoms if either the body is false or the head is true. Rules with empty bodies are called *facts*; their head should always true.

If a program Π contains no negated atoms ($\forall r \in \Pi \,.\, B^-(\Pi) = \emptyset$) its semantics is unambiguous and can easily be computed as the fixed point of the T_p(the immediate consequence) operator. Starting from the empty set, we check in each iteration which rule bodies are true. The heads of those rules are added to the set for the next iteration. This is a monotonic process, so we obtain a unique fixpoint. This fixpoint is called the *answer set*. For example, given the following program:

$$a \leftarrow b, c.$$
$$b \leftarrow c.$$
$$c \leftarrow .$$
$$d \leftarrow e.$$
$$e \leftarrow d.$$

the unique answer set is $\{a, b, c\}$, as $T_p(\emptyset) = \{c\}$, $T_p(\{c\}) = \{b, c\}$, $T_p(\{b, c\}) = \{a, b, c\}$ and $T_p(\{a, b, c\}) = \{a, b, c\}$. Note that d and e are not included in the model

---

[4] For example see: http://www.wikihow.com/Harmonise-a-Chorale-in-the-Style-of-Bach

as their is no way of concluding e without knowing d and vice versa. This is different to the classical interpretation of this program (via Clark's completion) which would have two models, one of which would contain d and e.

The natural mechanism for computing negation in logic programs in *negation as failure*, which tends to be characterised as epistemic negation ("we do not known this is true"), rather than classical negation ("we know that this is not true"). This correspondence is motivated by the intuition that we should only claim to know things that can be proven; thus anything that can not be proven is not known. To extend the semantics to support this type of negation, the *Gelfond-Lifschitz reduct* is used. This takes a set of proposed atoms and gives a reduced, positive program by removing any rule which depends on the negation of any atom in the set and dropping all other negative dependencies.

Definition 1. *Given an AnsProlog program Π and a set of atoms A, the Gelfond-Lifschitz transform of Π with respect to A is the following set of rules:*

$$\Pi^A = \{H(r) \leftarrow B^+(r) | r \in \Pi, B^-(r) \cap A = \emptyset\} \tag{1}$$

This allows us to define the concept of *answer sets*. Intuitively, these are sets of possible beliefs about the world which are consistent with all of the rules and have acyclic support for every atom that is known, and thus in the set.

Definition 2. *Given an AnsProlog program Π, A is an answer set of $\Pi \iff A$ is the unique answer set of Π^A.*

For example, the following program has two answer sets:

$$a \leftarrow \text{not } b.$$
$$b \leftarrow \text{not } a.$$
$$c \leftarrow \text{not } d.$$
$$d \leftarrow b.$$
$$d \leftarrow e, \text{not } a.$$
$$e \leftarrow d, \text{not } a.$$

$\{a, c\}$ and $\{b, c, d, e\}$. Computing the reduct with respect to $\{a, c\}$ gives:

$$a \leftarrow .$$
$$c \leftarrow .$$
$$d \leftarrow b.$$
$$d \leftarrow e.$$
$$e \leftarrow d.$$

which results in $T_p^\infty(\emptyset) = \{a, c\}$.

A given program will have zero or more answer sets and computing an answer set is NP complete.

When used as a knowledge representation language, *AnsProlog* is enhanced to contain constraints (e.g. : $-b$, not c) and choice rules (*e.g.* $\{a, b, c\} : -b$, not c). The former are rules with an empty head, stating that a valid answer set should not make the body true. The latter is a short hand notation for expression that a certain number of atoms need to be true under certain circumstances. These are syntactic sugar and can be removed with linear, modular transformations (see [11]). Variables and predicated rules are also used and are handled, at the theoretical level and in most implementations, by instantiation (referred to as *grounding*).

ASP is a programming paradigm in which a problem is *represented* as an *AnsProlog* program in such a way that the answer sets correspond to solutions. A reasoning engine is then used to produce the answer sets of the program. Typically these are composed of two components, a *grounder* which removes the variables from the program by instantiation and an *answer set solver* which compute answer sets of the propositional program. These answer sets are then *interpreted* to give solutions of the original problem. GRINGO[12] and LPARSE[13] are the grounders most commonly used and CLASP[14], SMODELS[15], CMODELS[16] and DLV[17] represent the state of the art of solver development.

ASP has been used to tackle a variety of problems, including: planning and diagnosis [18,19,20], modelling and rescheduling of the propulsion system of the NASA Space Shuttle [20], multi-agent systems [21,22,23], Semantic Web and web-related technologies [24,25], superoptimisation [26], reasoning about biological networks [27], voting theory [28] and investigating the evolution of language [29].

5   The ANTON System

What we are seeking to do, which is a new application in both music and computing, is to apply ASP techniques to compositional rules to produce a system which can be applied more widely and freely than has previously been possible. ASP is used to create a description of the rules that govern the melodic and harmonic properties of correct piece of music. The ASP program works as a model for music composition that can be used to assist the composer by suggesting, completing and verifying short pieces.

Rather than create a procedural or probabilistic algorithm for producing music, AN-TON takes the approach of representing the rules of what constitutes a valid piece and then searching for pieces that meet this specification. The rules of composition are modelled so that the *AnsProlog* program defines the requirements for a piece to be valid, and thus every answer set corresponds to a valid piece. In generating a new piece, the composition system simply has to generate an (arbitrary) answer set. Rather than the traditional problem/solution mapping of answer set programming, this is using an *AnsProlog* program to create a 'random' example of a complex, structured object.

Figure 1 presents a simplified fragment of the *AnsProlog* program used in ANTON. The model is defined over a number of time steps, given by the variable T. The key proposition is `chosenNote(P,T,N)` which represents the concept "At time T, part P plays note N". To encode the options for melodic progress ("the tune either steps up or down one note in the key, or it leaps more than one note"), choice rules are used.

```
% At every time step, every part either steps to the next note in the key
% or leaps to a further note in the key
1 { stepUp(P,T), stepDown(P,T), leapUp(P,T), leapDown(P,T) } 1 :- part(P), time(T).

% A leap can only be over a consonant interval (3,4,5,7 or 12 semitones)
1 { leapBy(P,T,I) : consonantInterval(I) } 1 :- leapUp(P,T).

% When a part leaps up by I, the note at time T+1 is I steps higher
% than the current note
choosenNote(P,T+1,N+I) :- choosenNote(P,T,N), leapBy(P,T,I).

% Every note must be in the chosen mode (major, minor, etc.)
:- choosenNote(P,T,N), mode(M), not inMode(N,M).

% The interval between parts must not be dissonant (non consonant)
:- choosenNote(P1,T,N1), choosenNote(P2,T,N2),
interval(N1,N2,C), not consonantInterval(C).
```

Fig. 1. A simplified ANTON fragment

To encode the melodic limits on the pattern of notes and the harmonic limits on which combinations of notes may be played at once, constraints are included.

To allow for verification and diagnosis, each rule is given an error message:

```
% No tri-tones
% No note can be within two notes of a tritone (a note +/- 6 semitones)
#const err_tt="Tri-tone".
reason(err_tt).
error(P,T,err_tt) :- choosenNote(P,T,N1), choosenNote(P,T+2,N1+6).
error(P,T,err_tt) :- choosenNote(P,T,N1), choosenNote(P,T+2,N1-6).
```

Depending on how you want to use the system, composition or diagnosis, you will either be interested in those pieces that do not results into errors or in an answer set that mentions the error messages. For the former we simply specify the constraint `:- error(P,T,R)`. For the latter we include the rules: `errorFound:-error(P,T,R)`. and `:- not errorFound`.

By adding constraints on which notes can be included, it is possible to specify part or all of a melody, harmony or complete piece. This allows ANTON to be used for a number of other tasks beyond automatic composition. By fixing the melody it is possible to use it as an automatic harmonisation tool. By fixing part of a piece, it can be used as computer aided composition tool. By fixing a complete piece, it is possible to check its conformance to the rules, for marking student compositions or harmonisations.

The complete system consists of three major phases; building the program, running the ASP program and interpreting the results. As a simple example suppose we wish to create a 4 bar piece in E major one would write

```
programBuilder.pl --task=compose --mode=major --time=16 > program
```

which builds the ASP program, giving the length and mode. Then

```
lparse -W all < program | ./shuffle.pl 6298 | smodels 1 > tunes
```

```
keyMode(lydian).
choosenNote(1,1,25).
choosenNote(1,2,24).
choosenNote(1,8,19).
choosenNote(1,9,20).
choosenNote(1,10,24).
choosenNote(1,14,29).
choosenNote(1,15,27).
choosenNote(1,16,25).
#const t=16.
configuration(solo).
part(1).
```

Fig. 2. musing.lp: An example of a partial piece

runs the ASP phase and generates a representation of the piece. We provide a number of output formats, one of which is a CSOUND [30] program with a suitable selection of sounds.

```
$ parse.pl --fundamental=e --output=csound < tunes > tunes.csd
```

generates the Csound input from the generic format, and then

```
$ csound tunes.csd -o dac
```

plays the melody. We provide in addition to Csound, output in text, ASP facts or the Lilypond score language, with MIDI under development. Naturally we provide scripts for all main ways of using the system.

Alternatively we could request the system to complete part of a piece. In order to do so, we provide the system with a set of ASP facts expressing the keyMode, the notes which are already fixed, the number of notes in your piece, the configuration and the number of parts. Figure 2 contains an example of such file. The format is the same as the one returned from the system except that all the notes in the piece will have been assigned.

We then run the system just as before with the exception of adding --piece=musing.lp when we run programBuilder.pl. The system will then return all possible valid composition that satisfy the criteria set out in the partial piece.

The *AnsProlog* programs used in ANTON contains just 191 lines (not including comments and empty lines) and encodes 28 melodic and harmonic rules. Once instantiated, the generated programs range from 3,500 atoms and 13,400 rules (a solo piece with 8 notes) to 11,000 atoms and 1,350,000 rules (a 16 note duet). Scripts are provided to convert the answer sets generated into output for the CSOUND synthesis system and the LILYPOND notation tool. The system is licensed under the GPL and is available, along with example pieces, from http://www.cs.bath.ac.uk/~mjb/ . Figure 3 contains an extract from a series of simple duets produced by the system.

It should be noted that the 500 lines of code here contrast with the 8000 lines in Strasheela[4] and 88000 in Bol[31]. For this reason we claim that our representation of the musical problem is easily read and understood.

6   Evaluation of ANTON

6.1   Practical Use

To assess the practicality of using answer set programming to create a composition system a number of tests were performed. Table 1 contains the times taken by a number of answer set solvers (SMODELS [15], SMODELS-IE [32], SMODELSCC [33], CMODELS [16] and CLASP [14]) in composing a single piece of a given length. Likewise Table 2 contains the times taken to compose a two part piece of a given length. LPARSE [13] was used to ground the programs and its run time, typically around 30-60 seconds, is omitted from the results.

All times where recorded using a 2.4GHz AMD Athlon X2 4600+ processor, running a 64 bit version of OpenSuSE 10.3. All solvers were built in 32 bit mode. Each run was limited to 20 minutes of CPU time and 2Gb of RAM. The *AnsProlog* programs used are available from `http://www.cs.bath.ac.uk/~mjb/`.

These results show that the system, when using the more powerful solvers, is fast enough to be used as a component in an interactive composition tool. Further work would be needed to support real time generation of music. It is also interesting to note that the only solvers able to generate longer sequences using two parts all implement clause learning strategies, suggesting that the problem is particularly susceptible to this kind of technique.

Table 1. Time taken (in seconds) for a number of solvers generating a solo piece

	smodels 2.32		smodels-ie 1.0.0		smodelscc 1.08	cmodels 3.75		clasp 1.0.5
Length	Default	Restarts	Default	Restarts	No lookahead	w/ zchaff	w/ MiniSAT	Default
4	1.02	1.03	0.09	0.09	1.17	0.33	0.39	0.22
6	2.43	2.43	0.38	0.38	2.58	0.64	0.85	0.46
8	5.16	5.16	1.03	1.04	4.94	1.06	1.62	1.01
10	12.25	11.72	2.58	2.59	8.55	1.54	2.63	1.33
12	28.25	46.13	8.08	15.14	11.36	2.42	4.04	2.27
14	40.62	140.00	10.50	43.54	18.78	3.14	6.05	3.48
16	101.05	207.25	29.40	69.53	27.94	4.01	9.40	4.62

Table 2. Time taken (in seconds) for a number of solvers generating a duet

	smodels 2.32		smodels-ie 1.0.0		smodelscc 1.08	cmodels 3.75		clasp 1.0.5
Length	Default	Restarts	Default	Restarts	No lookahead	w/ zchaff	w/ MiniSAT	Default
4	3.77	3.77	0.31	0.32	4.08	1.18	1.26	0.77
6	10.36	11.24	1.89	1.89	13.90	2.17	2.81	1.60
8	54.64	77.10	14.71	21.84	26.07	3.88	5.93	3.73
10	Time out	Time out	Time out	500.26	78.72	9.51	11.12	9.34
12	Time out	Time out	Time out	Time out	103.81	14.50	18.14	16.84
14	Time out	Time out	Time out	Time out	253.92	32.41	32.34	25.59
16	Time out	Time out	Time out	Time out	452.38	82.64	49.29	29.63

Twenty Short Pieces (extract)

Anton

Fig. 3. Part of a set of pieces composed by the system

6.2 Music Quality

The other way to evaluate the system is to judge the music it produces. This is less certain process, involving personal values. However we feel that the music is acceptable, at least of the quality of a student of composition, and at times capable of moments of excitement. The first composition, part of which is shown in Figure 3, consisting of twenty short melodies[5] shows promise with real musical moments, but the only real evaluation is for the reader to listen; the web site provides the sounds.

6.3 ASP as the Knowledge Representation Language

In constructing ANTON a number of advantages of using answer set programming have become clear; as have a number of limitations.

Firstly, *AnsProlog* is very fast to write and very compact. As well as the obvious benefits, this means it is possible to develop the system at the same time as undertaking knowledge capture and to prototype features in the light of the advice of domain experts. Part of the reason why it is so fast to use is that rules are fully declarative. Programming thus focuses on expressing the concepts that are being modelled rather than having to worry about which order to put things in - such as which rules should come first, which concepts have higher priority, which choices should be made first. This also makes incremental development easy as new constraints can be added one at a time, without having to consider how they affect the search strategy.

---

[5] We call this ANTON's Opus 1: Twenty Short Pieces.

Being able to add rules incrementally during development turns out to be extremely useful from a software engineering view point. During the development of ANTON, we experimented with a number of different development methodologies. The most effective approach was found to be first writing a script that translates answer sets to human readable score or output for a synthesiser. Next the choice rules were added to the *AnsProlog* program to create all possible pieces, valid or not. Finally the constraints were incrementally added to restrict the output to only valid sequences. By building up a library of valid pieces it was possible to perform regression testing at each step and thus isolate bugs as soon as they were introduced.

Using answer set programming was not without issue. One persistent problem was the lack of mature development support tools, particularly debugging tools. SPOCK [34] was used but as its focus is on computing the reasons behind the error, rather than the interface issues of explaining these reasons to the user, it was normally quicker to find bugs by looking at the last changes made and which regression tests failed. Generally, the bugs that where encountered where due to subtle mismatches between the intended meaning of a rule and the declarative reading of the rule used. For example the predicate stepUp(P,T) is used to represent the proposition "At time T, part P steps up to give the note at time T+1", however, it could easily be misinterpreted as "At time T-1, part P steps up to give the note at time T". Which of these is used is not important, as long as the same declarative reading is used for all rules. With the first "meaning" selected for ANTON, the rule:

```
chosenNote(P,T,N+S)  :- chosenNote(P,T-1,N),  stepUp(P,T),
                        stepBy(P,T,S).
```

would not encode the intended progression of notes. One possible way of supporting a programmer in avoiding these subtle errors would be to develop a system that translated rules into natural language, given the declarative reading of the propositions involved. It should then be relatively straightforward to check that the rule encoded what was intended.

7   Conclusions and Directions for Future Work

We have built a sophisticated composition system with adequate run time performance.

Using knowledge representation techniques it is possible to create an automatic composition system that is significantly smaller, simpler and more expressive than the current state of the art. The choice of using a pure declarative language, *AnsProlog*, allows the system to be flexible enough to be used as a platform for research into the rules of composition.

There are a number of possible lines of development for the ANTON system, both in terms of the musical rules it contains and the supporting system.

7.1   Music Research

The system provides a platform for a novel approach to music research. We can learn aspects of the rules, finding which are inconsistent or redundant, and can determine the importance of rules. We hope that this will throw light on the compositional process. We can see if there are any "unspoken" rules of composition, and also the related, finding unknown rules of composition. One particularly interesting possibility is using the system to generate a large set of pieces, acquiring human evaluations of the 'quality' of each and then using techniques such as inductive logic programming to infer rules for composing 'good' pieces.

The work so far has been limited to a particular style of Western music. However the framework should be applicable to other styles, especially formal ones. The rules of Hindustani classical music are taught to pupils in a traditional, oral, fashion, but we see no reason why this framework cannot capture these. Recent work [35] indicates that there are indeed universal melodic rules, and the combination of the ASP methodology with this musical insight is an intriguing one.

In real pieces some of the rules are sometimes broken. This could be simulated by one of a number of extensions to answer set semantics (preferences [36], consistency restoring rules, defensible rules, etc.). How to systematise the knowledge of when it is acceptable to break the rules and in which contexts it is 'better' to break them is an open problem.

One deliberate simplification of the current system is the lack of rhythm as the style of composition we are implementing traditionally contain few explicit restrictions. So all parts play all the time, with notes of equal duration. While usual in some styles, this obviates a whole range of interesting variety. We have not yet considered rhythm, but one of us is already researching rhythmic structures and performance gesture [37], so in the longer term this may be incorporated.

7.2 Systems Development

The current system can write short melodies effectively and efficiently. Development work is still needed to take this to entire pieces; we can start from these melodic fragments but a longer piece needs a variety of different harmonisations for the same melody, and related melodies with the same harmonic structure and a number of similar techniques. We have not solved the difficult global structure problem but it does create a starting point on which we can build a system that is hierarchical over time scales; we have a mechanism for building syntactically correct sentences, but these need to be built into paragraph and chapters, as it were.

The system performance currently seems to suggest that a real-time composition system is possible, which would open up the possibility for performance and improvisation. Profiling of the current system has indicated that some conceptually simple tasks like parsing are taking a disproportionate fraction of the run-time, and some engineering would assist in removing these problems. Clearly this is one of a number of system-like issues that need to be addressed. Also, the availability of a parallel answer set solver that implements clause learning would help in building this type of application.

An obvious extension to the composition of duets is to expand this to three and four parts, by adding inner voices. It should perhaps be noted that inner voices obey different rules, and these need to be implemented.

References

1. Chuang, J.: Mozart's Musikalisches Würfelspiel (1995),
   `http://sunsite.univie.ac.at/Mozart/dice/`
2. Xenakis, I.: Formalized Music. Bloomington Press, Stuyvesant (1992)
3. Cope, D.: A Musical Learning Algorithm. Computer Music Journal 28(3), 12–27 (Fall, 2006)
4. Anders, T.: Composing Music by Composing Rules: Design and Usage of a Generic Music Constraint System. Ph.D thesis, Queen's University, Belfast, Department of Music (2007)
5. Fux, J.: The Study of Counterpoint from Johann Joseph Fux's Gradus ad Parnassum. W.W. Norton (1965, orig 1725)
6. Thakar, M.: Counterpoint. New Haven (1990)
7. Brothwell, A., Ffitch, J.: An Automatic Blues Band. In: Barknecht, F., Rumori, M. (eds.) 6th International Linux Audio Conference, Kunsthochschule für Medien Köln, LAC 2008, pp. 12–17 (March 2008)
8. Leach, J.L.: Algorithmic Composition and Musical Form. Ph.D thesis, University of Bath, School of Mathematical Sciences (1999)
9. Ebcioğlu, K.: An Expert System for Harmonization of Chorales in the Style of J.S. Bach. Ph.D thesis, State University of New York, Buffalo, Department of Computer Science (1986)
10. Rohrmeier, M.: Towards modelling harmonic movement in music: Analysing properties and dynamic aspects of pc set sequences in Bach's chorales. Technical Report DCRR-004, Darwin College, University of Cambridge (2006)
11. Baral, C.: Knowledge Representation, Reasoning and Declarative Problem Solving, 1st edn. Cambridge University Press, Cambridge (2003)
12. Gebser, M., Schaub, T., Thiele, S.: GrinGo: A New Grounder for Answer Set Programming. In: Baral, C., Brewka, G., Schlipf, J.S. (eds.) LPNMR 2007. LNCS, vol. 4483, pp. 266–271. Springer, Heidelberg (2007)
13. Syrjänen, T.: Lparse 1.0 User's Manual. Helsinki University of Technology (2000)
14. Gebser, M., Kaufmann, B., Neumann, A., Schaub, T.: Conflict-Driven Answer Set Solving. In: Proceeding of IJCAI 2007, pp. 386–392 (2007)
15. Syrjänen, T., Niemelä, I.: The Smodels System. In: Codognet, P. (ed.) ICLP 2001. LNCS, vol. 2237. Springer, Heidelberg (2001)
16. Lierler, Y., Maratea, M.: Cmodels-2: SAT-based Answer Set Solver Enhanced to Non-tight Programs. In: Lifschitz, V., Niemelä, I. (eds.) LPNMR 2004. LNCS, vol. 2923, pp. 346–350. Springer, Heidelberg (2003)
17. Eiter, T., Leone, N., Mateis, C., Pfeifer, G., Scarcello, F.: The KR System dlv: Progress Report, Comparisons and Benchmarks. In: Cohn, A.G., Schubert, L., Shapiro, S.C. (eds.) KR 1998: Principles of Knowledge Representation and Reasoning, pp. 406–417. Morgan Kaufmann, San Francisco (1998)
18. Eiter, T., Faber, W., Leone, N., Pfeifer, G., Polleres, A.: The DLV^K Planning System. In: Flesca, S., Greco, S., Leone, N., Ianni, G. (eds.) JELIA 2002. LNCS (LNAI), vol. 2424, pp. 541–544. Springer, Heidelberg (2002)
19. Lifschitz, V.: Answer set programming and plan generation. J. of Artificial Intelligence 138(1-2), 39–54 (2002)
20. Nogueira, M., Balduccini, M., Gelfond, M., Watson, R., Barry, M.: A A-Prolog Decision Support System for the Space Shuttle. In: Answer Set Programming: Towards Efficient and Scalable Knowledge Represenation and Reasoning. American Association for Artificial Intelligence Press, Stanford (March 2001)
21. Baral, C., Gelfond, M.: Reasoning agents in dynamic domains. In: Logic-based artificial intelligence, pp. 257–279. Kluwer Academic Publishers, Dordrecht (2000)

22. Buccafurri, F., Caminiti, G.: A Social Semantics for Multi-agent Systems. In: Baral, C., Greco, G., Leone, N., Terracina, G. (eds.) LPNMR 2005. LNCS, vol. 3662, pp. 317–329. Springer, Heidelberg (2005)

23. Cliffe, O., De Vos, M., Padget, J.: Specifying and Analysing Agent-based Social Institutions using Answer Set Programming. In: Boissier, O., Padget, J., Dignum, V., Lindemann, G., Matson, E., Ossowski, S., Sichman, J., Vazquez-Salceda, J. (eds.) ANIREM 2005 and OOOP 2005. LNCS, vol. 3913, pp. 99–113. Springer, Heidelberg (2006)

24. Polleres, A.: Semantic Web Languages and Semantic Web Services as Application Areas for Answer Set Programming. In: Brewka, G., Niemelä, I., Schaub, T., Truszczyński, M. (eds.) Nonmonotonic Reasoning, Answer Set Programming and Constraints, Internationales Begegnungs- und Forschungszentrum für Informatik (IBFI), Schloss Dagstuhl, Germany. Dagstuhl Seminar Proceedings, vol. 05171 (2005)

25. Ruffolo, M., Leone, N., Manna, M., Saccà, D., Zavatto, A.: Exploiting ASP for Semantic Information Extraction. In: De Vos, M., Provetti, A. (eds.) Answer Set Programming. CEUR Workshop Proceedings, vol. 142, CEUR-WS.org (2005)

26. Brain, M., Crick, T., De Vos, M., Fitch, J.: TOAST: Applying Answer Set Programming to Superoptimisation. In: International Conference on Logic Programming. LNCS. Springer, Heidelberg (August 2006)

27. Grell, S., Schaub, T., Selbig, J.: Modelling biological networks by action languages via answer set programming. In: Etalle, S., Truszczyński, M. (eds.) ICLP 2006. LNCS, vol. 4079, pp. 285–299. Springer, Heidelberg (2006)

28. Konczak, K.: Voting Theory in Answer Set Programming. In: Fink, M., Tompits, H., Woltran, S. (eds.) Proceedings of the Twentieth Workshop on Logic Programming (WLP 2006). Number INFSYS RR-1843-06-02, Technical Report Series, pp. 45–53. Technische Universität Wien (2006)

29. Erdem, E., Lifschitz, V., Nakhleh, L., Ringe, D.: Reconstructing the Evolutionary History of Indo-European Languages Using Answer Set Programming. In: Dahl, V., Wadler, P. (eds.) PADL 2003. LNCS, vol. 2562, pp. 160–176. Springer, Heidelberg (2002)

30. Boulanger, R. (ed.): The Csound Book. MIT Press, Cambridge (2000)

31. Bel, B.: Migrating Musical Concepts: An Overview of the Bol Processor. Computer Music Journal 22(2), 56–64 (1998)

32. Brain, M., De Vos, M., Satoh, K.: Smodels-ie: Improving the Cache Utilisation of Smodels. In: Costantini, S., Watson, R. (eds.) Proceedings of the 4th Workshop on Answer Set Programming, pp. 309–314 (2007)

33. Ward, J., Schlipf, S.: Answer set programming with clause learning. In: Lifschitz, V., Niemelä, I. (eds.) LPNMR 2004. LNCS, vol. 2923, pp. 302–313. Springer, Heidelberg (2003)

34. Brain, M., Gebser, M., Pührer, J., Schaub, T., Tompits, H., Woltran, S.: "That is illogical captain!" – The Debugging Support Tool spock for Answer-Set Programs: System Description. In: De Vos, M., Schaub, T. (eds.) Proceedings of the Workshop on Software Engineering for Answer Set Programming (SEA 2007), pp. 71–85 (2007)

35. Endrich, A.: Building Musical Relationships. In: Preparation (manuscript, 2008)

36. Brain, M., De Vos, M.: Implementing OCLP as a Front End for Answer Set Solvers: From Theory to Practice. In: Proceedings of Answer Set Programming: Advances in Theory and Implementation (ASP 2003), Ceur-WS (September 2003)

37. Boenn, G.: Composing Rhythms Based Upon Farey Sequences. In: Digital Music Research Network Conference (July 2007)

On the Efficient Execution of ProbLog Programs

Angelika Kimmig[1], Vítor Santos Costa[2], Ricardo Rocha[2], Bart Demoen[1],
and Luc De Raedt[1]

[1] Departement Computerwetenschappen, K.U. Leuven
Celestijnenlaan 200A - bus 2402, B-3001 Heverlee, Belgium
{Angelika.Kimmig, Bart.Demoen, Luc.DeRaedt}@cs.kuleuven.be
[2] CRACS & Faculdade de Ciências, Universidade do Porto, Portugal
R. do Campo Alegre 1021/1055, 4169-007 Porto, Portugal
{vsc,ricroc}@dcc.fc.up.pt

Abstract. The past few years have seen a surge of interest in the field of probabilistic logic learning or statistical relational learning. In this endeavor, many probabilistic logics have been developed. ProbLog is a recent probabilistic extension of Prolog motivated by the mining of large biological networks. In ProbLog, facts can be labeled with mutually independent probabilities that they belong to a randomly sampled program. Different kinds of queries can be posed to ProbLog programs. We introduce algorithms that allow the efficient execution of these queries, discuss their implementation on top of the YAP-Prolog system, and evaluate their performance in the context of large networks of biological entities.

1 Introduction

In the past few years, a multitude of different formalisms combining probabilistic reasoning with logics, databases, or logic programming has been developed. Prominent examples include PHA [1], PRISM [2], SLPs [3], ProbView [4], CLP($\mathcal{BN}$) [5], CP-logic [6], Trio [7], probabilistic Datalog (pD) [8], and probabilistic databases [9]. Although these logics have been traditionally studied in the knowledge representation and database communities, the focus is now often on a machine learning perspective, which imposes new requirements. First, these logics must be simple enough to be learnable and at the same time sufficiently expressive to support interesting probabilistic inferences. Second, because learning is computationally expensive and requires answering long sequences of possibly complex queries, inference in such logics must be fast, although inference in even the simplest probabilistic logics is computationally hard.

In this paper, we study these problems in the context of a simple probabilistic logic, ProbLog [10], which has been used for learning in the context of large biological networks where edges are labeled with probabilities. Large and complex networks of biological concepts (genes, proteins, phenotypes, etc.) can be extracted from public databases, and probabilistic links between concepts can be obtained by various prediction techniques [11]. ProbLog is essentially an extension of Prolog where facts are labeled with the probability that they belong to a

M. Garcia de la Banda and E. Pontelli (Eds.): ICLP 2008, LNCS 5366, pp. 175–189, 2008.

randomly sampled program, and these probabilities are mutually independent. A ProbLog program thus specifies a probability distribution over all its possible non-probabilistic subprograms. The success probability of a query is defined as the probability that it succeeds in such a random subprogram. The semantics of ProbLog is not new: ProbLog programs define a distribution semantics [12]. This is a well-known semantics for probabilistic logics that has been (re)defined multiple times in the literature; see for instance the works of [13,1,8,14,9]. However, even though relying on the same semantics, in order to allow efficient inference, systems such as PRISM [12] and PHA [1] additionally require all proofs of a query to be mutually exclusive. Thus, they cannot easily represent the type of network analysis tasks that motivated ProbLog.

We contribute exact and approximate inference algorithms for ProbLog. We present algorithms for computing the success and explanation probabilities of a query, and show how they can be efficiently implemented combining Prolog inference with Binary Decision Diagrams (BDDs) [15]. In addition to an iterative deepening algorithm that computes an approximation along the lines of [16], we further adapt the Monte Carlo approach suggested by [13] and used also by [11] in the context of biological network inference. These two approximation algorithms compute an upper and a lower bound on the success probability. Furthermore, we also contribute an approximation algorithm that computes a lower bound only using the k-most likely proofs.

The key contribution of this paper is the tight integration of these algorithms in the state-of-the-art implementation of the YAP-Prolog system. This integration includes several improvements over the initial implementation used in [10], which enable the use of ProbLog to effectively query Sevon's Biomine network [11] containing about 1,000,000 nodes and 6,000,000 edges, as will be shown in the experiments.

This paper is organised as follows. After introducing ProbLog and its semantics in Section 2, we present several algorithms for exact and approximate inference in Section 3. Section 4 then discusses how these algorithms are implemented in YAP-Prolog, and Section 5 reports on experiments that validate the approach. Finally, Section 6 concludes and touches upon related work.

2   ProbLog

A ProbLog program consists of a set of labeled facts $p_i :: c_i$ together with a set of definite clauses. Each ground instance (that is, each instance not containing variables) of such a fact c_i is true with probability p_i, where all probabilities are assumed mutually independent. The definite clauses allow to add arbitrary *background knowledge* (BK).

Figure 1(a) shows a small probabilistic graph that we shall use as running example in the text. It can be encoded in ProbLog as follows:

$0.8 :: \mathsf{edge(a, c)}.$ $0.7 :: \mathsf{edge(a, b)}.$ $0.8 :: \mathsf{edge(c, e)}.$
$0.6 :: \mathsf{edge(b, c)}.$ $0.9 :: \mathsf{edge(c, d)}.$ $0.5 :: \mathsf{edge(e, d)}.$

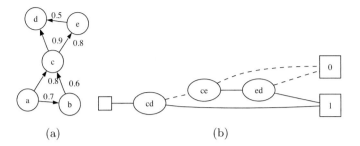

Fig. 1. (a) Example of a probabilistic graph: edge labels indicate the probability that the edge is part of the graph. (b) Binary Decision Diagram encoding the DNF formula $cd \lor (ce \land ed)$, corresponding to the two proofs of query *path(c,d)* in the graph. An internal node labeled xy represents the Boolean variable for the edge between x and y, solid/dashed edges correspond to values true/false.

Such a probabilistic graph can be used to sample subgraphs by tossing a coin for each edge. A ProbLog program $T = \{p_1 :: c_1, \cdots, p_n :: c_n\} \cup BK$ defines a probability distribution over subprograms $L \subseteq L_T = \{c_1, \cdots, c_n\}$:

$$P(L|T) = \prod_{c_i \in L} p_i \prod_{c_i \in L_T \setminus L} (1 - p_i).$$

We extend our example with the following background knowledge:

$$\texttt{path(X, Y)} : - \texttt{edge(X, Y)}.$$
$$\texttt{path(X, Y)} : - \texttt{edge(X, Z)}, \texttt{path(Z, Y)}.$$

We can then ask for the probability that there exists a path between two nodes, say c and d, in our probabilistic graph, that is, we query for the probability that a randomly sampled subgraph contains the edge from c to d, or the path from c to d via e (or both of these). Formally, the *success probability* $P_s(q|T)$ of a query q in a ProbLog program T is defined as

$$P_s(q|T) = \sum_{L \subseteq L_T} P(q|L) \cdot P(L|T), \tag{1}$$

where $P(q|L) = 1$ if there exists a θ such that $L \cup BK \models q\theta$, and $P(q|L) = 0$ otherwise. In other words, the success probability of query q is the probability that the query q is *provable* in a randomly sampled logic program.

As a consequence, the probability of a *specific* proof, also called *explanation*, is that of sampling a logic program L that contains all the facts needed in that explanation or proof. The *explanation probability* $P_x(q|T)$ is defined as the probability of the most likely explanation or proof of the query q

$$P_x(q|T) = \max_{e \in E(q)} P(e|T) = \max_{e \in E(q)} \prod_{c_i \in e} p_i, \tag{2}$$

where $E(q)$ is the set of all explanations for query q [17].

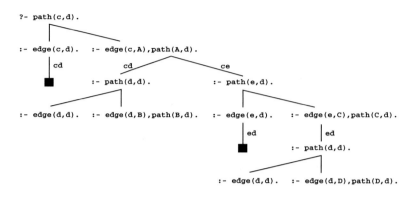

Fig. 2. SLD-tree for query $path(c, d)$

In our example, the set of all explanations for $path(c, d)$ contains the edge from c to d (with probability 0.9) as well as the path consisting of the edges from c to e and from e to d (with probability $0.8 \cdot 0.5 = 0.4$). Thus, $P_x(path(c, d)|T) = 0.9$.

The ProbLog semantics is essentially a distribution semantics [12]. Sato has rigorously shown that this class of programs defines a joint probability distribution over the set of possible least Herbrand models of the program, that is, of the background knowledge BK together with a subprogram $L \subseteq L_T$; for further details we refer to [12]. The distribution semantics has been used widely in the literature; see e.g. [13,1,8,14,9].

3   Inference in ProbLog

This section discusses algorithms for computing exactly and approximately the success and explanation probabilities of ProbLog queries. It additionally contributes a new algorithm for Monte Carlo approximation of success probabilities.

3.1   Exact Inference

Calculating the *success probability* of a query using Equation (1) directly is infeasible for all but the tiniest programs; [10] presents a method involving two steps. The first step computes the proofs of the query q in the logical part of the theory T, that is, in $BK \cup L_T$. This step is akin to that performed for pD by [8]. The result will be a DNF formula. The second component employs Binary Decision Diagrams [15] to compute the probability of this formula.

Following Prolog, we employ SLD-resolution to obtain all different proofs. As an example, the SLD-tree for the query ?- $path(c, d)$. is depicted in Figure 2. Each successful proof in the SLD-tree uses a set of facts $\{p_{i_1} :: c_{i_1}, \cdots, p_{i_k} :: c_{i_k}\} \subseteq T$. These facts are necessary for the proof, and the proof is independent of other probabilistic facts in T.

Let us now introduce a Boolean random variable b_i for each clause $p_i :: c_i \in T$, indicating whether c_i is in logic program, that is, b_i has probability p_i of being true. The probability of a particular proof involving clauses $\{p_{i_1} :: c_{i_1}, \cdots, p_{i_k} :: c_{i_k}\} \subseteq T$ is then the probability of the conjunctive formula $b_{i_1} \wedge \cdots \wedge b_{i_k}$. Since a goal can have multiple proofs, the success probability of query q equals the probability that the disjunction of these conjunctions is true. This yields

$$P_s(q|T) = P \left(\bigvee_{e \in E(q)} \bigwedge_{b_i \in cl(e)} b_i \right) \tag{3}$$

where $E(q)$ denotes the set of proofs or explanations of the goal q and $cl(e)$ denotes the set of Boolean variables representing ground facts used in the explanation e. Thus, the problem of computing the success probability of a ProbLog query can be reduced to that of computing the probability of a DNF formula. The formula corresponding to our example query $path(c, d)$ is $cd \vee (ce \wedge ed)$, where we use xy as Boolean variable representing $edge(x, y)$.

Computing the probability of DNF formulae is an NP-hard problem, as the different conjunctions need not be independent. Indeed, even under the assumption of independent variables used in ProbLog, the different conjunctions are not mutually exclusive and may overlap. Various algorithms have been developed to tackle this problem, which is known as the disjoint-sum-problem. The pD-engine HySpirit [8] uses the inclusion-exclusion principle, which is reported to scale to about ten proofs. For ICL, which extends PHA by allowing non-disjoint proofs, [14] proposes a symbolic disjoining algorithm, but does not report scalability results. Our implementation employs Binary Decision Diagrams (BDDs) [15], an efficient graphical representation of a Boolean function over a set of variables which scales to tens of thousands of proofs; see Section 4 for more details.

Calculating the *explanation probability* P_x, however, can easily be realized using a best-first search, guided by the probability of the current derivation, through standard logic programming techniques based on the SLD-tree [18].

3.2 Approximative Inference

As the size of the DNF formula grows with the number of proofs, its evaluation can become quite expensive, and finally infeasible. For instance, when searching for paths in graphs or networks, even in small networks with a few dozen edges there are easily $O(10^6)$ possible paths between two nodes. ProbLog therefore includes several approximation methods.

Bounded Approximation. The first approximation algorithm, similar to the one proposed in [10], uses DNF formulae to obtain both an upper and a lower bound on the probability of a query. It is related to work by [16] in the context of PHA, but adapted towards ProbLog. The algorithm uses an incomplete SLD-tree, i.e. an SLD-tree where branches are only extended up to a given probability threshold[1], to obtain DNF formulae for the two bounds. The lower bound formula d_1 represents all proofs with a probability above the current threshold.

---

[1] Using a probability threshold instead of the depth bound of [10] has been found to speed up convergence, as upper bounds are tighter on initial levels.

The upper bound formula d_2 additionally includes all derivations that have been stopped due to reaching the threshold, as these still *may* succeed. The algorithm proceeds in an iterative-deepening manner, starting with a high probability threshold and successively multiplying this threshold with a fixed shrinking factor until the difference between the current bounds becomes sufficiently small. As $d_1 \models d \models d_2$, where d is the formula corresponding to the full SLD-tree of the query, the success probability is guaranteed to lie in the interval $[P(d_1), P(d_2)]$.

As an illustration, consider a probability bound of 0.9 for the SLD-tree in Figure 2. In this case, d_1 encodes the left success path while d_2 additionally encodes the path up to $path(e, d)$, i.e. $d_1 = cd$ and $d_2 = cd \vee ce$, whereas the formula for the full SLD-tree is $d = cd \vee (ce \wedge ed)$.

K-Best. Using a fixed number of proofs to approximate the probability allows better control of the overall complexity, which is crucial if large numbers of queries have to be evaluated e.g. in the context of parameter learning. [19] therefore introduce the k-probability $P_k(q|T)$, which approximates the success probability by using the k best (that is, most likely) explanations instead of all proofs when building the DNF formula used in Equation (3):

$$P_k(q|T) = P \left(\bigvee_{e \in E_k(q)} \bigwedge_{b_i \in cl(e)} b_i \right) \tag{4}$$

where $E_k(q) = \{e \in E(q) | P_x(e) \geq P_x(e_k)\}$ with e_k the kth element of $E(q)$ sorted by non-increasing probability. Setting $k = \infty$ and $k = 1$ leads to the success and the explanation probability respectively. Finding the k best proofs can be realized using a simple branch-and-bound approach (cf. also [1]).

To illustrate k-probability, we consider again our example graph, but this time with query $path(a, d)$. This query has four proofs, represented by the conjunctions $ac \wedge cd$, $ab \wedge bc \wedge cd$, $ac \wedge ce \wedge ed$ and $ab \wedge bc \wedge ce \wedge ed$, with probabilities 0.72, 0.378, 0.32 and 0.168 respectively. As P_1 corresponds to the explanation probability P_x, we obtain $P_1(path(a, d)) = 0.72$. For $k = 2$, overlap between the best two proofs has to be taken into account: the second proof only adds information if the first one is absent. As they share edge cd, this means that edge ac has to be missing, leading to $P_2(path(a, d)) = P((ac \wedge cd) \vee (\neg ac \wedge ab \wedge bc \wedge cd)) = 0.72 + (1 - 0.8) \cdot 0.378 = 0.7956$. Similarly, we obtain $P_3(path(a, d)) = 0.8276$ and $P_k(path(a, d)) = 0.83096$ for $k \geq 4$.

Monte Carlo. As an alternative approximation technique without BDDs, we propose a Monte Carlo method. In this algorithm, we repeatedly sample a logic program from the ProbLog program and check for the existence of some proof of the query of interest. The fraction of samples where the query is provable is taken as an estimate of the query probability, and after each m samples the 95% confidence interval is calculated. Although confidence intervals do not directly correspond to the exact bounds used in our previous approximation algorithm, we employ the same stopping criterion, that is, we run the Monte Carlo simulation until the width of the confidence interval is at most δ. Such an algorithm

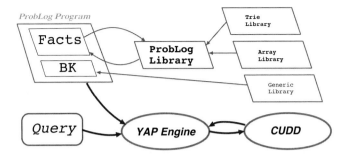

Fig. 3. ProbLog Implementation: A ProbLog program (top-left) requires the ProbLog library which in turn relies on functionality from the tries and array libraries. ProbLog queries (bottom-left) are sent to the YAP engine, and may require calling the BDD library CUDD.

(without the use of confidence intervals) was suggested already by Dantsin [13], although he does not report on an implementation. It was also used in the context of networks (not Prolog programs) by [11].

4   Implementation

This section discusses the main building blocks used to implement ProbLog on top of the YAP Prolog system. An overview is shown in Figure 3. On the top-left corner we show a typical ProbLog program, including ProbLog facts and background knowledge (BK).

The implementation requires ProbLog programs to use the `problog` module. Each program consists of a set of labeled ground facts and of unlabeled *background knowledge*, a generic Prolog program. Labeled ground facts are pre-processed as described below. Notice that the implementation currently only supports labeled *ground facts*.

In contrast to standard Prolog queries, where one is interested in answer substitutions, in ProbLog one is interested in a probability. As discussed before, two common ProbLog queries are the most likely explanation and its probability, and the probability of whether a query would have an answer substitution. We have discussed two very different approaches to the problem:

- In k best and bounded approximation, the engine explicitly reasons about probabilities of proofs. The challenge is how to compute the probability of each individual proof, store a large number of proofs, and compute the probability of sets of proofs.
- In Monte Carlo, the probabilities of facts are used to sample from ProbLog programs. The challenge is how to compute a sample quickly, in a way that inference can be as efficient as possible.

ProbLog programs execute from a ProbLog top-level query and proceed as follows:

- Initialise a new ProbLog query;
- While probabilistic inference did not converge:
  - set environment for new query;
  - call Prolog goal;
  - instrument every ProbLog call in the current proof: for example, a proof may be pruned immediately if its probability is lower than some bound;
  - process success or exit substitution;
- Call external solver, if required;

Notice that the current ProbLog implementation relies on Prolog's backtracking to explore the search space. On the other hand, and in contrast to most other probabilistic logic implementations, in ProbLog there is no clear separation between logical and probabilistic inference: in a fashion similar to constraint logic programming, probabilistic inference can drive logical inference.

Implementing ProbLog poses a number of interesting challenges. First, labeled facts have to be efficiently compiled to allow mutual calls between the Prolog BK and the ProbLog engine. Second, for k best and bounded inference, sets of proofs have to be manipulated and transformed into BDDs. Finally, Monte Carlo simulation requires representing and manipulating samples. We discuss these issues next.

Source-to-source transformation. We use the `term_expansion` mechanism to allow Prolog calls to labeled facts, and for labeled facts to call the ProbLog engine. As an example, the program:

$$0.715 :: \text{edge}('\text{PubMed\_2196878}', '\text{MIM\_609065}').$$
$$0.659 :: \text{edge}('\text{PubMed\_8764571}', '\text{HGNC\_5014}').$$

would be compiled as:

$$\text{edge}(A, B) : - \text{problog\_edge}(C, A, B, D),$$
$$\text{add\_to\_proof}(C, D).$$

$$\text{problog\_edge}(0, '\text{PubMed\_2196878}', '\text{MIM\_609065}', -0.3348).$$
$$\text{problog\_edge}(1, '\text{PubMed\_8764571}', '\text{HGNC\_5014}', -0.4166).$$

Thus, the internal representation of each fact contains an identifier, the original arguments, and the logarithm of the probability. The `add_to_proof` procedure updates the data structure representing the current path through the search space and its probability. Compared to the original meta-interpreter based implementation of [10], the main benefit of source-to-source transformation is faster execution time, which in turn improves scalability.

Tries. Manipulating proofs is critical in ProbLog. We represent each proof as a list containing the identifier of each different ground probabilistic fact used in the proof, ordered by first use. When manipulating proofs, the key operation is often *insertion*: we would like to add a proof to an existing set of proofs. Some algorithms, such as exact inference or Monte Carlo, only manipulate complete

proofs. Others, such as bounded approximation, require adding partial derivations too. The nature of the SLD-tree means that proofs tend to share both a
prefix and a suffix. Partial proofs tend to share prefixes only. This suggests using
tries to maintain the set of proofs. We use the YAP implementation of tries for
this task, based itself on XSB Prolog's work on tries of terms.

Binary Decision Diagrams. To efficiently compute the probability of a DNF
formula representing a set of proofs, our implementation represents this formula
as a Binary Decision Diagram (BDD) [15]. Given a fixed variable ordering, a
Boolean function f can be represented as a full Boolean decision tree, where each
node on the ith level is labeled with the ith variable and has two children called
low and high. Leaves are labeled by the outcome of f for the variable assignment
corresponding to the path to the leaf, where in each node labeled x, the branch
to the low (high) child is taken if variable x is assigned 0 (1). Starting from
such a tree, one obtains a BDD by merging isomorphic subgraphs and deleting
redundant nodes until no further reduction is possible. A node is redundant if
the subgraphs rooted at its children are isomorphic. Figure 1(b) shows the BDD
for the existence of a path between c and d in our earlier example.

Our implementation uses the C++ interface of the BDD package CUDD[2] to
construct and evaluate BDDs. More precisely, the trie representation of the DNF
is translated to C++ code that uses the CUDD primitives for building BDDs.
The program is executed via Prolog's shell utility, and results are reported via
shared files. We currently work on a tighter integration of BDDs into Prolog.

During the generation of the code, it is crucial to exploit the structure sharing
(prefixes and suffixes) already in the trie representation of a DNF formula, otherwise CUDD computation time becomes extremely long or memory overflows
quickly. Our translation starts by creating the C++ code for each single variable.
Since CUDD builds BDDs by joining smaller BDDs using logical operations, the
trie is traversed bottom-up to successively generate code for all its subtrees. Two
types of operations are used to combine nodes. First, all the children of a node
are combined as a disjunction resulting in a new child node. This child node is
then combined with the parent node as a conjunction. A subtree that occurs
multiple times in the trie is translated only once, and the resulting BDD is used
for all occurrences of that subtree. Because of the optimizations in CUDD, the
resulting BDD can have a very different structure than the trie.

After CUDD has generated the BDD, the probability of a formula is calculated
(also in C++) by traversing the BDD, in each node summing the probability
of the high and low child, weighted by the probability of the node's variable
being assigned true and false respectively. Intermediate results are cached, and
the algorithm has a time and space complexity linear in the size of the BDD.

Monte Carlo. Monte Carlo execution is quite different from the approaches
discussed before. Instead of combining large numbers of proofs, we now need to
be able to manipulate large numbers of different programs or samples.

Generating complete samples and checking for a proof does not scale to large
databases, even if proofs are cached in a trie to skip inference on a new sample

---

[2] http://vlsi.colorado.edu/~fabio/CUDD

by checking first whether a subsample is in the proof cache. In fact, already representing and generating the whole sample is a challenge for large databases. Within YAP, the efficient implementation of arrays offers the most compact way of representing large numbers of nodes. On the other hand, quite often proofs are local, i.e. we only need to verify whether facts from a small fragment of the database are in the sample. We take advantage of independence between facts to generate the sample *lazily*: we verify whether a fact is in the sample only when we need it for a proof. Samples are thus represented as a three-valued array: 0 means sampling was not asked yet, 1 means in sample, 2 means not in sample.

5   Experiments

We experiment our implementation of ProbLog in the context of the biological network obtained from the Biomine project [11]. We use two subgraphs extracted around three genes known to be connected to the Alzheimer disease (HGNC numbers 983, 620 and 582) as well as the full network. The smaller graphs are obtained querying Biomine for best paths of length 2 (resulting in graph SMALL) or all paths of length 3 (resulting in graph MEDIUM) starting at one of the three genes. SMALL contains 79 nodes and 144 edges, MEDIUM 5220 nodes and 11532 edges. We use SMALL for a first comparison of our algorithms on a small scale network where success probabilities can be calculated exactly. Scalability is evaluated using both MEDIUM and the entire BIOMINE network with roughly 1,000,000 nodes and 6,000,000 edges. In all experiments, we query for the probability that two of the gene nodes mentioned above are connected, that is, we use queries such as path('HGNC_983','HGNC_620',Path). We use the following definition of an acyclic path in our background knowledge:

$$path(X, Y, A) \quad : - path(X, Y, [X], A),$$
$$path(X, X, A, A).$$
$$path(X, Y, A, R) : - X \setminus == Y, edge(X, Z), absent(Z, A), path(Z, Y, [Z|A], R).$$

As list operations to check for the absence of a node get expensive for long paths, we consider an alternative definition for use in Monte Carlo. It provides cheaper testing by using the internal database of YAP to store nodes on the current path under key `visited`:

$$memopath(X, Y, A) \quad : - eraseall(visited), memopath(X, Y, [X], A).$$
$$memopath(X, X, A, A).$$
$$memopath(X, Y, A, R) : - X \setminus == Y, edge(X, Z), recordzifnot(visited, Z, \_),$$
$$memopath(Z, Y, [Z|A], R).$$

All experiments were performed on Core 2 Duo 3 GHz machines running Linux. All times reported are in `msec` and do not include the time to load the graph into Prolog. The latter takes 32, 192 and 66772 `msec` for SMALL, MEDIUM and BIOMINE respectively. We report T_P, the time spent by ProbLog to search

Table 1. k-probability on SMALL

path	983 − 620			983 − 582			620 − 582		
k	T_p	T_B	P	T_p	T_B	P	T_p	T_B	P
1	16	-	0.07	4	-	0.03	4	-	0.42
2	0	1613	0.08	0	1686	0.05	4	1511	0.66
4	4	1758	0.10	0	1519	0.06	4	1676	0.86
8	0	1590	0.11	0	1643	0.06	4	1778	0.92
16	4	1744	0.11	4	1536	0.06	4	1719	0.92
32	8	1839	0.11	12	1676	0.07	4	1681	0.96
64	24	1891	0.11	20	1665	0.09	12	1590	0.99
128	52	2054	0.11	32	2130	0.10	48	2286	1.00
256	212	2141	0.11	128	2039	0.10	76	1942	1.00
512	436	13731	0.11	209	2280	0.11	300	2245	1.00
1024	1837	3349	0.11	1372	2195	0.11	581	4080	1.00
exact	641	8343	0.11	5629	2716	0.11	496	2288	1.00

for proofs, as well as T_B, the time spent to compile and execute BDD programs (whenever meaningful). We also report the estimated probability P. For approximate inference using bounds, we report exact intervals for P, and also include the number n of BDDs constructed. We set both the initial threshold and the shrinking factor to 0.5. We compute k-probability for $k = 1, 2, \ldots, 1024$. Note that no BDDs are used for $k = 1$. In the bounding algorithms, we range the error interval between 10% and 1%. Monte Carlo recalculates confidence intervals after $m = 1000$ samples. We also report the number S of samples used.

Small Sized Sample. We first compare our algorithms on SMALL. Table 1 shows the results for k-probability and exact inference. Note that nodes 620 and 582 are close to each other, whereas node 983 is farther apart. Therefore, connections involving the latter are less likely. In this graph, we obtain good approximations using a small fraction of proofs (the queries have 13136, 155695 and 16048 proofs respectively). Our results also show a significant increase in running times as ProbLog explores more paths in the graph, both within the Prolog code and within the BDD code. The BDD running times can vary widely, we may actually have large running times for smaller BDDs, depending on BDD structure.

Table 2 gives corresponding results for bounded approximation. The algorithm converges quickly, as few proofs are needed and BDDs remain small. Note however that exact inference is competitive for this problem size. Moreover, we observe large speedups compared to the implementation with meta-interpreters used in [10], where total runtimes to reach $\delta = 0.01$ for these queries were 46234, 206400 and 307966 `msec` respectively. Table 3 shows the performance of the Monte Carlo estimator. On SMALL, Monte Carlo is the fastest approach. Already within the first 1000 samples a good approximation is obtained.

The experiments on SMALL thus confirm that the implementation on top of YAP-Prolog enables efficient probabilistic inference on small sized graphs.

Table 2. Inference using bounds on SMALL

path	983 − 620				983 − 582				620 − 582			
δ	T_p	T_B	n	P	T_p	T_B	n	P	T_p	T_B	n	P
0.1	0	5051	3	[0.07,0.12]	0	4994	3	[0.06,0.12]	12	1690	1	[0.99,1.00]
0.05	0	6504	4	[0.07,0.12]	40	10907	6	[0.06,0.11]	12	1751	1	[0.99,1.00]
0.01	8	9897	6	[0.10,0.11]	68	12684	7	[0.10,0.11]	12	1968	1	[0.99,1.00]

Table 3. Monte Carlo Inference on SMALL

path	983 − 620			983 − 582			620 − 582		
δ	S	T_p	P	S	T_p	P	S	T_p	P
0.1	1000	19	0.10	1000	21	0.10	1000	63	1.00
0.05	1000	19	0.10	1000	23	0.11	1000	59	1.00
0.01	16000	898	0.11	16000	1418	0.11	1000	59	1.00

Medium Sized Sample. For graph MEDIUM with around 11000 edges we impose a limit of one hour on running times. On this graph, exact inference is no longer feasible. Table 4 again shows results for the k-probability. Comparing these results with the corresponding values from Table 1, we observe that the estimated probability is higher now: this is natural, as the graph has both more nodes and is more connected, therefore leading to many more possible explanations. This also explains the increase in running times. Approximate inference using bounds only reached very loose bounds within the one hour timelimit, e.g. $[0.33, 0.90]$ for nodes 983 and 620. We found that this is due to the fact that BDDs representing upper bounds get very complex easily.

The Monte Carlo estimator using the standard definition of path/3 on MEDIUM did not converge within the time limit. A detailed analysis shows that this is caused by some queries backtracking too heavily. Table 5 therefore reports results using the memorising version memopath/3. With this improved definition, Monte Carlo performs well: it obtains a good approximation in a few seconds. Requiring tighter bounds however can increase runtimes significantly.

Biomine Database. The Biomine Database covers hundreds of thousands of entitities and millions of links. On BIOMINE, we therefore restrict our experiments to the approximations given by k-probability and Monte Carlo. Given the results on MEDIUM, we directly use memopath/3 for Monte Carlo. Tables 6 and 7 show the results on the large network. We observe that on this large graph, the number of possible paths is tremendous, which implies success probabilities practically equal to 1. Still, we observe that ProbLog's branch-and-bound search to find the best solutions performs reasonably also on this size of network. However, runtimes for obtaining tight confidence intervals with Monte Carlo explode quickly even with the improved path definition.

Altogether, the experiments confirm that our implementation provides good approximations of ProbLog probabilities and is able to deal with large graphs.

Table 4. k-probability on MEDIUM

path k	983 − 620			983 − 582			620 − 582		
	T_p	T_B	P	T_p	T_B	P	T_p	T_B	P
1	208	-	0.07	737	-	0.03	45	-	0.42
2	172	1591	0.11	725	1560	0.03	44	1599	0.47
4	200	1681	0.16	757	1738	0.05	60	1464	0.72
8	217	1691	0.25	744	1538	0.06	80	1778	0.92
16	284	1756	0.33	725	1508	0.10	100	1825	0.99
32	628	1855	0.38	753	1570	0.15	144	1578	1.00
64	717	1653	0.41	809	1684	0.23	200	1801	1.00
128	749	1715	0.42	933	1890	0.30	296	1734	1.00
256	849	1600	0.55	1044	1513	0.49	405	1904	1.00
512	2352	1696	0.64	2880	1598	0.53	576	2496	1.00
1024	6208	1849	0.70	5032	1728	0.56	2549	52250	1.00

Table 5. Monte Carlo Inference using `memopath/3` on MEDIUM

memo δ	983 − 620			983 − 582			620 − 582		
	S	T_p	P	S	T_p	P	S	T_p	P
0.1	1000	1319	0.77	1000	2364	0.76	1000	1878	1.00
0.05	2000	2682	0.76	2000	4766	0.76	1000	1805	1.00
0.01	29000	39687	0.76	29000	70183	0.77	1000	1970	1.00

Table 6. k-probability on BIOMINE

path k	983 − 620			983 − 582			620 − 582		
	T_p	T_B	P	T_p	T_B	P	T_p	T_B	P
1	5,445	-	0.09	1,248	-	0.11	10,189	-	0.59
2	5,472	1,611	0.12	1,313	1,563	0.17	2,288	1,570	0.63
4	5,989	1,735	0.13	13,729	1,986	0.28	600	1,545	0.65
8	7,016	1,656	0.16	19,885	1,878	0.38	929	1,792	0.66
16	10,012	1,980	0.50	30,338	1,816	0.53	1,557	1,644	0.92
32	14,857	1,872	0.57	35,134	1,657	0.56	2,484	1,922	0.95
64	19,770	1,642	0.80	36,995	1,737	0.65	4,425	1,925	0.95
128	23,165	1,892	0.88	163,242	1,835	0.76	8,472	2,117	0.98
256	35,395	2,149	0.95	292,054	1,463	0.85	16,390	4,935	1.00
512	170,438	3,148	0.98	489,254	15,410	0.88	29,525	7,693	1.00
1024	346,742	609,700	0.99	767,968	97,818	0.93	49,952	102,366	1.00

Table 7. Monte Carlo Inference using `memopath/3` on BIOMINE

memo δ	983 − 620			983 − 582			582 − 620		
	S	T_p	P	S	T_p	P	S	T_p	P
0.1	1000	2,714,781	1.00	1000	4,887,260	0.97	1000	4,709,921	0.99
0.05	1000	2,807,927	1.00	1000	4,769,216	0.98	1000	4,823,262	0.99
0.01	1000	2,686,881	1.00	4000	19,187,318	0.98	2000	9,406,026	0.99

6 Conclusions

ProbLog is an elegant probabilistic logic language that addresses the problem of representing uncertain knowledge by explicitely encoding uncertainty about the truth of facts. The language naturally extends Logic Programming languages such as Prolog. We present an implementation of the ProbLog language on top of the YAP Prolog system that is designed to scale for large sized problems. We show that ProbLog can indeed be used to obtain both explanation and (approximations of) success probabilities for queries on a large database. To the best of our knowledge, this is the first example of a probabilistic logic programming system that can execute queries on such large databases. Furthermore, compared to the initial implementation of ProbLog used in [10], the tight integration in YAP-Prolog leads to speedups in runtime of several orders of magnitude.

Although we focussed on connectivity queries and Biomine in this work, similar problems are found across many domains; we believe that the techniques presented so far apply to a variety of queries and databases. This is largely possible because ProbLog provides a clean separation between background knowledge and what is specific to the engine. As shown for Monte Carlo inference, such an interface can be very useful to improve performance as it allows incrementally refining background knowledge, e.g. graph procedures. Initial experiments with Dijkstra's algorithm for finding the explanation probability are very promising.

Compared to alternative formalisms such as PHA [1], PRISM [2], SLPs [3], CLP($\mathcal{BN}$) [5], and CP-logic [6], ProbLog is an extremely simple probabilistic logic. Yet, it has proven to be natural and convenient for modeling biological networks and as a vehicle for developing mining and machine learning approaches [17,20,19,21]. The efficiency of the probabilistic logic implementation is the most important factor determining the success and the performance of the learning approaches. Therefore, we expect the efficiency gains to open new possibilities for learning, and to increase the use of probabilistic logics in practical applications. Another possible use of a simple probabilistic logic, such as ProbLog, is as a target language in which other, possibly more complex, formalisms can be compiled. For instance, [22] shows how CP-logic [6] can be compiled into ProbLog, and SLPs [3] can be compiled in Sato's PRISM, which is closely related to ProbLog. Finally, as ProbLog, unlike PRISM and PHA, deals with the disjoint-sum-problem, it is interesting to study how program transformation and analysis techniques could be used to optimize ProbLog programs, by detecting and taking into account situations where some conjunctions are disjoint.

Acknowledgements. We would like to thank Hannu Toivonen for his many contributions to ProbLog and the Biomine team for the application. This work is partially supported by the GOA project 2008/08 Probabilistic Logic Learning. Angelika Kimmig is supported by the Research Foundation-Flanders (FWO-Vlaanderen). Vítor Santos Costa and Ricardo Rocha are partially supported by the research projects STAMPA (PTDC/EIA/67738/2006) and JEDI (PTDC/EIA/66924/2006) and by Fundação para a Ciência e Tecnologia.

References

1. Poole, D.: Probabilistic Horn abduction and Bayesian networks. Artificial Intelligence 64, 81–129 (1993)
2. Sato, T., Kameya, Y.: Parameter learning of logic programs for symbolic-statistical modeling. J. Artif. Intell. Res. (JAIR) 15, 391–454 (2001)
3. Muggleton, S.: Stochastic logic programs. In: De Raedt, L. (ed.) ILP (1995)
4. Lakshmanan, L.V.S., Leone, N., Ross, R.B., Subrahmanian, V.S.: ProbView: A flexible probabilistic database system. ACM Trans. Database Syst. 22(3), 419–469 (1997)
5. Santos Costa, V., Page, D., Qazi, M., Cussens, J.: CLP(BN): constraint logic programming for probabilistic knowledge. In: Meek, C., Kjærulff, U. (eds.) UAI, pp. 517–524. Morgan Kaufmann, San Francisco (2003)
6. Vennekens, J., Verbaeten, S., Bruynooghe, M.: Logic programs with annotated disjunctions. In: Demoen, B., Lifschitz, V. (eds.) ICLP 2004. LNCS, vol. 3132, pp. 431–445. Springer, Heidelberg (2004)
7. Widom, J.: Trio: A system for integrated management of data, accuracy, and lineage. In: CIDR, pp. 262–276 (2005)
8. Fuhr, N.: Probabilistic Datalog: Implementing logical information retrieval for advanced applications. JASIS 51(2), 95–110 (2000)
9. Dalvi, N.N., Suciu, D.: Efficient query evaluation on probabilistic databases. In: Nascimento, M.A., Özsu, M.T., Kossmann, D., Miller, R.J., Blakeley, J.A., Schiefer, K.B. (eds.) VLDB, pp. 864–875. Morgan Kaufmann, San Francisco (2004)
10. De Raedt, L., Kimmig, A., Toivonen, H.: ProbLog: A probabilistic Prolog and its application in link discovery. In: Veloso, M.M. (ed.) IJCAI, pp. 2462–2467 (2007)
11. Sevon, P., Eronen, L., Hintsanen, P., Kulovesi, K., Toivonen, H.: Link discovery in graphs derived from biological databases. In: Leser, U., Naumann, F., Eckman, B.A. (eds.) DILS 2006. LNCS (LNBI), vol. 4075, pp. 35–49. Springer, Heidelberg (2006)
12. Sato, T.: A statistical learning method for logic programs with distribution semantics. In: Sterling, L. (ed.) ICLP, pp. 715–729. MIT Press, Cambridge (1995)
13. Dantsin, E.: Probabilistic logic programs and their semantics. In: Voronkov, A. (ed.) RCLP 1990 and RCLP 1991. LNCS, vol. 592, pp. 152–164. Springer, Heidelberg (1992)
14. Poole, D.: Abducing through negation as failure: stable models within the independent choice logic. J. Log. Program. 44(1-3), 5–35 (2000)
15. Bryant, R.E.: Graph-based algorithms for boolean function manipulation. IEEE Trans. Computers 35(8), 677–691 (1986)
16. Poole, D.: Logic programming, abduction and probability. New Generation Computing 11, 377–400 (1993)
17. Kimmig, A., De Raedt, L., Toivonen, H.: Probabilistic explanation based learning. In: Kok, J.N., Koronacki, J., de Mántaras, R.L., Matwin, S., Mladenic, D., Skowron, A. (eds.) ECML 2007. LNCS, vol. 4701, pp. 176–187. Springer, Heidelberg (2007)
18. Lloyd, J.W.: Foundations of Logic Programming, 2nd edn. Springer, Berlin (1989)
19. Gutmann, B., Kimmig, A., Kersting, K., De Raedt, L.: Parameter learning in probabilistic databases: A least squares approach. In: Daelemans, W., Goethals, B., Morik, K. (eds.) ECML PKDD 2008, Part I. LNCS, vol. 5211, pp. 473–488. Springer, Heidelberg (2008)
20. De Raedt, L., Kersting, K., Kimmig, A., Revoredo, K., Toivonen, H.: Compressing probabilistic Prolog programs. Machine Learning 70(2-3), 151–168 (2008)
21. Kimmig, A., De Raedt, L.: Probabilistic local pattern mining. In: ILP (2008)
22. Riguzzi, F.: A top down interpreter for LPAD and CP-logic. In: Basili, R., Pazienza, M.T. (eds.) AI*IA 2007. LNCS, vol. 4733, pp. 109–120. Springer, Heidelberg (2007)

Engineering an Incremental ASP Solver

M. Gebser, R. Kaminski, B. Kaufmann, M. Ostrowski, T. Schaub, and S. Thiele

Institut für Informatik, Universität Potsdam, August-Bebel-Str. 89, D-14482 Potsdam, Germany

Abstract. Many real-world applications, like planning or model checking, comprise a parameter reflecting the size of a solution. In a propositional formalism like Answer Set Programming (ASP), such problems can only be dealt with in a bounded way, considering one problem instance after another by gradually increasing the bound on the solution size. We thus propose an incremental approach to both grounding and solving in ASP. Our goal is to avoid redundancy by gradually processing the extensions to a problem rather than repeatedly re-processing the entire (extended) problem. We start by furnishing a formal framework capturing our incremental approach in terms of module theory. In turn, we take advantage of this framework for guiding the successive treatment of program slices during grounding and solving. Finally, we describe the first integrated incremental ASP system, *iclingo*, and provide an experimental evaluation.

1   Introduction

Answer Set Programming (ASP; [1]) faces a growing range of applications. This is due to the availability of efficient ASP solvers and ASP's rich modeling language, jointly allowing for an easy yet efficient handling of knowledge-intensive applications. Among them, many real-world applications, like planning or model checking, comprise parameters reflecting solution sizes. However, in the propositional setting of ASP, such problems can only be dealt with in a bounded way by considering in turn one problem instance after another, gradually increasing the bound on the solution size. Such an approach can nonetheless be highly efficient as demonstrated by Satisfiability (SAT) solvers in the aforementioned application areas [2,3]. However, while SAT has its focus on solving, ASP is also concerned with grounding in view of its modeling language.

We address this by proposing an incremental approach to both grounding and solving in ASP. Our goal is to avoid redundancy by gradually processing the extensions to a problem rather than repeatedly re-processing the entire extended problem. To this end, we express a *(parametrized) domain description* as a triple (B, P, Q) of logic programs, among which P and Q contain a (single) parameter k ranging over the natural numbers. In view of this, we sometimes denote P and Q by $P[k]$ and $Q[k]$. The base program B is meant to describe static knowledge, independent of parameter k. The role of P is to capture knowledge accumulating with increasing k, whereas Q is specific for each value of k. Our goal is then to decide whether the program

$$R[k/i] = B \cup \bigcup_{1 \leq j \leq i} P[k/j] \cup Q[k/i] \tag{1}$$

has an answer set for some (minimum) integer $i \geq 1$. In what follows, we write $R[i]$ rather than $R[k/i]$ whenever clear from the context.

M. Garcia de la Banda and E. Pontelli (Eds.): ICLP 2008, LNCS 5366, pp. 190–205, 2008.

For illustration, consider an action description in $\mathcal{C}+$ [4], involving an action a and a fluent p, along with a query in $\mathcal{Q}_n$ [5] about trajectories of length n. We translate these statements into the following domain description:

$$
\left.\begin{array}{c}
a \text{ causes } p \\
\text{exogenous } a \\
\text{inertial } p
\end{array}\right\} \mapsto \left\{
\begin{array}{c}
B = \left\{\begin{array}{l}
p(0) \leftarrow not \; \neg p(0) \\
\neg p(0) \leftarrow not \; p(0) \\
\leftarrow p(0), \neg p(0)
\end{array}\right\} \\[3em]
P[k] = \left\{\begin{array}{l}
a(k) \leftarrow not \; \neg a(k) \\
\neg a(k) \leftarrow not \; a(k) \\
p(k) \leftarrow a(k) \\
p(k) \leftarrow p(k{-}1), not \; \neg p(k) \\
\neg p(k) \leftarrow \neg p(k{-}1), not \; p(k) \\
\leftarrow p(k), \neg p(k) \\
\leftarrow a(k), \neg a(k)
\end{array}\right\}
\end{array}\right.
\quad (2)
$$

$$
\left.\begin{array}{c}
\neg p \text{ holds at } 0 \\
p \text{ holds at } n \\
\neg a \text{ occurs at } n
\end{array}\right\} \mapsto \left\{ Q[k] = \left\{\begin{array}{l}
\leftarrow not \; \neg p(0) \\
\leftarrow not \; p(k) \\
\leftarrow not \; \neg a(k)
\end{array}\right\} \right. .
$$

This domain description induces no answer sets for $R[1]$, but we obtain a single one for $R[2]$, that is, $AS(R[2]) = \{\{\neg p(0), a(1), p(1), \neg a(2), p(2)\}\}$.

Such an answer is usually found by appeal to iterative deepening search. That is, one first checks whether $R[1]$ has an answer set, if not, the same is done for $R[2]$, and so on. For a given i, this approach re-processes B for i times and $(i{-}j{+}1)$ times each $P[j]$, where $1 \leq j \leq i$, while each $Q[j]$ is dealt with only once. Unlike this, we propose to compute answers sets of (1) in an incremental fashion, starting from $R[1]$ but then gradually dealing with the program slices $P[i]$ and $Q[i]$ rather than the entire program $R[i]$ in (1). However, B and the previously processed slices $P[j]$ and $Q[j]$, $1 \leq j < i$, must be taken into account when dealing with $P[i]$ and $Q[i]$: while the rules in $P[j]$ are accumulated, the ones in $Q[j]$ must be discarded. For accomplishing this, an ASP system has to operate in a "stateful way." That is, it has to maintain its previous state for processing the current program slices. In this way, all components, B, $P[j]$, and $Q[i]$, of (1) are dealt with only once, and duplicated work is avoided when increasing i.

Given that an ASP system is composed of a grounder and a solver, our incremental approach has the following specific advantages over the standard approach. As regards grounding, it reduces efforts by avoiding reproducing previous ground rules. Regarding solving, it reduces redundancy, in particular, if a learning ASP solver is used, given that previously gathered information on heuristics, conflicts, or loops (cf. [6]), respectively, remains available and can thus be continuously exploited. We provide some empirical evidence using the new incremental ASP system *iclingo* [7].

2   Background

Our language is built from a set $\mathcal{F}$ of *function* symbols (including the natural numbers), a set $\mathcal{V}$ of *variable* symbols, and a set $\mathcal{P}$ of *predicate* symbols. In view of our goal, $\mathcal{V}$ contains a distinguished parameter symbol k (varying over natural numbers). The set $\mathcal{T}$

of *terms* is the smallest set containing $\mathcal{V}$ and all expressions of the form $f(t_1, \ldots, t_n)$, where $f \in \mathcal{F}$ and $t_i \in \mathcal{T}$ for $1 \leq i \leq n$. The set $\mathcal{A}$ of *atoms* contains all expressions of the form $p(t_1, \ldots, t_n)$, where $p \in \mathcal{P}$ and $t_i \in \mathcal{T}$ for $1 \leq i \leq n$. A *literal* is an atom a or its (default) negation *not* a. Given a set L of literals, let $L^+ = \{a \in \mathcal{A} \mid a \in L\}$ and $L^- = \{a \in \mathcal{A} \mid not\ a \in L\}$. A *logic program* over $\mathcal{A}$ is a set of *rules* of the form $a \leftarrow b_1, \ldots, b_m, not\ c_{m+1}, \ldots, not\ c_n$, where $a, b_i, c_j \in \mathcal{A}$ for $0 < i \leq m < j \leq n$. The semantics of integrity constraints and choice rules is given through program transformations. For instance, $\{a\} \leftarrow$ is a shorthand for $a \leftarrow not\ a', a' \leftarrow not\ a$ and similarly $\leftarrow a$ for $a' \leftarrow a, not\ a'$, for a new atom a'. For a rule r, let $head(r) = a$ be the *head* of r, $body(r) = \{b_1, \ldots, b_m, not\ c_{m+1}, \ldots, not\ c_n\}$ be the *body* of r, and finally $atom(r) = \{head(r)\} \cup body(r)^+ \cup body(r)^-$. For a program P, define $head(P) = \{head(r) \mid r \in P\}$ and $atom(P) = \bigcup_{r \in P} atom(r)$. Given an expression $e \in \mathcal{T} \cup \mathcal{A}$, let $var(e)$ denote the set of all variables occurring in e; analogously, $var(r)$ gives all variables in rule r. Expression $e \in \mathcal{T} \cup \mathcal{A}$ is *ground*, if $var(e) = \emptyset$. The *ground instantiation* of a program P is defined as $grd(P) = \{r\theta \mid r \in P, \theta : var(r) \to \mathcal{U}\}$, where $\mathcal{U} = \{t \in \mathcal{T} \mid var(t) = \emptyset\}$; analogously, $grd(\mathcal{A}) = \{a \in \mathcal{A} \mid var(a) = \emptyset\}$.

A set $X \subseteq grd(\mathcal{A})$ is an *answer set* of a program P over $\mathcal{A}$, if X is the $\subseteq$-smallest model of $\{head(r) \leftarrow body(r)^+ \mid r \in grd(P), body(r)^- \cap X = \emptyset\}$. The set of answer sets of a program P is denoted $AS(P)$. Two programs, P and P', are *equivalent*, denoted by $P \equiv P'$, if $AS(P) = AS(P')$.

3   Semantic Underpinnings through Incremental Modularity

For providing a clear interface between program slices and guaranteeing their compositionality, we build upon the concept of a module developed in [8]: a *module* $\mathbb{P}$ is a triple (P, I, O) consisting of a (ground) program P over $grd(\mathcal{A})$ and sets $I, O \subseteq grd(\mathcal{A})$ such that $I \cap O = \emptyset$, $atom(P) \subseteq I \cup O$, and $head(P) \subseteq O$. The elements of I and O are called *input* and *output* atoms, also denoted by $I(\mathbb{P})$ and $O(\mathbb{P})$, respectively; similarly, we refer to P by $P(\mathbb{P})$. We say that $\mathbb{P}$ is *input-free*, if $I(\mathbb{P}) = \emptyset$.

For giving an incremental account of modularity, we begin with associating a (nonground) program P and a set I of (ground) input atoms with a module, denoted by $\mathbb{P}(I)$, imposing certain restrictions on the ground program induced by P. To this end, we define for a program P over $grd(\mathcal{A})$ and a set $X \subseteq grd(\mathcal{A})$, the set $P|_X$ of rules as

$$\{head(r) \leftarrow body(r)^+ \cup L \mid r \in P, body(r)^+ \subseteq X, L = \{not\ c \mid c \in body(r)^- \cap X\}\} .$$

Note that $P|_X$ projects the bodies of rules in P to the atoms of X. If a body contains an atom outside X, either the corresponding rule or literal is removed, depending on whether the atom occurs positively or negatively. This allows us to associate (nonground) programs with (ground) modules in the following way.

Definition 1. *Let P be a program over $\mathcal{A}$ and $I \subseteq grd(\mathcal{A})$. We define $\mathbb{P}(I)$ as the module $(\,grd(P)|_Y, I, head(grd(P)|_X)\,)$, where $X = I \cup head(grd(P))$ and $Y = I \cup head(grd(P)|_X)$.*

The full ground instantiation $grd(P)$ of P is projected onto inputs and atoms defined in $grd(P)$. The head atoms of this projection, viz., $head(grd(P)|_{I \cup head(grd(P))})$, serve as output atoms and are used to simplify $grd(P)$, sparing only input and output atoms.

As a simple example, consider $P[k] = \{p(k) \leftarrow p(Y), not\ p(2); p(k) \leftarrow p(2)\}$. Note that $grd(P[1])$ is infinite. However, for $X = \{p(0), p(1)\}$, we get

$$grd(P[1])|_X = \{p(1) \leftarrow p(0);\ p(1) \leftarrow p(1)\}\ \text{and}\ head(grd(P[1])|_X) = \{p(1)\}\ .$$

For $I = \{p(0)\}$, we obtain $I \cup head(grd(P[1])) = I \cup head(grd(P[1])|_X) = \{p(0)\} \cup \{p(1)\} = X$. Thus, $\mathbb{P}[1](\{p(0)\}) = (\ grd(P[1])|_{\{p(0),p(1)\}},\ \{p(0)\},\ \{p(1)\}\ )$, and $P(\mathbb{P}[1](I)) = grd(P[1])|_X$ is finite. Note that, if $p(1)$ had been in I, we would not have obtained a module since $P[1]$ defines $p(1)$. Hence, it must be an output atom.

Proposition 1. *Let P be a program over $\mathcal{A}$, $I \subseteq grd(\mathcal{A})$, and $\mathbb{P}(I) = (P', I, O)$. Then, we have $O \subseteq grd(\mathcal{A})$ and $atom(P') \subseteq I \cup O$.*

We define the *join* of two modules $\mathbb{P}$ and $\mathbb{Q}$, denoted by $\mathbb{P} \sqcup \mathbb{Q}$, as the module

$$(\ P(\mathbb{P}) \cup P(\mathbb{Q}),\ I(\mathbb{P}) \cup (I(\mathbb{Q}) \setminus O(\mathbb{P})),\ O(\mathbb{P}) \cup O(\mathbb{Q})\ ),$$

provided that $(I(\mathbb{P}) \cup O(\mathbb{P})) \cap O(\mathbb{Q}) = \emptyset$. This definition is simpler than the original one in [8], but also more restrictive. For instance, our definition does not permit (negative) recursion between two modules to be joined, similar to splitting [9]. (Note that positive and negative recursion are allowed within each module.) Also note that the join of $\mathbb{P}$ and $\mathbb{Q}$, as defined above, is not commutative: even if $\mathbb{P} \sqcup \mathbb{Q}$ is defined, $\mathbb{Q} \sqcup \mathbb{P}$ might be undefined. However, lacking commutativity is not an issue in our incremental context, where portions of a domain description are always processed in order.

We make use of the join to formalize the compositionality of modules induced by domain descriptions.

Definition 2. *A domain description $(B, P[k], Q[k])$ is modular, if the modules*

$$\mathbb{P}_i = \mathbb{P}_{i-1} \sqcup \mathbb{P}[i](O(\mathbb{P}_{i-1}))\qquad and\qquad \mathbb{Q}_i = \mathbb{P}_i \sqcup \mathbb{Q}[i](O(\mathbb{P}_i))$$

are defined for $i \geq 1$, where $\mathbb{P}_0 = \mathbb{B}(\emptyset)$.

The requirement of the join being defined demands that gradually obtained ground programs must define distinct atoms. Also, the directedness of the join, in a sense, permits an information flow between ground programs in increasing order of values substituted for k, but not the other way round.

As an example, consider $(B, P[k], Q[k])$ over $\mathcal{A}$, where:

$$\begin{aligned}
B &= \{\ dbl(0,0) \leftarrow\ \} \\
P[k] &= \{\ n(k) \leftarrow;\qquad dbl(k, 2*Y) \leftarrow n(Y), not\ n(Y+1)\ \} \\
Q[k] &= \{\ \leftarrow dbl(Y, k-1)\ \}\ .
\end{aligned} \qquad (3)$$

This domain description induces the following modules:[1]

$$\begin{aligned}
\mathbb{P}_0 &= (\ B = \{dbl(0,0) \leftarrow\},\ \emptyset,\ \{dbl(0,0)\}\ ), \\
\mathbb{P}_1 &= (\ B \cup \{n(1) \leftarrow;\ dbl(1,2) \leftarrow n(1)\},\ \emptyset,\ O(\mathbb{P}_0) \cup \{n(1), dbl(1,2)\}\ ), \\
\mathbb{Q}_1 &= (\ P(\mathbb{P}_1) \cup \{\leftarrow dbl(0,0)\},\ \emptyset,\ O(\mathbb{P}_1)\ ), \\
\mathbb{P}_2 &= (\ P(\mathbb{P}_2),\ \emptyset,\ O(\mathbb{P}_1) \cup \{n(2), dbl(2,2), dbl(2,4)\}\ )
\end{aligned}$$

$$\text{where } P(\mathbb{P}_2) = P(\mathbb{P}_1) \cup \{n(2) \leftarrow\} \cup \left\{ \begin{aligned} dbl(2,2) &\leftarrow n(1), not\ n(2) \\ dbl(2,4) &\leftarrow n(2) \end{aligned} \right\},$$

$$\mathbb{Q}_2 = (\ P(\mathbb{P}_2),\ \emptyset,\ O(\mathbb{P}_2)\ ),$$

---

[1] For simplicity, we evaluate arithmetic expressions.

$$\mathbb{P}_3 = (\ P(\mathbb{P}_3),\ \emptyset,\ O(\mathbb{P}_2) \cup \{n(3), dbl(3,2), dbl(3,4), dbl(3,6)\}\ )$$

$$\text{where } P(\mathbb{P}_3) = P(\mathbb{P}_2) \cup \{n(3) \leftarrow\} \cup \left\{ \begin{array}{l} dbl(3,2) \leftarrow n(1),\, not\ n(2) \\ dbl(3,4) \leftarrow n(2),\, not\ n(3) \\ dbl(3,6) \leftarrow n(3) \end{array} \right\},$$

$$\mathbb{Q}_3 = (\ \{\leftarrow dbl(1,2);\ \leftarrow dbl(2,2);\ \leftarrow dbl(3,2)\},\ \emptyset,\ O(\mathbb{P}_3)\ )\ ,\ \text{etc.}$$

All above modules are defined (in terms of the join) and input-free. Since this also applies to $\mathbb{P}_i$ and $\mathbb{Q}_i$ for every $i > 3$, we have that domain description (3) is modular. Hence, we can read off the results of the expressed queries from the answer sets of each $P(\mathbb{Q}_i)$. If $i \geq 1$ is odd, we get $AS(P(\mathbb{Q}_i)) = \emptyset$. Otherwise, if $i \geq 1$ is even, then $AS(P(\mathbb{Q}_i)) = \{\{dbl(0,0)\} \cup \{n(j), dbl(j, 2{*}j) \mid 1 \leq j \leq i\}\}$. In fact, for $1 \leq j \leq i$ and $Y = j$, literals $not\ n(Y{+}1)$ are removed from the body of the second rule in $P[k]$ during the incremental construction because the underlying atoms $n(j{+}1)$ are undefined in $P[j]$. In this way, the atoms $dbl(j, 2{*}j)$ are derived. Note that this is not possible for $j < i$ with program $\bigcup_{1 \leq j \leq i} P[j]$ in a non-incremental setting.

Proposition 2. *Let $(B, P[k], Q[k])$ be a modular domain description, and let $(\mathbb{P}_i)_{i \geq 0}$ and $(\mathbb{Q}_i)_{i \geq 1}$ as in Definition 2. Then, we have the following for $i \geq 1$:*

1. *$\mathbb{P}_i$ and $\mathbb{Q}_i$ are input-free;*
2. *$atom(P(\mathbb{P}_i)) \subseteq O(\mathbb{P}_i)$ and $atom(P(\mathbb{Q}_i)) \subseteq O(\mathbb{Q}_i)$;*
3. *$P(\mathbb{P}_i) = P(\mathbb{B}(\emptyset)) \cup \bigcup_{1 \leq j \leq i} P(\mathbb{P}[j](O(\mathbb{P}_{j-1})))$ and $P(\mathbb{Q}_i) = P(\mathbb{P}_i) \cup P(\mathbb{Q}[i](O(\mathbb{P}_i)))$;*
4. *$head(P(\mathbb{P}[i](O(\mathbb{P}_{i-1})))) \cap atom(P(\mathbb{P}_{i-1})) = \emptyset$ and $head(P(\mathbb{Q}[i](O(\mathbb{P}_i)))) \cap atom(P(\mathbb{P}_i)) = \emptyset$.*

The third item essentially states that the combined programs obtained for $i \geq 1$ equal the union of subprograms added for each $1 \leq j \leq i$. Importantly, the fourth item expresses that the head atoms of a newly added subprogram are different from all atoms encountered before. Hence, the sequence $(O(\mathbb{P}_i))_{i \geq 0}$ of output atoms amounts to a splitting sequence [9] for $\bigcup_{i \geq 0} P(\mathbb{P}_i)$. Nonetheless, we intentionally use modules and joins rather than splitting for formalizing our approach, as the composition of (ground) programs done in incremental steps is only indirectly addressed by splitting sequences.

Note that we only take advantage of module theory for establishing a well-defined formal setting for incremental ASP solving. Our computational approach deals directly with programs in order to exploit existing ASP technology. In view of this, the next result shows when the module-guarded formation of ground programs coincides with separate grounding. To this end, we define a domain description $(B, P[k], Q[k])$ as *bound*, if $atom(grd(B)) \subseteq head(grd(B))$ and $atom(grd(P[i])) \subseteq head(grd(B \cup \bigcup_{1 \leq j \leq i} P[j]))$ for all $i \geq 1$. With this concept at hand, we have the following result.

Theorem 1. *Let $(B, P[k], Q[k])$ be a bound modular domain description, and let $(\mathbb{P}_i)_{i \geq 0}$ and $(\mathbb{Q}_i)_{i \geq 1}$ as in Definition 2. Then, we have the following for $i \geq 1$:*

1. *$P(\mathbb{P}_i) \equiv grd(B \cup \bigcup_{1 \leq j \leq i} P[j]);$*
2. *$P(\mathbb{Q}_i) \equiv grd(B \cup \bigcup_{1 \leq j \leq i} P[j] \cup Q[i]).$*

That is, for bound modular domain descriptions, the same result is obtained when grounding is done either stepwise or in a single pass. Note that the domain description given in (2) is modular and bound. Likewise, the domain description in (3) is modular, but it is not bound because of $n(Y)$ and $n(Y{+}1)$ occurring in body literals of $P[k]$.

4   Incremental ASP Solving

The computation of answer sets consists of two phases: a *grounding* phase aiming at a compact ground instantiation of the original program and a *solving* phase computing the answer sets of the obtained ground program. As motivated in Section 1, our incremental approach is based on the idea that the grounder as well as the solver are implemented in a stateful way. Thus, both keep their previous states when increasing parameter k in (1). As regards grounding, at each step i, the goal is to produce only ground rules stemming from program slices $P[i]$ and $Q[i]$, without re-producing previous ground rules. The ground program slices are then gradually passed to the solver that accumulates all ground rules from $P[j]$, for $1 \leq j \leq i$, while discarding the rules from $Q[j]$, if $j < i$.

Grounding. Let us now characterize the consecutive program slices in terms of grounding programs. In practice, given a program P, the goal of a grounder is to produce a finite and compact yet equivalent representation of $grd(P)$ by applying answer set preserving simplifications (cf. [10,11]). In our context, $P[i]$ and $Q[i]$ are not grounded in isolation for $i \geq 1$. Rather, the ground programs obtained from previous program slices are augmented with newly derived ground rules. We thus assume a grounder to be stateful, where states are represented by the head atoms of ground rules belonging to the output of previous grounding steps.

Given a program P over $\mathcal{A}$ and $I \subseteq grd(\mathcal{A})$, we define an (*incremental*) *grounder* as a partial function ground : $(P, I) \mapsto (P', O)$, where P' is a program over $grd(\mathcal{A})$ and $O \subseteq grd(\mathcal{A})$. Thereby, P' stands for the ground program obtained from P, where the input atoms I provide domain information used to instantiate non-ground atoms in the rules of P. The output atoms in O essentially correspond to $head(P')$. Their main use is to carry state information, as O can serve as input to subsequent grounding steps. Also note that ground is not required to be total, given that existing grounders, like *lparse* [12] and *gringo* [7], impose certain restrictions on non-ground programs, such as being ω- or λ-restricted, not necessarily met by P.

Next, we formalize a grounder's *adequacy* to an incremental setting.

Definition 3. *A grounder* ground *is adequate, if for every program P over $\mathcal{A}$ and $I \subseteq grd(\mathcal{A})$ such that* ground$(P, I) = (P', O)$ *is defined, the following holds:*

1. $\big(P \cup \{\{a\} \leftarrow \ |\ a \in I\}\big) \equiv \big(P' \cup \{\{a\} \leftarrow \ |\ a \in I\}\big),$
2. $\bigcup_{X \in AS(P \cup \{\{a\} \leftarrow |a \in I\})}(X \setminus I) \subseteq O \subseteq head(grd(P)|_Y)$, *where* $Y = I \cup head(grd(P))$, *and*
3. *for every* $r' \in P'$, *there is some* $r \in grd(P)$ *such that* $head(r) = head(r')$ *and* $body(r)^+ \setminus (I \cup O) \subseteq body(r')^+$.

The first condition expresses that P and P', each augmented with any combination of input atoms in I, must be equivalent. The second condition stipulates that all non-input atoms belonging to some answer set X of $P \cup \{\{a\} \leftarrow \ |\ a \in I\}$ are contained in O. In addition, O must not exceed the head atoms of $grd(P)|_{I \cup head(grd(P))}$ in order to suitably restrict subsequently produced ground rules, using O as an input (cf. Definition 4). Finally, the third condition forbids the introduction of rules that cannot be obtained from $grd(P)$ via permissible simplifications. Clearly, an adequate grounder may apply answer-set preserving simplifications to compact its output.

For illustration, consider $P[k]$ in (3) along with $I = \{n(1)\}$. An adequate grounder could, for instance, map $(P[2], I)$ to $(P', O = \{n(2), dbl(2, 2), dbl(2, 4)\})$, where

$$P' = \{n(2) \leftarrow; \ dbl(2, 2) \leftarrow n(1), not \ n(2); \ dbl(2, 4) \leftarrow n(2), not \ n(3)\} \ . \quad (4)$$

Note that $AS(P' \cup \{\{n(1)\} \leftarrow\}) = \{\{n(1), n(2), dbl(2, 4)\}, \{n(2), dbl(2, 4)\}\} = AS(P[2] \cup \{\{n(1)\} \leftarrow\})$. Due to fact $n(2) \leftarrow$, the second rule could also be dropped from P'; similarly, $dbl(2, 2)$ could be removed from O. Furthermore, literals $n(2)$ and $not \ n(3)$ could be dropped from the last rule, still satisfying Definition 3. Note that it is crucial to restrict the atoms in O to $head(P')$. For instance, this forbids the inclusion of $n(3)$ in O, permitting further simplifications of P' wrt O.

The following definition specifies the (ground) program slices gradually obtained from a domain description using a (stateful) grounder.

Definition 4. *Let* $(B, P[k], Q[k])$ *be a domain description, and let* ground *be a grounder. We define for* $i \geq 1$:

$$(P_0, O_0) = (P_0'|_{O_0}, O_0) \, , \qquad \text{where } (P_0', O_0) = \text{ground}(B, \emptyset) \, ,$$
$$(P_i, O_i) = (P_i'|_{(\bigcup_{0 \leq j \leq i} O_j)}, O_i) \, , \qquad \text{where } (P_i', O_i) = \text{ground}(P[i], \bigcup_{0 \leq j < i} O_j) \, ,$$
$$(Q_i, O_i') = \text{ground}(Q[i], \bigcup_{0 \leq j \leq i} O_j) \, .$$

Note that the successively identified output atoms in O_j, for $0 \leq j \leq i$, are used to simplify ground programs P_i' by eliminating either rules or negative body literals. We thus obtain ground program slices P_i such that $\bigcup_{r \in P_i} (body(r)^+ \cup body(r)^-) \subseteq \bigcup_{0 \leq j \leq i} O_j$. This reduction is important in view of the compositional semantics of domain descriptions in Definition 2. For instance, if not done by ground itself, literal $not \ n(3)$ must a posteriori be removed from the body of the third rule in (4), in order to obtain the intended ground program slice. However, ground programs Q_i need not be reduced, since their rules are neither accumulated nor reused.

The next result links the semantics of modular domain descriptions to that of ground programs gradually produced by an adequate grounder.

Theorem 2. *Let* $(B, P[k], Q[k])$ *be a modular domain description and* ground *an adequate grounder. Let* $(\mathbb{P}_i)_{i \geq 0}$ *and* $(\mathbb{Q}_i)_{i \geq 1}$ *be as in Definition 2 and* $(P_i, O_i)_{i \geq 0}$ *and* $(Q_i, O_i')_{i \geq 1}$ *as in Definition 4. If* (P_j, O_j) *is defined for* $0 \leq j \leq i$, *we have for* $i \geq 1$:

1. $P(\mathbb{P}_0) \equiv P_0;$
2. $P(\mathbb{P}_i) \equiv \bigcup_{0 \leq j \leq i} P_j;$
3. $P(\mathbb{Q}_i) \equiv \bigcup_{0 \leq j \leq i} P_j \cup Q_i$, *provided that* (Q_i, O_i') *is defined.*

Recall that ground can be partial. In fact, existing grounders impose certain restrictions on the non-ground programs of a domain description, such as being ω- or λ-restricted, guaranteeing the finiteness of equivalent ground programs. Assuming that such requirements are met, we next detail how grounding output can be processed by an answer set solver.

Solving. As with grounding, special care must be taken for customizing existing ASP solving technology in an incremental setting. First, we have to guarantee the compositionality of successive program slices. Second, a solver has to respect the cumulative and volatile roles of P_j and Q_i, respectively. And finally, we have to furnish a clear interface between the grounding and the solving component.

For capturing compositionality, we rely on [13], characterizing the answer sets of a program P over $grd(\mathcal{A})$ by the (classical) models of its completion and loop formulas. For $Y \subseteq grd(\mathcal{A})$, define the *completion* of P, $CF(P, Y)$, as the set of formulas

$$a \leftrightarrow \bigvee_{r \in P, head(r)=a} \left(\bigwedge_{b \in body(r)^+} b \wedge \bigwedge_{c \in body(r)^-} \neg c \right),$$

for all $a \in Y$. Moreover, $Y \subseteq grd(\mathcal{A})$ is a *loop* of P, if $(Y, E = \{(head(r), b) \mid r \in P, head(r) \in Y, b \in body(r)^+ \cap Y\})$ is a strongly connected graph such that $E \neq \emptyset$. Then, the set of *loop formulas* for P, $LF(P)$, is given by the set of formulas

$$\bigvee_{a \in Y} a \rightarrow \bigvee_{r \in P, head(r) \in Y, body(r)^+ \cap Y = \emptyset} \left(\bigwedge_{b \in body(r)^+} b \wedge \bigwedge_{c \in body(r)^-} \neg c \right),$$

for all loops Y of P. As shown in [13], a set $X \subseteq grd(\mathcal{A})$ is an answer set of P iff $X \models CF(P, grd(\mathcal{A})) \cup LF(P)$.

For programs induced by modular domain descriptions, completion and loop formulas can be sliced as follows.

Theorem 3. *Let $(B, P[k], Q[k])$ be a modular domain description, let* ground *be an adequate grounder, and let $(P_i, O_i)_{i \geq 0}$ and $(Q_i, O_i')_{i \geq 1}$ as in Definition 4. If (P_j, O_j) is defined for $0 \leq j \leq i$ and if (Q_i, O_i') is defined, we have the following for $i \geq 1$:[2]*

$$CF(\textstyle\bigcup_{0 \leq j \leq i} P_j \cup Q_i, grd(\mathcal{A})) \equiv \bigcup_{0 \leq j \leq i} CF(P_j, O_j) \cup CF(Q_i, grd(\mathcal{A}) \setminus \bigcup_{0 \leq j \leq i} O_j)$$
$$LF(\textstyle\bigcup_{0 \leq j \leq i} P_j \cup Q_i) \equiv \bigcup_{0 \leq j \leq i} LF(P_j) \cup LF(Q_i|_{head(\bigcup_{0 \leq j \leq i} P_j \cup Q_i)}).$$

Recall that modular domain descriptions $(B, P[k], Q[k])$ induce splitting sequences [9]. This means that the answer sets of $\bigcup_{0 \leq j \leq i} P_j \cup Q_i$ can be decomposed into a sequence of answer sets for subprograms $P_0, \ldots, P_i, Q_i$. Theorem 3 reflects this decomposition in terms of completion and loop formulas, which are material to the data structures of ASP solvers. Thus, the practical consequence of the decomposability of completion and loop formulas is that a solver can successively build its data structures in a modular fashion. If this was not the case, it would be rather misleading to qualify an approach as incremental. Hence, a modularity condition is essential for incremental computations.

When processing consecutive program slices, we have to distinguish cumulative and volatile ones. That is, while the ground rules in P_j are accumulated within the solver for $0 \leq j \leq i$, the ones in Q_j must be discarded for $1 \leq j < i$ when Q_i is added. We accomplish this by adding to each rule in Q_j a new body atom α_j, along with rules achieving that α_j holds only at step j. To this end, we define the following set of rules for a program Q over $grd(\mathcal{A})$ and a new atom $\alpha \notin grd(\mathcal{A})$:

$$Q(\alpha) = \{head(r) \leftarrow body(r) \cup \{\alpha\} \mid r \in Q\}.$$

In our incremental setting, the addition of new atoms allows us to selectively (de)activate volatile program slices.

Proposition 3. *Let $(P_i)_{i \geq 0}$ and $(Q_i)_{i \geq 1}$ be sequences of programs over $grd(\mathcal{A})$, and let $F_j = \{\alpha_j \leftarrow\}$ for $\alpha_j \notin grd(\mathcal{A})$ and $j \geq 1$. Then, we have the following for $i \geq 1$:*

$$\textstyle\bigcup_{0 \leq j \leq i} P_j \cup Q_i \cup F_i \equiv P_0 \cup \bigcup_{1 \leq j \leq i} (P_j \cup Q_j(\alpha_j)) \cup F_i.$$

---

[2] We abuse notation and let $\equiv$ stand for classical equivalence here.

The addition of F_i on the left hand side is merely for establishing formal equivalence, considering that α_i occurs in $Q_i(\alpha_i)$ but not in Q_i. The fact that programs $Q_j(\alpha_j)$ behave neutrally, as long as α_j is underivable, provides us with a handle to control the effective program slices. In addition to activating some $Q_j(\alpha_j)$ for $j \geq 1$, we also have to deactivate it in subsequent steps. Thus, a solver cannot include α_j persistently as a fact. But rather than explicitly deleting any fact (or rule) previously passed to the solver, we build upon an interface supporting *assumptions*. This trims the required solver interface to only two functions:

- add(P) incorporates a ground logic program P into the rule database of the solver;
- solve(L) takes a set L of ground literals and computes the answer sets X of the ground program comprised in the solver that satisfy $L^+ \subseteq X$ and $L^- \cap X = \emptyset$.

This simple interface is similar to the one for incremental SAT solving given in [14]. The literals L passed to solve constitute assumptions, which can semantically be viewed as the set of integrity constraints $\{\leftarrow not\ a \mid a \in L^+\} \cup \{\leftarrow a \mid a \in L^-\}$. However, as regards *clasp* [6], the crucial difference between integrity constraints and assumptions is that the former give rise to program simplifications affecting internal data structures, while the effect of the latter is temporary, i.e., restricted to an invocation of solve. While former assumptions can easily be withdrawn, for a learning solver, it would be much harder to support an explicit deletion of obsolete problem parts [14].

Let us now situate the *solver* in our incremental context.

Definition 5. *Let $(R_i)_{i \geq 0}$ and $(L_i)_{i \geq 0}$ be sequences of programs and literals over* $grd(\mathcal{A}) \cup \{\alpha_i \mid i \geq 0\}$. *A solver is a pair of total functions* add $: R_i \mapsto S_i$ *and* solve $: L_i \mapsto X$, *where* $S_0 = R_0|_{head(R_0)}$, $S_i = S_{i-1} \cup R_i|_{head(S_{i-1} \cup R_i)}$ *for* $i \geq 1$, *and* $X \subseteq 2^{(grd(\mathcal{A}) \cup \{\alpha_i \mid i \geq 0\})}$.

Note that only add affects a solver's state, where added programs are subject to simplification. In fact, as with P_i for $i \geq 0$ in Definition 4, we assume that atoms not occurring as the head of any rule are eliminated. Even if such an atom becomes derivable later on when another program is added, it can thus not interact with the rules already present. The reason for this design decision is that, although operating in an open environment, the possible addition of information or program slices, respectively, should not force the solver to continuously rebuild its existent data structures. Of course, this necessitates program slices to be provided in a bottom-up manner. The second function, solve, leaves the accumulated program slices (logically) unaffected, that is, the passed literals are only assumed locally within solve.

The objective of maintaining program slices, once they have been added, also motivates the following definition of *soundness*.

Definition 6. *A solver as in Definition 5 is sound, if for all sequences $(R_i)_{i \geq 0}$ and $(L_i)_{i \geq 0}$ of programs and literals over $grd(\mathcal{A}) \cup \{\alpha_i \mid i \geq 0\}$, and for every $i \geq 0$, we have: $X \in$ solve(L_i) iff $L_i^+ \subseteq X \subseteq head(S_i) \setminus L_i^-$ such that $X \models \bigcup_{0 \leq j \leq i}(CF(R_j|_{head(S_j)}, head(R_j|_{Y_j})) \cup LF(R_j|_{head(S_j)}))$, where $Y_0 = head(R_0)$ and $Y_j = head(S_{j-1} \cup R_j)$ for $1 \leq j \leq i$.*

First, observe that literals passed as assumptions in L_i must be respected by solutions X returned by a sound solver. Second, X must satisfy the completion and loop formulas individually for each program slice, thereby, restricting the attention to the respective head atoms. This conception allows the solver to build its data structures in a modular way, without sacrificing soundness, but it also relocates the responsibility to properly partition a program away from the solver. However, as Theorem 3 shows, modular domain descriptions (along with an adequate grounder) permit the construction of a program's completion and loop formulas locally for program slices, obtaining the same answer sets as with the entire program.

We now define the program slices to be added to the solver for the ground rules obtained from a domain description.

Definition 7. *Let* $(B, P[k], Q[k])$ *be a domain description, let* ground *be a grounder, and let* $(P_i, O_i)_{i \geq 0}$ *and* $(Q_i, O'_i)_{i \geq 1}$ *as in Definition 4. If* (P_0, O_0), (P_j, O_j), *and* (Q_j, O'_j) *are defined for* $1 \leq j \leq i$, *we define a sequence* $(R_i)_{i \geq 0}$ *of programs and a sequence* $(L_i)_{i \geq 0}$ *of literals for* $1 \leq j \leq i$ *and* $\alpha_{j-1}, \alpha_j \notin grd(\mathcal{A})$ *by:*

$$R_0 = P_0 \qquad R_j = P_j \cup Q_j(\alpha_j) \cup \{\{\alpha_j\} \leftarrow\} \cup \{\leftarrow \alpha_{j-1}\}$$
$$L_0 = \emptyset \qquad L_j = \{\alpha_j\}.$$

The difference between the cumulative rules in P_j and the volatile ones in Q_j is that an additional atom α_j is appended to the bodies of the latter. Moreover, choice rule $\{\alpha_j\} \leftarrow$ nominally permits the unconditional inclusion of α_j in an answer set. However, upon the invocation of solve in step j, literal α_j is passed as assumption, so that answer sets must necessarily contain α_j. In contrast, in step $j + 1$, integrity constraint $\leftarrow \alpha_j$ is persistently added to the solver, forcing α_j to be false. Due to this, all rules in Q_j are deactivated in later steps. Notably, *clasp* eliminates such false atoms and rules with false bodies from its data structures, thus deleting a whole obsolete program Q_j.

In theory, no added rule is deleted later on. Thus, we require an additional condition.

Definition 8. *We define a domain description* $(B, P[k], Q[k])$ *as separated, if for all* $i \geq 1$ *and* $j > i$, $head(grd(Q[i])) \cap head(grd(P[j] \cup Q[j])) = \emptyset$.

Separation can easily be achieved by using distinct predicates and parameter k in the heads of rules in $Q[k]$ as well as in body atoms corresponding to such heads. The domain descriptions given in (2) and (3), trivially, are separated.

Using an adequate grounder and a sound solver, we finally establish that our incremental solving strategy leads to the desired outcomes for modular domain descriptions.

Theorem 4. *Let* $(B, P[k], Q[k])$ *be a separated modular domain description, let* ground *be an adequate grounder, and let* $(P_i, O_i)_{i \geq 0}$ *and* $(Q_i, O'_i)_{i \geq 1}$ *as in Definition 4. Furthermore, let* (add, solve) *be a sound solver,* $(R_i)_{i \geq 0}$ *and* $(L_i)_{i \geq 0}$ *as in Definition 7, and* $S_j = $ add(R_j) *for* $j \geq 0$ *as in Definition 5. If* (P_0, O_0), (P_j, O_j), *and* (Q_j, O'_j) *are defined for* $1 \leq j \leq i$, *we have the following for* $i \geq 1$:
$$X \in \text{solve}(L_i) \text{ iff } (X \setminus \{\alpha_i\}) \in AS(\textstyle\bigcup_{0 \leq j \leq i} P_j \cup Q_i).$$

Comparing with the third item in Theorem 2 shows that our approach, comprising incremental grounding and solving, matches exactly the semantics of (programs induced by) separated modular domain descriptions. In this context, the modularity condition in Definition 2 allows us to largely reuse existing ASP technology, as we see below.

Algorithm 1. combines our grounding and solving functions for successively computing the answer sets of programs induced by a domain description $(B, P[k], Q[k])$. To this end, isolve makes use of one instance of a grounder, denoted by GROUNDER, and one instance of a solver, viz., SOLVER. Programs B, $P[i]$, and $Q[i]$ are then gradually grounded by means of GROUNDER. Provided that GROUNDER can instantiate the given programs, i.e., if they satisfy any additional require-

---
Algorithm 1. isolve

Input   : A domain description $(B, P[k], Q[k])$.
Output : A nonempty set of answer sets.
Internal: A grounder GROUNDER.
Internal: A solver SOLVER.

1 $i \leftarrow 0$
2 $(P_0, O) \leftarrow$ GROUNDER.ground$(B, \emptyset)$
3 SOLVER.add(P_0)
4 **loop**
5     $i \leftarrow i + 1$
6     $(P_i, O_i) \leftarrow$ GROUNDER.ground$(P[i], O)$
7   SOLVER.add(P_i)
8     $O \leftarrow O \cup O_i$
9     $(Q_i, O_i') \leftarrow$ GROUNDER.ground$(Q[i], O)$
10   SOLVER.add$(Q_i(\alpha_i) \cup \{\{\alpha_i\} \leftarrow\} \cup \{\leftarrow \alpha_{i-1}\})$
11     $\mathcal{X} \leftarrow$ SOLVER.solve$(\{\alpha_i\})$
12   **if** $\mathcal{X} \neq \emptyset$ **then return** $\{X \setminus \{\alpha_i\} \mid X \in \mathcal{X}\}$

---

ments GROUNDER may impose, the obtained ground programs are fed into SOLVER through function add. In Line 7, 10, and 11 of Algorithm 1, cumulative and volatile program slices are handled according to the sequences of programs and assumptions, respectively, specified in Definition 7. Note that isolve terminates as soon as function solve of SOLVER reports some answer set. Otherwise, if no answer set is found in any step $i \geq 1$, isolve (in theory) loops forever on increasing values for k.

For illustrating isolve, reconsider the example in (2). We give in Figure 1 the accumulation of ground rules within the solver during the formation of the answer set containing $\{\neg p(0), a(1), p(1), \neg a(2), p(2)\}$. The left column shows the value of i in Algorithm 1, the middle one groups the rules added in Line 2, 7, and 10 of Algorithm 1, and the right one gives the assumption, α_i, used in each iteration. The rules accumulated within the solver at the end of the first iteration yield no answer set under assumption α_1, while the addition of the rules obtained in the next step yields the above answer set under assumption α_2. Note that this answer set also includes α_2, while it does not contain α_1 due to integrity constraint $\leftarrow \alpha_1$.

i		Rules	L
0	B	$p(0) \leftarrow not\ \neg p(0)$	
		$\neg p(0) \leftarrow not\ p(0)$	
		$\leftarrow p(0), \neg p(0)$	
1	$P[1]$	$a(1) \leftarrow not\ \neg a(1)$	
		$\neg a(1) \leftarrow not\ a(1)$	
		$p(1) \leftarrow a(1)$	
		$p(1) \leftarrow p(0), not\ \neg p(1)$	
		$\neg p(1) \leftarrow \neg p(0), not\ p(1)$	
		$\leftarrow p(1), \neg p(1)$	
		$\leftarrow a(1), \neg a(1)$	
	$Q[1](\alpha_1)$	$\leftarrow not\ \neg p(0), \alpha_1$	α_1
		$\leftarrow not\ p(1), \alpha_1$	
		$\leftarrow not\ \neg a(1), \alpha_1$	
		$\{\alpha_1\} \leftarrow$	
		$\leftarrow \alpha_0$	
2	$P[2]$	$a(2) \leftarrow not\ \neg a(2)$	
		$\neg a(2) \leftarrow not\ a(2)$	
		$p(2) \leftarrow a(2)$	
		$p(2) \leftarrow p(1), not\ \neg p(2)$	
		$\neg p(2) \leftarrow \neg p(1), not\ p(2)$	
		$\leftarrow p(2), \neg p(2)$	
		$\leftarrow a(2), \neg a(2)$	
	$Q[2](\alpha_2)$	$\leftarrow not\ \neg p(0), \alpha_2$	α_2
		$\leftarrow not\ p(2), \alpha_2$	
		$\leftarrow not\ \neg a(2), \alpha_2$	
		$\{\alpha_2\} \leftarrow$	
		$\leftarrow \alpha_1$	

Fig. 1. Tracing Algorithm 1: isolve

If GROUNDER is adequate and if SOLVER is sound, for a separated modular domain description $(B, P[k], Q[k])$ such that $P(\mathbb{Q}_i)$ (cf. Definition 2) has an answer set for some $i \geq 1$, isolve returns the answer sets of $P(\mathbb{Q}_i)$ for the least such $i \geq 1$.

Theorem 5. *Let $(B, P[k], Q[k])$ be a separated modular domain description, let* GROUNDER *be an adequate grounder, and let* SOLVER *be a sound solver. Let $(P_i, O_i)_{i \geq 0}$ and $(Q_i, O'_i)_{i \geq 1}$ be as in Definition 4 for* ground $=$ GROUNDER.ground, *and let $(\mathbb{Q}_i)_{i \geq 1}$ as in Definition 2. If (P_0, O_0), (P_i, O_i), and (Q_i, O'_i) are defined for all $i \geq 1$, we have* isolve$((B, P[k], Q[k])) = AS(P(\mathbb{Q}_i))$ *for the least $i \geq 1$ such that $AS(P(\mathbb{Q}_i)) \neq \emptyset$.*

Note that the above result builds upon the assumption that $(B, P[k], Q[k])$ is modular. When feeding a non-modular domain description (that GROUNDER can instantiate) into isolve, interpretations computed by SOLVER.solve do not necessarily match the answer sets of the combined program slices.

We next provide simple syntactic conditions under which B, $P[k]$, and $Q[k]$ assemble a modular domain description.

Proposition 4. *Let $(B, P[k], Q[k])$ be a domain description, and let $\mathbf{P} = \bigcup_{i \geq 1} P[i]$ and $\mathbf{Q} = \bigcup_{i \geq 1} Q[i]$. Then, $(B, P[k], Q[k])$ is modular if the following conditions hold*:

1. $atom(grd(B)) \cap (head(grd(\mathbf{P})) \cup head(grd(\mathbf{Q}))) = \emptyset$,
2. $atom(grd(\mathbf{P})) \cap head(grd(\mathbf{Q})) = \emptyset$, *and*
3. $\{head(grd(P[i])) \mid i \geq 1\}$ *is a partition of* $head(grd(\mathbf{P}))$.

Pragmatically, these conditions can be granted by using predicates not occurring in $B \cup P[k]$ for the heads of rules in $Q[k]$, and by including 0 as parameter in every atom of B as well as parameter k in the head of every rule in $P[k]$. Of course, parameter 0 can also be omitted in atoms of B if the corresponding predicates are not used in the heads of rules in $P[k]$. Recalling the domain descriptions given in (2) and (3), one can observe that the respective programs B, $P[k]$, and $Q[k]$ fit into this scheme. In fact, many problems over time parameters are naturally stated via modular domain descriptions.

5   Experiments with the Incremental ASP System *iclingo*

We implemented our approach to incremental ASP solving within the system *iclingo* by building on grounder *gringo* (2.0.0) and solver *clasp* (1.1.0) (all available at [7]). As input, *gringo* accepts λ-restricted programs, inducing finite equivalent ground programs. Procedurally, *iclingo* uses *gringo* as delineated in Algorithm 1. The customization of *clasp* conceptually affects two components, namely, the treatment of a program's completion and loop formulas, respectively. Note that neither of these adaptations would be necessary in a SAT solver, since the underlying semantics does not rely on Clark's completion. Over time, *clasp* accumulates ground program slices and, moreover, learns further constraints during solving. As a matter of fact, *clasp* is equipped with dynamic deletion and simplification techniques disposing of superfluous constraints.

Our experiments consider *iclingo* in four settings: keeping over successive solving steps *(1)* learned constraints, *(2)* learned constraints and heuristic values, *(3)* heuristic values only, and *(4)* neither. We compare these variants with iterative deepening search using *clingo*, the direct combination of *gringo* and *clasp* via an internal interface, as well as *gringo* and *clasp* via a textual interface (using the output language of *lparse* [12]). Except for using different communication channels, *clingo* as well as piped *gringo* and *clasp* run identically, and *clingo* is consistently faster at a fraction of run-time.

The benchmarks in Table 1 belong to four different classes. In the Blocksworld example, the goal is to reconstruct a tower of n blocks in inverse order, requiring a plan of length n. In the Queens example, we compute (at most) one answer set for each value of k, iterating from 1 to n. For Sokoban and Towers of Hanoi, we use handmade instances from [15,16], each instance requiring n steps for achieving its goal condition. With both of these planning problems, the default encoding includes the initial state in a base program B and the goal condition in a query program $Q[k]$. We also provide alternative encodings (attributed by "back" in Table 1), in which B contains the goal and $Q[k]$ the initial state. Table 1 summarizes run-time results in seconds, taking the average of three runs per instance. The rows marked with Σ show the sums of run-times over all instances of a benchmark class, also distinguishing encodings, with timeouts taken as 1200s. The last row $(\Sigma\Sigma)$ sums run-times over all benchmark classes. All benchmarks as well as extended results are available at [7].

On the Blocksworld and Queens examples, we see that *iclingo* clearly outperforms *clingo* by one order of magnitude, which is primarily due to reduced grounding overhead. In fact, the simple Blocksworld problems are solved without any search, but *clingo* has to redo full grounding and propagation in each iterative deepening step, working on ground programs of considerable size. For example, considering the Blocksworld problem with four blocks, viz., $n = 4$, *gringo* produces 158 ground rules in the first step and 236 ground rules for each further step. While *iclingo* adds this number of rules in each incremental step, resulting in $158 + (n-1) * 236 = 866$ ground rules for $n = 4$, *clingo* processes $n * 158 + (n * (n-1)/2) * 236 = 2048$ ground rules before obtaining a solution. Of course, the ratio of ground rules processed by *iclingo* gets even smaller as n increases, explaining the dramatic performance gains on Blocksworld. On the Queens example, we observe a similar effect, but here, *clasp* has to search for a solution for $n \geq 4$. Interestingly, *iclingo (1)*, keeping learned constraints, has a clear edge, but *iclingo (2)*, additionally keeping heuristic values, is by far the slowest among all *iclingo* variants. However, *iclingo (3)*, keeping heuristic values, is again consistently faster than *iclingo (4)*, keeping neither heuristic values nor learned constraints. This suggests that the strategy of *iclingo (2)* here tends to bias future runs too much, while a moderate amount of memory via either learned constraints or heuristic values is helpful.

Other than the simple Blocksworld and combinatorial Queens examples, Sokoban and Towers of Hanoi contain more realistic instances, shifting the focus to search for a plan. In fact, all systems underlie non-deterministic heuristic effects and traverse the search space differently. Though all systems spend most of their run-time in the solving component, the savings in grounding are still noticeable for *iclingo*, but smaller than on Blocksworld and Queens. On Sokoban, we observe varying relative performance of the considered systems on individual instances, which is due to the elevated difficulty of the problem. However, on the instance requiring the most steps, viz., $n = 21$, we have that the learning variants, *iclingo (1)* and *iclingo (2)*, perform much better than the

Table 1. Benchmark results on a 2.2GHz PC under Linux; each run limited to 1200s time

Name	n	iclingo (1)	iclingo (2)	iclingo (3)	iclingo (4)	clingo	gringo	clasp
Blocksworld	20	2.61	2.61	2.62	2.62	37.09		42.41
	25	6.78	6.84	6.80	6.80	124.35		138.68
	30	15.68	15.80	15.71	15.81	330.15		362.39
	35	32.43	32.36	32.29	32.31	753.90		821.96
	40	60.99	60.75	60.71	61.04	-		-
	Σ	118.49	118.36	118.13	118.58	2445.49		2565.44
Queens	80	19.46	65.83	39.98	47.79	144.28		153.61
	90	36.72	135.19	70.81	81.70	249.13		264.21
	100	49.25	227.69	111.99	128.62	409.69		431.23
	110	64.05	424.03	176.16	201.67	636.91		669.75
	120	99.54	612.76	274.29	354.00	958.34		1003.67
	Σ	269.02	1465.50	673.23	813.78	2398.35		2522.47
Sokoban	16	243.22	287.46	320.07	334.08	376.74		384.41
	12	26.50	37.55	50.61	28.19	27.83		28.43
	16	124.26	124.44	320.97	341.94	189.48		194.12
	16	135.72	164.70	128.66	183.74	120.60		123.57
	18	140.80	145.07	233.71	275.12	236.60		242.19
	16	26.86	40.60	29.41	27.88	45.94		47.04
	17	1165.67	906.00	734.44	730.09	887.26		904.75
	14	119.95	140.11	106.40	213.22	96.26		98.10
	14	35.42	42.74	58.79	46.81	70.16		71.81
	21	286.46	200.43	600.19	777.68	278.97		285.09
	17	120.33	140.44	139.19	156.85	171.01		174.90
	14	39.09	36.21	36.00	47.48	66.12		67.43
	Σ	2464.28	2265.75	2758.44	3163.08	2566.97		2621.84
Sokoban back	16	-	-	-	-	-		-
	12	51.23	44.62	98.09	57.42	72.59		74.30
	16	264.81	201.48	265.21	359.38	296.45		302.46
	16	148.19	121.19	150.06	145.40	148.25		151.43
	18	723.07		-	-	1059.02		1081.34
	16	243.81	185.00	340.97	190.32	402.27		410.72
	17	599.74	714.40	1051.60	825.61	-		-
	14	149.37	126.04	164.98	191.33	170.36		173.74
	14	29.73	69.46	73.03	28.04	43.06		43.89
	21	346.56	428.43	400.81	295.69	402.78		411.70
	17	181.00	143.20	172.83	317.82	234.21		239.56
	14	15.06	58.45	39.27	17.50	59.63		60.78
	Σ	3952.57	4492.27	5156.85	4828.51	5288.62		5349.92
Towers	33	38.00	42.96	48.46	27.15	31.98		32.76
	34	61.40	36.78	47.09	45.95	61.77		63.39
	36	81.26	60.77	88.52	131.29	86.56		88.46
	39	223.46	155.76	184.63	204.13	216.89		222.74
	41	429.82	327.74	392.47	342.11	459.97		471.22
	Σ	833.94	624.01	761.17	750.63	857.17		878.57
Towers back	33	4.62	6.42	5.68	5.80	12.59		12.79
	34	55.79	33.42	56.27	42.39	52.80		54.00
	36	16.66	16.46	14.69	17.11	24.81		25.38
	39	27.88	25.43	28.60	32.83	46.01		46.85
	41	48.20	36.38	62.75	40.62	83.78		85.60
	Σ	153.15	118.11	167.99	138.75	219.99		224.62
	$\Sigma\Sigma$	7791.45	9084.00	9635.81	9813.33	13776.59		14162.86

remaining ones, *iclingo (3)* and *iclingo (4)*, which are also outperformed by *clingo*. The "back" encoding of Sokoban does not yield overall performance gains for any of the considered systems, but we observe that *iclingo (1)* copes best with this encoding. Note that both the initial and the goal states of Sokoban instances are total. Hence, with both encodings, *clasp* searches for a trajectory from one complete state to another. Finally, on Towers of Hanoi, the differences between the systems are rather small, and all of them show significant gains on the "back" encoding. In contrast to Sokoban, goal conditions do here not define total states. Thus, learning may further constrain the goal in B, while the total initial state in $Q[k]$ can easily be propagated. The differences between Sokoban and Towers of Hanoi regarding the impact of encodings show that incremental problems constitute a whole new setting, different from traditional ones, and further investigations are needed for optimizing computational strategies to deal with them.

6 Discussion

We presented the first theoretical and practical account of incremental ASP solving. Our framework allows for tackling bounded problems in ASP, paving the way for more ambitious real-world applications. Our approach is driven by the desire to minimize redundancies while gradually treating program slices. However, fixing the incremental solving process required the integration and adaption of successive grounding and solving steps in a globally consistent way. To this end, we developed an incremental module theory guiding the formal setting of iterative grounding and solving by means of existing ASP grounders and solvers. Module theory does not only provide us with a natural semantics for non-ground, parametrized program slices but moreover makes precise their composition by appeal to input/output interfaces. Such compositionality provides the primary basis for incremental computations. Our experimental results indicate the computational impact of our incremental approach on parametrized domain descriptions. While savings in grounding are evident, on different encodings of search-intensive problems, we have seen that the effectiveness of solving techniques in an incremental setting is (currently) less predictable. Indeed, incremental problems differ from traditional ones, so that dedicated computational strategies for them can be developed and explored. In this respect, our system *iclingo* makes merely a first step. Future work also includes more elaborate incremental algorithms than isolve, allowing for non-elementary program slices while still guaranteeing optimality of solutions.

References

1. Baral, C.: Knowledge Representation, Reasoning and Declarative Problem Solving. Cambridge University Press, Cambridge (2003)
2. Kautz, H., Selman, B.: Planning as satisfiability. In: Proc. of ECAI 1992, pp. 359–363. Wiley, Chichester (1992)
3. Clarke, E., Biere, A., Raimi, R., Zhu, Y.: Bounded model checking using satisfiability solving. Formal Methods in System Design 19(1), 7–34 (2001)
4. Giunchiglia, E., Lee, J., Lifschitz, V., McCain, N., Turner, H.: Nonmonotonic causal theories. Artificial Intelligence 153(1-2), 49–104 (2004)
5. Gelfond, M., Lifschitz, V.: Action languages. Electron. Trans. on AI 3(6), 193–210 (1998)
6. Gebser, M., Kaufmann, B., Neumann, A., Schaub, T.: Conflict-driven answer set solving. In: Proc. of IJCAI 2007. AAAI Press, Menlo Park (2007)
7. http://www.cs.uni-potsdam.de/wv/software
8. Oikarinen, E., Janhunen, T.: Modular equivalence for normal logic programs. In: Proc. of ECAI 2006, pp. 412–416. IOS Press, Amsterdam (2006)
9. Lifschitz, V., Turner, H.: Splitting a logic program. In: Proc. of ICLP, pp. 23–37. MIT Press, Cambridge (1994)
10. Brass, S., Dix, J.: Semantics of (disjunctive) logic programs based on partial evaluation. Journal of Logic Programming 40(1), 1–46 (1999)

11. Eiter, T., Fink, M., Tompits, H., Woltran, S.: Simplifying logic programs under uniform and strong equivalence. In: Lifschitz, V., Niemelä, I. (eds.) LPNMR 2004. LNCS, vol. 2923, pp. 87–99. Springer, Heidelberg (2003)
12. http://www.tcs.hut.fi/Software
13. Lin, F., Zhao, Y.: ASSAT: computing answer sets of a logic program by SAT solvers. Artificial Intelligence 157(1-2), 115–137 (2004)
14. Eén, N., Sörensson, N.: Temporal induction by incremental SAT solving. Electronic Notes in Theoretical Computer Science 89(4) (2003)
15. http://www.ne.jp/asahi/ai/yoshio/sokoban/handmade/
16. http://asparagus.cs.uni-potsdam.de/

Concurrent and Local Evaluation of Normal Programs

Rui Marques[1] and Terrance Swift[2]

[1] CITI, Dep. Informática — FCT, Universidade Nova de Lisboa
[2] CENTRIA — Universidade Nova de Lisboa

Abstract. Tabled evaluations can incorporate a number of features, including tabled negation, reduction with respect to the well-founded model, tabled constraints and answer subsumption. Many of these features are most efficiently evaluated using the Local evaluation strategy, which fully evaluates each mutually dependent set of tabled subgoals before returning answers to other subgoals outside of that set. In this paper, we introduce a formalism, Concurrent Local SLG by which multiple threads of computation concurrently perform Local evaluation of the well-founded semantics, and which is a framework for multi-threaded tabling in the XSB system. We prove several properties of Local evaluation within single-threaded tabled computation. We then extend SLG to a model of concurrency and show that the completeness and complexity of SLG are retained when computed by multiple threads. Finally, we extend Local evaluation to concurrent SLG, and show that the properties of Local evaluation continue to hold under concurrency.

This paper provides an operational semantics for a type of concurrent TLP that relies on a scheduling strategy called Local evaluation [4]. The model of concurrency adopted is one in which threads of computation execute separate subgoals while sharing completed tables. The main idea behind Local evaluation is that it fully evaluates a single mutually dependent set of tabled subgoals before performing operations (such as returning answers) to subgoals outside of that set. Experiments in several implementations have shown that Local evaluation utilizes space efficiently (see e.g. [4,10]) and as a result it has been implemented for several Prologs.

Another feature of Local evaluation is shown in an example in [4] in which tabling was used to compute the shortest path between two nodes. When Local evaluation was used the shortest path could be computed in a time proportional to the number of nodes in the graph, while if a non-Local scheduling strategy was used the time was proportional to the number of *paths* in the graph – i.e. the time was exponential in the number of nodes. Comparing path lengths to compute a shortest path can be considered as an instance of *answer subsumption* in which answers are retained and propagated only if they are maximal over a partial order or are a monotonic function of answers so far produced.

Using SLG resolution [1] as a basis, this paper presents the following results about concurrent and Local evaluations.

M. Garcia de la Banda and E. Pontelli (Eds.): ICLP 2008, LNCS 5366, pp. 206–222, 2008.
© Springer-Verlag Berlin Heidelberg 2008

- As analysis of Local evaluation in the literature has been mostly empirical, Local SLG evaluation is formally defined in Section 2 and shown complete for queries to normal programs. Properties are derived about dependencies between subgoals in a Local evaluation, about the return of answers, and about the extent of non-completed subgoals in an evaluation.
- Section 3 presents SLG_C, an extension of SLG to concurrent evaluations in which completed tables are shared among threads. SLG_C is complete for queries to normal programs, and its abstract complexity is the same as SLG.
- Concurrent *Local* SLG (Local SLG_C) is then defined in Section 3.1. It is shown that properties of Local SLG evaluations extend to the sub-evaluations performed by each concurrently executing thread, and a property is derived about the structure of dependencies between threads.
- Section 4 sketches the implementation of Local SLG_C in XSB, where the engine design is directly motivated by the preceding results for subgoal and thread dependencies. In addition to having the properties of finite evaluations presented in this paper, XSB's implementation of Local SLG_C has been extended to support tabled constraints, answer subsumption, tabled dynamic code, and space reclamation.

We begin with a review of SLG evaluation.

1   SLG Evaluation

This presentation of SLG reformulates the operations of [1] using the model of a forest of trees. However, for reasons of space we make the following restrictions throughout this paper. First, the formal definitions in this paper consider only finite evaluations, although the statements of theorems that are true for transfinite evaluations are not restricted. Second, our definition of Completely Evaluated (Definition 4) does not permit Early Completion. And third, we do not formally define the concept of a supported answer. All of this formalism can be found in the full version of this paper, available at http://www.cs.sunysb.edu/~tswift/papers.html.

Terminology and assumptions. We assume the standard terminology of logic programming and an understanding of the well-founded semantics (see [12]). All programs discussed are normal, and defined over a countable language of predicates and function symbols. If L is a literal, the *underlying subgoal* of L is L if L is positive and S if $L = not\ S$. A *3-valued interpretation* I of a program P is a set of literals defined over the Herbrand base of P, H_P. For $A \in H_P$, if $A \in I$, A is true in I, and if $not\ A \in I$, A is false in I; otherwise A and $not\ A$ are undefined in I. When I is an interpretation and A is an atom, $I|_A$ refers to

$$\{L \mid L \in I \text{ and } (L{=}G \text{ or } L = not\ G) \text{ and } G \text{ is in the ground instantiation of } A\}$$

The well-founded model of a program P is denoted as $WFM(P)$. In the following sections, we use the terms *goal*, *subgoal*, and *atom* interchangeably. Variant terms are considered to be identical.

The nodes in SLG trees are built from atoms and default literals along with a special type of literal called a *delay* literal.

Definition 1 (Delay Literals). *A negative delay literal has the form not A, where A is a ground atom. A positive delay literal has the form A_{Ans}^{Subg}, where A is an atom whose truth value is based on that of some answer Ans for the subgoal Sub. If θ is a substitution, then $(A_{Ans}^{Subg})\theta = (A\theta)_{Ans}^{Subg}$.*

The annotations in positive delay literals are used to propagate truth values when a given answer to a given subgoal becomes unconditionally true or false.

Definition 2 (*SLG* Trees and Forest). *An SLG forest consists of a set of SLG trees. Nodes of SLG trees have the form:*

$$Answer\_Template :\text{-} DelaySet|GoalList$$

or simply fail. *In the first form, the Answer_Template is an atom, DelaySet is a set of delay literals and GoalList is a sequence of literals. The second form is called a* failure node.

An SLG tree T *is associated with a (possibly empty) marking sequence, which is a sequence of terms possibly preceded by the distinguished term* complete. *The first element of the marking sequence for* T *is denoted as* marking(T). *For a term t,* setMark(T, t) *prepends t to the marking sequence of* T.

A node N is an answer *when it is a leaf node for which* GoalList *is empty. If the DelaySet of an answer is empty it is termed an* unconditional answer, *otherwise, it is a* conditional answer.

The root node of a given SLG tree has the form $S :\text{-} |S$ where S is a subgoal — a property ensured by Definition 6. Thus, within a forest each tree and subgoal are uniquely associated, so when T is an SLG tree in a forest $\mathcal{F}$ whose root node is $S :\text{-} |S$ it is sometimes convenient to use the terminology S *is the root node for* T; T *is the tree for* S; and S *is in* $\mathcal{F}$. If $marking(T) = complete$, we refer to both S and T as *completed*. Until Section 3, marking sequences will either be empty or will contain only the term *complete*. Literals in a *GoalList* are resolved by an arbitrary but fixed literal selection strategy. For simplicity, throughout this paper literals are always selected in a left-to-right order.

SLG operations transform one forest of trees into another. One of the operations, ANSWER RETURN is based on answer resolution, which is extended to take account of delay literals.

Definition 3 (Answer Resolution). *Let N be a node $A :\text{-} D|L_1, ..., L_n$, where $n > 0$, and $Ans = A' :\text{-} D'|$ an answer whose variables have been standardized apart from N. N is SLG resolvable with Ans if $\exists i, 1 \leq i \leq n$, such that L_i and A' are unifiable with an mgu θ. The SLG resolvent of N and Ans on L_i is:*

$$(A :\text{-} D|L_1, ..., L_{i-1}, L_{i+1}, ..., L_n)\theta$$

if D' is empty; otherwise the resolvent has the form:

$$(A :\text{-} D, L_{iA'}^{L_i}|L_1, ..., L_{i-1}, L_{i+1}, ..., L_n)\theta$$

The SLG COMPLETION operation marks a set of trees as *complete* when they can produce no more useful answers – a condition captured as follows.

Definition 4 (Completely Evaluated). *A set S of subgoals in a forest $\mathcal{F}$ is completely evaluated if no $S \in S$ is completed; and if for each $S \in S$, for each node N in the tree for S:*

1. *The underlying subgoal of the selected literal of N is completed; or*
2. *There are no applicable* NEW SUBGOAL, PROGRAM CLAUSE RESOLUTION, ANSWER RETURN, NEGATION RETURN *or* DELAYING *operations (Definition 6) for N.*

In order to prevent S from being repeatedly completed, the preceding definition explicitly prohibits S from containing any completed subgoals.

SLG forests are related to interpretations in the following manner.

Definition 5. *Let $\mathcal{F}$ be a forest. The interpretation induced by $\mathcal{F}$, $I_\mathcal{F}$, is the smallest set such that:*

- *A (ground) atom $A \in I_\mathcal{F}$ iff A is in the ground instantiation of some unconditional answer Ans :- $\mid$ in $\mathcal{F}$.*
- *A (ground) literal not $A \in I_\mathcal{F}$ iff A is in the ground instantiation of a completely evaluated subgoal in $\mathcal{F}$, and A is not in the ground instantiation of any answer in $\mathcal{F}$.*

An atom S is successful *in $\mathcal{F}$ if some tree in $\mathcal{F}$ has an unconditional answer S. S is* failed *in $\mathcal{F}$ if S is completed and the tree for S contains no answers. An atom S is* successful *(failed) in $I_\mathcal{F}$ if S' (not S') is in $I_\mathcal{F}$ for every S' in the ground instantiation of S. A negative delay literal not D is successful (failed) in a forest $\mathcal{F}$ if D is failed (successful) in $\mathcal{F}$. Similarly, a positive delay literal D_{Ans}^{Subg} is successful in $\mathcal{F}$ if Subg has an unconditional answer Ans :- $\mid$ and failed if Subg has no answer with head Ans.*

Given these concepts, the SLG operations themselves can be stated.

Definition 6 (SLG Operations). *Given a forest $\mathcal{F}_n$ of a SLG evaluation of program P, $\mathcal{F}_{n+1}$ may be produced by one of the following operations.*

1. NEW SUBGOAL: *Let $\mathcal{F}_n$ contain a non-root node*
$$N = Ans \text{ :- } DelaySet \mid G, GoalList$$
   where G is the selected literal S or not S. Assume $\mathcal{F}_n$ contains no tree with root subgoal S. Then add the tree S :- $\mid S$ to $\mathcal{F}_n$.
2. PROGRAM CLAUSE RESOLUTION: *Let $\mathcal{F}_n$ contain a root node $N = S$:- $\mid S$ and C be a program clause Head :- Body such that Head unifies with S with mgu θ. Assume that in $\mathcal{F}_n$, N does not have a child $N_{child} = (S$:- $\mid Body)\theta$. Then add N_{child} as a child of N.*

3. ANSWER RETURN: *Let $\mathcal{F}_n$ contain a non-root node*
$$N = Ans \text{ :- } DelaySet|S, GoalList$$

whose selected literal S is positive. Let Ans be an answer node for S in $\mathcal{F}_n$ and N_{child} be the SLG resolvent of N and Ans on S. Assume that in $\mathcal{F}_n$, N does not have a child N_{child}. Then add N_{child} as a child of N.

4. NEGATION RETURN: *Let $\mathcal{F}_n$ contain a leaf node*
$$N = Ans \text{ :- } DelaySet|not\ S, GoalList.$$

whose selected literal not S is ground.
   (a) NEGATION SUCCESS: *If S is failed in $\mathcal{F}_n$, then create a child for N of the form: Ans :- DelaySet|GoalList.*
   (b) NEGATION FAILURE: *If S succeeds in $\mathcal{F}_n$, then create a child for N of the form* fail.

5. DELAYING: *Let $\mathcal{F}_n$ contain a leaf node $N = Ans \text{ :- } DelaySet|not\ S, GoalList$, such that the selected literal npt S is ground, S is in $\mathcal{F}_n$, but S is neither successful nor failed in $\mathcal{F}_n$. Then create a child for N of the form Ans :- DelaySet, not $S|GoalList$.*

6. SIMPLIFICATION: *Let $\mathcal{F}_n$ contain a leaf node $N = Ans \text{ :- } DelaySet|$, and let $L \in DelaySet$*
   (a) *If L is failed in $\mathcal{F}$ then create a child* fail *for N.*
   (b) *If L is successful in $\mathcal{F}$, then create a child Ans :- DelaySet'| for N, where $DelaySet' = DelaySet - L$.*

7. COMPLETION: *Given a completely evaluated set $\mathcal{S}$ of subgoals (Definition 4), for each $S \in \mathcal{S}$, setMark$(T, complete)$, where T is the tree for S.*

8. ANSWER COMPLETION: *Given a set of unsupported answers $\mathcal{UA}$, create a failure node as a child for each answer Ans $\in \mathcal{UA}$.*

In the above definition, the ANSWER COMPLETION operation relies on the concept of *unsupported answers*. Unsupported answers are conditional answers that are false in the well-founded model, and reflect certain unfounded sets in that model. While necessary for completeness of SLG, the ANSWER COMPLETION operation is not affected by local or concurrent evaluations, so for reasons of space, we omit its formal definition (see the full version of this paper).

SLG Evaluations. An SLG evaluation consists of a (possibly transfinite) sequence of forests. However as noted, we restrict definitions of evaluations to be finite for reasons of space (see the full version of this paper for the general case).

Definition 7 (SLG Evaluation). *Given a program P and goal G, an SLG evaluation $\mathcal{E}$ is a sequence of SLG forests $\mathcal{F}_0, \mathcal{F}_1, \ldots, \mathcal{F}_\beta$, such that:*

- *$\mathcal{F}_0$ is the forest containing a single tree G :- $|$ G*
- *For each successor ordinal, $n + 1 \leq \beta$, $\mathcal{F}_{n+1}$ is obtained from $\mathcal{F}_n$ by an application of an SLG operation from Definition 6.*

If no operation is applicable to $\mathcal{F}_\beta$, $\mathcal{F}_\beta$ is called a final forest *of $\mathcal{E}$. If $\mathcal{F}_\beta$ contains a leaf node with a non-ground selected negative literal, it is* floundered.

The correctness is formulated as follows for transfinite evaluations.

Theorem 1 ([1]). *Let $\mathcal{E}$ be an SLG evaluation of a goal to a program P. Then $\mathcal{E}$ has a final forest $\mathcal{F}$. Let A be an atom such that A :- $|A$ is the root of some tree in $\mathcal{F}$. Then if $\mathcal{F}$ is non-floundered, $WFM(P)|_A = I_{\mathcal{F}}|_A$.*

2   Local SLG Evaluations

As noted above, a Local SLG evaluation fully evaluates each mutually dependent set of tabled subgoals before performing operations to subgoals outside of that set. We begin to formalize that notion by defining what it means for one subgoal to depend on another.

Definition 8 (Subgoal Dependency Graph). *Let $\mathcal{F}$ be a forest, and let S_1 :- $|S_1$ be the root of a non-completed tree in $\mathcal{F}$. The subgoal S_1 directly depends on a subgoal S_2 iff S_2 is not completed in $\mathcal{F}$, and there is some node N in the tree for S_1 such that S_2 is the underlying subgoal of the selected literal of N.*
*   The Subgoal Dependency Graph of $\mathcal{F}$, SDG$(\mathcal{F})$ = (V,E), is a directed graph in which $(S_i, S_j) \in E$ iff subgoal S_i directly depends on subgoal S_j, and V is the underlying set of E. S_1 "depends on" S_2 in $\mathcal{F}$ is there is a path from S_1 to S_2 in $SDG(\mathcal{F})$.*

Since the SDG of a forest is a directed graph, it can be partitioned into disjoint sets of strongly connected components, or SCCs, where a node with no outgoing edges is considered to be in a *trivial* SCC. We refer to a given SCC by the set of its vertices (subgoals), and distinguish *independent* SCCs.

Definition 9 (Independent SCC). *A strongly connected component $\mathcal{S}$ is independent if $\forall S \in \mathcal{S}$: if S depends on some S', then $S' \in \mathcal{S}$.*

By Definition 9 it is straightforward that a trivial SCC is independent, and that each independent component is *maximal* — i.e. contained in no larger SCC. Local evaluation, then, performs operations on independent SCCs. Formally:

Definition 10 (Local SLG Evaluation). *Given a program P and goal G, a Local SLG evaluation $\mathcal{E}$ is a sequence of SLG forests $\mathcal{F}_0, \mathcal{F}_1, \ldots, \mathcal{F}_\beta$, such that:*

1. *$\mathcal{F}_0$ is the forest containing a single tree G :- $\mid G$*
2. *For each successor ordinal, $n + 1 \leq \beta$, $\mathcal{F}_{n+1}$ is obtained from $\mathcal{F}_n$ by an application of an SLG operation from Definition 6 such that:*
   (a) if a NEW SUBGOAL operation is applied to create a tree S :- $|S$ then S is the underlying subgoal of a selected literal in a tree whose root subgoal is in an independent SCC of SDG$(\mathcal{F}_n)$;
   (b) a PROGRAM CLAUSE RESOLUTION, ANSWER RETURN, NEGATION RETURN or DELAYING operation is only applied to a node on a tree whose root subgoal is in an independent SCC of SDG$(\mathcal{F}_n)$;

$\mathcal{E}$ is delay avoiding if no DELAYING operation is performed in a forest if any other operation is applicable.

In the transfinite extension of Definition 10, a Local (SLG) evaluation works as an unrestricted SLG evaluation whenever an independent SCC does not exist in a forest, leading to the following theorem.

Theorem 2 (Completeness of Local Evaluation). *Let P be a program and G a goal. Then there exists an SLG evaluation $\mathcal{E}$ of G against P with final forest $\mathcal{F}$ if and only if there exists a local SLG evaluation $\mathcal{E}^L$ of G against P with final forest $\mathcal{F}^L$ such that $I_\mathcal{F}|_G = I_{\mathcal{F}^L}|_G$.*

While Local evaluation is ideally complete for the well-founded semantics, its importance arises from its efficiency for certain classes of programs, along with properties that can be used to ensure the correctness of implementations. The first such property is:

Theorem 3. *Let $\mathcal{E}^L$ be a finite Local SLG evaluation. For each $\mathcal{F}$ in $\mathcal{E}^L$ $SDG(\mathcal{F})$ has one and only one independent SCC.*

Theorem 3 implies the following corollary which will be used by the implementation described in Section 4.

Corollary 1. *Let $\mathcal{E}^L$ be a finite Local SLG evaluation. For each $\mathcal{F}$ in $\mathcal{E}^L$ there is at most one incoming edge for each maximal SCC in $SDG(\mathcal{F})$.*

The following corollary captures the notion that in a Local evaluation, a subgoal may only return answers out of its SCC once its SCC has been completed.

Corollary 2. *In any forest $\mathcal{F}$ of a Local SLG evaluation, if an answer A is used in an* ANSWER RETURN *operation to a node in a tree with root subgoal S, then the tree for A has been completed, or is in the same SCC as S in $SDG(\mathcal{F})$.*

Corollary 2 has practical importance for answer subsumption since it implies that no answer A need be returned out of an SCC if the model entails an answer that is preferred to A – only the preferred answer need be returned. In addition, it is easy to see that if Local evaluation were extended to ensure that all appropriate SIMPLIFICATION and ANSWER COMPLETION operations are performed for an independent SCC just after it has been completed, the following statement also holds. If a forest in Local evaluation contains a conditional answer $A = S \text{ :- } D|$ and S is successful or failed in $\mathcal{F}$, A will never be propagated outside of the SCC. This strategy reduces the overall number of SIMPLIFICATION and ANSWER COMPLETION operations and has been adopted by the XSB engine when computing non-stratified programs. The space efficiency of Local evaluation is stated as follows:

Theorem 4. *Let $\mathcal{E}^L$ be a finite delay-avoiding Local evaluation of a goal G to a program P, and let $\mathcal{E}$ be an SLG evaluation of G to a P. Then for any forest $\mathcal{F}^L$ in $\mathcal{E}^L$, there exists a forest $\mathcal{F}$ in $\mathcal{E}$ such that $SDG(\mathcal{F}^L)$ is a subgraph of $SDG(\mathcal{F})$.*

3   Sharing Completed Tables in a Concurrent Evaluation

Rather than starting with a single top-level atomic query, a concurrent SLG, SLG_C, evaluation is initialized with a set of atomic queries, such that each atomic query is evaluated by a different thread of computation. In this model of concurrency, threads share only *completed* tables so that a thread is prevented from consuming answers from a (non-completed) table owned by another thread. This disallows consume-producer models of concurrency and implies that different threads may not collaborate to evaluate subgoals within a single SCC. However as discussed below, within a Local evaluation the restriction may not be binding since Local evaluations prevent consumer-producer models by their nature, and since the scope of an SCC in a Local evaluation is relatively small.

Formally, this model of concurrency marks every non-completed tree in a given forest with a *thread identifier* (cf. Definition 2). As terminology, if N is a node in a tree T, $marking(N)$ denotes $marking(T)$, and if S is a subgoal $marking(S)$ denotes $marking(T)$, where T is the tree for S.

Definition 11 (Thread). *A thread identifier is an element of a set of terms that does not include the term* complete. *Given an SLG forest $\mathcal{F}$ in an evaluation $\mathcal{E}$, a thread state is the maximal set $\mathcal{T}$ of trees in $\mathcal{F}$ such that for all $T \in \mathcal{T}$ $marking(T) = t$ where t is a thread identifier. A thread in $\mathcal{E}$ is the sequence of thread states for a given marking. A thread is* active *in $\mathcal{F}$ if its thread state in $\mathcal{F}$ is non-empty.*

Let S be a subgoal, T the tree for S, and N a node in a forest. N is thread compatible *with S if $marking(T) =$ complete *or $marking(T) = marking(N)$.*

SLG_C uses SLG forests and other notions from Definitions 1-5, but differs in that certain SLG_C operations may create or change thread markings, and markings may restrict the applicability of operations based on whether a node and subgoal are thread compatible according to the previous definition. Definition 12 presents a new operation called USURPATION, along with those operations that differ from Definition 6 where the difference in each altered operation is underlined.

Definition 12 (SLG_C Operations). *Given an SLG forest $\mathcal{F}_n$, $\mathcal{F}_{n+1}$ may be produced by one of the following operations.*

1. NEW SUBGOAL: *Let $\mathcal{F}_n$ contain a non-root node*
$$N = Ans \text{ :- } DelaySet | G, GoalList$$

   where G is the selected literal S or not S. Assume $\mathcal{F}_n$ contains no tree with root subgoal S. Then add the tree $T = S \text{ :- } | S$ to $\mathcal{F}_n$, and $\underline{setMark(T, marking(N))}$.

2. <u>ANSWER RETURN</u>: *Let $\mathcal{F}_n$ contain a non-root node*
$$N = Ans \text{ :- } DelaySet | S, GoalList$$

   whose selected literal S is positive. Let Ans be an answer node for S in $\mathcal{F}_n$ <u>such that N is thread compatible with S</u> and let N_{child} be the SLG resolvent of N and Ans on S. Assume that in $\mathcal{F}_n$, N does not have a child N_{child}. Then add N_{child} as a child of N.

3. NEGATION RETURN: *Let $\mathcal{F}_n$ contain a leaf node*
$$N = Ans :\text{-} DelaySet|not\ S, GoalList.$$

whose selected literal not S is ground where N is thread compatible with S.
  (a) NEGATION SUCCESS: *If S is failed in $\mathcal{F}_n$, then create a child for N of the form: Ans :- DelaySet|GoalList.*
  (b) NEGATION FAILURE: *If S succeeds in $\mathcal{F}_n$, then create a child for N of the form* fail.
4. COMPLETION: *Given a completely evaluated set $\mathcal{S}$ of subgoals such that for all $S \in \mathcal{S}, marking(S) = t$, then for each $S \in \mathcal{S}, setMark (T, complete)$, where T is the tree for S.*
5. USURPATION: *Let $\mathcal{S}$ be a set of subgoals in deadlock (Definition 13), $S_U \in \mathcal{S}$, and T_U the tree for S_U. For each $S \in \mathcal{S}, setMark(T, marking(T_U))$.*

The thread compatibility restrictions can mean that an SLG operation is applicable in a given forest, but that the corresponding SLG_C operation is not. The USURPATION operation is designed to address cases where SLG_C operations might get stuck – which are formalized as situations of deadlock.

Definition 13 (Deadlock). *A set $\mathcal{S}$ of subgoals in a forest $\mathcal{F}$ is in* deadlock *if:*

1. *For each $S \in \mathcal{S}$ there are no applicable* NEW SUBGOAL, PROGRAM CLAUSE RESOLUTION, ANSWER RETURN, NEGATION RETURN *or* DELAYING *operations of Definition 12; and*
2. *There exists no $\mathcal{S}'$ such that $\mathcal{S} \subseteq \mathcal{S}'$ and $\mathcal{S}'$ is completely evaluated in $\mathcal{F}$.*

Example 1. As defined, SLG_C evaluations may use any scheduling strategy, and are not restricted to Local evaluations. They also begin with a *set* of goals rather than with a single goal. Figure 1 illustrates a simple, non-Local, SLG_C evaluation of the goal $\{a(X), b(X)\}$ to the program P_2, where a(X) is initially marked with thread identifier 1 and b(X) with thread identifier 2. Through NEW SUBGOAL operations, trees for c(X) and e(X) are created and associated with thread identifier 1, while d(X) is created and associated with thread identifier 2. Evaluation continues until there is a deadlock, as shown in Figure 1b. Note in Figure 1b, that while there is an answer that could be returned to the node e(1):- |d(X) in a non-Local evaluation, the node is associated with thread identifier 1, while the answer is associated with thread identifier 2 so that the return is prohibited by the thread compatibility restrictions. USURPATION is the only operation applicable to this forest; assume that thread identifier 1 performs the USURPATION, marking trees for c(X), d(X), and e(X) with identifier 1. Afterward, an answer for e(1) is derived, leading to Figure 1c. Further ANSWER RETURN operations lead to Figure 1d.'v All of the subgals in thread identifier 1 have been completely evaluated, but the subgoal b(X) in thread identifier 2 cannot be completely evaluated until the answer for d(X) is resolved with the node b(X):- |d(X). Since a completed subgoal is thread compatible with any thread, once d(X) is completed, the answer for d(X) can be resolved.

```
a(X):- c(X).  b(X):- d(X).  c(X):- e(1),d(X).  d(X):- c(X).
                                                d(1).

e(1):- d(X)
```

(a) The Program P_2

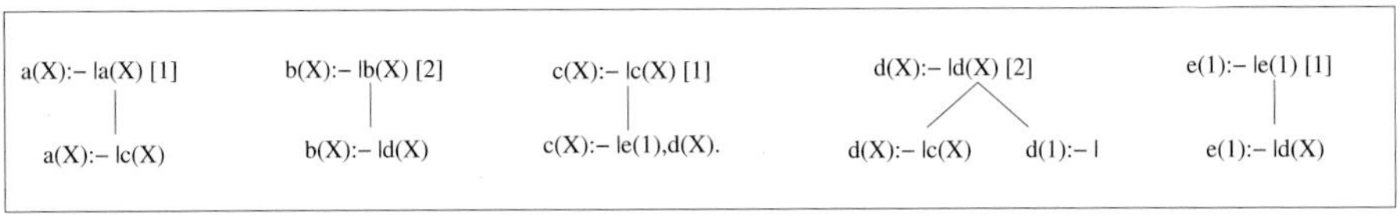

(b) State α: Deadlock

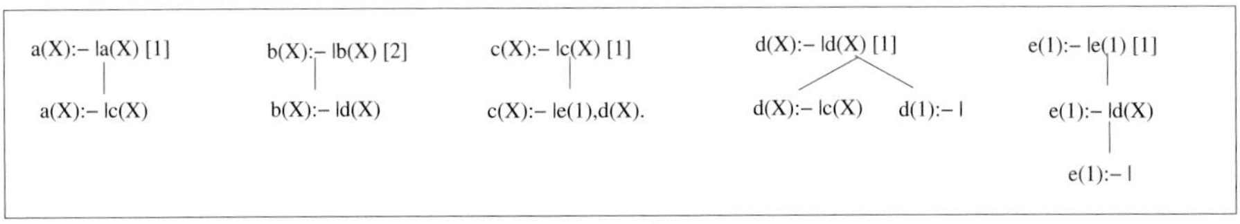

(c) State β: Answer for e(1)

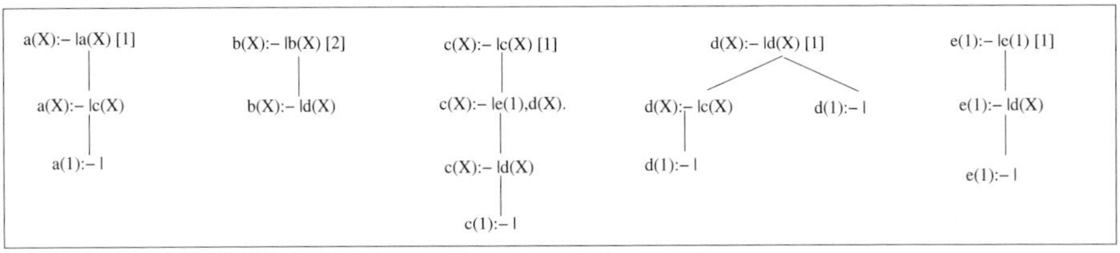

(d) State γ: Complete Evaluation for Thread Identifier 1

Fig. 1. A non-Local SLG_C Evaluation of P_2

The definition of a SLG_C evaluation is nearly the same as for SLG (Definition 7), but is initialized so that each atomic query in the set of goals it is presented with is marked with a different thread identifier (Its formal, transfinite, definition can be found in the full version of this paper). In addition, SLG_C forests are based on Definition 2, so the definition of an interpretation induced by a forest is identical in both frameworks, leading to the following theorem.

Theorem 5 (Correctness of SLG_C). *Let P be a program and $\mathcal{G}$ a finite non-empty set of goals. Then a SLG_C evaluation of $\mathcal{G}$ against P exists with final state $\widehat{\mathcal{F}}$, iff for every $G_i \in \mathcal{G}$ there exists an SLG evaluation of G_i against P with final state $\mathcal{F}^i$ and $I_{\widehat{\mathcal{F}}} = (\bigcup I_{\mathcal{F}^i})$.*

The completeness portion of the theorem follows from a demonstration that for any SLG operation on a forest, an equivalent SLG_C operation is applicable after zero or more USURPATION operations. The following theorem bounds the number of USURPATION operations in a finite evaluation, which implies that the abstract complexity of SLG_C is the same as that of SLG.

Theorem 6 (Complexity of USURPATION**).** *Let $\mathcal{E}$ be a finite SLG_C evaluation with final forest $\mathcal{F}$, and $S_\mathcal{F}$ the set of all subgoals in $\mathcal{F}$. Then there are at most $|S_\mathcal{F}|$ USURPATION operations performed.*

3.1   Concurrent Local Evaluations

In SLG_C the Subgoal Dependency Graph (Definition 8) can be partitioned into disjoint sub-graphs for each thread state of a forest.

Definition 14 (Thread Subgoal Dependency Graph). *For each thread state t in a forest $\mathcal{F}$, the* Thread Subgoal Dependency Graph *of t ($Thread\_SDG(\mathcal{F}, t)$) consists of the sub-graph of $SDG(\mathcal{F})$ determined by subgoals in $\mathcal{F}$ whose marking is t.*

Local SLG_C evaluation is based on independent SCCs within Thread SDGs, rather than within a global SDG.

Definition 15 (Local SLG_C). *Given a program P, a set $\mathcal{T}$ of thread identifiers, and a finite non-empty set G of goals, a Local SLG_C evaluation $\mathcal{E}$ is a sequence of forests $\mathcal{F}_0, \mathcal{F}_1, \ldots, \mathcal{F}_\beta$, such that:*

1. *$\mathcal{F}_0$ is a set-minimal forest containing the trees $T_i = G_i :- |G_i$, for each $G_i \in \mathcal{G}$, where for each T_i there is a $t_i \in \mathcal{T}$ such that $marking(T_i) = t_i$, and $t_i \neq t_j$ if $i \neq j$.*
2. *For each successor ordinal, $n + 1 \leq \beta$, $\mathcal{F}_{n+1}$ is obtained from $\mathcal{F}_n$ by an application of an operation from Definition 12 such that:*
   (a) *if a NEW SUBGOAL is applied to create a tree $T = S :- |S$ then S is the underlying subgoal of a selected literal in a tree whose root subgoal is in an independent SCC of $Thread\_SDG(\mathcal{F}_n, marking(T))$;*
   (b) *a PROGRAM CLAUSE RESOLUTION, ANSWER RETURN, NEGATION RETURN or DELAYING operation is only applied to a node on a tree whose root subgoal is in an independent SCC of $Thread\_SDG(\mathcal{F}_n, marking(T))$.*

This finitary definition can be extended to the transfinite evaluations, leading to the following theorem.

Theorem 7 (Correctness of Local SLG_C). *Let P be a program and $\mathcal{G}$ a finite non-empty set of goals. Then a Local SLG_C evaluation of $\mathcal{G}$ against P exists with final state $\widehat{\mathcal{F}}$, iff every $G_i \in \mathcal{G}$ there exists an SLG evaluation of G_i against P with final state $\mathcal{F}^i$ and $I_{\widehat{\mathcal{F}}} = (\bigcup I_{\mathcal{F}^i})$.*

The following theorem is an analogue of Theorem 3, and implies that each thread of an Local SLG_C evaluation has the dependency properties of Section 2.

Theorem 8. *Let $\mathcal{F}$ be a forest in a finite Local SLG_C evaluation. Then for each active thread t in $\mathcal{F}$, $Thread\_SDG(\mathcal{F}, t)$ has one and only one independent SCC.*

The Thread Dependency Graph can be seen as a homomorphism of the SDG of a given SLG_C forest.

Definition 16 (Thread Dependency Graph). *Let t_1 and t_2 be two active threads in a SLG forest $\mathcal{F}$. t_1 directly depends on t_2 if there exist a subgoal in t_1 that directly depends on a subgoal in t_2 (according to Definition 8). The Thread Dependency Graph $TDG(\mathcal{F}) = (V,E)$ of $\mathcal{F}$ is a directed graph where V is the set of active threads in $\mathcal{F}$ and $(t_i, t_j) \in E$ iff t_i directly depends on t_j.*

Based on the thread dependency graph, the following theorem shows that any thread depends on at most one other thread.

Theorem 9. *Let $\mathcal{F}$ be a forest in a finite Local SLG_C evaluation. Then for each node in $TDG(\mathcal{F})$ there is at most one outgoing edge.*

As a practical matter, this theorem indicates that each thread of computation will wait on the results from at most one other thread. so that the thread communication and dependency detection required to implement the USURPATION operation will be relatively simple.

4   Implementing SLG_C in the SLG-WAM

We summarize the changes made to XSB's SLG-WAM in order to implement Local SLG_C. Our discussion omits numerous optimizations required for efficiency. In particular, due to space restrictions we do not discuss the propagation of subgoal dependencies between threads, or the handling of subgoals that have been usurped multiple times (see [8] for details). We first describe Local SLG_C for definite programs before considering negation.

Since XSB's SLG-WAM implements Local evaluation, it is evident from Section 3 that the main addition is the USURPATION operation, which mainly affects the SLG-WAM tabletry instruction. This instruction occurs at the entry point of a tabled predicate when a tabled subgoal *Subg* is called.

In the sequential SLG-WAM tabletry is essentially responsible for determining whether a NEW SUBGOAL operation is required. The instruction first determines whether *Subg* is in the table using its representation in the WAM argument registers. If *Subg* is not in the table, a NEW SUBGOAL operation is effectively performed. *Subg* will have been copied to the table during the check; and a *generator* choice point is created to backtrack through program clauses, to check whether the subgoal's SCC has been fully evaluated, and to schedule ANSWER RETURN operations if the SCC is not fully evaluated. On the other hand, if *Subg* is in the table, tabletry creates a *consumer* choice point to backtrack through any answers to *Subg* in the table and thereby perform ANSWER RETURN operations.

Extensions to tabletry for Local SLG_C are summarized in Figure 2. If *Subg* is new, it is copied into the table as in the sequential case, but in order to represent the *TDG* a thread identifier is associated with *Subg*. For this association the *subgoal frame*, a structure containing information about each tabled subgoal, is extended with a *ThreadMark* cell. The essential difference from the sequential case of tabletry occurs when *Subg* is not new and is currently marked by

Instruction tabletry
/* $Subg$ is in argument registers; $T_{current}$ is current thread */
Perform the subgoal_check_insert($Subg$) operation in the table for this predicate
If $Subg$ is not new and is marked by another thread
    lock global TDG mutex
    If deadlock($T_{current}$,$Subg.ThreadMark$)
        /* all other threads in the independent SCC are suspended at deadlock */
        usurp($T_{current}$,$Subg.ThreadMark$)
    Else unlock TDG mutex; suspend the calling thread until $Subg$ completes
    Proceed as in the sequential case; if $Subg$ was usurped, treat it as a new subgoal

deadlock($T_{current}$,$depends\_thread$)
    while($depends\_thread \neq$ NULL)
        if($depends\_thread = T_{current}$) return true;
        else $depends\_thread \leftarrow depends\_thread.suspended\_on\_thread$);
    return false;

usurp($T_{current}$, $first\_usurped$)
    Traverse SCC_{dl} to reset $suspended\_on\_thread$ dependency of each usurped thread
    Unlock global TDG mutex
    Traverse SCC_{dl} to
        Propagate the proper subgoal dependency to each usupred thread
        Reset stacks of each (suspended) usurped thread

Fig. 2. Summary of Concurrent Local SLG implementation in the SLG-WAM

another thread (and therefore not marked as completed). In this case deadlock detection is performed: if a deadlock is not found, the calling thread $T_{current}$ suspends as it does not have any applicable Local SLG_C operations; otherwise $T_{current}$ performs a USURPATION operation. In addition to changes in tabletry, a change is made to the SLG-WAM completion instruction so that any thread suspended on $Subg$ is awakened when $Subg$ is completed (a condition variable based on the predicate symbol of $Subg$ is used for this awakening).

The design of deadlock detection in the SLG-WAM relies on Theorem 9, which states that each thread may be suspended on at most one other thread. The SLG-WAM adds a $suspended\_on\_thread$ field to the context of each thread to denote any thread dependency. As shown in Figure 2, when a thread $T_{current}$ performs deadlock detection, it starts by checking whether the thread marking $Subg$ is suspended using this $suspended\_on\_thread$ field: if the thread is not suspended, $T_{current}$ may suspend without fear of deadlock and it will be awakened when $Subg$ is completed. If the marker of $Subg$ is suspended, the deadlock detection code follows the $suspended\_on\_thread$ field. By Theorem 9, any loop in the TDG must be a simple cycle so that deadlock detection is a simple while loop that exits in one of two cases. If $T_{current}$ is found in the $suspended\_on\_thread$ field for one of the traversed threads, then $T_{current}$ depends (transitively) on itself and deadlock occurs; otherwise if the $suspended\_on\_thread$ field of a traversed thread is null, $T_{current}$ transitively depends on a subgoal that is actively being computed.

The fact that the thread dependencies for deadlocked threads form a simple cycle also underlies the control flow of the usurp() function which consists of two traversals of the deadlocked TDG cycle, denoted SCC_{dl}. Each traversal begins with the thread that marks $Subg$. In the first traversal, the usurping thread $T_{current}$ updates the TDG, setting the *suspended_on_thread* field of each usurped thread to its own id. Adjusting the TDG must be performed under global mutual exclusion: otherwise two concurrently usurping threads might produce an incoherent TDG. In the second traversal, which is not under mutual exclusion, the execution stacks in each usurped thread $T_{usurped}$ are examined and manipulated – an operation that is safe since $T_{usurped}$ has suspended on a subgoal due to thread compatibility restrictions. The manipulation ensures that $T_{usurped}$ will no longer generate answers for usurped subgoals that it has marked, but rather will be set to consume answers. This stack manipulation is considerably simplified by the property that the SDG for $T_{usurped}$ will depend on a *single* usurped subgoal $S_{T_{usurped}}$ – the first subgoal in SCC_{dl} that $T_{usurped}$ encountered. (the property is implied by Corollary 1 together with Theorem 8). However to determine $S_{T_{usurped}}$, both subgoal dependencies contained in $T_{usurped}$ and subgoal dependencies across usurped threads must be considered. Accordingly, usurp() also propagates cross-thread dependencies (the actual mechanism is not shown in this summary) and uses these dependencies when resetting the stacks of $T_{usurped}$. As a result, when $T_{usurped}$ is awakened it will call $S_{T_{usurped}}$ again from scratch and backtrack through the answers of the completed subgoal.

This approach has the virtue of conceptual simplicity, but any partial computations for the usurped subgoals are lost, and will be recomputed by the usurping thread. Theorem 6 states that the maximal number of USURPATION operations in a SLG$_C$ evaluation is linear in $atoms(P)$, the number of atoms in a program P. In [8] it is shown that USURPATION operations affect only constant-time operations so that even if answers for usurped subgoals are recomputed, the complexity of the well-founded semantics is unaffected.

Extensions for Negation and Answer Subsumption. As suggested by the changed operations in Definition 12, the SLG-WAM requires few modifications beyond those presented to extend Local SLG$_C$ to the well-founded semantics. Consider first stratified programs. In the SLG-WAM, if the underlying (tabled) subgoal $Subg$ of a selected negative literal is not new and not complete, the computation path "suspends" and resumes only when $Subg$ has been completed. These operations are essentially the same as the interactions between threads so far described. In the case of non-stratified negation the first new operation to consider is the DELAYING operation. If $Subg$ is involved in a loop through negation, the resumption mechanism is the same except that a bit in the subgoal frame of $Subg$ is set to indicate that $Subg$ was delayed rather than completed. Several cycles of delaying may be needed before $Subg$ is finally completed, but each cycle may be handled by the thread suspension and usurpation mechanisms described. When $Subg$ is completed, any SIMPLIFICATION operations for its SCC are performed before awakening any threads suspended on $Subg$, so that SIMPLIFICATION is not affected by the concurrency mechanisms. Beyond negation, answer subsumption is implemented as an extension to the SLG-WAM new_answer operation which is unaffected by Local SLG_C.

Performance Several performance studies have been made on tabling with Local SLG_C [6,8,7]. We focus on tests of scalability in which a list of M queries is distributed to N threads and the elapsed time measured. [7] measured the use of Local SLG_C on programs which analyzed configuration reachability for various extensions of Petri nets. Depending on particular formalism for the net, the programs were definite, or used well-founded negation, tabled constraints or answer subsumption. For nearly all of these benchmarks, left-recursive reachability of the form reachable(*bound,free*)) scaled perfectly to 4 processors (the number available for this experiment).

In contrast, [8] measured scalability on a worst case: where multiple threads concurrently evaluated right recursion on random graphs of varying densities, using queries of the form rightRec(*bound,free*). Observe that for right-recursion over a graph, the connectivity of the SDG directly reflects the connectivity of the graph. Consider properties of a random graph of V vertices (cf. [11]). If each vertex has at most 1 edge there can be no cycles; if each vertex has between 1 and $\ln(V)$ edges the graph (and SDG) is likely to be split up into several SCCs; while if each vertex has $\ln(V)$ or more edges the graph is likely to be connected, with the SDG consisting of a single SCC. While somewhat preliminary, [8] indicates that the number of deadlocks are relatively small. For graphs with between 1 and $\ln(V)$ edges per vertex, this is either because the graphs do not contain large SCCs or because the subgoals in these SCCs are quickly completed. For fully connected graphs, each thread is usurped at most once. As expected, scalability is poor for the connected graphs as usurped threads must wait for the SCC to be evaluated. However, the elapsed time for the Local SLG_C is never worse than that for a Local single-threaded evaluation on any graph. In other words, for these benchmarks the implementation of Local SLG_C is not affected by the cost of recomputing answers for usurped subgoals and degenerates into a mostly sequential evaluation where threads wait for the completion of SCCs.

5   Discussion

Local SLG_C is well suited for multi-threaded evaluations that benefit from Local evaluation and can provide speedups on problems that can be subdivided relatively easily. At the same time, Local SLG_C is not intended to support general table parallelism. Local evaluation itself prevents one thread from consuming answers concurrently produced by another thread if the consuming and producing subgoals are in different SCCs. Beyond this, a Local SLG_C evaluation may have a number of threads suspended on incomplete or usurped subgoals, although Theorem 6 puts a limit on the number of USURPATION operations.

We believe that a salient strength of Local SLG_C is its formal basis. By Theorem 7 several threads can cooperate to correctly compute the well-founded semantics, and by Theorem 6 the abstract complexity is the same as a sequential SLG evaluation. By Theorem 8 each thread in a Local SLG_C evaluation will have a single independent SCC, and so each thread will have properties of a Local evaluation, including the space efficiency property of Theorem 4. By Corollary 2 (and Theorem 8) each thread will only return answers from completed tables, a useful property for computing the well-founded semantics and answer subsumption. As noted in Section 4, the implementation of Local SLG_C directly relies on Theorem 9 and Corollary 1. As a result of the theory-oriented design, the implementation of Local SLG_C, although delicate, mainly requires about 300 lines of code to be added to the `tabletry` instruction: thus Local SLG_C should be relatively easy to port to other tabling engines that implement Local evaluation.

Related Work. These strengths and limitations distinguish (Local) SLG_C from previous work, which we briefly discuss (see [6] for more details). [5] presents an approach to distributed tabling in which the SDG (Definition 8) is distributed among threads, the dependencies partially represented by numerical encodings associated with subgoals, and a message-counting algorithm used for termination detection. Maintaining the distributed SDG leads to an approach that is cubic in the number of messages. SLG_C differs from [5] in being a more minimal extension of SLG requiring only the addition of markings and USURPATION, and in retaining the complexity of SLG. Another distributed tabling method, [2] avoids the cubic message complexity by using a centralized table manager to maintain dependency and other information and a credit-recovery algorithm to detect completion of the SCCs. SLG_C differs from [2] in not requiring an explicit table manager and in using the "optimistic" USURPATION operation to control concurrency, as well as in being a formalism sufficient for proving completeness and other properties. [9] presents algorithms for adding tabling to an or-parallel engine and implements these algorithms in YAP, with impressive results for definite programs. As mentioned above, unlike [9] Local SLG_C does not address general table parallelism, although it addresses normal programs and is based on a formalization which permits a concise implementation. Perhaps the closest work is [3] which allows threads to share answers when tables are not completed: Concurrent SLG differs from this work in using a simpler method of concurrency control, as well as in modeling normal rather than definite programs.

Acknowledgements. The authors thank Manuel Carro, Pablo Chico de Guzmán, and anonymous reviewers for their careful comments.

References

1. Chen, W., Warren, D.S.: Tabled Evaluation with Delaying for General Logic Programs. Journal of the ACM 43(1), 20–74 (1996)
2. Damásio, C.: A distributed tabling system. In: Proceedings of the 2nd Workshop on Tabulation in Parsing and Deduction, TAPD 2000, pp. 65–75 (2000)
3. Freire, J., Hu, R., Swift, T., Warren, D.S.: Parallelizing tabled evaluation. In: Swierstra, S.D. (ed.) PLILP 1995. LNCS, vol. 982, pp. 115–132. Springer, Heidelberg (1995)

4. Freire, J., Swift, T., Warren, D.S.: Beyond depth-first: Improving tabled logic programs through alternative scheduling strategies. JFLP 1998(3) (1998)
5. Hu, R.: Distributed Tabled Evaluation. Ph.D thesis, SUNY at Stony Brook (1997)
6. Marques, R.: Concurrent Tabling: Algorithms and Implementation. Ph.D thesis, Universidade Nova de Lisboa (2007)
7. Marques, R., Swift, T., Cunha, J.: Extending tabled logic programming with multi-threading: A systems perspective (2008)
8. Marques, R., Swift, T., Cunha, J.: A simple and efficient implementation of concurrent local tabling (2008), http://www.cs.sunysb.edu/~tswift
9. Rocha, R., Silva, F., Costa, V.S.: On applying or-parallelism and tabling to logic programs. Theory and Practice of Logic Programming 4(6) (2004)
10. Rocha, R., Silva, F., Santos Costa, V.: Dynamic mixed-strategy evaluation of tabled logic programs. In: Gabbrielli, M., Gupta, G. (eds.) ICLP 2005. LNCS, vol. 3668, pp. 250–264. Springer, Heidelberg (2005)
11. Spencer, J.: The Strange Logic of Random Graphs. Springer, Heidelberg (2000)
12. van Gelder, A., Ross, K.A., Schlipf, J.S.: Unfounded sets and well-founded semantics for general logic programs. Journal of the ACM 38(3), 620–650 (1991)

On the Continuity of Gelfond-Lifschitz Operator and Other Applications of Proof-Theory in ASP

V.W. Marek[1] and J.B. Remmel[2]

[1] Department of Computer Science
University of Kentucky
Lexington, KY 40506-0046, USA
[2] Department of Mathematics
University of California
La Jolla, CA 92093

Abstract. Using a characterization of stable models of logic programs P as satisfying valuations of a suitably chosen propositional theory, called the set of *reduced defining equations* $r\Phi_P$, we show that the finitary character of that theory $r\Phi_P$ is equivalent to a certain continuity property of the Gelfond-Lifschitz operator GL_P associated with the program P. The introduction of the formula $r\Phi_P$ leads to a double-backtracking algorithm for computation of stable models by reduction to satisfiability of suitably chosen propositional theories. This algorithm does not use the reduction via loop-formulas as proposed in [1] or its extension proposed in [2]. Finally, we discuss possible extensions of techniques proposed in this paper to the context of cardinality constraints.

1 Introduction

The use of proof theory in logic based formalisms for constraint solving is pervasive. For example, in Satisfiability (SAT), proof theoretic methods are used to find lower bounds on complexity of various SAT algorithms. However, proof-theoretic methods have not played as prominent role in Answer Set Programming (ASP) formalisms. This is not to say that there were no attempts to apply proof-theoretic methods in ASP. To give a few examples, Marek and Truszczynski in [3] used the proof-theoretic methods to characterize Reiter's extensions in Default Logic (and thus stable semantics of logic programs). Bonatti [4] and separately Milnikel [5] devised non-monotonic proof systems to study skeptical consequences of programs and default theories. Lifschitz [6] used proof-theoretic methods to approximate well-founded semantics of logic programs. Bondarenko et.al. [7] studied an approach to stable semantics using methods with a clear proof-theoretic flavor. Marek, Nerode, and Remmel in a series of papers, [8,9,10,11,12,13], developed proof theoretic methods to study what they termed *non-monotonic rule systems* which have as special cases almost all ASP formalisms that have been seriously studied in the literature. Recently the area of proof systems for ASP (and more generally, nonmonotonic logics) received a lot of attention [14,15]. It

M. Garcia de la Banda and E. Pontelli (Eds.): ICLP 2008, LNCS 5366, pp. 223–237, 2008.

is clear that the community feels that an additional attention to these area is necessary. Nevertheless, there is no clear classification of proof systems for nonmonotonic reasoning analogous to those in classical logic and SAT, in particular.

In this paper, we define a notion of P-proof schemes, which is a kind of a proof system that was previously used by Marek, Nerode, and Remmel to study complexity issues for stable semantics of logic programs [12]. This proof system abstracts of M-proofs of [3] and produces Hilbert-style proofs. The nonmonotonic character of our P-proofs is provided by the presence of guards, called the *support* of the proof scheme, to insure context-dependence. A different but equivalent, presentation of proof schemes, using a guarded resolution is also possible.

We shall show that we can use P-proof schemes to find a characterization of stable models via *reduced defining equations*. While in general these defining equations may be infinite, we study the case of programs for which all these equations are finite. This resulting class of programs, called FSP-programs, turns out to be characterized by a form of continuity of the Gelfond-Lifschitz operator.

Contributions of the Paper

The contributions of this paper consist, primarily, of investigations that elucidate the proof-theoretical character of the stable semantics for logic programs, an area with 20 years history [16]. The two principal results of this paper are the following.

1. We show that the Gelfond-Lifschitz operator GL_P is, in fact, a proof-theoretical construct (Proposition 7).
2. Given (1), we show that the upper-half continuity of that operator is equivalent to finiteness of (propositional) formulas in a certain class associated with the program P (Proposition 10).

These two results hold for arbitrary programs. A third contribution of this paper which is in a somewhat different direction from our first two results, is to show that in case of the finite programs P, we can use our proof theory techniques to construct a class of theories C_P, which we call the set of candidate theories associated with P, with the following properties: (i) the theories in C_P are of size linear in P, (ii) the propositional models of any $T \in C_P$ are stable models of P, and (iii) for every stable model M of P, there is $T \in C_P$ such that M is a model of T. Thus we can find stable models of P by using SAT solvers to find models of $T \in C_P$. This result shows how the exponential size of completion of P with loop formulas [1] can be traded for exponential number of linear-size propositional theories.

The outline of this paper is as follows. In section 2, we provide the necessary background on logic programs and stable models to present our results. In section 3, we introduce P-proof schemes and the reduced defining equations for a logic program P as well as certain associated equivalence theorems. In section 4, we discuss the continuity properties of operators. In section 5, we introduce an algorithm (and establish its correctness) for stable model computation that follows from the techniques outlined in earlier sections. In Section 6 we extend our techniques to the context of programs with cardinality constraints. Finally in Section 7, we have provide some conclusions and directions for future work.

2   Preliminaries

Let At be a countably infinite set of atoms. We will study programs consisting of clauses built of the atoms from At. A *program clause* C is a string of the form

$$p \leftarrow q_1, \ldots, q_m, \neg r_1, \ldots, \neg r_n \qquad (1)$$

The integers m or n or both can be 0. The atom p will be called the head of C and denoted $head(C)$. We let $PosBody(C)$ denote the set $\{q_1, \ldots, q_m\}$ and $NegBody(C)$ denote the set $\{r_1, \ldots, r_n\}$. For any set of atoms X, we let $\neg X$ denote the conjunction of negations of atoms from X. Thus, we can write clause (1) as

$$head(C) \leftarrow Posbody(C), \neg negBody(C).$$

Let us stress that the set $NegBody(C)$ is a set of atoms, not a set of negated atoms as is sometimes used in the literature. A normal propositional program is a set P of such clauses. For any $M \subseteq At$, we say that M is model of C if whenever $q_1, \ldots, q_m \in M$ and $\{r_1, \ldots, r_n\} \cap M = \emptyset$, then $p \in M$. We say that M is a model of a program P if M is a model of each clause $C \in P$. Horn clauses are clauses with no negated literals, i.e. clauses of the form (1) where $n = 0$. We will denote by $Horn(P)$ the part of the program P consisting of its Horn clauses. Horn programs are logic programs P consisting entirely of Horn clauses. Thus for a Horn program P, $P = Horn(P)$.

Each Horn program P has a least model in the Herbrand base and the least model of P is the least fixed point of a continuous operator T_P representing 1-step Horn clause logic deduction ([17]). That is, for any set $I \subseteq At$, we let $T_P(I)$ equal the set of all $p \in At$ such that there is a clause $C = p \leftarrow q_1, \ldots, q_m$ in P and $q_1, \ldots, q_m \in I$. Then T_P has a least fixed point F_P which is obtained by iterating T_P starting at the empty set for ω steps, i.e., $F_P = \bigcup_{n \in \omega} T_P^n(\emptyset)$ where for any $I \subseteq At$, $T_P^0(I) = I$ and $T_P^{n+1}(I) = T_P(T_P^n(I))$. Then F_P is the least model of P.

The semantics of interest for us is the *stable semantics* of normal programs, although we will discuss some extensions in Section 5. The stable models of a program P are defined as fixed points of the operator $T_{P,M}$. This operator is defined on the set of all subsets of At, $\mathcal{P}(At)$. If P is a program and $M \subseteq At$ is a subset of the Herbrand base, define operator $T_{P,M} \colon \mathcal{P}(At) \to \mathcal{P}(At)$ as follows:

$$T_{P,M}(I) = \{p \colon \text{there exist a clause } C = p \leftarrow q_1, \ldots, q_m, \neg r_1, \ldots, \neg r_n$$
$$\text{in } P \text{ such that } q_1 \in I, \ldots, q_m \in I, r_1 \notin M, \ldots, r_n \notin M\}$$

The following is immediate, see [18] for unexplained notions.

Proposition 1. *For every program P and every set M of atoms the operator $T_{P,M}$ is monotone and continuous.*

Thus the operator $T_{P,M}$ like all monotonic continuous operators, possesses a least fixed point $F_{P,M}$.

Given program P and $M \subseteq At$, we define the *Gelfond-Lifschitz reduct* of P, P_M, as follows. For every clause $C = p \leftarrow q_1, \ldots, q_m, \neg r_1, \ldots, \neg r_n$ of P, execute the following operations.

(1) If some atom r_i, $1 \leq i \leq n$, belongs to M, then eliminate C altogether.
(2) In the remaining clauses that have not been eliminated by operation (1), eliminate all the negated atoms.

The resulting program P_M is a Horn propositional program. The program P_M possesses a least Herbrand model. If that least model of P_M coincides with M, then M is called a *stable model* for P. This gives rise to an operator GL_P which associates to each $M \subseteq At$, the least fixed point of $T_{P,M}$. We will discuss the operator GL_P and its proof-theoretic connections in section 4.2.

3   Proof Schemes and Reduced Defining Equations

In this section we recall the notion of a *proof scheme* as defined in [8,3] and introduce a related notion of *defining equations*.

Given a propositional logic program P, a proof scheme is defined by induction on its length. Specifically, a proof scheme w.r.t. P (in short P-proof scheme) is a sequence $S = \langle\langle C_1, p_1\rangle, \ldots, \langle C_n, p_n\rangle, U\rangle$ subject to the following conditions:

(I) when $n = 1$, $\langle\langle C_1, p_1\rangle, U\rangle$ is a P-proof scheme if $C_1 \in P$, $p_1 = head(C_1)$, $PosBody(C_1) = \emptyset$, and $U = NegBody(C_1)$ and
(II) when $\langle\langle C_1, p_1\rangle, \ldots, \langle C_n, p_n\rangle, U\rangle$ is a P-proof scheme, $C = p \leftarrow PosBody(C), \neg NegBody(C)$ is a clause in the program P, and $PosBody(C) \subseteq \{p_1, \ldots, p_n\}$, then

$$\langle\langle C_1, p_1\rangle, \ldots, \langle C_n, p_n\rangle, \langle C, p\rangle, U \cup NegBody(C)\rangle$$

is a P-proof scheme.

When $S = \langle\langle C_1, p_1\rangle, \ldots, \langle C_n, p_n\rangle, U\rangle$ is a P-proof scheme, then we call (i) the integer n – the *length* of S, (ii) the set U – the *support* of S, and (iii) the atom p_n – the *conclusion* of S. We denote U by $supp(S)$.

Example 1. Let P be a program consisting of four clauses: $C_1 = p \leftarrow$, $C_2 = q \leftarrow p, \neg r$, $C_3 = r \leftarrow \neg q$, and $C_4 = s \leftarrow \neg t$. Then we have the following examples of P-proof schemes:

(a) $\langle\langle C_1, p\rangle, \emptyset\rangle$ is a P-proof scheme of length 1 with conclusion p and empty support.
(b) $\langle\langle C_1, p\rangle, \langle C_2, q\rangle, \{r\}\rangle$ is a P-proof scheme of length 2 with conclusion q and support $\{r\}$.
(c) $\langle\langle C_1, p\rangle, \langle C_3, r\rangle, \{q\}\rangle$ is a P-proof scheme of length 2 with conclusion r and support $\{q\}$.
(d) $\langle\langle C_1, p\rangle, \langle C_2, q\rangle, \langle C_3, r\rangle, \{q, r\}\rangle$ is a P-proof scheme of length 3 with conclusion r and support $\{q, r\}$.

Proof scheme in (c) is an example of a proof scheme with unnecessary items (the first term). Proof scheme (d) is an example of a proof scheme which is not internally consistent in that r is in the support of its proof scheme and is also its conclusion.   □

A P-proof scheme carries within itself its own applicability condition. In effect, a P-proof scheme is a *conditional* proof of its conclusion. It becomes applicable when all the constraints collected in the support are satisfied. Formally, for any set of atoms M, we say that a P-proof scheme S is M-*applicable* if $M \cap supp(S) = \emptyset$. We also say that M *admits* S if S is M-applicable.

The fundamental connection between proof schemes and stable models [8,3] is given by the following proposition.

Proposition 2. *For every normal propositional program P and every set M of atoms, M is a stable model of P if and only if the following conditions hold.*

(i) *For every $p \in M$, there is a P-proof scheme S with conclusion p such that M admits S.*

(ii) *For every $p \notin M$, there is no P-proof scheme S with conclusion p such that M admits S.*

Proposition 2 says that the presence and absence of the atom p in a stable model depends *only* on the supports of proof schemes. This fact naturally leads to a characterization of stable models in terms of propositional satisfiability. Given $p \in At$, the *defining equation* for p w.r.t. P is the following propositional formula:

$$p \Leftrightarrow (\neg U_1 \vee \neg U_2 \vee \ldots) \tag{2}$$

where $\langle U_1, U_2, \ldots \rangle$ is the list of all supports of P-proof schemes with conclusion p. Here for any finite set $S = \{s_1, \ldots, s_n\}$ of atoms, $\neg S = \neg s_1 \wedge \cdots \wedge \neg s_n$. If p is not the conclusion of any proof scheme, then we set the defining equation of p to be $p \Leftrightarrow \bot$. Also, in the case where all the supports of proof schemes of p are empty, we set the defining equation of p to be $p \Leftrightarrow \top$. Up to a total ordering of the finite sets of atoms such a formula is unique. For example, suppose we fix a total order on At, $p_1 < p_2 < \cdots$. Then given two sets of atoms, $U = \{u_1 < \cdots < u_m\}$ and $V = \{v_1 < \cdots < v_n\}$, we say that $U \prec V$, if either (i) $u_m < v_n$, (ii) $u_m = v_n$ and $m < n$, or (iii) $u_m = v_n$, $n = m$, and $(u_1, \ldots, u_n)$ is lexicographically less than $(v_1, \ldots, v_n)$. We say that (2) is the *defining equation* for p relative to P if $U_1 \prec U_2 \prec \cdots$. We will denote the defining equation for p with respect to P by Eq_p^P.

For example, if P is a Horn program, then for every atom p, either the support of all its proof schemes are empty or p is not the conclusion of any proof scheme. The first of these alternatives occurs when p belongs to the least model of P, $lm(P)$. The second alternative occurs when $p \notin lm(P)$. The defining equations are $p \Leftrightarrow \top$ (that is p) when $p \in lm(P)$ and $p \Leftrightarrow \bot$ (that is $\neg p$) when $p \notin lm(P)$. When P is a stratified program the defining equations are more complex, but the resulting theory is logically equivalent to

$$\{p : p \in Perf_P\} \cup \{\neg p : p \notin Perf_P\}$$

where $Perf_P$ is the unique stable model of P.

Let Φ_P be the set $\{Eq_p^P : p \in At\}$. We then have the following consequence of Proposition 2.

Proposition 3. *Let P be a normal propositional program. Then stable models of P are precisely the propositional models of the theory Φ_P.*

When P is *purely negative*, i.e. all clauses C of P have $PosBody(C) = \emptyset$, the stable and supported models of P coincide [19] and the defining equations reduce to Clark's completion [20] of P.

Let us observe that in general the propositional formulas on the right-hand-side of the defining equations may be infinite.

Example 2. Let P be an infinite program consisting of clauses $p \leftarrow \neg p_i$, for all $i \in n$. In this case, the defining equation for p in P is infinite. That is, it is

$$p \Leftrightarrow (\neg p_1 \vee \neg p_2 \vee \neg p_3 \vee \ldots)$$

□

The following observation is quite useful. If U_1, U_2 are two finite sets of propositional atoms then

$$U_1 \subseteq U_2 \text{ if and only if } \neg U_2 \models \neg U_1$$

Here $\models$ is the propositional consequence relation. The effect of this observation is that not all the supports of proof schemes are important, only the inclusion-minimal ones.

Example 3. Let P be an infinite program consisting of clauses $p \leftarrow \neg p_1, \ldots, \neg p_i$, for all $i \in N$. The defining equation for p in P is

$$p \Leftrightarrow [\neg p_1 \vee (\neg p_1 \wedge \neg p_2) \vee (\neg p_1 \wedge \neg p_2 \wedge \neg p_3) \vee \ldots]$$

which is infinite. But our observation above implies that this formula is *equivalent* to the formula

$$p \Leftrightarrow \neg p_1$$

□

Motivated by the Example 3, we define the *reduced defining equation* for p relative to P to be the formula

$$p \Leftrightarrow (\neg U_1 \vee \neg U_2 \vee \ldots) \tag{3}$$

where U_i range over *inclusion-minimal* supports of P-proof schemes for the atom p and $U_1 \prec U_2 \prec \cdots$. Again, if p is not the conclusion of any proof scheme, then we set the defining equation of p to be $p \Leftrightarrow \bot$. In the case, where there is a proof scheme of p with empty support, then we set the defining equation of p to be $p \Leftrightarrow \top$. We denote this formula as rEq_p^P, and define $r\Phi_P$ to be the theory consisting of rEq_p^P for all $p \in At$. We then have the following strengthening of Proposition 3.

Proposition 4. *Let P be a normal propositional program. Then stable models of P are precisely the propositional models of the theory $r\Phi_P$.*

In our Example 3, the theory Φ_P involved formulas with infinite disjunctions, but the theory $r\Phi_P$ contains only usual finite propositions.

Given a normal propositional program P, we say that P is a *finite support program* (FSP-program) if all the reduced defining equations for atoms with respect to P are finite propositional formulas. Equivalently, a program P is an *FSP*-program if for every atom p, there are only finitely many inclusion-minimal supports of P-proof schemes for p.

4 Continuity Properties of Operators and Proof Schemes

In this section we investigate continuity properties of operators and we will see that one of those properties characterizes the class of FSP programs.

4.1 Continuity Properties of Monotone and Antimonotone Operators

Let us recall that $\mathcal{P}(At)$ denotes the set of all subsets of At. We say that any function $O : \mathcal{P}(At) \to \mathcal{P}(At)$ is an operator on the set At of propositional atoms. An operator O is *monotone* if for all sets $X, Y \subseteq At$, $X \subseteq Y$ implies $O(X) \subseteq O(Y)$. Likewise an operator O is *antimonotone* if for all sets $X, Y \subseteq At$, $X \subseteq Y$ implies $O(Y) \subseteq O(X)$. For a sequence $\langle X_n \rangle_{n \in N}$ of sets of atoms, we say that $\langle X_n \rangle_{n \in N}$ is *monotonically increasing* if for all $i, j \in N$, $i \leq j$ implies $X_i \subseteq X_j$ and we say that $\langle X_n \rangle_{n \in N}$ is *monotonically decreasing* if for all $i, j \in N$, $i \leq j$ implies $X_j \subseteq X_i$.

There are four distinct classes of operators that we shall consider in this paper. First, we shall consider two types of monotone operators, upper-half continuous monotone operators and lower-half continuous monotone operators. That is, we say that a monotone operator O is *upper-half continuous* if for every monotonically increasing sequence $\langle X_n \rangle_{n \in N}$, $O(\bigcup_{n \in N} X_n) = \bigcup_{n \in N} O(X_n)$. We say that a monotone operator O is *lower-half continuous* if for every monotonically decreasing sequence $\langle X_n \rangle_{n \in N}$, $O(\bigcap_{n \in N} X_n) = \bigcap_{n \in N} O(X_n)$. In the Logic Programming literature the first of these properties is called *continuity*. The classic result due to van Emden and Kowalski is the following.

Proposition 5. *For every Horn program P, the operator T_P is upper-half continuous.*

In general, the operator T_P for Horn programs is *not* lower-half continuous. For example, let P be the program consisting of the clauses $p \leftarrow p_i$ for $i \in N$. Then the operator T_P is not lower-half continuous. That is, if $X_i = \{p_i, p_{i+1}, \ldots\}$, then clearly $p \in T_P(X_i)$ for all i. However, $\bigcap_i X_i = \emptyset$ and $p \notin T_P(\emptyset)$.

Lower-half continuous monotone operators have appeared in the Logic Programming literature [21]. Even more generally, for a monotone operator O, let us define its *dual* operator O^d as follows:

$$O^d(X) = At \setminus O(At \setminus X).$$

Then an operator O is upper-half continuous if and only if O^d is lower-half continuous [22]. Therefore, for any Horn program P, the operator T_P^d is lower-half continuous.

For antimonotone operators, we have two additional notions of continuity. We say that an antimonotone operator O is *upper-half* continuous if for every monotonically increasing sequence $\langle X_n \rangle_{n \in N}$, $O(\bigcup_{n \in N} X_n) = \bigcap_{n \in N} O(X_n)$. Similarly, we say an antimonotone operator O is *lower-half* continuous if for every monotonically decreasing sequence $\langle X_n \rangle_{n \in N}$, $O(\bigcap_{n \in N} X_n) = \bigcup_{n \in N} O(X_n)$.

4.2 Gelfond-Lifschitz Operator GL_P and Proof-Schemes

For the completeness sake, let us recall that the Gelfond-Lifschitz operator for a program P, which we denote GL_P, assigns to a set of atoms M the least fixpoint of the operator $T_{P,M}$ or, equivalently, the least model N_M of the program P_M which is the Gelfond-Lifschitz reduct of P via M [16]. The following fact is crucial.

Proposition 6 ([16]). *The operator GL is antimonotone.*

Here is a useful proof-theoretic characterization of the operator GL_P.

Proposition 7. *Let P be a normal propositional program and M be a set of atoms. Then*

$$GL_P(M) = \{p : \text{ there exists a } P\text{-proof scheme } S \text{ such that } M \text{ admits } S,$$
$$\text{and } p \text{ is the conclusion of } S\}$$

4.3 Continuity Properties of the Operator GL_P

In this subsection, we state our results on the continuity properties of the operator GL_P. First, it is easy to prove that for every program P, the operator GL_P is lower-half continuous. Moreover, we can prove that if f is a lower-half continuous antimonotone operator, then $f = GL_P$ for a suitably chosen program P. Finally, we can prove that the operator GL_P is upper-half continuous if and only if P is an *FSP*-program. That is, GL_P is upper-half continuous if for all atoms p the reduced defining equation for any p (w.r.t. P) is finite. Thus we have the following results.

Proposition 8. *For every normal program P, the operator GL_P is lower-half continuous.*

The lower-half continuity of antimonotone operators is closely related to programs, as shown in the following result.

Proposition 9. *Let At be a denumerable set of atoms. Let f be an antimonotone and lower-half continuous operator on $\mathcal{P}(At)$. Then there exists a normal logic program P such that $f = GL_P$.*

We are now ready to state one of the main result of this paper.

Proposition 10. *Let P be a normal propositional program. The following are equivalent:*

(a) P *is an* FSP-*program.*
(b) The operator GL_P is upper-half continuous, i.e.

$$GL_P\left(\bigcup_{n \in N} X_n\right) = \bigcap_{n \in N} GL_P(X_n)$$

for every monotonically increasing sequence $\langle X_n \rangle_{n \in N}$.

5 Computing Stable Models Via Satisfiability, but without Loop Formulas or Defining Equations

Proposition 3 characterized the stable models of a propositional program in terms of the collection of all propositional valuations of the underlying set of atoms. In this section, we give an alternative characterization in terms of the models of P, only. The proof of this characterization uses Proposition 3, but relates stable models of finite propositional programs P to models of theories of size $O(|P|)$. This is in contrast to Proposition 3 since the set of defining equations is, in general, of size exponential in $|P|$.

A *subequation* for an atom p is either a formula $\neg p$ or a formula

$$p \Leftrightarrow \neg S$$

where S is a support of a proof scheme for p. Here if $S = \emptyset$, then by convention we interpret $p \Leftrightarrow \neg S$ to be simply the atom p. The idea is that a subequation either asserts absence of the atom p in the putative stable model or provides the reason for the presence of p in the putative stable model. A *candidate theory* for program P is the union of P and a set of subequations, one for each $p \in At$. C_P is the class of all candidate theories for the program P.

The key to our algorithm is the following result.

Proposition 11. *1. Let $T \in C_P$. If T is consistent, then every propositional model of T is a stable model for P.*
2. For every stable model M of P, there is a theory $T \in C_P$ such that M is a model for T.

Proposition 11, similarly to [1] characterizes stable models of logic programs via propositional satisfiability, except that theories are smaller.

Next we give an example of our approach to reducing the computation of stable models to satisfiability of propositional theories. It will be clear from this example that our approach avoids having to compute the completion of the program and thus significantly reduces the size of the input theories.

Example 4. Let P be a propositional program as follows:

$$p \leftarrow t, \neg q$$
$$p \leftarrow \neg r$$
$$q \leftarrow \neg s$$
$$t \leftarrow$$

Let us observe that the atom p has two supports of minimal proof schemes: $\{q\}$ and $\{r\}$. The atom q has just one support: $\{s\}$, the atom t has a single support - the empty set. The atoms r and s have no support at all.

Thus there are *three* subequations for p:

$$p \Leftrightarrow \neg q$$
$$p \Leftrightarrow \neg r$$
$$\neg p$$

Now, q has just two subequations: $q \Leftrightarrow \neg s$, and $\neg q$, t has also two subequations, t and $\neg t$, but this second one leads to contradiction whenever chosen. Finally each of r and s have just one defining equation, $\neg r$, and $\neg s$, respectively.

First let us choose for p, the subequation $\neg p$, and for q, the subequation $q \Leftrightarrow \neg s$. The remaining subequations are forced to t, $\neg r$, and $\neg s$. The resulting theory has nine clauses, when we write our program in propositional form:

$$S = \{\neg p, \neg r, \neg s, t, q \Leftrightarrow \neg s\} \cup \{\neg t \vee p \vee q, r \vee p, s \vee q, t\}.$$

It is quite obvious that this theory is inconsistent. However, if we choose for p, the subequation $p \Leftrightarrow \neg r$ and for q, the subequation $q \Leftrightarrow \neg s$, then the resulting theory written out in propositional form is

$$S = \{p \Leftrightarrow \neg r, \neg r, \neg s, t, q \Leftrightarrow \neg s\} \cup \{\neg t \vee p \vee q, r \vee p, s \vee q, t\}.$$

In this case, $\{p, q, t\}$ is a model of S and hence, $\{p, q, t\}$ is a stable model of P. $\square$

Let us observe that our discussion above implies an algorithm for computing stable models. In this algorithm, we fix an order of propositional variables (atoms) and we

1. systematically generate proof-schemes for atoms,
2. then generate subequations (one per each atom), and
3. then submit the resulting theories to a SAT solver.

The algorithm described above can be implemented as a *two-tier backtracking search*, with the on-line computation of supports of proof schemes using resolution to collect the negative information derived from clauses, and the usual backtracking scheme of DPLL. This second backtracking can be implemented using any DPLL-based SAT-solver. Proposition 11 implies that the algorithm we outlined is both sound and complete. Indeed, if the SAT solver returns a model M of a theory T, then M is a stable model of P by Proposition 11(1). Otherwise we generate another candidate theory and loop through this process until one satisfying assignment is found. Proposition 11(2) guarantees the completeness of our algorithm.

Our algorithm is not using loop formulas like the algorithms of Lin and Zhao [1] or Giunchiglia, Lierare and Maratea [23], but systematically searches for supports of proof schemes, thus providing supports for atoms in the putative model. It also differs from the modified loop formulas approach of Ferraris, Lee and Lifschitz [2] in that we do not consider loops of the call-graph of P at all. Instead, we compute systematically proof schemes and their supports for atoms. While the time-complexity of our algorithm is significant, the space complexity is $O(|P|)$. This is the effect of not looking at loop formulas at all ([24]). The issue of the feasibility of practical implementation of the above algorithm is not clear at the time of writing of this paper.

6   Extensions to CC-Programs

In [25] Niemelä and coauthors defined a significant extension of logic programming with stable semantics which allows for programming with cardinality constraints, and, more generally, with weight constraints. This extension has been further studied in [26,27]. To keep things simple, we will limit our discussion to cardinality constraints only, although it is possible to extend our arguments to any class of convex constraints [28]. *Cardinality constraints* are expressions of the form lXu, where $l, u \in N, l \leq u$ and X is a finite set of atoms. The semantics of an atom lXu is that a set of atoms M satisfies lXu if and only if $l \leq |M \cap X| \leq u$. When $l = 0$, we do not write it, and, likewise, when $u \geq |X|$, we omit it, too. Thus an atom p has the same meaning as $1\{p\}$ while $\neg p$ has the same meaning as $\{p\}0$.

The stable semantics for CC-programs is defined via fixpoints of an analogue of the Gelfond-Lifschitz operator GL_P; see the details in [25] and [26]. The operator in question is neither monotone nor antimonotone. But when we limit our attention to the programs P where clauses have the property that the head consists of a single atom (i.e. are of the form $1\{p\}$), then one can define an operator $CCGL_P$ which is antimonotone and whose fixpoints are stable models of P. This is done as follows.

Given a clause C

$$p \leftarrow l_1 X_1 u_1, \ldots, l_m X_m u_m,$$

we transform it into the clause

$$p \leftarrow l_1 X_1, \ldots, l_m X_m, X_1 u_1, \ldots, X_m u_m \qquad (4)$$

[27]. We say that a clause C of the form (4) is a CC-Horn clause if it is of the form

$$p \leftarrow l_1 X_1, \ldots, l_m X_m. \qquad (5)$$

A CC-Horn program is a CC-program all of whose clauses are of the form (5). If P is a CC-Horn program, we can define the analogue of the one step provability operator T_P by defining that for a set of atom M,

$$T_P(M) = \{p : (\exists C = p \leftarrow l_1 X_1, \ldots, l_m X_m)(\forall i \in \{1, \ldots m\})(|X_i \cap M| \geq l_i)\} \quad (6)$$

It is easy to see that T_P is monotone operator and the least fixed point of T_P is given by

$$lfp(T_P) = \bigcup_{n \geq 0} T_P^n(\emptyset). \qquad (7)$$

We can define the analogue of the Gelfond-Lifschitz reduct of a CC-program, which we call the NSS-reduct of P, as follows. Let $\bar{P}$ denote the set of all transformed clauses derived from P. Given a set of atoms M, we eliminate from $\bar{P}$ those clauses where some upper-constraint $(X_i u_i)$ is not satisfied by M, i.e. $|M \cap X_i| > u_i$. In the remaining clauses, the constraints of the form $X_i u_i$ are eliminated altogether. This leaves us with a CC-Horn program P_M. We then define $CCGL_P(M)$ to be the least fixed point of T_{P_M} and say that M is a CC-stable model if M is a model of P and $M = CCGL_P(M)$. The equivalence of this construction and the original construction in [25] for normal CC-programs is shown in [27].

Next we define the analogues of P-proof schemes for normal CC-programs, i.e. programs which consists entirely of clauses of the form (4). This is done by induction as follows. When

$$C = p \leftarrow X_1 u_1, \ldots, X_k u_k$$

is a normal CC-clause without the cardinality-constraints of the form $l_i X_i$ then

$$\langle \langle C, p \rangle, \{X_1 u_1, \ldots, X_k u_k\} \rangle$$

is a P-CC-proof scheme with support $\{X_1 u_1, \ldots, X_k u_k\}$. Likewise, when

$$S = \langle \langle C_1, p_1 \rangle, \ldots, \langle C_n, p_n \rangle, U \rangle$$

is a P-CC-proof scheme,

$$p \leftarrow l_1 X_1, \ldots, l_m X_m, X_1 u_1, \ldots, X_m u_m$$

is a clause in P, and $|X_1 \cap \{p_1, \ldots, p_n\}| \geq l_1, \ldots, |X_m \cap \{p_1, \ldots, p_n\}| \geq l_m$, then

$$\langle \langle C_1, p_1 \rangle, \ldots, \langle C_n, p_n \rangle, \langle C, p \rangle, U \cup \{X_1 u_1, \ldots, X_m u_m\} \rangle$$

is a P-CC-proof scheme with support $U \cup \{X_1 u_1, \ldots X_m u_m\}$. The notion of admittance of a P-CC-proof scheme is similar to the notion of admittance of P-proof scheme for normal programs P. That is, if $\mathcal{S} = \langle \langle C_1, p_1 \rangle, \ldots, \langle C_n, p_n \rangle, \langle C, p \rangle, U \rangle$ is a CC-proof scheme with support $U = \{X_1 u_1, \ldots X_n u_n\}$, then $\mathcal{S}$ is admitted by M if for every $X_i u_i \in U$, $M \models X_i u_i$, i.e. $|M \cap X_i| \leq u_i$.

Similarly, we can associate a propositional formula ϕ_U so that M admits $\mathcal{S}$ if and only if $M \models \phi_U$ as follows:

$$\phi_U = \bigwedge_{i=1}^{n} \bigvee_{W \subseteq X_i, |W|=|X_i|-u_i} \neg W. \tag{8}$$

Then we can define a partial ordering on the set of possible supports of proof scheme by defining $U_1 \preceq U_2 \iff \phi_{U_2} \models \phi_{U_1}$. For example if $U_1 = \langle \{1, 2, 3\}2, \{4, 5, 6\}2 \rangle$ and $U_2 = \langle \{1, 2, 3, 4, 5, 6\}, 4 \rangle$, then

$$\phi_{U_1} = (\neg 1 \vee \neg 2 \vee \neg 3) \wedge (\neg 4 \vee \neg 5 \vee \neg 6)$$
$$\phi_{U_2} = \bigvee_{1 \leq i < j \leq 6} (\neg i \wedge \neg j).$$

Then clearly $\phi_{U_1} \models \phi_{U_2}$ so that $U_2 \preceq U_1$. We then define a normal propositional CC-program to be a *FPS CC-program* if for each $p \in At$, there are finitely many $\preceq$-minimal supports of P-CC-proof schemes with conclusion p.

We can also define analogue of the defining equation $CCEq_p^P$ of p relative to a normal CC-program P as

$$p \Leftrightarrow (\phi_{U_1} \vee \phi_{U_2} \vee \cdots) \tag{9}$$

where $\langle U_1, U_2, \ldots \rangle$ is a list of supports of all P-CC-proofs schemes with conclusion p. Again up to a total ordering of possible finite supports, this formula is unique. Let Φ_P be the set $\{CCEq_p^P : p \in At\}$. Similarly, we define the *reduced defining equation* for p relative to P to be the formula

$$p \Leftrightarrow (\neg \phi_{U_1} \vee \neg \phi_{U_2} \vee \ldots) \tag{10}$$

where U_i range over $\preceq$-*minimal* supports of P-CC-proof schemes for the atom p.

Then we have the following analogues of Propositions 2 and 3.

Proposition 12. *For every normal propositional CC-program P and every set M of atoms, M is a CC-stable model of P if and only if the following two conditions hold:*

(i) for every $p \in M$, there is a P-CC-proof scheme $\mathcal{S}$ with conclusion p such that M admits $\mathcal{S}$ and

(ii) for every $p \notin M$, there is no P-CC-proof scheme S with conclusion p such that M admits S.

Proposition 13. *Let P be a normal propositional CC-program. Then CC-stable models of P are precisely the propositional models of the theory Φ_P.*

We also can prove the analogues of Propositions 6 and 7.

Proposition 14. *For any CC-program P, the operator $CCGL_P$ is antimonotone.*

Proposition 15. *Let P be a normal propositional CC-program and M be a set of atoms. Then*

$$CCGL_P(M) = \{p : \text{ there exists a } P\text{-proof scheme } S \text{ such that } M \text{ admits } S,$$
$$\text{and } p \text{ is the conclusion of } S\}$$

We can also prove that analogue of Proposition 8.

Proposition 16. *For every normal CC-program P, the operator $CCGL_P$ is lower-half continuous.*

However, we can only prove the analogue of the first half of Proposition 10.

Proposition 17. *Let P be a normal propositional CC-program. Then if P is an FSP-program, the operator $CCGL_P$ is upper-half continuous, i.e.*

$$CCGL_P\left(\bigcup_{n \in N} X_n \right) = \bigcap_{n \in N} CCGL_P(X_n)$$

for every monotonically increasing sequence $\langle X_n \rangle_{n \in N}$.

We note that, alternatively, one can easily give a direct reduction of our CC-programs to normal logic programs using the methods of [29] and the distributivity result for disjunctions in the bodies of clauses of [30]. Such reductions, of course, lead to an exponential blow up in the size of the representation.

7   Conclusions

In this paper, we have explored the applications of P-proof schemes. We have shown that the Gelfond-Lifschitz operator GL_P is upper-half continuous if and only if for each atom p, there are only finitely many minimal supports of P-proof schemes for p. We also show how we can use P-proofs schemes to associate a natural defining equation for each atom of p and how we can use proof schemes to generate candidate theories whose propositional models correspond to stable models. This leads to an algorithm for finding stable models where we submit candidate theories to SAT solvers.

We note that the investigations of proof systems in a related area, SAT, have played a key role in establishing lower bounds on the complexity of algorithms for finding the models. We wonder if there are analogous results in ASP. In particular, are there proof systems for ASP that can be used to develop a deeper understanding of the complexity issues related to finding stable models? The P-proof schemes described in this paper represent one possible candidate of such a proof system for ASP.

Acknowledgments

The research of the first author was supported by the National Science Foundation under Grant IIS-0325063 and by the Kentucky Science and Engineering Foundation under Grant KSEF-1036-RDE-008. The research of the second author was supported by the National Science Foundation under Grant DMS 0654060.

References

1. Lin, F., Zhao, Y.: Assat: Computing answer sets of a logic program by sat solvers. In: Proceedings of AAAI 2002, pp. 112–117 (2002)
2. Ferraris, P., Lee, J., Lifschitz, V.: A generalization of Lin-Zhao theorem. Annals of Mathematics and Artificial Intelligence 47, 79–101 (2006)
3. Marek, V., Truszczyński, M.: Nonmonotonic Logic. Springer, Heidelberg (1993)
4. Bonatti, P.: Reasoning with infinite stable models. Artificial Intelligence Journal 156, 75–111 (2004)
5. Milnikel, R.: Sequent calculi for skeptical reasoning in predicate default logic and other nonmonotonic systems. Annals of Mathematics and Artificial Intelligence 44, 1–34 (2005)
6. Lifschitz, V.: Foundations of logic programming. In: Principles of Knowledge Representation, pp. 69–127. CSLI Publications (1996)
7. Bondarenko, A., Toni, F., Kowalski, R.: An assumption-based framework for non-monotonic reasoning. In: Proceedings of LPNMR 1993, pp. 171–189. MIT Press, Cambridge (1993)
8. Marek, W., Nerode, A., Remmel, J.: Nonmonotonic rule systems I. Annals of Mathematics and Artificial Intelligence 1, 241–273 (1990)
9. Marek, W., Nerode, A., Remmel, J.: Nonmonotonic rule systems II. Annals of Mathematics and Artificial Intelligence 5, 229–264 (1992)
10. Marek, W., Nerode, A., Remmel, J.: A context for belief revision: Normal logic programs. In: Proceedings, Workshop on Defeasible Reasoning and Constraint Solving, International Logic Programming Symposium (1991)
11. Marek, W., Nerode, A., Remmel, J.: How complicated is the set of stable models of a logic program? Annals of Pure and Applied Logic 56, 119–136 (1992)
12. Marek, W., Nerode, A., Remmel, J.: The stable models of predicate logic programs. Journal of Logic Programming 21, 129–154 (1994)
13. Marek, W., Nerode, A., Remmel, J.: Context for belief revision: Forward chaining-normal nonmonotonic rule systems. Annals of Pure and Applied Logic 67, 269–324 (1994)
14. Gebser, M., Schaub, T.: Generic tableaux for answer set programming. In: Proceedings of International Conference on Logic Programming, 2007, pp. 119–133 (2007)
15. Järvisalo, M., Oikarinen, E.: Extended asp tableaux and rule redundancy in normal logic programs. In: Dahl, V., Niemelä, I. (eds.) ICLP 2007. LNCS, vol. 4670, pp. 134–148. Springer, Heidelberg (2007)
16. Gelfond, M., Lifschitz, V.: The stable model semantics for logic programming. In: Proceedings of the International Joint Conference and Symposium on Logic Programming, pp. 1070–1080 (1988)
17. Lloyd, J.: Foundations of Logic Programming. Springer, Heidelberg (1989)
18. Apt, K.: Logic programming. In: van Leeuwen, J. (ed.) Handbook of Theoretical Computer Science, pp. 493–574. MIT Press, Cambridge (1990)
19. Dung, P., Kanchanasut, K.: On the generalized predicate completion of non-Horn programs. In: Logic programming. Proceedings of the North American Conference (1989)

20. Clark, K.: Negation as failure. In: Minker, J., Gallaire, H. (eds.) Logic and data bases, pp. 293–322. Plenum Press (1978)
21. Doets, K.: From Logic to Logic Programming. MIT Press, Cambridge (1994)
22. Jonsson, B., Tarski, A.: Boolean algebras with operators. American Journal of Mathematics 73, 891–939 (1951)
23. Giunchiglia, E., Lierler, Y., Maratea, M.: Answer set programming based on propositional satisfiability. Journal of Automated Reasoning 36, 345–377 (2006)
24. Lifschitz, V., Razborov, A.: Why are there so many loop formulas. Annals of Mathematics and Artificial Intelligence 7, 261–268 (2006)
25. Simons, P., Niemelä, I., Soininen, T.: Extending and implementing the stable model semantics. Artificial Intelligence Journal 138, 181–234 (2002)
26. Marek, V., Remmel, J.: Set constraints in logic programming. In: Lifschitz, V., Niemelä, I. (eds.) LPNMR 2004. LNCS (LNAI), vol. 2923, pp. 154–167. Springer, Heidelberg (2003)
27. Marek, V., Niemelä, I., Truszczyński, M.: Logic programs with monotone abstract constraint atoms. Theory and Practice of Logic Programming 8, 167–199 (2008)
28. Liu, L., Truszczyński, M.: Properties of programs with monotone and convex constraints. In: Proceedings of the 20th National Conference on Artificial Intelligence, pp. 701–706 (2005)
29. Ferraris, P., Lifschitz, V.: Weight constraints as nested expressions. Theory and Practice of Logic Programming 5, 45–74 (2005)
30. Lifschitz, V., Tang, L., Turner, H.: Nested expressions in logic programs. Annals of Mathematics and Artificial Intelligence 25, 369–389 (1999)

αleanTAP: A Declarative Theorem Prover for First-Order Classical Logic

Joseph P. Near*, William E. Byrd, and Daniel P. Friedman

Indiana University, Bloomington, IN 47405
{jnear,webyrd,dfried}@cs.indiana.edu

Abstract. We present αleanTAP, a declarative tableau-based theorem prover written as a pure relation. Like leanTAP, on which it is based, αleanTAP can prove ground theorems in first-order classical logic. Since it is declarative, αleanTAP *generates* theorems and accepts non-ground theorems and proofs. The lack of mode restrictions also allows the user to provide guidance in proving complex theorems and to ask the prover to instantiate non-ground parts of theorems. We present a complete implementation of αleanTAP, beginning with a translation of leanTAP into αKanren, an embedding of nominal logic programming in Scheme. We then show how to use a combination of tagging and nominal unification to eliminate the impure operators inherited from leanTAP, resulting in a purely declarative theorem prover.

1 Introduction

We present a declarative theorem prover for first-order classical logic. We call this prover αleanTAP, since it is based on the leanTAP [1] prover and written in αKanren [2]. Our prover is a pure relation and has no mode restrictions [3]; given a logic variable as the theorem to be proved, αleanTAP *generates* valid theorems.

leanTAP is a lean tableau-based theorem prover for first-order logic due to Beckert and Posegga [1]. Written in Prolog, it is extremely concise and is capable of a high rate of inference. leanTAP uses Prolog's cut (!) in three of its five clauses in order to avoid nondeterminism, and uses copy_term/2 to make copies of universally quantified formulas. Although Beckert and Posegga take advantage of Prolog's unification and backtracking features, their use of the impure cut and copy_term/2 makes leanTAP non-declarative.

We show how to eliminate these impure operators from leanTAP. To eliminate the use of Prolog's cut, we introduce a tagging scheme that makes our formulas unambiguous. To eliminate the use of copy_term/2, we use substitution instead of copying terms. Universally quantified formulas are used as templates, rather than instantiated directly; instead of representing universally quantified variables with logic variables, we use the noms of nominal logic [4]. We then use nominal unification [5] to write a substitution relation that replaces quantified variables with logic variables, leaving the original template untouched.

---

* Now at the Massachusetts Institute of Technology: jnear@csail.mit.edu

M. Garcia de la Banda and E. Pontelli (Eds.): ICLP 2008, LNCS 5366, pp. 238–252, 2008.
© Springer-Verlag Berlin Heidelberg 2008

The resulting declarative theorem prover is interesting for two reasons. First, because of the technique used to arrive at its definition: we use declarative substitution rather than copy_term/2. To our knowledge, there is no method for copying arbitrary terms declaratively. Our solution is not completely general but is useful when a term is used as a template for copying, as in the case of leanTAP. Second, because of the flexibility of the prover itself: αleanTAP is capable of instantiating non-ground theorems during the proof process, and accepts non-ground *proofs*, as well. Whereas leanTAP is fully automated and either succeeds or fails to prove a given theorem, αleanTAP can accept guidance from the user in the form of a partially-instantiated proof, regardless of whether the theorem is ground.

We present an implementation of αleanTAP, demonstrating our technique for eliminating cuts and copy_term/2 from leanTAP. Our implementation demonstrates our contributions: first, it illustrates a method for eliminating common impure operators, and demonstrates the use of nominal logic for representing formulas in first-order logic; second, it shows that the tableau process can be represented as a relation between formulas and their tableaux; and third, it demonstrates the flexibility of relational provers to mimic the full spectrum of theorem provers, from fully automated to fully dependent on the user.

We proceed as follows. In section 2 we provide a brief description of αKanren and describe the concept of tableau theorem proving. In section 3 we motivate our declarative prover by examining its declarative properties and the proofs it returns. In section 4 we present the implementation of αleanTAP. In section 5 we briefly examine αleanTAP's performance. In section 6, we discuss related work. Familiarity with αKanren and knowledge of tableau theorem proving would be helpful; for more on these topics, see the references given in section 2.

2 Preliminaries

We begin by presenting a brief overview of αKanren, the language in which αleanTAP is written. We also provide an introduction to tableau theorem proving and its implementation in leanTAP.

2.1 αKanren Refresher

αKanren is an embedding of nominal logic programming in Scheme. It extends the Scheme language with a term constructor ⋈ (pronounced "tie") and five operators: ≡, #, **exist**[1], **fresh**, and **cond**^{e}. In addition to these declarative operators, we use the impure operator **cond**^{a} to model Prolog's cut.

≡ unifies two terms using nominal unification. **exist** and **fresh**, which are syntactically similar to Scheme's **lambda** and whose bodies are conjoined, are used to introduce new lexical variables; those introduced by **exist** bind logic (or unification) variables, while those introduced by **fresh** bind *noms* (also called "names" or "atoms" in nominal logic). A nom unifies only with a logic variable

---

[1] The name **exist** is chosen to avoid conflict with R^{6}RS Scheme's [6] *exists*.

or with itself; in αlean*TAP*, noms represent variable names. $\#$ is a freshness constraint: $(\#\ a\ t)$ asserts that the nom a does *not* occur free in t. $\bowtie$ is a term constructor: $(\bowtie\ a\ t)$ creates a term in which all free occurrences of the nom a in t are considered bound. Thus $(\#\ a\ (\bowtie\ a\ t))$ always succeeds.

cond^e, which is syntactically similar to **cond**, expresses a disjunction of clauses. Each clause may contain arbitrarily many conjoined goals. **cond**^{a} is similar to **cond**^{e}, but only a single clause of a **cond**^{a} may succeed. The successful clause may succeed an arbitrary number of times, but once its first goal is successful, no other clause may succeed. This behavior is similar to placing a cut (!) before the first conjunct in the body of each relevant clause.

run provides an interface between Scheme and αKanren; it allows the user to limit the number of answers returned, and to specify a logic variable whose value should be *reified* to obtain answers. Reification is the process of replacing distinct logic variables in a term with unique names. The first such variable to be found is represented by the symbol $_{-0}$, the second by $_{-1}$, and so on. For example:

$$
\begin{aligned}
&(\textbf{run}^5\ (q) \\
&\quad (\textbf{exist}\ (x\ y\ z) \\
&\qquad (\textbf{cond}^e \\
&\qquad\quad ((\equiv x\ 3)\ (\equiv y\ 2)\ (\equiv z\ y)) \qquad\Rightarrow ((3\ 2\ 2)\ (_{-0}\ _{-0}\ _{-0})\ (_{-0}\ _{-1}\ _{-0})) \\
&\qquad\quad ((\equiv x\ y)\ (\equiv y\ z)) \\
&\qquad\quad ((\equiv x\ z))) \\
&\qquad (\equiv `(,x\ ,y\ ,z)^2\ q)))
\end{aligned}
$$

This **run** expression has three answers, each corresponding to one line of the **cond**^{e}. In the first answer, all three variables have been instantiated to ground values. In the second, the three variables have been unified with one another, so they have the same reified value. In the third, x and z share the same reified value, which is distinct from that of y.

Nominal unification equates α-equivalent binders:

$$(\textbf{run}^1\ (q)\ (\textbf{fresh}\ (a\ b)\ (\equiv (\bowtie\ a\ a)\ (\bowtie\ b\ b)))) \Rightarrow (_{-0})$$

Although the noms a and b are distinct and would therefore fail to unify, this **run** expression succeeds. Like the terms $\lambda a.a$ and $\lambda b.b$, the terms $(\bowtie\ a\ a)$ and $(\bowtie\ b\ b)$ bind in the same way and are thus α-equivalent.

For a more complete description of αKanren, see Byrd and Friedman [2]. A newer implementation of αKanren in R^{6}RS Scheme [6] was used in the development of αlean*TAP*^{3}; this version uses triangular substitutions [7] instead of idempotent substitutions and is significantly faster. αKanren is based on αProlog [8], which implements the nominal unification of Urban, Pitts, and Gabbay [5], and miniKanren, an earlier logic programming language [9,10].

---

[2] Here, backquote and comma are used to build a list of logic variables: the expression $`(,x\ ,y\ ,z)$ is equivalent to [X, Y, Z] in Prolog. Similarly, the expression $`(,x\ .\ ,y)$ constructs a pair, and is equivalent to [X|Y] in Prolog.

[3] The latest αKanren and αlean*TAP* source code is available at
https://code.launchpad.net/~jnear-csail/minikanren/alphaleanTAP

2.2   Tableau Theorem Proving

Tableau is a method of proving first-order theorems that works by refuting the theorem's negation. In our description we assume basic knowledge of first-order logic; for coverage of this subject and a more complete description of tableau proving, see Fitting [11]. For simplicity, we consider only formulas in Skolemized *negation normal form* (NNF). Converting a formula to this form requires removing existential quantifiers through Skolemization, reducing logical connectives so that only $\wedge$, $\vee$, and $\neg$ remain, and pushing negations inward until they are applied only to literals—see section 3 of Beckert and Posegga [1] for details.

To form a tableau, a compound formula is expanded into branches recursively until no compound formulas remain. The leaves of this tree structure are referred to as *literals*. leanTAP forms and expands the tableau according to the following rules. When the prover encounters a conjunction $x \wedge y$, it expands both x and y on the same branch. When the prover encounters a disjunction $x \vee y$, it splits the tableau and expands x and y on separate branches. Once a formula has been fully expanded into a tableau, it can be proved unsatisfiable if on each branch of the tableau there exist two complementary literals a and $\neg a$ (each branch is *closed*). In the case of propositional logic, syntactic comparison is sufficient to find complementary literals; in first-order logic, sound unification must be used. A closed tableau represents a proof that the original formula is unsatisfiable.

The addition of universal quantifiers makes the expansion process more complicated. To prove a universally quantified formula $\forall x.M$, leanTAP generates a logic variable v and expands M, replacing all occurrences of x with v (i.e., it expands M' where $M' = M[v/x]$). If leanTAP is unable to close the current branch after this expansion, it has the option of generating another logic variable and expanding the original formula again. When the prover expands the formula $\forall x.F(x) \wedge (\neg F(\mathsf{a}) \vee \neg F(\mathsf{b}))$, for example, $\forall x.F(x)$ must be expanded twice, since x cannot be instantiated to both a and b.

3   Introducing αleanTAP

We begin by presenting some examples of αleanTAP's abilities, both in proving ground theorems and in generating theorems. We also explore the proofs generated by αleanTAP, and show how passing partially-instantiated proofs to the prover can greatly improve its performance.

3.1   Running Forwards

Both leanTAP and αleanTAP can prove ground theorems; in addition, αleanTAP produces a proof. This proof is a list representing the steps taken to build a closed tableau for the theorem; Paulson [12] has shown that translation to a more standard format is possible. Since a closed tableau represents an unsatisfiable formula, such a list of steps proves that the negation of the formula is valid. If the list of steps is ground, the proof search becomes deterministic, and αleanTAP acts as a proof checker.

lean*TAP* encodes first-order formulas using Prolog terms. For example, the term (p(b),all(X,(-p(X);p(s(X))))) represents $p(b) \wedge \forall x.\neg p(x) \vee p(s(x))$. In our prover, we represent formulas using Scheme lists with extra tags:

(and (pos (app p (app b))) (forall (⋈ a (or (neg (app p (var a)))
                                        (pos (app p (app s (var a)))))))))

Consider Pelletier Problem 18 [13]: $\exists y. \forall x. F(y) \Rightarrow F(x)$. To prove this theorem in αlean*TAP*, we transform it into the following *negation* of the NNF:

(forall (⋈ a (and (pos (app f (var a))) (neg (app f (app g1 (var a)))))))

where (app g1 (var a)) represents the application of a Skolem function to the universally quantified variable a. Passing this formula to the prover, we obtain the proof (univ conj savefml savefml univ conj close). This proof lists the steps the prover (presented in section 4.3) follows to close the tableau. Because both conjuncts of the formula contain the nom a, we must expand the universally quantified formula more than once.

Partially instantiating the proof helps αlean*TAP* prove theorems with similar subparts. We can create a non-ground proof that describes in general how to prove the subparts and have αlean*TAP* fill in the trivial differences. This can speed up the search for a proof considerably. By inspecting the negated NNF of Pelletier Problem 21, for example, we can see that there are at least two portions of the theorem that will have the same proof. By specifying the structure of the first part of the proof and constraining the identical portions by using the same logic variable to represent both, we can give the prover some guidance without specifying the whole proof. We pass the following non-ground proof to αlean*TAP*:

(conj univ split (conj savefml savefml conj split x x)
    (conj savefml savefml conj split (close) (savefml split y y)))

On our test machine, our prover solves the original problem with no help in 68 milliseconds (ms); given the knowledge that the later parts of the proof will be duplicated, the prover takes only 27 ms. This technique also yields improvement when applied to Pelletier Problem 43: inspecting the negated NNF of the formula, we see two parts that look nearly identical. The first part of the negated NNF—the part representing the theorem itself—has the following form:

(and (or (and (neg (app Q (app g4) (app g3)))
              (pos (app Q (app g3) (app g4))))
         (and (pos (app Q (app g4) (app g3)))
              (neg (app Q (app g3) (app g4))))) ...)

Since we suspect that the same proof might suffice for both branches of the theorem, we give the prover the partially-instantiated proof (conj split x x). Given just this small amount of help, αlean*TAP* proves the theorem in 720 ms, compared to 1.5 seconds when the prover has no help at all. While situations in which large parts of a proof are identical are rare, this technique also allows us to handle situations in which different parts of a proof are merely similar by instantiating as much or as little of the proof as necessary.

3.2   Running Backwards

Unlike lean*TAP*, αlean*TAP* can generate valid theorems. Some interpretation of the results is required since the theorems generated are negated formulas in NNF.[4] In the example

> (**run**^{1} (q) (**exist** (x) (*prove*^{o} q '() '() '() x)))
> $\Rightarrow$ ((and (pos (app $_{-0}$)) (neg (app $_{-0}$))))

the reified logic variable $_{-0}$ represents any first-order formula p, and the entire answer represents the formula $p \wedge \neg p$. Negating this formula yields the original theorem: $\neg p \vee p$, or the law of excluded middle. We can also generate more complicated theorems; here we use the "generate and test" idiom to find the first theorem matching the negated NNF of the inference rule *modus ponens*:

> (**run**^{1} (q)
>   (**exist** (x)
>   (*prove*^{o} x '() '() '() q)
>   ($\equiv$ '(and (and (or (neg (app a)) (pos (app b))) (pos (app a)))
>   (neg (app b)))
> x)))
> $\Rightarrow$ ((conj conj split (savefml close) (savefml savefml close)))

This process takes about 5.1 seconds; *modus ponens* is the 173rd theorem to be generated, and the prover also generates a proof of its validity. When this proof is given to αlean*TAP*, *modus ponens* is the sixth theorem generated, and the process takes only 20 ms.

Thus the declarative nature of αlean*TAP* is useful both for generating theorems and for producing proofs. Due to this flexibility, αlean*TAP* could become the core of a larger proof system. Automated theorem provers like lean*TAP* are limited in the complexity of the problems they can solve, but given the ability to accept assistance from the user, more problems become tractable.

As an example, consider Pelletier Problem 47: Schubert's Steamroller. This problem is difficult for tableau-based provers like lean*TAP* and αlean*TAP*, and neither can solve it automatically [1]. Given some help, however, αlean*TAP* can prove the Steamroller. Our approach is to prove a series of smaller lemmas that act as stepping stones toward the final theorem; as each lemma is proved, it is added as an assumption in proving the remaining ones. The proof process is automated—the user need only specify which lemmas to prove and in what order. Using this strategy, αlean*TAP* proves the Steamroller in about five seconds; the proof requires twenty lemmas.

αlean*TAP* thus offers an interesting compromise between large proof assistants and smaller automated provers. It achieves some of the capabilities of a larger system while maintaining the lean deduction philosophy introduced by lean*TAP*. Like an automated prover, it is capable of proving simple theorems without user guidance. Confronted with a more complex theorem, however, the user can

---

[4] The full implementation of αlean*TAP* includes a simple declarative translator from negated NNF to a positive form.

provide a partially-instantiated proof; αleanTAP can then check the proof and fill in the trivial parts the user has left out. Because αleanTAP is declarative, the user may even leave required axioms out of the theorem to be proved and have the system derive them. This flexibility comes at no extra cost to the user—the prover remains both concise and reasonably efficient.

The flexibility of αleanTAP means that it could be made interactive through the addition of a read-eval-print loop and a simple proof translator between αleanTAP's proofs and a more human-readable format. Since the proof given to αleanTAP may be partially instantiated, such an interface would allow the user to conveniently guide αleanTAP in proving complex problems. With the addition of equality and the ability to perform single beta steps, this flexibility would become more interesting—in addition to reasoning about programs and proving properties about them, αleanTAP would instantiate non-ground programs during the proof process.

4   Implementation

We now present the implementation of αleanTAP. We begin with a translation of leanTAP from Prolog into αKanren. We then show how to eliminate the translation's impure features through a combination of substitution and tagging.

leanTAP implements both expansion and closing of the tableau. When the prover encounters a conjunction, it uses its argument UnExp as a stack (Figure 1): leanTAP expands the first conjunct, pushing the second onto the stack for later expansion. If the first conjunct cannot be refuted, the second is popped off the stack and expansion begins again. When a disjunction is encountered, the split in the tableau is reflected by two recursive calls. When a universal quantifier is encountered, the quantified variable is replaced by a new logic variable, and the formula is expanded. The FreeV argument is used to avoid replacing the free variables of the formula. leanTAP keeps a list of the literals it has encountered on the current branch of the tableau in the argument Lits. When a literal is encountered, leanTAP attempts to unify its negation with each literal in Lits; if any unification succeeds, the branch is closed. Otherwise, the current literal is added to Lits and expansion continues with a formula from UnExp.

4.1   Translation to αKanren

While αKanren is similar to Prolog with the addition of nominal unification, αKanren also uses a variant of interleaving depth-first search [14], so the order of $\mathbf{cond}^e$ clauses in αKanren is irrelevant. Because of Prolog's depth-first search, leanTAP must use VarLim to limit its search depth; in αKanren, VarLim is not necessary, and thus we omit it.

In Figure 1 we present mKleanTAP, our translation of leanTAP into αKanren; we label two clauses (①, ②), since we will modify these clauses later. To express Prolog's cuts, our definition uses $\mathbf{cond}^a$. The final two clauses of leanTAP do not contain Prolog cuts; in mKleanTAP, they are combined into a single clause containing a **cond**^{e}. In place of leanTAP's recursive call to `prove` to check the membership of Lit in Lits, we call *member*^{o}, which performs a membership check using sound unification.[5] Prolog's `copy_term/2` is not built into αKanren; this addition is available as part of the mKleanTAP source code.

```
prove((E1,E2),UnExp,Lits,
      FreeV,VarLim) :- !,
  prove(E1,[E2|UnExp],Lits,
        FreeV,VarLim).

prove((E1;E2),UnExp,Lits,
      FreeV,VarLim) :- !,
  prove(E1,UnExp,Lits,FreeV,VarLim),
  prove(E2,UnExp,Lits,FreeV,Varlim).

prove(all(X,Fml),UnExp,Lits,
      FreeV,VarLim) :- !,
  \+ length(FreeV,VarLim),
  copy_term((X,Fml,FreeV),
            (X1,Fml1,FreeV)),
  append(UnExp,[all(X,Fml)],UnExp1),
  prove(Fml1,UnExp1,Lits,
        [X1|FreeV],VarLim).

prove(Lit,_,[L|Lits],_,_) :-
  (Lit = -Neg; -Lit = Neg) ->
  (unify(Neg,L);
   prove(Lit,[],Lits,_,_)).

prove(Lit,[Next|UnExp],Lits,
      FreeV,VarLim) :-
  prove(Next,UnExp,[Lit|Lits],
        FreeV,VarLim).
```

$$(\textbf{define } prove^o$$
$$(\lambda \; (fml \; unexp \; lits \; freev)$$
$$(\textbf{cond}^a$$
$$((\textbf{exist} \; (e_1 \; e_2)$$
$$(\equiv \text{`(and ,}e_1 \text{ ,}e_2) \; fml)$$
$$(prove^o \; e_1 \text{ `(,}e_2 \text{ . ,}unexp) \; lits \; freev)))$$

$$((\textbf{exist} \; (e_1 \; e_2)$$
$$(\equiv \text{`(or ,}e_1 \text{ ,}e_2) \; fml)$$
$$(prove^o \; e_1 \; unexp \; lits \; freev)$$
$$(prove^o \; e_2 \; unexp \; lits \; freev)))$$

① $((\textbf{exist} \; (x \; x_1 \; body \; body_1 \; unexp_1)$
$$(\equiv \text{`(forall ,}x \text{ ,}body) \; fml)$$
$$(copy\text{-}term^o \text{ `(,}x \text{ ,}body \text{ ,}freev)$$
$$\text{`(,}x_1 \text{ ,}body_1 \text{ ,}freev))$$
$$(append^o \; unexp \text{ `(,}fml) \; unexp_1)$$
$$(prove^o \; body_1 \; unexp_1 \; lits$$
$$\text{`(,}x_1 \text{ . ,}freev))))$$

② $((\textbf{cond}^e$
$$((\textbf{exist} \; (neg)$$
$$(\textbf{cond}^a$$
$$((\equiv \text{`(not ,}neg) \; fml))$$
$$((\equiv \text{`(not ,}fml) \; neg)))$$
$$(member^o \; neg \; lits)))$$

$$((\textbf{exist} \; (next \; unexp_1)$$
$$(\equiv \text{`(,}next \text{ . ,}unexp_1) \; unexp)$$
$$(prove^o \; next \; unexp_1 \text{ `(,}fml \text{ . ,}lits)$$
$$freev)))))))))$$

Fig. 1. leanTAP and mKleanTAP: a translation from Prolog to αKanren

4.2   Eliminating *copy-term*^{o}

Since *copy-term*^{o} is an impure operator, its use makes *prove*^{o} non-declarative: reordering the goals in the prover can result in different behavior. For example, moving the call to *copy-term*^{o} after the call to *prove*^{o} causes the prover to diverge when given any universally quantified formula. To make our prover declarative, we must eliminate the use of *copy-term*^{o}.

Tagging the logic variables that represent universally quantified variables allows the use of a declarative technique that creates two pristine copies of the original term: one copy may be expanded and the other saved for later copying.

---

[5] We define *member*^{o} in Figure 3; it uses sound unification ($\equiv^{\checkmark}$).

Unfortunately, this copying examines the entire body of each quantified formula and instantiates the original term to a potentially invalid formula.

Another approach is to represent quantified variables with symbols or strings. When a new instantiation is needed, a new variable name can be generated, and the new name can be substituted for the old without affecting the original formula. This solution does not destroy the prover's input, but it is difficult to ensure that the provided data is in the correct form declaratively: if the formula to be proved is non-ground, then the prover must generate unique names. If the formula *does* contain these names, however, the prover must *not* generate new ones. This problem can be solved with a declarative preprocessor that expects a logical formula *without* names and puts them in place. If the preprocessor is passed a non-ground formula, it instantiates the formula to the correct form. The requirement of a preprocessor, however, means the prover itself is not declarative.

We use nominal logic [4] to solve the *copy-term^o* problem. Nominal logic is designed to handle the complexities of dealing with names and binders declaratively. Since noms represent unique names, we achieve the benefits of the symbol or string approach without the use of a preprocessor. We can generate unique names each time we encounter a universally quantified formula, and use nominal unification to perform the renaming of the quantified variable. If the original formula is uninstantiated, our newly-generated name is unique and is put in place correctly; we no longer need a preprocessor to perform this function.

Using the tools of nominal logic, we can modify mKlean*TAP* to represent universally quantified variables using noms and to perform substitution instead of copying. When the prover reaches a literal, however, it must replace each nom with a logic variable, so that unification may successfully compare literals. To accomplish this, we associate a logic variable with each unique nom, and replace every nom with its associated variable before comparing literals. These variables are generated each time the prover expands a quantified formula.

To implement this strategy, we change our representation of formulas slightly. Instead of representing $\forall x.F(x)$ as (forall x (f x)), we use a nom wrapped in a var tag to represent a variable reference, and the term constructor ⋈ to represent the $\forall$ binder: (forall (⋈ a (f (var a)))), where a is a nom. The var tag allows us to distinguish noms representing variables from other formulas. We now write a relation *subst-lit^o* to perform substitution of logic variables for tagged noms in a literal, and we modify the literal case of *prove^o* to use it. We also replace the clause handling forall formulas and define *lookup^o*. The two clauses of *lookup^o* overlap, but since each mapping in the environment is from a unique nom to a logic variable, a particular nom will never appear twice.

We present the changes needed to eliminate *copy-term^o* from mKlean*TAP* in Figure 2. Instead of copying the body of each universally quantified formula, we generate a logic variable x and add an association between the nom representing the quantified variable and x to the current environment. When we prepare to close a branch of the tableau, we call *subst-lit^o*, replacing the noms in the current literal with their associated logic variables.

① ((**fresh** (a)
   (**exist** $(x\ body\ unexp_1)$
    ($\equiv$ '(forall ,($\bowtie$ a $body$)) fml)
    ($append^o$ $unexp$ '($,fml$) $unexp_1$)
    ($prove^o$ $body$ $unexp_1$ $lits$
      '(($,a$. $,x$) . $,env$)))))

② ((**exist** (lit)
   ($subst\text{-}lit^o$ fml env lit)
   (**cond**^{e}
    ((**exist** (neg)
     (**cond**^{a}
      (($\equiv$ '(not $,neg$) lit))
      (($\equiv$ '(not $,lit$) neg)))
     ($member^o$ neg $lits$)))
    ((**exist** $(next\ unexp_1)$
     ($\equiv$ '($,next$. $,unexp_1$) $unexp$)
     ($prove^o$ $next$ $unexp_1$ '($,lit$. $,lits$)
      env))))))

(**define** $lookup^o$
  (λ $(a\ env\ out)$
   (**exist** $(first\ rest)$
    (**cond**^{e}
     (($\equiv$ '(($,a$. $,out$) . $,rest$) env))
     (($\equiv$ '($,first$. $,rest$) env)
      ($lookup^o$ a $rest$ out)))))))

(**define** $subst\text{-}lit^o$
  (λ $(fml\ env\ out)$
   (**cond**^{a}
    ((**exist** (a)
     ($\equiv$ '(var $,a$) fml)
     ($lookup^o$ a env out)))
    ((**exist** $(e_1\ e_2\ r_1\ r_2)$
     ($\equiv$ '($,e_1$. $,e_2$) fml)
     ($\equiv$ '($,r_1$. $,r_2$) out)
     ($subst\text{-}lit^o$ e_1 env r_1)
     ($subst\text{-}lit^o$ e_2 env r_2)))
    (($\equiv$ fml out)))))

Fig. 2. Changes to mKlean*TAP* to eliminate *copy-term*^{o}

The original `copy_term/2` approach used by lean*TAP* and mKlean*TAP* avoids replacing free variables by copying the list (x $body$ $freev$). The copied version is unified with the list (x_1 $body_1$ $freev$), so that *only* the variable x will be replaced by a new logic variable—the free variables will be copied, but those copies will be unified with the original variables afterwards. Since our substitution strategy does not affect free variables, the *freev* argument is no longer needed, and so we have eliminated it.

4.3   Eliminating cond^a

Both *prove*^{o} and *subst-lit*^{o} use **cond**^{a} because the clauses that recognize literals overlap with the other clauses. To solve this problem, we have designed a tagging scheme that ensures that the clauses of our substitution and *prove*^{o} relations do not overlap. To this end, we tag both positive and negative literals, applications, and variables. Constants are represented by applications of zero arguments. Our prover thus accepts formulas of the following form:

Fml $\rightarrow$ (and Fml Fml) | (or Fml Fml) | (forall ($\bowtie$ Nom Fml)) | Lit
Lit $\rightarrow$ (pos $Term$) | (neg $Term$)
$Term \rightarrow$ (var Nom) | (app $Symbol$ $Term^*$)

This scheme has been chosen carefully to allow unification to compare literals. In particular, the tags on variables *must* be discarded before literals are compared. Consider the two non-ground literals (not (f x)) and (f (p y)). These literals are complementary: the negation of one unifies with the other, associating x with (p y). When we apply our tagging scheme, however, these literals become (neg (app f (var x))) and (pos (app f (app p (var y)))), respectively, and are no longer complementary: their subexpressions (var x) and (app p (var y)) do not unify. To avoid this problem, our substitution relation discards the var tag when it replaces noms with logic variables.

```
(define proveᵒ
  (λ (fml unexp lits env proof)
    (condᵉ
      ((exist (e₁ e₂ prf)
        (≡ '(and ,e₁ ,e₂) fml)
        (≡ '(conj . ,prf) proof)
        (proveᵒ e₁ '(,e₂ . ,unexp)
                lits env prf)))
      ((exist (e₁ e₂ prf₁ prf₂)
        (≡ '(or ,e₁ ,e₂) fml)
        (≡ '(split ,prf₁ ,prf₂) proof)
        (proveᵒ e₁ unexp lits env prf₁)
        (proveᵒ e₂ unexp lits env prf₂)))
      ((fresh (a)
        (exist (x body unexp₁ prf)
          (≡ '(forall ,(⋈ a body)) fml)
          (≡ '(univ . ,prf) proof)
          (appendᵒ unexp '(,fml) unexp₁)
          (proveᵒ body unexp₁ lits
                  '((,a . ,x) . ,env) prf))))
      ((exist (lit)
        (subst-litᵒ fml env lit)
        (condᵉ
          ((exist (tm neg)
            (≡ '(close) proof)
            (condᵉ
              ((≡ '(pos ,tm) lit)
               (≡ '(neg ,tm) neg))
              ((≡ '(neg ,tm) lit)
               (≡ '(pos ,tm) neg)))
            (memberᵒ neg lits)))
          ((exist (next unexp₁ prf)
            (≡ '(,next . ,unexp₁) unexp)
            (≡ '(savefml . ,prf) proof)
            (proveᵒ next unexp₁ '(,lit . ,lits)
                    env prf)))))))))

(define memberᵒ
  (λ (x ls)
    (exist (a d)
      (≡ '(,a . ,d) ls)
      (condᵉ
        ((≡ᵛ a x))
        ((memberᵒ x d))))))
```

```
(define appendᵒ
  (λ (ls s out)
    (condᵉ
      ((≡ '() ls) (≡ s out))
      ((exist (a d r)
        (≡ '(,a . ,d) ls)
        (≡ '(,a . ,r) out)
        (appendᵒ d s r))))))

(define subst-litᵒ
  (λ (fml env out)
    (condᵉ
      ((exist (l r)
        (≡ '(pos ,l) fml)
        (≡ '(pos ,r) out)
        (subst-termᵒ l env r)))
      ((exist (l r)
        (≡ '(neg ,l) fml)
        (≡ '(neg ,r) out)
        (subst-termᵒ l env r))))))

(define subst-termᵒ
  (λ (fml env out)
    (condᵉ
      ((exist (a)
        (≡ '(var ,a) fml)
        (lookupᵒ a env out)))
      ((exist (f d r)
        (≡ '(app ,f . ,d) fml)
        (≡ '(app ,f . ,r) out)
        (subst-term*ᵒ d env r))))))

(define subst-term*ᵒ
  (λ (tm* env out)
    (condᵉ
      ((≡ '() tm*) (≡ '() out))
      ((exist (e₁ e₂ r₁ r₂)
        (≡ '(,e₁ . ,e₂) tm*)
        (≡ '(,r₁ . ,r₂) out)
        (subst-termᵒ e₁ env r₁)
        (subst-term*ᵒ e₂ env r₂))))))
```

Fig. 3. Final definition of αleanTAP

Given our new tagging scheme, we can easily rewrite our substitution relation without the use of **cond**^{a} . We simply follow the production rules of the grammar, defining a relation to recognize each.

Finally, we modify *prove*^{o} to take advantage of the same tags. We also add a *proof* argument to *prove*^{o}. We call this version of the prover αleanTAP, and present its definition in Figure 3. It is declarative, since we have eliminated the use of *copy-term*^{o} and every use of **cond**^{a}. In addition to being a sound and complete theorem prover for first-order logic, αleanTAP can now generate valid first-order theorems.

5   Performance

Like the original leanTAP, αleanTAP can prove many theorems in first-order logic. Because it is declarative, αleanTAP is generally slower at proving ground theorems than mKleanTAP, which is slower than the original leanTAP. Figure 4 presents a summary of αleanTAP's performance on the first 46 of Pelletier's 75 problems [13], showing it to be roughly twice as slow as mKleanTAP.

#	leanTAP	mKleanTAP	αleanTAP		#	leanTAP	mKleanTAP	αleanTAP
1	0.1	0.7	2.0		24	1.7	31.9	60.3
2	0.0	0.1	0.3		25	0.2	7.5	14.1
3	0.0	0.2	0.5		26	0.8	130.9	187.5
4	0.0	1.0	1.7		27	2.3	40.4	79.3
5	0.1	1.2	2.5		28	0.3	19.1	29.6
6	0.0	0.1	0.2		29	0.1	27.9	57.0
7	0.0	0.1	0.2		30	0.1	4.2	9.6
8	0.0	0.3	0.8		31	0.3	13.2	23.1
9	0.1	4.3	9.7		32	0.2	23.9	42.4
10	0.3	5.5	10.2		33	0.1	15.9	39.2
11	0.0	0.3	0.6		34	199129.0	7272.9	8493.5
12	0.6	17.7	31.9		35	0.1	0.5	1.1
13	0.1	3.7	8.2		36	0.2	6.7	12.4
14	0.1	4.2	9.7		37	0.8	123.3	169.2
15	0.0	0.8	1.9		38	8.9	4228.8	8363.8
16	0.0	0.2	0.6		39	0.0	1.1	2.8
17	1.1	9.2	18.1		40	0.2	8.1	19.2
18	0.1	0.5	1.2		41	0.1	6.9	17.0
19	0.3	15.1	33.5		42	0.4	15.0	32.1
20	0.5	8.1	12.7		43	43.2	668.4	1509.6
21	0.4	22.1	38.7		44	0.3	15.1	35.7
22	0.1	3.4	6.4		45	3.4	145.3	239.7
23	0.1	2.5	5.4		46	7.7	505.5	931.2

Fig. 4. Performance of leanTAP, mKleanTAP, and αleanTAP on the first 46 Pelletier Problems. All times are in milliseconds, averaged over 100 trials. All tests were run under Debian Linux on an IBM Thinkpad X40 with a 1.1GHz Intel Pentium-M processor and 768MB RAM. leanTAP tests were run under SWI-Prolog 5.6.55; mKleanTAP and αleanTAP tests were run under Ikarus Scheme 0.0.3+.

These performance numbers suggest that while there is a penalty to be paid for declarativeness, it is not so severe as to cripple the prover. The advantage mKlean*TAP* enjoys over the original lean*TAP* in Problem 34 is due to αKanren's interleaving search strategy; as the result for mKlean*TAP* shows, the original lean*TAP* is faster than αlean*TAP* for any given search strategy.

Many automated provers now use the TPTP problem library [15] to assess performance. Even though it is faster than αlean*TAP*, however, lean*TAP* solves few of the TPTP problems. The Pelletier Problems, on the other hand, fall into the class of theorems lean*TAP* was designed to prove, and so we feel they provide a better set of tests for the comparison between lean*TAP* and αlean*TAP*.

6   Related Work

Through his integration of lean*TAP* with the Isabelle theorem prover [12], Paulson shows that it is possible to modify lean*TAP* to produce a list of Isabelle tactics representing a proof. This approach could be reversed to produce a proof translator from Isabelle proofs to αlean*TAP* proofs, allowing αlean*TAP* to become interactive as discussed in section 3.2.

The lean*TAP* Frequently Asked Questions [16] states that lean*TAP* might be made declarative through the elimination of Prolog's cuts but does not address the problem of `copy_term/2` or specify how the cuts might be eliminated. Other provers written in Prolog include those of Manthey and Bry [17] and Stickel [18], but each uses some impure feature and is thus not declarative.

Christiansen [19] uses constraint logic programming and metavariables (similar to nominal logic's names) to build a declarative interpreter based on Kowalski's non-declarative `demonstrate` predicate [20]. This approach is similar to ours, but the Prolog-like language is not complicated by the presence of binders.

Higher-order abstract syntax (HOAS), presented in Pfenning and Elliott [21], can be used instead of nominal logic to perform substitution on quantified formulas. Felty and Miller [22] were among the first to develop a theorem prover using HOAS to represent formulas; Pfenning and Schurmann [23] also use a HOAS encoding for formulas.

Kiselyov [24] uses a HOAS encoding for universally quantified formulas in his original translation of lean*TAP* into miniKanren. Since miniKanren does not implement higher-order unification, the prover cannot generate theorems.

Lisitsa's λlean*TAP* [25] is a prover written in λProlog that addresses the problem of `copy_term/2` using HOAS, and is perhaps closest to our own work. Like αlean*TAP*, λlean*TAP* replaces universally quantified variables with logic variables using substitution. However, λlean*TAP* is not declarative, since it contains cuts. Even if we use our techniques to remove the cuts from λlean*TAP*, the prover does not generate theorems, since λProlog uses a depth-first search strategy. Generating theorems requires the addition of a tagging scheme and iterative deepening on *every clause* of the program. Even with these additions, however, λlean*TAP* often generates theorems that do not have the proper HOAS encoding, since that encoding is not specified in the prover.

7 Conclusion

We have presented αleanTAP, a declarative tableau theorem prover for first-order classical logic. Based on the concise but non-declarative prover leanTAP, αleanTAP retains leanTAP's minimalism without the use of Prolog's copy_term/2 or cut. To avoid the use of copy_term/2, we have represented universally quantified variables with noms rather than logic variables, allowing us to perform substitution instead of copying. To eliminate cuts, we have enhanced the tagging scheme for representing formulas.

Both of these transformations are broadly applicable. When cuts are used to handle overlapping clauses, a carefully crafted tagging scheme can often be used to eliminate overlapping. When terms must be copied, substitution can often be used instead of copy_term/2—in the case of αleanTAP, we use a combination of nominal unification and substitution.

The resulting theorem prover retains the strengths of leanTAP. It is slower than mKleanTAP, our translation of leanTAP, by a factor of two, but remains concise. In addition, its declarative nature makes it more flexible than leanTAP: given non-ground values for both the theorem to be proved *and* its proof, αleanTAP fills in the uninstantiated parts. Like leanTAP, αleanTAP has the capability of proving theorems on its own, and like a proof assistant, it can accept help from the user in proving theorems.

Acknowledgements

We thank Oleg Kiselyov for pointing out an alternative solution for making leanTAP declarative and for his helpful comments on a draft of this paper. We also thank Matthew Lakin for his comments on a later version. We are grateful to Ramana Kumar and Christian Urban for their work on the triangular substitution-based implementation of αKanren. We also thank Micah Linnemeier and Adam Hinz for their participation in the early stages of this research. We appreciate the many insightful comments provided by the anonymous referees.

References

1. Beckert, B., Posegga, J.: leanTAP: Lean tableau-based deduction. Journal of Automated Reasoning 15(3), 339–358 (1995)
2. Byrd, W.E., Friedman, D.P.: αKanren: A fresh name in nominal logic programming. In: Proceedings of the 2007 Workshop on Scheme and Functional Programming, Université Laval Technical Report DIUL-RT-0701, pp. 79–90 (2007), http://www.cs.indiana.edu/~webyrd
3. Mellish, C.S.: The Automatic Generation of Mode Declarations for Prolog Programs. Dept. of Artificial Intelligence, University of Edinburgh (1981)
4. Pitts, A.M.: Nominal logic: A first order theory of names and binding. In: Kobayashi, N., Pierce, B.C. (eds.) TACS 2001. LNCS, vol. 2215, pp. 219–242. Springer, Heidelberg (2001)

5. Urban, C., Pitts, A., Gabbay, M.: Nominal unification. Theoretical Computer Science 323(1-3), 473–497 (2004)
6. Sperber, M., Clinger, W., Dybvig, R., Flatt, M., van Straaten, A., Kelsey, R., Rees, J.: Revised 6 report on the algorithmic language Scheme (September 2007)
7. Baader, F., Snyder, W.: Unification theory. Handbook of Automated Reasoning 1, 446–533
8. Cheney, J., Urban, C.: αProlog: A logic programming language with names, binding and α-equivalence. In: Demoen, B., Lifschitz, V. (eds.) ICLP 2004. LNCS, vol. 3132, pp. 269–283. Springer, Heidelberg (2004)
9. Byrd, W.E., Friedman, D.P.: From variadic functions to variadic relations
10. Friedman, D.P., Byrd, W.E., Kiselyov, O.: The Reasoned Schemer. The MIT Press, Cambridge (2005)
11. Fitting, M.: First-Order Logic and Automated Theorem Proving. Springer, Heidelberg (1996)
12. Paulson, L.C.: A generic tableau prover and its integration with Isabelle. Journal of Universal Computer Science 5(3), 73–87 (1999)
13. Pelletier, F.: Seventy-five problems for testing automatic theorem provers. Journal of Automated Reasoning 2(2), 191–216 (1986)
14. Kiselyov, O., Shan, C., Friedman, D., Sabry, A.: Backtracking, interleaving, and terminating monad transformers (functional pearl). ACM SIGPLAN Notices 40(9), 192–203 (2005)
15. Sutcliffe, G., Suttner, C.: The TPTP Problem Library. Journal of Automated Reasoning 21(2), 135–277 (1998)
16. Beckert, B., Posegga, J.: The leanTAP-FAQ: Frequently asked questions about leanTAP, http://www.uni-koblenz.de/~beckert/pub/LeanTAP_FAQ.pdf
17. Manthey, R., Bry, F.: SATCHMO: A theorem prover implemented in Prolog. In: Proceedings of the 9th International Conference on Automated Deduction, pp. 415–434 (1988)
18. Stickel, M.: A Prolog technology theorem prover. In: Proceedings of the 9th International Conference on Automated Deduction, pp. 752–753 (1988)
19. Christiansen, H.: Automated reasoning with a constraint-based metainterpreter. The Journal of Logic Programming 37(1-3), 213–254 (1998)
20. Kowalski, R.A.: Logic for Problem Solving. Prentice Hall PTR, Upper Saddle River (1979)
21. Pfenning, F., Elliot, C.: Higher-order abstract syntax. In: Proceedings of the SIGPLAN Conference on Programming Language Design and Implementation, vol. 23(7), pp. 199–208 (1988)
22. Felty, A., Miller, D.: Specifying theorem provers in a higher-order logic programming language. In: Proceedings of the 9th International Conference on Automated Deduction, pp. 61–80 (1988)
23. Pfenning, F., Schurmann, C.: System description: Twelf—a meta-logical framework for deductive systems. In: Proceedings of the 16th International Conference on Automated Deduction, pp. 202–206 (1999)
24. Friedman, D.P., Kiselyov, O.: A declarative applicative logic programming system, http://kanren.sourceforge.net
25. Lisitsa, A.: λleanTAP: lean deduction in λProlog. Technical report, ULCS-03-017, University of Liverpool, Department of Computer Science (2003)

Towards Ludics Programming: Interactive Proof Search

Alexis Saurin

INRIA Saclay - Île-de-France & École polytechnique (LIX)
saurin@lix.polytechnique.fr

Abstract. Girard [1] introduced Ludics as an interactive theory aiming at overcoming the distinction between syntax and semantics in logic.

In this paper, we investigate how ludics could serve as a foundation for logic programming, providing a mechanism for interactive proof search, that is proof search by interaction (or proof search by cut-elimination).

Keywords: Ludics, Game Semantics, Logic Programming, Proof Search, Interaction, Proof Normalization.

1 Introduction

Proof Theory and Computation. Recent developments in proof theory have led to major advances in the theory of programming languages. The modelling of computation using proofs impacted deeply the foundational studies of programming languages as well as many of their practical issues by providing formal tools to analyze programs properties. Declarative programming languages have been related mainly in two ways to the mathematical theory of proofs: on the one hand, the "computation as proof normalization" paradigm provided a foundation for functional programming languages through the well-known Curry-Howard correspondence [2]. On the other hand the "computation as proof search" paradigm stands as a foundation for logic programming: the computation of a program is the search for a proof in some deductive system.

Computation as Proof Search. Uniform proofs and abstract logic programming languages [3] and focalization [4] in linear logic (LL) [5] allowed to consider computation as proof search for much richer fragments of logic than first-order Horn clauses with resolution (Hereditary Harrop formulas, higher order, LL) and to benefit from the structure of sequent calculus which enrich the dynamics of proof search. This impacted deeply the design of logic programming languages by allowing to model various programming primitives logically (HO programming, modules, resource management, concurrent primitives, ...). Nevertheless some essential programming constructions could not be dealt with logically, in particular when concerned with the control of computation [6,7] (cut predicate, (intelligent) backtracking, ...). As a consequence, some parts of the languages do not have a very well established nor declarative semantics, and thus it is

M. Garcia de la Banda and E. Pontelli (Eds.): ICLP 2008, LNCS 5366, pp. 253–268, 2008.
© Springer-Verlag Berlin Heidelberg 2008

difficult to analyze programs using those constructions even though they are extremely common in Prolog programming. A long-standing research direction on proof search is to treat those extra-logical primitives in a logical way in order to get closer to the "ideal" correspondence: "Algorithm = Logic" [8].

We can draw a comparison with functional programming: the extension of the Curry-Howard correspondence to classical logic allowed to capture logically several control operators that were used in practice (like call/cc) thanks to typing rules [9] or thanks to extensions of λ-calculus such as $\lambda\mu$-calculus [10]. However, corresponding extensions in logic programming could not be achieved up to now, this may be understood as the result of a mismatch between sequent calculus proof theory and logic programming: while in sequent calculus, we manipulate proofs, the process of searching for proofs does not deal with proofs until the computation is finished. Instead, the objects of proof search are partial proofs (or open proofs) which may end up not leading to a proof at all but to a failure. Such failed proofs are not part of the proof theory of sequent calculus.

Ludics and Interaction. Girard introduced Ludics [1] in which unfinished proofs are given a clear status being at the heart of this theory of interaction. Ludics is a logical theory that attempts to overcome the distinction between syntax and semantics by considering that interaction comes first and by building syntax and semantics afterwards. Ludics objects can be seen as intermediate objects "between" syntax (sequent proofs) and semantics (innocent strategies [11]).

Games and Logic Programming. Game-theoretic approaches to logic programming are fairly natural and however not as much developped as for functional programming [12,13]. Van Emden was the first to notice connections between logic programming computations and two-person games with $\alpha\beta$-algorithm [14], which was later studied in details by Loddo et al. [15,16,17]. Pym and Ritter [18,19] proposed a game semantics for uniform proofs and backtracking by relating intuitionnistic and classical provability while the author, Miller and Delande [20,21] developed a neutral approach to proofs and refutations based on games which was inspired by Prolog search engine [20]. More recently, Galanaki et al. [22] generalized van Emden's games for logic programs with (well-founded) negation.

Structure of the Paper. We investigate the use of Ludics as a foundation for proof search and logic programming by means of a model of interactive proof search (IPS). We first draw in section 2 the general picture of "computation as interactive proof search" (or proof search by cut-elimination). Basic Ludics definitions are introduced in section 3 while the heart of the paper is section 4 with the definition of the SLAM, an abstract machine for IPS and the explanation of how backtracking can be treated.

2   Logic Programming, Interactivity and Ludics

In the uniform-proof model, computation is modelled as a search for a proof of a sequent $\mathcal{P} \vdash G$ which is directed by the goal G, the logic program $\mathcal{P}$ being used only when the goal is an atomic formula. While the dynamics of proof search is concerned with partial proofs, sequent calculus theory is a theory of complete proofs: it is thus difficult to speak about failures, backtrack or pruning of the search tree [7] (like the `cut` in Prolog) in this setting.

We propose another approach which considers proof search interactively.

2.1 Searching for Proofs Interactively

The sequent $\mathcal{P} \vdash G$ is the current state of the computation but it is also a way to constrain the future of the computation. In the same way, restrictions on the logical rules that are allowed (like in linear logic) or proof strategies also impose constraints on proof search. These constraints on the dynamics of proof search are of different kinds and are uneasy to relate and compare.

The interactive approach to proof search we are investigating precisely aims at providing a uniform framework for expressing and analyzing the constraints on proof search: instead of building a proof depending on a given sequent, we shall consider building a proof that shall pass some tests, that shall be opposed to attempts to refute it. The tests will have the form of (para)proofs and thus will be built in the same system as the one in which we are searching for proofs.

IPS Computation. We shall develop a computational setting as follows. We are willing to search for a proof $\mathfrak{D}$ of $\vdash A$. Formula A is described as a set of tests: $(\mathfrak{E}_i)_{i \in I}$. Proof construction shall proceed by consensus with the tests: $\mathfrak{D}$ can be extended with rule R only if the extended object interacts well with all the tests. At some point, it may become impossible to extend $\mathfrak{D}$ further: *(i)* either $\mathfrak{D}$ cannot pass some of the tests *(ii)* or all tests are satisfied and no more constraint applies to $\mathfrak{D}$ so that there is no need (and no guideline) to extend it further. Case *(i)* is a failure while case *(ii)* is a success. In case of a failure $\mathfrak{D}_{\maltese}$, one may try another search. Apart from backtracking up to the last choice point and restarting the search, there is another option: to use $\mathfrak{D}_{\maltese}$ in order to provide new tests $\mathfrak{E}_j^{\mathfrak{D}_{\maltese}}$ to constrain the search even more.

2.2 Motivations and Intuitions for Ludics

We describe ludics intuitions, with connections towards logic programming:

Monism. Ludics has been introduced by Girard [1] as an interactive theory that aims at overcoming the traditional distinction between syntax and semantics by considering that interaction should come first and logic shall be reconstructed afterwards: designs can be viewed both as an abstraction of multiplicative additive linear logic (MALL) sequent proofs (syntactical viewpoint) and as a concrete presentation of game semantics innocent strategies [11] (semantical viewpoint).

Focalization. Andreoli's Focalization [4] is the root of a polarized approach to logic [23] and allows to define synthetic connectives and synthetic rules (which are clusters of connectives or rules of the same polarity) in MALL. MALL connectives can be classified in two sets of connectives: positive connectives ($\otimes, \oplus, \mathbf{1}, \mathbf{0}$) and negative ones ($\invamp, \&, \perp, \top$). Provability cannot be lost during the negative phase while it can be during the positive phase by making a wrong choice of rule. Thus there is clearly an active phase (positive) and a passive phase (negative) and when searching for a proof, one alternates between those two phases.

Proof Normalization. In the cut elimination process, a conversion step corresponds to the selection, by the positive rule, of a continuation for the normalization (*e.g.* selection of one of the &-premises by a ⊕-rule during cut-elimination). But there is still a problem for an interactive interpretation to hold: we cannot find a proof for both A and $A^{\perp}$. Notice that if there cannot be proofs for both a formula and its negation, it is perfectly legal to attempt to prove both A and $A^{\perp}$ [20,21]. A failed attempt to prove A is a tree with some open branches. Let us add a new rule, the **daimon**, to mark the fact that the search for a proof has been stopped: $\overline{\vdash \Gamma}$ ✠. We thus have paraproofs for any sequents, even for $\vdash$.

The normalization between two paraproofs is a ***process through which they test each other***. The one that is caught using ✠ is considered as the loser of the play and the play ends there. Notice that this normalization process is an exploration of the two paraproofs: the cut visits some parts of the paraproofs. When ✠ is reached, the paraproofs are said to be **orthogonal**. A paraproof that wins an interaction may still contain itself a daimon: it is simply not part of this precise interaction, but would be detected by some other interactions.

Locations. Whereas in functional programming it matters to know if the types of functions and arguments match, it is not relevant for proof search to know the complete structure of formulas to be proved: we only need to know enough to choose the next rule. In Ludics, we use addresses (or **loci**): a formula is dealt with through its address ξ and an inference rule R on ξ creates **subloci** $(\xi i, \xi j, \dots)$ which refer to *where* the subformulas are (not *what* they are).

Behaviours. A provable formula may be interpreted as the set of its proofs or rather its paraproofs. Actually things are even more drastic in Ludics: formulas are defined interactively by a standard technique of biorthogonality closure which defines the **behaviours**. Given a paraproof Π in behaviour **A** and a paraproof Π' in $\mathbf{A}^{\perp}$, a part of Π can be explored by normalization with Π'. Sometimes Π is entirely visited by some Π' but usually, there are parts of Π that cannot be explored, whatever $\Pi' \in \mathbf{A}^{\perp}$ you test it with. However, a class of paraproofs which is highly interesting is the class of paraproofs that can be completely visited during normalization with elements of $\mathbf{A}^{\perp}$, they are said to be **material**.

2.3   Searching for Proofs Interactively in MALL

Adding More Proofs: *MALL*✠. If we want to search for proofs by interaction, we need to have enough proof objects to interact with, as noticed in 2.2: we need to extend logic in order to have more proofs and provable formulas. In the following, we consider $MALL$✠ proofs which are built from unit-only $MALL$-formulas $(F ::= F \otimes F \mid F \oplus F \mid \mathbf{1} \mid \mathbf{0} \mid F \,\otimes\, F \mid F \,\&\, F \mid \perp \mid \top)$ by adding the ✠ rule to $MALL$ proof system, see Figure 1.

$$\cfrac{}{\vdash \mathbf{1}} \mathbf{1} \qquad \cfrac{\vdash \Gamma, A \quad \vdash \Delta, B}{\vdash \Gamma, \Delta, A \otimes B} \otimes \qquad \cfrac{\vdash \Gamma, A_i}{\vdash \Gamma, A_0 \oplus A_1} \oplus_i, \ i \in \{0,1\} \qquad \cfrac{\vdash \Gamma, A \quad \vdash \Delta, A^{\perp}}{\vdash \Gamma, \Delta} \ cut$$

$$\cfrac{}{\vdash \Gamma, \top} \top \qquad \cfrac{\vdash \Gamma}{\vdash \Gamma, \perp} \perp \qquad \cfrac{\vdash \Gamma, A, B}{\vdash \Gamma, A \,\wp\, B} \,\wp \qquad \cfrac{\vdash \Gamma, A \quad \vdash \Gamma, B}{\vdash \Gamma, A \,\&\, B} \ \& \qquad \cfrac{}{\vdash \Gamma} \maltese$$

Fig. 1. $MALL\maltese$ sequent calculus (In $\maltese$, Γ contains no negative formula)

$$\mathfrak{D}_2 = \cfrac{\cfrac{}{\vdash \mathbf{1}_0} \maltese}{\vdash \mathbf{1}_0 \,\&\, (\perp_{10} \oplus_1 \perp_{11})} \&|_0 \qquad\qquad \mathfrak{D}_3 = \cfrac{\cfrac{}{\vdash \perp_{10} \oplus \perp_{11}} \maltese}{\vdash \mathbf{1}_0 \,\&\, (\perp_{10} \oplus_1 \perp_{11})} \&|_1$$

Fig. 2. MALL$\maltese$ proofs with partial inferences

An Example of IPS in MALL$\maltese$. We can look for a paraproof $\mathfrak{D}$ that would pass tests $\mathfrak{D}_0$ and $\mathfrak{D}_1$ which are paraproofs of sequent [1] $\vdash \mathbf{1}_0 \,\&\, (\perp_{10} \oplus_1 \perp_{11})$:

$$\mathfrak{D}_i = \cfrac{\cfrac{}{\vdash \mathbf{1}_0} \mathbf{1} \quad \cfrac{\cfrac{\cfrac{}{\vdash} \maltese}{\vdash \perp_{1i}} \perp}{\vdash \perp_{10} \oplus_1 \perp_{11}} \oplus_i}{\vdash \mathbf{1}_0 \,\&\, (\perp_{10} \oplus_1 \perp_{11})} \& \qquad\qquad \text{with } i \in \{0,1\}$$

$\mathfrak{D}$ shall be a proof of sequent $\vdash \perp_0 \oplus (\mathbf{1}_{10} \,\&_1\, \mathbf{1}_{11})$ such that paraproofs built by cutting $\mathfrak{D}$ with any of the $\mathfrak{D}_i$s normalize:

$$\cfrac{\mathfrak{D}_i \vdash \mathbf{1}_0 \,\&\, (\perp_{10} \oplus_1 \perp_{11}) \quad \mathfrak{D} \vdash \perp_0 \oplus (\mathbf{1}_{10} \,\&_1\, \mathbf{1}_{11})}{\vdash} \ cut \qquad \leadsto_{cut-elim} \qquad \cfrac{}{\vdash} \maltese$$

Performing the cut reduction will impose constraints on $\mathfrak{D}$ that can be used as a guide to search for a paraproof on $\vdash \perp_0 \oplus (\mathbf{1}_{10} \,\&_1\, \mathbf{1}_{11})$. We end up with:

$$\mathfrak{D} = \cfrac{\cfrac{\cfrac{}{\vdash \mathbf{1}_{10}} \mathbf{1}^{\star_0} \quad \cfrac{}{\vdash \mathbf{1}_{11}} \mathbf{1}^{\star_1}}{\vdash \mathbf{1}_{10} \,\&_1\, \mathbf{1}_{11}} \&}{\vdash \perp_0 \oplus (\mathbf{1}_{10} \,\&_1\, \mathbf{1}_{11})} \oplus_1 \qquad \text{or} \qquad \mathfrak{D}' = \cfrac{\cfrac{\cfrac{}{\vdash} \maltese}{\vdash \perp_0} \perp}{\vdash \perp_0 \oplus (\mathbf{1}_{10} \,\&_1\, \mathbf{1}_{11})} \oplus_0$$

In $\mathfrak{D}$, the branch ending at $\star_i$ has been built thanks to $\mathfrak{D}_i$. $\mathfrak{D}'$ is a failure.

Beyond MALL$\maltese$. Finally, one could even imagine adding paraproofs of figure 2 (which use only partial $\&$ proof rules) to the set of tests. If $\mathfrak{D}_2$ is in the normalization environment then $\mathfrak{D}$ *is forced* to use $\oplus_0$ as a first rule while interactive search with $\mathfrak{D}_3$ would forbid the search of failure $\mathfrak{D}'$ by forcing the selection of $\oplus_1$. $\mathfrak{D}_2$ and $\mathfrak{D}_3$ can thus be used to forbid some interactions to occur.

This brief study shows the many possibilities to guide (or constrain) proof search interactively. However, it is needed to relax some of the logical principles. For instance, it is needed to add the daimon $\maltese$ which allows to prove any sequent, but it is also important to admit "partial" logical rules (see $\mathfrak{D}_2$ and $\mathfrak{D}_3$) and other principles of (linear) logic shall be reconsidered (the weakening for instance). This is one of the reasons why we go to Ludics which has a good theory of interaction.

The following section is devoted to the introduction of Ludics.

---

[1] We index formulas to identify them more easily, anticipating on the use of addresses.

3   Introduction to Ludics

Actions and Designs. In Ludics, proofs are replaced by designs and proof rules by actions while formulas are now accessed through their location.

An **address** (or **locus**) is a finite sequence of integers (written ξ). An **action** is either a pair of an address (the **focus**) and a finite set of integers together with a polarity (we write $(\xi, I)^+$ or $(\xi, I)^-$ and speak of **proper actions**) or the **daimon** ($\maltese$) which is positive. When forgetting the polarity of a proper action κ, we speak of a **neutral action** and write κ_ν. We say that $(\xi, I)^\epsilon$ **creates** addresses $\xi \star i$ ($i \in I$) and that action κ **justifies** κ' when they have opposite polarity and κ creates the focus of κ'. A **base** is a finite set of polarized addresses (ξ^+ or ξ^-) with at most one negative address and such that no address is prefix of another address. We write $\xi \vdash \Lambda$ (resp. $\vdash \Lambda$) for **negative** (resp. **positive**) **bases**. A singleton base $(\xi \vdash, \vdash \xi)$ is **atomic** and $\vdash$ is the **empty base**.

A **design** $\mathfrak{D}$ on a base β is a (possibly infinite) prefix-closed set of finite sequences of actions (*ie.* a forest of actions) such that:

Chronicles. Let $\chi = (\kappa_0, \ldots, \kappa_n) \in \mathfrak{D}$. In χ, actions have alternating polarities and addresses occur at most once. If $\kappa_i \in \chi$, either $\kappa_i = (\xi, I)^\epsilon$ and $\xi^\epsilon \in \beta$ or κ_i is justified by κ_j with $j < i$ ($j = i - 1$ for κ_i negative) or $\kappa_i = \maltese$ and $i = n$;

Positivity. The leaves of the forest are positive;

Positive branching. The tree only branches on positive actions: if $\chi_1, \chi_2 \in \mathfrak{D}$ are not prefix of each other, they first differ on negative actions;

Additive sharing. If κ_0, κ_1 are distinct actions with the same focus then the sequences leading to κ_0 and κ_1 first differ on negative actions with same focus;

Totality. If the base is positive, $\mathfrak{D} \neq \emptyset$.

A design is **positive or negative** according to its base. A **slice** is a design where no address occurs twice. A slice of a design $\mathfrak{D}$ is any slice included in $\mathfrak{D}$. In particular, a negative slice is a tree. When drawing designs and slices, we adopt **Faggian's convention**: positive actions are circled while negative actions (which are not branching) are not circled. We give in figure 3 and 4 examples of designs. Notice that $\mathfrak{D}_0, \mathfrak{D}_1$ are slices while $\mathfrak{D}$ is not in figure 3.

Another approach to designs is as **co-inductively generated** by a grammar:
$$\mathfrak{P} ::= \maltese^{\vdash \Gamma} \mid (\xi, I)^+ \cdot \{\mathfrak{N}_i^{\xi i \vdash \Gamma_i}, i \in I, i \neq j \Rightarrow \Gamma_i \cap \Gamma_j = \emptyset, \forall i \in I, \Gamma_i \subset \Gamma\}^{\vdash \xi, \Gamma}$$
$$\mathfrak{N} ::= \{(\xi, I)^- \cdot \mathfrak{P}_I^{\vdash \xi I, \Gamma_I}, I \in \mathcal{N} \subset \mathcal{P}_f(\omega), \forall I \in \mathcal{N}, \Gamma_I \subset \Gamma\}^{\xi \vdash \Gamma}$$
For instance, $\mathfrak{Far}_{\xi \vdash \xi'}$ is $\mathfrak{Far}_{\xi \vdash \xi'} = \{(\xi, I)^- \cdot (\xi', I)^+ \cdot \{\mathfrak{Far}_{\xi' i \vdash \xi i}, i \in I\}, I \in \mathcal{P}_f(\omega)\}$.

Normalization and Interaction. Interaction is built with cut-nets normalization which reflects linear logic cut-normalization. Designs are cut-free: a cut is the coincidence of a locus with opposite polarity in the base of two designs.

A **cut-net** $\mathfrak{R} = (\mathfrak{D}_i)_{i \in I}$ is a non-empty finite set of designs on bases $(\beta_i)_{i \in I}$ such that *(i)* the loci in $(\beta_i)_{i \in I}$ are either equal or disjoint; *(ii)* a locus ξ appears in at most two bases (then it occurs with different polarities and is called a **cut** in $\mathfrak{R}$) and *(iii)* the cuts define a binary relation over the designs which shall be connected and acyclic. The **base** of $\mathfrak{R}$ is the set of polarized loci of the $(\beta_i)_{i \in I}$

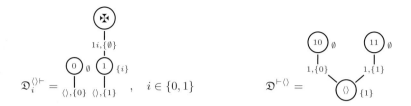

Fig. 3. Designs corresponding to MALL✠ proofs from section 2.3

Fig. 4. Important designs: $\mathfrak{Dai}, \mathfrak{Dai}^- \,\&\, \mathfrak{Far}$

which **are not** cuts. A net with empty base is **closed**. An action in $\mathfrak{R}$ is **visible** if it is ✠ or if its focus is not subloctus of a cut, otherwise it is **hidden**. In any cut-net, there is a **main design**: the only positive design of the net if such a design exists or the only negative design of base $\xi \vdash \Lambda$ such that ξ is not a cut.

Whereas in slices all actions are distinct, a design $\mathfrak{D}$ may contain several copies of the same action. To describe an action occurrence, we need additional information on the *position* of the action in the design: the branch leading to the action, called the **chronicle** for κ and written $Ch_{\mathfrak{D}}(\kappa)$. Views will allow to find the chronicle for an action provided we know a certain path in the design. The ***positive and negative views*** for a sequence of neutral actions are[2]: (i) $\ulcorner \epsilon \urcorner^+ = \ulcorner \epsilon \urcorner^- = \epsilon$; (ii) $\ulcorner s \cdot (\xi, I) \urcorner^+ = \ulcorner s \urcorner^- \cdot (\xi, I)^+$; (iii) $\ulcorner s \cdot (\xi, I) \urcorner^- = \ulcorner t \urcorner^+ \cdot (\xi, I)^-$ if $s = tu$ and u is the longest suffix of s such that no action in u creates ξ.

A path p in a slice $\mathfrak{S}$ (*ie.* a sequence of actions in $\mathfrak{S}$) is a **visit path** if it is: (i) of alternating polarities; (ii) made only of proper actions; (iii) downward closed (if $p' \cdot \kappa$ is a prefix of p, all actions below κ in $\mathfrak{S}$ are in p'). The polarity of p is its last action polarity. Given a path p, we write p_ν for the sequence of neutral actions canonically associated with p. Notice that a visit path cannot necessarily be realized by interaction. The following is an essential property of views: If p is a visit path in a slice $\mathfrak{S}$ with last action κ of polarity ϵ then $\ulcorner p_\nu \urcorner^\epsilon$ is the chronicle for κ in $\mathfrak{S}$, $Ch_{\mathfrak{S}}(\kappa)$.

The ***Loci Abstract Machine*** (LAM [24]), is an abstract machine that computes the interaction of a cut-net $\mathfrak{R}$, described as tokens[3] travelling on the cut-net. Let $\mathfrak{R}$ be a cut-net on a base β. Let $T_{\mathfrak{R}}$ be the set of all positions reached by the tokens during normalization.

---

[2] Notice that in case (iii), either t is empty or its last neutral action is (σ, J) with $\xi = \sigma j$ for some $j \in J$. Moreover, one can trivially extend positive views to sequences ending with the ✠: $\ulcorner s \cdot ✠ \urcorner^+ = \ulcorner s \urcorner^- \cdot ✠$.

[3] A **token** is a pair (s, κ) of a neutral sequence of actions s and an action κ, where s records the path followed by the token from the initial state up to κ.

- **Initialization.** If κ is at the root of the main design in $\mathfrak{R}$ the $(\epsilon, \kappa) \in T_{\mathfrak{R}}$;
- **Transitions.** Let $(s, \kappa) \in T_{\mathfrak{R}}$. There are 3 cases:
  - **Visible.** If κ is a visible action of polarity ϵ, then for each κ' such that $\ulcorner s\kappa\urcorner^{\epsilon}\kappa' \in \mathfrak{R}$, $(s\kappa, \kappa') \in T_{\mathfrak{R}}$ (notice $\ulcorner s\kappa\urcorner^{\epsilon}$ is the chronicle leading to κ);
  - **Up.** If κ is a hidden negative action, then let κ' be the successor of the extremal action of $\ulcorner s\kappa\urcorner^{-}$, we have $(s\kappa, \kappa') \in T_{\mathfrak{R}}$;
  - **Jump.** If κ is a hidden positive action, then let $\kappa' = \kappa^{-}$. If $\ulcorner s\kappa\urcorner^{-} \in \mathfrak{R}$ then $(s, \kappa') \in T_{\mathfrak{R}}$. Otherwise normalization fails.

Let $\mathfrak{R}$ be a cut-net and let $T_{\mathfrak{R}}$ be the positions reached by the tokens during normalization. A ***normalization path*** is the sequence of actions which are visited during the normalization of $\mathfrak{R}$: $Path(\mathfrak{R})$ is defined to be the set $\{s \cdot \kappa_{\nu}/(s, \kappa) \in T_{\mathfrak{R}}$ such that s is maximal$\}$. We also define $hide(p)$ to be the sequence obtained by removing all hidden actions in p and ***Hide($\mathfrak{R}$)*** to be the set $\{hide(p), p \in Path(\mathfrak{R})\}$. The ***normal form*** of a cut-net $\mathfrak{R}$ is the design defined to be[4]: $[\mathfrak{R}] = \{\chi/\chi$ is a prefix of p^{+} with $p \in \mathrm{Hide}(\mathfrak{R})\}$.

If $\mathfrak{R}$ is a closed cut-net, we call ***dispute*** the normalization path of $\mathfrak{R}$. If the net is $\{\mathfrak{D}, \mathfrak{E}\}$, we write $[\mathfrak{D} \rightleftharpoons \mathfrak{E}]$ for the dispute.

Orthogonality and Behaviours. Orthogonality describes those normalizations that were successful: designs $\mathfrak{D}, \mathfrak{E}$ are ***orthogonal*** if they form a cut-net and $[\mathfrak{D}, \mathfrak{E}] = \maltese$, written $\mathfrak{D} \perp \mathfrak{E}$. If $\mathfrak{D}$ has base $\xi_1^{\epsilon_1}, \ldots, \xi_n^{\epsilon_n}$ and $(\mathfrak{E}_{\xi_i})_{1 \leq i \leq n}$ are designs on atomic base $\xi_i^{-\epsilon_i}$, $(\mathfrak{D}, \mathfrak{E}_{\xi_1}, \ldots, \mathfrak{E}_{\xi_n})$ forms a closed cut-net; if $[\mathfrak{D}, \mathfrak{E}_{\xi_1}, \ldots, \mathfrak{E}_{\xi_n}] = \maltese$ we write $\mathfrak{D} \perp (\mathfrak{E}_{\xi_i})_{1 \leq i \leq n}$. The ***orthogonal*** of an atomic design $\mathfrak{D}$ is: $\mathfrak{D}^{\perp} = \{\mathfrak{E}/\mathfrak{D} \perp \mathfrak{E}\}$. A set of designs on the same atomic base, written **E**, is called an ***ethic*** and its orthogonal is $\mathbf{E}^{\perp} = \{\mathfrak{D}/\forall \mathfrak{E} \in \mathbf{E}, \mathfrak{D} \perp \mathfrak{E}\}$. $\prec$ is a relation on designs defined by: $\mathfrak{D} \prec \mathfrak{D}'$ if, and only if, $\mathfrak{D}^{\perp} \subseteq \mathfrak{D}'^{\perp}$. $\prec$ is actually a ***partial order*** (Separation theorem, [1]).

A ***behaviour*** **G** is an ethic which is equal to its bi-orthogonal: $\mathbf{G} = \mathbf{G}^{\perp\perp}$. It is immediate that ***the orthogonal of an ethic*** is a behaviour. Let $\mathfrak{D}$ be a design, the ***principal behaviour*** of $\mathfrak{D}$ is $\{\mathfrak{D}\}^{\perp\perp}$: it is the smallest behaviour containing $\mathfrak{D}$. If $\mathfrak{E} \in \mathbf{G}$, there exists a smallest design $\mathfrak{D} \subset \mathfrak{E}$ such that $\mathfrak{D} \in \mathbf{G}$. It is the ***incarnation*** of $\mathfrak{E}$ in **G** written $|\mathfrak{E}|_{\mathbf{G}}$. A design is said to be ***material*** in a behaviour when it is equal to its own incarnation.

4   Interactive Proof Search Algorithm

In this section, we give a machine inspired by Faggian's LAM, the Searching LAM (SLAM) allowing to build interactively designs by orthogonality to tests.

Idea of the algorithm. Before going to the formal definitions of IPS procedure, we sketch how IPS works on a simple example: consider the interactive search driven by one very simple design provided in figure 5 resulting in a design $\mathfrak{D}$.

0. To begin with, $\mathfrak{D}_0$ is empty and we have visited an empty path: $Path_0 = \epsilon$;
1. $\mathfrak{E}$ is a negative design so that it is a forest. It may begin with several negative

---

[4] We use notation $s^{+/-}$ to mean: $\epsilon^{+} = \epsilon^{-} = \epsilon$; $(s \cdot \kappa)^{+} = s^{-} \cdot \kappa^{+}$; $(s \cdot \kappa)^{-} = s^{+} \cdot \kappa^{-}$.

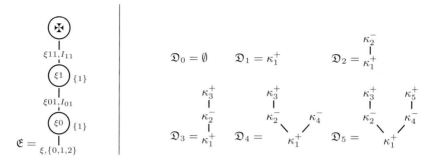

Fig. 5. Interactive search for $\mathfrak{D}$

actions on focus ξ, in $\text{Init}_{\mathfrak{E}} = \{(\xi, \{0,1,2\})^-\}$, one of which shall be followed during a normalization process. Choose some action κ_1^- in $\text{Init}_{\mathfrak{E}}$ and add $\kappa_{1\nu}$ to the normalization path and κ_1^+ as the first action of $\mathfrak{D}$: $Path_1 = \langle (\xi, \{0,1,2\}) \rangle$;

2. Design $\mathfrak{D}$ could have several negative actions above κ_1^+ but at this point, normalization would follow only one action which corresponds to the positive action after κ_1^- in $\mathfrak{E}$: $\kappa_2^+ = (\xi 0, \{1\})^+$ and $Path_2 = \langle \kappa_{1\nu}, \kappa_{2\nu} \rangle$;

3. In $\mathfrak{E}$, κ_2^+ is followed by actions in $\{(\xi 01, I_{01})^-\}$, we choose κ_3^- in this set and we extend $Path_2$ with $\kappa_{3\nu}$ and $\mathfrak{D}$ with κ_3^+: $Path_3 = \langle \kappa_{1\nu}, \kappa_{2\nu}, \kappa_{3\nu} \rangle$;

4. In $\mathfrak{E}$, κ_3^- is followed by $\kappa_4^+ = (\xi 1, \{1\})^+$ and thus, $Path_3$ is extended with $\kappa_{4\nu}$ and $\mathfrak{D}_4$ with κ_4^- which is put right above its justifyer. $Path_4 = \langle \kappa_{1\nu}, \kappa_{2\nu}, \kappa_{3\nu}, \kappa_{4\nu} \rangle$ and the branch leading to κ_4^- in $\mathfrak{D}$ is given by: $\ulcorner Path_4 \urcorner^- = \kappa_1^+, \kappa_4^-$;

5. In $\mathfrak{E}$, $Succ(\kappa_4^+) = \{(\xi 11, I_{11})^-\}$. $Path_5 = \langle \kappa_{1\nu}, \ldots, \kappa_{5\nu} \rangle$ and we add κ_5^+;

6. In $\mathfrak{E}$, κ_5^- is followed by a unique action, $\kappa_6^+ = \maltese$. The normalization ends with $\mathfrak{E}$ using a $\maltese$ and the final dispute is $[\mathfrak{D} \rightleftharpoons \mathfrak{E}] = \langle \kappa_{1\nu}, \ldots, \kappa_{5\nu}, \maltese \rangle$.

At the end of the IPS, we have built a design $\mathfrak{D}$ on $\vdash \xi$ such that $[\mathfrak{D}, \mathfrak{E}] = \maltese$ with $\maltese$ used by $\mathfrak{E}$. This example illustrates the basic mechanisms that we shall encounter while doing IPS. We now introduce formally the IPS process.

4.1   SLAM-1

We first introduce an abstract machine for interactive search of designs in the restricted case of 4, when the test-environment is made of only one design, $\mathfrak{E}$.

Definition 1 (States of SLAM-1). *States of SLAM-1 are triples $\langle p \bullet \mathbf{E} \mid \mathfrak{D}$ of a sequence of neutral actions p, a set of designs $\mathbf{E}$ (current test-environment) containing at most one positive design and a set of chronicles $\mathfrak{D}$ (the design under construction, for which p is a visit path). An **initial state** is of the form $\langle \epsilon \bullet \{\mathfrak{E}\} \mid \emptyset \rangle$. A **final state** of the form $\langle p \bullet \emptyset \mid \mathfrak{D} \rangle$.*

We saw in 4 that there may be choices to make during IPS when several negative actions are available. In order to define a deterministic search machine (for instance a depth-first search strategy with left most choice), we introduce **selection functions** which shall parametrize the abstract machine. Those selection functions take as input a state $\mathcal{S}$ of the machine together with a set of negative actions *Init* and return a subset of *Init* (which is not empy unless *Init* is itself empty). A selection function *Select* is said **deterministic** when $Select(\mathcal{S}, Init)$ is a singleton except when $Init = \emptyset$. When taking as selection function the second projection one has the fully non-deterministic machine. Moreover, the set *Init* of initial negative actions is obtained as follows: given a family of negative designs $\mathbf{E} = (\mathfrak{D}_i = \{\kappa_j^{i^-} \cdot \mathfrak{D}_j^i, j \in J_i\})_{i \in I}$, one sets $Init(\mathbf{E})$ to $\{\kappa_j^{i^-}, j \in J_i, i \in I\}$. Then, given a sequence of neutral actions p, a set of negative actions I and a set of chronicles $\mathfrak{D}$, one sets $\Im(p, I, \mathfrak{D})$ to be $\{\kappa \in Init \,/\, \kappa \text{ is justified by an action in } \ulcorner p \urcorner^-\}$.

Definition 2 (SLAM-1). *Let Select be a selection function and $\mathfrak{E}$ an atomic design. SLAM-1 is defined as follows:*

Initial State: $\langle \epsilon \bullet \{\mathfrak{E}\} \mid \emptyset \rangle$

Transitions: $\langle p \bullet \mathbf{E} \mid \mathfrak{D} \rangle \longrightarrow \langle p' \bullet \mathbf{E}' \mid \mathfrak{D}' \rangle$

- *If $\mathbf{E}$ contains a positive design $\mathfrak{D}^+ = \kappa^+ \cdot \{\mathfrak{D}'_j, j \in J\}$. If $\kappa^+ = \maltese$, then final state $\langle p \bullet \maltese \bullet \emptyset \mid \mathfrak{D} \rangle$ is reached. Otherwise, κ^+ is proper and we set **(i)** p' to $p \cdot \kappa$, **(ii)** $\mathbf{E}'$ to $\mathbf{E} \setminus \{\mathfrak{D}^+\} \cup \{\mathfrak{D}'_j, j \in J\}$ and **(iii)** $\mathfrak{D}'$ to $\mathfrak{D} \cup \{\ulcorner p \cdot \kappa \urcorner^-\}$.*

- *Otherwise $\mathbf{E} = (\mathfrak{D}_i = \{\kappa_j^{i^-} \cdot \mathfrak{D}_j^i, j \in J_i\})_{i \in I}$. Let $Ini = \Im(p, Init(\mathbf{E}), \mathfrak{D})$. If $Select(\langle p \bullet \mathbf{E} \mid \mathfrak{D} \rangle, Ini) \neq \emptyset$, one chooses some $\kappa \in Select(\langle p \bullet \mathbf{E} \mid \mathfrak{D} \rangle, Ini)$, and considers $\mathfrak{D}_i$ $(i \in I)$ the negative design of which κ is an initial action, and $\mathfrak{D}_j^i$ $(j \in J_i)$ the positive design immediately above κ in $\mathfrak{D}_i$ (ie. $\kappa = \kappa_j^i$). We set **(i)** p' to $p \cdot \kappa$, **(ii)** $\mathbf{E}'$ to $\mathbf{E} \setminus \{\mathfrak{D}_i\} \cup \{\mathfrak{D}_j^i\}$ and **(iii)** $\mathfrak{D}'$ to $\mathfrak{D} \cup \{\ulcorner p \cdot \kappa \urcorner^+\}$. If $Ini = \emptyset$, final state $\langle p \bullet \emptyset \mid \mathfrak{D} \cup \{\ulcorner p \cdot \maltese \urcorner^+\} \rangle$ is reached.*

   *A **result** of the machine consists in the third component of a final state.*

4.2   Properties of SLAM-1

We consider here an IPS with test environment $\mathbf{E}$. The sets of chronicles built by interaction during an evaluation of the machine satisfy the coherence conditions for designs in section 3:

Proposition 1. *The results of SLAM-1 executions are slices.*

Proposition 2. *If $\mathfrak{D}$ is a result of SLAM-1, then $\mathfrak{D} \in \mathbf{E}^\perp$. $\mathfrak{D}$ is material in $\mathbf{E}^\perp$.*

Definition 3 ($\mathfrak{D}_i^{\maltese}$). *If $(\langle p_i \bullet \mathbf{E}_i \mid \mathfrak{D}_i \rangle)_{0 \leq i \leq n}$ is a run of SLAM-1, then for $0 < i < n$ one may build a design $\mathfrak{D}_i^{\maltese}$ by adding a daimon if the last action visited is negative or replacing the last visited rule with a daimon if it is positive.*

$\mathfrak{D}_i^{\maltese}$ are more and more precise:

Proposition 3. *For $0 < i < n$, $\mathfrak{D}_i^{\maltese}$ is a slice, it is material in $\mathbf{E}^\perp$ and for $0 < i \leq j < n$, one has: $\{\mathfrak{D}_i^{\maltese}\}^{\perp\perp} \subseteq \{\mathfrak{D}_j^{\maltese}\}^{\perp\perp} \subseteq \mathbf{E}^\perp$.*

The IPS procedure described by SLAM-1 only produces slices as asserted by proposition 2. As a result, this setting is fairly restricted and moreover the test-environments considered are very constrained and as a conclusion do not allow much flexibility. For instance it does not allow to build proofs with additive branching and it does not allow to treat backtracking. For instance one would like to work with more general test environments such as the ones considered in section 2.3 when using $\mathfrak{D}_0$ and $\mathfrak{D}_1$ to build the two premisses of a with rule or with $\mathfrak{D}_2$ or $\mathfrak{D}_3$ to avoid visiting some branch. We shall now remove this restriction resulting in a more complex machine that we define in what follows.

4.3 SLAM-n

SLAM-n will consider states storing several tests and the interactive construction will depend on several designs and not only one: as a consequence there shall be a mechanism to synchronize the tests that contribute to the same branch. Moreover distinct parts of the test environment may contribute to different additive branches of the design; it is thus necessary to locate the interactions.

Definition 4 (SLAM-n States). *States have the form* $\langle (p_i \bullet (\mathbf{E}_E^{ij})_{j \in J_i})_{i \in I} \mid \mathfrak{D} \rangle$ *where* $(p_i)_{i \in I}$ *are pairwise incomparable sequences of neutral actions,* $(\mathbf{E}^{ij})_{i \in I, j \in J_i}$ *are sets of designs such that for* $i \in I$ *either all* $\mathbf{E}^{ij}$ *($j \in J_i$) contain one positive design or they contain only negative designs, and* $\mathfrak{D}$ *is a set of chronicles.*

Definition 5 (SLAM-n). *Let Select be a selection function and* $(\mathfrak{E}_j)_{j \in J}$ *be designs on some atomic base* $\xi \vdash$, *SLAM-n is defined as follows:*

Initial State: $\langle (\epsilon \bullet (\{\mathfrak{E}_j\})_{j \in J}) \mid \emptyset \rangle$

Transitions: $\langle (p_i \bullet (\mathbf{E}_E^{ij})_{j \in J_i})_{i \in I} \mid \mathfrak{D} \rangle \longrightarrow \langle (p_i' \bullet (\mathbf{E}_E'^{ij})_{j \in J_i'})_{i \in I'} \mid \mathfrak{D}' \rangle$
  One chooses some $i_0 \in I$ *such that the last action of* p_{i_0} *is not* $\maltese$.
- *If each* $\mathbf{E}_E^{i_0 j}$ *contains a positive design* $\mathfrak{D}_{i_0 j}^+ = \kappa_{i_0 j}^+ \cdot \{\mathfrak{D}_k', k \in K_{i_0 j}\}$ *then let* $J_{i_0}' = \{j \in J_{i_0}, \kappa_{i_0 j}^+$ *is a proper action}. One partitions* J_{i_0}' *in maximal non-empty subsets* $(J_{i_0}^l)_{l \in L}$ *such that if* $\forall l \in L, \forall m, n \in J_{i_0}^l, \kappa_{i_0 m}^+ = \kappa_{i_0 n}^+$ *(and thus if* $k \neq l, m \in J_{i_0}^k, n \in J_{i_0}^l$ *then* $\kappa_{i_0 m}^+ \neq \kappa_{i_0 n}^+$). *Let* $\kappa_{i_0 l}'$ *be the action canonically associated with* $J_{i_0}^l$.
  (i) If $\exists l \in L, \ulcorner p_{i_0} \cdot \kappa_{i_0 l}' \urcorner^- \in \mathfrak{D}$, *SLAM-n is* **stuck,** *(ii) otherwise:*

  - $I' = I \setminus \{i_0\} \cup L, J_i' = J_i$ *if* $i \in I \setminus \{i_0\}$ *and* $J_l' = J_{i_0 l}, l \in L$
  - $p_i' = p_i$ *if* $i \in I \setminus \{i_0\}, p_l' = p_{i_0} \cdot \kappa_{i_0 l}', l \in L$
  - $\mathbf{E}'^{ij} = \mathbf{E}^{ij}$ *if* $i \in I \setminus \{i_0\}, j \in J_i$
  - $\mathbf{E}'^{lj} = \mathbf{E}^{i_0 j} \setminus \{\mathfrak{D}_{i_0 j}^+\} \cup \{\mathfrak{D}_k', k \in K_{i_0 j}\}$ *for* $l \in L, j \in J_{i_0 l}$
  - $\mathfrak{D}' = \mathfrak{D} \cup \{\ulcorner p_{i_0} \cdot \kappa_{i_0 l}' \urcorner^-, l \in L\}$

- *If for any* $j \in J_{i_0}, \mathbf{E}^{i_0 j}$ *contains only negative designs:* $(\mathfrak{D}_{jl} = \{\kappa_k^{jl^-} \cdot \mathfrak{D}_k^{jl}, k \in K_{jl}\})_{l \in L_j} = \mathbf{E}^{i_0 j}$. *Let* $Init_j = Init(\mathbf{E}^{i_0 j})$ *and* $Init = \Im(p_{i_0}, \cap_{j \in J_{i_0}} Init_j, \mathfrak{D})$.
  (i) If $Init \neq \emptyset$, *let* κ *be some action in* $Select(\langle (p_i \bullet (\mathbf{E}^{ij})_{j \in J_i})_{i \in I} \mid \mathfrak{D} \rangle, Init)$, *and for every* $j \in J_{i_0}$, *one considers the negative design* $\mathfrak{D}_{jl}$ *of which* κ *is an initial action in* $\mathbf{E}^{i_0 j}$ *and* $k_0 \in K_{jl}$ *such that* $\mathfrak{D}_{k_0}^{jl}$ *is the positive design immediately above* κ *in* $\mathfrak{D}_{jl}$. *Then, with* $I' = I$ *and* $J_i' = J_i, \forall i \in I'$:

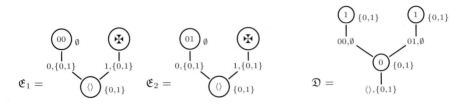

Fig. 6. An execution of SLAM-n from $\mathfrak{E}_1$ and $\mathfrak{E}_2$ not resulting in a design

- $p'_i = p_i$ for $i \neq i_0$ and $p'_{i_0} = p_{i_0} \cdot \kappa$
- $\mathbf{E}'^{ij} = \mathbf{E}^{ij}$ for $i \in I' \setminus \{i_0\}, j \in J'_i$ and $\mathbf{E}'^{i_0 j} = \mathbf{E}^{i_0 j} \setminus \{\mathfrak{D}_{jl}\} \cup \{\mathfrak{D}^{jl}_{k_0}\}, \forall j \in J_{i_0}$
- $\mathfrak{D}' = \mathfrak{D} \cup \{\ulcorner p_{i_0} \cdot \kappa \urcorner^+\}$

(ii) If $Init = \emptyset$, then we add chronicle $\ulcorner p_{i_0} \cdot \maltese \urcorner^+$ to the design under construction moving to the state: $\langle (p_i \bullet (\mathbf{E}^{ij}_E)_{j \in J_i})_{i \in I \setminus \{i_0\}} \mid \mathfrak{D} \cup \{\ulcorner p_{i_0} \cdot \maltese \urcorner^+\}\rangle$.

SLAM-n contains a case where the machine is stuck. Moreover, when the tests are chosen totally arbitrarily, the set of chronicles which is produced by SLAM-n may not be a design as examplified in figure 6: $\mathfrak{D}$ which results from IPS with $\mathfrak{E}_1$ and $\mathfrak{E}_2$, violates the ***additive sharing*** condition. In order to fix this problem, we slightly modify the definition of $\Im(p, I, \mathfrak{D})$ as follows: $\Im(p, I, \mathfrak{D}) = \{(\sigma, I)^- / (\sigma, I)^-$ is justified in $\ulcorner p \urcorner^-$ and if $\exists \chi \cdot (\sigma, L)^+ \in \mathfrak{D}$ then the first difference between χ and $\ulcorner p \urcorner^-$ involves negative actions on the same focus$\}$.

Proposition 4. *If $\langle (\epsilon \bullet \{(\mathfrak{E}_i)_{i \in I}\}) \mid \emptyset \rangle$ is an initial state, then an execution of SLAM-n that is never stuck (case 1.(i) is never encountered) results in a set of chronicles interactively built which is a design.*

Proposition 5. *A final state for an execution which is never **stuck** (case 1.(i) of SLAM-n) is of the form $\langle (p_i \cdot \maltese \bullet \emptyset)_{i \in I} \mid \mathfrak{D} \rangle$.*

4.4   Backtracking

In the present section we briefly explain how backtracking can be dealt with using generalized environments. We shall consider a final state $\mathcal{S}' = \langle (p_i \cdot \maltese \bullet \emptyset)_{i \in I} \mid \mathfrak{D} \rangle$ reached from an initial state $\mathcal{S} = \langle (\epsilon \bullet (\{\mathfrak{E}_j\})_{j \in J}) \mid \emptyset \rangle$. If $I \neq \emptyset$, then $\mathfrak{D}$ is a failure (it contains $\maltese$ at $\ulcorner p_i \cdot \maltese \urcorner^+$). One shall use those paths $p_i, i \in I$ to enrich the test environment with new designs.

Definition 6 ($\mathfrak{Test}(p)$). *If p is a sequence of neutral actions, $\mathfrak{Test}(p)$ is:*
$\mathfrak{Test}(\epsilon) = \emptyset$; $\mathfrak{Test}(\kappa) = \{\kappa^+\}$; $\mathfrak{Test}(s \cdot \kappa \cdot \kappa') = \{\ulcorner s \cdot \kappa \cdot \kappa' \urcorner^+, \ulcorner s \cdot \kappa \urcorner^-\} \cup \mathfrak{Test}(s)$.

Proposition 6. *$\mathfrak{Test}(p_i), i \in I$ is a slice. Moreover, $\mathfrak{Test}(p_i)$ is the smallest design (as sets of chronicles) realizing interaction $p_i \cdot \maltese$ with the final design $\mathfrak{D}$.*

In order to model the backtrack instruction, one shall use a variant of $\mathfrak{Test}(\_)$. Indeed, $\mathfrak{Test}(\_)$ contains both too many and too few chronicles to be used to backtrack: a backtrack design should not allow to interact along p_i up to reaching the daimon and it should be able to interact with any other design.

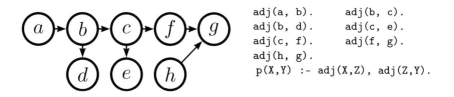

```
adj(a, b).        adj(b, c).
adj(b, d).        adj(c, e).
adj(c, f).        adj(f, g).
adj(h, g).
p(X,Y)  :- adj(X,Z), adj(Z,Y).
```

Fig. 7. Graph

Fig. 8. Designs $\mathfrak{E}_1$ and $\mathfrak{E}_2$ with $I_1 = \{a, b, c, d, g, h\}$, $I_2 = \{a, b, c, d, e, g\}$

Definition 7 ($\mathfrak{Backtrack}(p)$). $\mathfrak{Backtrack}(p)$ *is the smallest design such that:*

1. $\mathfrak{Backtrack}(p)$ *contains all positive chronicles of* $\mathfrak{Test}(p)$ *except* $\ulcorner p \urcorner^{\top+}$;
2. *if* $\chi \in \mathfrak{Backtrack}(p)$ *has last action* $(\xi, I)^+$, *then for any* $i \in I$ *and* $J \in \mathcal{P}_f(\omega)$
such that $\chi \cdot (\xi i, J)^- \notin \mathfrak{Test}(p)$, *one has* $\chi \cdot (\xi i, J)^- \cdot \maltese \in \mathfrak{Backtrack}(p)$.

Remark 1. In definition 7, $\mathfrak{Backtrack}(p)$ is drastically infinite because of all the $\chi \cdot$
$(\xi i, J)^- \cdot \maltese$ that are added. However, by collecting information during the search
(at step 1. of SLAM-n, when considering the set of initial positive actions in the
environment), one may retain the needed actions and build a finite $\mathfrak{Backtrack}(p)$
if original test-environments are made of finitely branching designs.

Proposition 7. $\langle (\epsilon \bullet (\{\mathfrak{E}_j\})_{j \in J} \cup (\{\mathfrak{Backtrack}(p_i)\})_{i \in I}) \mid \emptyset \rangle$ *is an initial state
that will not compute disputes* $(p_i)_{i \in I}$ *anymore.*

4.5   A Concrete Example

Let $\mathcal{G}$ be the graph represented in figure 7. We want to implement the search for
paths of length 2 in this graph using interactive proof search. This corresponds
to the predicates shown in figure 7. For instance, $p(c, g)$ could be represented
as the MALL formula: $\bigoplus_{x \in \{a,...,h\}} (adj(c, x) \;\&\; adj(x, g))$. The graph and the
path relation p shall be represented as counter-designs[5], as tests that will guide

---

[5] Here is how $\mathfrak{E}_1$ and $\mathfrak{E}_2$ are built: Let us choose a location p in which one shall locate
the designs of the environment (on base $p \vdash$) and the design to construct by ISP
(on base $\vdash p$). Let us suppose $a, b, \ldots, g, h$ are integer codes representing nodes of
the graph in the obvious way (one can choose arbitrary distinct integers). pe will
thus represent the formula $(adj(c, e) \;\&\; adj(e, g))$ and $pe1$ and $pe2$ will respectively
represent $(adj(c, e))$ and $(adj(e, g))$. $\mathfrak{E}_1$ represents the arcs having their origin in c and
$\mathfrak{E}_2$ represents the arcs having g as goal.

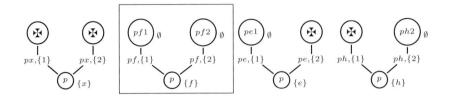

Fig. 9. The 8 possible results for an IPS with $\mathfrak{E}_1$ and $\mathfrak{E}_2$ ($x \in \{a, b, c, d, g\}$)

an interactive search for a design $\mathfrak{D}$. The counter-design environnement could be made of two designs $\mathfrak{E}_1$ and $\mathfrak{E}_2$ of figure 8.

There are 8 choices for the first action in constructing design $\mathfrak{D}$, but this leads then to the designs of figure 9 (8 possible computations) depending on the choice of the first action (only one being a success).

5   Conclusion

The aim of this paper was to introduce a novel approach to proof search as computation where the search is not guided by a sequent as in standard proof search but is contrained by an environment of tests.

Contributions. The contributions of the paper are the following: After motivating the need for an interactive approach for proof-search, we examplified a "concrete" approach to interactive proof-search on a sequent calculus derived from MALL sequent calculus. We then introduced ludics concepts by emphasizing those concepts that are the most relevant for the logic programming community. We introduced the SLAM, an abstract machine inspired by Faggian's LAM [24] and analyzed its search behaviour. Finally, we explained how to treat backtracking in interactive proof search by enriching the test-environment.

Related Works. In [24], Faggian introduced the LAM and studied some properties of its execution. Those results will be helpful to develop IPS. Pym and Ritter [18] give a semantics for proof search which is related with game semantics. They have a treatment of backtracking using relations between intuitionistic and classical proofs. We shall investigate the connections with our work.

Future Works. Lots of things are still to be done in order to have a computation model based on interactive proof search. First we shall develop the treatment of the cut and other pruning operations in the same way we did for backtracking. We shall work towards extending the expressiveness of interactive proof-search, mostly in two directions: first-order and exponentials. Fleury and Quatrini [25] proposed a theory of first-order in Ludics while Faggian and Basaldella proposed very recently an approach to the exponentials in Ludics that would allow using a formula (here, an action) several times. We shall investigate these two directions.

Aknowledgments. The author thanks Dale Miller for his advice and directions, Jean-Yves Girard for his comments on this project as well as Claudia Faggian for helpful discussions regarding the material in this paper.

References

1. Girard, J.Y.: Locus solum. Mathematical Structures in Computer Science 11(3) (2001)
2. Howard, W.A.: The formulae-as-type notion of construction, 1969. In: Seldin, Hindley (eds.) To H. B. Curry: Essays in Combinatory Logic, Lambda Calculus, and Formalism. Academic Press, New York (1980)
3. Miller, D., Nadathur, G., Pfenning, F., Scedrov, A.: Uniform proofs as a foundation for logic programming. Annals of Pure and Applied Logic 51 (1991)
4. Andreoli, J.M.: Logic programming with focusing proofs in linear logic. Journal of Logic and Computation 2(3) (1992)
5. Girard, J.Y.: Linear logic. Theoretical Computer Science 50 (1987)
6. Naish, L.: Negation and Control in Prolog. LNCS, vol. 238. Springer, Heidelberg (1986)
7. Naish, L.: Pruning in logic programming. Technical Report 95/16, Department of Computer Science, University of Melbourne, Australia (1995)
8. Miller, D.: Sequent calculus and the specification of computation. In: Berger, U., Schwichtenberg, H. (eds.) Computational Logic. Nato ASI Series, vol. 165. Springer, Heidelberg (1999)
9. Griffin, T.: A formulae-as-types notion of control. In: POPL 1990 (1990)
10. Parigot, M.: $\lambda\mu$-calculus: an algorithmic interpretation of classical natural deduction. In: Voronkov, A. (ed.) LPAR 1992. LNCS, vol. 624. Springer, Heidelberg (1992)
11. Faggian, C., Hyland, M.: Designs, disputes and strategies. In: Bradfield, J.C. (ed.) CSL 2002 and EACSL 2002. LNCS, vol. 2471, p. 442. Springer, Heidelberg (2002)
12. Abramsky, S., Jagadeesan, R.: Games and full completeness for multiplicative linear logic. Journal of Symbolic Logic 59(2) (1994)
13. Hyland, J.M.E., Ong, C.H.L.: On full abstraction for PCF. Information and Computation 163 (2000)
14. van Emden, M.H.: Quantitative deduction and its fixpoint theory. Journal of Logic Programming 3(1) (1986)
15. Cosmo, R.D., Loddo, J.V., Nicolet, S.: A game semantics foundation for logic programming. In: PLILP/ALP (1998)
16. Loddo, J.V., Cosmo, R.D.: Playing logic programs with the alpha-beta algorithm. In: Parigot, M., Voronkov, A. (eds.) LPAR 2000. LNCS, vol. 1955. Springer, Heidelberg (2000)
17. Loddo, J.V.: Généralisation des Jeux Combinatoires et Applications aux Langages Logiques. Ph.D thesis, Université Paris VII (2002)
18. Pym, D., Ritter, E.: Reductive Logic and Proof-search: proof theory, semantics, and control, vol. 45. Oxford Logic Guides, Oxford (2004)
19. Pym, D., Ritter, E.: A games semantics for reductive logic and proof-search. In: Ghica, D., McCusker, G. (eds.) GaLoP 2005 (2005)
20. Miller, D., Saurin, A.: A game semantics for proof search: Preliminary results. In: Proceedings of MFPS 2005. ENTCS, vol. 155 (2006)

21. Delande, O., Miller, D.: A neutral approach to proof and refutation in MALL. In: Pfenning, F. (ed.) LICS 2008. IEEE Computer Society Press, Los Alamitos (2008)

22. Galanaki, C., Rondogiannis, P., Wadge, W.W.: An infinite-game semantics for well-founded negation in logic programming. Annals of Pure and Applied Logic 151(2) (2008)

23. Laurent, O.: Étude de la polarisation en logique. Thèse de doctorat, Université Aix-Marseille II (2002)

24. Faggian, C.: Travelling on designs. In: Bradfield, J.C. (ed.) CSL 2002 and EACSL 2002. LNCS, vol. 2471. Springer, Heidelberg (2002)

25. Fleury, M.R., Quatrini, M.: First order in ludics. Mathematical Structures in Computer Science 14(2) (2004)

Declarative Semantics for Active Integrity Constraints

Luciano Caroprese[1] and Mirosław Truszczyński[2]

[1] Università della Calabria, 87030 Rende, Italy
[2] Department of Computer Science, University of Kentucky, Lexington, KY 40506, USA

Abstract. We study *active integrity constraints*, a formalism designed to describe integrity constraints on databases *and* to specify preferred ways to enforce them. The original semantics proposed for active integrity constraints is based on the concept of a *founded repair*. We point out that groundedness underlying founded repairs does not prevent cyclic justifications and so, may be inappropriate in some applications. Thus, using a different notion of grounding, with roots in logic programming and revision programming, we introduce two new semantics: of *justified weak repairs*, and of *justified repairs*. We study properties of these semantics, relate them to earlier semantics of active integrity constraints, and establish the complexity of basic decision problems.

1   Introduction

Integrity constraints are conditions on databases. If a database violates integrity constraints, it needs to be *repaired* — updated so that the integrity constraints hold again. Often there are several ways to enforce integrity constraints. The paper is concerned with the problem to specify preferred ways to update databases.

A database can be viewed formally as a finite set of ground atoms in the language of first-order logic determined by the database schema and an infinite countable set of constants. An *integrity constraint* is a formula in this language. A database *satisfies* an integrity constraint if it is its *Herbrand* model. Since databases and sets of integrity constraints are *finite*, without loss of generality, we will limit our attention to the case when databases are subsets of some finite set At of *propositional* atoms, and integrity constraints are clauses in the propositional language generated by At.

Let us consider the database $\mathcal{I} = \{a, b\}$ and the integrity constraint $\neg a \vee \neg b$. As, $\mathcal{I}$ does not satisfy $\neg a \vee \neg b$, it needs to be "repaired" — replaced by a database that satisfies the constraint. Assuming $At = \{a, b, c, d\}$, the databases $\emptyset$, $\{a\}$, $\{b\}$, $\{a, c\}$ are examples of databases that could be considered as replacements for $\mathcal{I}$. Since the class of replacements of $\mathcal{I}$ is quite large, the question arises whether there is a principled way to narrow it down. One of the most intuitive and commonly accepted postulates is that the change between the initial database $\mathcal{I}$ and the revised database $\mathcal{R}$, given by $\mathcal{I} \div \mathcal{R}$, be minimal (cf. [1]). In our case, the minimality of change narrows down the class of possible revisions to $\{a\}$ and $\{b\}$.

In some cases, the minimality of change is not specific enough and may leave too many candidate revisions. The problem can be addressed by formalisms that allow the database designer to formulate integrity constraints and, in addition, to state preferred ways for enforcing them. In this paper, we study a recent formalism of that type: *active integrity constraints* (*aic*'s, for short) [2].

M. Garcia de la Banda and E. Pontelli (Eds.): ICLP 2008, LNCS 5366, pp. 269–283, 2008.

Aic's *explicitly* encode both integrity constraints and preferred basic actions to repair them, when the constraints are violated. To specify the meaning of sets of aic's, [2] proposed the concept of *foundedness*, and combined it with the requirement of the minimality of change to get the semantics of *founded repairs*. Foundedness reflects a certain groundedness condition. We show that in some cases this groundedness condition is too weak to prevent *cyclic* justifications. To address the problem, we introduce a new semantics for aic's, which we call the semantics of *justified repairs*.

The semantics of *justified repairs* uses a stronger concept of groundedness than that behind founded repairs. In general, it is also too weak to imply the minimality of change property and so, we impose this property on justified repairs *explicitly*. We show that the class of justified repairs is a subclass of the class of founded repairs.

We also consider a broader class of ways to enforce integrity constraints by dropping the minimality of change postulate. We refer to the elements of that class as *weak repairs*. Combining the concept with the appropriate groundedness condition yields the semantics of *founded weak repairs* and *justified weak repairs*. While the minimality of change condition is a natural requirement to impose on preferred ways to enforce integrity constraints, including weak repairs in the considerations offers a richer perspective. In particular, it brings up the question of identifying classes of aic's, for which the groundedness condition alone is sufficient to guarantee change-minimality. We exhibit here two classes of aic's, for which the groundedness condition behind justified repairs ensures the minimality of change.

A fundamental property of semantics describing database updates is the invariance under *shifting* [3,4]. Informally, shifting consists of changing the membership status of some facts in a database and the corresponding modification (systematic renaming) of the integrity constraints. We show that all semantics of aic's we consider here are invariant under shifting.

Although we consider just the propositional case our results can be lifted to the first-order case via grounding (like in the case of stable-model semantics for Logic Programming). As a consequence, our framework is able to handle numerical expressions in the body of the constraints. Indeed, grounding eliminates them and leaves us with the basic propositional case presented here.

A richer field of semantics of database updates gives rise to a trade-off. On the one hand the semantics differ in how much they refine the class of (weak) repairs that enforce integrity constraints, and on the other hand, in the complexity of the existence of a repair problem. We discuss ways in which this trade-off can be exploited in practice.

The semantics discussed in the paper are motivated by connections to the semantics of answer sets for disjunctive logic programming on the one hand, and to revision programming [3], on the other. We exploit them to develop the definition of groundedness for justified weak repairs, and to establish the complexity of deciding the existence of repairs of particular types. We develop a detailed discussion of these connections in another paper [5]. Due to space limits, we omit the proofs (they can be found at www.cs.uky.edu/ai/aic-full.pdf).

2   Integrity Constraints and Database Repairs — Basic Concepts

We consider a finite set At of propositional atoms. We represent databases as subsets of At. Databases are *updated* by inserting and deleting atoms. An *update action* is an expression of the form $+a$ or $-a$, where $a \in At$. Update actions $+a$ and $-b$ state that a and b are to be inserted and deleted, respectively. We say that a set $\mathcal{U}$ of update actions is *consistent* if it does not contain update actions $+a$ and $-a$, for any $a \in At$.

Sets of update actions determine database updates. Let $\mathcal{D}$ be a database and $\mathcal{U}$ a consistent set of update actions. The result of *updating* $\mathcal{D}$ *by means of* $\mathcal{U}$ is the database

$$\mathcal{DB} \circ \mathcal{U} = (\mathcal{DB} \cup \{a \mid +a \in \mathcal{U}\}) \setminus \{a \mid -a \in \mathcal{U}\}.$$

We have the following straightforward property of the operator $\circ$, which asserts that if a set o update actions is consistent, the order in which they are executed is immaterial.

Proposition 1. *If $\mathcal{U}_1$ and $\mathcal{U}_2$ are sets of update actions such that $\mathcal{U}_1 \cup \mathcal{U}_2$ is consistent, then for every database $\mathcal{I}$, $\mathcal{I} \circ (\mathcal{U}_1 \cup \mathcal{U}_2) = (\mathcal{I} \circ \mathcal{U}_1) \circ \mathcal{U}_2$.*   □

It is common to impose on databases conditions, called *integrity constraints*, that must always be satisfied. In the propositional setting, an *integrity constraint* is a formula

$$r = L_1, \ldots, L_m \supset \perp, \tag{1}$$

where L_i, $1 \leq i \leq m$, are literals (expressions of the form a and *not a*, where a is an atom) and ',' stands for the conjunction. Any subset of At (and so, also any database) can be regarded as a propositional interpretation. We say that a database $\mathcal{I}$ *satisfies* an integrity constraint r, denoted by $\mathcal{I} \models r$, if $\mathcal{I}$ satisfies the propositional formula represented by r. In this way, an integrity constraint encodes a condition on databases: the conjunction of its literals must not hold (or equivalently, the disjunction of the corresponding dual literals must hold).

Any language of (propositional) logic could be used to describe integrity constraints (in the introduction we used the language with the connectives $\vee$ and $\neg$). Our present choice is reminiscent of the syntax used in logic programming. It is not coincidental. In the context of aic's the subject of this paper, the negation operator has some similarities to the default negation operator in logic programming and so, as it is common in the logic programming literature, we denote it with *not* rather than $\neg$.

Given a set η of integrity constraints and a database $\mathcal{I}$, the problem of *database repair* consists of updating $\mathcal{I}$ so that integrity constraints in η hold.

Definition 1. [WEAK REPAIR AND REPAIR] *Let $\mathcal{I}$ be a database and η a set of integrity constraints. A weak repair for $\langle \mathcal{I}, \eta \rangle$ is a consistent set $\mathcal{U}$ of update actions such that $(\{+a \mid a \in \mathcal{I}\} \cup \{-a \mid a \in At \setminus \mathcal{I}\}) \cap \mathcal{U} = \emptyset$ ($\mathcal{U}$ consists of "essential" update actions only), and $\mathcal{I} \circ \mathcal{U} \models \eta$ (constraint enforcement).*

A consistent set $\mathcal{U}$ of update actions is a repair for $\langle \mathcal{I}, \eta \rangle$ if it is a weak repair for $\langle \mathcal{I}, \eta \rangle$ and for every $\mathcal{U}' \subseteq \mathcal{U}$ such that $\mathcal{I} \circ \mathcal{U}' \models \eta$, $\mathcal{U}' = \mathcal{U}$ (minimality of change).   □

If an original database satisfies integrity constraints (formally, if $\mathcal{I} \models \eta$), then no change is needed to enforce the constraints and so $\mathcal{U} = \emptyset$ is the *only* repair for $\langle \mathcal{I}, \eta \rangle$. However, there may be other *weak* repairs for $\langle \mathcal{I}, \eta \rangle$. This points to the problem with weak repairs. They allow for the possibility of replacing $\mathcal{I}$ with a weak repair $\mathcal{I}'$ for $\langle \mathcal{I}, \eta \rangle$ even when $\mathcal{I}$ does not violate η. Thus, the minimality of change is a natural and useful property and, for the most part, we are interested in properties of repairs and their refinements. However, considering weak repairs explicitly is useful as it offers a broader perspective.

If a set η of integrity constraints is inconsistent, there is no database satisfying it (constraints cannot be enforced). In such case, the database repair problem is trivial and not interesting. However, assuming consistency of integrity constraints does not yield any significant simplifications. Therefore, we do not make this assumption here.

Finally, we note that the problem of the existence of a weak repair is NP-complete (it is just a simple reformulation of the SAT problem). Since repairs exist if and only if weak repairs do, the problem of the existence of a repair is NP-complete, too.

3   Active Integrity Constraints

Given no other information but integrity constraints, we have no reason to prefer one repair over another. If several repairs are possible, guidance on how to select a repair to execute could be useful. The formalism of *active integrity constraints* (*aic*'s, for short) [2] was designed to address this problem. We will now review it and offer a first extension by introducing the semantics of founded weak repairs.

For a propositional literal L, we write L^D for the dual literal to L. Further, if $L = a$, we define $ua(L) = +a$. If $L = not\,a$, we define $ua(L) = -a$. Conversely, for an update action $\alpha = +a$, we set $lit(\alpha) = a$ and for $\alpha = -a$, $lit(\alpha) = not\,a$. We call $+a$ and $-a$ the *duals* of each other, and write α^D to denote the update action dual to an update action α. Finally, we extend the notation introduced here to to sets of literals and sets of update actions, as appropriate.

An *active integrity constraint* (*aic*, for short) is an expression of the form

$$r = L_1, \ldots, L_m \supset \alpha_1 | \ldots | \alpha_k \tag{2}$$

where L_i are literals, α_j are update actions, and

$$\{lit(\alpha_1)^D, \ldots, lit(\alpha_k)^D\} \subseteq \{L_1, \ldots, L_m\} \tag{3}$$

The set $\{L_1, \ldots, L_m\}$ is the *body* of r; we denote it by $body(r)$. Similarly, the set $\{\alpha_1, \ldots, \alpha_k\}$ is the *head* of r; we denote it by $head(r)$.

An aic with the empty head can be regarded as an integrity constraint (and so, we write the empty head as $\bot$, for consistency with the notation of integrity constraints). An aic with a non-empty head functions as an integrity constraint (its body must be false) *and* it explicitly provides support for the use of update actions in its head (if its body is true).

The role of the condition (3) is to ensure that an aic supports only those update actions that can "fix" it (executing them ensures that the resulting database satisfies the constraint). The condition can be stated concisely as follows: $[lit(head(r))]^D \subseteq body(r)$. We call literals in $[lit(head(r))]^D$ *updatable* by r. They are precisely those literals that can be affected by an update action in $head(r)$. We call every literal in

$body(r) \setminus [lit(head(r))]^D$ *non-updatable* by r. We denote the set of literals updatable by r as $up(r)$ and the set of literals non-updatable by r as $nup(r)$.

With the notation we introduced, we can discuss the intended meaning of an aic r of the form (2) in more detail. First, r functions as an integrity constraint $L_1, \ldots, L_m \supset \bot$. Second, it provides support for one of the update actions α_i, *assuming all non-updatable literals in r hold in the repaired database*. In particular, the constraint $a, b \supset -a| - b$, given $\mathcal{I} = \{a, b\}$, provides the support for $-a$ or $-b$, independently of the repaired database, as it has no non-updatable literal. In the same context of $\mathcal{I} = \{a, b\}$, the constraint $a, b \supset -a$ provides support for $-a$ but only if b is present in the repaired database.

A database $\mathcal{I}$ satisfies an aic r, $\mathcal{I} \models r$, if it satisfies the corresponding integrity constraint. It is now straightforward to adapt the concept of a (weak) repair to the case of aic's. Specifically, a set $\mathcal{U}$ of update actions is a *(weak) repair* for a database $\mathcal{I}$ with respect to a set η of aic's if it is a (weak) repair for $\mathcal{I}$ with respect to the set of *standard* integrity constraints represented by η.

Let us consider the aic $r = a, b \supset -b$, and let $\mathcal{I} = \{a, b\}$ be a database. Clearly, $\mathcal{I}$ violates r as the condition expressed in the body of r is *true*. There are two possible repairs of $\mathcal{I}$ with respect to r or, more precisely, with respect to the integrity constraint encoded by r: performing the update action $-a$ (deleting a), and performing the update action $-b$ (deleting b). We select the latter as a preferred repair, since r provides support for the update action $-b$.

Repairs do not need to obey preferences expressed by the heads of aic's. To formalize the notion of "support" and translate it into a method to select "preferred" repairs, [2] proposed the concept of a *founded repair* — a repair that is *grounded* in ("implied" by) a set of aic's. The following definition, in addition to founded repairs, introduces a new semantics of founded *weak* repairs.

Definition 2. [FOUNDED (WEAK) REPAIR] *Let $\mathcal{I}$ be a database, η a set of aic's, and $\mathcal{U}$ a consistent set of update actions.*

1. *An update action α is* founded *with respect to $\langle \mathcal{I}, \eta \rangle$ and $\mathcal{U}$ if there is $r \in \eta$ such that $\alpha \in head(r)$, $\mathcal{I} \circ \mathcal{U} \models nup(r)$, and $\mathcal{I} \circ \mathcal{U} \models \beta^D$, for every $\beta \in head(r) \setminus \{\alpha\}$.*
2. *The set $\mathcal{U}$ is* founded *with respect to $\langle \mathcal{I}, \eta \rangle$ if every element of $\mathcal{U}$ is founded with respect to $\langle \mathcal{I}, \eta \rangle$ and $\mathcal{U}$.*
3. *$\mathcal{U}$ is a* founded (weak) repair *for $\langle \mathcal{I}, \eta \rangle$ if $\mathcal{U}$ is a (weak) repair for $\langle \mathcal{I}, \eta \rangle$ and $\mathcal{U}$ is founded with respect to $\langle \mathcal{I}, \eta \rangle$.* □

Foundedness is indeed a formalization of a certain notion of "groundedness". Let us assume that α is founded with respect to $\langle \mathcal{I}, \eta \rangle$ and $\mathcal{U}$ by means of an aic $r \in \eta$. Let us also assume that $\mathcal{I} \not\models r$, that is, $\mathcal{I} \models body(r)$. By the foundedness, all literals in $body(r)$, except possibly for $lit(\alpha^D)$, are satisfied in $\mathcal{I} \circ \mathcal{U}$. Thus, if $\mathcal{U}$ is to enforce r, it must contain α. We observe that the foundedness does not imply the constraint enforcement nor the minimality of change.

Example 1. Let $\mathcal{I} = \emptyset$ and η consist of the following aic's:
$$r_1 = not\ a \quad \supset +a$$
$$r_2 = not\ b, c \supset +b$$
$$r_3 = b, not\ c \supset +c.$$

The unique founded repair for $\langle \mathcal{I}, \eta \rangle$ is $\{+a\}$. The set $\{+a, +b, +c\}$ is founded, guarantees constraint enforcement (and so, it is a founded weak repair), but it it is *not* change-minimal. The set $\{+b, +c\}$ is founded but does not guarantee constraint enforcement. Therefore, in the definition of founded (weak) repairs, the property of being a (weak) repair must be enforced explicitly. We also note that foundedness properly narrows down the class of repairs. If $\eta = \{a, b \supset -b\}$, and $\mathcal{I} = \{a, b\}$ (an example we considered earlier), $\mathcal{U} = \{-a\}$ is a repair for $\langle \mathcal{I}, \eta \rangle$ but not a founded repair.   □

Next, we show that there could exist founded *weak* repairs even when no founded repair exists.

Example 2. Let $\mathcal{I} = \emptyset$ and η consist of the following aic's:

$$not\ a, b, c \supset +a \qquad\qquad not\ b, a, c \supset +b$$
$$not\ c, a, b \supset +c \qquad\qquad not\ a \qquad \supset \bot$$

One can check that the only founded sets of update actions are $\mathcal{U}_1 = \emptyset$ ($\emptyset$ is always vacuously founded) and $\mathcal{U}_2 = \{+a, +b, +c\}$. Moreover, $\mathcal{U}_3 = \{+a\}$ is a repair and $\mathcal{U}_2$ is a weak repair. Thus, $\mathcal{U}_2$ is a founded weak repair but, as it is not minimal, not a founded repair. In fact, there are no founded repairs in this example.   □

Finally, we discuss the key issue arising in the context of founded repairs that motivates much of the remainder of the paper. In some cases, founded repairs, despite combining foundedness with change-minimality, are still not grounded strongly enough. The problem is the circularity of support.

Example 3. Let $\mathcal{I} = \{a, b\}$ and let η_1 consist of the following aic's:

$$r_1 = a, b \qquad \supset -a$$
$$r_2 = a, not\ b \supset -a$$
$$r_3 = not\ a, b \supset -b.$$

One can check that $\mathcal{U} = \{-a, -b\}$ is a repair for $\langle \mathcal{I}, \eta_1 \rangle$. Moreover, it is a founded repair: $-a$ is founded with respect to $\langle \mathcal{I}, \eta_1 \rangle$ and $\mathcal{U}$, with r_2 providing the necessary support, while $-b$ is founded with respect to $\langle \mathcal{I}, \eta_1 \rangle$ and $\mathcal{U}$ because of r_3.

The problem is that, arguably, $\mathcal{U} = \{-a, -b\}$ supports itself through circular dependencies. The constraint r_1 is the only one violated by $\mathcal{I}$ and forcing the need for a repair. However, according to intuitions we discussed earlier, r_1 supports the foundedness of $-a$ *only if* b remains in the database. This is not the case here. Thus, the support for the foundedness of $-a$ in $\mathcal{U}$ must come entirely from r_2 and r_3. The same holds for $-b$ as it is not even mentioned in the head of r_1.

It follows that the foundedness of $-a$ is supported solely by r_2, and it *requires* that $-b$ be included in the repair. In the same way, the foundedness of $-b$ is supported solely by r_3, and it depends on $-a$ being included in the repair. Thus, the foundedness of $\{-a, -b\}$ is "circular": $-a$ is founded (and so included in $\mathcal{U}$) due to the fact that $-b$ has been included in $\mathcal{U}$, and $-b$ is founded (and so included in $\mathcal{U}$) due to the fact that $-a$ has been included in $\mathcal{U}$, but there is no independent justification for having any of these two actions included. As we noted, r_1 does not "found" any of $-a$ nor $-b$.   □

To summarize this section, the semantics of repairs for aic's enforces constraints and satisfies the minimality of change property. It has no groundedness properties beyond what is implied by the two requirements. The semantics of founded repairs gives preference to some ways of repairing constraints over others. It only considers repairs whose all elements are founded. However, foundedness may be circular and so the associated concept of groundedness is weak. We revisit this issue in the next section.

On the computational side, the complexity of the semantics of repairs is lower than that of founded repairs. From the result stated in the previous section, it follows that the problem of the existence of a repair is NP-complete, while the problem of the existence of a founded repair is Σ_P^2-complete [2]. For the sake of completeness, we also note that the problem of the existence of a founded weak repair is again "only" NP-complete (the proof is simple and we omit it).

4   Justified Repairs

In this section, we will introduce another semantics for aic's that captures a stronger concept of groundedness than the one behind founded repairs. The goal is to disallow circular dependencies like the one we discussed in Example 3.

We start by defining when a set of update actions is *closed* under aic's. Let η be a set of aic's and let $\mathcal{U}$ be a set of update actions. If $r \in \eta$, and for every *non-updatable* literal $L \in body(r)$ there is an update action $\alpha \in \mathcal{U}$ such that $lit(\alpha) = L$ then, after applying $\mathcal{U}$ or any of its consistent supersets to the initial database, the result of the update, say $\mathcal{R}$, satisfies all non-updatable literals in $body(r)$. To guarantee that $\mathcal{R}$ satisfies r, $\mathcal{R}$ must *falsify* at least one literal in $body(r)$. To this end $\mathcal{U}$ must contain at least one update action from $head(r)$.

Definition 3. [CLOSED SET OF UPDATE ACTIONS] *A set $\mathcal{U}$ of update actions is* closed *under an aic r if $nup(r) \subseteq lit(\mathcal{U})$ implies $head(r) \cap \mathcal{U} \neq \emptyset$. A set $\mathcal{U}$ of update actions is* closed *under a set η of aic's if it is closed under every $r \in \eta$.*   □

If a set of update actions is not closed under a set η of aic's, executing its elements may fail to enforce constraints. Therefore, closed sets of update actions are important. We regard *minimal* such sets as "forced" by η, as all elements in a minimal set of update actions closed under η are necessary (no nonempty subset can be dropped).

Another key notion in our considerations is that of *no-effect actions*. Let $\mathcal{I}$ be a database and $\mathcal{R}$ a result of updating $\mathcal{I}$. An update action $+a$ (respectively, $-a$) is a *no-effect* action with respect to $(\mathcal{I}, \mathcal{R})$ if $a \in \mathcal{I} \cap \mathcal{R}$ (respectively, $a \notin \mathcal{I} \cup \mathcal{R}$). Informally, a no-effect action does not change the status of its underlying atom. We denote by $ne(\mathcal{I}, \mathcal{R})$ the set of all no-effect actions with respect to $(\mathcal{I}, \mathcal{R})$. We note the following two simple properties reflecting the nature of no-effect actions — their redundancy.

Proposition 2. *Let $\mathcal{I}$ be a database. Then*

1. *For every database $\mathcal{R}$, $\mathcal{R} \circ ne(\mathcal{I}, \mathcal{R}) = \mathcal{R}$*
2. *For every set $\mathcal{E}$ of update actions such that $\mathcal{E} \cup ne(\mathcal{I}, \mathcal{I} \circ \mathcal{E})$ is consistent, $\mathcal{I} \circ \mathcal{E} = \mathcal{I} \circ (\mathcal{E} \cup ne(\mathcal{I}, \mathcal{I} \circ \mathcal{E}))$.*   □

Our semantics of justified repairs is based on the knowledge-representation principle (a form of the frame axiom) that remaining in the previous state requires no reason (persistence by inertia). Thus, when justifying update actions necessary to transform $\mathcal{I}$ into $\mathcal{R}$ based on η we assume the set $ne(\mathcal{I}, \mathcal{R})$ as given. This brings us to the notion of a justified weak repair.

Definition 4. [JUSTIFIED WEAK REPAIR] *Let $\mathcal{I}$ be a database and η a set of aic's. A consistent set $\mathcal{U}$ of update actions is a justified action set for $\langle \mathcal{I}, \eta \rangle$ if $\mathcal{U}$ is a minimal set of update actions containing $ne(\mathcal{I}, \mathcal{I} \circ \mathcal{U})$ and closed under η. If $\mathcal{U}$ is a justified action set for $\langle \mathcal{I}, \eta \rangle$, then $\mathcal{E} = \mathcal{U} \setminus ne(\mathcal{I}, \mathcal{I} \circ \mathcal{U})$ is a justified weak repair for $\langle \mathcal{I}, \eta \rangle$.* $\square$

Intuitively, a set $\mathcal{U}$ of update actions is a justified action set, if it is precisely the set of update actions forced or *justified* by η and the no-effect actions with respect to $\mathcal{I}$ and $\mathcal{I} \circ \mathcal{U}$. This "fixpoint" aspect of the definition is reminiscent of the definitions of semantics of several non-monotonic logics, including (disjunctive) logic programming with the answer-set semantics. The connection can be made more formal and we take advantage of it in the section on the complexity and computation.

We will now study justified action sets and justified weak repairs. We start with an alternative characterization of justified weak repairs.

Theorem 1. *Let $\mathcal{I}$ be a database, η a set of aic's and $\mathcal{E}$ a consistent set of update actions. Then $\mathcal{E}$ is a a justified weak repair for $\langle \mathcal{I}, \eta \rangle$ if and only if $\mathcal{E} \cap ne(\mathcal{I}, \mathcal{I} \circ \mathcal{E}) = \emptyset$ and $\mathcal{E} \cup ne(\mathcal{I}, \mathcal{I} \circ \mathcal{E})$ is a justified action set for $\langle \mathcal{I}, \eta \rangle$.* $\square$

Justified weak repairs have two key properties for the problem of database update: constraint enforcement (hence the term "weak repair") and foundedness.

Theorem 2. *Let $\mathcal{I}$ be a database, η a set of aic's, and $\mathcal{E}$ a justified weak repair for $\langle \mathcal{I}, \eta \rangle$. Then*

1. *For every atom a, exactly one of $+a$ or $-a$ is in $\mathcal{E} \cup ne(\mathcal{I}, \mathcal{I} \circ \mathcal{E})$*
2. $\mathcal{I} \circ \mathcal{E} \models \eta$
3. *$\mathcal{E}$ is founded for $\langle \mathcal{I}, \eta \rangle$.* $\square$

Theorem 2 directly implies that justified weak repairs are founded weak repairs.

Corollary 1. *Let $\mathcal{I}$ be a database, η a set of aic's, and $\mathcal{E}$ a justified weak repair for $\langle \mathcal{I}, \eta \rangle$. Then, $\mathcal{E}$ is a founded weak repair for $\langle \mathcal{I}, \eta \rangle$.* $\square$

The converse to Corollary 1 does not hold. That is, there are founded weak repairs that are not justified weak repairs.

Example 4. The database and aic's from Example 3 illustrate the point. As we noted there, $\mathcal{U} = \{-a, -b\}$ is a founded repair. Thus, it is also a founded weak repair.

As pointed out, the support for the foundedness of $\mathcal{U}$ is circular. The semantics of justified weak repairs resolves the problem. Indeed, $\mathcal{U}$ is not a justified weak repair for $\langle \mathcal{I}, \eta_1 \rangle$. One can check that $\mathcal{U} \cup ne(\mathcal{I}, \mathcal{I} \circ \mathcal{U})$ $(= \{-a, -b\})$ contains $ne(\mathcal{I}, \mathcal{I} \circ \mathcal{U})$ $(= \emptyset)$, and is closed under η. But it is not a minimal set of update actions containing $ne(\mathcal{I}, \mathcal{I} \circ \mathcal{U})$ and closed under η. Indeed, $\emptyset$ has these two properties, too. Thus, the notion of groundedness employed by justified weak repairs is stronger.

In Example 3, the problem is caused by r_1. Let us consider a situation, where r_1 is replaced with $r'_1 = a, b \supset -a| - b$. The constraint r'_1 provides support for $-a$ or $-b$ independently of the repaired database (as there are no non-updatable literals in r'_1). If $-a$ is selected (with support from r'_1), r_3 supports $-b$. If $-b$ is selected (with support from r'_1), r_2 supports $-a$, Thus the cyclic support given by r_2 and r_3 in the presence of r_1 is broken. Indeed, one can check that $\{-a, -b\}$ is a justified weak repair.   □

While stronger property than foundedness, being a justified weak repair still does not guarantee change-minimality (and so, the term *weak* cannot be dropped).

Example 5. Let $\mathcal{I}' = \emptyset$, and η_3 be a set of aic's consisting of

$$r_1 = not\ a, b \supset +a| - b$$
$$r_2 = a, not\ b \supset -a| + b$$

Let us consider the set of update actions $\mathcal{E} = \{+a, +b\}$. It is easy to verify that $\mathcal{E}$ is a justified weak repair for $\langle \mathcal{I}', \eta_3 \rangle$. Therefore, it ensures constraint enforcement and it is founded. However, $\mathcal{E}$ is not minimal as $\mathcal{I}'$ is consistent with η_3, and the empty set of update actions is its only repair.   □

Thus, to have change-minimality, it needs to be enforced directly as in the case of founded repairs. By doing so, we obtain the notion of *justified repairs*.

Definition 5. [JUSTIFIED REPAIR] *Let $\mathcal{I}$ be a database and η a set of aic's. A set $\mathcal{E}$ of update actions is a* justified repair *for $\langle \mathcal{I}, \eta \rangle$ if $\mathcal{E}$ is a justified weak repair for $\langle \mathcal{I}, \eta \rangle$, and for every $\mathcal{E}' \subseteq \mathcal{E}$ such that $\mathcal{I} \circ \mathcal{E}' \models \eta$, $\mathcal{E}' = \mathcal{E}$.*   □

Theorem 2 has yet another corollary, this time concerning justified and founded repairs.

Corollary 2. *Let $\mathcal{I}$ be a database, η a set of aic's, and $\mathcal{E}$ a justified repair for $\langle \mathcal{I}, \eta \rangle$. Then, $\mathcal{E}$ is a founded repair for $\langle \mathcal{I}, \eta \rangle$.*   □

Example 4 shows that the inclusion asserted by Corollary 2 is proper. Indeed, we argued there that $\{-a, -b\}$ is a founded repair but not a justified weak repair. Thus, $\{-a, -b\}$ is not a justified repair, either.

As illustrated by Example 5, in general, justified weak repairs form a proper subclass of justified repairs. However, in some cases the two concepts coincide — the minimality is a consequence of the groundedness underlying the notion of a justified weak repair. One such case is identified in the next theorem. The other important case is discussed in the next section.

Theorem 3. *Let $\mathcal{I}$ be a database and η a set of aic's such that for each update action $\alpha \in \bigcup_{r \in \eta} head(r)$, $\mathcal{I} \models lit(\alpha^D)$. If $\mathcal{E}$ is a justified weak repair for $\langle \mathcal{I}, \eta \rangle$, then $\mathcal{E}$ is a justified repair for $\langle \mathcal{I}, \eta \rangle$.*   □

This theorem concerns the case when each update action in the head of an aic, if executed, would change the status of the underlying atom in the database. For instance, if the initial database is empty and all update actions prescribed by aic's are insert actions, then justified weak repairs are guaranteed to be minimal and so, are justified repairs.

5   Normal Active Integrity Constraints and Normalization

An aic r is *normal* if $|head(r)| = 1$. We will now study properties of normal aic's. The next result shows that for that class of constraints, updating by justified weak repairs guarantees the minimality of change property and so, the explicit reference to the latter can be omitted from the definition of justified repairs.

Theorem 4. *Let $\mathcal{I}$ be a database and η a set of normal aic's. If $\mathcal{E}$ is a justified weak repair for $\langle \mathcal{I}, \eta \rangle$ then $\mathcal{E}$ is a justified repair for $\langle \mathcal{I}, \eta \rangle$.*   □

Next, we introduce the operation of *normalization* of aic's, which consists of eliminating disjunctions from the heads of rules. For an aic $r = \phi \supset \alpha_1 | \dots | \alpha_n$, by r^n we denote the set of *normal* aic's $\{\phi \supset \alpha_1, \dots, \phi \supset \alpha_n\}$. For a set η of aic's, we set $\eta^n = \bigcup_{r \in \eta} r^n$. It is shown in [6] that $\mathcal{E}$ is founded for $\langle \mathcal{I}, \eta \rangle$ if and only if $\mathcal{E}$ is a founded for $\langle \mathcal{I}, \eta^n \rangle$. Thus, $\mathcal{E}$ is a founded (weak) repair for $\langle \mathcal{I}, \eta \rangle$ if and only if $\mathcal{E}$ is a founded (weak) repair for $\langle \mathcal{I}, \eta^n \rangle$. For justified repairs, we have a weaker result. Normalization may eliminate some justified (weak) repairs.

Theorem 5. *Let $\mathcal{I}$ be a database and η a set of aic's.*

1. *If a set $\mathcal{E}$ of update actions is a justified repair for $\langle \mathcal{I}, \eta^n \rangle$, then $\mathcal{E}$ is a justified repair for $\langle \mathcal{I}, \eta \rangle$;*
2. *If a set $\mathcal{E}$ of update action is a justified weak repair for $\langle \mathcal{I}, \eta^n \rangle$, then $\mathcal{E}$ is a justified weak repair for $\langle \mathcal{I}, \eta \rangle$.*   □

The following example shows that the inclusion in the previous theorem is, in general, proper.

Example 6. Let us consider an empty database $\mathcal{I}' = \emptyset$, the set η_4 of aic's

$$r_1 = not\ a, not\ b \supset +a| + b$$
$$r_2 = a, not\ b \qquad \supset +b$$
$$r_3 = not\ a, b \qquad \supset +a$$

its normalized version η_4^n

$$r_{1,1} = not\ a, not\ b \supset +a \qquad r_{2,1} = a, not\ b \supset +b$$
$$r_{1,2} = not\ a, not\ b \supset +b \qquad r_{3,1} = not\ a, b \supset +a$$

and the set of update actions $\mathcal{E} = \{+a, +b\}$. It is easy to verify that $\mathcal{E}$ is a justified repair for $\langle \mathcal{I}', \eta_4 \rangle$. However, $\mathcal{E}$ is not a justified weak repair for $\langle \mathcal{I}', \eta_4^n \rangle$ (and so, not a justified repair for $\langle \mathcal{I}', \eta_4^n \rangle$). Indeed, it is not a minimal set containing $ne(\mathcal{I}', \mathcal{I}' \circ \mathcal{E}) = \emptyset$ and closed under η_4^n, as $\emptyset$ is also closed under η_4^n.   □

6   Shifting Theorem

We will now study the concept of shifting [3]. Shifting consists of transforming an instance $\langle \mathcal{I}, \eta \rangle$ of the database repair problem to a syntactically isomorphic instance $\langle \mathcal{I}', \eta' \rangle$ by changing integrity constraints to reflect the "shift" of $\mathcal{I}$ into $\mathcal{I}'$. A semantics for database repair problem has the *shifting property* if the repairs of the "shifted" instance of the database update problem are precisely the results of modifying the repairs of the original instance according to the shift from $\mathcal{I}$ to $\mathcal{I}'$. The shifting property is important. If a semantics of database updates has it, the study of that semantics can be reduced to the case when the input database is empty. In many cases it allows us to relate a semantics of database repairs to some semantics of logic programs with negation.

Example 7. Let $\mathcal{I} = \{a, b\}$ and let $\eta_5 = \{a, b \supset -a| - b\}$. There are two founded repairs for $\langle \mathcal{I}, \eta_5 \rangle$: $\mathcal{E}_1 = \{-a\}$ and $\mathcal{E}_2 = \{-b\}$. Let $\mathcal{W} = \{a\}$. We will now "shift" the instance $\langle \mathcal{I}, \eta_5 \rangle$ with respect to $\mathcal{W}$. To this end, we will first modify $\mathcal{I}$ by changing the status in $\mathcal{I}$ of elements in $\mathcal{W}$, in our case, of a. Since $a \in \mathcal{I}$, we will remove it. Thus, $\mathcal{I}$ "shifted" with respect to $\mathcal{W}$ becomes $\mathcal{J} = \{b\}$. Next, we will modify η_5 correspondingly, replacing literals and update actions involving a by their duals. That results in $\eta_5' = \{not\ a, b \supset +a| - b\}$. One can check that the resulting instance $\langle \mathcal{J}, \eta_5' \rangle$ of the update problem has two founded repairs: $\{+a\}$ and $\{-b\}$. Moreover, they can be obtained from the founded repairs for $\langle \mathcal{I}, \eta_5 \rangle$ by consistently replacing $-a$ with $+a$ and $+a$ with $-a$ (the latter does not apply in this example). In other words, the original update problem and its shifted version are isomorphic. □

The situation presented in Example 7 is not coincidental. In this section we present results showing that the semantics of (weak) repairs, founded (weak) repairs and justified (weak) repairs satisfy the shifting property. We start by observing that *shifting* a database $\mathcal{I}$ to a database $\mathcal{I}'$ can be modeled by means of the symmetric difference operator. Namely, we have $\mathcal{I}' = \mathcal{I} \div \mathcal{W}$, where $\mathcal{W} = \mathcal{I} \div \mathcal{I}'$. This identity shows that one can shift any database $\mathcal{I}$ into any database $\mathcal{I}'$ by forming a symmetric difference of $\mathcal{I}$ with some set of atom $\mathcal{W}$ (specifically, $\mathcal{W} = \mathcal{I} \div \mathcal{I}'$). We will now extend the operation of shifting a database with respect to $\mathcal{W}$ to the case of literals, update actions and aic's. To this end, we introduce a *shifting* operator $T_{\mathcal{W}}$.

Definition 6. *Let $\mathcal{W}$ be a database and ℓ a literal or an update action. We define*

$$T_{\mathcal{W}}(\ell) = \begin{cases} \ell^D & \text{if the atom of } \ell \text{ is in } \mathcal{W} \\ \ell & \text{if the atom of } \ell \text{ is not in } \mathcal{W} \end{cases}$$

and we extend this definition to sets of literals or update actions, respectively. Furthermore, if op is an operator on sets of literals or update actions (such as conjunction or disjunction), for every set X of literals or update actions, we define $T_{\mathcal{W}}(op(X)) = op(T_{\mathcal{W}}(X))$. Finally, for an aic $r = \phi \supset \psi$, we set $T_{\mathcal{W}}(r) = T_{\mathcal{W}}(\phi) \supset T_{\mathcal{W}}(\psi)$ and we extend the notation to sets aic's in the standard way. □

To illustrate the last two parts of the definition, we note that when op stands for the conjunction of a set of literals and $X = \{L_1, \ldots, L_n\}$, where every L_i is a literal, $T_{\mathcal{W}}(op(X)) = op(T_{\mathcal{W}}(X))$ specializes to $T_{\mathcal{W}}(L_1, \ldots, L_n) = T_{\mathcal{W}}(L_1), \ldots, T_{\mathcal{W}}(L_n)$. Similarly, for an aic $r = L_1, \ldots, L_n \supset \alpha_1| \ldots |\alpha_m$ we obtain

$$T_{\mathcal{W}}(r) = T_{\mathcal{W}}(L_1), \ldots, T_{\mathcal{W}}(L_n) \supset T_{\mathcal{W}}(\alpha_1)| \ldots |T_{\mathcal{W}}(\alpha_m).$$

Clearly, we overload the notation $T_{\mathcal{W}}$ and interpret it based on the type of the argument. We have the following two results.

Theorem 6. [SHIFTING THEOREM FOR (WEAK) REPAIRS AND FOUNDED (WEAK) REPAIRS] *Let $\mathcal{I}$ and $\mathcal{W}$ be databases. For every set η of aic's and for every consistent set $\mathcal{E}$ of update actions, we have*

1. *$\mathcal{E}$ is a weak repair for $\langle \mathcal{I}, \eta \rangle$ if and only if $T_{\mathcal{W}}(\mathcal{E})$ is a weak repair for $\langle \mathcal{I} \div \mathcal{W}, T_{\mathcal{W}}(\eta) \rangle$*
2. *$\mathcal{E}$ is a repair for $\langle \mathcal{I}, \eta \rangle$ if and only if $T_{\mathcal{W}}(\mathcal{E})$ is a repair for $\langle \mathcal{I} \div \mathcal{W}, T_{\mathcal{W}}(\eta) \rangle$*
3. *$\mathcal{E}$ is founded for $\langle \mathcal{I}, \eta \rangle$ if and only if $T_{\mathcal{W}}(\mathcal{E})$ is founded for $\langle \mathcal{I} \div \mathcal{W}, T_{\mathcal{W}}(\eta) \rangle$.*
4. *$\mathcal{E}$ is a founded (weak) repair for $\langle \mathcal{I}, \eta \rangle$ if and only if $T_{\mathcal{W}}(\mathcal{E})$ is a founded (weak) repair for $\langle \mathcal{I} \div \mathcal{W}, T_{\mathcal{W}}(\eta) \rangle$.* □

Theorem 7. [SHIFTING THEOREM FOR JUSTIFIED (WEAK) REPAIRS] *Let $\mathcal{I}$ and $\mathcal{W}$ be databases. For every set η of aic's and for every set $\mathcal{E}$ of update actions, $\mathcal{E}$ is an justified (weak) repair for $\langle \mathcal{I}, \eta \rangle$ if and only if $T_{\mathcal{W}}(\mathcal{E})$ is a justified (weak) repair for $\langle \mathcal{I}, T_{\mathcal{W}}(\eta) \rangle$.* □

Theorems 6 and 7 imply that in the context of (weak) repairs, founded (weak) repairs or justified (weak) repairs, an instance $\langle \mathcal{I}, \eta \rangle$ of the database update problem can be shifted to the instance the empty initial database. That property simplifies studies of these semantics as it allows us to eliminate one parameter (the initial database) from considerations.

Corollary 3. *Let $\mathcal{I}$ be a database and η a set of aic's. Then $\mathcal{E}$ is a weak repair (repair, weak repair, founded weak repair, founded repair, justified weak repair, justified repair, respectively) for $\langle \mathcal{I}, \eta \rangle$ if and only if $T_{\mathcal{I}}(\mathcal{E})$ is a weak repair (repair, weak repair, founded weak repair, founded repair, justified weak repair, justified repair, respectively) for $\langle \emptyset, T_{\mathcal{I}}(\eta) \rangle$.* □

Example 8. Let us look at one of the instances of the database repair problem considered in Example 4, specifically, at $\langle \mathcal{I}, \eta_2 \rangle$. We recall that $\mathcal{I} = \{a, b\}$ and η_2 consists of the constraints:

$$a, b \quad \supset -a | - b$$
$$a, not\ b \supset -a$$
$$not\ a, b \supset -b.$$

The set $\{-a, -b\}$ is the only weak repair for $\langle \mathcal{I}, \eta_2 \rangle$ and, as we noted earlier, it is a (weak) founded repair and a (weak) justified repair for $\langle \mathcal{I}, \eta_2 \rangle$, as well. Let us "shift" this instance to $\mathcal{I}' = \emptyset$, To this end, we shift with respect to $W = \mathcal{I} \div \mathcal{I}' = \{a, b\}$. One can check that $\emptyset = T_{\{a,b\}}(\{a, b\})$, that is, $\mathcal{I}' = T_{\mathcal{W}}(\mathcal{I})$. Moreover, $T_{\mathcal{W}}(\eta_2) = \eta_4$, where η_4 is the set of aic's considered in Example 6 above. Thus, indeed, by shifting $\langle \mathcal{I}, \eta_2 \rangle$ with respect to W, we obtain the database repair problem $\langle \mathcal{I}', \eta_4 \rangle$. It is easy to verify that $T_{\{a,b\}}(\{-a, -b\}) = \{+a, +b\}$ and that $\{+a, +b\}$ is the only (weak) repair for $\langle \mathcal{I}', \eta_4 \rangle$, which happens also to be a (weak) founded repair and a (weak) justified repair for $\langle \mathcal{I}', \eta_4 \rangle$, in agreement with the results of this section. □

7   Complexity and Computation

We noted earlier that the problem of the existence of a (weak) repair is NP-complete, and the same is true for the problem of the existence of founded weak repairs. On the other hand, the problem of the existence of a founded repair is Σ_P^2-complete [2]. In this section, we study the problem of the existence of justified (weak) repairs.

For our hardness results, we will use problems in logic programming. We will consider disjunctive and normal logic programs that satisfy some additional syntactic constraints. Namely, we will consider only programs without rules which contain multiple occurrences of the same atom (that is, in the head and in the body, negated or not; or in the body — both positively and negatively). We call such programs *simple*. It is well known that the problem of the existence of a stable model of a normal logic program is NP-complete [7], and of the disjunctive logic program — Σ_2^P-complete [8]. The proofs in [7,8] imply that the results hold also under the restriction to simple normal and simple disjunctive programs, respectively (in the case of disjunctive logic programs, a minor modification of the construction is required). Let ρ be a logic programming rule, say

$$\rho = a_1|\ldots|a_k \leftarrow \beta.$$

We define

$$aic(\rho) = not\ a_1, \ldots, not\ a_k, \beta \supset +a_1|\ldots|+a_k.$$

We extend the operator $aic(\cdot)$ to logic programs in a standard way. We note that if a rule ρ is simple then $body(aic(\rho))$ is consistent and $nup(aic(\rho)) = body(\rho)$.

We recall that a set M of atoms is an answer set of a disjunctive logic program P if M is a minimal set closed under the reduct P^M, where P^M consists of the rules obtained by dropping all negative literals from those rules in P that do not contain a literal $not\ a$ in the body, for any $a \in M$ (we refer to [9] for details). The following result states a property of the translation needed for hardness arguments.

Theorem 8. *Let P be a simple disjunctive logic program. A set M of atoms is an answer set of P if and only if $ua(M)$ is a justified weak repair for $\langle\emptyset, aic(P)\rangle$.*   □

Example 9. Let us consider Example 6. We observe that η_4 is equal to $aic(P)$ where P is the simple disjunctive logic program consisting of the rules: $\rho_1 = a \mid b$, $\rho_2 = b \leftarrow a$ and $\rho_3 = a \leftarrow b$. We know that $\mathcal{E} = \{+a, +b\}$ is the unique justified repair for $\langle\mathcal{I}', \eta_4\rangle$, where $\mathcal{I}' = \emptyset$. Moreover, one can check that $M = \{a, b\}$, for which $\mathcal{E} = ua(M)$, is the unique answer set of P. Furthermore, since the instance $\langle I', \eta_4\rangle$ is the result of shifting $\langle\mathcal{I}, \eta_2\rangle$, also the repairs of $\langle\mathcal{I}, \eta_2\rangle$ can be expressed in terms of answer sets of the disjunctive logic program $aic(P)$. This points to a general translation of instances of the database repair problem into disjunctive logic programs by combining shifting with the mapping aic. A detailed study of this relationship is a subject of a separate paper.   □

We now state main results of the section.

Theorem 9. *Let $\mathcal{I}$ be a database and η a set of normal aic's. Then checking if there exists a justified repair (justified weak repair, respectively) for $\langle\mathcal{I}, \eta\rangle$ is an NP-complete problem.*   □

Theorem 10. *Let $\mathcal{I}$ be a database and η a set of aic's. The problem of the existence of a justified weak repair for $\langle\mathcal{I}, \eta\rangle$ is a Σ_2^P-complete problem.*   □

Theorem 11. *Let $\mathcal{I}$ be a database and η a set of aic's. The problem of the existence of a justified repair for $\langle \mathcal{I}, \eta \rangle$ is a Σ_2^P-complete problem.* $\qquad\qquad\square$

8   Discussion

We recall that given a database $\mathcal{I}$ and a set η of aic's, the goal is to replace $\mathcal{I}$ with $\mathcal{I}'$ so that $\mathcal{I}'$ satisfies η. The set of update actions needed to transform $\mathcal{I}$ into $\mathcal{I}'$ must at least be a repair for $\langle \mathcal{I}, \eta \rangle$ (assuming we insist on change-minimality, which normally is the case). However, it should also obey preferences captured by the heads of constraints in η. Let us denote by $\mathbf{R}(\mathcal{I}, \eta)$, $\mathbf{WR}(\mathcal{I}, \eta)$, $\mathbf{FR}(\mathcal{I}, \eta)$, $\mathbf{FWR}(\mathcal{I}, \eta)$, $\mathbf{JR}(\mathcal{I}, \eta)$, and $\mathbf{JWR}(\mathcal{I}, \eta)$ the classes of repairs, weak repairs, founded repairs, founded weak repairs, justified repairs and justified weak repairs for $\langle \mathcal{I}, \eta \rangle$, respectively. Figure 1 shows the relationships among these classes, with all inclusions being in general proper.

$$\mathbf{FR}(\mathcal{I}, \eta^n)$$
$$\|$$
$$\mathbf{JR}(\mathcal{I}, \eta^n) \subseteq \mathbf{JR}(\mathcal{I}, \eta) \subseteq \mathbf{FR}(\mathcal{I}, \eta) \subseteq \mathbf{R}(\mathcal{I}, \eta) = \mathbf{R}(\mathcal{I}, \eta^n)$$
$$\| \qquad\qquad \cap \qquad\qquad \cap \qquad\qquad \cap \qquad\qquad \cap$$
$$\mathbf{JWR}(\mathcal{I}, \eta^n) \subseteq \mathbf{JWR}(\mathcal{I}, \eta) \subseteq \mathbf{FWR}(\mathcal{I}, \eta) \subseteq \mathbf{WR}(\mathcal{I}, \eta) = \mathbf{WR}(\mathcal{I}, \eta^n)$$
$$\|$$
$$\mathbf{FWR}(\mathcal{I}, \eta^n)$$

Fig. 1. Relationships among classes of repairs

Thus, given an instance $\langle \mathcal{I}, \eta \rangle$ of the database repair problem, one might first attempt to select a repair for $\langle \mathcal{I}, \eta \rangle$ from the most restricted set of repairs, $\mathbf{JR}(\mathcal{I}, \eta^n)$. Not only these repairs are strongly tied to preferences expressed by η — the related computational problems are relatively easy. The problem to decide whether this set is empty is NP-complete. However, the class $\mathbf{JR}(\mathcal{I}, \eta^n)$ is narrow and it may be that $\mathbf{JR}(\mathcal{I}, \eta^n) = \emptyset$. If it is so, the next step might be to try to repair $\mathcal{I}$ by selecting a repair from $\mathbf{JR}(\mathcal{I}, \eta)$. This class of repairs for $\langle \mathcal{I}, \eta \rangle$ reflects the preferences captured by η. Since it is broader than the previous one, there is a better possibility it will be non-empty. However, the computational complexity grows — the existence problem for $\mathbf{JR}(\mathcal{I}, \eta)$ is Σ_P^2-complete. If also $\mathbf{JR}(\mathcal{I}, \eta) = \emptyset$, it still may be that founded repairs exist. Moreover, deciding whether a founded repair exists is not harder than the previous step. Finally, if there are no founded repairs, one still may consider just a repair. This is not quite satisfactory as it ignores the preferences encoded by η and concentrates only on the constraint enforcement. However, deciding whether a repair exists is "only" NP-complete. Moreover, this class subsumes all other classes of repairs and offers the best chance of success.

We note that if we fail to find a justified or founded repair in the process described above, we may decide that respecting preferences encoded in aic's is more important than the minimality of change postulate. In such case, rather to proceed to seek a repair, as discussed above, we also have an option to consider justified weak repairs of $\langle \mathcal{I}, \eta \rangle$, where the existence problem is Σ_2^P-complete and, then founded weak repairs for $\langle \mathcal{I}, \eta \rangle$, where the existence problem is NP-complete.

9   Conclusion

We studied the formalism of aic's [2], designed for enforcing integrity constraints on databases in the presence of preferences on alternative ways to do so. The original semantics proposed for aic's is based on the concept of a *founded repair*. Founded repairs are sets of update actions to be performed over the database in order to make it consistent. They are minimal w.r.t. change and supported by aic's. In some cases, elements of founded repairs cyclically support each other, which often is undesirable. Therefore, we introduced several new semantics for aic's. Two most important of them are the semantics of justified weak repairs and justified repairs. They are based on the concept of groundedness similar to that underlying the answer-set semantics of logic programs. We established the relationship of the two new semantics to that of founded repairs. For each semantics we determined the complexity of the basic existence of repair problem. Furthermore, we proved that each semantics satisfies the *shifting property*. Shifting consists of transforming an instance of a database repair problem to another syntactically isomorphic one by changing aic's to reflect the "shift" from the original database to the new one. These latter results are essential for relating repair formalism we studied with the formalism of Lifschitz-Woo programs [10], a subject of our future work.

Acknowledgments

This work was partially supported by the NSF grant IIS-0325063 and the KSEF grant KSEF-1036-RDE-008.

References

1. Winslett, M.: Updating Logical Databases. Cambridge University Press, Cambridge (1990)
2. Caroprese, L., Greco, S., Sirangelo, C., Zumpano, E.: Declarative semantics of production rules for integrity maintenance. In: Etalle, S., Truszczyński, M. (eds.) ICLP 2006. LNCS, vol. 4079, pp. 26–40. Springer, Heidelberg (2006)
3. Marek, W., Truszczyński, M.: Revision programming. Theoretical Computer Science 190, 241–277 (1998)
4. Pivkina, I.: Revision programming: a knowledge representation formalism. PhD thesis, Department of Computer Science, University of Kentucky (2001),
   http://lib.uky.edu/ETD/ukycosc2001d00022/pivkina.pdf
5. Caroprese, L., Truszczyński, M.: Declarative Semantics for Revision Programming and Connections to Active Integrity Constraints. In: Hölldobler, S., Lutz, C., Wansing, H. (eds.) JELIA 2008. LNCS, vol. 5293. Springer, Heidelberg (2008)
6. Caroprese, L., Greco, S., Zumpano, E.: Active integrity constraints for database consistency maintenance, Manuscript, IEEE TKDE (submitted, 2008)
7. Marek, W., Truszczyński, M.: Autoepistemic logic. Journal of the ACM 38, 588–619 (1991)
8. Eiter, T., Gottlob, G.: On the computational cost of disjunctive logic programming: propositional case. Annals of Mathematics and Artificial Intelligence 15, 289–323 (1995)
9. Gelfond, M., Lifschitz, V.: Classical negation in logic programs and disjunctive databases. New Generation Computing 9, 365–385 (1991)
10. Lifschitz, V., Woo, T.: Answer sets in general nonmonotonic reasoning. In: Proceedings of KR 1992, pp. 603–614. Morgan Kaufmann, San Francisco (1992)

A Folding Algorithm for Eliminating Existential Variables from Constraint Logic Programs

Valerio Senni[1], Alberto Pettorossi[1], and Maurizio Proietti[2]

[1] DISP, University of Rome Tor Vergata, Via del Politecnico 1, I-00133 Rome, Italy
{senni,pettorossi}@disp.uniroma2.it
[2] IASI-CNR, Viale Manzoni 30, I-00185 Rome, Italy
proietti@iasi.cnr.it

Abstract. The existential variables of a clause in a constraint logic program are the variables which occur in the body of the clause and not in its head. The elimination of these variables is a transformation technique which is often used for improving program efficiency and verifying program properties. We consider a folding transformation rule which ensures the elimination of existential variables and we propose an algorithm for applying this rule in the case where the constraints are linear inequations over rational or real numbers. The algorithm combines techniques for matching terms modulo equational theories and techniques for solving systems of linear inequations. We show that an implementation of our folding algorithm performs well in practice.

1 Introduction

Constraint logic programming is a very expressive language for writing programs in a declarative way and for specifying and verifying properties of software systems [1]. When writing programs in a declarative style or writing specifications, one often uses *existential variables*, that is, variables which occur in the body of a clause and not in its head. For instance, the formula $\forall N \, (N > 0 \rightarrow p(N))$, specifying "the predicate $p(N)$ holds for every positive number N", can be written by using the following two clauses:

$$prop \leftarrow \neg q \qquad\qquad q \leftarrow N > 0 \wedge \neg p(N)$$

where N is an existential variable. However, the use of existential variables may give rise to inefficient or even nonterminating computations (and this may happen when an existential variable denotes an intermediate data structure or when an existential variable ranges over an infinite set). For this reason some transformation techniques have been proposed for eliminating those variables from logic programs and constraint logic programs [2,3]. In particular, in [3] it has been shown that by eliminating the existential variables from a constraint logic program defining a nullary predicate, like *prop* above, one may obtain a propositional program and, thus, decide whether or not that predicate holds.

M. Garcia de la Banda and E. Pontelli (Eds.): ICLP 2008, LNCS 5366, pp. 284–300, 2008.
© Springer-Verlag Berlin Heidelberg 2008

The transformation techniques for the elimination of the existential variables make use of the *unfolding* and *folding* rules which have been first proposed in the context of functional programming by Burstall and Darlington [4], and then extended to logic programming [5] and to constraint logic programming [6,7,8,9]. In the techniques for eliminating existential variables a particularly relevant role is played by the folding rule, which can be defined as follows.

Let (i) H and K be atoms, (ii) c and d be constraints, and (iii) G and B be goals (that is, conjunctions of literals). Given two clauses γ: $H \leftarrow c \wedge G$ and δ: $K \leftarrow d \wedge B$, if there exist a constraint e, a substitution ϑ, and a goal R such that $H \leftarrow c \wedge G$ is equivalent (w.r.t. a given theory of constraints) to $H \leftarrow e \wedge (d \wedge B)\vartheta \wedge R$, then γ is folded into the clause η: $H \leftarrow e \wedge K\vartheta \wedge R$. In order to use the folding rule to eliminate existential variables we also require that the variables occurring in $K\vartheta$ are a subset of the variables occurring in H.

In the literature, no algorithm is provided to determine whether or not, given a theory of constraints, the suitable e, ϑ, and R which are required for folding, do exist. In this paper we propose an algorithm based on linear algebra and term rewriting techniques for computing e, ϑ, and R, if they exist, in the case when the constraints are linear inequations over the rational numbers (however, the techniques we will present are valid without relevant changes also when the inequations are over the real numbers).

For instance, let us consider the clauses:

$$\gamma: \quad p(X_1, X_2, X_3) \leftarrow X_1 < 1 \wedge X_1 \geq Z_1 + 1 \wedge Z_2 > 0 \wedge q(Z_1, f(X_3), Z_2) \wedge r(X_2)$$
$$\delta: \quad s(Y_1, Y_2, Y_3) \leftarrow W_1 < 0 \wedge Y_1 - 3 \geq 2W_1 \wedge W_2 > 0 \wedge q(W_1, Y_3, W_2)$$

and suppose that we want to fold γ using δ for eliminating the existential variables Z_1 and Z_2 occurring in γ. Our folding algorithm **FA** computes (see Examples 1–3 in Section 4): (i) the constraint e: $X_1 < 1$, (ii) the substitution ϑ: $\{Y_1/2X_1+1, Y_2/a, Y_3/f(X_3), W_1/Z_1, W_2/Z_2\}$, where a is an arbitrary constant, and (iii) the goal R: $r(X_2)$, and the clause derived by folding γ using δ is:

$$\eta: \quad p(X_1, X_2, X_3) \leftarrow X_1 < 1 \wedge s(2X_1 + 1, a, f(X_3)) \wedge r(X_2)$$

which has no existential variables. (The correctness of this folding can easily be checked by unfolding η w.r.t. $s(2X_1+1, a, f(X_3))$.) In general, there may be zero or more triples $\langle e, \vartheta, R \rangle$ that satisfy the conditions for the applicability of the folding rule. For this reason, our folding algorithm is nondeterministic and in different runs it may compute different folded clauses.

The paper is organized as follows. In Section 2 we introduce some basic definitions concerning constraint logic programs. In Section 3 we present the folding rule which we use for eliminating existential variables. In Section 4 we describe our algorithm for applying the folding rule and we prove the soundness and completeness of this algorithm with respect to the declarative specification of the rule. In Section 5 we analyze the complexity of our folding algorithm. We also describe an implementation of that algorithm and we present an experimental evaluation of its performance. Finally, in Section 6 we discuss related work and we suggest some directions for future investigations.

2   Preliminary Definitions

In this section we recall some basic definitions concerning constraint logic programs, where the constraints are conjunctions of linear inequations over the rational numbers. As already mentioned, the results we will present in this paper are valid also when the constraints are conjunctions of linear inequations over the real numbers. For notions not defined here the reader may refer to [1,10].

Let us consider a first order language $\mathcal{L}$ given by a set *Var* of variables, a set *Fun* of function symbols, and a set *Pred* of predicate symbols. Let $+$ denote addition, $\cdot$ denote multiplication, and $\mathbb{Q}$ denote the set of rational numbers. We assume that $\{+,\cdot\} \cup \mathbb{Q} \subseteq \textit{Fun}$ (in particular, every rational number is assumed to be a 0-ary function symbol). We also assume that the predicate symbols $\geq$ and $>$ denoting inequality and strict inequality, respectively, belong to *Pred*.

In order to distinguish terms representing rational numbers from other terms (which, in general, may be considered as finite trees), we assume that $\mathcal{L}$ is a typed language [10] with two basic types: rat, which is the type of rational numbers, and tree, which is the type of finite trees. We also consider types constructed from basic types by using the type constructors $\times$ and $\rightarrow$. A variable $X \in \textit{Var}$ has either type rat or type tree. We denote by $\textit{Var}_{\text{rat}}$ and $\textit{Var}_{\text{tree}}$ the set of variables of type rat and tree, respectively. A predicate symbol of arity n and a function symbol of arity n in $\mathcal{L}$ have types of the form $\tau_1 \times \cdots \times \tau_n$ and $\tau_1 \times \cdots \times \tau_n \rightarrow \tau_{n+1}$, respectively, for some types $\tau_1, \ldots, \tau_n, \tau_{n+1} \in \{\text{rat}, \text{tree}\}$. In particular, the predicate symbols $\geq$ and $>$ have type $\text{rat} \times \text{rat}$, the function symbols $+$ and $\cdot$ have type $\text{rat} \times \text{rat} \rightarrow \text{rat}$, and the rational numbers have type rat. The function symbols in $\{+,\cdot\} \cup \mathbb{Q}$ are the only symbols whose type is $\tau_1 \times \cdots \times \tau_n \rightarrow \text{rat}$, for some types $\tau_1, \ldots, \tau_n$, with $n \geq 0$.

A *term* u is either a *term of type* rat or a *term of type* tree. A term p of type rat is a *linear polynomial* of the form $a_1 X_1 + \ldots + a_n X_n + a_{n+1}$, where $a_1, \ldots, a_{n+1}$ are rational numbers and $X_1, \ldots, X_n$ are variables in $\textit{Var}_{\text{rat}}$ (a *monomial* of the form aX stands for the term $a \cdot X$). A term t of type tree is either a variable X in $\textit{Var}_{\text{tree}}$ or a term of the form $f(u_1, \ldots, u_n)$, where f is a function symbol of type $\tau_1 \times \cdots \times \tau_n \rightarrow \text{tree}$, and $u_1, \ldots, u_n$ are terms of type $\tau_1, \ldots, \tau_n$, respectively.

An *atomic constraint* is a linear inequation of the form $p_1 \geq p_2$ or $p_1 > p_2$. A *constraint* is a conjunction $c_1 \wedge \ldots \wedge c_n$, where $c_1, \ldots, c_n$ are atomic constraints. When $n = 0$ we write $c_1 \wedge \ldots \wedge c_n$ as *true*. A constraint of the form $p_1 \geq p_2 \wedge p_2 \geq p_1$ is abbreviated as the equation $p_1 = p_2$ (which, thus, is not an atomic constraint). We denote by $LIN_{\mathbb{Q}}$ the set of all constraints.

An *atom* is of the form $r(u_1, \ldots, u_n)$, where r is a predicate symbol, not in $\{\geq, >\}$, of type $\tau_1 \times \ldots \times \tau_n$ and $u_1, \ldots, u_n$ are terms of type $\tau_1, \ldots, \tau_n$, respectively. A *literal* is either an atom (called a *positive literal*) or a negated atom (called a *negative literal*). A *goal* is a conjunction $L_1 \wedge \ldots \wedge L_n$ of literals, with $n \geq 0$. Similarly to the case of constraints, the conjunction of 0 literals is denoted by *true*. A *constrained goal* is a conjunction $c \wedge G$, where c is a constraint and G is a goal. A *clause* is of the form $H \leftarrow c \wedge G$, where H is an atom and $c \wedge G$ is a constrained goal. A *constraint logic program* is a set of clauses. A *formula* of the language $\mathcal{L}$ is constructed as usual in first order logic from the symbols of $\mathcal{L}$ by using the logical connectives $\wedge$, $\vee$, $\neg$, $\rightarrow$, $\leftarrow$, $\leftrightarrow$, and the quantifiers $\exists$, $\forall$.

If e is a term or a formula then by $Vars_{\mathtt{rat}}(e)$ and $Vars_{\mathtt{tree}}(e)$ we denote, respectively, the set of variables of type $\mathtt{rat}$ and of type $\mathtt{tree}$ occurring in e. By $Vars(e)$ we denote the set of all variables occurring in e, that is, $Vars_{\mathtt{rat}}(e) \cup Vars_{\mathtt{tree}}(e)$. Similar notation will also be used for sets of terms or sets of formulas. Given a clause $\gamma: H \leftarrow c \wedge G$, by $EVars(\gamma)$ we denote the set of the *existential variables* of γ, that is, $Vars(c \wedge G) - Vars(H)$. The *constraint-local* variables of γ are the variables in the set $Vars(c) - Vars(\{H, G\})$. Given a set $X = \{X_1, \ldots, X_n\}$ of variables and a formula φ, by $\forall X \varphi$ we denote the formula $\forall X_1 \ldots \forall X_n \varphi$ and by $\exists X \varphi$ we denote the formula $\exists X_1 \ldots \exists X_n \varphi$. By $\forall(\varphi)$ and $\exists(\varphi)$ we denote the *universal closure* and the *existential closure* of φ, respectively. In what follows we will use the notion of *substitution* as defined in [10] with the following extra condition: for any substitution $\{X_1/t_1, \ldots, X_n/t_n\}$, for $i = 1, \ldots, n$, the type of X_i is equal to the type of t_i.

Let $\mathcal{L}_{\mathtt{rat}}$ denote the sublanguage of $\mathcal{L}$ given by the set $Var_{\mathtt{rat}}$ of variables, the set $\{+, \cdot\} \cup \mathbb{Q}$ of function symbols, and the set $\{\geq, >\}$ of predicate symbols. We denote by $\mathcal{Q}$ the interpretation which assigns to every function symbol or predicate symbol of $\mathcal{L}_{\mathtt{rat}}$ the usual function or relation on $\mathbb{Q}$. For a formula φ of $\mathcal{L}_{\mathtt{rat}}$ (in particular, for a constraint), the satisfaction relation $\mathcal{Q} \models \varphi$ is defined as usual in first order logic. A $\mathcal{Q}$-*interpretation* is an interpretation I for the typed language $\mathcal{L}$ which agrees with $\mathcal{Q}$ for each formula φ of $\mathcal{L}_{\mathtt{rat}}$, that is, for each φ of $\mathcal{L}_{\mathtt{rat}}$, $I \models \varphi$ iff $\mathcal{Q} \models \varphi$. The definition of a $\mathcal{Q}$-interpretation for typed languages is a straightforward extension of the one for untyped languages [1]. We say that a $\mathcal{Q}$-interpretation I is a $\mathcal{Q}$-*model* of a program P if for every clause $\gamma \in P$ we have that $I \models \forall(\gamma)$. Similarly to the case of logic programs, we can define *stratified* constraint logic programs and we have that every such program P has a *perfect* $\mathcal{Q}$-model [1,6,9], denoted by $M(P)$.

A *solution* of a set C of constraints is a ground substitution σ of the form $\{X_1/a_1, \ldots, X_n/a_n\}$, where $\{X_1, \ldots, X_n\} = Vars(C)$ and $a_1, \ldots, a_n \in \mathbb{Q}$, such that $\mathcal{Q} \models c\sigma$ for every $c \in C$. A set of constraints is said to be *satisfiable* if it has a solution. We assume that we are given a function *solve* that takes a set C of constraints in $LIN_{\mathbb{Q}}$ as input and returns a solution σ of C, if C is satisfiable, and **fail** otherwise. The function *solve* can be implemented, for instance, by using the Fourier-Motzkin or the Khachiyan algorithms [11]. We assume that we are also given a function *project* such that for every constraint $c \in LIN_{\mathbb{Q}}$ and for every finite set of variables $X \subseteq Var_{\mathtt{rat}}$, $\mathcal{Q} \models \forall X ((\exists Y c) \leftrightarrow project(c, X))$, where $Y = Vars(c) - X$ and $Vars(project(c, X)) \subseteq X$. The *project* function can be implemented, for instance, by using the Fourier-Motzkin variable elimination algorithm or the algorithm presented in [12].

A clause $\gamma: H \leftarrow c \wedge G$ is said to be in *normal form* if (i) every term of type $\mathtt{rat}$ occurring in G is a variable, (ii) each variable of type $\mathtt{rat}$ occurs at most once in G, (iii) $Vars_{\mathtt{rat}}(H) \cap Vars_{\mathtt{rat}}(G) = \emptyset$, and (iv) γ has no constraint-local variables. It is always possible to transform any clause γ_1 into a clause γ_2 in normal form such that γ_1 and γ_2 have the same $\mathcal{Q}$-models. (In particular, the constraint-local variables of any given clause can be eliminated by applying the *project* function.) The clause γ_2 is called *a normal form of* γ_1. Without loss of generality, when presenting the folding rule and the corresponding algorithm for its application, we will assume that the clauses are in normal form.

Given two clauses γ_1 and γ_2, we write $\gamma_1 \cong \gamma_2$ if there exist a normal form $H \leftarrow c_1 \wedge B_1$ of γ_1, a normal form $H \leftarrow c_2 \wedge B_2$ of γ_2, and a variable renaming ρ such that: (1) $H = H\rho$, (2) $B_1 =_{AC} B_2\rho$, and (3) $\mathcal{Q} \models \forall (c_1 \leftrightarrow c_2\rho)$, where $=_{AC}$ denotes equality modulo the equational theory of associativity and commutativity of conjunction. We refer to this theory as the $AC_\wedge$ *theory* [13].

Proposition 1. (i) $\cong$ *is an equivalence relation.* (ii) *If* $\gamma_1 \cong \gamma_2$ *then, for every* $\mathcal{Q}$-*interpretation* I, $I \models \gamma_1$ *iff* $I \models \gamma_2$. (iii) *If* γ_2 *is a normal form of* γ_1 *then* $\gamma_1 \cong \gamma_2$.

3   The Folding Rule

In this section we introduce our folding transformation rule which is a variant of the rules considered in the literature [6,7,8,9]. In particular, by using our variant of the folding rule we may replace a constrained goal occurring in the body of a clause where some existential variables occur, by an atom which has no existential variables in the folded clause.

Definition 1 (Folding Rule). Let γ: $H \leftarrow c \wedge G$ and δ: $K \leftarrow d \wedge B$ be clauses in normal form without variables in common. Suppose also that there exist a constraint e, a substitution ϑ, and a goal R such that: (1) $\gamma \cong H \leftarrow e \wedge d\vartheta \wedge B\vartheta \wedge R$; (2) for every variable X in $EVars(\delta)$, the following conditions hold: (2.1) $X\vartheta$ is a variable not occurring in $\{H, e, R\}$, and (2.2) $X\vartheta$ does not occur in the term $Y\vartheta$, for every variable Y occurring in $d \wedge B$ and different from X; (3) $Vars(K\vartheta) \subseteq Vars(H)$. By *folding clause* γ *using clause* δ we derive the clause η: $H \leftarrow e \wedge K\vartheta \wedge R$.

Condition (3) ensures that no existential variable of η occurs in $K\vartheta$. However, in e or R some existential variables may still occur. These variables may be eliminated by further folding steps using clause δ again or other clauses. In Theorem 1 below we establish the correctness of the folding rule w.r.t. the perfect model semantics. That correctness follows immediately from [7,8,9].

A *transformation sequence* is a sequence $P_0, \ldots, P_n$ of programs such that, for $k = 0, \ldots, n-1$, program P_{k+1} is derived from program P_k by an application of one of the following transformation rules: *definition, unfolding, folding*. For a detailed presentation of the definition and unfolding rules we refer to [9]. An application of the folding rule is defined as follows. For $k = 0, \ldots, n$, by $Defs_k$ we denote the set of clauses introduced by the definition rule during the construction of $P_0, \ldots, P_k$. Program P_{k+1} is derived from program P_k by an application of the folding rule if $P_{k+1} = (P_k - \{\gamma\}) \cup \{\eta\}$, where γ is a clause in P_k, δ is a clause in $Defs_k$, and η is the clause derived by folding γ using δ as indicated in Definition 1.

Theorem 1. [9] *Let* P_0 *be a stratified program and let* $P_0, \ldots, P_n$ *be a transformation sequence. Suppose that, for* $k = 0, \ldots, n-1$, *if* P_{k+1} *is derived from* P_k *by folding clause* γ *using clause* $\delta \in Defs_k$, *then there exists* j, *with* $0 < j < n$, *such* *that $\delta \in P_j$ and P_{j+1} is derived from P_j by unfolding δ w.r.t. a positive literal in its body. Then $P_0 \cup Defs_n$ and P_n are stratified and $M(P_0 \cup Defs_n) = M(P_n)$.*

4   An Algorithm for Applying the Folding Rule

Now we will present an algorithm for determining whether or not a clause $\gamma : H \leftarrow c \wedge G$ can be folded using a clause $\delta : K \leftarrow d \wedge B$, according to Definition 1. The objective of our folding algorithm is to find a constraint e, a substitution ϑ, and a goal R such that $\gamma \cong H \leftarrow e \wedge d\vartheta \wedge B\vartheta \wedge R$ holds (see Point (1) of Definition 1), and also Points (2) and (3) of Definition 1 hold. Our algorithm computes e, ϑ, and R, if they exist, by applying two procedures: (i) the *goal matching procedure*, called **GM**, which matches the goal G against B and returns a substitution α and a goal R such that $G =_{AC} B\alpha \wedge R$, and (ii) the *constraint matching procedure*, called **CM**, which matches the constraint c against $d\alpha$ and returns a substitution β and a new constraint e such that c is equivalent to $e \wedge d\alpha\beta$ in the theory of constraints. The substitution ϑ to be found is $\alpha\beta$, that is, the composition of the substitutions α and β. The output of the folding algorithm is either the clause $\eta \colon H \leftarrow e \wedge K\vartheta \wedge R$, or **fail** if folding is not possible. Since Definition 1 does not determine e, ϑ, and R in a unique way, our folding algorithm is nondeterministic and, as already said, in different runs it may compute different output clauses.

4.1   Goal Matching

Let us now present the goal matching procedure **GM**. This procedure uses the notion of binding which is defined as follows: a *binding* is a pair of the form e_1/e_2, where e_1, e_2 are either both goals or both terms. Thus, the notion of *set of bindings* is a generalization of the notion of substitution.

Goal Matching Procedure: GM

Input: two clauses in normal form without variables in common $\gamma \colon H \leftarrow c \wedge G$ and $\delta \colon K \leftarrow d \wedge B$.

Output: a substitution α and a goal R such that: (1) $G =_{AC} B\alpha \wedge R$; (2) for every variable X in $EVars(\delta)$, the following conditions hold: (2.1) $X\alpha$ is a variable not occurring in $\{H, R\}$, and (2.2) $X\alpha$ does not occur in the term $Y\alpha$, for every variable Y occurring in $d \wedge B$ and different from X; (3) $Vars_{\text{tree}}(K\alpha) \subseteq Vars(H)$. If such α and R do not exist, then **fail**.

Consider a set $Bnds$ of bindings initialized to the singleton $\{B/G\}$. Consider also the following rewrite rules (i)–(x). When the left hand side of a rule is written as $Bnds_1 \cup Bnds_2 \Longrightarrow \ldots$ then we assume that $Bnds_1 \cap Bnds_2 = \emptyset$.

(i) $\{(L_1 \wedge B_1) / (G_1 \wedge L_2 \wedge G_2)\} \cup Bnds \Longrightarrow \{L_1/L_2, \; B_1/(G_1 \wedge G_2)\} \cup Bnds$
   where: (1) L_1 and L_2 are both positive or both negative literals and have the same predicate symbol with the same arity, and (2) B_1, G_1, and G_2 are goals (possibly, the empty conjunction *true*);

(ii) $\{\neg A_1/\neg A_2\} \cup Bnds \Longrightarrow \{A_1/A_2\} \cup Bnds$;

(iii) $\{a(s_1, \ldots, s_n)/a(t_1, \ldots, t_n)\} \cup Bnds \Longrightarrow \{s_1/t_1, \ldots, s_n/t_n\} \cup Bnds$;

(iv) $\{a(s_1, \ldots, s_m)/b(t_1, \ldots, t_n)\} \cup Bnds \Longrightarrow \mathbf{fail}$, if a is syntactically different from b or $m \neq n$;

(v) $\{a(s_1, \ldots, s_n)/X\} \cup Bnds \Longrightarrow \mathbf{fail}$, if X is a variable;

(vi) $\{X/s\} \cup Bnds \Longrightarrow \mathbf{fail}$, if X is a variable and $X/t \in Bnds$ for some t syntactically different from s;

(vii) $\{X/s\} \cup Bnds \Longrightarrow \mathbf{fail}$, if $X \in EVars(\delta)$ and one of the following three conditions holds: (1) s is not a variable, or (2) $s \in Vars(H)$, or (3) there exists $Y \in Vars(d \wedge B)$ different from X such that: (3.1) $Y/t \in Bnds$, for some term t, and (3.2) $s \in Vars(t)$;

(viii) $\{X/s,\ true/G_2\} \cup Bnds \Longrightarrow \mathbf{fail}$, if $X \in EVars(\delta)$ and $s \in Vars(G_2)$;

(ix) $\{X/s\} \cup Bnds \Longrightarrow \mathbf{fail}$, if $X \in Vars_{\mathtt{tree}}(K)$ and $Vars(s) \not\subseteq Vars(H)$;

(x) $Bnds \Longrightarrow \{X/s\} \cup Bnds$, where s is an arbitrary ground term of type $\mathtt{tree}$, if $X \in Vars_{\mathtt{tree}}(K) - Vars(B)$ and there is no term t such that $X/t \in Bnds$.

IF there exist a set of bindings α (which, by construction, is a substitution) and a goal R such that: (c1) $\{B/G\} \Longrightarrow^* \{true/R\} \cup \alpha$ (where $true/R \notin \alpha$), (c2) no α' exists such that $\alpha \Longrightarrow \alpha'$, and (c3) α is different from $\mathbf{fail}$ (that is, α is a maximally rewritten, non-failing set of bindings such that (c1) holds) THEN return α and R ELSE return $\mathbf{fail}$.

Rule (i) associates each literal in B with a literal in G in a nondeterministic way. Rules (ii)–(vi) are a specialization to our case of the usual rules for matching [14]. Rules (vii)–(x) ensure that any pair $\langle \alpha, R \rangle$ computed by $\mathbf{GM}$ satisfies Conditions (2) and (3) of the folding rule, or if no such pair exists, then $\mathbf{GM}$ returns $\mathbf{fail}$.

Example 1. Let us apply the procedure $\mathbf{GM}$ to the clauses γ and δ presented in the Introduction, where the predicates p, q, r, and s are of type $\mathtt{rat} \times \mathtt{tree} \times \mathtt{tree}$, $\mathtt{rat} \times \mathtt{tree} \times \mathtt{rat}$, $\mathtt{tree}$, and $\mathtt{rat} \times \mathtt{tree} \times \mathtt{tree}$, respectively, and the function f is of type $\mathtt{tree} \to \mathtt{tree}$. The clauses γ and δ are in normal form and have no variables in common. The procedure $\mathbf{GM}$ performs the following rewritings, where the arrow $\overset{r}{\Longrightarrow}$ denotes an application of the rewrite rule r:

$$\{q(W_1, Y_3, W_2)/(q(Z_1, f(X_3), Z_2) \wedge r(X_2))\}$$
$$\overset{i}{\Longrightarrow} \{q(W_1, Y_3, W_2)/q(Z_1, f(X_3), Z_2),\ true/r(X_2)\}$$
$$\overset{iii}{\Longrightarrow} \{W_1/Z_1,\ Y_3/f(X_3),\ W_2/Z_2,\ true/r(X_2)\}$$
$$\overset{x}{\Longrightarrow} \{W_1/Z_1,\ Y_3/f(X_3),\ W_2/Z_2,\ Y_2/a,\ true/r(X_2)\}$$

In the final set of bindings, the term a is an arbitrary constant of type $\mathtt{tree}$. The output of $\mathbf{GM}$ is the substitution $\alpha\colon \{W_1/Z_1, Y_3/f(X_3), W_2/Z_2, Y_2/a\}$ and the goal $R\colon r(X_2)$.

The termination of the goal matching procedure can be shown via an argument based on the multiset ordering of the size of the bindings. Indeed, each of the rules (i)–(ix) replaces a binding by a finite number of smaller bindings, and rule (x) can be applied at most once for each variable in the head of clause δ.

4.2   Constraint Matching

Given two clauses in normal form $\gamma\colon H \leftarrow c \wedge G$ and $\delta\colon K \leftarrow d \wedge B$, if the goal matching procedure **GM** returns the substitution α and the goal R, then we can construct two clauses in normal form: $H \leftarrow c \wedge B\alpha \wedge R$ and $K\alpha \leftarrow d\alpha \wedge B\alpha$ such that $G =_{AC} B\alpha \wedge R$. The constraint matching procedure **CM** takes in input these two clauses, which, for reasons of simplicity, we now rename as $\gamma'\colon H \leftarrow c \wedge B' \wedge R$ and $\delta'\colon K' \leftarrow d' \wedge B'$, respectively, and returns a constraint e and a substitution β such that: (1) $\gamma' \cong H \leftarrow e \wedge d'\beta \wedge B' \wedge R$, (2) $B'\beta = B'$, (3) $Vars(K'\beta) \subseteq Vars(H)$, and (4) $Vars(e) \subseteq Vars(\{H, R\})$. If such e and β do not exist, then the procedure **CM** returns **fail**.

Now, let $\widetilde{e}$ denote the constraint $project(c, X)$, where $X = Vars(c) - Vars(B')$ (see Section 2 for the definition of the $project$ function). Lemma 1 below shows that, for any substitution β, if there exists a constraint e satisfying Conditions (1)–(4) above, then we can always take e to be the constraint $\widetilde{e}$. Thus, by Lemma 1 the procedure **CM** should only search for a substitution β such that $\mathcal{Q} \models \forall(c \leftrightarrow (\widetilde{e} \wedge d'\beta))$.

Lemma 1. *Let $\gamma'\colon H \leftarrow c \wedge B' \wedge R$ and $\delta'\colon K' \leftarrow d' \wedge B'$ be the input clauses of the constraint matching procedure. For every substitution β, there exists a constraint e such that: (1) $\gamma' \cong H \leftarrow e \wedge d'\beta \wedge B' \wedge R$, (2) $B'\beta = B'$, (3) $Vars(K'\beta) \subseteq Vars(H)$, and (4) $Vars(e) \subseteq Vars(\{H, R\})$ iff $\mathcal{Q} \models \forall(c \leftrightarrow (\widetilde{e} \wedge d'\beta))$ and Conditions (2) and (3) hold.*

Now we introduce some notions and we state some properties (see Lemma 2 and Theorem 2) which will be exploited by the constraint matching procedure **CM** for reducing the equivalence between c and $\widetilde{e} \wedge d'\beta$, for a suitable β, to a set of equivalences between the atomic constraints occurring in c and $\widetilde{e} \wedge d'\beta$.

A conjunction $a_1 \wedge \ldots \wedge a_m$ of (not necessarily distinct) atomic constraints is said to be *redundant* if there exists i, with $0 \leq i \leq m$, such that $\mathcal{Q} \models \forall((a_1 \wedge \ldots \wedge a_{i-1} \wedge a_{i+1} \wedge \ldots \wedge a_m) \rightarrow a_i)$. In this case we also say that a_i is redundant in $a_1 \wedge \ldots \wedge a_m$. Thus, the empty conjunction *true* is non-redundant and an atomic constraint a is redundant iff $\mathcal{Q} \models \forall(a)$. Given a redundant constraint c, we can always derive a non-redundant constraint c' which is equivalent to c, that is, $\mathcal{Q} \models \forall(c \leftrightarrow c')$, by repeatedly eliminating from the constraint at hand an atomic constraint which is redundant in that constraint.

Without loss of generality we can assume that any given constraint c is of the form $p_1 \, \rho_1 \, 0 \wedge \ldots \wedge p_m \, \rho_m \, 0$, where $m \geq 0$ and $\rho_1, \ldots, \rho_m \in \{\geq, >\}$. We define the *interior* of c, denoted $interior(c)$, to be the constraint $p_1 > 0 \wedge \ldots \wedge p_m > 0$. A constraint c is said to be *admissible* if both c and $interior(c)$ are satisfiable and non-redundant. For instance, the constraint $c_1\colon X - Y \geq 0 \wedge Y \geq 0$ is admissible, while the constraint $c_2\colon X - Y \geq 0 \wedge Y \geq 0 \wedge X > 0$ is not admissible (indeed, c_2 is non-redundant and $interior(c_2)\colon X - Y > 0 \wedge Y > 0 \wedge X > 0$ is redundant). The following Lemma 2 characterizes the equivalence of two constraints when one of them is admissible.

Lemma 2. *Let us consider an admissible constraint a of the form $a_1 \wedge \ldots \wedge a_m$ and a constraint b of the form $b_1 \wedge \ldots \wedge b_n$, where $a_1, \ldots, a_m, b_1, \ldots, b_n$ are atomic constraints (in particular, they are not equalities). We have that $\mathcal{Q} \models \forall (a \leftrightarrow b)$ holds iff there exists an injection $\mu : \{1, \ldots, m\} \rightarrow \{1, \ldots, n\}$ such that for $i = 1, \ldots, m$, $\mathcal{Q} \models \forall (a_i \leftrightarrow b_{\mu(i)})$ and for $j = 1, \ldots, n$, if $j \notin \{\mu(i) \mid 1 \leq i \leq m\}$, then $\mathcal{Q} \models \forall (a \rightarrow b_j)$.*

In order to see that admissibility is a needed hypothesis for Lemma 2, let us consider the non-admissible constraint $c_3 : X - Y \geq 0 \wedge Y \geq 0 \wedge X + Y > 0$. We have that $\mathcal{Q} \models \forall (c_2 \leftrightarrow c_3)$ and yet there is no injection which has the properties stated in Lemma 2.

Lemma 2 will be used to show that if there exists a substitution β such that $\mathcal{Q} \models \forall (c \leftrightarrow (\tilde{e} \wedge d'\beta))$, where c is an admissible constraint and $\tilde{e}$ is defined as in Lemma 1, then **CM** computes such a substitution β. Indeed, given the constraint c, of the form $a_1 \wedge \ldots \wedge a_m$, and the constraint $\tilde{e} \wedge d'$, of the form $b_1 \wedge \ldots \wedge b_n$, **CM** computes: (1) an injection μ from $\{1, \ldots, m\}$ to $\{1, \ldots, n\}$, and (2) a substitution β such that: (2.i) for $i = 1, \ldots, m$, $\mathcal{Q} \models \forall (a_i \leftrightarrow b_{\mu(i)}\beta)$, and (2.ii) for $j = 1, \ldots, n$, if $j \notin \{\mu(i) \mid 1 \leq i \leq m\}$, then $\mathcal{Q} \models \forall (c \rightarrow b_j\beta)$.

In order to compute β satisfying the property of Point (2.i), we make use of the following Property $P1$: given the satisfiable, non-redundant constraints $p > 0$ and $q > 0$, we have that $\mathcal{Q} \models \forall (p > 0 \leftrightarrow q > 0)$ holds iff there exists a rational number $k > 0$ such that $\mathcal{Q} \models \forall (kp - q = 0)$ holds. Property $P1$ holds also if we replace $p > 0$ and $q > 0$ by $p \geq 0$ and $q \geq 0$, respectively.

Finally, in order to compute β satisfying the property of Point (2.ii), we make use of the following Theorem 2 which is a generalization of the above Property $P1$ and it is an extension of Farkas' Lemma to the case of systems of weak and strict inequalities [11].

Theorem 2. *Suppose that $p_1 \rho_1 0, \ldots, p_m \rho_m 0, p_{m+1} \rho_{m+1} 0$ are atomic constraints such that, for $i = 1, \ldots, m + 1$, $\rho_i \in \{\geq, >\}$ and $\mathcal{Q} \models \exists (p_1 \rho_1 0 \wedge \ldots \wedge p_m \rho_m 0)$. Then $\mathcal{Q} \models \forall (p_1 \rho_1 0 \wedge \ldots \wedge p_m \rho_m 0 \rightarrow p_{m+1} \rho_{m+1} 0)$ iff there exist $k_1 \geq 0, \ldots, k_{m+1} \geq 0$ such that: (i) $\mathcal{Q} \models \forall (k_1 p_1 + \cdots + k_m p_m + k_{m+1} = p_{m+1})$, and (ii) if ρ_{m+1} is $>$ then $(\sum_{i \in I} k_i) > 0$, where $I = \{i \mid 1 \leq i \leq m+1, \rho_i \text{ is } >\}$.*

As we will see below, the constraint matching procedure **CM** may generate *bilinear* polynomials (see rules (i)–(iii)), that is, non-linear polynomials of a particular form, which we now define. Let p be a polynomial and $\langle P_1, P_2 \rangle$ be a partition of a (proper or not) superset of $Vars(p)$. The polynomial p is said to be *bilinear in the partition* $\langle P_1, P_2 \rangle$ if the monomials of p are of the form: *either* (i) $k \, XY$, where k is a rational number, $X \in P_1$, and $Y \in P_2$, *or* (ii) $k \, X$, where k is a rational number and X is a variable, *or* (iii) k, where k is a rational number. Let us consider a polynomial p which is bilinear in the partition $\langle P_1, P_2 \rangle$ where $P_2 = \{Y_1, \ldots, Y_m\}$. The *normal form* of p, denoted $nf(p)$, w.r.t. a *given ordering* $Y_1, \ldots, Y_m$ *of the variables in* P_2, is a bilinear polynomial which is derived by: (i) computing the bilinear polynomial $p_1 Y_1 + \cdots + p_m Y_m + p_{m+1}$ such that $\mathcal{Q} \models \forall (p_1 Y_1 + \cdots + p_m Y_m + p_{m+1} = p)$, and (ii) erasing from that bilinear polynomial every summand $p_i Y_i$ such that $\mathcal{Q} \models \forall (p_i = 0)$.

Constraint Matching Procedure: CM

Input: two clauses in normal form $\gamma': H \leftarrow c \wedge B' \wedge R$ and $\delta': K' \leftarrow d' \wedge B'$.
Output: a constraint e and a substitution β such that: (1) $\gamma' \cong H \leftarrow e \wedge$ $d'\beta \wedge B' \wedge R$, (2) $B'\beta = B'$, (3) $Vars(K'\beta) \subseteq Vars(H)$, and (4) $Vars(e) \subseteq$ $Vars(\{H, R\})$. If such e and β do not exist, then **fail**.

IF c is unsatisfiable THEN return an arbitrary ground, unsatisfiable constraint e and a substitution β of the form $\{U_1/a_1, \ldots, U_s/a_s\}$, where $\{U_1, \ldots, U_s\} = Vars_{\mathtt{rat}}(K')$ and $a_1, \ldots, a_s$ are arbitrary rational numbers ELSE, if c is satisfiable, we proceed as follows.

Let X be the set $Vars(c) - Vars(B')$, Y be the set $Vars(d') - Vars(B')$, and Z be the set $Vars_{\mathtt{rat}}(B')$. Let e be the constraint $project(c, X)$. Without loss of generality, we may assume that: (i) c is a constraint of the form $p_1 \rho_1 0 \wedge \ldots \wedge p_m \rho_m 0$, where for $i = 1, \ldots, m$, p_i is a linear polynomial and $\rho_i \in \{\geq, >\}$, and (ii) $e \wedge d'$ is a constraint of the form $q_1 \pi_1 0 \wedge \ldots \wedge q_n \pi_n 0$, where for $j = 1, \ldots, n$, q_i is a linear polynomial and $\pi_i \in \{\geq, >\}$.

Let us consider the following rewrite rules (i)–(v) which are all of the form:
$$\langle f_1 \leftrightarrow g_1, \; S_1, \; \sigma_1 \rangle \Longrightarrow \langle f_2 \leftrightarrow g_2, \; S_2, \; \sigma_2 \rangle$$
where: (1) $f_1, g_1, f_2,$ and g_2 are constraints, (2) S_1 and S_2 are sets of constraints, and (3) σ_1 and σ_2 are substitutions. In the rewrite rules (i)–(v) below, whenever S_1 is written as $A \cup B$, we assume that $A \cap B = \emptyset$.

(i) $\langle p\,\rho\,0 \wedge f \leftrightarrow g_1 \wedge q\,\rho\,0 \wedge g_2, \; S, \; \sigma \rangle \Longrightarrow$
$\langle f \leftrightarrow g_1 \wedge g_2, \; \{nf(V p - q) = 0, V > 0\} \cup S, \; \sigma \rangle$
where V is a new variable and $\rho \in \{\geq, >\}$;

(ii) $\langle \mathit{true} \leftrightarrow q \geq 0 \wedge g, \; S, \; \sigma \rangle \Longrightarrow$
$\langle \mathit{true} \leftrightarrow g, \; \{nf(V_1 p_1 + \ldots + V_m p_m + V_{m+1} - q) = 0,$
$V_1 \geq 0, \ldots, V_{m+1} \geq 0\} \cup S, \; \sigma \rangle$
where $V_1, \ldots, V_{m+1}$ are new variables;

(iii) $\langle \mathit{true} \leftrightarrow q > 0 \wedge g, \; S, \; \sigma \rangle \Longrightarrow$
$\langle \mathit{true} \leftrightarrow g, \; \{nf(V_1 p_1 + \ldots + V_m p_m + V_{m+1} - q) = 0,$
$V_1 \geq 0, \ldots, V_{m+1} \geq 0, (\sum_{i \in I} V_i) > 0\} \cup S, \; \sigma \rangle$
where $V_1, \ldots, V_{m+1}$ are new variables and $I = \{i \mid 1 \leq i \leq m+1, \rho_i$ is $>\}$;

(iv) $\langle f \leftrightarrow g, \; \{p U + q = 0\} \cup S, \; \sigma \rangle \Longrightarrow \langle f \leftrightarrow g, \; \{p = 0, q = 0\} \cup S, \; \sigma \rangle$
if $U \in X \cup Z$;

(v) $\langle f \leftrightarrow g, \; \{a U + q = 0\} \cup S, \; \sigma \rangle \Longrightarrow$
$\langle f \leftrightarrow (g\{U/-\frac{q}{a}\}), \; \{nf(p\{U/-\frac{q}{a}\})\rho\,0 \mid p\,\rho\,0 \in S\}, \; \sigma\{U/-\frac{q}{a}\}\rangle$
if $U \in Y$, $Vars(q) \cap Vars(R) = \emptyset$, and $a \in (\mathbb{Q} - \{0\})$;

IF there exist a set C of constraints and a substitution σ_Y such that: (c1) $\langle c \leftrightarrow e \wedge d', \emptyset, \emptyset \rangle \Longrightarrow^* \langle \mathit{true} \leftrightarrow \mathit{true}, C, \sigma_Y \rangle$, (c2) there is no triple T such that $\langle \mathit{true} \leftrightarrow \mathit{true}, C, \sigma_Y \rangle \Longrightarrow T$, (c3) for every constraint $f \in C$, we have that $Vars(f) \subseteq W$, where W is the set of the new variables introduced during the rewriting steps from $\langle c \leftrightarrow e \wedge d', \emptyset, \emptyset \rangle$ to $\langle \mathit{true} \leftrightarrow \mathit{true}, C, \sigma_Y \rangle$, and (c4) C is satisfiable and $solve(C) = \sigma_W$,
THEN construct a substitution σ_G of the form $\{U_1/a_1, \ldots, U_s/a_s\}$, where $\{U_1, \ldots, U_s\} = Vars_{\mathtt{rat}}(K'\sigma_Y\sigma_W) - Vars(H)$ and $a_1, \ldots, a_s$ are arbitrary rational numbers, and return the constraint e and the substitution $\beta = \sigma_Y\sigma_W\sigma_G$
ELSE return **fail**.

Note that in order to apply rules (iv) and (v), pU and aU, respectively, should be the leftmost monomials. The procedure **CM** is nondeterministic (see rule (i)). By induction on the number of rule applications, we can show that the polynomials occurring in the second components of the triples are all bilinear in the partition $\langle W, X \cup Y \cup Z \rangle$, where W is the set of the new variables introduced during the application of the rewrite rules. The normal forms of the bilinear polynomials which occur in the rewrite rules are all computed w.r.t. the fixed variable ordering $Z_1, \ldots, Z_h, Y_1, \ldots, Y_k, X_1, \ldots, X_l$, where $\{Z_1, \ldots, Z_h\} = Z$, $\{Y_1, \ldots, Y_k\} = Y$, and $\{X_1, \ldots, X_l\} = X$.

The termination of the procedure **CM** is a consequence of the following facts: (1) each application of rules (i), (ii), and (iii) reduces the number of atomic constraints occurring in the first component of the triple $\langle f \leftrightarrow g, \ S, \ \sigma \rangle$ at hand; (2) each application of rule (iv) does not modify the first component of the triple at hand, does not introduce any new variables, and replaces an equation occurring in the second component of the triple at hand by two smaller equations; (3) each application of rule (v) does not modify the number of atomic constraints in the first component of the triple at hand and eliminates all occurrences of a variable. Thus, the termination of **CM** can be proved by a lexicographic combination of two linear orderings and a multiset ordering.

Example 2. Let us consider again the clauses γ and δ of the Introduction and let α be the substitution computed by applying the procedure **GM** to γ and δ as shown in Example 1. Let us also consider the clauses γ' and δ', where γ' is γ and δ' is $\delta\alpha$, that is,

δ': $s(Y_1, a, f(X_3)) \leftarrow Z_1 < 0 \wedge Y_1 - 3 \geq 2Z_1 \wedge Z_2 > 0 \wedge q(Z_1, f(X_3), Z_2)$

Now we apply the procedure **CM** to clauses γ' and δ'. The constraint $X_1 < 1 \wedge X_1 \geq Z_1 + 1 \wedge Z_2 > 0$ occurring in γ' is satisfiable. The procedure **CM** starts off by computing the constraint e as follows:

$$e = project(X_1 < 1 \wedge X_1 \geq Z_1 + 1 \wedge Z_2 > 0, \{X_1\}) = X_1 < 1$$

Now **CM** performs the following rewritings, where: (i) all polynomials are bilinear in $\langle \{V_1, \ldots, V_7\}, \{X_1, Y_1, Z_1, Z_2\} \rangle$, (ii) their normal forms are computed w.r.t. the variable ordering Z_1, Z_2, Y_1, X_1, and (iii) $\overset{r}{\Longrightarrow}^k$ denotes k applications of rule r. (We have underlined the constraints that are rewritten by an application of a rule. Note also that the atomic constraints occurring in the initial triple are the ones in γ' and δ', rewritten into the form $p > 0$ or $p \geq 0$.)

$\langle (\underline{1 - X_1 > 0} \wedge X_1 - Z_1 - 1 \geq 0 \wedge Z_2 > 0) \leftrightarrow$
$\quad (\underline{1 - X_1 > 0} \wedge -Z_1 > 0 \wedge Y_1 - 3 - 2Z_1 \geq 0 \wedge Z_2 > 0), \ \emptyset, \ \emptyset \rangle$

$\overset{i}{\Longrightarrow} \langle (\underline{X_1 - Z_1 - 1 \geq 0} \wedge Z_2 > 0) \leftrightarrow (-Z_1 > 0 \wedge \underline{Y_1 - 3 - 2Z_1 \geq 0} \wedge Z_2 > 0),$
$\quad \{(1 - V_1)X_1 + V_1 - 1 = 0, V_1 > 0\}, \ \emptyset \rangle$

$\overset{i}{\Longrightarrow} \langle \underline{Z_2 > 0} \leftrightarrow (-Z_1 > 0 \wedge \underline{Z_2 > 0}),$
$\quad \{(1 - V_1)X_1 + V_1 - 1 = 0, V_1 > 0, \ (2 - V_2)Z_1 - Y_1 + V_2 X_1 - V_2 + 3 = 0, V_2 > 0\}, \ \emptyset \rangle$

$\overset{i}{\Longrightarrow} \langle true \leftrightarrow \underline{-Z_1 > 0},$
$\quad \{(1 - V_1)\underline{X_1} + V_1 - 1 = 0, V_1 > 0, \ (2 - V_2)Z_1 - Y_1 + V_2 X_1 - V_2 + 3 = 0, V_2 > 0,$

$$(V_3-1)Z_2=0, V_3>0\}, \quad \emptyset\rangle$$

$$\overset{iii}{\Longrightarrow} \langle true \leftrightarrow true,$$
$$\{(1-V_1)X_1+V_1-1=0, V_1>0, \ (2-V_2)Z_1-Y_1+V_2X_1-V_2+3=0, V_2>0,$$
$$\overline{(V_3-1)Z_2=0, V_3>0}, \ (1-V_5)Z_1+V_6Z_2+(V_5-V_4)X_1+V_4-V_5+V_7=0,$$
$$V_4\geq0, V_5\geq0, V_6\geq0, V_7\geq0, \ V_4+V_6+V_7>0\}, \ \emptyset\rangle$$

$$\overset{iv}{\Longrightarrow}^6 \langle true \leftrightarrow true,$$
$$\{1-V_1=0, V_1-1=0, V_1>0, \ 2-V_2=0, \underline{-Y_1+V_2X_1-V_2+3=0}, V_2>0,$$
$$V_3-1=0, V_3>0, \ 1-V_5=0, V_6=0, V_5-V_4=0, V_4-V_5+V_7=0,$$
$$V_4\geq0, V_5\geq0, V_6\geq0, V_7\geq0, \ V_4+V_6+V_7>0\}, \ \emptyset\rangle$$

$$\overset{v}{\Longrightarrow} \langle true \leftrightarrow true,$$
$$\{1-V_1=0, V_1-1=0, V_1>0, \ 2-V_2=0, V_2>0,$$
$$V_3-1=0, V_3>0, \ 1-V_5=0, V_6=0, V_5-V_4=0, V_7-V_5+V_4=0,$$
$$V_4\geq0, V_5\geq0, V_6\geq0, V_7\geq0, \ V_4+V_6+V_7>0\}, \ \{Y_1/V_2X_1-V_2+3\}\rangle$$

Let C be the second component of the final triple of the above sequence of rewritings. We have that C is satisfiable and has a unique solution given by the following substitution: $\sigma_W = solve(C) = \{V_1/1, V_2/2, V_3/1, V_4/1, V_5/1, V_6/0, V_7/0\}$. The substitution σ_Y computed in the third component of the final triple of the above sequence of rewritings is $\{Y_1/V_2X_1-V_2+3\}$. Since $Vars_{\text{rat}}(s(Y_1, a, f(X_3))\sigma_Y\sigma_W)-Vars(H) = \{X_1, X_3\}-\{X_1, X_2, X_3\}=\emptyset$, we have that σ_G is the identity substitution. Thus, the output of the procedure **CM** is the constraint $e = X_1<1$ and the substitution $\beta = \sigma_Y\sigma_W\sigma_G = \{Y_1/2X_1+1\}\cup\sigma_W$.

4.3   The Folding Algorithm

Now we are ready to present our folding algorithm.

Folding Algorithm: FA

Input: two clauses in normal form without variables in common $\gamma\colon H \leftarrow c\wedge G$ and $\delta\colon K \leftarrow d\wedge B$.

Output: the clause $\eta\colon H \leftarrow e \wedge K\vartheta \wedge R$, if it is possible to fold γ using δ according to Definition 1, and **fail**, otherwise.

IF there exist a substitution α and a goal R which are the output of an execution of the procedure **GM** when given in input the clauses γ and δ
AND there exist a constraint e and a substitution β which are the output of an execution of the procedure **CM** when given in input the clauses $\gamma'\colon H \leftarrow c \wedge B\alpha \wedge R$ and $\delta'\colon K\alpha \leftarrow d\alpha \wedge B\alpha$
THEN return the clause $\eta\colon H \leftarrow e \wedge K\alpha\beta \wedge R$ ELSE return **fail**.

The following theorem states that the folding algorithm **FA** terminates (Point 1), it is sound (Point 2), and, if the constraint c is admissible, then **FA** is complete (Point 3). The proof of this result can be found in [15].

Theorem 3 (Termination, Soundness, and Completeness of FA). *Let the input of the algorithm **FA** be two clauses γ and δ in normal form without variables in common. Then: (1) **FA** terminates; (2) if **FA** returns a clause η,* *then η can be derived by folding γ using δ according to Definition 1; (3) if it is possible to fold γ using δ according to Definition 1 and the constraint occurring in γ is either unsatisfiable or admissible, then* **FA** *does not return* **fail**.

Example 3. Let us consider clause γ: $p(X_1, X_2, X_3) \leftarrow X_1 < 1 \wedge X_1 \geq Z_1 + 1 \wedge Z_2 > 0 \wedge q(Z_1, f(X_3), Z_2) \wedge r(X_2)$ and clause δ: $s(Y_1, Y_2, Y_3) \leftarrow W_1 < 0 \wedge Y_1 - 3 \geq 2W_1 \wedge W_2 > 0 \wedge q(W_1, Y_3, W_2)$ of the Introduction. Let the substitution α : $\{W_1/Z_1, Y_3/f(X_3), W_2/Z_2, Y_2/a\}$ and the goal R : $r(X_2)$ be the result of applying the procedure **GM** to γ and δ as shown in Example 1, and let the constraint e : $X_1 < 1$ and the substitution β : $\{Y_1/2X_1 + 1\} \cup \sigma_W$ be the result of applying the procedure **CM** to γ and $\delta\alpha$ as shown in Example 2. Then, the output of the folding algorithm **FA** is the clause η : $p(X_1, X_2, X_3) \leftarrow e \wedge s(Y_1, Y_2, Y_3)\alpha\beta \wedge R$, that is: η : $p(X_1, X_2, X_3) \leftarrow X_1 < 1 \wedge s(2X_1 + 1, a, f(X_3)) \wedge r(X_2)$.

5   Complexity of the Algorithm and Experimental Results

Let us first analyze the time complexity of our folding algorithm **FA** by assuming that: (i) each rule application during the goal matching procedure **GM** and the constraint matching procedure **CM** takes constant time, and (ii) each computation of the functions *nf*, *solve*, and *project* takes constant time. In these hypotheses our **FA** algorithm is in NP (w.r.t. the number of occurrences of symbols in the input clauses). To show this result, it is sufficient to show that both the goal matching procedure **GM** and the constraint matching procedure **CM** are in NP.

We have that **GM** is in NP w.r.t. the number of occurrences of symbols in the two goals B and G appearing in the input clauses. Indeed, rule (i) of **GM** chooses a mapping from the set of the occurrences of the literals of B to the set of occurrences of the literals of G and each application of any other rule of **GM** consumes at least one symbol of the input clauses.

We have that also **CM** is in NP w.r.t. the number N of occurrences of symbols in the initial triple $\langle c \leftrightarrow e \wedge d', \emptyset, \emptyset \rangle$. Indeed, rule (i) of **CM** chooses a mapping from the set of occurrences of the atomic constraints in c to the set of occurrences of the atomic constraints in $e \wedge d'$. Moreover, the length of any sequence of applications of the other rules of **CM** is polynomial in N as we now show. First, we may assume that the applications of rules (iv) and (v) are done after the applications of rules (i), (ii), and (iii). Since each application of rules (i), (ii), and (iii) reduces the number of constraints occurring in the first component of the triple at hand, we may have at most N applications of these three rules. Moreover, each application of rules (i), (ii), and (iii) introduces at most $m + 1$ new variables, with $m + 1 \leq N$. Hence, at most N^2 new variables are introduced. Rule (iv) can be applied at most M times, where M is the number of variable occurrences in the second component of the triple at hand. Finally, each application of rule (v) eliminates all occurrences of one variable in Y, which is a subset of the variables occurring in the input triple and, therefore, this rule can be applied at most N times. Moreover, for each application of rule (v), the cardinality of the second component of the triple at hand does not change and the number of variable occurrences in each constraint in that component is bounded by the cardinality of $X \cup Y \cup Z$ (which is at most N). Thus, M is bounded by a polynomial of the value of N.

A more detailed time complexity analysis of our folding algorithm **FA** where we do *not* assume that the functions *nf*, *solve*, and *project* are computed in constant time, is as follows. (i) *nf* takes polynomial time in the size of its argument, (ii) *solve* takes polynomial time in the number of variables of its argument by using Khachiyan's method [11], and (iii) *project* takes $O(2^v)$ time, where $v = |Vars(c) \cap Vars(B')|$ (see [12] for the complexity of variable elimination from linear constraints). Since the *project* function is applied only once at the beginning of the procedure **CM**, we get that the computation of our **FA** algorithm requires nondeterministic polynomial time plus $O(2^v)$ time.

Note that since matching modulo the equational theory $AC_\wedge$ is NP-complete [13,16], one cannot hope for a folding algorithm whose asymptotic time complexity is significantly better than our **FA** algorithm.

In the following Table 1 we report some experimental results for our algorithm **FA**, implemented in SICStus Prolog 3.12, on a Pentium IV 3GHz. We have considered the example $D0$ of the Introduction, the four examples $D1$–$D4$ for which folding can be done in one way only (*Number of Foldings* $= 1$), and the four examples $N1$–$N4$ for which folding can be done in more than one way (*Number of Foldings* > 1).

The *Number of Variables* row indicates the number of variables in clause γ (to be folded) plus the number of variables in clause δ (used for folding). The *Time* row indicates the seconds required for finding the folded clause (or the first folded clause, in examples $N1$–$N4$). The *Total-Time* row indicates the seconds required for finding all folded clauses. (Note that even when there exists one folded clause only, *Total-Time* is greater than *Time* because, after the folded clause has been found, **FA** checks that no other folded clauses can be computed.)

In example $D1$ clause γ is $p(A) \leftarrow A < 1 \wedge A \geq B+1 \wedge q(B)$ and clause δ is $r(C) \leftarrow D < 0 \wedge C-3 \geq 2D \wedge q(D)$. In example $N1$ clause γ is $p \leftarrow A > 1 \wedge 3 > A \wedge B > 1 \wedge 3 > B \wedge q(A) \wedge q(B)$ and clause δ is $r \leftarrow C > 1 \wedge 3 > C \wedge D > 1 \wedge 3 > D \wedge q(C) \wedge q(D)$. Similar clauses (with more variables) have been used in the other examples.

Our algorithm **FA** performs reasonably well in practice. However, when the number of variables (and, in particular, the number of variables are of type `rat`) increases, the performance rapidly deteriorates.

Table 1. Execution times of the folding algorithm **FA** for various examples

Example	$D0$	$D1$	$D2$	$D3$	$D4$	$N1$	$N2$	$N3$	$N4$
Number of Foldings	1	1	1	1	1	2	4	4	16
Number of Variables	10	4	8	12	16	4	8	12	16
Time (in seconds)	0.01	0.01	0.08	3.03	306	0.02	0.08	0.23	1.09
Total-Time (in seconds)	0.02	0.02	0.14	4.89	431	0.03	49	1016	11025

6   Related Work and Conclusions

The elimination of existential variables from logic programs and constraint logic programs is a program transformation technique which has been proposed for improving program performance [2] and for proving program properties [3]. This technique makes use of the definition, unfolding, and folding rules [5,6,7,8,9]. In this paper we have considered constraint logic programs, where the constraints are linear inequations over the rational (or real) numbers, and we have focused on the problem of automating the application of the folding rule. Indeed, the applicability conditions of the many folding rules for transforming constraint logic programs which have been proposed in the literature [3,6,7,8,9], are specified in a declarative way and no algorithm is given to determine whether or not, given a clause γ to be folded by using a clause δ, one can actually perform that folding step. The problem of checking the applicability conditions of the folding rule is not trivial (see, for instance, the example presented in the Introduction).

In this paper we have considered a folding rule which is a variant of the rules proposed in the literature, and we have given an algorithm, called **FA**, for checking its applicability conditions. To the best of our knowledge, ours is the first algorithmic presentation of the folding rule. The applicability conditions of our rule consist of the usual conditions (see, for instance, [9]) together with the extra condition that, after folding, the existential variables should be eliminated. Thus, our algorithm **FA** is an important step forward for the full automation of the above mentioned program transformation techniques [2,3] which improve program efficiency or prove program properties by eliminating existential variables.

We have proved the termination and the soundness of our algorithm **FA**. We have also proved that if the constraint appearing in the clause γ to be folded is *admissible*, then **FA** is complete, that is, it does not return **fail** whenever folding is possible. The class of admissible constraints is quite large. We have also implemented the folding algorithm and our experimental results show that it performs reasonably well in practice.

Our algorithm **FA** consists of two procedures: (i) the *goal matching* procedure, and (ii) the *constraint matching* procedure. The *goal matching* procedure solves a problem similar to the problem of matching two terms modulo an associative, commutative (AC, for short) equational theory [17,18]. However, in our case we have the extra conditions that: (i.1) the matching substitution should be consistent with the types (either rational numbers or trees), and (i.2) after folding, the existential variables should be eliminated. Thus, we could not directly use the AC-matching algorithms available in the literature.

The *constraint matching* procedure solves a generalized form of the matching problem, modulo the equational theory $\mathcal{Q}$ of linear inequations over the rational numbers. That problem can be seen as a *restricted unification* problem [19]. In [19] it is described how to obtain, under certain conditions, an algorithm for solving a restricted unification problem from an algorithm that solves the corresponding unrestricted unification problem. To the best of our knowledge, for the theory $\mathcal{Q}$ of constraints a solution is provided in the literature neither for the restricted unification problem nor for the unrestricted one. Moreover, one cannot apply the so called *combination methods* either [20]. These methods consist in constructing a matching algorithm for a given theory which is the combination of simpler theories, starting from the matching algorithms for those simpler theories. Unfortunately, as we said, we cannot use these combination methods for the theory $\mathcal{Q}$ because some applicability conditions are not satisfied and, in particular, $\mathcal{Q}$ is neither *collapse-free* nor *regular* [20].

In the future we plan to adapt our folding algorithm **FA** to other constraint domains such as the linear inequations over the integers. We will also perform a more extensive experimentation of our folding algorithm using the MAP program transformation system [21].

Acknowledgements

We thank the anonymous referees for helpful suggestions. We also thank John Gallagher for comments on a draft of this paper.

References

1. Jaffar, J., Maher, M.: Constraint logic programming: A survey. Journal of Logic Programming 19/20, 503–581 (1994)
2. Proietti, M., Pettorossi, A.: Unfolding-definition-folding, in this order, for avoiding unnecessary variables in logic programs. Theo. Comp. Sci. 142(1), 89–124 (1995)
3. Pettorossi, A., Proietti, M., Senni, V.: Proving properties of constraint logic programs by eliminating existential variables. In: Etalle, S., Truszczyński, M. (eds.) ICLP 2006. LNCS, vol. 4079, pp. 179–195. Springer, Heidelberg (2006)
4. Burstall, R.M., Darlington, J.: A transformation system for developing recursive programs. Journal of the ACM 24(1), 44–67 (1977)
5. Tamaki, H., Sato, T.: Unfold/fold transformation of logic programs. In: Tärnlund, S.Å. (ed.) Proc. ICLP 1984, pp. 127–138. Uppsala University, Uppsala (1984)
6. Maher, M.J.: A transformation system for deductive database modules with perfect model semantics. Theoretical Computer Science 110, 377–403 (1993)
7. Etalle, S., Gabbrielli, M.: Transformations of CLP modules. Theoretical Computer Science 166, 101–146 (1996)
8. Bensaou, N., Guessarian, I.: Transforming constraint logic programs. Theoretical Computer Science 206, 81–125 (1998)
9. Fioravanti, F., Pettorossi, A., Proietti, M.: Transformation rules for locally stratified constraint logic programs. In: Lau, K.K., Bruynooghe, M. (eds.) Program Development in Computational Logic. LNCS, vol. 3049, pp. 292–340. Springer, Heidelberg (2004)
10. Lloyd, J.W.: Foundations of Logic Programming, 2nd edn. Springer, Heidelberg (1987)
11. Schrijver, A.: Theory of Linear and Integer Programming. J. Wiley & Sons, Chichester (1986)
12. Weispfenning, V.: The complexity of linear problems in fields. J. Symb. Comput. 5(1-2), 3–27 (1988)

13. Baader, F., Snyder, W.: Unification theory. In: Robinson, A., Voronkov, A. (eds.) Handbook of Automated Reasoning, vol. I, pp. 445–532. Elsevier Science, Amsterdam (2001)
14. Terese: Term Rewriting Systems. Cambridge University Press (2003)
15. Senni, V.: Transformation Techniques for Constraint Logic Programs with Application to Protocol Verification. PhD thesis, University of Rome "Tor Vergata", Rome, Italy (2008)
16. Benanav, D., Kapur, D., Narendran, P.: Complexity of matching problems. Journal of Symbolic Computation 3(1-2), 203–216 (1987)
17. Livesey, M., Siekmann, J.: Unification of A+C Terms (Bags) and A+C+I Terms (Sets). TR 3/76, Institut für Informatik I, Universität Karlsruhe (1976)
18. Stickel, M.E.: A unification algorithm for associative-commutative functions. J. ACM 28(3), 423–434 (1981)
19. Bürckert, H.J.: Some relationships between unification, restricted unification, and matching. In: Siekmann, J.H. (ed.) CADE 1986. LNCS, vol. 230, pp. 514–524. Springer, Heidelberg (1986)
20. Ringeissen, C.: Matching in a class of combined non-disjoint theories. In: Baader, F. (ed.) CADE 2003. LNCS, vol. 2741, pp. 212–227. Springer, Heidelberg (2003)
21. The MAP transformation system, http://www.iasi.cnr.it/~proietti/system.html

Negative Ternary Set-Sharing*

Eric Trias,[1,2,**] Jorge Navas,[1] Elena S. Ackley,[1] Stephanie Forrest[1],
and M. Hermenegildo[1,3]

[1] University of New Mexico, USA
[2] Air Force Institute of Technology, USA
[3] Technical U. of Madrid (Spain) and IMDEA-Software

Abstract. The Set-Sharing domain has been widely used to infer at compile-
time interesting properties of logic programs such as occurs-check reduction,
automatic parallelization, and finite-tree analysis. However, performing abstract
unification in this domain requires a closure operation that increases the number
of sharing groups exponentially. Much attention has been given to mitigating this
key inefficiency in this otherwise very useful domain. In this paper we present
a novel approach to Set-Sharing: we define a new representation that leverages
the complement (or negative) sharing relationships of the original sharing set,
without loss of accuracy. Intuitively, given an abstract state $sh_\mathcal{V}$ over the finite
set of variables of interest $\mathcal{V}$, its negative representation is $\wp(\mathcal{V}) \setminus sh_\mathcal{V}$. Using
this encoding during analysis dramatically reduces the number of elements that
need to be represented in the abstract states and during abstract unification as the
cardinality of the original set grows toward $2^{|\mathcal{V}|}$. To further compress the num-
ber of elements, we express the set-sharing relationships through a set of ternary
strings that compacts the representation by eliminating redundancies among the
sharing sets. Our experiments show that our approach can compress the number
of relationships, reducing significantly the memory usage and running time of all
abstract operations, including abstract unification.

1 Introduction

In abstract interpretation [11] of logic programs *sharing* analysis has received considerable attention. Two or more variables in a logic program are said to *share* if in some
execution of the program they are bound to terms that contain a common variable. A
variable in a logic program is said to be *ground* if it is bound to a term that does not
contain free variables in all possible executions of the program. *Set-Sharing* is an important type of combined sharing and groundness analysis. It was originally introduced
by Jacobs and Langen [17,19] and its abstract values are sets of sets of variables that
keep track in a compact way of the sharing patterns among variables.

* The authors gratefully acknowledge the support of the National Science Foundation (grants
CCR-0331580 and CCR-0311686, and DBI-0309147), the Santa Fe Institute, the Air
Force Institute of Technology, the Prince of Asturias Chair in Information Science and
Technology at UNM, and by EU projects 215483 *S-Cube*, IST-15905 *MOBIUS*, Span-
ish projects ITEA2/PROFIT FIT-340005-2007-14 *ES_PASS*, MEC TIN2005-09207-C03-01
MERIT/COMVERS, and Comunidad de Madrid project S-0505/TIC/0407 *PROMESAS*.
** The views expressed in this article are those of the author and do not reflect the official policy
or position of the United States Air Force, Department of Defense, or the U.S. Government.

M. Garcia de la Banda and E. Pontelli (Eds.): ICLP 2008, LNCS 5366, pp. 301–316, 2008.
© Springer-Verlag Berlin Heidelberg 2008

Example 1 (Set-Sharing abstraction). Let $V = \{X_1, X_2, X_3, X_4\}$ be a set of variables. The abstraction in Set-Sharing of a substitution $\theta = \{X_1 \mapsto f(U_1, U_2, V_1, V_2, W_1),$ $X_2 \mapsto g(V_1, V_2, W_1), X_3 \mapsto g(W_1, W_1), X_4 \mapsto a\}$ will be $\{\{X_1\}, \{X_1, X_2\}, \{X_1,$ $X_2, X_3\}\}$. Sharing group $\{X_1\}$ in the abstraction represents the occurrence of run-time variables U_1 and U_2 in the concrete substitution, $\{X_1, X_2\}$ represents V_1 and V_2, and $\{X_1, X_2, X_3\}$ represents W_1. Note that X_4 does not appear in the sharing groups because X_4 is ground. Note also that the number of (occurrences of) shared run-time variables is abstracted away.

Set-Sharing has been used to infer several interesting properties and perform optimization and verification of programs at compile-time, most notably but not limited to: occurs-check reduction (e.g., [27]), automatic parallelization (e.g., [25,6]), and finite-tree analysis (e.g., [2]). The accuracy of Set-Sharing has been improved by extending it with other kinds of information, the most relevant being *freeness* and *linearity* information [24,17,25,9,15], and also information about *term structure* [25,18,3,23]. Sharing in combination with other abstract domains has also been studied [8,14,10]. The significance of Set-Sharing is that it keeps track of sharing among sets of variables more accurately than other abstract domains such as e.g. *Pair-Sharing* [27] due to better groundness propagation and other factors that are relevant in some of its applications [5]. In addition, Set-Sharing has attracted much attention [7,10] because its algebraic properties allow elegant encodings into other efficient implementations (e.g., *ROBDDs* [4]). In [25],the first comparatively efficient algorithms were presented for the basic operations needed for set sharing-based analyses.

However, Set-Sharing has a key computational disadvantage: the *abstract unification* (*amgu*, for short) implies potentially exponential growth in the number of sharing groups due to the *up-closure* (also called *star-union*) operation which is the heart of that operation. Considerable attention has been given in the literature to reducing the impact of the complexity of this operation. In [29], Zaffanella et al. extended the Set-Sharing domain for inferring pair-sharing to support *widening*. Although significant efficiency gains are achieved, this approach loses precision with respect to the original Set-Sharing. A similar approach is followed in [26] but for inferring set-sharing in a *top-down* framework. Other relevant work was presented in [21] in which the up-closure operation was delayed and full sharing information was recovered lazily. However, this interesting approach shares some of the disadvantages of Zaffanella's widening. Therefore, the authors refined the idea in [20] reformulating the amgu in terms of the *closure under union* operation, collapsing those closures to reduce the total number of closures and applying them to smaller descriptions without loss of accuracy. In [10] the authors show that the Set-Sharing domain is isomorphic to the dual negative of *Pos* [1], denoted by $\overline{coPos}$. This insight improved the understanding of Set-Sharing analysis, and led to an elegant expression of the combination with groundness dependency analysis based on the reduced product of Sharing and Pos. In addition, this work pointed out the possible implementation of $\overline{coPos}$ through ROBDDs leading to more efficient implementations of Set-Sharing analyses, although this point was not investigated further.

In this paper we introduce a novel approach to Set-Sharing: we define a new representation that leverages the complement (or negative) sharing relationships of the original sharing set, without loss of accuracy. Intuitively, given an abstract state $sh_\mathcal{V}$ over the finite set of variables of interest $\mathcal{V}$, its negative representation is $\wp(\mathcal{V}) \setminus sh_\mathcal{V}$. Using this encoding during analysis dramatically reduces the number of elements that need to be represented in the abstract states and during abstract unification as the cardinality of the original set grows toward $2^{|\mathcal{V}|}$. To further compress the number of elements, we express the set-sharing relationships through a set of ternary strings that compacts the representation by eliminating redundancies among the sharing sets. It is important to notice that our work is not based on [10]. Although they define the dual negated positive Boolean functions, $\overline{coPos}$ does not represent the entire complement of the positive set. Moreover, they do not use $\overline{coPos}$ as a means of compressing relationships but as a way of representing Sharing through Boolean functions. We also represent Sharing through Boolean functions, but that is where the similarity ends.

2   Set-Sharing Encoded by Binary Strings

The presentation here follows that of [29,10] since the notation used and the abstract unification operation obtained are rather intuitive, but adapted for handling binary strings rather than sets of sets of variables.

Therefore, unless otherwise stated, here and in the rest of paper we will represent the set-sharing domain using a set of strings rather than a set of sets of variables. An algorithm for this conversion and examples are presented in [28].

Definition 1 (Binary sharing domain, bSH). Let alphabet $\Sigma = \{0, 1\}$, $\mathcal{V}$ be a fixed and finite set of variables of interest in arbitrary order, and Σ^l the finite set of all strings over Σ with length l, $0 \le l \le |\mathcal{V}|$. Let $bSH^l = \wp^0(\Sigma^l)$ be the *proper power set* (i.e., $\wp(\Sigma^l) \setminus \{\emptyset\}$) that contains all possible combinations over Σ with length l. Then, the *binary sharing domain* is defined as $bSH = \bigcup_{0 \le l \le |\mathcal{V}|} bSH^l$.   ∎

Let $\mathcal{F}$ and $\mathcal{P}$ be sets of ranked (i.e., with a given arity) functors of interest; e.g., the function symbols and the predicate symbols of a program. We will use $Term$ to denote the set of terms constructed from $\mathcal{V}$ and $\mathcal{F} \cup \mathcal{P}$. Although somehow unorthodox, this will allow us to simply write $g \in Term$ whether g is a term or a predicate atom, since all our operations apply equally well to both classes of syntactic objects. We will denote by $\hat{t}$ the binary representation of the set of variables of $t \in Term$ according to a particular order among variables. Since $\hat{t}$ will be always used by a bitwise operation with some string of length l, the length of $\hat{t}$ must be l. If not, $\hat{t}$ is adjusted with 0's in those positions associated with variables represented in the string but not in t.

Definition 2 (Binary relevant sharing $rel(bsh, t)$, irrelevant sharing $irrel(bsh, t)$). Given $t \in Term$, the set of binary strings in $bsh \in bSH^l$ of length l that are relevant with respect to t is obtained by a function $rel(bsh, t) : bSH^l \times Term \rightarrow bSH^l$ defined as:
$$rel(bsh, t) = \{s \mid s \in bsh, (s \wedge \hat{t}) \ne 0^l\}$$

where $\wedge$ represents the bitwise AND operation and 0^l is the all-zeros string of length l. Consequently, the set of binary strings in $bsh \in bSH^l$ that are *irrelevant with respect to t* is a function $irrel(bsh, t) : bSH^l \times Term \rightarrow bSH^l$ where $irrel(bsh, t)$ is the *complement of $rel(bsh, t)$, i.e., $bsh \setminus rel(bsh, t)$.*   ∎

Definition 3 (Binary cross-union, $\boxtimes$). Given $bsh_1, bsh_2 \in bSH^l$, their *cross-union* is a function $\boxtimes : bSH^l \times bSH^l \rightarrow bSH^l$ defined as

$$bsh_1 \boxtimes bsh_2 = \{s \mid s = s_1 \bigvee s_2, s_1 \in bsh_1, s_2 \in bsh_2\}$$

where $\bigvee$ represents the bitwise OR operation. ∎

Definition 4 (Binary up-closure, $(.)^*$). Let l be the length of strings in $bsh \in bSH^l$, then the *up-closure* of bsh, denoted bsh^* is a function $(.)^* : bSH^l \rightarrow bSH^l$ that represents the smallest superset of bsh such that $s_1 \bigvee s_2 \in bsh^*$ whenever $s_1, s_2 \in bsh^*$:

$$bsh^* = \{s \mid \exists n \geq 1 \, \exists t_1, \ldots, t_n \in bsh, s = t_1 \bigvee \ldots \bigvee t_n\}$$

∎

Definition 5 (Binary abstract unification, $amgu$). The abstract unification is a function $amgu : \mathcal{V} \times Term \times bSH^l \rightarrow bSH^l$ defined as

$$amgu(x, t, bsh) = irrel(bsh, x = t) \cup (rel(bsh, x) \boxtimes rel(bsh, t))^*$$

∎

The design of the analysis must be completed by defining the following abstract operations that are required by an analysis engine: $init$ (initial abstract state), $equivalence$ (between two abstract substitutions), $join$ (defined as the union), and $project$. In the interest of brevity, we define only the $project$ operation because the other three operations are trivial. We refer the reader to [28] for the rest of operations.

Definition 6 (Binary projection, $bsh|_t$). The *binary projection* is a function $bsh|_t$: $bSH^l \times Term \rightarrow bSH^k$ ($k \leq l$) that removes the i-th positions from all strings (of length l) in $bsh \in bSH^l$, if and only if the i-th positions of $\hat{t}$ (denoted by $\hat{t}[i]$) is 0, and it is defined as $\qquad bsh|_t = \{s' \mid s \in bsh, s' = \pi(s, t)\}$

where $\pi(s, t)$ is the binary string projection defined as

$$\pi(s, t) = \begin{cases} \epsilon, & \text{if } s = \epsilon, \text{ the empty string} \\ \pi(s', t), & \text{if } s = s'a_i \text{ and } \hat{t}[i] = 0 \\ \pi(s', t)a_i, & \text{if } s = s'a_i \text{ and } \hat{t}[i] = 1 \end{cases}$$

and $s'a_i$ is the concatenation of character a to string s' at position i. ∎

3   Ternary Set-Sharing

In this section, we introduce a more efficient representation for the Set-Sharing domain defined in Sec. 2 to accommodate a larger number of variables for analysis. We extend the binary string encoding discussed above to the ternary alphabet $\Sigma_* = \{0, 1, *\}$, where the $*$ symbol denotes both 0 and 1 bit values. This representation effectively compresses the number of elements in the set into fewer strings without changing what is represented (i.e., without loss of accuracy). To handle the ternary alphabet, we redefine the binary operations covered in Sec. 2.

Definition 7 (Ternary Sharing Domain, tSH). Let alphabet $\Sigma_* = \{0, 1, *\}$, $\mathcal{V}$ be a fixed and finite set of variables of interest in an arbitrary order as in Def. 1, and Σ_*^l the finite set of all strings over Σ_* with length l, $0 \leq l \leq |\mathcal{V}|$. Then, $tSH^l = \wp^0(\Sigma_*^l)$ and hence, the *ternary sharing domain* is defined as $tSH = \bigcup_{0 \leq l \leq |\mathcal{V}|} tSH^l$. ∎

Prior to defining how to transform the binary string representation into the corresponding ternary string representation, we introduce two core definitions, Def. 8 and Def. 9, for comparing ternary strings. These operations are essential for the conversion and set operations. In addition, they are used to eliminate redundant strings within a set and to check for equivalence of two ternary sets containing different strings.

Definition 8 (Match, $\mathcal{M}$). Given two ternary strings, $x, y \in \Sigma_*^l$, of length l, *match* is a function $\mathcal{M} : \Sigma_*^l \times \Sigma_*^l \to \mathcal{B}$, such that $\forall i \ 1 \leq i \leq l$,

$$x \mathcal{M} y = \begin{cases} \text{true, if } (x[i] = y[i]) \vee (x[i] = *) \vee (y[i] = *) \\ \text{false, otherwise} \end{cases} \qquad \blacksquare$$

Definition 9 (Subsumed_By $\not\subseteq$ and Subsumed_In $\not\subseteq$). Given two ternary strings s_1, $s_2 \in \Sigma_*^l$, $\not\subseteq : \Sigma_*^l \times \Sigma_*^l \to \mathcal{B}$ is a function such that $s_1 \not\subseteq s_2$ if and only if every string matched by s_1 is also matched by s_2 ($s_1 \not\subseteq s_2 \iff \forall s \in tSH^l, \ if \ s_1 \mathcal{M} s \ then \ s_2 \mathcal{M} s$). For convenience, we augment this definition to deal with sets of strings. Given a ternary string $s \in \Sigma_*^l$ and a ternary sharing set, $tsh \in tSH^l$, $\not\subseteq : \Sigma_*^l \times tSH^l \to \mathcal{B}$ is a function such that $s \not\subseteq tsh$ if and only if there exists some element $s' \in tsh$ such that $s \not\subseteq s'$. $\blacksquare$

Figure 1 gives the pseudo code for an algorithm which converts a set of binary strings into a set of ternary strings. The function Convert evaluates each string of the input and attempts to introduce $*$ symbols using PatternGenerate, while eliminating redundant strings using ManagedGrowth.

PatternGenerate evaluates the input string bit-by-bit to determine where the $*$ symbol can be introduced. The number of $*$ symbols introduced depends on the sharing set represented and k, the desired minimum number of specified bits, where $0 \leq k \leq l$ (the string length). For a given set of strings of length l, parameter k controls the compression of the set. For $k = l$ (all bits specified), there is no compression and $tsh = bsh$. For a non-empty bsh, $k = 1$ introduces the maximum number of $*$ symbols. For now, we will assume that $k = 1$, and experimental results in Sec. 5 shows the best overall k value for a given l. The Specified function returns the number of specified bits (0 or 1) in x.

ManagedGrowth checks if the input string y subsumes other strings from tsh. If no redundant string exists, then y is appended to tsh only if y itself is not redundant to an existing string in tsh. Otherwise, y replaces all the redundant strings.

Example 2 (Conversion from bSH to tSH). Assume the following sharing set of binary strings $bsh = \{1000, 1001, 0100, 0101, 0010, 0001\}$. Then, a ternary string representation produced by applying Convert is $tsh = \{100*, 0010, 010*, *001\}$.

Definition 10 (Ternary-or $\bigvee$ and Ternary-and $\bigwedge$). Given two ternary strings, $x, y \in \Sigma_*^l$ of length l, *ternary-or* and *ternary-and* are two bitwise-or functions defined as $\bigvee, \bigwedge : \Sigma_*^l \times \Sigma_*^l \to \Sigma_*^l$ such that $z = x \bigvee y$ and $w = x \bigwedge y$, $\forall i \ 1 \leq i \leq l$, where:

$$z[i] = \begin{cases} * \text{ if } (x[i] = * \wedge y[i] = *) \\ 0 \text{ if } (x[i] = 0 \wedge y[i] = 0) \\ 1 \ otherwise \end{cases} \qquad w[i] = \begin{cases} * \text{ if } (x[i] = * \wedge y[i] = *) \\ 1 \text{ if } (x[i] = 1 \wedge y[i] = 1) \\ \vee \ (x[i] = 1 \wedge y[i] = *) \\ \vee \ (x[i] = * \wedge y[i] = 1) \\ 0 \ otherwise \end{cases} \qquad \blacksquare$$

0 Convert(bsh, k)	15 PatternGenerate(tsh, x, k)
1 $tsh \leftarrow \emptyset$	16 $m \leftarrow$ Specified(x)
2 **foreach** $s \in bsh$	17 $i \leftarrow 0$
3 $y \leftarrow$ PatternGenerate(tsh, s, k)	18 $x' \leftarrow x$
4 $tsh \leftarrow$ ManagedGrowth(tsh, y)	19 $l \leftarrow length(x)$
5 **return** tsh	20 **while** $m > k$ and $i < l$
6 ManagedGrowth(tsh, y)	21 Let b_i be the value of x' at position i
7 $S_y = \{s \mid s \in tsh, s \underline{\underline{\subseteq}} y\}$	22 **if** $b_i = 0$ or $b_i = 1$ **then**
8 **if** $S_y = \emptyset$ **then**	23 $x' \leftarrow x'$ with position i replaced by $\overline{b_i}$
9 **if** $y \underline{\underline{\not\subseteq}} tsh$ **then**	24 **if** $x' \underline{\subseteq} tsh$ **then**
10 append y to tsh	25 $x' \leftarrow x'$ with position i replaced by $*$
11 **else**	26 **else**
12 remove S_y from tsh	27 $x' \leftarrow x'$ with position i replaced by b_i
13 append y to tsh	28 $m \leftarrow$ Specified(x')
14 **return** tsh	29 $i \leftarrow i + 1$
	30 **return** x'

Fig. 1. A deterministic algorithm for converting a set of binary strings bsh into a set of ternary strings tsh, where k is the desired minimum number of specified bits (non-*) to remain

Definition 11 (Ternary set intersection, $\cap$). Given $tsh_1, tsh_2 \in tSH^l$, $\cap : tSH^l \times tSH^l \rightarrow tSH^l$ is defined as

$$tsh_1 \cap tsh_2 = \{r \mid r = s1 \bigwedge s2, s1 \mathcal{M} s2, s1 \in tsh1, s2 \in tsh2\} \qquad \blacksquare$$

For convenience, we define two binary patterns, 0-mask and 1-mask, in order to simplify further operations. The former takes an l-length binary string s and returns a set with a single string having a 0 where $s[i] = 1$ and $*$'s elsewhere, $\forall i\ 1 \leq i \leq l$. The latter also takes an l-length binary string s, but returns a set of strings with a 1 where $s[i] = 1$ and $*$'s elsewhere, $\forall i\ 1 \leq i \leq l$. For instance, 0-mask($0110$) and 1-mask($0110$) return $\{*00*\}$ and $\{*1**, **1*\}$, respectively.

Definition 12 (Ternary relevant sharing $rel(tsh, t)$, irrelevant sharing $irrel(tsh, t)$). Given $t \in Term$ with length l and $tsh \in tSH^l$ with strings of length l, the set of strings in tsh that are *relevant* with respect to t is obtained by a function $rel(tsh, t) : tSH^l \times Term \rightarrow tSH^l$ defined as

$$rel(tsh, t) = tsh \cap \text{1-mask}(\hat{t})$$

In addition, $irrel(tsh, t)$ is defined as

$$irrel(tsh, t) = (tsh \cap \text{1-mask}(\overline{\hat{t}})) \cap \text{0-mask}(\hat{t}) \qquad \blacksquare$$

Ternary cross-union, $\bowtie$, and ternary up-closure, $(.)^*$, operations are as defined in Def. 3 and in Def. 4, respectively, except the binary version of the bitwise OR operator is replaced with its ternary counterpart defined in Def. 10 in order to account for the $*$ symbol. In addition, the ternary abstract unification ($amgu$) is defined exactly as the binary version, Def.5, using the corresponding ternary definitions.

Example 3 (Ternary abstract unification). Let $tsh = \{100*, 010*, 0010, *001\}$ as in Example 2. Consider again the analysis of $X_1 = f(X_2, X_3)$, the result is:

$$
\begin{aligned}
A &= rel(tsh, X_1) & &= \{100*\} \\
B &= rel(tsh, f(X_2, X_3)) & &= \{010*, 0010\} \\
A \bowtie B & & &= \{110*, 101*\} \\
(A \bowtie B)^* & & &= \{110*, 101*, 111*\} \\
C &= irrel(tsh, X_1 = f(X_2, X_3)) & &= \{0001\} \\
amgu(X_1, f(X_2, X_3), tsh) &= C \cup (A \bowtie B)^* &&= \{0001, 110*, 101*, 111*\}
\end{aligned}
$$

Here briefly, we describe the ternary projection. The other ternary operations required by any analysis framework can be be found in [28]. The ternary projection, $tsh|_t$, is defined similarly as binary projection, see Def. 6. However, the projection domain and range is extended to accommodate the $*$ symbol. For example, let $tsh = \{100*, 010*, 0010, *001\}$ as in Example 2. Then, the projection of tsh over the term $t = f(X_1, X_2, X_3)$ is $tsh|_t = \{100, 010, 001\}$. Note that since all zeros is meaningless in a set-sharing representation, it is not included here.

4   Negative Ternary Set-Sharing

In this section, we extend the use of the ternary representation discussed in the previous section.[1] In certain cases, a more compact representation of sharing relationships among variables can be captured equivalently by working with the complement (or negative) set of the original sharing set. A ternary string t can either be *in* or *not in* the set $tsh \in tSH$. This mutual exclusivity together with the finiteness of $\mathcal{V}$ allows for checking t's membership in tsh by asking if t is in tsh, or, equivalently, if t is *not* in its complement, $\overline{tsh}$. The same reasoning is applicable to binary strings (i.e., bSH). Given a set of l-bit binary strings, its complement or negative set contains *all* the l-bit ternary strings *not* in the original set. Therefore, if the cardinality of a set is greater than half of the maximum size (i.e., $2^{|\mathcal{V}|-1}$), then the size of its complement will not be greater than $2^{|\mathcal{V}|-1}$. It is this size differential that we exploit. In Set-Sharing analysis, as we consider programs with larger numbers of variables of interest, the potential number of sharing groups grows exponentially toward $2^{|\mathcal{V}|}$, whereas the number of sharing groups not in the sharing set decreases toward 0.

The idea of a negative set representation and its associated algorithms extends the work by Esponda et al. in [12,13]. In that work, a negative set is generated from the original set in a similar manner to the conversion algorithms shown in Figs. 1 and 2. However, they produce a negative set with unspecified bits in random positions and with less emphasis on managing the growth of the resulting set. The technique was originally introduced as a means of generating Boolean satisfiability (SAT) formulas where, by leveraging the difficulty of finding solutions to hard SAT instances, the contents of the original set are obscured without using encryption [12]. In addition, these hard-to-reverse negative sets are still able to answer membership queries efficiently while remaining intractable to reverse (i.e., to obtain the contents of the original set). In this paper, we are not interested in this security property, but use the negative approach simply to address the efficiency issues faced by traditional Set-Sharing domain.

---

[1] Note that we could have also used the binary representation described in Sec. 2 but we chose the ternary encoding in order to achieve more compactness.

0 NegConvert(sh, k)	0 NegConvertMissing(bsh, k)
1 $tnsh \leftarrow \mathcal{U}$	1 $tnsh \leftarrow \emptyset$
2 **foreach** $t \in sh$	2 $bnsh \leftarrow \mathcal{U} \setminus bsh$
3 $tnsh \leftarrow$ Delete($tnsh, t, k$)	3 **foreach** $t \in bnsh$
4 **return** $tnsh$	4 $tnsh \leftarrow$ Insert($tnsh, t, k$)
	5 **return** $tnsh$

10 Delete($tnsh, x, k$)
11 $D_x \leftarrow \forall t \in tnsh, x \mathfrak{M} t$
12 $tnsh' \leftarrow tnsh$ with D_x removed
13 **foreach** $y \in D_x$
14   **foreach** unspecified bit position q_i of y
15   **if** b_i (the ith bit of x) is specified, **then**
16          $y' \leftarrow y$ with position q_i replaced by $\overline{b_i}$
17          $tnsh' \leftarrow$ Insert($tnsh', y', k$)
18 **return** $tnsh'$

20 Insert($tnsh, x, k$)
21 $m \leftarrow$ Specified(x)
22 **if** $m < k$ **then**
23    $P \leftarrow$ select $(k - m)$ unspecified bit positions in x
24    $V_P \leftarrow$ every possible bit assignment of length $|P|$
25   **foreach** $v \in V_P$
26       $y \leftarrow x$ with positions P replaced by v
27       $tnsh' \leftarrow$ ManagedGrowth($tnsh, y$)
28 **else**
29    $y \leftarrow$ PatternGenerate($tnsh, x, k$)
30    $tnsh' \leftarrow$ ManagedGrowth($tnsh, y$)
31 **return** $tnsh'$

Fig. 2. NegConvert, NegConvertMissing, Delete and Insert algorithms used to transform positive to negative representation; k is the desired number of specified bits (non-*'s) to remain

The conversion to the negative set can be accomplished using the two algorithms shown in Figure 2. NegConvert uses the Delete operation to remove input strings of the set sh from $\mathcal{U}$, the set of all l-bit strings $\mathcal{U} = \{*^l\}$, and then, the Insert operation to return $\mathcal{U} \setminus sh$ which represents all strings *not* in the original input. Alternatively, NegConvertMissing uses the Insert operation directly to append each string *missing* from the input set to an empty set resulting in a representation of all strings *not* in the original input. Although as shown in Table 1 both algorithms have similar complexities, depending on the size of the original input it may be more efficient to find all the strings missing from the input and transform them with NegConvertMissing, rather than applying NegConvert to the input directly. Note that the resulting negative set will use the same ternary alphabet described in Def. 7. For clarity, we will denote it by $tNSH$ such that $tNSH \equiv tSH$.

For simplicity, we describe only NegConvert since NegConvertMissing uses the same machinery. Assume a transformation from bsh to $tnsh$ calling NegConvert with $k = 1$. We begin with $tnsh = \mathcal{U} = \{* * **\}$ (line 1), then incrementally Delete each element of bsh from $tnsh$ (line 2-3). Delete removes all strings matched by x from

Table 1. Summary of conversions: l-length strings; $\alpha = |Result| \cdot l$; if $m < k$ then $\delta = k - m$ else $\delta = 0$, where m = minimum specified bits in entire set, k = number of specified bits desired; $bnsh = \mathcal{U} \setminus bsh$; $\beta = O(2^l)$ time to find $bnsh$

Transformation	Time Complexity	Size Complexity
$bSH \rightarrow tSH$	$O(|bsh|\alpha l)$	$O(|bsh|)$
$bSH/tSH \rightarrow tNSH$	$O(|bsh|\alpha(\alpha 2^\delta + 1))$	$O(|tnsh|(l - m)2^\delta)$
$tNSH \rightarrow tSH$	$O(|tnsh|\alpha(\alpha 2^\delta + 1))$	$O(|tsh|(l - m)2^\delta)$
$bSH \rightarrow tNSH$	$O(\beta + |bnsh|(\alpha 2^\delta + 1))$	$O(|bnsh|2^\delta)$

$tnsh$ (line 11-12). If the set of matched strings, D_x, contains unspecified bit values (* symbols), then all string combinations *not* matching x must be re-inserted back into $tnsh$ (line 13-17). Each string y' not matching x is found by setting the unspecified bit to the opposite bit value found in $x[i]$ (line 16). Then, Insert ensures string y' has at least k specified bits (line 22-26). This is done by specifying $k - m$ unspecified bits (line 23) and appending each to the result using ManagedGrowth (line 24-26). If string x already has at least k specified bits, then the algorithm attempts to introduce more * symbols using PatternGenerate (line 28) and appends it while removing any redundancy in the resulting set using ManagedGrowth (line 29).

Example 4 (Conversion from bSH to tNSH). Consider the same sharing set as in Example 2: $bsh = \{1000, 1001, 0100, 0010, 0101, 0001\}$. A negative ternary string representation is generated by applying the NegConvert algorithm to obtain $\{0000, 11^{**}, 1^*1^*, {}^*11^*, {}^{**}11\}$. Since a string of all 0's is meaningless in a set-sharing representation, it is removed from the set. Thus, $tnsh = \{11^{**}, 1^*1^*, {}^*11^*, {}^{**}11\}$.

NegConvertMissing would return the same result for Example 4, and, in general, an equivalent negative representation. Table 1 illustrates the different transformation functions and their complexities for a given input. Transformation $bSH \rightarrow tSH$ can be performed by the Convert algorithm described in Fig. 1. Transformations $bSH/tSH \rightarrow tNSH$ and $bSH \rightarrow tNSH$ are done by NegConvert and NegConvertMissing, respectively. Both transformations show that we can convert a positive representation into negative with corresponding difference in time and memory complexity. Depending on the size of the original input we may prefer one transformation over another. If the input size is relatively small, less than 50% of the maximum size, then NegConvert is often more efficient than NegConvertMissing. Otherwise, we may prefer to insert those strings missing in the input set. In our implementation, we continuously track the size of the relationships to choose the most efficient transformation. Finally, transformation $tNSH \rightarrow tSH$ is performed by NegConvert to revert back to the ternary positive from a negative representation.

Consider now the same set of variables and order among them as in Example 4 but with a slightly different set of sharing groups encoded as $bsh = \{1000, 1100, 1110\}$ or $tsh = \{1^*00, 1110\}$. Then, a negative ternary string representation produced by NegConvert is $tnsh = \{00^{**}, 01^{**}, 0^*1^*, 0^{**}1, 1^{**}1, {}^*01^*\}$. This example shows that the number of elements, or size, of the negative result can be greater than the positive, $|tnsh| = 6 > |bsh| = 3$ and $|tsh| = 2$, unlike Example 4 where $|bsh| = 6$, and $|tnsh| = 4 < |bsh|$. As the size of $|bsh|$ increases, the complement set that the negative must represent $(2^{|\mathcal{V}|} - |bsh|)$ decreases. This illustrates how selecting the appropriate set-sharing representation affects the size of the converted result. Thus, the size of the original sharing set at specific program points will be used by the analysis to produce the most compact working set. The negative sharing set representation allows us to represent more variables of interest enabling larger problem instances to be evaluated.

We now define the negative abstract unification operations, along with key ancillary operations required by our engine to use the negative representation.

Definition 13 (Negative relevant sharing and irrelevant sharing). Given $t \in Term$ and $tnsh \in tNSH^l$ with strings of length l, the set of strings in $tnsh$ that are *negative relevant* with respect to t is obtained by a function $\overline{rel}(tnsh, t) : tNSH^l \times Term \rightarrow tNSH^l$ defined as:

$$\overline{rel}(tnsh, t) = tnsh \,\overline{\sqcap}\, \texttt{0-mask}(\hat{t}),$$

In addition, $\overline{irrel}(tnsh, t)$ is defined as:

$$\overline{irrel}(tnsh, t) = tnsh \,\overline{\sqcap}\, \texttt{1-mask}(\hat{t}).$$

where $\overline{\sqcap} \equiv \sqcup$ and defined in [13]. ■

Because the negative representation is the complement, it is not only more compact for large positive set-sharing instances, but also, and perhaps more importantly, it enables us to use inverse operations that are more memory- and computationally efficient than in the positive representation. However, the negative representation does have its limitations. Certain operations that are straightforward in the positive representation are $\mathcal{NP}$-Hard in the negative representation [12,13].

A key observation given in [12] is that there is a mapping from Boolean formulas to the negative set-sharing domain such that finding which strings are not represented is equivalent to finding satisfying assignments to the corresponding Boolean formula. This is known to be an $\mathcal{NP}$-Hard problem. As mentioned before, this fact is exploited in [12] for privacy enhancing applications. In [28] we show that negative cross-union, $\boxtimes$, is $\mathcal{NP}$-Complete.

Due to the interdependent nature of the relationship between the elements of a negative set, it is unclear how a precise negative cross-union can be accomplished without going through a positive representation. Therefore, we accomplish the negative cross-union by first identifying the represented positive strings and then applying cross-union accordingly. Rather than iterating through all possible strings in $\mathcal{U}$ and performing cross-union on strings not in $tnsh$, we achieve a more efficient negative cross-union, $\boxtimes$, by converting $tnsh$ to tsh first, i.e., using **NegConvert** from Table 1 and performing ternary cross-union on strings $t \in tsh$. In this way, the ternary representation continues to provide a compressed representation of the sharing set. Note that the negative up-closure operation, $\overline{*}$, suffers the same drawback as cross-union. Therefore, it is handled the same way as negative cross-union.

Definition 14 (Negative union, $\overline{\sqcup}$). Given two negative sets with same length strings, $tnsh_1$ and $tnsh_2$, the *Negative Union* returns a negative set representing the set union of $tnsh_1 \overline{\sqcup} tnsh_2$, and is defined in [13] as:

$$tnsh_1 \overline{\sqcup} tnsh_2 = \{z | (x \mathcal{M} y) \Rightarrow z = x \bigwedge y, x \in tnsh_1, y \in tnsh_2\}$$

where $\bigwedge$ is the ternary AND operator. ∎

Definition 15 (Negative abstract unification, $\overline{amgu}$). The *negative abstract unification* is a function $\overline{amgu} : \mathcal{V} \times Term \times tNSH^l \to tNSH^l$ defined as

$$\overline{amgu}(x, t, tnsh) = \overline{irrel}(tnsh, x = t) \overline{\sqcup} \left(\overline{rel}(tnsh, x) \overline{\boxtimes} \overline{rel}(tnsh, t) \right)^{\overline{*}},$$ ∎

Example 5 (Negative abstract unification). Let $tnsh = \{11**, 1*1*, *11*, **11\}$ be the same sharing set as in Example 4. Consider the analysis of $X_1 = f(X_2, X_3)$:

$$
\begin{aligned}
A &= \overline{rel}(tnsh, X_1) & &= \{11**, 1*1*, *11*, **11, 0***\} \\
B &= \overline{rel}(tnsh, f(X_2, X_3)) & &= \{11**, 1*1*, *11*, **11, *00*\} \\
A \overline{\boxtimes} B & & &= \{00**, 01**, 0*0*, *00*\} \\
(A \overline{\boxtimes} B)^{\overline{*}} & & &= \{01**, 0*1*, 100*\} \\
C &= \overline{irrel}(tnsh, X_1 = f(X_2, X_3)) & &= \{11**, 1*1*, *11*, **11, 1***, \\
& & & \quad *1**, **1*\} \\
& & &= \{1***, *1**, **1*\} \\
\overline{amgu}(X_1, f(X_2, X_3), tnsh) &= C \overline{\sqcup} (A \overline{\boxtimes} B)^{\overline{*}} & &= \{01**, 0*1*, 0**0, 100*\}
\end{aligned}
$$

Here, we define the negative projection and refer the reader to [28] for the remaining operations:

Definition 16 (Negative projection, $\overline{tnsh|_t}$). The *negative projection* is a function $\overline{tnsh|_t}: tNSH^l \times Term \to tNSH^k$ ($k \leq l$) that selects elements of $tnsh$ projected onto the binary representation of $t \in Term$ and is defined as

$$\overline{tnsh|_t} = \overline{\pi}(tnsh, \Upsilon_t),$$

$\Upsilon_t =$ positions where $\hat{t}[i] = 1, \forall i 1 \leq i \leq l$ and *Negative Project* $\overline{\pi}$ as defined in [13]. ∎

We find that the resulting negative set will contain strings that have a bit value projected in column(s) specified by Υ if and only if all possible binary combination of all strings created with the projected column(s) appear in the negative set. For example, given $tnsh = \{000, 011, 10*, 11*\}$, the $\overline{\pi}_{\Upsilon=1,2}(tnsh) = \{10, 11\}$.

5 Experimental Results

We developed a proof-of-concept implementation to measure experimentally the relative efficiency in terms of running time and memory usage obtained with the two new representations, tSH and $tNSH$. Our first objective is to study the implications of the conversions in the representation for analysis. Note that although both tSH and $tNSH$ do not imply a loss of precision, the sizes of the resulting representations and their conversion times can vary significantly from one to another. An essential issue is to determine experimentally the best overall k parameter for the conversion algorithms. Second, we study the core abstract operation of the traditional set-sharing, $amgu$, under two different metrics. One is the running time to perform the abstract unification. The other metric expresses the memory usage through the size of the representation in terms

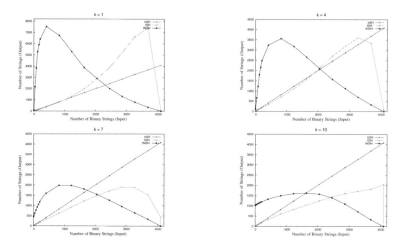

Fig. 3. Compression level after conversions from bSH to tSH and $tNSH$ for k = 1, 4, 7 & 10

of number of strings during key steps in the unification. All experiments have been conducted on an Intel^R Core^{TM} Duo CPU T2350 at 1.86GHz with 1GB of RAM running Ubuntu 7.04, and were performed with 12-bit strings since we consider this value large enough to show all the relevant features of our approach. In general, within some upper bound, the more variables considered the better the expected efficiency.

The first experiment determines the best k value suitable for the conversion algorithms, shown in Figs. 1 and 2. We submit a set of 12-bit strings in random order using different k values. We evaluate size of the output (see Fig. 3) for a given k value. As expected, bSH ($x = y$ line) results in no compression; tSH slowly increases with increasing input size, remaining below bSH (for $k = 7$ and $k = 10$) due to the compression provided by the $*$ symbol and by having little redundancy; $tNSH$, the complement set, starts larger than bSH but quickly tapers off as the input size increases past 50% of $|\mathcal{U}|$. Since the k parameter helps determine the minimum number of specified bits in the set, there is a direct relationship between the k parameter and the size of the output due to compression by the $*$ symbol. A smaller k value, i.e., $k = 1$, introduces the maximum number of $*$ symbols in the set. However, for a given input, a small k value does not necessarily result in the best compression factor (see $k = 1$ of Fig. 3). This result may be counter-intuitive, but it is due to the potentially larger number of unmatched strings that must be re-inserted back into the set determined by all the strings that must be represented by the converted result, see line 13-17 of Fig. 2. In addition, a small k value results in a set with more ternary strings than the number of binary strings represented. This occurs when multiple ternary strings, none of which subsumes any other, represent the same binary string. This redundancy in the ternary representation is not prevented by ManagedGrowth, and is apparent in Fig. 3 when $|tSH|$ and $|tNSH|$ exceed the maximum size of binary sharing relationships (i.e., 4096). One way to reduce the number of redundant strings is to sort the binary input by *Hamming distance* before conversion. In the subsequent tests, sorting was performed to maximize compression. We have found empirically that a k setting near (or slightly larger than) $l/2$ is the best

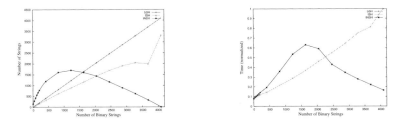

Fig. 4. Memory usage (avg. # of strings) and time normalized for conversions with $k = 7$

overall value considering both the result size and time complexity. We use $k = 7$ in the following experiments. It is interesting to note that a k value of $log_2(l)$ results in polynomial time conversion of the input (see the Complexity column of Table 1) but it may not result in the maximum compression of the set (see $k = 4$ of Fig. 3). Therefore, k may be adjusted to produce results based on acceptable performance level depending on which parameter is more important to the user, the level of compression (memory constraints) or execution time.

Our second experiment shows the comparison in terms of memory usage (Fig. 4, left) and running time (Fig. 4, right) of the conversion algorithms for transforming an initial set of binary strings, bSH, into its corresponding set of ternary strings, tSH, or its complement (negative), $tNSH$. We generated random sets of binary strings (over 30 runs) using $k = 7$ and we converted the set of binary strings using the **Convert** algorithm described in Fig. 1 for tSH, and **NegConvertMissing** in Fig. 2 for $tNSH$. The plot on the left shows that the number of positive ternary strings, $|tSH|$, used for encoding the input binary strings always remains below $|bSH|$, and this number increases slowly with increasing input size. It important to notice that for large values of $|bSH|$, tSH compacts worse than expected and the compression factor is lower. The main cause is the use of the parameter $k = 7$ that implies only the use of 5 or less $*$ symbols for compression. Conversely, the number of negative sharing relationships, $|tNSH|$, is greater than $|bSH|$ and $|tSH|$ up to between 40% and 50%, respectively. However, when the load exceeds those thresholds $tNSH$ compresses much better than its alternatives. For instance, for the maximum number of binary sharing relationships, $tNSH$ compresses them to only one negative string. On the other hand, the rightmost plot shows the average time consumed over 30 runs for both conversion algorithms. Again, $tNSH$ scales better than the positive ternary solution, tSH, after a threshold established around 50% of the maximum number of binary sharing relationships. Our proof-of-concept implementation is not really optimized, since our objective is to study the *relative* performance between the three representations, and thus times are normalized to the range $[0, 1]$. We argue that comparisons that we report between representations are fair since the three cases have been implemented with similar efficiency, and useful since the absolute performance of the base representation is well understood.

Finally, our third experiment shows the efficiency in terms of the memory usage (in Fig. 5, left) and running time (in Fig. 5, right) when performing the abstract unification for $k = 7$. Several characteristics of the abstract unification influence the memory usage and its performance. Given an arbitrary set of variables of interest $\mathcal{V}$ ($|\mathcal{V}| = 12$),

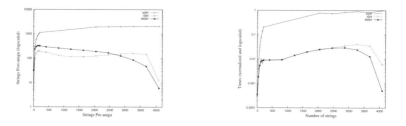

Fig. 5. Memory usage (avg. # of strings) and time normalized for amgu over 30 runs with $k = 7$

we constructed $x \in V$ by selecting one variable and $t \in Term$ as a term consisting of a subset of the remaining variables, i.e., $V \setminus \{x\}$. We tested with different values of t. Another important aspect is the input sharing set, bSH. Again, we reduced the influence of this factor by generating randomly 30 different sets. In the leftmost plot, the x-axis illustrates the number of input binary strings considered during the $amgu$. In the case of the positive and negative ternary $amgu$, the input binary strings were first converted to their corresponding compressed representations. The y-axis shows the number of strings after the unification. The plot shows that exceeding a threshold lower than 500 in the number of input binary sharing relationships, both tSH and $tNSH$ yield a significant smaller number of strings than the binary solution after unification. Moreover, when the number of the input binary strings is smaller than 50% of its maximum value, tSH compresses more efficiently than $tNSH$. However, if this value is exceeded then this trend is reversed: the negative encoding yields a better compression as the cardinality of the original set grows toward $2^{|V|}$. The rightmost plot shows the size of the random binary input sets in the x-axis, and the average time consumed for performing the abstract unification in its y-axis, normalized again from 0 to 1. This graph shows that the execution times behave similarly to the memory usage during abstract unification. Both tSH and $tNSH$ run much faster than bSH. The differences are significant (a factor of 10) for most x-values, reaching a factor of 1000 for large values of $|bSH|$. When the load exceeds a $50 - 60\%$-threshold, $tNSH$ scales better than tSH by a factor of 10. The main difference with respect to the memory usage depicted in the leftmost plot is that for a smaller load, tSH runs as fast as $tNSH$ during unification. The main reason is that the ternary relevant and irrelevant sharing operations are less efficient than their negative counterparts, i.e., intersection is an expensive operation in the positive whereas negative intersection is very efficient (positive union).

6   Conclusions

We have presented a novel approach to Set-Sharing that leverages the complement (negative) sharing relationships of the original sharing set, without any loss of accuracy. In this work, we based the negative representation on ternary strings. We also showed that the same ternary representation can be used as a positive encoding to efficiently compact the original binary sharing set. This provides the user the option of working with whichever set sharing representation is more efficient for a given problem instance.

The capabilities of our negative approach to compress sharing relationships are orthogonal to the use of the ternary representation. Hence, the negative relationships may be encoded using other representations such as BDDs [16]. Concretely, *Zero-suppressed BDDs* [16] are particularly interesting because they were designed to represent sets of combinations (i.e., sets of sets). In addition, ZBDDs may be also applicable to similar sharing-related analyses in object-oriented languages (e.g., [22]).

Our experimental evaluation has shown that our approach can reduce significantly the memory usage of the sharing relationships and the running time of the abstract operations, including the abstract unification. Our experiments also show how to set up key parameters in our algorithms in order to control the desired compression and time complexities. We have shown that we can obtain a reasonable compression in polynomial time by tuning appropriately those parameters. Thus, we believe our results can contribute to the practical, scalable application of Set-Sharing.

References

1. Armstrong, T., Marriott, K., Schachte, P., Søndergaard, H.: Boolean functions for dependency analysis: Algebraic properties and efficient representation. In: LeCharlier, B. (ed.) SAS 1994. LNCS, vol. 864. Springer, Heidelberg (1994)
2. Bagnara, R., Gori, R., Hill, P.M., Zaffanella, E.: Finite-tree analysis for constraint logic-based languages. Information and Computation 193(2), 84–116 (2004)
3. Bruynooghe, M., Codish, M., Mulkers, A.: Abstract unification for a composite domain deriving sharing and freeness properties of program variables. Verification and Analysis of Logic Languages (1994)
4. Bryant, R.E.: Symbolic Boolean Manipulation with Ordered Binary-Decision Diagrams. ACM Comput. Surv. 24(3), 293–318 (1992)
5. Bueno, F., García de la Banda, M.: Set-Sharing is not always redundant for Pair-Sharing. In: Kameyama, Y., Stuckey, P.J. (eds.) FLOPS 2004. LNCS, vol. 2998. Springer, Heidelberg (2004)
6. Bueno, F., García de la Banda, M., Hermenegildo, M.: Effectiveness of Global Analysis in Strict Independence-Based Automatic Program Parallelization. In: 1994 Intl. Symposium on Logic Programming (1994)
7. Codish, M., Lagoon, V., Bueno, F.: An algebraic approach to sharing analysis of logic programs. In: Proc. of the Fourth Intl. Static Analysis Symposium (1997)
8. Codish, M., Mulkers, A., Bruynooghe, M., García de la Banda, M., Hermenegildo, M.: Improving Abstract Interpretations by Combining Domains. In: PEPM 1993 (1993)
9. Codish, M., Dams, D., Filé, G., Bruynooghe, M.: On the design of a correct freeness analysis for logic programs. The Journal of Logic Programming 28(3), 181–206 (1996)
10. Codish, M., Søndergaard, H., Stuckey, P.J.: Sharing and groundness dependencies in logic programs. ACM Transactions on Prog. Languages and Systems 21(5), 948–976 (1999)
11. Cousot, P., Cousot, R.: Abs Interp: a Unified Lattice Model for Static Analysis of Programs by Construction or Approx of Fixpoints. In: POPL 1977 (1977)
12. Esponda, F., Ackley, E.S., Forrest, S., Helman, P.: On-line negative databases (with experimental results). Intl. Journal of Unconventional Computing 1(3), 201–220 (2005)
13. Esponda, F., Trias, E.D., Ackley, E.S., Forrest, S.: A relational algebra for negative databases. Technical Report TR-CS-2007-18, University of New Mexico (2007)
14. Fecht, C.: An efficient and precise sharing domain for logic programs. In: Kuchen, H., Swierstra, S.D. (eds.) PLILP 1996. LNCS, vol. 1140, pp. 469–470. Springer, Heidelberg (1996)

15. Hill, P.M., Zaffanella, E., Bagnara, R.: A correct, precise and efficient integration of set-sharing, freeness and linearity for the analysis of finite and rational tree languages. In: TPLP 2004 (2004)
16. Minato, S.: ZBDDs for Set Manipulation in Combinatorial Problems. In: DAC 1993 (1993)
17. Jacobs, D., Langen, A.: Static Analysis of Logic Programs for Independent And-Parallelism. Journal of Logic Programming 13(2, 3), 291–314 (1992)
18. King, A., Soper, P.: Depth-k Sharing and Freeness. In: ICLP 1994 (1994)
19. Langen, A.: Advanced techniques for approximating variable aliasing in Logic Programs. PhD thesis, Computer Science Dept., University of Southern CA (1990)
20. Li, X., King, A., Lu, L.: Collapsing Closures. In: Etalle, S., Truszczyński, M. (eds.) ICLP 2006. LNCS, vol. 4079. Springer, Heidelberg (2006)
21. Li, X., King, A., Lu, L.: Lazy Set-Sharing Analysis. In: Hagiya, M., Wadler, P. (eds.) FLOPS 2006. LNCS, vol. 3945. Springer, Heidelberg (2006)
22. Méndez-Lojo, M., Hermenegildo, M.: Precise Set Sharing Analysis for Java-style Programs. In: Logozzo, F., Peled, D.A., Zuck, L.D. (eds.) VMCAI 2008. LNCS, vol. 4905. Springer, Heidelberg (2008)
23. Mulkers, A., Simoens, W., Janssens, G., Bruynooghe, M.: On the Practicality of Abstract Equation Systems. In: ICLP 1995 (1995)
24. Muthukumar, K., Hermenegildo, M.: Combined Determination of Sharing and Freeness of Program Variables Through Abstract Interpretation. In: ICLP 1991 (1991)
25. Muthukumar, K., Hermenegildo, M.: Compile-time Derivation of Variable Dependency Using Abstract Interpretation. JLP 13(2/3), 315–347 (1992)
26. Navas, J., Bueno, F., Hermenegildo, M.: Efficient top-down set-sharing analysis using cliques. In: Van Hentenryck, P. (ed.) PADL 2006. LNCS, vol. 3819. Springer, Heidelberg (2005)
27. Søndergaard, H.: An application of abstract interpretation of logic programs: occur check reduction. In: Robinet, B., Wilhelm, R. (eds.) ESOP 1986. LNCS, vol. 213. Springer, Heidelberg (1986)
28. Trias, E., Navas, J., Ackley, E.S., Forrest, S., Hermenegildo, M.: Efficient Representations for Set-Sharing Analysis. TR-CLIP9/2008.0, Univ. of New Mexico (2008)
29. Zaffanella, E., Bagnara, R., Hill, P.M.: Widening Sharing. In: Nadathur, G. (ed.) PPDP 1999. LNCS, vol. 1702. Springer, Heidelberg (1999)

Termination of Narrowing
Using Dependency Pairs*

María Alpuente, Santiago Escobar, and José Iborra

Technical University of Valencia (UPV), Spain
{alpuente,sescobar,jiborra}@dsic.upv.es

Abstract. In this work, we extend the dependency pair approach for automated proofs of termination in order to prove the termination of narrowing. Our extension of the dependency pair approach generalizes the standard notion of dependency pairs by taking specifically into account the dependencies between the left-hand side of a rewrite rule and its own argument subterms. We demonstrate that the new *narrowing dependency pairs* exactly capture the narrowing termination behavior and provide an effective termination criterion which we prove to be sound and complete. Finally, we discuss how the problem of analyzing narrowing chains can be recast as a standard analysis problem for traditional (rewriting) chains, so that the proposed technique can be effectively mechanized by reusing the standard DP infrastructure.

1 Introduction

In recent years, the dependency pair (DP) method for automating the termination proofs of term rewriting has achieved tremendous success, as witnessed by the large number of publications and tools since its introduction in [6] and subsequent reformulation in [9] (see [11,13] for extensive references thereof).

Narrowing is a generalization of term rewriting that allows free variables in terms (as in logic programming) and replaces pattern matching by syntactic unification so that it subsumes both rewriting and SLD-resolution [12]. Narrowing has many important applications including execution of functional–logic programming languages [12], verification of security policies [15] and cryptographic protocols [8], equational unification [14], and symbolic reachability [16], among others. Termination of narrowing itself is, therefore, of great interest to these applications.

Termination of narrowing is a more restrictive property than termination of rewriting or termination of pure logic programs due to the high degree of non-determinism caused by the interaction of rule selection, redex selection, and unification. In recent works [2,4], we identified some non–trivial classes of TRSs where narrowing terminates. The results in [4] generalize previously known criteria for termination of narrowing, which were essentially restricted before to

---

* This work has been partially supported by the EU (FEDER) and Spanish MEC project TIN2007-68093-C02-02, Integrated Action Hispano-Alemana HA2006-0007, and UPV-VIDI grant 3249 PAID0607.

M. Garcia de la Banda and E. Pontelli (Eds.): ICLP 2008, LNCS 5366, pp. 317–331, 2008.
© Springer-Verlag Berlin Heidelberg 2008

either confluent term rewriting systems (TRSs) [14] or to left–flat TRSs (i.e., each argument of the left–hand side of a rewrite rule is either a variable or a ground term) that are compatible with a termination ordering [7], among other applicability conditions. Roughly speaking, we proved in [4] that confluence is a superfluous requirement for the termination of narrowing. We also weakened the left–flatness condition required in [7] to the requirement that every non-ground, strict subterm of the left–hand side (lhs) of every rewrite rule must be a *rigid normal form,* i.e., unnarrowable. Finally, in [2] we proved modular termination of a restriction of narrowing, called basic narrowing [14], in several hierarchical combinations of TRSs, which provides new algorithmic criteria to prove termination of narrowing via termination of basic narrowing (cf. [4]).

In [17], the notions of dependency pairs and dependency graphs, which were originally developed for term rewriting, were adapted to the logic programming domain, leading to automated termination analyses that are directly applicable to any definite logic program. Two different adaptations of the DP technique for narrowing have been proposed recently. In [18,19], the original dependency pair technique of [6] was adapted to the termination of narrowing, whereas [20] adapts the logic programming dependency pair approach of [17] instead, to prove termination of narrowing w.r.t. a given set of queries that are supplemented with *call modes.* Unfortunately, these two methods apply only to two particular classes of TRSs: right–linear TRSs (i.e., no repeated variables occur in the right–hand sides of the rules) or constructor systems (the arguments of the lhs's of the rules are constructor –i.e., data– terms). These two classes are overly restrictive for many practical uses of narrowing, such as the applications mentioned above. In this work, we are interested in developing automatable methods for proving termination of narrowing in TRSs that resist all previous techniques.

Example 1. Consider our running example, which is the non–right–linear, non–constructor–based, non–confluent TRS, adapted from [15], that is shown in Figure[1] 1. This TRS models a security (filtering) and routing policy that allows packets coming from external networks to be analyzed. We do not describe the intended meaning of each symbol since it is not relevant for this work, but note the kind of expressivity that is assumed in the domain of rule–based policy specification, that does not fit in the right–linear restriction or the constructor discipline. Narrowing is terminating for this TRS, but it cannot be proved by using any of the existing methods [2,4,18,19,20]. In this paper, we provide techniques that allow us to prove it automatically.

The main contributions of this paper are as follows:

– We present a new method for proving the termination of narrowing that is based on a suitable extension of the DP technique to narrowing that is applicable to any class of TRSs. Our method generalizes the standard notion of dependency pairs to narrowing by taking the dependencies between the lhs of a rewrite rule and its own argument subterms specifically into account.

---

[1] In this paper, variables are written in italic font and function symbols are in typewriter font.

```
filter(pckt(src, dst, established))         →   accept
filter(pckt(eth0, dst, new))                →   accept
filter(pckt(194.179.1.x:port, dst, new))    →   filter(pckt(secure, dst, new))
filter(pckt(158.42.x.y:port, dst, new))     →   filter(pckt(secure, dst, new))
filter(pckt(secure, dst:80, new))           →   accept
filter(pckt(secure, dst:other, new))        →   drop
filter(pckt(ppp0, dst, new))                →   drop
filter(pckt(123.123.1.1:port, dst, new))    →   accept
pckt(10.1.1.1:port, ppp0, s)                →   pckt(123.23.1.1:port, ppp0, s)
pckt(10.1.1.2:port, ppp0, s)                →   pckt(123.23.1.1:port, ppp0, s)
pckt(src, 123.123.1.1:port, new)            →   natroute(pckt(src, 10.1.1.1:port, established),
                                                         pckt(src, 10.1.1.2:port, established))
natroute(a, b)                              →   a
natroute(a, b)                              →   b
```

Fig. 1. The *FullPolicy* TRS

- We demonstrate that the new *narrowing dependency pairs* exactly capture the termination of narrowing behavior. We provide a termination criterion based on *narrowing chains* which we demonstrate to be sound and complete.
- This allows us to develop a technique that is more general in all cases and, for general calls (i.e., without considering call modes) strictly subsumes the DP methods for proving termination of narrowing of [18,19,20], as well as all previous (decidable) termination of narrowing criteria [2,4,7,14].
- We have implemented a tool for proving the termination of narrowing automatically that is based on our technique, and we made it publicly available.

Plan of the Paper

After recalling some preliminaries in Section 2, in Section 3 we discuss the problem of *echoing*, which we identify as being ultimately responsible for the non–termination of narrowing. In Section 4, we develop the notion of narrowing dependency pairs and provide a sound and complete criterion for the termination of narrowing that is based on analyzing narrowing chains. In Section 5, we discuss the effective automation of our method, which mainly consists of two steps: DP extraction and argument filtering transformation. Section 6 concludes. More details and proofs of all technical results can be found in [3].

2   Preliminaries

In this section, we briefly recall the essential notions and terminology of term rewriting. For missing notions and definitions on equations, orderings and rewriting, we refer to [21].

$\mathcal{V}$ denotes a countably infinite set of variables, and Σ denotes a set of function symbols, or signature, each of which has a fixed associated arity. Terms are viewed as labelled trees in the usual way, where $\mathcal{T}(\Sigma, \mathcal{V})$ and $\mathcal{T}(\Sigma)$ denote the non-ground term algebra and the ground algebra built on $\Sigma \cup \mathcal{V}$ and Σ, respectively. Positions are defined as sequences of natural numbers used to address subterms of a term, with ϵ as the root (or top) position (i.e., the empty sequence). Concatenation of positions p and q is denoted by $p.q$, and $p < q$ is the usual prefix ordering. The root symbol of a term is denoted by root(t). Given

$S \subseteq \Sigma \cup \mathcal{V}$, $\mathcal{P}os_S(t)$ denotes the set of positions of a term t that are rooted by function symbols or variables in S. $\mathcal{P}os_{\{f\}}(t)$ with $f \in \Sigma \cup \mathcal{V}$ will be simply denoted by $\mathcal{P}os_f(t)$, and $\mathcal{P}os_{\Sigma \cup \mathcal{V}}(t)$ will be simply denoted by $\mathcal{P}os(t)$. $t|_p$ is the subterm at the position p of t. $t[s]_p$ is the term t with the subterm at the position p replaced with term s. By $Var(s)$, we denote the set of variables occurring in the syntactic object s. By $\bar{x}$, we denote a tuple of pairwise distinct variables. A *fresh* variable is a variable that appears nowhere else. A *linear* term is one where every variable occurs only once.

A *substitution* σ is a mapping from the set of variables $\mathcal{V}$ into the set of terms $\mathcal{T}(\Sigma, \mathcal{V})$ with a (possibly infinite) domain $D(\sigma)$, and image $I(\sigma)$. A substitution is represented as $\{x_1 \mapsto t_1, \ldots, x_n \mapsto t_n\}$ for variables $x_1, \ldots, x_n$ and terms $t_1, \ldots, t_n$. The application of a substitution θ to term t is denoted by $t\theta$, using postfix notation. Composition of substitutions is denoted by juxtaposition, i.e., the substitution $\sigma\theta$ denotes $(\theta \circ \sigma)$. We write $\theta_{\upharpoonright Var(s)}$ to denote the restriction of the substitution θ to the set of variables in s; by abuse of notation, we often simply write $\theta_{\upharpoonright s}$. Given a term t, $\theta = \nu\,[t]$ iff $\theta_{\upharpoonright Var(t)} = \nu_{\upharpoonright Var(t)}$, that is, $\forall x \in Var(t)$, $x\theta = x\nu$. A substitution θ is more general than σ, denoted by $\theta \leq \sigma$, if there is a substitution γ such that $\theta\gamma = \sigma$. A *unifier* of terms s and t is a substitution ϑ such that $s\vartheta = t\vartheta$. The *most general unifier* of terms s and t, denoted by $mgu(s,t)$, is a unifier θ such that for any other unifier θ', $\theta \leq \theta'$.

A *term rewriting system* (TRS) $\mathcal{R}$ is a pair (Σ, R), where R is a finite set of rewrite rules of the form $l \to r$ such that $l, r \in \mathcal{T}(\Sigma, \mathcal{V})$, $l \notin \mathcal{V}$, and $Var(r) \subseteq Var(l)$. For TRS $\mathcal{R}$, $l \to r \ll \mathcal{R}$ denotes that $l \to r$ is a new variant of a rule in $\mathcal{R}$ such that $l \to r$ contains only *fresh* variables, i.e., contains no variable previously met during any computation (standardized apart). We will often write just $\mathcal{R}$ or (Σ, R) instead of $\mathcal{R} = (\Sigma, R)$. A TRS $\mathcal{R}$ is called *left–linear* (respectively *right–linear*) if, for every $l \to r \in \mathcal{R}$, l (respectively r) is a linear term. Given a TRS $\mathcal{R} = (\Sigma, R)$, the signature Σ is often partitioned into two disjoint sets $\Sigma = \mathcal{C} \uplus \mathcal{D}$, where $\mathcal{D} = \{f \mid f(t_1, \ldots, t_n) \to r \in R\}$ and $\mathcal{C} = \Sigma \setminus \mathcal{D}$. Symbols in $\mathcal{C}$ are called *constructors*, and symbols in $\mathcal{D}$ are called *defined functions*. The elements of $\mathcal{T}(\mathcal{C}, \mathcal{V})$ are called *constructor terms*. We let $Def(\mathcal{R})$ denote the set of defined symbols in $\mathcal{R}$. A constructor system is a TRS whose lhs's are terms of the form $f(c_1, \ldots, c_k)$ where $f \in \mathcal{D}$ and $c_1, \ldots, c_k$ are constructor terms. A term whose root symbol is a defined function is called *root-defined*.

A rewrite step is the application of a rewrite rule to an expression. A term $s \in \mathcal{T}(\Sigma, \mathcal{V})$ *rewrites* to a term $t \in \mathcal{T}(\Sigma, \mathcal{V})$, denoted by $s \xrightarrow{p}_{\mathcal{R}} t$, if there exist $p \in \mathcal{P}os_\Sigma(s)$, $l \to r \in \mathcal{R}$, and substitution σ such that $s|_p = l\sigma$ and $t = s[r\sigma]_p$. When no confusion can arise, we omit the subscript in $\to_{\mathcal{R}}$. We also omit the reduced position p when it is not relevant. A term s is a *normal form* w.r.t. the relation $\to_{\mathcal{R}}$ (or simply a normal form), if there is no term t such that $s \to_{\mathcal{R}} t$. A term is a reducible expression or *redex* if it is an instance of the left hand side of a rule in $\mathcal{R}$. A term s is a *head normal form* if there are no terms t, t' s.t. $s \to^*_{\mathcal{R}} t' \xrightarrow{\epsilon}_{\mathcal{R}} t$. A term t is said to be *terminating* w.r.t. R if there is no infinite reduction sequence $t \to_{\mathcal{R}} t_1 \to_{\mathcal{R}} t_2 \to_{\mathcal{R}} \ldots$. A TRS $\mathcal{R}$ is *(→)-terminating* (also called strongly normalizing or noetherian) if every term is terminating w.r.t. R.

A TRS $\mathcal{R}$ is *confluent* if, whenever $t \to_{\mathcal{R}}^* s_1$ and $t \to_{\mathcal{R}}^* s_2$, there exists a term w s.t. $s_1 \to_{\mathcal{R}}^* w$ and $s_2 \to_{\mathcal{R}}^* w$.

A term $s \in \mathcal{T}(\Sigma, \mathcal{V})$ narrows to a term $t \in \mathcal{T}(\Sigma, \mathcal{V})$, denoted by $s \overset{p}{\leadsto}_{\theta, \mathcal{R}} t$, if there exist $p \in \mathcal{P}os_{\Sigma}(s)$, $l \to r \ll \mathcal{R}$, and substitution θ such that $\theta = mgu(s|_p, l)$ and $t = (s[r]_p)\theta$. We use $\overset{>\epsilon}{\to}_{\mathcal{R}}$ (resp. $\overset{>\epsilon}{\leadsto}_{\theta, \mathcal{R}}$) to denote steps in which the selected redex (resp. *narrex*, i.e. narrowable expression) is below the root.

3   The *echoing* Problem

The dependency pair technique [6] is one of the most powerful methods for automated termination analyses. The technique focuses on the dependency relations between defined function symbols, paying particular attention to strongly connected components within a graph of functional dependencies, in order to produce automated termination proofs. The dependency graph is typically extracted by considering the dependencies between the lhs's of a rewrite rule and all proper subterms of the rhs of the rule.

An adaptation of the DP method to narrowing is given in [19] that requires the TRS to have the so-called *Top Reduced Almost Terminating* (TRAT) property, defined as follows. Given a property P on terms, a term t is said to be a *minimal P term* if t satisfies P but none of the proper subterms of t does. Given a TRS $\mathcal{R}$ and a binary relation $\Rightarrow$ (being $\to_{\mathcal{R}}$ or $\leadsto_{\mathcal{R}}$), an infinite derivation $t \Rightarrow t_1 \Rightarrow t_2 \ldots$ is called *almost terminating* if t is a minimal non–terminating term w.r.t. $\Rightarrow$. An almost terminating derivation $t \Rightarrow t_1 \Rightarrow t_2 \ldots$ is called *top reduced* if it contains a derivation step at the root position. We say that $\Rightarrow$ has the TRAT property if, for every non-terminating term t, there exists a top reduced almost-terminating sequence stemming from one subterm of t.

Let us briefly recall the notion of *context*. A context is a term with several occurrences of a fresh symbol $\square$. If $C[\ ]$ contains k occurrences of symbol $\square$ at positions $p_1, \ldots, p_k$, we write $C[t_1, \ldots, t_k]$ to denote the term $(C[t_1]_{p_1}) \cdots [t_k]_{p_k}$.

In [19] it is proved that every monotone relation has the TRAT property. Since the rewriting relation is monotone (i.e., $t \to_{\mathcal{R}} s$ implies $C[t] \to_{\mathcal{R}} C[s]$), then it has the TRAT property for every TRS $\mathcal{R}$ (cf. [13, Lemma 1]). In term rewriting this ensures that, in every almost terminating, infinite term rewriting derivation, a rewriting step is given at the root. Unfortunately, the narrowing relation is not monotone: $t \leadsto_{\sigma, \mathcal{R}} s$ does not entail $C[t] \leadsto_{\sigma, \mathcal{R}} C[s]$ but $C[t] \leadsto_{\sigma, \mathcal{R}} (C\sigma)[s]$ instead.

Example 2. [7] Consider the TRS consisting of the rule $f(f(x)) \to x$, and the non–linear term $c(f(x), x)$. Then there does not exist an infinite narrowing derivation for the subterms, $f(x)$ and x, whereas $c(f(x), x)$ is infinitely narrowed without ever performing a narrowing step at the root:

$$c(\underline{f(x)}, x) \leadsto_{\{x \mapsto f(x')\}} c(x', \underline{f(x')}) \leadsto_{\{x' \mapsto f(x'')\}} c(\underline{f(x'')}, x'') \ldots$$

As shown by the above example, in the presence of non linearity the non–monotony of narrowing has undesirable effects for its termination, since *narrexes* can be brought into the context by the substitution computed at the preceding narrowing step, thus causing other terms in the context to grow. This *echoing* effect plays a fatal role in the (non–) termination of narrowing.

There are some classes of TRSs in which narrowing exhibits a monotone or monotone–like behaviour and thus enjoys the TRAT property. [19] considers two such classes: right–linear TRS (w.r.t. linear goals), and constructor systems. We note that these two classes are a particular case of a larger characterization of narrowing termination that we formalized in [4] by the QSRNC (*Quasi stable rigidly normalized condition*), though in [4] we do not make the relation with TRAT explicit.

The inspiration for this work comes from realizing that monotonicity is not really a *necessary* condition for the termination of narrowing, provided the partially computed substitutions do not *echo*, i.e., they do not bring narrexes into the context that might either introduce a term that does not terminate or *echo* again. Let us introduce the idea by means of one example.

Example 3. Consider the non–linear input call $c(f(x), x)$ in the non–constructor TRS consisting of rules $f(g(x)) \to x$ and $g(x) \to x$. The only possible derivation for this term is finite, whereas the TRS, together with the considered non–linear input term, do not fit in any of the characterizations given for TRAT [18,19,20] or any decidable criteria for the termination of narrowing [2,4,7,14]. Note that the argument $g(x)$ of the lhs of the first rule is a narrex.

Let us start with some lessons learnt from the termination of rewriting that would be good to transfer to the termination of narrowing. In rewriting (and narrowing), if a TRS is not terminating then there must be a minimal non-terminating term. In rewriting such a minimal non-terminating term is rooted by a defined symbol but this is not true for narrowing. As in [13], let us denote the set of all minimal non-terminating terms w.r.t. rewriting (resp. narrowing) by $\mathcal{T}^\infty$ (resp. $\mathcal{T}_{\rightsquigarrow}^\infty$). The following definition is crucial.

Definition 1 (Echoing terms). *Let $\mathcal{R}$ be a TRS. We define the set of minimal echoing terms w.r.t. $\mathcal{R}$, denoted by $\mathcal{T}^\circlearrowleft$, as follows: $s \in \mathcal{T}^\circlearrowleft$ if, given a fresh binary symbol c and a variable $x \in Var(s)$, then $c(s, x) \in \mathcal{T}_{\rightsquigarrow}^\infty$ but $s \notin \mathcal{T}_{\rightsquigarrow}^\infty$, and there is no proper subterm s' of s such that $s' \in \mathcal{T}^\circlearrowleft$.*

Now, we provide our key result for the termination of narrowing. We write $s \trianglerighteq t$ to denote that t is a subterm of s, and $s \triangleright t$ if t is a proper subterm of s.

Lemma 1. *Let $\mathcal{R}$ be a TRS. For every term $t \in \mathcal{T}_{\rightsquigarrow}^\infty$, we have that either*

1. (TOP) *there exists a rewrite rule $l \to r \in \mathcal{R}$, substitutions σ, ρ, a term t', and a non-variable subterm u of r such that $t \overset{\geq \epsilon *}{\underset{\rho, \mathcal{R}}{\rightsquigarrow}} t' \overset{\epsilon}{\underset{\sigma, l \to r}{\rightsquigarrow}} r\sigma \trianglerighteq u$ and $u \in \mathcal{T}_{\rightsquigarrow}^\infty$;*
2. (HYBRID) *there are terms t', t'', u, substitutions ρ, σ, a position p, and a variable x such that $t \overset{\geq \epsilon *}{\underset{\rho, \mathcal{R}}{\rightsquigarrow}} t' \overset{p}{\underset{\sigma, \mathcal{R}}{\rightsquigarrow}} t''$, $x \in Var(t'|_p)$, $x\sigma \trianglerighteq u$, and $u \in \mathcal{T}_{\rightsquigarrow}^\infty$;*
3. (ECHOING) *there are terms t', t'', u, substitutions ρ, σ, a position p, and a variable x such that $t \overset{\geq \epsilon *}{\underset{\rho, \mathcal{R}}{\rightsquigarrow}} t' \overset{p}{\underset{\sigma, \mathcal{R}}{\rightsquigarrow}} t''$, $x \in Var(t'|_p)$, $x\sigma \trianglerighteq u$, and $t'|_p, u \in \mathcal{T}^\circlearrowleft$.*

Informally, the lemma above distinguishes three different kinds of minimal non–terminating terms. The TOP case is the usual one shared by rewriting and narrowing non–termination; the other two cases are due to non–monotonicity and thus unique to narrowing. In the pure ECHOING case, the narrowing of an echoing subterm introduces into the context a new echoing subterm that reproduces the process again, as in Example 2. In the HYBRID echoing case, the reduction of an echoing subterm introduces into the context a minimal non–terminating narrex that spawns an infinite narrowing derivation, as in Example 4 below.

Example 4. Consider the following TRS:

$$\mathtt{f}(\mathtt{g}(x)) \to \mathtt{a} \qquad\qquad \mathtt{g}(x) \to \mathtt{g}(x)$$

$\mathtt{g}(x) \in \mathcal{T}_{\leadsto}^{\infty}$ is a minimal non–terminating term for rewriting. $\mathtt{f}(x) \notin \mathcal{T}_{\leadsto}^{\infty}$, since only the derivation $\mathtt{f}(x) \leadsto_{\{x \mapsto \mathtt{g}(x')\}} \mathtt{a}$ can be proven. However, given a fresh symbol $\mathtt{c}$, there is a HYBRID infinite narrowing derivation stemming from the term $\mathtt{c}(\mathtt{f}(x), x) \in \mathcal{T}_{\leadsto}^{\infty}$. Therefore, $\mathtt{f}(x) \in \mathcal{T}^{\circlearrowleft}$.

4   Narrowing Dependency Pairs

In this section, we develop the notion of narrowing dependency pairs, and provide a sound and complete criterion for the termination of narrowing that is based on analyzing narrowing chains.

The intuitive idea behind our method is as follows. In order to construct the set of dependency pairs, we not only relate the lhs of each rule with the root–defined subterms occurring in the corresponding rhs, as in standard rewriting DP, but also with its *own* root–defined subterms, i.e., those terms whose root symbol is a defined function. The resulting set of dependency pairs faithfully captures the behaviour of infinite narrowing derivations which incrementally compute an infinite substitution, or more precisely, where the substitution computed by narrowing contains an infinite term.

Suppose we split the substitution σ computed by a narrowing step $t \leadsto_{l \to r, \sigma} s$ into two pieces, $\sigma \equiv \sigma_{\restriction l} \uplus \sigma_{\restriction t}$. The $\sigma_{\restriction l}$ part of the substitution has the usual effect of propagating narrexes from the left hand side to the right hand side of the rule. On the other hand, the $\sigma_{\restriction t}$ part is responsible for the echoing of *narrexes* to the context that can fire a new narrowing step. These narrexes come from the subterms of the left hand side of the rule, as in Example 2 above, or from the term being narrowed itself, e.g. when $\mathtt{c}(z, \mathtt{h}(\mathtt{g}(x), z))$ is narrowed to $\mathtt{c}(\mathtt{g}(x), 0)$ by using the rule $\mathtt{h}(y, y) \to 0$ and most general unifier $\{z \mapsto \mathtt{g}(x), y \mapsto \mathtt{g}(x)\}$.

Although the narrexes coming from proper subterms of the narrex selected at the preceding step might cause non–termination, standard (rewriting) termination analyses already cope with them. However, narrexes coming from proper subterms of the lhs of the rules are specific to narrowing, and thus we focus on them in our notion of narrowing dependency pairs.

$$
\begin{array}{ll}
(1) & \texttt{filter}^{\#}(\texttt{pckt}(194.179.1.x{:}p, dst, \texttt{new})) \;\rightarrow\; \texttt{filter}^{\#}(\texttt{pckt}(\texttt{secure}, dst, \texttt{new})) \\
(2) & \texttt{filter}^{\#}(\texttt{pckt}(194.179.1.x{:}p, dst, \texttt{new})) \;\rightarrow\; \texttt{pckt}^{\#}(\texttt{secure}, dst, \texttt{new}) \\
(3) & \texttt{filter}^{\#}(\texttt{pckt}(158.42.x.y{:}p, dst, \texttt{new})) \;\rightarrow\; \texttt{filter}^{\#}(\texttt{pckt}(\texttt{secure}, dst, \texttt{new})) \\
(4) & \texttt{filter}^{\#}(\texttt{pckt}(158.42.x.y{:}p, dst, \texttt{new})) \;\rightarrow\; \texttt{pckt}^{\#}(\texttt{secure}, dst, \texttt{new}) \\
(5) & \texttt{pckt}^{\#}(10.1.1.1{:}p, \texttt{ppp0}, s) \;\rightarrow\; \texttt{pckt}^{\#}(123.23.1.1{:}p, \texttt{ppp0}, s) \\
(6) & \texttt{pckt}^{\#}(10.1.1.2{:}p, \texttt{ppp0}, s) \;\rightarrow\; \texttt{pckt}^{\#}(123.23.1.1{:}p, \texttt{ppp0}, s) \\
(7) & \texttt{filter}^{\#}(\texttt{pckt}(123.123.1.1{:}p, dst, \texttt{new})) \;\rightarrow\; \texttt{pckt}^{\#}(123.123.1.1{:}p, dst, \texttt{new}) \\
(8) & \texttt{pckt}^{\#}(src, 123.123.1.1{:}p, \texttt{new}) \;\rightarrow\; \texttt{pckt}^{\#}(src, 10.1.1.1{:}p, \texttt{established}) \\
(9) & \texttt{pckt}^{\#}(src, 123.123.1.1{:}p, \texttt{new}) \;\rightarrow\; \texttt{pckt}^{\#}(src, 10.1.1.2{:}p, \texttt{established}) \\
(10) & \texttt{filter}^{\#}(\texttt{pckt}(src, dst, \texttt{established})) \;\rightarrow\; \texttt{pckt}^{\#}(src, dst, \texttt{established}) \\
(11) & \texttt{filter}^{\#}(\texttt{pckt}(\texttt{eth0}, dst, \texttt{new})) \;\rightarrow\; \texttt{pckt}^{\#}(\texttt{eth0}, dst, \texttt{new}) \\
(12) & \texttt{filter}^{\#}(\texttt{pckt}(194.179.1.x{:}p, dst, \texttt{new})) \;\rightarrow\; \texttt{pckt}^{\#}(194.179.1.x{:}p, dst, \texttt{new}) \\
(13) & \texttt{filter}^{\#}(\texttt{pckt}(158.42.x.y{:}p, dst, \texttt{new})) \;\rightarrow\; \texttt{pckt}^{\#}(158.42.x.y{:}p, dst, \texttt{new}) \\
(14) & \texttt{filter}^{\#}(\texttt{pckt}(\texttt{secure}, dst{:}80, \texttt{new})) \;\rightarrow\; \texttt{pckt}^{\#}(\texttt{secure}, dst{:}80, \texttt{new}) \\
(15) & \texttt{filter}^{\#}(\texttt{pckt}(\texttt{secure}, dst{:}\texttt{other}, \texttt{new})) \;\rightarrow\; \texttt{pckt}^{\#}(\texttt{secure}, dst{:}\texttt{other}, \texttt{new}) \\
(16) & \texttt{filter}^{\#}(\texttt{pckt}(\texttt{ppp0}, dst, \texttt{new})) \;\rightarrow\; \texttt{pckt}^{\#}(\texttt{ppp0}, dst, \texttt{new}) \\
(17) & \texttt{pckt}^{\#}(src, 123.123.1.1{;}p, \texttt{new}) \rightarrow \texttt{natroute}^{\#}(\; \texttt{pckt}(src, 10.1.1.1{:}p, \texttt{established}), \\
& \hspace{5.5cm} \texttt{pckt}(src, 10.1.1.2{:}p, \texttt{established}))
\end{array}
$$

Fig. 2. Dependency pairs of *FullPolicy*

Notation Let $\mathcal{R}$ be a TRS defined over a signature $\Sigma = \mathcal{D} \uplus \mathcal{C}$. Let $\Sigma^{\#}$ denote the extension of Σ with $\{f^{\#} \mid f \in \mathcal{D}\}$, where $f^{\#}$ is a fresh symbol with the same arity as f. If $t \in \mathcal{T}(\Sigma, \mathcal{V})$ is of the form $\texttt{f}(s_1, \ldots, s_n)$ with $\texttt{f}$ a defined symbol, then $t^{\#}$ denotes the term $\texttt{f}^{\#}(s_1, \ldots, s_n)$.

The following definition extends the traditional, vanilla DPs with a novel kind of dependency pairs, which we call *ll–dependency pairs*.

Definition 2 (Narrowing Dependency Pair). *Given a TRS $\mathcal{R}$, we have two types of narrowing dependency pairs:*

- *a lr–dependency pair (or standard[2] DP) of $\mathcal{R}$ is a pair $l^{\#} \to t^{\#}$ where $l \to r \in \mathcal{R}$, $r \trianglerighteq t$, and $root(t) \in \mathcal{D}$.*
- *a ll–dependency pair (ll-DP) of $\mathcal{R}$ is a pair $l^{\#} \to u^{\#}$ where $l \to r \in \mathcal{R}$, $l \triangleright u$, and $root(u) \in \mathcal{D}$.*

The set of all (narrowing) dependency pairs of $\mathcal{R}$ is denoted by $NDP_{\mathcal{R}}$.

Example 5. The TRS $\texttt{f}(\texttt{f}(x)) \to x$ of Example 2 has no lr–dependency pairs and the single ll–dependency pair $\texttt{f}^{\#}(\texttt{f}(x)) \to \texttt{f}^{\#}(x)$.

Example 6. For the TRS of Example 1 we obtain the narrowing dependency pairs shown in Figure 2.

Recall that our purpose is to prove that there are no infinite narrowing derivations. Since dependency pairs model all function calls in $\mathcal{R}$, this is equivalent to proving that there are no infinite *chains* of narrowing dependency pairs.

For narrowing we consider suitable the following definition of chain. As in [11,19], we assume that different occurrences of dependency pairs are variable disjoint. In the following, $\mathcal{P}$ is usually a set of dependency pairs.

---

[2] Modern formulations exclude pairs $l^{\#} \to u^{\#}$ when $l \triangleright u$. This refinement could be applied to lr-DPs in our definition, but the pair would not be actually discarded, since it is also computed as a ll-DP.

Definition 3 (Narrowing Chain). *Let* $\mathcal{P}, \mathcal{R}$ *be two TRS's. A (possibly infinite) sequence of narrowing dependency pairs* $s_1 \to t_1, s_2 \to t_2, \ldots, s_n \to t_n \in \mathcal{P}$ *is called a* $(\mathcal{P}, \mathcal{R})$-*narrowing chain if there exist terms* $u_1, u_2, \ldots, u_n$ *and substitutions* $\sigma_1, \rho_1, \sigma_2, \rho_2, \ldots, \sigma_n, \rho_n$ *s.t.* $u_1 \overset{\epsilon}{\rightsquigarrow}_{\sigma_1, s_1 \to t_1} t_1 \sigma_1 \overset{\geq \epsilon *}{\rightsquigarrow}_{\rho_1, \mathcal{R}} u_2 \overset{\epsilon}{\rightsquigarrow}_{\sigma_2, s_2 \to t_2}$ $t_2 \sigma_2 \overset{\geq \epsilon *}{\rightsquigarrow}_{\rho_2, \mathcal{R}} u_3 \cdots u_n \overset{\epsilon}{\rightsquigarrow}_{\sigma_n, s_n \to t_n} t_n \sigma_n.$

We often omit the $(\mathcal{P}, \mathcal{R})$ prefix when referring to narrowing chains when it is clear from the context. The following result establishes the soundness of analyzing narrowing chains.

Lemma 2. *Let* $\mathcal{R}$ *be a TRS. For every* $(NDP_{\mathcal{R}}, \mathcal{R})$-*narrowing chain* $s_1 \to t_1,$ $\ldots, s_n \to t_n$, *there exists a narrowing derivation in* $\mathcal{R}$ *which gives at least one reduction step for every pair in the chain.*

Namely, there are contexts $C_1[\,], \ldots, C_{n+1}[\,]$, *positions* $p_1, \ldots, p_{n+1}$, *terms* $u_1,$ $\ldots, u_n$, *and substitutions* $\tau_1, \ldots, \tau_n, \rho_1, \ldots, \rho_{n-1}$ *s.t.* $\tau_i = mgu(u_i, s_i)$ *for* $i \in$ $\{1, \ldots, n\}$, *and* $C_1[u_1]_{p_1} \overset{p_1}{\rightsquigarrow}_{\tau_1, \mathcal{R}} C_2[t_1 \tau_1]_{p_2} \overset{\geq p_2 *}{\rightsquigarrow}_{\rho_1, \mathcal{R}} C_2 \rho_1[u_2]_{p_2} \overset{p_2}{\rightsquigarrow}_{\tau_2, \mathcal{R}} C_3[t_2 \tau_2]_{p_3}$ $\overset{\geq p_3 *}{\rightsquigarrow}_{\rho_2, \mathcal{R}} C_3 \rho_2[u_3]_{p_3} \cdots C_n \rho_{n-1}[u_n]_{p_n} \overset{p_n}{\rightsquigarrow}_{\tau_n, \mathcal{R}} C_{n+1}[t_n \tau_n]_{p_{n+1}}.$

Now we are able to show that, whenever there are no infinite narrowing chains, narrowing does terminate.

Theorem 1 (Termination Criterion). *A TRS* $\mathcal{R}$ *is terminating for narrowing if and only if no infinite* $(NDP_{\mathcal{R}}, \mathcal{R})$-*narrowing chain exists.*

Example 7. Consider the ll-DP $d \equiv f^{\#}(f(x)) \to f^{\#}(x)$ of Example 5. There is a narrowing chain $f^{\#}(x) \rightsquigarrow_{\{x \mapsto f(x')\}, d} f^{\#}(x') \rightsquigarrow_{\{x' \mapsto f(x'')\}, d} f^{\#}(x'') \cdots.$

5   Automating the Method

In order to automate the task of proving the absence of narrowing chains, it would be very convenient to reformulate the problem using only rewriting chains, as it is done e.g. in [19,20,17], since this allows us to reuse existing tools and techniques of the rewriting DP literature. We develop our method inspired by [18] but we provide all results without requiring TRAT, which is the main novel contribution of this section. Let us recall the notion of argument filtering.

Definition 4 (Argument Filtering). [6] *An argument filtering (AF) for a signature* Σ *is a mapping* π *that assigns to every* n-*ary function symbol* $f \in \Sigma$ *an argument position* $i \in \{1, \ldots, n\}$, *or a (possibly empty) list* $[i_1, \ldots, i_m]$ *of argument positions with* $1 \leq i_i < \ldots < i_m \leq n$. *The signature* Σ_π *consists of all function symbols* f *s.t.* $\pi(f)$ *is some list* $[i_1, \ldots, i_m]$, *where in* Σ_π *the arity of* f *is* m. *Every AF* π *induces a mapping from* $\mathcal{T}(\Sigma, \mathcal{V})$ *to* $\mathcal{T}(\Sigma_\pi, \mathcal{V})$:

$$\pi(t) = \begin{cases} t & \textit{if } t \textit{ is a variable} \\ \pi(t_i) & \textit{if } t = f(t_1, \ldots, t_n) \textit{ and } \pi(f) = i \\ f(\pi(t_{i_1}), \ldots, \pi(t_{i_m})) & \textit{if } t = f(t_1, \ldots, t_n) \textit{ and } \pi(f) = [i_1, \ldots, i_m] \end{cases}$$

We extend π to a TRS $\mathcal{R}$ as $\pi(\mathcal{R}) = \{\pi(l) \to \pi(r) \mid l \to r \in \mathcal{R} \text{ and } \pi(l) \neq \pi(r)\}$. For any argument filtering π and ordering $>$, we define $s \geq_\pi t \iff \pi(s) > \pi(t)$ or $\pi(s) \equiv \pi(t)$. We also define the filtering of a position p w.r.t. a term t as follows. Given a n-ary symbol $f \in \Sigma$ and $i \in \{1, \ldots, n\}$, $\pi(i, f) = j$ if $\pi(f) = [i_1, \ldots, i_j, \ldots, i_k]$, $i_j = i$. Given a term t and a position $p \in \mathcal{P}os(t)$, the filtering of p w.r.t. t is defined as follows:

$$\pi(p, t) = \begin{cases} \epsilon & \text{if } p = \epsilon \\ \pi(q, t) & \text{if } p = q.i, i \in \mathbb{N}, \pi(root(t|_q)) = i \\ \pi(q, t).\pi(i, root(t|_q)) & \text{if } p = q.i, i \in \mathbb{N}, \pi(root(t|_q)) = [i_1, .., i, .., i_k] \end{cases}$$

Example 8. Consider the TRS of Example 1 and the argument filtering $\pi(\texttt{pckt})$ $= [1, 3]$ and $\pi(f) = [1, \ldots, ar(f)]$ for any other $f \in \Sigma$. Let us consider the term t = $\texttt{filter(pckt(secure}, dst, \texttt{new}))$, its filtered version is $\pi(t)$ = $\texttt{filter(pckt(secure, new))}$ and the filtering of position 1.3 is $\pi(1.3, \pi(t)) = 1.2$ where $\pi(1.2, \pi(t))$ is undefined.

Definition 5. *Given a TRS $\mathcal{R}$ and an AF π, we say that π is a sound AF for $\mathcal{R}$ iff $\pi(\mathcal{R})$ is a TRS, i.e., the rhs's of the rules do not contain extra variables not appearing in the corresponding lhs.*

Our main result in this section is Theorem 2 below that relates infinite narrowing $(\mathcal{P}, \mathcal{R})$–chains to infinite rewriting $(\pi(\mathcal{P}), \pi(\mathcal{R}))$–chains. In order to prove this result, we first need two auxiliary lemmata. The first one establishes a correspondence between rewriting derivations in $\mathcal{R}$ and derivations in the filtered TRS $\pi(\mathcal{R})$.

Lemma 3. *Given a TRS $\mathcal{R}$, a sound AF π, and terms s and t, $s \to_\mathcal{R}^* t$ implies $\pi(s) \to_{\pi(\mathcal{R})}^* \pi(t)$. Moreover, the derivation in $\pi(\mathcal{R})$ uses the same rules in the same order at the corresponding filtered positions (whenever the filtered position exists).*

The next lemma extends the correspondence established in Lemma 3 to narrowing, which can be done only when the original filtered term is ground. The key point is that the correspondence holds *regardless* of the substitution computed by narrowing. It is in fact a (one-way) lifting lemma from narrowing derivations in $\mathcal{R}$ to rewriting sequences in $\pi(\mathcal{R})$.

Lemma 4. *Given a TRS $\mathcal{R}$ and a sound AF π, let s and t be terms s.t. $\pi(s)$ is ground. Then $s \leadsto_{\sigma, \mathcal{R}}^* t$ implies $\pi(s) \to_{\pi(\mathcal{R})}^* \pi(t)$. Moreover, the derivation in $\pi(\mathcal{R})$ uses the same rules in the same order at the corresponding filtered positions (whenever the filtered position exists).*

Let us recall here the standard definition of chain for rewriting.

Definition 6 (Chain). [6,11] *Let $\mathcal{P}, \mathcal{R}$ be two TRS's. A (possibly infinite) sequence of pairs $s_1 \to t_1, s_2 \to t_2, \ldots$ from $\mathcal{P}$ is a $(\mathcal{P}, \mathcal{R})$–chain if there exists a substitution σ with $t_i\sigma \to_\mathcal{R} s_{i+1}$ for all i.*

The following result allows us to prove the absence of narrowing chains by analyzing standard rewriting chains. This is very useful because it means that we can reuse all the DP infrastructure available for rewriting.

Theorem 2. *Let $\mathcal{R}$ be a TRS over a signature Σ, $\mathcal{P}$ be a TRS over a signature $\Sigma^{\#}$, and π a sound AF over $\Sigma^{\#}$ s.t. $\pi(t)$ is ground for at least one pair $s \rightarrow t \in \mathcal{P}$ in every $(\mathcal{P},\mathcal{R})$–narrowing chain. If there exists no infinite $(\pi(\mathcal{P}), \pi(\mathcal{R}))$–chain, then there exists no infinite $(\mathcal{P},\mathcal{R})$–narrowing chain.*

The following straightforward consequence of Theorems 1 and 2 characterizes termination of narrowing as a rewriting problem.

Corollary 1. *Let $\mathcal{R}$ be a TRS over a signature Σ, and π a sound AF over $\Sigma^{\#}$ s.t. $\pi(t)$ is ground for at least one pair $s \rightarrow t \in NDP_{\mathcal{R}}$ in every $(NDP_{\mathcal{R}},\mathcal{R})$– narrowing chain. If there exists no infinite $(\pi(NDP_{\mathcal{R}}), \pi(\mathcal{R}))$–chain, then narrowing terminates in $\mathcal{R}$.*

5.1   Extending the DP Framework to Narrowing

By means of Theorem 2, it is possible now to recast the problem of termination of narrowing in the DP *framework* of [9]. In this framework a DP *problem* is a tuple $(\mathcal{P}, \mathcal{R})$ of two TRSs, $\mathcal{R}$ and $\mathcal{P}$, where initially $\mathcal{P} = NDP_{\mathcal{R}}$. If there is no associated infinite narrowing chain, we say that the problem is *finite*. Termination methods are then formulated as *DP processors* that take a DP problem and return a new set of DP problems. A DP processor is *sound* if the input problem is finite whenever all the output problems are. We speak of *narrowing DP problems* to distinguish them from the standard ones.

   In the usual style [20,17], we show here how to adapt a few of the most important DP processors, and then give one that transforms a narrowing DP problem into a rewriting one, which allows us to use any of the existing DP processors for termination of rewriting.

   The following definition adapts the standard notion of dependency graph to our setting by simply considering narrowing dependency pairs instead of vanilla DPs.

Definition 7 (Dependency Graph). *Given a (narrowing) DP problem $\langle \mathcal{P}, \mathcal{R} \rangle$ its (resp. narrowing) dependency graph is the directed graph where the nodes are the elements of $\mathcal{P}$, and there is an edge from $s \rightarrow t \in \mathcal{P}$ to $u \rightarrow v \in \mathcal{P}$ if $s \rightarrow t, u \rightarrow v$ is a (resp. narrowing) chain from $\mathcal{P}$.*

The theorem below establishes that the narrowing dependency graph of a narrowing DP problem is equal to the dependency graph of the rewriting DP problem defined by the same TRS and DP set.

Theorem 3. *Given a narrowing DP problem $\langle \mathcal{P}, \mathcal{R} \rangle$, its narrowing dependency graph is the same as the dependency graph of the rewriting DP problem defined by $\langle \mathcal{P}, \mathcal{R} \rangle$.*

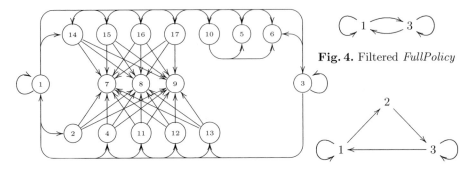

Fig. 4. Filtered *FullPolicy*

Fig. 3. Estimated dependency graph of *FullPolicy*   **Fig. 5.** Dependency Graph

It is well known that computing the exact dependency graph is undecidable and thus several approximations [11] are used to compute an *estimated* dependency graph which includes the exact graph. The following approximation is commonly used.

Definition 8 (Estimated Dependency Graph). [9] *Let $\langle \mathcal{P}, \mathcal{R} \rangle$ be a DP problem. Let* $\mathsf{CAP}_\mathcal{R}(t)$ *be the result of replacing* [3] *all the proper subterms of t with a defined root symbol by a fresh variable, and* $\mathsf{REN}(t)$ *the linearization of t (replacing all ocurrences of a non linear variable with independent fresh variables). The nodes of the estimated dependency graph (EDG) are the pairs of $\mathcal{P}$ and there is an edge from $s^{\#} \to t^{\#}$ to $u^{\#} \to v^{\#}$ iff* $\mathsf{REN}(\mathsf{CAP}_\mathcal{R}(t))$ *and u are unifiable.*

Example 9. For the problem of Example 1 and the set of DPs obtained in Example 6, the EDG is shown in Figure 5.1.

For finite TRSs, infinite chains show up as cycles in the dependency graph[4]. We can analyze separately every chain, that is, every cycle in the dependency graph. This is accomplished by the following DP processor.

Theorem 4 (Dependency Graph Processor). [9] *For a DP problem $\langle \mathcal{P}, \mathcal{R} \rangle$, let Proc be the processor that returns problems $\{\langle \mathcal{P}_1, \mathcal{R} \rangle, \ldots, \langle \mathcal{P}_n, \mathcal{R} \rangle\}$, where $\mathcal{P}_1, \ldots, \mathcal{P}_n$ are the sets of nodes of every cycle in the estimated dependency graph. Proc is sound.*

Example 10. In the graph obtained in the EDG of Example 9, the only cycle consists of (1) and (3). Thus the dependency graph processor deletes all the other dependency pairs, and returns the problems $\{ (\{(1),(3)\}, \mathcal{R}), (\{(1)\}, \mathcal{R}), (\{(3)\}, \mathcal{R}) \}$ corresponding to the graph shown in Figure 4.

---

[3] This function was first defined for approximating loops in dependency graphs in [5], where it is called $\overset{\circ}{t}$.

[4] The converse does not hold, not every cycle corresponds to an infinite chain.

The next processor we adapt is the standard reduction pair processor. The following is the standard notion of reduction pair.

Definition 9 (Reduction Pair). *A reduction pair* $(\succeq, \succ)$ *consists of a quasi-rewrite ordering* $\succeq$ *and an ordering* $\succ$ *with the following properties: (i)* $\succ$ *is closed under substitutions and well founded, and (ii)* $(\succ \circ \succeq) \subseteq \succ$.

For a narrowing DP problem $\langle \mathcal{P}, \mathcal{R} \rangle$, this processor tries to find a reduction pair $(\succeq, \succ)$ and a suitable filtering π s.t. all the filtered $\mathcal{R}$-rules are weakly decreasing w.r.t. $\succeq$, and all filtered $\mathcal{P}$ pairs are weakly or strictly decreasing. For any TRS $\mathcal{P}$ and relation $\succ$, let $\mathcal{P}_\succ = \{s \to t \mid s \succ t\}$.

Theorem 5 (Reduction Pair processor). *Let* $(\mathcal{P}, \mathcal{R})$ *be a narrowing DP problem s.t.* $\mathcal{P}$ *is a cycle[5],* $(\succeq, \succ)$ *be a reduction pair, and* π *be an argument filtering s.t.* $\pi(t)$ *is ground for at least one pair* $s \to t \in \pi(\mathcal{P})$. *Then* $Proc_\pi(\mathcal{P}, \mathcal{R})$ *returns* $\{(\mathcal{P} \setminus \mathcal{P}_{\succ_\pi}, \mathcal{R})\}$ *if* $\mathcal{P}_{\succ_\pi} \cup \mathcal{P}_{\succeq_\pi} = \mathcal{P}$, $\mathcal{P}_{\succ_\pi}$ *is not empty, and* $\mathcal{R}_{\succeq_\pi} = \mathcal{R}$; $\{(\mathcal{P}, \mathcal{R})\}$ *otherwise.*

Note that it is not enough to consider all the pairs in a strongly connected component (SCC) at once, as it is commonly done in rewriting, and that we consider cycles instead. The reason is that the condition of Theorem 2, groundness of one DP rhs per chain (cycle), would not be ensured when working with SCCs instead.

Example 11. Consider a TRS $\mathcal{R}$ with the Dependency Graph of Figure 5. Our dependency graph processor decomposes this problem into three subproblems corresponding to the cycles $\{1\}$, $\{3\}$ and $\{1,2,3\}$. A SCC problem would consider only the last of these three. Suppose we did indeed use SCCs. The reduction pair processor defined above can synthetize a filtering π_2 s.t. the rhs of (2) is ground and an ordering s.t. (3) can be oriented strictly; upon doing so it will remove (3) of the DP problem, thus leaving only $\{1,2\}$. This eliminates two cycles at once, $\{3\}$ and $\{1,2,3\}$. But this is unsound, since we cannot eliminate the cycle in $\{3\}$ unless we find an argument filtering π_3 s.t. the rhs of (3) is ground and there is a suitable ordering.

We claim that it is straightforward to adapt most of the standard DP processors in order to deal with the grounding AF requirement, and due to lack of space we will present only one more processor, which can be used to transform a narrowing DP problem into an ordinary one. Afterwards, any existing DP processor for rewriting becomes applicable.

Theorem 6 (Argument Filtering Processor). *Let* $(\mathcal{P}, \mathcal{R})$ *be a narrowing DP problem s.t.* $\mathcal{P}$ *is a cycle, and* π *be an argument filtering s.t.* $\pi(t)$ *is ground for at least one pair* $s \to t \in \pi(\mathcal{P})$. *Then,* $Proc_\pi(\mathcal{P}, \mathcal{R}) = \{(\mathcal{P}_\pi, \pi(\mathcal{R}))\}$, *where* $\mathcal{P}_\pi$ *is defined as* $\mathcal{P}_\pi = \{\pi(l) \to \pi(r) \mid l \to r \in \mathcal{P}, l \not\trianglerighteq r\}$. $Proc_\pi$ *is a sound narrowing DP processor.*

---

[5] Note that this requirement is easily fulfilled by running the dependency graph processor first.

Finally, we include the subterm refinement in the AF processor as it can be the case that the rhs of a DP becomes a subterm of the lhs after the filtering.

Example 12. The set of narrowing DP problems resulting of Example 10 can be solved by using the AF processor to transform them into rewriting problems.

- $(\{(1)\}, \mathcal{R})$ For this problem soundness requires that $\pi(\mathtt{pckt}) = [1, 3]$. Using the identity for all other symbols, we get the following (rewriting) DP problem that is finite, as one can easily check with a modern termination tool implementing the DP method such as Aprove [10], or Mu-Term [1]:
  $(\{\mathtt{filter}^\#(\mathtt{pckt}(194.179.1.}x\mathtt{:}p, \mathtt{new})) \to \mathtt{filter}^\#(\mathtt{pckt}(\mathtt{secure}, \mathtt{new})\}, \mathcal{R})$
- $(\{(3)\}, \mathcal{R})$ In this case, we proceed in a similar way, and the same AF π allows us to transform the current subproblem into a finite (rewriting) DP problem.
- $(\{(1),(3)\}, \mathcal{R})$ Finally, by using the same AF π, we get a finite DP problem.

This finally proves that the FullPolicy TRS is terminating for narrowing.

6   Conclusion

We have introduced a new technique for termination proofs of narrowing via termination of rewriting that is based on a suitable generalization of dependency pairs. Although several refinements of the notion of dependency pairs such as [11,13] had been proposed previously for termination analysis of TRSs, this is the first time that the notion of dependency pair has been *extended* to deal with narrowing on arbitrary TRSs and queries. This is possible because we first identified the problem of *echoing*, which is ultimately responsible for narrowing non–termination. Our contribution is threefold: 1) we ascertained the suitable notions that allow us to detect when the terms in a narrowing derivation actually do echo; 2) our approach leads to much weaker conditions for verifying the termination of narrowing that subsume all previously known termination of narrowing criteria; 3) the resulting method can be effectively mechanized. We have implemented our technique in a tool that is publicly available[6]. and satisfactorily evaluated this tool on large example sets.

References

1. Alarcón, B., Gutiérrez, R., Iborra, J., Lucas, S.: Proving termination of context-sensitive rewriting with Mu–Term. ENTCS 188, 105–115 (2007)
2. Alpuente, M., Escobar, S., Iborra, J.: Modular Termination of Basic Narrowing. In: Voronkov, A. (ed.) RTA 2008. LNCS, vol. 5117, pp. 1–16. Springer, Heidelberg (2008)
3. Alpuente, M., Escobar, S., Iborra, J.: Dependency Pairs for the Termination of Narrowing. Technical Report DSIC-II/08/08, DSIC-UPV (2008)

---

[6] http://www.dsic.upv.es/users/elp/soft/narradar

4. Alpuente, M., Escobar, S., Iborra, J.: Termination of Narrowing revisited. Theor. Comput. Sci. (to appear, 2008)
5. Alpuente, M., Falaschi, M., Vidal, G.: Compositional Analysis for Equational Horn Programs. In: Rodríguez-Artalejo, M., Levi, G. (eds.) ALP 1994. LNCS, vol. 850, pp. 77–94. Springer, Heidelberg (1994)
6. Arts, T., Giesl, J.: Termination of Term Rewriting using Dependency Pairs. Theor. Comput. Sci. 236(1-2), 133–178 (2000)
7. Christian, J.: Some termination criteria for narrowing and e-narrowing. In: Kapur, D. (ed.) CADE 1992. LNCS, vol. 607, pp. 582–588. Springer, Heidelberg (1992)
8. Escobar, S., Meadows, C., Meseguer, J.: A Rewriting-Based Inference System for the NRL Protocol Analyzer and its Meta-Logical Properties. Theor. Comput. Sci. 367(1-2), 162–202 (2006)
9. Giesl, J., Thiemann, R., Schneider-Kamp, P.: The dependency pair framework: Combining techniques for automated termination proofs. In: Baader, F., Voronkov, A. (eds.) LPAR 2005. LNCS, vol. 3452, pp. 301–331. Springer, Heidelberg (2005)
10. Giesl, J., Thiemann, R., Schneider-Kamp, P., Falke, S.: Automated termination proofs with AProVe. In: van Oostrom, V. (ed.) RTA 2004. LNCS, vol. 3091, pp. 210–220. Springer, Heidelberg (2004)
11. Giesl, J., Thiemann, R., Schneider-Kamp, P., Falke, S.: Mechanizing and Improving Dependency Pairs. J. Autom. Reasoning 37(3), 155–203 (2006)
12. Hanus, M.: The Integration of Functions into Logic Programming: From Theory to Practice. J. Log. Program. 19-20, 583–628 (1994)
13. Hirokawa, N., Middeldorp, A.: Dependency pairs revisited. In: van Oostrom, V. (ed.) RTA 2004. LNCS, vol. 3091, pp. 249–268. Springer, Heidelberg (2004)
14. Hullot, J.-M.: Canonical Forms and Unification. In: Bibel, W. (ed.) CADE 1980. LNCS, vol. 87, pp. 318–334. Springer, Heidelberg (1980)
15. Kirchner, C., Kirchner, H., Santana de Oliveira, A.: Analysis of Rewrite-Based Access Control Policies. In: 3rd Int'l Workshop on Security and Rewriting Techniques, SecreT 2008. ENTCS (to appear, 2008)
16. Meseguer, J., Thati, P.: Symbolic reachability analysis using narrowing and its application to verification of cryptographic protocols. Higher-Order and Symbolic Computation 20(1-2), 123–160 (2007)
17. Nguyen, M.T., Schneider-Kamp, P., de Schreye, D., Giesl, J.: Termination Analysis of Logic Programs based on Dependency Graphs. In: King, A. (ed.) LOPSTR 2007. LNCS, vol. 4915, pp. 8–22. Springer, Heidelberg (2008)
18. Nishida, N., Miura, K.: Dependency graph method for proving termination of narrowing. In: 8th Int'l Workshop on Termination, WST 2006 (2006)
19. Nishida, N., Sakai, M., Sakabe, T.: Narrowing-based simulation of term rewriting systems with extra variables. ENTCS 86(3) (2003)
20. Nishida, N., Vidal, G.: Termination of Narrowing via Termination of Rewriting (2008), http://www.dsic.upv.es/~gvidal
21. TeReSe (ed.): Term Rewriting Systems. Cambridge University Press, Cambridge (2003)

Dynamic Analysis of Bounds Versus Domain Propagation

Christian Schulte[1] and Peter J. Stuckey[2]

[1] ICT, KTH - Royal Institute of Technology, Sweden
cschulte@kth.se
[2] National ICT Australia, Victoria Laboratory,
Department of Computer Science and Software Engineering,
University of Melbourne, Australia
pjs@cs.mu.oz.au

Abstract. Constraint propagation solvers interleave propagation (removing impossible values from variable domains) with search. Previously, Schulte and Stuckey introduced the use of static analysis to determine where in a constraint program domain propagators can be replaced by more efficient bounds propagators and still ensure that the same search space is traversed.

This paper introduces a dynamic yet considerably simpler approach to uncover the same information. The information is obtained by a linear time traversal of an analysis graph that straightforwardly reflects the properties of propagators implementing constraints. Experiments confirm that the simple dynamic method is efficient and that it can be used interleaved with search, taking advantage of the simplification of the constraint graph that arises from search.

1 Introduction

In building a finite domain constraint programming solution to a combinatorial problem a tradeoff arises in the choice of propagation that is used for each constraint: stronger propagation methods are more expensive to execute but may detect failure earlier; weaker propagation methods are (generally) cheaper to execute but may (exponentially) increase the search space explored to find an answer. In this paper we investigate the possibility of dynamically analysing finite domain constraint problems and determining whether the propagation methods used for some constraints could be replaced by simpler, and more efficient alternatives without increasing the size of the search space.

Example 1. Consider the following constraints where $x_1, \ldots, x_4$ range over integer values -3 to 3 (the constraint graph is shown in Fig. 1):

$$x_1 = |x_2|, \quad x_2 \neq x_3, \quad 2x_3 + 3x_4 = 3, \quad x_4 \geq x_1$$

Each constraint could be implemented using domain propagation or bounds propagation. If each constraint uses domain propagation we have stronger information, and the search space explored in order to find all solutions for the

M. Garcia de la Banda and E. Pontelli (Eds.): ICLP 2008, LNCS 5366, pp. 332–346, 2008.

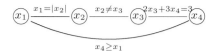

Fig. 1. Binary constraint graph for $x_1 = |x_2|, x_2 \neq x_3, 2x_3 + 3x_4 = 3, x_4 \geq x_1$

problem will be no larger than if we used bounds propagation. The question we ask is: can we get the same search space with bounds propagation?

Domain propagation on $x_4 \geq x_1$ is equivalent to bounds propagation since the constraint only places upper and lower bounds on its variables. This is not the case for the remaining constraints: If $x_2 = 2$ and $x_3 \in [-3 .. 3]$ then domain propagation on $x_2 \neq x_3$ determines that $x_3 \in \{-3, -2, -1, 0, 1, 3\}$ whereas bounds propagation infers nothing. Similarly if $x_1 \in \{0, 2, 3\}$ and $x_2 \in [-3 .. 3]$ then domain propagation on $x_1 = |x_2|$ determines that $x_2 \in \{-3, -2, 0, 2, 3\}$ but bounds propagation infers nothing. From the initial set of values domain propagation determines that $x_3 \in \{-3, 0, 3\}$ and $x_4 \in \{-1, 1, 3\}$ while bounds propagation determines that $x_3 \in [-3 .. 3]$ and $x_4 \in [-1 .. 3]$.

Suppose that we use a labelling strategy that either assigns a variable to its lower bound, or constrains it to be greater than its lower bound. Then none of the constraints added during search creates holes in the domains and depends only on the variable bounds. This is in contrast to a strategy that assigns a variable to its middle domain value, or excludes its middle domain value.

Domain propagation and bounds propagation differs if changing the bounds of some variable (by search) causes change in the bounds of some variable by domain propagation which is not found by bounds propagation.

Suppose search sets $x_3 = 0$, then bounds and domain propagation of $2x_3 + 3x_4 = 3$ sets $x_4 = 1$. Bounds (and domain, as it is identical) propagation of $x_4 \geq x_1$ forces $x_1 \in [-3 .. 0]$. Bounds and domain propagation on $x_1 = |x_2|$ forces $x_2 \in [-1 .. 1]$. Bounds propagation on $x_2 \neq x_3$ makes no changes, resulting in a fixpoint for bounds propagation. Domain propagation on $x_2 \neq x_3$ makes $x_2 \in \{-1, 1\}$. Domain propagation on $x_1 = |x_2|$ then forces $x_1 = 1$. The resulting bounds for x_1 have changed, hence future search is affected.

But we do not need to use domain propagation for all constraints. Domain propagation on $x_2 \neq x_3$ and $x_1 = |x_2|$ is vital, as the above discussion shows. Domain propagation on $2x_2 + 3x_3 = 3$ is not required. As discussed above, the bounds of x_2 and x_3 after domain or bounds propagation are identical, and indeed we can prove this is always the case. Neither of the other constraints on x_2 and x_3 can propagate information from holes in their domains, hence the resulting propagation will be the same.   □

Previously [1] we introduced a static analysis of a finite domain CLP program that was able to determine when to replace domain propagators by bounds propagators without increasing search space. This paper provides a dynamic linear time analysis of the propagation graph that determines whether domain propagators can be replaced by bounds propagators without increasing search space. The approach simplifies and generalizes the previous approach.

Example 2. Consider the constraints

$$x_1 = |x_2|, \quad x_2 \neq x_3, \quad 2x_3 + 3x_4 = x_5, \quad x_4 \geq x_1, \quad x_5 \neq x_4 - 1, \quad x_5 \geq x_2$$

where $x_1, \ldots, x_5$ range over integers from -3 to 3. Analysis using the method of [1] or this paper determines that no domain propagator can be replaced by a bounds propagator. But if search sets $x_5 = 3$ the constraints of Example 1 are obtained, since x_5 is replaced by 3 in $2x_3 + 3x_4 = x_5$, and the redundant constraints $x_5 \neq x_4 - 1$ and $x_5 \geq x_2$ are removed. A dynamic analysis can now detect that bounds propagation can be used for $2x_3 + 3x_4 = 3$.   □

The contributions of this paper are:

- A linear time analysis of the propagation graph that determines whether bounds propagators can be replaced by domain propagators without increasing search space.
- The analysis is dynamic, that is it can be run at any stage during the search. Since propagators become simpler as search proceeds this provides more scope for optimization than a static analysis before search begins.
- We show examples where our analysis detects search space equivalent replacements for both static and dynamic uses and show the possible performance benefits that arise.

2   Propagation-Based Constraint Solving

This section defines our terminology for the basic components of a constraint propagation engine. In this paper we restrict ourselves to finite domain integer constraint solving. Almost all the discussion applies to other forms of finite domain constraint solving such as for sets and multisets.

Domains. A *domain* D is a complete mapping from a fixed (finite) set of variables $\mathcal{V}$ to finite sets of integers. A *false domain* D is a domain with $D(x) = \emptyset$ for some $x \in \mathcal{V}$. A variable $x \in \mathcal{V}$ is *fixed* by a domain D, if $|D(x)| = 1$. The *intersection* of domains D_1 and D_2, denoted $D_1 \sqcap D_2$, is defined by the domain $D(x) = D_1(x) \cap D_2(x)$ for all $x \in \mathcal{V}$. By $-\{x\}$ we denote the variable set $\mathcal{V} - \{x\}$.

A domain D_1 is *stronger* than a domain D_2, written $D_1 \sqsubseteq D_2$, if $D_1(x) \subseteq D_2(x)$ for all $x \in \mathcal{V}$. A domain D_1 is stronger than (equal to) a domain D_2 w.r.t. variables V, denoted $D_1 \sqsubseteq_V D_2$ (resp. $D_1 =_V D_2$), if $D_1(x) \subseteq D_2(x)$ (resp. $D_1(x) = D_2(x)$) for all $x \in V$.

A range is a contiguous set of integers, we use *range* notation $[l .. u]$ to denote the range $\{d \in \mathbb{Z} \mid l \leq d \leq u\}$ when l and u are integers. A domain is a *range domain* if $D(x)$ is a range for all x. Let $D' = \text{range}(D)$ be the smallest range domain containing D, that is, the unique domain $D'(x) = [\inf D(x) .. \sup D(x)]$ for all $x \in \mathcal{V}$. A domain D is *bounds equivalent* to a domain D', written $D \overset{B}{=} D'$ iff $\text{range}(D) = \text{range}(D')$.

Valuations and Constraints. An *integer valuation* θ is a mapping of variables to integer values, written $\{x_1 \mapsto d_1, \ldots, x_n \mapsto d_n\}$. We extend the valuation θ to map expressions and constraints involving the variables in the natural way.

Let vars be the function that returns the set of variables appearing in a valuation. We define a valuation θ to be an element of a domain D, written $\theta \in D$, if $\theta(x_i) \in D(x_i)$ for all $x_i \in \text{vars}(\theta)$.

The *infimum* and *supremum* of an expression e with respect to a domain D are defined as $\inf_D e = \inf \{\theta(e)|\theta \in D\}$ and $\sup_D e = \sup \{\theta(e)|\theta \in D\}$.

A *constraint* c over variables $x_1, \ldots, x_n$ is a set of valuations θ such that $\text{vars}(\theta) = \{x_1, \ldots, x_n\}$. We also define $\text{vars}(c) = \{x_1, \ldots, x_n\}$.

Propagators. We will *implement* a constraint c by a set of propagators $\text{prop}(c)$ that map domains to domains. A *propagator* f is a monotonically decreasing function from domains to domains: $f(D) \sqsubseteq D$, and $f(D_1) \sqsubseteq f(D_2)$ whenever $D_1 \sqsubseteq D_2$. For the purposes of this paper we also assume that propagators are *idempotent*, that is $f(f(D)) = f(D)$ for all domains D. This assumption is just required for defining the edges in the analysis graph correctly, it is not important for the actual execution.

A propagator f is *correct* for a constraint c iff $\{\theta \mid \theta \in D\} \cap c = \{\theta \mid \theta \in f(D)\} \cap c$ for all domains D. This restriction is very weak, for example the identity propagator is correct for all constraints.

The *variables* $\text{vars}(f)$ of a propagator f are $\{x \in \mathcal{V} \mid \exists D. \ f(D)(x) \neq D(x)\} \cup \{x \in \mathcal{V} \mid \exists D_1, D_2. \ D_1 =_{-\{x\}} D_2, f(D_1) \neq_{-\{x\}} f(D_2)\}$. The set includes the variables that can change as a result of applying f, and the variables that can modify the result of f.

Example 3. For the constraint $c \equiv x_1 \leq x_2 + 1$ the function f_1 defined by $f_1(D)(x_1) = \{d \in D(x_1) \mid d \leq \sup_D x_2 + 1\}$ and $f(D)(v) = D(v), v \neq x_1$ is a correct propagator for c. Its variables are x_1 whose domain can be modified by f_1 (the first case of the definition above) and x_2 which can cause the modification of the domain of x_1 (the second case of the definition above). So $\text{vars}(f_1) = \{x_1, x_2\}$. Let $D_1(x_1) = \{1, 5, 8\}$ and $D_1(x_2) = \{1, 5\}$, then $f(D_1) = D_2$ where $D_2(x_1) = D_2(x_2) = \{1, 5\}$. The propagator is idempotent. □

A *propagation solver* $\text{solv}(F, D)$ for a set of propagators F and an initial domain D finds the greatest mutual fixpoint of all the propagators $f \in F$. In other words, $\text{solv}(F, D)$ returns a new domain defined by

$$\text{solv}(F, D) = \text{gfp}(\lambda d.\, \text{iter}(F, d))(D) \qquad \text{iter}(F, D) = \bigsqcap_{f \in F} f(D)$$

where gfp denotes the greatest fixpoint w.r.t $\sqsubseteq$ lifted to functions.

Domain and Bounds Propagators. A consistency notion C gives a condition on domains with respect to constraints. A set of propagators F maintains C-*consistency* for a constraint c, if for a domain D where $f(D) = D, f \in F$ is always C consistent for c. Many propagators in practice are designed to maintain some form of consistency: usually domain or bounds.

The most prominent consistency technique is *arc consistency* [2], which ensures that for each binary constraint, every value in the domain of the first variable has a supporting value in the domain of the second variable that satisfies the constraint. Arc consistency can be naturally extended to *domain consistency* for constraints with more than two variables. A domain D is *domain consistent* for a constraint c if D is the least domain containing all solutions $\theta \in D$ of c. That is, there does not exist $D' \sqsubset D$ such that $\theta \in D \wedge \theta \in c \rightarrow \theta \in D'$.

Define the *domain propagator* $\mathrm{dom}(c)$, for a constraint c as

$$\mathrm{dom}(c)(D)(x) = \{\theta(x) \mid \theta \in D \wedge \theta \in c\} \quad \text{where } x \in \mathrm{vars}(c)$$
$$\mathrm{dom}(c)(D)(x) = D(x) \quad\quad\quad\quad\quad \text{otherwise}$$

Bounds consistency relaxes the consistency requirement to apply only to the lower and upper bounds of each variable x. There are a number of different notions of bounds consistency [3], we give the two most common here.

A domain D is bounds($\mathbb{Z}$) *consistent* for a constraint c if for each $x_i \in \{x_1, \ldots, x_n\} = \mathrm{vars}(c)$, $1 \le i \le n$ and for each $d_i \in \{\inf_D x_i, \sup_D x_i\}$ there exist *integers* d_j with $\inf_D x_j \le d_j \le \sup_D x_j$, $1 \le j \le n, j \ne i$ such that $\theta = \{x_1 \mapsto d_1, \ldots, x_n \mapsto d_n\}$ is an *integer solution* of c.

A domain D is bounds($\mathbb{R}$) *consistent* for a constraint c if for each $x_i \in \{x_1, \ldots, x_n\} = \mathrm{vars}(c)$, $1 \le i \le n$ and for each $d_i \in \{\inf_D x_i, \sup_D x_i\}$ there exist *real numbers* d_j with $\inf_D x_j \le d_j \le \sup_D x_j$, $1 \le j \le n, j \ne i$ such that $\theta = \{x_1 \mapsto d_1, \ldots, x_n \mapsto d_n\}$ is a *real solution* of c.

A propagator f is a *bounds propagator* if it only relies on bounds and creates new bounds

$$\forall D.\ f(D) = \mathrm{range}(f(\mathrm{range}(D))) \sqcap D$$

We can define bounds propagators for the two consistency notions above. A bounds($\mathbb{Z}$) *propagator*, $\mathrm{zbnd}(c)$ for a constraint c ensures that $\mathrm{zbnd}(c)(D)$ is bounds($\mathbb{Z}$) consistent with c, while a bounds($\mathbb{R}$) *propagator*, $\mathrm{rbnd}(c)$ ensures bounds($\mathbb{R}$) consistency.

3   An Abstraction of Propagation

The aim of this paper is to find where we can replace a propagator f by a bounds propagator f^B without changing the search space, under the assumption that

$$\forall D.\ f(\mathrm{range}(D))) \overset{B}{=} f^B(D)$$

That is, applied to range domains the propagators give the same bounds. Note that if $f = \mathrm{dom}(c)$ and $f^B = \mathrm{zbnd}(c)$ then this property holds. We will not attempt to replace domain propagators by bounds($\mathbb{R}$) propagators since the property does not hold.

Example 4. Consider the constraint $c \equiv x = 3y + 5z$, and the range domain $D(x) = [2 .. 7]$, $D(y) = [0 .. 2]$ and $D(z) = [-1 .. 2]$, then $\mathrm{dom}(c)(D)(x) = \{3, 5, 6\}$ while $\mathrm{rbnd}(c)(D)(x) = [2 .. 7]$. The bounds are different.   □

In order to detect that we can replace domain propagators by bounds propagators, we build an analysis graph that shows how each propagator reacts to holes and creates holes in the domain of its variables. The analysis graph is in some sense an abstraction of the constraint (hyper)graph where an edge is an abstract propagator. Analysis of the graph corresponds to executing the abstract propagators to fixpoint, hence is an abstract propagation process.

The nodes of an analysis graph G are labelled by variables $v \in \mathcal{V}$, as well as the special nodes $source \oplus$ and $sink \ominus$. The analysis graph G for a set of propagators F contains directed edges for each propagator f as follows:

- An edge $x \xrightarrow{f} y$ between two variables x and y labelled by a propagator f indicates that f can propagate holes in the domain of x to the domain of y.

  There is an edge $x \xrightarrow{f} y$ in G, iff there exist domains D, D' and variables $S \subseteq \mathcal{V}$ with $D' =_{\mathcal{V}-S} D$, $D \overset{B}{=} D'$, $D'(x) \neq D(x)$, and $x \in S$ such that $f(D')(y) \neq f(D)(y) \cap D'(y)$. That is, D' differs from D only because of the removal of internal values for variables S including x.

- An edge $x \xrightarrow{f} \ominus$ between variable x and the sink indicates that by propagating f, holes in the domain of x can cause bounds changes on other variables.

  There is an edge $x \xrightarrow{f} \ominus$ in G, iff there exist domains D, D' and variables $S \subseteq \mathcal{V}$ with $D' =_{\mathcal{V}-S} D$, $D \overset{B}{=} D'$, $D'(x) \neq D(x)$, and $x \in S$ such that $f(D') \overset{B}{\neq} f(D)$.

- An edge $\oplus \xrightarrow{f} x$ between the source and variable x indicates that the propagator f can create holes in the domain of x from a range domain.

  There is an edge $\oplus \xrightarrow{f} x$ in G, iff there exists a range domain D (that is, $D = \text{range}(D)$) such that $f(D)(x) \neq \text{range}(f(D))(x)$. That is, applying f to a range domain D can create a hole in the domain of x.

As an example, let us consider the edges in the analysis graph for some common domain propagators (a full list is given in Table 1):

$\text{dom}(x = y + k)$ $(x, y \in \mathcal{V}, k \in \mathbb{Z})$: $\{x \xrightarrow{f} y, y \xrightarrow{f} x\}$. Holes are propagated, but neither created nor converted to bounds.

$\text{dom}(x \neq y)$ $(x, y \in \mathcal{V})$: $\{\oplus \xrightarrow{f} x, \oplus \xrightarrow{f} y\}$. Holes are not propagated, but created.

$\text{dom}(x = k \times y)$ $(x, y \in \mathcal{V}, k \in \mathbb{Z})$: $\{x \xrightarrow{f} y, y \xrightarrow{f} x, \oplus \xrightarrow{f} x\}$. Holes are propagated and holes for x are created (as only multiples of k are kept for x).

$\text{dom}(x = |y|)$ $(x, y \in \mathcal{V})$: $\{x \xrightarrow{f} y, y \xrightarrow{f} x, \oplus \xrightarrow{f} y, y \xrightarrow{f} \ominus\}$. Holes are transmitted, holes for y are created (by bounds of x), and holes in y can change bounds (for x).

$\text{dom}(\sum_{i=1}^{n} x_i \leq k)$ $(x_i \in \mathcal{V}, k \in \mathbb{Z})$: $\{\}$. No holes are created or transmitted.

$\text{dom}(\sum_{i=1}^{n} x_i = k)$ $(x_i \in \mathcal{V}, k \in \mathbb{Z})$: $\{x_i \xrightarrow{f} x_j \mid 1 \leq i \neq j \leq n\}$. Holes are transmitted between each pair of variables.

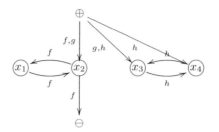

Fig. 2. Analysis graph for $x_1 = |x_2|$, $x_2 \neq x_3$, $2x_3 + 3x_4 = 3$, $x_4 \geq x_1$

$\mathrm{dom}(b \Leftrightarrow x = y)$ $(b, x, y \in \mathcal{V}$, b Boolean): $\{x \xrightarrow{f} y, y \xrightarrow{f} x, \oplus \xrightarrow{f} x, \oplus \xrightarrow{f} y, x \xrightarrow{f} \ominus, y \xrightarrow{f} \ominus\}$. Unsurprisingly the union of $x = y$ and $x \neq y$, except that holes in x and y can create bounds changes in b. For example, $D(x) = \{1, 3, 5\}$ and $D(y) = \{2, 4, 6\}$ yields $b = 0$.

$\mathrm{dom}(\mathtt{alldifferent}(x_1, \ldots, x_n))$ $(x_i \in \mathcal{V})$: $\{x_i \xrightarrow{f} x_j \mid 1 \leq i \neq j \leq n\} \cup \{\oplus \xrightarrow{f} x_i, x_i \xrightarrow{f} \ominus \mid 1 \leq i \leq n\}$. The propagator can do everything. But we should be careful, we do have a bounds($\mathbb{Z}$) propagator that will give the same bounds, if no other propagator causes holes in the domains.

$\mathrm{dom}(x = \min(y, z))$ $(x, y, z \in \mathbb{Z})$: $\{x \xrightarrow{f} y, y \xrightarrow{f} x, x \xrightarrow{f} z, z \xrightarrow{f} x, y \xrightarrow{f} \ominus, z \xrightarrow{f} \ominus\}$. There is no direct transmission from y to z, and no changes of ranges from holes. Notice that for $D(x) = \{1, 3, 4\}$, $D(y) = \{1, 3, 5\}$, $D(z) = \{2, 4, 6\}$ the constraint includes the solutions $(1, 1, 2), (3, 3, 4), (4, 5, 4), (3, 3, 6)$. But changing $D(z)$ to $\{2, 6\}$ changes the upper bound of x.

Example 5. The analysis graph for the problem of Example 1 is shown in Figure 2, where $f = \mathrm{dom}(x_1 = |x_2|)$, $g = \mathrm{dom}(x_2 \neq x_3)$, $h = \mathrm{dom}(2x_3 + 3x_4 = 3)$ and $\mathrm{dom}(x_4 \geq x_1)$ does not generate any edges. The reasoning in Example 1 is now explicitly viewable. The path from $\oplus \xrightarrow{g} x_2 \xrightarrow{f} \ominus$ shows that holes created by g can cause bounds to change through f as illustrated in Example 1.

While h can create new holes (edges from $\oplus$ to x_3 and x_4), these holes can never change the bounds of a variable (reach $\ominus$). Hence h can be replaced by a bounds($\mathbb{Z}$) propagator, without changing propagation. □

In order to replace propagators we have to take into account the constraints that will be added by search. Edges are added corresponding to the behaviour of the search procedure. If search relies (f refers to the labelling):

- on bounds information to make decisions and only adds bounds constraints, no edges are added (e.g. standard $\mathtt{labelling}(x_1, \ldots, x_n)$);
- on all domain information to make decisions but only add bounds constraints, $\{x_i \xrightarrow{f} \ominus \mid 1 \leq i \leq n\}$ are added (e.g. $\mathtt{labellingff}(x_1, \ldots, x_n)$ for first-fail labelling);
- on all domain information and may add constraints that add holes to domains, $\{\oplus \xrightarrow{f} x_i, x_i \xrightarrow{f} \ominus \mid 1 \leq i \leq n\}$ are added (e.g. middle out labelling $\mathtt{labellingmid}(x_1, \ldots, x_n)$).

Table 1. The table lists analysis graph edges for primitive constraints and some labellings, where $N \xrightarrow{f} M$ with $N \subseteq \{\oplus\} \cup \mathcal{V}$ and $M \subseteq \{\ominus\} \cup \mathcal{V}$ denotes the set $\{n \xrightarrow{f} m \mid n \in N, m \in M, n \neq m\} - \{\oplus \xrightarrow{f} \ominus\}$. The last column shows whether a bounds($\mathbb{Z}$) propagator for the constraint is commonly available.

Constraint	G	zbnd
$\sum_{i=1}^{n} a_i x_i \leq d$	$\emptyset$	✔
$x_0 = d$	$\emptyset$	✔
$a_1 x_1 + a_2 x_2 = d, \|a_i\| = 1$	$\{x_1 \xrightarrow{f} x_2, x_2 \xrightarrow{f} x_1\}$	✔
$a_1 x_1 + a_2 x_2 = d$	$\{x_1 \xrightarrow{f} x_2, x_2 \xrightarrow{f} x_1, \oplus \xrightarrow{f} x_1, \oplus \xrightarrow{f} x_2\}$	✔
$\sum_{i=1}^{n} a_i x_i = d, n > 2,$	$\{\oplus, x_1, \ldots, x_n\} \xrightarrow{f} \{x_1, \ldots, x_n, \ominus\}$	
$\sum_{i=1}^{n} a_i x_i = d, n > 2, \|a_i\| = 1$	$\{x_1, \ldots, x_n\} \xrightarrow{f} \{x_1, \ldots, x_n\}$	✔
$\sum_{i=1}^{n} a_i x_i \neq d$	$\{\oplus\} \xrightarrow{f} \{x_1, \ldots, x_n\}$	✔
$x_0 \Leftrightarrow \sum_{i=1}^{n} a_i x_i \leq d$	$\emptyset$	✔
$x_0 \Leftrightarrow \sum_{i=1}^{n} a_i x_i = d$	$\{\oplus, x_1, \ldots, x_n\} \xrightarrow{f} \{x_1, \ldots, x_n, \ominus\}$	
$x_1 = \neg x_2$	$\emptyset$	✔
$x_1 = (x_2 \wedge x_3)$	$\emptyset$	✔
$x_1 = x_2 \times x_3$	$\{\oplus, x_1, x_2, x_3\} \xrightarrow{f} \{x_1, x_2, x_3, \ominus\}$	
$x_1 = x_2 \times x_2 \wedge x_2 \geq 0$	$\{x_1 \xrightarrow{f} x_2, x_2 \xrightarrow{f} x_1, \oplus \xrightarrow{f} x_1\}$	✔
$x_1 = x_2 \times x_2$	$\{x_1 \xrightarrow{f} x_2, x_2 \xrightarrow{f} x_1, \oplus \xrightarrow{f} x_1, x_2 \xrightarrow{f} \ominus\}$	✔
$x_1 = \|x_2\|$	$\{x_1 \xrightarrow{f} x_2, x_2 \xrightarrow{f} x_1, \oplus \xrightarrow{f} x_2, x_2 \xrightarrow{f} \ominus\}$	✔
$x_0 = \min(x_1, \ldots, x_n)$	$\{x_0\} \xrightarrow{f} \{x_1, \ldots, x_n, \ominus\} \cup \{x_1, \ldots, x_n\} \xrightarrow{f} \{x_0\}$	✔
$\texttt{alldifferent}(x_1, \ldots, x_n)$	$\{\oplus, x_1, \ldots, x_n\} \xrightarrow{f} \{x_1, \ldots, x_n, \ominus\}$	✔
$\texttt{default}(x_1, \ldots, x_n)$	$\{\oplus, x_1, \ldots, x_n\} \xrightarrow{f} \{x_1, \ldots, x_n, \ominus\}$	
$\texttt{labelling}(x_1, \ldots, x_n)$	$\emptyset$	
$\texttt{labellingff}(x_1, \ldots, x_n)$	$\{x_1, \ldots, x_n\} \xrightarrow{f} \{\ominus\}$	
$\texttt{labellingmid}(x_1, \ldots, x_n)$	$\{\oplus\} \xrightarrow{f} \{x_1, \ldots, x_n\} \cup \{x_1, \ldots, x_n\} \xrightarrow{f} \{\ominus\}$	

4   Main Result

A path from $\oplus$ to $\ominus$ is evidence of where bounds information can create holes in domains, and where holes then can change bounds. We must keep track of the holes in the domains in order to have accurate bounds information.

Theorem 1. *Let G be the analysis graph for a set of propagators F. Let $B \subseteq F$ be the set of propagators such that G contains no paths from $\oplus$ to $\ominus$ labelled with two or more propagators. Then $F' = \{f^B \mid f \in B\} \cup \{f \mid f \in F - B\}$ is such that $\text{solv}(F, D_0) \stackrel{B}{=} \text{solv}(F', D_0)$ for all range domains D_0.*

Proof. The proof is by induction. Let f_1, f_2, ..., f_n be the sequence of propagators applied in calculating $\text{solv}(F, D_0)$. Let

$$D_1 = f_1(D_0), D_2 = f_2(D_1), \ldots, D_n = f_n(D_{n-1}) = \text{solv}(F, D_0)$$

We let g_i be the corresponding propagator to f_i in F', that is $g_i = f_i$ if $f_i \in F - B$ and $g_i = f_i^B$ if $f_i \in B$. Define

$$D_0' = D_0, D_1' = g_1(D_0'), D_2' = g_2(D_1'), \ldots, D_n' = g_n(D_{n-1}')$$

be the analogous sequence of propagators in F'. Note that since $\forall D''. f_i(D'') \sqsubseteq g_i(D'')$ we have that $D_i \sqsubseteq D_i'$. We show that $D_i \overset{B}{=} D_i'$ for $0 \leq i \leq n$.

We show by induction: for each $0 \leq i \leq n$ that $D_i \overset{B}{=} D_i'$, and for each $v \in \mathcal{V}$ where $D_i(v)$ is not a range then there is a path from $\oplus$ to v in the analysis graph.

Clearly the induction hypothesis holds for $D_0 = D_0'$. Assume the hypothesis holds for $0 \leq i < K$.

Suppose to the contrary that $D_K \overset{B}{\neq} D_K'$. If $D_{K-1} =_{\text{vars}(f_K)} \text{range}(D_{K-1})$ then $D_K = f_K(D_{K-1}) = f_K(\text{range}(D_{K-1})) \overset{B}{=} g_K(D_{K-1}) \overset{B}{=} g_k(D_{K-1}') = D_K'$. Contradiction. Hence there exists $v \in \text{vars}(f_K)$ such that $D_{K-1}(v)$ is not a range. By the induction hypothesis, there is a path from $\oplus$ to v. And by definition $v \overset{f_K}{\rightarrow} \ominus$ is in the analysis graph G. The witnesses for D', D, S and x in the definition of $v \overset{f_K}{\rightarrow} \ominus$ are $D' = D_{K-1}$, $D = D_{K-1}'$, $S = \text{vars}(f_K)$ and $x = v$. Hence all propagators modifying the interior of the domain of v are either f_K or are not in B. In the first case, since f_K is idempotent $f_k(D_{K-1}) = f_K(\text{range}(D_{K-1})$ as no other propagators have changed the interior of the domains of $\text{vars}(f_K)$. Thus $D_K = f_K(D_{K-1}) = f_K(\text{range}(D_{K-1})) \overset{B}{=} g_K(D_{K-1}') = D_K'$. Contradiction. In the second case since all propagators acting on the interior of domains of $\text{vars}(f_K)$ are in $F - B$ we have that $D_{K-1} =_{\text{vars}(f_K)} D_{K-1}'$, and $f_K = g_K$ hence $D_K \overset{B}{=} D_K'$. Contradiction. As a result we have that $D_K \overset{B}{=} D_K'$.

Suppose that $D_K(v)$ is not a range, and $D_K(v) \neq D_{K-1}(v)$

If $D_{K-1} =_{\text{vars}(f_K)} \text{range}(D_{K-1})$ then we have an edge $\oplus \overset{f_K}{\rightarrow} v$ in the analysis graph G. The witnesses D and x in the definition of $\oplus \overset{f_K}{\rightarrow} v$ are $D = \text{range}(D_{K-1})$ and $x = v$, since $D = \text{range}(D)$ and $f_K(D)(v) = f_K(D_{K-1})(v) \neq \text{range}(f_K(D))(v)$.

Otherwise $D_{K-1} \neq_{\text{vars}(f_K)} \text{range}(D_{K-1})$, and so there exists $u \in \text{vars}(f_K)$ where $D_{K-1}(u)$ is not a range. Then we have an edge $u \overset{f_K}{\rightarrow} v$ in the analysis graph G. The witnesses are $D' = D_{K-1}$ and $D = \text{range}(D_{K-1})$, $S = \text{vars}(f_K)$, $x = u$ and $y = v$. By the induction hypothesis there is a path from $\oplus$ to u in the analysis graph, and hence also to v.

As a result of the proof by induction we have that $D_n \overset{B}{=} D_n'$. Then since D_n is a fixpoint for all f_i, and since g_i where they differ from f_i only depend on bounds, we have that D_n is a fixpoint for all g_i. Now $\text{solv}(F', D_0)$ is the greatest fixpoint of F' less than D_0 and since D_n is such a fixpoint we have that $D_n \sqsubseteq \text{solv}(F', D_0) \sqsubseteq D_n'$ and hence $\text{solv}(F, D_0) = D_n \overset{B}{=} \text{solv}(F', D_0)$. $\square$

Note that the proof can be applied for *non-range* domains D, by adding artificial propagators f that remove the internal values of range(D) to give D. In effect we add edges $\oplus \xrightarrow{f} v$ for each v where $D(v) \neq$ range(D)(v).

Importantly the theorem is based on propagators rather than constraints, hence we might have bounds propagators in the original set of propagators F we are trying to improve.

Example 6. Consider propagators for the SEND+MORE=MONEY problem: $f = \text{dom}(\texttt{alldifferent}(S, E, N, D, M, O, R, Y))$, a large linear bounds propagator rbnd($SEND + MORE = MONEY$), dom($S > 0$), and dom($M > 0$). The only edges are $\{x \xrightarrow{f} y \mid x, y \in \{S, E, N, D, M, O, R, Y\}, x \neq y\} \cup \{\oplus \xrightarrow{f} x, x \xrightarrow{f} \ominus \mid x \in \{S, E, N, D, M, O, R, Y\}\}$. All propagators can be replaced by bounds propagators. If the long linear constraint used domain propagation the propagator for the `alldifferent` constraint could not be improved. □

5   Finding Which Propagators to Replace

In order to use Theorem 1 we need to determine which propagators appear on paths from $\oplus$ to $\ominus$, involving at least two propagators. Rather than track (a possibly exponential number of) paths explicitly, we mark each variable x by the propagators on paths from $\oplus$ to x, and by the propagators on paths from x to $\ominus$. We can check each edge for a propagator f to see whether it causes f to be on a path from $\oplus$ to $\ominus$, involving at least two propagators.

The algorithm is shown in Figure 3. Assuming that munion(m_1, m_2) is simply defined as $m_1 \cup m_2$, the propagators on a path from $\oplus$ to n are stored in source[n], while sink[n] holds the propagators on a path from n to $\ominus$. The **forward** marking starts from all variables adjacent to $\oplus$ and marks them, and then follows any edges. It checks if the variable has been marked previously with the current set and if so immediately returns. The **backward** marking works analogously. Finally the new propagator set F' is constructed by checking each edge for propagator f, and if f takes part in a path from $\oplus$ to $\ominus$ involving at least two propagators, adding the original version f to F', otherwise adding the bounds version f^B.

Theorem 2. *Let G be the analysis graph for F. Let B be the set of propagators $f \in F$ such that G contains no paths from $\oplus$ to $\ominus$ labelled with two or more propagators. Then* analyse(F) $= \{f^B \mid f \in B\} \cup \{f \mid f \in F - B\}$ *and the complexity of* analyse(F) *is $O(G)$.*

Proof. (Sketch) Under the assumption that munion(m_1, m_2) is simply defined as $m_1 \cup m_2$ it is easy to see that variables source[n] and sink[n] contain the set of propagators appearing in paths from $\oplus$ to n and n to $\ominus$ respectively. The domain-test $|\text{source}[n_1] \cup \{f\} \cup \text{sink}[n_2]| > 1$ correctly determines if f appears on a path from $\oplus$ to $\ominus$ involving at least two propagators.

Now consider the actual definition of munion(m_1, m_2). This is in effect an abstraction of the original algorithm where all sets of cardinality greater than 1 are

$\mathsf{munion}(m_1,m_2)$
  if $(|m_1 \cup m_2| > 1)$ **return** F **else return** $m_1 \cup m_2$

$\mathsf{forward}(x,m)$
  if $(m \subseteq \mathrm{source}[x])$ **return**
  $\mathrm{source}[x] \leftarrow \mathsf{munion}(\mathrm{source}[x],m)$
  for $(x \xrightarrow{g} y \in G)$
    $\mathsf{forward}(y,\mathsf{munion}(\mathrm{source}[x],\{g\}))$

$\mathsf{backward}(x,m)$
  if $(m \subseteq \mathrm{sink}[x])$ **return**
  $\mathrm{sink}[x] \leftarrow \mathsf{munion}(\mathrm{sink}[x],m)$
  for $(y \xrightarrow{g} x \in G)$
    $\mathsf{backward}(y,\mathsf{munion}(\mathrm{sink}[x],\{g\}))$

$\mathsf{domain}(f,G)$
  return $\exists n_1 \xrightarrow{f} n_2 \in G.\ |\mathsf{munion}(\mathrm{source}[n_1], \mathsf{munion}(\{f\}, \mathrm{sink}[n_2]))| > 1$

$\mathsf{analyse}(F)$
  let G be the analysis graph for F
  for $(n \in \mathcal{V} \cup \{\oplus, \ominus\})$
    $\mathrm{source}[n] \leftarrow \mathrm{sink}[n] \leftarrow \emptyset$
  for $(\oplus \xrightarrow{f} x \in G)$
    $\mathsf{forward}(x,\{f\})$
  for $(x \xrightarrow{f} \ominus \in G)$
    $\mathsf{backward}(x,\{f\})$
  return $\{f \mid f \in F \land \mathsf{domain}(f,G)\} \cup \{f^B \mid f \in F \land \neg\mathsf{domain}(f,G)\}$

Fig. 3. Propagation analysis of the set of propagators F

replaced by F. This does not change the result of the domain-test. For the test to fail, $\mathrm{source}[n_1]$ and $\mathrm{sink}[n_2]$ are either $\{f\}$ or $\emptyset$, and these results are maintained by the actual definition of $\mathsf{munion}(m_1,m_2)$. For the test to pass $|\mathrm{source}[n_1] \cup \{f\} \cup \mathrm{sink}[n_2]| > 1$ and hence also $|\mathsf{munion}(\mathrm{source}[n_1], \mathsf{munion}(\{f\}, \mathrm{sink}[n_2]))| > 1$. Hence the algorithm is correct.

The complexity result follows since $\mathsf{forward}$ can only update $\mathrm{source}[n]$ at most twice, after which $\mathrm{source}[n] = F$ and all further calls immediately return. Hence the complexity of all calls to $\mathsf{forward}$ is $O(G)$. The same reasoning applies to $\mathsf{backward}$ and hence to $\mathsf{analyse}$.   □

The astute reader will have noticed that, while $\mathsf{analyse}$ is linear in the size of the analysis graph, the analysis graph may be quadratically larger in size than the constraint graph, since some propagators add edges $\{x_i \xrightarrow{f} x_j \mid 1 \le i \ne j \le n\}$. This is fixed by replacing $\{x_i \xrightarrow{f} x_j \mid 1 \le i \ne j \le n\}$ by $\{x_i \xrightarrow{f} z, z \xrightarrow{f} x_i \mid 1 \le i \le n\}$ where z is a new variable. The resulting analysis graph is linear in the size of the constraint graph and gives the same results as the original graph.

Implementation. The algorithm in Figure 3 has been implemented in Gecode, but the decisions made in the implementation should readily carry over to other constraint programming systems.

While treatment of variables is generic in the analysis algorithm, the way how propagators are analysed depends on the particular propagator. Propagators are implemented as objects in Gecode. Propagators provide methods for propagation, creation, deletion, and so on. For analysis, we add an `analyse` method that can be implemented for each individual propagator: execution of the method adds the edges for the propagator to the analysis graph.

The values of source[x] and sink[x] are directly stored in the variable x. Rather than storing a set of propagators F for source[x] and sink[x], it is sufficient to use a pointer to a propagator f (if $F = \{f\}$) and two special marks $\langle 0 \rangle$ ($|F| = 0$) and $\langle 2 \rangle$ ($|F| \geq 2$). Then $\mathsf{munion}(m_1, m_2)$ returns m as follows: if $m_1 = m_2$ then $m = m_1$; if $m_1 = \langle 2 \rangle$ or $m_2 = \langle 2 \rangle$ then $m = \langle 2 \rangle$; if $m_1 = \langle 0 \rangle$ then $m = m_2$; if $m_2 = \langle 0 \rangle$ then $m = m_1$.

6   Experimental Evaluation

All experiments use Gecode, a C++-based constraint programming library [4]. Gecode is one of the fastest constraint programming systems currently available, benchmarks comparing Gecode to other systems can be found on Gecode's webpage. The version used here corresponds to Gecode 2.1.1. Gecode has been compiled with the Microsoft Visual Studio Express Edition 2008 (32 bit).

All examples have been run on a Mac Pro with two 2.8 GHz Quad Core Xeon 5400 CPUs and 8192 MB main memory running 64 bit Windows Vista. Runtimes are the average of 25 runs with a coefficient of deviation less than 3%.

Static Analysis. Table 2 shows the runtime (time, in milliseconds), which percentage of the runtime is spent on the analysis in the optimized case, and the number of nodes during search (as to be expected, the same for both). Examples with a – as entry have been stopped after a runtime of one hour. The examples

Table 2. Static analysis

	original	optimized		both	
Example	time	time		analysis	nodes
is-20	127.800	0.054	(−100.0%)	15.1%	13
is-40	–	0.162	(−100.0%)	17.5%	28
vc-20	87.680	0.029	(−100.0%)	27.8%	4
vc-40	–	0.076	(−100.0%)	36.9%	6
photo-eq	890.400	429.240	(−51.8%)	0.0%	5 472
photo-lq	714.480	78.800	(−89.0%)	0.0%	10 350
money	0.020	0.017	(−18.0%)	5.6%	4
donald	21.722	21.220	(−2.3%)	0.0%	5 788
magic-5	1 324.880	1 103.920	(−16.7%)	0.0%	89 016

are chosen to provide for a direct comparison with the results reported in [1], there also more information on the benchmarks can be found.

The examples is-n (independent sets) and vc-n (vertex cover) for random graphs with n nodes are modeled in the natural way using Boolean variables. The constraints are all inequalities except the objective function which is defined using a large linear equation with unit coefficients (optimized by analysis). photo-* are simple placement problems and use reified constraints for expressing satisfaction of preferences with a Boolean variable. The total satisfaction then is computed by a large linear equation ranging over these Boolean variables. While photo-eq uses reified linear equations, photo-lq uses reified linear inequalities to express preferences. Analysis shows for photo-eq that bounds propagation can be used on the large linear equation. For photo-lq, bounds propagation can also be used for the single occurring alldifferent constraint. The well-known examples money (see Example 6), donald ($DONALD + GERALD = ROBERT$), and magic square magic-5 use bounds propagation for linear equations with more than three variables. Analysis shows that bounds propagation can be used for the single alldifferent constraint in each example.

The analysis is run before evaluating solv for the first time (such that infeasible domain propagators could be optimized away). The benefit of the analysis clearly outweighs its cost (for already medium sized examples the cost is zero). This is true for the expensive (exponential) and often infeasible domain propagators for long linear equations (for example, is-n and vc-n) but also for feasible domain propagators such as alldifferent.

Dynamic Analysis and Analysis Cost. In the following we evaluate a variation of the analysis in order to assess its cost and benefit. We assume that the feasibility of domain propagation is classified as follows. For a constraint c (or for a propagator f implementing c) a predicate feasible(c) holds, iff domain propagation is sufficiently efficient for c. For example, one could define feasible($\sum_{i=1}^{n} a_i x_i = d$) to hold iff $n \leq 3$, and feasible(alldifferent($x_1, \ldots, x_n$)) to always hold.

Initially, all constraints are propagated by bounds propagators. Propagators might become feasible during search(e.g., some x_i in $\sum_{i=1}^{n} a_i x_i = d$ become fixed). A bounds propagator will be replaced by a domain propagator, if it is feasible and the analysis shows that domain propagation might be beneficial. Hence, we construct the analysis graph G as follows: if the propagator is a domain propagator, the edges are entered as before. If the propagator is a feasible bounds propagator for the constraint c, the edges for dom(c) are entered. After running the analysis phase, domain propagators are replaced by bounds propagators if possible as before. If domain(f, G) holds for a feasible bounds propagator f, it is replaced by a corresponding domain propagator.

By this, only bounds propagators that are feasible *and can potentially improve propagation* are replaced by domain propagators. Just using feasibility alone would, in all benchmark examples discussed above, immediately replace the bounds propagator for alldifferent by a useless domain propagator. Note that as search proceeds, a bounds propagator for a constraint can be replaced by

Table 3. Dynamic analysis and analysis cost

Example	$n = 1$		$n = 5$		$n = 10$		$n = 25$	
	nodes	time	nodes	time	nodes	time	nodes	time
(a) analysis with optimization								
alpha	−80.7%	−40.7%	−72.8%	−43.0%	−68.4%	−9.9%	−32.6%	−4.5%
money-c	±0.0%	+45.6%	±0.0%	+11.0%	±0.0%	+5.9%	±0.0%	+3.5%
donald-c	−7.5%	+117.7%	−6.5%	+37.9%	−2.8%	+25.0%	−0.9%	+12.6%
magic-4	−15.2%	+485.3%	−6.5%	+314.0%	−3.4%	+209.1%	−1.7%	+120.5%
(b) only analysis								
alpha	±0.0%	+91.8%	±0.0%	+20.8%	±0.0%	+10.7%	±0.0%	+5.1%
money-c	±0.0%	+43.0%	±0.0%	+10.6%	±0.0%	+6.0%	±0.0%	+2.5%
donald-c	±0.0%	+99.8%	±0.0%	+22.7%	±0.0%	+12.7%	±0.0%	+4.7%
magic-4	±0.0%	+94.7%	±0.0%	+20.8%	±0.0%	+10.9%	±0.0%	+5.3%

a domain propagator when becoming feasible, and later be replaced by a bounds propagator when the analysis finds that bounds propagation is sufficient.

Table 3 shows the runtime and the number of nodes during search relative to execution of the examples without running any analysis and using bounds propagators. The analysis is run every n-th time before solv is computed by the solver, where for (a) bounds and domain propagators are replaced, while for (b) the analysis results are ignored (measuring analysis cost). It is important that the analysis is run before solv is evaluated as the replacement of bounds by domain propagators might require re-evaluation of solv. The examples all use an alldifferent constraint and some linear equations (money-c and donald-c use several linear equations for a model using carries in the letter equation).

Clearly, running the analysis before every evaluation of solv is infeasible, however running it every 10 times reduces the overhead to around 10%: that means the analysis is efficient enough to be actually run dynamically. It may be that an incremental version of the analysis could reduce this overhead substantially. In cases where replacing bounds by domain propagators is useful as the search space shrinks, the additional cost of domain propagation might still be too high. There is at least some evidence (alpha) that dynamic analysis can be beneficial, and we have just scratched the surface of possibilities for automatic selection of propagation style.

7   Conclusion and Related Work

The original work on analysing when domain propagation could be replaced by bounds propagation [1] works in a completely different way. Propagators are classified as *bounds-preserving*: meaning that on range domains they always give range domains; and *endpoint-relevant*: meaning that the bounds resulting from applying the propagator only depend on the bounds it is applied to. Bounds preserving propagators are propagators with no edges $\oplus \xrightarrow{f} x$, while endpoint-relevant propagators are propagators with no edges $x \xrightarrow{f} \ominus$. Two analyses are undertaken to find (Boolean) bounds preservation and endpoint relevant descriptions for the context of each constraint. Each constraint is then given the appropriate propagator by examining its context. The algorithms used in the approach are $O(nm)$ where n is the size of the constraint graph and m is the number of constraints. The analysis is substantially more complicated to implement than the approach in this paper, and indeed has never been implemented.

The approach of this paper is

- considerably simpler, easier to prove, and implemented;
- $O(n)$ where n is the size of the constraint graph; and
- more expressive, although this does not lead to more replacement of domain propagators by bounds propagators. An example is the description for $\mathrm{dom}(x_1 = |x_2|)$ which in the new approach tracks the behaviour of x_1 and x_2 more accurately than is possible in the old approach.

As future work we will consider proving and implementing a stronger version of Theorem 1 where we let B be the set of all propagators where there is no path from $\oplus$ to $\ominus$ where adjacent edges have to be from different propagators.

Example 7. Consider the propagators $f = \mathrm{dom}(x_1 = x_2)$, $g = \mathrm{dom}(x_2 = |x_3|)$, and $h = \mathrm{dom}(x_3 = x_4)$, which generate the analysis graph $x_1 \overset{f}{\to} x_2$, $x_2 \overset{f}{\to} x_1$, $\oplus \overset{g}{\to} x_2$, $x_2 \overset{g}{\to} x_3$, $x_3 \overset{g}{\to} x_2$, $x_3 \overset{g}{\to} \ominus$, $x_3 \overset{h}{\to} x_4$, $x_4 \overset{h}{\to} x_3$. The analysis detects that nothing can be a bounds propagator. But indeed all could be replaced because any holes generated by g are only fed back to itself, and hence cannot change bounds. There are no alternating paths from $\oplus$ to $\ominus$. □

Acknowledgements. Part of the work has been carried out while the first author has been a visiting researcher at the NICTA Victoria research laboratory, Melbourne, Australia. The authors thank Mikael Z. Lagerkvist, Guido Tack, and the anonymous reviewers for helpful comments.

References

1. Schulte, C., Stuckey, P.J.: When do bounds and domain propagation lead to the same search space? ACM Trans. Program. Lang. Syst. 27(3), 388–425 (2005)
2. Mackworth, A.K.: Consistency in networks of relations. Artificial Intelligence 8(1), 99–118 (1977)
3. Choi, C.W., Harvey, W., Lee, J.H.M., Stuckey, P.J.: Finite domain bounds consistency revisited. In: Sattar, A., Kang, B.-h. (eds.) AI 2006. LNCS, vol. 4304, pp. 49–58. Springer, Heidelberg (2006)
4. Gecode Team: Gecode: Generic constraint development environment (2006), http://www.gecode.org

Lparse Programs Revisited: Semantics and Representation of Aggregates

Guohua Liu and Jia-Huai You

Department of Computing Science
University of Alberta
Edmonton, Alberta, Canada
{guohua,you}@cs.ualberta.ca

Abstract. Lparse programs are logic programs with weight constraints as implemented in the SMODELS system, which constitute an important class of logic programs with constraint atoms. To effectively apply lparse programs to problem solving, a clear understanding of its semantics and representation power is indispensable. In this paper, we study the semantics of lparse programs, called the *lparse semantics*. We show that for a large class of programs, called *strongly satisfiable programs*, the lparse semantics agrees with the semantics based on conditional satisfaction. However, when the two semantics disagree, a stable model admitted by the lparse semantics may be circularly justified. We then present a transformation, by which an lparse program can be transformed to a strongly satisfiable one, so that no circular models may be generated under the current implementation of SMODELS. This leads to an investigation of a methodological issue, namely the possibility of compact representation of aggregate programs by lparse programs. We present some experimental results to compare this approach with the ones where aggregates are more explicitly handled.

1 Introduction

Lparse programs are logic programs with weight constraints implemented in the SMODELS system [15], which have been considered one of the most important recent extensions to answer set programming (ASP). Since weight constraints can be nonmonotone, lparse programs constitute a class of logic programs with constraints beyond monotone constraints.

In a related development, ASP has been extended to support abstract constraint atoms, called *c-atoms* for short, for representation and reasoning with constraints on sets of atoms [11,12]. Many constraints studied in the past, such as weight constraints, aggregates, and what are called global constraints in the Constraint Satisfaction Problem (CSP) [1,19] can be represented by c-atoms. In this sense, logic programs with c-atoms subsume lparse programs and logic programs with aggregates and global constraints. One focus in the study of logic programs with c-atoms is on the semantics, with a number of proposals for programs with various kinds of c-atoms, such as [10] for monotone c-atoms, [5,7,14,17] for aggregates, and [9,12,16] for arbitrary constraint atoms. All of these semantics agree on programs with monotone c-atoms. When nonmonotone c-atoms are present, they may admit different sets of stable models. The relationships between these semantics have been investigated in [16].

M. Garcia de la Banda and E. Pontelli (Eds.): ICLP 2008, LNCS 5366, pp. 347–361, 2008.
© Springer-Verlag Berlin Heidelberg 2008

Despite of being one of the most popular systems, the semantics of lparse programs has not been fully studied. In [11], it is shown that lparse programs can be transformed to logic programs with monotone weight constraints while preserving the lparse semantics. Based on this result, in [10] weight constraints are translated to pseudo-boolean constraints. We do not know of any study that addresses the lparse semantics itself. For instance, since lparse programs are logic programs with constraint atoms, question arises as how the lparse semantics is related to the semantics for logic programs with constraint atoms. If differences exist, what are the nature of the differences and their potential implications in applications. These questions are important since SMODELS has been used for benchmarks and serious applications involving cardinality and weight constraints (e.g. [8,20]), and will likely be adopted in further endeavors in applying the ASP technology to real world applications.

In this paper, we study the semantics of lparse programs by investigating the relationship between it and the semantics proposed for logic programs with c-atoms. It turns out that the lparse semantics differs from all the other semantics. However, we show that for a large class of lparse programs, called *strongly satisfiable programs*, the lparse semantics agrees with the semantics based on conditional satisfaction [16]. For example, lparse programs where weight constraints are upper bound free are all strongly satisfiable. This result is useful in that we are now sure that the known properties of the latter semantics also hold for these programs. One important property is that any answer set is a *well-supported model* [16], ensuring that any conclusion must be supported by a non-circular justification in the sense of Fages [6].

Our study further reveals that for lparse programs where the two semantics disagree, lparse-stable models may be circularly justified, based on a formal notion of circular justification. We then show that there exists a transformation from lparse programs to strongly satisfiable programs, which provides a way to run lparse programs under the current implementation of SMODELS without generating circular models.

The SMODELS system has been used to run logic programs with aggregates (or called aggregate programs). A methodological question of interest is whether the standard aggregates can be effectively encoded by weight constraints[1], and if so, what are the advantages. It turns out that most aggregates proposed for ASP can be encoded by weight constraints in linear size. Most of these encodings are straightforward and already widely used in SMODELS' applications (e.g., [8]), with the exception of the MAX/MIN constraints, which are more involved. In this sense, SMODELS can be seen as a system for aggregate programs already.

To evaluate this approach to representing and computing with aggregates, we have conducted a preliminary round of experiments. We compare SMODELS with SMODELS[A] and DLV[A] on logic programs with standard aggregates. Our experiments show that lparse programs often run faster, sometimes substantially faster, than the two aggregate systems for the benchmarks tested. This suggests that representing aggregates by weight constraints is a promising alternative to the explicit handling of aggregates in logic programs. Besides efficiency, another advantage is at the system level: an aggregate language can be built on top of SMODELS by a simple front end to essentially

---

[1] In this paper, by *effective* or *compact* encoding of a constraint by weight constraints, we mean the collective size of the encoded weight constraints is linear in the size of constraint's *domain*.

transform standard aggregates to weight constraints in linear time. This is in contrast with the state of the art in handling aggregates in ASP, which typically requires a more explicit implementation.

The next section gives some preliminary definitions. Section 3 shows that the lparse semantics is closely related to the semantics based on conditional satisfaction. The differences between these two semantics are studied in Section 4, whereas Section 5 presents a transformation which closes the gap between the two semantics. In section 6, encodings of standard aggregates by weight constraints are presented, which provide necessary information for the experiments that are reported in Section 7. Section 8 concludes the paper and proposes issues that require further investigation.

2 Preliminaries

Throughout the paper, we assume a fixed propositional language with a countable set of propositional atoms.

2.1 Lparse Semantics

A *weight constraint* is of the form

$$l\,[a_1{=}w_{a_1}, ..., a_n{=}w_{a_n}, \text{not } b_1{=}w_{b_1}, ..., \text{not } b_m{=}w_{b_m}]\,u \tag{1}$$

where each a_i, b_j is an atom, and each atom and not-atom (negated atom) is associated with a *weight*. Atoms and not-atoms are also called *literals* (the latter may be emphasized as *negative* literals). The literal set of a weight constraint W, denoted $lit(W)$, is the set of literals occurring in W. The numbers l and u are the *lower* and *upper bounds*, respectively. The weights and bounds are real numbers (only integers are supported by smodels). Either of the bounds may be omitted in which case the missing lower bound is taken to be $-\infty$ and the missing upper bound by ∞.

A set of atoms M satisfies a weight constraint W of the form (1), denoted $M \models W$, if (and only if) $l \leq w(W, M) \leq u$, where

$$w(W, M) = \sum_{a_i \in M} w_{a_i} + \sum_{b_i \notin M} w_{b_i} \tag{2}$$

M satisfies a set of weight constraints Π if $M \models W$ for every $W \in \Pi$.

A weight constraint W is *monotone* if for any two sets R and S, if $R \models W$ and $R \subseteq S$, then $S \models W$; otherwise, W is *nonmonotone*. There are some special classes of nonmonotone weight constraints. W is *antimonotone* if for any R and S, $S \models W$ and $R \subseteq S$ imply $R \models W$; W is *convex* if for any R and S such that $R \subseteq S$, if $S \models W$ and $R \models W$, then for any I such that $R \subseteq I \subseteq S$, we have $I \models W$.

An *lparse program* is a finite set of rules of the form

$$W_0 \leftarrow W_1, ..., W_n \tag{3}$$

where each W_i is a weight constraint.

We will use $At(P)$ to denote the set of the atoms appearing in a program P.

If every weight constraint is of the form $1\,[l = 1]\,1$ where l is a literal, then an lparse program is essentially a normal program. The weight constraint $1\,[l = 1]\,1$ will be simply written as l.

As pointed out in [15], negative weights and negative literals are closely related in that they can replace each other and that one is inessential when the other is available.

Negative weights can be eliminated by applying the following transformation: For a weight constraint W of the form (1), if $w_{a_i} < 0$, then replace $a_i = w_{a_i}$ with $\text{not } a_i = |w_{a_i}|$ and increase the lower bound to $l + |w_{a_i}|$ and the upper bound to $u + |w_{a_i}|$; if $w_{b_i} < 0$, then replace $\text{not } b_i = w_{b_i}$ with $b_i = |w_{b_i}|$ and increase the lower bound to $l + |w_{b_i}|$ and the upper bound to $u + |w_{b_i}|$.

For instance, the weight constraint

$$-1 \, [a_1 = -1, a_2 = 2, \text{not } b_1 = 1, \text{not } b_2 = -2] \, 1$$

can be transformed to

$$2 \, [\text{not } a_1 = 1, a_2 = 2, \text{not } b_1 = 1, b_2 = 2] \, 4$$

From now on, we assume that weights are non-negative if not said otherwise.

The stable models of lparse programs are defined using the reduct of weight constraints, which is defined as follows: The *reduct* of a weight constraint W of the form (1) w.r.t. a set of atoms M, denoted by W^M, is the constraint

$$l' \, [a_1 = w_{a_1}, ..., a_n = w_{a_n}] \tag{4}$$

where $l' = l - \sum_{b_i \notin M} w_{b_i}$.

Let P be an lparse program and M a set of atoms. The reduct P^M of P, w.r.t. M, is defined by

$$P^M = \{p \leftarrow W_1^M, ..., W_n^M \mid W_0 \leftarrow W_1, ... W_n \in P,$$
$$p \in lit(W_0) \cap M \text{ and } w(W_i, M) \le u \text{ for all } i \ge 1\} \tag{5}$$

Definition 1. [15] *Let P be an lparse program and $M \subseteq At(P)$. M is an lparse-stable model of P iff the following two conditions hold:*

1. *$M \models P$,*
2. *M is the least model of P^M.*

Note that P^M is an lparse program where all constraints are monotone and the head of each rule is an atom. Thus its least model can be computed by a fixpoint construction.

2.2 Semantics of Logic Programs with Constraint Atoms

An *abstract constraint atom* (or *c-atom*) is of the form (D, C), where D is a set of atoms called the *domain* of the c-atom, and C a collection of the subsets from 2^D, consisting of the *admissible solutions* to the constraint. Given a c-atom $A = (D, C)$, We use A_d and A_c to refer to D and C, respectively.

A logic program with c-atoms is a collection of rules of the form: $C_0 \leftarrow C_1, ..., C_k$, where each C_i is a c-atom.

For a rule r of the above form, the *head* of r, denoted by $hd(r)$ is C_0, and the *body*, denoted by $bd(r)$ is the set $\{C_1, ..., C_k\}$.

A set of atoms M satisfies a c-atom A, written $M \models A$, if $M \cap A_d \in A_c$. M is a *model* of a program P if for every rule $r \in P$, either $M \models hd(r)$ or $M \not\models bd(r)$. If a c-atom is not satisfied by any set of atoms (such as c-atoms of the form $(D, \emptyset)$) and appears in the head of a rule, we may write a special symbol $\perp$ instead. A c-atom A is said to be *elementary* if it is of the form $(\{a\}, \{\{a\}\})$, which is just written as a. A rule is said to be *basic* if its head is either elementary or $\perp$. A program is *basic* if every rule in it is basic.

Abstract constraint atoms are introduced to represent constraints on sets. In practical constraint systems however, constraints are concrete and *language supported*, such as weight constraints, aggregates, and global constraints. The satisfaction of such a concrete constraint is pre-defined in the given language. We can associate a concrete constraint C in a given language with a c-atom C' such that C'_d is the same as the domain of C, and for any set of atoms M, $M \models C$ if and only if $M \models C'$. In this case, we call C' a *c-atom representation* of C.

For instance, for a weight constraint W of the form (1), a c-atom representation of W is a c-atom A whose domain A_d is the set of atoms appearing in W and A_c consists of those $S \subseteq A_d$ such that $S \models W$. Under this setting, lparse programs constitute a class of logic program with c-atoms, where c-atoms are just weight constraints.

The definition of answer sets in [16] is based on the abstract form of constraint atoms. It is notationally important to lift this definition to cover all constraint atoms, be they in the abstract form or in a language supported form.

In the sequel, a c-atom refers to a constraint atom, either in the abstract form or in a language supported form. We use $dom(C)$ to denote the domain of a c-atom, particularly, if A is a weight constraint, $dom(C) = \{a \mid a \in lit(A) \text{ or } \text{not } a \in lit(A)\}$.

Answer sets for logic programs with c-atoms are defined in two steps. In the first, answer sets for basic programs are defined, based on *conditional satisfaction*.

Definition 2. *Let M and S be sets of atoms and W be a c-atom. The set S conditionally satisfies W w.r.t. M, denoted by $S \models_M W$, if $S \models W$ and for every I such that $S \cap dom(W) \subseteq I \subseteq M$, we have $I \models W$.*

Given sets R and S, and a basic program P, the operator $T_P(R, S)$ is defined as:

$$T_P(R, S) = \{a : \exists r \in P, hd(r) = a \neq \perp, R \models_S bd(r)\}.$$

T_P is monotone w.r.t. its first argument, given that the second argument is fixed.

Definition 3. *Let M be a model of a basic program P. M is an answer set for P iff $M = T_P^\infty(\emptyset, M)$, where $T_P^0(\emptyset, M) = \emptyset$ and $T_P^{i+1}(\emptyset, M) = T_P(T_P^i(\emptyset, M), M)$, for all $i \geq 0$.*

In the second step, a logic program with c-atoms is represented by its instances in the form of basic programs, and the answer sets of the former are defined in terms of the ones of the latter.

Let P be a program with c-atoms and $r \in P$. By an abuse of notation, assume $hd(r)$ is a c-atom representation of the constraint in the head of rule r. Then, for each $\pi \in hd(r)_c$, the *instance* of r w.r.t. π is the set of rules consisting of

1. $b \leftarrow bd(r)$, for each $b \in \pi$, and
2. $\perp \leftarrow d, bd(r)$, for each $d \in hd(r)_d \setminus \pi$.

An *instance of P* is a basic program obtained by replacing each rule of P with one of its instances.

Definition 4. [16] *Let P be a logic program with c-atoms and $M \subseteq At(P)$. M is an answer set for P iff M is an answer set for one of its instances.*

From now on, *answer sets* of logic programs with c-atoms or c-atom representation of weight constraints refer to Definition 4 if not said otherwise.

3   Coincidence between Semantics

We show that, for a large class of lparse programs, the lparse semantics coincides with that of [16].

Notation: Given a weight constraint W of the form (1) and a set of atoms M, we define $M_a(W) = \{a_i \in M \mid a_i \in lit(W)\}$ and $M_b(W) = \{b_i \in M \mid \text{not } b_i \in lit(W)\}$. Since W is always clear by context, we will simply write M_a and M_b.

Let M be a set of atoms and W a weight constraint of the form (1). W is said to be *strongly satisfiable by M* if $M \models W$ implies that for any $V \subseteq M_b$, $w(W, M \setminus V) \leq u$. W is *strongly satisfiable* if for any set of atoms M, W is strongly satisfiable by M. An lparse program is *strongly satisfiable* if every weight constraint that appears in the body of a rule in it is strongly satisfiable.

Strongly satisfiable lparse programs constitute an interesting class of programs. In particular, weight constraints W that possess one of the following syntactically checkable conditions are strongly satisfiable.

– $lit(W)$ contains only atoms;
– $\sum_1^n w_{a_i} + \sum_1^m w_{b_i} \leq u$.

For example, the following constraints are all strongly satisfiable: $1 [a = 1, b = 2] 2$, $1 [a = 1, \text{not } b = 2] 3$, and $1 [a = 1, \text{not } b = 2]$. But $1 [a = 1, \text{not } b = 2] 2$ is not, since it is satisfied by $\{a, b\}$ but not by $\{a\}$.

Strongly satisfiable constraints are not necessarily convex or monotone.

Example 1. Let $A = 2[a = 1, b = 1, \text{not } c = 1]$ be a weight constraint. Since A is upper bound free, it is strongly satisfiable. But A is neither monotone nor convex, since $\{a\} \models A$, $\{a, c\} \not\models A$, and $\{a, b, c\} \models A$.   □

Theorem 1. *Let P be an lparse program and $M \subseteq At(P)$. Suppose for any weight constraint W appearing in the body of a rule in P, W is strongly satisfiable by M. Then, M is an lparse-stable model of P iff M is an answer set for P.*

The theorem can be proved as follows. Let M and S be two sets of atoms such that $S \subseteq M$, and P be a program in which the weight constraints that appear in the bodies of rules in P are strongly satisfiable by M. We will prove a key lemma below which relates $S \models_M W$ with $S \models W^M$. The goal is to ensure a one-to-one correspondence between the derivations based on conditional satisfaction (Definition 3) and the derivations in the construction of the least model (Definition 1). Then it can be shown, by induction on the length of derivations, that an lparse-stable model of P is an answer set for an instance of P, and vice versa.

Lemma 1. *Let W be a weight constraint of the form (1), and S and M be sets of atoms such that $S \subseteq M$. Then,*

(i) *If $S \models_M W$ then $S \models W^M$ and $w(W, M) \leq u$.*
(ii) *If $S \models W^M$ and W is strongly satisfiable by M, then $S \models_M W$.*

The proof of (i) is routine, but the proof of (ii) involves some subtleties.

Proof. (ii) Assume $S \not\models_M W$ and W is strongly satisfiable by M. We show $S \not\models W^M$.

We have either $S \models W$ or $S \not\models W$. If $S \not\models W$ then clearly $S \not\models W^M$. Assume $S \models W$. Then from $S \not\models_M W$, we have $\exists I, S \cap dom(W) \subset I \subseteq M$, such that $I \not\models W$. Since W is strongly satisfiable by M, if $M \models W$ then for any $R = M \setminus V$, where $V \subseteq M_b$, $w(W, R) \leq u$. Assume $M \models W$. Let R be such that $R_b = I_b$ and $I_a \subseteq R_a$. It's clear that $w(W, R) \leq u$ leads to $w(W, I) \leq u$. Thus, since $M \models W$, that $I \not\models W$ is due to the violation of the lower bound, i.e., $w(W, I) < l$.

Now consider $I' = S_a \cup M_b$; i.e., we restrict I_a to S_a and expand I_b to M_b. Note that by construction, it still holds that $S \cap dom(W) \subset I' \subseteq M$. Clearly, $I \not\models W$ leads to $I' \not\models W$, which is also due to the violation of the lower bound, as $w(W, I') \leq w(W, I)$, i.e., we have $w(W, I') < l$. By definition, we have $w(W^{I'}, I') < l'$, where $l' = l - \sum_{b_i \notin I'} w_{b_i}$. Note that since $I'_b = M_b$, we have $l' = l - \sum_{b_i \notin M} w_{b_i}$. Since $I'_a = S_a$, it follows that $w(W^{I'}, S) < l'$. Now since $W^{I'}$ is precisely the same constraint as W^M, we have $w(W^{I'}, S) = w(W^M, S)$, and therefore $w(W^M, S) < l'$. This shows $S \not\models W^M$. $\square$

By Theorem 1 and the definition of strongly satisfiable programs, we can show the following.

Theorem 2. *Let P be a strongly satisfiable lparse program, and $M \subseteq At(P)$ be a set of atoms. M is an lparse-stable model of P iff M is an answer set for P.*

4   When the Semantics Disagree

The following theorem can be proved using Lemma 1 and Example 2 below.

Theorem 3. *Every answer set of an lparse program P is an lparse-stable model of P, but the converse does not hold.*

Question: What happens to the lparse programs that are not strongly satisfiable.

Example 2. Let P be a program consisting of a single rule: $a \leftarrow [\text{not } a = 1]\, 0$ and $M_1 = \emptyset$ and $M_2 = \{a\}$ be two sets. The weight constraint $[\text{not } a = 1]\, 0$ in P is not strongly satisfiable, since although M_2 satisfies the upper bound, its subset M_1 does not. By Definition 1, P has two lparse stable models: M_1 and M_2. But, by Definition 4, M_1 is an answer set for P and M_2 is not. Note that M_2 is not a minimal model.

The reason that M_2 is not an answer set for P is due to the fact that a is derived by its being in M_2. This kind of circular justification can be seen more clearly below.

– The weight constraint is substituted with an equivalent aggregate:
$$a \leftarrow COUNT(\{X \mid X \in D\}) = 1, \text{ where } D = \{a\}.$$

- The weight constraint is substituted with its c-atom representation:
$$a \leftarrow (\{a\}, \{\{a\}\}).$$
- The weight constraint is transformed to an equivalent one without negative literal, but with a negative weight, according to [15]:[2]
$$a \leftarrow [a = -1] - 1.$$

For the claim of equivalence, note that for any set of atoms M, we have: $M \models [\text{not } a = 1]0$ iff $[a = -1] - 1$ iff $M \models COUNT(\{X \mid X \in D\}) = 1$ (where $D = \{a\}$) iff $M \models (\{a\}, \{\{a\}\})$.   □

The type of circular justification observed here is similar to "answer sets by reduct" in dealing with nonmonotone c-atoms [16]. But the constraint $[\text{not } a = 1]\,0$ is actually monotone! One may think that the culprit for M_2 above is because it is not a minimal model. However, the following example shows that lparse-stable models that are also minimal models may still be circularly justified.

Example 3. Consider the following lparse program P (which is obtained from the one in Example 2 by adding the second rule):

$$a \leftarrow [\text{not } a = 1]\,0 \qquad f \leftarrow \text{not } f, \text{not } a$$

Now, $M = \{a\}$ is a minimal model of P, and also an lparse-stable model of P, but clearly a is justified by its being in M.   □

We now give a more formal account of circular justification for lparse-stable models, borrowing the idea of *unfounded sets* previously used for normal programs [18] and logic programs with monotone and antimonotone aggregates [3].

Definition 5. *Let P be an lparse program and M an lparse-stable model of P. M is said to be* circularly justified, *or simply* circular, *if there exists a non-empty set $U \subseteq M$ such that $\forall \phi \in U$, $M \setminus U$ does not satisfy the body of any rule in P where ϕ is in the literal set of the head of the rule.*

Theorem 4. *Let P be an lparse program and M an lparse-stable model of P. If M is an answer set for P, then M is not circular.*

Example 2 shows that extra lparse-stable models (lparse-stable models that are not answer sets) of a program may be circular. However, not all extra lparse-stable models are necessarily circular.

Example 4. Consider an lparse program P that consists of three rules.

$$a \leftarrow \qquad b \leftarrow 2[a = 1, \text{not } b = 1] \qquad b \leftarrow [a = 1, \text{not } b = 1]1$$

$M = \{a, b\}$ is an lparse-stable model but not an answer set for P. However, it can be verified that M is not circular under our definition (Definition 5).[3]   □

---

[2] Caution: Due to an internal bug, SMODELS produces $\emptyset$ as the only stable model, which is inconsistent with the lparse semantics defined in [15].

[3] It appears that the notion of circular justification is still an open issue; there could be different intuitions and definitions.

5   Transformation to Strongly Satisfiable Programs

In this section we show that all lparse programs can be transformed to strongly satisfiable programs. This is achieved by replacing each weight constraint of form (1) in a
given program by two upper bound-free weight constraints.

Let W be a weight constraint of form (1). The *strongly satisfiable encoding* of W,
denoted by (W_1, W_2) consists of the following constraints:

$$W_1 : l[a_1 = w_{a_1}, ..., a_n = w_{a_n}, \text{not } b_1 = w_{b_1}, \text{not } b_1 = w_{b_m}]$$

$$W_2 : -u + \sum_{i=1}^{n} w_{a_i} + \sum_{i=1}^{m} w_{b_i} [\text{not } a_1 = w_{a_1}, ..., \text{not } a_n = w_{a_n}, b_1 = w_{b_1}, ..., b_m = w_{b_m}]$$

Intuitively, W_1 and W_2 are to code the lower and upper bound constraints of W, respectively. It is easy to verify that the encoding is satisfaction-preserving, as shown in
the following lemma.

Lemma 2. *Let W be a weight constraint, (W_1, W_2) be its strongly satisfiable encoding, and M be a set of atoms. $M \models W$ iff $M \models W_1$ and $M \models W_2$.*

By Lemmas 1 and 2, the following result can be established.

Theorem 5. *Let W be a weight constraint, (W_1, W_2) be the strongly satisfiable encoding of W, and S and M be two sets of atoms, such that $S \subseteq M$. $S \models_M W$ iff $S \models W_1^M$
and $S \models W_2^M$.*

Theorem 5 guarantees the one-to-one correspondence between the derivations based on
conditional satisfaction (Definition 3) and the derivations in the construction of the least
model (Definition 1).

Theorem 6. *Let P be an lparse program, $Tr(P)$ be the program obtained by replacing
each W in the body of rules in P by the strongly satisfiable encoding of W, and M be
a set of atoms. M is an answer set for P iff M is an lparse stable model of $Tr(P)$.*

Example 5. Consider a program P with a single rule: $a \leftarrow 0[\text{not } a = 3]2$. Then,
$Tr(P)$ consists of

$$a \leftarrow 0[\text{not } a = 3], 1[a = 3].$$

The weight constraints in $Tr(P)$ are all upper bound-free, hence $Tr(P)$ is strongly
satisfiable. Both $\emptyset$ and $\{a\}$ are lparse-stable models of P, but $\emptyset$ is the only lparse-stable
model of $Tr(P)$, which is also the only answer set for P.   □

6   Logic Programs with Aggregates

Aggregates as weight constraints:

Aggregates are constraints on sets taking the form

$$aggr(\{X \mid p(X)\}) \text{ op } Result \tag{6}$$

where $aggr$ is an *aggregate function*, p is a predicate symbol, and X is a variable which takes value from a set $D(X) = \{a_1, ..., a_n\}$, called the *variable domain*. The standard aggregate functions are those in $\{SUM, COUNT, AVG, MAX, MIN\}$. The relational operator op is from $\{=, \neq, <, >, \leq, \geq\}$ and $Result$ is a numeric constant.

The domain of an aggregate A, denoted $Dom(A)$, is the set of atoms $\{p(a) \mid a \in D(X)\}$. The size of an aggregate is $|Dom(A)|$. Let $M \subseteq Dom(A)$. M is a *model* of an aggregate A, denoted $M \models A$, if $aggr(\{a \mid p(a) \in M\})$ op $Result$ holds.

Let A be an aggregate in the form (6). A set of weight constraints $\{W_1, ..., W_n\}$ is an *encoding* of A, denoted $e(A)$, if for any model M of A, there is a model M' of $e(A)$ such that $M'_{|Dom(A)} = M$ and for any model M' of $e(A)$, $M'_{|Dom(A)}$ is a model of A, where $M'_{|S}$ denotes $M' \cap S$.

We show the encodings of aggregates of the form (6), where the operator op is $\geq$. The encodings can be easily extended to other relational operator except for $\neq$ (more on $\neq$ later in this section). For example, aggregate $SUM(\{X \mid p(X)\}) > k$ can be encoded as $SUM(\{Y \mid p(Y)\}) \geq k + 1$.

The encodings work for the aggregates whose variable domain contains only integers. For the aggregates whose variable domain contains real numbers, each real number can be converted to an integer by multiplying a factor. In this case, the $Result$ also needs to be processed correspondingly.

For convenience, below we may write negative weights in weight constraints. Recall that negative weights can be eliminated by a simple transformation.

$SUM, COUNT, AVG$. These aggregates can be encoded by weight constraints rather directly. For instance, $SUM(\{X \mid p(X)\}) \geq k$ can be represented by

$$k \, [p(a_1) = a_1, ..., p(a_n) = a_n]. \tag{7}$$

We note that aggregates $COUNT(\{X \mid p(X)\}) \geq k$ and $AVG(\{X \mid p(X)\}) \geq k$ can be encoded simply by substituting the weights in (7) with 1 and $a_i - k$ (for AVG the lower bound k is also replaced by zero), respectively.

MAX. Let $A = MAX(\{X \mid p(X)\}) \geq k$ be an aggregate. The idea in the encoding of A is that for a set of numbers $S = \{a_1, ..., a_n\}$, the maximum number in S is greater than or equal to k if and only if

$$\sum_{i=1}^{n} (a_i - k + 1) > -\sum_{i=1}^{n} |a_i - k + 1|. \tag{8}$$

For each atom $p(a_i)$, two new literals $p^+(a_i)$ and $p^-(a_i)$ are introduced. The encoding $e(A)$ consists of the following constraints.

$$0 \, [p(a_i) = -1, p^+(a_i) = 1, p^-(a_i) = 1] \, 0, \ 1 \leq i \leq n \tag{9}$$

$$0 \, [p(a_i) = -d_i, p^+(a_i) = d_i], \ 1 \leq i \leq n \tag{10}$$

$$0 \, [p(a_i) = d_i, p^-(a_i) = -d_i], \ 1 \leq i \leq n \tag{11}$$

$$1 \, [p(a_1) = d_1, p^+(a_1) = d_1, p^-(a_1) = -d_1,$$
$$..., p(a_n) = d_n, p^+(a_n) = d_n, p^-(a_n) = -d_n] \tag{12}$$

$$1 \, [p(a_1) = 1, ..., p(a_n) = 1] \tag{13}$$

where $d_i = a_i - k + 1$.

In the following presentation, for any model M of the encoding, $a = 1$ means $a \in M$ and $a = 0$ means $a \notin M$.

The constraints (9), (10) and (11) are used to encode $|a_i - k + 1|$. Clearly, if $a_i > k - 1$, we have $p^+(a_i) = p(a_i)$ and $p^-(a_i) = 0$; if $a_i < k - 1$, we have $p^-(a_i) = p(a_i)$ and $p^+(a_i) = 0$; and if $a_i = k - 1$, we have $p^+(a_i) = p(a_i)$ or $p^-(a_i) = p(a_i)$.

The constraint (12) encodes the relation (8) and the constraint (13) guarantees that a model of $e(A)$ is not an empty set.

MIN. Let $A = MIN(\{X \mid p(X)\}) \geq k$ be an aggregate. The idea in the encoding of A is that for a set of numbers $S = \{a_1, ..., a_n\}$, the minimal number in S is greater than or equal to k if and only if

$$\sum_{i=1}^{n} (a_i - k) = \sum_{i=1}^{n} |a_i - k|. \tag{14}$$

Similar to MAX, the constraint in (14) can be encoded by weight constraints.

We note that all the encodings above result in weight constraints whose collective size is linear in the size of the domain of the aggregate being encoded.

In the encoding of MAX (similarly for MIN), the first three constraints are the ones between the newly introduced literals $p^+(a_i)$, $p^-(a_i)$ and the literal $p(a_i)$. We call them *auxiliary constraints*. The last two constraints code the relation between $p(a_i)$ and $p(a_j)$, where $i \neq j$. We call them *relation constraints*. Let A be an aggregate, we denote the set of auxiliary constraints in $e(A)$ by $a(A)$ and the relation constraints by $r(A)$. If A is aggregate $SUM, COUNT$, or AVG, we have that $r(A) = e(A)$, because no new literals are introduced in the encodings.

For a given aggregate A, the constraints in $e(A)$ can be transformed to strongly satisfiable weight constraints. In the sequel, we assume $e(A)$ contains only strongly satisfiable weight constraints.

Programs with Aggregates to lparse Programs

A logic program with aggregates is a set of rules of the form $h \leftarrow A_1, ..., A_n$, where h is an atom and A_i are aggregates from $\{SUM, COUNT, AVG, MIN, MAX\}$.

We will represent a logic program with aggregates P by an lparse program, denoted $\tau(P)$, as follows:

1. For each rule of the above form in P, we have an lparse rule of the form

    $$h \leftarrow r(A_1), ..., r(A_n) \tag{15}$$

    in $\tau(P)$. In the formula (15), we use $r(A_i)$ to denote the conjunction of all the weight constraints in $r(A_i)$, and
2. If there are newly introduced literals in the encoding of aggregates, the *auxiliary rule* of the form

    $$W \leftarrow p(a_i) \tag{16}$$

    is included in $\tau(P)$, for each auxiliary constraint W of each atom $p(a_i)$ in the aggregates.

Theorem 7. *Let P be a logic program with aggregates where the relational operator is not $\neq$. For any lparse-stable model M of $Tr(\tau(P))$, $M_{|At(P)}$ is an answer set for P (as defined in Definition 4). For any answer set M for P, there is an lparse-stable model M' of $Tr(\tau(P))$ such that $M'_{|At(P)} = M$.*

When an aggregate is encoded by a conjunction of weight constraints, logic equivalence leads to equivalence under conditional satisfaction. This is why in the encodings so far we only need to ensure that an encoding is satisfaction-preserving. But this is not the case when disjunction is involved, which causes problem in dealing with the relational operator $\neq$.

Example 6. Let $A = SUM(\{X \,|p(X)\}) \neq -1$, $A_1 = SUM(\{X \,|p(X)\}) > -1$ and $A_2 = SUM(\{X \,|p(X)\}) < -1$. Note that A is logically equivalent to $A_1 \vee A_2$. Consider $S = \{p(1)\}$ and $M = \{p(1), p(2), p(-3)\}$. While S conditionally satisfies A w.r.t. M (i.e., $S \models_M A$), it is not the case that S conditionally satisfies A_1 w.r.t. M or S conditionally satisfies A_2 w.r.t. M.   □

Since the answer set existence problem under the lparse semantics is *NP*-complete, and the transformation to strongly satisfiable programs is a polynomial time reduction, our transformation enables a computational mechanism for a large class of logic programs with aggregates whose complexity falls into *NP*-completeness.[4]

7   Experiments

We code logic programs with aggregates as lparse programs and use SMODELS 2.32 for the stable model computation. If a benchmark program is not already strongly satisfiable, it will be transformed into one, thus we can use the current implementation of SMODELS for our experiments.

   We compare our approach with two systems, SMODELS^A and DLV^A. The lparse programs are run on Linux AS release 4 with 1GHz CPU and 512MB RAM. The reported execution time of SMODELS consists of the transformation time (from aggregates to weight constraints), the grounding time (calling to lparse), and the search (by SMODELS) time. The execution time of smodels^A consists of grounding time, search time and unfolding time (computing the solutions to aggregates). The execution time of DLV^A, includes the grounding time and search time (the grounding phase is not separated from the search in DLV^A).

   We list the results reported in [4] and [2] for comparison. Thus, the comparison of the execution time is only indicative, since the platforms are similar but not the same.

Comparison with Smodels^A
We compare our approach to the unfolding approach implemented in the system SMODELS^A [4].[5]

---

[4] This is closely related to a result of [17], which shows that although the existence problem is in general in NP^{co-NP}, the same problem is in *NP* if neither $SUM(.) \neq k$ nor $AVG(.) \neq k$ is present in the program.

[5] The benchmarks and programs can be found at www.cs.nmsu.edu/~ielkaban/asp-aggr.html.

Table 1. Benchmarks used by SMODELS^A

Program	Sample Size	smodels	smodels^A
Company Contr.	20	0.03	0.09
Company Contr.	40	0.18	0.36
Company Contr.	80	0.87	2.88
Company Contr.	120	2.40	12.14
Employee Raise	15/5	0.01	0.69
Employee Raise	21/15	0.05	4.65
Employee Raise	24/20	0.05	5.55
Party Invit.	80	0.02	0.05
Party Invit.	160	0.07	0.1
NM1	125	0.61	0.21
NM1	150	0.75	0.29
NM2	125	0.65	2.24
NM2	150	1.08	3.36

The aggregates used in the first and second set of problems (the company control and employee raise problems) are SUM; the third set of problems (the party invitation problems) are $COUNT$, and the fourth and fifth set of problems (the NM1 and NM2, respectively) are MAX and MIN, respectively.

The experimental results are reported in Table 1, where the sample size is measured by the argument used to generate the test cases. The execution times are the average of one hundred randomly generated instances for each sample size. The results show that SMODELS is often faster than SMODELS^A, even though both use the same search engine.

Scale-up could be a problem for SMODELS^A, due to exponential blowup. For instance, for an aggregate like $COUNT(\{a|a \in S\}) \geq k$, SMODELS^A would list all *aggregate solutions* in the unfolded program, whose number is $C^k_{|S|}$. For a large domain S and k being around $|S|/2$, this is a huge number. If one or a few solutions are needed, SMODELS takes little time to compute the corresponding weight constraints.

Comparison with DLV^A

In [2] the seating problem was chosen to evaluate the performance of DLV^A[6]. The problem is to generate a sitting arrangement for a number of guests, with m tables and n chairs per table. Guests who like each other should sit at the same table; guests who dislike each other should not sit at the same table. The aggregate used in the problem is $COUNT$.

We use the same setting to the problem instances as in [2]. The results are shown in Table 2. The instance size is the number of atom occurrences in the ground programs. We report the result of the average over one hundred randomly generated instances for each problem size.

The experiments show that, by encoding logic programs with aggregates as lparse programs, SMODELS solves the problem efficiently. For large instances, the execution time of SMODELS is about one order of magnitude lower than that of DLV^A and the sizes of the instances are also smaller than those in the language of DLV^A.

---

[6] The program contains disjunctive head, but it can be easily transformed to a non-disjunctive program.

Table 2. Seating

C	T	Execution Time		Instance Size	
		smodels	DLV^A	smodels	DLV^A
4	3	0.1	0.01	293	248
4	4	0.2	0.01	544	490
5	5	0.58	0.02	1213	1346
5	10	0.35	0.31	6500	7559
5	15	1.24	1.88	18549	22049
5	20	3.35	7.08	40080	47946
5	25	8.19	64.29	73765	88781
5	30	16.42	152.45	12230	147567

Table 3. Pigeon-hole

p	h	Execution Time		Instance Size	
		Lparse	Normal	Lparse	Normal
5	4	0.00	0.01	98	345
6	5	0.01	0.01	142	636
7	6	0.01	0.06	194	1057
8	7	0.09	0.49	254	1632
9	8	0.74	4.38	322	2385
10	9	6.89	43.66	398	3340
11	10	71.92	480.19	482	4521
12	11	827.85	5439.09	574	5952

Lparse Programs vs. Normal Programs for Global Constraints
Some global constraints can be encoded by weight constraints compactly. We have
experimented with the pigeon-hole problem modeled by the *AllDifferent* constraint. The
lparse program that encodes *AllDifferent* is about one order of magnitude smaller than
the normal program encoding [13] in the size and the execution of the lparse program
is 6-7 times faster than its normal program counterpart for hard unsatisfiable instances
(where the number of holes is one less than the number of pigeons), which are run on
the same machine under the default setting. See Table 3 for the results.

8   Conclusions and Future Work

We have shown that for a large class of lparse programs the lparse semantics coincides
with the semantics based on conditional satisfaction. In general, answer sets admitted
by the latter are all lparse-stable models. When an lparse-stable model is not an answer
set, it may be circularly justified. We have proposed a transformation, by which an
lparse program can be translated to another one, such that all lparse-stable models are
answer sets and thus well-supported models.

As an issue of methodology, we have shown that most standard aggregates can be
encoded by weight constraints and SMODELS can be applied to efficiently compute the
answer sets of aggregate programs with almost all standard aggregates.

Our work has left some aspects unexplored. As we have shown, lparse-stable models that are not sanctioned by the semantics based on conditional satisfaction may or
may not be circular under our definition of circular justification. This left the question
of what would be the desired semantics for lparse programs unanswered. It seems that
the notion of unfounded sets can serve as a basis for a new semantics for lparse programs, since it appears to separate the desired lparse-stable models from the undesired
ones. Then, a question is whether a transformation exists that eliminates only circular
models.

Among the types of aggregates proposed in the literature, the only ones that cannot be encoded compactly by weight constraints are the *product constraints*, such as
$TIMES(\{X \mid p(X)\}) \geq k$, due to the non-linear nature of the expressions involved.

Plus the difficulty in encoding aggregates involving the relational operator $\neq$, this shows the limit of using SMODELS to run aggregate programs.

References

1. Aggoun, A., Beldiceanu, N.: Extending CHIP in order to solve complex scheduling and placement problems. J. Mathematical and Computer Modelling 17(7), 57–73 (1993)
2. Armi, D., Faber, W., Ielpa, G.: Aggregate functions in disjunctive logic programming: Semantics, complexity, and implementation in DLV*. In: IJCAI 2003, pp. 847–852 (2003)
3. Calimeri, F., Faber, W., Leone, N., Perri, S.: Declarative and computational properties of logic programs with aggregates. In: IJCAI 2005, pp. 406–411 (2005)
4. Elkabani, I., Pontelli, E., Son, T.C.: $Smodels^A$ – a system for computing answer sets of logic programs with aggregates. In: Baral, C., Greco, G., Leone, N., Terracina, G. (eds.) LPNMR 2005. LNCS, vol. 3662, pp. 427–431. Springer, Heidelberg (2005)
5. Faber, W., Leone, N., Pfeifer, G.: Recursive aggregates in disjunctive logic programs. In: Alferes, J.J., Leite, J. (eds.) JELIA 2004. LNCS, vol. 3229, pp. 200–212. Springer, Heidelberg (2004)
6. Fages, F.: Consistency of Clark's completion and existence of stable models. J. Methods of Logic in Computer Science 1, 51–60 (1994)
7. Ferraris, P.: Answer sets for propositional theories. In: Baral, C., Greco, G., Leone, N., Terracina, G. (eds.) LPNMR 2005. LNCS, vol. 3662, pp. 119–131. Springer, Heidelberg (2005)
8. Gebser, M., Liu, L., Namasivayam, G., Neumann, A., Schaub, T., Truszczyński, M.: The first answer set programming system competition. In: Baral, C., Brewka, G., Schlipf, J. (eds.) LPNMR 2007. LNCS, vol. 4483, pp. 1–17. Springer, Heidelberg (2007)
9. Liu, L., Pontelli, E., Son, T.C., Truszczyński, M.: Logic programs with abstract constraint atoms: The role of computations. In: Dahl, V., Niemelä, I. (eds.) ICLP 2007. LNCS, vol. 4670, pp. 286–301. Springer, Heidelberg (2007)
10. Liu, L., Truszczyński, M.: Properties and applications of programs with monotone and convex constraints. J. Artificial Intelligence Research 7, 299–334 (2006)
11. Marek, V., Niemelä, I., Truszczyński, M.: Logic programs with monotone abstract constraint atoms. J. Theory and Practice of Logic Programming 8(2), 167–199 (2008)
12. Marek, V.W., Remmel, J.B.: Set constraints in logic programming. In: Lifschitz, V., Niemelä, I. (eds.) LPNMR 2004. LNCS, vol. 2923, pp. 167–179. Springer, Heidelberg (2003)
13. Niemelä, I.: Logic programs with stable model semantics as a constraint programming paradigm. Annals of Math. and Artificial Intelligence 25(3-4), 241–273 (1999)
14. Pelov, N., Denecker, M., Bruynooghe, M.: Well-founded and stable semantics of logic programs with aggregates. J. Theory and Practice of Logic Programming 7, 301–353 (2007)
15. Simons, P., Niemelä, I., Soininen, T.: Extending and implementing the stable model semantics. Artificial Intelligence 138(1-2), 181–234 (2002)
16. Son, T.C., Pontelli, E., Tu, P.H.: Answer sets for logic programs with arbitrary abstract constraint atoms. J. Artificial Intelligence Research 29, 353–389 (2007)
17. Son, T.C., Pontelli, E.: A constructive semantic characterization of aggregates in answer set programming. J. Theory and Practice of Logic Programming 7, 355–375 (2006)
18. van Gelder, A., Ross, K., Schlipf, J.: The well-founded semantics for general logic programs. J. ACM 38(3), 620–650 (1991)
19. van Hoeve, W.-J., Katriel, I.: Global constraints. In: Rossi, F., van Beek, P., Walsh, T. (eds.) Handbook of Constraint Programming, Ch. 7. Elsevier, Amsterdam (2006)
20. Wu, G., You, J., Lin, G.: Quartet based phylogeny reconstruction with answer set programming. IEEE/ACM Transactions on Computational Biology and Bioinformatics 4(1), 139–152 (2007)

Compiling Fuzzy Answer Set Programs to Fuzzy Propositional Theories

Jeroen Janssen[1,*], Stijn Heymans[2,*], Dirk Vermeir[1], and Martine De Cock[2]

[1] Dept. of Computer Science, Vrije Universiteit Brussel
{jeroen.janssen, dvermeir}@vub.ac.be
[2] Dept. of Applied Mathematics and Computer Science, Universiteit Gent
{stijn.heymans, martine.decock}@ugent.be

Abstract. We show how a fuzzy answer set program can be compiled to an equivalent fuzzy propositional theory whose models correspond to the answer sets of the program. This creates a basis for constructing fuzzy answer set solvers, such as solvers based on fuzzy SAT-solvers or on linear programming.

Keywords: answer set programming, fuzzy logic, Clark's completion, fuzzy ASSAT.

1 Introduction

Fuzzy answer set programming (FASP, see e.g. [1,2,3]) is a form of many-valued logic programming (see e.g. [4,5,6]) that extends answer set programming (ASP) to handle vague predicates, partial satisfaction of rules, and, in the case of [3], the notion of quality of an answer set, i.e. a solution may be an answer set to a certain degree. This makes it possible to provide approximate answers, e.g. for problems that do not have a perfect solution. For many application areas, this is a desirable feature.

As an example, consider the problem of arranging a group of people such that friends are seated close to each other. Clearly, the input predicate *friend* is vague, with *friend*(a, b) indicating the degree of friendship between a and b, e.g. on a scale from 0 to 1. Likewise, the second input predicate, *near*, is also vague, with *near*(s, z) representing the proximity between the seats s and z.

The following (ungrounded)[1] FASP program P_{intro} defines (and solves) the problem where "←" and "," are interpreted as the indicated fuzzy implicator and t-norm respectively, and 0 and 1 stand for the minimal ("false") and maximal ("true") truth value, see Section 2.

$$
\begin{array}{ll}
(choice) & sit(P, S) \leftarrow_{\rightsquigarrow^m, \wedge^m} 1 \\
(c_1) & 0 \leftarrow_{\rightsquigarrow^m, \wedge^m} sit(P, S), sit(P', S), P \neq P' \\
(c_2) & 0 \leftarrow_{\rightsquigarrow^m, \wedge^m} sit(P, S), sit(P, S'), S \neq S'
\end{array}
$$

---

* Funded by Research Foundation–Flanders
[1] Grounding is performed as usual, except that for input predicates, the actual value of the literal is substituted, e.g. *near*(s, z) might be replaced by .7.

M. Garcia de la Banda and E. Pontelli (Eds.): ICLP 2008, LNCS 5366, pp. 362–376, 2008.

$$
\begin{aligned}
(crisp) & & 0 &\leftarrow_{\rightsquigarrow^m,\curlywedge^m} sit(P,S), not_{\sim^s} sit(P,S) \\
(u)\ unhappy(P) &\leftarrow_{\rightsquigarrow^m,\curlywedge^m} & & sit(P,S), sit(P',S'), friend(P,P'), not_{\sim^s} near(S,S') \\
(q) & & 0 &\leftarrow_{\rightsquigarrow^l,\curlywedge^l} unhappy(P) \\
(sit)\ seated(P) &\leftarrow_{\rightsquigarrow^m,\curlywedge^m} & & sit(P,S) \\
(all) & & 0 &\leftarrow_{\rightsquigarrow^m,\curlywedge^m} not\ seated(P)
\end{aligned}
$$

The following aggregator specifies the quality of the solution[2] as a monotonic function on the degrees of satisfaction of the rules:

$$
\mathcal{A}_{P_{intro}} = ((c_1 \curlywedge^m c_2 \curlywedge^m crisp \curlywedge^m sit \curlywedge^m all \curlywedge^m u) \geq 1) \curlywedge^m q
$$

The (choice) rules generate a seating arrangement which is completely arbitrary, since the degree of satisfaction of the (choice) rules does not influence $\mathcal{A}_{P_{intro}}$. Thus, an instantiation

$$
(choice\langle p,s \rangle)\ \ sit(p,s) \leftarrow_{\rightsquigarrow^m,\curlywedge^m} 1
$$

of (choice) with p a person and s a seat, can be used to motivate any literal $sit(p,s)^l$ with l an arbitrary truth value[3], hence the name for these rules. Indeed, having $sit(p,s)^l$ with $l \in [0..1[$ implies that $(choice\langle p,s \rangle)$ is only satisfied to degree l, but this has no impact on the value of $\mathcal{A}_{P_{intro}}$, which is independent of the degrees of satisfaction of the (choice) rule instantiations.

However, the constraints (c_1), (c_2), (crisp) and (all), which $\mathcal{A}_{P_{intro}}$ forces to be fully satisfied, ensure that only arrangements where each person fully occupies exactly one seat can appear in an answer set. Why particular operators are being used for specific rules is explained in Section 3. The overall quality of the solution is represented by the degree of satisfaction of the (q) constraint which itself depends on the vague output predicate unhappy defined by the (u) rules. Thus, friends that sit far apart will weaken the satisfaction of a (q) rule and hence give rise to an answer set with a lower aggregated value.

As an example, consider a case where there are three available seats s_1, s_2, and z, only two of which are relatively near to each other, namely $near(s_1,s_2)^{.8}$, and three people connected by friendship with $friend(a,b)^{.8}$ and $friend(a,c)^{.5}$. Obviously, there exists no perfect arrangement that puts a close to both of her friends. However, an arrangement such as

$$
I_1 = \{\ sit(a,s_1)^1, sit(b,s_2)^1, sit(c,z)^1, unhappy(a)^{.5}, \ldots \} \tag{1}
$$

is still better than e.g. the arrangement

$$
I_2 = \{\ sit(a,s_1)^1, sit(b,z)^1, sit(c,s_2)^1, unhappy(a)^{.8}, \ldots \} \tag{2}
$$

In accordance with this intuition, I_1 yields a .5-answer set of the FASP program P_{intro}, while I_2 corresponds to a .2-answer set only, as we explain in Section 3.

---

[2] In the grounded version, each ungrounded rule (r) in $\mathcal{A}_{P_{intro}}$ is replaced by $\bigsqcap\{r_i | r_i \in r\}$ where r represents the set of grounded instances of the rule.

[3] We use l^u to denote that a literal l holds to degree u. The default value for any atom is 0.

In this paper, we make an important contribution towards the implementation of a fuzzy answer set solver. In particular, we show how FASP programs (in the sense of [3], but this can be readily adapted to other approaches such as e.g. [1,2] as these can be translated to the FASP framework used in this paper) can be implemented by translating them to an equivalent formula in a fuzzy propositional logic, such that the answer sets of the program correspond to models of the formula. The latter can be computed using a fuzzy satisfiability (FSAT) solver or, subject to restrictions on the choice of connectives used in the program, by translating the formula, e.g. using tableau methods such as proposed in [7,8,9], to a linear programming problem that can itself be solved using standard tools.

The remainder of the paper is organized as follows. Section 2 contains preliminaries, while Section 3 introduces the fuzzy answer set programming [3] formalism being used. A fuzzy propositional logic framework is presented in Section 4. In Section 5, we extend to FASP programs the well-known translation of regular logic programs to a propositional theory called "Clark's completion" [10]. This translation forms the basis of many algorithms for finding answer sets such as those based on linear programming [11] or those using SAT-solvers [12]. We show that, under certain conditions, the models of our fuzzy completion and the fuzzy answer sets of a program coincide.

However, as in the boolean case, not every model of the fuzzy completion is an answer set. In Section 6, we remedy the situation by adding "loop formulas" to the completion, thus extending a similar approach for traditional answer set programs from [12]. We also show that the procedure proposed by [12] to iteratively compute such loop formulas "on demand" can be extended to fuzzy answer set programs. Finally, section 7 presents conclusions and directions for further research.

Due to space restrictions, all proofs have been omitted. They can be obtained from the full paper at http://tinf2.vub.ac.be/~jeroen/papers/ICLP08/ICLP08-full.pdf

2   Preliminaries

The traditional logical operations of negation, conjunction, disjunction, and implication are generalised to logical operators acting on $[0, 1]$ in the usual way (see e.g. [13]). A *negator* is any anti-monotone $[0, 1] \rightarrow [0, 1]$ mapping $\sim$ satisfying $\sim 0 = 1$ and $\sim 1 = 0$. A negator $\sim$ is called *involutive* iff $\forall x \in [0, 1] \cdot \sim\sim x = x$. A *triangular norm*, t-norm for short, is any commutative and associative $[0, 1]^2 \rightarrow [0, 1]$ (infix) operator λ satisfying $\forall x \in [0, 1] \cdot 1 \lambda x = x$. Moreover we require λ to be increasing in both of its arguments, i.e.[4] for $x_1, x_2 \in [0, 1]$, $x_1 \leq x_2$ implies $x_1 \lambda y \leq x_2 \lambda y$. Intuitively, a t-norm corresponds to conjunction. In this paper, we restrict ourselves to continuous t-norms. As the most often used t-norms are continuous, this is not a burdensome restriction.

---

[4] Note that the monotonicity of the second component immediately follows from that of the first component due to the commutativity.

An *implicator* $\rightsquigarrow$ is any $[0,1]^2 \rightarrow [0,1]$ (infix) operator $\rightsquigarrow$ satisfying $0 \rightsquigarrow 0 = 1$, and $\forall x \in [0,1] \cdot 1 \rightsquigarrow x = x$. Moreover $\rightsquigarrow$ must be decreasing in its first, and increasing in its second argument. Every t-norm $\curlywedge$ induces a *residual implicator* defined by $x \rightsquigarrow y = \sup\{\, \lambda \in [0,1] \mid x \curlywedge \lambda \leq y \,\}$. When the partial mappings of a t-norm $\curlywedge$ are supmorphisms[5], then $\curlywedge$ and its residual implicator $\rightsquigarrow$ satisfy the *residual property*, i.e. $\forall x, y, z \in [0,1] \cdot x \curlywedge y \leq z \equiv x \leq y \rightsquigarrow z$. Throughout this paper we only consider such residual pairs.

Well-known fuzzy logical operators on $[0,1]$ include the *minimum t-norm* $x \curlywedge^m y = \min(x, y)$, its residual implicator (also known as the "Gödel implicator") $x \rightsquigarrow^m y = 1$ if $x \leq y$, and $x \rightsquigarrow^m y = y$ otherwise, the *Lukasiewicz t-norm* $x \curlywedge^l y = \max(x + y - 1, 0)$, and its residual implicator $x \rightsquigarrow^l y = \min(1 - x + y, 1)$. For negation, often the *standard negator* $\sim^s x = 1 - x$ is used.

Fuzzy equivalence is denoted as $\approx$ and defined as $a \approx b = (a \rightsquigarrow b) \curlywedge (b \rightsquigarrow a)$, where $\curlywedge$ is a t-norm and $\rightsquigarrow$ its residual implicator. If we want to denote the use of a specific t-norm together with its residual implicator, we do so by superscripting the $\approx$-symbol as in $\approx^m = (a \rightsquigarrow^m b) \curlywedge^m (b \rightsquigarrow^m a)$.

An *fuzzy set* A over some (ordinary) set X is an $X \rightarrow [0,1]$ mapping. For x in X, $A(x)$ is called the *membership degree* of x in A. We also use $\mathcal{F}(X)$ to denote the set of all fuzzy sets over X. The *support* of a fuzzy set A is defined by $supp(A) = \{\, x \mid A(x) > 0 \,\}$. Fuzzy set inclusion is also defined as usual by $A \subseteq B$, iff $\forall x \in X \cdot A(x) \leq B(x)$. Fuzzy set intersection (union) is defined by $(A \cap B)(x) = A(x) \sqcap B(x)$ $((A \cup B)(x) = A(x) \sqcup B(x))$. This is extended to sets of fuzzy sets in the usual way, i.e. $\bigcap\{\, A_1, \ldots, A_n \,\} = A_1 \cap \ldots \cap A_n$ and $\bigcup\{\, A_1, \ldots, A_n \,\} = A_1 \cup \ldots \cup A_n$. Lastly the fuzzy set difference we will be using in this paper is $(A \setminus B)(x) = |A(x) - B(x)|$.

3 Fuzzy Answer Set Programming

Fuzzy answer set programming [3] is an extension of regular answer set programming (see e.g. [14]), a declarative formalism based on the stable model semantics for logic programming [15].

Definition 1 (FASP program). *A literal[6] is an atom a or a constant from $[0,1]$. An extended literal is either an atom or of the form $not_\sim a$, with a an atom and $\sim$ a negator, representing negation as failure (naf). A rule r is of the form*

$$a \leftarrow_{\rightsquigarrow, \curlywedge} b_1, \ldots, b_n, not_{\sim_1} c_1, \ldots, not_{\sim_m} c_m$$

where $n \geq 0$, $m \geq 0$ and a, $\{\, b_i \mid 1 \leq i \leq n \,\}$, and $\{\, c_j \mid 1 \leq j \leq m \,\}$ are (sets of) literals; $\sim_1, \ldots, \sim_m$ are negators and $\rightsquigarrow$ and $\curlywedge$ are resp. a residual implicator and a t-norm. The literal a is called the head, *denoted r_h of the rule r, while $\{\, b_1 \ldots, b_n, not \ c_1, \ldots, not \ c_m \,\}$ is called the* body *r_b of r. We use $Lit(r_b)$ to*

---

[5] The partial mappings of a t-norm $\curlywedge$ are called supmorphisms when for an arbitrary index set J it holds that $\sup\{\, x_i \curlywedge y \mid i \in J \,\} = \sup\{\, x_i \mid i \in J \,\} \curlywedge y$.

[6] As usual, we will assume that programs have already been grounded.

denote the set of regular literals $\{ b_1, \ldots, b_n \}$ *from* r_b. *A* constraint *is a rule* r
where $r_h \in [0, 1]$.

For a rule r, we use $\curlywedge_{r_b}$ *and* $\rightsquigarrow_r$ *to denote the rule's t-norm* $\curlywedge$, *and implicator*
$\rightsquigarrow$, *respectively. We also use* $\curlywedge_r$ *to denote the t-norm of which* $\rightsquigarrow_r$ *is the residual
implicator.*

A (FASP) program P *is a finite set of rules. The set of all literals that occur
in* P *is called the* Herbrand Base $\mathcal{B}_P$ *of* P. *The set of all rules in* P *that have
the literal* l *in the head is denoted as* P_l.

A rule-interpretation *is a function* $\rho : P \rightarrow [0, 1]$ *that associates a degree of
satisfaction* $\rho(r)$ *to each rule* $r \in P$. *With every FASP program, the programmer
must define a monotonic* aggregator *function* $\mathcal{A}_P : (P \rightarrow [0, 1]) \rightarrow [0, 1]$, *which
aggregates the values of all rules into a single degree of rule satisfaction for the
program.*

Definition 2 (Interpretation of a FASP program). *Let* P *be a FASP
program. An* interpretation *of* P *is any fuzzy set* $I \in \mathcal{F}(\mathcal{B}_P)$. *Interpretations
are extended to constants, extended literals and rules in a straightforward way:
for a constant* $c \in [0, 1]$, *define* $I(c) = c$. *For extended literals, we define
$I(not_{\sim} a) = \sim I(a)$. For a rule* $r = a \leftarrow_{\rightsquigarrow, \curlywedge} b_1, \ldots, b_n, not_{\sim_1} c_1, \ldots, not_{\sim_m} c_m$, *the
extension to the rule body* r_b *is defined as:* $I(r_b) = I(b_1) \curlywedge \ldots \curlywedge I(b_n) \curlywedge I(not_{\sim_1} c_1) \curlywedge
\ldots \curlywedge I(not_{\sim_m} c_m)$, *yielding the degree of satisfaction of* r *as* $I(r) = I(r_b) \rightsquigarrow I(r_h)$.

For every interpretation I *there is a corresponding rule interpretation* I_ρ,
defined by $I_\rho(r) = I(r)$ *for all* r *from* P.

Example 1. Consider a grounded version of the program P_{intro} from Section 1,
with the seat constants, person constants, the *near* and *friend* predicates as
given in the introduction, and the interpretations I_1 and I_2 as given in (1)-
(2). Interpretation I_1 satisfies the constraint $0 \leftarrow_{\rightsquigarrow^l, \curlywedge^l} unhappy(a)$ to degree
$I_1(unhappy(a)) \rightsquigarrow^l 0 = \min(1 - .5 + 0, 1) = .5$, while interpretation I_2 satisfies this constraint only to degree .2. Note that the choice of the Łukasiewicz
implicator $\rightsquigarrow^l$ in this constraint is crucial to preserve the gradual character of
the vague *unhappy* predicate in the rule satisfaction. Using the Gödel implicator
$\rightsquigarrow^m$ e.g. would force this rule to be evaluated in a crisp way (either the rule is
fully satisfied or it is not satisfied at all), hence loosing the nuance.

In the (*crisp*) rules on the contrary, the choice for the residual pair $\curlywedge^m$ and
$\rightsquigarrow^m$ allows to enforce that a given person either sits on a given seat or not.
Indeed, a constraint like $0 \leftarrow_{\rightsquigarrow^m, \curlywedge^m} sit(a, s_1), not_{\sim^s} sit(a, s_1)$ is only satisfied to
degree 1 when the rule body is satisfied to degree 0. Since the minimum t-norm
does not have zero divisors, this situation only occurs when either $I(sit(a, s_1)) =
0$, i.e. a does not sit on seat s_1, or when $I(not_{\sim^s} sit(a, s_1)) = 0$, i.e. $I(sit(a, s_1)) =
1$, in other words a sits on seat s_1.

Residual implicators adhere to the property that $x \rightsquigarrow y = 1$ iff $x \leq y$. In other
words, according to Definition 2, an interpretation fully satisfies a rule whenever
it satisfies the head at least as much as the body. The interpretation

$$I_3 = \{ sit(a, s_1)^1, sit(b, s_2)^1, sit(c, z)^1, unhappy(a)^{.9}, \ldots \} \tag{3}$$

fully satisfies the rule

$$unhappy(a) \leftarrow_{\rightsquigarrow^m, \curlywedge^m} sit(a, s_1), sit(c, z), friend(a, c), not_{\sim^s} near(s_1, z)$$

since $.9 \geq \min(1, 1, .5, 1)$. However, assigning $.5$ to $unhappy(a)$ would already be sufficient to fully satisfy the rule; in other words the desire to fully satisfy this rule does not provide sufficient justification to assign to $unhappy(a)$ a degree higher than $.5$. To ensure that we only derive a minimal knowledge set from our programs, we use the so called "support" of an interpretation with respect to a given rule and relative to a given rule interpretation. Intuitively, this is the lowest possible value that can be assigned to the head of the rule such that the rule is satisfied to at least the degree that is required by the given rule interpretation.

Definition 3 (Support). *Let P be a FASP program. We define the* support *of an interpretation I of P with respect to the rule $r \in P$ and relative to the rule interpretation ρ of P as:*

$$I_s(r, \rho) = \inf\{\, k \in [0, 1] \mid I(r_b) \rightsquigarrow_r k \geq \rho(r)\,\}$$

We abbreviate $I_s(r, I_\rho)$ as $I_s(r)$.

Theorem 1. *Let P be a FASP program. For any interpretation I of P, rule $r \in P$, and rule interpretation ρ of P the following holds:*

$$I_s(r, \rho) = I(r_b) \curlywedge_r \rho(r)$$

For $\rho = I_\rho$ we have the following result:

$$I_s(r) = I(r_b) \sqcap I(r_h)$$

The definition of fuzzy answer sets relies on the notion of *unfounded sets*, which, intuitively, are sets of "assumption" literals that have no proper motivation from the program.

Definition 4 (Unfounded-free interpretation). *Let I be an interpretation of a program P. A set $Y \subseteq \mathcal{B}_P$ is called* unfounded *w.r.t. I iff for each literal $l \in Y$ and rule $r \in P_l$ it holds that either:*

- $Y \cap Lit(r_b) \neq \emptyset$ *or*
- $I(l) > I_s(r)$ *or*
- $I(r_b) = 0$

An interpretation I of P is unfounded-free *iff $supp(I) \cap Y = \emptyset$ for any unfounded set Y w.r.t. I.*

The first condition in Definition 4 prevents circular motivation between assumptions. The second condition prohibits assumptions motivated by rules that are not applied conservatively, i.e. a rule r is used to motivate a truth value of the head in excess of the support that is actually available (from $I_s(r)$). The third condition finally helps to ensure that Definition 4 is a proper generalization of the classical definition of unfounded sets [16].

Example 2. Consider an interpretation $I = \{\, a^{0.5}, b^{0.5}\,\}$ for program P_2, defined below.

$$r_1 : a \leftarrow_{\leadsto m, \lambda m} b$$
$$r_2 : b \leftarrow_{\leadsto m, \lambda m} a$$

As there is no rule supporting the fact that $I(a) = 0.5$ or $I(b) = 0.5$, this interpretation contains more knowledge than what is inferable from the program and is therefore unwanted. In fact e.g. $Y = \{\, a, b\,\}$ is an unfounded set because both $Y \cap Lit(r_1) \neq \emptyset$ and $Y \cap Lit(r_2) \neq \emptyset$. Since $supp(I) \cap Y \neq \emptyset$, I is not unfounded-free.

Answer sets of FASP programs are unfounded-free interpretations reflecting the intuition that each literal in an answer set should have a proper motivation in the program. Moreover, the rules of the program should be satisfied to a desired degree.

Definition 5 (y-answer set). *Let P be a FASP program and $y \in [0, 1]$. An interpretation I of P is called a y-answer set iff I is unfounded-free and $\mathcal{A}_P(I_\rho) \geq y$.*

Example 3. Consider program P_{intro} from Section 1 and its interpretations I_1, I_2, and I_3 as given in (1)–(3). The set $\{\, unhappy(a)\,\}$ is unfounded w.r.t. I_3 as for each grounded instance r of the (u) rules with $unhappy(a)$ in the head, it holds that $I_3(unhappy(a)) > (I_3)_s(r)$. Hence I_3 is not unfounded-free. Interpretations I_1 and I_2 on the other hand are unfounded-free. Furthermore one can verify that $\mathcal{A}_{P_{intro}}((I_1)_\rho) \geq .5$ and $\mathcal{A}_{P_{intro}}((I_2)_\rho) \geq .2$, in other words I_1 and I_2 are resp. a .5-answer set and a .2-answer set of P_{intro}.

4 Fuzzy Propositional Logic

We build a fuzzy propositional logic starting from a set of t-norms $\{\, \lambda_1, \ldots, \lambda_n\,\}$, their residual implicators $\{\, \leadsto_1, \ldots, \leadsto_n\,\}$ and a set of negators $\{\, \sim_1, \ldots, \sim_k\,\}$, all of which are defined over $[0, 1]$. Furthermore there is a set of variable symbols $\{\, v_1, \ldots, v_l\,\}$. Further connectives are $\approx$, $\sqcup$ and $\sqcap$, where $\sqcup$ and $\sqcap$ are the infix supremum and infimum resp. and where $\approx$ is defined as $p \approx q = (p \leadsto q) \lambda (q \leadsto p)$, for λ a t-norm and $\leadsto$ its residual implicator.

The syntax of this fuzzy propositional logic is defined as follows. A *proposition* is either a constant from $[0, 1]$, a variable, or an expression of one of the following forms, where p and q are propositions: $p \lambda_i q$, where $i \in 1 \ldots n$, $p \leadsto_i q$, where $i \in 1 \ldots n$, $\sim_i p$, where $i \in 1 \ldots k$, $p \approx_i q$, where $i \in 1 \ldots n$, $p \sqcup q$, or $p \sqcap q$. A *theory* is a set of propositions.

The semantics of this logic is defined in a straightforward way. Let I be a fuzzy set over the variables of a proposition. Then I is inductively extended to propositions as follows: let p and q be fuzzy propositions and I an interpretation over the variables of p and q, then $I(l) = l$, where $l \in [0, 1]$, $I(p \lambda q) = I(p) \lambda I(q)$, $I(p \leadsto q) = I(p) \leadsto I(q)$, $I(\sim p) =\sim I(p)$, $I(p \sqcup q) = I(p) \sqcup I(q)$ and $I(p \sqcap q) = I(p) \sqcap I(q)$. A fuzzy set over the variables of a proposition is then called an *interpretation* of this proposition.

We say that an interpretation I is a model of a theory P, whenever $\forall p \in P \cdot I(p) = 1$ and denote this as $I \models P$.

5   Fuzzy Completion

In this section we show how certain fuzzy answer set programs can be translated to fuzzy theories such that the models of these theories will be y-answer sets and vice versa.

Definition 6 (Fuzzy y-completion). *Let P be a FASP program with aggregator $\mathcal{A}_P$ and let $y \in [0, 1]$. The fuzzy completion of the body of a rule $r \in P$, with $r = a \leftarrow_{\leadsto, \lambda} b_1, \ldots, b_n, not_{\sim_1} c_1, \ldots, not_{\sim_m} c_m$, is the propositional formula*

$$Comp(r_b) = b_1 \curlywedge_{r_b} \ldots \curlywedge_{r_b} b_n \curlywedge_{r_b} \sim_1 c_1 \curlywedge_{r_b} \ldots \curlywedge_{r_b} \sim_m c_m$$

The completion of the rule r is defined as:

$$Comp(r) = Comp(r_b) \sqcap r_h$$

Assume that the aggregator is representable as a fuzzy propositional formula, i.e. that a proposition $Comp_y(\mathcal{A}_P)$ exists such that for any interpretation I of P, $\mathcal{A}_P(I_\rho) \geq y$ iff $I \models Comp_y(\mathcal{A}_P)$. The fuzzy y-completion of the program P is then defined as:

$$Comp_y(P) = \{\, l \approx \bigsqcup \{\, Comp(r) \mid r \in P_l \,\} \mid l \in \mathcal{B}_P \,\} \cup Comp_y(\mathcal{A}_P)$$

for $\approx$ an arbitrary equivalence relation.

Note that the y in the completion is the same y we use for y-answer sets, thus the intention is that the models of the y-completion of a program will be the y-answer sets of the program.

Example 4. Consider the following program P:

$$r_1 : a \leftarrow_{\leadsto^m, \lambda^m} not_{\sim^s} b$$
$$r_2 : b \leftarrow_{\leadsto^m, \lambda^m} not_{\sim^s} a$$

with aggregator $\mathcal{A}_P(\rho) = \inf\{\, \rho(r) \mid r \in P \,\}$. The aggregator of this program is representable in fuzzy propositional logic as the formula $y \leadsto (\sim^s b \leadsto^m a) \sqcap (\sim^s a \leadsto^m b)$. The completion of this program will then be the following fuzzy propositional theory:

$$a \approx^m ((\sim^s b) \sqcap a)$$
$$b \approx^m ((\sim^s a) \sqcap b)$$
$$y \leadsto^m (\sim^s b \leadsto^m a) \sqcap (\sim^s a \leadsto^m b)$$

It is easy to see that the interpretation $I = \{\, a^{0.8}, b^{0.2} \,\}$ is a 1-answer set of this program and will also be a model of the completion $Comp_1(P)$.

Readers familiar with the completion in traditional logic programming may wonder why our completion uses $Comp(r_b) \sqcap r_h$ instead of the more usual $Comp(r_b)$ in the right-hand side of the equations. This is necessary in order to support the partial satisfaction of rules. Indeed, using $Comp(r_b)$ would force rules to be fully satisfied, while using $Comp(r_b) \sqcap r_h$ allows interpretations for which $I(r_h) < I(r_b)$, leading to $(I(r_b) \leadsto_r I(r_h)) < 1$, hence interpretations that only partially satisfy rules.

In the fuzzy y-completion of a program P, we do not introduce a separate proposition for literals l that do not appear in the head of any rule from P, since these will be subsumed by the introduction of $l \approx \bigsqcup \emptyset$ (with our choice of equivalence relations), which is equivalent to $l \approx 0$ by definition of $\bigsqcup$. No separate propositions are added for constraints, i.e. rules with a value from $[0, 1]$ in the head, either, since constraints are only used to determine the aggregated satisfaction value of the program and hence are only needed in the aggregator proposition.

Finally, the condition on aggregators to be representable in fuzzy propositional logic is necessary to solve programs using SAT-solvers. That this condition still allows for sufficient expressiveness is illustrated by the fact that the aggregator of the program in the introduction can be represented as

$$Comp_y(\mathcal{A}_{P_{intro}}) = [1 \leadsto^m (c_1 \wedge^m c_2 \wedge^m crisp \wedge^m sit \wedge^m all \wedge^m u)] \sqcap [y \leadsto^l q]$$

One can now show that any y-answer set of a program P is a model of its completion $Comp_y(P)$.

Theorem 2. *Let P be a FASP program. Then if the aggregator is representable in fuzzy propositional logic, any y-answer set of P is a model of $Comp_y(P)$.*

The reverse of Theorem 2 is not true in general, since it is already invalid for classical answer set programming. The problem is with the completion of programs that have "loops", as shown in the following example.

Example 5. Consider P_2 from Example 2. The y-completion of this program is:

$$a \approx b \sqcap a$$
$$b \approx a \sqcap b$$
$$y \leadsto^m (a \leadsto^m b) \sqcap (b \leadsto^m a)$$

The interpretation $I = \{ a^1, b^1 \}$, is a model of $Comp_y(P_2)$, but it is not a y-answer set of P_2, as the only y-answer set (with $y > 0$) of this program is $\{ a^0, b^0 \}$.

As in the crisp case, when a program has no loops in its positive dependency graph however, the models of the y-completion and the y-answer sets do coincide. First we define what a loop of a logic program actually means and then we formally state that the aforementioned holds.

Definition 7 (Loop). *Let P be a FASP program. The positive dependency graph of P is then a directed graph $G_P = (\mathcal{B}_P, R)$ where $a R b \equiv \exists r \in P_a \cdot$*

$b \in Lit(r_b)$. *We denote this relation also with* $G_P(a, b)$ *for any literals* a *and* b
in the Herbrand base of P. *We call a non-empty set* $L \subseteq \mathcal{B}_P$ *a loop iff for all*
literals a *and* b *in* L *there is a path (with length* > 0*) from* a *to* b *in* G_P *such*
that all vertices on this path are elements of L.

Using this definition, one can easily see that the program from Example 2 contains the loop $L = \{\, a, b \,\}$.

Theorem 3. *Let* P *be a FASP program. If* P *has no loops in its positive de-*
pendency graph and its aggregator is representable in fuzzy propositional logic, it
holds that I *is a* y*-answer set of* P *iff* $I \models Comp_y(P)$.

6   Solving the Loop Problem

As mentioned in the previous section, sometimes the models of the y-completion
are not y-answer sets, which hinders the possibility of using the y-completion of
a program to e.g. compute y-answer sets using a fuzzy satisfiability solver. In this
section, we investigate how the solution for boolean answer set programming,
which consists of adding loop formulas to the completion [12], can be extended
to fuzzy answer set programs.

For this extension, we will start from a partition of the rules whose heads
are in a loop, for a given loop L. Based upon this partition, we will then define
a condition that must be fulfilled and can be expressed in fuzzy propositional
logic, such that any model of the y-completion satisfying it, will no longer have
the problem of attaching a value that is too high to atoms that occur in a loop.

For any program P and loop L we consider the following partition of rules
with heads in the loop of P (due to [12]):

$$R_P^+(L) = \{\, a \leftarrow B \mid (a \leftarrow B) \in P \wedge a \in L \wedge B \cap L \neq \emptyset \,\}$$
$$R_P^-(L) = \{\, a \leftarrow B \mid (a \leftarrow B) \in P \wedge a \in L \wedge B \cap L = \emptyset \,\}$$

Intuitively, this means that $R_P^+(L)$ contains the rules that are "in" the loop L,
i.e. that are responsible for the creation of the loop in the positive dependency
graph, whereas the rules in $R_P^-(L)$ are the rules that are outside of this loop. We
will refer to them as "loop rules", resp. "non-loop rules". Recalling the program
from Example 2, the partitions of rules with respect to the loop $L = \{\, a, b \,\}$
would be $R_P^+(L) = \{\, a \leftarrow_{\rightsquigarrow m, \lambda m} b, b \leftarrow_{\rightsquigarrow m, \lambda m} a \,\}$ and $R_P^-(L) = \emptyset$.

All literals in the support of a y-answer set are derived using rules that are
not contained in any loop. Therefore, like in [12], this motivates the use of "loop
formulas" to eliminate any model of the completion in which the value of a
literal is derived using only loop rules (or is higher than what the non-loop rules
could conclude). Considering Example 2 once again, one can see that for the
interpretation $I_0 = \{\, a^1, b^1 \,\}$, the loop rules were used to attach the high values
to a and b. The only interpretation that does not use the loop rules would be
$I_1 = \{\, a^0, b^0 \,\}$.

There is thus a problem when the values of literals in a loop are only
supported by other literals in the loop. This is the case when their value is

only supported by loop rules, as the support of these rules is by definition always based on literals in the loop. Hence to solve this problem, we should require that at least one non-loop rule supports the value of loop literals. Only one rule's support is needed as this support propagates through the loop.

Example 6. As an illustration of the above remark, consider program P_6.

$$r_1 : a \leftarrow_{\leadsto^m, \lambda^m} 0.8$$
$$r_2 : a \leftarrow_{\leadsto^m, \lambda^m} b$$
$$r_3 : b \leftarrow_{\leadsto^m, \lambda^m} a$$

with aggregator $\mathcal{A}_P(\rho) = \inf\{\, \rho(r) \mid r \in P_6 \,\}$.

There is a loop $L = \{\, a, b \,\}$ in P_6, with loop sets $R_{P_6}^+(L) = \{\, r_2, r_3 \,\}$ and $R_{P_6}^-(L) = \{\, r_1 \,\}$. The interpretation $I = \{\, a^1, b^1 \,\}$ is a model of $Comp_1(P_6)$ since $I \models a \approx (0.8 \sqcap a) \sqcup (a \sqcap b)$ as $(0.8 \sqcap I(a)) \sqcup (I(b) \sqcap I(a)) = 1$, $I \models b \approx b \sqcap a$ likewise and $I \models 1 \leadsto^m (0.8 \leadsto^m a) \sqcap (b \leadsto^m a) \sqcap (a \leadsto^m b)$ as $0.8 \leadsto^m I(a) = 1$ since $0.8 \le I(a)$ and likewise $(I(b) \leadsto^m I(a)) = 1$ and $(I(a) \leadsto^m I(b)) = 1$. I is not a 1-answer set of P_6 however, as $L \cap supp(I) \ne \emptyset$ and L is unfounded due to $I(a) > 0.8$, $Lit(r_{2b}) \cap L \ne \emptyset$ and $Lit(r_{3b}) \cap L \ne \emptyset$. In other words, I has only used loop rules to determine the values of a and b.

The set $I' = \{\, a^{0.8}, b^{0.8} \,\}$ is however a 1-answer set as the non-loop rule r_1 was used to derive the value of literal a. Since the value of b is derived from this non-loop-derived value of a, the use of the loop rule r_3 to determine the value of b then poses no problem.

Summing all of this up, the definition then becomes:

Definition 8 (Loop formula). *Let P be a FASP program and $L = \{\, l_1, \ldots, l_m \,\}$ a loop in the positive dependency graph of P. Suppose that $R_P^-(L) = \{\, r_1, \ldots, r_n \,\}$. Then the loop formula associated with the loop L, denoted by $\mathrm{LF}(L, P)$, is the following fuzzy proposition:*

$$l_1 \sqcup \ldots \sqcup l_m \leadsto Comp(r_1) \sqcup \ldots \sqcup Comp(r_n)$$

If $R_P^-(L) = \emptyset$, the loop formula becomes:

$$l_1 \sqcup \ldots \sqcup l_m \leadsto 0$$

The loop formula proposed for boolean answer set programs in [12] is of the form

$$\neg(\bigwedge B_{11} \vee \ldots \vee \bigwedge B_{1k_1} \vee \ldots \vee \bigwedge B_{n1} \vee \ldots \vee \bigwedge B_{nk_n}) \Rightarrow (\neg l_1 \wedge \ldots \wedge \neg l_m)$$

It can easily be seen that our loop formulas are a straightforward generalisation of this loop formula as the latter is equivalent to

$$(l_1 \vee \ldots \vee l_m) \Rightarrow (\bigwedge B_{11} \vee \ldots \vee \bigwedge B_{1k_1} \vee \ldots \vee \bigwedge B_{n1} \vee \ldots \vee \bigwedge B_{nk_n})$$

Furthermore, since $I \models l_1 \sqcup \ldots \sqcup l_m \leadsto 0$ only when $I(l_1) \sqcup \ldots \sqcup I(l_m) \le 0$, it is easy to see that in the case where no rules exist outside of the loop, the maximum amount of knowledge we can derive from our program is that the literals in the loop are all "false" (0).

Example 7. Consider program P_2 from Example 2 again. There is a loop $L = \{a, b\}$ in G_P with as loop formula $a \sqcup b \leadsto^m 0$, since the set $R_P^-(L) = \emptyset$. $I_0 = \{a^1, b^1\}$ is not a model of this formula, as $I_0(a) \sqcup I_0(b) \leadsto 0 = 1 \equiv I_0(a) \sqcup I_0(b) \leq 0$. Hence, only the interpretation $I_1 = \{a^0, b^0\}$ is a model of this loop formula, which is the intended behaviour.

Considering program P_6 from Example 6, we can see that the loop $L = \{a, b\}$ has the loop formula $a \sqcup b \leadsto a \sqcap 0.8$. Since $I \models a \sqcup b \leadsto^m a \sqcap 0.8$ only if $a \leq 0.8$ and $b \leq a \sqcap 0.8$, interpretation I from Example 6 is eliminated as a model while I' is preserved.

We now show that by adding loop formulas to the completion of a program, we get a propositional theory that is both sound and complete with respect to the answer set semantics. First we show that this procedure is complete.

Theorem 4. *Let P be a FASP program and let $\mathrm{LF}(P)$ be the set of all loop formulas of P, i.e. the set of loop formulas for any loop L in P. Then for any interpretation I of P it holds that if I is a y-answer set of P, then $I \models \mathrm{LF}(P) \cup Comp_y(P)$.*

Secondly we show that it is sound.

Theorem 5. *Let P be a FASP program and $\mathrm{LF}(P)$ be the set of all loop formulas of P. Then for any interpretation I of P it holds that if $I \models \mathrm{LF}(P) \cup Comp_y(P)$, then I is a y-answer set of P.*

A straightforward procedure for finding answer sets would now be to extend the completion of a program with all possible loop formulas and let a fuzzy SAT solver generate models of the resulting propositional theory. The models of the propositional theory that we get this way will be y-answer sets of the program, as ensured by Theorems 4 and 5. This however has a potential drawback, as the amount of loops can grow exponentially. In [12] a procedure to overcome this problem was proposed, where loop formulas are added iteratively, when a model of the completion generated by a SAT-solver violates a loop formula. We will show that the same procedure can be used for finding fuzzy answer sets. For this, we need a characterization of answer sets in terms of the consequence operator.

Definition 9 (Consequence operator). *Let P be a FASP program and let ρ be a rule interpretation of P. The consequence operator of P and ρ is defined as follows:*

$$\Pi_{P,\rho} : (\mathcal{B}_P \to [0, 1]) \to \mathcal{B}_P \to [0, 1]$$

$$\Pi_{P,\rho}(I)(l) = \sup_{r \in P_l} I_s(r, \rho)$$

This operator is monotonic and thus has a least fixpoint [17], denoted as $lfp(\Pi_{P,\rho})$. Furthermore, a reduct is defined as follows:

Definition 10 (Reduct). *Let P be a FASP program. Then the reduct of a rule $r \in P$, where $r = a \leftarrow_{\leadsto,\curlywedge} b_1, \ldots, b_n, not_{\sim_1} c_1, \ldots, not_{\sim_m} c_m$, with respect to* *an interpretation I is denoted as r^I and defined as $r^I = a \leftarrow_{\rightsquigarrow,\curlywedge} b_1, \ldots, b_n, \sim_1 I(c_1), \ldots, \sim_m I(c_m)$. The reduct of a program P w.r.t. an interpretation I is denoted as P^I and defined as $P^I = \{ r^I \mid r \in P \}$.*

It can then be shown that a fixpoint characterisation exists for fuzzy answer sets, as follows:

Theorem 6. *Let P be a FASP program. Then I is a y-answer set of P iff $I = \mathit{lfp}(\Pi_{P^I, I_\rho})$ and $\mathcal{A}_P(I_\rho) \geq y$.*

Using this characterisation of fuzzy answer sets, we have a quick way of checking whether a model of the y-completion is a y-answer set. In case it is not a y-answer set, the following theorem shows us that this means there is at least one loop whose loop formula is violated. Furthermore, it identifies a set of literals that contains the loop, enabling us to reduce the search space for finding the loops.

Theorem 7. *Let P be a FASP program. If an interpretation I of P is a model of $Comp_y(P)$ and $I \neq \mathit{lfp}(\Pi_{P^I, I_\rho})$, then some $L \subseteq supp(I \setminus \mathit{lfp}(\Pi_{P^I, I_\rho}))$ must exist such that L is a loop and $I \not\models \mathrm{LF}(L, P)$.*

Now, we can extend the ASSAT-procedure proposed in [12] to fuzzy answer set programs. The main idea of this method is to use a fuzzy SAT-solver to find models of the fuzzy propositional theory constructed from the completion and the loop formulas of some maximal loops. If the model generated is not an answer set, then the loop that is violated is sought and added to the theory and the process is started again. The algorithm thus becomes:

1. Initialize $Loops = \emptyset$.
2. Generate a model I of $Comp_y(P) \cup \mathrm{LF}(Loops, P)$, where $\mathrm{LF}(Loops, P)$ is the set of loop formulas of all loops in $Loops$.
3. If $I = \mathit{lfp}(\Pi_{P^I, I_\rho})$, return I as it is a y-answer set. Else, find the loops occurring in $supp(I \setminus \mathit{lfp}(\Pi_{P^I, I_\rho}))$, add them to $Loops$ and go to step 2.

As we only need to search for the loops of a subset of all literals due to Theorem 7, which only needs to be done when a model is generated that is not an answer set, this procedure does not need to add an exponential number of loop formulas at the start. Based on the experimental results in [12], we would expect a similar improvement when finding fuzzy answer sets using fuzzy SAT-solvers.

7   Conclusions and Future Work

We defined a fuzzy version of Clark's completion, creating a basis for different kinds of (fuzzy) answer set solvers. Furthermore, we defined loop formulas that ensure that the completion semantics coincide with the program semantics in the presence of loops in the positive dependency graph. We have also shown how, similar to the ASSAT procedure for answer set programs, loop formulas of fuzzy answer set programs can be computed "on the fly", thus avoiding a possibly exponential blow-up of the number of loop formulas to consider.

As algorithms for solving the fuzzy SAT problem, with restrictions on the operators used, have been developed [7,8,9], the results of this paper thus effectively create a basis for practical implementations of the FASP paradigm. This is enhanced by the possibility of iteratively adding loop formulas, as in the ASSAT procedure for crisp answer set programming.

In the future, we intend to investigate solving the completion proposition using a combination of a translation to linear programming and tableaux, as in [7,9], but with less restrictions on the operators. Related with this, we intend to investigate the possibilities in directly solving the program using mixed integer programming as in [11].

A first prototype FASPMIP[7] has already been developed It supports a simple concrete syntax to express a limited set of connectives and a restricted set of aggregator functions.

As an example, the source (not including the "data") for the program P_{intro} from Section 1 is shown below.

```
sit(P,S) :/ Person(P),Seat(S). % choice
:- sit(P,S),sit(PP,S), P /= PP.
:- sit(P,S),sit(P,SS), S /= SS.
:- sit(P,S),not sit(P,S). % crispify sit/2
unhappy(P) :- sit(P,S), sit(PP,SS), friend(P,PP), not near(S,SS).
:~ unhappy(P). % score
seated(P) :- sit(P,S). :- not seated(P),Person(P). % all seated
```

To compute the semantics of an input program, FASPMIP parses and grounds the rules in the usual way. Then the program is translated to a set of linear programming constraints corresponding to the y-completion of the program, see also [11]. The resulting linear programming model is then written to a file using the *MathProg* modeling language. The file serves as input for the LP/MIP *glpsol* solver[8], which computes a minimal y-answer set.

The output (for selected predicates) of FASPMIP for a 0.5-answer set of the program P_{intro} from Section 1 is shown below.

```
[(near(s1,s2),0.8), (friend(a,c),0.5),(friend(a,b),0.8),
 (unhappy(a),0.5),(sit(c,s3),1.0),(sit(b,s2),1.0),(sit(a,s1),1.0)]
```

References

1. Lukasiewicz, T.: Fuzzy description logic programs under the answer set semantics for the semantic web. In: Proceedings of the Second International Conference on Rules and Rule Markup Languages for the Semantic Web (RuleML 2006), pp. 89–96. IEEE Computer Society, Los Alamitos (2006)

---

[7] Available from `http://tinf2.vub.ac.be/faspsolver/faspmip-0.1.tar.gz`.

[8] *glpsol* is part of GLPK, the GNU Linear Programming Kit, see `http://www.gnu.org/software/glpk/glpk.html`.

2. Lukasiewicz, T., Straccia, U.: Tightly integrated fuzzy description logic programs under the answer set semantics for the semantic web. In: Marchiori, M., Pan, J.Z., de Sainte Marie, C. (eds.) RR 2007. LNCS, vol. 4524, pp. 289–298. Springer, Heidelberg (2007)

3. Van Nieuwenborgh, D., De Cock, M., Vermeir, D.: An introduction to fuzzy answer set programming. Annals of Mathematics and Artificial Intelligence 50(3-4), 363–388 (2007)

4. Damásio, C., Medina, J., Ojeda-Aciego, M.: Sorted multi-adjoint logic programs: termination results and applications. In: Alferes, J.J., Leite, J. (eds.) JELIA 2004. LNCS, vol. 3229, pp. 260–273. Springer, Heidelberg (2004)

5. Kifer, M., Subrahmanian, V.S.: Theory of generalized annotated logic programming and its applications. Journal of Logic Programming 12(3-4), 335–367 (1992)

6. Straccia, U.: Annotated answer set programming. In: Proceedings of the 11th International Conference on Information Processing and Management of Uncertainty in Knowledge-Based Systems, IPMU 2006 (2006)

7. Hähnle, R.: Many-valued logic and mixed integer programming. Annals of Mathematics and Artificial Intelligence 12(3-4), 231–263 (1994)

8. Lepock, C., Pelletier, F.J.: Fregean algebraic tableaux: Automating inferences in fuzzy propositional logic. In: Sutcliffe, G., Voronkov, A. (eds.) LPAR 2005. LNCS, vol. 3835, pp. 43–48. Springer, Heidelberg (2005)

9. Straccia, U.: Reasoning and experimenting within Zadeh's fuzzy propositional logic. Technical report, Paris, France (2000)

10. Clark, K.L.: Negation as failure. In: Logic and Databases, pp. 293–322. Plenum Press, New York (1978)

11. Bell, C., Nerode, A., Ng, R.T., Subrahmanian, V.S.: Mixed integer programming methods for computing nonmonotonic deductive databases. Journal of the ACM 41(6), 1178–1215 (1994)

12. Lin, F., Zhao, Y.: ASSAT: computing answer sets of a logic program by sat solvers. Artificial Intelligence 157(1-2), 115–137 (2004)

13. Novák, V., Perfilieva, I., Močkoř, J.: Mathematical Principles of Fuzzy Logic. Kluwer Academic Publishers, Dordrecht (1999)

14. Baral, C.: Knowledge Representation, Reasoning and Declarative Problem Solving. Cambridge University Press, Cambridge (2003)

15. Gelfond, M., Lifschitz, V.: The stable model semantics for logic programming. In: Proceedings of the Fifth International Conference and Symposium on Logic Programming (ICLP/SLP 1988), ALP, IEEE, pp. 1081–1086. The MIT Press, Cambridge (1988)

16. van Gelder, A., Ross, K.A., Schlipf, J.S.: The well-founded semantics for general logic programs. Journal of the Association for Computing Machinery 38(3), 620–650 (1991)

17. Tarski, A.: A lattice theoretical fixpoint theorem and its application. Pacific Journal of Mathematics 5, 285–309 (1955)

Abstract Answer Set Solvers

Yuliya Lierler

University of Texas at Austin
yuliya@cs.utexas.edu

Abstract. Nieuwenhuis, Oliveras, and Tinelli showed how to describe enhancements of the Davis-Putnam-Logemann-Loveland algorithm using transition systems, instead of pseudocode. We design a similar framework for three algorithms that generate answer sets for logic programs: SMODELS, ASP-SAT with Backtracking, and a newly designed and implemented algorithm SUP. This approach to describing answer set solvers makes it easier to prove their correctness, to compare them, and to design new systems.

1 Introduction

Most state-of-the-art Satisfiability (SAT) solvers are based on variations of the Davis-Putnam-Logemann-Loveland (DPLL) procedure [1]. Usually enhancements of DPLL are described fairly informally with the use of pseudocode. It is often difficult to understand the precise meaning of these modifications and to prove their properties on the basis of such informal descriptions. In [2], the authors proposed an alternative approach to describing DPLL and its enhancements (for instance, backjumping and learning). They describe each variant of DPLL by means of a transition system that can be viewed as an abstract framework underlying DPLL computation. The authors further extend the framework to the algorithms commonly used in Satisfiability Modulo Background Theories.

The abstract framework introduced in [2] describes what "states of computation" are, and which transitions between states are allowed. In this way, it defines a directed graph such that every execution of the DPLL procedure corresponds to a path in this graph. Some edges may correspond to unit propagation steps, some to branching, some to backtracking. This allows the authors to model a DPLL algorithm by a mathematically simple and elegant object, graph, rather than a collection of pseudocode statements. Such an abstract way of presenting DPLL simplifies the analysis of its correctness and facilitates formal reasoning about its properties. Instead of reasoning about pseudocode constructs, we can reason about properties of a graph. For instance, by proving that the graph corresponding to a version of DPLL is acyclic we demonstrate that the algorithm always terminates. On the other hand, by checking that every terminal state corresponds to a solution we establish the correctness of the algorithm.

The graph introduced in [2] is actually an imperfect representation of DPLL in the sense that some paths in the graph do not correspond to any execution of DPLL (for example, paths in which branching is used even though unit propagation is applicable). But this level of detail is irrelevant when we talk about correctness. Furthermore, it

M. Garcia de la Banda and E. Pontelli (Eds.): ICLP 2008, LNCS 5366, pp. 377–391, 2008.

makes our correctness theorems more general. These theorems cover not only executions of the pseudo-code, but also some computations that are prohibited by its details.

In this paper we take the abstract framework for describing DPLL-like procedures for SAT solvers as a starting point and design a similar framework for three algorithms that generate answer sets for logic programs. The first one is the SMODELS algorithm [3], implemented in one of the major answer set solvers[1]. The other algorithm is called SUP and can be seen as a simplification of SMODELS algorithm.[2] We implemented this algorithm in the new, previously unpublished system SUP[3]. The last algorithm that we describe is ASP-SAT with Backtracking[4] [4]. It computes models of the completion of the given program using DPLL and tests them until an answer set is found.

We start by reviewing the abstract framework for DPLL developed in [2] in a form convenient for our purposes. We demonstrate how this framework can be modified to describe an algorithm for computing supported models of a logic program, and then extend it to the SMODELS algorithm for computing answer sets. We show that for a large class of programs, called tight, the graph representing SMODELS is closely related to the graph representing the application of DPLL to the completion of the program. As a step towards extending these ideas to ASP-SAT with Backtracking, we analyze a modification of the original DPLL graph that includes testing the models found by DPLL. We then show how a special case of this construction corresponds to ASP-SAT with Backtracking.

We hope that the analysis of algorithms for computing answer sets in terms of transition systems described in this paper will contribute to clarifying computational principles of answer set programming and to the development of new systems.

2   Review: Abstract DPLL

For a set σ of atoms, a *state* relative to σ is either a distinguished state *FailState* or a list M of literals over σ such that M contains no repetitions, and each literal in M has an *annotation*, a bit that marks it as a *decision* literal or not. For instance, the states relative to a singleton set $\{a\}$ of atoms are

$$FailState, \quad \emptyset, \quad a, \quad \neg a, \quad a^d, \quad \neg a^d, a \neg a, \quad a^d \neg a,$$
$$a \neg a^d, \quad a^d \neg a^d, \neg a\, a, \quad \neg a^d\, a, \quad \neg a\, a^d, \quad \neg a^d\, a^d,$$

where by $\emptyset$ we denote the empty list. The concatenation of two such lists is denoted by juxtaposition. Frequently, we consider M as a set of literals, ignoring both the annotations and the order between its elements. We write l^d to emphasize that l is a decision literal. A literal l is *unassigned by* M if neither l nor $\bar{l}$ belongs to M.

---

[1] SMODELS: http://www.tcs.hut.fi/Software/smodels

[2] The idea of simplifying the SMODELS algorithm in this manner was suggested to us by Mirosław Truszczyński (August 2, 2007).

[3] SUP: http://www.cs.utexas.edu/users/tag/sup. In fact, SUP implements a more sophisticated form of the algorithm that is enhanced with learning.

[4] A more sophisticated form of this algorithm, ASP-SAT with Learning, is implemented in system CMODELS: http://www.cs.utexas.edu/users/tag/cmodels

If C is a disjunction (conjunction) of literals then by $\overline{C}$ we understand the conjunction (disjunction) of the complements of the literals occurring in C. We will sometimes identify C with the set of its elements.

For any CNF formula F (a set of clauses), we will define its *DPLL graph* DP_F. The set of nodes of DP_F consists of the states relative to the set of atoms occurring in F. We use the terms "state" and "node" interchangeably. If a state is consistent and complete then it represents a truth assignment for F.

The set of edges of DP_F is described by a set of "transition rules". Each transition rule has the form $M \implies M'$ followed by a condition, so that

- M and M' are symbolic expressions for nodes of DP_F, and
- if the condition is satisfied there is an edge between node M and M' in the graph.

There are four transition rules that characterize the edges of DP_F:

$$\textit{Unit Propagate: } M \implies M\,l \text{ if } C \vee l \in F \text{ and } \overline{C} \subseteq M$$

$$\textit{Decide:} \qquad M \implies M\,l^d \text{ if } l \text{ is unassigned by } M$$

$$\textit{Fail:} \qquad M \implies \textit{FailState} \text{ if } \begin{cases} M \text{ is inconsistent, and} \\ M \text{ contains no decision literals} \end{cases}$$

$$\textit{Backtrack:} \quad P\,l^d\,Q \implies P\,\overline{l} \text{ if } \begin{cases} P\,l^d\,Q \text{ is inconsistent, and} \\ Q \text{ contains no decision literals.} \end{cases}$$

Note that an edge in the graph may be justified by several transition rules.

This graph can be used for deciding the satisfiability of a formula F simply by constructing an arbitrary path leading from node $\emptyset$ until a terminal node M is reached. The following proposition shows that this process always terminates, that F is unsatisfiable if M is *FailState*, and that M is a model of F otherwise.

Proposition 1. *For any CNF formula F,*

(a) graph DP_F is finite and acyclic,
(b) any terminal state of DP_F other than FailState is a model of F,
(c) FailState is reachable from $\emptyset$ in DP_F if and only if F is unsatisfiable.

For instance, let F be the set consisting of the clauses

$$a \vee b$$
$$\neg a \vee c.$$

Here is a path in DP_F with every edge annotated by the name of a transition rule that justifies the presence of this edge in the graph:

$$\begin{array}{lll} \emptyset & \implies & (\textit{Decide}) \\ a^d & \implies & (\textit{Unit Propagate}) \\ a^d\,c & \implies & (\textit{Decide}) \\ a^d\,c\,b^d & & \end{array} \qquad (1)$$

Since the state $a^d \, c \, b^d$ is terminal, Proposition 1(b) asserts that $\{a, c, b\}$ is a model of F. Here is another path in DP_F from $\emptyset$ to the same terminal node:

$$
\begin{array}{ll}
\emptyset & \Longrightarrow (\textit{Decide}) \\
a^d & \Longrightarrow (\textit{Decide}) \\
a^d \, \neg c^d & \Longrightarrow (\textit{Unit Propagate}) \\
a^d \, \neg c^d \, c \Longrightarrow (\textit{Backtrack}) \\
a^d \, c & \Longrightarrow (\textit{Decide}) \\
a^d \, c \, b^d &
\end{array}
\tag{2}
$$

Path (1) corresponds to an execution of DPLL; path (2) does not, because it uses *Decide* instead of *Unit Propagate*.

Note that the graph DP_F is a modification of the *classical DPLL* graph defined in [2, Section 2.3]. It is different in three ways. First, the description of the classical DPLL graph involves a "PureLiteral" transition rule, which we have dropped. Second, its states are pairs $M \parallel F$ for all CNF formulas F. For our purposes, it is not necessary to include F. Third, in the definition of that graph, each M is required to be consistent. In case of the DPLL, due to the simple structure of a clause, it is possible to characterize the applicability of *Backtrack* in a simple manner: when some of the clauses become inconsistent with the current partial assignment, *Backtrack* is applicable. In ASP, it is not easy to describe the applicability of *Backtrack* if only consistent states are taken into account. We introduced inconsistent states in the graph DP_F to facilitate our work on extending this graph to model the SMODELS algorithm.

3   Background: Logic Programs

A *(propositional) logic program* is a finite set of rules of the form

$$
a_0 \leftarrow a_1, \ldots, a_m, not \, a_{m+1}, \ldots, not \, a_n,
\tag{3}
$$

where each a_i is an atom. By $Bodies(\Pi, a)$ we denote the (multi-)set of the bodies of all rules of Π with head a. We will identify the body of (3) with the conjunction of literals

$$
a_1 \wedge \ldots \wedge a_m \wedge \neg a_{m+1} \wedge \ldots \neg a_n.
$$

and (3) with the implication

$$
a_1 \wedge \ldots \wedge a_m \wedge \neg a_{m+1} \wedge \ldots \neg a_n \rightarrow a_0.
$$

For any set M of literals, by M^+ we denote the set of positive literals from M. We assume that the reader is familiar with the definition of an answer set (stable model) of a logic program [5]. For any consistent and complete set M of literals (*assignment*), if M^+ is an answer set for a program Π, then M is a model of Π. Moreover, in this case M is a *supported* model of Π, in the sense that for every atom $a \in M$, $M \models B$ for some $B \in Bodies(\Pi, a)$.

4   Generating Supported Models

In the next section we will define, for an arbitrary program Π, a graph SM_Π representing the application of the SMODELS algorithm to Π; the terminal nodes of SM_Π are answer sets of Π. As a step in this direction, we describe here a simpler graph ATLEAST_Π. The terminal nodes of ATLEAST_Π are supported models of Π.

The set of nodes of ATLEAST_Π consists of the states relative to the set of atoms occurring in Π. The edges of the graph ATLEAST_Π are described by the transition rules *Decide*, *Fail*, *Backtrack* introduced above in the definition of DP_F and the additional transition rules[5]:

Unit Propagate LP: $M \implies M\,a$ if $a \leftarrow B \in \Pi$ and $B \subseteq M$

All Rules Cancelled: $M \implies M\,\neg a$ if $\overline{B} \cap M \neq \emptyset$ for all $B \in Bodies(\Pi, a)$,

Backchain True: $M \implies M\,l$ if $\begin{cases} a \leftarrow B \in \Pi, \\ a \in M, \\ \overline{B'} \cap M \neq \emptyset \text{ for all } B' \in Bodies(\Pi, a) \setminus B, \\ l \in B \end{cases}$

Backchain False: $M \implies M\,\bar{l}$ if $\begin{cases} a \leftarrow l, B \in \Pi, \\ \neg a \in M, \text{ and} \\ B \subseteq M. \end{cases}$

Note that each of the rules *Unit Propagate LP* and *Backchain False* is similar to *Unit Propagate*: the former corresponds to *Unit Propagate* on $C \vee l$ where l is the head of the rule, and the latter corresponds to *Unit Propagate* on $C \vee l$ where $\bar{l}$ is an element of the body of the rule.

This graph can be used for deciding whether program Π has a supported model by constructing a path from $\emptyset$ to a terminal node:

Proposition 2. *For any program Π,*

(a) graph ATLEAST_Π is finite and acyclic,

(b) any terminal state of ATLEAST_Π other than FailState is a supported model of Π,

(c) FailState is reachable from $\emptyset$ in ATLEAST_Π if and only if Π has no supported models.

For instance, let Π be the program

$$\begin{aligned} a &\leftarrow not\ b \\ b &\leftarrow not\ a \\ c &\leftarrow a \\ d &\leftarrow d. \end{aligned} \tag{4}$$

---

[5] The names of some of these rules follow [6].

Here is a path in ATLEAST$_\Pi$:

$$
\begin{array}{lll}
\emptyset & \Longrightarrow & (Decide) \\
a^d & \Longrightarrow & (Unit\ Propagate\ LP) \\
a^d\ c & \Longrightarrow & (All\ Rules\ Cancelled) \\
a^d\ c\ \neg b & \Longrightarrow & (Decide) \\
a^d\ c\ \neg b\ d^d &&
\end{array}
\tag{5}
$$

Since the state $a^d\ c\ \neg b\ d^d$ is terminal, Proposition 2(b) asserts that $\{a,c,\neg b,d\}$ is a supported model of program Π.

The assertion of Proposition 2 will remain true if we drop the transition rules *Backchain True* and *Backchain False* from the definition of ATLEAST$_\Pi$.

The transition rules defining ATLEAST$_\Pi$ are closely related to procedure *Atleast* [3, Sections 4.1], which is one of the core procedures of the SMODELS algorithm.

5   Smodels

Recall that a set U of atoms occurring in a program Π is said to be *unfounded* [7] on a consistent set M of literals w.r.t. Π if for every $a \in U$ and every $B \in Bodies(\Pi,a)$, $M \models \neg B$ or $U \cap B^+ \neq \emptyset$.

We now describe the graph SM$_\Pi$ that represents the application of the SMODELS algorithm to program Π. SM$_\Pi$ is a graph whose nodes are the same as the nodes of the graph ATLEAST$_\Pi$. The edges of SM$_\Pi$ are described by the transition rules of ATLEAST$_\Pi$ and the additional transition rule:

$$
Unfounded: M \Longrightarrow M\ \neg a \ \text{if} \ \begin{cases} M \text{ is consistent, and} \\ a \in U \text{ for a set } U \text{ unfounded on } M \text{ w.r.t. } \Pi \end{cases}
$$

This transition rule of SM$_\Pi$ is closely related to procedure *Atmost* [3, Sections 4.2], which together with the procedure *Atleast* forms the core of the SMODELS algorithm.

The graph SM$_\Pi$ can be used for deciding whether program Π has an answer set by constructing a path from $\emptyset$ to a terminal node:

Proposition 3. *For any program Π,*

(a) graph SM$_\Pi$ is finite and acyclic,
(b) for any terminal state M of SM$_\Pi$ other than FailState, M^+ is an answer set of Π,
(c) FailState is reachable from $\emptyset$ in SM$_\Pi$ if and only if Π has no answer sets.

To illustrate the difference between SM$_\Pi$ and ATLEAST$_\Pi$, assume again that Π is program (4). Path (5) in the graph ATLEAST$_\Pi$ is also a path in SM$_\Pi$. But state $a^d\ c\ \neg b\ d^d$, which is terminal in ATLEAST$_\Pi$, is not terminal in SM$_\Pi$. This is not surprising, since the set $\{a,c,d\}$ of atoms that belongs to this state is not an answer set of Π. To get to a state that is terminal in SM$_\Pi$, we need two more steps:

$$
\begin{array}{ll}
\ \ \vdots \\
a^d\ c\ \neg b\ d^d & \Longrightarrow \ (Unfounded,\ U = \{d\}) \\
a^d\ c\ \neg b\ d^d\ \neg d & \Longrightarrow \ (Backtrack) \\
a^d\ c\ \neg b\ \neg d.
\end{array}
\tag{6}
$$

Proposition 3(b) asserts that $\{a,c\}$ is an answer set of Π.

The assertion of Proposition 3 will remain true if we drop the transition rules *All Rules Cancelled*, *Backchain True*, and *Backchain False* from the definition of SM_Π.

6   Sup

In this section we show how to extend the graph ATLEAST_Π by the modification of transition rule *Unfounded* so that terminal nodes of the resulting graph correspond to answer sets of Π.

The graph SUP_Π is the subgraph of SM_Π such that its nodes are the same as the nodes of the graph SM_Π and its edges are described by the transition rules of ATLEAST_Π and the following modification of the rule *Unfounded* of SM_Π:

$$\text{Unfounded SUP: } M \implies M \neg a \text{ if } \begin{cases} \text{no literal is unassigned by } M, \\ M \text{ is consistent, and} \\ a \in U \text{ for a set } U \text{ unfounded on } M \text{ w.r.t. } \Pi. \end{cases}$$

This graph can be used for deciding whether a program Π has an answer set by constructing a path from $\emptyset$: Proposition 3 remains correct after replacing graph SM_Π with SUP_Π.

The only difference between SUP_Π and SM_Π is due to the additional restriction in *Unfounded SUP*: it is applicable only to the states that assign all atoms in Π. To illustrate the difference between SUP_Π and SM_Π, assume that Π is program (4). Path (6) in SM_Π is also a path in SUP_Π. On the other hand the path

$$\emptyset \underset{\neg d}{\implies} (\textit{Unfounded}, U = \{d\})$$

of SM_Π does not belong to SUP_Π

We can view the graph SUP_Π as a description of a particular strategy for traversing SM_Π, i.e., an edge corresponding to an application of *Unfounded* to a state in SM_Π is considered only if a transition rule *Decide* is not applicable in this state. Note that system SMODELS implements the opposite strategy, i.e., an edge corresponding to an application of *Decide* is considered only if *Unfounded* is not applicable. Nevertheless, the strategy described by SUP_Π may be reasonable for many problems. For instance, it is easy to see that transition rule *Unfounded* is redundant for tight programs. Furthermore, the analogous strategy has been successfully used in SAT-based answer set solvers ASSAT[6] [8] and CMODELS (see Footnote 4) [4]. These systems first compute the completion of a program and then test each model of the completion whether it is an answer set (this can be done by testing whether it contains unfounded sets). In fact, the work on ASSAT and CMODELS inspired the development of system SUP. Unlike ASSAT and CMODELS, SUP does not compute the completion of a program but performs its inference directly on the the program by means of transition rules of the graph SUP_Π.

We have implemented system SUP (see Footnote 3), whose underlying algorithm is modelled by the graph SUP_Π. In the implementation, we used

---

[6] ASSAT: http://assat.cs.ust.hk/

- the interface of SAT-solver MINISAT[7] (v1.12b) that supports non-clausal constraints [9] in order to implement inferences described by *Unit Propagate LP*, *All Rules Cancelled*, *Backchain True*, *Backchain False*, *Decide*, and *Fail*,
- parts of the CMODELS code that support transition rule *Unfounded SUP*.

Note that system SUP also implements conflict-driven backjumping and learning. Preliminary results available at SUP web site (see Footnote 3) comparing SUP with other answer set solvers are promising.

The implementation of SUP proofs that the abstract framework for answer set solvers introduced in this work may suggest new designs for solvers.

7   Tight Programs

We now recall the definitions of the positive dependency graph and a tight program. The *positive dependency graph* of a program Π is the directed graph G such that

- the nodes of G are the atoms occurring in Π, and
- G contains the edges from a_0 to a_i ($1 \leq i \leq m$) for each rule (3) in Π.

A program is *tight* if its positive dependency graph is acyclic. For instance, program (4) is not tight since its positive dependency graph has a cycle due to the rule $d \leftarrow d$. On the other hand, the program constructed from (4) by removing this rule is tight.

Recall that for any program Π and any assignment M, if M^+ is an answer set of Π then M is a supported model of Π. For the case of tight programs, the converse holds also: M^+ is an answer set for Π if and only if M is a supported model of Π [10].

It is also well known that the supported models of a program can be characterized as models of its completion in the sense of [11]. It turns out that for tight programs the graph SM_Π is "almost identical" to the graph DP_F, where F is the (clausified) completion of Π. To make this claim precise, we need the following terminology.

We say that an edge $M \implies M'$ in the graph SM_Π is *singular* if

- the only transition rule justifying this edge is *Unfounded*, and
- some edge $M \implies M''$ can be justified by a transition rule other than *Unfounded*.

For instance, let Π be the program

$$a \leftarrow b$$
$$b \leftarrow c.$$

The edge

$$a^d \, b^d \, \neg c^d \implies (Unfounded, \ U = \{a,b\})$$
$$a^d \, b^d \, \neg c^d \, \neg a$$

in the graph SM_Π is singular, because the edge

$$a^d \, b^d \, \neg c^d \implies (All \ Rules \ Cancelled)$$
$$a^d \, b^d \, \neg c^d \, \neg b$$

belongs to SM_Π also.

---

[7] MINISAT: http://minisat.se/

From the point of view of actual execution of the SMODELS algorithm, singular edges of the graph SM_Π are inessential: SMODELS never follows a singular edge. By SM_Π^- we denote the graph obtained from SM_Π by removing all singular edges.

Recall that for any program Π, its completion consists of Π and the formulas that can be written as

$$\neg a \vee \bigvee_{B \in Bodies(\Pi,a)} B \tag{7}$$

for every atom a in Π. *CNF-Comp*(Π) is the completion converted to CNF using straightforward equivalent transformations. In other words, *CNF-Comp*(Π) consists of clauses of two kinds:

1. the rules $a \leftarrow B$ of the program written as clauses

$$a \vee \overline{B}, \tag{8}$$

2. formulas (7) converted to CNF using the distributivity of disjunction over conjunction[8].

Proposition 4. *For any tight program Π, the graph SM_Π^- is equal to each of the graphs* ATLEAST$_\Pi$ *and* DP$_{CNF\text{-}Comp(\Pi)}$.

For instance, let Π be the program

$$a \leftarrow b, \, not \, c$$
$$b.$$

This program is tight. Its completion is

$$(a \leftrightarrow b \wedge \neg c) \wedge b \wedge \neg c,$$

and *CNF-Comp*(Π) is

$$(a \vee \neg b \vee c) \wedge (\neg a \vee b) \wedge (\neg a \vee \neg c) \wedge b \wedge \neg c.$$

Proposition 4 asserts that, for this formula F, SM_Π^- coincides with DP$_F$ and with ATLEAST$_\Pi$.

From Proposition 4, it follows that applying the SMODELS algorithm to a tight program essentially amounts to applying DPLL to its completion. A similar relationship, in terms of pseudocode representations of SMODELS and DPLL, is established in [12].

8 Generate and Test

In this section, we present a modification of the graph DP$_F$ that includes testing the models of F found by DPLL. Let F be a CNF formula, and let X be a set of models

---

[8] It is essential that repetitions are not removed in the process of clausification. For instance, *CNF-Comp*$(a \leftarrow not \, a)$ is the formula $(a \vee a) \wedge (\neg a \vee \neg a)$.

of F. The terminal nodes of the graph $\text{GT}_{F,X}$ defined below are models of F that belong to X.

The nodes of the graph $\text{GT}_{F,X}$ are the same as the nodes of the graph DP_F. The edges of $\text{GT}_{F,X}$ are described by the transition rules of DP_F and the additional transition rules:

$$\textit{Fail GT:} \quad M \implies \textit{FailState} \text{ if } \begin{cases} \text{no literal is unassigned by } M, \\ M \notin X, \\ M \text{ contains no decision literals} \end{cases}$$

$$\textit{Backtrack GT:} \; P\, l^d\, Q \implies P\, \bar{l} \text{ if } \begin{cases} \text{no literal is unassigned by } P\, l^d\, Q, \\ P\, l^d\, Q \notin X, \\ Q \text{ contains no decision literals.} \end{cases}$$

It is easy to see that the graph DP_F is a subgraph of $\text{GT}_{F,X}$. Furthermore, when the set X coincides with the set of all models of F the graphs are identical. This graph can be used for deciding whether a formula F has a model that belongs to X by constructing a path from $\emptyset$ to a terminal node:

Proposition 5. *For any CNF formula F and any set X of models of F,*

(a) *graph $\text{GT}_{F,X}$ is finite and acyclic,*
(b) *any terminal state of $\text{GT}_{F,X}$ other than FailState belongs to X,*
(c) *FailState is reachable from $\emptyset$ in $\text{GT}_{F,X}$ if and only if X is empty.*

Note that to verify the applicability of the new transition rules *Fail GT* and *Backtrack GT* we need a procedure for testing whether a set of literals belongs to X, but there is no need to have the elements of X explicitly listed.

ASP-SAT with Backtracking [4] is a procedure that computes models of the completion of the given program using DPLL, and tests them until an answer set is found. The application of the ASP-SAT with Backtracking algorithm to a program Π can be viewed as constructing a path from $\emptyset$ to a terminal node in the graph $\text{GT}_{F,X}$, where

- F is the completion of Π converted to conjunctive normal form, and
- X is the set of all assignments corresponding to answer sets of Π.

9   Related Work

Simons [3] described the SMODELS algorithm by means of a pseudocode and demonstrated its correctness. Gebser and Schaub [13] provided a deductive system for describing inferences involved in computing answer sets by tableaux methods. The abstract framework presented in this paper can be viewed as a deductive system also, but it is a very different system. For instance, we describe backtracking by an inference rule, and the Gebser-Schaub system doesn't. Accordingly, the derivations considered in this paper describe search process, and derivations in the Gebser-Schaub system don't. Also, the abstract framework discussed here doesn't have any inference rule similar to Cut; this is why its derivations are paths, rather than trees.

10   Proofs

Due to the lack of space, some proofs are omitted.[9]

Lemma 1. *For any CNF formula F and a path from $\emptyset$ to a state $l_1 \ldots l_n$ in DP_F, every model X of F satisfies l_i if it satisfies all decision literals l_j^d with $j \leq i$.*

Proof. By induction on the length of a path. Since the property trivially holds in the initial state $\emptyset$, we only need to prove that all transition rules of DP_F preserve it.

Consider an edge $M \Longrightarrow M'$ where M is a sequence $l_1 \ldots l_k$ such that every model X of F satisfies l_i if it satisfies all decision literals l_j^d with $j \leq i$.

Unit Propagate: M' is $M\, l_{k+1}$. Take any model X of F such that X satisfies all decision literals l_j^d with $j \leq k+1$. By the inductive hypothesis, $X \models M$. From the definition of *Unit Propagate*, for some clause $C \vee l_{k+1} \in F$, $\overline{C} \subseteq M$. Consequently, $M \models \neg C$. It follows that $X \models l_{k+1}$.

Decide: M' is $M\, l_{k+1}^d$. Obvious.

Fail: Obvious.

Backtrack: M has the form $P\, l_i^d\, Q$ where Q contains no decision literals. M' is $P\, \overline{l_i}$. Take any model X of F such that X satisfies all decision literals l_j^d with $j \leq i$. We need to show that $X \models \overline{l_i}$. By contradiction. Assume that $X \models l_i$. Since Q does not contain decision literals, X satisfies all decision literals in $P\, l_i^d\, Q$. By the inductive hypothesis, it follows that X satisfies $P\, l_i^d\, Q$, that is, M. This is impossible because M is inconsistent.

Proof of Proposition 1.   (a) The finiteness of DP_F is obvious. For any list N of literals by $|N|$ we denote the length of N. Any state M, other than *FailState*, has the form $M_0\, l_1\, M_1 \ldots l_p\, M_p$, where $l_1 \ldots l_p$ are all desicion literals of M; we define $\alpha(M)$ as the sequence of nonnegative integers $|M_0|, |M_1|, \ldots, |M_p|$, and $\alpha(FailState) = \infty$. For any states M and M' of DP_F, we understand $\alpha(M) < \alpha(M')$ as the lexicographical order. By the definition of the transition rules defining the edges of DP_F, if there is an edge from a state M to M' in DP_F, then $\alpha(M) < \alpha(M')$. It follows that if a state M' is reachable from M then $\alpha(M) < \alpha(M')$. Consequently, the graph is acyclic.

(b) Consider any terminal state M other than *FailState*. From the fact that *Decide* is not applicable, we derive that M assigns all literals. Similarly, since neither *Backtrack* nor *Fail* is applicable, M is consistent. Consequently, M is an assignment. Consider any clause $C \vee l$ in F. It follows that if $\overline{C} \not\subseteq M$ then $C \cap M \neq \emptyset$. Since *Unit Propagate* is not applicable, it follows that if $\overline{C} \subseteq M$ then $l \in M$. We derive that $M \models C \vee l$. Hence, M is a model of F.

(c) Left-to-right: Since *FailState* is reachable from $\emptyset$, there is an inconsistent state M without decision literals such that there exists a path from $\emptyset$ to M. By Lemma 1, any model of F satisfies M. Since M is inconsistent we conclude that F has no models.

Right-to-left: From (a) it follows that there is a path from $\emptyset$ to some terminal state. By (b), this state cannot be different from *FailState*, because F is unsatisfiable.

Lemma 2. *For any program Π and a path from $\emptyset$ to a state $l_1 \ldots l_n$ in $\mathrm{ATLEAST}_\Pi$, every supported model X for Π satisfies l_i if it satisfies all decision literals l_j^d with $j \leq i$.*

---

[9] http://www.cd.utexas.edu/users/yuliya/papers/aasp-full.ps
contains a full version of the paper.

Proof. By induction on the length of the path. Similar to the proof of Lemma 1. We will show that the property in question is preserved by the four new rules.

Unit Propagate LP: M' is $M\ a$. Take any model X of Π such that X satisfies all decision literals l_j^d with $j \leq k$. From the inductive hypothesis it follows that $X \models M$. By the definition of *Unit Propagate LP*, $B \subseteq M$ for some rule $a \leftarrow B$. Consequently, $M \models B$. Since X is a model of Π we derive that $X \models a$.

All Rules Cancelled: M' is $M\ \neg a$, such that $\overline{B} \cap M \neq \emptyset$ for every $B \in Bodies(\Pi, a)$. Consequently, $M \models \neg B$ for every $B \in Bodies(\Pi, a)$. Take any model X of Π such that X satisfies all decision literals l_j^d with $j \leq k$. We need to show that $X \models \neg a$. By contradiction. Assume that $X \models a$. By the inductive hypothesis, $X \models M$. Therefore, $X \models \neg B$ for every $B \in Bodies(\Pi, a)$. We derive that X is not a supported model of Π.

Backchain True: M' is $M\ l$. Take any supported model X of Π such that X satisfies all decision literals l_j^d with $j \leq k$. We need to show that $X \models l$. By contradiction. Assume $X \models \overline{l}$. Consider the rule $a \leftarrow B$ corresponding to this application of *Backchain True*. Since $l \in B$, $X \models \neg B$. By the definition of *Backchain True*, $\overline{B'} \cap M \neq \emptyset$ for every B' in $Bodies(\Pi, a) \setminus B$. Consequently, $M \models \neg B'$ for every B' in $Bodies(\Pi, a) \setminus B$. By the inductive hypothesis, $X \models M$. It follows that $X \models \neg B'$ for every B' in $Bodies(\Pi, a) \setminus B$. Hence X is not supported by Π.

Backchain False: M' is $M\ \overline{l}$. Take any model X of Π such that X satisfies all decision literals l_j^d with $j \leq k$. We need to show that $X \models \overline{l}$. By contradiction. Assume that $X \models l$. By the definition of *Backchain False* there exists a rule $a \leftarrow l, B$ in Π such that $\neg a \in M$ and $B \subseteq M$. Consequently, $M \models \neg a$ and $M \models B$. By the inductive hypothesis, $X \models M$. It follows that $X \models \neg a$ and $X \models B$. Since $X \models l$, X does not satisfy the rule $a \leftarrow l, B$, so that it is not a model of Π.

Proof of Proposition 2. Parts (a) and (c) are proved as in the proof of Proposition 1, using Lemma 2.

(b) Let M be a terminal state. It follows that none of the rules are applicable. From the fact that *Decide* is not applicable, we derive that M assigns all literals. Since neither *Backtrack* nor *Fail* is applicable, M is consistent. Since *Unit Propagate LP* is not applicable, it follows that for every rule $a \leftarrow B \in \Pi$, if $B \subseteq M$ then $a \in M$. Consequently, if $M \models B$ then $M \models a$. We derive that M is a model of Π. We now show that M is a supported model of Π. By contradiction. Suppose that M is not a supported model. Then, there is an atom $a \in M$ such that $M \not\models B$ for every $B \in Bodies(\Pi, a)$. Since M is consistent, $\overline{B} \cap M \neq \emptyset$ for every $B \in Bodies(\Pi, a)$. Consequently, *All Rules Cancelled* is applicable. This contradicts the assumption that M is terminal.

We say that a model X of a program Π is *unfounded-free* if no non-empty subset of X is an unfounded set on X w.r.t. Π.

Lemma 3 (Theorem 4.6 [14]). *For any model X of a program Π, X^+ is an answer set for Π if and only if X is unfounded-free.*

Lemma 4. *For any unfounded set U on a consistent set Y of literals w.r.t. a program Π, and any assignment X, if $X \models Y$ and $X \cap U \neq \emptyset$, then X^+ is not an answer set for Π.*

Proof. Assume that X^+ is an answer set for Π. Then X is a model of Π. By Lemma 3, it follows that X^+ is unfounded-free. Since $X \cap U \neq \emptyset$ it follows that $X \cap U$ is not unfounded on X. This means that for some rule $a \leftarrow B$ in Π such that $a \in X \cap U$, $X \not\models \neg B$ and $X \cap U \cap B^+ = \emptyset$. Since $X \models Y$, it follows that $Y \not\models \neg B$. Since X satisfies B, $B^+ \subseteq X$ and consequently $U \cap B^+ = X \cap U \cap B^+ = \emptyset$. It follows that set U is not an unfounded set on Y.

Lemma 5. *For any program Π and a path from $\emptyset$ to a state $l_1 \ldots l_n$ in SM_Π, and any assignment X, if X^+ is an answer set for Π then X satisfies l_i if it satisfies all decision literals l_j^d with $j \leq i$.*

Proof. By induction on the length of a path. Recall that for any assignment X, if X^+ is an answer set for Π, then X is a supported model of Π, and that the transition system SM_Π extends ATLEAST_Π by the transition rule *Unfounded*. Given our proof of Lemma 2, we only need to demonstrate that application of *Unfounded* preserves the property.

Consider a transition $M \Longrightarrow^{Unfounded} M'$, where M is a sequence $l_1 \ldots l_k$. M' is $M \neg a$, such that $a \in U$, where U is an unfounded set on M w.r.t Π. Take any assignment X such that X^+ is an answer set for Π and X satisfies all decision literals l_j^d with $j \leq k$. By the inductive hypothesis, $X \models M$. Then $X \models \neg a$. Indeed, otherwise a would be a common element of X and U, and $X \cap U$ would be non-empty, which contradicts Lemma 4 with M as Y.

Since the graph SUP_Π is a subgraph of SM_Π, Lemma 5 immediately holds for SUP_Π.

Proposition 3. *For any program Π,*

(a) *graph SM_Π [SUP_Π] is finite and acyclic.*
(b) *for any terminal state M of SM_Π [SUP_Π] other than FailState, M^+ is an answer set of Π.*
(c) *FailState is reachable from $\emptyset$ in SM_Π [SUP_Π] if and only if Π has no answer sets.*

Proof. Parts (a) and (c) are proved as in the proof of Proposition 1, using Lemma 5.
(b) As in the proof of Proposition 2(b) we derive that M is a model of Π. Assume that M^+ is not an answer set. Then, by Lemma 3, there is a non-empty unfounded set U on M w.r.t. Π such that $U \subseteq M$. It follows that *Unfounded* [*Unfounded SUP*] is applicable (with an arbitrary $a \in U$). This contradicts the assumption that M is terminal.

Lemma 6. *For any CNF formula F and a set X of models of F, and a path from $\emptyset$ to a state $l_1 \ldots l_n$ in $\text{GT}_{F,X}$, any model $Y \in X$ satisfies l_i if it satisfies all decision literals l_j^d with $j \leq i$.*

Proof. Similar to the proof of Lemma 1. There are two more rules to consider:
    Fail GT: Obvious.
    Backtrack GT: M has the form $P \, l_i^d \, Q$ where Q contains no decision literals, $M \not\in X$. Then, M' is $P \, \bar{l}_i$. Take any model E of F in X such that E satisfies all decision literals l_j^d with $j \leq i$. We need to show that $E \models \bar{l}_i$. By contradiction. Assume $E \models l_i$. By the inductive hypothesis, and the fact that M' is $P \, l_i^d \, Q$ where Q contains no decision literals, it follows that $E \models M$. Since M has no unassigned literals, $E = M$. This contradicts the assumption that $M \not\in X$.

Proof of Proposition 5. Part (a) and part (c) right-to-left are proved as in the proof of Proposition 1.

(b) Let M be any terminal state other than *FailState*. As in the proof of Proposition 1(b) it follows that M is a model of F. Neither *Fail GT* nor *Backtrack GT* is applicable. Then, M belongs to X.

(c) Left-to-right: Since *FailState* is reachable from $\emptyset$, there is a state M without decision literals such that it is reachable from $\emptyset$ and either transition rule *Fail* or *Fail GT* is applicable.

Case 1. *Fail* is applicable. Then, M is inconsistent. By Lemma 6, any model of F in X satisfies M. Since M is inconsistent we conclude that X is empty.

Case 2. *Fail GT* is applicable. Then, M assigns all literals and $M \notin X$. From Lemma 6, it follows that for any $Y \in X$, $Y = M$. Since $M \notin X$, we conclude that X is empty.

11 Conclusions

In this paper we showed how to model algorithms for computing answer sets of a program by means of simple mathematical objects, graphs. This approach simplifies the analysis of the correctness of algorithms and allows us to study the relationship between various algorithms using the structure of the corresponding graphs. For example, we used this method to establish that applying the SMODELS algorithm to a tight program essentially amounts to applying DPLL to its completion. It also suggests new designs for answer set solvers, as can be seen from our work on SUP. In the future we will investigate the generalization of this framework to backjumping and learning performed by the SMODELS$_{cc}$ algorithm [6], to SUP with Learning, and to ASP-SAT with Learning [4]. We also would like to generalize this approach to the algorithms used in disjunctive answer set solvers.

Acknowledgements. We are grateful to Marco Maratea for bringing to our attention the work by Nieuwenhuis et al. (2006), to Vladimir Lifschitz for the numerous discussions, to Martin Gebser and Michael Gelfond for valuable comments. The author was supported by the National Science Foundation under Grant IIS-0712113.

References

[1] Davis, M., Logemann, G., Loveland, D.: A machine program for theorem proving. Communications of ACM 5(7), 394–397 (1962)

[2] Nieuwenhuis, R., Oliveras, A., Tinelli, C.: Solving SAT and SAT modulo theories: From an abstract Davis-Putnam-Logemann-Loveland procedure to DPLL(T). Journal of the ACM 53(6), 937–977 (2006)

[3] Simons, P.: Extending and Implementing the Stable Model Semantics. PhD thesis, Helsinki University of Technology (2000)

[4] Giunchiglia, E., Lierler, Y., Maratea, M.: Answer set programming based on propositional satisfiability. Journal of Automated Reasoning 36, 345–377 (2006)

[5] Gelfond, M., Lifschitz, V.: The stable model semantics for logic programming. In: Kowalski, R., Bowen, K. (eds.) Proceedings of International Logic Programming Conference and Symposium, pp. 1070–1080. MIT Press, Cambridge (1988)

[6] Ward, J.: Answer Set Programming with Clause Learning. PhD thesis, The University of Cincinnati (2004)

[7] Van Gelder, A., Ross, K., Schlipf, J.: The well-founded semantics for general logic programs. Journal of ACM 38(3), 620–650 (1991)

[8] Lin, F., Zhao, Y.: ASSAT: Computing answer sets of a logic program by SAT solvers. Artificial Intelligence 157, 115–137 (2004)[10]

[9] Een, N., Sörensson, N.: An extensible sat-solver. In: Giunchiglia, E., Tacchella, A. (eds.) SAT 2003. LNCS, vol. 2919. Springer, Heidelberg (2004)

[10] Fages, F.: Consistency of Clark's completion and existence of stable models. Journal of Methods of Logic in Computer Science 1, 51–60 (1994)

[11] Clark, K.: Negation as failure. In: Gallaire, H., Minker, J. (eds.) Logic and Data Bases, pp. 293–322. Plenum Press, New York (1978)

[12] Giunchiglia, E., Maratea, M.: On the relation between answer set and SAT procedures (or, between smodels and cmodels). In: Gabbrielli, M., Gupta, G. (eds.) ICLP 2005. LNCS, vol. 3668, pp. 37–51. Springer, Heidelberg (2005)

[13] Gebser, M., Schaub, T.: Tableau calculi for answer set programming. In: Etalle, S., Truszczyński, M. (eds.) ICLP 2006. LNCS, vol. 4079, pp. 11–25. Springer, Heidelberg (2006)

[14] Leone, N., Rullo, P., Scarcello, F.: Disjunctive stable models: Unfounded sets, fixpoint semantics, and computation. Information and Computation 135(2), 69–112 (1997)

---

[10] Revised version:
http://www.cs.ust.hk/faculty/flin/papers/assat-aij-revised.pdf

Partial Functions and Equality in Answer Set Programming

Pedro Cabalar*

Department of Computer Science,
Corunna University (Corunna, Spain)
cabalar@udc.es

Abstract. In this paper we propose an extension of Answer Set Programming (ASP) [1], and in particular, of its most general logical counterpart, Quantified Equilibrium Logic (QEL) [2], to deal with partial functions. Although the treatment of equality in QEL can be established in different ways, we first analyse the choice of decidable equality with complete functions and Herbrand models, recently proposed in the literature [3]. We argue that this choice yields some counterintuitive effects from a logic programming and knowledge representation point of view. We then propose a variant called $\mathrm{QEL}_{\mathcal{F}}^{=}$ where the set of functions is partitioned into *partial* and Herbrand functions (we also call *constructors*). In the rest of the paper, we show a direct connection to Scott's *Logic of Existence* [4] and present a practical application, proposing an extension of normal logic programs to deal with partial functions and equality, so that they can be translated into function-free normal programs, being possible in this way to compute their answer sets with any standard ASP solver.

1 Introduction

Since its introduction two decades ago, the paradigm of *Answer Set Programming* (ASP) [5] has gradually become one of the most successful and practical formalisms for Knowledge Representation due to its flexibility, expressiveness and current availability of efficient solvers. This success can be easily checked by the continuous and plentiful presence of papers on ASP in the main conferences and journals on Logic Programming, Knowledge Representation and Artificial Intelligence during the last years. The declarative semantics of ASP has allowed many syntactic extensions that have simplified the formalisation of complex domains in different application areas like constraint satisfaction problems, planning or diagnosis.

In this paper we consider one more syntactic extension that is an underlying feature in most application domains: the use of *(partial) functions*. Most ASP programs include some predicates that are nothing else than relational representations of functions from the original domain being modelled. For instance,

---

* This research was partially supported by Spanish MEC project TIN-2006-15455-C03-02 and Xunta de Galicia project INCITE08-PXIB105159PR.

when modelling the typical educational example of family relationships, we may use a predicate $mother(X, Y)$ to express that X's mother is Y, but of course, we must add an additional constraint to ensure that Y is unique wrt X, i.e., that the predicate actually acts as the function $mother(X) = Y$. In fact, it is quite common that first time Prolog students use this last notation as their first attempt. Functions are not only a natural element for knowledge representation, but can also simplify in a considerable way ASP programs. Apart from avoiding constraints for uniqueness of value, the possibility of nesting functional terms like in $W = mother(father(mother(X)))$ allows a more compact and readable representation than the relational version $mother(X, Y), father(Y, Z), mother(Z, W)$ involving extra variables, which may easily mean a source of formalisation errors. Similarly, as we will see later, the use of partial functions can also save the programmer from including explicit conditions in the rule bodies to check that the rule head is actually defined.

The addition of functions to ASP is not new at all, although there exist two different ways in which functions are actually understood. Most of the existing work in the topic (like the general approaches [6,7,8] or the older use of function *Result* for Situation Calculus inside ASP [9]) treat functions in the same way as Prolog, that is, they are just a way for *constructing* the Herbrand universe, and so they satisfy the unique names assumption – e.g. $mother(john) = mary$ is always false. A different alternative is dealing with functions in a more similar way to Predicate Calculus, as done for instance in *Functional Logic Programming* [10]. The first and most general approach in this direction is due to the logical characterisation of ASP in terms of *Equilibrium Logic* [11] and, in particular, to its extension to first order theories, *Quantified Equilibrium Logic* (QEL) [2]. As a result of this characterisation, the concept of stable model is now defined for any theory from predicate calculus with equality. In fact, stable models can be alternatively described by a second-order logic operator [12] quite close to Circumscription [13], something that has been already used, for instance, to study strong equivalence for programs with variables [3].

As we will explain in the next section, we claim that the exclusive use of Herbrand functions and the currently proposed interpretation of equality in QEL with the requirement for functions to be complete yield some counterintuitive results when introducing functions for knowledge representation. To solve these problems, we propose a variation of QEL that uses a similar structure to the logical characterisation [14] for functional logic programs, where we separate Herbrand functions (or constructors) from partial functions. We further show how our semantics for partial functions has a direct relation to the *Logic of Existence* (or E-logic) proposed by Scott [4].

The rest of the paper is organized as follows. In the next section, we informally consider some examples of knowledge representation with functions in ASP, commenting the apparently expected behaviour and the problems that arise when using the current proposal for QEL. In Section 3, we introduce our variant called $QEL_{\mathcal{F}}^{=}$. Section 4 defines some useful derived operators, many of them directly extracted from E-logic and showing the same behaviour. In Section 5 we consider a syntactic subclass of logic programs with partial functions and Herbrand constants, and show how they can be translated into (non-functional) normal logic programs afterwards. Finally, Section 6 contains a brief discussion about related work and Section 7 concludes the paper.

2   A Motivating Example

Consider the following simple scenario with a pair of rules.

Example 1. When deciding the second course of a given meal once the first course is fixed, we want to apply the following criterion: on Fridays, we repeat the first course as second one; the rest of week days, we choose *fish* if the first was *pasta*.   □

A straightforward encoding of these rules[1] into ASP would correspond to the program Π_1:

$$second(fish) \leftarrow first(pasta) \land \neg friday \tag{1}$$
$$second(X) \leftarrow first(X) \land friday \tag{2}$$
$$\bot \leftarrow first(X) \land first(Y) \land X \neq Y \tag{3}$$
$$\bot \leftarrow second(X) \land second(Y) \land X \neq Y \tag{4}$$

where the last two rules just represent that each course is unique, i.e., $first(salad)$ and $first(pasta)$ cannot be simultaneously true, for instance. In fact, these constraints immediately point out that $first$ and $second$ are 0-ary functions. A very naive attempt to use these functions for representing our example problem could be the pair of formulas Π_2:

$$second = fish \leftarrow first = pasta \land \neg friday \tag{5}$$
$$second = first \leftarrow friday \tag{6}$$

Of course, Π_2 is not a logic program, but it can still be given a logic programming meaning by interpreting it under Herbrand models of QEL, or the equivalent recent characterisation of stable models for first order theories [12]. Unfortunately, the behaviour of Π_2 in QEL with Herbrand models will be quite different to that of Π_1 by several reasons that can be easily foreseen. First of all, there exists now a qualitative difference between functions $first$ and $second$ with respect to $fish$ and $pasta$. For instance, while it is clear that $fish = pasta$ must be false, we should allow $second = first$ to cope with our Fridays criterion. If we deal with Herbrand models or unique names assumption, the four constants would be pairwise different and (5) would be equivalent to $\bot \leftarrow \bot$, that is, a tautology, whereas (6) would become the constraint $\bot \leftarrow friday$.

---

[1] As a difference wrt to the typical ASP notation, we use $\neg$ to represent default negation and, instead of a comma, we use $\land$ to separate literals in the body.

Even after limiting the unique names assumption only to constants $fish$ and $pasta$, new problems arise. For instance, the approaches in [2,12,3,15] deal with complete functions and the axiom of *decidable equality*:

$$x = y \vee \neg(x = y) \tag{DE}$$

This axiom is equivalent to $x = y \leftarrow \neg\neg(x = y)$ which informally implies that we always have a justification to assign any value to any function. Thus, for instance, if it is not Friday and we do not provide any information about the first course, i.e., no atom $first(X)$ holds, then Π_1 will not derive any information about the second course, that is, no atom $second(X)$ is derived. In Π_2, however, functions $first$ and $second$ must *always* have a value, which is further justified in any stable model by (DE). As a result, we get that a possible stable model is, for instance, $first = fish$ and $second = pasta$. A related problem of axiom (DE) is that it allows rewriting a rule like (5) as the constraint:

$$\bot \leftarrow first = pasta \wedge \neg friday \wedge \neg(second = fish)$$

whose relational counterpart would be

$$\bot \leftarrow first(pasta) \wedge \neg friday \wedge \neg second(fish) \tag{7}$$

and whose behaviour in logic programming is very different from the original rule (1). As an example, while $\Pi_1 \cup \{first(pasta)\}$ entails $second(fish)$, the same program after replacing (1) by (7) has no stable models.

Finally, even after removing decidable equality, we face a new problem that has to do with directionality in the equality symbol when used in the rule heads. The symmetry of '=' allows rewriting (6) as:

$$first = second \leftarrow friday \tag{8}$$

that in a relational notation would be the rule:

$$first(X) \leftarrow second(X) \wedge friday \tag{9}$$

which, again, has a very different meaning from the original (2). For instance $\Pi_1 \cup \{friday, second(fish)\}$ does not entail anything about the first course, whereas if we replace in this program (2) by (9), we obtain $first(fish)$. This is counterintuitive, since our program was intended to derive facts about the second course, and not about the first one. To sum up, we will need some kind of new directional operator to specify the function value in a rule head.

3   Quantified Equilibrium Logic with Partial Functions

The definition of propositional Equilibrium Logic [11] relied on establishing a selection criterion on models of the intermediate logic, called the logic of *Here-and-There* (HT) [16]. The first order case [2] followed similar steps, introducing a quantified version of HT, called SQHT$^=$ that stands for *Quantified HT with static domains*[2] *and equality.* In this section we describe the syntax and semantics of a variant, called SQHT$^=_{\mathcal{F}}$, for dealing with partial functions.

We begin by defining a first-order language by its *signature*, a tuple $\Sigma = \langle \mathcal{C}, \mathcal{F}, \mathcal{P} \rangle$ of disjoint sets where $\mathcal{C}$ and $\mathcal{F}$ are sets of *function names* and $\mathcal{P}$ a set of *predicate names*. We assume that each function (resp. predicate) name has the form f/n where f is the function (resp. predicate) symbol, and $n \geq 0$ is an integer denoting the number of arguments (or *arity*). Elements in $\mathcal{C}$ will be called *Herbrand functions* (or *constructors*), whereas elements in $\mathcal{F}$ will receive the name of *partial functions*. The sets $\mathcal{C}_0$ (Herbrand constants) and $\mathcal{F}_0$ (partial constants) respectively represent the elements of $\mathcal{C}$ and $\mathcal{F}$ with arity 0. We assume $\mathcal{C}_0$ contains at least one element.

First-order formulas are built up in the usual way, with the same syntax of classical predicate calculus with equality $=$. We assume that $\neg\varphi$ is defined as $\varphi \to \bot$ whereas $x \neq y$ just stands for $\neg(x = y)$. Given any set of functions $\mathcal{A}$ we write $Terms(\mathcal{A})$ to stand for the set of ground terms built from functions (and constants) in $\mathcal{A}$. In particular, the set of all possible ground terms for signature $\Sigma = \langle \mathcal{C}, \mathcal{F}, \mathcal{P} \rangle$ would be $Terms(\mathcal{C} \cup \mathcal{F})$ whereas the subset $Terms(\mathcal{C})$ will be called the *Herbrand Universe* of $\mathcal{L}$. The *Herbrand Base* $HB(\mathcal{C}, \mathcal{P})$ is a set containing all atoms that can be formed with predicates in $\mathcal{P}$ and terms in the Herbrand Universe, $Terms(\mathcal{C})$.

From now on, we assume that all free variables are implicitly universally quantified. We use letters x, y, z and their capital versions to denote variables, t to denote terms, and letters c, d to denote ground terms. Boldface letters like $\mathbf{x}, \mathbf{t}, \mathbf{c}, \ldots$ represent tuples (in this case of variables, terms and ground terms, respectively). The corresponding semantics for SQHT$^=_{\mathcal{F}}$ is described as follows.

Definition 1 (state). *A state for a signature $\Sigma = \langle \mathcal{C}, \mathcal{F}, \mathcal{P} \rangle$ is a pair (σ, A) where $A \subseteq HB(\mathcal{C}, \mathcal{P})$ is a set of atoms from the Herbrand Base and $\sigma : Terms (\mathcal{C} \cup \mathcal{F}) \to Terms(\mathcal{C}) \cup \{\mathsf{u}\}$ is a function assigning to any ground term in the language some ground term in the Herbrand Universe or the special value $\mathsf{u} \notin Terms(\mathcal{C} \cup \mathcal{F})$ (standing for* undefined*). Function σ must satisfy:*

(i) $\sigma(c) = c$ *for all* $c \in Terms(\mathcal{C})$.

(ii) $\sigma(f(t_1, \ldots, t_n)) = \begin{cases} \mathsf{u} & \text{if } \sigma(t_i) = \mathsf{u} \text{ for some } i = 1 \ldots n \\ \sigma(f(\sigma(t_1), \ldots, \sigma(t_n))) & \text{otherwise} \end{cases}$

$\square$

As we can see, our domain is exclusively formed by the terms from the Herbrand Universe, $Terms(\mathcal{C})$. These elements are used as arguments of ground atoms in the set A, that collects the *true* atoms in the state. Similarly, the value of any functional term is an element from $Terms(\mathcal{C})$, excepting the cases in which partial functions are left undefined – if so, they are assigned the special element u (different from any syntactic symbol) instead. Condition (i) asserts, as expected,

---

[2] The term *static domain* refers to the fact that the universe is shared among all worlds in the Kripke frame.

that any term c from the Herbrand Universe has the fixed valuation $\sigma(c) = c$. Condition (ii) guarantees, on the one hand, that a functional term with an undefined argument becomes undefined in its turn, and on the other hand, that functions preserve their interpretation through subterms – for instance, if we have $\sigma(f(a)) = c$ we expect that $\sigma(g(f(a))$ and $\sigma(g(c))$ coincide. It is easy to see that (ii) implies that σ is completely determined by the values it assigns to all terms like $f(\mathbf{c})$ where f is any partial function and $\mathbf{c}$ a tuple of elements in $Terms(\mathcal{C})$.

Definition 2 (Ordering $\preceq$ among states). *We say that state $S = (\sigma, A)$ is smaller than state $S' = (\sigma', A')$, written $S \preceq S'$, when both:*

i) $A \subseteq A'$.
ii) $\sigma(d) = \sigma'(d)$ *or* $\sigma(d) = \mathbf{u}$, *for all* $d \in Terms(\mathcal{C} \cup \mathcal{F})$.   □

We write $S \prec S'$ when the relation is strict, that is, $S \preceq S'$ and $S \neq S'$. The intuitive meaning of $S \preceq S'$ is that the former contains *less information* than the latter, so that any true atom or defined function value in S must hold in S'.

Definition 3 (HT-interpretation). *An HT interpretation I for a signature $\Sigma = \langle \mathcal{C}, \mathcal{F}, \mathcal{P} \rangle$ is a pair of states $I = \langle S^h, S^t \rangle$ with $S^h \preceq S^t$.*   □

The superindices h, t represent two worlds (respectively standing for *here* and *there*) with a reflexive ordering relation further satisfying $h \leq t$. An interpretation like $\langle S^t, S^t \rangle$ is said to be *total*, referring to the fact that both states contain the same information[3].

Given an interpretation $I = \langle S^h, S^t \rangle$, with $S^h = (\sigma^h, I^h)$ and $S^t = (\sigma^t, I^t)$, we define when I *satisfies* a formula φ at some world $w \in \{h, t\}$, written $I, w \models \varphi$, inductively as follows:

- $I, w \models p(t_1, \ldots, t_n)$ if $p(\sigma^w(t_1), \ldots, \sigma^w(t_n)) \in I^w$;
- $I, w \models t_1 = t_2$ if $\sigma^w(t_1) = \sigma^w(t_2) \neq \mathbf{u}$;
- $I, w \not\models \bot$; $I, w \models \top$;
- $I, w \models \alpha \wedge \beta$ if $I, w \models \alpha$ and $I, w \models \beta$;
- $I, w \models \alpha \vee \beta$ if $I, w \models \alpha$ or $I, w \models \beta$;
- $I, w \models \alpha \rightarrow \beta$ if for all w' s.t. $w \leq w'$: $I, w' \not\models \alpha$ or $I, w' \models \beta$;
- $I, w \models \forall x\, \alpha(x)$ if for each $c \in Terms(\mathcal{C})$: $I, w \models \alpha(c)$;
- $I, w \models \exists x\, \alpha(x)$ if for some $c \in Terms(\mathcal{C})$: $I, w \models \alpha(c)$.   □

An important observation is that the first condition above implies that an atom with an undefined argument will always be valuated as false since, by definition, $\mathbf{u}$ never occurs in ground atoms of I^h or I^t. Something similar happens with equality: $t_1 = t_2$ will be false if any of the two operands, or even both, are undefined. As usual, we say that I is a *model* of a formula φ, written $I \models \varphi$, when $I, h \models \varphi$. Similarly, I is a *model* of a theory Γ when it is a model of all of its formulas. The next definition introduces the idea of equilibrium models for $\mathrm{SQHT}^=_{\mathcal{F}}$.

---

[3] Note that by *total* we do not mean that functions cannot be left undefined. We may still have some term d for which $\sigma^t(d) = \mathbf{u}$.

Definition 4 (Equilibrium model). *A model* $\langle S^t, S^t \rangle$ *of a theory* Γ *is an equilibrium model if there is no strictly smaller state* $S^h \prec S^t$ *that* $\langle S^h, S^t \rangle$ *is also model of* Γ. □

The Quantified Equilibrium Logic with partial functions (QEL$_{\mathcal{F}}^{=}$) is the logic induced by the SQHT$_{\mathcal{F}}^{=}$ equilibrium models.

4   Useful Derived Operators

From the SQHT$_{\mathcal{F}}^{=}$ semantics, it is easy to see that the formula $(t = t)$, usually included as an axiom for equality, is not valid in SQHT$_{\mathcal{F}}^{=}$. In fact, $I, w \models (t = t)$ iff $\sigma^w(t) \neq \mathbf{u}$, that is, term t is defined. In this way, we can introduce Scott's [4] *existence* operator[4] in a standard way: $E\ t \stackrel{\text{def}}{=} (t = t)$. Condition (ii) in Definition 1 implies the *strictness* condition of E-logic, formulated by the axiom $E\ f(t) \rightarrow E\ t$. As happens with $(t = t)$, the substitution axiom for functions:

$$t_1 = t_2 \rightarrow f(t_1) = f(t_2)$$

is not valid, since it may be the case that the function is undefined. However, the following weaker version is an SQHT$_{\mathcal{F}}^{=}$ tautology:

$$t_1 = t_2 \wedge E\ f(t_1) \rightarrow f(t_1) = f(t_2)$$

To represent the *difference* between two terms, we may also have several alternatives. The straightforward one is just $\neg(t_1 = t_2)$, usually abbreviated as $t_1 \neq t_2$. However, this formula can be satisfied when any of the two operands is undefined. We may sometimes want to express a stronger notion of difference that behaves as a positive formula (this is usually called *apartness* in the intuitionistic literature [17]). In our case, we are especially interested in an apartness operator $t_1 \# t_2$ where both arguments are required to be defined:

$$t_1 \# t_2 \stackrel{\text{def}}{=} E\ t_1 \wedge E\ t_2 \wedge \neg(t_1 = t_2)$$

To understand the meaning of this operator, consider the difference between $\neg(King(France) = LouisXIV)$ and $King(Spain)\#LouisXIV$. The first expression means that we cannot prove that the King of France is Louis XIV, what includes the case in which France has not a king. The second expression means that we can prove that the King of Spain (and so, such a concept exists) is not Louis XIV.

The next operator we introduce has to do with definedness of rule heads in logic programs. The inclusion of a formula in the consequent of an implication may have an undesired effect when thinking about its use as a rule head. For

---

[4] Contrarily to the original Scott's E-logic, variables in SQHT$_{\mathcal{F}}^{=}$ are always defined. This is not an essential difference: terms may be left undefined instead, and so most theorems, like $(x = y) \rightarrow (y = x)$ are expressed here using metavariables for terms $(t_1 = t_2) \rightarrow (t_2 = t_1)$.

instance, consider the rule $visited(next(x)) \leftarrow visited(x)$ and assume we have the fact $visited(1)$ but there is no additional information about $next(1)$. We would expect that the rule above does not yield any particular effect on $next(1)$. Unfortunately, as $visited(next(1))$ must be true, the function $next(1)$ must become defined and, as a collateral effect, it will be assigned some arbitrary value, say $next(1) = 10$ so that $visited(10)$ is made true. To avoid this problem, we will use a new operator $:-$ to define a different type of implication where the consequent is only forced to be true when all the functional terms that are "necessary to build" the atoms in the consequent are defined. Given a term t we define its set of *structural arguments* $Args(t)$ as follows. If t has the form $f(t_1, \ldots, t_n)$ for any partial function $f/n \in \mathcal{F}$, then $Args(t) \overset{\text{def}}{=} \{t_1, \ldots, t_n\}$; otherwise, $Args(t) \overset{\text{def}}{=} t$. We extend this definition for any atom A, so that its set of structural arguments $Args(A)$ corresponds to:

$$Args(P(t_1, \ldots, t_n)) \overset{\text{def}}{=} \{t_1, \ldots, t_n\}$$
$$Args(t = t') \overset{\text{def}}{=} Args(t) \cup Args(t')$$

In our previous example, $Args(visited(next(x))) = \{next(x)\}$. Notice that, for an equality atom $t = t'$, we do not consider $\{t, t'\}$ as arguments as we have done for the rest of predicates, but go down one level instead, considering $Args(t) \cup Args(t')$ in its turn. For instance, if A is the atom $friends(mother(x), mother(y))$, then $Args(A)$ would be $\{mother(x), mother(y)\}$, whereas for an equality atom A' like $mother(x) = mother(y)$, $Args(A') = \{x, y\}$. We define $[\varphi]$ as the result of replacing each atom A in φ by the conjunction of all $E\,t \to A$ for each $t \in Args(A)$. We can now define the new implication operator as follows $\varphi :- \psi \overset{\text{def}}{=} \psi \to [\varphi]$. Back to the example, if we use now $visited(next(x)) :- visited(x)$ we obtain, after applying the previous definitions, that it is equivalent to:

$$visited(x) \to [visited(next(x))]$$
$$\leftrightarrow visited(x) \to (E\ next(x) \to visited(next(x)))$$
$$\leftrightarrow visited(x) \wedge E\ next(x) \to visited(next(x))$$

Another important operator will allow us to establish a direction in a rule head assignment – remember the discussion about distinguishing between (6) and (8) in Section 2. We define this *assignment* operator as follows:

$$f(\mathbf{t}) := t' \overset{\text{def}}{=} E\ t' \to f(\mathbf{t}) = t'$$

Now, our Example 1 would be encoded with the pair of formulas:

$$second := fish :- first = pasta \wedge \neg friday \qquad second := first :- friday$$

that, after some elementary transformations, lead to:

$$second = fish \leftarrow first = pasta \wedge \neg friday$$
$$second = first \leftarrow E\ first \wedge friday$$

Using these operators, a compact way to fix a default value t' for a function $f(\mathbf{t})$ would be $f(\mathbf{t}) := t' \ :- \ \neg(f(\mathbf{t})\#t')$. Finally, we introduce a nondeterministic choice assignment with the following set-like expression:

$$f(\mathbf{t}) \in \{x \mid \varphi(x)\} \tag{10}$$

where $\varphi(x)$ is a formula (called the set *condition*) that contains the free variable x. The intuitive meaning of (10) is self-explanatory. As an example, the formula $a \in \{x \mid \exists y\ Parent(x, y)\}$ means that a should take a value among those x that are parents of some y. Expression (10) is defined as the conjunction of:

$$\forall x\ (\varphi(x) \rightarrow f(\mathbf{t}) = x \vee f(\mathbf{t}) \neq x) \tag{11}$$
$$\neg\exists x\ (\varphi(x) \wedge f(\mathbf{t}) = x) \rightarrow \bot \tag{12}$$

Other typical set constructions can be defined in terms of (10):

$$f(\mathbf{t}) \in \{t'(\mathbf{y}) \mid \exists \mathbf{y}\ \varphi(\mathbf{y})\} \stackrel{\text{def}}{=} f(\mathbf{t}) \in \{x \mid \exists \mathbf{y}\ (\varphi(\mathbf{y}) \wedge t'(\mathbf{y}) = x)\}$$
$$f(\mathbf{t}) \in \{t'_1, \dots, t'_n\} \stackrel{\text{def}}{=} f(\mathbf{t}) \in \{x \mid t'_1 = x \vee \cdots \vee t'_n = x\}$$

It must be noticed that variable x in (10) is not free, but quantified and local to this expression. Note that $\varphi(x)$ may contain other quantified and/or free variables. For instance, observe the difference between:

$$Person(y) \rightarrow a(y) \in \{x \mid Parent(x, y)\} \tag{13}$$
$$Person(y) \rightarrow a(y) \in \{x \mid \exists y\ Parent(x, y)\} \tag{14}$$

In (13) we assign, per each person y, one of her parents to $a(y)$, whereas in (13) we are assigning *any* parent as, in fact, we could change the set condition to $\exists z\ Parent(x, z)$.

At a first sight, it could seem that the formula $\exists x(\varphi(x) \wedge f(\mathbf{t}) = x)$ could capture the expected meaning of $f(\mathbf{t}) \in \{x \mid \varphi(x)\}$ in a more direct way. Unfortunately, such a formula would not "pick" a value x among those that satisfy $\varphi(x)$. For instance, if we translate $a \in \{x \mid \exists y\ Parent(x, y)\}$ as $\exists x(\exists y\ Parent(x, y) \wedge a = x)$ we would allow the free addition of facts for $Parent(x, y)$. Notice also that a formula like $a \in \{t\}$ is stronger than an assignment $a := t$ since when t is undefined, the former is always false, regardless the value of a (it would informally correspond to an expression like $a \in \emptyset$).

5   Logic Programs with Partial Functions

In this section we consider a subset of $QEL_{\mathcal{F}}^{=}$ which corresponds to a certain kind of logic program that allow partial functions but not constructors other than a finite set of Herbrand constants $\mathcal{C} = \mathcal{C}_0$. The interest of this syntactic class is that it can be translated into ground normal logic programs, and so, equilibrium models can be computed by any of the currently available answer set provers. From now on, we assume that any function f/n with arity $n > 0$ is partial, $f/n \in \mathcal{F}$, and any constant c is a constructor, $c \in \mathcal{C}$, unless we include a declaration $c/0 \in \mathcal{F}$. As usual in logic programming notation, we use in this section capital letters to represent variables.

In what follows we will use the tag 'FLP' to refer to functional logic programming definitions, and 'LP' to talk about the more restrictive syntax of normal logic programs (without functions). An FLP-*atom* has the form[5] $p(\mathbf{t})$ or $t_1 = t_2$, where p is a predicate name, $\mathbf{t}$ a tuple of terms and t_1, t_2 a pair of terms. An FLP-*literal* is an atom A or its default negation $\neg A$. We call LP-*terms* (resp. LP-*atoms*, resp. LP-*literals*) to those not containing partial function symbols.

An FLP-*rule* is an implication $\alpha :\!- \beta$ where β (called *body*) is a conjunction of literals, and α (called *head*) has the form of one the following expressions:

- an atom $p(\mathbf{t})$;
- the truth constant $\bot$;
- an assignment $f(\mathbf{t}) := t'$ with $f \in \mathcal{F}$;
- or a *choice* like $f(\mathbf{t}) \in \{x \mid \varphi(x)\}$ with $f \in \mathcal{F}$ and $\varphi(x)$ a conjunction of literals. We call x the *choice variable* and $\varphi(x)$ the choice condition.

A *choice rule* is a rule with a *choice* head. A *functional logic program* is a set of FLP-rules. A rule is said to be *safe* when: (1) if a variable x is the term t' or one of the terms in $\mathbf{t}$, or occurs in the scope of negation, or in a choice condition (excepting the choice variable), then it also occurs in some positive literal in the body; and (2) if x is a choice variable, then it occurs in some positive literal of the choice condition $\varphi(x)$. For instance, the rules $p(f(X), Y) :\!- q(Y)$ and $f \in \{Y \mid p(Y)\}$ are safe, whereas the rules $f(Z) := 0$ or $f \in \{Y \mid \neg p(Y)\}$ are not safe. A safe program is a set of safe rules. The following is an example of a program in FLP syntax:

Example 2 (Hamiltonian cycles). Let Π_2 be the FLP-program:

$$\bot :\!- next(X) = next(Y) \wedge X \neq Y \tag{15}$$

$$next(X) \in \{Z \mid arc(X, Z)\} :\!- node(X) \tag{16}$$

$$visited(1) \tag{17}$$

$$visited(next(X)) :\!- visited(X) \tag{18}$$

$$\bot :\!- \neg visited(X) \wedge node(X). \tag{19}$$

An LP-*rule* is such that its body exclusively contains LP-literals and its head is either $\bot$ or an LP-atom $p(\mathbf{t})$. An LP-*program* is a set of LP-rules. It is easy to see that, for LP-rules, $\alpha :\!- \beta$ is equivalent to $\beta \rightarrow \alpha$. Thus, an LP-program has the form of a (standard) normal logic program with constraints and without partial functions. The absence of partial functions guarantees that $QEL_{\mathcal{F}}^{=}$ and QEL coincide for this kind of program:

Proposition 1. *$QEL_{\mathcal{F}}^{=}$ equilibrium models of an LP-program Π correspond to QEL equilibrium models of Π.*

---

[5] Expressions like $t_1 \# t_2$ are left for a future work.

Furthermore, it is also very easy to see that, for LP-programs, the definition of *safeness* we provided generalises the standard definition for normal logic programs. As a result, this means in particular that when an LP-program Π is safe, $QEL_{\mathcal{F}}^{=}$ equilibrium models coincide with the set of stable models of the grounded version of Π, since QEL satisfies this property.

The translation of an FLP-program Π will be done in two steps. In a first step, we will define a QEL theory $\Gamma(\Pi)$ for a different signature and prove that it is $SQHT_{\mathcal{F}}^{=}$ equivalent modulo the original signature. This theory $\Gamma(\Pi)$ is not an LP-program, but can be easily translated into an LP-program Π^* applying some simple transformations that preserve equivalence wrt equilibrium models (even in QEL). The main idea of the translation is that, for each partial function $f/n \in \mathcal{F}$ occurring in Π we will handle a predicate like $holds\_f(X_1, \ldots, X_n, V)$ in Π^*, or $holds\_f(\mathbf{X}, V)$ for short. The technique of converting a function into a predicate and shifting the function value as an extra argument is well known in Functional Logic Programming and has received the name of *flattening* [18,19]. Obviously, once we deal with a predicate, we will need that no two different values are assigned to the same function. This can be simply captured by:

$$\bot \leftarrow holds\_f(\mathbf{X}, V) \wedge holds\_f(\mathbf{X}, W) \wedge \neg(V = W) \tag{20}$$

with variables V, W not included in $\mathbf{X}$.

Given the original signature $\Sigma = \langle \mathcal{C}, \mathcal{F}, \mathcal{P} \rangle$ for program Π, the theory $\Gamma(\Pi)$ will deal with a new signature $\Sigma^* = \langle \mathcal{C}, \emptyset, \mathcal{P}^* \rangle$ where $\mathcal{P}^*$ consists of $\mathcal{P}$ plus a new predicate $holds\_f/(n+1)$ per each partial function $f/n \in \mathcal{F}$.

Definition 5 (Correspondence of interpretations). *Given an HT interpretation $I = \langle S^h, S^t \rangle$ for signature $\Sigma = \langle \mathcal{C}, \mathcal{F}, \mathcal{P} \rangle$ we define a corresponding interpretation $I^* = \langle (\sigma^h, J^h), (\sigma^t, J^t) \rangle$ for signature $\Sigma^* = \langle \mathcal{C}, \emptyset, \mathcal{P}^* \rangle$ so that, for any $f/n \in \mathcal{F}$, any tuple $\mathbf{c}$ of n elements from $\mathcal{C}$, any predicate $p/n \in \mathcal{P}$ and any $w \in \{h, t\}$:*

1. *$holds\_f(\mathbf{c}, d) \in J^w$ iff $\sigma^w(\mathbf{c}) = d$ with $d \in \mathcal{C}$.*
2. *$p(\mathbf{c}) \in J^w$ iff $p(\mathbf{c}) \in I^w$.*   □

Once (20) is fixed, the correspondence between I and I^* is bidirectional:

Proposition 2. *Given signature $\Sigma = \langle \mathcal{C}, \mathcal{F}, \mathcal{P} \rangle$ and an interpretation J for Σ^* satisfying (20), then there exists an interpretation I for Σ such that $I^* = J$.*

Definition 6 (Translation of terms). *We define the translation of a term t as the triple $\langle t^*, \Phi(t) \rangle$ where t^* is an LP-term and $\Phi(t)$ is a formula s.t.:*

1. *For an LP-term t, then $t^* \stackrel{\text{def}}{=} t$ and $\Phi(t) \stackrel{\text{def}}{=} \top$.*
2. *When $t = f(\mathbf{t})$ with f a partial function, then $t^* \stackrel{\text{def}}{=} X_t$ and $\Phi(t) \stackrel{\text{def}}{=} \Phi(\mathbf{t}) \wedge holds\_f(\mathbf{t}^*, X_t)$ where X_t is a new fresh variable and $\Phi(\mathbf{t})$ stands for the conjunction of all $\Phi(t_i)$ for all terms t_i in the tuple $\mathbf{t}$.*   □

For 0-ary partial functions, we would have that $\mathbf{t}$ is empty – in this case we just assume that $\Phi(\mathbf{t}) = \top$. We introduce now some additional notation. Given a term t, $subterms(t)$ denotes all its subterms, including t itself. Given a set of terms T, by T^* we mean $\{t^* \mid t \in S\}$. If ρ is a replacement of variables by Herbrand constants $[\mathbf{X} \leftarrow \mathbf{c}]$, we write $I, w, \rho \models \varphi$ to stand for $I, w \models \varphi[\mathbf{X} \leftarrow \mathbf{c}]$. Given a conjunction of literals $B = L_1 \wedge \cdots \wedge L_n$, we denote $B^* \stackrel{\text{def}}{=} L_1^* \wedge \cdots \wedge L_n^*$.

Definition 7 (Translation of literals). *The* translation of an atom *(or positive literal)* A *is a formula* A^* *defined as follows:*

1. *If* $A = p(\mathbf{t})$, *then* $A^* \stackrel{\text{def}}{=} \exists \mathbf{X}\big(p(\mathbf{t}^*) \wedge \Phi(\mathbf{t}) \big)$ *where* $\mathbf{X}$ *is the set of new fresh variables in* $subterms(\mathbf{t})^*$ *(those not occurring in the original literal).*
2. *If* $A = (t_1 = t_2)$, *then* $A^* \stackrel{\text{def}}{=} \exists \mathbf{X}\big(t_1^* = t_2^* \wedge \Phi(t_1) \wedge \Phi(t_2) \big)$ *where* $\mathbf{X}$ *is the set of new fresh variables in* $subterms(t_1)^* \cup subterms(t_1)^*$.

The translation of a negative literal $L = \neg A$ *is the formula* $L^* \stackrel{\text{def}}{=} \neg A^*$. ☐

Definition 8 (Translation of rules). *The* translation of an (FLP) rule r *like* H :- B *is a conjunction of formulas* $\Gamma(r)$ *defined as follows:*

1. *If* $H = \bot$, *then* $\Gamma(r)$ *is the formula* $\bot \leftarrow B^*$.
2. *If* H *is like* $p(\mathbf{t})$ *then* $\Gamma(r)$ *is the formula* $p(\mathbf{t}^*) \leftarrow \Phi(\mathbf{t}) \wedge B^*$
3. *If* H *has the form* $f(\mathbf{t}) := t'$ *then* $\Gamma(r)$ *is the formula* $holds\_f(\mathbf{t}^*, t'^*) \leftarrow \Phi(\mathbf{t}) \wedge \Phi(t') \wedge B^*$
4. *If* H *has the form* $f(\mathbf{t}) \in \{X \mid \varphi(X)\}$ *then* $\Gamma(r)$ *is the conjunction of:*

$$holds\_f(\mathbf{t}^*, X) \vee \neg holds\_f(\mathbf{t}^*, X) \leftarrow \Phi(\mathbf{t}) \wedge B^* \wedge \varphi(X)^* \tag{21}$$
$$\bot \leftarrow \neg \exists X (holds\_f(\mathbf{t}^*, X) \wedge \varphi(X)^*) \wedge \Phi(\mathbf{t}) \wedge B^* \tag{22}$$

where we assume that, if X *happened to occur in* B, *we have previously replaced it in the choice by a new fresh variable symbol, say* $\{Y \mid \varphi(Y)\}$.

Definition 9 (Translation of a program $\Gamma(\Pi)$**).** *The* translation of an FLP program Π *is a theory* $\Gamma(\Pi)$ *consisting of the union of all* $\Gamma(r)$ *per each rule* $r \in \Pi$ *plus, for each partial function* f/n, *the schemata* (20). ☐

Theorem 1 (Correctness of $\Gamma(\Pi)$**).** *For any FLP-program* Π *with signature* $\Sigma = \langle \mathcal{C}, \mathcal{F}, \mathcal{P} \rangle$ *any pair of interpretations* I *for* Σ *and* J *for* Σ^* *such that* $J = I^*$: $I, w \models \Pi$ *iff* $I^*, w \models \Gamma(\Pi)$. ☐

As an example, the translation of Π_2 is the theory $\Gamma(\Pi_2)$:

$$\bot \leftarrow holds\_next(X, X_0) \wedge holds\_next(Y, X_1) \wedge X_0 = X_1 \wedge \neg(X = Y) \tag{23}$$
$$holds\_next(X, Z) \vee \neg holds\_next(X, Z) \leftarrow arc(X, Z) \wedge node(X) \tag{24}$$
$$\bot \leftarrow \neg \exists Z (holds\_next(X, Z) \wedge arc(X, Z)) \wedge node(X) \tag{25}$$
$$visited(1) \tag{26}$$
$$visited(X_2) \leftarrow holds\_next(X, X_2) \wedge visited(X) \tag{27}$$
$$\bot \leftarrow \neg visited(X) \wedge node(X) \tag{28}$$
$$\bot \leftarrow holds\_next(X, V) \wedge holds\_next(X, W) \wedge \neg(V = W) \tag{29}$$

Of course, $\Gamma(\Pi)$ is not a normal logic program, since it contains disjunction and negation in the head of "rules", whereas it may also contain expressions like $\exists X(\varphi(X))$ with $\varphi(X)$ a conjunction of literals. However, we can build an LP-program Π^* by removing these constructions and introducing new auxiliary predicates. For instance, a formula like $p \vee \neg p \leftarrow \alpha$ is equivalent (w.r.t. equilibrium models) to the pair of rules $(p \leftarrow \neg aux \wedge \alpha)$ and $(aux \leftarrow \neg p \wedge \alpha)$ where aux is a new auxiliary predicate. Similarly, we can replace a formula $\exists X(\varphi(X))$ in a rule body by a new auxiliary predicate aux', and include a rule $(aux' \leftarrow \varphi(X))$ for its definition. In our example, these transformations would replace (24) by:

$$holds\_next(X, Z) \leftarrow \neg aux(X, Z) \wedge arc(X, Z) \wedge node(X)$$
$$aux(X, Z) \leftarrow \neg holds\_next(X, Z) \wedge arc(X, Z) \wedge node(X)$$

and (25) by the rules:

$$aux'(X) \leftarrow holds\_next(X, Z) \wedge arc(X, Z) \wedge node(X)$$
$$\bot \leftarrow \neg aux'(X) \wedge node(X)$$

where, of course, the auxiliary predicates must incorporate as arguments all the free variables of the original expression they replace.

Proposition 3. *If Π is safe then Π^* is safe.* $\square$

6   Related Work

The present approach has incorporated many of the ideas previously presented in [20,21]. With respect to other logical characterisations of Functional Programming languages, the closest one is [14], from where we extracted the separation of constructors and partial functions. The main difference is that $QEL_{\mathcal{F}}^=$ provides a completely logical description of all operators that allows an arbitrary syntax (including rules with negation, disjunction in the head, etc).

Scott's E-Logic is not the only choice for logical treatment of partial functions. A related approach is the so-called *Logic of Partial Functions* (LPF) [22]. The main difference is that LPF is a three-valued logic – formulas containing undefined terms have a third, undefined truth value. The relation to (relational) ASP in this way in much more distant than the current approach, since stable models and their logical counterpart, equilibrium models, are two-valued[6].

As for the relation to other approaches exclusively dealing with Herbrand functions [6,7,8] it seems that they should be embeddable in $QEL^=$, which corresponds to the fragment of $QEL_{\mathcal{F}}^=$ without partial functions. In a similar way, the recent approach in [15] seems to correspond to the fragment of $QEL_{\mathcal{F}}^=$ with complete functions (that is, the addition of decidable equality). Formal comparisons are left for future work.

---

[6] Note that in this work we are not considering explicit negation.

7   Conclusions

This paper has tried to clarify some relevant aspects related to the use of functions in ASP for Knowledge Representation. These aspects include definedness, the treatment of equality or the directionality in function assignments. Although, as we have shown, the proposed approach can be translated into relational ASP and thus considered as *syntactic sugar*, we claim that the use of functions may provide a more natural, compact and readable way of representing many scenarios. The previous experience with a very close language to that of Section 5, implemented in an online interpreter[7] and used for didactic purposes, shows that the functional notation helps the student concentrate on the mathematical definition of the domain to be represented, and forget some low level representation tasks typically present in ASP programming, like adding constraints for uniqueness of value, using extra variables to replace the ability of nesting functional terms, or adding conditions to check that function-like predicates are defined.

We also hope that the current approach will help to integrate, in the future, the explicit treatment of arithmetic functions made by some ASP tools, that are currently handled *outside* the formal setting. For instance, the ASP grounder `lparse`[8] syntactically accepts a program like $p(div(10, X)) \leftarrow q(X)$ but raises a "divide by zero" runtime error if fact $q(0)$ is added to the program. On the other hand, when div is replaced by a non-built-in function symbol, say f, the meaning is quite different, and we get $\{p(f(10,0)), q(0)\}$ as a stable model. In this paper we have also identified and separated evaluable and (possibly) partial functions (like div above) from constructors (like f in the previous example).

We have provided a translation of our functional language into normal logic programs to show that: (1) it can be implemented with current ASP solvers; but more important (2) that the proposed semantics is *sensible* with respect to the way in which we usually program in the existing ASP paradigm. A topic for future study is the implementation of a solver that directly handles the functional semantics. Other open topics are the axiomatisation of the current logical framework or the addition of a second, explicit (or strong) negation.

Acknowledgements. Many thanks to Joohyung Lee and Yunsong Meng for detecting some technical errors in a preliminary version of this work, and to the anonymous referees for their helpful suggestions.

References

1. Gelfond, M., Lifschitz, V.: The stable model semantics for logic programming. In: Proc. of the 5th Intl. Conf. on Logic Programming, pp. 1070–1080 (1988)
2. Pearce, D., Valverde, A.: Towards a first order equilibrium logic for nonmonotonic reasoning. In: Alferes, J.J., Leite, J. (eds.) JELIA 2004. LNCS, vol. 3229, pp. 147–160. Springer, Heidelberg (2004)

---

[7] Available at `http://www.dc.fi.udc.es/~cabalar/fal/`

[8] Available at `http://www.tcs.hut.fi/Software/smodels/`

3. Lifschitz, V., Pearce, D., Valverde, A.: A characterization of strong equivalence for logic programs with variables. In: Baral, C., Brewka, G., Schlipf, J. (eds.) LPNMR 2007. LNCS, vol. 4483, pp. 188–200. Springer, Heidelberg (2007)
4. Scott, D.: Identity and existence in intuitionistic logic. Lecture Notes in Mathematics 753, 660–696 (1979)
5. Marek, V., Truszczyński, M.: Stable models and an alternative logic programming paradigm. In: The Logic Programming Paradigm: a 25-year Perspective, pp. 169–181. Springer, Heidelberg (1999)
6. Syrjänen, T.: Omega-restricted logic programs. In: Eiter, T., Faber, W., Truszczyński, M. (eds.) LPNMR 2001. LNCS, vol. 2173, pp. 267–279. Springer, Heidelberg (2001)
7. Bonatti, P.A.: Reasoning with infinite stable models. Artificial Intelligence 156, 75–111 (2004)
8. Šimkus, M., Eiter, T.: Decidable non-monotonic disjunctive logic programs with function symbols. In: Dershowitz, N., Voronkov, A. (eds.) LPAR 2007. LNCS, vol. 4790, pp. 514–530. Springer, Heidelberg (2007)
9. Gelfond, M., Lifschitz, V.: Representing action and change by logic programs. Journal of Logic Programming 17, 301–321 (1993)
10. Hanus, M.: The integration of functions into logic programming: from theory to practice. Journal of Logic Programming 19(20), 583–628 (1994)
11. Pearce, D.: A new logical characterisation of stable models and answer sets. In: Dix, J., Przymusinski, T.C., Moniz Pereira, L. (eds.) NMELP 1996. LNCS (LNAI), vol. 1216. Springer, Heidelberg (1997)
12. Ferraris, P., Lee, J., Lifschitz, V.: A new perspective on stable models. In: Proc. of the International Joint Conference on Artificial Intelligence (IJCAI 2007), pp. 372–379 (2004)
13. McCarthy, J.: Circumscription: A form of non-monotonic reasoning. Artificial Intelligence 13, 27–39 (1980)
14. Almendros-Jiménez, J.M., Gavilanes-Franco, A., Gil-Luezas, A.: Algebraic semantics for functional logic programming with polymorphic order-sorted types. In: Hanus, M., Rodríguez-Artalejo, M. (eds.) ALP 1996. LNCS, vol. 1139. Springer, Heidelberg (1996)
15. Lin, F., Wang, Y.: Answer set programming with functions. In: Proc. of the 11th Intl. Conf. on Principles of Knowledge Representation and Reasoning, KR 2008 (to appear, 2008)
16. Heyting, A.: Die formalen Regeln der intuitionistischen Logik. Sitzungsberichte der Preussischen Akademie der Wissenschaften, Physikalisch-mathematische Klasse, 42–56 (1930)
17. Heyting, A.: Intuitionism. An Introduction. North-Holland, Amsterdam (1956)
18. Naish, L.: Adding equations to NU-Prolog. In: Małuszyński, J., Wirsing, M. (eds.) PLILP 1991. LNCS, vol. 528, pp. 15–26. Springer, Heidelberg (1991)
19. Rouveirol, C.: Flattening and saturation: Two representation changes for generalization. Machine Learning 14(1), 219–232 (1994)
20. Cabalar, P., Lorenzo, D.: Logic programs with functions and default values. In: Alferes, J.J., Leite, J. (eds.) JELIA 2004. LNCS, vol. 3229, pp. 294–306. Springer, Heidelberg (2004)
21. Cabalar, P.: A functional action language front-end. In: 3rd Workshop on Answer Set Programming, ASP 2005 (2005), http://www.dc.fi.udc.es/ai/~cabalar/asp05_C.pdf/
22. Barringer, H., Cheng, H., Jones, C.B.: A logic covering undefinedness in program proofs. Acta Informatica 21, 251–269 (1984)

Computable Functions in ASP: Theory and Implementation*

Francesco Calimeri, Susanna Cozza, Giovambattista Ianni, and Nicola Leone

Department of Mathematics, University of Calabria, I-87036 Rende (CS), Italy
{calimeri,cozza,ianni,leone}@mat.unical.it

Abstract. Disjunctive Logic Programming (DLP) under the answer set semantics, often referred to as Answer Set Programming (ASP), is a powerful formalism
for knowledge representation and reasoning (KRR). The latest years witness an
increasing effort for embedding functions in the context of ASP. Nevertheless,
at present no ASP system allows for a reasonably unrestricted use of function
terms. Functions are either required not to be recursive or subject to severe syntactic limitations, if allowed at all in ASP systems.

In this work we formally define the new class of finitely-ground programs,
allowing for a powerful (possibly recursive) use of function terms in the full ASP
language with disjunction and negation. We demonstrate that finitely-ground programs have nice computational properties: (i) both brave and cautious reasoning
are decidable, and (ii) answer sets of finitely-ground programs are computable.
Moreover, the language is highly expressive, as any computable function can be
encoded by a finitely-ground program. Due to the high expressiveness, membership in the class of finitely-ground program is clearly not decidable (we prove
that it is semi-decidable). We single out also a subset of finitely-ground programs,
called finite-domain programs, which are effectively recognizable, while keeping
computability of both reasoning and answer set computation.

We implement all results in DLV, further extending the language in order
to support list and set terms, along with a rich library of built-in functions for
their manipulation. The resulting ASP system is very powerful: any computable
function can be encoded in a rich and fully declarative KRR language, ensuring termination on every finitely-ground program. In addition, termination is "a
priori" guaranteed if the user asks for the finite-domain check.

1 Introduction

Disjunctive Logic Programming (DLP) under the answer set semantics, often referred
to as Answer Set Programming (ASP) [1,2,3,4,5], evolved significantly during the last
decade, and has been recognized as a convenient and powerful method for declarative
knowledge representation and reasoning. Several systems supporting ASP have been
implemented so far, thereby encouraging a number of applications in many real-world
contexts ranging, e.g., from information integration, to frauds detection, to software

* Supported by M.I.U.R. within projects "Potenziamento e Applicazioni della Programmazione
Logica Disgiuntiva" and "Sistemi basati sulla logica per la rappresentazione di conoscenza:
estensioni e tecniche di ottimizzazione."

M. Garcia de la Banda and E. Pontelli (Eds.): ICLP 2008, LNCS 5366, pp. 407–424, 2008.
© Springer-Verlag Berlin Heidelberg 2008

configuration, and many others. On the one hand, the above mentioned applications have confirmed the viability of the exploitation of ASP for advanced knowledge-based tasks. On the other hand, they have evidenced some limitations of ASP languages and systems, that should be overcome to make ASP better suited for real-world applications even in industry. One of the most noticeable limitations is the fact that complex terms like functions, sets and lists, are not adequately supported by current ASP languages/systems. Therefore, even by using state-of-the-art systems, one cannot directly reason about recursive data structures and infinite domains, such as XML/HTML documents, lists, time, etc. This is a strong limitation, both for standard knowledge-based tasks and for emerging applications, such as those manipulating XML documents.

The strong need to extend DLP by functions is clearly perceived in the ASP community, and many relevant contributions have been recently done in this direction [6,7,8,9,10]. However, we still miss a proposal which is fully satisfactory from a linguistic viewpoint (high expressiveness) and suited to be incorporated in the existing ASP systems. Indeed, at present no ASP system allows for a reasonably unrestricted use of function terms. Functions are either required not to be recursive or subject to severe syntactic limitations, if allowed at all in ASP systems.

This paper aims at overcoming the above mentioned limitations, toward a powerful enhancement of ASP systems by functions. The contribution is both theoretical and practical, and leads to the implementation of a powerful ASP system supporting (recursive) functions, sets, and lists, along with libraries for their manipulations. The main results can be summarized as follows:

▶ We formally define the new class of *finitely-ground* ($\mathcal{FG}$) DLP programs. This class allows for (possibly recursive) function symbols, disjunction and negation. We demonstrate that $\mathcal{FG}$ programs enjoy many relevant computational properties:
  • both brave and cautious reasoning are computable, even for non-ground queries;
  • answer sets are computable;
  • each computable function can be expressed by a $\mathcal{FG}$ program.

▶ Since $\mathcal{FG}$ programs express any computable function, membership in this class is obviously not decidable (we prove that it is semi-decidable). For users/applications where termination needs to be "a priori" guaranteed, we define the class of *finite-domain* ($\mathcal{FD}$) programs:
  • both reasoning and answer set generation are computable for $\mathcal{FD}$ programs (they are a subclass of $\mathcal{FG}$ programs), and, in addition,
  • recognizing whether a program is an $\mathcal{FD}$ program is decidable.

▶ We extend the language with list and set terms, along with a rich library of built-in functions for lists and sets manipulations.

▶ We implement all results and the full (extended) language in DLV, obtaining a very powerful system where the user can exploit the full expressiveness of $\mathcal{FG}$ programs (able to encode any computable function), or require the finite-domain check, getting the guarantee of termination. The system is available for downloading [11]; it is already in use in many universities and research centers throughout the world.

For space limitations, we cannot include detailed proofs. Further documentation and examples are available on the web site [11].

2   DLP with Functions

This section reports the formal specification of the DLP language with function symbols allowed.

Syntax and notations. A *term* is either a *simple term* or a *functional term*. A *simple term* is either a constant or a variable. If $t_1 \ldots t_n$ are terms and f is a function symbol (*functor*) of arity n, then: $f(t_1, \ldots, t_n)$ is a *functional term*. Each t_i, $1 \leq i \leq n$, is a subterm of $f(t_1, \ldots, t_n)$. The subterm relation is reflexive and transitive, that is: (i) each term is also a subterm of itself; and (ii) if t_1 is a subterm of t_2 and t_2 is subterm of t_3 then t_1 is also a subterm of t_3.

Each predicate p has a fixed arity $k \geq 0$; by $p[i]$ we denote its i-th argument. If $t_1, \ldots, t_k$ are terms, then $p(t_1, \ldots, t_k)$ is an *atom*. A *literal* l is of the form a or not a, where a is an atom; in the former case l is *positive*, and in the latter case *negative*. A *rule* r is of the form $\alpha_1 \vee \cdots \vee \alpha_k :\!- \beta_1, \ldots, \beta_n, \text{not } \beta_{n+1}, \ldots, \text{not } \beta_m.$ where $m \geq 0$, $k \geq 0$; $\alpha_1, \ldots, \alpha_k$ and $\beta_1, \ldots, \beta_m$ are atoms. We define $H(r) = \{\alpha_1, \ldots, \alpha_k\}$ (the *head* of r) and $B(r) = B^+(r) \cup B^-(r)$ (the *body* of r), where $B^+(r) = \{\beta_1, \ldots, \beta_n\}$ (the *positive body* of r) and $B^-(r) = \{\text{not } \beta_{n+1}, \ldots, \text{not } \beta_m\}$ (the *negative body* of r). If $H(r) = \emptyset$ then r is a *constraint*; if $B(r) = \emptyset$ and $|H(r)| = 1$ then r is referred to as a *fact*.

A rule is safe if each variable in that rule also appears in at least one positive literal in the body of that rule. For instance, the rule $p(X, f(Y, Z)) :\!- q(Y), \text{not } s(X).$ is not safe, because of both X and Z. From now on we assume that all rules are safe and there is no constraint.[1] A DLP program is a finite set P of rules. As usual, a program (a rule, a literal) is said to be *ground* if it contains no variables. Given a program P, according with the database terminology, a predicate occurring only in facts is referred to as an *EDB* predicate, all others as *IDB* predicates. The set of all facts of P is denoted by Facts(P); the set of instances of all EDB predicates is denoted by EDB(P) (note that EDB(P) $\subseteq$ Facts(P)). The set of all head atoms in P is denoted by $Heads(P) = \bigcup_{r \in P} H(r)$.

Semantics. The most widely accepted semantics for DLP programs is based on the notion of answer-set, proposed in [3] as a generalization of the concept of stable model [2].

Given a program P, the *Herbrand universe* of P, denoted by U_P, consists of all (ground) terms that can be built combining constants and functors appearing in P. The *Herbrand base* of P, denoted by B_P, is the set of all ground atoms obtainable from the atoms of P by replacing variables with elements from U_P. A *substitution* for a rule $r \in P$ is a mapping from the set of variables of r to the set U_P of ground terms. A *ground instance* of a rule r is obtained applying a substitution to r. Given a program P the *instantiation (grounding) grnd(P)* of P is defined as the set of all ground instances of its rules. Given a ground program P, an *interpretation* I for P is a subset of B_P. A positive literal $l = a$ (resp., a negative literal $l = \text{not } a$) is true w.r.t. I if $a \in I$ (resp., $a \notin I$); it is false otherwise. Given a ground rule r, we say that r is satisfied w.r.t.

---

[1] Under Answer Set semantics, a constraint :- B(r) can be simulated through the introduction of a standard rule fail :- B(r), not fail, where fail is a fresh predicate not occurring elsewhere in the program.

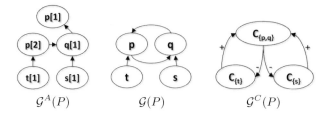

Fig. 1. *Argument, Dependency* and *Component* Graphs of the program in Example 1

I if some atom appearing in $H(r)$ is true w.r.t. I or some literal appearing in $B(r)$ is false w.r.t. I. Given a ground program P, we say that I is a *model* of P, iff all rules in $grnd(P)$ are satisfied w.r.t. I. A model M is *minimal* if there is no model N for P such that $N \subset M$.

The *Gelfond-Lifschitz reduct* [3] of P, w.r.t. an interpretation I, is the positive ground program P^I obtained from $grnd(P)$ by: (i) deleting all rules having a negative literal false w.r.t. I; (ii) deleting all negative literals from the remaining rules. $I \subseteq B_P$ is an *answer set* for a program P iff I is a minimal model for P^I. The set of all answer sets for P is denoted by $AS(P)$.

Dependency Graphs. We next define three graphs that point out dependencies among arguments, predicates, and components of a program.

Definition 1. The *Argument Graph* $\mathcal{G}^A(P)$ of a program P is a directed graph containing a node for each argument $p[i]$ of an IDB predicate p of P; there is an edge $(q[j], p[i])$ iff there is a rule $r \in P$ such that: (a) an atom $p(\bar{t})$ appears in the head of r; (b) an atom $q(\bar{v})$ appears in $B^+(r)$; (c) $p(\bar{t})$ and $q(\bar{v})$ share the same variable within the i-th and j-th term, respectively.

Given a program P, an argument $p[i]$ is said to be recursive with $q[j]$ if there exists a cycle in $\mathcal{G}^A(P)$ involving both $p[i]$ and $q[j]$. Roughly speaking, this graph keeps track of (body-head) dependencies between the arguments of predicates sharing some variable. It is actually a more detailed version of the commonly used (predicate) dependency graph, defined below.

Definition 2. The *Dependency Graph* $\mathcal{G}(P)$ of P is a directed graph whose nodes are the IDB predicates appearing in P. There is an edge (p_2, p_1) in $\mathcal{G}(P)$ iff there is some rule r with p_2 appearing in $B^+(r)$ and p_1 in $H(r)$, respectively.

The graph $\mathcal{G}(P)$ suggests to split the set of all predicates of P into a number of sets (called components), one for each strongly connected component (SCC)[2] of the graph itself. Given a predicate p, we denote its component by $comp(p)$; with a small abuse of notation, we define also $comp(l)$ and $comp(a)$, where l is a literal and a is an atom, accordingly.

In order to single out dependencies among components, a proper graph is defined next.

---

[2] We recall here that a strongly connected component of a directed graph is a maximal subset S of the vertices, such that each vertex in S is reachable from all other vertices in S.

Definition 3. Given a program P and its Dependency Graph $\mathcal{G}(P)$, the *Component Graph* of P, denoted $\mathcal{G}^C(P)$, is a directed labelled graph having a node for each strongly connected component of $\mathcal{G}(P)$ and: (i) an edge (B, A), labelled "+", if there is a rule r in P such that there is a predicate $q \in A$ occurring in the head of r and a predicate $p \in B$ occurring in the positive body of r; (ii) an edge (B, A), labelled "-", if there is a rule r in P such that there is a predicate $q \in A$ occurring in the head of r and a predicate $p \in B$ occurring in the negative body of r, and there is no edge (B, A), with label "+". Self-cycles are not considered.

Example 1. Consider the following program P, where a is an EDB predicate:

$$q(g(3)).$$
$$p(X, Y) :\text{-} q(g(X)), t(f(Y)). \qquad s(X) \vee t(f(X)) :\text{-} a(X), \text{not } q(X).$$
$$q(X) :\text{-} s(X), p(Y, X).$$

Graphs $\mathcal{G}^A(P), \mathcal{G}(P)$ and $\mathcal{G}^C(P)$ are respectively depicted in Figure 1. There are three SCC in $\mathcal{G}(P)$: $C_{\{s\}} = \{s\}, C_{\{t\}} = \{t\}$ and $C_{\{p,q\}} = \{p, q\}$ which are the three nodes of $\mathcal{G}^C(P)$.

An ordering among the rules, respecting dependencies pointed out by $\mathcal{G}^C(P)$, is defined next.

Definition 4. A path in $\mathcal{G}^C(P)$ is *strong* if all its edges are labelled with "+". If, on the contrary, there is at least an edge in the path labelled with "-", the path is *weak*. A *component ordering* for a given program P is a total ordering $\langle C_1, \ldots, C_n \rangle$ of all components of P s.t., for any C_i, C_j with $i < j$, both the following conditions hold: (i) there are no strong paths from C_j to C_i; (ii) if there is a weak path from C_j to C_i, then there must be a weak path also from C_i to C_j.[3]

Example 2. Consider the graph $\mathcal{G}^C(P)$ of previous example. Both $C_{\{s\}}$ and $C_{\{t\}}$ are connected to $C_{\{p,q\}}$ through a strong path, while a weak path connects: $C_{\{s\}}$ to $C_{\{t\}}$, $C_{\{t\}}$ to $C_{\{s\}}, C_{\{p,q\}}$ to $C_{\{s\}}$ and $C_{\{p,q\}}$ to $C_{\{t\}}$. Both $\gamma_1 = \langle C_{\{s\}}, C_{\{t\}}, C_{\{p,q\}} \rangle$ and $\gamma_2 = \langle C_{\{t\}}, C_{\{s\}}, C_{\{p,q\}} \rangle$ constitute component orderings for the program P.

By means of the graphs defined above, it is possible to identify a set of subprograms (also called *modules*) of P, allowing for a modular bottom-up evaluation. We say that a rule $r \in P$ *defines* a predicate p if p appears in $H(r)$. Once a component ordering $\gamma = \langle C_1, \ldots, C_n \rangle$ is given, for each component C_i we define the *module* of C_i, denoted by $P(C_i)$, as the set of all rules r defining some predicate $p \in C_i$ excepting those that define also some other predicate belonging to a lower component (i.e., certain C_j with $j < i$ in γ).

Example 3. Consider the program P of Example 1. If we consider the component ordering γ_1, the corresponding modules are:

$$P(C_{\{s\}}) = \{ s(X) \vee t(f(X)) :\text{-} a(X), \text{not } q(X). \}, \qquad P(C_{\{t\}}) = \emptyset,$$
$$P(C_{\{p,q\}}) = \{p(X, Y) :\text{-} q(g(X)), t(f(Y))., q(X) :\text{-} s(X), p(Y, X)., q(g(3)). \}.$$

---

[3] Note that, given the component ordering γ, C_i stands for the i-th component in γ, and $C_i < C_j$ means that C_i precedes C_j in γ (i.e., $i < j$).

The modules of P are defined, according to a component ordering γ, with the aim of properly instantiating all rules. It is worth remembering that we deal only with safe rules, i.e., all variables appear in the positive body; it is therefore enough to instantiate the positive body. Furthermore, any component ordering γ guarantees that, when $r \in P(C_i)$ is instantiated, each nonrecursive predicate p appearing in $B^+(r)$ is defined in a lower component (i.e., in some C_j with $j < i$ in γ). It is also worth remembering that, according to how the modules of P are defined, if r is a disjunctive rule, then it is associated only to a unique module $P(C_i)$, chosen in such a way that, among all components C_j such that $comp(a) = C_j$ for some $a \in H(r)$, it always holds $i \leq j$ in γ (that is, the disjunctive rule is associated only to the (unique) module corresponding to the lowest component among those "covering" all predicates featuring some instance in the head of r). This implies that the set of the modules of P constitute an exact partition for it.

3   Finitely-Ground Programs

In this section we introduce a subclass of DLP programs, namely finitely-ground ($\mathcal{FG}$) programs, having some nice computational properties.

Since the set of ground instances of a rule might be infinite (because of the presence of function symbols), it is crucial to try to identify those that really matter in order to compute answer sets. Supposing that S contains all atoms that are potentially true, next definition singles out the relevant instances of a rule.

Definition 5. Given a rule r and a set S of ground atoms, an *S-restricted* instance of r is a ground instance r' of r such that $B^+(r') \subseteq S$. The set of all S-restricted instances of a program P is denoted as $Inst_P(S)$.

Note that, for any $S \subseteq B_P$, $Inst_P(S) \subseteq grnd(P)$. Intuitively, this helps selecting, among all ground instances, those somehow *supported* by a given set S.

Example 4. Consider the following program P:

$t(f(1)).$ $t(f(f(1))).$ $p(1).$ $p(f(X)) :- p(X), t(f(X))).$

The set $Inst_P(S)$ of all S-restricted instances of P, w.r.t. $S = Facts(P)$ is:

$t(f(1)).$ $t(f(f(1))).$ $p(1).$ $p(f(1)) :- p(1), t(f(1)).$

The presence of negation allows for identifying some further rules which do not matter for the computation of answer sets, and for simplifying the bodies of some others. This can be properly done by exploiting a modular evaluation of the program that relies on a component ordering.

Definition 6. Given a program P, a component ordering $\langle C_1, \ldots, C_n \rangle$, a set S_i of ground rules for C_i, and a set of ground rules R for the components preceding C_i, the *simplification* $Simpl(S_i, R)$ of S_i w.r.t. R is obtained from S_i by:

1. *deleting* each rule whose body contains some negative body literal not a s.t. $a \in Facts(R)$, or whose head contains some atom $a \in Facts(R)$;

2. *eliminating* from the remaining rules each literal l s.t.:
   - $l = a$ is a positive body literal and $a \in Facts(R)$, or
   - $l = $ not a is a negative body literal, $comp(a) = C_j$ with $j < i$, and $a \notin Heads(R)$.

Assuming that R contains all instances of the modules preceding C_i, $Simpl(S_i, R)$ deletes from S_i all rules whose body is certainly false or whose head is certainly already true w.r.t. R, and simplifies the remaining rules by removing from the bodies all literals that are true w.r.t. R.

Example 5. Consider the following program P:

$$t(1). \qquad s(1). \qquad s(2).$$
$$q(X) :\text{-} t(X). \qquad p(X) :\text{-} s(X), \text{not } q(X).$$

It is easy to see that $\langle C_1 = \{q\}, C_2 = \{p\}\rangle$ is the only component ordering for P. If we consider $R = EDB(P) = \{ t(1)., s(1)., s(2). \}$ and $S_1 = \{q(1):\text{-}t(1).\}$, then $Simpl(S_1, R) = \{q(1).\}$ (i.e., $t(1)$ is eliminated from body). Considering then $R = \{t(1)., s(1)., s(2)., q(1).\}$ and $S_2 = \{ p(1):\text{-} s(1), \text{not } q(1)., p(2):\text{-} s(2), \text{not } q(2). \}$, after the simplification we have $Simpl(S_2, R) = \{p(2).\}$. Indeed, $s(2)$ is eliminated as it belongs to $Facts(R)$ and not $q(2)$ is eliminated because $comp(q(2)) = C_1$ precedes C_2 in the component ordering and the atom $q(2) \notin Heads(R)$; in addition, rule $p(1):\text{-} s(1), \text{not } q(1).$ is deleted, since $q(1) \in Facts(R)$.

We are now ready to define an operator Φ that acts on a module of a program P in order to: (i) select only those ground rules whose positive body is contained in a set of ground atoms consisting of the heads of a given set of rules; (ii) perform a further simplification among these rules by means of the $Simpl$ operator.

Definition 7. Given a program P, a component ordering $\langle C_1, \ldots, C_n\rangle$, a component C_i, the module $M = P(C_i)$, a set X of ground rules of M, and a set R of ground rules belonging only to EDB(P) or to modules of components C_j with $j < i$, let $\Phi_{M,R}(X)$ be the transformation defined as follows: $\Phi_{M,R}(X) = Simpl(Inst_M(Heads(R \cup X)), R)$.

Example 6. Let P be the program of Example 1 where the extension of EDB predicate a is $\{a(1)\}$. Considering the component $C_1 = \{s\}$, the module $M = P(C_1)$, and the sets $X = \emptyset$ and $R = \{a(1)\}$, we have:
$$\Phi_{M,R}(X) = Simpl(Inst_M(Heads(R \cup X)), R) =$$
$$= Simpl(Inst_M(\{a(1)\}), \{a(1).\}) =$$
$$= Simpl(\{s(1) \lor t(f(1)):\text{-} a(1), \text{not } q(1).\}, \{a(1).\}) =$$
$$= \{s(1) \lor t(f(1)):\text{-} \text{not } q(1).\}.$$

The operator defined above has the following important property.

Proposition 1. $\Phi_{M,R}$ always admits a least fixpoint $\Phi_{M,R}^\infty(\emptyset)$.

Proof. (Sketch) The statement follows from Tarski's theorem [12]), noting that $\Phi_{M,R}$ is a monotonic operator and that a set of rules forms a meet semilattice under set containment. □

By properly composing consecutive applications of Φ^∞ to a component ordering, we can obtain an instantiation which drops many useless rules w.r.t. answer sets computation.

Definition 8. Given a program P and a component ordering $\gamma = \langle C_1, \ldots, C_n \rangle$ for P, the *intelligent instantiation* P^γ of P for γ is the last element S_n of the sequence s.t. $S_0 = EDB(P)$, $S_i = S_{i-1} \cup \Phi^\infty_{M_i, S_{i-1}}(\emptyset)$, where M_i is the program module $P(C_i)$.

Example 7. Let P be the program of Example 1 where the extension of EDB predicate a is $\{a(1)\}$; considering the component ordering $\gamma = \langle C_1 = \{s\}, C_2 = \{t\}, C_3 = \{p, q\} \rangle$ we have:

- $S_0 = \{a(1).\}$;
- $S_1 = S_0 \cup \Phi^\infty_{M_1, S_0}(\emptyset) = \{a(1)., \ s(1) \vee t(f(1)) :\!\!- \text{not } q(1).\}$;
- $S_2 = S_1 \cup \Phi^\infty_{M_2, S_1}(\emptyset) = \{a(1)., \ s(1) \vee t(f(1)) :\!\!- \text{not } q(1).\}$;
- $S_3 = S_2 \cup \Phi^\infty_{M_3, S_2}(\emptyset) = \{a(1)., \ s(1) \vee t(f(1)) :\!\!- \text{not } q(1).,$
$$q(g(3))., \ p(3,1) :\!\!- q(g(3)), t(f(1))., \ q(1) :\!\!- s(1), p(3,1).\}.$$

Thus, the resulting intelligent instantiation P^γ of P for γ is:

$$a(1). \qquad q(g(3)). \qquad s(1) \vee t(f(1)) :\!\!- \text{not } q(1).$$
$$p(3,1) :\!\!- q(g(3)), t(f(1)). \qquad q(1) :\!\!- s(1), p(3,1).$$

We are now ready to define the class of $\mathcal{FG}$ programs.

Definition 9. A program P is *finitely-ground* ($\mathcal{FG}$) if P^γ is finite, for every component ordering γ for P.

Example 8. The program of Example 1 is $\mathcal{FG}$: P^γ is finite both when $\gamma = \langle C_{\{s\}}, C_{\{t\}}, C_{\{p,q\}} \rangle$ and when $\gamma = \langle C_{\{t\}}, C_{\{s\}}, C_{\{p,q\}} \rangle$ (i.e., for the both of two component orderings for P).

4   Properties of Finitely-Ground Programs

In this section the class of $\mathcal{FG}$ programs is characterized by identifying some key properties.

The next theorem shows that we can compute the answer sets of an $\mathcal{FG}$ program by considering intelligent instantiations, instead of the theoretical (possibly infinite) ground program.

Theorem 1. Let P be an $\mathcal{FG}$ program and P^γ be the intelligent instantiation of P w.r.t. a component ordering γ for P. Then, $AS(P) = AS(P^\gamma)$ (i.e., P and P^γ have the same answer sets).

Proof. (Sketch) Given $\gamma = \langle C_1, \ldots, C_n \rangle$, let denote, as usual, by M_i the program module $P(C_i)$, and consider the sets $S_0, \ldots, S_n$ as defined in Definition 8. Since $P = \bigcup_{i=0}^{n} M_i$ the theorem can be proven by showing that:

$$AS(S_k) = AS(\textstyle\bigcup_{i=0}^{k} M_i) \text{ for } 1 \leq k \leq n$$

where M_0 denotes $EDB(P)$. The equation clearly holds for $k = 0$. Assuming that it holds for all $k \leq j$, we can show that it holds for $k = j + 1$. The equation above can be rewritten as:

$$AS(S_{k-1} \cup \Phi^\infty_{M_k, S_{k-1}}(\emptyset)) = AS(\bigcup_{i=0}^{k-1} M_i \cup M_k)) \text{ for } 1 \leq k \leq n$$

The induction hypothesis allows us to assume that the equivalence $AS(S_{k-1}) = AS(\bigcup_{i=0}^{k-1} M_i)$ holds. A careful analysis is needed of the impact that the addition of M_k to $\bigcup_{i=0}^{k-1} M_i$ has on answer sets of S_k; in order to prove the theorem, it is enough to show that the set $\Phi^\infty_{M_k, S_{k-1}}(\emptyset)$ does not drop any "meaningful" rule w.r.t. M_k.

If we disregard the application of the $Simpl$ operator, i.e. we consider the operator Φ performing only $Inst_{M_k}(Heads(S_{k-1} \cup \emptyset))$, then $\Phi^\infty_{M_k, S_{k-1}}(\emptyset)$ clearly generates all rules having a chance to have a true body in any answer set; omitted rules have a false body in every answer set, and are therefore irrelevant.

The application of $Simpl$ does not change the scenario: it relies only on previously derived facts, and on the absence of atoms from heads of previously derived ground rules.[4] If a fact q has been derived in a previous component, then any rule featuring q in the head or not q in the body is deleted, as it is already satisfied and cannot contribute to any answer set. The simplification operator also drops, from the bodies, positive atoms of lower components appearing as facts, as well as negative atoms belonging to lower components which do not appear in the head of any already generated ground rule. The presence of facts in the bodies is obviously irrelevant, and the deleted negative atoms are irrelevant as well. Indeed, by construction of the component dependency graph, while instantiating a module, all rules defining atoms of lower components have been already instantiated. Thus, atoms of lower components not appearing in the head of any generated rule, have no chances to be true in any answer set. □

Corollary 1. An $\mathcal{FG}$ program has finitely many answer sets, and each of them is finite.

Theorem 2. Given an $\mathcal{FG}$ program P, $AS(P)$ is computable.

Proof. Note that by Theorem 1, answer sets of P can be obtained by computing the answer sets of P^γ for a component ordering γ of choice, which can be easily computed. Then, P^γ can be obtained by computing the sequence of fixpoints of Φ specified in Definition 8. Each fixpoint is guaranteed to be finitely computable, since the program is finitely-ground. □

From this property, the main result below immediately follows.

Theorem 3. Cautious and brave reasoning over $\mathcal{FG}$ programs are computable. Computability holds even for non-ground queries.

As the next theorem shows, the class of $\mathcal{FG}$ programs allows for the encoding of any computable function.

---

[4] Note that, due to the elimination of true literals performed by the simplification operator $Simpl$, the intelligent instantiation of a rule with a non empty body may generate some facts.

Theorem 4. Given a recursive function f, there exists a DLP program P_f such that, for any input x for f, $P_f \cup \theta(x)$ is finitely-ground and $AS(P_f \cup \theta(x))$ encodes $f(x)$, for θ a simple function encoding x by a set of facts.

Proof. (Sketch) We can build a positive program P_f, which encodes the Turing machine M_f corresponding to f (see [11]). For any input x to M_f, $(P_f \cup \theta(x))^\gamma$ is finite for any component ordering γ, and $AS(P_f \cup \theta(x))$ contains an appropriate encoding of $f(x)$.   □

Note that recognizing $\mathcal{FG}$ programs is semi-decidable, yet not decidable:

Theorem 5. Recognizing whether P is an $\mathcal{FG}$ program is R.E.-complete.

Proof. (Sketch) Semi-decidability is shown by implementing an algorithm evaluating the sequence given in Definition 8, and answering "yes" if the sequence converges in finite time.

On the other hand, given a Turing machine M and an input tape x, it is possible to write a corresponding program P_M and a set $\theta(x)$ of facts encoding x, such that M halts on input x iff $P_M \cup \theta(x)$ is finitely-ground. The program P_M is the same as in the proof of Theorem 4 and reported in [11].   □

5   Finite-Domain Programs

In this section we single out a subclass of $\mathcal{FG}$ programs, called finite-domain ($\mathcal{FD}$) programs, which ensures the decidability of recognizing membership in the class.

Definition 10. Given a program P, the set of *finite-domain arguments ($\mathcal{FD}$ arguments)* of P is the maximal (w.r.t. inclusion) set $FD(P)$ of arguments of P such that, for each argument $q[k] \in FD(P)$, every rule r with head predicate q satisfies the following condition. Let t be the term corresponding to argument $q[k]$ in the head of r. Then,

1. either t is variable-free, or
2. t is a subterm [5] of (the term of) some $\mathcal{FD}$ argument of a positive body predicate, or
3. every variable appearing in t also appears in (the term of) a $\mathcal{FD}$ argument of a positive body predicate which is not recursive with $q[k]$.

If all arguments of the predicates of P are $\mathcal{FD}$, then P is said to be an $\mathcal{FD}$ *program.*

Intuitively, $\mathcal{FD}$ arguments can range only on a finite set of different ground values. Observe that $FD(P)$ is well-defined; indeed, it is easy to see that there always exists, and it is unique, a maximal set satisfying Definition 10 (trivially, given two sets A_1 and A_2 of $\mathcal{FD}$ arguments for a program P, the set $A_1 \cup A_2$ is also a set of $\mathcal{FD}$ arguments for P).

Example 9. The following is an example of $\mathcal{FD}$ program:

$$q(f(0)). \qquad q(X) :\!- q(f(X)).$$

---

[5] The condition can be made less strict considering other notions, as, e.g., the *norm* of a term [13,14,15].

Indeed q[1] is the only argument in the program and it is an $\mathcal{FD}$ argument, since the two occurrences of $q[1]$ in a rule head satisfy first and second condition of Definition 10, respectively.

Example 10. The following is not an $\mathcal{FD}$ program:

$$q(f(0)). \qquad\qquad q(X) :\!\!- q(f(X)).$$
$$s(f(X)) :\!\!- s(X). \qquad v(X) :\!\!- q(X),\ s(X).$$

We have that all arguments belong to $FD(P)$, except for $s[1]$. Indeed, $s[1]$ appears as head argument in the third rule with term $f(X)$, and: (i) $f(X)$ is not variable-free; (ii) $f(X)$ is not a subterm of some term appearing in a positive body $\mathcal{FD}$ argument; (iii) there is no positive body predicate which is not recursive with s and contains X.

By the following theorems we now point out two key properties of $\mathcal{FD}$ programs.

Theorem 6. Recognizing whether P is an $\mathcal{FD}$ program is decidable.

Proof. (Sketch) An algorithm deciding whether P is $\mathcal{FD}$ or not can be defined as follows. Arguments of predicates in P are all supposed to be $\mathcal{FD}$ at first. If at least one rule is found, such that for an argument of an head predicate none of the three conditions of Definition 10 holds, then P is recognized as not being an $\mathcal{FD}$ program. If no such rule is found, the answer is positive. □

Theorem 7. Every $\mathcal{FD}$ program is an $\mathcal{FG}$ program.

Proof. (Sketch) Given an $\mathcal{FD}$ program P, it is possible to find *a priori* an upper bound for the maximum nesting level[6] of the terms appearing in P^γ, for any component ordering γ for P. This is given by $max\_nl = (n+1) * m$, where m is the maximum nesting level of the terms in P, and n is the number of components in γ. Indeed, given that P is an $\mathcal{FD}$ program, it is easy to see that the maximum nesting level cannot increase because of recursive rules, since, in this case, the second condition of Definition 10 forces a sub-term relationships between head and body predicates. Hence, the maximum nesting level can increase only because of body-head dependencies among predicates of different components. We can now compute the set of all possible ground terms t obtained by combining all constants and function symbols appearing in P, such that the nesting level of t is less or equal to max_nl. This is a finite set, and clearly a superset of the ground terms appearing in P^γ. Thus, P^γ is necessarily finite. □

The results above allow us to state the following properties for $\mathcal{FD}$ programs.

Corollary 2. Let P be an $\mathcal{FD}$ program, then:

1. P has finitely many answer sets, and each of them is finite.
2. $AS(P)$ is computable;
3. skeptical and credulous reasoning over P are computable. Computability holds even if the query at hand is not ground.

---

[6] The nesting level of a ground term is defined inductively as follows: (i) a constant term has nesting level zero; (ii) a functional term $f(t_1, \ldots, t_n)$ has nesting level equal to the maximum nesting level among $t_1, \ldots, t_n$ plus one.

6 An ASP System with Functions, Sets, and Lists

In this section we briefly illustrate the implementation of an ASP system supporting the language herein presented. Such system actually features an even richer language, that, besides functions, explicitly supports also complex terms such as lists and sets, and provides a large library of built-in predicates for facilitating their manipulation. Thanks to such extensions, the resulting language becomes even more suitable for easy and compact knowledge representation tasks.

Language. We next informally point out the peculiar features of the fully extended language, with the help of some sample programs.

In addition to simple and functional terms, there might be also *list* and *set* terms; a term which is not simple is said to be *complex*. A list term can be of two different forms: (i) $[t_1, \ldots, t_n]$, where t_1, ..., t_n are terms; (ii) $[h|t]$, where h (the head of the list) is a term, and t (the tail of the list) is a list term. Examples for list terms are: $[jan, feb, mar, apr, may, jun]$, $[jan \mid [feb, mar, apr, may, jun]]$, $[[jan, 31] \mid$ $[[feb, 28], [mar, 31], [apr, 30], [may, 31], [jun, 30]]]$.

Set terms are used to model collections of data having the usual properties associated with the mathematical notion of set. They satisfy idempotence (i.e., sets have no duplicate elements) and commutativity (i.e., two collections having the same elements but with a different order represent the same set) properties. A *set term* is of the form: $\{t_1, \ldots, t_n\}$, where t_1, ..., t_n are ground terms. Examples for set terms are: $\{red, green, blue\}$, $\{[red, 5], [blue, 3], [green, 4]\}$, $\{\{red, green\}, \{red, blue\},$ $\{green, blue\}\}$. Note that duplicated elements are ignored, thus the sets: $\{red, green, blue\}$ and $\{green, red, blue, green\}$ are actually considered as the same.

As already mentioned, in order to easily handle list and set terms, a rich set of built-in functions and predicates is provided. Functional terms prefixed by a $\#$ symbol are *built-in* functions. Such kind of functional terms are supposed to be substituted by the values resulting from the application of a functor to its arguments, according to some predefined semantics. For this reason, built-in functions are also referred to as *interpreted* functions. Atoms prefixed by $\#$ are, instead, instances of *built-in* predicates. Such kind of atoms are evaluated as true or false by means of operations performed on their arguments, according to some predefined semantics[7]. Some simple built-in predicates are also available, such as the comparative predicates equality, less-than, and greater-than $(=, <, >)$ and arithmetic predicates like successor, addition or multiplication, whose meaning is straightforward. A pair of simple examples about complex terms and proper manipulation functions follows. Another interesting example, i.e., the Hanoi Tower problem, is reported in [11].

Example 11. Given a directed graph, a *simple path* is a sequence of nodes, each one appearing exactly once, such that from each one (but the last) there is an edge to the next in the sequence. The following program derives all simple paths for a directed graph, starting from a given *edge* relation:

$path([X, Y]) :\text{-} edge(X, Y).$
$path([X|[Y|W]]) :\text{-} edge(X, Y), path([Y|W]), \text{not } \#member(X, [Y|W]).$

---

[7] The specification of the entire library for lists and sets manipulation is available at [11].

The first rule builds a simple path as a list of two nodes directly connected by an edge. The second rule constructs a new path adding an element to the list representing an existing path. The new element will be added only if there is an edge connecting it to the head of an already existing path. The external predicate $\#member$ (which is part of the above mentioned library for lists and sets manipulation) allows to avoid the insertion of an element that is already included in the list; without this check, the construction would never terminate in the presence of circular paths. Even if not an $\mathcal{FD}$ program, it is easy to see that this is an $\mathcal{FG}$ program; thus, the system is able to effectively compute the (in this case, unique) answer set.

Example 12. Let us imagine that the administrator of a social network wants to increase the connections between users. In order to do that, (s)he decides to propose a connection to pairs of users that result, from their personal profile, to share more than two interests. If the data about users are given by means of EDB atoms of the form $user(id, \{interest_1, \ldots, interest_n\})$, the following rule would compute the set of common interests between all pairs of users:

$$sharedInterests(U_1, U_2, \#intersection(S_1, S_2)) :\!\!- user(U_1, S_1), user(U_2, S_2), U_1 \neq U_2.$$

where the interpreted function $\#intersection$ takes as input two sets and returns their intersection. Then, the predicate selecting all pairs of users sharing more than two interests could be defined as follows:

$$proposeConnection(pair(U_1, U_2)) :\!\!- sharedInterests(U_1, U_2, S), \#card(S) > 2.$$

Here, the interpreted function $\#card$ returns the cardinality of a given set, which is compared to the constant 2 by means of the built-in predicate ">".

Implementation. The presented language has been implemented on top of the state-of-the-art ASP system DLV [16]. Complex terms have been implemented by using a couple of built-in predicates for packing and unpacking them (see below). These functions, along with the library for lists and sets manipulation have been incorporated in DLV by exploiting the framework introduced in [17].

In particular, support for complex terms is actually achieved by suitably rewriting the rules they appear in. The resulting rewritten program does not contain complex terms any more, but a number of instances of proper built-in predicates. We briefly illustrate in the following how the rewriting is performed in case of functional terms; the cases of list and set terms are treated analogously. Firstly, any functional term $t = f(X_1, \ldots, X_n)$, appearing in some rule $r \in P$, is replaced by a fresh variable Ft and then, one of the following atom is added to $B(r)$:

- $\#function\_pack(Ft, f, X_1, \ldots, X_n)$ if t appears in $H(r)$;
- $\#function\_unpack(Ft, f, X_1, \ldots, X_n)$ if t appears in $B(r)$.

This transformation is applied to the rule r until no functional terms appear in it. The role of an atom $\#function\_pack$ is to build a functional term starting from a functor and its arguments; while an atom $\#function\_unpack$ acts unfolding a functional term to give values to its arguments. So, the former binds the Ft variable, provided that all other terms are already bound, the latter binds (checks values, in case they are already bound) the $X_1, \ldots, X_n$ variables according to the binding for the Ft variable (the whole functional term).

Example 13. The rule: $p(f(f(X))) \coloneq q(X, g(X, Y))$.   will be rewritten as follow:

$$p(Ft_1) \coloneq \#function\_pack(Ft_1, f, Ft_2), \#function\_pack(Ft_2, f, X),$$
$$q(X, Ft_3), \#function\_unpack(Ft_3, g, X, Y).$$

Note that rewriting the nested functional term $f(f(X))$ requires two $\#function\_pack$ atoms in the body: (i) for the inner f function having X as argument and (ii) for the outer f function having as argument the fresh variable Ft_2, representing the inner functional term.

The resulting ASP system is indeed very powerful: the user can exploit the full expressiveness of $\mathcal{FG}$ programs (plus the ease given by the availability of complex terms), at the price of giving the guarantee of termination up. In this respect, it is worth stating that the system grounder fully complies with the definition of *intelligent* instantiation introduced in this work (see Section 3 and Definition 8). This implies, among other things, that the system is guaranteed to terminate and correctly compute all answer sets for any program resulting as finitely-ground. Nevertheless, the system features a syntactic $\mathcal{FD}$ programs recognizer, based on the algorithm sketched in Theorem 6. This kind of finite-domain check, which is active by default, ensures a priori computability for all accepted programs.

The system prototype, called DLV-complex, is available at [11]; the above mentioned library for list and set terms manipulation is available for free download as well, together with a reference guide and a number of examples. Some preliminary tests have been carried out in order to measure how much the new features cost in terms of performances: rewriting times are negligible; the cost of evaluating function terms (pack/unpack functions) is low (about 1.5 times a comparison built-in as '$<$'); there is no overhead at all on answer-sets computation. Therefore, the system can profitably deal with real-world problems. For instance, in the area of self-healing Web Services DLV-complex is already exploited for the computation of minimum cardinality diagnoses [18], and functional terms are here employed to replace existential quantification. In summary, the introduction of functions brings only a little overhead, while it offers a significant gain in terms of knowledge-modeling power and program clarity. In some cases, the better problem encoding obtained through functions can bring also a significant computational gain.[8]

7   Related Works

Functional terms are widely used in logic formalisms stemming from first order logic. Introduction and treatment of functional terms (or similar constructs) have been studied

---

[8] For instance, the encoding for Tower of Hanoi reported in [11] against the classical guess-and-check encoding (a disjunctive version of the Smodels program exploited for the First ASP competition [19]) allows one to enjoy nice speedups and to scale much better while increasing the number of disks.

indeed in several fields, such as Logic Programming and Deductive Databases. In the ASP community, the treatment of functional terms has recently received quite some attention [6,7,8,9,10]. We next focus on the main proposals for introducing functional terms in ASP.

Finitary Programs [10,6] are a major contribution to the introduction of recursive functional terms (and thus infinite domains) in logic programming under stable model semantics.

Given a normal (or-free) program P, a labelled dependency graph $LDG(P)$ is associated to $grnd(P)$. The set of nodes consists of the (infinite) set of atoms in B_P; there is an edge (A, B) (from A to B) if there is a rule $r \in grnd(P)$ such that $A \in H(r)$ and $B \in B(r)$; in particular, the edge is labelled $\neg$ if $B \in B^-(r)$. Program P is finitary if: *(i)* from any node in $LDG(P)$ only a finite sets of nodes is reachable (i.e., the program is *finitely recursive*, as any atom depends only on a finite set of other atoms), and *(ii)* the dependency graph $LDG(P)$ has only a finite number of cycles with an odd number of negated ($\neg$) edges (called *odd-cycles*).

The class of finitary programs can be seen as a "dual" notion of the class of finitely-ground programs. The former is suitable for a top-down evaluation, while the latter allows for a bottom-up computation. Comparing the computational properties of the two classes, we observe:

– Both finitary programs and finitely-ground programs can express any computable function.
– Ground queries are decidable for both finitary and finitely-ground programs; however, for finitary programs, to obtain decidability one needs to additionally know ("a priori") what is the set of atoms involved in odd-cycles [20].
– Answer sets on finitely-ground programs are computable, while they are not computable on finitary programs. The same holds for nonground queries.
– Recognizing if a program is finitely-ground is semi-decidable; while recognizing if a program is finitary is undecidable.[9]

Finitary and $\mathcal{FG}$ programs are not comparable: there are finitary programs that are not finitely-ground, and finitely-ground programs that are not finitary. The syntactic restrictions imposed by the two notions somehow come from the underlying computational approaches (top-down vs bottom-up). Finitary programs impose that all rule variables must occur in the head; while finitely-ground programs require that all rule variables occur in the positive body. Therefore, $p(X, Y) :\!- q(X).$ is safe for finitary programs, while it is not for finitely-ground programs (as Y is not range-restricted). On the contrary, $p(X, Y) :\!- q(X, V), r(V, Y)$ is safe for finitely-ground programs, while it is not admissible for finitary programs (because of the "local" variable V). Similarly, for the nesting level of the functions: it cannot increase head-to-body for finitary programs, while it cannot increase body-to-head for finitely-ground programs. For instance, $p(X) :\!- p(f(X)).$ is not finitary, while $p(f(X)) :\!- p(X).$ is not finitely-ground.

---

[9] Indeed, recognizing a finitary program has not been proven to be semi-decidable. In particular, recognizing the validity of the first condition of finitary programs (finite-recursion) has been proven to be not decidable (see [10], Theorem 26), while recognizing the second condition (finite odd cycles) has been proven to be not semi-decidable (see [10], Theorem 27).

Importantly, finitary programs are or-free; while finitely-ground programs allow for disjunctive rules. The class of finitary programs has been extended to the disjunctive case in [21]. To this end, a third condition on the disjunctive heads is added to the definition of finitary programs, in order to guarantee the decidability of ground querying.

Concluding, we observe that the bottom-up nature of the notion of $\mathcal{FG}$ programs allows for an immediate implementation of this class in ASP systems (as ASP instantiators are based on a bottom-up computational model). Indeed, we were able to enhance DLV to deal with finitely-ground by small changes in its instantiator, keeping the database optimization techniques which rely on the bottom-up model and significantly improve the efficiency of the instantiation. While an ASP instantiator should be replaced by a top-down grounder to deal with finitary programs.

ω-restricted Programs [9] allow for function symbols under Answer Set semantics. They have been effectively implemented into SMODELS [22] - a very popular ASP system. The notion of ω-restricted program relies on the concept of ω-stratification. An ω-stratification corresponds, essentially, to a traditional stratification (i.e., a function mapping each predicate name to a *level* number) w.r.t. negation, extended by the (uppermost) ω-stratum, which contains all predicates depending negatively on each other (basically, this stratum contains entirely the unstratified part of the program). In order to avoid infiniteness/undecidability, programs must fulfill some syntactic conditions w.r.t. an ω-stratification. In particular, each variable appearing in a rule must also occur in a positive body literal belonging to a *strictly* lower stratum than the head. The above restrictions are strong enough to guarantee the computability of answer sets, yet losing recursive completeness. Thus, ω-restricted programs are strictly less expressive than both finitary and $\mathcal{FG}$ programs (which can express all computable functions). From a merely syntactic viewpoint, the class of ω-restricted programs is uncomparable with that of finitary programs, while it is strictly contained in the class of $\mathcal{FD}$ programs (and thus, of $\mathcal{FG}$ programs). Indeed, if a program P is ω-restricted, then each variable appearing in a rule head fulfills Condition 3 of Definition 10 (thus, P is $\mathcal{FD}$). On the contrary, there are $\mathcal{FD}$ programs that are not ω-restricted: for instance, the $\mathcal{FD}$ program made of the single rule $p(X) :\!- p(f(X))$ is $\mathcal{FD}$ but it is not ω-restricted.

FDNC *programs* [7] allow for function symbols in DLP programs. In order to retain the decidability of the standard reasoning tasks, the structure of any rule must be chosen among one out of seven predefined forms. These syntactic restrictions ensure that programs have a *forest-shaped model* property. Answer sets of FDNC programs are in general infinite, but have a finite representation which can be exploited for knowledge compilation and fast query answering. The class of FDNC programs is less expressive than both finitary and finitely-ground programs. From a syntactic viewpoint, FDNC programs are uncomparable with both finitary and finitely-ground programs. Notably, FDNC programs are finitely recursive, but not necessarily finitary.

Other works. Recently, in [8], functions have been proposed as a tool for obtaining a more direct and compact representation of problems, and for improving the performance of ASP computation by reducing the size of resulting ground programs. The class of programs which is considered is strictly contained in ω-restricted programs:

indeed, predicates as well as functions must range over finite domains, which must be explicitly (and extensively) provided.

The idea of $\mathcal{FG}$ programs is also related to termination studies of SLD-resolution for Prolog programs (see e.g. [15,13,14]). In this context, several notion of *norm* for complex terms were introduced. Intuitively, proving that norms of sub-goals are non-increasing during top-down evaluation ensures decidability of a given program. Note that such techniques can not be applied in a straightforward way to our setting, for a series of technical differences. First, propagation of norm information should be studied from rules bodies to heads while traditional termination analysis works the other way around. Also, top-down termination analysis often integrates right recursion avoidance techniques, which are not required in the context of ASP.

As for the deductive database field, we recall that one of the first comprehensive proposals has been $\mathcal{LDL}$ [23], a declarative language featuring a non-disjunctive logic programming paradigm based on bottom-up model query evaluation. $\mathcal{LDL}$ provides a rich data model including the possibility to manage complex objects, lists and sets. The language allows for a stratified form of negation, while functional terms are managed by means of "infinite" base relations computed by external procedures; proper restrictions (called constraints) and checks based on structural properties of the program (interdependencies between arguments) ensure that a finite number of tuples are generated for each relation.

With respect to the enriched language presented in Section 6, it is worth remembering that the book [1] showed examples of how certain kinds of reasoning about sets and lists could be captured by propositional ASPs, thus giving examples of programs with function symbols that can be rewritten as propositional ASPs.

8   Conclusions

We have formally defined the class of $\mathcal{FG}$ programs, which allows for (possibly recursive) complex terms in the full ASP language (logic programs with disjunction and negation). We have proven that, for each program P in this class, there exists a finite subset P' of its instantiation having precisely the same answer sets as P. Importantly, such a subset P' is computable for $\mathcal{FG}$ programs. It turns out that: (i) both cautious and brave reasoning tasks are computable for finitely ground programs, even if the query is not ground, (ii) the answer sets of the program are computable as well. We have also demonstrated that $\mathcal{FG}$ programs can express every computable function. We have singled out also a subclass of $\mathcal{FG}$ programs, called finite-domain programs, which are efficiently recognizable, while keeping the computability of the reasoning tasks. We have implemented all results in the DLV system, further extending the language with list and set terms, along with a rich library for their manipulation. The resulting system is very powerful: it combines the expressiveness of functions, sets, and lists, with the knowledge modeling features of ASP in a fully declarative framework. The system is available for downloading from [11], where the user can find also a manual and further examples; DLV-complex is already successfully used in many universities and research institutes. Ongoing work focuses on the extensions of the classes of finitely-ground and finitely-domain programs and on their combinations with the notion of finitary and $\mathbb{FDNC}$ programs.

References

1. Baral, C.: Knowledge Representation, Reasoning and Declarative Problem Solving. In: CUP (2003)
2. Gelfond, M., Lifschitz, V.: The Stable Model Semantics for Logic Programming. In: ICLP/SLP 1988, pp. 1070–1080. MIT Press, Cambridge (1988)
3. Gelfond, M., Lifschitz, V.: Classical Negation in Logic Programs and Disjunctive Databases. NGC 9, 365–385 (1991)
4. Lifschitz, V.: Answer Set Planning. In: Schreye, D.D. (ed.) ICLP 1999, pp. 23–37 (1999)
5. Marek, V.W., Truszczyński, M.: Stable Models and an Alternative Logic Programming Paradigm. In: The Logic Programming Paradigm – A 25-Year Perspective, pp. 375–398 (1999)
6. Baselice, S., Bonatti, P.A., Criscuolo, G.: On Finitely Recursive Programs. In: Dahl, V., Niemelä, I. (eds.) ICLP 2007. LNCS, vol. 4670, pp. 89–103. Springer, Heidelberg (2007)
7. Simkus, M., Eiter, T.: FDNC: Decidable Non-monotonic Disjunctive Logic Programs with Function Symbols. In: Dershowitz, N., Voronkov, A. (eds.) LPAR 2007. LNCS, vol. 4790, pp. 514–530. Springer, Heidelberg (2007)
8. Lin, F., Wang, Y.: Answer Set Programming with Functions. In: KR 2008 (to appear, 2008)
9. Syrjänen, T.: Omega-restricted logic programs. In: Eiter, T., Faber, W., Truszczyński, M. (eds.) LPNMR 2001. LNCS, vol. 2173. Springer, Heidelberg (2001)
10. Bonatti, P.A.: Reasoning with infinite stable models. Artificial Intelligence 156(1), 75–111 (2004)
11. Calimeri, F., Cozza, S., Ianni, G., Leone, N.: DLV-Complex homepage (since 2008), http://www.mat.unical.it/dlv-complex
12. Tarski, A.: A lattice-theoretical fixpoint theorem and its applications. Pacific J. Math. 5, 285–309 (1955)
13. Bossi, A., Cocco, N., Fabris, M.: Norms on Terms and their use in Proving Universal Termination of a Logic Program. Theoretical Computer Science 124(2), 297–328 (1994)
14. Bruynooghe, M., Codish, M., Gallagher, J.P., Genaim, S., Vanhoof, W.: Termination analysis of logic programs through combination of type-based norms. ACM TOPLAS 29(2), 10 (2007)
15. Schreye, D.D., Decorte, S.: Termination of Logic Programs: The Never-Ending Story. JLP 19/20, 199–260 (1994)
16. Leone, N., Pfeifer, G., Faber, W., Eiter, T., Gottlob, G., Perri, S., Scarcello, F.: The DLV System for Knowledge Representation and Reasoning. ACM TOCL 7(3), 499–562 (2006)
17. Calimeri, F., Cozza, S., Ianni, G.: External sources of knowledge and value invention in logic programming. AMAI 50(3-4), 333–361 (2007)
18. Friedrich, G., Ivanchenko, V.: Diagnosis from first principles for workflow executions. Tech. Rep., http://proserver3-iwas.uni-klu.ac.at/download_area/Technical-Reports/technical_report_2008_02.pdf
19. Gebser, M., Liu, L., Namasivayam, G., Neumann, A., Schaub, T., Truszczyński, M.: The first answer set programming system competition. In: Baral, C., Brewka, G., Schlipf, J. (eds.) LPNMR 2007. LNCS, vol. 4483, pp. 3–17. Springer, Heidelberg (2007)
20. Bonatti, P.A.: Erratum to: Reasoning with infinite stable models. Artificial Intelligence Forthcoming
21. Bonatti, P.A.: Reasoning with infinite stable models II: Disjunctive programs. In: Stuckey, P.J. (ed.) ICLP 2002. LNCS, vol. 2401, pp. 333–346. Springer, Heidelberg (2002)
22. Simons, P., Niemelä, I., Soininen, T.: Extending and Implementing the Stable Model Semantics. Artificial Intelligence 138, 181–234 (2002)
23. Naqvi, S., Tsur, S.: A logical language for data and knowledge bases. CS press, New York (1989)

Composing Normal Programs with Function Symbols

Sabrina Baselice and Piero A. Bonatti

Università di Napoli Federico II

Abstract. Several expressive, decidable fragments of Answer Set Programming with function symbols have been identified over the past years. Undecidability results suggest that there are no maximal decidable program classes encompassing all these fragments; this raises a sort of interoperability question: Given two programs belonging to different fragments, does their union preserve the nice computational properties of each fragment? In this paper we give a positive answer to this question and outline two of its possible applications. First, membership to a "good" fragment can be checked once and independently for each program module; this allows modular answer set programming with function symbols. As a second application, we extend known decidability results, by showing how different forms of recursion can be simultaneously supported.

1 Introduction

Answer Set Programming (ASP) is one of the most interesting achievements in the area of Logic Programming and Nonmonotonic Reasoning. It is a declarative problem solving paradigm, mainly centered around some well-engineered implementations of the stable model semantics of logic programs [1,2], such as SMODELS and DLV [3,4].

The existing ASP languages are being extended with function symbols to overcome several drawbacks of Datalog versions, related to expressiveness, encoding style, and memory requirements [5]. However, function symbols cannot be freely used because reasoning would otherwise become highly undecidable [6,7]; it is necessary to restrict program syntax so as to guarantee the decidability of the reasoning tasks of interest. Some of the main approaches in this direction are ω-restricted programs [8], finitary programs [5], and FDNC programs [9].

These "good" fragments of ASP are mutually incomparable. Moreover, the class of finitary programs is undecidable [5], therefore one can only *approximately* check whether a given program is finitary, and no best approximation exists (even worse, there exist infinitely many incomparable implementations of the membership check). Then an important question is: Can one safely compose a program out of modules that have been independently proven to belong to different "good" ASP fragments, thereby taking the best out of each approach? By "safely" we mean that the compound program should preserve the good computational properties of the constituent programs.

M. Garcia de la Banda and E. Pontelli (Eds.): ICLP 2008, LNCS 5366, pp. 425–439, 2008.

Of course, a positive answer to this question would imply that membership of a given ASP library to one of the good fragments needs to be checked only once and that the library—roughly speaking—is guaranteed to be usable in every context. A second implication is that the decidability results for individual fragments could be extended to hybrid compound programs that belong to none of the fragments that component programs belong to. In other words, it would be possible to systematically derive new good fragments from the known ones.

In this paper, we make a first step along these lines by identifying a range of "good" composition patterns that preserve decidability under fairly general conditions. As a consequence, for these kinds of composition, program checking can be modularized and new decidability results can be systematically derived.

In this paper we deal with compositions of finitary, ω-restricted, and *finitely triggering* modules. Finitely triggering modules support recursion patterns complementary to those allowed in finitary programs.

We shall first prove that the property of being finitely recursive or finitary is preserved by domain extensions in most cases. Then we shall apply this persistency result to prove decidability results for suitable combinations of finitary and non-finitary programs.

The paper is organized as follows. After a section on preliminaries, we prove in Section 3 that the classes of finitely recursive and finitary programs are closed under domain extensions. Section 4 introduces finitely triggering programs and a generalization thereof, covering also ω-restricted programs. The forms of module compositions we deal with and some properties of homogeneous module composition are introduced in Section 5. Then Section 6 completes the analysis with decidability and undecidability results for the possible forms of composition. A final discussion of the results and directions for future work can be found in Section 7.

2   Preliminaries

We assume the reader to be familiar with classical logic programming [10].

(Normal) logic programs are sets of rules

$$A \leftarrow L_1, ..., L_n \quad (n \geq 0),$$

where A is a logical atom and each L_i $(i = 1, ..., n)$ is a *literal*, that is, either a logical atom B or a negated atom $\texttt{not } B$.

If r is a rule with the above structure, then let $head(r) = A$ and $body(r) = \{L_1, ..., L_n\}$. Moreover, let $body^+(r)$ (respectively $body^-(r)$) be the set of all atoms B s.t. B (respectively $\texttt{not } B$) belongs to $body(r)$.

The ground instantiation of a program P is denoted by $\mathsf{Ground}(P)$, and the set of atoms occurring in $\mathsf{Ground}(P)$ is denoted by $atom(P)$. Similarly, $atom(r)$ denotes the set of atoms occurring in a rule r.

A Herbrand model M of P is a *stable model* of P iff $M = \mathsf{lm}(P^M)$, where $\mathsf{lm}(X)$ denotes the least model of a positive program X, and P^M is the *Gelfond-Lifschitz transformation* of P, obtained from $\mathsf{Ground}(P)$ by

i) removing all rules r such that $body^-(r) \cap M \neq \emptyset$, and
ii) removing all negative literals from the body of the remaining rules [1,2].

Normal programs may have one, none, or multiple stable models. We say that a program is *consistent* if it has at least one stable model; otherwise the program is *inconsistent*. A *skeptical* consequence of a program P is any formula satisfied by all the stable models of P. A *credulous* consequence of P is any formula satisfied by at least one stable model of P.

The *dependency graph of a program* P is a labelled directed graph, denoted by $DG(P)$, whose vertices are the ground atoms of P's language. Moreover,

i) there exists an edge labelled '+' (called positive edge) from A to B iff for some rule $r \in \mathsf{Ground}(P)$, $A = \mathsf{head}(r)$ and $B \in body(r)$;
ii) there exists an edge labelled '-' (called negative edge) from A to B iff for some rule $r \in \mathsf{Ground}(P)$, $A = \mathsf{head}(r)$ and $\mathtt{not}\, B \in body(r)$.

An atom A *depends positively* (respectively *negatively*) on B if there is a directed path from A to B in the dependency graph with an even (respectively odd) number of negative edges. Moreover, each atom depends positively on itself. A *depends* on B if A depends positively or negatively on B.

An *odd-cycle* is a cycle in the dependency graph with an odd number of negative edges. A ground atom is *odd-cyclic* if it occurs in an odd-cycle. Note that there exists an odd-cycle iff some ground atom A depends negatively on itself.

Definition 1. *A program P is* finitely recursive *iff each ground atom A depends on finitely many ground atoms in $DG(P)$.*

Decidability results will involve an important subclass of finitely recursive programs:

Definition 2 (Finitary programs). *We say that a normal program P is* finitary *if the following conditions hold:*

1. *P is finitely recursive.*
2. *There are finitely many odd-cyclic atoms in the dependency graph $DG(P)$.*

For example, most standard list manipulation programs (`member`, `append`, `remove` etc.) are finitely recursive. The reader can find numerous examples of finitely recursive programs in [5]. Finitary programs have very good computational properties. In particular, given a finitary program P and the set of its odd-cyclic atoms, both skeptical and credulous ground inferences are decidable [11]).

Definition 3 (Splitting set and bottom program [12],[13]). *A* splitting set *of a logic program P is any set U of atoms such that, for all rules $r \in \mathsf{Ground}(P)$, if $head(r) \in U$ then $atom(r) \subseteq U$. If U is a splitting set for P, we also say that U splits P. The set of rules $r \in \mathsf{Ground}(P)$ such that $head(r) \in U$ is called the* bottom *of P relative to the splitting set U and is denoted by $bot_U(P)$.*

The bottom program provides the projection of P's stable models on the language determined by the splitting set. The top module determines the rest of each stable model; for this purpose it should be partially evaluated w.r.t. the stable models of the bottom.

Definition 4 (Partial evaluation [12],[13]). *The partially evaluated top of a logic program P with splitting set U w.r.t. a set of ground atoms X is the program $top_U(P, X) =$*

$$\{r' \mid \text{there exists } r \in \text{Ground}(P) \setminus bot_U(P) \text{ s.t. } head(r') = head(r),$$
$$(body^+(r) \cap U) \subseteq X \text{ and } (body^-(r) \cap U) \cap X = \emptyset,$$
$$body^+(r') = body^+(r) \setminus U \text{ and } body^-(r') = body^-(r) \setminus U\}.$$

We are finally ready to formulate the splitting theorem (and hence the modular construction of stable models based on the top and bottom programs) in formal terms.

Theorem 5 (Splitting theorem [13]). *Let U be a splitting set for a logic program P. An interpretation M is a stable model of P iff $M = J \cup I$, where*

1. *I is a stable model of $bot_U(P)$, and*
2. *J is a stable model of $top_U(P, I)$.*

3   Persistency of the Finitely Recursiveness Property

We start by proving some important auxiliary results of independent interest, namely, that under mild restrictions both finitely recursive program and finitary programs remain such when their domain is extended with new terms.

Let P and Q be logic programs and $\text{Ground}(P, Q)$ be the set of all instances of P's rules that belong to $\text{Ground}(P \cup Q)$. Intuitively, $\text{Ground}(P, Q)$ is the ground instantiation of P w.r.t. an extended language, comprising both the symbols occurring in P and those occurring in Q.

First we need to link each path in a dependency graph to the (nonground) rules that generate it.

Definition 6. *A dependency sequence for a program P is a (possibly infinite) sequence of (possibly nonground) atoms $A_1, A_2, \ldots, A_i, \ldots$ such that there exists a corresponding sequence of rules $R_1, R_2, \ldots R_i, \ldots$ with the following properties:*

1. *each R_i is an instance of a rule in P;*
2. *for all A_i in the sequence but the last element (if any), $A_i = \text{head}(R_i)$ and A_{i+1} occurs in $\text{body}(R_i)$ (possibly in the scope of a negation symbol).*

Note that every path in the dependency graph is a dependency sequence.

A dependency sequence Δ is *odd-cyclic* if $\Delta = A_1, \ldots, A_n, A_1$ and the number of indexes i such that B_i occurs negated in $\text{body}(R_i)$ (cf. condition c) is odd.

Lemma 7 (Lifting). *For all paths π in the dependency graph of $\mathsf{Ground}(P,Q)$ there exist a dependency sequence Δ for P and a substitution σ such that $\Delta\sigma = \pi$. Moreover all the constants and function symbols in Δ occur in P.*

To prove this lemma we need some additional terminology. The set of *P-external terms* of an expression E, denoted by $xt_P(E)$, is the set of all terms $f(t)$ occurring in E such that f does not occur in P, and such that for some occurrence of $f(t)$ in E, no term enclosing this occurrence has the same property (in other words, in all the enclosing terms, the most external symbol is in P's language).

Proof. Let $\pi = A_1, A_2, \ldots, A_i, \ldots$ be a (possibly infinite) path in the dependency graph of $\mathsf{Ground}(P,Q)$. By definition, there must be a set of rules $R_1, R_2, \ldots, R_i, \ldots$ and substitutions $\theta_1, \theta_2, \ldots, \theta_i, \ldots$ such that for all $i > 0$

a) $R_i \in P$;
b) $\mathsf{head}(R_i)\theta_i = A_i$;
c) there exists an atom B_i occurring (possibly negated) in $\mathsf{body}(R_i)$ such that $B_i\theta_i = A_{i+1}$.

For each P-external term t occurring in the range of some θ_i (more precisely, $t \in \bigcup_{i>0} \bigcup_{u \in range(\theta_i)} xt_P(u)$), introduce a new, distinct variable v_t. Let σ be the substitution mapping each v_t on the corresponding term t.

Now each θ_i can be expressed as $\theta'_i\sigma$, where θ'_i is obtained from θ_i by replacing each P-external term t in its range with v_t.

Since by b) and c) $B_i\theta_i = \mathsf{head}(R_{i+1})\theta_{i+1} = A_{i+1}$, after replacing each external term t with v_t, we have that for all $i > 0$, $B_i\theta'_i = \mathsf{head}(R_{i+1})\theta'_{i+1}$. Then the sequence $\Delta = \langle \mathsf{head}(R_i)\theta'_i \rangle_{i>0}$ is a dependency sequence for P induced by rules

$$R_1\theta'_1, R_2\theta'_2, \ldots, R_i\theta'_i, \ldots$$

and clearly $\Delta\sigma = \pi$. Moreover, since all P-external terms have been removed by the above construction, all the constants and function symbols occurring in Δ occur also in P. □

A similar result holds for odd-cycles.

Lemma 8. *For all programs P and Q, if the dependency graph of $\mathsf{Ground}(P,Q)$ has an odd cycle with P-external terms then P has a nonground dependency sequence based on the same rules that generate the odd cycle.*

Proof. Let $\pi = A_1, \ldots, A_n, A_1$ be an odd-cyclic path for $\mathsf{Ground}(P,Q)$ containing some P-external terms. By Lemma 7, there exist a dependency sequence Δ for P and a substitution Σ such that $\Delta\sigma = \pi$ and Δ contains no occurrences of P-external terms. Since π contains some P-external terms, it follows that σ must be nontrivial and Δ nonground. Moreover, as illustrated in the proof of Lemma 7, Δ is based on the same sequence of rules that generate π. □

Now we prove that the class of finitely recursive programs *with infinite domains* is closed under domain extensions.

Theorem 9. *If P is finitely recursive and has an infinite Herbrand domain then for all programs Q, Ground(P, Q) is finitely recursive.*

Proof. Suppose not. Then either the dependency graph of P has an infinite path π, or some of its nodes (atoms) A is infinitely branching. First assume that π is a path in the dependency graph of Ground(P, Q) containing infinitely many distinct atoms. By Lemma 7, there exists a dependency sequence Δ whose constants and functions occur in P, and there exists a substitution σ such that $\Delta\sigma = \pi$. Now, since π contains infinitely many distinct atoms, there are only two possibilities:

a) there is no upper bound to the nesting level of the atoms in Δ, or
b) there is no upper bound to the number of distinct variables occurring in Δ.

In the first case, by binding any constant in P's vocabulary to the variables in Δ we necessarily obtain a path in Ground(P) with infinitely many distinct atoms with unbounded depth, which contradicts the hypothesis that P is finitely recursive.

Similarly, in the second case, we can bind the infinitely many variables occurring in Δ to larger and larger ground terms taken from the Herbrand domain of P, thereby obtaining a path in Ground(P) with infinitely many distinct atoms with unbounded depth. Then case b) contradicts the hypothesis, too.

Now, suppose some ground atom A is infinitely branching in the dependency graph. Then, there must be a rule r whose body contains a variable X not occurring in head(r). Consequently, A must be infinitely branching also in the dependency graph of Ground(P), because its Herbrand domain is infinite. This contradicts the hypothesis that P is finitely recursive.   □

When a program's domain is *finite* we need some restriction on its *local variables*. Recall that a local variable of a rule R is a variable that occurs in body(R) and not in head(R).

Theorem 10. *If P is a Datalog program without local variables, then for all programs Q, Ground(P, Q) is finitely recursive.*

Proof. Suppose not. As in the previous theorem we have to consider two cases. Let π be a path in the dependency graph of Ground(P, Q) containing infinitely many distinct atoms. By Lemma 7, there is a dependency sequence Δ whose constants and functions occur in P, and there exists a substitution σ such that $\Delta\sigma = \pi$. Now consider the rules R_i ($i > 0$) underlying Δ (cf. Def. 6). Since P has no local variables, the same must be true of the instances R_i, and hence for all $i > 0$, the variables occurring in A_{i+1} occur also in A_i. It follows that all the variables occurring in Δ occur also in its first element A_1. Moreover, since function and constant symbols come from P, which is function-free, we have that the nesting depth of all atoms is 1. Since both the number of distinct variables and atom nesting depth are bounded in Δ it follows that Δ contains finitely many distinct atoms. But this implies that also $\Delta\sigma$—and hence π—can only contain finitely many distinct atoms, and this contradicts the assumption.

Now, suppose some atom A is infinitely branching. Then P should contain a rule with a local variable—a contradiction. □

The restriction on local variables is necessary: Consider a simple finitely recursive Datalog program $P = \{p(X) \leftarrow q(X, Y)\}$ with a local variable Y and a program $Q = \{r(f(0))\}$. In $\mathsf{Ground}(P, Q)$, each atom $p(t)$ depends on infinitely many atoms $q(t, u)$ where $u = 0, f(0), f(f(0)), \dots$ therefore P is not persistently finitely recursive.

Of course, the classes of finitely recursive and finitary programs are closed also under program inclusion.

Proposition 11. *If $P \supseteq Q$ and P is finitely recursive (resp. finitary) then Q is finitely recursive (resp. finitary).*

Proof. $P \supseteq Q$ implies that any set of paths in the dependency graph of Q that violate the definition of finitely recursive (resp. finitary) programs must occur in the dependency graph of P, too. This immediately entails the contrapositive of the proposition, which is equivalent to what is to be proved. □

We are finally ready to state the main theorem of this section, that follows easily from the above results.

Definition 12. *A logic program P is persistently FR iff for all programs Q, $\mathsf{Ground}(P, Q)$ is finitely recursive. Moreover P is persistently finitary iff for all programs Q, $\mathsf{Ground}(P, Q)$ is finitary.*

Theorem 13. *P is persistently FR iff some of the following conditions hold:*

a) P is a finitely recursive program with an infinite Herbrand domain;
b) P is Datalog and has no local variables.

Moreover, P is persistently finitary iff some of the following conditions hold:

c) P is a finitary program with an infinite Herbrand domain;
d) P is a Datalog programs with no local variables and ground odd-cyclic dependency sequences only.

This theorem is very important as it proves that most programs (in particular those with function symbols, that are in the main focus of this paper) locally retain their properties when they are included as subprograms in larger sets of rules. In the rest of the paper we shall identify the forms of compositions with other subprograms that preserve the good computational properties of finitely recursive and finitary programs at the level of the entire program.

4   Programs with Finite Semantics

Most of the finitary programs of practical interest that can be found in the literature are finitely recursive because during any top-down recursive computation some group of arguments becomes smaller and smaller at each recursive call, as in the following program:

$$nat(0).$$
$$nat(s(X)) \leftarrow nat(X).$$

Now we introduce a class of programs based on the opposite principle, that is, during any top-down recursion some group of arguments becomes larger and larger. Therefore, any bottom-up computation converges.

Definition 14. *A program P is* finitely triggering *(FT for short) iff for each ground atom A in the Herbrand base of P, only finitely many other atoms depend on A.*

Example 15. The program

$$p(a). \quad p(f(f(b))). \quad p(f(f(f(c)))).$$
$$p(X) \leftarrow p(f(X)).$$

is finitely triggering. To prove this, it suffices to note that an atom $p(t)$ depends on $p(u)$ iff t is a strict subterm of u.

Clearly, if P is finitely triggering and safe,[1] then for all finite interpretations I, a bottom-up evaluation of P^I terminates after a finite number of steps and produces a finite model. As a consequence:

Theorem 16. *Let P be a safe, finitely triggering program. Then*

a) *P has finitely many stable models, and each of them is finite;*
b) *the set of stable models of P is decidable, and so are credulous and skeptical inferences from P.*

By analogy with finitely recursive and finitary programs, we can prove that the class of finitely triggering programs is closed under domain extensions. In this case, the extra restrictions needed for Datalog programs concern those variables that occur only in the head (and make a rule unsafe).

Note that, if all facts in a finitely triggering program P are ground then P is safe. Indeed, since for each ground atom A in Ground(P) only finitely many ground atoms depend on A, it is necessary that, for all rule r in P, any ground substitution for body(r) is a ground substitution for head(r).

Definition 17. *P is* persistently FT *iff for all programs Q, Ground(P,Q) is finitely triggering.*

Theorem 18. *P is persistently FT iff some of the following conditions hold:*

a) *P is a finitely triggering program with an infinite Herbrand domain;*
b) *P is Datalog and safe.*

The property of having a finite semantics (in the sense of Theorem 16) is shared by ω-restricted programs [8]. In the rest of the paper we will abstract all these program classes by means of the following notion:

---

[1] Recall that P is safe iff for every rule $R \in P$, each variable occurring in head(R) occurs also in body$^+$(R).

Definition 19. *A class of programs C has the* computable finite semantics property *(CFSP for short) iff (i) for all P in C, P has finitely many stable models each of which is finite, and (ii) there exists a computable function f mapping each member of C onto its set of stable models.*

C has the persistent CFSP *(PCFSP for short) iff C has the CFSP and is closed under domain extensions.*

Safe finitely triggering programs enjoy the PCFSP by Theorem 18. By a simple recursion on ω-stratifications [8], it can be easily shown that ω-restricted programs enjoy the PCFSP, too.

5   Program Module Composition

Classes of logic programs such as finitary programs, finitely triggering programs, ω-restricted programs, etc. guarantee good computational properties by imposing different restrictions on their programs. If P and Q are two normal programs belonging to these classes, is it possible to reason on the program $P \cup Q$ by taking advantage of properties of P and Q? The idea is to *"compose"* P and Q to obtain a program $P \cup Q$ that, as a whole, might not be subject to the restrictions on P or Q (in particular this happens when P and Q belong to different classes) but that again enjoys good computational properties.

To do this it is necessary to identify the relationship between the predicates defined in P and those defined in Q. If P can call predicates defined in Q without redefining them, in that case P *depends on* Q (slight variations of this notion have been introduced for different purposes in [14,15]). If the predicates defined in Q do not occur in P and vice versa, then P and Q are *independent*. Next we formalize these intuitive concepts.

Metavariables P and Q are supposed to range over normal programs. $\mathsf{Def}(P)$ denotes the set of predicates *defined in P*, that is, the set of all predicate symbols occurring in the head of some rule in P, while $\mathsf{Called}(P)$ is the set of predicates *called by P*, that is, the set of all predicate symbols occurring in the body of some rule in P.

Now, the dependency relations for normal logic programs can be defined as follows:

P depends on Q, in symbols $P \rhd Q$, if and only if

$$\mathsf{Def}(P) \cap \mathsf{Def}(Q) = \emptyset\,, \tag{1}$$
$$\mathsf{Def}(P) \cap \mathsf{Called}(Q) = \emptyset\,, \tag{2}$$
$$\mathsf{Called}(P) \cap \mathsf{Def}(Q) \neq \emptyset\,. \tag{3}$$

Conversely, *P and Q are independent* (equivalently, P is independent of Q), in symbols $P \| Q$, if and only if

$$\mathsf{Def}(P) \cap \mathsf{Def}(Q) = \emptyset\,, \tag{4}$$
$$\mathsf{Def}(P) \cap \mathsf{Called}(Q) = \emptyset\,, \tag{5}$$
$$\mathsf{Called}(P) \cap \mathsf{Def}(Q) = \emptyset\,. \tag{6}$$

Note that $P\|Q$ if and only if $Q\|P$, while $\triangleright$ is asymmetric.

Nested compositions of homogeneous modules can be collapsed into a single module of the same kind (this will allow us to focus on compositions of heterogeneous modules later on). First consider compositions of finitary programs. We need four auxiliary results:

Lemma 20. *If P is persistently FR then for all $P' \subseteq P$, P' is persistently FR.*

Proof. Suppose that there exists a subset P' of P s.t. P' is not persistently FR. Then there exists Q s.t. $\mathsf{Ground}(P', Q)$ is not finitely recursive, i.e., its dependency graph contains either an infinite path or an infinitely branching node. However, the dependency graph of $\mathsf{Ground}(P', Q)$ is a subgraph of the dependency graph of $\mathsf{Ground}(P, Q)$. This implies that $\mathsf{Ground}(P, Q)$ is not a FR program, either. This contradicts the hypothesis. $\qquad\square$

Theorem 21. *Suppose that $P \triangleright Q$ or $P\|Q$. Then $P \cup Q$ is persistently FR iff both P and Q are persistently FR.*

Proof. The only-if-part of theorem follows from Lemma 20. Now consider the opposite implication.

By Theorem 13 P (resp. Q) is persistently FR iff some of the following conditions hold:

a) it is finitely recursive with an infinite Herbrand domain;
b) it is Datalog and has no local variables.

We will prove the if-part by considering all the possible combinations of programs satisfying conditions a) or b).

Suppose that both P and Q are datalog without local variables. Clearly, $P \cup Q$ has the same property, therefore, by Theorem 13, it is persistently FR.

Next, if P and Q are persistently FR and at least one of them satisfies condition a), we will prove that $P \cup Q$ is finitely recursive with an infinite Herbrand domain by proving that the union of two persistently FR programs, for which a dependency relation holds, is always a finitely recursive program. Then the observation that if P or Q has an infinite Herbrand domain also $P \cup Q$ has, concludes the proof.

If P and Q are persistently FR then $\mathsf{Ground}(P, Q)$ and $\mathsf{Ground}(Q, P)$ are finitely recursive and, for each atom A in $\mathsf{Ground}(P \cup Q)$, if there are some atoms which A depends on, the predicate symbol of A either belongs to $\mathsf{Def}(Q)$ or belongs to $\mathsf{Def}(P)$. If the predicate symbol of A belongs to $\mathsf{Def}(Q)$ then A depends on finitely many atoms because $\mathsf{Ground}(Q, P)$ is finitely recursive and, by definition of dependency relations, A cannot depend on atoms in $\mathsf{Ground}(P, Q)$ not occurring in $\mathsf{Ground}(Q, P)$.

If the predicate symbol of A belongs to $\mathsf{Def}(P)$ then, in $\mathsf{Ground}(P \cup Q)$, A depends on the finite set of ground atoms $S_0 = \{B_1, B_2, \ldots, B_k\}$ in the finitely recursive program $\mathsf{Ground}(P, Q)$, and on the finitely many and finite sets of ground atoms $S_1, \ldots, S_k$ on which each B_i in S_0 depends in the finitely recursive program $\mathsf{Ground}(Q, P)$. Note that the predicate symbol in A does not belong to

$\mathsf{Def}(Q)$ and that if the predicate symbol of B_i belongs to $\mathsf{Def}(Q)$ then it does not depends on atoms in $\mathsf{Ground}(P, Q)$, otherwise S_i is empty.   □

Let $\mathsf{OC}(P)$ be the set of the predicate symbols of the odd-cyclic atoms occurring in the dependency graph $DG(P)$ of P. The following proposition easily follows from the definitions:

Proposition 22. *If $P \triangleright Q$ or $P\|Q$ then $\mathsf{OC}(Q) \cap \mathsf{OC}(P) = \emptyset$.*

Corollary 23. *If $P \triangleright Q$ or $P\|Q$ then $\mathsf{OC}(P \cup Q) = \mathsf{OC}(Q) \cup \mathsf{OC}(P)$*

Finally we can prove the main result:

Theorem 24. *Suppose that $P \triangleright Q$ or $P\|Q$. Then $P \cup Q$ is persistently finitary iff both P and Q are persistently finitary.*

Proof. By Theorem 21, $P \cup Q$ is persistently FR iff P and Q are persistently FR. Now, we have to prove only that, for any program Q', $\mathsf{Ground}(P \cup Q, Q')$ contains only finitely many odd-cyclic atoms iff $\mathsf{Ground}(P, Q')$ and $\mathsf{Ground}(Q, Q')$ do.

By Proposition 22 and Corollary 23, if $P \triangleright Q$ or $P\|Q$, the set of odd-cyclic atoms in $\mathsf{Ground}(P \cup Q)$ is the union of the set of odd-cyclic atoms in $\mathsf{Ground}(P)$ and the set of odd-cyclic atoms in $\mathsf{Ground}(Q)$.

Since definitions of dependency relations are only syntactic, if $P \triangleright Q$ or $P\|Q$ then, for any program Q', $\mathsf{Ground}(P, Q') \triangleright \mathsf{Ground}(Q, Q')$ or $\mathsf{Ground}(P, Q')\|$ $\mathsf{Ground}(Q, Q')$, respectively. It follows that Proposition 22 and Corollary 23 again hold for $\mathsf{Ground}(P, Q')$ and $\mathsf{Ground}(Q, Q')$, and then $\mathsf{Ground}(P \cup Q, Q')$ contains finitely many odd-cyclic atoms iff $\mathsf{Ground}(P, Q')$ and $\mathsf{Ground}(Q, Q')$ contain finitely many odd-cyclic atoms.   □

The above results show that program modules that have been independently proved to be finitary or finitely recursive can be freely composed as their union preserves their properties. *In particular, if both programs are finitary then reasoning in the union program is decidable* (given the odd-cycles of the two modules).

Moreover, as a consequence of the above theorem, finitary modules with no interposed non-finitary module can be dealt with as a single finitary module. Next we prove that similar properties hold for program classes enjoying the PCFSP. We start again with some preliminary results.

Lemma 25. *If $P\|Q$, then a set of ground atoms M is a stable model of $P \cup Q$ if and only if $M = M_Q \cup M_P$ where:*

- *M_Q is a stable model of $\mathsf{Ground}(Q, P)$, and*
- *M_P is a stable model of $\mathsf{Ground}(P, Q)$.*

Proof. By definition of dependency relations we can derive that $\mathsf{Ground}(Q, P) = bot_{atom(\mathsf{Ground}(Q,P))}(P \cup Q)$. So, by the splitting theorem, M is a stable model of $P \cup Q$ iff $M = M_Q \cup M_P$ where M_Q is a stable model of $\mathsf{Ground}(Q, P)$ and M_P is a stable model of $top_{atom(\mathsf{Ground}(Q,P))}(\mathsf{Ground}(P, Q), M_Q)$.

Note that $top_{atom(\mathsf{Ground}(Q,P))}(\mathsf{Ground}(P, Q), M_Q) = \mathsf{Ground}(P, Q)$ because, by definition of independency relation, M_Q cannot contain atoms that occur in the body of some rule of $\mathsf{Ground}(P, Q)$. Then M_P is also a stable model of $\mathsf{Ground}(P, Q)$.   □

The result we were aiming at immediately follows as a corollary:

Corollary 26. *If P and Q belong to a program class with the PCFSP and $P\|Q$, then*

a) *$P \cup Q$ has the PCFSP;*
b) *the set of stable models of $P \cup Q$, as well as its skeptical and credulous consequences are all decidable.*

For the special case of finitely triggering programs, we can extend the above result to $\triangleright$ dependencies using dependency sequences, by analogy with the proof for finitary programs:

Theorem 27. *If P and Q are persistently FT programs and $P \triangleright Q$ or $P\|Q$, then $P \cup Q$ is persistently FT.*

It can be shown that the result for $P \triangleright Q$ cannot be extended to PCFSP classes such as ω-restricted programs (hint: when P depends on the ω-stratum of Q the composite program is generally not ω-restricted).

6   Decidability and Undecidability Results

Here we discuss which kinds of compositions lead to decidable inference problems. We start with the homogeneous composition of finitary programs.

Theorem 28. *Given two persistently finitary programs P and Q such that either $P \triangleright Q$ or $P\|Q$, and given the sets of odd-cyclic atoms of the two programs, $\mathsf{OC}(P)$ and $\mathsf{OC}(Q)$, both the set of ground skeptical consequences and the set of ground credulous consequences of $P \cup Q$ are decidable.*

Proof. By Theorem 24, $P \cup Q$ is persistently finitary. Note that its (finite) set of odd-cyclic atoms is $\mathsf{OC}(P) \cup \mathsf{OC}(Q)$, which is effectively computable from $\mathsf{OC}(P)$ and $\mathsf{OC}(Q)$. Then the skeptical and the credulous consequences of $P \cup Q$ are decidable as proved in [5].   □

We can compose a finitary program with one with the PCFSP only in the following cases:

Theorem 29. *Let Q belong to a class with the PCFSP, let P be persistently finitary, and suppose that either $P \triangleright Q$ or $P\|Q$. Then the problems of checking whether a given ground goal G is a skeptical, resp. credulous consequence of $P\cup Q$ given the set of odd-cyclic atoms of P is decidable.*

Proof. (Sketch) If $P\|Q$ then exploit Lemma 25 and the separate decidability results for classes with the PCFSP and for finitary programs.

   If $P \triangleright Q$, note that by the splitting set theorem, the problem of reasoning with $P \cup Q$ can be reduced to reasoning with the partial evaluation of P w.r.t. the stable models of $\mathsf{Ground}(Q, P)$, that are finitely many, finite, and effectively computable by definition. Note that the partial evaluation of a finitary program is still finitary and that in this particular kind of compositions the set of odd-cyclic atoms is not changed by the partial evaluation, therefore the problem of reasoning with $P \cup Q$ is reduced to a finite number of decidable reasoning problems over computable finitary programs.   □

In general the opposite dependency $(Q \triangleright P)$ leads to undecidable reasoning problems. We show it by simulating any given Turing machine $\mathcal{M}$ with a FT program $Q_{\mathcal{M}}$. The tape will be encoded with three terms representing the tape on the left of the current symbol v, the current symbol itself, and the tape on the right of v. Each configuration is encoded by an atom $c(s, l, v, r, n)$ where s is the current state, the triple (l, v, r) encodes the tape, and n is a counter which is decremented at each computation step. The simulation of $\mathcal{M}$ halts when n reaches zero. For each transition from a current state s and v to a state s', that rewrites v with v' and moves the head to the right, $Q_{\mathcal{M}}$ contains the following rules:

$$c(s', [v' \mid L], X, R, N) \leftarrow c(s, L, v, [X \mid R], s(N))$$
$$c(s', [v' \mid L], blank, [], N) \leftarrow c(s, L, v, [], s(N))$$

The rules for transitions that move the head to the left are symmetric. Furthermore, $Q_{\mathcal{M}}$ contains m rules:

$$terminate \leftarrow c(f_i, L, V, R, 0) \qquad (i = 1, \ldots, m)$$

where $f_1, \ldots, f_m$ are the final states of $\mathcal{M}$. Finally, $Q_{\mathcal{M}}$ contains

$$c(s_0, [], v_0, [v_1, \ldots, v_n], N) \leftarrow nat(N)$$

where s_0 is the initial state of $\mathcal{M}$. Clearly, $terminate$ is a logical consequence of $Q_{\mathcal{M}} \cup \{nat(s^n(0))\}$ iff $\mathcal{M}$ terminates in n steps on input $\boldsymbol{v} = v_0, \ldots, v_n$. Note that $Q_{\mathcal{M}}$ is finitely triggering due to the counter, and this property is persistent because the domain is infinite. Now it suffices to compose $Q_{\mathcal{M}}$ with the persistently finitary program P:

$$nat(0).$$
$$nat(s(X)) \leftarrow nat(X).$$

to obtain a composition $Q_{\mathcal{M}} \triangleright P$ where $Q_{\mathcal{M}}$ has the PCFSP, P is persistently finitary, and inference is undecidable, as $terminate$ is a logical consequence of the compound program iff $\mathcal{M}$ terminates on input $\boldsymbol{v} = v_0, \ldots, v_n$. Furthermore, by extending $Q_{\mathcal{M}}$ with

$$diverge \leftarrow \mathbf{not}\ terminate$$

we obtain a co-r.e.-hard goal $(diverge)$. Therefore, the complexity of reasoning with this kind of compositions is not semidecidable either.

We are left to consider the homogeneous composition of programs belonging to a class with the PCFSP. When $P \| Q$, inferences are decidable by Corollary 26.

When $P \triangleright Q$, the definition of PCFSP is too abstract to prove general results. Here we provide a decidability result for finitely triggering programs:

Theorem 30. *Given two safe, persistently FT programs P and Q such that either $P \triangleright Q$ or $P \| Q$, both the set of skeptical consequences and the set of credulous consequences of $P \cup Q$ are decidable.*

Proof. A straightforward consequence of Theorem 27 and Theorem 16.

7   Conclusions and Future Work

Under mild restrictions on local variables (that can be relaxed as shown in [5] by binding local variables with generalized domain predicates) finitary programs can be freely composed without affecting their good properties. We proved also that in some cases hybrid compositions are possible, thereby supporting decidable reasoning in the presence of different forms of recursion covering both finitely recursive and finitely triggering patterns. Our decidability results are summarized in the following table.

	Persis. Finitary	PCFSP
Persis. Finitary	*decidable*	*decidable*
PCFSP	*undecidable*	*dec. for Persis. FT*

To prove these results we showed that the class of finitely recursive programs with infinite domains is closed under domain extensions, which is of independent theoretical interest.

According to the above table and the results on homogeneous composition (Theorem 24, Corollary 26, and Theorem 27) we can currently handle compound programs consisting of a bottom layer of modules with the PCFSP, and a free upper network of persistently finitary modules. In the bottom layer independent modules can be freely added, while dependencies must be limited to persistently FT programs only, according to our current results.

It is worth pointing out that the definitions and results of this paper can be extended to disjunctive logic programs with minor modifications. Since the notion of finitary programs can be extended to disjunctive logic programs in several possible ways, space limitations induced us to postpone their treatment to a future journal version.

Our analysis should be extended to explore compositions involving FDNC modules. FDNC programs [9] are a recently introduced fragment of the class of finitely recursive programs, where inference decidability derives from a certain guarded structure of programs rather than consistency results and restrictions on odd-cycles. Since interesting fragments of description logics (and nonmonotonic extensions thereof) can be encoded into FDNC programs, their inclusion in our composition framework is of particular interest and may have an impact on rule-based semantic web approaches.

Acknowledgements

This work is partially supported by the PRIN project *Enhancement and Applications of Disjunctive Logic Programming*, funded by the Italian Ministry of Research (MIUR). The authors are grateful to the anonymous referees for their constructive comments.

References

1. Gelfond, M., Lifschitz, V.: The stable model semantics for logic programming. In: Proc. of the 5th ICLP, pp. 1070–1080. MIT Press, Cambridge (1988)
2. Gelfond, M., Lifschitz, V.: Classical negation in logic programs and disjunctive databases. New Generation Computing 9(3-4), 365–386 (1991)
3. Niemelä, I., Simons, P.: Smodels - an implementation of the stable model and well-founded semantics for normal lp. [16], 421–430
4. Eiter, T., Leone, N., Mateis, C., Pfeifer, G., Scarcello, F.: A deductive system for non-monotonic reasoning. [16], 364–375
5. Bonatti, P.A.: Reasoning with infinite stable models. Artif. Intell. 156(1), 75–111 (2004)
6. Marek, V.W., Nerode, A., Remmel, J.B.: The stable models of a predicate logic program. J. Log. Program. 21(3), 129–153 (1994)
7. Marek, V.W., Remmel, J.B.: On the expressibility of stable logic programming. [17], 107–120
8. Syrjänen, T.: Omega-restricted logic programs. [17], 267–279
9. Simkus, M., Eiter, T.: FDNC: Decidable non-monotonic disjunctive logic programs with function symbols. In: Dershowitz, N., Voronkov, A. (eds.) LPAR 2007. LNCS, vol. 4790, pp. 514–530. Springer, Heidelberg (2007)
10. Lloyd, J.W.: Foundations of Logic Programming, 1st edn. Springer, Heidelberg (1984)
11. Baselice, S., Bonatti, P.A., Criscuolo, G.: On finitely recursive programs. In: Dahl, V., Niemelä, I. (eds.) ICLP 2007. LNCS, vol. 4670, pp. 89–103. Springer, Heidelberg (2007)
12. Baral, C.: Knowledge Representation, Reasoning and Declarative Problem Solving. Cambridge University Press, Cambridge (2003)
13. Lifschitz, V., Turner, H.: Splitting a Logic Program. In: Proceedings of the 12th International Conference on Logic Programming, Kanagawa 1995. MIT Press Series Logic Program, pp. 581–595. MIT Press, Cambridge (1995)
14. Eiter, T., Gottlob, G., Mannila, H.: Disjunctive datalog. ACM Trans. Database Syst. 22(3), 364–418 (1997)
15. Eiter, T., Leone, N., Saccà, D.: On the partial semantics for disjunctive deductive databases. Ann. Math. Artif. Intell. 19(1-2), 59–96 (1997)
16. Dix, J., Furbach, U., Nerode, A. (eds.): LPNMR 1997. LNCS, vol. 1265. Springer, Heidelberg (1997)
17. Eiter, T., Faber, W., Truszczynski, M. (eds.): LPNMR 2001. LNCS, vol. 2173. Springer, Heidelberg (2001)

Verification from Declarative Specifications Using Logic Programming

Marco Montali[1], Paolo Torroni[1], Marco Alberti[2], Federico Chesani[1],
Marco Gavanelli[2], Evelina Lamma[2], and Paola Mello[1]

[1] DEIS, University of Bologna. V.le Risorgimento 2, 40136 Bologna, Italy
[2] ENDIF, University of Ferrara. V. Saragat 1, 44100 Ferrara, Italy

Abstract. In recent years, the declarative programming philosophy has had a visible impact on new emerging disciplines, such as heterogeneous multi-agent systems and flexible business processes. We address the problem of formal verification for systems specified using declarative languages, focusing in particular on the Business Process Management field. We propose a verification method based on the g-SCIFF abductive logic programming proof procedure and evaluate our method empirically, by comparing its performance with that of other verification frameworks.

1 Introduction

Since its introduction, the declarative programming paradigm has been successfully adopted by IT researchers and practitioners. As in the case of logic programming, the separation of logic aspects from control aspects long advocated by Kowalski [1] enables the programmer to more easily write correct programs, improve and modify them. In recent years, the declarative programming philosophy has had a visible impact on new emerging disciplines. Examples are multi-agent interaction protocol specification languages, which rely on declarative concepts such as commitments [2] or expectations [3] and make an extensive use of rules, business rules [4] and declarative Business Process (BP) specification languages such as ConDec [5]. In ConDec, business processes are specified following an open and declarative approach: rather than completely fix the control flow among activities, ConDec focuses on the (minimal) set of constraints that must be satisfied during the execution, providing an high degree of flexibility.

Although declarative technologies improve readability and modifiability, and help reducing programming errors, what makes systems trustworthy and reliable is formal verification. Since the temporal dimension plays in these settings a fundamental role, a natural choice would be to model such systems using temporal logic specifications. In particular, ConDec models can be represented as a conjunction of (propositional) Linear Temporal Logic (LTL, [6]) formulae, each one formalizing a specific constraint in the model [5]. By adopting this choice, the problem of consistency and properties verification can be cast as a satisfiability problem. This problem, in turn, is often reduced to model checking [7]. However, it is well known that the construction of the input for model checking algorithms takes a considerable amount of resources. This is especially true if we consider

M. Garcia de la Banda and E. Pontelli (Eds.): ICLP 2008, LNCS 5366, pp. 440–454, 2008.
© Springer-Verlag Berlin Heidelberg 2008

declarative specifications such as the ones of ConDec, in which the system is not represented as a Kripke structure, but it is itself specified as an LTL formula; the translation of an LTL formula into an automaton is exponential in the size of the formula, and it becomes undecidable for variants of temporal logic with explicit time, such as Metric Temporal Logic (MTL) with dense time [8].

Unlike model checking, by adopting an approach based on Logic Programming (LP) a system's specifications can be directly represented as a logic formula, handled by a proof system with no need for a translation. Hence, we address the verification problem by using Abductive Logic Programming (ALP, [9]), and in particular the SCIFF framework [3]. SCIFF is an ALP rule-based language and family of proof procedures for the specification and verification of event-based systems. The language describes which events are expected (not) to occur when certain other events happen; it includes universally and existentially quantified variables, constraint logic programming (CLP) constraints and quantifier restrictions [10]. It has an explicit representation of time, which can be modelled as a discrete or as a dense variable, depending on the constraint solver of choice. Two different proof procedures can be then used to verify SCIFF specifications, ranging from run-time/a-posteriori compliance verification (SCIFF proof procedure) to static verification of properties (g-SCIFF proof procedure).

We focus on the last point, addressing the problem of ConDec static verification by (i) automatically translating ConDec models into the SCIFF framework (following the mapping proposed in [11]) and (ii) using g-SCIFF for reasoning. Via g-SCIFF, we can carry out a goal-directed verification task, without having to generate an intermediate format (as in model checking, where the formula specifying the system must be translated into an automaton). In this setting, abduction is used to generate (simulate) partially specified execution traces which comply with the specification and entail the goal of interest. The experiments we run to compare the performance of g-SCIFF and that of other verification tools support our claims and motivate us to pursue this line of research.

The paper is organized as follows. In Section 2 we discuss the application domains, proposing some examples of specification and verification in the context of Business Process Management (BPM). Section 3 presents the SCIFF framework and our verification method based on g-SCIFF. Section 4 evaluates it experimentally, in relation with other verification techniques. Related work is described in Section 5. Finally, Section 6 discusses advantages and limits of g-SCIFF and concludes the paper by outlining future work.

2   Declarative Business Processes: Specification and Verification

If we skim through recent BPM, Web Service choreography, and Multi-Agent System literature, we will find a strong push for declarativeness. In the BPM context, van der Aalst and Pesic recently proposed a declarative flow language (ConDec, [5]) to specify, enact, and monitor business processes. Their claim is that declarative languages fit better with complex, unpredictable processes,

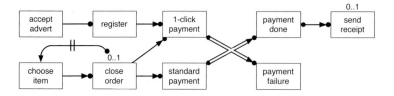

Fig. 1. A ConDec model

where a good balance between support and flexibility is of key importance. To motivate their claim, the authors show a simple example with two activities, A and B, which can be executed multiple times but exclude each other, i.e., if A is executed B cannot be executed and vice-versa. In procedural languages, such as Petri nets, it is difficult to specify the above process without introducing additional assumptions and choice points, which lead to pointlessly complicate the model. This constraint can instead be easily expressed via a simple declarative LTL expression: $\neg(\Diamond A \wedge \Diamond B)$. This is also true for LP rules. For example, in SCIFF we could use two ICs, $\mathbf{H}(a, T) \Rightarrow \mathbf{EN}(b, T')$ and $\mathbf{H}(b, T) \Rightarrow \mathbf{EN}(a, T')$, to define precisely the intended model without introducing additional constraints.

2.1   A ConDec Example

In this article, we focus on the BPM domain. We use ConDec [5] as a declarative process specification language. Fig. 1 shows the ConDec specification of a payment protocol. Boxes represent instances of activities. Numbers (e.g., 0; N..M) above the boxes are cardinality constraints that tell how many instances of the activity have to be done (e.g., never; between N and M). Edges and arrows represent relations between activities. Double line arrows indicate alternate execution (after A, B must be done before A can be done again), while barred arrows and lines indicate negative relations (doing A disallows doing B). Finally, a solid circle on one end of an edge indicates which activity activates the relation associated with the edge. For instance, the execution of accept advert in Fig. 1 does not activate any relation, because there is no circle on its end (a valid model could contain an instance of accept advert and nothing else), register instead activates a relation with accept advert (a model is not valid if it contains only register). If there is more than one circle, the relation is activated by each one of the activities that have a circle. Arrows with multiple sources and/or destinations indicate temporal relations activated/satisfied by either of the source/destination activities. The parties involved—a merchant, a customer, and a banking service to handle the payment—are left implicit.

In our example, the six left-most boxes are customer actions, payment done/ payment failure model a banking service notification about the termination status of the payment action, and send receipt is a merchant action. The ConDec chart specifies relations and constraints among such actions. If register is done (once or more than once), then also accept advert must be done (before or after register) at least once. No temporal ordering is implied by such a relation. Conversely,

Fig. 2. Two sample queries: checking (a) existential and (b) universal properties

the arrow from choose item to close order indicates that, if close order is done, choose item must be done at least once before close order. However, due to the barred arrow, close order cannot be followed by (any instance of) choose item. The 0..1 cardinality constraints say that close order and send receipt can be done at most once. 1-click payment must be preceded by register and by close order, whereas standard payment needs to be preceded only by close order (registration is not required). After 1-click or standard payment, either payment done or payment failure must follow, and no other payment can be done, before either of payment done/failure is done. After payment done there must be at most one instance of send receipt and before send receipt there must be at least a payment done. Sample valid models are: the empty model (no activity executed), a model containing one instance of accept advert and nothing else, and a model containing 5 instances of choose item followed by a close order. A model containing only one instance of 1-click payment instead is not valid.

2.2   Static Verification of ConDec Models

Let us consider some examples of verification on the model. A first, simple type of verification is known as checking for dead activities [12]. We want to check whether a given activity, say send receipt, can be executed. To verify the query, we add a 1..* cardinality constraint on the activity. If the extended specification is unfeasible, it means that send receipt cannot be executed in any possible valid model, indicating that probably there is a mistake in the design. In our example, a verifier should return a positive answer, together with a sample valid execution, such as: choose item → close order → standard payment → payment done → send receipt, which amounts to a proof that send receipt is not a dead activity.

   Let us consider a more elaborated example. We want to check whether it is still possible to have a complete transaction, if we add some constraints such as: the customer does not accept to receive ads, and the merchant does not offer standard payment. To verify the query, we add a 0 cardinality constraint on accept advert and on standard payment, and a 1..* cardinality constraint on send receipt, expressing that we want to obtain a complete transaction (see Fig. 2(a))[1]. Such an extended specification is unsatisfiable: a verifier should return a negative answer.

   Let us now consider another complex property. A merchant wants to make sure that during a transaction with 1-click payment a receipt is always sent *after* the customer has accepted the ads. Since the query is, in this case, universal,

---

[1] This technique is also used to avoid vacuous answers, in which the model is trivially satisfied if nothing happens.

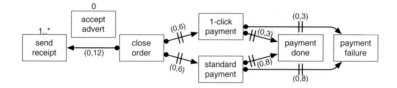

Fig. 3. Sample query concerning verification of properties on models with explicit time

to verify we have extend the specifications with the query's negation, which is an existential query (*"does there exist a transaction executing 1-click payment in which accept advert is not executed before send receipt?"*). The negated query corresponds to the relations shown in Fig. 2(b). Given the model, this query should succeed, since there is no temporal constraint associated with accept advert, thus accept advert does not have to be executed *before* send receipt in all valid models. The success of the existential negated query amounts to a counterexample against the initial (universal) query. A verifier should produce such a counterexample: choose item → close order → register → 1-click payment → payment done → send receipt → accept advert. That could lead a system designer to decide to improve the model, for example, by introducing an arrow from accept advert to send receipt.

Let us finally consider an example of a query with explicit time; we adopt an extended ConDec notation, proposed in [11]. In such a notation, arrows can be labeled with (*start time, end time*) pairs. The meaning of an arrow labelled (T_s, T_e) linking two activities A and B is: B must be done between T_s and T_e time units after A. A labeled barred arrow instead indicates that B cannot be executed between T_s and T_e time units after A. In this way we can express minimum and maximum latency constraints. For instance, the query depicted in Fig. 3 contains a $(0, 12)$ labelled barred arrow, expressing that B must occur after A and at most 12 time units after A (maximum latency constraint on the sequence $A \ldots B$). The query also contains a 0 cardinality constraint on accept advert (the customer does not accept ads). The intuition behind the whole query is: *"is there a transaction with no accept advert, terminating with a send receipt within 12 time units as of close order, given that close order, 1-click payment, and standard payment cause a latency of 6, 3, and 8 time units?"*. It turns out that the specification is unfeasible, because the 0 cardinality constraint on accept advert rules out the 1-click payment path, and the standard payment path takes more than 12 time units. A verifier should return failure.

3   The SCIFF Framework

SCIFF was initially proposed to specify and verify agent interaction protocols [3], but it has also been successfully applied in the context of service choreographies, electronic contracts and, in particular, declarative business processes [13,11].

3.1   The SCIFF Language

SCIFF specifications consist of an abductive logic program, i.e., a triplet $\langle \mathcal{P}, \mathcal{IC},$ $\mathcal{A} \rangle$ where $\mathcal{P}$ is a logic program (a collection of clauses), $\mathcal{IC}$ is a set of integrity constraints (IC) and $\mathcal{A}$ is a set of abducible predicates. SCIFF considers events as first class objects. Events can be, for example, sending a message, or starting an action, and they are associated with a time point. Events are identified by a special functor, **H**, and are described by an arbitrary term (possibly containing variables). SCIFF uses ICs to model relations among events and expectations about events. Expectations are abducibles identified by functors **E** and **EN**. **E** are "positive" expectations, and indicate events to be expected. **EN** are "negative" expectations and model events that are expected not to occur. Happened events and expectations explicitly contain a time variable, to represent when the event occurred/is expected (not) to occur. Event and time variables can be constrained by means of Prolog predicates or CLP constraints [14]; the latter are especially useful to specify orderings between events and quantitative time constraints (such as delays and deadlines). An IC is a forward *body* $\Rightarrow$ *head* rule which links happened events and expectations. Typically, the *body* contains a conjunction of happened events, whereas the *head* is a disjunction of conjunctions of positive and negative expectations. ICs are interpreted in a reactive manner; the intuition is that when the body of a rule becomes true (i.e., the involved events occur), then the rule fires, and the expectations in the head are generated by abduction. For example, $\mathbf{H}(a, T) \Rightarrow \mathbf{EN}(b, T')$ defines a relation between events a and b, saying that if a occurs at time T, b should not occur at any time. Instead, $\mathbf{H}(a, T) \Rightarrow \mathbf{E}(b, T') \wedge T' \leq T + 300$ says that if a occurs, then an event b should occur no later than 300 time units after a.

To exhibit a correct behavior, given a goal $\mathcal{G}$ and a triplet $\langle \mathcal{P}, \mathcal{IC}, \mathcal{A} \rangle$, a set of abduced expectations must be *fulfilled* by corresponding events. The concept of fulfillment is formally captured by the SCIFF declarative semantics [3], which intuitively states that $\mathcal{P}$, together with the abduced literals, must entail $\mathcal{G} \wedge \mathcal{IC}$, positive expectations must have a corresponding matching happened event, and negative expectations must not have a corresponding matching event.

3.2   Static Verification Using g-SCIFF

The SCIFF framework includes two different proof procedures to perform verification. The SCIFF proof procedure checks the compliance of a narrative of events with the specification, by matching events with expectations during the execution (run-time monitoring) or a-posteriori. The g-SCIFF proof procedure is a "generative" extension of the SCIFF proof procedure whose purpose is to prove system properties at design time (static verification), or to generate counterexamples of properties that do not hold.

The proof procedures are implemented in SICStus 4 and are freely available[2]. Their implementation features a unique design, that has not been used before in other abductive proof procedures. First, the various transitions in the operational

---

[2] See http://lia.deis.unibo.it/sciff/

semantics are implemented as constraint handling rules (CHR, [15])[3]. The second important feature is their ability to interface with constraint solvers: both with the CLP(FD) solver and with the CLP($\mathcal{R}$) solver embedded in SICStus. The user can thus choose the most suitable solver for the application at hand, which is an important issue in practice. It is well known, in fact, that no solver dominates the other, and we measured, in different applications, orders of magnitude of improvements by switching solver. In this paper we discuss static verification, reporting the results obtained with the CLP($\mathcal{R}$) solver, which is based on the simplex algorithm, and features a complete propagation of linear constraints.

Existing formal verification tools rely on model checking or theorem proving. However, a drawback of most model checking tools is that they typically only accommodate discrete time and finite domains. Moreover, the cardinality of domains impacts heavily on the performance of the verification process, especially in relation to the production of a model consisting of a state automaton. On the other hand, theorem proving in general has a low level of automation, and it may be hard to use, because it heavily relies on the user's expertise [17]. g-SCIFF presents interesting features from both approaches. Like theorem proving, its performance is not heavily affected by domain cardinality, and it accommodates domains with infinite elements, such as dense time. Similarly to model checking, it works in a push-button style, thus offering a high level of automation.

In the style of [18], we do verification by abduction: in g-SCIFF, event occurrences are abduced as well as expectations, in order to model all the possible evolutions of the system being verified. More specifically, g-SCIFF works by applying the transitions sketched in the following, until a fix-point is reached:

Unfolding substitutes an atom with its definitions in $\mathcal{P}$;

Propagation given an implication $(\mathbf{a}(X) \wedge R) \Rightarrow H$ and an abduced literal $\mathbf{a}(Y)$, generates the implication $(X = Y \wedge R) \Rightarrow H$;

Case Analysis Given an implication $(c(X) \wedge R) \Rightarrow H$ in which c is a constraint (possibly the equality constraint '='), generates two children: $c(X) \wedge (R \Rightarrow H)$ and $\neg c(X)$;

Splitting distributes conjunctions and disjunctions;

Logical Equivalences performs usual replacements: $true \Rightarrow A$ with A, etc.;

Constraint Solving posts constraints to the constraint solver of choice;

Fulfilment declares fulfilled;
- an expectation $\mathbf{E}(p, t)$ if there is a corresponding literal $\mathbf{H}(p, t)$, or
- an expectation $\mathbf{EN}(p, t)$ if there is no matching literal $\mathbf{H}(p, t)$ and it cannot happen in the sequel (e.g., because a deadline has expired);

Violation declares violated an expectation: symmetrical to fulfilment;

Fulfiller if an expectation $\mathbf{E}(p, t)$ is not fulfilled, abduces an event $\mathbf{H}(p, t)$;

Consistency imposes consistency of the set of expectations, by which $\mathbf{E}(p, t)$ and $\mathbf{EN}(p, t)$ cause failure.

---

[3] Other proof procedures [16] have been implemented on top of CHR, but with a different design: they map integrity constraints (instead of transitions) into constraint handling rules. This choice gives more efficiency, but less flexibility.

Most of the transitions above are the same as the ones of the SCIFF proof procedure. The main difference with g-SCIFF stands in the *fulfiller* transition, that is not applied in SCIFF, by only in g-SCIFF. In particular, g-SCIFF uses *fulfiller* to generate narratives of events (*"histories"*) starting from the specification (and the query of interest): abduction is used to simulate executions of the system which comply with the specification and entail the query. To do so, it applies the rule $\mathbf{E}(P, T) \rightarrow \mathbf{H}(P, T)$, which fulfills an expectation by abducing a matching event (possibly with variables). *Fulfiller* is applied only at the fix-point of the other transitions. SCIFF and g-SCIFF also exploit an implementation of reified unification (a solver on equality/disequality of terms) which takes into consideration quantifier restrictions [10] and variable quantification. Histories are thus generated intensionally, and hypothetical events can contain variables, possibly subject to CLP constraints.

Verification of properties is conducted as follows. An existential property can be passed to g-SCIFF as a goal containing positive expectations: if the g-SCIFF proof procedure succeeds in proving the goal, the generated history proves that there exists a way to obtain the goal via a valid execution of the activities. A universal property Q can be negated (as in model checking), and then passed to g-SCIFF. If the g-SCIFF proof procedure succeeds in finding a history which satisfies the negated property, such a history is a counterexample against Q.

The examples shown in Section 2.1 are correctly handled by g-SCIFF. The first one (check for dead activity) completes in 10ms[4], the second one (Fig. 2(a)), in 20ms, the third one (Fig. 2(b)) in 420ms, and the last one (Fig. 3) in 80ms.

4   Experimental Evaluation

A ConDec chart is a good starting point to compare two verification methods: satisfiability checking LTL formulas via model checking, and g-SCIFF.

Indeed, the semantics of ConDec can be given both in terms of LTL formulae [5,11] and of SCIFF programs [11]. By adopting LTL, each ConDec constraint is associated with a formula; the conjunction of all formulae (*"conjunction formula"*) gives the semantics of the entire chart. In SCIFF the approach is similar: each ConDec constraint is mapped to a set of ICs, and the entire model is represented by the union of all ICs.

For example, the relation between accept advert and register corresponds to the LTL formula $(\Diamond \text{register}) \Rightarrow (\Diamond \text{accept advert})$ and to the following IC:

$$\mathbf{H}(register, T) \Rightarrow \mathbf{E}(acceptAdvert, T').$$

The barred arrow from close order to choose item corresponds to the LTL formula $\Box(\text{close order} \Rightarrow \neg(\Diamond \text{choose item}))$ and to the following IC:

$$\mathbf{H}(closeOrder, T) \Rightarrow \mathbf{EN}(chooseItem, T') \wedge T' > T.$$

---

[4] Experiments have been performed on a MacBook Intel CoreDuo 2 GHz machine.

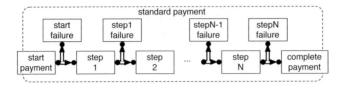

Fig. 4. Parametric extension to the model presented in Fig.1

Finally, the relation between payment done and send receipt corresponds to the LTL formula ($\Box$(payment done $\Rightarrow$ $\Diamond$send receipt)) $\wedge$ (($\Diamond$send receipt) $\Rightarrow$ (($\neg$send receipt)$\mathcal{U}$payment done)) and to the following two ICs:

$$\mathbf{H}(paymentDone, T) \Rightarrow \mathbf{E}(receipt, T') \wedge T' > T$$
$$\mathbf{H}(receipt, T) \Rightarrow \mathbf{E}(paymentDone, T') \wedge T' < T.$$

We run an extensive experimental evaluation to compare g-SCIFF with model checking techniques. To the best of our knowledge, there are no benchmarks on the verification of declarative business process specifications. We created our own, starting from the sample model introduced in Section 2.1, Fig. 1, and extending the standard payment activity as follows. Instead of a single activity, standard payment consists of a chain of N activities in alternate succession: start payment $\bullet\!\!\!\to\!\bullet$ step 1 $\bullet\!\!\!\to\!\bullet$ step 2 $\bullet\!\!\!\to\!\bullet$ ... $\bullet\!\!\!\to\!\bullet$ step N $\bullet\!\!\!\to\!\bullet$ complete payment in which every two consecutive steps are linked by an alternate succession relation. Moreover, we model a possible failure at each of these steps (start failure, step 1 failure, ...). This extension to the model is depicted in Fig. 4. Additionally, we add a K..* cardinality constraint on action payment failure, meaning that payment failure must occur at least K times. The new model is thus parametric on N and K. We complicated the model in such a way to stress g-SCIFF and emphasize its performance results in both favorable and unfavorable cases.

4.1   Verifying ConDec Models with g-SCIFF and Model Checking Techniques

To verify ConDec models with g-SCIFF, we adopted the following methodology. Given a ConDec specification $\mathcal{S}$ and a query (negated query, if the query is universal) $\mathcal{Q}$:

1. Build a SCIFF specification which formalizes $\mathcal{S}$, following the translation described in [11]; do the same with $\mathcal{Q}$.
2. Run g-SCIFF with the translation of $\mathcal{Q}$ as goal: if the query is entailed by $\mathcal{Q}$, then g-SCIFF generates an execution trace which complies with $\mathcal{S}$ and, at the same time, satisfies $\mathcal{Q}$.

In the LTL setting, the problem of static verification is cast as a satisfiability problem, which in turn can be reduced to model checking [7]:

1. Map activities to boolean variables (1=execution);
2. Build a "conjunction-formula" ϕ of $\mathcal{S}$ and $\mathcal{Q}$, following the translation described in [5];
3. Build a universal model $\mathcal{M}$, capable to generate all the activity execution traces;
4. Model check $\neg\phi$ against $\mathcal{M}$: if the model checker finds a counterexample, ϕ is satisfiable and the counterexample is in fact an execution trace satisfying both $\mathcal{S}$ and $\mathcal{Q}$.

In order to choose a suitable model checker, we followed on the results of an experimental investigation conducted by Rozier and Vardi on LTL satisfiability checking [7], by which it emerges that the symbolic approach is clearly superior to the explicit approach, and that NuSMV [19] is the best performing model checker in the state of the art for the benchmarks they considered. We thus chose to run our benchmarks to compare g-SCIFF with NuSMV[5].

Unfortunately, the comparison could not cover all relevant aspects of the language, such as some temporal aspect, because neither NuSMV nor any other model checker cited in [7] offers all of the features offered by SCIFF. As a future work, we plan to compare the performance of g-SCIFF against that of other model checkers for MTL [8]. However, since existing MTL tools seem to use classical model checking and not symbolic model checking, our feeling is that g-SCIFF would largely outperform them on these instances.

4.2 Experimental Results

We compared g-SCIFF with NuSMV on two sets of benchmarks:

1. the existential query presented in Section 2.1, Fig. 2(a)[6];
2. a variation of the above, without the 0 cardinality constraint on std payment.

Of the two benchmarks, the first one concerns verification of unsatisfiable specifications and the second one verification of satisfiable specifications. The latter requires producing an example demonstrating satisfiability, which generally increases the runtime. The input files are available on a Web site[7]. The runtime resulting from the benchmarks is reported in Table 1 and Table 2. Fig. 5 shows the ratio NuSMV/g-SCIFF runtime, in Log scale.

It turns out that g-SCIFF outperforms NuSMV in most cases, up to several orders of magnitude. This is especially true for the first benchmark, for which g-SCIFF is able to complete the verification task always in less than 0.15s, while NuSMV takes up to 136s. For the second benchmark, g-SCIFF does comparatively better as N increases, for a given K, whereas NuSMV improves with respect to g-SCIFF and eventually outperforms it, for a given N, as K increases. This

---

[5] It is worth noticing that explicit model checkers, such as SPIN, in our experiments could not handle in reasonable time a ConDec chart such as the one we described earlier.

[6] The 0 cardinality constraint is set on the start payment activity.

[7] See http://www.lia.deis.unibo.it/research/climb/iclp08benchmarks.zip

Table 1. Results of first benchmark (SCIFF/NuSMV), in seconds

$K \setminus N$	0	1	2	3	4	5
0	0.01/0.20	0.02/0.57	0.03/1.01	0.02/3.04	0.02/6.45	0.03/20.1
1	0.02/0.35	0.03/0.91	0.03/2.68	0.04/4.80	0.04/8.72	0.04/29.8
2	0.02/0.46	0.04/1.86	0.05/4.84	0.05/10.8	0.07/36.6	0.07/40.0
3	0.03/0.54	0.05/2.40	0.06/8.75	0.07/20.1	0.09/38.6	0.10/94.8
4	0.05/0.63	0.05/2.34	0.08/9.51	0.10/27.1	0.11/56.63	0.14/132
5	0.05/1.02	0.07/2.96	0.09/8.58	0.12/29.0	0.14/136	0.15/134

Table 2. Results of second benchmark (SCIFF/NuSMV), in seconds

$K \setminus N$	0	1	2	3	4	5
0	0.02/0.28	0.03/1.02	0.04/1.82	0.05/5.69	0.07/12.7	0.08/37.9
1	0.06/0.66	0.06/1.67	0.07/4.92	0.08/9.21	0.11/17.3	0.15/57.39
2	0.14/0.82	0.23/3.44	0.33/8.94	0.45/22.1	0.61/75.4	0.91/72.86
3	0.51/1.01	1.17/4.46	1.87/15.87	3.77/41.2	5.36/79.2	11.4/215
4	1.97/1.17	4.79/4.43	10.10/17.7	26.8/52.2	61.9/116	166/268
5	5.78/2.00	16.5/5.71	48.23/16.7	120/60.5	244/296	446/259

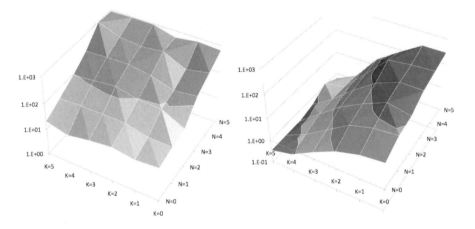

Fig. 5. Charts showing the ratio NuSMV/g-SCIFF runtime, in Log scale

is the case, because NuSMV's runtime is somehow proportional to the size of the LTL formula to be checked, whereas the runtime of g-SCIFF, which follows a "simulation by abduction" approach, heavily depends on the type of query it has to answer to, rather than on its length, and on the order of clauses and on the type of functors used in the SCIFF program. This suggests that suitable heuristics that choose how to explore the search tree could help improve the g-SCIFF performance. This is subject for future research.

5   Related Work

We discuss other related approaches to verification, starting by those using ALP. Alessandra Russo et al. [18] exploit abduction for verification of declarative specifications expressed in terms of required reactions to events. They use the event calculus (EC) and include an explicit time structure. Global systems invariants are proved by refutation, and adopting a goal-driven approach similar to ours. The main difference concerns the underlying specification language: while Russo et al. rely on a general purpose ALP proof procedure which handles EC specifications and requirements, we adopt a language which directly captures the notion of occurred events and expectations, whose temporal relationships are mapped on CLP constraints. In this way, for the time structure we can rely on a variety of CLP domains (e.g., integers, reals, just to mention the two most relevant ones).

Another system aimed at proving properties of graphical specifications translated to logic programming formalisms is West2East [20], where interaction protocols modeled in Agent UML are translated to a Prolog program representing the corresponding finite state machine, whose properties can be verified exploiting the Prolog meta-programming facilities. However, the focus of that work is more on agent oriented software engineering, rather than verification: the system allows (conjunctions of) existential or universal queries about the exchanged messages (i.e., to check if a given message is guaranteed to be exchanged in at least one or all of the possible protocol instatiations) or guard conditions, and it is not obvious how to express and verify more complex properties.

In [21], the authors propose a mixed informal-formal approach to BP design and verification. Differently from this work, they consider a procedural language for the specification of business processes (XPDL). Verification is carried on, formally, by exploiting the Situation Calculus, a dialect of First Order Logic, and its Golog interpreter in particular.

In [22], Fisher and Dixon propose a clausal temporal resolution method to prove satisfiability of arbitrary propositional LTL formulae. The approach is twofold: first, the LTL formula is translated into a standard normal form (SNF), which preserves satisfiability; then a resolution method, encompassing classical as well as temporal resolution rules, is applied until either no further resolvents can be generated or *false* is derived, in which case the formula is unsatisfiable. From a theoretical point of view, clausal temporal resolution always terminates, while avoiding the state-explosion problem; however, the translation to SNF produces large formulas, and finding suitable candidates for applying a temporal resolution step makes the resolution procedure exponential in the size of the formula. Furthermore, in case of satisfiability no example is produced.

Differently from the approach here presented, in other works LP and CLP have been exploited to implement model checking techniques. Of course, since they mimic model checking, they inherit the same drawbacks of classical model checkers when applied for the static verification of ConDec models.

For example, Delzanno and Podelski [23] propose to translate a procedural system specification into a CLP program. Safety and liveness properties, expressed in Computation Tree Logic, are checked by composing them with the translated program, and by calculating the least and the greatest fix-point sets.

In [24], Gupta and Pontelli model the observed system through an automaton, and convert it into CLP. As in our approach, they cannot handle infinite sequences without the intervention of the user: the user is supposed to provide a predicate that generates a finite number of sequences of events representing all the possible evolutions of the system.

6   Discussion and Conclusion

A most prominent feature and, in our opinion, a major advantage of the approach we present, with respect to other approaches to verification in the same application domains, is the language, as we have discussed earlier. It is declarative and it accommodates explicit time and dense domains. A software engineer can specify the system using a compact, intuitive graphical language such as ConDec, then the specification is mapped automatically to a SCIFF program. Using g-SCIFF, It is possible to verify the specification's properties. Using the SCIFF proof procedure it is possible to monitor and verify at run-time that the execution of an implemented system complies with the specifications. This eliminates the problem of having to produce two sets of specifications (one for static and one for run-time verification) and of verifying that they are equivalent.

Apart from the language, the main difference with model checking is that queries are evaluated top-down, i.e., starting from a goal. No model needs to be generated, which eliminates a computationally expensive step. By going top-down, the verification algorithm only considers relevant portions of the search space, which can boost performance. On the downside, the performance strongly depends on the way SCIFF programs are written w.r.t. the property. Due to the left-most, depth-first search tree exploration strategy inherited from Prolog by SCIFF, the order of clauses influences the performance, and so does the ordering of atoms inside the clauses. However, this does not impact on soundness.

A major drawback of our approach is that it does not always guarantee termination, as opposed to unbounded model checkers, which typically guarantee that the verification algorithm terminates even when checking formulae producing models of infinite length, such as, for instance, $\Box(a \rightarrow \Diamond a)$. In general, g-SCIFF would not terminate in such a case - although it does terminate if it is used with finite domains, such as discrete time and limited time span. However, g-SCIFF implements a work-around to address this deficiency, similar to the one used in bounded model checking. In particular, g-SCIFF can be invoked in bounded mode, which restricts the number of actions generated by g-SCIFF. In this way, g-SCIFF does not guarantee completeness in the general case, but it is still able to say that, for example, a query fails with models consisting of at most N actions. Another technique implemented by SCIFF is iterative deepening, which can be used to address similar cases at the cost of a worse performance. However, we emphasize that we are proposing g-SCIFF for use in application domains in which interactions are expected to eventually terminate. A typical ConDec model does not contain infinite loops—at least, not intentionally. In particular, all ConDec relations individually produce loop-free SCIFF programs, and specifications such as the one we presented earlier do not have this problem. Thus, although a combination of ConDec relations can indeed produce infinite loops, we can consider them to be uncommon cases which can be identified through a pre-processing phase and verified by using g-SCIFF with iterative deepening. A promising approach to deal with infinite computations during verification seems to be Coinductive Logic Programming [25,26], since Coinductive LP extends the usual operational semantics of logic programming to allow reasoning over infinite and cyclic structures and properties. It might be, therefore, a useful approach to deal with models which lead to infinite g-SCIFF computations. This issue, together with a more extensive theoretical and experimental evaluation, will be our next research direction.

Acknowledgments. This work has been partially supported by the FIRB project *TOCAI.IT*.

References

1. Kowalski, R.A.: Algorithm = logic + control. Communications of the ACM 22(7), 424–436 (1979)
2. Singh, M.P.: Agent communication language: rethinking the principles. IEEE Computer, 40–47 (December 1998)
3. Alberti, M., Chesani, F., Gavanelli, M., Lamma, E., Mello, P., Torroni, P.: Verifiable agent interaction in abductive logic programming: the SCIFF framework. ACM Transactions on Computational Logic 9(4), 1–43 (2008)
4. Nalepa, G.: Proposal of business process and rules modeling with the xtt method. In: International Symposium on Symbolic and Numeric Algorithms for Scientific Computing (SYNASC), pp. 500–506 (2007)
5. Pesic, M., van der Aalst, W.M.P.: A declarative approach for flexible business processes management. In: Eder, J., Dustdar, S. (eds.) BPM Workshops 2006. LNCS, vol. 4103, pp. 169–180. Springer, Heidelberg (2006)
6. Emerson, E.A.: Temporal and modal logic. In: Handbook of Theoretical Computer Science, Volume B: Formal Models and Sematics (B), pp. 995–1072. MIT Press, Cambridge (1990)
7. Rozier, K.Y., Vardi, M.Y.: LTL satisfiability checking. In: Model Checking Software. In: Bošnački, D., Edelkamp, S. (eds.) SPIN 2007. LNCS, vol. 4595, pp. 149–167. Springer, Heidelberg (2007)
8. Alur, R., Henzinger, T.A.: Real-time logics: complexity and expressiveness. Information and Computation 104, 35–77 (1993)
9. Kakas, A.C., Kowalski, R.A., Toni, F.: Abductive logic programming. J. Log. Comput. 2(6), 719–770 (1992)
10. Bürckert, H.: A resolution principle for constrained logics. Artificial Intelligence 66, 235–271 (1994)
11. Montali, M., Pesic, M., van der Aalst, W.M., Chesani, F., Mello, P., Storari, S.: Declarative specification and verification of service choreographies. ACM Transaction on the Web (submitted, 2008)

12. Pesic, M., Schonenberg, H., van der Aalst, W.: Declare: Full support for loosely-structured processes. In: 11th IEEE International Enterprise Distributed Object Computing Conference (EDOC 2007), Annapolis, Maryland, USA, October 15-19, 2007, pp. 287–300. IEEE Computer Society, Los Alamitos (2007)

13. Bryl, V., Mello, P., Montali, M., Torroni, P., Zannone, N.: B-Tropos: Agent-oriented requirements engineering meets computational logic for declarative business process modeling and verification. In: Sadri, F., Satoh, K. (eds.) CLIMA VIII. LNCS (LNAI), vol. 5056, pp. 157–176. Springer, Heidelberg (2008)

14. Jaffar, J., Maher, M.: Constraint logic programming: a survey. Journal of Logic Programming 19(20), 503–582 (1994)

15. Frühwirth, T.: Theory and practice of constraint handling rules. Journal of Logic Programming 37(1-3), 95–138 (1998)

16. Christiansen, H., Dahl, V.: HYPROLOG: A new logic programming language with assumptions and abduction. In: Gabbrielli, M., Gupta, G. (eds.) ICLP 2005. LNCS, vol. 3668, pp. 159–173. Springer, Heidelberg (2005)

17. Halpern, J.Y., Vardi, M.Y.: Model checking vs. theorem proving: A manifesto. In: Artificial intelligence and mathematical theory of computation: papers in honor of John McCarthy, pp. 151–176 (1991)

18. Russo, A., Miller, R., Nuseibeh, B., Kramer, J.: An abductive approach for analysing event-based requirements specifications. In: Stuckey, P. (ed.) ICLP 2002. LNCS, vol. 2401, pp. 22–37. Springer, Heidelberg (2002)

19. Cimatti, A., Clarke, E.M., Giunchiglia, F., Roveri, M.: NuSMV: a new symbolic model checker. International Journal on Software Tools for Technology Transfer 2(4), 410–425 (2000)

20. Casella, G., Mascardi, V.: West2east: exploiting web service technologies to engineer agent-based software. IJAOSE 1(3/4), 396–434 (2007)

21. Li, B., Iijima, J.: Architecture on a hybrid business process design and verification system. In: International Conference on Wireless Communications, Networking and Mobile Computing (WiCom), pp. 6199–6204 (2007)

22. Fisher, M., Dixon, C., Peim, M.: Clausal temporal resolution. ACM Transactions on Computational Logic 2(1), 12–56 (2001)

23. Delzanno, G., Podelski, A.: Model checking in clp. In: Cleaveland, W.R. (ed.) TACAS 1999. LNCS, vol. 1579, pp. 223–239. Springer, Heidelberg (1999)

24. Gupta, G., Pontelli, E.: A constraint-based approach for specification and verification of real-time systems. In: Proceedings of the 18th IEEE Real-Time Systems Symposium (RTSS 1997), pp. 230–239. IEEE Computer Society, Los Alamitos (1997)

25. Gupta, G., Bansal, A., Min, R., Simon, L., Mallya, A.: Coinductive logic programming and its applications. In: Dahl, V., Niemelä, I. (eds.) ICLP 2007. LNCS, vol. 4670, pp. 27–44. Springer, Heidelberg (2007)

26. Jaffar, J., Santosa, A.E., Voicu, R.: A clp proof method for timed automata. In: Proceedings of the 25th IEEE Real-Time Systems Symposium (RTSS 2004), pp. 175–186. IEEE Computer Society, Los Alamitos (2004)

Prolog Based Description Logic Reasoning

Gergely Lukácsy, Péter Szeredi, and Balázs Kádár

Budapest University of Technology and Economics
Department of Computer Science and Information Theory
1117 Budapest, Magyar tudósok körútja 2., Hungary
{lukacsy,szeredi}@cs.bme.hu

Abstract. In this paper we present the recent developments of the DLog system, an ABox reasoning engine for the the $\mathcal{SHIQ}$ description logic language. DLog differs from traditional description logic reasoners in that it transforms description logic axioms into a Prolog program. The transformation is done independently from the ABox, i.e. the set of assertions about the individuals. This makes it possible to store the ABox assertions in a database, rather than in memory. This approach results in better scalability and helps using description logic ontologies directly on top of existing information sources.

The transformation involves several optimisation steps, which aim at producing more efficient Prolog programs. In this paper we focus on the partial evaluation technique we apply to obtain programs that do not use logic variables. This simplifies the implementation, improves performance and opens up the possibility of compiling into Mercury code.

In the paper we also present the recent architectural changes in the DLog system, summarise the most important features of the implementation and evaluate the performance of DLog by comparing it to the best available description logic reasoners.

Keywords: description logic, logic programming, resolution, large data sets.

1   Introduction

Description Logics (DLs) are becoming widespread as more and more systems start using semantic technologies. Similarly to [1], the motivation for our work comes from the realisation that DLs are, or soon will be, used to reason on large amounts of data. On the Web, for example, we already have tremendous amounts of meta-information. Obviously, such information sources cannot be stored directly in memory.

Thus, we are interested in querying DL concepts where the assertions about the individuals – the so called ABox – may be stored externally, e.g. in databases. We found that most existing DL reasoners are not suitable for this task, as the traditional algorithms for querying DL concepts need to examine the whole ABox to answer a query. This results in scalability problems and undermines the point of using databases.

M. Garcia de la Banda and E. Pontelli (Eds.): ICLP 2008, LNCS 5366, pp. 455–469, 2008.

We have developed an approach where the inference algorithm is divided into two phases. From the given terminological knowledge, without accessing the underlying data set, we first create a *query-plan*, in the form of a Prolog program. Subsequently, this query-plan can be run on the ABox data, to obtain the required results. This algorithm has been incorporated in the ABox reasoning engine *DLog*, which is available at http://dlog-reasoner.sourceforge.net.

In this paper we focus on the recent developments of the DLog system, which include a partial evaluation technique we apply to avoid using logic variables in the Prolog programs generated, as well as the architectural redesign of the system. The complete description of other aspects of DLog, including the detailed explanation of the optimisation techniques, can be found in [2].

This paper is structured as follows. In Section 2 we introduce Description Logics and summarise existing theorem proving approaches for DLs. Section 3 gives an overview of the DLog approach. Section 4 discusses a new optimisation technique, called unfolding. Section 5 presents the architecture and the implementation details of the *DLog server* extension. Finally, before concluding the paper, we compare the performance of DLog with other reasoning systems.

2   Preliminaries and Related Work

Description Logics [3] are a family of simple logic languages used for knowledge representation. DLs are used for describing various kinds of knowledge of a selected field as well as of general nature. The Description Logic approach uses *concepts* to represent sets of *objects* i.e. unary relations, and *roles* to describe binary relations between objects. Objects are the instances occurring in the modelled application field, and thus are also called *instances* or *individuals*.

A DL knowledge base is a set of DL axioms consisting of two disjoint parts: the *TBox* and the *ABox*. The TBox (terminology box) contains terminological axioms, such as $C \sqsubseteq D$ (concept C is subsumed by concept D). The ABox (assertion box) stores knowledge about the individuals in the world, e.g. the concept assertion $C(i)$ states that individual i is an instance of the concept C.

Concepts and roles may either be *atomic* or *composite*. A composite concept is built from atomic concepts using *constructors*. The expressiveness of a DL language depends on the constructors allowed for building composite concepts or roles. We use the DL language $\mathcal{SHIQ}$ in this paper which is one the most widely used DL variant. For more details we refer the reader to the first two chapters of [3].

In this paper, we will deal with two ABox-reasoning problems: instance check and instance retrieval. In an *instance check* problem, a *query-concept* C and an individual i is given. The question is whether $C(i)$ is entailed by the TBox and the ABox. In an *instance retrieval* problem the task is to retrieve all the instances of a query-concept C, entailed by the given TBox and ABox.

Traditionally, ABox-reasoning is based on the *tableau inference* algorithm. An individual i is inferred to be an instance of a concept C, if the tableau algorithm reports inconsistency for the given TBox and ABox, when the latter is extended with the indirect assertion $\neg C(i)$. This approach cannot be directly used for high volume instance retrieval, because it requires checking all instances in the ABox. Novel techniques have been developed recently, such as [4], to overcome this drawback of the tableau approach. These techniques have been incorporated in the state-of-the-art DL reasoners, such as RacerPro and Pellet, the two tableau reasoners used in our performance evaluation in Section 6.

In [5], a resolution-based inference algorithm is described, which is not as sensitive to the increase of the ABox size as the tableau-based methods. However, this approach still requires the input of the *whole content* of the ABox before attempting to answer any queries. The KAON2 system [1] provides an implementation of this approach.

Article [6] introduces the term Description Logic Programming. This idea uses a direct transformation of $\mathcal{ALC}$ concepts into definite Horn-clauses, and poses some restrictions on the form of the knowledge base, which disallow axioms requiring disjunctive reasoning. Further important work on Description Logic Programming includes [7,8,9].

The Prolog Technology Theorem Prover approach (PTTP) was developed by Mark E. Stickel in the late 1980's [10], providing a theorem prover for First Order Logic (FOL) on top of Prolog. This means that an arbitrary FOL formula is transformed into a set of Horn-clauses, and FOL reasoning is performed using Prolog execution. In PTTP, each first order clause gives rise to a number of Horn-clauses, the so-called *contrapositives*. By using contrapositives each literal of a FOL clause will appear in the head of a Horn clause, ensuring that it can participate in a resolution step in spite of the restricted selection rule of Prolog.

In the PTTP approach, ancestor resolution is used instead of *factoring* inference rule. Ancestor resolution is implemented in Prolog by building an *ancestor list* which contains *open* predicate calls (i.e. calls which were entered or re-entered, but have not been exited yet, according to the Procedure-Box model of Prolog execution). If the ancestor list contains a literal which can be unified with the negation of the current goal literal, then the goal literal succeeds and the unification with the ancestor element is performed. Note that in order to retain completeness, as an alternative to ancestor resolution, one has to try to prove the current goal using normal resolution as well.

There are two further features to make the PTTP approach complete. First, to avoid infinite loops, iterative deepening is used as opposed to the standard depth-first Prolog search strategy. Second, in contrast with Prolog, PTTP uses occurs check during unification.

3   An Overview of the DLog Approach

In this section we give a high level overview of the DLog reasoner. Let us consider the following DL knowledge base example:

```
1  ∃hasFriend.Alcoholic  ⊑  ¬Alcoholic
2  ∃hasParent.¬Alcoholic  ⊑  ¬Alcoholic

3  hasParent(i1, i2)     hasParent(i1, i3)     hasFriend(i2, i3)
```

The axiom in line 1 states that if someone has a friend who is alcoholic, then he is not alcoholic. Line 2 states that if someone has a parent, who is not an alcohol addict, then he is not alcoholic either. The ABox in line 3 contains assertions for the `hasParent` and `hasFriend` relations, but nothing about someone being alcoholic or non-alcoholic. Interestingly, it is possible to conclude that `i1` is non-alcoholic as one of his parents has to be non-alcoholic.

The common properties of such problems is that solving them requires *case analysis* and therefore the trivial Prolog translation usually does not work.

The first step of our sound and complete $\mathcal{SHIQ}$ to Prolog transformation process is to convert a $\mathcal{SHIQ}$ knowledge base to a set of first order clauses of a specific form. Here we rely on the saturation techniques described in [1] and [11]. In the present paper we only make use of the fact that the output of these transformations takes a specific form: [1] and [11] prove that for an arbitrary $\mathcal{SHIQ}$ knowledge base KB, the resulting set of first-order clauses, denoted by $DL(KB)$, only contains clauses of the form listed in Figure 1.

---

(1) $\neg R(x, y) \lor S(y, x)$

(2) $\neg R(x, y) \lor S(x, y)$

(3) $\mathbf{P}(x)$

(4) $\bigvee_{i,j,k} \neg R_k(x_i, x_j) \lor \bigvee_i \mathbf{P}(x_i) \lor \bigvee_{i,j}(x_i = x_j)$

(5) $R(a, b)$

(6) $C(a)$

Fig. 1. The format of FOL clauses generated from $\mathcal{SHIQ}$ knowledge bases

Here clause types (1)–(4) correspond to the TBox, while (5) and (6) are ABox clause templates. $\mathbf{P}(x)$ denotes a nonempty disjunction of possibly negated unary literals: $(\neg)P_1(x) \lor \ldots \lor (\neg)P_n(x)$. A clause of type (4) has further properties: it contains at least one negative binary literal, and at least one unary literal, but the set of variable equalities may be empty. Also, its negative binary literals contain all the variables of the clause. Furthermore, if we build a graph from the binary literals by converting $R(x, y)$ to an edge $x \rightarrow y$, this graph will be a tree.

Note that, in contrast with [1], all clauses containing function symbols are eliminated: the resulting clauses can be resolved further only with ABox clauses. This forms the basis of a pure two phase reasoning framework, where every possible ABox-independent reasoning step is performed before accessing the ABox itself, allowing us to store the content of the ABox in an external database.

Actually, in the general transformation, we use only certain properties of the clauses in Figure 1. These properties are satisfied by a subset of first order clauses that is, in fact, larger than the set of clauses that can be generated from a $\mathcal{SHIQ}$ KB. We call these clauses *DL clauses*. As a consequence of this, our results can be used for DL knowledge bases that are more expressive than $\mathcal{SHIQ}$. This includes the use of certain role constructors, such as union. Furthermore, some parts of the knowledge base can be supplied by the user directly in the form of first order clauses. More details can be found in [2].

As the clauses of a $\mathcal{SHIQ}$ knowledge base KB are normal first-order clauses we can apply the PTTP technology (cf. Section 2) directly on these. This involves the generation of contrapositives of $DL(KB)$, which also requires the introduction of new predicate names for negated literals.

We have simplified the PTTP approach for the special case of DL clauses. The following list is a brief summary of the principles we use in the execution of DL predicates, in comparison with their counterparts in PTTP:

- DLog uses normal Prolog unification, rather than occurs check;
- DLog uses loop elimination, instead of iterative deepening;
- DLog eliminates contrapositives with negated binary literals in the head;
- DLog does not apply ancestor resolution for roles;
- DLog uses deterministic ancestor resolution.

In [2], we have proved that these modifications result in a reasoner on DL clauses, which is sound and complete.

We have implemented the specialised PTTP approach as follows. First, we transform the DL clauses to a *DL predicate* format simply by generating all contrapositives and grouping these into predicates. For very simple knowledge bases, not requiring ancestor resolution nor loop elimination, the DL predicate translation produces a sound, executable Prolog code. For more complex knowledge bases, such as the alcoholic example, one has to include loop elimination and ancestor resolution in the DL predicates themselves.[1] The complete and formalised transformation process is presented in [2].

As an example, the DL predicate format of the above alcoholic problem is shown below:

```
1  alcoholic(A) :- hasParent(B, A), alcoholic(B).

2  not_alcoholic(A) :- hasParent(A, B), not_alcoholic(B).
3  not_alcoholic(A) :- hasFriend(A, B), alcoholic(B).
4  not_alcoholic(A) :- hasFriend(B, A), alcoholic(B).

5  hasParent(i1, i2). hasParent(i1, i3). hasFriend(i2, i3).
```

Figure 2 shows the executable Prolog code generated for the DL predicate alcoholic, as shown in line 1 above. Lines 1 and 2 of the figure implement loop elimination and ancestor resolution, respectively. Line 3 is derived from the single DL clause of alcoholic, by extending the head and appropriate body calls with an additional argument, storing the ancestor list.

Note that an additional clause is required in the Prolog code, if the ABox contains assertions for the given unary predicate. For example, if there were assertions for alcoholic in the ABox, then the alcoholic predicate would have a fourth clause of form: alcoholic(A, _) :- alcoholic(A).

---

[1] Another option is to use an interpreter catering for loop elimination and ancestor resolution, see [12].

```
1 alcoholic(A, B) :- member(C, B), C == alcoholic(A), !, fail.
2 alcoholic(A, B) :- memberchk(not_alcoholic(A), B).
3 alcoholic(A, B) :- C = [alcoholic(A)|B], hasParent(D,A), alcoholic(D,C).
```

Fig. 2. The Prolog translation of the predicate `alcoholic`

4 Unfolding

The present section discusses an important optimisation in the translation of
DL predicates to Prolog code. This transformation uses well known partial evaluation techniques to produce Prolog code that is both more efficient and uses
simpler data structures, relying on the specific features of DL predicates.

4.1 Motivation and Goals

Recall that DL predicates contain body goals with at most two arguments, and
that only unary predicates require ancestor resolution and loop elimination.
These two execution elements rely on maintaining a list of (unary) ancestor
goals, which, in general, are not necessarily ground.

Non-ground ancestors can only be created in the early phase of execution. As
soon as a binary goal exits successfully, or a unary goal succeeds and instantiates
its argument, the query variable is instantiated and from this point onwards all
unary goal invocations, as well as the ancestor list, are ground. This is because
such goals are brought to the front of the clause body the goal ordering algorithm,
as described in [2].

The main goal of the unfolding transformation is to eliminate the phase involving non-ground ancestors. This is achieved by repeatedly unfolding clauses
with unary goals only, until an invocation of either a binary goal, or of a unary
ABox predicate, i.e. a predicate which is defined solely by ABox facts, appears
in the body. Naturally, in the process of unfolding both ancestor resolution and
loop elimination has to be taken care of.

This transformation has several advantages. Performing ancestor resolution at
compile time obviously saves runtime. What is more important, it may well be
the case that ancestor resolution can be fully eliminated for certain predicates,
thus also avoiding the need for building ancestor lists for these predicates. Even
when ancestor lists are needed, they are ground, and thus no logic variables occur
in the DLog code. This means the DL predicates can be potentially compiled to
Mercury, rather than to plain Prolog, with obvious efficiency implications. Unfolding also opens the possibility for a more efficient implementation of ancestor
storage, such as hash tables[2].

---

[2] Hash tables have already been introduced in the previous version of DLog. However
there we had to rely on the so called superset transformation, cf. Section 3, to
ensure that all unary goals are ground. By the use of unfolding, the calculation of
the superset, a potentially expensive operation, can be avoided.

4.2 An Example

Let us consider the following simple TBox:

$$\neg\text{Alcoholic} \sqsupseteq \text{Worried} \sqcap \text{Happy} \tag{1}$$

$$\text{Happy} \sqsupseteq \text{Worried} \sqcap \exists\text{hasFriend}.\top \tag{2}$$

$$\text{Worried} \sqsupseteq \neg\text{Happy} \tag{3}$$

$$\text{Worried} \sqsupseteq \exists\text{hasFriend}.\text{Alcoholic} \tag{4}$$

The DL predicates corresponding to the above TBox are shown below. Comments indicate which DL axiom gives rise to the given clause. Clauses which are contrapositives of "main" translations are shown in italics.

```
not_alcoholic(X) :-    worried(X), happy(X).                    (1)
not_alcoholic(Y) :-    hasFriend(X, Y), not_worried(X).        (4)

happy(X) :-            worried(X), hasFriend(X, _).            (2)
happy(X) :-            not_worried(X).                          (3)

worried(X) :-          not_happy(X).                           (3)
worried(X) :-          hasFriend(X, Y), alcoholic(Y).          (4)

not_worried(X) :-      happy(X), alcoholic(X).                 (1)
not_worried(X) :-      not_happy(X), hasFriend(X, _).          (2)

not_happy(X) :-        worried(X), alcoholic(X).               (1)
```

Note that the above code cannot be directly executed in Prolog. Because `alcoholic` can be called within `not_alcoholic`, the invocation of the latter has to be put on the ancestor list, while the definition of the former has to cater for ancestor resolution. The same holds for the `happy`–`not_happy` pair of predicates. Therefore, similarly to the Prolog code in Figure 2, a second argument is added to these predicates to store the ancestor list, and their definition is extended by a clause performing the ancestor resolution.

In contrast with this fairly complex translation, the unfolding optimisation results in Prolog code that does not require ancestor resolution. The *executable* Prolog code resulting from the optimisation is shown below, under the assumption that the ABox only contains facts for `hasFriend` and `worried`.

```
happy(A) :-            hasFriend(A, _).

not_alcoholic(A) :-    worried(A), hasFriend(A, _).
not_alcoholic(A) :-    hasFriend(A, A).
```

4.3 The Process of Transformation

The unfolding transformation takes a set of DL predicates and an ABox signature (the list of functors present in the ABox), and produces an equivalent set of *annotated* DL predicates, i.e. DL predicates in which each goal is associated with an explicit ancestor list. This list contains the terms that have to be added to the ancestor list, maintained by the DLog execution, when the given goal is invoked. Note that this annotation is implicit in the input DL predicates, as each goal is assumed to be annotated with its parent goal.

In general, each unary input predicate p/1 is duplicated in the output: there is an *entry* version, named p/1, and an *inner* version, named 'p$'/1. The inner version is equivalent to the original, while the entry version is a specialisation of the inner predicate, under the assumption that the ancestor list supplied to the predicate is empty. Note that this is the case when the given predicate is invoked from outside.

The entry version of a predicate is omitted from the output, if it has no clauses, and the inner version is only included if it is invoked (perhaps indirectly, through other inner predicates) from one of the entry predicates. For instance, consider the unfolded code of the example at the end of Section 4.2. This Prolog program does not contain the entry predicate not_worried/1 because all its clauses fail, when called with an empty ancestor list. Furthermore, the code contains no inner predicates, because none is invoked from the entry ones.

The transformation process consists of the following phases, discussed below in detail.

1. Equivalence transformations:
   (a) primary and secondary unfolding,
   (b) simplification
2. Specialisation of entry predicates
3. Composing the target program.

Primary unfolding is a process applied to each unary DL predicate. We start with a most general invocation of the given predicate, say p(X), and repeatedly expand the goal sequence at hand by nondeterministically replacing a unary goal with a clause body of its definition. The expansion goes on until a binary or an ABox predicate invocation appears in the sequence (recall that this ensures that ancestor lists are ground). Depending on the option settings, the expansion will continue after this minimal objective is achieved, but only for those unary goals whose argument is the same variable as that of the original goal (i.e. X in our example). Having enumerated all expansions B of goal p(X), the set of clauses 'p(X) :- B.' forms the result of the primary unfolding.

For example, let us consider the following simple program:

```
p(X) :- q(X), r(X).

q(X) :- a(X).

q(X) :- b(X,Y), p(Y).
```

The minimal primary unfolding of p/1 is the following (assuming a/1 is an ABox predicate, and ignoring annotations for the moment):

```
p(X) :- a(X), r(X).
p(X) :- b(X,Y), p(Y), r(X).
```

If multiple unary goals are available for expansion, as e.g. in q(X),r(X) after the first expansion of p(X), we select the goal whose definition is the smallest (in terms of clauses). Thus, if r/1 had only a single clause, then we would have chosen to expand the goal r(X), rather than q(X), in the above example.

In addition to using the clauses of its predicate definition, a goal can also be satisfied through ABox assertions or using ancestor resolution. Primary unfolding has to take this into account. If, for example, q/1 is present in the ABox signature, i.e. there are some ABox assertions of form q(...), then a third clause for p/1 is generated:

$$p(X) \; :- \; q_{abox}(X), \; r(X).$$

The $_{abox}$ subscript indicates here that it is not the whole q/1 predicate which is to be called, only its ABox assertions. The above clause can obviously be treated as satisfying the minimal unfolding objective.

Furthermore, if q/1 can succeed via ancestor resolution (i.e. it can be reached from not_q/1) then a fourth clause is added:

$$p(X) \; :- \; \text{'\$checkanc'}(not\_q(X)), \; r(X).$$

Here the '$checkanc' goal indicates that an ancestor check has to be performed: if not_q(X) unifies with an element on the current ancestor list, then this call should succeed; otherwise it should fail. Note that a clause containing the special '$checkanc' goal is treated as satisfying the minimal unfolding requirement, as it will always be removed at entry predicate specialisation (see below).

Also note that these additional clauses, generated during primary unfolding, correspond to the additional clauses in the Prolog translation, cf. Figure 2.

During primary unfolding an ancestor list is maintained. Each time an expansion is performed, the goal being expanded is added to the ancestor list. The goals in the unfolded clauses are annotated with their ancestor lists. In the above example this results in the following (the ancestors are shown as subscripts):

$$p(X) \; :- \; a(X), \; r_{p(X)}(X). \tag{5}$$

$$p(X) \; :- \; b(X,Y), \; p_{p(X),q(X)}(Y), \; r_{p(X)}(X). \tag{6}$$

Note that no ancestors are given for the goals a and b, as these predicate invocations access the ABox only, and so are not dependent on the ancestor list.

The ancestor list maintained during unfolding is also needed to perform the loop elimination and ancestor resolution operations. For example, assume that the predicate q/1 has a third clause: 'q(X) :- p(X).' When unfolding this clause within p/1, we detect that its body, p(X), is bound to fail, because of loop elimination. Correspondingly, in spite of the third clause for q/1, the unfolded p/1 will still contain the clauses (5) and (6) only.

Similarly, if the third clause added to q/1 is 'q(X) :- not_p(X).', then primary unfolding will determine that a successful ancestor resolution can be applied at this point. Thus the unfolded p/1 is extended with a third clause:

$$p(X) \; :- \; r_{p(X)}(X). \tag{7}$$

Note that both (5) and (6) are consequences of the above clause. This is detected in the program simplification phase, and both clauses are removed. Thus, in this last variant, the unfolded Prolog code for p/1 contains a single clause only, (7). Primary unfolding is performed only once, at the beginning of the optimisation.

Secondary unfolding is the expansion of a unary goal in a unary clause, where the goal argument is different from the head variable. We apply secondary unfolding only in the deterministic case. This means that secondary unfolding is applicable to $q_{Ancs}(Y)$ if:

- q/1 cannot succeed via ancestor resolution, has no ABox clauses, but does have a *single* TBox clause, and, furthermore, the Ancs ancestor list has no member with the functor q/1, (i.e. we are not inside another primary or secondary unfolding for q/1); or
- q/1 cannot succeed via ancestor resolution, has no TBox clauses, but does have ABox clauses; or
- q/1 has no TBox and no ABox clauses, but it can succeed via ancestor resolution.

In the first case the goal $q_{Ancs}(Y)$ is expanded to the body of the single clause of predicate q/1. In the second case the goal is replaced by $q_{abox}(Y)$. Finally, in the third case, the goal in question is replaced by '$checkanc'(not_q(Y)), provided no member of the ancestor list Ancs has the functor not_q/1. Otherwise, if Ancs has a member not_q(Z)[3], then we still have two cases. Let p/1 denote the functor of the predicate in which the given invocation of q/1 is found. If p/1 cannot be reached from not_q/1, then the goal can only succeed if Y and Z are the same. Therefore the goal is replaced by the unification Y = Z. Otherwise, a goal '$checkanc'(not_q(Y), not_q(Z)) is generated, whose task is either to unify its two arguments, or to unify the first argument with a member of the current ancestor list.

The main purpose of secondary unfolding is to clarify the ancestor resolution dependencies in the program. When the goal in question succeeds through the ABox, it becomes clear that it does not need the ancestor list argument. Similarly, if the third case is resolved through the unification of two variables, the ancestor list argument becomes unnecessary.

Secondary unfolding is first performed together with primary unfolding, but it is then repeated, possibly several times, within program simplification.

Program simplification is the phase of the transformation where redundancies are removed. There are three basic simplifications:

- removal of a group of goals posing a constraint which is *weaker* than some other group of goals in the same clause body,
- removal of a clause whose body poses a *stronger* constraint than some other body in the same predicate,
- removal of unnecessary ancestor annotations.

The essence of the first two simplifications is best illustrated with an example. Consider a clause body containing the following two groups of goals:

---

[3] Each functor can occur only once on an Ancs ancestor list, because nested unfolding of the same predicate is disallowed, cf. the first case of secondary unfolding.

b(X, Y), q(Y) and b(X, Z), q(Z), r(Z).

Assuming that variables Y and Z do not occur elsewhere, we can notice that
the first group of goals poses a *weaker* constraint than the second group, and
therefore the first group is unnecessary. For the same reason, if the above two
goal groups occur as complete clause bodies within the same predicate, then the
clause with the second, stronger constraint will be removed.

Regarding the third simplification, let us note that a term p(X) is included in
the ancestor annotation of a goal q(Y) for the purpose of being put on the ancestor list of q. However, there is no need to include p(X) in the ancestor list of q if
there are no goals reachable from within q that may make use of this ancestor (i.e.
goals invoking the predicate not_p/1 or being of form '$checkanc'(p(_)...)).
Note also that there are several optimisations which result in the removal of goals
and clauses. This means that even if p(X) was considered a necessary ancestor
at an earlier stage, it may become superfluous later, when no more goals making
use of it are reachable from q. To cater for this, simplifications and secondary
unfolding are performed repeatedly, until a fixpoint is reached. At this point the
first phase, that of equivalence transformations, is completed.

Specialisation of entry predicates is the second phase. Here we specialise the
output of phase 1 under the assumption that the ancestor list of the predicate
is empty (which is the case for entry predicates). Although the optimisation is
driven by this assumption, we keep track of the functors whose absence from the
ancestor list is really needed for the given optimisation to work. If the optimised
entry version of p/1 is not guaranteed to work correctly for an invocation where
q(_) is present on p/1's ancestor list, p/1 is said to be *sensitive* to q/1. For each
predicate, we keep track of the predicate functors it is sensitive to.

We start the phase by removing all clauses that contain a '$checkanc'/1
or '$checkanc'/2 goal. Obviously, when the enclosing predicate is called with
an empty ancestor list, these goals will fail. Whenever we remove a clause of
a predicate p/1, because of the presence of a '$checkanc'(q(_)...) goal, we
note that p/1 is sensitive to q/1.

When clauses are removed, some predicates may become empty. If such a
predicate, say r/1, has no ABox clauses either, it will always fail, unless called
with a goal in its ancestor list to which it is sensitive. Consequently, if a clause C
of another predicate t/1 calls r_{Ancs}(Y), where Ancs does not contain any goals
to which r/1 is sensitive, then C can be removed. Note that at the same time
t/1 inherits the sensitivity of r/1, i.e. it becomes sensitive to all the predicates
r/1 is sensitive to. This process is continued until a fixpoint is reached.

The next task of this phase is the identification of the *query predicates*, i.e.
non-recursive predicates which need no ancestor resolution at all. A query predicate can only call ABox predicates and query predicates. Thus a list of query
predicates is built, again iteratively, until a fixpoint is reached. Note that we
assign a cumulated sensitivity to each query predicate, which is the union of
its own sensitivity and the sensitivities of any predicates it calls, directly or
indirectly. This will be used in the next, final phase.

Composing the target program means putting together the entry predicates, as produced by phase 2, with inner predicates, which are the output of phase 1. More precisely, the set of inner predicates is obtained by renaming: p/1 becomes 'p$'/1. Note that all goals in the entry predicate bodies also undergo this renaming, as do the terms on the ancestor lists.

Next, as the final optimisation, we revert some goals to call the entry, rather than the inner version. Namely, if p/1 is a query predicate, which is called by a goal in a context where none of the functors of the cumulated sensitivity of p/1 can appear on the ancestor list of the goal, then this invocation can call the entry version of p/1, instead of its renamed, inner version.

Having performed this optimisation we can remove those inner predicates which are never called.

Status of the implementation. The unfold optimisation has been implemented and is being integrated into the DLog system. At present we are capable of executing queries for those knowledge bases whose optimised form consists of query predicates only. This is the case, for example, for the LUBM test suite; its performance is evaluated in Section 6.

5   DLog Server Architecture

We have extended the DLog implementation, as described in [2], into a server architecture which supports multiple interfaces such as DIG, OWL, etc., and is capable of operating in a server mode, as required by popular tools such as the Protégé ontology editor. DLog was originally developed in SICStus Prolog, and has been recently ported to the open source SWI Prolog.

The general architecture of the DLog system is shown in Figure 3. Here, the rectangles with rounded corners represent the modules of the DLog system. The logger and configuration modules, used by all other modules, are not shown in the figure. The configuration module manages both global settings (such as server ports), and knowledge base specific settings (such as the selection of optimisations to use). The modular structure of the DLog system makes implementing new features (such as new interfaces) fairly easy.

The system provides a console interface to access all features locally, and server interfaces for other applications (for example, the DIG interface [13] used by Protégé). The input arriving from these sources may contain TBox axioms, ABox assertions, queries, or control messages (e.g. creating a new database or setting system parameters). After transforming the input to an internal representation, the interfaces pass it to the knowledge base manager, which executes the command. The system can manage multiple knowledge bases simultaneously.

The *ABox translator* module processes the *ABox*, which either contains the assertions themselves, or the description of how to access the databases containing the assertions. It produces *ABox code*, which is a Prolog module containing either the assertions themselves or the appropriate database access predicates. The ABox translator also generates the signature of the ABox, as required by the *TBox translator*. The TBox axioms are first processed by the DL translator

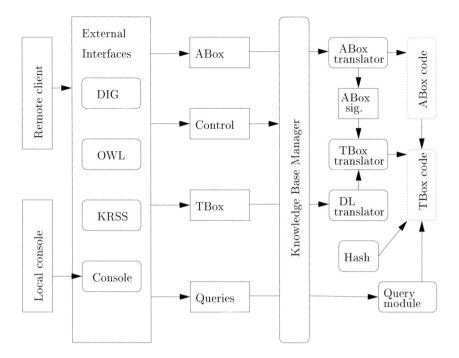

Fig. 3. The architecture of the DLog system

module, which transforms the DL formulae to a set of DL clauses [11]. The results are passed on to the TBox translator module which generates the *TBox code*, a Prolog program that can be directly executed to answer instance check and instance retrieval queries. The queries are executed by the *Query module* by using this program. The Prolog program generated as *TBox code* relies on the *Hash* module, which implements a hash table in C, to speed up loop elimination and ancestor resolution.

6   Evaluation

We have compared our system with three state-of-the-art ABox reasoners: RacerPro 1.9.0, Pellet 1.5.0, and the latest version of KAON2 (August 2007). For the benchmark we have used publicly available benchmark ontologies (LUBM and VICODI), as well as the ontology corresponding to the Iocaste problem introduced in [2]. The tests were performed on a Fujitsu-Siemens S7020 laptop with 1.25GB memory.

A sample of the test results is presented in Table 1. Here the values are given in seconds and dash (-) indicates a timeout of 600 seconds. For the LUBM test cases we show the DLog execution with the unfolding optimisation turned off and on (the latter is denoted by the UF suffix). The fastest total time in each

Table 1. Sample results of performance evaluation

Test		Iocaste10	Iocaste1000	LUBM1	LUBM1UF	LUBM4	LUBM4UF	VICODI
DLog	load	0.07	0.33	6.96	7.06	21.34	21.44	8.61
	runtime	0.00	0.01	0.26	0.23	1.32	1.10	0.05
	total	**0.07**	**0.34**	**7.22**	7.29	**22.66**	22.54	8.66
KAON2	load	0.45	-	6.56	N/A	28.73	N/A	5.88
	runtime	0.72	-	0.70	N/A	1.69	N/A	0.36
	total	1.17	-	7.26	N/A	30.42	N/A	**6.24**
RacerPro	load	0.01	0.51	24.28	N/A	-	N/A	34.96
	runtime	0.07	1.68	117.89	N/A	-	N/A	76.48
	total	0.08	2.19	142.17	N/A	-	N/A	111.44
Pellet	load	1.27	2.19	16.76	N/A	-	N/A	-
	runtime	0.19	456.40	31.93	N/A	-	N/A	-
	total	1.46	458.58	48.69	N/A	-	N/A	-

column is set in boldface (except for the results with unfolding). For detailed performance evaluation, including tests with ABoxes stored in databases, see [2].

We found that the larger the ABox, the better DLog performs compared to its peers. Our implementation of unfolding, still in its prototype stage produces 10-15% speed-up at runtime, with a constant (approx. 0.1 sec) cost at load time, which we believe is very promising.

7   Conclusions

In this paper we have presented the Description Logic reasoning system DLog. Unlike the traditional Tableau based approach, DLog determines the instances of a given $\mathcal{SHIQ}$ concept by transforming the knowledge base into a Prolog program. This technique allows us to use top-down query execution and to store the content of the ABox externally in a database, something which is essential when large amounts of data are involved.

Following an overview of other optimisation techniques we presented the newly introduced unfolding optimisation. This is basically a partial evaluation technique used to unfold clauses containing no binary literals. As a result we can obtain programs where we no longer need to cater for executing unary predicates with uninstantiated arguments (except for the outermost query predicate).

We have compared DLog with the best available ABox reasoning systems. From the test results we can conclude that in all of the scenarios DLog is significantly faster than traditional reasoning systems.

As an overall conclusion, we believe that our results are very promising and clearly show that Description Logic is an interesting application field for Prolog and logic programming.

Acknowledgements

The authors acknowledge the support of the Hungarian NKFP programme for the SINTAGMA project under grant no. 2/052/2004. We are also grateful to Tamás Benkő and the anonymous reviewers for their comments on earlier versions of the paper. Thanks are due to Zsolt Zombori for his work [11] on the design and implementation of critical components of the DLog system.

References

1. Motik, B.: Reasoning in Description Logics using Resolution and Deductive Databases. Ph.D thesis, Universität Karlsruhe, Karlsruhe, Germany (2006)
2. Lukácsy, G., Szeredi, P.: Efficient description logic reasoning in Prolog: the DLog system. Technical report, Budapest University of Technology and Economics, Theory and Practice of Logic Programming (submitted, 2008), http://sintagma.szit.bme.hu/lukacsy/publikaciok/dlog_tplp.pdf
3. Baader, F., Nutt, W.: Basic description logics. In: Baader, F., Calvanese, D., McGuinness, D.L., Nardi, D., Patel-Schneider, P.F. (eds.) Description Logic Handbook. Cambridge University Press, Cambridge (2003)
4. Haarslev, V., Möller, R.: Optimization techniques for retrieving resources described in OWL/RDF documents: First results. In: Proc. KR 2004, Whistler, BC, Canada, June 2-5, 2004, pp. 163–173 (2004)
5. Hustadt, U., Motik, B., Sattler, U.: Reasoning for Description Logics around SHIQ in a resolution framework. Technical report, FZI, Karlsruhe (2004)
6. Grosof, B.N., Horrocks, I., Volz, R., Decker, S.: Description logic programs: Combining logic programs with description logic. In: Proc. of WWW 2003, pp. 48–57. ACM, New York (2003)
7. Hustadt, U., Motik, B., Sattler, U.: Data complexity of reasoning in very expressive description logics. In: Proceedings of IJCAI 2005, pp. 466–471 (2005)
8. Samuel, K., Obrst, L., Stoutenburg, S., Fox, K., Franklin, P., Johnson, A., Laskey, K.J., Nichols, D., Lopez, S., Peterson, J.: Translating OWL and Semantic Web Rules into Prolog: Moving toward Description Logic Programs. TPLP 8(3), 301–322 (2008)
9. Motik, B., Rosati, R.: A Faithful Integration of Description Logics with Logic Programming. In: Veloso, M.M. (ed.) Proc. of the 20th Int. Joint Conference on Artificial Intelligence (IJCAI 2007), Hyderabad, India, pp. 477–482. Morgan Kaufmann Publishers, San Francisco (2007)
10. Stickel, M.E.: A Prolog technology theorem prover: a new exposition and implementation in Prolog. Theoretical Computer Science 104(1), 109–128 (1992)
11. Zombori, Z.: Efficient two-phase data reasoning for Description Logics. In: Proceedings of the IFIP International Conference on Artificial Intelligence, Milan, Italy (2008), http://www.cs.bme.hu/~zombori/BME/dlog/dl_reasoning.pdf
12. Nagy, Z., Lukácsy, G., Szeredi, P.: Translating description logic queries to Prolog. In: Van Hentenryck, P. (ed.) PADL 2006. LNCS, vol. 3819, pp. 168–182. Springer, Heidelberg (2005)
13. Bechhofer, S.: The DIG interface (2006), http://dig.cs.manchester.ac.uk/

Resource Management Policy Handling Multiple Use-Cases in MPSoC Platforms Using Constraint Programming

Luca Benini[1], Davide Bertozzi[2], and Michela Milano[1]

[1] DEIS, University of Bologna
V.le Risorgimento 2, 40136, Bologna, Italy
{luca.benini, michela.milano}@unibo.it
[2] Dipartimento di Ingegneria, University of Ferrara
V. Saragat 1, 41100, Ferrara, Italy
dbertozzi@ing.unife.it

Abstract. Multi-processor system-on-chip (MPSoC) technology is finding widespread application in the embedded system domain, like in cell phones, automotive control units or avionics. Once deployed in field, these devices always run the same set of applications, in a well-characterized context. It is therefore possible to spend a large amount of time for off-line software optimization and then deploy the results on the field. Each possible set of applications that can be active simultaneously in an MPSoC platform leads to a different use-case that the system has to be verified and tested for. Above all, smooth switching between use-cases falls within the scope of the resource manager, since users should not experience artifacts or delays when a transition between any two consecutive use-cases takes place. In this paper, we propose a semi-static approach to the resource management problem, where the allocation and scheduling solutions for the tasks in each use-case are computed off-line via a Logic Based Benders Decomposition approach using Constraint Programming and stored for use in run-time mapping decisions. The solutions are logically organized in a lattice, so that the transition costs between any two consecutive use-cases can be bound. The resulting framework exhibits both a high level of flexibility and orders of magnitude speed ups w.r.t. monolithic approaches that do not exploit decomposition.

1 Introduction

The ever increasing hardware/software parallelism of digital integrated systems raises new challenges for optimization techniques in the field of electronic design automation. In essence, applications are increasingly developed as a set of concurrent tasks executed onto an hardware platform consisting of parallel computation units [2]. This paradigm is at the core of Multi-Processor System-on-Chip (MPSoC) technology.

Mapping several tens or even hundreds of tasks onto a parallel hardware architecture has been faced either via fast heuristic algorithms [15] or exact approaches [14,18,19,8]. The former ones provide very limited or no information on the distance between the best computed solution and the optimal one, and sometimes they even fail to find existing feasible solutions. In contrast, the latter ones provide the optimal solution but exhibit

M. Garcia de la Banda and E. Pontelli (Eds.): ICLP 2008, LNCS 5366, pp. 470–484, 2008.
© Springer-Verlag Berlin Heidelberg 2008

exponential worst case complexity. The effort in developing exact methods is to devise algorithms that are efficient in practice.

This paper moves a significant step further with respect to previous work. In fact, here we consider that in state-of-the-art MPSoC platforms multiple applications with different performance requirements and resource utilization needs might run in parallel [5]. Even focusing on a single application, there are a number of execution modes associated with the different user-tunable options (multiple resolution video processing capabilities, multiple video recording features [3,4]). This leads to the proliferation of possible use-cases (or compound modes) that the system has to be verified and tested for [1].

The number of active applications in each compound mode depends on the application domain and on the computation power provided by the underlying hardware platforms. In high-end modern television platforms, up to 60 applications can run simultaneously, corresponding to an order of 2^{60} possible use cases. No mature methodology can handle even the design-time analysis of such a huge use-case space. Dynamic resource management schemes are used in practice in these platforms [9,7], which take purely on-line allocation and scheduling decisions. Unfortunately, these approaches do not provide any guarantee on optimal allocation of system resources, hence the system must be significantly over-designed, with undesirable cost implications.

In low-end MPSoC platforms, from a couple up to a dozen of active applications might be running in parallel in each compound mode. For instance, a mobile phone should be able to run concurrent applications such as listening to MP3 music, sending an sms and downloading some Java applications in the background [10]. Moreover, 4 categories of use-cases were identified for ambient intelligence in [11].

Many critical challenges still have to be addressed by system designers when developing admission control and resource management policies for their MPSoCs. Smooth switching between use-cases has to be enforced, so that users do not experience any noticeable artifacts or delays when a transition between any two consecutive use-cases takes place. On the other hand, the higher the mode switching overhead to reconfigure the system and adapt it to the new working conditions, the higher the efficiency of the system in the new execution scenario. Finally, since the number of use-cases is exponential in the number of applications in the system, finding a design-time mapping of applications on the processors for each use-case requires computation-efficient optimization engines.

This paper proposes a semi-static approach to the resource management problem for low- to medium-end MPSoC platforms. We model applications with exposed task level parallelism as generic task graphs, and compute off-line optimal allocations and schedules for each use-case. The allocation and scheduling is faced using a Logic Based Benders Decomposition approach based on Constraint Programming achieving orders of magnitude speed ups with respect to monolithic approaches using either Constraint Programming or Integer Programming [19]. Computed system configurations are stored for use in run-time mapping decisions. Our approach features two basic innovations with respect to previous work.

First, we assume a target MPSoC platform supporting run-time migration of tasks from their native execution processor to a destination one featuring a lower workload.

This feature provides additional degrees of freedom for system reconfiguration during use-case switchings. This however complicates the resource management strategy and the associated optimization problem, which must trade-off the migration cost with the efficiency of the new execution scenario.

Second, we do not compute task allocations and schedules for each use-case in isolation, but pose a bound on the transition cost to the next possible use-cases. This is accomplished by logically organizing use-case specific mapping problems in a lattice. The lattice can be built around the critical use-cases that absolutely require optimal system configuration for their execution. Depending on system requirements, they might be the worst case execution scenario where all applications are active or the most frequent use-cases.

2   Logic Based Benders Decomposition

The technique we use in this paper is derived from a method, known in Operations Research as Benders Decomposition [16], and refined by [17] with the name of Logic-based Benders Decomposition. The classical Benders Decomposition method decomposes a problem into two loosely connected subproblems. It enumerates values for the connecting variables. For each set of values enumerated, it solves the subproblem that results from fixing the connecting variables to these values. Solution of the subproblem generates a Benders cut that the connecting variables must satisfy in all subsequent solutions enumerated. The process converges providing the optimal solution of the problem overall. The classical Benders approach, however, requires that the subproblem be a continuous linear or nonlinear programming problem. Scheduling is a combinatorial problem that has no practical linear or nonlinear programming model. Therefore, the Benders decomposition idea can be extended to a logic-based form (Logic Based Benders Decomposition - LBBD) that accommodates an arbitrary subproblem, such as a discrete scheduling problem. More formally, as introduced in [17], a problem can be written as

$$\min f(y) \tag{1}$$
$$s.t \; p_i(y) \quad i \in I_1 \; \text{Master Problem Constraints} \tag{2}$$
$$g_i(x) \quad i \in I_2 \; \text{Subproblem Constraints} \tag{3}$$
$$q_i(y) \rightarrow h_i(x) \quad i \in I_3 \; \text{Conditional Constraints} \tag{4}$$
$$y \in Y \; \text{Master Problem Variables} \tag{5}$$
$$x_j \in D_i \; \text{Subproblem Variables} \tag{6}$$

We have master problem constraints, subproblem constraints and conditional constraints linking the two models. If we solve the master problem to optimality, we obtain values for variables y in I_1, namely $\bar{y}$ and the remaining problem is a feasibility problem:

$$g_i(x) \; i \in I_2 \; \text{Subproblem Constraints} \tag{7}$$
$$q_i(\bar{y}) \rightarrow h_i(x) \; i \in I_3 \; \text{Conditional Constraints} \tag{8}$$
$$x_j \in D_i \; \text{Subproblem Variables} \tag{9}$$

We can add to this problem a secondary objective function, say $f_1(x)$ to discriminate among feasible solutions. If the problem is infeasible, a Benders cut $B_y(y)$ is created constraining variables y.

In practice, to avoid the generation of master problem solutions that are trivially infeasible for the subproblem, it is worth adding a relaxation of the subproblem to the master problem.

Deciding to use the LBBD to solve a combinatorial optimization problem implies a number of design choices that strongly affect the overall performance of the algorithm. Design choices are:

– how to decompose the problem, i.e., which constraints are part of the master problem and which instead are part of the subproblem;
– which technique and which model to chose for each component
– which Benders cuts to use, establishing the interaction between the master and the subproblem;
– which relaxation to use so as to avoid the generation of trivially infeasible solutions in the master problem.

3   Migration-Enabled MPSoC Architecture and Use-Cases

The resource management strategy proposed in this work targets the MPSoC architecture template illustrated in Fig. 1, which matches several recently proposed industrial MPSoC platforms [12]. It consists of a configurable number of processor cores. Each processor core has its own private memory which can be accessed in a contention-free regime. It can be used to store task code and private data, as well as to store communication queues between tasks mapped on the same processor. In contrast, the processor cores compete to access the system shared memory, which serves as the mailbox for inter-processor communication or to store global data structures. The system interconnect can be a shared bus, in case the private memories are local to their processors, or a crossbar where each private memory resides on a separate branch. This way, communication parallelism can take place.

Applications for this kind of systems are represented as directed acyclic task graphs where nodes represent application functional blocks and arcs are data-dependencies due to communication and synchronization. We suppose we have a number of task graphs representing single applications that might be active at the samne time on the target platform.

In principle, every possible combination of applications (use-case) can be optimized in isolation. Allocation of tasks to processors, memory requirements to memory slots and communication requirements to system interconnects is performed along with a schedule of the overall use-case. The objective function that we consider in this paper is the communication cost. In practice, however, the optimization of each use-case is not independent from the others. The efficient execution of the new scenario might in fact require background tasks (those that remain active in two consecutive use-cases) to be redistributed throughout the system so to efficiently allocate newly activated tasks and optimally execute the new global task set. This can be achieved by means of a

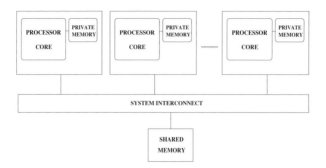

Fig. 1. Reference MPSoC platform

task migration mechanism, provided the associated transition cost remains within pre-defined bounds. In fact, a task which migrates from one core to another one needs to be temporarily suspended. Moreover, a migration event induces a traffic peak on the bus, which might impair execution quality of other running tasks. These fluctuations need to be controlled not to significantly impact user-perceived performance.

Task migration has been traditionally used in computer clusters. Its feasibility in the context of performance sensitive and power constrained MPSoCs has been proved by [13]. The migration software support considered in this paper is based on the same principles and implementation.

4   Handling Multiple Use-Cases

In the context of multiple use-cases, we have to find the optimal allocation and scheduling for each of them. The aim is not to consider each use-case in isolation, but to place them all in a lattice where every transition between use-cases has a bounded migration cost. The purpose is on one hand to meet migration cost bound for the entire life time of the system, and to obtain on the other hand a flexible and reliable design methodology.

A use-case is composed by a number of task graphs. Each task graph g has a number of tasks NT_g. Each task t has memory requirement mem_t, a state $state_t$ that should be possibly migrated during use-case transitions, a communication requirement with the preceding task com_t and a duration dur_t, including the time to acquire input data, for executing and for writing output data. Each task graph has an associated deadline. In this paper we consider pipelined task graphs where communicating tasks are those with consecutive indexes. In addition we consider the pipeline at working rate. Therefore, we always consider a number of pipeline iterations equal to the number of tasks in the pipeline.

The problem we face is to allocate tasks to processors, memory requirement to storage devices and schedule the overall application so as to minimize the communication cost (bus utilization) for each use case and have bounded migration cost transitions between use cases.

Let us consider a simple example. Suppose we have an MPSoC platform with three processors running at 400 MHz, three 500 KB private memories, and a 1 MB shared

Table 1. Task requirement of task graph A

t	t_0^A	t_1^A	t_2^A	t_3^A	t_4^A	t_5^A	t_6^A	t_7^A
dur_t	3.0	2.5	1.0	1.0	2.0	0.65	1.5	1.0
$state_t$	50	40	100	50	20	10	50	40
mem_t	20	80	30	150	30	110	40	10
com_t	0	35	60	20	30	20	10	30

Table 2. Task requirement of task graph B

t	t_0^B	t_1^B	t_2^B	t_3^B	t_4^B
dur_t	8.0	6.0	9.0	7.0	8.0
$state_t$	10	10	30	20	10
mem_t	10	50	30	30	20
com_t	0	30	50	10	40

Table 3. Task requirement of task graph C

t	t_0^C	t_1^C	t_2^C	t_3^C	t_4^C	t_5^C
dur_t	0.9	1.6	0.4	0.5	0.8	0.7
$state_t$	10	10	30	20	30	15
mem_t	10	50	30	30	15	20
com_t	0	30	50	10	40	20

memory divided in 3 mailboxes (333 KB each). The real time constraint for all task graphs be 33 ms. We have three pipelined task graphs, A, B and C. A contains 8 tasks, B 5 tasks, while C has 6 tasks. In tables 1, 2 and 3 we model their requirements (durations are in milliseconds, all other values in KB).

The optimal mapping for task graph A in isolation (leading to a feasible schedule) is the following: from t_0^A to t_4^A on one processor (say P1), and t_5^A, t_6^A and t_7^A on a second processor (say P2). Clearly, mapping all tasks on a single processor is infeasible for the deadline constraint. The notation we use to express this solution is the following $Sol_A = [\{t_0^A, t_1^A, t_2^A, t_3^A, t_4^A\}, \{t_5^A, t_6^A, t_7^A\}]$. Note that the allocation of groups of tasks to processor is subject to permutation symmetries. In this mapping, the communication cost of the task graph A is 320. In fact, t_4^A and t_5^A communicate with a cost of 20 that should be multiplied by the number of pipeline iterations (8) equal to the number of tasks in the task graph and multiplied by 2 for the writing and reading activities.

The optimal mapping for task graph B in isolation is the following: t_0^B, t_1^B and t_2^B on one processor (say P1), t_3^B and t_4^B on a second processor (say P2), i.e. $Sol_B = [\{t_0^B, t_1^B, t_2^B\}, \{t_3^B, t_4^B\}]$. In this mapping, the communication cost of the task graph B is 100.

The optimal solution for task graph C maps all tasks on a single processor with zero communication cost.

If more than one use-case can be active at the same time, we cannot simply optimize single task graphs in isolation, but we have to take into account all their combinations.

One possibility, explained in this example, is to start optimizing the maximum load use-case where all three task graphs are running at the same time. The optimal solution for use-case ABC is

$$Sol_{ABC} = [\{t_0^A, t_5^A, t_2^B, t_4^B, t_5^C\}, \{t_1^A, t_2^A, t_6^A, t_7^A, t_0^B, t_3^B, t_1^C, t_3^C\}, \{t_3^A, t_4^A, t_1^B, t_0^C, t_2^C, t_4^C\}]$$

with a communication cost of 4460. Starting from the optimal mapping for ABC, we can compute all transitions if one application completes its execution and shuts down, i.e., transitions from ABC to AB, to AC and to BC. Again, starting from each configuration with two task graphs, we can compute the transitions when one task graph is deactivated, i.e., transitions to use-cases A, B and C. At each transition, we compute the optimal mapping for the new system configuration while bounding the switching (migration) cost with respect to the old configuration. The migration cost is obtained by summing the amount of data (the *state* of each task) to be migrated between the two configurations.

It is worth noting for allocating and scheduling task graph A we have to consider two transitions: one from AB and one from AC. It is often the case that we obtain two different mappings for A, but in order to save memory for the storage of off-line computed mappings, we would like to obtain the same mapping for A by switching from both AB and AC. To achieve this, in the problem formulation for computing the optimal mapping for A we have two migration cost bounds: one bounding the cost for switching from A to AB and the second bounding the cost from A to AC.

We therefore obtain a lattice. The lattice we build has a structure of 7 nodes corresponding to all possible use cases (configuration of task graphs running on the

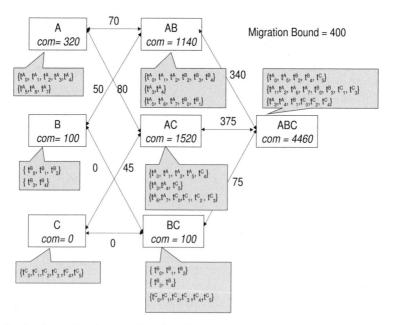

Fig. 2. Lattice for a migration cost bound of 400kB. For each node, the optimal mapping is reported. Migration costs are reported on each transition edge.

Table 4. Communication costs in lattice nodes when varying the migration cost bound

MB	ABC	AB	AC	BC	A	B	C
0	4460	2660	3160	3100	1360	1300	1800
50	4460	1760	2080	940	1040	100	240
100	4460	1760	1720	100	1040	100	120
200	4460	1460	1830	100	880	100	0
300	4460	1300	1830	100	800	100	0
400	4460	1140	1520	100	320	100	0

Table 5. Migration costs for use-case switchings (lattice arcs) for different migration cost bounds

MB	ABC → AB	ABC → AC	ABC → BC	AB → A	AB → B	BC → B	BC → C	AC → A	AC → C
0	0	0	0	0	0	0	0	0	0
50	30	50	40	10	10	0	20	10	40
100	30	80	75	10	10	0	50	10	65
200	180	145	75	80	70	0	0	70	45
300	230	145	75	220	80	0	0	300	45
400	340	375	75	70	50	0	0	80	45

architecture). In Fig. 2 we show the lattice obtained when the migration cost bound on all arcs is 400 kB. In this case, the cost bound is large enough to obtain, for each node, the optimal mapping that allows the system to best execute that use-case. Even augmenting the cost bound to 500 or 1000 KB, the lattice would not change.

The opposite holds when we have a zero migration cost bound. We basically have a lattice where transitions among nodes leave the background tasks (common to the new use-case) unchanged, i.e., no migration events are triggered. Clearly, we have solutions for intermediate migration cost bounds. For lack of space we do not report them in pictures with the corresponding mappings, but we only report communication and migration costs in the tables 4 and 5. We show in table 4 different communication costs we obtain for lattice nodes when decreasing the bound on the migration cost, referred in the table as MB. In table 5 we report the migration cost for nodes transitions in the above mentioned lattice.

The total number of optimization problems, and consequently the total number of nodes in the lattice, is bound to $\sum_{i=1}^{n} \binom{n}{i} = 2^n$ where n is the overall number of task graphs. It is indeed a large number, but for large n we could decide to reach only a limited subset of possible configurations (e.g., the mission-critical use-cases, those needing prompt activations, the most frequent ones, etc.). Moreover, the higher computation efficiency of our basic optimization engine with respect to traditional Integer Linear Programming formulations (see section 6.2) extends the range of applicability of our methodology to all reasonable low- to medium-end MPSoC platforms.

5 CP Logic Based Benders Decomposition

In this section, we present the basic block of our framework, namely, the optimization problem arising at use-case switchings. Clearly, to build the lattice we have to take into account when a new application starts or stops its execution on top of a platform where other applications are running. For instance, we have the configuration where task graphs A and B are concurrently running and task graph C starts its execution. We have to accommodate task graph C on the platform, possibly migrating tasks belonging to task graphs A and B (subject to a migration cost bound) and optimize the new run-time scenario. Since we have to solve the allocation of tasks to resources and their scheduling, we use Logic based Benders Decomposition [17] that has been proven very effective in similar problems [19]. We divide the problem into two parts: mapping (i.e., allocation) and scheduling. The two solvers are *interleaved* so as to exchange solutions and no-goods (Benders cuts) and converge to an *optimal* solution for the *problem overall*.

Activation of a New Application. We have a set S_{TG} of task graphs already running on the platform, and a new task graph G_{new} starting its execution. For sake of brevity we call $S_{new} = S_{TG} \cup \{G_{new}\}$. Each task graph g has a number of tasks NT_g. As stated in section 4, each task t has memory requirement mem_t, a state $state_t$, a communication requirement com_t and a duration dur_t. In this paper we consider pipelined task graphs, but the model can be easily extended to generic task graphs. In pipelined task graphs communicating tasks are those with consecutive indexes.

We divide the problem into two parts: mapping for the master problem and scheduling for the subproblem.

Master Problem Model. In the mapping model, we have variables T_{tp}^g (for each task graph $g \in S_{new}$, for each task $t = 1..NT_g$, and for each processor $p = 1..NP$) that take value 1 if task t of the task graph g runs on processor p; in addition, we have variables X_{tp}^g that take value 1 if task t of the task graph g runs on processor p while $t - 1$ of the same task graph g (communicating with t) does not. Basically, variables X are used to model communication.

Since we start from a platform configuration where some applications are already running, we have some additional instantiated variables $T_{t\bar{p}}^g$ (for each $t = 1..NT_g$, $p = 1..NP$, $g \in S_{TG}$) stating which processor runs each background task before the new task graph G_{new} is admitted into the system. These background tasks should possibly be migrated.

Let us now focus on the model constraints: each task should run on one and only one processor.

$$\sum_{p=1}^{P} T_{tp}^g = 1 \quad \forall g \in S_{new} \ \forall t = 1..NT_g$$

Variables T and X should be linked. Therefore we should add to the model the following constraints

$$X_{tp}^g = |T_{tp}^g - T_{t-1p}^g| \forall g \in S_{new} \ \forall t = 1..NT_g \ \forall p = 1..NP$$

We then have constraints on the memory capacity. Private memories should be able to store task data and code, as well as queues for communicating tasks running on the same processor:

$$\sum_{g \in S_{new}} \sum_{t=1}^{NT_g} mem_t * T_{tp}^g + com_t * (1 - X_{tp}^g) \leq MemCap_p \quad \forall p = 1..NP$$

We also have mailbox capacity constraints in shared memory. Each processor has a fixed size mailbox for incoming communications to tasks running onto it:

$$\sum_{g \in Snew} \sum_{t=1}^{NT_g} com_t * X_{tp}^g \leq MboxCap_p \quad \forall p = 1..NP$$

In this model we have to minimize the communication cost, i.e., the traffic on the bus due to data transfers between communicating tasks allocated on different processors, while bounding the migration cost, i.e., the traffic generated in case an already running task (i.e., belonging to S_{TG}) is migrated to more efficiently accommodate the new scenario S_{new}. The objective function is therefore

$$min \sum_{p=1}^{NP} \sum_{g \in Snew} \sum_{t=1}^{NT_g} 2 * rep * com_t * X_{tp}^g$$

The repetition number rep we consider is equal to the number of tasks of the considered task graph NT_g. The motivation is that we need to have the pipeline at working rate. The parameter 2 is due to the fact that for each communication, we have a task writing data in the mailbox and one task reading the same data from the mailbox.

The migration cost bound constraint on the overall migration cost $BoundMigr$ at use-case switching is:

$$\sum_{g \in S_{new}} \sum_{t=1}^{NT_g} state_t(1 - T_{tp}^g) \leq BoundMigr \quad \forall p = 1..NP$$

Note that, among all solutions with the minimum communication cost, with a bounded migration cost, we can choose the one that minimizes also the migration cost, as a secondary objective function.

Subproblem Relaxation. In the mapping model we need to take into account a relaxation of the scheduling problem to avoid the generation of trivially infeasible mappings. A simple but effective relaxation takes into account the sum of task durations for all tasks allocated on each processor, which should be bounded by the real time constraint of the specific processor.

$$\sum_{g \in Snew} \sum_{t=1}^{NT_g} dur_t * T_{tp}^g \leq RealTime_p \quad \forall p = 1..NP$$

In addition we have added symmetry breaking constraints that avoid the useless and time consuming search for symmetric solutions.

Subproblem model. Once the optimal allocation is decided, we start solving the scheduling problem with fixed allocations of tasks to processors and of memory requirements to storage devices. Each task t is associated to three variables $StartIN_t$, $Start_t$, $StartOUT_t$ representing respectively the starting time of the reading activity of the task, the starting time of its execution and the starting time of the writing activity of the task t. Each activity has a duration dIN_t, d_T and $dOUT_t$, respectively. The durations of the input and output activities depend on the mapping of the previous and the next task in the pipeline. If they are all allocated on the same processor, then their sum is equal to the duration used for the relaxation in the mapping model $dIN_t + d_T + dOUT_t = dur_t$, otherwise their sum is strictly greater than dur_t.

We have to express the precedence constraints among activities of the same task and of different tasks in the pipeline.

In particular, for all tasks t belonging to $g \in S_{new}$ we impose:

$StartIN_t + dIN_t = Start_t$

$Start_t + d_t = StartOUT_t$

$StartOUT_{t-1} + dOUT_{t-1} \leq StartIN_t$

Also, for all tasks running on the same processor we have to respect the real time constraint.

$$StartOUT_{last_p} + dOUT_{last_p} - StartIN_{first_p} \leq RealTime_p \; \forall p = 1..P$$

where the $last_p$ and $first_p$ index represent the last and the first task running on the processor p. All these constraints should hold for each repetition of the pipeline. In addition, we have to express the constraint that tasks on each processor should never overlap. We use the well known global constraint *cumulative* available in most commercial Constraint Programming solvers that enables the representation of limited resource capacity constraints. Its parameters are: a list of variables $[S_1, \ldots, S_n]$ representing the starting time of all activities sharing the resource, their duration $[D_1, \ldots, D_n]$, the resource consumption for each activity $[R_1, \ldots, R_n]$ and the available resource capacity C. Clearly this constraint holds if in any time step where at least one activity is running the sum of the required resource is less than or equal to the available capacity. We use this constraint on a list of start time variables $Start_p$ of all the reading, writing and executing activities allocated on processor p, on a list of their durations Dur_p, on a list of the same length of ones [1] and on the capacity of each processor, 1. We impose:

$$cumulative(Start_p, Dur_p, [1], 1)$$

Finally we model the bus with an additive model already presented and validated in [19]. Again we use the cumulative constraint working on the starting times of the reading and writing activities that use the bus, i.e., those communication between tasks allocated on different processors, $Start_{com}$, their durations Dur_{com}, their resource requirement $Band$ and the maximum bus bandwidth $MaxBand$

$$cumulative(Start_{com}, Dur_{com}, Band, MaxBand)$$

Benders Cuts. If the scheduling part is feasible, we have an optimal solution since the objective function depends only on allocation problem variables. If, instead, the scheduling is infeasible given the mapping proposed by the first model, we have to generate a no-good, i.e., a constraint, that removes a set of solutions that are provably infeasible. In particular, we select all the resources that provoke a failure, e.g., either resources whose capacity is violated, or resources that lead to a violation of the real time constraints. We call them *conflicting resources*, CR. Then, we impose that for each resource in $R \in CR$ the set of tasks ST_R allocated to R should not be reassigned to the same resource in the next iteration. For example if a conflicting resource R is a processor and ST_R the set of tasks previously allocated to it, the resulting no-good is:

$$\sum_{g \in Snew} \sum_{i \in ST_R} T_{iR}^g \leq |ST_R| - 1 \quad \forall R \in CR$$

Shut Down of an Application. We have a set S_{new} of Task Graphs already running on the platform, and a task graph G_{new} completing its execution. We should therefore find the optimal mapping and scheduling on the remaining task graphs in the set $S_{TG} = S_{new} \setminus \{G_{new}\}$. The model for this optimization problem is identical to the model used when a new task graph is activated. The only difference is that we have to replace S_{new} with S_{TG} in all constraints and in the objective function. In fact, the only tasks we want to allocate, schedule and possibly migrate are those belonging to S_{TG}.

6 Advantages of the Approach

6.1 Flexibility

The developed framework provides the needed flexibility to system designers. In the example described in section 4 we made two assumptions: the first one is that the migration cost bound is the same on each transition arc in the lattice. Indeed, we could use different cost bounds for different transitions. Suppose, in fact, that the transition between use-case A and AB is more frequent or must be faster than the transition between B and AB. We can then allow a higher cost bound for the transition between B and AB and a tighter bound for the transition A, AB.

The second assumption concerned our choice to optimize the maximum load use-case and to build the lattice around it. In this case, it is always possible to *complete* the lattice, i.e., to find optimal mappings for all configurations of task graphs subject to migration cost bounds. In fact, it is always possible to complete a lattice with zero migration cost transitions by simply removing tasks from the optimal maximum load allocation.

This is not always the case. For instance, let us build the lattice around the intermediate nodes in Fig. 2, namely use-cases AB, AC and BC. This might be desirable in order to have the system optimally running not just one use-case (e.g., the maximum load one), but many of them, such as the most frequent or mission-critical use-cases. In this case, it is not always possible to complete the lattice satisfying the migration cost bound.

Let us go through an example. In the task set considered in section 4, suppose the designer wants to optimize use-cases AB (with minimum communication cost of 1140 kB with optimal mapping), AC (min. communication cost: 1520 kB) and BC (100 kB). In addition, the designer imposes a migration cost constraint of 100 kB at each use-case switching. The problem overall ends up being over-constrained, and some constraints have to be relaxed with designer assistance.

If we relax the migration cost bound, we obtain a lattice where all transition costs fulfil the constraint except one, i.e., the transition between AC and ABC whose cost is 115. An alternative is to relax the constraint of having three system configurations that must optimally run their use-cases, while still keeping the migration bound unaltered. If optimal execution is required only for AB, there is no chance to complete the lattice anyway. Therefore, system configuration in AB should be sub-optimal. It turns out that we have two possibilities to complete the lattice: make the system optimally run BC or AC. The two approaches to constraint relaxation can be interleaved.

These choices are in charge of the designer and depend on the specific performance activation/deactivation-cost requirements for the applications at hand. This design methodology can also be easily automated by means of an interactive tool.

6.2   Scalability

In Fig. 3 we show the scalability of our approach on a single optimization problem. The tests are run on ILOG Solver and Scheduler 6.3. The number of tasks on the X axis represents the sum of the number of tasks in the task graphs we consider in the problem at hand, including reading, computation and writing activities. On the Y axis we report the computational time in seconds. Each result is the mean on 20 instances.

From this graph, we can see that in each lattice (counting as a worst case 2^n problems) we start from small problems (those containing one or few task graphs) to larger problems (corresponding to the maximum load for the system).

In addition, being this an off-line approach, we can spend quite a large amount of time in generating the complete lattice and then be able, at run time, to switch between pre-computed mappings and scheduling with minimum reconfiguration overhead.

It is worth noting that having organized the solver in a Logic Based Benders Decomposition framework speeds up the solution process of some orders of magnitudes. Neither a Constraint Programming approach nor an Integer Programming approach working on the problem overall (i.e., without decomposition) could even solve the smallest instances (50 tasks) within the timeout set to 15 minutes, while the decomposition approach takes few seconds.

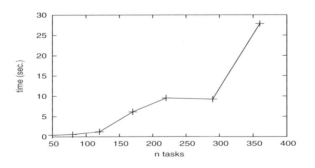

Fig. 3. Scalability analysis

7   Related Work

With the advent of MPSoC technology, a lot of effort is being devoted to mapping a single application with exposed task level parallelism onto a parallel hardware platform. Approaches range from Integer Programming modeling and solving frameworks [14,18] to heuristic search techniques [15], which are less computation demanding but also unable to provide optimality guarantees. The extension of such guarantees to a broader range of problem instances was achieved in [19,8], by leveraging an optimization engine based on Logic-based Benders Decomposition. Even though its worst case run-time is obviously exponential, it is computationally efficient in practice, dealing with instance sizes that are much larger than those that could be handled in the past by complete search algorithms. The optimization problems tackled by the above works prove not capable of capturing the complexity of resource management decisions in state-of-the-art MPSoC devices, where a number of applications could have to be executed in parallel, giving rise to *execution scenarios* or *use-cases*. The research on resource management strategies handling multiple use-cases is still in the early stage. The multi-use case mapping problem is addressed in [6] with reference to a Network on Chip (NoC) communication infrastructure. The approach is based on building a synthetic worst case use-case that includes the constraints of all the use-cases and to design and optimize the NoC based on this. Unfortunately, the worst case use-case has highly over-specified constraints leading to NoC overdesign. The work in [5] improves upon this methodology. Instead of using a synthetic worst case use-case, separate data structures are maintained for the different use-cases. Although more scalable, this approach limits only to NoC reconfiguration (core mapping across use-cases is fixed) and simply prevents such a reconfiguration during mode switching as the only way to achieve smooth switching.

When the number of use-cases becomes enormous (for instance in digital TV platforms), then composability has been proposed as a way of analysing applications in isolation while still reasoning about their overall behaviour [7]. Then, a composition function is used to compute total requirements of the system. However, this approach heavily suffers from the lack of performance predictability and requires the resource manager to impose specified utilizations or time-budgets.

8   Conclusion

In this paper we target MPSoC systems with task migration support and running multiple use-cases. We propose a semi-static approach to the dynamic resource management problem, where the allocation and scheduling solutions for the tasks in each use-case are computed off-line and stored for use in run-time mapping decisions. The solutions are logically organized in a lattice, so that the transition costs between any two consecutive use-cases can be bound.

Acknowledgement

The work described in this publication was partially supported by the PREDATOR Project funded by the European Community's 7th Framework Programme, Contract FP7-ICT-216008.

References

1. Mathys, Y., Chatelain, A.: Verification Strategy for Integration 3G Baseband SoC. In: Design and Automation Conference, pp. 7–10. ACM, New York (2003)
2. Horowitz, H., Alon, E., Patil, D., Naffziger, S., Kumar, R., Bernstein, K.: Scaling, Power, and the Future of CMOS. In: IEEE International Electron Devices Meeting, IEDM, pp. 9–15. IEEE Press, Los Alamitos (2005)
3. Philips, Nexperia PNX8550 Home Entertainment Engine (December 2003)
4. Dutta, S., Jensen, R., Rieckmann, A.: Viper: A Multiprocessor SoC for Advanced Set-Top-Box and Digital TV Systems. In: IEEE Design and Test of Computers, pp. 21–31 (2001)
5. Murali, S., Coenen, M., Radulescu, A., Goossens, K.: A Methodology for Mapping Multiple Use-Cases onto Networks on Chips. In: Design Automation and Test in Europe Conference, pp. 118–123. IEEE Press, Los Alamitos (2006)
6. Murali, S., Coenen, M., Radulescu, A., Goossens, K.: Mapping and Configuration Methods for Multi-Use-Case Networks on Chips. In: Asia and South Pacific Conference on Design Automation, pp. 146–151 (2006)
7. Kumar, A., Mesman, B., Corporaal, H., van Meerbergen, J., Yajun, H.: Global Analysis of Resource Arbitration for MPSoC. In: 9th Euromicro Conference on Digital System Design (2006)
8. Ruggiero, M., Pari, G., Guerri, A., Bertozzi, D., Milano, M., Benini, L., Andrei, A.: A Cooperative, Accurate Solving Framework for Optimal Allocation, Scheduling and Frequency Selection on Energy- Efficient MPSoCS. In: IEEE International SOC Conference (2006)
9. Moreira, O., Mol, J.D., Bekooij, M., van Meerbergen, J.: Multiprocessor Resource Allocation for Hard-Real Time Streaming with a Dynamic Job-Mix. In: IEEE Real Time on Embedded Technology and Applications Symposium, pp. 332–341 (2005)
10. Wolf, W.: The Future of Multiprocessor Systems-on-Chip. In: Design and Automation Conference, pp. 681–685. ACM Press, New York (2004)
11. Kaasinen, E., Tuomisto, T., Vaelkkynen, P.: Ambient Functionality - Use Cases. In: Joint sOc-EUSAI Conference, pp. 51–56 (2005)
12. ARM11 MPCore, http://www.arm.com/products/CPUs/ARM11MPCoreMulti processor.html
13. Bertozzi, S., Acquaviva, A., Poggiali, A., Bertozzi, D.: Supporting Task Migration in MP-SoCs: A Feasibility Study. In: Design Automation and Test in Europe Conference, pp. 15–20 (2006)
14. Prakash, S., Parker, A.: SOS: Synthesis of Application-Specific Heterogeneous Multiprocessor Systems. Journal of Parallel and Distributed Computing, 338–351 (1992)
15. Axelsson, J.: Architecture Synthesis and Partitioning of Real-Time Synthesis: a Comparison of 3 Heuristic Search Strategies. In: 5th International Workshop on Hardware/Software Codesign (CODES/CASHE 1997), pp. 161–166 (1997)
16. Benders, J.F.: Partitioning procedures for solving mixed-variables programming problems. Numerische Mathematik, 238–252 (1962)
17. Hooker, J.N., Ottosson, G.: Logic-based Benders decomposition. Mathematical Programming, 33–60 (2003)
18. Bender, A.: MILP based Task Mapping for Heterogeneous Multiprocessor Systems. In: EURO-DAC96/EURO-VHDL 1996: Conference on European Design Automation, pp. 190–197 (1996)
19. Ruggiero, M., Guerri, A., Bertozzi, D., Poletti, F., Milano, M.: Communication-Aware Allocation and Scheduling Framework for Stream-Oriented Multi-Processor Systems-on-Chip. In: Design Automation and Test in Europe Conference, pp. 3–8 (2006)

Optimization of CHR Propagation Rules

Peter Van Weert[*]

Department of Computer Science, K.U.Leuven, Belgium
Peter.VanWeert@cs.kuleuven.be

Abstract. Constraint Handling Rules (CHR) is an elegant, high-level programming language based on multi-headed, forward chaining rules. To ensure CHR propagation rules are applied at most once with the same combination of constraints, CHR implementations maintain a so-called *propagation history*. The performance impact of this history can be significant. We introduce several optimizations that, for the majority of CHR rules, eliminate this overhead. We formally prove their correctness, and evaluate their implementation in two state-of-the-art CHR systems.

1 Introduction

Constraint Handling Rules (CHR) [1,2] is a high-level committed-choice CLP language, based on multi-headed, guarded multiset rewrite rules. Originally designed for the declarative specification of constraint solvers, it is increasingly used for general purposes, in a wide range of applications. Efficient implementations exist for several host languages, including Prolog [3], Haskell, and Java [4].

An important, distinguishing feature of CHR are *propagation rules*. Unlike most rewrite rules, propagation rules do not remove the constraints matched by their head. To avoid trivial non-termination, each CHR rule is therefore applied at most once with the same combination of constraints. This requirement stems from the formal study of properties such as termination and confluence [1], and is reflected in most current CHR implementations.

To prevent reapplication, a CHR runtime system maintains a so-called *propagation history*, containing a tuple for each constraint combination that fired a rule. Efficiently implementing a propagation history is challenging. Even with the implementation techniques proposed in e.g. [5,6,7], maintaining a propagation history remains expensive. Our empirical observations reveal that the history often has a significant impact on both space and time performance. Existing literature on CHR compilation nevertheless pays only scant attention to history-related optimizations. This paper resolves this discrepancy by introducing several novel approaches to resolve history-related performance issues. We show that, for almost all CHR rules, the propagation history can be eliminated completely. We either use innovative, alternate techniques to prevent rule reapplication, or prove that reapplication has no observable effect. Experimental results confirm the relevance and effectiveness of our optimizations.

---

[*] Research Assistant of the Research Foundation – Flanders (FWO-Vlaanderen).

M. Garcia de la Banda and E. Pontelli (Eds.): ICLP 2008, LNCS 5366, pp. 485–500, 2008.
© Springer-Verlag Berlin Heidelberg 2008

Overview. Section 3 discusses *non-reactive* CHR rules—rules that are not re-considered when built-in constraints are added—and shows that their history can always be eliminated without affecting the program's operational seman-tics. More precisely, we prove that reapplication of non-reactive rules is either impossible, or that it can be prevented using a novel, more efficient technique.

Section 4 introduces the notion of *idempotence*. We prove that reapplying idempotent rules has no observable effect, and thus that their history can be eliminated as well, even if the rule is reactive. Together, the optimizations of Sections 3 and 4 cover the majority of the rules found in existing CHR programs.

We implemented the proposed optimizations in two state-of-the-art CHR im-plementations. Section 5 reports on the significant performance gains obtained. Section 6, finally, reviews some related work and concludes.

For self-containedness, we first briefly review CHR's syntax and operational semantics in Section 2. Gentler introductions are found for instance in [1,5,6].

2   Preliminaries

2.1   CHR Syntax

CHR is embedded in a host language $\mathcal{H}$. A *constraint type* c/n is denoted by a functor/arity pair; *constraints* $c(x_1, \ldots, x_n)$ are atoms constructed from these symbols. Their arguments x_i are instances of data types offered by $\mathcal{H}$. Many CHR systems support type and mode declarations for constraint arguments.

There are two classes of constraints: *built-in constraints*, solved by an under-lying constraint solver of the host language $\mathcal{H}$, and *CHR constraints*, handled by a CHR program. A CHR program $\mathcal{P}$, also called a *CHR handler*, is a sequence of CHR rules. The generic syntactic form of a CHR rule is:

$$\rho @ H_k \setminus H_r \Leftrightarrow G \mid B$$

The rule's unique *name* ρ is optional; if omitted a name is assigned implicitly. The *head* consists of two conjunctions of CHR constraints, H_k and H_r. Their conjuncts are called *occurrences* (*kept* and *removed occurrences* resp.). If H_k is empty, the rule is a *simplification rule*. If H_r is empty, it is a *propagation rule*, and '$\Rightarrow$' is used instead of '$\Leftrightarrow$'. If both are non-empty, the rule is a *simpagation* rule. The *guard* G is a conjunction of built-in constraints, the *body* B a conjunction of CHR and built-in constraints. A trivial guard 'true $\mid$' may be omitted.

Example 1. Fig. 1 shows a classic CHR handler, called LEQ. It defines a sin-gle CHR constraint, a less-than-or-equal constraint, using four CHR rules. All three kinds of rules are present. All constraint arguments are logical variables. The handler uses a built-in equality constraint =/2 (e.g. Prolog's built-in uni-fication). The first two rules remove redundant constraints. The `antisymmetry` rule replaces the CHR constraints matched by its head with a built-in equality constraint. The `transitivity` propagation rule adds implied CHR constraints.

```
reflexivity    @ leq(X, X) ⇔ true.
idempotence    @ leq(X, Y) \ leq(X, Y) ⇔ true.
antisymmetry   @ leq(X, Y), leq(Y, X) ⇔ X = Y.
transitivity   @ leq(X, Y), leq(Y, Z) ⇒ leq(X, Z).
```

Fig. 1. LEQ, a CHR program for the less-than-or-equal constraint

Head Normal Form In the Head Normal Form of a CHR program $\mathcal{P}$, denoted HNF($\mathcal{P}$), variables occur at most once in a rule's head. For instance in HNF(LEQ), the normalized form of the **transitivity** rule from Fig. 1 is:

```
transitivity @ leq(X, Y), leq(Y₁, Z) ⇒ Y = Y₁ | leq(X, Z).
```

2.2   CHR's Refined Operational Semantics

The behavior of most current CHR implementations is captured formally by the *refined operational semantics* [8], commonly denoted as ω_r. The ω_r semantics is formulated as a state transition system, in which *transition rules* define the relation between subsequent *execution states*. The version presented here follows [5,6], which is a slight refinement of the original specification [8].

Notation. Sets, multisets and sequences (ordered multisets) are defined as usual. We use $S[i]$ to denote the i'th element of a sequence S, $+\!+$ for sequence *concatenation*, and $[e|S]$ to denote $[e] +\!+ S$. The *disjoint union* of sets is defined as: $\forall X, Y, Z : X = Y \sqcup Z \leftrightarrow X = Y \cup Z \wedge Y \cap Z = \emptyset$. For a logical expression X and a set V of variables, $vars(X)$ denotes the set of *free variables*, and *constraint projection* is defined as $\pi_V(X) \leftrightarrow \exists v_1, \ldots, v_n : X$ with $\{v_1, \ldots, v_n\} = vars(X) \setminus V$.

Execution States. An execution state of ω_r is a tuple $\langle \mathbb{A}, \mathbb{S}, \mathbb{B}, \mathbb{T} \rangle_n$. The role of the *execution stack* $\mathbb{A}$ is explained below. The ω_r semantics is multiset-based. To distinguish between otherwise identical constraints, the *CHR constraint store* $\mathbb{S}$ is a set of *identified* CHR constraints, denoted $c\#i$, where each CHR constraint c is associated with a unique integer number i, called a *constraint identifier*. The projection operators CHR($c\#i$) = c and ID($c\#i$) = i are extended to sequences and sets in the obvious manner. The integer n represents the next available constraint identifier. The *built-in constraint store* $\mathbb{B}$ is a conjunction containing all built-in constraints passed to the built-in solver. Their meaning is determined by the built-in constraint theory $\mathcal{D}_{\mathcal{H}}$ (see e.g. [6] for a rigorous definition of $\mathcal{D}_{\mathcal{H}}$). The *propagation history* $\mathbb{T}$, finally, is a set of tuples, each recording a sequence of identifiers of CHR constraints that fired a rule, and the name of that rule.

Transition Rules. Fig. 2 lists the transition rules of ω_r. Execution proceeds by exhaustively applying these transitions, starting from an *initial execution state* $\langle Q, \emptyset, \text{true}, \emptyset \rangle_1$. The constraint sequence Q is called the initial *query* Q.

CHR constraints are assigned unique identifiers and added to $\mathbb{S}$ in **Activate** transitions. The execution stack $\mathbb{A}$ is a sequence used to treat constraints as procedure calls. The top-most element of $\mathbb{A}$ is called the *active constraint*. When

---

1. Solve $\langle[b|\mathbb{A}], \mathbb{S}, \mathbb{B}, \mathbb{T}\rangle_n \rightarrowtail_\mathcal{P} \langle S \mathbin{+\!\!+} \mathbb{A}, \mathbb{S}, b \wedge \mathbb{B}, \mathbb{T}\rangle_n$ if b is a built-in constraint. For the set of *reactivated constraints* $S \subseteq \mathbb{S}$, the following bounds hold: lower bound: $\forall H \subseteq \mathbb{S} : (\exists K, R : H = K \mathbin{+\!\!+} R \wedge \exists \rho \in \mathcal{P} : \neg appl(\rho, K, R, \mathbb{B}) \wedge appl(\rho, K, R, b \wedge \mathbb{B})) \rightarrow (S \cap H \neq \emptyset)$ and upper bound: $\forall c \in S : vars(c) \not\subseteq fixed(\mathbb{B})$.

---

2. Activate $\langle[c|\mathbb{A}], \mathbb{S}, \mathbb{B}, \mathbb{T}\rangle_n \rightarrowtail_\mathcal{P} \langle[c\#n : 1|\mathbb{A}], \{c\#n\} \sqcup \mathbb{S}, \mathbb{B}, \mathbb{T}\rangle_{n+1}$ if c is a CHR constraint (which has not yet been active or stored in $\mathbb{S}$).

---

3. Reactivate $\langle[c\#i|\mathbb{A}], \mathbb{S}, \mathbb{B}, \mathbb{T}\rangle_n \rightarrowtail_\mathcal{P} \langle[c\#i : 1|\mathbb{A}], \mathbb{S}, \mathbb{B}, \mathbb{T}\rangle_n$ if c is a CHR constraint (re-added to $\mathbb{A}$ by a **Solve** transition but not yet active).

---

4. Simplify $\langle[c\#i : j|\mathbb{A}], \mathbb{S}, \mathbb{B}, \mathbb{T}\rangle_n \rightarrowtail_\mathcal{P} \langle B \mathbin{+\!\!+} \mathbb{A}, K \sqcup S, \theta \wedge \mathbb{B}, \mathbb{T}'\rangle_n$ with $\mathbb{S} = \{c\#i\} \sqcup K \sqcup R_1 \sqcup R_2 \sqcup S$, if the j-th occurrence of c in $\mathcal{P}$ occurs in rule ρ, and θ is a matching substitution such that $apply(\rho, K, R_1 \mathbin{+\!\!+} [c\#i] \mathbin{+\!\!+} R_2, \mathbb{B}, \theta) = B$. Let $t = (\rho, \mathrm{ID}(K \mathbin{+\!\!+} R_1) \mathbin{+\!\!+} [i] \mathbin{+\!\!+} \mathrm{ID}(R_2))$, then $t \notin \mathbb{T}$ and $\mathbb{T}' = \mathbb{T} \cup \{t\}$.

---

5. Propagate $\langle[c\#i : j|\mathbb{A}], \mathbb{S}, \mathbb{B}, \mathbb{T}\rangle_n \rightarrowtail_\mathcal{P} \langle B \mathbin{+\!\!+} [c\#i : j|\mathbb{A}], \mathbb{S} \setminus R, \theta \wedge \mathbb{B}, \mathbb{T}'\rangle_n$ with $\mathbb{S} = \{c\#i\} \sqcup K_1 \sqcup K_2 \sqcup R \sqcup S$, if the j-th occurrence of c in $\mathcal{P}$ occurs in rule ρ, and θ is a matching substitution such that $apply(\rho, K_1 \mathbin{+\!\!+} [c\#i] \mathbin{+\!\!+} K_2, R, \mathbb{B}, \theta) = B$. Let $t = (\rho, \mathrm{ID}(K_1) \mathbin{+\!\!+} [i] \mathbin{+\!\!+} \mathrm{ID}(K_2 \mathbin{+\!\!+} R))$, then $t \notin \mathbb{T}$ and $\mathbb{T}' = \mathbb{T} \cup \{t\}$.

---

6. Drop $\langle[c\#i : j|\mathbb{A}], \mathbb{S}, \mathbb{B}, \mathbb{T}\rangle_n \rightarrowtail_\mathcal{P} \langle\mathbb{A}, \mathbb{S}, \mathbb{B}, \mathbb{T}\rangle_n$ if c has no j-th occurrence in $\mathcal{P}$.

---

7. Default $\langle[c\#i : j|\mathbb{A}], \mathbb{S}, \mathbb{B}, \mathbb{T}\rangle_n \rightarrowtail_\mathcal{P} \langle[c\#i : j + 1|\mathbb{A}], \mathbb{S}, \mathbb{B}, \mathbb{T}\rangle_n$ if the current state cannot fire any other transition.

Fig. 2. The transition rules of the refined operational semantics ω_r

active, a CHR constraint performs a search for applicable rules. The ω_r semantics specifies that occurrences in a handler are tried in a top-down, right-to-left order. To realize this order in ω_r, identified constraints on the execution stack are *occurrenced*. If an occurrenced identified CHR constraint $c\#i : j$ is active, only matches with the j'th occurrence of c's constraint type are considered. Interleaving a sequence of **Default** transitions, all applicable rules are thus fired in **Propagate** and **Simplify** transitions. A rule is applicable if the store contains matching *partner constraints* for all remaining occurrences in its head. Formally:

Definition 1. *Given a conjunction of built-in constraints $\mathbb{B}$, a rule ρ is applicable with sequences of identified CHR constraints K and R, denoted $appl(\rho, K, R, \mathbb{B})$, iff a matching substitution θ exists for which $apply(\rho, K, R, \mathbb{B}, \theta)$ is defined. The latter partial function is defined as $apply(\rho, K, R, \mathbb{B}, \theta) = B$ iff $K \cap R = \emptyset$ and, renamed apart, ρ is of form "ρ @ $H_k \setminus H_r \Leftrightarrow G \mid B$" ($H_k$ or H_r may be empty) with $\mathrm{CHR}(K) = \theta(H_k)$, $\mathrm{CHR}(R) = \theta(H_r)$, and $\mathcal{D}_\mathcal{H} \models \mathbb{B} \rightarrow \pi_{vars(\mathbb{B})}(\theta \wedge G)$.*

If the top-most element of $\mathbb{A}$ is a built-in constraint, this constraint is passed to the built-in solver in a **Solve** transition. As this may affect the entailment of guards, all CHR constraints for which additional rules might have become applicable have to be put back on the execution stack. These then cause **Reactivate** transitions to reinitiate searches for applicable rules. Constraints with fixed arguments are not reactivated, as no additional guards can become entailed.

Definition 2. *A variable v is* fixed *by constraint conjunction B, or $v \in$ fixed(B), iff $\mathcal{D}_{\mathcal{H}} \models \forall \theta ((\pi_{\{v\}}(B) \wedge \pi_{\{\theta(v)\}}(\theta(B))) \rightarrow v = \theta(v))$ for any variable renaming θ.*

When a rule fires, its body is executed. By putting the body on the activation stack, the different conjuncts of the body are activated (for CHR constraints) or solved (for built-in constraints) in a left-to-right order. Control only returns to the original active constraint *after* the body is completely executed.

Derivations. For a CHR operational semantics ω, an ω-derivation D is a (possibly infinite) sequence of ω_r states, with $D[1]$ an initial execution state for some query Q, and $D[i] \rightarrowtail_{\mathcal{P}} D[i+1]$ valid ω transitions. We use the notational abbreviation $\sigma_1 \rightarrowtail_{\mathcal{P}}^{\star} \sigma_n$ to denote a *finite* derivation $[\sigma_1, \ldots, \sigma_n]$.

3   Non-reactive Propagation Rules

Section 3.1 introduces *non-reactive CHR rules*, rules that are never matched by a reactivated constraint, and illustrates that a substantial portion of CHR rules is non-reactive. In Section 3.2, we prove that the history of certain non-reactive propagation rules can be eliminated, as CHR's operational semantics ensures these rules are never matched by the same constraint combination. For the remaining non-reactive rules, we introduce an innovative, more efficient technique to prevent rule reapplication in Section 3.3, and prove its soundness.

3.1   Introduction: From Fixed to Non-reactive CHR

Non-reactive CHR constraints are never reactivated when built-in constraints are added. Formally:

Definition 3. *A CHR constraint type c/n is* non-reactive *in a program $\mathcal{P}$ under a refined operational semantics $\omega_r^{\star}$ (ω_r or any of its refinements: see further) iff for any* **Solve** *transitions of the form $\langle [b|\mathbb{A}], \mathbb{S}, \mathbb{B}, \mathbb{T} \rangle_n \rightarrowtail_{\mathcal{P}} \langle S \mathbin{+\!\!+} \mathbb{A}, \mathbb{S}, b \wedge \mathbb{B}, \mathbb{T} \rangle_n$ in any $\omega_r^{\star}$-derivation D the set of reactivated constraints $S \subseteq \mathbb{S}$ does not contain constraints of type c/n. A rule $\rho \in \mathcal{P}$ is* non-reactive *iff all constraint types that occur in its head are non-reactive in $\mathcal{P}$.*

The simplest instances are so-called *fixed* constraints. A CHR constraint type c/n is fixed iff $vars(c) \subseteq fixed(\emptyset)$ (see Definition 2) for all constraints c of this type. Clearly, if all constraint arguments are fixed, no additional rule becomes applicable when adding built-in constraints. Which CHR constraints are fixed is derived from their mode declarations, or using static *groundness analysis* [9].

Example 2. The FIBBO handler depicted in Fig. 3, performs a bottom-up computation of all Fibonacci numbers up to a given number. The constraint declarations[1] specify that all arguments are fixed instances of the host language's **int** type (the '+' mode declaration indicates a constraint's argument is fixed).

---

[1] The syntax is inspired by that of the K.U.Leuven CHR system [3,6].

```
:- chr_constraint up_to(+int), fib(+int,+int).

up_to(U) ⇒ fib(0,1), fib(1,1).
up_to(U), fib(N - 1,M₁), fib(N,M₂) ⇒ N < U | fib(N + 1,M₁ + M₂).
```

Fig. 3. This handler, referred to as FIBBO, performs a bottom-up computation of all Fibonacci numbers up to a given number. All constraint arguments are fixed integers.

```
:- chr_constraint fib(+int,?int).

memoization  @ fib(N,M₁) \ fib(N,M₂) ⇔ M₁ = M₂.
base_case    @ fib(N,M) ⇒ N ≤ 1 | M = 1.
recursion    @ fib(N,M) ⇒ N > 1 | fib(N-1,M₁), fib(N-2,M₂), M = M₁ + M₂.
```

Fig. 4. A CHR handler that computes Fibonacci numbers using a top-down computation strategy with memoization

Under ω_r, a CHR constraint type is non-reactive iff it is fixed. The following example though shows why the class of non-reactive constraints should be larger:

Example 3. Fig. 4 contains an alternative Fibonacci handler, this time using a top-down computation strategy with memoization. The `fib/2` constraint is not fixed, and is typically called with a free (logical) variable as second argument— hence also the '?' mode declaration. Reactivating `fib/2` constraints is nevertheless pointless, as there are *no guards* constraining its second argument. Additional built-in constraints therefore never result in additional applicable rules.

All theoretical results in this section apply to non-reactive rules only. Under ω_r, however, constraints such as `fib/2` are not non-reactive. As using unbound, unguarded arguments to retrieve results is very common in CHR, a minor refinement ω_r is required to increase the practical relevance of our results.

In general, CHR constraints should only be reactivated if extra built-in constraints may cause more guards to become entailed. We therefore reintroduce the concept of *anti-monotonicity* [7,10]:

Definition 4. *A conjunction of built-in constraints B is* anti-monotone *in a set of variables V iff* $\forall B_1, B_2((\pi_{vars(B)\setminus V}(B_1 \wedge B_2) \leftrightarrow \pi_{vars(B)\setminus V}(B_1))$
$$\rightarrow ((\mathcal{D}_\mathcal{H} \not\models B_1 \rightarrow B) \rightarrow (\mathcal{D}_\mathcal{H} \not\models B_1 \wedge B_2 \rightarrow B)))$$

Definition 5. *A CHR program $\mathcal{P}$ is* anti-monotone *in the i'th argument of a CHR constraint type c/n, if and only if for every occurrence $c(x_1, \ldots, x_i, \ldots, x_n)$ in HNF($\mathcal{P}$), the guard of the corresponding rule is anti-monotone in $\{x_i\}$.*

Any CHR program is anti-monotone in both fixed and unguarded constraint arguments. Moreover, several typical built-ins are anti-monotone in their arguments. In Prolog, for instance, `var(X)` is anti-monotone in $\{X\}$. Using anti-monotonicity, we now define ω'_r, a slight refinement of ω_r[2]:

---

[2] We refer to [7, Appendix A] for a formal proof that ω'_r is indeed an instance of ω_r.

```
:- chr_constraint account(+client_id, +float), sum(+client_id, ?float).
:- chr_constraint gen(+client_id), sum(+float), get(?float).

sum_balances @  sum(C, Sum) ⇔ gen(C), get(Sum).
generate     @  gen(C), account(C,B) ⇒ sum(B).
simplify     @  sum(B₁), sum(B₂) ⇔ sum(B₁ + B₂).
retrieve     @  get(Q), gen(_), sum(Sum) ⇔ Q = Sum.
```

Fig. 5. CHR rules computing the sum of the account balances of a given client. These rules may be part of some larger CHR handler modeling a banking application.

Definition 6. *Let delay_vars$_\mathcal{P}(c)$ denote the set of variables in which $\mathcal{P}$ is not anti-monotone that occur in an (identified) CHR constraint c. Then ω'_r is obtained from ω_r by replacing the upper bound on the set of reactivated constraints S in its* **Solve** *transition with "$\forall c \in S : delay\_vars_\mathcal{P}(c) \not\subseteq fixed(\mathbb{B})$".*

Most rules in general-purpose CHR programs are non-reactive under ω'_r. Several CHR systems, including the K.U.Leuven CHR and JCHR systems [3,4], implement ω'_r. Doing so, may already improve performance considerably (see [10]). In the following two subsections, we prove that for non-reactive CHR rules the expensive maintenance of a propagation history can always be avoided.

3.2 Propagation History Elimination

Because non-reactive CHR constraints are only active once, non-reactive propagation rules often do not require a history:

Example 4. The sum/2 constraint in Fig. 5 computes the sum of a client's account balances using a common CHR programming idiom to compute *aggregates*: a (typically non-reactive) propagation rule generates a number of constraints, from which, after simplification to a single constraint, the result can be retrieved.

When the active gen/1 constraint considers the *generate* rule, it iterates over candidate account/2 partner constraints. Assuming this iteration does not contain duplicates (a property formalized shortly in Definition 8), the *generate* rule never fires with the same constraint combination under ω_r, even if no propagation history is maintained. Indeed, the *generate* rule only adds sum/1 constraints, which, as there is no get/1 constraint yet in the store (the body of the *sum_balances* rule is executed from left to right), only fire the *simplify* rule.

The history, however, is not superfluous for all non-reactive CHR rules, as shown by the following example:

Example 5. Reconsider the FIBBO handler of Fig. 3. If an up_to(U) constraint is told, the first rule propagates two fib/2 constraints. After this, the second rule propagates all required fib/2 constraints, each time with a fib/2 constraint as the active constraint. Next, control returns to the up_to(U) constraint, and advances to its second occurrence. Some mechanism is then required to prevent the second (non-reactive) propagation rule to add erroneous fib/2 constraints.

So, non-reactive propagation rules can match the same constraint combination more than once. This occurs if one or more partner constraints for an active constraint in rule ρ were added by firing ρ or some earlier rule, whilst the same constraint was already active. We say these partner constraints *observe* the corresponding occurrence of the active constraint in ρ (cf. also [9]). Formally:

Definition 7. *Let the k'th occurrence of a rule ρ's head be the j'th occurrence of constraint type c/n. Then this occurrence is* unobserved *under a refined operational semantics $\omega_r^\star$ iff for all* **Activate** *or* **Default** *transitions of the form[3]:*

$$\langle \mathbb{A}_0, \mathbb{S}, \mathbb{B}, \mathbb{T} \rangle_- \rightarrowtail_{\mathcal{P}} \langle [c\#i:j|\mathbb{A}], \mathbb{S}, \mathbb{B}, \mathbb{T} \rangle_-$$

($\mathbb{A}_0[1] = c\#i$ or $\mathbb{A}_0[1] = c\#i:j-1$) the following holds: $\forall(\rho, I) \in \mathbb{T} : I[k] \neq i$, and similarly for all transition sequences starting with a **Propagate** *transition*

$$\langle \mathbb{A}, \mathbb{S}, \mathbb{B}, \mathbb{T} \rangle_- \rightarrowtail_{\mathcal{P}} \langle B + \!\!+ \,\mathbb{A}, \mathbb{S}', \mathbb{B}', \mathbb{T}' \rangle_- \rightarrowtail_{\mathcal{P}}^\star \langle \mathbb{A}, \mathbb{S}'', \mathbb{B}'', \mathbb{T}'' \rangle_-$$

with $\mathbb{A}[1] = c\#i:j$, $\forall(\rho, I) \in \mathbb{T}'' \backslash \mathbb{T}' : I[k] \neq i$.

Let $\omega_r^\dagger$ denote the semantics obtained from ω_r' by adding the following condition to its **Propagate** and **Simplification** transitions: "*If the j'th occurrence of c is unobserved under ω_r', then $\mathbb{T}' = \mathbb{T}$*". Also, to prevent trivial reapplication in a consecutive sequence of **Propagate** transitions (see e.g. Example 4), propagation in $\omega_r^\dagger$ is defined to be *duplicate-free*:

Definition 8 (Duplicate-free Propagation). *Propagation in a refined operational semantics $\omega_r^\star$ is* duplicate-free *iff for all $\omega_r^\star$-derivations D of a CHR program $\mathcal{P}$ where the j'th occurrence of c is kept, the following holds:*

$$if \quad \begin{cases} \sigma_1 \rightarrowtail_{\mathcal{P}} \sigma_2 \rightarrowtail_{\mathcal{P}}^\star \sigma_1' \rightarrowtail_{\mathcal{P}} \sigma_2' \text{ is part of } D \\ \sigma_1 = \langle [c\#i:j|\mathbb{A}], \mathbb{S}, \ldots \rangle_- \text{ and } \sigma_1' = \langle [c\#i:j|\mathbb{A}], \mathbb{S}', \ldots \rangle_- \\ \sigma_1 \rightarrowtail_{\mathcal{P}} \sigma_2 \text{ is a } \textbf{Propagate} \text{ transition applied with constraints } H \subseteq \mathbb{S} \\ \sigma_1' \rightarrowtail_{\mathcal{P}} \sigma_2' \text{ is a } \textbf{Propagate} \text{ transition applied with constraints } H' \subseteq \mathbb{S}' \\ \text{between } \sigma_2 \text{ and } \sigma_1' \text{ no } \textbf{Default} \text{ transition occurs of the form} \\ \quad \sigma_2 \rightarrowtail_{\mathcal{P}}^\star \langle [c\#i:j|\mathbb{A}], \ldots \rangle_- \rightarrowtail_{\mathcal{P}} \langle [c\#i:j+1|\mathbb{A}], \ldots \rangle_- \rightarrowtail_{\mathcal{P}}^\star \sigma_1' \end{cases}$$

then $H \neq H'$.

The following theorem establishes the equivalence of $\omega_r^\dagger$ and ω_r', thus proving the soundness of eliminating the history of unobserved CHR rules:

Theorem 1. *Define the mapping function $\alpha^\dagger$ as follows:*

$$\alpha^\dagger(\langle \mathbb{A}, \mathbb{S}, \mathbb{B}, \mathbb{T} \rangle_n) = \langle \mathbb{A}, \mathbb{S}, \mathbb{B}, \{(\rho, I) \in \mathbb{T} \mid \rho \text{ is not unobserved}\} \rangle_n$$

If D is an ω_r' derivation, then $\alpha^\dagger(D)$ is an $\omega_r^\dagger$ derivation. Conversely, if D is an $\omega_r^\dagger$ derivation, then there exists an ω_r' derivation D' such that $\alpha^\dagger(D) = D'$.

Proof. See [11]. $\qquad\qquad\qquad\qquad\qquad\qquad\qquad\qquad\qquad\qquad\qquad\qquad\qquad\square$

---

[3] We use '_' to denote that we are not interested in the identifier counter.

Implementation. The main difficulty in the implementation of this optimization is deriving that a rule is unobserved (enforcing duplicate-free propagation is
typically straightforward, as shown in Section 3.3). The abstract interpretation-
based late storage analysis of [9], which derives a similar observation property,
can be adapted for this purpose. The details are beyond the scope of this paper.

3.3   Optimized Reapplication Avoidance

Non-reactive CHR rules that are not unobserved, such as the second rule in the
FIBBO handler of Example 5, do require some mechanism to prevent reapplication. Moreover, even if a rule is unobserved, this does not mean the compiler's
analysis is capable of deriving it. In this section we therefore present a novel,
very efficient technique that prevents the reapplication of any non-reactive propagation rule without maintaining a costly propagation history.

The central observation is that, when a non-reactive rule is applied, the active
constraint is always more recent than its partner constraints:

Lemma 1. *Let $\mathcal{P}$ be an arbitrary CHR program, with $\rho \in \mathcal{P}$ a non-reactive rule,
and D an arbitrary ω_r' derivation with this program. Then for each* **Simplify** *or*
Propagate *transition in D of the form*

$$\langle[c\#i:j|\mathbb{A}], \mathbb{S}, \mathbb{B}, \mathbb{T}\rangle_n \rightarrowtail_{\mathcal{P}} \langle\mathbb{A}', \mathbb{S}', \mathbb{B}', \mathbb{T} \sqcup \{(\rho, I_1 +\!\!+ [i] +\!\!+ I_2)\}\rangle_n \qquad (1)$$

the following holds: $\forall i' \in I_1 \cup I_2 : i' < i$.

Proof. Assume $i' = \max(I_1 \sqcup I_2)$ with $i' \geq i$. By Definition 1 of rule applicability,
$i' \neq i$, and $\exists c'\#i' \in \mathbb{S}$. This $c'\#i'$ partner constraint must have been stored in an
Activate transition. Since $i' = \max(I_1 \sqcup \{i\} \sqcup I_2)$, in D, this transition came *after*
the **Activate** transitions of all other partners, including $c\#i$. In other words, all
constraints in the matching combination of transition (1) were stored prior to
the activation of $c'\#i'$. Also, in (1), $c\#i$ is back on top of the activation stack.
Because c is non-reactive, and thus never put back on top by a **Reactivate**
transition, the later activated $c'\#i'$ must have been removed from the stack
in a **Drop** transition. This implies that all applicable rules matching c' must
have fired. As all required constraints were stored (see earlier), this includes the
application of ρ in (1). By contradiction, our assumption is false, and $i' < i$. □

Let $\omega_r^{\ddagger}$ denote the semantics obtained from ω_r' by replacing the propagation
history condition in its **Simplify** and **Propagate** transitions with the following:

> If ρ is non-reactive, then $\forall i' \in \mathrm{ID}(H_1 \cup H_2) : i' < i$ and $\mathbb{T}' = \mathbb{T}$. *Otherwise,*
> let $t = (\rho, \mathrm{ID}(H_1) +\!\!+ [i] +\!\!+ \mathrm{ID}(H_2))$, then $t \notin \mathbb{T}$ and $\mathbb{T}' = \mathbb{T} \cup \{t\}$.

Propagation in $\omega_r^{\ddagger}$ is again duplicate-free, as defined by Definition 8. Similarly
to Theorem 1, the following theorem proves that ω_r' and $\omega_r^{\ddagger}$ are equivalent:

Theorem 2. *Define the mapping function $\alpha^{\ddagger}$ as follows:*

$$\alpha^{\ddagger}(\langle\mathbb{A}, \mathbb{S}, \mathbb{B}, \mathbb{T}\rangle_n) = \langle\mathbb{A}, \mathbb{S}, \mathbb{B}, \{(\rho, I) \in \mathbb{T} \mid \rho \text{ is a reactive CHR rule}\}\rangle_n$$

*If D is an ω_r' derivation, then $\alpha^{\ddagger}(D)$ is an $\omega_r^{\ddagger}$ derivation. Conversely, if D is an
$\omega_r^{\ddagger}$ derivation, then there exists an ω_r' derivation D' such that $\alpha^{\ddagger}(D) = D'$.*

Proof. See [7] or [11].   □

```
procedure up_to(U)#ID : 2
   foreach fib(N,M₂)#ID₂ in ...
      foreach fib(N-1,M₁)#ID₁ in ...
         if N < U
            if ID < ID₁ and ID < ID₂
               ⋱
```

```
procedure up_to(U)#ID : 2
   foreach fib(N,M₂)#ID₂ in ...
      if ID < ID₂ and N < U
         foreach fib(N-1,M₁)#ID₁ in ...
            if ID < ID₁
               ⋱
```

(a) Efficient reapplication avoidance   (b) After *Loop-invariant Code Motion*
using identifier comparisons

Fig. 6. Pseudocode for the second occurrence of the up_to/1 constraint of Fig. 3

Implementation. The standard CHR compilation scheme (see e.g. [5,6]) generates for each occurrence a nested iteration that looks for matching partner constraints for the active constraint. If a matching combination is found, and the active constraint is not removed, the constraint iterators are suspended and the rule's body is executed. Afterwards, the nested iteration is simply resumed.

Example 6. Fig. 6(a) shows the generated code for the second occurrence of the up_to/1 constraint in Fig. 3. For the query up_to(U), the propagation history for the corresponding rule would require $\mathcal{O}(U)$ space. Because all constraints are non-reactive, however, no propagation history has to be maintained. Simply comparing constraint identifiers suffices.

If all iterators return candidate partner constraints at most once, propagation is guaranteed to be duplicate-free (see Definition 8). Most iterators used by CHR implementations have this property. If not, a temporary history can for instance be maintained whilst the active constraint is considering an occurrence.

Loop-Invariant Code Motion. Most CHR compilers perform so-called *Loop-invariant Code Motion* optimization to check guard entailment as soon as possible (e.g. 'N < U' in Fig. 6(b)). Contrary to a propagation history check, identifier comparisons enable additional code motion, as illustrated in Fig. 6(b). This may prune the search space of candidate partner constraints considerably.

Note furthermore that Lemma 1 does not only apply to propagation rules, but also to simplification and simpagation rules. Whilst maintaining a history for non-propagation rules is pointless, comparing partner constraint identifiers in outer loops is not, as they may avoid redundant iterations of nested loops.

4 Idempotence

Constraints in CHR handlers that specify traditional constraint solvers, such as the leq/2 constraint of Example 1, typically range over unbound variables, and are thus highly reactive. Without a history, constraint reactivations may cause reactive propagation rules to fire multiple times with the same combination. For constraint solvers, however, such additional rule applications typically have no effect, as they only add redundant constraints that are immediately removed. For such rules, the propagation history may be eliminated as well.

Example 7. Suppose the reactive `transitivity` propagation rule of Fig. 1 is allowed to fire a second time with the same constraint combination matching its head, thus adding a `leq(X,Z)` constraint for the second time. If the earlier told duplicate is still in the store, this redundant `leq(X,Z)` constraint is immediately removed by the *idempotence* rule. Otherwise, the former duplicate must have been removed by either the *reflexivity* or the *antisymmetry* rule. It is easy to see that in this case X = Z, and thus that the new, redundant `leq(X,Z)` constraint is again removed immediately by the *reflexivity* rule.

We say the `leq/2` constraint of the above example is *idempotent*. With $live(\mathbb{T}, \mathbb{S})$ $= \{(\rho, I) \in \mathbb{T} \mid I \subseteq \text{ID}(\mathbb{S})\}$, *idempotence* is defined formally as:

Definition 9. *A CHR constraint type c/n is* idempotent *in a CHR program $\mathcal{P}$ under a refined semantics $\omega_r^\star$ iff for any state $\sigma = \langle [c|\mathbb{A}], \mathbb{S}, \mathbb{B}, \mathbb{T} \rangle_n$ in a $\omega_r^\star$ derivation D with c a CHR constraint, the following holds: if earlier in D a state $\langle [c'|\mathbb{A}'], \mathbb{S}', \mathbb{B}', \mathbb{T}' \rangle_{n'}$ occurs with $\mathcal{D}_\mathcal{H} \models \mathbb{B} \to c = c'$, then $\sigma \rightarrowtail_\mathcal{P}^\star \langle \mathbb{A}, \mathbb{S}'', \mathbb{B}'', \mathbb{T}'' \rangle_{n''}$ with $\mathbb{S}'' = \mathbb{S}$, $live(\mathbb{T}'', \mathbb{S}) = live(\mathbb{T}, \mathbb{S})$, and $\mathcal{D}_\mathcal{H} \models \pi_{vars(\mathbb{B}) \cup vars(D[1])}(\mathbb{B}'') \leftrightarrow \mathbb{B}$.*

In other words, an idempotent constraint c for which a syntactically equal constraint c' was told earlier in the same derivation, is removed without making any observable state change. Since '$\rightarrowtail_\mathcal{P}^\star$' denotes a finite derivation, telling duplicate idempotent CHR constraints also does not affect termination.

We do not consider arbitrary, extra-logical host language statements here, and assume all built-in constraints b are idempotent, that is: $\forall b : \mathcal{D}_\mathcal{H} \models b \wedge b \leftrightarrow b$. By adding "*If* $\mathcal{D}_\mathcal{H} \models (\mathbb{B} \wedge b) \leftrightarrow \mathbb{B}$, *then* $S = \emptyset$" to the **Solve** transition of ω_r (or any of its refinements from Section 3), we avoid redundant constraint reactivations when idempotent built-in constraints are told. This is correct, as **Solve**'s upper bound on S already specifies that any matching already possible prior to b's addition may be omitted from S. Most CHR systems already implement this optimization. Denote the resulting semantics ω_r^{idem}.

Definition 10. *A CHR rule $\rho \in \mathcal{P}$ is* idempotent *under ω_r^{idem} iff all CHR constraint types that occur in its body are idempotent in $\mathcal{P}$ under ω_r^{idem}.*

We now prove that an idempotent propagation rule may be fired more than once with the same combination of constraints, without affecting a program's operational semantics. Let $\omega_r^{idem'}$ denote the semantics obtained by adding the following phrase to the **Simplify** and **Propagate** transitions of ω_r^{idem}:

If the rule ρ is idempotent, then $\mathbb{T}' = \mathbb{T}$; *otherwise,* ... *(as before)*

Assuming furthermore that propagation for $\omega_r^{idem'}$ is duplicate-free[4] in the sense of Definition 8, the $\omega_r^{idem'}$ semantics is equivalent to ω_r^{idem}. More precisely:

Theorem 3. *If D' is an $\omega_r^{idem'}$ derivation, then there exists an ω_r^{idem} derivation D with $D[1] = D'[1]$ such that a monotonic function α can be defined from the states in D to states in D' for which*

---

[4] In this case a *finite* number of duplicate propagations would also not be a problem.

- $\alpha(D[1]) = D'[1]$
- if $\alpha(D[i]) = D'[k]$ and $\alpha(D[j]) = D'[l]$ with $i < j$, then $k < l$
- if $\alpha(\langle \mathbb{A}, \mathbb{S}, \mathbb{B}, \mathbb{T} \rangle_n) = \langle \mathbb{A}', \mathbb{S}', \mathbb{B}', \mathbb{T}' \rangle_{n'}$, then $\mathcal{D}_{\mathcal{H}} \models \pi_{vars(\mathbb{B}) \cup vars(D[1])}(\mathbb{B}') \leftrightarrow \mathbb{B}$, $\mathbb{A}' = \mathbb{A}$, $\mathbb{S}' = \mathbb{S}$, and $live(\mathbb{T}', \mathbb{S}) = live(\mathbb{T}, \mathbb{S}) \setminus \{(\rho, I) \in \mathbb{T} \mid \rho \text{ is idempotent}\}$.

Conversely, if D is an ω_r^{idem} derivation, then an $\omega_r^{idem'}$ derivation D' exists with $D'[1] = D[1]$ for which a function with these same properties can be defined.

Proof Sketch. An $\omega_r^{idem'}$ derivation D' only differs from the corresponding ω_r^{idem} derivation D when a **Propagate** transition fires an idempotent propagation rule ρ using a combination of constraints that fired ρ before. This $\omega_r^{idem'}$ transition has form $\sigma_0 = \langle \mathbb{A}, \mathbb{S}, \mathbb{B}, \mathbb{T} \rangle_n \rightarrowtail_{\mathcal{P}} \langle B \mathbin{+\!+} \mathbb{A}, \mathbb{S}, \mathbb{B}, \mathbb{T} \rangle_n = \sigma_1$. Because ρ's body B is idempotent, it follows from Definition 9 that the remainder of D' begins with $\sigma_1 \rightarrowtail_{\mathcal{P}}^{\star} \sigma_0' = \langle \mathbb{A}, \mathbb{S}, \mathbb{B}', \mathbb{T}' \rangle_n$, with $\mathcal{D}_{\mathcal{H}} \models \pi_{vars(\mathbb{B}) \cup vars(D[1])}(\mathbb{B}') \leftrightarrow \mathbb{B}$, and $live(\mathbb{T}', \mathbb{S}) = live(\mathbb{T}, \mathbb{S})$. Because σ_0' is thus essentially equivalent to σ_0, we simply omit states σ_1 to σ_0' in the corresponding ω_r^{idem} derivation D.

Given above observations it is straightforward to construct the mapping function α and the required derivations for both directions of the proof. $\square$

For multi-headed propagation rules, reapplication is often cheaper than maintaining and checking a history. The experimental results of Section 5 confirm this. Of course, reapplying a body can be arbitrarily expensive. To estimate the cost of reapplication versus the cost of maintaining a history, heuristics can be used.

4.1   Deriving Idempotence

The main challenge lies in automatically deriving that a CHR constraint is idempotent. A wide class of idempotent CHR constraints should be covered:

Example 8. Many constraint solvers contain a rule such as:

```
in(X,L₁,U₁) \ in(X,L₂,U₂) ⇔ L₂ ≤ L₁, U₂ ≥ U₁ | true.
```

Here, 'in(X,L,U)' denotes that the variable X lies in the interval $[L, U]$. The in/3 constraint is probably idempotent (it depends on the preceding rules). There is an important difference though with the leq/2 constraint in Example 7: by the time the constraint is told for the second time, the earlier told duplicate may now be replaced with a *syntactically different* constraint—in this case: a constraint representing a smaller interval domain.

Theorem 4 provides a sufficiently strong syntactic condition for determining the idempotence of a CHR constraint. It uses arbitrary preorders on the constraint's arguments. For the three arguments of the in/3 constraint in Example 8 for instance, the preorders $=$, $\leq$ and $\geq$ can be used respectively.

Let $bi(B)$ and $chr(B)$ denote the conjunction of built-in respectively CHR constraints that occur in a constraint conjunction B. Then:

Theorem 4. *A CHR constraint type c/n is idempotent in $\mathcal{P}$ under ω_r^{idem} if for preorders $\lhd_1, \ldots, \lhd_n$:*

1. *There exists a rule of the form "$c(y_1, \ldots, y_n) \setminus c(x_1, \ldots, x_n) \Leftrightarrow G \mid true."*
   in HNF($\mathcal{P}$) with $\mathcal{D}_{\mathcal{H}} \models (x_1 \lhd_1 y_1 \wedge \ldots \wedge x_n \lhd_n y_n) \rightarrow G$.
   Let ρ be the first such rule occurring in the HNF($\mathcal{P}$) sequence.
2. *All rules in HNF($\mathcal{P}$) prior to ρ that contain an occurrence of c/n have a*
   trivial body 'true', and do not contain any removed occurrences apart from
   possibly that c/n occurrence.

Consider a set of n mutually distinct variables $V = \{x_1, \ldots, x_n\}$. For all removed
occurrences of c/n in HNF($\mathcal{P}$) that can be renamed to the form

$$H_k \setminus H_{r_1}, c(x_1, \ldots, x_n), H_{r_2} \Leftrightarrow G \mid B$$

(H_k, H_{r_1}, and H_{r_2} may be empty), such that $\neg \exists c(y_1, \ldots, y_n) \in H_k \cup chr(B)$:
$\mathcal{D}_{\mathcal{H}} \models G \wedge bi(B) \rightarrow (x_1 \lhd_1 y_1 \wedge \ldots \wedge x_n \lhd_n y_n)$, define $\Phi = \pi_V(G \wedge bi(B))$. For
each of these occurrences, either $\mathcal{D}_{\mathcal{H}} \models \Phi \leftrightarrow false$, or conditions 3 and 4 hold:

3. *There exists a rule in HNF($\mathcal{P}$) that can be renamed such that it has form*
   "$c(x_1, \ldots, x_n) \Leftrightarrow G \mid B$", with $bi(B) = B$ and $\mathcal{D}_{\mathcal{H}} \models \Phi \rightarrow (G \wedge B)$.
   Let ρ' be the first such rule occurring in the HNF($\mathcal{P}$) sequence.
4. *All rules in HNF($\mathcal{P}$) prior to ρ' that contain an occurrence of c/n can be*
   renamed to "$H_k \setminus H_r \Leftrightarrow G \mid B$" with $H_k \mathbin{++} H_r = H_1 \mathbin{++} [c(x_1, \ldots, x_n)] \mathbin{++} H_2$,
   such that either
     - *$\mathcal{D}_{\mathcal{H}} \models \Phi \rightarrow \neg G$; or*
     - *$H_r \subseteq [c(x_1, \ldots, x_n)] \wedge (bi(B) = B) \wedge \mathcal{D}_{\mathcal{H}} \models (\Phi \wedge G) \rightarrow B$; or*
     - *$\exists c(y_1, \ldots, y_n) \in H_1 \cup H_2 : \mathcal{D}_{\mathcal{H}} \models (\Phi \wedge G) \rightarrow (x_1 \lhd_1 y_1 \wedge \ldots \wedge x_n \lhd_n y_n)$.*

Proof Sketch. By Definition 9, we have to show that adding a c/n constraint makes no essential changes to the execution state if a duplicate constraint was added earlier in the same derivation. The proof considers two cases: either the duplicate constraint, or a constraint derived from it, is still in the store, or it has been removed. We show that, if the theorem's conditions hold, in both these cases the newly told duplicate is removed, and that it only makes idempotent state changes before that. The complete, formal proof can be found in [11].   □

5   Evaluation

We implemented the optimizations introduced in this paper in the K.U.Leuven CHR system [3,6] for SWI-Prolog, and in the K.U.Leuven JCHR system [4] for Java, and evaluated them using typical CHR benchmarks and constraint solvers[5]. Benchmark timings are given in Tables 1 and 2. The *history* columns give the reference timings (in milliseconds) when using a propagation history.

The *non-react* columns in Table 1 contain the results when the optimizations of Section 3 are used. For the *non-react+* measurements, loop-invariant code motion was applied to the identifier comparisons (see Section 3.3; currently

---

[5] Information on the benchmarks and the platform used is found in [11, Appendix B].

Table 1. Benchmark results (in average milliseconds) for non-reactive CHR rules

	SWI		JCHR			total #	n-headed propagation rules			
	history	non-react	history	non-react	non-react+	rules	$n=1$	$n=2$	$n=3$	$n>3$
FIBBO(1000)	15,929	4,454 (28%)	70	67 (95%)	21 (30%)	3	1	-	1	-
FIBBO(3000)	*timeout*	*timeout*	542	464 (85%)	153 (28%)	3	1	-	1	-
FLOYD-WARSH(30)	11,631	9,706 (83%)	368	188 (51%)	186 (51%)	21	3	2	1	-
INTERPOL(8)	5,110	1,527 (30%)	43	41 (95%)	37 (86%)	5	-	2	-	-
MANNERS(128)	849	561 (66%)	328	322 (98%)	317 (97%)	8	-	-	1	-
NSP_GRND(12)	547	169 (31%)	10	6 (60%)	5 (50%)	3	1	1	-	-
NSP_GRND(36)	81,835	10,683 (13%)	1,434	502 (35%)	494 (34%)	3	1	1	-	-
SUM(1000,100)	6,773	3,488 (51%)	215	135 (63%)	*N/A*	4	-	1	-	-
TURING(20)	10,372	7,387 (71%)	761	280 (37%)	276 (36%)	11	1	4	1	5
WFS(200)	2,489	2,143 (86%)	71	67 (94%)	67 (94%)	44	-	4	-	-

Table 2. Benchmark results (in average milliseconds) for idempotent propagation rules. The '#' columns give the number of propagation rules over the total number of rules.

	SWI		JCHR		#			SWI		JCHR		#
	history	idempotence	hist.	idempot.				history	idempotence	hist.	idempot.	
INTERVAL(21)	22,622	17,611 (78%)	8	5 (62%)	15/27	EQ(35)		3,465	1,931 (56%)	47	19 (40%)	1/4
INTERVAL(42)	*timeout*	*timeout*	54	28 (52%)	15/27	LEQ(70)		3,806	1,236 (32%)	85	35 (41%)	1/4
NSP_GRND(12)	547	164 (30%)	10	6 (60%)	2/3	NSP(12)		1,454	1,036 (71%)	12	8 (67%)	2/3
NSP_GRND(36)	81,835	10,485 (13%)	1,365	496 (36%)	2/3	NSP(36)		*timeout*	*timeout*	1,434	621 (43%)	2/3
TIMEPOINT(16)	1,684	1,312 (78%)	404	317 (78%)	2/7	MINMAX(15)		4,826	3,631 (75%)	133	82 (61%)	6/54

only implemented in JCHR[6]). Only for the SUM benchmark the the history was eliminated using the optimization of Section 3.2 (code motion is of course not applicable (*N/A*) in this case). Table 2 shows the results for the idempotence-based history elimination of Section 4.

Significant performance gains are measured all optimizations. The selected benchmarks run about two times faster on average, and scale better as well. Even though no numbers are shown, it is moreover clear that the space complexity of the propagation histories has become optimal. Unoptimized, the worst-case space consumption of a propagation history is linear in the number of rule applications (cf. Example 6). Using our optimizations, histories consume no space at all. In extreme cases, this even improves the space complexity of the entire handler.

6   Conclusions

Related Work. A preliminary version of this paper covering only Section 3.3 of the present paper appeared in [7]. The present paper completes this earlier work by introducing propagation history elimination based on unobservedness and idempotence, and by providing a more extensive experimental evaluation.

Section 3.2 can be seen as an extension and formalization of an optimization briefly presented in [5]. This ad-hoc optimization was restricted to fixed CHR constraints, and lacked a formal correctness proof.

---

[6] In JCHR, after code motion, identifier comparisons are integrated in the constraint iterators themselves. These iterators moreover exploit the fact that the stored constraints are often sorted on their identifiers. This can further improve performance.

Since the propagation history contributes to significant performance issues when implementing CHR in a tabling environment (see e.g. [12]), [13] proposes an alternative set-based CHR semantics, and argues that it does not need a propagation history. Our results, however, show that abandoning CHR's familiar multiset-based semantics is not necessary: indeed, our optimizations eliminate the history-related performance issues whilst preserving the ω_r-semantics.

Conclusions. Whilst there is a vast research literature on CHR compilation and optimization, propagation histories never received much attention. Maintaining a propagation history, however, comes at a considerable runtime cost, both in time and in space. In this work, we resolved this discrepancy by introducing several innovative optimization techniques that circumvent the maintenance of a history for the majority of CHR propagation rules:

- For *non-reactive* CHR propagation rules, we showed that very cheap constraint identifier comparisons can be used. These comparisons can moreover be moved early in the generated nested iterations, thus pruning the search space of possible partner constraints. We also formally identified the class of non-reactive rules for which the history can simply be eliminated.
- Whilst rules in general-purpose CHR programs are mostly non-reactive, CHR handlers that specify a constraint solver are typically highly reactive. We therefore introduced the concept of *idempotence*, and found that most rules in the latter handlers are idempotent. We showed that if a propagation rule is idempotent, the rule may safely be applied more than once matching the same combination of constraints. Interestingly, reapplication is mostly cheaper than maintaining and checking a history. We also presented a sufficient syntactic condition for the idempotence of a CHR constraint.

We proved the correctness of all our optimizations and analyses in the formal framework of CHR's refined operational semantics [8], and implemented them in two state-of-the-art CHR systems [3,4]. Our experimental results show significant performance gains for all benchmarks containing propagation rules.

Acknowledgments. The author thanks Tom Schrijvers for his invaluable aid in the implementation of the optimizations in the K.U.Leuven CHR system. Thanks also to Bart Demoen and the anonymous referees of CHR 2008 and ICLP 2008 for their useful comments on earlier versions of this paper.

References

1. Frühwirth, T.: Theory and practice of Constraint Handling Rules. J. Logic Programming, Special Issue on Constraint Logic Programming 37(1–3), 95–138 (1998)
2. Sneyers, J., Van Weert, P., Schrijvers, T., De Koninck, L.: As time goes by: Constraint Handling Rules – A survey of CHR research between 1998 and 2007. Journal of Theory and Practice of Logic Programming (submitted, 2008)
3. Schrijvers, T., Demoen, B.: The K.U.Leuven CHR system: Implementation and application. In: CHR 2004: Selected Contributions, Ulm, Germany, pp. 8–12 (2004)

4. Van Weert, P., Schrijvers, T., Demoen, B.: K.U.Leuven JCHR: a user-friendly, flexible and efficient CHR system for Java. In: CHR 2005: Proc. 2nd Workshop on Constraint Handling Rules, Sitges, Spain, pp. 47–62 (2005)
5. Duck, G.J.: Compilation of Constraint Handling Rules. Ph.D thesis, University of Melbourne, Australia (December 2005)
6. Schrijvers, T.: Analyses, optimizations and extensions of Constraint Handling Rules. Ph.D thesis, K.U.Leuven, Belgium (June 2005)
7. Van Weert, P.: A tale of histories. In: CHR 2008: Proc. 5th Workshop on Constraint Handling Rules, Hagenberg, Austria, pp. 79–94 (2008)
8. Duck, G.J., Stuckey, P.J., García de la Banda, M., Holzbaur, C.: The refined operational semantics of Constraint Handling Rules. In: [14], pp. 90–104
9. Schrijvers, T., Stuckey, P.J., Duck, G.J.: Abstract interpretation for Constraint Handling Rules. In: Barahona, P., Felty, A. (eds.) PPDP 2005: Proc. 7th Intl. Conf. Princ. Pract. Declarative Programming, Lisbon, Portugal, pp. 218–229. ACM, New York (2005)
10. Schrijvers, T., Demoen, B.: Antimonotony-based delay avoidance for CHR. Technical Report CW 385, K.U.Leuven, Dept. Computer Science (July 2004)
11. Van Weert, P.: Optimization of CHR propagation rules: Extended report. Technical Report CW 519, K.U.Leuven, Dept. Computer Science (August 2008)
12. Schrijvers, T., Warren, D.S.: Constraint Handling Rules and tabled execution. In: [14], pp. 120–136
13. Sarna-Starosta, B., Ramakrishnan, C.: Compiling Constraint Handling Rules for efficient tabled evaluation. In: Hanus, M. (ed.) PADL 2007. LNCS, vol. 4354, pp. 170–184. Springer, Heidelberg (2006)
14. Demoen, B., Lifschitz, V. (eds.): ICLP 2004. LNCS, vol. 3132. Springer, Heidelberg (2004)

Termination Analysis of CHR Revisited

Paolo Pilozzi[*] and Danny De Schreye

Dept. of Computer Science, K.U.Leuven, Belgium
paolo.pilozzi@cs.kuleuven.be, danny.deschreye@cs.kuleuven.be

Abstract. Today, two distinct direct approaches to prove termination of CHR programs exist. The first approach, by *T. Frühwirth*, proves termination of CHR programs without propagation. The second, by *Voets et al.*, deals with programs that contain propagation. It is however less powerful on programs without propagation. In this paper, we present new termination conditions that are strictly more powerful than those from previous approaches and that are also applicable to a new class of programs. Furthermore, we present a new representation for CHR states for which size-decreases between consecutive states correspond to termination. Both contributions are linked: our termination conditions correspond to the existence of a well-founded order on the new state representation, which decreases for consecutive computation states.

Keywords: Constraint Handling Rules, Termination Analysis.

1 Introduction

Constraint Handling Rules [1] is a declarative programming language. It was designed and proved successful for efficiently implementing various kinds of constraint solvers (see e.g. [2,3]). The language is closely related to Logic Programming (LP) and to lesser extent to Term-Rewrite Systems (TRS). Relating it to LP, its most distinguishing features are that:

- its rules do not act on goals of sequentially ordered atoms, but on multi-sets of constraints (*constraint stores*),
- the rules are multi-headed and introduce new constraints depending on the presence of a multi-set of constraints in the store that match the head.
- in addition to multi-headed variants of LP-clauses (*simplification rules*), it also supports *propagation rules*, which do not remove any constraints from the store, but only add new constraints conditional on the presence of others.

It is mostly the latter feature of the language that makes termination analysis of CHR an interesting and difficult problem. Consider a propagation rule:

$$a(s(N)) \Rightarrow a(N).$$

Here, $a/1$ is a constraint, $s/1$ a functor and N a variable. Given a constraint, say $a(s(s(0)))$, in the store, the rule adds a constraint $a(s(0))$. Because propagation

---

[*] Supported by I.W.T. Flanders - Belgium.

rules do not remove constraints, to avoid trivial non-termination, they must respect a *fire-once* policy: they can only be activated *once* on any matching multi-set of constraints. Under this restriction and taking into account that CHR uses matching instead of unification, a program consisting only of the above rule is terminating for any given constraint store.

Now consider a slight variant:

$$a(s(N)), a(N) \Rightarrow a(N).$$

Here, the comma denotes conjunction. Based on LP-termination intuition, one would be inclined to think that this rule is terminating as well. We have only strengthened the precondition of the rule and there is still a decrease in the overall "size" between the heads and the body of the rule. The latter rule, however, is non-terminating for any constraint store on which it can be activated at least once. The reason is that each time the rule is activated, say on a constraint store $a(s(s(0))), a(s(0))$, it adds a new constraint $a(s(0))$. This "fresh" copy of $a(s(0))$ recombines with $a(s(s(0)))$ to fire the rule again. Thus, we get non-termination.

Formally modelling and analyzing these aspects of CHR-termination has proven to be difficult. The first approach, by T. Frühwirth in [4], adapts LP termination analysis to the CHR context. The work succeeded in showing that such an adaption can elegantly and effectively be done. However, its focus is on CHR without propagation, as such avoiding the problems illustrated above.

Recently, in [5], new termination criteria have been proposed, which are applicable to CHR programs with propagation. The conditions proposed in this approach are of a very different nature than those of LP termination analysis or of [4]. In particular, the approach does not reason in terms of decreases in size of consecutive computation states, as it is most often the case in termination analysis. In fact, in the presence of propagation rules, it is a non-trivial problem to come up with a representation of a computation state which can easily be seen to decrease in size for terminating computations. For instance, it is clear that the constraint store itself is insufficient for this purpose. By any application of a propagation rule, information is added to the store, while none is removed.

Voets et al. [5] addresses the general setting of the full CHR-language, but is less precise on programs without propagation. We introduce examples of and discuss causes for this in the remainder of the paper. So, we currently have two approaches to prove termination, successful on *different* classes of programs.

One of the goals of the current paper is to present a new termination condition which is more powerful than both [4] and [5]. So, if any of the techniques in [4] or [5] is able to prove a program terminating, then our approach will succeed as well. Moreover, we will show that there is a class of programs that is not in the scope of [4] nor [5], and for which our technique succeeds also. So, we provide strictly more powerful conditions than both existing approaches.

A second goal of our work is to address the problem of finding a representation for CHR computation states, for which decreases in size of consecutive states correspond to termination of the computation. For this purpose, we complement the constraint store with two additional structures:

- the token store, which keeps track of which propagation rules are still allowed to fire on which multi-subsets of the constraint store,
- the propagation store, which collects all constraints that can be added to the current constraint store by exhaustively applying all propagation rules.

Finally, the two contributions of the paper are linked: our new termination conditions constructively imply the existence of a well-founded order on the state representation that decreases for consecutive states.

The paper is organized as follows. In the next section, we discuss CHR syntax and adapt concepts from LP termination analysis to CHR. Then, a brief explanation on the existing approaches to termination analysis of CHR is given. Section 3 covers CHR semantics, where we introduce the token store to model a fire-once policy for propagation rules. Section 4 discusses termination of propagation rules. There, we define the notion of propagation safeness and introduce the *propagation store*. In Section 5, we come to the heart of our approach: we present our new representation for CHR states that can be shown to decrease in size for terminating programs containing also propagation rules. Then, we formulate verifiable conditions, which imply such decreases. In Section 6, we discuss our approach and conclude.

2   Preliminaries

CHR [1,6] manipulates a conjunction of *constraints* $c(t_1, \ldots, t_n)$ of arity $n \geq 0$, that are collected in a constraint store S. As CHR is built on top of a host-language, there are pre-defined *built-in constraints* that are solved by an underlying solver CT and there are user-defined *CHR constraints* that are solved by the rules of a CHR program P. A CHR program consists of a finite set of rules, syntactically named by *"rulename @"*. There are essentially two kinds of rules in a CHR program. The next example program illustrates their use.

Example 1 (Primes [7]).

> $test @ primes(M) \setminus primes(N) \Leftrightarrow N > M, N \ mod \ M \ is \ 0 \mid true.$
> $generate @ primes(N) \Rightarrow N > 2 \mid Np \ is \ N - 1, primes(Np).$

The *test* rule is a *simplification rule*. In general, a simplification rule takes the form $H_k \setminus H_r \Leftrightarrow G \mid B, C$, where H_k, H_r and C are conjunctions of CHR constraints and G and B conjunctions of built-in constraints. However, when no kept heads are present, we write it as $H_r \Leftrightarrow G \mid B, C$. The *test* rule verifies, using a guard $N > M, N \ mod \ M \ is \ 0$, whether the removed head constraint $primes(N)$ can be divided by the kept head constraint $primes(M)$. If so, $primes(N)$ is replaced by a built-in *true*. The *generate* rule is a *propagation rule*. In general a propagation rule takes the form $H_k \Rightarrow G \mid B, C$, where H_k and C are conjunctions of CHR constraints and G and B conjunctions of built-in constraints. The *generate* rule adds decreasing numbers. Given the guard $N > 2$ of the propagation rule, only numbers greater than 2 can fire the rule. Therefore, no number lower than 2 is added, given the added built-in $Np \ is \ N - 1$.   □

In CHR, we denote by $Term_P$ and Con_P the sets of respectively all terms and all constraints that can be constructed from the alphabet underlying a CHR program P. These constraints are interpreted by a *level mapping* to natural numbers, which is a function defined in terms of *norms* [8,9].

Definition 1 (Norm, level mapping). *Let P be a CHR program. Then, a norm is a function $\|.\| : Term_P \to \mathbb{N}$ and a level mapping $|.| : Con_P \to \mathbb{N}$.* □

There are several examples of norms and level mappings in literature on LP termination analysis [8]. Two well-known norms are *list-length* and *term-size*. The value that a level mapping assigns to a constraint is refered to as a *level value*. It was demonstrated by Frühwirth in [4], that for CHR programs without propagation, the sizes of consecutive computation states can be compared using a multi-set order on the *level values* of the constraints in the constraint store.

In multi-sets, multiple instances of a same element are allowed. When joining two multi-sets, denoted by ⊎, the elements of both multi-sets are added together. An order can be defined on multi-sets, corresponding to an order on its elements.

Definition 2 (Multi-set order adapted from [10]). *Assume a partial order $>$ for the elements of two multi-sets X and Y and let n_r^X be the number of elements in X of level value r. Then X is strictly larger than Y, denoted by $X \succ_m Y$, if there exists a level value r, such that $n_r^X > n_r^Y$ and $\forall q > r : n_q^X = n_q^Y$.* □

Multi-set order has been shown to be well-founded if the order of its elements is well-founded [10]. Therefore, if a decrease can be shown for successive computation states, and thus on changes in the state caused by rules, we prove that a program must terminate. We illustrate this in the next example.

Example 2 (Termination of CHR programs without propagation [4]).

$$R_1 @ a(s(N)), a(N), a(N) \Leftrightarrow a(s(N)), a(N). \qquad R_2 @ a(s(N)) \Leftrightarrow a(N).$$

Termination is shown by proving multi-set size decreases for the constraint store, using a level mapping $|a(N)| = \|N\|_{ts}$, where $\|.\|_{ts}$ is term-size. □

For CHR programs with propagation, the above approach cannot be used due to explicit increases in the constraint store caused by propagation. For such programs, termination is currently proved using a different approach [5].

The conditions for CHR programs with propagation from [5], compare the sizes of individual constraints, rather than multi-sets of constraints. Propagation rules may only add constraints with strictly lower level values than any of the heads used in the rule. A simplification rule must remove more constraints of the maximally occurring level value, than it adds constraints of that value.

Example 3 (Termination of CHR programs with propagation [5]).

$$R_1 @ a(s(s(N))) \Rightarrow a(s(N)), a(N). \qquad R_2 @ a(s(N)) \Leftrightarrow a(N).$$

Termination of the program is shown for ground queries, using a level mapping $|a(N)| = \|N\|_{ts}$. The first rule only adds constraints with a level value which is strictly lower than that of the constraint that fired the rule. In the second rule, the constraint with the maximal level value is in the head. Thus the number of constraints with maximal level value decreases.   □

Notice that the condition on simplification is a strengthened variant of multi-set order. Therefore, in the case of a program with only simplification rules, the condition for CHR without propagation covers more programs.

Example 4 (Revisiting Example 2).

$$R_1 @ a(s(N)), a(N), a(N) \Leftrightarrow a(s(N)). \qquad R_2 @ a(s(N)) \Leftrightarrow a(N).$$

Termination cannot be shown using [5] since its condition on simplification rules requires that $|a(s(N))| > |a(N)|$ for R_2. As such, no decrease in the number of constraints with maximal level value can be shown for R_1. One reason for the stronger condition from [5] is that in the case of a propagation rule, e.g. $R_2 @ a(s(N)) \Rightarrow a(N)$, we obtain a non-terminating program.   □

3   CHR Semantics

Declaratively, simplification corresponds to a logical equivalence between removed constraints H_r and added constraints $B \wedge C$, provided presence of the kept constraints H_k and satisfiability of the guard G: $G \to (H_k \to H_r \leftrightarrow B \wedge C)$. Propagation on the other hand completes state information. Given the presence of constraints, new constraints are added: $G \to (H \to B \wedge C)$.

Operationally, rules are applied exhaustively on the CHR constraints in the *constraint store*. Rule application is non-deterministic. Any applicable rule can be fired. This is however a committed choice, it cannot be undone [1, 11, 12, 6]. We will study termination for all possible non-deterministic choices.

Definition 3 (Constraint store). *The constraint store is a set S of uniquely labeled CHR constraints $c\sharp i$ and built-in constraints b. We define $chr(c\sharp i) = c$ to obtain the constraint and $id(c\sharp i) = i$ to obtain the label.*   □

Labeling constraints is required to prevent *trivial non-termination*, caused by propagation. We label CHR constraints to keep track of combinations of constraints that can still fire propagation rules. As such, a *fire-once policy* is introduced on combinations of constraints. To this end, we consider a token store.

Definition 4 (Token store). *Let P be a CHR program and S a constraint store. Then the token store T given S, is the set of tokens $(R_i, id_1, \ldots, id_n)$, where $(R_i @ h_1, \ldots, h_n \Rightarrow G \mid B, C)$ is a propagation rule in P and where $c_j \sharp id_j$ are constraints in S, such that $CT \models \exists \sigma\theta : c_1 = h_1\sigma \wedge \cdots \wedge c_n = h_n\sigma \wedge G\sigma\theta$. Here, σ is a match substitution and θ an answer substitution for the guard.*   □

The elements of a token store are tokens which represent the possibility to apply a propagation rule on constraints in the constraint store. Once the propagation rule has been applied to these constraints, the corresponding token is removed, so that the rule is no longer applicable on the same combination of constraints. Whenever the application of a rule causes CHR constraints to be added to the constraint store, new tokens $T^A_{(D,S)}$ enter the token store.

Definition 5 (Addition of tokens). *Let P be a CHR program, S a constraint store and D a labeled CHR constraint, added to the constraint store S, then*

$$T^A_{(D,S)} = \{ (R, i_1, \ldots, i_n) \mid (R @ h_1, \ldots, h_n \Rightarrow G \mid B, C) \in P, \text{ where}$$
$$\{c_1 \sharp i_1, \ldots, c_n \sharp i_n\} \subseteq \{D\} \cup S \text{ such that } D \in \{c_1 \sharp i_1, \ldots, c_n \sharp i_n\} \text{ and}$$
$$CT \models \exists \sigma \theta : (c_1 = h_1 \sigma) \wedge \cdots \wedge (c_n = h_n \sigma) \wedge G \sigma \theta \}$$

If multiple labeled constraints $D = \{D^1, \ldots, D^n\}$ are added, then

$$T^A_{(D,S)} = T^A_{(D^1,S)} \cup T^A_{(D^2,\{D^1\} \cup S)} \cup \cdots \cup T^A_{(D^n,\{D^1,\ldots,D^{n-1}\} \cup S)}$$

Where σ is a match substitution and θ an answer substitution. □

Tokens $T^E_{(D,S)}$ in the token store T may become invalid as a consequence of removing constraints D from the constraint store S.

Definition 6 (Elimination of tokens). *Let T be a token store and $D = \{D^1, \ldots, D^n\}$ labeled CHR constraints removed from the constraint store S, then*

$$T^E_{(D,S)} = \{(R, i_1, \ldots, i_n) \in T \mid \exists D^j \in D : id(D^j) \in \{i_1, \ldots, i_n\}\}$$ □

The rules in a CHR program define a state transition system [1, 11, 12, 6]. We define states and transitions.

Definition 7 (CHR state). *A CHR state is a tuple $\langle S, T \rangle_\nu$, where S is the constraint store and T the token store. Every state is annotated with a fresh integer ν, not yet assigned to a constraint. An* initial state *or* query *is a tuple $\langle S, T^A_{(S,\emptyset)} \rangle_\nu$, with v a fresh integer value.* □

The *transition relation $\mathscr{T}$* between CHR states, given CT for built-ins and P for CHR constraints, is defined as follows [1, 11, 12, 6].

Definition 8 (Transition relation). *Let $H_k = h_1, \ldots, h_j$, $H_r = h_{j+1}, \ldots, h_n$ and $C = c_1, \ldots, c_m$ denote conjunctions of CHR constraints, let G and B denote conjunctions of built-in constraints, let σ be a match substitution for the heads of the rule R and let θ be an answer substitution for the guard. Then, $\mathscr{T}$ is:*

[SOLVE] Solving built-in constraints
    IF $S = b \cup S_\rho$, where b is a built-in constraint such that $CT \models \exists \beta : b\beta$
    THEN there exists a transition $\mathscr{T} : \langle S, T \rangle_\nu \rightarrow \langle S_\rho \beta, T \rangle_\nu$

[SIMPLIFY] Simplification of CHR constraints

IF $(R_s \ @ \ H_k \setminus H_r \Leftrightarrow G \mid B, C)$ *is a fresh variant of a rule in* P *and* $S = H'_k \cup H'_r \cup S_\rho$, *with* $H'_k = \{d_1 \sharp i_1, \ldots, d_j \sharp i_j\}$ *and* $H'_r = \{d_{j+1} \sharp i_{j+1}, \ldots, d_n \sharp i_n\}$ *such that* $CT \models \exists \sigma\theta : (d_1 = h_1\sigma) \wedge \cdots \wedge (d_n = h_n\sigma) \wedge G\sigma\theta$

THEN *there exists a transition* $\mathcal{T} : \langle S, T \rangle_\nu \to \langle S', T' \rangle_{\nu+m}$

where $S' = (H'_k \cup S_\rho \cup B \cup \{c_1 \sharp \nu, \ldots, c_m \sharp (\nu + m - 1)\})\sigma\theta$ *and*

where $T' = (T \setminus T^E_{(H'_r, S)}) \cup T^A_{(\{c_1 \sharp \nu, \ldots, c_m \sharp (\nu+m-1)\}, H'_k \cup S_\rho)}$

[PROPAGATE] Propagation of CHR constraints

IF $(R_p \ @ \ H_k \Rightarrow G \mid B, C)$ *is a fresh variant of a rule in* P *and* $S = H'_k \cup S_\rho$, *with* $H'_k = \{d_1 \sharp i_1, \ldots, d_j \sharp i_j\}$ *and* $T = \{(R_p, i_1, \ldots, i_j)\} \cup T_\rho$ *such that* $CT \models \exists \sigma\theta : (d_1 = h_1\sigma) \wedge \cdots \wedge (d_j = h_j\sigma) \wedge G\sigma\theta$

THEN *there exists a transition* $\mathcal{T} : \langle S, T \rangle_\nu \to \langle S', T' \rangle_{\nu+m}$

where $S' = (S \cup B \cup \{c_1 \sharp \nu, \ldots, c_m \sharp (\nu + m - 1)\})\sigma\theta$ *and*

where $T' = T_\rho \cup T^A_{(\{c_1 \sharp \nu, \ldots, c_m \sharp (\nu+m-1)\}, S)}$ $\qquad \square$

The next example computation for Primes (Example 1), illustrates the transition relation.

Example 5 (Executing Primes). For a query $\langle \{primes(7)\sharp 1\}, \{(R_2, 1)\} \rangle_2$, we get as a possible computation:

$$I_0 = \langle \{primes(7)\sharp 1\}, \{(R_2, 1)\} \rangle_2 \xrightarrow{R_2}$$
$$I_1 = \langle \{primes(7)\sharp 1, primes(6)\sharp 2\}, \{(R_2, 2)\} \rangle_3 \xrightarrow{R_2}$$
$$I_2 = \langle \{primes(7)\sharp 1, primes(6)\sharp 2, primes(5)\sharp 3\}, \{(R_2, 3)\} \rangle_4 \xrightarrow{R_2}$$
$$I_3 = \langle \{primes(7)\sharp 1, primes(6)\sharp 2, primes(5)\sharp 3, primes(4)\sharp 4\}, \{(R_2, 4)\} \rangle_5 \xrightarrow{R_2}$$
$$I_4 = \langle \{primes(7)\sharp 1, primes(6)\sharp 2, primes(5)\sharp 3, primes(4)\sharp 4, primes(3)\sharp 5\}, \{(R_2, 5)\} \rangle_6 \xrightarrow{R_1}$$
$$I_5 = \langle \{primes(7)\sharp 1, primes(5)\sharp 3, primes(4)\sharp 4, primes(3)\sharp 5\}, \{(R_2, 5)\} \rangle_6 \xrightarrow{R_2}$$
$$I_6 = \langle \{primes(7)\sharp 1, primes(5)\sharp 3, primes(4)\sharp 4, primes(3)\sharp 5, primes(2)\sharp 6\}, \emptyset \rangle_7 \xrightarrow{R_1}$$
$$I_7 = \langle \{primes(7)\sharp 1, primes(5)\sharp 3, primes(3)\sharp 5, primes(2)\sharp 6\}, \emptyset \rangle_7$$

Note that we have omitted discussion of the solve transition. $\qquad \square$

A *final state* or *answer* is a state in which no more transitions are possible. It is therefore necessarily of the form $\langle S, \emptyset \rangle_v$. A transition in CHR is called a computation step and a sequence of transitions, a computation. If all computations are finite, a CHR program terminates.

Definition 9 (Termination of a CHR program). *We say that a CHR program* P *terminates for a query* I *iff all computations of* P *for* I *are finite.* $\qquad \square$

Termination of CHR programs, executed under an operational semantics as described above, corresponds to the notion of universal termination.

As in LP [8], we wish to describe by a call set, the constraints that participate in computations of a CHR program P, given a query I. As such, we can establish interpretations that are *rigid* w.r.t. the constraints represented by the call set: the interpretation of constraints cannot alter under substitution.

Definition 10 (Call set). *Let* $I \subseteq Con_P$. *Then by* $Call(P, I)$, *we denote the subset of* Con_P, *where* $C \in Call(P, I)$ *if* C *is a constraint used in the application of a rule in some computation of* P *for* I. $\qquad \square$

4   Propagation in CHR

4.1   Motivation

Example 5 confirms our earlier observation that the constraint store is insufficient to monitor the size-decreases in CHR-computations. In the example, with each propagation step, the constraint store grows. The example also suggests that the full state representation $\langle S, T \rangle_\nu$, is appropriate to observe decreases. To illustrate this, we first introduce an ordering on tokens.

Definition 11 (Token mapping). *Given a level mapping $|.|$, the associated token mapping is a function $|.|_\tau$ from tokens to $\mathbb{N}$, such that for every state $\langle S, T \rangle_\nu$ and token $t = (R_p, i_1, \ldots, i_n)$ in T: $|t|_\tau = min(\{|c_{i_1}|, \ldots, |c_{i_j}|\})$, where $c_{i_j} = chr(id^{-1}(i_j))$.* $\qquad\square$

Returning to Example 5, we can now easily define a decreasing well-founded order on states $\langle S, T \rangle_\nu$, by taking a lexicographic order, based on ordered pairs (T, S). The lexicographic order uses multi-set order of token values on T and multi-set order of level values on S. In the example, in propagation steps, the size of T decreases (while that of S increases); in simplification steps the size of T is constant, while that of S decreases.

Unfortunately, such behavior is not always the case.

Example 6 (Counter example).

$$R_1 @ a, a, a \Leftrightarrow b, b. \qquad R_2 @ b \Rightarrow a.$$

We execute the program with a query $\langle \{a\sharp 1, a\sharp 2, a\sharp 3\}, \{\} \rangle_4$:

$$\langle \{a\sharp 1, a\sharp 2, a\sharp 3\}, \{\} \rangle_4 \xrightarrow{R_1} \langle \{b\sharp 4, b\sharp 5\}, \{(R_2, 4), (R_2, 5)\} \rangle_6 \xrightarrow{R_2}$$
$$\langle \{a\sharp 6, b\sharp 4, b\sharp 5\}, \{(R_2, 5)\} \rangle_7 \xrightarrow{R_2} \langle \{a\sharp 7, a\sharp 6, b\sharp 4, b\sharp 5\}, \{\} \rangle_8$$

Note that here, contrary to Example 5, in simplification steps, T does not remain constant during decreases of S. So, a lexicographic order as suggested above does not decrease. $\qquad\square$

To solve this, we will introduce a third component in our state representation: the *propagation store*. This component is redundant: it is computable from S and T. However, it simplifies defining a decreasing lexicographic order.

4.2   Propagation Safe CHR Programs

We introduce some more compact notations. We will denote a state $< S, T >_\nu$ by $\mathscr{S}$, possibly with sub- or superscripts. Given $\mathscr{S} = < S, T >_\nu$, we introduce argument selectors: $cs(\mathscr{S}) = S$ and $ts(\mathscr{S}) = T$. Given a state $\mathscr{S}$, a propagation rule R_p, a token t and substitutions σ and θ, we write $\mathscr{T}_{R_p, t, \sigma, \theta}(\mathscr{S})$ to denote the state $\mathscr{T}(\mathscr{S})$, where the transition has applied R_p using token t and match and answer substitution σ and θ. Likewise, given a state $\mathscr{S}$, a simplification rule R_s and substitutions σ and θ, we write $\mathscr{T}_{R_s, \sigma, \theta}(\mathscr{S})$ to denote the resulting state $\mathscr{T}(\mathscr{S})$ after simplification. Without loss of generality, we will regard computations as subsequences of simplification steps, interleaved with sequences of zero or more propagation steps:

$$\mathscr{S}_{(1,1)} \xrightarrow{\mathscr{T}_{R_{p(1,1)},t_{(1,1)},\sigma_{(1,1)},\theta_{(1,1)}}} \mathscr{S}_{(1,2)} \xrightarrow{\mathscr{T}_{R_{p(1,2)},t_{(1,2)},\sigma_{(1,2)},\theta_{(1,2)}}} \dots \xrightarrow{\mathscr{T}_{\mathbf{R_{s_1}},\sigma_1,\theta_1}}$$

$$\mathscr{S}_{(2,1)} \xrightarrow{\mathscr{T}_{R_{p(2,1)},t_{(2,1)},\sigma_{(2,1)},\theta_{(2,1)}}} \mathscr{S}_{(2,2)} \xrightarrow{\mathscr{T}_{R_{p(2,2)},t_{(2,2)},\sigma_{(2,2)},\theta_{(2,2)}}} \dots \xrightarrow{\mathscr{T}_{\mathbf{R_{s_2}},\sigma_2,\theta_2}} \dots$$

Within this setting, we distinguish two different kinds of CHR states in computations. A *fully propagated state* is a state with an empty token store. Therefore, no propagation rule is applicable on a fully propagated state. A *partially propagated state* is a state which does contain tokens. By the action of *full propagation* and *partial propagation*, we refer to sequences of propagation steps, originating from a CHR state and ending in a fully or partially propagated state, respectively. Notice that full propagation may correspond to an infinite sequence.

To guarantee termination of CHR programs, we will first guarantee finiteness of full propagation sequences. To this end, we consider the token store. We measure the token store as the multi-set of token values of its tokens. Therefore, if we guarantee that all applications of propagation rules decrease the size of the token store, then we prove that all sequences of propagation steps in computations of the program must be finite. This is the case if none of the tokens added can be of higher token value than the token removed by propagation.

Definition 12 (Propagation safe). *A CHR program P is propagation safe for a query I iff there exists a level mapping $|.|$ with associated token mapping $|.|_\tau$, such that for every application of a propagation rule $\mathscr{T}_{R_p,t,\sigma,\theta}$ on a state $\mathscr{S} = \langle S, T \rangle_\nu$ in some computation of P for I: $\forall t' \in T^A_{(C\sigma\theta,S)} : |t|_\tau > |t'|_\tau$.*

Recall that, in our notation for propagation rules, the C above denotes the added constraints of R_p. □

If a CHR program is propagation safe, then all propagation sequences are finite, because the size of the token store cannot infinitely decrease.

Proposition 1. *If a CHR program P is propagation safe for a query I, then there are no infinite sequences of propagation steps in computations of P for I.*

As a consequence, for CHR programs without simplification rules, propagation safeness implies program termination.

Corrolary 1. *If a CHR program P without simplification is propagation safe for a query I, then the program is terminating for I.*

We demonstrate this on a program for calculating Fibonacci numbers [7].

Example 7 (Fibonacci). The first rules resolve base cases, while the third rule adds Fibonacci constraints.

$R_1 @ fib(N,M) \Rightarrow N = 0 \mid M = 0.$
$R_2 @ fib(N,M) \Rightarrow N = s(0) \mid M = 1.$
$R_3 @ fib(s(s(N)),M_1), fib(s(N),M_2) \Rightarrow fib(N,M), M_1 \text{ is } M_2 + M.$

We query the program with constraints $fib(N,M)$, where N is ground. We use the level mapping $|fib(N,M)| = \|N\|_{ts}$. R_1 and R_2 are trivially propagation safe as these do not introduce tokens. For R_3, the token removed is of a strictly higher token value than any of the tokens added. So the program terminates. □

4.3 Full Propagation

We now define the notion of full propagation more formally.

Definition 13 (One-layer propagation). *Let P be a program, I a query and $\mathscr{S} = \langle S, T \rangle_\nu$ a state in a computation of P for I, where $T = \{t_1, t_2, \ldots, t_n\}$ with $n \neq 0$. Let $(t_1, t_2, \ldots, t_n)$ be any fixed ordering on the elements of T, then the one-layer propagation on $\mathscr{S}$ is:*

$$\mathscr{P}(\mathscr{S}) = \mathscr{T}_{R_{p_n}, t_n, \sigma_n, \theta_n}(\ldots \mathscr{T}_{R_{p_2}, t_2, \sigma_2, \theta_2}(\mathscr{T}_{R_{p_1}, t_1, \sigma_1, \theta_1}(\mathscr{S})))$$

where R_{p_i}, σ_i and θ_i are the propagation rule, match and answer substitutions corresponding to t_i, with $i = 1, \ldots, n$. □

The result of one-layer propagation is not independent of the selected ordering $(t_1, t_2, \ldots, t_n)$ on T. However, taking two different orders, the resulting states only differ in the labels they assign to the constraints.

Definition 14 (Label-equivalent state). *Two CHR states $\mathscr{S}_1$ and $\mathscr{S}_2$ are label-equivalent, denoted by $\mathscr{S}_1 \approx \mathscr{S}_2$, iff there exists a one-to-one mapping Ψ from labels to labels, such that $\Psi(\mathscr{S}_1) = \mathscr{S}_2$.* □

Proposition 2. *Let $\mathscr{S} = \langle S, T \rangle_\nu$ be a state in a computation of P for I and let $(t_1, t_2, \ldots, t_n)$ and $(t'_1, t'_2, \ldots, t'_n)$, $n > 0$, be two orderings on T. Let $\mathscr{P}(\mathscr{S})$ denote the result of one-layer propagation with $(t_1, t_2, \ldots, t_n)$ and $\mathscr{P}'(\mathscr{S})$ that with $(t'_1, t'_2, \ldots, t'_n)$, then $\mathscr{P}(\mathscr{S}) \approx \mathscr{P}'(\mathscr{S})$.* □

In what follows, we will omit to make an explicit distinction between label-equivalent states and abuse the notation $\mathscr{P}(\mathscr{S})$ to denote some representant, using some order, of the equivalence class of the result of one-layer propagation.

We have the following properties.

Proposition 3. *Let $\mathscr{S} = \langle S, T \rangle_\nu$ be a state in a computation of P for I and $T \neq \emptyset$. Then, $S \subseteq cs(\mathscr{P}(\mathscr{S}))$ and $T \cap ts(\mathscr{P}(\mathscr{S})) = \emptyset$* □

One-layer propagation removes all tokens of T from the token store, but it may add new ones. As a result, there can be further propagation after the application of $\mathscr{P}$. We therefore define powers of $\mathscr{P}$.

Definition 15 (Powers of $\mathscr{P}$). *Let $\mathscr{S}$ be a state in a computation of P for I:*

If $ts(\mathscr{S}) \neq \emptyset$, then $\mathscr{P}^1(\mathscr{S}) = \mathscr{P}(\mathscr{S})$
If $ts(\mathscr{P}^{n-1}(\mathscr{S})) \neq \emptyset$, then $\mathscr{P}^n(\mathscr{S}) = \mathscr{P}(\mathscr{P}^{n-1}(\mathscr{S})), n > 1$. □

In principal, one could try to define an order on the set of all states, such that it becomes a complete lattice and such that $\mathscr{P}$ is monotonic and continuous on it. Full propagation would then correspond to the least fixpoint. However, since we are interested in termination analysis, we are only interested in finitely terminating propagation. By requiring propagation safeness, we can characterize full propagation on the basis of finite powers of $\mathscr{P}$.

Proposition 4. *Let $\mathscr{S}$ be a state in a computation of P for I. If P is propagation safe for I, then there exists $n_0 \in \mathbb{N}$ such that: $ts(\mathscr{P}^{n_0}(\mathscr{S})) = \emptyset$.* □

The proposition follows immediately from Proposition 1. So, assuming propagation safeness, we characterize full propagation on a state $\mathscr{S}$ as $\mathscr{P}^{n_0}(\mathscr{S})$.

4.4   The Propagation Store

From now on, we assume propagation safeness of P for I. We are ready to define the third component in our state representation: the propagation store. Intuitively, it is the multi-set of all constraints that are added by full propagation.

Definition 16 (Propagation store). *Let* $\mathscr{S} = \langle S, T \rangle_\nu$ *be a state in some computation of a propagation safe CHR program* P *for a query* I. *Then, the propagation store of* $\mathscr{S}$ *is* $U = chr(cs(\mathscr{P}^{n_0}(\mathscr{S})) \setminus S)$. $\qquad\square$

Example 8 (Executing Primes). We revisit the computation of Primes from Example 5 and represent for it the propagation store:

$$\langle \{primes(7)\sharp 1\}, \{\mathbf{primes(6)}, \mathbf{primes(5)}, \mathbf{primes(4)}, \mathbf{primes(3)}, \mathbf{primes(2)}\}, \{(R_2, 1)\}\rangle_2$$
$$\langle \{primes(7)\sharp 1, primes(6)\sharp 2\}, \{\mathbf{primes(5)}, \mathbf{primes(4)}, \mathbf{primes(3)}, \mathbf{primes(2)}\}, \{(R_2, 2)\}\rangle_3$$
$$\langle \{primes(7)\sharp 1, primes(6)\sharp 2, primes(5)\sharp 3\}, \{\mathbf{primes(4)}, \mathbf{primes(3)}, \mathbf{primes(2)}\}, \{(R_2, 3)\}\rangle_4$$
$$\langle \{primes(7)\sharp 1, primes(6)\sharp 2, primes(5)\sharp 3, primes(4)\sharp 4\}, \{\mathbf{primes(3)}, \mathbf{primes(2)}\}, \{(R_2, 4)\}\rangle_5$$
$$\langle \{primes(7)\sharp 1, primes(6)\sharp 2, primes(5)\sharp 3, primes(4)\sharp 4, primes(3)\sharp 5\}, \{\mathbf{primes(2)}\}, \{(R_2, 5)\}\rangle_6$$
$$\langle \{primes(7)\sharp 1, primes(5)\sharp 3, primes(4)\sharp 4, primes(3)\sharp 5\}, \{\mathbf{primes(2)}\}, \{(R_2, 5)\}\rangle_6$$
$$\langle \{primes(7)\sharp 1, primes(5)\sharp 3, primes(4)\sharp 4, primes(3)\sharp 5, primes(2)\sharp 6\}, \{\}, \{\}\rangle_7$$
$$\langle \{primes(7)\sharp 1, primes(5)\sharp 3, primes(3)\sharp 5, primes(2)\sharp 6\}, \{\}, \{\}\rangle_7$$

Note that we have left out state names as well as transitions due to space restrictions. The propagation store together with the constraint store remains constant when propagation occurs. When simplifying, their combined size decreases. It turns out that this is typical for terminating programs. $\qquad\square$

By proposition 2 we know that the result of one-layer propagation is unique up to label-equivalence. Therefore, the propagation store, as the result of a finite sequence of one-layer propagations, is also unique up to label-equivalence.

Corrolary 2. *For any state* $\mathscr{S}$ *in a computation of* P *for* I, *the propagation store* U *is well-defined up to label-equivalence.* $\qquad\square$

To avoid misunderstanding, note that our introduction of the propagation store does not mean that we restrict our attention to computation rules in which simplification is interleaved with full propagation. We will still allow that propagation is interrupted by simplification. So, there is no restriction on the computation rule. However, if we do interrupt full propagation by applying a simplification rule, this affects the propagation store. That is, if constraints are removed from the constraint store, some tokens may become invalid and as a consequence also constraints in the propagation store become invalid. When adding constraints to the constraint store, new tokens are added to the token store and as a result, new constraints are also added to the propagation store.

We will not explicitly define the added and eliminated elements of the propagation store due to a simplification step, because they are not needed in the termination conditions that we will propose. Moreover, the propagation store is redundant anyway. So the new propagation store can always be determined by computing full propagation on a newly obtained state.

5   Termination of CHR

5.1   CHR State Ordering

We now come to the heart of our approach. As we have already illustrated in Example 8, the combined size of constraint and propagation store $chr(S) \uplus U$ remains equal when propagating, while the size of the token store T decreases. We furthermore have illustrated that $chr(S) \uplus U$ decreases in size when simplifying the program. We can therefore define a lexicographical order on states that can be shown to decrease for every application of a rule.

Definition 17 (CHR state ordering). *To any state $\mathscr{S} = \langle S, T \rangle_\nu$ we associate a tuple $\langle S \uplus U, T \rangle$, where U is the propagation store of $\mathscr{S}$. We order the tuples using lexicographical order, based on multi-set order of level values on $chr(S) \uplus U$ and multi-set order on token values on T.* □

Obviously, since level and token values are well-founded, the CHR state ordering is a well-founded order. We will introduce sufficient conditions on CHR rules that imply decreases of all consecutive computation states under this order.

5.2   The Ranking Condition on Propagation Rules

First, we observe that propagation steps do not affect the order of the $chr(S) \uplus U$ component in our lexicographical order. It is the essence of the meaning of a propagation store that it collects all the constraints that can be added to the constraint store by upcoming propagation steps. Therefore, applying a propagation rule moves constraints from U to S. More precisely, we have the following.

Proposition 5. *Let $\mathscr{T}_{R_p, t, \sigma\theta} : \langle S, T \rangle_\nu \to \langle S', T' \rangle_{\nu'}$ be a propagation transition with associated propagation stores U and U', then $chr(S) \uplus U = chr(S') \uplus U'$* □

Next, note that propagation safeness is a condition that explicitly requires a decrease of the multi-set order of the token values in T with any application of a propagation rule. We therefore introduce a ranking condition (RC) on propagation rules that implies propagation safeness. As a result, the CHR state ordering decreases with propagation transitions if this ranking condition holds.

Definition 18 (RC on propagation rules). *Let $R_p @ h_1, \ldots, h_n \Rightarrow G \mid B, c_1, \ldots, c_m$ be a propagation rule in a CHR program P, I a query and σ a match substitution for the heads of R_p and θ an answer substitution for $G\sigma$ such that $CT \models G\sigma\theta$ holds. Then, the RC on propagation rules is satisfied w.r.t. a rigid level mapping $|.|$ for $Call(P, I)$ iff $\forall h_i, c_j : |h_i\sigma| > |c_j\sigma\theta|$.* □

Proposition 6. *If a CHR program P satisfies the RC on propagation rules w.r.t. a rigid level mapping $|.|$ for $Call(P, I)$, then P is propagation safe for I.*

Example 9 (Fibonacci revisited). We recall the third rule from Example 7:

$$R_3 @ fib(s(s(N)), M_1), fib(s(N), M_2) \Rightarrow fib(N, M), M_1 \text{ is } M_2 + M.$$

R_3 satisfies the RC on propagation rules if $|fib(s(s(N)), M_1)| > |fib(N, M)|$ and $|fib(s(N), M)| > |fib(N, M)|$. Using the level mapping $|fib(N, M)| = \|N\|_{ts}$, it can be verified that this is indeed the case for all instances of the rule, using ground first arguments for $fib/2$. For the other rules in Example 7, the RC is trivially satisfied. The program is therefore propagation safe.   □

5.3   The Ranking Condition on Simplification Rules

We now want to introduce a condition on simplification rules, such that for every application of a simplification rule, the multi-set order of level values of consecutive $chr(S) \uplus U$ multi-sets decreases. However, we do not want to reason explicitly of the propagation store. Full propagation may require many iterations of the $\mathscr{P}$ operator and we do not want to compute them all.

It turns out that, assuming propagation safeness for the propagation rules, if there is a multi-set order decrease on $chr(S) \uplus chr(cs(\mathscr{P}^1(\langle S, T \rangle_\nu) \setminus S))$, then there is also a decrease on $chr(S) \uplus U$. As a result, we only need to consider the first-layer propagation. We need the following notation.

Definition 19 (Propagation layers). *Let $\mathscr{S} = \langle S, T \rangle_\nu$ be a computation state of P for I, we denote: $U^0 = chr(S)$ and $U^i = chr(cs(\mathscr{P}^i(\mathscr{S}))) \setminus U^{i-1}, i > 0$.* □

With this notation, $U = U^1 \uplus \cdots \uplus U^{n_0}$ is the disjoint union of consecutive propagation layers. We formulate the following lemma.

Lemma 1. *Let P be propagation safe for I given a level mapping $|.|$. Let $\mathscr{S}$ be a computation state in a computation of P for I. Then, there exists a constraint $D \in U^1$, such that $\forall 1 < i \leq n_0, \forall D' \in U^i : |D'| < |D|$.*   □

Intuitively, if all constraints in U^1 are smaller than some given value, then all constraints in U are smaller than that value. The reason being that propagation safeness imposes further decreases on following layers U^i, $i > 1$.

Our ranking condition is a refinement of the ranking condition for simplification rules defined in [4]. We first recall that condition.

Definition 20 (RC on simplification rules from [4]). *Let $R_s @ H_k \setminus H_r \Leftrightarrow G \mid B, C$ be a simplification rule in a CHR program P. Let σ be a match substitution for the head constraints and θ an answer substitution for $G\sigma$ such that $CT \models G\sigma\theta$ holds and let $|.|$ be a rigid level mapping w.r.t. a CHR program P and a query I, such that the added constraints $C\sigma\theta$ and removed constraints $H_r\sigma$ in R_s have ranks $r_1 > r_2 > ... > r_k$ and such that n_i^a and n_i^e represent respectively the number of constraints of rank r_i in $C\sigma\theta$ and in $H_r\sigma$. Then, R_s satisfies the RC on simplification rules w.r.t. $|.|$ iff $\exists r_j : n_j^e > n_j^a$ and $\forall r_i > r_j : n_i^e = n_i^a$.*   □

We refine this condition by additionally imposing that all first-layer propagations that can follow the application of the simplification rule and consume an added constraint of the simplification rule also only introduce constraints with a level value smaller than r_j.

Definition 21 (RC on simplification rules). *Let* R_s @ $H_k \setminus H_r \Leftrightarrow G_s \mid B, c_{(s,1)}, \ldots, c_{(s,m_s)}$ *be a simplification rule in a CHR program* P *and let* $|.|$ *be a rigid level mapping w.r.t.* $Call(P, I)$, *where* I *is a query. Assume that* R_s *satisfies the RC on simplification rules of [4] and let* σ *and* θ *be a matching and answer substitution as in Definition 20 and* r_j *the level value of Definition 20. Then* P *satisfies the ranking condition on simplification rules for* I *iff for all propagation rules* R_p @ $h_{(p,1)}, \ldots, h_{(p,n)} \Leftrightarrow G_s \mid B, c_{(p,1)}, \ldots, c_{(p,m_p)}$ *and* $\forall i, 1 \leq i \leq n$:

> **If** $\exists k, 1 \leq k \leq m_s$ **and** μ, σ', θ' *are such that*
> $$CT \models G_s \sigma\theta \wedge (b_{(s,i)}\sigma\theta = h_{(p,k)}\mu) \wedge G_p\mu\sigma'\theta',$$
> **then** $\forall l, 1 \leq l \leq m_p : |b_{(p,l)}\mu\sigma'\theta'| < r_j.$ □

What is expressed in the condition is that each time that a head constraint in a propagation rule matches an added constraint of the simplification rule, it can only add constraints of lower level value than r_j. Therefore, we are considering every possible activation of a propagation rule following the simplification rule and consuming some of its added constraints. We illustrate the condition with an example which is outside the scope of both [4] and [5].

Example 10 (Problem case for [4] and [5]).

> R_1 @ $a(s(N)), a(N) \Leftrightarrow a(s(N)).$ R_2 @ $a(s(s(M))), a(s(s(M))) \Rightarrow a(M).$

We consider any finite query consisting of ground instances of $a(N)$, using terms constructed from $s/1$ and 0. $Call(P, I)$ is the set of all such atoms. The level mapping $|a(N)| = \|N\|_{ts}$ is rigid on $Call(P, I)$.

The rule R_2 satisfies the RC on propagation rules: $|a(s(s(M)))| > |a(M)|$ for all considered instances. Note that R_1 does not satisfy the RC of [5]: the number of atoms with maximal level value (which is $|a(s(N))|$) does not decrease.

To verify our RC on simplification rules, first note that the RC of [4] (Definition 20 above) is satisfied: the number of constraints of level value $|s(s(N))|$ remains equal in head and body, but the number of constraints of level value $|a(N)|$ decreases. The r_j in Definition 20 and 21 has the value $|a(N)|$.

Verifying the second part of Definition 21, we need to consider every possible match of a head constraint of R_2 with a body constraint of R_1, given that we start off from an activated (thus ground) instance of R_1. There are two possible matches, treated identically: $a(s(s(M))) = a(s(N))$, so $s(M)$ is instantiated to N. For the body constraint in R_2, we then get $|a(M)| < |a(s(M))| = |a(N)| = r_j$. Thus, the condition holds and we prove termination.   □

By imposing both the RC on propagation rules and the RC on simplification rules, we now obtain a decreasing lexicographical ordering on the structure $\langle chr(S) \uplus U, T \rangle$. Therefore, our main result follows.

Theorem 1. *If a CHR program* P *satisfies the RC on propagation rules and the RC on simplification rules for a query* I, *then* P *terminates for* I.   □

6   Discussion and Conclusions

We have introduced a new termination condition for CHR programs. Our condition is strictly more powerful than both of the existing approaches. We are more powerful than [4], because on programs with simplification only, our conditions coincide, while programs including propagation are outside the scope of [4].

In the case of [5], for programs with propagation only, our approach is identical to [5]. For programs with simplification, if they are in the scope of [5], then the number of constraints of maximal level value decreases from head to body. As a result, 1) the multi-set order decreases as well (first part of our RC on simplification rules), 2) due to the RC on propagation rules, the extra condition of one-layer propagation trivially holds. Thus, these programs are also in the scope of our approach. Furthermore,Our condition can deal with programs that are outside the scope of both [4] and [5], as was explained in Example 10.

We have also introduced a new representation for CHR states and a class of orderings on this representation which facilitate reasoning about termination of CHR computations. Our termination conditions are strongly based on this new representation and its orderings. Our termination conditions correspond to imposing decreases of the ordering over these representations of consecutive computation states.

References

1. Frühwirth, T.: Theory and practice of constraint handling rules. J. Logic Programming 37(1–3), 95–138 (1998)
2. Abdennadher, S., Marte, M.: University course timetabling using constraint handling rules. Applied Artificial Intelligence 14(4), 311–325 (2000)
3. Frühwirth, T., Brisset, P.: Optimal placement of base stations in wireless indoor telecommunication. In: Maher, M.J., Puget, J.-F. (eds.) CP 1998. LNCS, vol. 1520, pp. 476–480. Springer, Heidelberg (1998)
4. Frühwirth, T.: Proving termination of constraint solver programs. In: New Trends in Constraints, pp. 298–317 (2000)
5. Voets, D., Pilozzi, P., De Schreye, D.: A new approach to termination analysis of constraint handling rules. In: Pre-proceedings of LOPSTR 2008, pp. 28–42 (2008)
6. Schrijvers, T.: Analyses, optimizations and extensions of constraint handling rules: Ph.D summary. In: Gabbrielli, M., Gupta, G. (eds.) ICLP 2005. LNCS, vol. 3668, pp. 435–436. Springer, Heidelberg (2005)
7. WebCHR, http://www.cs.kuleuven.be/~dtai/projects/chr/
8. De Schreye, D., Decorte, S.: Termination of logic programs: the never-ending story. J. of Logic Programming 19–20, 199–260 (1994)
9. Dershowitz, N.: Termination of rewriting. J. of Symbolic Computation 3(1–2), 69–116 (1987)
10. Dershowitz, N., Manna, Z.: Proving termination with multiset orderings. Commun. ACM 22(8), 465–476 (1979)
11. Abdennadher, S.: Operational semantics and confluence of constraint propagation rules. In: Smolka, G. (ed.) CP 1997. LNCS, vol. 1330, pp. 252–266. Springer, Heidelberg (1997)
12. Duck, G., Stuckey, P., García de la Banda, M., Holzbaur, C.: The refined operational semantics of constraint handling rules. In: Demoen, B., Lifschitz, V. (eds.) ICLP 2004. LNCS, vol. 3132, pp. 90–104. Springer, Heidelberg (2004)

Transactions in Constraint Handling Rules

Tom Schrijvers[1,*] and Martin Sulzmann[2]

[1] Department of Computer Science, K.U.Leuven, Belgium
tom.schrijvers@cs.kuleuven.be
[2] ITU, Copenhagen, Denmark
martin.sulzmann@gmail.com

Abstract. CHR is a highly concurrent language, and yet it is by no means a trivial task to write correct concurrent CHR programs. We propose a new semantics for CHR, which allows specifying and reasoning about *transactions*. Transactions alleviate the complexity of writing concurrent programs by offering entire derivations to run atomically and in isolation.

We derive several program transformations based on our semantics that transform particular classes of transitional CHR programs to non-transactional ones. These transformations are useful because they obviate a general purpose transaction manager, and may lift unnecessary sequentialization present in the transactional semantics.

1 Introduction

Constraint Handling Rules (CHR) [1] is a concurrent committed-choice constraint logic programming language. Each CHR rewrite rule specifies an atomic and isolated transformation step (rewriting) among a multi-set of constraints. Although this greatly facilitates writing concurrent programs, often we wish for entire derivations of CHR rewrite steps to be executed atomically and in isolation. For this purpose we propose CHR$^{\clubsuit}$, an extension of CHR where the user can group together sets of goals (constraints) in a transaction. Like database transactions, atomically executed transactions provide an "all-or-nothing" guarantee. The effects of the transaction are visible either in their entirety or the transaction has no effect. Further, transaction are executed in isolation from other transactions. That is, no intermediate state is observable by another transaction.

The efficient implementation of transactions is quite challenging: the amount of concurrency should be maximized with a minimum of synchronization overhead. For this purpose, non-interfering transactions should be identified for concurrent scheduling on different processors or processor cores. The current state of the art for dealing with concurrent transactions is *optimistic concurrency control*. In essence, each transaction is executed under the optimistic assumption that concurrent transactions do not interfere with each other. Each transaction's updates are logged and only committed once the transaction is fully executed, and

---

* Post-doctoral researcher of the Fund for Scientific Research - Flanders.

only no update conflicts with other transactions. In theory, this method supports a high-level of concurrency. Unfortunately, in practice many "false" conflicts may arise in case the objects protected by transactions are subject to a high-level of contention. The consequence is a significantly lower level of concurrency. This is a serious problem for the practical acceptance of transactions in the programming language setting.

Our novel idea is that instead of being concerned with a generic and efficient execution scheme for CHR$^{\bullet}$ which enables a high level of concurrency, we investigate meaning-preserving transformation methods of CHR$^{\bullet}$ to plain CHR programs. The advantages of this approach are that there is no overhead caused by a concurrency control scheme for transactions and "false" conflicts are completely avoided. Furthermore, resulting plain CHR programs enjoy a high-level of concurrency. In some cases, we can apply domain-specific optimizations to even further boost the level of concurrency. The correctness of our transformation methods is based on well-defined criteria and formal reasoning techniques. Our criteria and techniques cover a certain, we claim significant, class of CHR$^{\bullet}$ programs.

In summary, we make the following contributions:

- We introduce CHR$^{\bullet}$ (pronounce: Atom CHR) an extension of CHR with atomic transactions and develop the meta-theory for such a calculus (Section 4). We demonstrate the usefulness of CHR$^{\bullet}$ via a number of examples.
- We devise an execution scheme for CHR$^{\bullet}$ where transactions must be executed sequentially to guarantee atomicity and isolation but plain CHR derivations can be executed concurrently whenever possible (Section 5).
- Our approach to unlock concurrency in CHR$^{\bullet}$ works by means of transformation to plain CHR. Specifically, we consider transformation methods (Section 6) which cover
  - bounded transactions,
  - (partially) confluent transactions, and
  - domain-specific transaction synchronization and recovery.

Section 2 provides an overview of our work. Section 3 gives background material on the CHR language. CHR follows Prolog syntax conventions, where identifiers starting with a lower case letter indicate predicates and function symbols, and identifiers starting with upper case are variables. We will stick to this convention throughout the paper. Discussion of related work is deferred until Section 7. Section 8 concludes.

Additional material such as examples are given in an accompanying technical report [2].

2   Overview

In this section, we present two examples to motivate CHR$^{\bullet}$ and our transformation methods. In the first example, we see a bounded transaction, i.e. whose number of derivation steps is bounded. In the second example, transactions are unbounded.

Table 1. Non-atomic transfer

```
    balance(acc1,2000) ∧ balance(acc2,0) ∧ balance(acc3,1000)
  ∧ transfer(acc1,acc2,1000)
  ∧ transfer(acc1,acc3,1500)
↦ (unfold transfer x2)
    balance(acc1,2000) ∧ balance(acc2,0) ∧ balance(acc3,1000)
  ∧ withdraw(acc1,1000) ∧ deposit(acc2,1000)
  ∧ withdraw(acc1,1500) ∧ deposit(acc3,1500)
↦ (deposit(acc2,1000))
    balance(acc1,2000) ∧ balance(acc2,1000) ∧ balance(acc3,1000)
  ∧ withdraw(acc1,1000)
  ∧ withdraw(acc1,1500) ∧ deposit(acc3,1500)
↦ (deposit(acc3,1500))
    balance(acc1,500) ∧ balance(acc2,1000) ∧ balance(acc3,1000)
  ∧ withdraw(acc1,1000)
  ∧ deposit(acc3,1500)
↦ (deposit(acc3,1500))
    balance(acc1,500) ∧ balance(acc2,1000) ∧ balance(acc3,2500)
  ∧ withdraw(acc1,1000)
```

2.1   Bounded Transaction: Bank Transfer

Consider these (plain) CHR rules for updating a bank account:

```
balance(Acc,Bal), deposit(Acc,Amount)  <=>
                          balance(Acc,Bal+Amount).
balance(Acc,Bal), withdraw(Acc,Amount) <=>
                    Bal > Amount | balance(Acc,Bal-Amount).
```

The balance/2 constraint is a data constraint, and the deposit/2 and withdraw/2 constraints are operation constraints. The guard ensures that a withdraw is only possible if the amount in the account is sufficient. In the concurrent CHR semantics, rules can be applied simultaneously, as long as they operate on non-overlapping parts of the constraint store. Simultaneous deposit or withdrawal from distinct accounts is therefore possible.

The transfer constraint/rule combines deposit and withdraw among two accounts.

```
transfer(Acc1,Acc2,Amount) <=>
                  withdraw(Acc1,Amount) ∧ deposit(Acc2,Amount).
```

Suppose, we wish to perform two transfers where three accounts are involved.

```
      balance(acc1,2000) ∧ balance(acc2,0) ∧ balance(acc3,1000)
  ∧ transfer(acc1,acc2,1000)
  ∧ transfer(acc1,acc3,1500)
```

Table 1 shows a possible derivation. We simulate concurrency using an interleaving semantics. The point to note is that we cannot execute withdraw(acc1,1000) because of insufficient funds. The result is a "non-atomic" execution of the first transfer operations. We only manage to deposit but fail to withdraw. This is clearly not the desired behavior of a transfer.

In CHR$^{\clubsuit}$, such problems can be avoided by guarding each `transfer` constraint with an `atomic()` wrapper. In general, `atomic()` can be wrapped around any constraint C (possibly consisting of a conjunction of constraints). We refer to `atomic(`C`)` as a *transaction*. The CHR$^{\clubsuit}$ semantics guarantees that transactions are executed atomically and in isolation from other transactions. Informally, this means that all constraints (and also those occurring in subderivations) are either executed exhaustively or not at all. Any store updates are only visible once the transaction is completed.

Next, we consider transformation of the above CHR$^{\clubsuit}$ program to plain CHR. In this example, derivation steps within a transaction are bounded. By performing a simple unfolding of CHR, we can replace the atomic transfer rule by the following single rule.

```
balance(Acc1,Amt1),balance(Acc2,Amt2),transfer(Acc1,Acc2,Amt)
<=> Amt1 > Amt | balance(Acc1,Amt1-Amt) ∧ balance(Acc2,Amt2+Amt)
```

Immediately, this multi-headed rule expresses the fact that an atomic transfer requires exclusive access to both accounts involved. Section 6.1 contains the details of the transformation method for bounded transactions.

2.2   Unbounded Transaction: Shared Linked List

In this example, we consider linked lists of distinct elements (numbers) in increasing order. A list is made up of four kinds of data constraints:

- We write `node(X,P,Q)` to represent a node with value X at location (cfr. pointer address) P whose tail is at location Q.
- We write `nil(P)` to represent an empty list at location P.
- We write `found(X)` and `notfound(X)` to indicate that either a value X is part of the list or not.

Two operation constraints inspect and modify a list:

- The `find(X,P)` operation searches for the element X starting from the location P.
- Operation `insert(X,P)` adds the element X to the linked list at the proper position (if not already present).

The program is:

```
f1 @ node(X,P,Next) \ find(X,P) <=> found(X).
f2 @ nil(P) \ find(Y,P) <=> notfound(Y).
f3 @ node(X,P,Next) \ find(Y,P) <=> X < Y | find(Y,Next).
f4 @ node(X,P,Next) \ find(Y,P) <=> X > Y | notfound(Y).

i1 @ node(X,P,Next) \ insert(X,P) <=> true.
i2 @ node(X,P,Next) \ insert(Y,P) <=> X < Y | insert(Y,Next).
i3 @ node(X,P,Next),  insert(Y,P) <=> X > Y |
        fresh(NewP) ∧ node(Y,P,NewP) ∧ node(X,NewP,Next).
i4 @ nil(P),          insert(X,P) <=>
        fresh(NewP) ∧ node(X,P,NewP) ∧ nil(NewP).
```

For brevity's sake, we assume the existence of the primitive `fresh` for the generation of fresh locations. This could be encoded via additional CHR rules.

In $CHR^{\clubsuit}$, we can then specify the atomic and isolated execution of operations, for example (we omit the data store holding the linked list for simplicity)

$$\texttt{atomic(find(50,root))} \land \texttt{atomic(insert(2,root))} \qquad (***)$$

Transactions are unbounded because operations traverse a dynamic data structure. It is a well-known fact that in case the linked list is subject to a high-level of contention, an optimistic concurrency control scheme for transactions does not exhibit a high-level of concurrency due to many "false" conflicts. Details are in Section 5.1.

To safely remove `atomic()` wrappers (and thus avoiding "false" conflicts) we establish criteria which guarantee that the resulting program still behaves atomically and does not violate isolation. One of the key criteria is partial confluence of the primitive operations (i.e. plain CHR rules) out of which transactions are composed of. Partial confluence means that non-joinable critical pairs are either ruled out because they disobey an invariant (i.e. they are observably confluent [3]), or non-joinability can be explained as a specific serial (in essence indeterministic) execution of the (atomic) operations. The above linked list rules are partially confluent which therefore guarantees that isolation is not violated once we remove the `atomic()` wrappers in (***). Details are in Section 6 where we also discuss more complex transactions and the impact of additional operations such as delete.

3   Preliminaries: Concurrent CHR

We assume that the reader is already familiar with CHR ([1]), and restrict ourselves here to the conventions used in this paper.

The Concurrent CHR language. For the purpose of this paper, we consider only a subset the CHR language, with the following two restrictions.

Firstly, programs do not involve Prolog-style logical variables and built-in constraint solvers over these logical variables. In other words, all CHR constraints range over ground terms.

Secondly, CHR constraint symbols $\mathcal{C}$ are partitioned into two classes $\mathcal{C}_D$ and $\mathcal{C}_O$. The former are *data* constraints and the latter *operation* constraints, according to the terminology of [4]. The head of each CHR rule must consist of exactly one operation constraint and zero or more data constraints, i.e. it is of the form $O, D_1, \ldots, D_n$ with $n \geq 0$. Thus, each rule can be viewed as an operation. See Fig. 1 for the notational conventions used in this paper.

Neither of these restrictions is very demanding. In fact, Sneyers et al [5] show that this fragment of the CHR language is Turing-complete: their RAM machine simulator works on ground constraints and the program counter constraint can be considered the operation constraint while the other constraints are data constraints.

Operational Semantics. Frühwirth [6] proposes a (non-transactional) concurrent operational semantics for CHR (bottom of Fig. 1) on top of the basic rule application (middle of Fig. 1). Rule MONOTONICITY encodes the monotonicity property of CHR, which is also part of the sequential CHR semantics. Rule

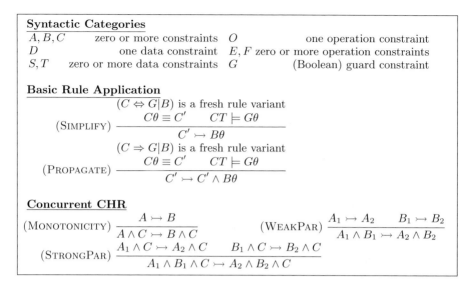

Fig. 1. Concurrent CHR

WEAKPAR is the traditional compositionality property, which allows for derivations to run fully isolated and their results to be merged. The rule STRONGPAR is proposed by Fruehwirth in [6]. It allows for a stronger form of concurrency, as both subderivations may share the same unmodified context E.

A CHR derivation starting from constraints C_0 yields after exhaustive application of the rules of Fig. 1 the constraints C_n. Such a derivation is denoted as $C_0 \rightarrowtail^* C_n$. As the CHR semantics is nondeterministic there may be many derivations, with different final constraints C_n, starting from the same C_0. We denote $\mathcal{S}[\![P]\!](C_0)$ the set $\{C_n \mid C_0 \rightarrowtail^* C_n\}$ wrt. CHR program P, i.e. the set of different possible final constraints.

4   The CHR$^{\clubsuit}$ Language

We propose CHR$^{\clubsuit}$ (pronounce: Atom CHR), a new extension of CHR with atomic transactions. An atomic transaction is denoted as $\texttt{atomic}(C)$ where C is a conjunction of CHR constraints. Atomic transactions may appear in queries and rule bodies, in addition to ordinary (non-transactional) constraints.

The semantics of CHR$^{\clubsuit}$ is an extension of the ordinary CHR semantics of Figure 1. It requires only one more rule:

$$(\text{ATOMIC}) \quad \frac{T \wedge S_i \wedge C_i \rightarrowtail^* T \wedge S_i' \text{ for } i = 1, ..., n}{T \wedge \bigwedge_{i=1}^{n} S_i \wedge \bigwedge_{i=1}^{n} \texttt{atomic}(C_i) \rightarrowtail T \wedge \bigwedge_{i=1}^{n} S_i'}$$

The ATOMIC rule is quite general in nature. It defines a derivation step that runs any number of atomic transactions $\texttt{atomic}(C_i)$ in parallel.

Each transaction is *isolated* from the others: the parallel step considers the separate evaluation of each C_i in isolation from the other C_j. The different transactions only share the common data, in our case constraints, $T \wedge \bigwedge_i S_i$. However, note that none of the transactions should observe updates S_i' from the other transactions to these common constraints.

Moreover, each transaction should run its full course, and not get stuck, i.e. no operation constraints should be left. This ensures that the context $T \wedge \bigwedge S_i$ provides sufficient data for the atomic derivation to have its intended effect. Without this condition, we could assume the context $T \wedge \bigwedge S_i$ to be empty, and thus lift the `atomic` wrapper and subsequently run the atomic derivation in a non-atomic manner.

The notation $\mathcal{S}^{\clubsuit}[\![P]\!](C)$ for CHR$^{\clubsuit}$ has the same meaning as $\mathcal{S}[\![P]\!](C)$ for plain CHR.

In Section 2, we have seen several examples showing the usefulness of CHR$^{\clubsuit}$. We refer to [2] for a more extensive collection of examples.

4.1   Properties of CHR$^{\clubsuit}$

An important property of transactions in general is *serializability*: for each parallel execution of transactions there is a sequential execution with the same outcome [7]. This serializability property also holds for CHR$^{\clubsuit}$.

Theorem 1 (Serializability). *For each* ATOMIC *derivation step* $C_1 \rightarrowtail C_2$ *with n concurrent transactions, there is a corresponding derivation* $C_1 \rightarrowtail^n C_2$ *of n consecutive* ATOMIC *steps each with only one transaction.*

The proof is straightforward, and the n transactions can be serialized in any order. A corollary of serializability is that in the worst case of any CHR$^{\clubsuit}$ derivation involves no concurrency at all.

While CHR$^{\clubsuit}$ is a syntactic and semantic extension of CHR, the `atomic` keyword in fact restricts the possible derivations for a query with respect to concurrent CHR. For this purpose we define the notion of erasure, which drops the `atomic` keyword from a syntactic object:

Definition 1 (Erasure). *The erasure from a syntactic CHR object o is denoted as:*

$$\epsilon(C) = C \, (\textit{where } C \textit{ atomic} - \textit{free}) \qquad \epsilon(C_1 \wedge C_2) = \epsilon(C_1) \wedge \epsilon(C_2)$$
$$\epsilon(\texttt{atomic}(C)) = C \qquad \epsilon(C_1 \texttt{ <=> } C_2) = C_1 \texttt{ <=> } \epsilon(C_2)$$
$$\epsilon(C_1 \texttt{ ==> } C_2) = C_1 \texttt{ ==> } \epsilon(C_2) \qquad \epsilon(C_1 \rightarrowtail C_2) = \epsilon(C_1) \rightarrowtail \epsilon(C_2)$$

We say that C is fully erased *iff $\epsilon(C) \equiv C$.*

Theorem 2 (Soundness under Erasure). *If $C_0 \rightarrowtail^* C_n$ is an CHR$^{\clubsuit}$ derivation wrt. program P, then $\epsilon(C_0 \rightarrowtail^* C_n)$ is a plain CHR derivation wrt. $\epsilon(P)$.*

Corollary 1. *The set of resulting constraints of an CHR$^{\clubsuit}$ program P is a subset of its erased form: $\forall P, \forall C. \mathcal{S}^{\clubsuit}[\![P]\!](C) \subseteq \mathcal{S}[\![\epsilon(P)]\!](\epsilon(C))$.*

Note that vice versa, i.e. by adding the `atomic` keyword to a concurrent CHR derivation, we do not necessarily obtain a valid CHR$^{\clubsuit}$ derivation. In Section 6 we will see cases where it is valid to do so. Of course, for fully erased programs both CHR$^{\clubsuit}$ and CHR yield the same result:

Theorem 3 (Completeness of Fully Erased Programs). *If CHR$^{\leftrightarrow}$ program P and constraints C_0 are fully erased, then $\mathcal{S}^{\leftrightarrow}[\![P]\!](C_0) = \mathcal{S}[\![P]\!](C_0)$.*

5   CHR$^{\leftrightarrow}$ Execution Schemes

We first sketch a possible optimistic concurrency control scheme for CHR$^{\leftrightarrow}$. The common problem of all optimistic concurrency methods is that the read logs of long running transactions may cause "false" conflicts with the write logs of other transactions. These conflicts lead to a roll back and therefore decreases the level of concurrency significantly as we will explain shortly. We therefore argue for a simple CHR$^{\leftrightarrow}$ execution scheme where transactions are executed sequentially but which allows for concurrent execution of CHR derivation steps whenever possible. To unlock concurrency in CHR$^{\leftrightarrow}$ programs, we investigate several transformation schemes from CHR$^{\leftrightarrow}$ to CHR programs in the upcoming Section 6.

5.1   Optimistic Concurrency in CHR$^{\leftrightarrow}$ and Its Problem

Optimistic Concurrency in CHR$^{\leftrightarrow}$ We apply the principle of optimistic concurrency control to CHR$^{\leftrightarrow}$ as follows. Each transaction is executed optimistically, keeping a log of all reads and writes to the shared store. At the end of a transaction, we check for conflicts with the read/write logs of other transactions. For example, a conflict arises if the read log of a transaction overlaps with the write log of another transaction. In this case, it is the transaction manager's duty to resolve the conflict by for example rolling back one transaction, i.e. we restart the transaction with an empty log, and letting the other transaction commit its write log.

The Problem   In case shared data objects are subject to a high level of contention, optimistic concurrency control of atomic transactions degenerates to a sequential execution scheme.

Example 1. Let's consider the earlier shared linked list example from Section 2.2. Suppose, we execute the two transactions `atomic(find(50,n`$_1$`))` $\wedge$ `atomic(insert(2,n`$_1$`))` on the shared store

`node(1,n`$_1$`,n`$_3$`)` $\wedge$ `node(3,n`$_3$`,n`$_4$`)` $\wedge$ `...` `node(50,n`$_{50}$`,n`$_{51}$`)` $\wedge$ `nil(n`$_{51}$`)`

The first transaction will search through the entire list whereas the second transaction will insert a new node containing 2 in between the first and second node. Both transactions "overlap". That is, the read log of the first transaction conflicts with the write log of the second transaction. When searching for (the last) element 50, we will read the entire list, among others `node(1,n`$_1$`,n`$_3$`)`. However, the second transaction will re-write this constraint to `node(1,n`$_1$`,n`$_2$`)`, and adds `node(2,n`$_2$`,n`$_3$`)`. This is a conflict between the read of the first transaction and the write of the second. Assuming that the second transaction commits first, we are forced to roll back the first transaction. In other words, the sequential execution of both transactions is enforced. This is unfortunate because the read/write conflict is a "false" conflict. The result of the find transaction is independent of the insertion of node 2. Hence, we would expect that both transactions can be executed concurrently.

5.2   A Simple CHR* Execution Scheme

We consider a simple, sequential execution scheme for CHR* programs but which allows for concurrent execution of CHR derivation steps whenever possible. The idea is to collect atomic transactions and process them sequentially. Thus, we trivially guarantee the atomic and isolated execution of transactions. The semantics of such a restricted CHR* calculus is given in Fig. 2. We define a rewrite relation $\rightarrowtail_{SeqACHR}$ among configurations C, AT where C is as before and AT refers to a conjunction of transactions. Rule SEQUENTIALATOMIC schedules a single transaction for (sequential) execution. Like in the case of rule ATOMIC, we need to ensure that operations within transactions are fully executed and do not get stuck. Rule COLLECTATOMIC collects all newly derived transactions. Rule CONCURRENTCHR switches to the concurrent CHR system. The intial, starting configuration is $C, True$.

In a concrete implementation, we could for example use a stack to systematically execute transactions. However, we wish to obtain a calculus in which we can represent all possible serializations of atomic transactions.

Theorem 4 (Equivalence). *We have that $C \rightarrowtail C'$ is derivable in the CHR* calculus from Section 4 iff $C, True \rightarrowtail_{SeqACHR} C'', S$ is derivable where $C' = C'' \wedge S$.*

$$\text{Transactions}\quad AT ::= \texttt{atomic}(C) \wedge AT \mid True$$

$$\text{CONCURRENTCHR} \qquad \frac{C \rightarrowtail_{CHR} C'}{C, AT \rightarrowtail_{SeqACHR} C', AT}$$

$$\text{SEQUENTIALATOMIC} \qquad \frac{\forall C. C \wedge C_1 \wedge C_2 \rightarrowtail^{*}_{SeqACHR} C \wedge C_3}{C_1, \texttt{atomic}(C_2) \wedge AT \rightarrowtail_{SeqACHR} C_3, AT}$$

$$\text{COLLECTATOMIC} \quad C_1 \wedge \texttt{atomic}(C_2), AT \rightarrowtail_{SeqACHR} C_1, \texttt{atomic}(C_2) \wedge AT$$

Fig. 2. Sequential CHR* and Concurrent CHR Calculus

6   From CHR* to CHR by Transformation

Our goal is to erase all (or as many as possible) $\texttt{atomic}()$ wrappers from CHR* programs such that we can execute them in the concurrent CHR fragment. Of course, simply erasing the $\texttt{atomic}()$ wrappers is not sound: the atomicity and isolation properties are easily lost.

Hence, in order to preserve atomicity and isolation of transactions under erasure, we not only erase the $\texttt{atomic}()$ wrappers, but also perform other transformation steps on the program. These proposed transformations are detailed in the following subsections.

Some of our proposed transformations are applicable statically (off-line), others are only valid if the execution environment satisfies certain conditions. We could either check for these conditions dynamically, that is, we apply transformations online, or the programmer gurantees that under all execution paths the conditions are

met. The techniques employed to carry out and verify the transformations range
from simple unfolding methods to more sophisticated confluence analyses.

As a guideline for the correctness of transformations, we have the following
generic criterion.

Definition 2 (Erasure Correctness Criterion). *A plain CHR program P'
is correct erased form of an $CHR^{\maltese}$ program P, iff $\forall C.\mathcal{S}^{\maltese}[\![P]\!](C) = \mathcal{S}[\![P']\!](\epsilon(C))$.*

As we observed earlier in Theorem 2, usually $\epsilon(P)$ (erasing the `atomic()` wrapper) does not satisfy the Erasure Correctness Criterion (ECC) as we only have
that $\mathcal{S}^{\maltese}[\![P]\!](C) \subseteq \mathcal{S}[\![\epsilon(P)]\!](\epsilon(C))$. Hence, we consider more sophisticated transformations and conditions below.

Some transformations do not directly establish the ECC: they only eliminate
particular atomic transaction wrappers. In such cases a more compositional approach is interesting: several transformations are combined to eliminate all transactions. Hence, we will usually prove a weaker criterion.

Definition 3 (Partial Erasure Correctness Criterion). *An $CHR^{\maltese}$ program
P' is correct partially erased form of an $CHR^{\maltese}$ program P, iff*

$$\forall C.\mathcal{S}^{\maltese}[\![P]\!](C) = \mathcal{S}^{\maltese}[\![P']\!](\epsilon(C))$$

By combining multiple transformations, we may end up with a fully erased
program. Hence, from Theorem 3 and the Partial Erasure Correctness of each
individual transformation, it then follows that the ECC holds.

For instance, a rather trivial form of erasure is erasure of operation-free
atomic transactions. In other words, let $\epsilon'(o)$ be defined as $\epsilon(o)$, except that
only $\epsilon'(\texttt{atomic}(S)) = S$ and not the more general $\epsilon'(\texttt{atomic}(C)) = C$. For this
operation-free erasure we get trivially:

Theorem 5 (Correctness of Operation-Free Erasure).

$$\forall P.\forall C.\mathcal{S}^{\maltese}[\![P]\!](C) = \mathcal{S}^{\maltese}[\![\epsilon'(P)]\!](\epsilon'(C))$$

While the transformation is trivial, it nevertheless is a useful building block for composite transformations. The more interesting transformations are discussed below.

6.1   Bounded Transactions as Multi-headed CHR Rules

We formalize the observations from the earlier Section 2.1 which observed that
bounded transactions can be replaced by multi-headed CHR rules.

Definition 4 (Bounded Transaction Elimination). *A* bounded *transaction
is one that performs a finite, statically known number of derivation steps.*

*Let $\beta(P)$ be the elimination of bounded transactions from P obtained by ap-
plying the following steps to each bounded transaction in P.*

1. *Replace a bounded atomic transaction* `atomic(G)` *by a new operation constraint C, where C has the same formal parameters as G.*
2. *Add a rule r to the program of the form C `<=>` G.*
3. *Unfold the rule r, until no more operation constraints appear in its body. We
   refer to [8] for a formal treatment of unfolding in CHR.*

In summary, we can make the following general claim.

Theorem 6. *The bounded transaction elimination $\beta(P)$ of an $CHR^{\clubsuit}$ program P satisfies the Partial Erasure Correctness Criterion, i.e. $\forall C.\mathcal{S}^{\clubsuit}[\![P]\!](C) = \mathcal{S}^{\clubsuit}[\![\beta(P)]\!](C)$.*

Numerous examples satisfy this criterion. We refer to [2] for details.

6.2   From CHR$^{\clubsuit}$ to CHR Via Confluence Analysis

We only consider atomic transactions that are well-behaved, i.e. do not get stuck:

Definition 5 (Well-Behaved Constraints). *We say that C is well-behaved wrt. program P iff $\mathcal{S}^{\clubsuit}[\![P]\!](C)$ only contains data constraints, and no operation constraints or atomic transactions.*

The motivation for this is that, in general (e.g. for unbounded transactions), we cannot model stuck atomic transactions by dropping the `atomic()` wrapper.

An example of a stuck transaction is a bank transfer (Section 2.1) that attempts to overdraw an account. This transaction can be made into a well-behaved transaction, if we drop the guard in the withdraw rule and hence allow negative balances:

```
balance(Acc,Bal), withdraw(Acc,Amount) <=> balance(Acc,Bal-Amount).
```

In the remainder of this paper, we assume that the programmer ensures well-behavedness, and focus on ensuring isolation for well-behaved constraints.

With the new semantics of withdrawal, the `atomic()` seems superfluous: any two consecutive transfers *commute*. Regardless of the order they are performed in, they yield the same final result. Hence, we can safely erase the wrapper which then leads to

$$\wedge \quad \begin{array}{l} \texttt{transfer(a1,a2, 100)} \wedge \texttt{transfer(a3,a4,150)} \\ \texttt{transfer(a5,a2, 200)} \wedge \texttt{transfer(a6,a1, 50)} \end{array}$$

We can now concurrently execute `transfer(a3,a4,150)` and `transfer(a6, a1,50)` and then sequentially execute the remaining transfers.

The generalized notion of the above commutativity is *confluence* [9]. A CHR program is confluent if any derivation from the same initial goal yields the same final result, i.e. $\forall C \exists C'.\mathcal{S}[\![P]\!](C) = \{C'\}$.

Hence, we get the following result if an erased program is confluent:

Theorem 7 (Erasure for Confluent Transactions). *If the erasure $\epsilon(P)$ of an $CHR^{\clubsuit}$ program P is confluent, then the ECC is satisfied for all well-behaved constraints, i.e. $\forall C.\mathcal{S}^{\clubsuit}[\![P]\!](C) = \mathcal{S}[\![\epsilon(P)]\!](\epsilon(C))$, where C is well-behaved.*

6.3   Relaxing Confluence

Confluence is a very strong assumption and guarantees that isolation is not violated once `atomic()` wrappers are removed. In practice, confluence is not satisfied by many programs where the non-determinism is acceptable. In case (non)confluence can be explained as a non-deterministic, serial execution of critical pairs among atomic operations, it is still safe to drop the `atomic()` wrapper.

Example 2. ecall the earlier shared-linked list example from Section 2.2. Most of the critical pairs among find and insert operations are observably joinable assuming that the data structure is a sorted linked list. The only non-joinable critical pair arises in case the insertion takes place on a "found" node: `nil(P)` $\wedge$ `insert(X,P)` $\wedge$ `find(X,P)` and `node(Y,P,Next)` $\wedge$ `insert(X,P)` $\wedge$ `find(X,P)` where `Y < X`. Depending on the order of execution we obtain different results. For example, for the first case the find fails if the insert is performed last. For the second case, it is the other way around. Yet each execution path corresponds to a valid serial execution of an atomic execution of find and an atomic execution of insert on a shared linked list. Hence, we argue that we can safely drop the `atomic()` wrapper around single find and insert operations.

We can restate Theorem 7 for partially confluent programs under two additional conditions.

Definition 6. *A CHR program P is* partially confluent *iff all critical pairs are either observably joinable [3] wrt. an invariant (sortedness in the above case), or non-joinability can be explained as a non-deterministic, serial execution of the operations involved.*

Definition 7. *A constraint C satisfies the* single atomic operation property *(SAOP) iff each* `atomic()` *wrapper contains at most one operation constraint and zero or more data constraints.*

An CHR$^{\bullet\!\!\!\bullet}$ *program P satisfies the* single atomic operation property *iff for each initial constraint satisfying SAOP, all constraints in intermediate derivations satisfy SAOP as well.*

Theorem 8 (Erasure for Partially Confluent SAOP Transactions). *If the erasure $\epsilon(P)$ of an CHR*$^{\bullet\!\!\!\bullet}$ *program P is partially confluent and P satisfies SAOP, then ECC is satisfied for all well-behaved, SAOP constraints, i.e. $\forall C.\mathcal{S}^{\bullet\!\!\!\bullet}[\![P]\!](C) = \mathcal{S}[\![\epsilon(P)]\!](\epsilon(C))$, where C is well-behaved and satisfies SAOP.*

Example 3. The restriction to SAOP, only single atomic operations in all derivation steps, is essential. Execution of

$$\text{node}(1,\text{p},\text{q}) \ \wedge \ \text{nil}(\text{q}) \ \wedge \ \text{atomic}(\text{insert}(2,\text{p}) \ \wedge \ \text{insert}(4,\text{p}))$$
$$\wedge \ \text{atomic}(\text{find}(2,\text{p}) \ \wedge \ \text{find}(4,\text{p}))$$

has two possible outcomes. We either find 2 and 4 or we find none of the two values. If we naively drop the `atomic()` wrappers it would however be possible to observe an intermediate of the first transaction where we find 2 but not 4.

We conclude that partial confluence is only a sufficient criteria to guarantee isolation for SAOP transactions (of course also in subsequent derivation steps). More complex transactions require a more involved confluence analysis.

6.4   Completion for Stuck Transactions

Confluence analysis is also useful to recover from stuck operations.

Example 4. Consider the extension of the linked list program with the operation `delete(X,P)`, which deletes X from the list (if present). This operation is implemented by the rules:

```
d1 @ node(X,P,Q), node(Y,Q,Next), delete(X,P) <=> node(Y,P,Next).
d2 @ node(X,P,Q), nil(Q), delete(X,P) <=> nil(P).
d3 @ node(X,P,Q) \ delete(Y,P) <=> X < Y | delete(Y,Q).
d4 @ node(X,P,Q) \ delete(Y,P) <=> X > Y | true.
d5 @ nil(P) \ delete(X,P) <=> true.
```

Adding these rules, leads to additional critical pairs. Several are of the kind discussed in the previous section, e.g. a find before or after a delete yields a different result, but both are acceptable.

However, we get a new kind of critical pair, where an operation gets stuck. For instance, consider the goal where for simplicity, we don't show nodes beyond Q.

$$node(X,P,Q) \land node(Z,Q,R) \land find(Y,Q) \land delete(Y,Q)$$

where $X < Y < Z$. If the find makes step first and then the delete removes the node, we get $node(X,P,R) \land find(Z,R)$ and the find can continue looking at the nodes not shown. However, if the delete goes first, the find is stuck: $node(X,P,R) \land find(Z,Q)$. The problem is that there is no more node Q to look at, and so the find does not know how to proceed.

Such a critical pair is undesirable and has to be eliminated. We do so by a form of domain-specific *completion*, i.e. we add rules to the program that identify the stuck state and get out of it. Firstly, to facilitate recognizing (potentially) stuck states, the delete operation should leave a trace of its operation: the delnode(Q,P) data constraint denotes that there previously was a node at location P with predecessor at Q.

```
d1 @ node(X,P,Q), node(Y,Q,Next), delete(X,P) <=>
       node(Y,P,Next) ∧ delNode(Q,P).
d2 @ node(X,P,Q), nil(Q), delete(X,P) <=>
       nil(P) ∧ delNode(Q,P).
```

Now the stuck operation can be detected by matching against the appropriate delnode constraint, and the operation can continue properly.

```
f5 @ nodeDel(P,Q) \ find(X,P) <=> find(X,Q).
i5 @ nodeDel(P,Q) \ insert(X,P) <=> insert(X,Q).
d6 @ nodeDel(P,Q) \ delete(X,P) <=> delete(X,Q).
```

The above rules perform a *smart* retry. Instead of restarting (failing) the entire transaction from scratch, only a small number of steps are required to recover and continue the transaction. A similar form of domain-specific completion has been performed by Frühwirth for the "union transaction" of a parallel union-find algorithm [6]. In essence, Frühwirth's starting point is a correct, parallel union-find implementation in CHR$^{\vee}$, although this is implicit in his work. He then performs sophisticated transformations to obtain a version in plain CHR.

7   Related Work

The idea of using semantic analysis to achieve greater concurrency and better failure recovery for transactions can already be found in the database literature [10,11]. Our contributions is to transfer these ideas to the programming language, specifically, Constraint Handling Rules setting.

Several other works enrich an existing programming language calculus with transactions, e.g. the work in [12] considers a process calculus extended with atomic transactions whereas the work on transaction logic [13] adds transactional state updates to a Horn logic calculus. None of these works consider meaning-preserving transformation methods from the transactional calculus to the plain calculus. Yet many of the examples found in the above works belong to the class of bounded transactions and can therefore be transformed to plain multi-headed CHR rules.

Support for transactions is now generally available in many programming languages. The issue of "false" conflicts (see Section 5.1) is well-recognized but we are only aware of a few works [14,15,16] which address this important problem. They appear to be complementary to our work, i.e. the methods proposed could be integrated with our transformational approach. We discuss them in turn below.

One possible approach to avoid "false" conflicts is to release read logs early, e.g. see [14]. The problem with this method is that it requires great care by the programmer to preserve atomicity and isolation.

A more principled approach proposed in [15] is to re-run only those parts of a transaction which have been actually affected by "real" conflicts. This approach is well-suited for side-effect free, declarative languages such as CHR but still requires to keep track of read/write logs to infer the (un)affected parts.

Fairly close in spirit is the work in [16] which establishes formal criteria to boost the level of concurrency of transactional code. The starting point is a language with support for highly concurrent linearizable operations to which then transactions are added such that the transactional code exhibits the same level of concurrency as the underlying operations. In the context of our work, a highly concurrent linearizable operation can be viewed as a multi-headed CHR rule. If the operations commute, i.e. are confluent, they can be scheduled for concurrent execution. The main differences are that the work in [16] still requires a transaction manager to detect conflicts between non-commutative operations (and there is the potential of deadlocks as pointed out in [16]). Our goal is to avoid as much as possible the need for a transaction manager by performing the opposite transformation, from transactional to non-transactional code. In general, our approach cannot deal with non-commutative operations, we require the stronger condition of partial confluence. On the other hand, we can easily perform domain-specific optimizations by providing specialized synchronization and recovery rules (see Section 6.4).

8   Conclusion and Future Work

We have presented the CHR$^{\text{♣}}$ calculus for CHR with atomic and isolated transactions. To execute CHR$^{\text{♣}}$ efficiently, we propose a simple execution scheme, that sequentializes atomic transactions. In order to improve concurrency, we propose several transformation methods that replace transactions by plain CHR goals. The methods are based on well-established concepts: unfolding and confluence analysis of CHR.

In future work, we plan to investigate further transformations and to what extent they can be automated. The addition of transaction combinators such as `orelse()` [17] should be straightforward by extending CHR$^{\text{♣}}$ with a choice operator along the lines of [18].

Acknowledgments. We thank the reviewers for their helpful comments.

References

1. Frühwirth, T.: Theory and practice of constraint handling rules. Journal of Logic Programming, Special Issue on Constraint Logic Programming 37(1-3), 95–138 (1998)
2. Schrijvers, T., Sulzmann, M.: Transactions in Constraint Handling Rules. Technical Report (2008), http://www.cs.kuleuven.be/~toms/transactions.pdf
3. Duck, G.J., Stuckey, P.J., Sulzmann, M.: Observable confluence for Constraint Handling Rules. In: Dahl, V., Niemelä, I. (eds.) ICLP 2007. LNCS, vol. 4670, pp. 224–239. Springer, Heidelberg (2007)
4. Schrijvers, T., Frühwirth, T.: Optimal union-find in Constraint Handling Rules. TPLP 6(1-2), 213–224 (2006)
5. Sneyers, J., Schrijvers, T., Demoen, B.: The computational power and complexity of Constraint Handling Rules. ACM TOPLAS (accepted, 2008)
6. Frühwirth, T.: Parallelizing union-find in Constraint Handling Rules using confluence. In: Gabbrielli, M., Gupta, G. (eds.) ICLP 2005. LNCS, vol. 3668, pp. 113–127. Springer, Heidelberg (2005)
7. Weikum, G., Vossen, G.: Transactional Information Systems: Theory, Algorithms, and the Practice of Concurrency Control and Recovery. Morgan Kaufmann, San Francisco (2002)
8. Tacchella, P., Gabbrielli, M., Meo, M.C.: Unfolding in CHR. In: Leuschel, M., Podelski, A. (eds.) PPDP 2007, pp. 179–186. ACM Press, New York (2007)
9. Abdennadher, S., Frühwirth, T., Meuss, H.: Confluence and semantics of constraint simplification rules. Constraints 4(2), 133–165 (1999)
10. Weihl, W.E.: Data-dependent concurrency control and recovery. SIGOPS Oper. Syst. Rev. 19(1), 19–31 (1985)
11. Korth, H.F., Levy, E., Silberschatz, A.: A formal approach to recovery by compensating transactions. Technical report (1990)
12. Acciai, L., Boreale, M., Dal-Zilio, S.: A concurrent calculus with atomic transactions. In: De Nicola, R. (ed.) ESOP 2007. LNCS, vol. 4421, pp. 48–63. Springer, Heidelberg (2007)
13. Bonner, A.J., Kifer, M.: Transaction logic programming. In: Proc. of ICLP 1993, pp. 257–279 (1993)
14. Ni, Y., Menon, V.S., Adl-Tabatabai, A.R., Hosking, A.L., Hudson, R.L., Moss, J.E.B., Saha, B., Shpeisman, T.: Open nesting in software transactional memory. In: Proc. of PPoPP 2007, pp. 68–78. ACM Press, New York (2007)
15. Harris, T., Stipic, S.: Abstract nested transactions. In: TRANSACT 2007: The Second ACM SIGPLAN Workshop on Transactional Computing (2007)
16. Herlihy, M., Koskinen, E.: Transactional boosting: a methodology for highly-concurrent transactional objects. In: Proc. of PPoPP 2008, pp. 207–216. ACM Press, New York (2008)
17. Harris, T., Marlow, S., Peyton Jones, S., Herlihy, M.: Composable memory transactions. In: Proc. of PPoPP 2005, pp. 48–60. ACM Press, New York (2005)
18. Abdennadher, S., Schütz, H.: CHRv: A flexible query language. In: Andreasen, T., Christiansen, H., Larsen, H.L. (eds.) FQAS 1998. LNCS, vol. 1495, pp. 1–14. Springer, Heidelberg (1998)

Cadmium: An Implementation of ACD Term Rewriting

Gregory J. Duck[1], Leslie De Koninck[2,⋆], and Peter J. Stuckey[1]

[1] National ICT Australia (NICTA)[⋆⋆]
Department of Computer Science and Software Engineering
University of Melbourne
{gjd,pjs}@cs.mu.oz.au
[2] Department of Computer Science, K.U.Leuven, Belgium
Leslie.DeKoninck@cs.kuleuven.be

Abstract. Cadmium is a rule based programming language for compiling solver independent constraint models to various solver dependent back-ends. Cadmium is based on a hybrid between Constraint Handling Rules (CHR) and term rewriting modulo Associativity, Commutativity and a restricted form of Distributivity (ACD) called Conjunctive Context (CC). Experience with using Cadmium in the G12 project shows that CC is a powerful language feature, as local model mapping can depend on some non-local context, such as variable declarations or other constraints. However, CC significantly complicates the Cadmium normalisation algorithm, since the normal form of a term may depend on what context it appears in. In this paper we present an implementation of Cadmium based on classic bottom-up evaluation, but modified to handle CC matching. We evaluate the performance of the new implementation compared to earlier prototype normalisation algorithms. We show that the resulting system is fast enough to run "real-world" Cadmium applications.

1 Introduction

Cadmium is high-level rule based programming language based on ACD Term Rewriting (ACDTR) [4] – a generalisation of Constraint Handling Rules (CHR) [5] and Associative Commutative (AC) term rewriting systems [1]. Cadmium's main application is the G12 project [10], where it is used to map high-level models of satisfaction and optimisation problems to low-level executable models. The flexibility and expressiveness of Cadmium allows us to map the same high-level model to different low-level models with very succinct programs (see e.g. [6,2]).

⋆ Research funded by a Ph.D. grant of the Institute for the Promotion of Innovation through Science and Technology in Flanders (IWT-Vlaanderen).
⋆⋆ NICTA is funded by the Australian Government as represented by the Department of Broadband, Communications and the Digital Economy and the Australian Research Council through the ICT Centre of Excellence program.

M. Garcia de la Banda and E. Pontelli (Eds.): ICLP 2008, LNCS 5366, pp. 531–545, 2008.

Associative Commutative (AC) term rewriting allows implicit reordering of AC operators before applying rules. An AC operator $\oplus$ satisfies the axioms:

$$(associativity) \quad (X \oplus Y) \oplus Z = X \oplus (Y \oplus Z)$$
$$(commutativity) \qquad X \oplus Y = Y \oplus X$$

For example, the rewrite rule $r = (X \wedge \neg X \rightarrow false)$ will not match the term $T = \neg a \wedge a$ under non-AC term rewriting because the order of the conjunction is different. However, since $\wedge$ is *commutative*, T is equivalent to $T' = a \wedge \neg a$. Since $T \equiv_{AC} T'$ and T' matches r (i.e. AC matching), T can be rewritten to $false$ under AC term rewriting.

ACD term rewriting [4] extends AC term rewriting with $\wedge$-Distributivity using the following axiom for all functors f:

$$(distribution) \quad P \wedge f(Q_1, \ldots, Q_i, \ldots Q_n) = P \wedge f(Q_1, \ldots, P \wedge Q_i, \ldots, Q_n)$$

It represents the fact that if some property P holds in the context of a term $f(Q_1, \ldots, Q_i, \ldots Q_n)$ it also holds in the context of all the subterms. We can then define the *conjunctive context* (CC)[1] of a term T as the conjunction of all terms that appear conjoined with a parent of that term, i.e. all terms that can $\wedge$-distribute to T.

Example 1. The CC of the boxed occurrence of x in the term

$$(x = 3) \wedge (x^2 > y \ \vee \ (\boxed{x} = 4) \wedge U \ \vee \ V) \wedge W$$

is $(x = 3) \wedge U \wedge W$. $\qquad\qquad\qquad\qquad\qquad\qquad\qquad\qquad\qquad$ □

We introduce CC matching rules of the form $(C \setminus H \iff B)$ which say we can rewrite the term H to B if H appears in a position where its conjunctive context is $C \wedge D$ for some D. Thus we can match on any term appearing in the conjunctive context of H.

Example 2. For example, CC matching can be used to specialise constraints based on variable types.

$$int(X) \wedge int(Y) \ \setminus \ X \le Y \iff intleq(X, Y)$$
$$real(X) \wedge real(Y) \ \setminus \ X \le Y \iff realleq(X, Y)$$
$$pair(X, A, B) \wedge pair(Y, C, D) \ \setminus \ X \le Y \iff (A \le C \vee (A = C \wedge B \le D))$$

Given the term $x \le y \wedge int(b) \wedge int(d) \wedge pair(x, a, b) \wedge pair(y, c, d)$ the conjunctive context of $x \le y$ is the remainder of the conjunction. Therefore the term $pair(x, a, b) \wedge pair(y, c, d)$ appears in the conjunctive context of $x \le y$ so the last rule is applicable. In the resulting term, $x \le y$ is replaced by the right hand side of the rule obtaining:

$$int(b) \wedge int(d) \wedge pair(x, a, b) \wedge pair(y, c, d) \wedge (a \le c \vee (a = c \wedge intleq(b, d)))$$

---

[1] We will use CC as shorthand for "conjunctive context" in the rest of the paper.

Now $int(b) \wedge int(d)$ appears in the CC of $b \leq d$ and hence the first rule applies to that term:

$$int(b) \wedge int(d) \wedge pair(x, a, b) \wedge pair(y, c, d) \wedge (a \leq c \vee (a = c \wedge intleq(b, d))$$

This term is now in *normal form*, i.e. no more rules are applicable.   □

One simple normalisation algorithm is *strict evaluation*, i.e. to normalise a term $f(T_1, ..., T_n)$, we first normalise each $T_1, ..., T_n$ to $U_1, ..., U_n$, and then test rules against $f(U_1, ..., U_n)$. If a rule $(f(H_1, ..., H_n) \Longleftrightarrow B)$ matches $f(U_1, ..., U_n)$, then any variable V in $H_1, ..., H_n$ must be bound to a normalised term. This is an important property, since it means V's value can be copied to the rule body without the need for further work.

Example 3. Consider the rule $(f(X) \Longleftrightarrow g(X))$. To ensure the body $g(X)$ is normalised it is sufficient to only check the rules for $g/1$, rather than normalise X first. Under strict evaluation X must already be in normal form.   □

A normalisation algorithm for Cadmium is more complex because of CC matching. It is possible that terms matched in the CC are not in normal form.

Example 4. Consider the following Cadmium program consisting of three rules:

```
X = Y \ X <=> var(X) | Y.     pass <=> true.     eq(X,Y) <=> X = Y.
```

This is an example of actual Cadmium code. Cadmium term syntax follows Prolog term syntax: any name starting with a capital letter represents a variable. The first rule implements substitution using CC matching – i.e. given an X where X=Y holds, then substitute X with Y. Like Prolog, Cadmium allows variables to appear in the goal. We will examine distinct problems with two different goals.

Early Application : Consider the goal $G_1 = $ (A ∧ A=pass). Under left-to-right strict evaluation, conjunct A with A=pass in its CC will be normalised first. Since A=pass can be rewritten to A=true, the CC is not in normal form. If we apply the first rule to A, and copy variables from the matching to the body as per Example 3, then the result is the unnormalised term pass. This is called *early application* since the result is unnormalised because a rule was *applied* with an unnormalised CC.

Early Failure : Consider the goal $G_2 = $ (A ∧ eq(A,true)). Conjunct A with eq(A,true) in its CC is normalised first. Again, the CC is unnormalised, since eq(A,true) can be rewritten to A=true. In this case the first rule does not match, since the substitution rule expects a =-term, not an eq-term. If eq(A,true) was normalised first, then the rule would match. This is called *early failure* since a rule *failed* to match because the CC was unnormalised.   □

So why not simply normalise the CC before it is used? In general it is impossible to force the CC to be normalised before it is used.

Example 5. Consider the program from Example 4 and the goal X=Y ∧ Y=X. Under the ACDTR semantics, only two rule applications are possible:

1. variable Y (inside conjunct X=Y) with CC Y=X rewrites to X; or
2. variable X (inside conjunct Y=X) with CC X=Y rewrites to Y.

The CC for (1) is unnormalised, because by (2) we have that Y=X can be rewritten to Y=Y. Likewise the CC for (2) is unnormalised because of (1). Either way a rule is applied with unnormalised CC. Therefore, in general it is impossible to guarantee a normalised CC.   □

A prototype basic normalisation algorithm that accounts for unnormalised CC first appeared in [4]. The main contributions of this paper are:

– we show that the basic normalisation algorithm, whilst simple to implement, is too inefficient to be practical on some "real-world" applications;
– we analyse the causes for incomplete normalisation (e.g. Example 4) and show how the basic algorithm handles these cases;
– we use this information to derive a more efficient normalisation algorithm used in the G12 Cadmium implementation of ACDTR;
– we also show how the information can be used to compile the bodies of rules into more efficient executable code.

2   Preliminaries

The syntax of Cadmium closely resembles that of Constraint Handling Rules [5]. There are two[2] types of rules; they have the following form:

$$(simplification) \quad H \iff g \mid B$$
$$(simpagation) \quad C \setminus H \iff g \mid B$$

where *head H*, *conjunctive context C*, *guard g*, and *body B* are arbitrary terms. A program P is a set of rules. Essentially a rule works as follows: given a term $t[h]$ and matching substitution θ where $h = H\theta$ such that $g\theta$ is true, and $C\theta$ appears in the conjunctive context of h, then we obtain the term $t[B\theta]$. ACDTR rules can be applied to any subterm of the goal, unlike in CHR.

For space reasons, we refer the reader to [4] for details about the declarative and operational semantics of Cadmium. A general understanding of term rewriting is sufficient to follow the paper, all important differences w.r.t. standard term rewriting are illustrated by examples.

2.1   Basic Normalisation with Conjunctive Context

In this section we present a version of the basic normalisation algorithm for ACDTR that first appeared in [4]. The basic algorithm is shown in Figure 1. The function normalise_acdtr(T,CC) normalises some term T with respect to the current CC and some compiled version of the program. For the initial goal $CC = \wedge$, i.e. an empty conjunction. Normalisation works in two parts: the first part handles conjunction and the second part handles all other terms.

---

[2] The original ACDTR [4] semantics also included a generalisation of *propagation rules*. However, these are not implemented in Cadmium.

```
normalise_acdtr(T,CC)
    if T = ∧(...)                    /* Conjunction */
        Acc := T
        repeat
            let Acc = ∧(T₁,...,Tₙ)
            Acc := ∧
            rulefired := false
            forall 1 ≤ i ≤ n
                CC' := flatten(∧(Acc, Tᵢ₊₁,...,Tₙ, CC))
                Uᵢ := normalise_acdtr(Tᵢ,CC')
                if (Uᵢ ≠ Tᵢ) rulefired := true
                Acc := flatten(Acc ∧ Uᵢ)
        until not rulefired
        return call_∧(Acc, CC)
    if T = f(T₁,...,Tₙ)      /* Other terms */
        forall 1 ≤ i ≤ n
            Uᵢ := normalise_acdtr(Tᵢ,CC)
        if isAC(f)
            U := flatten(f(U₁,...,Uₙ))
            return call_f(U, CC)
        else return call_f(U₁,...,Uₙ, CC)
    else
        return T
```

Fig. 1. Basic ACDTR normalisation algorithm

To begin with, let us consider the second part, which implements basic normalisation for AC term rewriting using a strict evaluation strategy. To normalise a (non-conjunction) term $T = f(T_1, \ldots, T_n)$, we first normalise each argument $T_1, \ldots, T_n$ to $U_1, \ldots, U_n$ respectively, and then normalise $U = f(U_1, \ldots, U_n)$ by calling a compiled procedure call_f that applies any rule that matches f/n terms, or returns U if no such rule exists. Details about the compiled procedures can be found in Section 4.

The calling conventions for AC and non-AC operators are different. For the AC case, the term $U = f(U_1, \ldots, U_n)$ must be created and *flattened* before the procedure call_f is called. The idea behind flattening is to represent a nested binary AC expression as a "flat" n-ary term. For example, the equivalent AC terms $(1+2)+3$ and $1+(2+3)$ are represented as $+(1, 2, 3)$ in flattened form. As with the binary-+, the n-ary + is also commutative, i.e. $+(\ldots, U_i, \ldots, U_j, \ldots) \equiv +(\ldots, U_j, \ldots, U_i, \ldots)$. The motivation for flattening is to simplify the AC matching implementation (see [8] for a more detailed discussion). For the rest of the paper, we may switch between binary and flattened notation for AC terms whenever convenient.

Conjunction is normalised differently from other (AC) terms. A conjunction $T = \wedge(T_1, \ldots, T_n)$ is normalised over several passes by the **repeat** loop, which works as follows. The **let** matching is assumed to return all conjuncts $T_1, \ldots, T_n$ of Acc, where Acc is initially set to T (the input conjunction), and to the accumulated result from the previous pass of the **repeat** loop in all further passes. For each pass, this may be a different set. Next Acc and *rulefired* are initialised, followed by the **forall** loop, which normalises each conjunct T_i of T with respect to CC', which is CC extended by all other conjuncts of T excluding T_i. The new conjuncts U_i are accumulated into variable Acc. One complication is that each U_i may itself be a conjunction, so flatten is used to ensure Acc remains in flattened form. We also compare the old T_i against its normalised version U_i. If there is a difference, then a rule has fired, and *rulefired* is set to *true*, which ensures another pass of the repeat loop. Note that the Cadmium implementation tracks rule firings explicitly rather than actually comparing (potentially large) terms. Finally, once Acc has reached a fixed point, i.e. $\neg rulefired$ holds, the procedure call_∧ is run. Each pass of the **repeat**-loop is referred to as a *conjunction pass*.

The intuition behind the normalise_acdtr algorithm is as follows. If a T_i changes to a U_i, then the CC of all T_j where $j \neq i$ has also changed – i.e. the CC contained T_i but now contains U_i. The next pass of the repeat loop ensures each T_j is *woken-up* with respect to the up-to-date CC containing U_i. Here, the terminology *wake-up* means a conjunct is renormalised with a new CC in the next conjunction pass.

Example 6 (Early Application). Consider the program and goal G_1 from Example 4. The first pass of the normalise_acdtr algorithm is (1) A with CC A=pass is rewritten to pass (early application), then (2) A=pass (with CC pass) is rewritten to A=true. After the first pass the conjunction Acc is pass ∧ A=true.

Since a rule has fired, the conjunction is normalised again. This time (3) pass (with CC A=true) is rewritten to true, then (4) A=true (with CC true) remains unchanged. After the second pass the conjunction Acc is true ∧ A=true. Since again a rule has fired, the conjunction is renormalised once more. This time no rule fires, since the conjunction is already in normal form. The $\neg rulefired$ test succeeds, and true ∧ A=true is ultimately returned.   □

Example 7 (Early Failure). Consider the program and goal G_2 from Example 4. The normalise_acdtr algorithm works as follows: (1) A with CC eq(A,true) remains unchanged (early failure), then (2) eq(A,true) (with CC A) is rewritten to A=true. After the first pass the conjunction Acc is A ∧ A=true.

Since a rule has fired, the conjunction is normalised again. This time (3) A with CC A=true is rewritten to true, then (4) A=true (with CC true) remains unchanged. After the second pass the conjunction Acc is true ∧ A=true. Another pass is tried, but since the conjunction is already in normal form, no more rewrites take place, and true ∧ A=true is returned.   □

3   Improved Normalisation

Algorithm normalise_acdtr is relatively simple and was used in earlier versions of the Cadmium implementation. However, the algorithm is still very "coarse" in the sense that *any* change of a conjunct results in the *entire conjunction being processed again*. Clearly this is sub-optimal, as it is probable that some changes in the CC do not affect the normalisation status of other conjuncts. An extreme example of this situation occurs when all rules in a program are simplification rules, and thus do not depend on the CC at all. In this case, conjunction can be treated the same as any other AC functor, hence only one pass is required to ensure a normal form.

Even if the program contains simpagation rules, the number of conjuncts that need to be woken-up per pass can often be reduced.

Example 8 (Early Failure). For example, consider the following rule that simplifies less-than constraints if the negation greater-than is present in the CC.

```
X > Y \  X < Y <=> false.
```

Suppose that the goal is `A<B` $\land$ `f(A,B)`. Clearly the normal form of the `A<B` conjunct only depends on the presence/absence of `A>B` in its CC.

During the initial conjunction pass of normalise_acdtr, conjunct `A<B` will not be rewritten because `A>B` does not appear in the CC (i.e. early failure). Then `A<B` will only need to *wake-up* iff a `A>B` term is subsequently added to the CC. Any other change to the CC can be safely ignored, since this would not affect the applicability of the above rule.   □

By definition, early failure means a conjunct C is not rewritten because some term T was not in its CC. Thus, we only need to wake-up C if a suitable T is subsequently added to C's CC. Likewise, a wake-up for early application is sometimes not necessary.

Example 9 (Early Application). Consider the following rules for Zinc expression manipulation in Cadmium.

```
decl(T,X) /\ decl(T,Y) /\ decl(T,Z) \ X*(Y+Z) <=> X*Y+X*Z.
int <=> float.
```

Here, `decl`(T,V) encodes a Zinc variable declaration, where T is the type and V is the variable. Consider the goal

```
A*(B+C) ∧ decl(int,A) ∧ decl(int,B) ∧ decl(int,C)
```

During the first conjunction pass, conjunct `A*(B+C)` is rewritten to `A*B+A*C` with the reaminder of the goal as CC. The CC is not in normal form since subterm(s) `int` are not in normal form, hence this is a case of early application.

However, `A*B+A*C` is in normal form and therefore does not need to be woken-up again. This is because the rule body depended only on program variables also appearing in the rule head, i.e. `X`, `Y`, and `Z`, but not `T`. Therefore if `X`, `Y`, and `Z` are in normal form, the new term `A*B+A*C` will also be in normal form.   □

The basic idea of the refined algorithm is to only wake up conjuncts if there is actually a need to do so.

Events and Wake-up Conditions. *Wake-up conditions* are conditions associated to conjuncts in conjunctions. An *event* declares that a wake-up condition has become satisfied. During normalisation, if an event occurs satisfying a wake-up condition, then any associated conjunct will be woken-up during the next conjunction pass.

```
normalise_cadmium(T,Curr,CC)
    if T = ∧(...)
        Acc := T
        repeat
            let Acc = ∧(T₁,...,Tₙ)
            Acc := ∧
            Prev := Curr ∪ {redo}
            Curr := ∅
            forall 1 ≤ i ≤ n
                if wakeup_conds(Tᵢ) ∩ Prev ≠ ∅
                    CC' := flatten(∧(Acc,Tᵢ₊₁,...,Tₙ,CC))
                    Uᵢ := normalise_cadmium(Tᵢ,∅,CC')
                    if (Uᵢ ≠ Tᵢ) Curr := createtop(Uᵢ) ∪ Curr
                    Acc := flatten(Acc ∧ Uᵢ)
                else Acc := flatten(Acc ∧ Tᵢ)
            until Curr = ∅
            return call_∧(Acc,CC)
    if T = f(T₁,...,Tₙ) ... /* As in Figure 1 */
```

Fig. 2. Improved normalisation algorithm from the Cadmium implementation

The Cadmium implementation uses the following wake-up conditions:

Case	Condition/Event
Early Application	redo
Early Failure	create(f/a)

Condition redo means that the conjunct is always to be woken-up during the next pass. It will be associated to a conjunct C if C is not in normal form due to early application. Early application does not always result in a redo condition, as was the case in Example 9. Condition create(f/a) means that the conjunct will be woken-up if some term with functor/arity f/a is added to the CC. This condition is useful for early failure. For example, in Example 8, the conjunct A<B needs to be woken up if a A>B term is added to its CC. We can approximate this precise condition with a create(>/2) wake-up condition. In general, determining the precise conditions is undecidable, so some approximation is always required.

The improved algorithm is described in Figure 2. This version is called normalise_cadmium because it is the actual normalisation algorithm used by the Cadmium implementation. The main difference between this version and the previous algorithm is the tracking of events and wake-up conditions. $Prev$ and $Curr$ are sets of events. $Prev$ contains all events that occurred during the previous pass and a redo event. Each new pass generates this event. $Curr$ accumulates the events that occur during the current pass. Note that initially $Curr$ is an argument to normalise_cadmium. For now, we can assume that the value passed in through $Curr$ is always the empty set. This will change later in Section 4.

The function $wakeup\_conds(T_i)$ returns the set of wake-up conditions associated to a given conjunct T_i. If T_i has not been normalised yet (i.e. in the initial pass), then its set of wake-up conditions is assumed to be {redo}. If T_i is subsequently normalised to U_i, then the wake-up conditions for U_i are roughly determined as follows:

1. *Early Application*: If an early application resulted in an unnormalised sub-term of U_i, then `redo` $\in$ *wakeup_conds*(U_i).
2. *Early Failure*: If a simpagation rule $(C \backslash H \Longleftrightarrow G|B)$ failed to fire on some subterm S of T_i, and S also appears in U_i, then

$$\{\texttt{create}(f_1/a_1), \ldots, \texttt{create}(f_n/a_n)\} \subseteq \textit{wakeup\_conds}(U_i)$$

where the f_i/a_i are the functor/arity pairs of the conjuncts in C.

Note that wake-up conditions propagate upwards, i.e. if the normalisation of some subterm S of T_i generates a wake-up condition C, then C is propagated upwards and attached to U_i. For nested conjunctions, C will be propagated upwards to every conjunct S appeared in. The exact mechanism for generating wakeup conditions is the role of the Cadmium compiled code, i.e. in the `call_f` procedures. This will explained in Section 4.2.

Wake-up conditions are used to prevent unnecessary renormalisation during the second or later conjunction passes. Conjunct T_i will only wake-up if there exists an event in *Prev* that is also present in *wakeup_conds*(T_i). Otherwise, the conjunct is already in normal form, and the old value can be used.

If a conjunct T_i is renormalised to U_i where $T_i \neq U_i$, the call `createtop`(U_i) will generate an appropriate set of `create` events. If $U_i = \wedge(V_1, \ldots, V_n)$, then `createtop`$(U_i)$ generates $\{\texttt{create}(f_1/a_1), \ldots, \texttt{create}(f_n/a_n)\}$, where $f_1/a_1, \ldots, f_n/a_n$ are the functor/arities of $V_1, \ldots, V_n$. Otherwise, if $U_i = g(W_1, \ldots, W_n)$ where $g \neq \wedge$, then `createtop`(U_i) generates the singleton set $\{\texttt{create}(g/n)\}$. The generated events are accumulated into *Curr* and used as *Prev* during the next pass.

Example 10. Consider the following three rule program.

```
(1)    X > Y \ X < Y <=> false.
(2)    gt(X,Y) <=> X > Y.
(3)    h(_) \ f(X) <=> g(X).
```

Rule (1) is the rule from Example 8. Rule (2) rewrites an auxiliary term into a >/2 term. Rule (3) is an artificial rule which depends on the CC.

Consider the execution of the goal term: $\texttt{h(1)} \wedge \texttt{wrap(f(x<y)} \wedge \texttt{gt(x,y))}$. There are two levels of nested conjunction, with the inner conjunction inside the `wrap/1` term. Assume execution proceeds from left-to-right. First `h(1)` is normalised and remains unchanged. Next the `wrap/1` term and the inner conjunction are normalised. The inner conjunct `f(x<y)` is normalised first. As normalisation proceeds bottom-up, the following wake-up conditions are generated:

1. Subterm `x<y` could potentially fire Rule (1), given a `x>y` term in the CC. Thus a `create(>/2)` waking condition is generated for this term.
2. Term `f(x<y)` fires rule (3) to give `g(x<y)`. Since the body is independent of the CC, no `redo` waking condition needs to be generated for this term.

Thus, the set of waking conditions attached to the first inner conjunct g(x<y) is {create(>/2)}.

Next, the second inner conjunct gt(x,y) is normalised to x>y. This generates a create(>/2) event, which is recorded in *Curr*, but no wake-up conditions are recorded for this term. The intermediate result after the first pass is: h(1) ∧ wrap(g(x<y) ∧ x>y).

In the second pass, the inner conjunct g(x<y) is renormalised to g(false), since the attached wake-up condition create(>/2) matches an event that occurred during the previous pass. The second inner conjunct, x>y, will not be woken up since it has no wake-up conditions. Normalisation proceeds without any more rule applications, thus the final result is: h(1) ∧ wrap(g(false) ∧ x > y).   □

4   Implementation

In this section we discuss some details about the Cadmium implementation.

The current Cadmium implementation compiles rules of the form $(C \setminus H \iff B)$ into a low-level byte-code for a simple virtual machine. There are two parts to compilation: compiling the matching $(C \setminus H)$, and compiling the body B.

Matching. Matching in Cadmium is similar to matching in any other declarative programming language, such as Prolog. For example, the rule (f(g(X,Y),h) <=> ...) can be compiled directly into a Prolog clause (call_f(g(X,Y),h) :- !, ...) that uses Prolog unification for matching. The cut is necessary since Cadmium rules are committed choice.

Compiling AC matching is somewhat more complicated, as it involves non-deterministically trying combinations of matchings – i.e. the different permutations of the arguments of an AC term. This can be implemented in Prolog as backtracking search. CC matching is essentially the same as AC matching, except we match against the accumulated *CC* rather than a term matching the rule head.

Body. The simplest version of rule body compilation is to call the Cadmium normalisation procedure. For example, given (f(X,Y,Z) <=> g(h(X,Y),a(1,Z))) then the compiled rule in Prolog is

```
call_f(X,Y,Z,Ret) :- !, normalise(g(h(X,Y),a(1,Z)),Ret)
```

where normalise implements the Cadmium normalisation algorithm. This will cause each term matching X, Y, Z to be renormalised again, which is inefficient.

A better (and more standard) approach is to eliminate all calls to the normalise procedure by iteratively unfolding its application, and to substitute matching variables directly rather than renormalising them. For example, after one unfolding step we have:

```
normalise(g(h(X,Y),a(1,Z))) ≡ call_g(normalise(h(X,Y)),normalise(a(1,Z)))
```

After completely unfolding normalise, the rule code becomes:

```
call_f(X,Y,Z,Ret) :- !, call_h(X,Y,RH), call_a(1,Z,RA), call_g(RH,RA,Ret).
```

4.1   Compiling Conjunction in the Body

Compiling conjunction in the rule body is the same as before, i.e. iterative unfolding of the call to the `normalise` procedure. However, because of CC, the `normalise` procedure cannot be unfolded any deeper than any top-most conjunction appearing in the rule body. For example, consider the rule:

```
f(X,Y) <=> g(X) /\ f(Y).
```

According to the Cadmium normalisation algorithm, `g(X)` and all of its subterms must be (re)normalised with `f(Y)` in the CC, and vice versa. Therefore, unfolding `normalise` directly will not work, i.e.,

$$normalise(g(X) \wedge f(Y)) \not\equiv call\_\wedge(normalise(g(X)), normalise(f(Y)))$$

since the latter does not handle CC correctly.

The basic approach for handling conjunctions is to unfold `normalise` *as much as possible*, but stopping at the top-most conjunction. This conjunction is simply constructed, then passed to `normalise` to be executed as if it were a fresh goal. For example, the compiled version of the above rule is:

```
call_f(X,Y,Ret) :- !, C1 = g(X), C2 = f(Y), wakeup_on(redo,C1),
           wakeup_on(redo,C2), normalise(C1 /\ C2,Ret).
```

This clause constructs `g(X) /\ f(Y)` and passes it to `normalise`. The built-in `wakeup_on/2` attaches a `redo` wake-up condition to each conjunct to force normalisation via wake-up. Without the `redo`, `normalise` will skip each conjunct.

Conjunction Collector Optimisation. Under the basic approach, each conjunct in a rule body is completely (re)normalised again, which in some cases is inefficient. However, sometimes we can avoid wake-up in a rule body. Consider the following rule from the MiniZinc to FlatZinc mapping [6,2]:

```
cons(X) /\ cons(Y) /\ Z <=> cons(X /\ Y) /\ Z.
```

Here $cons(X)$ represents a Zinc constraint item (`constraint X`). The body of the rule contains two conjuncts: `cons(X /\ Y)` and `Z`. In this rule, `Z` will always match a conjunction – i.e. the "rest" of the conjunction matching the rule head minus `cons(X)` and `cons(Y)`. Furthermore, thanks to bottom-up evaluation, `Z` must already be normalised, so each conjunct in `Z` already has a set of wake-up conditions attached to it. We can use these tighter wake-up conditions instead of attaching a `redo` condition as was the case above. This can potentially avoid a lot of unnecessary renormalisation.

Example 11. Consider the constraint item collection rule from above. When this rule is applied, the CC of the conjuncts in `Z` remains unchanged save for the removal/addition of some `cons/1` terms. Therefore, only the conjuncts with a `create(cons/1)` wake-up condition need be renormalised.

The optimised code of the constraint item collection rule is:

```
call_/\(Conj,Ret) :- /* Code for matching */ !,
          C1 = cons(X /\ Y), wakeup_on(redo,C1),
          normalise(C1 /\ Z,[create(cons/1)],Ret).
```

Notice that (1) there is no `redo` wake-up condition attached to Z, and (2) we now pass the initial event `create(cons/1)` to the `normalise` procedure, since a new `cons/1` term was added to the conjunction. This will cause any conjunct with a `create(cons/1)` in Z to be renormalised as expected.   □

4.2   Generating Wake-Up Conditions

In this section we explain how wake-up conditions are generated in the compiled code. This depends on the type of condition being generated.

Wake-up Condition `redo`: The `normalise_cadmium` algorithm returns either a normalised term, or an unnormalised term because of early application. In the latter case, a `redo` wake-up condition must be generated to ensure overall completeness after subsequent passes of the super conjunctions.[3] A `redo` wake-up condition is therefore needed when the body B from a rule $(C \backslash H \Longleftrightarrow G | B)$ contains a variable X such that X is also in C, but not in H. Note that if X also appears in H, then because X was processed before its super term H, we can assume X is in normal form, or `redo` has already been generated.

Example 12. Consider the following rules:

```
X > Y \ X < Y <=> false.
X = Y \ X <=> var(X) | Y.
decl(T,X) /\ decl(T,Y) /\ decl(T,Z) \ X*(Y+Z) <=> X*Y+X*Z.
```

from Examples 8, 4, and 9 respectively. The body of the first rule does not contain any variables, thus is independent of the CC. The body of the second rule does depend on the CC through variable Y. The body of the third rule shares variables X, Y, and Z with the CC; however these variables also appear in the rule head. Therefore, only the second rule is required to generate a `redo` wake-up condition. The code for the second rule is therefore:

```
call_var(X,Ret) :- /* Matching */, !, wakeup_lift([redo]), Ret = Y.
```

Here, the call `wakeup_lift`(C) lifts wake-up conditions C to any conjunct containing the term matching X.   □

Wake-up Condition `create`: The `create` wake-up conditions are generated after all rules for a particular term fail to match. The compiler assumes that any simpagation rule matching failure is caused by *early failure*.

---

[3] Early application implies there is at least one super conjunction, since otherwise the CC will be empty.

Bench.	Maude	Cadmium
qsort(216)	1.12s	1.20s
qsort(343)	6.37s	6.74s
msort(729)	4.27s	4.28s
msort(1000)	12.56s	11.64s
bsort(240)	1.65s	1.78s
bsort(360)	7.67s	8.52s
rev	0.83s	1.25s
taut_hard(2)	0.13s	3.84s
taut_hard(3)	0.36s	37.82s
perm(8)	0.38s	0.27s
perm(9)	6.79s	3.71s

(a) Maude vs. Cadmium

Bench.	−events	+events
queens(8)	2.61s	2.74s
queens(9)	40.70s	43.69s
cnf_conversion(19)	11.07s	9.36s
cnf_conversion(20)	15.42s	12.97s
substitution(22)	1.54s	0.92s
substitution(23)	3.13s	2.04s
warehouses.mzn	5.14s	0.57s
langford.mzn	>300s	33.42s
packing.mzn	0.96s	0.23s
timetabling.mzn	9.19s	0.76s
radiation.mzn	37.58s	2.47s
Geom. mean[5]	6.57s	36.76%

(b) Cadmium ±events

Fig. 3. Experiments comparing the run-time performance of Cadmium

Example 13. Consider the following program which contains two rules for f/2.

g(X) \ f(X,Y) <=> i(Y).   g(Y) /\ h(Y,Y) \ f(1,Y) <=> Y.

Consider the compiled version of this program, where procedure call_f checks these rules. If both rules fail to match, then call_f will simply construct the f/2 term, but will also generate the appropriate create wake-up conditions:

```
...     /* Code for rules 1-2. */
call_f(X,Y,Ret) :- !, wakeup_lift([create(g/1),create(h/2)]), Ret = f(X,Y).
```

In general this approach is an over-approximation. For example, call_f(2,Y) will never apply the second rule. However the compiler still assumes early failure has occurred, and generates a create(h/2) wake-up condition accordingly. This may result in some unnecessary wake-ups.

5   Experiments

Cadmium is part of the G12 project [10]. Its main application is mapping Zinc models, represented as terms, into various solver-dependent back-ends and/or to FlatZinc [6].

Two sets of benchmarks are tested.[4] The first set in Figure 3(a) compare Cadmium versus the Maude 2.3 system [3]. The second set in Figure 3(b) compare the Cadmium implementation using normalisation with/without events. All timings are an average over 10 runs on an Intel E8400 clocked at 3.6GHz.

The benchmarks from Figure 3(a) originate from the second *Rewriting Engines Competition* [7]. Note that the remaining examples from [7] could not be

---

[4] Benchmarks are available at http://www.cs.mu.oz.au/~gjd/download/iclp2008.tar.gz

used for various reasons, e.g. running too fast/slow on both systems, or testing confluence (not supported in Cadmium). The benchmarks show that Cadmium is competitive compared to an established implementation on pure (AC) term rewriting problems. The exception is taut_hard, where Cadmium is slower than Maude, because of differences in the implementation of AC indexing. The taut_hard causes worst-case behaviour for Cadmium's AC index structures. For the perm benchmark, which also uses AC matching, Cadmium improves upon Maude. Note that none of these benchmarks use CC matching, hence the CC optimisations shown in Figure 3(b) are not applicable here.

To test CC normalisation with/without events the benchmarks are as follows: Benchmark queens(n) finds all solutions to the n-queens problem. Benchmark cnf_conversion(n) converts the following Boolean formula into conjunctive normal form $\bigwedge_{i=1}^{n} \bigvee_{j=i+1}^{n} x_i \oplus x_j$. using a generic CNF conversion algorithm. Benchmark substitution(n) applies the substitution rule (Example 4) to the conjunction: $\bigwedge_{i=1}^{n} X_i = [X_{i+1}, \ldots, X_n]$ /\ f(X_i). Finally, the *.mzn benchmarks test MiniZinc to FlatZinc flattening in Cadmium [6]. These benchmarks are the most important, since they are a "real-world" Cadmium application doing what Cadmium was intended to do – i.e. rewrite (Mini)Zinc models. Note that the mapping used is further developed than earlier versions appearing in [6,2].

Figure 3(b) compares Cadmium normalisation without events (−*events*) versus with events (+*events*). Overall, normalisation *with* events is significantly better, with a 63% improvement.[5] The MiniZinc flattening benchmarks showed the largest gains. This is especially true for langford.mzn, where the −*events* version is too slow to be practical. On the other hand, the queens benchmarks were better off without events. In this case, the +*events* version avoided almost no wake-ups, so the extra overhead of tracking events causes a slow-down.

6   Related Work and Conclusions

Cadmium is a powerful rewriting language that implements rewriting based on non-local information in the form of Conjunctive Context. However, CC complicates any potential Cadmium normalisation algorithm, since the CC must be distributed to everywhere it is used. Furthermore, there are no guarantees the context itself is normalised, so traditional bottom-up evaluation strategies do not work. We have presented a normalisation algorithm based on waking-up conjuncts whose context may have changed in a way that affects rule application. By tracking wake-up conditions and events, renormalisation because of context changes can be significantly decreased. Experiments show speed-ups in real-world Cadmium applications such as Zinc model flattening.

There exist several other implementations of term rewriting, such as Maude [3], and others. Like Cadmium, matching modulo AC is a standard feature. The main difference between Cadmium and other implementations is the native support for CC normalisation.

---

[5]   Excluding langford.mzn.

Unification (and therefore matching) modulo distribution, i.e. $x * (y + z) = x * y + x * z$, has also been studied, e.g. in [9]. However, this work is not relevant to CC-distribution, which is based on a different axiom, e.g. $x \wedge f(y) = x \wedge f(x \wedge y)$.

For future work we intend to further improve the performance of Cadmium. We believe it is possible to refine the normalisation algorithm further, i.e. to avoid even more wake-ups by refining events, and to specialise the renormalisation that occurs during wake-up.

References

1. Baader, F., Nipkow, T.: Term rewriting and all that. Cambridge Univ. Press, Cambridge (1998)
2. Brand, S., Duck, G.J., Puchinger, J., Stuckey, P.J.: Flexible, Rule-based Constraint Model Linearisation. In: Hudak, P., Warren, D.S. (eds.) PADL 2008. LNCS, vol. 4902, pp. 68–83. Springer, Heidelberg (2008)
3. Clavel, M., Durán, F., Eker, S., Lincoln, P., Martí-Oliet, N., Meseguer, J., Talcott, C.: The Maude 2.0 System. In: Nieuwenhuis, R. (ed.) RTA 2003. LNCS, vol. 2706, pp. 76–87. Springer, Heidelberg (2003)
4. Duck, G.J., Stuckey, P.J., Brand, S.: ACD Term Rewriting. In: Etalle, S., Truszczyński, M. (eds.) ICLP 2006. LNCS, vol. 4079, pp. 117–131. Springer, Heidelberg (2006)
5. Frühwirth, T.: Theory and practice of constraint handling rules. Journal of Logic Programming 37, 95–138 (1998)
6. Nethercote, N., Stuckey, P.J., Becket, R., Brand, S., Duck, G.J., Tack, G.: MiniZinc: Towards a Standard CP Modelling Language. In: Bessière, C. (ed.) CP 2007. LNCS, vol. 4741, pp. 529–543. Springer, Heidelberg (2007)
7. Rewriting Engines Competition,
   http://www.lcc.uma.es/~duran/rewriting_competition/
8. Eker, S.M.: Associative-Commutative Matching Via Bipartite Graph Matching. Computer Journal 38(5), 381–399 (1995)
9. Schmidt-Schauß, M.: Decidability of Unification in the Theory of One-Sided Distributivity and a Multiplicative Unit. Journal of Symbolic Computation 22(3), 315–344 (1997)
10. Stuckey, P.J., García de la Banda, M., Maher, M., Marriott, K., Slaney, J., Somogyi, Z., Wallace, M., Walsh, T.: The G12 project: Mapping solver independent models to efficient solutions. In: Gabbrielli, M., Gupta, G. (eds.) ICLP 2005. LNCS, vol. 3668, pp. 9–13. Springer, Heidelberg (2005)

Quantified Equilibrium Logic and Foundations for Answer Set Programs

David Pearce[1,*] and Agustín Valverde[2,*]

[1] Universidad Rey Juan Carlos, Madrid, Spain
davidandrew.pearce@urjc.es
[2] Universidad de Málaga, Málaga, Spain
a_valverde@ctima.uma.es

Abstract. **QHT** is a first-order super-intuitionistic logic that provides a foundation for answer set programming (ASP) and a useful tool for analysing and transforming non-ground programs. We recall some properties of **QHT** and its nonmonotonic extension, quantified equilibrium logic (QEL). We show how the proof theory of **QHT** can be used to extend to non-ground programs previous results on the completeness of θ-subsumption. We also establish a reduction of **QHT** to classical logic and show how this can be used to obtain and extend classical encodings for concepts such as the strong equivalence of programs and theories. We pay special attention to a class of general (disjunctive) logic programs that capture all universal theories in QEL.

1 Introduction

Answer set programming (ASP) [1] is now becoming an established paradigm of logic-based, declarative programming with promising applications in areas such planning, diagnosis, information management, program verification, logical agents, Web reasoning and others. Until now ASP solvers have reduced programs with variables to the propositional case by a costly grounding or instantiation process. However, it is likely that future generation systems will operate directly at the first-order level as in traditional logic programming. In particular, formal methods will need to be developed that will provide for program transformation and optimisation and will delay or virtually eliminate the grounding process. Already, there is considerable interest in foundational concepts and methods for non-ground programs, see eg. [2,3,4,5,6].

There are two viable approaches to developing such formal methods. One of them is direct and based on a logical system called *quantified here-and-there logic*, **QHT**, and its non-monotonic extension *quantified equilibrium logic*, QEL. Its close relation to non-ground logic programs under answer set semantics has been studied in [7,8,9,10]. Since this is the logic that determines when programs are strongly equivalent or interchangeable in any context, it guarantees robust, semantics-preserving transformations.

* We gratefully acknowledge support from the Spanish MEC (now MCI) under the projects TIN2006-15455-CO3 and Agreement Technologies, Consolider CSD2007-00022, and the Junta de Andalucia, project P6-FQM-02049. We would also like to thank the anonymous referees for helpful comments that we hope have led to improvements in the paper.

M. Garcia de la Banda and E. Pontelli (Eds.): ICLP 2008, LNCS 5366, pp. 546–560, 2008.

A second approach to ASP foundations is more indirect and involves classical logic. Its primary advantage is its familiarity, its wealth of results and its suitability for rapid prototyping. Its drawback is that it lies one level removed from the action. We first have to translate and manipulate expressions before we obtain relevant representations in classical logic that in some cases could have been obtained in simpler fashion using **QHT**. This can sometimes add an *ad hoc* flavour to the modelling and make it hard to understand why a given representation works correctly.

The present paper has four main parts. In the first (§2) we recall the main features of **QHT** and QEL and their relevance for ASP foundations; and we show how a class of general logic programs can capture any universal theory in QEL. In the next section we illustrate how **QHT** can be applied to an important topic in ASP foundations, that of rule redundancy in programs, previously studied for the non-ground case in [2,11,3]. We show how to capture a general form of rule redundancy, θ-subsumption, and extend a subsumption result of [12] to the first-order case. In Section 4 we show how classical logic can be applied (indirectly) in ASP in virtue of a reduction relation that can be established from **QHT** to classical logic. This extends the reduction of propositional here-and-there logic studied in [13] and it yields an easy method of implementing a prototype **QHT** theorem prover. Lastly, in Section 5 we show how this reduction technique can be used to derive some classical encodings of key properties and concepts in ASP, from that of stable model in the sense of [4] to that of strong equivalence and its complexity, studied in [14].

2 Review of Quantified Equilibrium Logic and Answer Sets

For the propositional version of the logic **HT** of here-and-there and an overview of propositional equilibrium logic, see [15]. We denote by $\models_{\mathbf{HT}}$ the deduction relation for **HT**. Usually in quantified equilibrium logic we consider a full first-order language allowing function symbols and we include a second, strong negation operator as occurs in several ASP dialects. In this paper we shall restrict attention to the function-free language with a single negation symbol, '$\neg$'. In particular, we shall work with a quantified version of the logic **HT** of *here-and-there*. In other respects we follow the treatment of [10].

For the remainder of the paper we consider function-free first order languages $\mathcal{L} = \langle C, P \rangle$ built over a set of *constant* symbols, C, and a set of *predicate* symbols, P. The sets of $\mathcal{L}$-formulas, $\mathcal{L}$-sentences and atomic $\mathcal{L}$-sentences are defined in the usual way. We work here with *sentences*. If D is a non-empty set, we denote by $At_D(C, P)$ the set of ground atomic sentences of $\mathcal{L}' = \langle C \cup D, P \rangle$ ie. the extension of $\mathcal{L}$ with additional constant symbols for each element of D. By an $\mathcal{L}$-*interpretation* I over a set D we mean a subset I of $At_D(C, P)$. A *classical* $\mathcal{L}$-*structure* can be regarded as a tuple $\mathcal{M} = \langle (D, \sigma), I \rangle$ where I is an $\mathcal{L}$-interpretation over D. On the other hand, a *here-and-there* $\mathcal{L}$-structure with static domains, or $\mathbf{QHT}^s(\mathcal{L})$-*structure*, is a tuple $\mathcal{M} = \langle (D, \sigma), I_h, I_t \rangle$ where

- D is a non-empty set, called the *domain* of $\mathcal{M}$.
- σ is a mapping: $C \cup D \rightarrow D$ called the *assignment* such that $\sigma(d) = d$ for all $d \in D$. If $D = C$ and $\sigma = id$, $\mathcal{M}$ is a *Herbrand structure*.
- I_h, I_t are $\mathcal{L}$-interpretations over D such that $I_h \subseteq I_t$.

Thus we can think of a here-and-there structure $\mathcal{M}$ as similar to a first-order classical model, but having two parts, or components, h and t that correspond to two different points or "worlds", 'here' and 'there', in the sense of Kripke semantics for intuitionistic logic [16], where the worlds are ordered by $h \leq t$. At each world $w \in \{h, t\}$ one verifies a set of atoms I_w in the expanded language for the domain D. We call the model static, since, in contrast to say intuitionistic logic, the same domain serves each of the worlds. Since $h \leq t$, whatever is verified at h remains true at t. The satisfaction relation for $\mathcal{M}$ is defined so as to reflect the two different components, so we write $\mathcal{M}, w \models \varphi$ to denote that φ is true in $\mathcal{M}$ with respect to the w component. Evidently we should require that an atomic sentence is true at w just in case it belongs to the w-interpretation. Formally, if $p(t_1, \ldots, t_n) \in \mathrm{At}_D$ then

$$\mathcal{M}, w \models p(t_1, \ldots, t_n) \quad \text{iff} \quad p(\sigma(t_1), \ldots, \sigma(t_n)) \in I_w. \tag{1}$$

Then $\models$ is extended recursively as follows[1]:

- $\mathcal{M}, w \models \varphi \wedge \psi$ iff $\mathcal{M}, w \models \varphi$ and $\mathcal{M}, w \models \psi$.
- $\mathcal{M}, w \models \varphi \vee \psi$ iff $\mathcal{M}, w \models \varphi$ or $\mathcal{M}, w \models \psi$.
- $\mathcal{M}, t \models \varphi \rightarrow \psi$ iff $\mathcal{M}, t \not\models \varphi$ or $\mathcal{M}, t \models \psi$.
- $\mathcal{M}, h \models \varphi \rightarrow \psi$ iff $\mathcal{M}, t \models \varphi \rightarrow \psi$ and $\mathcal{M}, h \not\models \varphi$ or $\mathcal{M}, h \models \psi$.
- $\mathcal{M}, w \models \neg\varphi$ iff $\mathcal{M}, t \not\models \varphi$.
- $\mathcal{M}, t \models \forall x \varphi(x)$ iff $\mathcal{M}, t \models \varphi(d)$ for all $d \in D$.
- $\mathcal{M}, h \models \forall x \varphi(x)$ iff $\mathcal{M}, t \models \forall x \varphi(x)$ and $\mathcal{M}, h \models \varphi(d)$ for all $d \in D$.
- $\mathcal{M}, w \models \exists x \varphi(x)$ iff $\mathcal{M}, w \models \varphi(d)$ for some $d \in D$.

Truth of a sentence in a model is defined as follows: $\mathcal{M} \models \varphi$ iff $\mathcal{M}, w \models \varphi$ for each $w \in \{h, t\}$. A sentence φ is valid if it is true in all models, denoted by $\models \varphi$. A sentence φ is a consequence of a set of sentences Γ, denoted $\Gamma \models \varphi$, if every model of Γ is a model of φ. In a model $\mathcal{M}$ we also use the symbols H and T, possibly with subscripts, to denote the interpretations I_h and I_t respectively; so, an $\mathcal{L}$-structure may be written in the form $\langle U, H, T \rangle$, where $U = (D, \sigma)$.

The resulting logic is called *Quantified Here-and-There Logic with static domains*, and denoted in [5] by $\mathbf{QHT}^s$. In terms of satisfiability and validity this logic is equivalent to the logic previously introduced in [8]. To simplify notation we drop the superscript 's' and refer to this logic simply as quantified here-and-there, $\mathbf{QHT}$.

A complete axiomatisation of $\mathbf{QHT}$ can be obtained as follows [5]. We take the axioms and rules of first-order intuitionistic logic [16] and add the axiom of Hosoi

$$\alpha \vee (\neg\beta \vee (\alpha \rightarrow \beta))$$

which determines 2-element here-and-there models in the propositional case, together with the axiom:

$$\exists x(\alpha(x) \rightarrow \forall x \alpha(x)).$$

In the context of logic programs, the following assumptions often play a role. In the case of both classical and $\mathbf{QHT}$ models, we say that the *parameter names assumption*

---

[1] The following corresponds to the usual Kripke semantics for intuitionistic logic given our assumptions about the two worlds h and t and the single domain D, see e.g. [16].

(PNA) applies in case $\sigma|_C$ is surjective, i.e., there are no unnamed individuals in D; the *unique names assumption (UNA)* applies in case $\sigma|_C$ is injective; in case both the PNA and UNA apply, the *standard names assumption (SNA)* applies, i.e. $\sigma|_C$ is a bijection. In the following, we will speak about PNA-, UNA-, or SNA-models, respectively, depending on σ.

Equilibrium Models. As in the propositional case, quantified equilibrium logic is based on a suitable notion of minimal model.

Definition 1. *Among* **QHT**-*structures over a given language we define the order* $\trianglelefteq$ *by:* $\langle(D,\sigma),H,T\rangle \trianglelefteq \langle(D',\sigma'),H',T'\rangle$ *if* $D = D'$, $\sigma = \sigma'$, $T = T'$ *and* $H \subseteq H'$. *If the subset relation is strict, we write* '$\triangleleft$'.

Definition 2. *Let* Γ *be a set of sentences and* $\mathcal{M} = \langle(D,\sigma),H,T\rangle$ *a model of* Γ. $\mathcal{M}$ *is said to be* total *if* $H = T$. $\mathcal{M}$ *is said to be an* equilibrium *model of* Γ *if it is minimal under* $\trianglelefteq$ *among models of* Γ, *and it is total.*

Notice that a total **QHT** model of a theory Γ is equivalent to a classical first order model of Γ.

Answer Set Semantics. We consider a general form of non-ground disjunctive logic programs where negation is allowed in both rule heads and bodies, interpreted under the answer set semantics [17].[2] A *general* program Π consists of a set of rules of the form

$$a_1 \vee a_2 \vee \ldots \vee a_k \vee \neg a_{k+1} \vee \ldots \vee \neg a_l \leftarrow b_1, \ldots, b_m, \neg b_{m+1}, \ldots, \neg b_n \qquad (2)$$

where a_i ($i \in \{1, \ldots, l\}$) and b_j ($j \in \{1, \ldots, n\}$) are atoms, called head (body, respectively) atoms of the rule, in a function-free first-order language $\mathcal{L} = \langle C, P \rangle$ without equality. $C_\Pi \subseteq C$ is the set of constants which appear in Π. Rules where each variable appears in $b_1, \ldots, b_m$ are called *safe*. A program is *safe* if all its rules are safe. An (ordinary) disjunctive program is one whose rules contain no occurrences of negation in the head, ie. where $k = l$ in (2).

The *grounding* $gr_U(\Pi)$ of Π wrt. a universe $U = (D, \sigma)$ denotes the set of all rules obtained as follows: For $r \in \Pi$, replace (i) each constant c appearing in r with $\sigma(c)$ and (ii) each variable with some element in D. Observe that thus $gr_U(\Pi)$ is a ground program over the atoms in $At_D(C, P)$.

For a ground program Π and first-order structure $\mathcal{I}$ the *reduct* $\Pi^\mathcal{I}$ consists of rules

$$a_1 \vee a_2 \vee \ldots \vee a_k \leftarrow b_1, \ldots, b_m$$

obtained from all rules of the form (2) in Π for which $\mathcal{I} \models a_i$ for all $k < i \leq l$ and $\mathcal{I} \not\models b_j$ for all $m < j \leq n$.

Answer set semantics is usually defined in terms of *Herbrand structures* over $\mathcal{L} = \langle C, P \rangle$. Herbrand structures have a fixed universe, the *Herbrand universe* $\mathcal{H} = (C, id)$, where id is the identity function. For a Herbrand structure $\mathcal{I} = \langle \mathcal{H}, I \rangle$, I can be viewed

---

[2] We follow here largely the exposition from [18].

as a subset of the *Herbrand base*, $\mathcal{B}$, which consists of the ground atoms of $\mathcal{L}$. Note that by definition of $\mathcal{H}$, Herbrand structures are SNA-structures. A Herbrand structure $\mathcal{I}$ is an *answer set* [17] of Π if $\mathcal{I}$ is subset minimal among the structures satisfying $gr_{\mathcal{H}}(\Pi)^{\mathcal{I}}$. Two variations of this semantics, the open [19] and generalised open answer set [20] semantics, consider open domains, thereby relaxing the PNA. An *extended Herbrand structure* is a first-order structure based on a universe $U = (D, id)$, where $D \supseteq C$.

Definition 3. *A first-order $\mathcal{L}$-structure $\mathcal{I} = \langle U, I \rangle$ is called a* generalised open answer set *of Π if $\mathcal{I}$ is subset minimal among the structures satisfying all rules in $gr_U(\Pi)^{\mathcal{I}}$. If, additionally, $\mathcal{I}$ is an extended Herbrand structure, then $\mathcal{I}$ is an* open answer set *of Π.*

Note that in the case of open answer set semantics the UNA applies. The following facts are straightforward (see eg [18] for proofs).

- If $\mathcal{M}$ is an answer set of Π then $\mathcal{M}$ is also an open answer set of Π.
- Let Π be a safe program over $\mathcal{L} = \langle C, P \rangle$ with $\mathcal{M} = \langle U, I \rangle$ a (generalised) open answer set over universe $U = (D, \sigma)$. Then, for any atom from $At_D(C, P)$ such that $\mathcal{M} \models p(d_1, \ldots, d_n)$, there exist $c_i \in C_{\Pi}$ such that $\sigma(c_i) = d_i$ for each $1 \leq i \leq n$. Consequently:
- $\mathcal{M}$ is an (generalised) open answer set of a *safe* program Π if and only if $\mathcal{M}$ is an (generalised) answer set of Π.

Answer Sets and Equilibrium Models. In the propositional case it is well-known that equilibrium models coincide with answer sets [21]. For the present version of QEL the correspondence to answer sets can be described as follows.

Proposition 1 ([10]). *Let Γ be a universal theory in $\mathcal{L} = \langle C, P \rangle$. Let $\langle U, T, T \rangle$ be a total **QHT** model of Γ. Then $\langle U, T, T \rangle$ is an equilibrium model of Γ iff $\langle T, T \rangle$ is a propositional equilibrium model of $gr_U(\Gamma)$.*

By convention, when Π is a logic program with variables we consider the models and equilibrium models of its universal closure expressed as a set of logical formulas. So, from Proposition 1 we obtain:

Corollary 1. *Let Π be a logic program. A total **QHT** model $\langle U, T, T \rangle$ of Π is an equilibrium model of Π iff it is a generalised open answer set of Π.*

If we assume all models are UNA-models, we obtain the version of QEL found in [8]. There, the relation of QEL to (ordinary) answer sets for logic programs with variables was established.

Proposition 2. *[8, Corol. 7.7] Let Π be a logic program. A total UNA-**QHT** model $\langle U, T, T \rangle$ of Π is an equilibrium model of Π iff it is an open answer set of Π.*

2.1   Strong Equivalence and Normal Forms

The study of strong equivalence for logic programs and nonmonotonic theories was initiated in [9]. Programs or theories Π_1 and Π_2 are said to be strongly equivalent if and only if for any set of rules Σ, $\Pi_1 \cup \Sigma$ and $\Pi_2 \cup \Sigma$ have the same answer sets. Strong equivalence has also been defined and studied for logic programs with variables and first-order nonmonotonic theories under the stable model or equilibrium logic semantics [22,2,5,10]; it has become an important tool in ASP as a basis for program transformation and optimisation. In equilibrium logic we say that two (first-order) theories Π_1 and Π_2 are strongly equivalent if and only if for any theory Σ, $\Pi_1 \cup \Sigma$ and $\Pi_2 \cup \Sigma$ have the same equilibrium models [5,10]. Under this definition we have:

Theorem 1 ([5,10]). *Two (first-order) theories Π_1 and Π_2 are strongly equivalent if and only if they are equivalent in* **QHT**.

The proof contained in [10] shows that if theories are not strongly equivalent, the set of formulas Σ such that $\Pi_1 \cup \Sigma$ and $\Pi_2 \cup \Sigma$ do not have the same equilibrium models can be chosen to have the form of implications $(p \rightarrow q)$ where p and q are atomic. So if we are interested in the case where Π_1 and Π_2 are sets of rules, Σ can also be regarded as a set of rules.

A sentence is said to be in *prenex* form if it has the following shape, for some $n \geq 0$:

$$Q_1 x_1 \ldots Q_n x_n \alpha \tag{3}$$

where Q_i is $\forall$ or $\exists$ and α is quantifier-free. A sentence is said to be *universal* if it is in prenex form and all quantifiers are universal. A universal theory is a set of universal sentences. For **QHT**, normal forms such as prenex and Skolem forms were studied in [8]. In particular we have there the following property.

Theorem 2 ([8]). *In* **QHT** *every sentence is logically equivalent to a sentence in prenex form.*

Suppose that we convert a sentence φ into one in prenex form of kind (3). Since the matrix α is quantifier-free, we can apply equivalences from propositional logic to convert α into a special reduced form. The appropriate transformations are described in detail in [23]. They allow us to convert α into a logically equivalent general rule of form (2). In other words the matrix has precisely the form of a rule of a general logic program. So combining the transformations of [23] with Theorem 2 we obtain a normal form for theories in **QHT**. This resembles the form of general logic programs except that existential quantifiers may appear in front of rules.[3] On the other hand if Π is a universal theory in **QHT**, it is equivalent to a set of universal sentences and hence to a logic program in this general form. So we obtain:

Proposition 3. *Any universal theory is equivalent in* **QHT** *to a general logic program, hence in QEL any universal theory is strongly equivalent to some general program.*

3   Rule Redundancy and θ-Subsumption

We continue our analysis of general programs comprising rules of form (2) that represent a normal form for universal sentences in **QHT**. Instead of writing expressions

---

[3] A similar observation regarding first-order formulas under the new stable model semantics of [4] is made in [24].

of type (2), we shall consider a rule as a logical formula $\forall x r$, where $r = B^+(r) \wedge \neg B^-(r) \rightarrow Hd^+(r) \vee \neg Hd^-(r)$

$$B^+(r) = \bigwedge p_i(\mathbf{t}_i), \ B^-(r) = \bigvee p_i(\mathbf{t}_i), \ Hd^+(r) = \bigvee p_i(\mathbf{t}_i), \ Hd^-(r) = \bigwedge p_i(\mathbf{t}_i),$$

every $\mathbf{t}_i$ is a vector of terms, ie. either variables or constants, and $\mathbf{x}$ is the vector of variables in r.

For non-ground disjunctive programs under answer set semantics, various types of transformations and programs simplifications have been studied, eg. in [2,11,3]. Special cases arise when eg. a tautological rule may simply be dropped from a program, or one rule is more 'specific' than another so that removing the latter in the presence of the former results in a strongly equivalent program. In light of our results about **QHT** it is clear that a rule $\forall x r$ is tautological if and only if is valid in **QHT**, ie. $\models_{\mathbf{QHT}} \forall x r$. Similarly, in the general case a rule $\forall x r$ is redundant in the presence of another rule $\forall \mathbf{x} s$ if

$$\forall \mathbf{x} s \models_{\mathbf{QHT}} \forall \mathbf{x} r \tag{4}$$

When (4) holds it is clear that the rule $\forall x r$ can be dropped from any program containing $\forall \mathbf{x} s$ without loss, ie. the reduced program is strongly equivalent to the original.

In the works mentioned, one aim is to characterise such properties in terms of relations between the various elements in the bodies and heads of rules. We shall also consider here some aspects of rule redundancy, but our approach differs from that of [2,11,3] in two main ways. First, we consider general rules, where $Hd^-(r)$ need not be empty. Secondly, the works mentioned do not make use of properties such as (4). As a consequence, the methods they use for proving properties of rule transformations are different from those obtained by applying the logic **QHT**. An advantage of using (4) is that by completeness we have a sound and complete calculus for deduction in **QHT**. We can also of course use the reduction of **QHT** to classical logic, however here it will be convenient to work directly with proof systems for **QHT**.

In the rest of the section we need to use substitutions. As usual, a substitution ϑ is a map from the set of variables to the set of terms, ie. variables and constants; if α is a formula, $\alpha\vartheta$ is obtained by replacing every free variable x by $\vartheta(x)$.

Lemma 1. *A rule $\forall x r$ is a tautology iff either $B^+(r) \cap B^-(r) \neq \emptyset$, or $B^+(r) \cap Hd^+(r) \neq \emptyset$, or $B^-(r) \cap Hd^-(r) \neq \emptyset$.*

Proof: The "if" condition is trivial. To prove the "only if", let us assume that r is a tautology and let C_r be the set of constants in r and V_r the set of variables in r. Let us consider the assignment (D, σ), where $D = C_r \cup V_r$ and $\sigma = id \colon C_r \rightarrow D$ and the substitution $\vartheta = id \colon V_r \rightarrow D$. If r is a tautology, then $r\vartheta$ is true in the assignment (D, σ). Applying the propositional characterisation to the quantifier-free formula $r\vartheta$, we obtain the conclusion. □

Aside from tautologies, various different kind of rule elimination are studied in [11]. Since the most general of these is subsumption, we focus here on this property. First we establish a key result about substitutions.

Theorem 3. *Let $\forall x r$ and $\forall \mathbf{x} s$ be two rules; let C be the set of constants in r or s, V_r the set of variables in r and V_s the set of variables in s. Then, the following conditions are equivalent*

1. $\{\forall \mathbf{x} s, \forall \mathbf{x} r\} \equiv_s \forall \mathbf{x} s.$
2. $\forall \mathbf{x} s \models_{\mathbf{QHT}} \forall \mathbf{x} r$
3. $\{s\vartheta \mid \vartheta \colon V_s \to C \cup V_r\} \models_{\mathbf{HT}} r$

In item 3, we use the propositional entailment relation, $\models_{\mathbf{HT}}$, because the involved formulas are quantifier free and thus we only need to use propositional interpretations, where the first order atomic formulas are considered as propositional atoms.

To prove the theorem, we shall use a tableau system for $\mathbf{QHT}$. This system is constructed by extending the propositional system introduced in [25] based on the many-valued semantics of HT. The labels of the expansion rules are *regular* sets of truth values: $[> j] = \{i \mid i > j\}$, $[< j] = \{i \mid i < j\}$. The quantifiers in $\mathbf{QHT}$ are also regular and thus the expansion rules for them are the following:

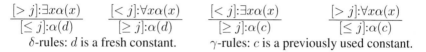

$$\frac{[> j]{:}\exists x \alpha(x)}{[\le j]{:}\alpha(d)} \qquad \frac{[< j]{:}\forall x \alpha(x)}{[\ge j]{:}\alpha(d)} \qquad \frac{[< j]{:}\exists x \alpha(x)}{[\ge j]{:}\alpha(c)} \qquad \frac{[> j]{:}\forall x \alpha(x)}{[\le j]{:}\alpha(c)}$$

δ-rules: d is a fresh constant. γ-rules: c is a previously used constant.

The general proof of the soundness and completeness theorem for the tableau system can be found in [26].

Proof of theorem 3: (1)$\Leftrightarrow$(2) is trivial. To prove (2)$\Leftrightarrow$(3) we use the semantic tableaux system for $\mathbf{QHT}$. $\forall \mathbf{x} s \models_{\mathbf{QHT}} \forall \mathbf{x} r$ if and only if $\{\{2\}{:}\forall \mathbf{x} s, [< 2]{:}\forall \mathbf{x} r\}$ can be extended to a closed tableau. The δ-formula $[< 2]{:}\forall \mathbf{x} r$ is expanded by replacing every variable in $\mathbf{x}$ by a fresh parameter; we can do that eliminating the universal quantifiers and treating the variables in r as new parameters. So, $\{\{2\}{:}\forall \mathbf{x} s, [< 2]{:}\forall \mathbf{x} r\}$ can be extended to a closed tableau if and only if $\{\{2\}{:}\forall \mathbf{x} s, [< 2]{:}r\}$ can; in this tableau, the rule r is considered ground. This tableau contains a finite set of parameters and constants, $C \cup V_r$, and thus, $\{\{2\}{:}s\vartheta \mid \vartheta \colon V_s \to C \cup V_r\} \cup \{[< 2]{:}r\}$ is finite and can be extended to a closed tableau if and only if $\{\{2\}{:}\forall \mathbf{x} s, [< 2]{:}r\}$ can. The tableau $\{\{2\}{:}s\vartheta \mid \vartheta \colon V_s \to C \cup V_r\} \cup \{[< 2]{:}r\}$ does not contain quantifiers, and thus, it may be considered as a propositional tableau. Therefore, $\{\{2\}{:}s\vartheta \mid \vartheta \colon V_s \to C \cup V_r\} \cup \{[< 2]{:}r\}$ can be extended to a closed tableau if and only if

$$\{s\vartheta \mid \vartheta \colon V_s \to C \cup V_r\} \models_{\mathbf{HT}} r \qquad \qquad \Box$$

As a consequence of this result, we can conclude that the checking whether a rule r entails another rule s is decidable, because the set of premises in condition 3 is finite.

It is not true that, in general, there is a single substitution θ_0 such that $s\theta_0 \models_{\mathbf{HT}} r$ if and only if $\{\forall \mathbf{x} s, \forall \mathbf{x} r\} \equiv_s \forall \mathbf{x} s$. For example,

$$\forall x(p(a, x) \to p(x, b)) \models p(a, a) \to p(b, b)$$

however there is no instance of $p(a, x) \to p(x, b)$ implying $p(a, a) \to p(b, b)$. Therefore, as for clauses in classical logic, we can not improve the previous characterisation.

As a consequence of Theorem 3, we have that, if $s\vartheta \models_{\mathbf{HT}} r$, then $\forall \mathbf{x} s \models_{\mathbf{QHT}} \forall \mathbf{x} r$ and by the completeness results for subsumption found in [12,27], $s\vartheta$ subsumes r. This justifies the following definition as a suitable notion of subsumption for extended rules using a single substitution.

Definition 4. *For every pair of fundamental rules r and s we say that s θ-subsumes r if there exists a substitution $\vartheta: V_s \to C \cup V_r$ such that:*

1. $B^-(s\vartheta) \subseteq B^-(r)$
2. $Hd^-(s\vartheta) \subseteq Hd^-(r) \cup B^+(r)$
3. $B^+(s\vartheta) \subseteq B^+(r) \cup Hd^-(r)$
4. $Hd^+(s\vartheta) \subseteq Hd^+(r) \cup B^-(r)$
5. *Either $B^+(s\vartheta) \cap Hd^-(r) = \emptyset$ or $Hd^+(s\vartheta) \cap Hd^+(r) = \emptyset$.*

For ordinary disjunctive rules this corresponds to the property $s \leq r$ studied in [3].

Example 1. The rule $s = p(x) \wedge \neg q(x, y) \to u(y)$ θ-subsumes $r = \neg q(x, a) \wedge \neg u(x) \to \neg p(a)$, because the substitution ϑ such that $\vartheta(x) = a$ and $\vartheta(y) = x$ satisfies the conditions in the previous definition; hence in any program containing both rules, r can be eliminated. This is verified as follows:

1. $B^-(s\vartheta) = \{q(x, a)\} = B^-(r)$
2. $Hd^-(s\vartheta) = \{u(x)\} = Hd^-(r)$
3. $B^+(s\vartheta) = \{p(a)\} = Hd^-(r)$
4. $Hd^+(s\vartheta) = \{u(x)\} \subseteq B^-(r)$
5. $Hd^+(s\vartheta) \cap Hd^+(r) = \emptyset$.

Proposition 4. *If s θ-subsumes r, then $\forall \mathbf{x} s \models_{\mathbf{QHT}} \forall \mathbf{x} r$.*

And finally, with the following result, we extend to non-ground programs the completeness results for subsumption found in [12,27].

Proposition 5. *s θ-subsumes r if there exists a substitution $\vartheta: V_s \to C \cup V_r$ such that $s\theta \models_{\mathbf{HT}} r$.*

4   Reduction of QHT to Classical Logic

In this section we show how the deduction problem for **QHT** can be reduced to an equivalent problem in classical predicate logic. This result has two main uses. First, since **QHT** is a pivotal tool for analysing answer set programs, it is useful to develop automated deduction methods for it. Reduction to classical logic provides such a method and allows for rapid prototyping and checking of properties of **QHT**. Secondly, classical logic is already being used as a foundational approach to ASP. This can be seen for example in the work of Ferraris, Lee, and Lifschitz [4] giving a new definition of stable model for first-order formulas, in the work of Lin [22] reducing the strong equivalence of programs to a satisfiability problem in classical logic, to extensions of this work by Traxler [14,11] implementing a strong equivalence checker using a classical logic theorem prover, and in many other cases. However, it is not always easy to understand from a conceptual point of view exactly why these applications of classical logic work the way they do. By establishing a general reduction of **QHT** to classical logic, we obtain almost immediately the equivalent classical formulations of certain key concepts and problems and explain easily why these representations function as they do.

Our aim is, given first order formulas φ, ψ to find a formula Φ such that $\varphi \models_{\mathbf{QHT}} \psi$ if and only if Φ is classically valid. In the absence of dedicated theorem provers for $\mathbf{QHT}$, this approach will nevertheless provide a proxy by allowing us to apply classical provers. We use notation essentially following [5].

If p and q are predicate constants of the same arity then $p \leq q$ stands for

$$\forall \mathbf{x}(p(\mathbf{x}) \to q(\mathbf{x})),$$

where $\mathbf{x}$ is a tuple of distinct object variables. If $\mathbf{p}$ and $\mathbf{q}$ are tuples $p_1, \ldots, p_n$ and $q_1, \ldots, q_n$ of predicate constants then $\mathbf{p} \leq \mathbf{q}$ stands for

$$p_1 \leq q_1 \wedge \cdots \wedge p_n \leq q_n.$$

Let $\mathcal{L}$ be a language containing the predicate constants $p_1, \ldots, p_n$ and φ a formula in $\mathcal{L}$. Denote by $\mathcal{L}(\bar{\mathbf{p}})$ the expansion of $\mathcal{L}$ by adding a new predicate $\bar{p}_i$ of the same arity for each predicate symbol p_i of $\mathcal{L}$. Define φ^* inductively as follows.

- $p_i(t_1, \ldots, t_m)^* = \bar{p}_i(t_1, \ldots, t_m)$
- $\bot^* = \bot$;
- $(\varphi \odot \psi)^* = \varphi^* \odot \psi^*$, where $\odot \in \{\wedge, \vee\}$;
- $(\varphi \to \psi)^* = (\varphi^* \to \psi^*) \wedge (\varphi \to \psi)$;
- $(Qx\varphi)^* = Qx\varphi^*$, where $Q \in \{\forall, \exists\}$.

(There is no clause for negation here, because $\neg\varphi$ is treated as shorthand for $\varphi \to \bot$.)

We define a function f which maps a classical structure $\mathcal{M}$ for $\mathcal{L}(\bar{\mathbf{p}})$ to a triple $f(\mathcal{M}) = (U, H, T)$ where $U = U_{\mathcal{M}}$; $T = \{p_i(\mathbf{d}) : \mathbf{d} \in \mathcal{M}(p_i)\}$; $H = \{p_i(\mathbf{d}) : \mathbf{d} \in \mathcal{M}(\bar{p}_i)\}$. Note that

$$\mathcal{M} \models \bar{\mathbf{p}} \leq \mathbf{p} \Leftrightarrow f(\mathcal{M}) \text{ is a } \mathbf{QHT} \text{ structure for } \mathcal{L}. \tag{5}$$

Moreover, it is evident that by the construction of $f(\mathcal{M})$, for any $\mathcal{L}$-formula φ, we have

$$\langle U, H, T \rangle, t \models \varphi \Leftrightarrow \mathcal{M} \upharpoonright \mathcal{L} \models \varphi \Leftrightarrow \mathcal{M} \models \varphi \tag{6}$$

Likewise we define a translation τ from $\mathcal{L}$ formulas to $\mathcal{L}(\bar{\mathbf{p}})$ formulas by setting $\tau(\varphi) = \bar{\mathbf{p}} \leq \mathbf{p} \wedge \varphi^*$.

Lemma 2. *For all models $\mathcal{M}$ and $\mathcal{L}$-formulas φ:*

$$f(\mathcal{M}) \models \varphi \Leftrightarrow \mathcal{M} \models \tau(\varphi).$$

Proof: We only need to prove that $f(\mathcal{M}), h \models \varphi$ if and only if $\mathcal{M} \models \tau(\varphi)$ and we do that by induction on φ:

(i) If $\varphi = p_i(d_1, \ldots, d_k)$, then the property holds immediately by the definition of τ.

(ii) Let ψ_1 and ψ_2 be such that, for $i = 1, 2$,

$$\langle U, H, T \rangle, h \models \psi_i \quad \text{iff} \quad \mathcal{M} \models \tau(\psi_i). \tag{7}$$

- For $\varphi = \psi_1 \wedge \psi_2$:

$$\langle U, H, T \rangle, h \models \psi_1 \wedge \psi_2 \Leftrightarrow \langle U, H, T \rangle, h \models \psi_1 \text{ and } \langle U, H, T \rangle, h \models \psi_2$$
$$\Leftrightarrow \mathcal{M} \models \tau(\psi_1) \text{ and } \mathcal{M} \models \tau(\psi_2) \quad \Leftrightarrow \mathcal{M} \models \overline{\mathbf{p}} \leq \mathbf{p} \wedge \psi_1^* \wedge \overline{\mathbf{p}} \leq \mathbf{p} \wedge \psi_2^*$$
$$\Leftrightarrow \mathcal{M} \models \overline{\mathbf{p}} \leq \mathbf{p} \wedge (\psi_1 \wedge \psi_2)^* \quad \Leftrightarrow \mathcal{M} \models \tau(\psi_1 \wedge \psi_2).$$

- For $\varphi = \psi_1 \vee \psi_2$ is similar.
- For $\varphi = \psi_1 \rightarrow \psi_2$:

$$\langle U, H, T \rangle, h \models \psi_1 \rightarrow \psi_2 \Leftrightarrow$$
$$\Leftrightarrow \langle U, H, T \rangle, t \models \psi_1 \rightarrow \psi_2 \text{ and, } \langle U, H, T \rangle, h \not\models \psi_1 \text{ or } \langle U, H, T \rangle, h \models \psi_2$$
$$\Leftrightarrow \mathcal{M} \models \overline{\mathbf{p}} \leq \mathbf{p} \wedge (\psi_1 \rightarrow \psi_2) \text{ (by (5) and (6)) and,}$$
$$\mathcal{M} \not\models \tau(\psi_1) \text{ or } \mathcal{M} \models \tau(\psi_2)$$
$$\Leftrightarrow \mathcal{M} \models \overline{\mathbf{p}} \leq \mathbf{p} \wedge (\psi_1 \rightarrow \psi_2) \text{ and, } \mathcal{M} \not\models \psi_1^* \text{ or } \mathcal{M} \models \psi_2^*$$
$$\Leftrightarrow \mathcal{M} \models \overline{\mathbf{p}} \leq \mathbf{p} \wedge (\psi_1 \rightarrow \psi_2) \text{ and, } \mathcal{M} \models \psi_1^* \rightarrow \psi_2^*$$
$$\Leftrightarrow \mathcal{M} \models \overline{\mathbf{p}} \leq \mathbf{p} \wedge (\psi_1 \rightarrow \psi_2)^*$$
$$\Leftrightarrow \mathcal{M} \models \tau(\psi_1 \rightarrow \psi_2)$$

Let ψ be such that, for every $d \in D$: $\langle U, H, T \rangle, h \models \psi(d)$ iff $\mathcal{M} \models \tau(\psi(d))$.

- For $\varphi = \forall x \psi(x)$:

$$\langle U, H, T \rangle, h \models \forall x \psi(x) \Leftrightarrow \langle U, H, T \rangle, h \models \psi(d) \text{ for all } d \in D$$
$$\Leftrightarrow \mathcal{M} \models \tau(\psi(d)) \text{ for all } d \in D \quad \Leftrightarrow \mathcal{M} \models \overline{\mathbf{p}} \leq \mathbf{p} \wedge \psi(d)^* \text{ for all } d \in D$$
$$\Leftrightarrow \mathcal{M} \models \overline{\mathbf{p}} \leq \mathbf{p} \wedge \forall x \psi(x)^* \quad \Leftrightarrow \mathcal{M} \models \overline{\mathbf{p}} \leq \mathbf{p} \wedge (\forall x \psi(x))^*$$
$$\Leftrightarrow \mathcal{M} \models \tau(\forall x \psi(x))$$

- For $\varphi = \exists x \psi(x)$ is similar. $\qquad \square$

Lemma 3. *Let K be the class of models $\mathcal{M}$ such that $\mathcal{M} \models \overline{\mathbf{p}} \leq \mathbf{p}$. The mapping f restricted to K is a bijection of K onto the* **QHT** *structures for $\mathcal{L}$.*

By Lemma 2 we obtain immediately the following reduction of the deduction problem for **QHT**.

Theorem 4. $\varphi \models_{\mathbf{QHT}} \psi \Leftrightarrow \tau(\varphi) \models \tau(\psi)$.

By the strong completeness theorem for **QHT**, proved in [5], we know that for any φ and set Γ

$$\Gamma \vdash_{\mathbf{QHT}} \varphi \Leftrightarrow \Gamma \models_{\mathbf{QHT}} \varphi$$

Since derivations are finite, it follows that **QHT** has the following compactness property: Suppose $\Gamma \models_{\mathbf{QHT}} \varphi$, then there is a finite subset Γ' of Γ such that $\Gamma' \models_{\mathbf{QHT}} \varphi$. Using the compactness property, we can extend Theorem 4 to:

Theorem 5. *Let Π be a theory in $\mathcal{L}$ and set $\tau(\Pi) = \{\tau(\psi) : \psi \in \Pi\}$. Then $\Pi \models_{\mathbf{QHT}} \varphi \Leftrightarrow \tau(\Pi) \models \tau(\varphi)$.*

In order to express validity in **QHT** in terms of classical logic, we use Lemma 3 to conclude:

Theorem 6. $\models_{\mathbf{QHT}} \varphi \Leftrightarrow \overline{\mathbf{p}} \leq \mathbf{p} \models \tau(\varphi)$.

But clearly we can now simplify the right hand side and state:

$$\models_{\mathbf{QHT}} \varphi \Leftrightarrow \overline{\mathbf{p}} \leq \mathbf{p} \models \varphi^*.$$

5   Classical Encodings of Stable Models and Strong Equivalence

Our reduction technique can be easily implemented and combined with a classical theorem prover to yield a method for automated deduction in **QHT**.[4] As remarked earlier our reduction also allows us to derive classical encodings of key concepts and properties, including stable model and strong equivalence. Let us start with the case of equilibrium model. Recall that a model of φ is in equilibrium if there is no 'smaller' model, that is, a model with the same 'there' part but with less atoms in the 'here' part. By the reduction technique we have seen that the 'here' part can be reconstructed from the evaluation of the new atoms $\overline{p}$ and thus, to obtain a smaller model, we need $\overline{\mathbf{p}} < \mathbf{p}$ and φ^* to be satisfiable. Therefore the equilibrium models of φ are those which cannot be extended to the atoms $\overline{\mathbf{p}}$ to obtain a model of $\overline{\mathbf{p}} < \mathbf{p} \wedge \varphi^*$. This property is expressed by a second order formula: the equilibrium models of φ are the classical models of

$$\varphi \wedge \neg \exists \overline{\mathbf{p}}(\overline{\mathbf{p}} < \mathbf{p} \wedge \varphi^*)$$

This formula is denoted by $\mathrm{SM}[\varphi]$ in [4] and is exactly the new definition of stable model for arbitrary first-order formulas by Ferraris, Lee, and Lifschitz.[5] In a sequel to that paper, Lee, Lifschitz and Palla [6] have applied the new definition and made the following refinements. The *stable models* of a formula are defined as in [4] while the *answer sets* of a formula are those Herbrand models of the formula that are stable in the sense of [4]. Using this new terminology, it follows that in general stable models and equilibrium models coincide, while answer sets are equivalent to SNA-**QHT** models that are equilibrium models.

Let us return to the subject of strong equivalence as characterised in Theorem 1. There have been several similar proposals for encoding the property of strong equivalence for logic programs into classical logic. For the propositional case, see for example [13,22,12,28]. Extensions to the case of non-ground programs can be found in [22,14,2,11,4]. Combining Theorem 1 with Theorems 4 and 5 we can obtain very simply the main encodings of strong equivalence for the non-ground case, as well as extend them to more general classes of programs and theories. In addition, these encodings no longer have an *ad hoc* flavour: they appear precisely as a result of the fact that **QHT** can be reduced as above to classical logic.

---

[4] For a prototype implementation of the **QHT** reduction using Prover9 see The Equilubrium Logic Workbench: a selection of tools facilitating reasoning with here-and-there and equilibrium logic; http://www.equilibriumlogic.net.

[5] In [4] it is also shown that this new notion of stable model is equivalent to that of equilibrium model defined here.

Let us start with [4] where Ferraris, Lee, and Lifschitz give a (first-order) characterisation in classical logic of strong equivalence for formulas under their new stable model semantics. We can derive a simple proof of this characterisation by applying Theorems 4 and 1 to obtain.

Proposition 6 ([4]). φ *is strongly equivalent to* ψ *if and only if the formula*

$$\overline{\mathbf{p}} \leq \mathbf{p} \rightarrow (\varphi^* \leftrightarrow \psi^*)$$

is logically valid (where φ, ψ *are formulas of the language* $\mathcal{L}$ *above and* $\mathbf{p}$ *is the list of predicate symbols appearing in at least one of* φ, ψ*).*

As a second example let's consider how Theorem 5 can be used to generalise the characterisation of strong equivalence by Lin [22] and refined and applied by Traxler [14,11] to implement a strong equivalence checker using a classical theorem prover (see also [2]). Traxler considers finite disjunctive logic programs under the variant of stable model semantics that works with Herbrand models. His stable models correspond therefore to equilibrium models that are SNA-models of **QHT**. Using a variant of the characterisation of strong equivalence for propositional programs due to Lin [22], he shows that the non strong equivalence of two programs can be reduced to the satisfiability of a first-order formula of a special form, called a Bernays-Schönfinkel formula, whose shape is

$$\exists x_1 \ldots x_m \forall y_1 \ldots y_n \varphi(x_1, \ldots, x_m, y_1, \ldots, y_n) \tag{8}$$

He observes that the satisfiability problem for such formulas is NEXPTIME-complete, while testing the strong equivalence of such datalog programs is coNEXPTIME-complete (a result previously obtained by Eiter et al [2]).

Suppose we deal with finite sets of universal sentences $\forall \mathbf{x}\varphi$ and $\forall \mathbf{x}\psi$ where $\mathbf{p}$ is the list of predicate symbols appearing in at least one of φ, ψ. Applying Theorem 4 or its corollary Proposition 6, theories φ and ψ are not strongly equivalent if and only if

$$\forall \mathbf{x}(\overline{\mathbf{p}} \leq \mathbf{p}) \wedge \forall \mathbf{x}\varphi^* \wedge \neg\forall \mathbf{x}\psi^* \tag{9}$$

is satisfiable or

$$\forall \mathbf{x}(\overline{\mathbf{p}} \leq \mathbf{p}) \wedge \forall \mathbf{x}\psi^* \wedge \neg\forall \mathbf{x}\varphi^* \tag{10}$$

is satisfiable. By classical logic, (9) is equivalent to $\forall \mathbf{x}(\overline{\mathbf{p}} \leq \mathbf{p}) \wedge \forall \mathbf{x}\varphi^* \wedge \exists \mathbf{y}\neg\psi^*$ which is in turn equivalent to

$$\exists \mathbf{y}\forall \mathbf{x}(\overline{\mathbf{p}} \leq \mathbf{p} \wedge \varphi^* \wedge \neg\psi^*). \tag{11}$$

Likewise (10) is equivalent to

$$\exists \mathbf{y}\forall \mathbf{x}(\overline{\mathbf{p}} \leq \mathbf{p} \wedge \psi^* \wedge \neg\varphi^*). \tag{12}$$

This yields two Bernays-Schönfinkel formulas of kind (8) to be tested for satisfiability. This test is NEXPTIME-complete [29]. It follows that for finite universal theories the complexity of testing strong equivalence in QEL is the same as that of Datalog programs ([2]):

Theorem 7. *For finite universal theories without function symbols or equality the complexity of checking strong equivalence in QEL is coNEXPTIME-complete.*

The formulas obtained by Traxler are a special case of (11) and (12) where φ, ψ are disjunctive logic programs and the transformation '$*$' is expanded.[6]

6   Conclusions

The intermediate predicate logic **QHT** provides a useful tool for program analysis and transformation in ASP. As we have seen, this is true not only for the case of normal and disjunctive programs usually handled by current ASP systems, but also for more general classes of programs discussed here. The case of stable models for arbitrary first-order formulas [4] is also covered, due to the correspondence with quantified equilibrium logic. We have illustrated how the proof theory of **QHT** can be used to analyse some types of rule redundancy for non-ground answer set programs and yield some novel results on θ-subsumption. We have also provided a reduction of **QHT** to classical logic. This can be used for automating deduction in **QHT** by means of classical theorem provers. The reduction is also useful for reproducing and extending many key concepts and properties of ASP expressed in terms of classical logic.

A prototype implementation of the **QHT** reduction is now available (see note 8). In the future we hope this may shed light on more complex kinds of rule redundancy and valid program transformations in ASP. One area of future work will be to analyse the new variant of the ASP language called RASPL-1 [6] which extends the syntactic class of general programs by allowing restricted use of existential quantification.

References

1. Baral, C.: Knowledge Representation, Reasoning and Declarative Problem Solving. Cambridge University Press, Cambridge (2002)
2. Eiter, T., Fink, M., Tompits, H., Woltran, S.: Strong and uniform equivalence in answer-set programming: Characterizations and complexity results for the non-ground case. In: AAAI 2005, Proceedings, pp. 695–700. AAAI Press/The MIT Press (2005)
3. Fink, M., Pichler, R., Tompits, H., Woltran, S.: Complexity of rule redundancy in non-ground answer-set programming over finite domains. In: Baral, C., Brewka, G., Schlipf, J. (eds.) LPNMR 2007. LNCS, vol. 4483, pp. 123–135. Springer, Heidelberg (2007)
4. Ferraris, P., Lee, J., Lifschitz, V.: A new perspective on stable models. In: IJCAI 2007, Proceedings, pp. 372–379 (2007)
5. Lifschitz, V., Pearce, D., Valverde, A.: A characterization of strong equivalence for logic programs with variables. In: Baral, C., Brewka, G., Schlipf, J. (eds.) LPNMR 2007. LNCS, vol. 4483, pp. 188–200. Springer, Heidelberg (2007)
6. Lee, J., Lifschitz, V., Palla, R.: A reductive semantics for counting and choice in answer set programming. In: AAAI 2008, Proceedings, pp. 472–479. AAAI Press, Menlo Park (2008)
7. Pearce, D., Valverde, A.: Towards a first order equilibrium logic for nonmonotonic reasoning. In: Alferes, J.J., Leite, J. (eds.) JELIA 2004. LNCS, vol. 3229, pp. 147–160. Springer, Heidelberg (2004)

---

[6] Additionally Traxler converts the matrix in each case to (a satisfiability equivalent) conjunctive normal form in order for it be processed by the classical theorem prover. Since he applies the unique name assumption, Traxler's formulas involve additional 'naming' predicates for each constant of the language, a technique found already in [22].

8. Pearce, D., Valverde, A.: A first order nonmonotonic extension of constructive logic. Studia Logica 80(2-3), 321–346 (2005)
9. Lifschitz, V., Pearce, D., Valverde, A.: Strongly equivalent logic programs. ACM Trans. Comput. Log. 2(4), 526–541 (2001)
10. Pearce, D., Valverde, A.: Quantified equilibrium logic. Technical report, Universidad Rey Juan Carlos (2006),
    http://www.matap.uma.es/investigacion/tr/ma06_02.pdf
11. Traxler, P.: Techniques for simplifying disjunctive datalog programs with negation. Magisterarbeit, TU Wien (January 2006)
12. Lin, F., Chen, Y.: Discovering classes of strongly equivalent logic programs. In: IJCAI 2005, Proceedings, Professional Book Center, pp. 516–521 (2005)
13. Pearce, D., Tompits, H., Woltran, S.: Encodings for equilibrium logic and logic programs with nested expressions. In: Brazdil, P.B., Jorge, A.M. (eds.) EPIA 2001. LNCS, vol. 2258, pp. 306–320. Springer, Heidelberg (2001)
14. Traxler, P.: Testing strong equivalence of datalog programs - implementation and examples. Technical report, TU Wien (September 2004)
15. Pearce, D.: Equilibrium logic. Ann. Math. Artif. Intell. 47(1-2), 3–41 (2006)
16. van Dalen, D.: Logic and Structure, 3rd edn. Springer, Heidelberg (1997)
17. Lifschitz, V., Woo, T.Y.C.: Answer sets in general nonmonotonic reasoning (preliminary report). In: KR, pp. 603–614 (1992)
18. de Bruijn, J., Pearce, D., Polleres, A., Valverde, A.: Quantified equilibrium logic and hybrid rules. In: Marchiori, M., Pan, J.Z., Marie, C.d.S. (eds.) RR 2007. LNCS, vol. 4524, pp. 58–72. Springer, Heidelberg (2007)
19. Heymans, S., Nieuwenborgh, D.V., Vermeir, D.: Open answer set programming with guarded programs. ACM Trans. Comput. Log. 9(4) (2008)
20. Heymans, S., Predoiu, L., Feier, C., de Bruijn, J., Nieuwenborgh, D.V.: G-hybrid knowledge bases. In: ALPSWS 2006, Proceedings. CEUR Workshop Proceedings, CEUR-WS.org., vol. 196, pp. 39–54 (2006)
21. Pearce, D.: A new logical characterization of stable models and answer sets. In: Dix, J., Przymusinski, T.C., Moniz Pereira, L. (eds.) NMELP 1996. LNCS, vol. 1216, pp. 57–70. Springer, Heidelberg (1997)
22. Lin, F.: Reducing strong equivalence of logic programs to entailment in classical propositional logic. In: KR 2002, Proceedings, pp. 170–176. Morgan Kaufmann, San Francisco (2002)
23. Cabalar, P., Pearce, D., Valverde, A.: Reducing propositional theories in equilibrium logic to logic programs. In: Bento, C., Cardoso, A., Dias, G. (eds.) EPIA 2005. LNCS, vol. 3808, pp. 4–17. Springer, Heidelberg (2005)
24. Lee, J., Palla, R.: Yet another proof of the strong equivalence between propositional theories and logic programs. In: CENT 2007, Proceedings. CEUR Workshop Proceedings, CEUR-WS.org. vol. 265 (2007)
25. Pearce, D., de Guzmán, I.P., Valverde, A.: A tableau calculus for equilibrium entailment. In: Dyckhoff, R. (ed.) TABLEAUX 2000. LNCS, vol. 1847, pp. 352–367. Springer, Heidelberg (2000)
26. Hähnle, R.: Automated Deduction in Multiple-Valued Logics. International Series of Monographs on Computer Science, vol. 10. Oxford University Press, Oxford (1994)
27. Cabalar, P., Pearce, D., Valverde, A.: Minimal logic programs. In: Dahl, V., Niemelä, I. (eds.) ICLP 2007. LNCS, vol. 4670, pp. 104–118. Springer, Heidelberg (2007)
28. Pearce, D., Tompits, H., Woltran, S.: Chatacterising equilibrium logic and nested logic programs: reductions and complexity. Technical Report GIA 2007-01-12, Universidad Rey Juan Carlos (2007); (to appear in Theory and Practice of Logic programming)
29. Papadimitriu, C.: Comptuational Complexity. Addison-Wesley, Reading (1994)

Elimination of Disjunction and Negation in Answer-Set Programs under Hyperequivalence⋆

Jörg Pührer, Hans Tompits, and Stefan Woltran

Institut für Informationssysteme, Technische Universität Wien,
Favoritenstraße 9–11, A–1040 Vienna, Austria
{puehrer,tompits}@kr.tuwien.ac.at,
woltran@dbai.tuwien.ac.at

Abstract. The study of different notions of equivalence is one of the corner-stones of current research in answer-set programming. This is mainly motivated by the needs of program simplification and modular programming, for which or-dinary equivalence is insufficient. A recently introduced equivalence notion in this context is *hyperequivalence*, which includes as special cases strong, uniform, and ordinary equivalence. We study in this paper the question of replacing pro-grams by syntactically simpler ones preserving hyperequivalence (we refer to such a replacement as a *casting*). In particular, we provide necessary and suffi-cient semantic conditions under which the elimination of disjunction, negation, or both, in programs is possible, preserving hyperequivalence. In other words, we characterise in model-theoretic terms when a disjunctive logic program can be replaced by a hyperequivalent normal, positive, or Horn program, respectively. Furthermore, we study the computational complexity of the considered tasks and, based on similar results for strong equivalence developed in previous work, we provide methods for constructing the respective hyperequivalent programs. Our results contribute to the understanding of problem settings in logic programming in the sense that they show in which scenarios the usage of certain constructs are superfluous or not.

1 Introduction

Answer-set programming (ASP) is an important logic-programming paradigm [1] that is based on principles of nonmonotonic reasoning and became popular for its fully declarative semantics [2]. An important research field in ASP is the study of equivalence of answer-set programs. Given the nonmonotonic nature of logic programs under the answer-set semantics, ordinary equivalence (which holds between two programs if their answer sets coincide) is too weak to yield a replacement property similar to the one of classical logic. That is to say, given a program $P = Q \cup R$, when replacing Q with an ordinarily equivalent program Q', it is not guaranteed that $Q' \cup R$ is ordinarily equivalent to P. This led to the introduction of stricter notions of equivalence, in particular *strong* and *uniform equivalence*: two programs, P and Q, are strongly equivalent [3] if $P \cup R$ and $Q \cup R$ have the same answer sets for any program R, called the *context*, while

---

⋆ This work was partially supported by the Austrian Science Fund (FWF) under projects P18019 and P20704.

M. Garcia de la Banda and E. Pontelli (Eds.): ICLP 2008, LNCS 5366, pp. 561–575, 2008.

they are uniformly equivalent [4] if the context is restricted to sets of facts. Recently, Woltran [5] introduced *hyperequivalence*, or *head-body relativised equivalence*, which is a parametrised notion that subsumes as special cases strong, uniform, and ordinary equivalence. It allows for specifying, on the one hand, the atoms which are permitted to occur in the rule heads of context programs and, on the other hand, the atoms allowed in the rule bodies. Besides generalising various equivalence notions, hyperequivalence can be parametrised for application-specific equivalence tests [6].

In this paper, we are interested in the question whether a given disjunctive logic program P can be replaced by a program Q that is from a syntactically simpler program class than P preserving hyperequivalence (we refer to Q as a *casting* of P). In particular, we are interested in the questions whether a given program can be casted (i) to a program without disjunctions, (ii) to a program without negations, and (iii) to a program without both disjunctions and negations. There is previous work addressing these questions for the notions of strong and uniform equivalence [7,8], introducing model-theoretic characterisations when a casting is possible. We will introduce such conditions for the general case of hyperequivalence, and thereby obtain proper generalisations of the old concepts. More specifically, our main contributions are the following:

- We introduce necessary and sufficient conditions for deciding whether, for a given program, a hyperequivalent normal, positive, or Horn program exists. These conditions are model-theoretic, operating on sets of SE-interpretations [9], which are well-known structures derived from the logical underpinning of strong equivalence [3].
- We provide methods that allow the construction of a casting, whenever a given program is castable. That is, if a program satisfies one of our model-theoretic conditions, we give a constructive method for finding a desired hyperequivalent program.
- We analyse the complexity of the casting problems under consideration. It turns out that these are located on the second and third level of the polynomial hierarchy.

In many situations, our results allow for program simplifications that are not possible under stronger notions of equivalence. For example, the program $P_{ex} = \{f \leftarrow b, not\ n;\ n \leftarrow p;\ b \vee p\}$ cannot be replaced by a program Q without negations such that $P_{ex} \cup R$ and $Q \cup R$ have the same answer sets for every program R. However, such a Q exists whenever atoms b and n do not occur in the head of any rule of R.

Casting under hyperequivalence is also essential for program simplification and modular programming: Depending on the atoms permitted to occur in the rule heads and rule bodies in the context, a module can faithfully be replaced by a simpler one. Moreover, understanding under which circumstances such a replacement is possible gives insight into which roles negation and disjunction play in a certain program.

2   Preliminaries

We deal with finite propositional disjunctive logic programs containing *rules* (over a set At of atoms) of form $a_1 \vee \cdots \vee a_l \leftarrow b_1, \ldots, b_m, not\ b_{m+1}, \ldots, not\ b_n$, where $l \geq 0, n \geq m \geq 0$, all a_i, b_j are from At, and *not* denotes default negation. A rule r as described is *normal*, if $l \leq 1$; *positive*, if $m = n$; and a *fact*, if $l = 1$ and $m = n = 0$. A rule is *Horn* if it is positive and normal. The *head* of r is the set $H(r) = \{a_1, \ldots, a_l\}$; the *body* of r is $B(r) = \{b_1, \ldots, b_m, not\ b_{m+1}, \ldots, not\ b_n\}$. We also define $B^+(r) = \{b_1, \ldots, b_m\}$ and $B^-(r) = \{b_{m+1}, \ldots, b_n\}$. A *disjunctive logic program* (DLP) over At, or simply a *program*, is a finite set of rules over At. A DLP P is a *normal logic program* (NLP) if every rule in P is normal. Likewise, P is a *positive logic program* (PLP) if every rule in P is normal, and it is a *Horn program* if every rule in it is Horn. We denote the class of all DLPs (resp., NLPs, PLPs, Horn programs) by $\mathcal{DLP}$ (resp., $\mathcal{NLP}, \mathcal{PLP}, \mathcal{HORN}$). Furthermore, $atm(P)$ stands for the set of all atoms occurring in P, and we define $H(P) = \bigcup_{r \in P} H(r)$ and $B(P) = \bigcup_{r \in P}(B^+(r) \cup B^-(r))$.

Let I be an *interpretation*, i.e., a set of atoms. I *satisfies* a rule r, symbolically $I \models r$, iff $I \cap H(r) \neq \emptyset$ whenever $B^+(r) \subseteq I$ and $I \cap B^-(r) = \emptyset$ jointly hold. Furthermore, I is a *model* of a program P, symbolically $I \models P$, iff $I \models r$, for all $r \in P$. I is an *answer set* [2] of a program P iff I is a minimal model of P^I, where $P^I = \{H(r) \leftarrow B^+(r) \mid r \in P,\ B^-(r) \cap I = \emptyset\}$ is the *reduct* of P relative to I.

We recall the recently introduced notion of *hyperequivalence*, also called *head-body-relativised equivalence* [5]. The idea is to restrict the alphabets of rule heads and rule bodies of the context programs, and thereby limiting the nonmonotonic side-effects of putting a program in some context. For alphabets $\mathcal{H}, \mathcal{B} \subseteq At$, let $\mathcal{DLP}_\mathcal{B}^\mathcal{H}$ denote the class of all programs P such that $H(P) \subseteq \mathcal{H}$ and $B(P) \subseteq \mathcal{B}$. Then, two programs P, Q over At are *hyperequivalent relative to* $\langle \mathcal{H}, \mathcal{B} \rangle$, or $\langle \mathcal{H}, \mathcal{B} \rangle$-*equivalent*, in symbols $P \equiv_\mathcal{B}^\mathcal{H} Q$, iff, for each $R \in \mathcal{DLP}_\mathcal{B}^\mathcal{H}$, it holds that $\mathcal{AS}(P \cup R) = \mathcal{AS}(Q \cup R)$. Hyperequivalence includes well-known equivalence notions as special cases: *strong equivalence* [3] coincides with $\langle At, At \rangle$-equivalence; *uniform equivalence* [4] coincides with $\langle At, \emptyset \rangle$-equivalence; and *ordinary equivalence* coincides with $\langle \emptyset, \emptyset \rangle$-equivalence.

Following Turner [9], strong equivalence can model-theoretically be characterised in terms of *SE-models*: First of all, by an *SE-interpretation* we understand a pair (X, Y), where $X, Y \subseteq At$ are sets of atoms such that $X \subseteq Y$. If $X = Y$, then (X, Y) is *total*, otherwise (X, Y) is *non-total*. An SE-interpretation (X, Y) is an *SE-model* of a program P over At if $Y \models P$ and $X \models P^Y$. It then holds that two programs P and Q are strongly equivalent iff they possess the same set of SE-models. In view of the logical underpinning of strong equivalence [3], viz., the logic of here-and-there [10] (also known as Gödel's three-valued logic [11]), the first component of an SE-interpretation is identified with the world "here", whilst the second component refers to the world "there". We write $SE(P)$ to refer to the set of all SE-models of a program P.

A semantical characterisation for hyperequivalence, similar to that using SE-models for strong equivalence, is given by the concept of an *HE-model* [5].[1] For $\mathcal{H}, \mathcal{B}, X, Y \subseteq At$, an SE-interpretation (X, Y) is an *HE-model relative to* $\langle \mathcal{H}, \mathcal{B} \rangle$ of a DLP P over At, or an $\langle \mathcal{H}, \mathcal{B} \rangle$-*model* of P for short, iff (i) $Y \models P$, (ii) for all $Y' \subset Y$ with $Y' \cap \mathcal{H} = Y \cap \mathcal{H}$, it holds that $Y' \not\models P^Y$, (iii) if $X \subset Y$, there is an $X' \subset Y$ with $X' \cap (\mathcal{H} \cup \mathcal{B}) = X$ such that $X' \models P^Y$, and (iv) if $X \subset Y$, for each $X' \subset Y$ with $(X \cap \mathcal{H}) \subseteq (X' \cap \mathcal{H})$, $(X' \cap \mathcal{B}) \subseteq (X \cap \mathcal{B})$, and $X \neq X' \cap (\mathcal{H} \cup \mathcal{B})$, it holds that $X' \not\models P^Y$. The set of all $\langle \mathcal{H}, \mathcal{B} \rangle$-models of a program P is denoted by $HE_\mathcal{B}^\mathcal{H}(P)$. Note that, for every non-total $\langle \mathcal{H}, \mathcal{B} \rangle$-model (X, Y) of P, it holds that $(X \cap \mathcal{H}) \subset (Y \cap \mathcal{H})$ and $X \subset Y \cap (\mathcal{H} \cup \mathcal{B})$.

---

[1] We slightly rephrase the original definition of an HE-model.

Proposition 1 ([5]). *For all programs P, Q over At and every $\mathcal{H}, \mathcal{B} \subseteq At$, $P \equiv_{\mathcal{B}}^{\mathcal{H}} Q$ iff $HE_{\mathcal{B}}^{\mathcal{H}}(P) = HE_{\mathcal{B}}^{\mathcal{H}}(Q)$.*

3   Setting the Stage: Casting under Strong Equivalence

The main question addressed in this paper is expressed by the following parametrised decision problem:

Definition 1. *Let $\mathcal{C}$ be a class of programs over some set At of atoms. Then, $\text{CAST}(\mathcal{C})$ is the problem of deciding whether, for a given DLP P over At and sets $\mathcal{H}, \mathcal{B} \subseteq At$ of atoms, there exists a program $Q \in \mathcal{C}$ with $P \equiv_{\mathcal{B}}^{\mathcal{H}} Q$.*

If a program P together with sets $\mathcal{H}, \mathcal{B}$ of atoms constitute a yes-instance of $\text{CAST}(\mathcal{C})$, we say that P is *castable to $\mathcal{C}$ under $\langle \mathcal{H}, \mathcal{B} \rangle$-equivalence*. Furthermore, a program $Q \in \mathcal{C}$ with $P \equiv_{\mathcal{B}}^{\mathcal{H}} Q$ is called an *$\langle \mathcal{H}, \mathcal{B} \rangle$-casting of P to $\mathcal{C}$*. In this paper, we are interested in those versions of $\text{CAST}(\mathcal{C})$ where $\mathcal{C} \in \{\mathcal{NLP}, \mathcal{PLP}, \mathcal{HORN}\}$. Our aim is to find model-theoretic conditions precisely characterising the yes-instances of $\text{CAST}(\mathcal{C})$. We do so by providing, for each class $\mathcal{C}$ as above and sets $\mathcal{H}, \mathcal{B}$ of atoms, a property $\phi_{\mathcal{B},\mathcal{C}}^{\mathcal{H}}(\cdot)$ satisfying the following key condition:

($\star$) $\phi_{\mathcal{B},\mathcal{C}}^{\mathcal{H}}(\mathcal{S})$ holds iff there exists a program $Q \in \mathcal{C}$ with $\mathcal{S} = HE_{\mathcal{B}}^{\mathcal{H}}(Q)$, for each set $\mathcal{S}$ of SE-interpretations.

From this, we immediately get that, for a given DLP P, $\phi_{\mathcal{B},\mathcal{C}}^{\mathcal{H}}(HE_{\mathcal{B}}^{\mathcal{H}}(P))$ holds iff there exists a program $Q \in \mathcal{C}$ such that $HE_{\mathcal{B}}^{\mathcal{H}}(P) = HE_{\mathcal{B}}^{\mathcal{H}}(Q)$, which in turn implies that $\phi_{\mathcal{B},\mathcal{C}}^{\mathcal{H}}(HE_{\mathcal{B}}^{\mathcal{H}}(P))$ holds iff P together with $\mathcal{H}$ and $\mathcal{B}$ is a yes-instance of $\text{CAST}(\mathcal{C})$, representing our desired characterisation. In addition to deciding whether an $\langle \mathcal{H}, \mathcal{B} \rangle$-casting of P exists, we also provide constructive methods to obtain such castings.

As a preparatory step towards the general setting, in this section we deal with the case where $\mathcal{H} = \mathcal{B} = At$, corresponding to casting under strong equivalence, which was already studied in the literature [12,8,7]. In particular, we will provide a special case of Condition ($\star$), in terms of a property $\varphi_{\mathcal{C}}(\cdot)$, amounting to $\phi_{At,\mathcal{C}}^{At}(\cdot)$, as follows:

($\star_{SE}$) $\varphi_{\mathcal{C}}(\mathcal{S})$ holds iff there exists a program $Q \in \mathcal{C}$ with $SE(Q) = \mathcal{S}$, for each set $\mathcal{S}$ of SE-interpretations.

We start with the following concept: A set $\mathcal{S}$ of SE-interpretations is *well-defined* iff, for each $(X,Y) \in \mathcal{S}$, also $(Y,Y) \in \mathcal{S}$. A well-defined set $\mathcal{S}$ of SE-interpretations is *complete* iff, for each $(X,Y) \in \mathcal{S}$, also $(X,Z) \in \mathcal{S}$, for any $Y \subseteq Z$ with $(Z,Z) \in \mathcal{S}$.

Proposition 2 ([12]). *For each DLP P, $SE(P)$ is complete. Moreover, for any complete set $\mathcal{S}$ of SE-interpretations (over At), there is a DLP Q (over At) such that $SE(Q) = \mathcal{S}$.*

Eiter, Tompits, and Woltran [12] describe, for a given complete set $\mathcal{S}$ of SE-interpretations, a concrete way for obtaining a DLP, $\text{CP}_{\mathcal{S}}$, such that $SE(\text{CP}_{\mathcal{S}}) = \mathcal{S}$ holds, which we refer to as the *canonical program* for $\mathcal{S}$. In fact, $\text{CP}_{\mathcal{S}}$ is composed of rules $\leftarrow Y, not\,(At \setminus Y)$, for each $Y \subseteq At$ such that $(Y,Y) \notin \mathcal{S}$, and of rules $\bigvee_{p \in (Y \setminus X)} p \leftarrow X, not\,(At \setminus Y)$, for each $X \subset Y$ such that $(X,Y) \notin \mathcal{S}$ and $(Y,Y) \in \mathcal{S}$.

To characterise programs castable to $\mathcal{NLP}$, we need an additional criterion on SE-interpretations: A set $\mathcal{S}$ of SE-interpretations is *closed under here-intersection*, or *HI-closed*, iff, whenever $(X, Y) \in \mathcal{S}$ and $(X', Y) \in \mathcal{S}$, then $(X \cap X', Y) \in \mathcal{S}$. This property results from the facts that the reduct of a program relative to a set of atoms is a Horn program if disjunction is not involved, and that the models of Horn theories are closed under intersection.

The characterising property for DLPs that can be casted to $\mathcal{PLP}$ under strong equivalence is called *here-totality*: A set $\mathcal{S}$ of SE-interpretations is here-total iff, for any pair $(X, Y) \in \mathcal{S}$, it holds that $(X, X) \in \mathcal{S}$.

In order for a DLP P to be castable to $\mathcal{HORN}$ under strong equivalence, it is not sufficient that $SE(P)$ is both HI-closed and here-total. In fact, the transformations to an NLP introduce in general negations, and those to a PLP disjunctions. Additionally, it turns out that the property of *closure under there-intersection* is required: A set $\mathcal{S}$ of SE-interpretations is closed under there-intersection, or *TI-closed*, iff, whenever $(X, X) \in \mathcal{S}$ and $(Y, Y) \in \mathcal{S}$, then $(X \cap Y, X \cap Y) \in \mathcal{S}$. Note that a set of SE-interpretations which is here-total and TI-closed is also HI-closed.

The next proposition states how the defined properties characterise castable DLPs.

Proposition 3 ([8,7]). *Let P be a DLP over set of atoms At. Then, there exists (i) an NLP Q with $P \equiv_{At}^{At} Q$ iff $SE(P)$ is HI-closed, (ii) a PLP Q' with $P \equiv_{At}^{At} Q'$ iff $SE(P)$ is here-total, and (iii) a Horn program Q'' with $P \equiv_{At}^{At} Q''$ iff $SE(P)$ is here-total and TI-closed.*

Example 1. Consider programs $P_1 = \{b \vee c \leftarrow a; \ a \leftarrow not\ b; \ b \leftarrow not\ a; \ b \leftarrow not\ c\}$ and $P_2 = \{a \vee b \leftarrow c; \ b \leftarrow a; \ a \leftarrow b, not\ c; \ c \leftarrow b, not\ a; \ \leftarrow a, b, c\}$ over $\{a, b, c\}$. The sets of SE-models of these programs are[2]

$$SE(P_1) = \{(b, b), (b, ab), (ab, ab), (ac, ac), (b, bc), (bc, bc),$$
$$(\emptyset, abc), (b, abc), (c, abc), (ab, abc), (ac, abc), (bc, abc), (abc, abc)\} \text{ and}$$

$$SE(P_2) = \{(\emptyset, \emptyset), (\emptyset, ab), (ab, ab), (\emptyset, bc), (bc, bc)\}.$$

$SE(P_1)$ is not HI-closed as it contains (ab, abc), (ac, abc), but not (a, abc). Hence, for each NLP Q, $P_1 \not\equiv_{At}^{At} Q$. $SE(P_2)$ is HI-closed and $P_2 \equiv_{At}^{At} P_2'$ holds for NLP $P_2' = \{a \leftarrow b, not\ c; \ c \leftarrow b, not\ a; \ b \leftarrow a; \ b \leftarrow c; \ \leftarrow a, b, c\}$.

For creating a strongly equivalent NLP for a given DLP P with $SE(P)$ being HI-closed, we refer to a known technique for removing disjunctions under strong equivalence [8].

Example 2. For program P_1 from Example 1, $SE(P_1)$ is not here-total, since, e.g., $(\emptyset, abc) \in SE(P_1)$ but $(\emptyset, \emptyset) \notin SE(P_1)$. Hence, there is no strongly equivalent PLP. Consider program $P_3 = \{a \leftarrow not\ b; \ b \leftarrow not\ a; \ \leftarrow a, b\}$ over $\{a, b\}$ with $SE(P_3) = \{(a, a), (b, b)\}$ that is here-total. P_3 can be replaced by the strongly equivalent PLP $P_3' = \{a \vee b \leftarrow; \ \leftarrow a, b\}$.

Note that P_3' is obtained from P_3 by moving all atoms from $B^-(r)$ of each rule r to $H(r)$. This transformation is called the *left-shift* of a program. Generally, the left-shift of any DLP P, where $SE(P)$ is here-total, is strongly equivalent to P.

---

[2] We write "abc" instead of "$\{a, b, c\}$", "a" instead of "$\{a\}$", etc.

Example 3. For program P_2 from Example 1, $SE(P_2)$ is HI-closed, here-total, but not TI-closed, as $(ab, ab), (bc, bc) \in SE(P_2)$ but $(b, b) \notin SE(P_2)$. Hence, there is no Horn program which is strongly equivalent to P_2. Consider program $P_4 = \{a \vee b \leftarrow; a \leftarrow b, not\ c; \leftarrow b, c\}$ over $\{a, b, c\}$, where $SE(P_4) = \{(a, a), (a, ab), (ab, ab), (a, ac), (ac, ac)\}$ is both here-total and TI-closed. P_4 can be replaced by the strongly equivalent Horn program $P_4' = \{a \leftarrow; \leftarrow b, c\}$.

To obtain a Horn program Q such that $P \equiv^{\mathcal{H}}_{\mathcal{B}} Q$ for a given DLP P, we proceed in two steps. First, a left-shift is applied on P to obtain a strongly equivalent PLP. Then, the remaining disjunctions can be eliminated by removing atoms from rule heads, as suggested by the following theorem.

Theorem 1. *For every PLP P such that $SE(P)$ is TI-closed, a Horn program P' such that $P \equiv^{At}_{At} P'$ can be obtained by removing all but one atom, a, from the head of each rule $r \in P$ with $|H(r)| > 1$. Thereby, a has to be chosen in such a way that, for every model Y of P with $B(r) \subseteq Y$, $a \in Y$ holds.*

For lifting the results for strong equivalence to general hyperequivalence, we will need the following consequence of Propositions 2 and 3.

Theorem 2. *Let $\mathcal{S}$ be a set of SE-interpretations. Then, there exists*

- *an NLP Q with $SE(Q) = \mathcal{S}$ iff $\mathcal{S}$ is complete and HI-closed,*
- *a PLP Q' with $SE(Q') = \mathcal{S}$ iff $\mathcal{S}$ is complete and here-total, and*
- *a Horn program Q'' with $SE(Q'') = \mathcal{S}$ iff $\mathcal{S}$ is complete, here-total, and TI-closed.*

4   Main Results

We now lift the results for strong equivalence to hyperequivalence. Note that Theorem 2 provides us with the special case $(\star_{SE})$ of our key condition $(\star)$, expressing that a property $\varphi_{\mathcal{C}}(\mathcal{S})$ holds iff there exists a program $Q \in \mathcal{C}$ with $SE(Q) = \mathcal{S}$, for each $\mathcal{C} \in \{\mathcal{NLP}, \mathcal{PLP}, \mathcal{HORN}\}$. We will use this property for proving the general case of Condition $(\star)$, thus establishing our main results, as outlined in the beginning of Section 3. This is achieved as follows: First of all, for each $\mathcal{C}$ as above, we define the corresponding property $\phi^{\mathcal{H}}_{\mathcal{B},\mathcal{C}}(\cdot)$ together with a function $\tau^{\mathcal{H}}_{\mathcal{B},\mathcal{C}}(\cdot)$ from sets of SE-interpretations to sets of SE-interpretations, which we refer to as a *completion transformation*, such that the following properties hold:

(i) if, for a set $\mathcal{S}$ of SE-interpretations, $\phi^{\mathcal{H}}_{\mathcal{B},\mathcal{C}}(\mathcal{S})$ holds, then $\varphi_{\mathcal{C}}(\tau^{\mathcal{H}}_{\mathcal{B},\mathcal{C}}(\mathcal{S}))$ holds;
(ii) if, for a set $\mathcal{S}$ of SE-interpretations, $\phi^{\mathcal{H}}_{\mathcal{B},\mathcal{C}}(\mathcal{S})$ holds and there exists a program $Q \in \mathcal{C}$ such that $\tau^{\mathcal{H}}_{\mathcal{B},\mathcal{C}}(\mathcal{S}) = SE(Q)$, then $HE^{\mathcal{H}}_{\mathcal{B}}(Q) = \mathcal{S}$;
(iii) for every program $Q \in \mathcal{C}$, $\phi^{\mathcal{H}}_{\mathcal{B},\mathcal{C}}(HE^{\mathcal{H}}_{\mathcal{B}}(Q))$ holds.

From these properties, $(\star)$ can then be established as follows: Assume that $\phi^{\mathcal{H}}_{\mathcal{B},\mathcal{C}}(\mathcal{S})$ holds. Then, by (i), so does $\varphi_{\mathcal{C}}(\tau^{\mathcal{H}}_{\mathcal{B},\mathcal{C}}(\mathcal{S}))$. From property $(\star_{SE})$ it follows that there is a program $Q \in \mathcal{C}$ with $SE(Q) = \tau^{\mathcal{H}}_{\mathcal{B},\mathcal{C}}(\mathcal{S})$. Hence, by (ii), $HE^{\mathcal{H}}_{\mathcal{B}}(Q) = \mathcal{S}$. Conversely, let $Q \in \mathcal{C}$ be a program with $HE^{\mathcal{H}}_{\mathcal{B}}(Q) = \mathcal{S}$. By (iii), $\phi^{\mathcal{H}}_{\mathcal{B},\mathcal{C}}(HE^{\mathcal{H}}_{\mathcal{B}}(Q))$ holds. Since

$HE_{\mathcal{B}}^{\mathcal{H}}(Q) = \mathcal{S}$, we get that $\phi_{\mathcal{B},\mathcal{C}}^{\mathcal{H}}(\mathcal{S})$ holds. Hence, $(\star)$ holds. As argued in Section 3, $(\star)$ in turn implies our main result expressing that, for each $\mathcal{C} \in \{\mathcal{NLP}, \mathcal{PLP}, \mathcal{HORN}\}$, $\phi_{\mathcal{B},\mathcal{C}}^{\mathcal{H}}(HE_{\mathcal{B}}^{\mathcal{H}}(P))$ holds iff P, $\mathcal{H}$, and $\mathcal{B}$ constitute a yes-instance of $\mathrm{CAST}(\mathcal{C})$.

In the remainder of this section we will show, for each individual class $\mathcal{C}$, how $\phi_{\mathcal{B},\mathcal{C}}^{\mathcal{H}}(\cdot)$ and $\tau_{\mathcal{B},\mathcal{C}}^{\mathcal{H}}(\cdot)$ are defined. We will provide the main proofs for the case of casting to $\mathcal{NLP}$ but only show the constructions and formulate the main results for the cases of casting to $\mathcal{PLP}$ and $\mathcal{HORN}$ due to space limitations.

4.1 Completeness for Hyperequivalence Models

First, we will introduce the notion of $\langle \mathcal{H}, \mathcal{B} \rangle$-*completeness*, a property of sets of SE-interpretations which is characteristic for the set of all $\langle \mathcal{H}, \mathcal{B} \rangle$-models of a program.

Definition 2. *Let* $\mathcal{H}, \mathcal{B}$ *be sets of atoms and* $\mathcal{S}$ *a set of SE-interpretations. Then,* $\mathcal{S}$ *is* $\langle \mathcal{H}, \mathcal{B} \rangle$-*well-defined if, for each* $(X, Y) \in \mathcal{S}$ *such that* $X \subset Y$, *it holds that (i)* $(Y, Y) \in \mathcal{S}$, *(ii)* $X \subset (Y \cap (\mathcal{H} \cup \mathcal{B}))$, *(iii)* $(X \cap \mathcal{H}) \subset (Y \cap \mathcal{H})$, *and (iv) there is no* $(X', Y) \in \mathcal{S}$ *with* $X' \subset Y$, $(X \cap \mathcal{H}) \subseteq (X' \cap \mathcal{H})$, $(X' \cap \mathcal{B}) \subseteq (X \cap \mathcal{B})$, *and* $X \neq X'$.
Moreover, $\mathcal{S}$ *is* $\langle \mathcal{H}, \mathcal{B} \rangle$-*complete if* $\mathcal{S}$ *is* $\langle \mathcal{H}, \mathcal{B} \rangle$-*well-defined and, for all* X, Y, Z *such that* (X, Y), $(Z, Z) \in \mathcal{S}$ *and* $Y \subset Z$, *there is some* $X' \subset Z$ *such that* $(X', Z) \in \mathcal{S}$, $(X \cap \mathcal{H}) \subseteq (X' \cap \mathcal{H})$, *and* $(X' \cap \mathcal{B}) \subseteq (X \cap \mathcal{B})$.

Condition (i) of $\langle \mathcal{H}, \mathcal{B} \rangle$-well-definedness subsumes well-definedness. Conditions (ii) and (iii) reflect that the "there"-component Y of an $\langle \mathcal{H}, \mathcal{B} \rangle$-model of P is a model of P^Y, minimal amongst the models sharing the same atoms from $\mathcal{H}$, and express that the "here"-component of non-total $\langle \mathcal{H}, \mathcal{B} \rangle$-models is a subset of $\mathcal{H} \cup \mathcal{B}$. Observe that Condition (iv) expresses an optimality property of non-total $\langle \mathcal{H}, \mathcal{B} \rangle$-models with respect to sets $\mathcal{H}$ and $\mathcal{B}$. For relating $\langle \mathcal{H}, \mathcal{B} \rangle$-models to SE-models, this optimality criterion is also captured in the following notion:

Definition 3. *Let* $\mathcal{H}, \mathcal{B}$ *be sets of atoms and* $\mathcal{S}$ *a set of SE-interpretations. Then, a non-total SE-interpretation* $(X, Y) \in \mathcal{S}$ *is* $\langle \mathcal{H}, \mathcal{B} \rangle$-*optimal in* $\mathcal{S}$ *if there is no* $X' \subset Y$ *such that* $(X', Y) \in \mathcal{S}$, $(X \cap \mathcal{H}) \subseteq (X' \cap \mathcal{H})$, $(X' \cap \mathcal{B}) \subseteq (X \cap \mathcal{B})$, *and* $X \cap (\mathcal{H} \cup \mathcal{B}) \neq X' \cap (\mathcal{H} \cup \mathcal{B})$.

The following two lemmas express relations between SE-models and HE-models.

Lemma 1. *Let* $\mathcal{H}, \mathcal{B} \subseteq At$ *be sets of atoms, P a DLP over At, and (X, Y) a non-total SE-model of P that is* $\langle \mathcal{H}, \mathcal{B} \rangle$-*optimal in $SE(P)$. If $(Y, Y) \in HE_{\mathcal{B}}^{\mathcal{H}}(P)$, then* $(X \cap (\mathcal{H} \cup \mathcal{B}), Y) \in HE_{\mathcal{B}}^{\mathcal{H}}(P)$.

Lemma 2. *Let* $\mathcal{H}, \mathcal{B} \subseteq At$ *be sets of atoms and P a DLP over At. If (Y, Y) is an* $\langle \mathcal{H}, \mathcal{B} \rangle$-*model of P, then (Y, Y) is an SE-model of P. If (X, Y) is a non-total $\langle \mathcal{H}, \mathcal{B} \rangle$-model of P, then, for some $X' \subset Y$ with $X = X' \cap (\mathcal{H} \cup \mathcal{B})$, $(X', Y) \in SE(P)$ and (X', Y) is* $\langle \mathcal{H}, \mathcal{B} \rangle$-*optimal in $SE(P)$.*

With Lemmas 1 and 2 at hand, we can show the following result for DLPs.

Theorem 3. *Let* $\mathcal{H}, \mathcal{B} \subseteq At$ *be sets of atoms and P a DLP over At. Then, $HE_{\mathcal{B}}^{\mathcal{H}}(P)$ is* $\langle \mathcal{H}, \mathcal{B} \rangle$-*complete.*

Proof. First, we show that $HE_{\mathcal{B}}^{\mathcal{H}}(P)$ is $\langle \mathcal{H}, \mathcal{B} \rangle$-well-defined. Consider some $X \subset Y$ with $(X, Y) \in HE_{\mathcal{B}}^{\mathcal{H}}(P)$. Conditions (i) and (ii) of the definition of an $\langle \mathcal{H}, \mathcal{B} \rangle$-model are satisfied for (Y, Y). As (Y, Y) is total, also Conditions (iii) and (iv) hold, and consequently $(Y, Y) \in HE_{\mathcal{B}}^{\mathcal{H}}(P)$. Since (X, Y) is non-total, we have that $(X \cap \mathcal{H}) \subset (Y \cap \mathcal{H})$ and $X \subset Y \cap (\mathcal{H} \cup \mathcal{B})$. Towards a contradiction, assume that there is some $(U, Y) \in HE_{\mathcal{B}}^{\mathcal{H}}(P)$ with $U \subset Y$, $(X \cap \mathcal{H}) \subseteq (U \cap \mathcal{H})$, $(U \cap \mathcal{B}) \subseteq (X \cap \mathcal{B})$, and $X \neq U$. From $(U, Y) \in HE_{\mathcal{B}}^{\mathcal{H}}(P)$ it follows from Condition (iii) of the definition of an $\langle \mathcal{H}, \mathcal{B} \rangle$-model of P that there is some $U' \subset Y$ with $U' \models P^Y$ and $U' \cap (\mathcal{H} \cap \mathcal{B}) = U$. From the latter and $X \neq U$, we get $X \neq U' \cap (\mathcal{H} \cap \mathcal{B})$. Furthermore, it holds that $(X \cap \mathcal{H}) \subseteq (U' \cap \mathcal{H})$ and $(U' \cap \mathcal{B}) \subseteq (X \cap \mathcal{B})$. Since $(X, Y) \in HE_{\mathcal{B}}^{\mathcal{H}}(P)$, we get by Condition (iv) that $U' \not\models P^Y$, being a contradiction to our previous result that $U' \models P^Y$. Hence, $HE_{\mathcal{B}}^{\mathcal{H}}(P)$ is $\langle \mathcal{H}, \mathcal{B} \rangle$-well-defined. Towards a contradiction, assume there is a DLP P such that $HE_{\mathcal{B}}^{\mathcal{H}}(P)$ is not $\langle \mathcal{H}, \mathcal{B} \rangle$-complete. Observe that there must be some X, Y, Z with $Y \subset Z$ such that $(X, Y), (Z, Z) \in HE_{\mathcal{B}}^{\mathcal{H}}(P)$ and, for every $X' \subset Z$ with $(X \cap \mathcal{H}) \subseteq (X' \cap \mathcal{H})$ and $(X' \cap \mathcal{B}) \subseteq (X \cap \mathcal{B})$, it holds that $(X', Z) \notin HE_{\mathcal{B}}^{\mathcal{H}}(P)$. Now we show that there is some $X' \subset Z$ such that $X' \cap (\mathcal{H} \cup \mathcal{B}) = X \cap (\mathcal{H} \cup \mathcal{B})$ and $(X', Z) \in SE(P)$. Consider the case that $X = Y$. We know from Lemma 2 that (X, X) and (Z, Z) are SE-models of P. By completeness of SE-models, we get that $(X, Z) \in SE(P)$. Note that $X \subset Z$. Now assume that $X \subset Y$. Then, by Lemma 2, there is a $U \subset Z$ with $X = U \cap (\mathcal{H} \cup \mathcal{B})$ such that $(U, Y) \in SE(P)$. Thus, since $(Z, Z) \in SE(P)$ and it holds that $Y \subseteq Z$, we get by completeness of SE-models that $(U, Z) \in SE(P)$. Consequently, in either case, there exists some $X' \subset Z$ such that $X' \cap (\mathcal{H} \cup \mathcal{B}) = X \cap (\mathcal{H} \cup \mathcal{B})$ and $(X', Z) \in SE(P)$. From that, and by definition of $\langle \mathcal{H}, \mathcal{B} \rangle$-optimality, there exists an $\langle \mathcal{H}, \mathcal{B} \rangle$-optimal $X_{opt} \subset Z$ in $SE(P)$ with $(X \cap \mathcal{H}) \subseteq (X_{opt} \cap \mathcal{H})$ and $(X_{opt} \cap \mathcal{B}) \subseteq (X \cap \mathcal{B})$. By $\langle \mathcal{H}, \mathcal{B} \rangle$-optimality of X_{opt} in $SE(P)$, since $(Z, Z) \in HE_{\mathcal{B}}^{\mathcal{H}}(P)$, we get by Lemma 1 that $(X_{opt} \cap (\mathcal{H} \cup \mathcal{B}), Z) \in HE_{\mathcal{B}}^{\mathcal{H}}(P)$. However, as $(X \cap \mathcal{H}) \subseteq (X_{opt} \cap \mathcal{H})$ and $(X_{opt} \cap \mathcal{B}) \subseteq (X \cap \mathcal{B})$, this is a contradiction to our observation. Hence, $HE_{\mathcal{B}}^{\mathcal{H}}(P)$ is $\langle \mathcal{H}, \mathcal{B} \rangle$-complete. □

Next, we show that, conversely, for every $\langle \mathcal{H}, \mathcal{B} \rangle$-complete set $\mathcal{S}$ of SE-interpretations, there is a DLP P such that $HE_{\mathcal{B}}^{\mathcal{H}}(P) = \mathcal{S}$. To this end, we define a mapping $c_{\mathcal{H}, \mathcal{B}}(\cdot)$, representing the completion transformation $\tau_{\mathcal{B}, \mathcal{C}}^{\mathcal{H}}(\cdot)$ for the case $\mathcal{C} = \mathcal{NLP}$ mentioned at the beginning of this section, assigning sets of SE-interpretations to sets of SE-interpretations, serving a double role: On the one hand, it is a device to construct a DLP from any $\langle \mathcal{H}, \mathcal{B} \rangle$-complete set $\mathcal{S}$ of SE-interpretations. On the other hand, the rewriting is designed such that $c_{\mathcal{H}, \mathcal{B}}(\mathcal{S})$ is HI-closed iff $\mathcal{S}$ is $\langle \mathcal{H}, \mathcal{B} \rangle$-closed under here-intersection, a property that is described later in this section.

Definition 4. *Let $\mathcal{H}, \mathcal{B}$ be sets of atoms. For every set $\mathcal{S}$ of SE-interpretations, let $c_{\mathcal{H}, \mathcal{B}}(\mathcal{S})$ be given by $\{(Y, Y) \mid (Y, Y) \in \mathcal{S}\} \cup \{(X, Y) \mid X \subset Y, (X \cap \mathcal{H}) \subseteq (X' \cap \mathcal{H}), (X' \cap \mathcal{B}) \subseteq (X \cap \mathcal{B}), (X', Y) \in \mathcal{S}, X' \subset Y\}$.*

Note that whenever $(X, Y) \in \mathcal{S}$, also $(X, Y) \in c_{\mathcal{H}, \mathcal{B}}(\mathcal{S})$.

Lemma 3. *Let $\mathcal{H}, \mathcal{B}$ be sets of atoms and $\mathcal{S}$ a set of SE-interpretations. If $\mathcal{S}$ is $\langle \mathcal{H}, \mathcal{B} \rangle$-complete, then $c_{\mathcal{H}, \mathcal{B}}(\mathcal{S})$ is complete.*

Proof. Assume that S is $\langle \mathcal{H}, \mathcal{B} \rangle$-complete. First, we show that $c_{\mathcal{H},\mathcal{B}}(S)$ is well-defined. Consider some $(X, Y) \in c_{\mathcal{H},\mathcal{B}}(S)$ with $X \subset Y$. By Definition 4, there is some $(X', Y) \in S$. Since S is well-defined, we also have $(Y, Y) \in S$ and therefore $(Y, Y) \in c_{\mathcal{H},\mathcal{B}}(S)$. So, $c_{\mathcal{H},\mathcal{B}}(S)$ is well-defined. Towards a contradiction, assume that $c_{\mathcal{H},\mathcal{B}}(S)$ is not complete. There must be some interpretations X, Y, Z with $Y \subseteq Z$ such that $(X, Y), (Z, Z) \in c_{\mathcal{H},\mathcal{B}}(S)$ and $(X, Z) \notin c_{\mathcal{H},\mathcal{B}}(S)$. Note that by Definition 4, it holds that $(Z, Z) \in S$. From $(X, Y) \in c_{\mathcal{H},\mathcal{B}}(S)$, it follows that $X \subseteq Y$. Furthermore, it must hold that $Y \subset Z$, as otherwise $(X, Z) = (X, Y) \in c_{\mathcal{H},\mathcal{B}}(S)$. In case that $X = Y$, we get by Definition 4 that $(X, X) \in S$. Since $(Z, Z) \in S$, by $\langle \mathcal{H}, \mathcal{B} \rangle$-completeness of S there is an $X' \subset Z$, where $(X', Z) \in S$, $(X \cap \mathcal{H}) \subseteq (X' \cap \mathcal{H})$ and $(X' \cap \mathcal{B}) \subseteq (X \cap \mathcal{B})$. In case that $X \subset Y$, we get by Definition 4 that there is some $(X'', Y) \in S$ such that $(X \cap \mathcal{H}) \subseteq (X'' \cap \mathcal{H})$ and $(X'' \cap \mathcal{B}) \subseteq (X \cap \mathcal{B})$. Since $(Z, Z) \in S$, by $\langle \mathcal{H}, \mathcal{B} \rangle$-completeness of S, there is again an $X' \subset Z$ with $(X', Z) \in S$, where $(X \cap \mathcal{H}) \subseteq (X'' \cap \mathcal{H}) \subseteq (X' \cap \mathcal{H})$ and $(X' \cap \mathcal{B}) \subseteq (X'' \cap \mathcal{B}) \subseteq (X \cap \mathcal{B})$. Therefore, in both cases, we have $(X, Z) \in c_{\mathcal{H},\mathcal{B}}(S)$, being a contradiction to $(X, Z) \notin c_{\mathcal{H},\mathcal{B}}(S)$. Hence, $c_{\mathcal{H},\mathcal{B}}(S)$ is complete. $\qquad\square$

The next lemma shows that a program having $c_{\mathcal{H},\mathcal{B}}(S)$ as its set of SE-models is guaranteed to have S as its set of $\langle \mathcal{H}, \mathcal{B} \rangle$-models. This is the case since all freshly introduced SE-interpretations either lack $\langle \mathcal{H}, \mathcal{B} \rangle$-optimality in $c_{\mathcal{H},\mathcal{B}}(S)$ or are already represented by an SE-interpretation in S.

Lemma 4. *Let* $\mathcal{H}, \mathcal{B} \subseteq At$ *be sets of atoms,* S *a set of SE-interpretations, and* P *a DLP over* At. *If* $SE(P) = c_{\mathcal{H},\mathcal{B}}(S)$ *and* S *is* $\langle \mathcal{H}, \mathcal{B} \rangle$-*complete, then* $HE_{\mathcal{B}}^{\mathcal{H}}(P) = S$.

Now we put things together. By using Proposition 2 and Lemmas 3 and 4 we get the following result:

Theorem 4. *Let* $\mathcal{H}, \mathcal{B} \subseteq At$ *be sets of atoms. Then, for every* $\langle \mathcal{H}, \mathcal{B} \rangle$-*complete set* S *of SE-interpretations, there is a DLP* P *over* At *such that* $HE_{\mathcal{B}}^{\mathcal{H}}(P) = S$.

4.2   Elimination of Disjunction

While $\langle \mathcal{H}, \mathcal{B} \rangle$-completeness generally characterises sets of SE-interpretations that are $\langle \mathcal{H}, \mathcal{B} \rangle$-models of a DLP, we now define a supplementary property for NLPs.

Definition 5. *Let* $\mathcal{H}$ *and* $\mathcal{B}$ *be sets of atoms. A set* S *of SE-interpretations is* $\langle \mathcal{H}, \mathcal{B} \rangle$-*closed under here-intersection, or* $\langle \mathcal{H}, \mathcal{B} \rangle$-*HI-closed, if, whenever* $(X_1, Y) \in S$ *and* $(X_2, Y) \in S$, *with* $X_1 \subset Y$ *and* $X_2 \subset Y$, *there is some* $X' \subset Y$ *such that* $(X', Y) \in S$, $(X_1 \cap X_2) \cap \mathcal{H} \subseteq (X' \cap \mathcal{H})$, *and* $(X' \cap \mathcal{B}) \subseteq (X_1 \cap X_2) \cap \mathcal{B}$.

In terms of the discussion from the beginning of this section, the joint stipulation of $\langle \mathcal{H}, \mathcal{B} \rangle$-completeness and $\langle \mathcal{H}, \mathcal{B} \rangle$-closure under here-intersection amounts to condition $\phi_{\mathcal{B},\mathcal{C}}^{\mathcal{H}}(\cdot)$ for $\mathcal{C} = \mathcal{NLP}$.

Theorem 5. *Let* $\mathcal{H}, \mathcal{B} \subseteq At$ *be sets of atoms and* P *an NLP over* At. *Then,* $HE_{\mathcal{B}}^{\mathcal{H}}(P)$ *is* $\langle \mathcal{H}, \mathcal{B} \rangle$-*HI-closed.*

Proof. Towards a contradiction, assume $HE_{\mathcal{B}}^{\mathcal{H}}(P)$ is not $\langle \mathcal{H}, \mathcal{B} \rangle$-HI-closed. Then, there must be some X_1, X_2, Y such that $(X_1, Y), (X_2, Y) \in HE_{\mathcal{B}}^{\mathcal{H}}(P)$ with $X_1 \subset Y$ and $X_2 \subset Y$, but there is no $X' \subset Y$ such that $(X', Y) \in HE_{\mathcal{B}}^{\mathcal{H}}(P)$, $(X_1 \cap X_2 \cap \mathcal{H}) \subseteq (X' \cap \mathcal{H})$, and $(X' \cap \mathcal{B}) \subseteq (X_1 \cap X_2 \cap \mathcal{B})$. Note that therefore $(X_1 \cap X_2, Y) \notin HE_{\mathcal{B}}^{\mathcal{H}}(P)$. Moreover, from well-definedness of $HE_{\mathcal{B}}^{\mathcal{H}}(P)$ and $(X', Y) \in HE_{\mathcal{B}}^{\mathcal{H}}(P)$, it follows that $(Y, Y) \in HE_{\mathcal{B}}^{\mathcal{H}}(P)$. By Lemma 2, there are SE-models $(X_1', Y), (X_2', Y)$ of P such that $X_1' \subset Y$, $X_2' \subset Y$, $X_1 = (X_1' \cap (\mathcal{H} \cup \mathcal{B}))$, and $X_2 = (X_2' \cap (\mathcal{H} \cup \mathcal{B}))$. As P is an NLP, from Theorem 2 it follows that $SE(P)$ is HI-closed. Therefore, $(X_1' \cap X_2', Y) \in SE(P)$ holds. Note that Conditions (i) and (ii) of the definition for being an $\langle \mathcal{H}, \mathcal{B} \rangle$-model of P are satisfied by $(X_1 \cap X_2, Y)$ since $(Y, Y) \in HE_{\mathcal{B}}^{\mathcal{H}}(P)$. Furthermore, from $(X_1' \cap X_2') \subset Y$, $(X_1' \cap X_2' \cap (\mathcal{H} \cup \mathcal{B})) = (X_1 \cap X_2)$, and $X_1' \cap X_2' \models P^Y$, it follows that Condition (iii) holds. Since $(X_1 \cap X_2, Y) \notin HE_{\mathcal{B}}^{\mathcal{H}}(P)$, Condition (iv) must be violated. Hence, there is some $X' \subset Y$ with $(X_1 \cap X_2 \cap \mathcal{H}) \subseteq (X' \cap \mathcal{H})$, $(X' \cap \mathcal{B}) \subseteq (X_1 \cap X_2 \cap \mathcal{B})$, and $(X_1 \cap X_2) \neq X' \cap (\mathcal{H} \cup \mathcal{B})$ such that $X' \models P^Y$, and thus $(X', Y) \in SE(P)$. Consider an $\langle \mathcal{H}, \mathcal{B} \rangle$-optimal SE-interpretation (X_{opt}, Y) in $SE(P)$ having these properties. Then, since $(Z, Z) \in HE_{\mathcal{B}}^{\mathcal{H}}(P)$, we get by Lemma 1 that $(X_{opt} \cap (\mathcal{H} \cup \mathcal{B}), Y) \in HE_{\mathcal{B}}^{\mathcal{H}}(P)$. We end up in a contradiction, as $X_{opt} \cap (\mathcal{H} \cup \mathcal{B}) \subset Y$, $(X_1 \cap X_2 \cap \mathcal{H}) \subseteq (X_{opt} \cap \mathcal{H})$, and $(X_{opt} \cap \mathcal{B}) \subseteq (X_1 \cap X_2 \cap \mathcal{B})$. Hence, $HE_{\mathcal{B}}^{\mathcal{H}}(P)$ is $\langle \mathcal{H}, \mathcal{B} \rangle$-HI-closed. □

As shown next, for an $\langle \mathcal{H}, \mathcal{B} \rangle$-complete set $\mathcal{S}$ of SE-interpretations that is $\langle \mathcal{H}, \mathcal{B} \rangle$-HI-closed, $c_{\mathcal{H}, \mathcal{B}}(\mathcal{S})$ is the set of SE-models of a normal logic program. New non-total SE-interpretations are introduced in $c_{\mathcal{H}, \mathcal{B}}(\mathcal{S})$ that, as we will see below, guarantee that $c_{\mathcal{H}, \mathcal{B}}(\mathcal{S})$ is HI-closed.

Lemma 5. *Let $\mathcal{H}, \mathcal{B}$ be sets of atoms and $\mathcal{S}$ a set of SE-interpretations. If $\mathcal{S}$ is $\langle \mathcal{H}, \mathcal{B} \rangle$-HI-closed, then $c_{\mathcal{H}, \mathcal{B}}(\mathcal{S})$ is HI-closed.*

Proof. Let $\mathcal{S}$ be $\langle \mathcal{H}, \mathcal{B} \rangle$-HI-closed. Consider some $(X_1, Y), (X_2, Y) \in c_{\mathcal{H}, \mathcal{B}}(\mathcal{S})$. We show that $(X_1 \cap X_2, Y) \in c_{\mathcal{H}, \mathcal{B}}(\mathcal{S})$. First, consider the case that $X_1 = Y$ or $X_2 = Y$. Without loss of generality, assume $X_2 = Y$. Then, we have $(X_1 \cap X_2, Y) \in c_{\mathcal{H}, \mathcal{B}}(\mathcal{S})$ since $X_1 = (X_1 \cap X_2)$. Now assume $X_1 \subset Y$ and $X_2 \subset Y$. From $\mathcal{S}$ being $\langle \mathcal{H}, \mathcal{B} \rangle$-HI-closed, it follows that there is some $X' \subset Y$ such that $(X', Y) \in \mathcal{S}$, $(X_1 \cap X_2 \cap \mathcal{H}) \subseteq (X' \cap \mathcal{H})$, and $(X' \cap \mathcal{B}) \subseteq (X_1 \cap X_2 \cap \mathcal{B})$. From Definition 4, we conclude $(X_1 \cap X_2, Y) \in c_{\mathcal{H}, \mathcal{B}}(\mathcal{S})$. □

We now state our main result for casting to $\mathcal{NLP}$ under hyperequivalence. Its proof follows the general argumentation for establishing $(\star)$ in the beginning of this section, using the preceding results.

Theorem 6. *For sets $\mathcal{H}, \mathcal{B} \subseteq At$ and a DLP P over At, there exists an NLP Q over At such that $P \equiv_{\mathcal{B}}^{\mathcal{H}} Q$ iff $HE_{\mathcal{B}}^{\mathcal{H}}(P)$ is $\langle \mathcal{H}, \mathcal{B} \rangle$-HI-closed.*

Example 4. Reconsider program P_1 from Example 1 and recall that there is no NLP that is strongly equivalent to P_1. We now weaken the notion of equivalence, by banning b from the bodies of rules in potential context programs. So, for sets $\mathcal{H} = \{a, b, c\}$ and $\mathcal{B} = \{a, c\}$, we have $HE_{\mathcal{B}}^{\mathcal{H}}(P_1) = \{(b, b), (b, ab), (ab, ab), (ac, ac), (b, bc), (bc, bc), (b, abc), (ab, abc), (ac, abc), (bc, abc), (abc, abc)\}$. As $HE_{\mathcal{B}}^{\mathcal{H}}(P_1)$ is $\langle \mathcal{H}, \mathcal{B} \rangle$-HI-closed, there is an NLP that is $\langle \mathcal{H}, \mathcal{B} \rangle$-equivalent to P_1, e.g., $P_1' = \{a \leftarrow not\ b;\ b \leftarrow not\ a;\ b \leftarrow not\ c;\ c \leftarrow not\ b\}$.

4.3 Elimination of Negation

Similarly to closure under here-intersection, we now generalise the notion of here-totality.

Definition 6. *Let $\mathcal{H}, \mathcal{B}$ be sets of atoms. A set $\mathcal{S}$ of SE-interpretations is $\langle \mathcal{H}, \mathcal{B} \rangle$-here-total if, for any pair $(X, Y) \in \mathcal{S}$ with $X \subset Y$, there is some $X' \subset Y$ such that $(X', X') \in \mathcal{S}$ and $X = X' \cap (\mathcal{H} \cup \mathcal{B})$.*

Concerning condition $\phi_{\mathcal{B},\mathcal{C}}^{\mathcal{H}}(\cdot)$ from the beginning of this section, its realisation in case $\mathcal{C} = \mathcal{PLP}$ is now given by conjoining $\langle \mathcal{H}, \mathcal{B} \rangle$-completeness and $\langle \mathcal{H}, \mathcal{B} \rangle$-here-totality.

Theorem 7. *Let $\mathcal{H}, \mathcal{B} \subseteq At$ be sets of atoms and P a PLP over At. Then, $HE_{\mathcal{B}}^{\mathcal{H}}(P)$ is $\langle \mathcal{H}, \mathcal{B} \rangle$-here-total.*

For casting a DLP to $\mathcal{PLP}$, another kind of completion is needed. We aim at mapping an $\langle \mathcal{H}, \mathcal{B} \rangle$-complete set of SE-interpretations being $\langle \mathcal{H}, \mathcal{B} \rangle$-here-total to a complete set of SE-interpretations that is here-total.

Definition 7. *For any set $\mathcal{S}$ of SE-interpretations, let $\hat{c}(\mathcal{S})$ be given by $\{(X, Y) \mid X \subseteq Y, (X, X), (Y, Y) \in \mathcal{S}\}$.*

Note that $\hat{c}(\cdot)$ represents the completion transformation $\tau_{\mathcal{B},\mathcal{C}}^{\mathcal{H}}(\cdot)$ for $\mathcal{C} = \mathcal{PLP}$.
  The main result for casting DLPs to $\mathcal{PLP}$ is formulated as follows:

Theorem 8. *Let $\mathcal{H}, \mathcal{B} \subseteq At$ be sets of atoms and P a DLP over At. Then, there exists a PLP Q over At such that $P \equiv_{\mathcal{B}}^{\mathcal{H}} Q$ iff $HE_{\mathcal{B}}^{\mathcal{H}}(P)$ is $\langle \mathcal{H}, \mathcal{B} \rangle$-here-total.*

Example 5. Again, consider program P_1 from Example 1 and recall that there is no PLP that is strongly equivalent to P_1. For sets $\mathcal{H} = \{a\}$ and $\mathcal{B} = \{a, c\}$, we have $HE_{\mathcal{B}}^{\mathcal{H}}(P_1) = \{(b, b), (\emptyset, ab), (ab, ab), (ac, ac)\}$. $HE_{\mathcal{B}}^{\mathcal{H}}(P_1)$ is $\langle \mathcal{H}, \mathcal{B} \rangle$-here-total, and thus there is a PLP that is $\langle \mathcal{H}, \mathcal{B} \rangle$-equivalent to P_1, e.g., $P_1'' = \{a \vee b \leftarrow; \ b \vee c \leftarrow\}$.

4.4 Joint Elimination of Disjunction and Negation

The characterising property of DLPs being castable to $\mathcal{HORN}$ is independent of the body alphabet. In conjunction with $\langle \mathcal{H}, \mathcal{B} \rangle$-completeness, it constitutes $\phi_{\mathcal{B},\mathcal{HORN}}^{\mathcal{H}}(\cdot)$.

Definition 8. *For a set $\mathcal{H}$ of atoms, a set $\mathcal{S}$ of SE-interpretations is $\mathcal{H}$-closed under there-intersection, or $\mathcal{H}$-TI-closed, if, whenever $(X, X) \in \mathcal{S}$ and $(Y, Y) \in \mathcal{S}$, there is a $(Z, Z) \in \mathcal{S}$ such that $Z \subseteq (X \cap Y)$ and $(Z \cap \mathcal{H}) = (X \cap Y) \cap \mathcal{H}$.*

Theorem 9. *Let $\mathcal{H}, \mathcal{B} \subseteq At$ be sets of atoms and P a Horn program over At. Then, $HE_{\mathcal{B}}^{\mathcal{H}}(P)$ is $\mathcal{H}$-TI-closed.*

The completion transformation for casting to $\mathcal{HORN}$, defined next, reuses the completion $\hat{c}(\cdot)$ from Definition 7. However, a refinement is necessary for guaranteeing closure under there-intersection of the respective mapping.

Definition 9. *Let $\mathcal{H} \subseteq At$ be a set of atoms. For every set $\mathcal{S}$ of SE-interpretations, let $\tilde{c}_{\mathcal{H}}(\mathcal{S})$ be given by $\hat{c}(\{(Z', Z') \mid (Z, Z) \in \mathcal{S}, Z \subseteq Z' \subseteq At, (Z' \cap \mathcal{H}) = (Z \cap \mathcal{H})\})$.*

As in the previous cases, $\tilde{c}_{\mathcal{H}}(\cdot)$ represents $\tau_{\mathcal{B},\mathcal{C}}^{\mathcal{H}}(\cdot)$ for $\mathcal{C} = \mathcal{HORN}$. As well, in Section 5 we will summarise the role of the completion transformations $c_{\mathcal{H},\mathcal{B}}(\cdot)$, $\hat{c}(\cdot)$, and $\tilde{c}_{\mathcal{H}}(\cdot)$ for computing a casting of a given program.

Theorem 10. *Let $\mathcal{H}, \mathcal{B} \subseteq At$ be sets of atoms and P a DLP over At. Then, there is a Horn program Q over At with $P \equiv_{\mathcal{B}}^{\mathcal{H}} Q$ iff $HE_{\mathcal{B}}^{\mathcal{H}}(P)$ is $\langle \mathcal{H}, \mathcal{B} \rangle$-here-total and $\mathcal{H}$-TI-closed.*

Example 6. Consider program P_2 from Example 1 and recall from Example 3 that there is no Horn program strongly equivalent to P_2. For sets $\mathcal{H} = \{a, c\}$ and $\mathcal{B} = \{a, b, c\}$, we have $HE_{\mathcal{B}}^{\mathcal{H}}(P_1) = \{(\emptyset, \emptyset), (\emptyset, ab), (ab, ab), (\emptyset, bc), (bc, bc)\}$. $HE_{\mathcal{B}}^{\mathcal{H}}(P_2)$ is $\langle \mathcal{H}, \mathcal{B} \rangle$-here-total and $\langle \mathcal{H}, \mathcal{B} \rangle$-TI-closed. Thus, there is a Horn program that is $\langle \mathcal{H}, \mathcal{B} \rangle$-equivalent to P_2, e.g., $P_2' = \{b \leftarrow a;\ b \leftarrow c;\ \leftarrow a, c\}$.

4.5   Special Cases

We briefly discuss our results with respect to important corner cases of hyperequivalence. Naturally, for strong equivalence, the introduced characterisations reduce to the notions presented in Section 3. Hence, we provided proper generalisations of the concepts known for this special case. For identical head and body alphabets, hyperequivalence reduces to relativised strong equivalence as introduced by Woltran [13]. Interestingly, $\langle A, A \rangle$-closure under here-intersection reduces to ordinary closure under here-intersection for $\langle A, A \rangle$-well-defined sets of SE-interpretations. Consequently, for relativised strong equivalence, we get the following refinement of Theorem 6:

Theorem 11. *Let $A \subseteq At$ be a set of atoms and P a DLP over At. Then, there exists an NLP Q over At such that $P \equiv_A^A Q$ iff $HE_A^A(P)$ is HI-closed.*

5   Computational Aspects of Program Casting

In this section, we first summarise how program castings can be computed, and afterwards we discuss the complexity of casting under hyperequivalence.

Let $\mathcal{H}, \mathcal{B} \subseteq At$ be sets of atoms. For obtaining an $\langle \mathcal{H}, \mathcal{B} \rangle$-casting of a given DLP P over At to class $\mathcal{C}$ with (i) $\mathcal{C} = \mathcal{NLP}$, (ii) $\mathcal{C} = \mathcal{PLP}$, or (iii) $\mathcal{C} = \mathcal{HORN}$, respectively, where P is castable to $\mathcal{C}$ under $\langle \mathcal{H}, \mathcal{B} \rangle$-equivalence, one can proceed as follows:

1. Compute $HE_{\mathcal{B}}^{\mathcal{H}}(P)$.
2. Depending on the class $\mathcal{C}$ of programs, compute (i) $\mathcal{S} = c_{\mathcal{H},\mathcal{B}}(HE_{\mathcal{B}}^{\mathcal{H}}(P))$, (ii) $\mathcal{S} = \hat{c}(HE_{\mathcal{B}}^{\mathcal{H}}(P))$, or (iii) $\mathcal{S} = \tilde{c}_{\mathcal{H}}(HE_{\mathcal{B}}^{\mathcal{H}}(P))$.
3. Compute the canonical program $CP_{\mathcal{S}}$ for $\mathcal{S}$.
4. Apply techniques to remove (i) disjunctions, (ii) negations, or (iii) negations and disjunctions from $CP_{\mathcal{S}}$, preserving strong equivalence, as discussed in Section 3.

For analysing the complexity of $CAST(\mathcal{C})$ for $\mathcal{C} \in \{\mathcal{NLP}, \mathcal{PLP}, \mathcal{HORN}\}$, we need the following membership result for $\langle \mathcal{H}, \mathcal{B} \rangle$-model checking.

Theorem 12. *The problem of deciding whether $(X, Y) \in HE_{\mathcal{B}}^{\mathcal{H}}(Q)$, for given $X, Y, \mathcal{H}, \mathcal{B} \subseteq At$ and DLP Q over At, is in Δ_2^P.*

The following relationship between $\langle \mathcal{H}, \mathcal{B} \rangle$-models and SE-models is essential for efficiently checking whether a DLP can be replaced by a hyperequivalent NLP.

Lemma 6. *Let* $X, Y, \mathcal{H}, \mathcal{B} \subseteq At$ *be sets of atoms, and* P *a DLP over* At *such that* $X \subseteq (\mathcal{H} \cup \mathcal{B})$. *If* $(Y, Y) \in HE_{\mathcal{B}}^{\mathcal{H}}(P)$, *then the following statements are equivalent:*

- *there is some* $X' \subset Y$ *with* $(X', Y) \in HE_{\mathcal{B}}^{\mathcal{H}}(P)$, $(X \cap \mathcal{H}) \subseteq (X' \cap \mathcal{H})$, *and* $(X' \cap \mathcal{B}) \subseteq (X \cap \mathcal{B})$;
- *there is some* $X'' \subset Y$ *with* $(X'', Y) \in SE(P)$, $(X \cap \mathcal{H}) \subseteq (X'' \cap \mathcal{H})$, *and* $(X'' \cap \mathcal{B}) \subseteq (X \cap \mathcal{B})$.

Theorem 13. *Deciding* CAST$(\mathcal{NLP})$ *is* Π_2^P*-complete. Moreover, the problem remains* Π_2^P*-hard if we restrict it to instances where* $\mathcal{H} = \mathcal{B}$ *holds.*

Proof (Sketch). For membership, we show that the complementary problem, i.e., deciding whether $HE_{\mathcal{B}}^{\mathcal{H}}(P)$ is not $\langle \mathcal{H}, \mathcal{B} \rangle$-HI-closed, is in Σ_2^P. Note that $HE_{\mathcal{B}}^{\mathcal{H}}(Q)$ is $\langle \mathcal{H}, \mathcal{B} \rangle$-HI-closed iff $HE_{\mathcal{B}}^{\mathcal{H}}(Q) \cap (atm(Q) \times atm(Q))$ is $\langle \mathcal{H}, \mathcal{B} \rangle$-HI-closed. We can nondeterministically guess some $X_1, X_2, Y \subseteq atm(Q)$. By Theorem 12, a polynomial number of NP-oracle calls suffice to decide whether $(X_1, Y) \in HE_{\mathcal{B}}^{\mathcal{H}}(Q)$ and $(X_2, Y) \in HE_{\mathcal{B}}^{\mathcal{H}}(Q)$. As a consequence of Lemma 6, an NP-oracle can be used to check whether there is no $X' \subset Y$ with $(X', Y) \in HE_{\mathcal{B}}^{\mathcal{H}}(Q)$, $(X_1 \cap X_2) \cap \mathcal{H} \subseteq (X' \cap \mathcal{H})$, and $(X' \cap \mathcal{B}) \subseteq (X_1 \cap X_2) \cap \mathcal{B}$. Thus, a nondeterministic algorithm with access to an NP-oracle solves the complementary problem in polynomial time.

We show hardness by a reducing the problem of deciding the truth of a quantified Boolean formula (QBF) to checking whether $HE_{\mathcal{B}}^{\mathcal{H}}(P)$ is not $\langle \mathcal{H}, \mathcal{B} \rangle$-HI-closed. Consider a QBF $\Phi = \exists K \forall L \delta_1 \vee \cdots \vee \delta_r$, where each δ_i is a conjunction of literals over $K \cup L$. We assume that $K \neq \emptyset$ and $L \neq \emptyset$. For every $x \in K \cup L$, we denote by $\overline{x}$ a globally new atom not appearing anywhere in ϕ. Given a set X of atoms, we define $\overline{X} = \{\overline{x} \mid x \in X\}$. Finally, for each conjunction $\delta = a_1 \wedge \cdots \wedge a_h \wedge \neg a_{h+1} \wedge \neg a_n$ of literals, we denote by $\delta^{\dagger}$ the sequence $a_1, \ldots, a_h, \overline{a_{h+1}}, \ldots, \overline{a_n}$ and define program P_{Φ}, using further new atoms a, b, w, as follows.

$$P_{\Phi} = \{k \leftarrow not\ \overline{k};\ \overline{k} \leftarrow not\ k;\ \leftarrow k, \overline{k} \mid k \in K\} \cup$$
$$\{l \vee \overline{l} \leftarrow;\ w \leftarrow l, \overline{l};\ l \leftarrow w;\ \overline{l} \leftarrow w; \mid l \in L\} \cup$$
$$\{a \vee b \leftarrow \delta_i^{\dagger};\ w \leftarrow \delta_i^{\dagger}; \mid 1 \leq i \leq r\}.$$

For $A = K \cup \overline{K} \cup \{a, b\}$, it can be shown that Φ is true iff $HE_A^A(P_{\Phi})$ is not HI-closed, and therefore, by Theorem 11, not $\langle A, A \rangle$-HI-closed. Since deciding the truth of a QBF of form Φ is Σ_2^P-hard, the assertion follows from that. □

It was shown [8] that there is no rewriting f from DLPs to NLPs such that $P \equiv_{\emptyset}^{At} f(P)$, where $f(P)$ is polynomial in the size of P, for every program P, unless the polynomial hierarchy (PH) collapses. Hence, there is also no polynomial rewriting from DLPs to NLPs for the general case of hyperequivalence, unless the PH collapses.

It turns out that checking whether a DLP can be replaced by a hyperequivalent PLP is computationally more expensive than deciding whether there is a corresponding NLP.

Theorem 14. *Deciding* CAST$(\mathcal{PLP})$ *is* Π_3^P*-complete. Moreover, the problem remains* Π_3^P*-hard if we restrict it to instances where* $\mathcal{B} \subseteq \mathcal{H}$ *holds.*

Proof (Sketch). We only show the hardness part. Consider a QBF $\Phi = \exists K \forall L \exists M \phi$, where ϕ is a formula in CNF over the set $K \cup L \cup M$ of atoms. We assume that $K \neq \emptyset$, $L \neq \emptyset$, and $M \neq \emptyset$. As before, for every $x \in K \cup L \cup M$, we denote by $\overline{x}$ a globally new atom not appearing anywhere in ϕ, and we define $\overline{X} = \{\overline{x} \mid x \in X\}$ for every set X of atoms. Finally, for each clause $\gamma = x_1 \vee \cdots \vee x_k \vee \neg x_{k+1} \vee \cdots \vee \neg x_n$, we denote by $\gamma^{\ddagger}$ the sequence $\overline{x}_1, \ldots, \overline{x}_k, x_{k+1}, \ldots, x_n$, and define a program P_{Φ}, using a further new atom w, as follows:

$$P_{\Phi} = \{j \vee \overline{j} \leftarrow; \ o \leftarrow j, \overline{j}; \ \overline{o} \leftarrow j, \overline{j} \mid j \in K \cup L, o \in K \cup L \cup M\} \cup$$
$$\{m \vee \overline{m} \leftarrow; \ w \leftarrow m, \overline{m}; \ m \leftarrow w; \ \overline{m} \leftarrow w \mid m \in M\} \cup$$
$$\{w \leftarrow \gamma^{\ddagger} \mid \text{ for each clause } \gamma \text{ in } \phi\} \cup \{w \leftarrow not\ w\}.$$

For $\mathcal{B} \subseteq \mathcal{H} = K \cup \overline{K}$, it can be shown that Φ is true iff $HE_{\mathcal{B}}^{\mathcal{H}}(P_{\Phi})$ is not $\langle \mathcal{H}, \mathcal{B} \rangle$-here-total. As deciding the truth of a QBF of form Φ is Σ_3^P-hard, the assertion follows.   □

Theorem 15. *Given set At of atoms, there is no rewriting $f : \mathcal{DLP} \times At \times At \to \mathcal{PLP}$ such that, for given sets $\mathcal{H}, \mathcal{B} \subseteq At$ of atoms and a DLP P that is castable to $\mathcal{PLP}$, $P \equiv_{\mathcal{B}}^{\mathcal{H}} f(P, \mathcal{H}, \mathcal{B})$ and $f(P, \mathcal{H}, \mathcal{B})$ is polynomial in the size of P, unless the polynomial hierarchy collapses. The result also holds under the restriction $\mathcal{B} \subseteq \mathcal{H}$.*

Proof. Let $\mathcal{H}, \mathcal{B}$ be sets of atoms such that $\mathcal{B} \subseteq \mathcal{H}$. Assume that a polynomial-size rewriting f of the described kind exists. We can guess a PLP P', polynomial in the size of P, in nondeterministic polynomial time. Since checking $P' \equiv_{\mathcal{B}}^{\mathcal{H}} P$ is in Π_2^P [5], a nondeterministic algorithm with access to a Σ_2^P-oracle can decide CAST($\mathcal{PLP}$). This yields membership of CAST($\mathcal{PLP}$) in Σ_3^P, which is a contradiction to the Π_3^P-hardness of the problem, unless the polynomial hierarchy collapses.   □

Finally, we have the following result for the Horn case:

Theorem 16. *Deciding CAST($\mathcal{HORN}$) is in Π_3^P.*

6   Discussion

We studied casting of disjunctive answer-set programs under hyperequivalence and provided necessary and sufficient semantical conditions, deciding for a program P, whether there exists a program Q of a given syntactic subclass of DLPs which is hyper-equivalent to P. Moreover, we provided methods for constructing such a Q and studied the complexity of deciding whether casting can be applied. Here, an open issue is determining exact complexity bounds for CAST($\mathcal{HORN}$).

Other open issues concern the canonical program we used to obtain our results. First of all, it would be valuable to have canonical programs which are "class sensitive", i.e., given a set $\mathcal{S}$ of SE-interpretations, the associated canonical program is one which is exactly in that class which is characterised by $\mathcal{S}$. This would circumvent the fourth and last step of our program casting algorithm as sketched in Section 5. Secondly, having a canonical program *directly* for HE-models rather than for SE-models would further simplify the task.

An interesting application of casting under hyperequivalence is modular programming, when modules are to be replaced by syntactically simpler programs. As it is typically known which atoms are allowed to occur in the heads and bodies of rules in context modules, adequate casting can be applied even when impossible under strong equivalence. Furthermore, casting under hyperequivalence gives insight into when a syntactical class is intrinsically needed, or contrarily, when connectives like disjunction and negation are dispensable. By varying the hyperequivalence parameters, atoms which are responsible for the need of a connective can be identified. Based on the notions developed, in a next step, properties can be extracted which allow for constructing methods for determining the strongest equivalence notion under which casting is possible. That is, for a given program P and syntactic class $\mathcal{C}$, find $\mathcal{H}$ and $\mathcal{B}$ such that P is castable to $\mathcal{C}$ under $\langle \mathcal{H}, \mathcal{B} \rangle$-equivalence and $\mathcal{H}$ and $\mathcal{B}$ satisfy some optimality condition.

Another crucial matter for future work is research into casting with equivalence under projection [12], where answer sets need to be identical only on selected atoms. Usually, one is interested in the behaviour of a program with respect to distinguished input and output atoms. By varying parameters $\mathcal{H}$ and $\mathcal{B}$, $\langle \mathcal{H}, \mathcal{B} \rangle$-equivalence allows for specifying the input part. Projection, on the other hand, is needed for determining output atoms. Once conditions for casting with projections are defined, it can be decided whether the respective task allows for replacing a program by a simpler one.

References

1. Baral, C.: Knowledge Representation, Reasoning and Declarative Problem Solving. Cambridge University Press, Cambridge (2003)
2. Gelfond, M., Lifschitz, V.: Classical negation in logic programs and disjunctive databases. New Generation Computing 9, 365–385 (1991)
3. Lifschitz, V., Pearce, D., Valverde, A.: Strongly equivalent logic programs. ACM Transactions on Computational Logic 2(4), 526–541 (2001)
4. Eiter, T., Fink, M.: Uniform equivalence of logic programs under the stable model semantics. In: Palamidessi, C. (ed.) ICLP 2003. LNCS, vol. 2916, pp. 224–238. Springer, Heidelberg (2003)
5. Woltran, S.: A common view on strong, uniform, and other notions of equivalence in answer-set programming. Theory and Practice of Logic Programming 8(2), 217–234 (2008)
6. Truszczyński, M., Woltran, S.: Relativized hyperequivalence of logic programs for modular programming. In: de la Banda, M.G., Pontelli, E. (eds.) ICLP 2008. LNCS, vol. 5366, pp. 576–590. Springer, Heidelberg (2008)
7. Eiter, T., Fink, M., Tompits, H., Woltran, S.: Simplifying logic programs under uniform and strong equivalence. In: Baral, C., Brewka, G., Schlipf, J. (eds.) LPNMR 2007. LNCS, vol. 4483, pp. 87–99. Springer, Heidelberg (2007)
8. Eiter, T., Fink, M., Tompits, H., Woltran, S.: On eliminating disjunctions in stable logic programming. In: Proc. KR 2004, pp. 447–458. AAAI Press, Menlo Park (2004)
9. Turner, H.: Strong equivalence made easy: Nested expressions and weight constraints. Theory and Practice of Logic Programming 3(4-5), 602–622 (2003)
10. Heyting, A.: Die formalen Regeln der intuitionistischen Logik. Sitzungsberichte, physik.-math. Klasse, preußische Akademie der Wissenschaften (1930)
11. Gödel, K.: Zum intuitionistischen Aussagenkalkül. Anzeiger Akademie der Wissenschaften in Wien, math.-naturwiss. Klasse 69, 65–66 (1932)
12. Eiter, T., Tompits, H., Woltran, S.: On solution correspondences in answer set programming. In: Proc. IJCAI 2005, pp. 97–102 (2005)
13. Woltran, S.: Characterizations for relativized notions of equivalence in answer set programming. In: Alferes, J.J., Leite, J. (eds.) JELIA 2004. LNCS, vol. 3229, pp. 161–173. Springer, Heidelberg (2004)

Relativized Hyperequivalence of Logic Programs for Modular Programming

Mirosław Truszczyński[1] and Stefan Woltran[2]

[1] Department of Computer Science, University of Kentucky, Lexington, KY 40506, USA
[2] Institut für Informationssysteme 184/2, Technische Universität Wien, Favoritenstraße 9-11, A-1040 Vienna, Austria

Abstract. A recent framework of relativized hyperequivalence of programs offers a unifying generalization of strong and uniform equivalence. It seems to be especially well suited for applications in program optimization and modular programming due to its flexibility that allows us to restrict, independently of each other, the head and body alphabets in context programs. We study relativized hyperequivalence for the three semantics of logic programs given by stable, supported and supported minimal models. For each semantics, we identify four types of contexts, depending on whether the head and body alphabets are given directly or as the *complement* of a given set. Hyperequivalence relative to contexts where the head and body alphabets are specified directly has been studied before. In this paper, we establish the complexity of deciding relativized hyperequivalence wrt the three other types of context programs.

1 Introduction

We study variants of relativized hyperequivalence that are relevant for the development and analysis of logic programs with modular structure. Our main results concern the complexity of deciding relativized hyperequivalence for the three major semantics of logic programs given by stable, supported and supported minimal models.

Logic programming with the semantics of stable models, nowadays often referred to as *answer-set programming*, is a computational paradigm for knowledge representation, as well as modeling and solving of constraint problems [1,2,3,4]. In recent years, it has been steadily attracting more attention. One reason is that answer-set programming is truly declarative. Unlike in, say, Prolog, the order of rules in programs and the order of literals in rules have no effect on the meaning of the program. Secondly, the efficiency of the latest tools for processing programs, especially solvers, reached the level that makes it feasible to use them for problems of practical importance [5].

It is broadly recognized in software engineering that modular programs are easier to design, analyze and implement. Hence, essentially all programming languages and environments support the development of modular programs. Accordingly, there has been much work recently to establish foundations of *modular* answer-set programming. One line of investigations has focused on the notion of an answer-set program *module* [6,7,8,9]. This work builds on ideas for compositional semantics of logic programs proposed in [10] and encompasses earlier results on stratification and *program splitting* [11].

The other main line of research, to which our paper belongs, has centered on program equivalence and, especially, on the concept of equivalence for substitution. Programs P

M. Garcia de la Banda and E. Pontelli (Eds.): ICLP 2008, LNCS 5366, pp. 576–590, 2008.
© Springer-Verlag Berlin Heidelberg 2008

and Q are *equivalent for substitution* wrt a class C of programs called *contexts*, if for every context $R \in C$, $P \cup R$ and $Q \cup R$ have the same stable models. Thus, if a logic program is the union of programs P and R, where $R \in C$, then P can be replaced with Q, with the guarantee that the semantics is preserved no matter what R is (as long as it is in C) precisely when P and Q are equivalent for substitution wrt C. If C contains the empty program (which is typically the case), the equivalence for substitution wrt C implies the standard equivalence under the stable-model semantics.[1] *The converse is not true.* We refer to these stronger forms of equivalence collectively as *hyperequivalence*.

Hyperequivalence wrt the class of *all* programs, known more commonly as *strong equivalence*, was proposed and studied in [12]. That work prompted extensive investigations of the concept that resulted in new characterizations [13,14] and connections to certain non-standard logics [15]. Hyperequivalence wrt contexts consisting of facts was studied in [16,17]. This version of hyperequivalence, known as *uniform equivalence*, appeared first in the database area in the setting of DATALOG and query equivalence [18]. Hyperequivalence wrt contexts restricted to a given alphabet, or *relativized* hyperequivalence, was proposed in [17,19]. It was generalized in [20] to allow contexts that use (possibly) different alphabets for the heads and bodies of rules. The approach offers a unifying framework for strong and uniform equivalence. Hyperequivalence, in which one compares projections of answer sets on some designated sets of atoms rather than entire answer sets was investigated in [21,22].

All those results concern the stable-model semantics of programs. There has been little work on other semantics, with [23] long being a notable single exception. Recently however, [24] introduced and investigated relativized hyperequivalence of programs under the semantics of supported models [25] and supported minimal models, two other major semantics of logic programs. [24] characterized these variants of hyperequivalence and established the complexity of some associated decision problems.

In this paper, we continue research of relativized hyperequivalence under all three major semantics of logic programs. As in [20,24], we focus on contexts of the form $\mathcal{HB}(A, B)$, where $\mathcal{HB}(A, B)$ stands for the set of all programs that use elements from A in the heads and atoms from B in the bodies of rules. Our main goal is to establish the complexity of deciding whether two programs are hyperequivalent (relative to a specified semantics) wrt $\mathcal{HB}(A, B)$. We consider the cases when A and B are either specified directly or in terms of their complement. As we point out in the following section, such contexts arise naturally when we design modular logic programs.

2   Motivation

In the paper we consider finite propositional programs only, all over a fixed countable infinite set of atoms At. For a set of atoms X, we define $X^c = At \setminus X$.

A logic program is *A-defining* if it specifies the definitions of atoms in A. The definitions may be recursive, they may involve *interface* atoms, that is, atoms defined in other modules, as well as atoms used locally to represent some needed auxiliary concepts. Let L be the set of local atoms, and let P be a particular logic program expressing the

---

[1] Two programs are equivalent under the stable-model semantics if they have the same stable models.

definitions. For P to behave properly when combined with other programs, these "context" programs must not have any occurrences of atoms from L and must have no atoms from A in the heads of their rules. In our terminology, these are precisely programs in $\mathcal{HB}((A \cup L)^c, L^c)$.[2]

The definitions of atoms in A can in general be captured by several different A-defining programs. A key question concerning such programs is whether they are equivalent. Clearly, two A-defining programs P and Q, both using atoms from L to represent local auxiliary concepts, should be regarded as equivalent if they behave in the same way in the context of any program from $\mathcal{HB}((A \cup L)^c, L^c)$. In other words, the notion of equivalence that is appropriate in our setting is hyperequivalence wrt $\mathcal{HB}((A \cup L)^c, L^c)$ under a selected semantics (stable, supported or supported-minimal).

Example 1. Let us assume that $A = \{a, b\}$ and that c and d are interface atoms (atoms defined elsewhere). We need a module that works as follows:

1. If c and d are both true, exactly one of a and b must be true
2. If c is true and d is false, only a must be true
3. If d is true and c is false, only b must be true
4. If c and d are both false, a and b must be false.

We point out that c and d may depend on a and b and so, in some cases the overall program may have no models of a particular type (to be concrete, for a time being we fix attention to stable models).

One way to express above conditions is by means of the following $\{a, b\}$-defining program P (in this example we assume programs without local atoms, that is, $L = \emptyset$):

$$a \leftarrow c, not\ b; \quad b \leftarrow d, not\ a.$$

Combining P with programs that specify facts: $\{c, d\}, \{c\}, \{d\}$ and $\emptyset$, it is easy to see that P behaves as required. For instance, $P \cup \{c\}$ has exactly one stable model $\{a, c\}$.

However, P may also be combined with more complex programs. For instance, let us consider the program $R = \{c \leftarrow not\ d; \ d \leftarrow a, not\ c\}$. Here, d can only be true if a is true and c is false. But then b must be true and a must be *false*, a contradiction. Thus, d must be false and c must be true. According to the specifications, there should be exactly one stable model for $P \cup R$ in this case: $\{a, c\}$. It is easy to verify that it is indeed the case.

The specifications for a and b can also be expressed by other $\{a, b\}$-defining programs, in particular, by the following program Q:

$$a \leftarrow c, d, not\ b; \quad b \leftarrow c, d, not\ a; \quad a \leftarrow c, not\ d; \quad b \leftarrow d, not\ c.$$

The question arises whether Q behaves in the same way as P relative to programs from $\mathcal{HB}(\{a, b\}^c, \emptyset^c) = \mathcal{HB}(\{a, b\}^c, At)$. For all contexts considered earlier, it is the case. However, in general, it is not so. For instance, if $R = \{c \leftarrow ; \ d \leftarrow a\}$ then, $\{a, c, d\}$ is a stable model of $P \cup R$, while $Q \cup R$ has no stable models. Thus, P and Q cannot be viewed as equivalent $\{a, b\}$-defining programs.   □

A similar scenario is as follows: We call a program A-*completing* if it completes partial and non-recursive definitions of atoms in A given elsewhere in the overall program

---

[2] A-defining programs were introduced in [26]. However, that work considered more restricted classes of programs with which A-defining programs could be combined.

(which, for instance, might specify the base conditions for a recursive definition of atoms in A). Assuming that P is an implementation of such a module (again with L as a set of local atoms), P can be combined with any program R that has no occurrences of atoms from L and no occurrences of atoms from A in the bodies of its rules. This is precisely the class $\mathcal{HB}(L^c, (A \cup L)^c)$.

One can also construct scenarios that give rise to hyperequivalence wrt context classes $\mathcal{HB}(A, B)$, where A or B is specified directly. Thus, hyperequivalence wrt context classes $\mathcal{HB}(A, B)$, where each of A and B is specified directly or in terms of its complement is of interest. Our goal is to study the complexity of deciding whether two programs are hyperequivalent relative to such classes of contexts.

3   Technical Preliminaries

Basic logic programming notation and definitions. *Disjunctive logic programs* (programs, for short) are sets of (program) *rules* — expressions of the form

$$a_1 | \ldots | a_k \leftarrow b_1, \ldots, b_m, not\, c_1, \ldots, not\, c_n, \tag{1}$$

where a_i, b_i and c_i are atoms in At, '$|$' stands for the disjunction, ',' stands for the conjunction, and *not* is the *default* negation. If $k = 0$, the rule is a *constraint*. If $k \leq 1$, the rule is *normal*. Programs consisting of normal rules are called *normal*.

We often write the rule (1) as $H \leftarrow B^+, not\, B^-$, where $H = \{a_1, \ldots, a_k\}$, $B^+ = \{b_1, \ldots, b_m\}$ and $B^- = \{c_1, \ldots, c_n\}$. We call H the *head* of the rule, and the conjunction $B^+, not\, B^-$, the *body* of the rule. The sets B^+ and B^- form the positive and negative body of the rule. Given a rule r, we write $H(r)$, $B(r)$, $B^+(r)$ and $B^-(r)$ to denote the head, the body, the positive body and the negative body of r, respectively. For a program P, we set $H(P) = \bigcup_{r \in P} H(r)$, and $B^{\pm}(P) = \bigcup_{r \in P} B^+(r) \cup B^-(r)$.

For an interpretation $M \subseteq At$ and a rule r, we define entailments $M \models B(r)$, $M \models H(r)$ and $M \models r$ in the standard way. An interpretation $M \subseteq At$ is a *model* of a program P ($M \models P$), if $M \models r$ for every $r \in P$.

The *reduct* of a disjunctive logic program P wrt a set M of atoms, denoted by P^M, is the program $\{H(r) \leftarrow B^+(r) \mid r \in P,\ M \cap B^-(r) = \emptyset\}$. A set M of atoms is a *stable model* of P if M is a minimal model (wrt inclusion) of P^M.

If a set M of atoms is a minimal hitting set of $\{H(r) \mid r \in P,\ M \models B(r)\}$, then M is a *supported model* of P. M is a *supported minimal model* of P if it is a supported model of P and a minimal model of P. We recall that each stable model is also supported, but (generally) not vice versa. Supported models of a *normal* logic program P have a useful characterization in terms of the (partial) one-step provability operator T_P, defined as follows. For $M \subseteq At$, if there is a constraint $r \in P$ such that $M \models B(r)$ (that is, $M \not\models r$), then $T_P(M)$ is undefined. Otherwise, $T_P(M) = \bigcup\{H(r) \mid r \in P,\ M \models B(r)\}$. Whenever we use $T_P(M)$ in a relation such as (proper) inclusion, equality or inequality, we always implicitly assume that $T_P(M)$ is defined.

It is well known that M is a model of P if and only if $T_P(M) \subseteq M$ (that is, T_P is defined for M and satisfies $T_P(M) \subseteq M$). Similarly, M is a *supported* model of P if $T_P(M) = M$ (that is, T_P is defined for M and satisfies $T_P(M) = M$) [27].

For a rule $r = a_1 | \ldots | a_k \leftarrow B$, where $k \geq 1$, a *shift* of r is a normal program rule of the form

$$a_i \leftarrow B, \, not \, a_1, \ldots, \, not \, a_{i-1}, \, not \, a_{i+1}, \ldots, \, not \, a_k,$$

where $i = 1, \ldots, k$. If r is normal, the only *shift* of r is r itself. A program consisting of all shifts of rules in a program P is the *shift* of P. We denote it by $sh(P)$. It is evident that a set M of atoms is a (minimal) model of P if and only if M is a (minimal) model of $sh(P)$. It is easy to check that M is a supported (minimal) model of P if and only if it is a supported (minimal) model of $sh(P)$. Moreover, M is a supported model of P if and only if $T_{sh(P)}(M) = M$. Thus, in all results concerning supported models, we will use implicitly the shift of programs involved (see also [24] for further details).

Characterizations of hyperequivalence of programs. Let $\mathcal{C}$ be a class of (disjunctive) logic programs. Programs P and Q are *supp-equivalent* (*suppmin-equivalent, stable-equivalent*, respectively) relative to $\mathcal{C}$ if for every program $R \in \mathcal{C}$, $P \cup R$ and $Q \cup R$ have the same supported (supported minimal, stable, respectively) models.

In this paper, we are interested in equivalence of all three types relative to classes of programs defined by the *head* and *body* alphabets. Let $A, B \subseteq At$. By $\mathcal{HB}(A, B)$ we denote the class of all programs P such that $H(P) \subseteq A$ and $B^{\pm}(P) \subseteq B$. Hence, the empty program is contained in any such $\mathcal{HB}(A, B)$.

For supp-equivalence and suppmin-equivalence, we need the following concept introduced in [24]. Given a program P, and a set $A \subseteq At$, we define

$$Mod_A(P) = \{Y \subseteq At \mid Y \models P \text{ and } Y \setminus T_P(Y) \subseteq A\}.$$

Theorem 1. *Let P and Q be programs, $A \subseteq At$, and $\mathcal{C}$ a class of programs such that $\mathcal{HB}(A, \emptyset) \subseteq \mathcal{C} \subseteq \mathcal{HB}(A, At)$. Then, P and Q are supp-equivalent relative to $\mathcal{C}$ if and only if $Mod_A(P) = Mod_A(Q)$ and for every $Y \in Mod_A(P)$, $T_P(Y) = T_Q(Y)$.*

To characterize suppmin-equivalence, we use the set $Mod_A^B(P)$ (following [24]), which consists of all pairs (X, Y) such that

1. $Y \in Mod_A(P)$
2. $X \subseteq Y|_{A \cup B}$
3. for each $Z \subset Y$ such that $Z|_{A \cup B} = Y|_{A \cup B}$, $Z \not\models P$
4. for each $Z \subset Y$ such that $Z|_B = X|_B$ and $Z|_A \supseteq X|_A$, $Z \not\models P$
5. if $X|_B = Y|_B$, then $Y \setminus T_P(Y) \subseteq X$.

Theorem 2. *Let $A, B \subseteq At$ and let P, Q be programs. Then, P and Q are suppmin-equivalent relative to $\mathcal{HB}(A, B)$ if and only if $Mod_A^B(P) = Mod_A^B(Q)$ and for every $(X, Y) \in Mod_A^B(P)$, $T_P(Y)|_B = T_Q(Y)|_B$.*

Relativized stable-equivalence of programs was characterized in [20]. We define $SE_A^B(P)$ to consist of all pairs (X, Y) such that:[3]

1. $Y \models P$
2. $X = Y$ or jointly $X \subseteq Y|_{A \cup B}$ and $X|_A \subset Y|_A$
3. for each $Z \subset Y$ such that $Z|_A = Y|_A$, $Z \not\models P^Y$
4. for each $Z \subset Y$ such that $Z|_B \subseteq X|_B$, $Z|_A \supseteq X|_A$, and either $Z|_B \subset X|_B$ or $Z|_A \supset X|_A$, $Z \not\models P^Y$
5. there is $Z \subseteq Y$ such that $X|_{A \cup B} = Z|_{A \cup B}$ and $Z \models P^Y$.

---

[3] We use a slightly different presentation than [20].

Theorem 3. *Let $A, B \subseteq At$ and let P, Q be programs. Then, P and Q are stable-equivalent relative to $\mathcal{HB}(A, B)$ if and only if $SE_A^B(P) = SE_A^B(Q)$.*

Decision problems. We study problems of deciding hyperequivalence relative to program classes $\mathcal{HB}(A', B')$, where A' and B' stand either for finite sets or for complements of finite sets. In the former case, the set is given *directly*. In the latter, it is specified by its finite *complement* (the set itself is infinite). Thus, we obtain the classes of *direct-direct*, *direct-complement*, *complement-direct* and *complement-complement* decision problems. We denote them using strings of the form $\text{SEM}_{\delta,\varepsilon}(\alpha, \beta)$, where (1) SEM stands for SUPP, SUPPMIN or STABLE and identifies the semantics relative to which we define hyperequivalence; (2) δ and ε stand for d or c (direct and complement, respectively), and specify one of the four classes of problems mentioned above; (3) α is either $\cdot$ or A, where $A \subseteq At$ is finite. If $\alpha = A$, then α specifies a *fixed* alphabet for the heads of rules in contexts: either A or the complement A^c of A, depending on whether $\delta = d$ or c. The parameter does not belong to and does not vary with input. If $\alpha = \cdot$, then the specification A of the head alphabet is part of the input and defines it as A or A^c, again according to δ; (4) β is either $\cdot$ or B, where $B \subseteq At$ is finite. It obeys the same conventions as α but defines the body alphabet according to the value of ε.

For instance, $\text{SUPPMIN}_{d,c}(A, \cdot)$, where $A \subseteq At$ is finite, stands for the following problem: given programs P and Q, and a set B, decide whether P and Q are suppmin-equivalent wrt $\mathcal{HB}(A, B^c)$. With some abuse of notation, we often talk about "the problem $\text{SEM}_{\delta,\varepsilon}(A, B)$" as a shorthand for "an arbitrary problem of the form $\text{SEM}_{\delta,\varepsilon}(A, B)$ with fixed finite sets A and B"; likewise we do so for $\text{SEM}_{\delta,\varepsilon}(\cdot, B)$ and $\text{SEM}_{\delta,\varepsilon}(A, \cdot)$.

As we noted, for supp- and suppmin-equivalence, there is no difference between normal and disjunctive programs. For stable-equivalence, allowing disjunctions in the heads of rules affects the complexity. Thus, in the case of stable-equivalence, we distinguish versions of the problems $\text{STABLE}_{\delta,\varepsilon}(\alpha, \beta)$, where the input programs are normal.[4] We denote these problems by $\text{STABLE}_{\delta,\varepsilon}^n(\alpha, \beta)$.

Direct-direct problems for the semantics of supported and supported minimal models were considered in [24] and their complexity was fully determined there. The complexity of problems $\text{STABLE}_{d,d}(\cdot, \cdot)$, was established in [20], and problems similar to $\text{STABLE}_{c,c}(A, A)$ were already studied in [17]. In this paper, we complete the results on the complexity of problems $\text{SEM}_{\delta,\varepsilon}(\alpha, \beta)$ for all three semantics. In particular, we establish the complexity of the problems with at least one of δ and ε being equal to c.

The complexity of problems involving the complement of A or B is not a straightforward consequence of the results on direct-direct problems. In the direct-direct problems, the class of context programs is essentially finite, as the head and body alphabets for rules are finite. It is no longer the case for the three remaining problems, where at least one of the alphabets is infinite and so, the class of contexts is infinite, as well.

Finally, we note that when we change A or B to $\cdot$ in the problem specification, the resulting problem is at least as hard as the original one. Indeed for each such pair of problems, there are some straightforward reductions from one to the other. We illustrate these relationships in Figure 1.

---

[4] We can also restrict the programs used as contexts to normal ones, since this makes no difference, cf. [20].

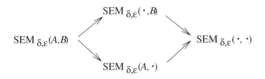

Fig. 1. A simple comparison of the hardness of problems

4   Supp-Equivalence

As the alphabet for the bodies of context programs plays no role in supp-equivalence (cf. Theorem 1), the complexity of $\text{SUPP}_{d,c}(A, \beta)$ and $\text{SUPP}_{d,c}(\cdot, \beta)$ is already solved (β is $\cdot$ or a set B of atoms) by the complexity of the corresponding direct-direct problems which have been shown coNP-complete in [24]. It remains to consider $\text{SUPP}_{c,d}(A, \beta)$ and $\text{SUPP}_{c,d}(\cdot, \beta)$ (which coincide with $\text{SUPP}_{c,c}(A, \beta)$, and respectively, $\text{SUPP}_{c,c}(\cdot, \beta)$).

First, we prove an upper bound on the complexity of the problem $\text{SUPP}_{c,d}(\cdot, \cdot)$.

Theorem 4. *The problem* $\text{SUPP}_{c,d}(\cdot, \cdot)$ *is in the class coNP.*

Proof: It is sufficient to show that $\text{SUPP}_{c,d}(\cdot, \emptyset)$ is in coNP, since (P, Q, A) is a YES instance of $\text{SUPP}_{c,d}(\cdot, \emptyset)$ if and only if (P, Q, A, B) is a YES instance of $\text{SUPP}_{c,d}(\cdot, \cdot)$.

Let $Y' = Y \cap (At(P) \cup A)$. We will show that $Y \in Mod_{A^c}(P)$ if and only if $Y' \in Mod_{A^c}(P)$. First, we note that $T_P(Y) = T_P(Y')$. If $Y \in Mod_{A^c}(P)$, then $Y \models P$ and $Y \setminus T_P(Y) \subseteq A^c$. The former property implies that $Y' \models P$. Since $Y' \setminus T_P(Y') = Y' \setminus T_P(Y) \subseteq Y \setminus T_P(Y)$, the latter one implies that $Y' \setminus T_P(Y') \subseteq A^c$. Thus, $Y' \in Mod_{A^c}(P)$.

Conversely, let $Y' \in Mod_{A^c}(P)$. Then $Y' \models P$ and, consequently, $Y \models P$. Moreover, we also have $Y' \setminus T_P(Y') \subseteq A^c$. Let $y \in Y \setminus T_P(Y)$. If $y \notin Y'$, then $y \notin A$, that is, $y \in A^c$. If $y \in Y'$, then $y \in Y' \setminus T_P(Y')$ (we recall that $T_P(Y) = T_P(Y')$). Hence, $y \in A^c$ in this case, too. It follows that $Y \setminus T_P(Y) \subseteq A^c$ and so, $Y \in Mod_{A^c}(P)$.

Next, we prove that $Mod_{A^c}(P) \neq Mod_{A^c}(Q)$ or, for some $Y \in Mod_{A^c}(P)$, $T_P(Y) \neq T_Q(Y)$ if and only if there is $Y' \subseteq At(P \cup Q) \cup A$ such that Y' belongs to exactly one of $Mod_{A^c}(P)$ and $Mod_{A^c}(Q)$, or Y' belongs to both $Mod_{A^c}(P)$ and $Mod_{A^c}(Q)$ and $T_P(Y') \neq T_Q(Y')$. Clearly, we need to prove the "only-if" implication. To this end, we note that if $Mod_{A^c}(P) \neq Mod_{A^c}(Q)$, then by the observation proved above, there is $Y' \subseteq At(P \cup Q) \cup A$ with that property. Thus, assume that $Mod_{A^c}(P) = Mod_{A^c}(Q)$. If for some $Y \in Mod_{A^c}(P)$, $T_P(Y) \neq T_Q(Y)$ then, Y belongs to both $Mod_{A^c}(P)$ and $Mod_{A^c}(Q)$. By the argument given above, $Y' = Y \cap (At(P \cup Q) \cup A)$ belongs to both $Mod_{A^c}(P)$ and $Mod_{A^c}(Q)$, and $T_P(Y') \neq T_Q(Y')$.

Thus, to decide the complementary problem, we nondeterministically guess $Y \subseteq At(P \cup Q) \cup A$, and verify that Y belongs to exactly one of $Mod_{A^c}(P)$ and $Mod_{A^c}(Q)$, or that Y belongs to $Mod_{A^c}(P)$ and $Mod_{A^c}(Q)$, and that $T_P(Y) \neq T_Q(Y)$.

Checking $Y \models P$ and $Y \models Q$ can be done in polynomial time. Similarly, for $R = P$ or Q, $Y \setminus T_R(Y) \subseteq A^c$ if and only if $(Y \setminus T_R(Y)) \cap A = \emptyset$. Thus, checking $Y \setminus T_R(Y) \subseteq A^c$ can be done in polynomial time, too, and so the algorithm is polynomial. Hence, the complementary problem is in NP, which implies the assertion.   □

For the lower bound we use the problem $\text{SUPP}_{c,d}(A, B)$.

Theorem 5. *The problem* $\text{SUPP}_{c,d}(A, B)$ *is coNP-hard.*

Proof: Let us consider a CNF φ, let Y be the set of atoms in φ, and let $Y' = \{y' \mid y \in Y\}$ be a set of new atoms. We define

$$P(\varphi) = \{y \leftarrow not\ y';\ y' \leftarrow not\ y \mid y \in Y\} \cup \{\leftarrow \hat{c} \mid c \text{ is a clause in } \varphi\}$$

where, for each clause $c \in \varphi$, say $c = y_1 \vee \cdots \vee y_k \vee \neg y_{k+1} \vee \cdots \vee \neg y_m$, $\hat{c}$ denotes the the sequence $y'_1, \ldots, y'_k, y_{k+1}, \ldots, y_m$. To simplify the notation, we write P for $P(\varphi)$. One can check that φ has a model if and only if P has a model. Moreover, for every model M of P such that $M \subseteq At(P)$, M is a *supported* model of P and, consequently, satisfies $M = T_P(M)$.

Next, let Q consist of f and $\leftarrow f$. As Q has no models, Theorem 1 implies that Q is supp-equivalent to P relative to $\mathcal{HB}(A^c, B)$ if and only if $Mod_{A^c}(P) = \emptyset$. If $M \in Mod_{A^c}(P)$, then there is $M' \subseteq At(P)$ such that $M' \in Mod_{A^c}(P)$. Since every model M' of P such that $M' \subseteq At(P)$ satisfies $M' = T_P(M')$, it follows that $Mod_{A^c}(P) = \emptyset$ if and only if P has no models. Thus, φ is unsatisfiable if and only if Q is supp-equivalent to P relative to $\mathcal{HB}(A^c, B)$, and the assertion follows. □

We combine Theorems 4 and 5 via the relations depicted in Figure 1 and obtain:

Corollary 1. *The problem* $\text{SUPP}_{\delta,\varepsilon}(\alpha, \beta)$ *is coNP-complete, for any combination of* $\delta, \varepsilon \in \{c, d\}$, $\alpha \in \{A, \cdot\}$, $\beta \in \{B, \cdot\}$.

5   Suppmin-Equivalence

In this section, we establish the complexity for direct-complement, complement-direct and complement-complement problems of deciding suppmin-equivalence. The complexity of direct-direct problems was determined in [24].

Upper bounds. The argument consists of a series of auxiliary results. Due to space restrictions, we omit some of the proofs. The first two lemmas are concerned with the basic problem of deciding whether $(X, Y) \in Mod^{B'}_{A'}(P)$, where A' and B' stand for A or A^c and B or B^c, respectively.

Lemma 1. *The following problems are in the class coNP: Given a program P, and sets X, Y, A, and B, decide whether (i) $(X, Y) \in Mod^{B}_{A^c}(P)$; (ii) $(X, Y) \in Mod^{B^c}_{A}(P)$; (iii) $(X, Y) \in Mod^{B^c}_{A^c}(P)$.*

Proof: We first show that the complementary problem to decide whether $(X, Y) \notin Mod^{B}_{A^c}(P)$ is in NP. To this end, we observe that $(X, Y) \notin Mod^{B}_{A^c}(P)$ if and only if at least one of the following conditions holds: (1) $Y \notin Mod_{A^c}(P)$, (2) $X \not\subseteq Y|_{A^c \cup B}$ (3) there is $Z \subset Y$ such that $Z|_{A^c \cup B} = Y|_{A^c \cup B}$ and $Z \models P$, (4) there is $Z \subset Y$ such that $Z|_B = X|_B$, $Z|_{A^c} \supseteq X|_{A^c}$ and $Z \models P$, (5) $X|_B = Y|_B$ and $Y \setminus T_P(Y) \not\subseteq X$. We note that verifying any condition involving A^c can be reformulated in terms of A. For instance, for every set V, we have $V|_{A^c} = V \setminus A$, and $V \subseteq A^c$ if and only if $V \cap A = \emptyset$. Thus, the conditions (1), (2) and (5) can be decided in polynomial time. Conditions (3) and (4) can be decided by a nondeterministic polynomial time algorithm. Indeed, once we nondeterministically guess Z, all other tests can be decided in polynomial time. The proofs for the remaining two claims use the same ideas and differ only in technical details depending on which of A and B is subject to the complement operation.   □

Lemma 2. *For every finite set $B \subseteq At$, the following problems are in the class Pol: given a program P, and sets X, Y and A, decide whether (i) $(X, Y) \in Mod_{A^c}^{B^c}(P)$; (ii) $(X, Y) \in Mod_{A}^{B^c}(P)$.*

Proof: In each case, the argument follows the same lines as that for Lemma 1. The difference is in the case of the conditions (3) and (4). Under the assumptions of this lemma, they can be decided in *deterministic* polynomial time. Indeed, let us note that there are no more than $2^{|B|}$ sets Z such that $Z|_{A^c \cup B^c} = Y|_{A^c \cup B^c}$ (or, for the second problem, such that $Z|_{A \cup B^c} = Y|_{A \cup B^c}$). Since B is finite and fixed, the condition (3) can be checked in polynomial time by a simple enumeration of all possible sets Z such that $Z \subset Y$ and $Z|_{A^c \cup B^c} = Y|_{A^c \cup B^c}$ and checking for each of them whether $Z \models P$. For the condition (4), the argument is similar. Since Z is constrained by $Z|_{B^c} = X|_{B^c}$, there are no more than $2^{|B|}$ possible candidate sets Z to consider in this case, too.   □

The role of the next lemma is to show that $(X, Y) \in Mod_A^B(P)$ implies constraints on X and Y.

Lemma 3. *Let P be a program and $A, B \subseteq At$. If $(X, Y) \in Mod_A^B(P)$ then $X \subseteq Y \subseteq At(P) \cup A$.*

Lemma 3 is too weak for the membership results for complement-direct and complement-complement problems, as for these two types of problems, it only limits Y to subsets of $At(P) \cup A^c$, which is infinite. To handle these two classes of problems we use the following lemma that can be derived from Theorem 2.

Lemma 4. *Let P, Q be programs and $A, B \subseteq At$. If $(X, Y) \in Mod_{A^c}^B(P) \setminus Mod_{A^c}^{B^c}(Q)$ then there is $(X', Y') \in Mod_{A^c}^B(P) \setminus Mod_{A^c}^B(Q)$ such that $Y' \subseteq At(P \cup Q) \cup A$. If $(X, Y) \in Mod_{A^c}^B(P)$ and $T_P(Y)|_B \neq T_Q(Y)|_B$, then there is $(X', Y') \in Mod_{A^c}^B(P)$ such that $T_P(Y')|_B \neq T_Q(Y')|_B$ and $Y' \subseteq At(P \cup Q) \cup A$.*

Theorem 6. *The following problems are contained in the class Π_2^P: SUPPMIN$_{c,d}(\cdot, \cdot)$, SUPPMIN$_{c,c}(\cdot, \cdot)$ and SUPPMIN$_{d,c}(\cdot, \cdot)$. The following problems are in the class coNP: SUPPMIN$_{d,c}(\cdot, B)$, SUPPMIN$_{c,c}(\cdot, B)$, SUPPMIN$_{c,c}(\emptyset, \cdot)$ and SUPPMIN$_{c,d}(\emptyset, \cdot)$.*

Proof: We provide a detailed argument for the problem SUPPMIN$_{c,d}(\cdot, \cdot)$. Clearly, P and Q are not suppmin-equivalent relative to $\mathcal{HB}(A^c, B)$ if and only if there is $(X, Y) \in Mod_{A^c}^B(P) \div Mod_{A^c}^B(Q)$, or $(X, Y) \in Mod_{A^c}^B(P)$ and $T_P(Y)|_B \neq T_Q(Y)|_B$. By Lemma 4, P and Q are not suppmin-equivalent relative to $\mathcal{HB}(A^c, B)$ if and only if there is (X, Y) such that $X \subseteq Y \subseteq At(P \cup Q) \cup A$ and $(X, Y) \in Mod_{A^c}^B(P) \div Mod_{A^c}^B(Q)$, or $(X, Y) \in Mod_{A^c}^B(P)$ and $T_P(Y)|_B \neq T_Q(Y)|_B$.

Thus, to decide the complementary problem, it suffices to guess $X, Y \subseteq At(P \cup Q) \cup A$ and check that $(X, Y) \in Mod_{A^c}^B(P) \div Mod_{A^c}^B(Q)$, or that (X, Y) is in both sets and $T_P(Y)|_B \neq T_Q(Y)|_B$. The first task can be decided by NP oracles (Lemma 1(i)) and testing $T_P(Y)|_B \neq T_Q(Y)|_B$ can be accomplished in polynomial time.

The remaining arguments are similar. The only differences are: For $\text{SUPPMIN}_{d,c}(\cdot,\cdot)$ and $\text{SUPPMIN}_{d,c}(\cdot, B)$ we use Lemma 3 to ensure that the decision algorithm can restrict in the guessing phase to pairs (X, Y) with $Y \subseteq At(P \cup Q) \cup A$; for $\text{SUPPMIN}_{d,c}(\cdot,\cdot)$ and $\text{SUPPMIN}_{c,c}(\cdot,\cdot)$, we use Lemma 1(ii)-(iii); to obtain a stronger upper bound for $\text{SUPPMIN}_{d,c}(\cdot, B)$ and $\text{SUPPMIN}_{c,c}(\cdot, B)$, we make use of Lemma 2. The result for $\text{SUPPMIN}_{c,d}(\emptyset, \cdot)$ was settled in [24] (although not directly, the case of $\text{SUPPMIN}_{c,c}(\emptyset, \cdot)$ follows also from [24]; we provide details in the full version). For problems involving B^c, we test $T_P(Y)|_{B^c} = T_Q(Y)|_{B^c}$ by comparing $T_P(Y) \setminus B$ and $T_Q(Y) \setminus B$.   □

Suppmin-equivalence — lower bounds and exact complexity results. To illustrate methods we use to obtain our results, we will provide full details for the case of direct-complement problems. For the other two types of problems, we only state the results.

Theorem 7. *The problem* $\text{SUPPMIN}_{d,c}(A, \cdot)$ *is* Π_2^P*-hard.*

Proof: Let $\forall Y \exists X \varphi$ be a QBF, where φ is a CNF formula over $X \cup Y$. We can assume that $A \cap X = \emptyset$ (if not, variables in X can be renamed). Next, we can assume that $A \subseteq Y$ (if not, add "dummy" tautology clauses to φ). We will construct programs $P(\varphi)$ and $Q(\varphi)$, and a set B, so that $\forall Y \exists X \varphi$ is true if and only if $P(\varphi)$ and $Q(\varphi)$ are suppmin-equivalent relative to $\mathcal{HB}(A, B^c)$. Since the problem to decide whether a given QBF $\forall Y \exists X \varphi$ is true is Π_2^P-complete, the assertion will follow.

For every atom $z \in X \cup Y$, we introduce a fresh atom z'. Given a set of "non-primed" atoms Z, we define $Z' = \{z' \mid z \in Z\}$. In particular, $A \cap (Y' \cup X') = \emptyset$. We use $\hat{c}$ as in the proof of Theorem 5 and define the following programs:

$$P(\varphi) = \{z \leftarrow not\ z';\ z' \leftarrow not\ z \mid z \in X \cup Y\} \cup \{\leftarrow y, y' \mid y \in Y\} \cup$$
$$\{x \leftarrow u, u';\ x' \leftarrow u, u' \mid x, u \in X\} \cup$$
$$\{x \leftarrow \hat{c};\ x' \leftarrow \hat{c} \mid x \in X, c\ \text{is a clause in}\ \varphi\};$$
$$Q(\varphi) = \{z \leftarrow not\ z';\ z' \leftarrow not\ z \mid z \in X \cup Y\} \cup \{\leftarrow z, z' \mid z \in X \cup Y\} \cup$$
$$\{\leftarrow \hat{c} \mid c\ \text{is a clause in}\ \varphi\}.$$

To simplify notation, from now on we write P for $P(\varphi)$ and Q for $Q(\varphi)$. We also define $B = X \cup X' \cup Y \cup Y'$. We observe that $At(P) = At(Q) = B$.

One can check that the models of Q contained in B are sets of type

1. $I \cup (Y \setminus I)' \cup J \cup (X \setminus J)'$, where $J \subseteq X$, $I \subseteq Y$ and $I \cup J \models \varphi$.

Each model of Q is also a model of P but P has additional models contained in B, viz.

2. $I \cup (Y \setminus I)' \cup X \cup X'$, for *each* $I \subseteq Y$.

Clearly, for each model M of Q such that $M \subseteq B$, $T_Q(M) = M$. Similarly, for each model M of P such that $M \subseteq B$, $T_P(M) = M$.

From these comments, it follows that for every model M of Q (resp. P), $T_Q(M) = M \cap B$ (resp. $T_P(M) = M \cap B$). Thus, for every model M of both P and Q, $T_Q(M)|_{B^c} = T_P(M)|_{B^c}$. It follows that P and Q are suppmin-equivalent with respect to $\mathcal{HB}(A, B^c)$ if and only if $Mod_A^{B^c}(P) = Mod_A^{B^c}(Q)$ (indeed, we recall that if $(N, M) \in Mod_A^{B^c}(R)$ then M is a model of R).

Let us assume that $\forall Y \exists X \varphi$ is false. Hence, there exists an assignment $I \subseteq Y$ to atoms Y such that for every $J \subseteq X$, $I \cup J \not\models \varphi$. Let $N = I \cup (Y \setminus I)' \cup X \cup X'$. We will show that $(N|_{A \cup B^c}, N) \in Mod_A^{B^c}(P)$.

Since N is a supported model of P, $N \in Mod_A(P)$. The requirement (2) for $(N|_{A \cup B^c}, N) \in Mod_A^{B^c}(P)$ is evident. The requirement (5) holds, since $N \setminus T_P(N) = \emptyset$. By the property of I, N is a minimal model of P. Thus, the requirements (3) and (4) hold, too. It follows that $(N|_{A \cup B^c}, N) \in Mod_A^{B^c}(P)$, as claimed. Since N is not a model of Q, $(N|_{A \cup B^c}, N) \notin Mod_A^{B^c}(Q)$.

Let us assume that $\forall Y \exists X \varphi$ is true. First, observe that $Mod_A^{B^c}(Q) \subseteq Mod_A^{B^c}(P)$. Indeed, let $(M, N) \in Mod_A^{B^c}(Q)$. It follows that N is a model of Q and, consequently, of P. From our earlier comments, it follows that $T_Q(N) = T_P(N)$. Since $N \setminus T_Q(N) \subseteq A$, $N \setminus T_P(N) \subseteq A$. Thus, $N \in Mod_A(P)$. Moreover, if $M|_{B^c} = N|_{B^c}$ then $N \setminus T_Q(N) \subseteq M$ and, consequently, $N \setminus T_P(N) \subseteq M$. Thus, the requirement (5) for $(M, N) \in Mod_A^{B^c}(P)$ holds. The condition $M \subseteq N|_{A \cup B^c}$ is evident (it holds as $(M, N) \in Mod_A^{B^c}(Q)$). Since N is a model of Q, $N = N' \cup V$, where N' is a model of type 1 and $V \subseteq At \setminus B$. Thus, every model $Z \subset N$ of P is also a model of Q. It implies that the requirements (3) and (4) for $(M, N) \in Mod_A^{B^c}(P)$ hold. Hence, $(M, N) \in Mod_A^{B^c}(P)$ and, consequently, $Mod_A^{B^c}(Q) \subseteq Mod_A^{B^c}(P)$.

We will now use the assumption that $\forall Y \exists X \varphi$ is true to prove the converse inclusion. To this end, let us consider $(M, N) \in Mod_A^{B^c}(P)$. If $N = N' \cup V$, where N' is of type 1 and $V \subseteq At \setminus B$, then arguing as above, one can show that $(M, N) \in Mod_A^{B^c}(Q)$. Therefore, let us assume that $N = N' \cup V$, where N' is of type 2 and $V \subseteq At \setminus B$. More specifically, let $N' = I \cup (Y \setminus I)' \cup X \cup X'$. By our assumption, there is $J \subseteq X$ such that $I \cup J \models \varphi$. That is, $Z = I \cup (Y \setminus I)' \cup J \cup (X \setminus J)'$ is a model of P. Clearly, $Z \subset N$. Moreover, since $Z, N \subseteq B$, we have $Z|_{A \cup B^c} = N|_{A \cup B^c}$. Since $(M, N) \in Mod_A^{B^c}(P)$, the requirement (3) implies that Z is not a model of P, a contradiction. Hence, the latter case is impossible and $Mod_A^{B^c}(P) \subseteq Mod_A^{B^c}(Q)$ follows.

We proved that $\forall Y \exists X \varphi$ is true if and only if $Mod_A^{B^c}(P) = Mod_A^{B^c}(Q)$. This completes the proof of the assertion. $\qquad\square$

Theorem 8. *The problem* SUPPMIN$_{d,c}(A, B)$ *is coNP-hard.*

Proof: Consider a CNF φ over atoms Y, and the programs $P(\varphi)$ and $Q = \{f \leftarrow; \leftarrow f\}$ from the proof of Theorem 5. We use P for $P(\varphi)$ in the following. We already know that P has a model if and only if φ is true. We now show that $Mod_A^{B^c}(P) \neq \emptyset$ if and only if φ is true. Since $Mod_A^{B^c}(Q) = \emptyset$ holds (as is easily seen), the assertion follows by Theorem 2.

Let us assume that P has a model. Then P has a model, say M, such that $M \subseteq Y \cup Y'$. We show that $(M, M) \in Mod_A^{B^c}(P)$. Indeed, since $T_P(M) = M$, $M \in Mod_A(P)$. Also, since $Y \cup Y' \subseteq B^c$, $M|_{A \cup B^c} = M$ and so, $M \subseteq M|_{A \cup B^c}$. Lastly, $M \setminus T_P(M) = \emptyset \subseteq M$. Thus, the conditions (1), (2) and (5) for $(M, M) \in Mod_A^{B^c}(P)$ hold. Since $M|_{A \cup B^c} = M$ and $M|_{B^c} = M$, there is no $Z \subset M$ such that $Z|_{A \cup B^c} = M|_{A \cup B^c}$ or $Z|_{B^c} = M|_{B^c}$. Thus, also conditions (3) and (4) hold, and $Mod_A^{B^c}(P) \neq \emptyset$ follows. Conversely, let $Mod_A^{B^c}(P) \neq \emptyset$ and let $(N, M) \in Mod_A^{B^c}(P)$. Then $M \in Mod_A(P)$ and, in particular, M is a model of P. $\qquad\square$

Combining Theorems 7 and 8 with Theorem 6 yields the following result that fully determines the complexity of direct-complement problems.

Corollary 2. *The problems* SUPPMIN$_{d,c}(A, \cdot)$ *and* SUPPMIN$_{d,c}(\cdot, \cdot)$ *are* Π_2^P-*complete. The problems* SUPPMIN$_{d,c}(A, B)$ *and* SUPPMIN$_{d,c}(\cdot, B)$ *are coNP-complete.*

This concludes the more detailed discussion on the direct-complement problems. Next, we just give the corresponding results for the remaining settings we have to study for suppmin-equivalence, complement-complement and complement-direct problems.

Theorem 9. *With* $A \neq \emptyset$, SUPPMIN$_{c,c}(A, \cdot)$ *and* SUPPMIN$_{c,d}(A, B)$ *are* Π_2^P-*hard. The problems* SUPPMIN$_{c,c}(\emptyset, \cdot)$ *and* SUPPMIN$_{c,c}(A, B)$ *are coNP-hard.*

Combining Theorem 9 with Theorem 6 yields the following corollary completing the picture of the complexity for suppmin-equivalence. The coNP-completeness results for the complement-direct problems were already proved in [24].

Corollary 3. *The problems* SUPPMIN$_{c,c}(\cdot, \cdot)$, SUPPMIN$_{c,d}(\cdot, B)$ *and* SUPPMIN$_{c,d}(\cdot, \cdot)$ *are* Π_2^P-*complete. For* $A \neq \emptyset$, *also the problems* SUPPMIN$_{c,c}(A, \cdot)$, SUPPMIN$_{c,d}(A, B)$ *and* SUPPMIN$_{c,d}(A, \cdot)$, *are* Π_2^P-*complete. Moreover, the following problems are coNP-complete:* SUPPMIN$_{c,c}(\emptyset, \cdot)$, SUPPMIN$_{c,c}(A, B)$, SUPPMIN$_{c,c}(\cdot, B)$, SUPPMIN$_{c,d}(\emptyset, \cdot)$ *and* SUPPMIN$_{c,d}(\emptyset, B)$.

6   Stable-Equivalence

We turn now to stable-equivalence. Here we also consider direct-direct problems as, in the case of fixed alphabets, they were not considered in [20].

Upper bounds. The following lemmas mirror the respective results from the previous section but show some interesting differences.

Lemma 5. *The following problems are in the class* D^P *in general[5] and in the class Pol for normal programs: Given a program P, and sets X, Y, A, and B, decide whether (i)* $(X, Y) \in SE_A^B(P)$; *(ii)* $(X, Y) \in SE_{A^c}^B(P)$; *(iii)* $(X, Y) \in SE_A^{B^c}(P)$; *(iv)* $(X, Y) \in SE_{A^c}^{B^c}(P)$.

Lemma 6. *For every finite sets $A, B \subseteq At$, the following problem is in the class Pol: given a program P, and sets X, Y decide whether* $(X, Y) \in SE_{A^c}^{B^c}(P)$.

Hence, polynomial-time model-checking for *disjunctive* programs is only possible for the set $SE_{A^c}^{B^c}(P)$. Compared to Lemma 2, this is due to the more involved condition (4) for $SE_{A^c}^{B^c}(P)$. For *normal* programs the reduct P^Y is a Horn program, which is essential for the tractability results in Lemma 5.

  The following lemmas hold for both disjunctive and normal programs.

Lemma 7. *Let P be a program and $A, B \subseteq At$. If $(X, Y) \in SE_A^B(P)$ then $X \subseteq Y \subseteq At(P) \cup A$.*

---

[5] The class D^P consists of all problems expressible as the conjunction of a problem in NP and a problem in coNP. However, this slight increase of complexity compared to Lemma 1 does not influence the subsequent Π_2^P-membership results, since a D^P-oracle amounts to an NP-oracle.

Lemma 8. *Let P, Q be programs and $A, B \subseteq At$. If $(X, Y) \in SE^B_{A^c}(P) \setminus SE^B_{A^c}(Q)$ then there is $(X', Y') \in SE^B_{A^c}(P) \setminus SE^B_{A^c}(Q)$ such that $Y' \subseteq At(P \cup Q) \cup A$.*

We can now use the similar arguments in the previous section to obtain the following collection of membership results:

Theorem 10. *The problem* STABLE$_{\delta, \varepsilon}(\cdot, \cdot)$, *is contained in the class Π^P_2, for any $\delta, \varepsilon \in \{c, d\}$;* STABLE$_{c,c}(A, B)$ *is contained in the class coNP. The problem* STABLE$^n_{\delta, \varepsilon}(\cdot, \cdot)$, *is contained in the class coNP for any $\delta, \varepsilon \in \{c, d\}$.*

Stable-equivalence — lower bounds and exact complexity results. We start with hardness for normal programs.

Theorem 11. *The problem* STABLE$^n_{\delta, \varepsilon}(A, B)$ *is coNP-hard for any $\delta, \varepsilon \in \{c, d\}$.*

Proof sketch: We use the standard reduction of UNSAT, thus let $P(\varphi)$ and Q be as in the proof of Theorem 5. It can be shown that $P(\varphi)$ has a stable model iff φ is satisfiable. Moreover, $P(\varphi) \cup R$ has no stable model (for arbitrary R) iff φ is not satisfiable. On the other hand, $Q \cup R$ has no stable model, for any R. Thus P is stable equivalent to Q relative to $\mathcal{C}$ iff φ is unsatisfiable, where $\mathcal{HB}(\emptyset, \emptyset) \subseteq \mathcal{C} \subseteq \mathcal{HB}(At, At)$, and thus where $\mathcal{C}$ is an arbitrary class. Hence, the result holds in particular for the desired classes. □

We now turn to the case of disjunctive programs. We note that coNP-hardness for STABLE$_{c,c}(A, B)$ follows immediately from the previous result. The remaining hardness results can be shown by suitable adaptations of the reductions used in [17].

Theorem 12. *The following problems are hard for the class Π^P_2:* STABLE$_{d,d}(A, B)$, STABLE$_{c,d}(A, B)$, STABLE$_{d,c}(A, B)$, STABLE$_{c,c}(A, \cdot)$, *and* STABLE$_{c,c}(\cdot, B)$.

Combining Theorems 11 and 12 with Theorem 10 yields the following corollary for the complete picture of the complexity for stable-equivalence.

Corollary 4. *The following problems are Π^P_2-complete for any combination of $\delta, \varepsilon \in \{c, d\}$:* STABLE$_{\delta, \varepsilon}(\cdot, \cdot)$, STABLE$_{\delta, \varepsilon}(A, \cdot)$, STABLE$_{\delta, \varepsilon}(\cdot, B)$. *As well,* STABLE$_{d,d}(A, B)$, STABLE$_{c,d}(A, B)$ *and* STABLE$_{d,c}(A, B)$ *are Π^P_2-complete, while* STABLE$_{c,c}(A, B)$ *is coNP-complete. The problem* STABLE$^n_{\delta, \varepsilon}(\alpha, \beta)$ *is coNP-complete, for any combination of $\delta, \varepsilon \in \{c, d\}$, $\alpha \in \{A, \cdot\}$, $\beta \in \{B, \cdot\}$.*

7   Discussion

We studied the complexity of deciding relativized hyperequivalence of programs under the semantics of stable, supported and supported minimal models. We focused on problems SEM$_{\delta, \epsilon}(\alpha, \beta)$, where at least one of δ and ϵ equals c, that is, at least one of the alphabets for the context problems is determined as the complement of the corresponding set A or B. As we noted, such problems arise naturally in the context of modular design of logic programs, yet they have received essentially no attention so far.

Table 1 summarizes the results. It shows that the problems concerning supp-equivalence (no normality restriction), and stable-equivalence for normal programs are all

Table 1. Complexity of $\mathrm{SEM}_{\delta,\varepsilon}(\alpha,\beta)$; all entries are completeness results

δ	ε	α	β	SUPP	SUPPMIN	STABLE	STABLE^n
d	c		$\cdot$	coNP	Π_2^P	Π_2^P	coNP
d	c		B	coNP	coNP	Π_2^P	coNP
c	c	$\cdot$ or $A \neq \emptyset$	$\cdot$	coNP	Π_2^P	Π_2^P	coNP
c	c	$\emptyset$	$\cdot$	coNP	coNP	Π_2^P	coNP
c	c	$\cdot$	B	coNP	coNP	Π_2^P	coNP
c	c	A	B	coNP	coNP	coNP	coNP
c	d	$\cdot$ or $A \neq \emptyset$		coNP	Π_2^P	Π_2^P	coNP
c	d	$\emptyset$		coNP	coNP	Π_2^P	coNP

coNP-complete (as are the corresponding direct-direct problems, studied in [24] and here). The situation is more diversified for suppmin-equivalence and stable-equivalence (no normality restriction) with some problems being coNP- and others Π_2^P-complete. For suppmin-equivalence lower complexity requires that B be a part of problem specification, or that A be a part of problem specification and be set to $\emptyset$. For stable-equivalence, the lower complexity only holds for the complement-complement problem with both A and B fixed as part of the problem specification. We also note that the complexity of problems for stable-equivalence is always at least that for suppmin-equivalence. Furthermore, our complexity results suggest possible algorithms for testing the equivalence notions under consideration. One such approach is to reduce the given characterizations to quantified Boolean formulas (QBFs) along the lines of previous work, e.g. [22], and then use extant solvers for QBFs to decide equivalence.

There are several questions worthy of further investigations. For instance, while stable-equivalence when only parts of models are compared was studied [21,22], no similar results are available for supp- and suppmin-equivalence. Also the complexity of the corresponding complement-direct, direct-complement and complement-complement problems for the three semantics in that setting has yet to be established.

Acknowledgments

We acknowledge support from the NSF (grant IIS-0325063), the KSEF (grant KSEF-1036-RDE-008), and the Austrian Science Fund (grants P18019-N04, P20704-N18).

References

1. Marek, V., Truszczyński, M.: Stable models and an alternative logic programming paradigm. In: Apt, K., Marek, W., Truszczyński, M., Warren, D. (eds.) The Logic Programming Paradigm: A 25-Year Perspective, pp. 375–398. Springer, Berlin (1999)
2. Niemelä, I.: Logic programming with stable model semantics as a constraint programming paradigm. Annals of Mathematics and Artificial Intelligence 25, 241–273 (1999)
3. Gelfond, M., Leone, N.: Logic programming and knowledge representation – the A-prolog perspective. Artificial Intelligence 138, 3–38 (2002)
4. Baral, C.: Knowledge Representation, Reasoning and Declarative Problem Solving. Cambridge University Press, Cambridge (2003)

5. Gebser, M., Liu, L., Namasivayam, G., Neumann, A., Schaub, T., Truszczyński, M.: The first answer set programming system competition. In: Baral, C., Brewka, G., Schlipf, J. (eds.) LPNMR 2007. LNCS, vol. 4483, pp. 3–17. Springer, Heidelberg (2007)
6. Gelfond, M.: Representing knowledge in A-Prolog. In: Kakas, A., Sadri, F. (eds.) Computational Logic: Logic Programming and Beyond. LNCS, vol. 2408, pp. 413–451. Springer, Heidelberg (2002)
7. Janhunen, T.: Some (in)translatability results for normal logic programs and propositional theories. Journal of Applied Non-Classical Logics 16, 35–86 (2006)
8. Oikarinen, E., Janhunen, T.: Modular equivalence for normal logic programs. In: Proceedings of ECAI 2006, pp. 412–416. IOS Press, Amsterdam (2006)
9. Janhunen, T., Oikarinen, E., Tompits, H., Woltran, S.: Modularity aspects of disjunctive stable models. In: Baral, C., Brewka, G., Schlipf, J. (eds.) LPNMR 2007. LNCS, vol. 4483, pp. 175–187. Springer, Heidelberg (2007)
10. Gaifman, H., Shapiro, E.: Fully abstract compositional semantics for logic programs. In: Proceedings of POPL 1989, pp. 134–142 (1989)
11. Lifschitz, V., Turner, H.: Splitting a logic program. In: Proceedings of ICLP 1994, pp. 23–37 (1994)
12. Lifschitz, V., Pearce, D., Valverde, A.: Strongly equivalent logic programs. ACM Transactions on Computational Logic 2(4), 526–541 (2001)
13. Lin, F.: Reducing strong equivalence of logic programs to entailment in classical propositional logic. In: Proceedings of KR 2002, pp. 170–176. Morgan Kaufmann, San Francisco (2002)
14. Turner, H.: Strong equivalence made easy: nested expressions and weight constraints. Theory and Practice of Logic Programming 3, 609–622 (2003)
15. de Jongh, D., Hendriks, L.: Characterizations of strongly equivalent logic programs in intermediate logics. Theory and Practice of Logic Programming 3, 259–270 (2003)
16. Eiter, T., Fink, M.: Uniform equivalence of logic programs under the stable model semantics. In: Palamidessi, C. (ed.) ICLP 2003. LNCS, vol. 2916, pp. 224–238. Springer, Heidelberg (2003)
17. Eiter, T., Fink, M., Woltran, S.: Semantical characterizations and complexity of equivalences in answer set programming. ACM Transactions on Computational Logic 8, 53 (2007)
18. Sagiv, Y.: Optimizing datalog programs. In: Minker, J. (ed.) Foundations of Deductive Databases and Logic Programming, pp. 659–698. Morgan Kaufmann, San Francisco (1988)
19. Inoue, K., Sakama, C.: Equivalence of logic programs under updates. In: Alferes, J.J., Leite, J. (eds.) JELIA 2004. LNCS, vol. 3229, pp. 174–186. Springer, Heidelberg (2004)
20. Woltran, S.: A common view on strong, uniform, and other notions of equivalence in answer-set programming. Theory and Practice of Logic Programming 8, 217–234 (2008)
21. Eiter, T., Tompits, H., Woltran, S.: On solution correspondences in answer-set programming. In: Proceedings of IJCAI 2005, pp. 97–102. Morgan Kaufmann, San Francisco (2005)
22. Oetsch, J., Tompits, H., Woltran, S.: Facts do not cease to exist because they are ignored: Relativised uniform equivalence with answer-set projection. In: Proceedings of AAAI 2007, pp. 458–464. AAAI Press, Menlo Park (2007)
23. Cabalar, P., Odintsov, S., Pearce, D., Valverde, A.: Analysing and extending well-founded and partial stable semantics using partial equilibrium logic. In: Etalle, S., Truszczyński, M. (eds.) ICLP 2006. LNCS, vol. 4079, pp. 346–360. Springer, Heidelberg (2006)
24. Truszczyński, M., Woltran, S.: Hyperequivalence of logic programs with respect to supported models. In: Proceedings of AAAI 2008, pp. 560–565. AAAI Press, Menlo Park (2008)
25. Clark, K.: Negation as failure. In: Gallaire, H., Minker, J. (eds.) Logic and Data Bases, pp. 293–322. Plenum Press, New York (1978)
26. Erdogan, S., Lifschitz, V.: Definitions in answer set programming. In: LPNMR 2004. LNCS (LNAI), vol. 2923, pp. 114–126. Springer, Heidelberg (2004)
27. Apt, K.: Logic programming. In: van Leeuven, J. (ed.) Handbook of Theoretical Computer Science, pp. 493–574. Elsevier, Amsterdam (1990)

Program Correspondence under the Answer-Set Semantics: The Non-ground Case*

Johannes Oetsch and Hans Tompits

Institut für Informationssysteme,
Arbeitsbereich Wissensbasierte Systeme 184/3,
Technische Universität Wien,
Favoritenstraße 9-11, A-1040 Vienna, Austria
{oetsch,tompits}@kr.tuwien.ac.at

Abstract. The study of various notions of equivalence between logic programs in the area of answer-set programming (ASP) gained increasing interest in recent years. The main reason for this undertaking is that ordinary equivalence between answer-set programs fails to yield a replacement property similar to the one of classical logic. Although many refined program correspondence notions have been introduced in the ASP literature so far, most of these notions were studied for propositional programs only, which limits their practical usability as concrete programming applications require the use of variables. In this paper, we address this issue and introduce a general framework for specifying parameterised notions of program equivalence for non-ground disjunctive logic programs under the answer-set semantics. Our framework is a generalisation of a similar one defined previously for the propositional case and allows the specification of several equivalence notions extending well-known ones studied for propositional programs. We provide semantic characterisations for instances of our framework generalising uniform equivalence, and we study decidability and complexity aspects. Furthermore, we consider axiomatisations of such correspondence problems by means of polynomial translations into second-order logic.

1 Introduction

Logic programs under the answer-set semantics are an established means for declarative knowledge representation and nonmonotonic reasoning as well as for declarative problem solving. Their characteristic feature regarding the way problems are represented, viz. that *models* represent solutions to problems and not *proofs* as in traditional logic-oriented languages (hence, the intended models are the "answer sets" for the problem), led to the coinage of the term *answer-set programming* (ASP) for this particular paradigm. Several highly sophisticated ASP solvers exist, like DLV [1] or GNT [2], and typical application areas of ASP are configuration, information integration, security analysis, agent systems, Semantic Web, and planning.

A recent line of research in ASP deals with the investigation of different notions of equivalence between answer-set programs, initiated by the seminal paper by Lifschitz, Pearce, and Valverde [3] on *strong equivalence*. The main reason for the introduction of

---

* This work was partially supported by the Austrian Science Fund (FWF) under grant P18019.

M. Garcia de la Banda and E. Pontelli (Eds.): ICLP 2008, LNCS 5366, pp. 591–605, 2008.

these notions is the fact that *ordinary equivalence*, which checks whether two programs have the same answer sets, is too weak to yield a replacement property similar to the one of classical logic. That is to say, given a program R along with some subprogram $P \subseteq R$, when replacing P with an equivalent program Q, it is not guaranteed that $Q \cup (R \setminus P)$ is equivalent to R. Clearly, this is undesirable for tasks like modular programming or program optimisation. Strong equivalence does circumvent this problem, essentially by definition—two programs P, Q are strongly equivalent iff, for any program R (the "context program"), $P \cup R$ and $Q \cup R$ have the same answer sets—, but is too restrictive for certain aspects. A more liberal notion is *uniform equivalence* [4], which is defined similar to strong equivalence but where the context programs are restricted to contain facts only.[1] However, both notions do not take standard programming techniques like the use of local predicates into account, which may occur in subprograms but which are ignored in the final computation. Thus, these notions do not admit the *projection* of answer sets to a set of designated output letters. For example, consider the two programs $P = \{r(x) \leftarrow s(x)\}$ and $Q = \{aux(x) \leftarrow s(x); \ r(x) \leftarrow aux(x)\}$. While P expresses that $r(x)$ is selected whenever $s(x)$ is known, Q yields the selection of $r(x)$ via the auxiliary predicate $aux(x)$. P and Q are not uniformly equivalent (as P and Q conjoined with any fact $aux(\cdot)$ have differing answer sets), and hence they are not strongly equivalent, but they are if the context programs do not contain aux which also has to be ignored in the comparison of the answer sets.

To accommodate such features, strong and uniform equivalence were further relaxed and generalised. On the one hand, Woltran [7] introduced *relativised* versions thereof, where the alphabet of the context can be parameterised (e.g., in the above example, we could specify contexts disallowing the use of the predicate symbol aux). On the other hand, Eiter *et al.* [8] introduced a general framework for specifying parameterisable program correspondence notions, allowing not only relativised contexts but also answer-set projection. Other forms of refined program equivalence are, e.g., *modular equivalence* [9] and *update equivalence* [10].

However, most of the above mentioned notions were introduced and analysed for propositional programs only, which is clearly a limiting factor given that practical programming purposes require the use of variables. In this paper, we address this point and introduce a general program correspondence framework for the non-ground case, lifting the propositional one by Eiter *et al.* [8]. Similar to the latter, program correspondence notions can be parameterised along two dimensions: one for specifying the kind of programs that are allowed as context for program comparison, and one for specifying a particular comparison relation between answer sets, determining which predicates should be considered for the program comparison. The framework allows to capture a range of different program equivalence notions, including the propositional ones mentioned above as well as non-ground versions of strong and uniform equivalence studied already in the literature [11,12,13].

We pay particular attention to correspondence problems which we refer to as *generalised query inclusion problems* (GQIPs) and *generalised query equivalence problems*

---

[1] We note that the concept of strong equivalence was actually first studied in the context of (negation free) datalog programs by Maher [5] using the term "equivalence as program segments", and likewise uniform equivalence was first studied for datalog programs by Sagiv [6].

(GQEPs), respectively. These are extensions of notions studied in previous work [14] for propositional programs (there termed PQIPs and PQEPs—*propositional query inclusion problems* and *propositional query equivalence problems*). A GQEP basically amounts to *relativised uniform equivalence with projection*, whilst in a GQIP, set equality is replaced by set inclusion. Intuitively, if Q corresponds to P under a GQIP, then Q can be seen as a sound approximation of P under brave reasoning and P as a sound approximation of Q under cautious reasoning. GQEPs and GQIPS are relevant in a setting where programs are seen as queries over databases and one wants to decide whether two programs yield the same output database on each input database. Indeed, query equivalence as well as program equivalence emerge as special cases. Also, such versions of generalised uniform equivalence are appropriate in cases where programs are composed out of modules, arranged in layers, such that each module of a certain layer gets its input from higher-layered modules and provides its output to lower-layered modules.

We provide semantic characterisations of GQIPs and GQEPs in terms of structures associated with each program such that a GQIP holds iff the structures meet set inclusion, and a GQEP holds iff the associated structures coincide. Our characterisation differs from the well-known characterisation of (relativised) uniform equivalence in terms of (relativised) UE-models [4,7] in case the projection set is unrestricted. Furthermore, we study decidability and complexity issues for correspondence problems, showing in particular that relativised strong equivalence is undecidable, which is, in some sense, surprising because usual (unrelativised) strong equivalence is decidable both in the propositional and the non-ground case.

Finally, we study axiomatisations of GQIPs and GQEPs in terms of second-order logic (SOL), which is in the spirit of providing logical characterisations of program equivalence, following the seminal result by Lifschitz, Pearce, and Valverde [3] that strong equivalence between propositional programs coincides with equivalence in the logic of here-and-there, which is intermediate between classical logic and intuitionistic logic. Indeed, the use of SOL recently gained increasing interest in ASP as Ferraris, Lee, and Lifschitz [15] defined an answer-set semantics for general first-order theories in terms of SOL, avoiding the need of an explicit grounding step. As well, our SOL characterisations generalise results for axiomatising PQIPs and PQEPs by means of quantified propositional logic, which is just a restricted form of SOL.

2   Preliminaries

2.1   Logic Programs

We deal with *disjunctive logic programs* (DLPs) formulated in a function-free first-order language. Such a language is based on a vocabulary $\mathcal{V}$ defined as a pair $(\mathbb{P}, \mathbb{D})$, where $\mathbb{P}$ fixes a countable set of predicate symbols and $\mathbb{D}$, called the *LP-domain*, or simply *domain*, fixes a countable and non-empty set of constants.

As usual, each $p \in \mathbb{P}$ has an associated non-negative integer, called the *arity* of p. An *atom over* $\mathcal{V} = (\mathbb{P}, \mathbb{D})$ is an expression of form $p(t_1, \ldots, t_n)$, where p is a n-ary predicate symbol from $\mathbb{P}$ and each t_i, $0 \le i \le n$, is either from $\mathbb{D}$ or a variable. An atom is *ground* if it does not contain variables. By $HB_{\mathcal{V}}$ we denote the *Herbrand base* of $\mathcal{V}$, i.e., the set of all ground atoms over $\mathcal{V}$. For a set $A \subseteq \mathbb{P}$ of predicate symbols and a set $C \subseteq \mathbb{D}$ of constants, we also write $HB_{A,C}$ to denote the set of all ground atoms constructed from the predicate symbols from A and the constants from C.

A *rule over* $\mathscr{V}$ is an expression of form

$$a_1 \vee \cdots \vee a_l \leftarrow a_{l+1}, \ldots, a_m, \text{not } a_{m+1}, \ldots, \text{not } a_n, \tag{1}$$

where $n \geq m \geq l \geq 0$, $n > 0$, and all a_i, $0 \leq i \leq n$, are atoms over $\mathscr{V}$. A rule is *positive* if $m = n$, *normal* if $l = 1$, and *Horn* if it is positive and normal. A rule of form (1) with $l = m = n = 1$ is a *fact*; we usually identify a fact $a \leftarrow$ with the atom a. For each rule r of form (1), we call $\{a_1, \ldots, a_l\}$ the *head of r*. Moreover, we call $\{a_{l+1}, \ldots, a_m\}$ the *positive body of r* and $\{a_{m+1}, \ldots, a_n\}$ the *negative body of r*. A rule r is *safe* iff all variables that occur in the head of r or in the negative body of r also occur in the positive body of r. Finally, a rule is ground if it contains only ground atoms.

A program, P, is a finite set of safe rules over $\mathscr{V}$. We say that P is positive (resp., normal, Horn, ground) if all rules in P are positive (resp., normal, Horn, ground). Sometimes, we will call ground programs (resp., rules, atoms) *propositional*. For any program P, a predicate symbol p that does not occur in the head of any rule in P is *extensional* (in P), and *intensional* otherwise. We denote by $PS(P)$ the set of all predicate symbols occurring in a program P, and say that P is *over A* if $PS(P) \subseteq A$. The *Herbrand universe* of P, HU_P, is the set of all constant symbols occurring in P. For technical reasons, we assume that HU_P contains an arbitrary element from the domain of $\mathscr{V}$ in case P does not contain any constant symbol.

For any set $C \subseteq \mathbb{D}$ and any rule r, we define the *grounding of r with respect to C*, denoted by $grd(r,C)$, as the set of all rules obtained from r by uniformly replacing all variables occurring in r by constants from C. Furthermore, for a program P, the *grounding of P with respect to C*, denoted by $grd(P,C)$, is $\bigcup_{r \in P} grd(r,C)$. An *interpretation I* over a vocabulary $\mathscr{V}$ is a set of ground atoms over $\mathscr{V}$. Moreover, I is a *model* of a ground rule r, symbolically $I \models r$, iff, whenever the positive body of r is a subset of I and no elements from the negative body of r are in I, then some element from the head of r is in I. I is a model of a ground program P, in symbols $I \models P$, iff $I \models r$, for all r in P.

Following Gelfond and Lifschitz [16], the *reduct* P^I, where I is an interpretation and P is a ground program, is the program obtained from P by (i) deleting all rules containing a default negated atom not a such that $a \in I$ and (ii) deleting all default negated atoms in the remaining rules. An interpretation I is an *answer set* of a ground program P iff I is a subset-minimal model of the reduct P^I. The answer sets of a non-ground program P are the answer sets of the grounding of P with respect to the Herbrand universe of P. The collection of all answer sets of a program P is denoted by $AS(P)$.

For a vocabulary $\mathscr{V} = (\mathbb{P}, \mathbb{D})$ and a set $A \subseteq \mathbb{P}$, by $\mathscr{P}_{\mathscr{V}}^A$ we denote the set of all programs over $\mathscr{V}$ that contain only predicate symbols from A. The set $\mathscr{F}_{\mathscr{V}}^A$ is defined analogously except that the programs are additionally required to contain only facts. Note that since we assume safety of rules in programs, the facts in the elements of $\mathscr{F}_{\mathscr{V}}^A$ are therefore ground. When omitting A in $\mathscr{P}_{\mathscr{V}}^A$ or $\mathscr{F}_{\mathscr{V}}^A$, we assume that $A = \mathbb{P}$. We also use the following notation: For an interpretation I and a set S of interpretations, $S|_I$ is defined as $\{Y \cap I \mid Y \in S\}$. For a singleton set $S = \{Y\}$, we also write $Y|_I$ instead of $S|_I$.

We recall some basic equivalence notions for logic programs. To begin with, two programs P and Q are *ordinarily equivalent* iff $AS(P) = AS(Q)$. The more restrictive notions of *strong* and *uniform equivalence*, originally defined for propositional programs by Lifschitz, Pearce, and Valverde [3] and Eiter and Fink [4], respectively, are given as follows [12]: Let $\mathscr{V} = (\mathbb{P}, \mathbb{D})$ be a vocabulary and P, Q two programs over $\mathscr{V}$. Then, P and Q are strongly equivalent iff $AS(P \cup R) = AS(Q \cup R)$, for any program $R \in \mathscr{P}_\mathscr{V}$, and P and Q are uniformly equivalent iff $AS(P \cup F) = AS(Q \cup F)$, for any $F \in \mathscr{F}_\mathscr{V}$. We also recall two further equivalence notions, especially important in the context of deductive databases: *query equivalence* and *program equivalence*. Let $\mathscr{E}$ be the set of the extensional predicates of $P \cup Q$. Then, P and Q are query equivalent with respect to a predicate p iff, for any set $F \in \mathscr{F}_\mathscr{V}^\mathscr{E}$, $AS(P \cup F)|_{HB_{\{p\}, \mathbb{D}}} = AS(Q \cup F)|_{HB_{\{p\}, \mathbb{D}}}$. Furthermore, P and Q are program equivalent iff, for any set $F \in \mathscr{F}_\mathscr{V}^\mathscr{E}$, $AS(P \cup F) = AS(Q \cup F)$.

2.2 Second-Order Logic

Classical second-order logic (SOL) extends classical first-order logic (FOL) by admitting quantifications over predicate and function variables. For our purposes, it suffices to consider a version of SOL without function variables. More formally, we assume that the vocabulary of SOL contains denumerable sets of *individual variables*, *predicate variables*, *predicate constants*, and *individual constants*, as well as the truth constants $\top$ and $\bot$, the usual connectives $\neg$, $\wedge$, $\vee$, $\rightarrow$, and $\leftrightarrow$, and the quantifiers $\forall$ and $\exists$. Each predicate variable and predicate constant is assumed to have a non-negative arity.

We use $QX_1 \cdots X_n \Phi$, for $Q \in \{\forall, \exists\}$, as an abbreviation of $QX_1 \cdots QX_n \Phi$. Moreover, for any set $X = \{X_1, \ldots, X_n\}$ of variables, $QX\Phi$, $Q \in \{\forall, \exists\}$, abbreviates $QX_1 \cdots X_n \Phi$.

The semantics of SOL is defined in terms of *SOL-frames*. A SOL-frame is a tuple $\langle D, m \rangle$, where D is a non-empty set, called the *SOL-domain*, and m is an *interpretation function* that maps any predicate constant with arity n to a subset of D^n and any individual constant to an element of D. An *assignment over M* is a function a that maps any predicate variable with arity n to a subset of D^n and any individual variable to an element of D. If the domain of a SOL-frame M is countable and M meets the unique-names assumption, i.e., different constant symbols are interpreted by different objects from the domain, then M is a *Herbrand frame*. Constant symbols are interpreted by themselves in a Herbrand frame. The *truth-value* of a formula Φ in a SOL-frame M with respect to an assignment a over M is denoted by $V_a^M(\Phi)$ and is defined as usual.

A formula Φ is *satisfied* in a SOL-frame M by an assignment a over M iff $V_a^M(\Phi) = 1$. Moreover, Φ is *true* in M iff Φ is satisfied in M by every assignment over M. If Φ is true in M, M is a *model* of Φ. A formula is *satisfiable* iff it possesses at least one model and *unsatisfiable* otherwise. A formula that is true in all frames is called *valid*. A formula Φ is *consequence* of a set A of formulae, symbolically $A \models \Phi$ iff, for each SOL-frame M, Φ is true in M whenever each formula in A is true in M.

We tacitly assume in what follows that each variable in a program vocabulary $\mathscr{V}$ is an individual variable in our SOL-vocabulary, each predicate symbol in $\mathscr{V}$ is a predicate variable, and each constant in $\mathscr{V}$ is an individual constant.

3 A Unifying Correspondence-Framework

In this section, we introduce the central concept of our work, a general framework for specifying parameterised notions of program correspondence for non-ground programs, which allows to capture a range of different equivalence notions defined in the literature in a uniform manner. We first discuss the basic definitions and some elementary properties, afterwards we concentrate on a specific instance of our method, viz. on correspondence notions generalising uniform equivalence. We then provide model-theoretic characterisations for this particular family of correspondences and analyse some computational properties.

3.1   The Basic Framework and Its Instances

We start with our central definition, which is a lifting of a correspondence framework introduced by Eiter *et al.* [8] for propositional programs to the non-ground setting.

Definition 1. *By a* correspondence frame, *or simply a* frame, *F, we understand a triple $(\mathcal{V},\mathcal{C},\rho)$, where (i) $\mathcal{V}$ is a vocabulary, (ii) $\mathcal{C} \subseteq \mathcal{P}_{\mathcal{V}}$, called the* context class *of F, and (iii) $\rho \subseteq 2^{2^{HB_{\mathcal{V}}}} \times 2^{2^{HB_{\mathcal{V}}}}$.*

*For every program $P,Q \in \mathcal{P}_{\mathcal{V}}$, we say that P and Q are F-*corresponding, *symbolically $P \simeq_F Q$, iff, for all $R \in \mathcal{C}$, $(AS(P \cup R), AS(Q \cup R)) \in \rho$.*

In a frame $F = (\mathcal{V},\mathcal{C},\rho)$, $\mathcal{V}$ fixes the language under consideration, $\mathcal{C}$ is the class of possible extensions of the programs that are to be compared, and ρ represents the comparison relation between the sets of answer sets of the two programs.

Following Eiter *et al.* [8], a *correspondence problem*, Π, over a vocabulary $\mathcal{V}$ is a tuple $(P,Q,\mathcal{C},\rho)$, where P and Q are programs over $\mathcal{V}$ and $(\mathcal{V},\mathcal{C},\rho)$ is a frame. We say that $(P,Q,\mathcal{C},\rho)$ *holds* iff $P \simeq_{(\mathcal{V},\mathcal{C},\rho)} Q$.

Important instances of frames are those where the comparison relation is given by projective versions of set equality and set inclusion, where projection allows to ignore auxiliary ("local") atoms during comparison, and the context class is parameterised by a set of predicate symbols. More formally, for sets S,S' of interpretations, an interpretation B, and $\odot \in \{\subseteq,=\}$, we define $S \odot_B S'$ as $S|_B \odot S'|_B$. For any vocabulary $\mathcal{V} = (\mathbb{P},\mathbb{D})$ and any set $B \subseteq \mathbb{P}$, the relation $\sqsubseteq_{\mathcal{V}}^B$ is defined as $\subseteq_{HB_{B,\mathbb{D}}}$, and $=_{\mathcal{V}}^B$ denotes $=_{HB_{B,\mathbb{D}}}$. If B is omitted, it is assumed that $B = \mathbb{P}$. We call a correspondence problem over $\mathcal{V}$ of form $(P,Q,\mathcal{P}_{\mathcal{V}}^A,\sqsubseteq_{\mathcal{V}}^B)$ an *inclusion problem* and one of form $(P,Q,\mathcal{P}_{\mathcal{V}}^A,=_{\mathcal{V}}^B)$ an *equivalence problem*, for $A,B \subseteq \mathbb{P}$. Furthermore, for a correspondence problem of form $\Pi = (P,Q,\mathcal{C},=_{\mathcal{V}}^B)$, we set $\Pi_{\sqsubseteq} =_{df} (P,Q,\mathcal{C},\sqsubseteq_{\mathcal{V}}^B)$ and $\Pi_{\sqsupseteq} =_{df} (Q,P,\mathcal{C},\sqsubseteq_{\mathcal{V}}^B)$. Clearly, Π holds iff $\Pi_{\sqsubseteq}$ and $\Pi_{\sqsupseteq}$ jointly hold.

Example 1. Consider the programs P and Q from the introduction. The claim is that, for any program M with $P \subseteq M$, P can be replaced by Q within M without changing the answer sets of M, provided M does not contain $aux(\cdot)$ which is also ignored concerning the answer sets of M. This is represented in our framework by the fact that the correspondence problem $\Pi = (P,Q,\mathcal{P}_{\mathcal{V}}^A,=_{\mathcal{V}}^B)$, with $A = B = \{r,s\}$, holds.   □

With the above notation at hand, it is quite straightforward to express the equivalence notions introduced earlier:

Theorem 1. *Let P,Q be programs over a vocabulary $\mathcal{V}$ and $\mathcal{E}$ the set of the extensional predicates of $P \cup Q$. Then, P and Q are*

- *ordinarily equivalent iff* $(P,Q,\{\emptyset\},=)$ *holds,*
- *strongly equivalent iff* $(P,Q,\mathscr{P}_{\mathscr{V}},=)$ *holds,*
- *uniformly equivalent iff* $(P,Q,\mathscr{F}_{\mathscr{V}},=)$ *holds,*
- *query equivalent with respect to a predicate p iff* $(P,Q,\mathscr{F}_{\mathscr{V}}^{\mathscr{E}},\equiv_{\mathscr{V}}^{\{p\}})$ *holds, and*
- *program equivalent iff* $(P,Q,\mathscr{F}_{\mathscr{V}}^{\mathscr{E}},=)$ *holds.*

We mentioned that our definition of correspondence frames lifts that of Eiter *et al.* [8] introduced for propositional programs. Let us elaborate this point in more detail. A frame in the sense of Eiter *et al.* [8] (which we henceforth will refer to as a *propositional frame*) is a tuple $F = (\mathscr{U},\mathscr{C},\rho)$, where $\mathscr{U}$ is a set of propositional atoms, $\mathscr{C}$ is a set of propositional programs over $\mathscr{U}$, and $\rho \subseteq 2^{2^{\mathscr{U}}} \times 2^{2^{\mathscr{U}}}$ is a comparison relation. As in our case, two programs P and Q are F-corresponding, in symbols $P \simeq_F Q$, iff, for any $R \in \mathscr{C}$, $(AS(P \cup R), AS(Q \cup R)) \in \rho$. Consider now a propositional frame $F = (\mathscr{U},\mathscr{C},\rho)$ and define the vocabulary $\mathscr{V}_0 = (\mathscr{U},\mathbb{D})$, where the arity of each $p \in \mathscr{U}$ is 0, thus $\mathbb{D}$ has no influence on the language and can be fixed arbitrarily (but, of course, $\mathbb{D}$ is assumed to be non-empty). Then, $HB_{\mathscr{V}_0} = \mathscr{U}$, and so $F_0 = (\mathscr{V}_0,\mathscr{C},\rho)$ is a frame in the sense of Definition 1. Furthermore, for every program P,Q over $\mathscr{U}$, $P \simeq_F Q$ iff $P \simeq_{F_0} Q$.

Consequently, every equivalence notion expressible in terms of propositional frames is also expressible in terms of frames in our sense. Indeed, propositional frames capture the following notions from the literature defined for propositional programs only so far:

- *Relativised strong and uniform equivalence* [7]: Let $\mathscr{U}$ be a set of propositional atoms, $A \subseteq \mathscr{U}$, $\mathscr{P}^A$ the set of all propositional programs constructed from atoms in A, and $\mathscr{F}^A$ the subclass of $\mathscr{P}^A$ containing all programs over A comprised of facts only. Then, two programs P and Q over $\mathscr{U}$ are strongly equivalent relative to A iff they are $(\mathscr{U},\mathscr{P}^A,=)$-corresponding. Moreover, they are uniformly equivalent relative to A iff they are $(\mathscr{U},\mathscr{F}^A,=)$-corresponding. Clearly, if $A = \mathscr{U}$, relativised strong and uniform equivalence collapse to the usual versions of strong and uniform equivalence, respectively.
- *Propositional query equivalence and inclusion problems* [14]: Let $\mathscr{U}$ be a set of propositional atoms. A propositional query inclusion problem (PQIP) over $\mathscr{U}$ is defined as a correspondence problem of form $(P,Q,\mathscr{F}^A,\subseteq_B)$ over $\mathscr{U}$, and a propositional query equivalence problem (PQEP) over $\mathscr{U}$ is defined as a correspondence problem of form $(P,Q,\mathscr{F}^A,=_B)$ over $\mathscr{U}$, where P and Q are propositional programs over $\mathscr{U}$, $A,B \subseteq \mathscr{U}$, and $\mathscr{F}^A$ is as above. Clearly, for $B = \mathscr{U}$, the latter problems turn into checking uniform equivalence relative to A.

Hence, these notions are then just special cases of correspondence problems according to Definition 1. In what follows, we will in particular be interested in analysing non-ground pendants of PQIPs and PQEPs. We thus define:

Definition 2. *Let* $\mathscr{V} = (\mathbb{P},\mathbb{D})$ *be a vocabulary,* $A,B \subseteq \mathbb{P}$, *and* $P,Q \in \mathscr{P}_{\mathscr{V}}$. *Then,* $(P,Q,\mathscr{F}_{\mathscr{V}}^A,\subseteq_{\mathscr{V}}^B)$ *is a* generalised query inclusion problem *(GQIP) over* $\mathscr{V}$ *and* $(P,Q,\mathscr{F}_{\mathscr{V}}^A,\equiv_{\mathscr{V}}^B)$ *is a* generalised query equivalence problem *(GQEP) over* $\mathscr{V}$.

Hence, for a GQEP $\Pi = (P,Q,\mathscr{F}_{\mathscr{V}}^A,\equiv_{\mathscr{V}}^B)$, if $A = B = \mathbb{P}$, Π coincides with testing uniform equivalence between P and Q, and if just $B = \mathbb{P}$, Π amounts to testing the extension of relativised uniform equivalence for non-ground programs.

Example 2. Consider the following two programs:

$$P = \left\{ \begin{array}{l} sel(x) \vee nsel(x) \leftarrow s(x);\ \bot \leftarrow sel(x), sel(y), \text{not } eq(x,y); \\ some \leftarrow sel(x);\ \bot \leftarrow \text{not } some;\ eq(x,x) \leftarrow s(x) \end{array} \right\},$$

$$Q = \left\{ \begin{array}{l} nsel(x) \vee nsel(y) \leftarrow s(x), s(y), \text{not } eq(x,y); \\ sel(x) \leftarrow s(x), \text{not } nsel(x);\ eq(x,x) \leftarrow s(x) \end{array} \right\}.$$

Program P takes as input facts over s and non-deterministically selects one element of the set implicitly defined by s, i.e., each answer set of P contains exactly one fact $sel(c)$ where c is from that set. Program Q, being more compact than P, aims at the same task, but does it the same job for every input? To answer this question, consider the GQEP $\Pi = (P, Q, \mathscr{F}_{\mathscr{V}}^A, \equiv_{\mathscr{V}}^B)$, for $A = \{s\}$ and $B = \{sel\}$. Since $AS(P) = \emptyset$ but $AS(Q) = \{\emptyset\}$, it follows that Π does not hold. Having only *non-empty* input regarding s in mind, we can verify that $\Pi' = (P \cup \{s(a)\}, Q \cup \{s(a)\}, \mathscr{F}_{\mathscr{V}}^A, \equiv_{\mathscr{V}}^B)$ holds.   □

The next properties generalise similar results from the propositional setting [8].

Theorem 2 (Anti-Monotony). *Let F be a correspondence frame of form $(\mathscr{V}, \mathscr{C}, \equiv_{\mathscr{V}}^B)$. If two programs are F-corresponding, then they are also F'-corresponding, for any frame $F' = (\mathscr{V}, \mathscr{C}', \equiv_{\mathscr{V}}^{B'})$ with $\mathscr{C}' \subseteq \mathscr{C}$ and $B' \subseteq B$.*

Theorem 3 (Projective Invariance). *Let $\mathscr{V} = (\mathbb{P}, \mathbb{D})$ be a vocabulary and F a correspondence frame of form $(\mathscr{V}, \mathscr{P}_{\mathscr{V}}, =)$. Then, two programs are F-corresponding iff they are F'-corresponding, for any frame $F' = (\mathscr{V}, \mathscr{P}_{\mathscr{V}}, \equiv_{\mathscr{V}}^B)$ with $B \subseteq \mathbb{P}$.*

Note that the last result states that strong equivalence coincides with strong equivalence with projection, no matter what projection set is used.

3.2 Model-Based Characterisations of GQIPs and GQEPs

We now provide necessary and sufficient conditions for deciding GQIPs and GQEPs, based on model-theoretic concepts. This is along the lines of characterising strong equivalence in terms of *SE-models* [17] and uniform equivalence in terms of *UE-models* [4]. However, our characterisations of GQIPs and GQEPs are based on structures which are, in some sense, orthogonal to SE- and UE-models, extending the concepts introduced in previous work for propositional programs [14].

We start with introducing objects witnessing the failure of a GQIP or GQEP.

Definition 3. *A counterexample for a GQIP $\Pi = (P, Q, \mathscr{F}_{\mathscr{V}}^A, \sqsubseteq_{\mathscr{V}}^B)$ over some vocabulary $\mathscr{V}$ is a pair (X, Y) such that (i) $X \in \mathscr{F}_{\mathscr{V}}^A$, (ii) $Y \in AS(P \cup X)$, and (iii) there exists no interpretation Z over $\mathscr{V}$ such that $Z \equiv_{\mathscr{V}}^B Y$ and $Z \in AS(Q \cup X)$. Furthermore, a counterexample for a GQEP Π is a pair which is a counterexample for one of $\Pi_{\sqsubseteq}$ or $\Pi_{\sqsupseteq}$.*

Obviously, given a problem $\Pi = (P, Q, \mathscr{F}_{\mathscr{V}}^A, \odot_{\mathscr{V}}^B)$, where $\odot \in \{\sqsubseteq, \equiv\}$, Π does not hold iff there exists a counterexample for Π.

Example 3. Recall problem Π from Example 2, which does not hold. The pair $(\emptyset, \emptyset)$ is a counterexample for $\Pi_{\sqsupseteq}$ since $AS(Q \cup \emptyset) = \{\emptyset\}$ but $AS(P \cup \emptyset) = \emptyset$. On the other hand, $\Pi' = (P \cup \{s(a)\}, Q \cup \{s(a)\}, \mathscr{F}_{\mathscr{V}}^A, \equiv_{\mathscr{V}}^B)$ from the same example does hold and, accordingly, has no counterexamples.   □

Next, we introduce structures assigned to programs, rather than to PQIPs or PQEPs as counterexamples are, yielding our desired model-theoretic characterisation.

Definition 4. *Let* $\mathcal{V} = (\mathbb{P}, \mathbb{D})$ *be a vocabulary, $A, B \subseteq \mathbb{P}$, and P a program over $\mathcal{V}$. An A-B-wedge of P over $\mathcal{V}$ is a pair (X, Y) such that $X \in \mathscr{F}_{\mathcal{V}}^A$ and $Y \in AS(P \cup X)|_{HB_{B,\mathbb{D}}}$. The set of all A-B-wedges of P is denoted by $\omega_{A,B}(P)$.*

It is straightforward to check that there exists a counterexample for a GQIP $\Pi = (P, Q, \mathscr{F}_{\mathcal{V}}^A, \sqsubseteq_{\mathcal{V}}^B)$ iff an A-B-wedge of P exists that is not an A-B-wedge of Q. Hence:

Theorem 4. *For $\Pi = (P, Q, \mathscr{F}_{\mathcal{V}}^A, \odot_{\mathcal{V}}^B)$, with $\odot \in \{\sqsubseteq, \equiv\}$, we have that (i) Π holds iff $\omega_{A,B}(P) \subseteq \omega_{A,B}(Q)$, if $\odot$ is $\sqsubseteq$, and (ii) Π holds iff $\omega_{A,B}(P) = \omega_{A,B}(Q)$, if $\odot$ is $\equiv$.*

Example 4. Consider again problem Π' from Example 3. Then, $\omega_{A,B}(P) = \omega_{A,B}(Q) = \{(\emptyset, \{sel(a)\}), (\{s(a)\}, \{sel(a)\}), (\{s(a), s(b)\}, \{sel(a)\}), (\{s(a), s(b)\}, \{sel(b)\}), \dots\}$, witnessing that Π' holds.   □

We finally give a characterisation of wedges in terms of classical models of program reducts, extending a similar one for the propositional case [14].

Theorem 5. *Let $\mathcal{V} = (\mathbb{P}, \mathbb{D})$ be a vocabulary and P a program over $\mathcal{V}$. Then, (X, Y) is an A-B-wedge of P iff (i) $X \in \mathscr{F}_{\mathcal{V}}^A$, (ii) $Y \subseteq HB_{B,\mathbb{D}}$, and (iii) there exists an interpretation Y' over $\mathcal{V}$ such that $X \subseteq Y'$, $Y' \equiv_{\mathcal{V}}^B Y$, $Y' \models grd(P, HU_{P \cup X})$, and, for each X' with $X \subseteq X' \subset Y'$, $X' \not\models grd(P, HU_{P \cup X})^{Y'}$.*

3.3 Computability Issues

We continue with an analysis of the computational complexity of deciding correspondence problems. In particular, our primary aim is to draw a border between decidable and undecidable instances of the framework.

It was shown by Shmueli [18] that query equivalence for Horn programs over infinite domains is undecidable. This undecidability result was subsequently extended by Eiter *et al.* [12] to program equivalence and uniform equivalence for disjunctive logic programs under the answer-set semantics. Since these notions can be formulated as special instances within our framework, we immediately get the following result:

Theorem 6. *The problem of determining whether a given correspondence problem over some vocabulary holds is undecidable in general, even if the programs under consideration are positive or normal.*

Some important decidable instances of the framework are obtained by imposing certain restrictions on the language of the programs under consideration. First of all, if we only consider propositional frames, checking inclusion and equivalence problems is decidable; in fact, this task is Π_4^P-complete in general [8]. Moreover, the complexity of checking PQIPs and PQEPs is Π_3^P-complete [14].

Also, for vocabularies with a finite domain, correspondence problems are decidable. In such a setting, programs are compact representations of their groundings over that domain. Since the size of a grounding of a program is, in general, exponential in the size of the program, for problems over a finite domain, we immediately obtain an upper complexity bound for correspondence checking which is increased by one exponential compared to the propositional case. That is, for a vocabulary $\mathscr{V}$ with a finite domain, checking inclusion and equivalence problems over $\mathscr{V}$ has co-NEXPTIME$^{\Sigma_3^P}$ complexity, and checking GQIPs and GQEPs over $\mathscr{V}$ has co-NEXPTIME$^{\Sigma_2^P}$ complexity.

More relevant in practice than frames over finite domains or propositional vocabularies are frames over infinite domains. For this setting, some decidable instantiations were already singled out in the literature. For example, checking ordinary equivalence is decidable, being co-NEXPTIME^{NP}-complete [19]. Furthermore, it was shown that deciding strong equivalence of two programs over an infinite domain is co-NEXPTIME-complete [12]. If we factor in Theorem 3, we obtain the following result:

Theorem 7. *Deciding whether a problem of form* $(P, Q, \mathscr{P}_{\mathscr{V}}, \odot_{\mathscr{V}}^B)$, *for* $\odot \in \{\sqsubseteq, \equiv\}$, *over some* $\mathscr{V} = (\mathbb{P}, \mathbb{D})$ *holds is co-NEXPTIME-complete, for any* $B \subseteq \mathbb{P}$.

One could conjecture that relativised strong equivalence is decidable as well, since both "ends" of the parametrisation, viz. ordinary equivalence and strong equivalence, are decidable. Interestingly, this is not the case.

Lemma 1. *Let P and Q be two programs over a vocabulary* $\mathscr{V}$ *and* $\mathscr{E}$ *the set of the extensional predicates of* $P \cup Q$. *Then,* $P \simeq_{(\mathscr{V}, \mathscr{F}_{\mathscr{V}}^{\mathscr{E}}, =)} Q$ *iff* $P \simeq_{(\mathscr{V}, \mathscr{P}_{\mathscr{V}}^{\mathscr{E}}, =)} Q$.

As $(\mathscr{V}, \mathscr{F}_{\mathscr{V}}^{\mathscr{E}}, =)$-correspondence coincides with program equivalence (cf. Theorem 1), and program equivalence is undecidable, we immediately obtain the following result:

Theorem 8. *The problem of determining whether a given correspondence problem of form* $(P, Q, \mathscr{P}_{\mathscr{V}}^A, =)$ *over some vocabulary* $\mathscr{V}$ *holds is undecidable.*

Thus, although testing relativised strong equivalence is decidable in the propositional case [7], it is undecidable in the general non-ground setting.

Finally, it is to mention that the important case of uniform equivalence, which is undecidable in general, is decidable for Horn programs [6]. Furthermore, Eiter *et al.* [20] give a detailed exposition of the complexity of strong and uniform equivalence with respect to restricted syntactic classes of programs. Although lower bounds for analogous classes could be obtained from these results, they do not shift the border between decidable and undecidable instantiations of our framework.

4   Translations into Second-Order Logic

In this section, we introduce encodings of GQIPs and GQEPs in terms of second-order logic (SOL). We start with some aspects concerning the choice of SOL as target formalism, rather than of FOL, and afterwards we present the encodings.

4.1   A Case for Second-Order Logic

SOL is a highly expressive formalism—too expressive for effective computing—yet with important applications in knowledge representation (KR) and nonmonotonic reasoning. Besides McCarthy's well-known circumscription formalism [21], SOL recently gained increased interest in the ASP area by using it to define a generalised answer-set semantics for first-order theories (which is actually closely related to circumscription) [15]. Also, many encodings of different KR formalisms into quantified propositional logic were developed, which is just a decidable fragment of SOL. Indeed, in previous work [14], polynomial translations of PQIPs and PQEPs into quantified propositional logic were developed, and therefore translating GQIPs and GQEPs into SOL is a natural lifting. Nevertheless, one may seek translations into FOL for them. In what follows, we show some undesired feature of such an endeavour.

Let us understand by an *FOL-translation* of a class S of correspondence problems a function assigning to each element of S a FOL-formula. An FOL-translation T of S is *faithful* iff, for any $\Pi \in S$, $T(\Pi)$ is valid iff Π holds.

Now consider the class U of problems of form $(P, Q, \mathscr{F}_\mathscr{V}, =)$, i.e., problems testing for uniform equivalence, where the domain of $\mathscr{V}$ is denumerable, and assume that T_U is an FOL-translation of S_U which is both faithful and computable. Define $C \subseteq S_U$ as the set containing all the problems in S_U that hold and let $\bar{C} = S_U \setminus C$. We first show that C is recursively enumerable. Consider the following algorithm: Let $\Pi \in S_U$. (i) Compute $\varphi = T_U(\Pi)$. (ii) Take any sound and complete calculus for FOL, and start to enumerate all proofs. If a proof for φ is found, terminate. If φ is valid, this method will terminate after a finite number of steps (by completeness of the calculus), otherwise the method will loop forever (by soundness of the calculus). Hence, C is indeed recursively enumerable.

Next, we show that $\bar{C}$ is recursively enumerable as well. Consider the following algorithm: Take a problem $\Pi = (P, Q, \mathscr{F}_\mathscr{V}, =)$ from S_U. Start enumerating $\mathscr{F}_\mathscr{V}$. For each such $X \in \mathscr{F}_\mathscr{V}$, if $AS(P \cup X) \neq AS(Q \cup X)$, terminate. If Π does not hold, there exists a counterexample for Π and the algorithm will terminate after a finite number of steps, otherwise it will loop forever. Thus, $\bar{C}$ is also recursively enumerable. Since both C and $\bar{C}$ are recursively enumerable, S_U must be decidable. But this is a contradiction since S_U is not decidable. We showed the following result:

Theorem 9. *Let S_U be the class of problems of form $(P, Q, \mathscr{F}_\mathscr{V}, =)$, where the domain of $\mathscr{V}$ is denumerable. Then, any FOL-translation of S_U is either not faithful or not computable.*

Theorem 9 applies for any logic possessing sound and complete calculi and extends to any class of correspondence problems that allows to decide uniform equivalence. Hence, characterising correspondence problems is indeed a case for full SOL; not only undecidability but also incompleteness with respect to deduction is inherent for verifying program correspondences in general.

4.2 Translating GQIPs and GQEPs

In the sequel, we will make use of superscripts as a renaming schema for predicate variables and formulae. Formally, for any set V of predicate variables, we assume pairwise disjoint sets $V^i = \{v^i \mid v \in V\}$ of predicate variables, for every $i \geq 1$. For a formula ϕ and every $i \geq 1$, ϕ^i is the formula obtained from ϕ by uniformly replacing each occurrence of an atomic formula $a(t_1, \ldots, t_n)$ in ϕ by $a^i(t_1, \ldots, t_n)$. Consider a vocabulary $\mathscr{V} = (\mathbb{P}, \mathbb{D})$. For any rule r over $\mathscr{V}$ of form (1), we define $H(r) = a_1 \vee \cdots \vee a_l$, $B^+(r) = a_{l+1} \wedge \cdots \wedge a_m$, and $B^-(r) = \neg a_{m+1} \wedge \cdots \wedge \neg a_n$. We identify empty disjunctions with $\bot$ and empty conjunctions with $\top$.

Next, we introduce some building blocks for our encodings. These are basically lifted versions of ones used to characterise different notions of program correspondence for propositional programs by means of quantified propositional logic [22,14].

We will relate sets of ground atoms with assignments over Herbrand frames in the following way: Let X be a set of predicate variables and a an assignment over a Herbrand frame M. Moreover, consider a program vocabulary $\mathscr{V}$. Then, for any integer i, $a|X^i| = \{x(t_1,\ldots,t_n) \mid x^i \in X^i, (t_1,\ldots,t_n) \in a(x^i)\}$, and, syntactically, $a|X^i|$ is assumed to be a set of ground atoms over $\mathscr{V}$.

Definition 5. *Let P be a program over a vocabulary $\mathscr{V}$ and $i,j \geq 1$. Then, $P^{\langle i,j \rangle} =_{df} \bigwedge_{r \in P} r^{\langle i,j \rangle}$, where $r^{\langle i,j \rangle} =_{df} \forall X \left((B^+(r^i) \wedge B^-(r^j)) \rightarrow H(r^i) \right)$ and X is the set of all variables occurring in r.*

Theorem 10. *Let P be a program over a vocabulary $\mathscr{V} = (\mathbb{P},\mathbb{D})$, $V = PS(P)$, M a Herbrand frame along with an assignment a over M, and $X,Y \subseteq HB_{\mathscr{V}}$ such that for some i,j, $X = a|V^i|$ and $Y = a|V^j|$. Then, $X \models grd(P,\mathbb{D})^Y$ iff $P^{\langle i,j \rangle}$ is satisfied in M by a.*

Example 5. Let $P = \{p(x) \leftarrow q(x), \text{not } q(a); \; q(x) \leftarrow p(x), \text{not } q(b)\}$ be a program over a vocabulary $\mathscr{V} = (\mathbb{P},\mathbb{D})$, $\mathbb{P} = \{p,q\}$, $\mathbb{D} = \{a,b\}$, and let $X = \{p(a),q(a),q(b)\}$ and $Y = \{q(a)\}$ be interpretations over $\mathscr{V}$. Observe that $X \models grd(P,\mathbb{D})^Y$. Furthermore, consider a Herbrand frame M and an assignment a over M such that $a|\{p,q\}^1| = X$ and $a|\{p,q\}^2| = Y$. It can be verified that $P^{\langle 1,2 \rangle} = \forall x(q^1(x) \wedge \neg q^2(a) \rightarrow p^1(x)) \wedge \forall x(p^1(x) \wedge \neg q^2(b) \rightarrow q^1(x))$ is satisfied in M by a.

We also make use of the following abbreviations for sets of predicate variables: Let p be a predicate variable of arity n. For any two integers $i,j \geq 1$, define $p^i \leq p^j =_{df} \forall x_1 \cdots x_n(p^i(x_1,\ldots x_n) \rightarrow p^j(x_1,\ldots x_n))$. Furthermore, let P be a finite set of predicate variables and let $i,j \geq 1$ be integers. Then, $(P^i \leq P^j) =_{df} \bigwedge_{p \in P}(p^i \leq p^j)$, $(P^i < P^j) =_{df}$ $(P^i \leq P^j) \wedge \neg(P^j \leq P^i)$, and $(P^i = P^j) =_{df} (P^i \leq P^j) \wedge (P^j \leq P^i)$.

We proceed with our central encoding, which captures the notion of an A-B-wedge.

Definition 6. *Let P be a program over a vocabulary $\mathscr{V} = (\mathbb{P},\mathbb{D})$. Furthermore, let A,B be finite subsets of $\mathbb{P}$ and $V = PS(P) \cup A \cup B$. Then, $TR_{\mathscr{V}}^{(A,B)}(P)$ is given by*

$$\exists V^3 \left((B^3 = B^1) \wedge (A^2 \leq A^3) \wedge P^{\langle 3,3 \rangle} \wedge \forall V^4 \left(((A^2 \leq A^4) \wedge (V^4 < V^3)) \rightarrow \neg P^{\langle 4,3 \rangle} \right) \right).$$

Lemma 2. *Let P be a program over a vocabulary $\mathscr{V} = (\mathbb{P},\mathbb{D})$, A,B finite subsets of $\mathbb{P}$, and $V = PS(P) \cup A \cup B$. Then, for any finite Herbrand frame M and an assignment a over M such that $X = a|A^2|$ and $Y = a|B^1|$, it holds that (X,Y) is an A-B-wedge of P iff $TR_{\mathscr{V}}^{(A,B)}(P)$ is satisfied in M by a.*

To give an intuition of the above encoding, recall the characterisation of wedges in terms of interpretations from Theorem 5. If we take the semantics of our building blocks into account, Definition 6 basically encodes Conditions (i)–(iii) of Theorem 5 by means of SOL. In particular, the interpretations Y, X, Y', and X' from Theorem 5 are captured by the sets B^1, A^2, V^3, and V^4 of variables in $TR_{\mathscr{V}}^{(A,B)}(P)$.

Next, we introduce two axioms that make some assumptions explicit. The first one captures the well-known *unique-names assumption*.

Definition 7. *For any program P over vocabulary $\mathscr{V}$, the* unique-names axiom *for P is given by* $UNA(P) =_{df} \bigwedge_{a,b \in HU_P, a \neq b} \neg(a = b)$.

We consider only finite sets in the context class of frames, hence we need as second axiom one which imposes finite SOL-domains for the models which will correspond to the domains of the programs and the sets of facts from the context class.

Definition 8. *Let $\mathscr{V} = (\mathbb{P}, \mathbb{D})$ be a vocabulary. Then, $FDA(\mathbb{D})$ is given as follows:*

1. *If $\mathbb{D}$ is finite, then $FDA(\mathbb{D}) =_{df} \forall x (\bigvee_{c \in \mathbb{D}} (x = c))$.*
2. *If $\mathbb{D}$ is denumerable, then $FDA(\mathbb{D}) =_{df} \exists S (\forall x S(x) \wedge \forall R (PO(R,S) \rightarrow MAX(R,S)))$, where*

$$PO(R,S) =_{df} \forall xyz \Big(S(x) \wedge S(y) \wedge S(z) \rightarrow (R(x,x) \wedge$$
$$(R(x,y) \wedge R(y,z) \rightarrow R(x,z)) \wedge (R(x,y) \wedge R(y,x) \rightarrow x = y)) \Big) \text{ and}$$
$$MAX(R,S) =_{df} \exists m (S(m) \wedge \forall x (S(x) \wedge R(m,x) \rightarrow m = x)).$$

The intuition of the first item should be clear: The SOL-domain of any model does not contain more objects than enumerated by the finite disjunction over the elements from the LP-domain $\mathbb{D}$. Hence, $FDA(\cdot)$ turns into the customary *domain-closure axiom*. If $\mathbb{D}$ is denumerable, the intuition of the second item is the following: $PO(R,S)$ is true if R is a partial order on S, and $MAX(R,S)$ is true if S contains a maximal element with respect to R. Hence, $FDA(\mathbb{D})$ encodes that there exists a set S such that each element of the SOL-domain in any model is in S and, for each partial order on S, S contains a maximal element with respect to that order. The latter is a well-known set-theoretic condition that ensures that S is finite. Since, for each model, any element from the SOL-domain is in S, it follows that each model is finite as well.

We are now in a position to state the main characterisation in SOL.

Theorem 11. *Let Π be a correspondence problem of form $(P,Q,\mathscr{F}_{\mathscr{V}}^A, \odot_{\mathscr{V}}^B)$, where $\mathscr{V} = (\mathbb{P}, \mathbb{D})$ and $\odot \in \{\sqsubseteq, \equiv\}$, and let $V = PS(P \cup Q)$, $A' = A|_V$, and $B' = B|_V$. Then:*

(i) *Π holds iff $UNA(P \cup Q), FDA(\mathbb{D}) \models TR_{\mathscr{V}}^{(A',B')}(P) \rightarrow TR_{\mathscr{V}}^{(A',B')}(Q)$, if $\odot$ is $\sqsubseteq$.*
(ii) *Π holds iff $UNA(P \cup Q), FDA(\mathbb{D}) \models TR_{\mathscr{V}}^{(A',B')}(P) \leftrightarrow TR_{\mathscr{V}}^{(A',B')}(Q)$, if $\odot$ is $\equiv$.*

That $FDA(\cdot)$ is indeed required can be seen as follows: For a vocabulary with a denumerable domain, define the programs

$$P = \left\{ \begin{array}{l} s(a); \ r(x,y) \vee r(y,x) \leftarrow s(x), s(y); \\ r(x,z) \leftarrow r(x,y), r(y,z); \ p(x,y) \leftarrow r(x,y), \text{not } r(y,x); \\ \bar{g}(x) \leftarrow p(x,y); \ g \leftarrow s(x), \text{not } \bar{g}(x) \end{array} \right\}, \ Q = P \cup \{\leftarrow \text{not } g\}.$$

The intuition behind program P is that, for any set X of facts over s, each answer set from $P \cup X$ contains g (the greatest element) iff X is finite. This is realised by formalising the property that any strict total order on a non-empty set S induces a greatest element with respect to this order relation iff S is finite. On the other hand, program $Q \cup X$ has no answer sets iff X is infinite. This is realised by defining Q as P augmented with the rule $\leftarrow$ not g that eliminates any answer set not containing g. In a nutshell, programs P and Q show that the answer-set semantics is expressible enough to distinguish whether the domain of X is finite. Now consider the problem $\Pi = (P, Q, \mathscr{F}_{\mathscr{V}}^A, \sqsubseteq_{\mathscr{V}}^B)$, where $A = \{s\}$, $B = \{g\}$, and $\mathscr{V}$ is a vocabulary with a denumerable domain. It is easy to see that Π holds since any answer set of P and Q contains g when joined with finite sets of facts over $\{s\}$. Nevertheless, $UNA(P \cup Q) \models TR_{\mathscr{V}}^{(A,B)}(P) \rightarrow TR_{\mathscr{V}}^{(A,B)}(Q)$ does not hold since there exist models of infinite size that correspond, roughly speaking, to infinite counterexamples.

Finally, one may wonder why $FDA(\cdot)$ comes in two guises, depending on the cardinality of the LP-domain. Let us assume that $FDA(\cdot)$ would be defined only by Item 2 of Definition 8, irrespective of the cardinality of $\mathbb{D}$. We use FDA' to refer to this version of $FDA(\cdot)$. Consider the following two programs: $P = \{eq(x,x) \leftarrow s(x)\}$ and $Q = P \cup \{\leftarrow s(x), s(y), \text{not } eq(x,y)\}$. Program P expresses that any element in the set implicitly defined by s is equal to itself; program Q is defined as P plus a rule expressing that Q has no answer set iff the set implicitly defined by s has more than one element. Hence, the problem $\Pi = (P, Q, \mathscr{F}_{\mathscr{V}}^A, \sqsubseteq_{\mathscr{V}}^B)$, for $A = \{s\}$ and $B = \emptyset$, holds only if the vocabulary $\mathscr{V}$ has a domain with less than two elements. Assume that $\mathscr{V}$ is such a vocabulary. However, $UNA(P \cup Q), FDA' \models TR_{\mathscr{V}}^{(A,B)}(P) \rightarrow TR_{\mathscr{V}}^{(A,B)}(Q)$ does not hold since FDA' only ensures that all models are finite but it makes no commitment about their cardinalities.

5   Conclusion

The focus of our work is on notions of program correspondence for non-ground logic programs under the answer-set semantics. Previously, refined equivalence notions taking answer-set projection and relativised contexts into account were defined and studied for propositional programs only. Indeed, the framework introduced in this paper is a lifting of a framework due to Eiter *et al.* [8] defined for specifying parameterised program correspondence notions for propositional programs. Our framework allows to capture several well-known equivalence notions in a uniform manner and, moreover, allows to directly extend notions studied so far for propositional programs only to the general non-ground case. In particular, we introduced GQIPs and GQEPs as generalisations of PQIPs and PQEPs, respectively, which in turn generalise uniform equivalence as well as query and program equivalence. We provided model-theoretic characterisations for GQIPs and GQEPs—in the spirit of characterising uniform equivalence in terms of UE-models—and axiomatised them in terms of second-order logic.

We plan to provide characterisations similar to those given for GQIPs and GQEPs to correspondence problems capturing relativised strong equivalence with projection (recall that GQEPs amount to relativised uniform equivalence with projection). A further point will be to study the generalised answer-set semantics recently introduced by Ferraris, Lee, and Lifschitz [15] in connection with our correspondence framework—in particular, to characterise equivalence notions for this semantics in terms of second-order logic, as that semantics is itself defined by means of second-order logic.

References

1. Leone, N., Pfeifer, G., Faber, W., Eiter, T., Gottlob, G., Perri, S., Scarcello, F.: The DLV System for Knowledge Representation and Reasoning. ACM TOCL 7(3), 499–562 (2006)
2. Janhunen, T., Niemelä, I., Seipel, D., Simons, P.: Unfolding Partiality and Disjunctions in Stable Model Semantics. ACM TOCL 7(1), 1–37 (2006)

3. Lifschitz, V., Pearce, D., Valverde, A.: Strongly Equivalent Logic Programs. ACM TOCL 2(4), 526–541 (2001)
4. Eiter, T., Fink, M.: Uniform Equivalence of Logic Programs under the Stable Model Semantics. In: Palamidessi, C. (ed.) ICLP 2003. LNCS, vol. 2916, pp. 224–238. Springer, Heidelberg (2003)
5. Maher, M.J.: Equivalences of logic programs. In: Minker, J. (ed.) Foundations of Deductive Databases and Logic Programming, pp. 627–658. Morgan Kaufmann, San Francisco (1988)
6. Sagiv, Y.: Optimizing Datalog Programs. In: Minker, J. (ed.) Foundations of Deductive Databases and Logic Programming, pp. 659–698. Morgan Kaufmann, San Francisco (1988)
7. Woltran, S.: Characterizations for Relativized Notions of Equivalence in Answer Set Programming. In: Alferes, J.J., Leite, J. (eds.) JELIA 2004. LNCS, vol. 3229, pp. 161–173. Springer, Heidelberg (2004)
8. Eiter, T., Tompits, H., Woltran, S.: On Solution Correspondences in Answer-Set Programming. In: 19th International Joint Conference on Artificial Intelligence, pp. 97–102 (2005)
9. Oikarinen, E., Janhunen, T.: Modular Equivalence for Normal Logic Programs. In: 17th European Conference on Artificial Intelligence, pp. 412–416. IOS Press, Amsterdam (2006)
10. Inoue, K., Sakama, C.: Equivalence of Logic Programs Under Updates. In: Alferes, J.J., Leite, J. (eds.) JELIA 2004. LNCS, vol. 3229, pp. 174–186. Springer, Heidelberg (2004)
11. Lin, F.: Reducing Strong Equivalence of Logic Programs to Entailment in Classical Propositional Logic. In: 8th International Conference on Principles of Knowledge Representation and Reasoning, pp. 170–176. Morgan Kaufmann, San Francisco (2002)
12. Eiter, T., Fink, M., Tompits, H., Woltran, S.: Strong and Uniform Equivalence in Answer-Set Programming: Characterizations and Complexity Results for the Non-Ground Case. In: 20th National Conference on Artificial Intelligence, pp. 695–700. AAAI Press, Menlo Park (2005)
13. Lifschitz, V., Pearce, D., Valverde, A.: A Characterization of Strong Equivalence for Logic Programs with Variables. In: Baral, C., Brewka, G., Schlipf, J. (eds.) LPNMR 2007. LNCS, vol. 4483, pp. 188–200. Springer, Heidelberg (2007)
14. Oetsch, J., Tompits, H., Woltran, S.: Facts do not Cease to Exist Because They are Ignored: Relativised Uniform Equivalence with Answer-Set Projection. In: 22nd National Conference on Artificial Intelligence, pp. 458–464. AAAI Press, Menlo Park (2007)
15. Ferraris, P., Lee, J., Lifschitz, V.: A New Perspective on Stable Models. In: 20th International Joint Conference on Artificial Intelligence, pp. 372–379 (2007)
16. Gelfond, M., Lifschitz, V.: Classical Negation in Logic Programs and Disjunctive Databases. New Generation Computing 9, 365–385 (1991)
17. Turner, H.: Strong Equivalence Made Easy: Nested Expressions and Weight Constraints. Theory and Practice of Logic Programming 3(4-5), 602–622 (2003)
18. Shmueli, O.: Decidability and Expressiveness Aspects of Logic Queries. In: 6th ACM SIGACT-SIGMOD-SIGART Symposium on Principles of Database Systems, pp. 237–249. ACM, New York (1987)
19. Dantsin, E., Eiter, T., Gottlob, G., Voronkov, A.: Complexity and Expressive Power of Logic Programming. ACM Computing Surveys 33(3), 374–425 (2001)
20. Eiter, T., Fink, M., Tompits, H., Woltran, S.: Complexity Results for Checking Equivalence of Stratified Logic Programs. In: 20th International Joint Conference on Artificial Intelligence, pp. 330–335 (2007)
21. McCarthy, J.: Circumscription—A Form of Non-Monotonic Reasoning. Artificial Intelligence 13, 27–39 (1980)
22. Tompits, H., Woltran, S.: Towards Implementations for Advanced Equivalence Checking in Answer-Set Programming. In: Gabbrielli, M., Gupta, G. (eds.) ICLP 2005. LNCS, vol. 3668, pp. 189–203. Springer, Heidelberg (2005)

Efficient Algorithms for Functional Constraints[*]

Yuanlin Zhang[1], Roland H.C. Yap[2],
Chendong Li[1], and Satyanarayana Marisetti[1]

[1] Texas Tech University, USA
[2] National University of Singapore, Singapore

Abstract. *Functional constraints* are an important constraint class in Constraint Programming (CP) systems, in particular for Constraint Logic Programming (CLP) systems. CP systems with finite domain constraints usually employ CSP-based solvers which use local consistency, e.g. arc consistency. We introduce a new approach which is based instead on *variable substitution*. We obtain efficient algorithms for reducing systems involving functional and *bi-functional constraints* together with other non-functional constraints. It also solves globally any CSP where there exists a variable such that any other variable is reachable from it through a sequence of functional constraints. Our experiments show that variable elimination can significantly improve the efficiency of solving problems with functional constraints.

1 Introduction

Functional constraints are a common class of constraints occurring in Constraint Satisfaction Problem(s) (CSP) [10,11,7]. In Constraint Programming (CP) systems such as Constraint Logic Programming (CLP), functional constraints also naturally arise as primitive constraints and from unification. Finite domain is a widely used and successful constraint domain for CLP. In this context, functional constraints (e.g., those in CHIP [11]), as primitive constraints, can facilitate the development of more efficient constraint solvers underlying CLP systems. In CLP, when reducing a goal, unification can also lead to functional constraints. For example, when matching $p(Z^2 + 1)$ with a rule on $p(X)$ where both X and Z are finite domain variables, a functional constraint $X = Z^2 + 1$ is produced.

Most work on functional constraints follows the approach in CSP which is based on arc or path consistency [11,3]. In this paper, we propose a new method — *variable substitution* — to process functional constraints. The idea is that if a constraint is functional on a variable, this variable in another constraint can be substituted using the functional constraint without losing any solution.

Given a variable, the *variable elimination* method substitutes this variable in *all* constraints involving it such that it is effectively "eliminated" from the problem. This idea is applied to reduce any problem containing non-functional

[*] Part of this work was supported by National Univ. of Singapore, grant 252-000-303-112.

M. Garcia de la Banda and E. Pontelli (Eds.): ICLP 2008, LNCS 5366, pp. 606–620, 2008.

constraints into a canonical form where some variables can be safely ignored when solving the problem. We design an efficient algorithm to reduce, in $\mathcal{O}(ed^2)$ where e is the number of constraints and d the size of the largest domain of the variables, a general binary CSP containing functional constraints into a canonical form. This reduction simplifies the problem and makes the functional portion trivially solvable. When the functional constraints are also bi-functional, then the algorithm is linear in the size of the CSP.

Many CLP systems with finite domains make use of constraint propagation algorithms such as arc consistency. Our experiments show that the substitution based "global" treatment of functional constraints can significantly speed up propagation based solvers.

In the rest of the paper, background on CSPs and functional constraints is given in Section 2. Variable substitution for binary functional constraints is introduced and studied in Section 3. Section 4 presents results on algorithms for variable elimination in general CSPs containing functional constraints. Section 5 presents an experimental study. Functional elimination is extended to non-binary constraints in Section 6. Related work is discussed in Section 7 and concluded in Section 8.

2   Preliminaries

We begin with the basic concepts and notation used in this paper.

A binary *Constraint Satisfaction Problem (CSP)* (N, D, C) consists of a finite set of variables $N = \{1, \cdots, n\}$, a set of domains $D = \{D_1, \cdots, D_n\}$, where D_i is the domain of variable i , and a set of constraints each of which is a binary relation between two variables in N.

A constraint between two variables i and j is denoted by c_{ij}. Symbols a and b possibly with subscript denote the values in a domain. A constraint c_{ij} is a set of allowed tuples. We assume testing whether a tuple belongs to a constraint takes constant time. For $a \in D_i$ and $b \in D_j$, we use either $(a, b) \in c_{ij}$ or $c_{ij}(a, b)$ to denote that a and b satisfy the constraint c_{ij}. For the problems of interest here, we require that for all $a \in D_i$ and $b \in D_j$, $(a, b) \in c_{ij}$ if and only if $(b, a) \in c_{ji}$. If there is no constraint on i and j, c_{ij} denotes a universal relation, i.e., $D_i \times D_j$.

A constraint graph $G = (V, E)$, where $V = N$ and $E = \{\{i, j\} \mid \exists c_{ij} \in C\}$, is usually used to describe the topological structure of a CSP. A *solution* of a constraint satisfaction problem is an assignment of a value to each variable such that the assignment satisfies all the constraints in the problem. A CSP is *satisfiable* if it has a solution. The *solution space* of a CSP is the set of all its solutions. Two CSPs are *equivalent* if and only if they have the same solution space. Throughout this paper, n represents the number of variables, d the size of the largest domain of the variables, and e the number of constraints in C.

We need two operations on constraints in this paper. One is the intersection of two constraints (intersection of the sets of tuples) that constrain the same set of variables. The other operation is the composition, denoted by the symbol "$\circ$," of two constraints sharing a variable. The composition of two relations is:

$$c_{jk} \circ c_{ij} = \{(a, c) \mid \exists b \in D_j, such \ that \ (a, b) \in c_{ij} \wedge (b, c) \in c_{jk}\}.$$

Composition is a basic operation in our variable substitution method. Composing c_{ij} and c_{jk} gives a new constraint on i and k.

Example. Consider constraints $c_{ij} = \{(a_1, b_1), (a_2, b_2), (a_2, b_3)\}$ and $c_{jk} = \{(b_1, c_1), (b_2, c_2), (b_3, c_2)\}$. The composition of c_{ij} and c_{jk} is a constraint on i and k: $c_{ik} = \{(a_1, c_1), (a_2, c_2)\}$. □

A constraint c_{ij} is *functional* on j if for any $a \in D_i$ there exists at most one $b \in D_j$ such that $c_{ij}(a, b)$. c_{ij} is *functional* on i if c_{ji} is functional on i. Given a constraint c_{ij} functional on j and a value $a \in D_i$, we assume throughout the paper that in constant time we can find the value $b \in D_j$, if there is one, such that $(a, b) \in c_{ij}$.

A special case of functional constraints are equations. These are ubiquitous in CLP. A typical functional constraint in arithmetic is a binary linear equation like $2x = 5 - 3y$ which is functional on x and on y. Functional constraints do not need to be linear. For example, a nonlinear equation $x^2 = y^2$ where $x, y \in 1..10$ is also functional on both x and y. In scene labeling problems [7], there are many functional constraints and other special constraints. □

When a constraint c_{ij} is functional on j, for simplicity, we say c_{ij} is functional by making use of the fact that the subscripts of c_{ij} are an ordered pair. When c_{ij} is functional on i, c_{ji} is said to be functional. That c_{ij} is functional does not mean c_{ji} is functional. In this paper, the definition of functional constraints is different from the one in [12,11] where constraints are functional on each of its variables, leading to the following notion.

A constraint c_{ij} is *bi-functional* if c_{ij} is functional on i and on j. A bi-functional constraint is called *bijective* in [3]. For functional constraints, we have the following property on their composition and intersection: 1) If c_{ij} and c_{jk} are functional on j and k respectively, their composition remains functional; and 2) The intersection of two functional constraints remains functional.

3 Variable Substitution and Elimination Using Binary Functional Constraints

We introduce the idea of variable substitution. Given a CSP (N, D, C), a constraint $c_{ij} \in C$ that is functional on j, and a constraint c_{jk} in C, we can substitute i for j in c_{jk} by composing c_{ij} and c_{jk}. If there is already a constraint $c_{ik} \in C$, the new constraint on i and k is simply the intersection of c_{ik} and $c_{jk} \circ c_{ij}$.

Definition 1. *Consider a CSP (N, D, C), a constraint $c_{ij} \in C$ functional on j, and a constraint $c_{jk} \in C$. To substitute i for j in c_{jk}, using c_{ij}, is to get a new CSP where c_{jk} is replaced by $c'_{ik} = c_{ik} \cap (c_{jk} \circ c_{ij})$. The variable i is called the substitution variable.*

A fundamental property of variable substitution is that it preserves the solution space of the problem.

Property 1. Given a CSP (N, D, C), a constraint $c_{ij} \in C$ functional on j, and a constraint $c_{jk} \in C$, the new problem obtained by substituting i for j in c_{jk} is equivalent to (N, D, C).

Proof. Let the new problem after substituting i for j in c_{jk} be (N, D, C') where $C' = (C - \{c_{jk}\}) \cup \{c'_{ik}\}$ and $c'_{ik} = c_{ik} \cap (c_{jk} \circ c_{ij})$.

Assume $(a_1, a_2, \cdots, a_n)$ is a solution of (N, D, C). We need to show that it satisfies C'. The major difference between C' and C is that C' has new constraint c'_{ik}. It is known that $(a_i, a_j) \in c_{ij}$, $(a_j, a_k) \in c_{jk}$, and if there is c_{ik} in C, $(a_i, a_k) \in c_{ik}$. The fact that $c'_{ik} = (c_{jk} \circ c_{ij}) \cap c_{ik}$ implies $(a_i, a_k) \in c'_{ik}$. Hence, c'_{ik} is satisfied by $(a_1, a_2, \cdots, a_n)$.

Conversely, we need to show that any solution $(a_1, a_2, \cdots, a_n)$ of (N, D, C') is a solution of (N, D, C). Given the difference between C' and C, it is sufficient to show the solution satisfies c_{jk}. We have $(a_i, a_j) \in c_{ij}$ and $(a_i, a_k) \in c'_{ik}$. Since $c'_{ik} = (c_{jk} \circ c_{ij}) \cap c_{ik}$, there must exist $b \in D_j$ such that $(a_i, b) \in c_{ij}$ and $(b, a_k) \in c_{jk}$. As c_{ij} is functional, b has to be a_j. Hence, a_j and a_k satisfy c_{jk}. □

Based on variable substitution, we can eliminate a variable from a problem so that no constraint will be on this variable (except the functional constraint used to substitute it).

Definition 2. *Given a CSP (N, D, C) and a constraint $c_{ij} \in C$ functional on j, to* eliminate j using c_{ij} *is to substitute i for j, using c_{ij}, in every constraint $c_{jk} \in C$ (except c_{ji}).*

We can also substitute i for j in c_{ji} to obtain c'_{ii} and then intersect c'_{ii} with the identity relation on D_i, equivalent to a direct revision of the domain of i with respect to c_{ij}. This would make the algorithms presented in this paper more uniform, i.e., only operations on constraints are used. Since in most algorithms we want to make domain revision explicit, we choose not to substitute i for j in c_{ji}.

Given a functional constraint c_{ij} of a CSP (N, D, C), let C_j be the set of all constraints involving j, except c_{ij}. The elimination of j using c_{ij} results in a new problem (N, D, C') where

$$C' = (C - C_j) \cup \{c'_{ik} \mid c'_{ik} = (c_{jk} \circ c_{ij}) \cap c_{ik}, c_{jk} \in C\}.$$

In the new problem, there is only one constraint c_{ij} on j and thus j can be regarded as being "eliminated".

Example. Consider a problem with three constraints whose constraint graph is shown in Figure 1 (a). Let c_{ij} be functional. The CSP after j has been eliminated using c_{ij} is shown in Figure 1 (b). In the new CSP, constraints c_{jk} and c_{jl} are discarded, and new constraints $c_{ik} = c_{jk} \circ c_{ij}$ and $c_{il} = c_{jl} \circ c_{ij}$ are added. □

The variable elimination involves "several" substitutions and thus preserves the solution space of the original problem by Property 1.

Property 2. Given a CSP (N, D, C) and a functional constraint $c_{ij} \in C$, the new problem (N, D, C') obtained by the elimination of variable j using c_{ij} is equivalent to (N, D, C).

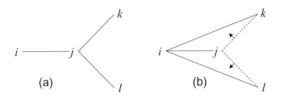

Fig. 1. (a): A CSP with a functional constraint c_{ij}. (b): The new CSP after eliminating the variable j using c_{ij}.

4   Elimination Algorithms for CSPs with Functional Constraints and Non-functional Constraints

We now extend variable elimination to general CSPs with functional and non-functional constraints. The idea of variable elimination (Definition 2 in Section 3) can be used to reduce a CSP to the following canonical functional form.

Definition 3. *A CSP (N, D, C) is in* canonical functional form *if for any constraint $c_{ij} \in C$ functional on j, the following conditions are satisfied: 1) if c_{ji} is also functional on i(i.e., c_{ij} is bi-functional), either i or j is not constrained by any other constraint in C; 2) otherwise, j is not constrained by any other constraint in C.*

As a trivial example, a CSP without any functional constraint is in canonical functional form. If a CSP contains some functional constraints, it is in canonical functional form intuitively if for any functional constraint c_{ij}, there is only one constraint on j. As an exception, the first condition in the definition implies that when c_{ij} is bi-functional, one variable of $\{i, j\}$ might have several bi-functional constraints on it.

In a canonical functional form CSP, *the functional constraints form disjoint star graphs*. A *star graph* is a tree where there exists a node, called the *center*, such that there is an edge between this center node and every other node. We call the variable at the center of a star graph, a *free variable*, and other variables in the star graph *eliminated variables*. Fig. 1(b) is a star graph, assuming c_{jk} and c_{jl} are functional on k and l respectively, with free variable i. The constraint between a free variable i and an eliminated variable j is functional on j, but it may or may not be functional on i. In the special case that the star graph contains only two variables i and j and c_{ij} is bi-functional, any one of the variables can be called a free variable while the other is called an eliminated variable.

If a CSP is in canonical functional form, all functional constraints and the eliminated variables can be *ignored* when we try to find a solution for this problem. Thus, to solve a CSP (N, D, C) in canonical functional form whose non-eliminated variables are NE, we only need to solve a smaller problem (NE, D', C') where D' is the set of domains of the variables NE and $C' = \{c_{ij} \mid c_{ij} \in C$ and $i, j \in NE\}$.

Proposition 1. *Consider a CSP $P_1 = (N, D, C)$ in a canonical functional form and a new CSP $P_2 = (NE, D', C')$ formed by ignoring the eliminated variables in P_1. For any free variable $i \in N$ and any constraint $c_{ij} \in C$ functional on j, assume any value of D_i has a support in D_j and this support can be found in constant time. Any solution of P_2 is extensible to a unique solution of P_1 in $\mathcal{O}(|N - NE|)$ time. Any solution of P_1 can be obtained from a solution of P_2.*

Proof. Let $(a_1, a_2, \cdots, a_{|NE|})$ be a solution of (NE, D', C'). Consider any eliminated variable $j \in N - NE$. In C, there is only one constraint on j. Let it be c_{ij} where i must be a free variable. By the assumption of the proposition, the value of i in the solution has a unique support in j. This support will be assigned to j. In this way, a unique solution for (N, D, C) is obtained. The complexity of this extension is $\mathcal{O}(|N - NE|)$.

Let S be a solution of (N, D, C) and S' the portion of S restricted to the variables in NE. S' is a solution of (NE, D', C') because $C' \subseteq C$. The unique extension of S' to a solution of P_1 is exactly S. □

Any CSP with functional constraints can be transformed into canonical functional form by variable elimination using the algorithm in Fig. 2. Given a constraint c_{ij} functional on j, Line 1 of the algorithm substitutes i for j in all constraints involving j. Note the arc consistency on c_{ik}, for all neighbor k of i, is enforced by line 3.

```
algorithm Variable-Elimination(inout (N, D, C), out consistent) {
        L ← N;
        while ( There is c_ij ∈ C functional on j where i, j ∈ L and i ≠ j){
            // Eliminate variable j,
1.          C ← {c'_ik | c'_ik ← (c_jk ∘ c_ij) ∩ c_ik, c_jk ∈ C, k ≠ i} ∪ (C − {c_jk ∈ C | k ≠ i});
2.          L ← L − {j};
3.          Revise the domain of i wrt c_ik for every neighbour k of i;
            if (D_i is empty) then { consistent ← false; return }
        }
        consistent ← true;
}
```

Fig. 2. A variable elimination algorithm to transform a CSP into a canonical functional form.

Theorem 1. *Given a CSP (N, D, C), `Variable-Elimination` transforms the problem into a canonical functional form in $\mathcal{O}(n^2 d^2)$.*

Proof. Assume `Variable-Elimination` transforms a CSP $P_1 = (N, D, C)$ into a new problem $P_2 = (N, D', C')$. We show that P_2 is of canonical functional form. For any variable $j \in N$, if there is a constraint $c_{ij} \in C'$ functional on j, there are two cases. Case 1: $j \notin L$ when the algorithm terminates. This means that c_{ij} is the functional constraint that is used to substitute j in other constraints

(Line 1). After substitution, c_{ij} is the unique constraint on j. Case 2: $j \in L$ when the algorithm terminates. Variable i must not be in L (otherwise, j will be substituted by Line 1). This implies that i was substituted using c_{ji}. Thus, c_{ji} is the only functional constraint on i in P_2. Hence, c_{ij} is bi-functional and i is not constrained by any other constraints.

Next, we show the complexity of Variable-Elimination. It eliminates any variable in N at most once (Line 2). For each variable j and a constraint c_{ij} functional on j, there are at most $n - 2$ other constraints on j. The variable j in those constraints needs to be substituted. The complexity of the substitution for each constraint is $\mathcal{O}(d^2)$. The elimination of j (Line 1) takes $\mathcal{O}(nd^2)$. There are at most $n - 1$ variables to eliminate and thus the worst case complexity of the algorithm is $\mathcal{O}(n^2d^2)$.   □

It is worth noting that the variable elimination algorithm is able to globally solve some CSPs containing non-functional constraints.

Example. Consider a simple example where there are three variables i, j, and k whose domains are $\{1, 2, 3\}$ and the constraints are $i = j$, $i = k + 1$, and $j \neq k$. Note that although the constraints are listed in an equational form, the actual constraints are explicit and discrete, thus normal equational reasoning might not be applicable. By eliminating j using c_{ij}, c_{ik} becomes $\{(2, 1), (3, 2)\}$, and the domain of i becomes $\{2, 3\}$. The non-functional constraint c_{jk} is gone. The problem is in canonical functional form. A solution can be obtained by letting i be 2 and consequently $j = 2$ and $k = 1$.   □

By carefully choosing an ordering of the variables to eliminate, a faster algorithm can be obtained. The intuition is that once a variable i is used to substitute for other variables, i itself should not be substituted by any other variable later.

Example. Consider a CSP with functional constraints c_{ij} and c_{jk}. Its constraint graph is shown in Fig. 3(a) where a functional constraint is represented by an arrow. If we eliminate k and then j, we first get c_{jl_1} and c_{jl_2}, and then get c_{il_1} and c_{il_2}. Note that j is first used to substitute for k and later is substituted by i. If we eliminate j and then k, we first get c_{ik}, and then get c_{il_1} and c_{il_2}. In this way, we reduce the number of compositions of constraints.   □

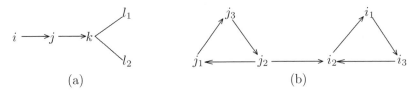

$$(a) \qquad\qquad\qquad\qquad (b)$$

Fig. 3. (a) The constraint graph of a CSP with functional constraints c_{ij} and c_{jk}. (b) A directed graph.

Given a CSP $P = (N, D, C)$, P^F is used to denote its directed graph (V, E) where $V = N$ and $E = \{(i, j) \mid c_{ij} \in C$ and c_{ij} is functional on $j\}$. Non-functional constraints in C do not appear in P^F. A subgraph of a directed graph is *strongly connected* if for any two vertices of the subgraph, any one of them is reachable from the other. A *strongly connected component* of a directed graph is a maximum subgraph that is strongly connected. To describe our algorithm we need the following notation.

Definition 4. *Given a directed graph* (V, E)*, a sequence of the nodes of* V *is a* functional elimination ordering *if for any two nodes* i *and* j*,* i *before* j *in the sequence implies that there is a path from* i *and* j*. A functional elimination ordering of a CSP problem* P *is a functional elimination ordering of* P^F*.*

The functional elimination ordering is used to overcome the redundant computation shown in the example on Fig. 3(a). Given a directed graph G, a functional elimination ordering can be found by: 1) finding all the strongly connected components of G; 2) modifying G by taking every component as one vertex with edges changed and/or added accordingly; 3) finding a topological ordering of the nodes in the new graph; and 4) replacing any vertex v in the ordering by any sequence of the vertices of the strongly connected component represented by v.

To illustrate the process, consider the example in Fig. 3(b) which can be taken as P^F for some CSP problem P. All strongly connected components are $\{j_1, j_2, j_3\}$, denoted by c_1, and $\{i_1, i_2, i_3\}$, denoted by c_2. We construct the new graph by replacing the components by vertices: $(\{c_1, c_2\}, \{(c_1, c_2)\})$. We have the edge (c_1, c_2) because the two components are connected by (j_2, i_2). The topological ordering of the new graph is $\langle c_1, c_2 \rangle$. Now we can replace c_1 by any sequence of j's and c_2 by any sequence of i's. For example, we can have a functional elimination ordering $\langle j_3, j_2, j_1, i_2, i_3, i_1 \rangle$.

The algorithm `Linear-Elimination` in Fig. 4 first finds a functional elimination ordering (Line 1). Line 4 and 6 are to *process* all the variables in O. Every variable i of O is *processed* as follows: i will be used to substitute for all the variables *reachable* from i *through constraints that are functional in* C^0 *and still exist in the current* C. Those constraints are called *qualified* constraints. Specifically, L initially holds the immediate reachable variables through qualified constraints (Line 8). Line 9 is a loop to eliminate all variables reachable from i. The loop at Line 11 is to eliminate j using i from the current C. In this loop, if a constraint c_{jk} is qualified (Line 14), k is reachable from i through qualified constraints. Therefore, it is put into L (Line 15).

To illustrate the ideas underlying the algorithm, consider the example in Fig. 3(b). Now, we assume the edges in the graph are the only constraints in the problem. Assume the algorithm finds the ordering given earlier: $O = \langle j_3, j_2, j_1, i_2, i_3, i_1 \rangle$. Next, it starts from j_3. The qualified constraints leaving j_3 are $c_{j_3 j_2}$ only. So, the immediate reachable variables through qualified constraints are $L = \{j_2\}$. Take and delete j_2 from L. Substitute j_3 for j_2 in constraints $c_{j_2 i_2}$ and $c_{j_2 j_1}$. As a result, constraints $c_{j_2 i_2}$ and $c_{j_2 j_1}$ are removed from C while $c_{j_3 j_1} = c_{j_3 j_1} \cap (c_{j_2 j_1} \circ c_{j_3 j_2})$ and new constraint $c_{j_3 i_2} = c_{j_2 i_2} \circ c_{j_3 j_2}$ is introduced to C. One can verify that both $c_{j_2 j_1}$ and $c_{j_2 i_2}$ are qualified. Hence, variables j_1 and i_2 are reachable from j_3 and thus are put into L. Assume j_1 is selected from L. Since there are no other constraints on j_1, nothing is done. Variable i_2 is then selected from L. By eliminating i_2 using j_3, $c_{i_2 i_1}$ and $c_{i_2 i_3}$ are removed from C and $c_{j_3 i_1}$ and $c_{j_3 i_3}$ are added to C. Constraint $c_{i_2 i_1}$ is qualified, and thus

---

algorithm Linear-Elimination(**inout** (N, D, C)) {
1. Find a functional elimination ordering O of the problem;
2. Let C^0 be C; any c_{ij} in C^0 is denoted by c_{ij}^0;
3. For each $i \in N$, it is marked as not *eliminated*;
4. **while** (O is not empty) {
      Take and delete the first variable i from O;
6.   **if** (i is **not** *eliminated*) {
8. $L \leftarrow \{j \mid (i, j) \in C$ and c_{ij}^0 is functional$\}$;
9.   **while** (L not empty) {
          Take and delete j from L;
11.   **for** any $c_{jk} \in C - \{c_{ji}\}$ { // Substitute i for j in c_{jk};
             $c_{ik}' \leftarrow c_{jk} \circ c_{ij} \cap c_{ik}$;
             $C \leftarrow C \cup \{c_{ik}'\} - \{c_{jk}\}$;
14.   **if** (c_{jk}^0 is functional) **then**
15. $L \leftarrow L \cup \{k\}$;
         }
16.   Mark j as *eliminated*;
      } // loop on L
    }
 } // loop on O
} // end of algorithm

Fig. 4. A variable elimination algorithm of complexity $O(ed^2)$

i_1 is added to L. Note that $c_{i_2 i_3}$ is not qualified because it is not functional on i_3 in terms of the graph. We take out the only variable i_1 in L. After i_1 is eliminated using j_3, $c_{i_1 i_3}$ is removed from C, and constraint $c_{j_3 i_3}$ is updated to be $c_{j_3 i_3} \cap (c_{i_1 i_3} \circ c_{j_3 i_1})$. Since $c_{i_1 i_3}$ is qualified, i_3 is added to L. One can see that although i_3 was not reachable when i_2 was eliminated, it finally becomes reachable because of i_1. In general, all variables in a strongly connected component are reachable from the variable under processing if one of them is reachable. Now, take i_3 out of L, and nothing is done because there are no other constraints incident on it. Every variable except j_3 is marked as *eliminated* (Line 16), the **while** loop on O (Line 4 and 6) terminates.

Theorem 2. *Given a CSP problem, the worst case time complexity of* Linear-Elimination *is* $O(ed^2)$ *where e is the number of constraints and d the size of maximum domain in the problem.*

Proof. To find a functional elimination ordering involves the identification of strongly connected components and topological sorting. Each of two operations takes linear time. Therefore, Line 1 of the algorithm takes $\mathcal{O}(n + e)$.

The **while** loop of Line 4 takes $\mathcal{O}(ed^2)$. Assume that there is a unique identification number associated with each constraint in C. After some variable of a constraint is substituted, the constraint's identification number refers to the new constraint. For any identification number α, let its first associated constraint be c_{jk}. Assuming j is substituted by some other variable i, we can show that i

will be never be substituted later in the algorithm. By the algorithm, i is selected at Line 6. So, all variables before i in O have been processed. Since i is not eliminated, it is not reachable from any variable before it (in terms of O) through qualified constraints (due to loop of Line 9). Hence, there are two cases: 1) there is no constraint c_{mi} of C such that c_{mi}^0 is functional on i, 2) there is at least one constraint c_{mi} of C such that c_{mi}^0 is functional on i. In the first case, our algorithm will never substitute i by any other variable. By definition of functional elimination ordering, case 2 implies that i belongs to a strongly connected component whose variables have not been eliminated yet. Since all variables in the component will be substituted by i, after the loop of Line 9, there is no constraint c_{mi} of C such that c_{mi}^0 is functional on i. Hence, i will never be substituted. In a similar fashion, if variable k is substituted by l, l will never be substituted later by the algorithm. So, there are at most two substitutions occurring to α. By definition, substitution involves a functional constraint, its complexity is $O(d^2)$ in the worst case. Since there is a unique identification number for each constraint, the time taken by **while** loop at Line 4 is $O(ed^2)$.

In summary, the worst case time complexity of the algorithm is $O(ed^2)$. □

To characterize the property of `Linear-Elimination`, we need the following notation.

Definition 5. *Given a problem P, let C^0 be the constraints before* `Linear-Elimination` *and C the constraints of the problem at any moment during the algorithm. A constraint c_{ij} of C is* trivially functional *if it is functional and satisfies the condition: c_{ij}^0 is functional or there is a path $i_1(=i), i_2, \cdots, i_m(=j)$ in C_0 such that $c_{i_k i_{k+1}}^0 (k \in 1..m-1)$ is functional on i_{k+1}.*

Theorem 3. *Algorithm* `Linear-Elimination` *transforms a CSP (N, D, C) into a canonical functional form if all newly produced functional constraints (due to substitution) are trivially functional.*

The proof of this result is straightforward and thus omitted here.

Corollary 1. *For a CSP problem with non-functional constraints and bi-functional constraints, the worst case time complexity of algorithm* `Linear-Elimination` *is linear to the problem size.*

This result follows the observation below. When the functional constraint involved in a substitution is bi-functional, the complexity of the composition is linear to the constraints involved. From the proof of Theorem 2, the complexity of the algorithm is linear to the size of all constraints, i.e., the problem size.

Corollary 2. *Consider a CSP with both functional and non-functional constraints. If there is a variable of the problem such that every variable of the CSP is reachable from it in P^F, the satisfiability of the problem can be decided in $\mathcal{O}(ed^2)$ using* `Linear-Elimination`.

For a problem with the property given in the corollary, its canonical functional form becomes a star graph. So, any value in the domain of the free variable is extensible to a solution if we add (arc) consistency enforcing during `Linear-Elimination`. The problem is not satisfiable if a domain becomes empty during the elimination process.

5   Experimental Results

We investigate to see the effectiveness of variable elimination on problem solving. In our experiments, a problem is either directly solved by a general solver or variable elimination is invoked before the solver.

Since there are no publicly available benchmarks on functional constraints, we generate random problems $\langle n, d, e, nf, t \rangle$ where n is the number of variables, d domain size, e the number of constraints, nf the number of functional constraints, and t the tightness of non-functional constraints. Tightness r is defined as the percentage of allowed tuples over d^2. Except the nf functional constraints, all other constraints are non-functional. Each functional constraint is made to have d allowed tuples. Our implementation allows other tightness for functional constraints. However, we observed from the experiments that if we make the number of allowed tuples less than d, the problems are easy (i.e., with very few backtracks) to solve.

We selected meaningful problems from the ones generated to do benchmarking. In the context of random problems, the tightness $1/d$ of functional constraints is rather tight. Therefore, when we increase nf, the "hardness" of the problems drops correspondingly. In our experiments, we systematically examine the problems with the following setting: n, d are 50, e varies from 100 to 710 with step size 122 (10% of all possible constraints), nf varies from 2 to 12, and t varies from 0.2 to 1.0 with step size 0.05. When nf is small (e.g, 2), there are so many hard problems that we can only scan a small portion of the problems (we stop running when the time limit $4 * 10^4$s is reached). When nf is large (e.g., 12), even for the most difficult problem instances, the number of backtracks is small and thus they are simple. For example, when $nf = 12$, the most difficult problems are with $e = 710$. The table below shows the hardness of the problems, with $nf = 12$ and $e = 710$, in terms of number of backtracks (#bt) needed. When t is from 0.2 to 0.65, #bt is 0. For the most difficult case of t being 0.8, #bt is small (around 1000). On the other hand, when nf is small, one can expect that the application of elimination may not make much difference.

t	$0.2 - 0.65$	0.7	0.75	0.8	0.85	$0.9 - 0.95$
#bt	0	5.7	22.9	1023	0.2	0

Due to the observations above, we evaluate the algorithm on non-trivial cases (e.g., trivial cases include few backtracks or very small number of functional constraints). We study the effectiveness of variable elimination for each nf on the most difficult problems as we discovered in the exploration process above. The results with nf varying from 6 to 12 are shown in Fig. 5. The results were obtained on a DELL PowerEdge 1850 (two 3.6GHz Intel Xeon CPUs) in Linux. We implement both the elimination algorithm and a general solver in C++. The

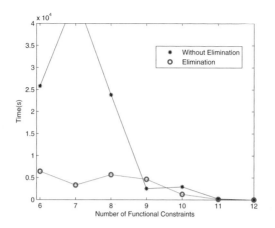

Fig. 5. Performance of the algorithms on random problems. When $nf = 7$, time limit is reached by the solver without variable elimination.

solver uses the standard backtracking algorithm. During the search, a variable with maximum degree is selected first with tie broken by lexicographical order while the value of a variable is selected in a lexicographical order.

For the problem instances used in Figure 5, the time to transform the instances into their canonical forms is negligible compared to the time solving the problems. There are two reasons. First, the number of constraints involved in the elimination is relatively small compared to the total number of constraints in the problems. Second, the algorithm is as efficient as the optimal general arc consistency algorithm used in the solver. Thirdly, the elimination is applied only once before the backtracking search.

The results show that the variable elimination can significantly speed up problem solving by more than 5 times on difficult problems where a lot of backtracks occur. As the number of functional constraints increases, one would assume that the variable elimination should be more effective. However, we notice that as the number of functional constraints increases, the random problems become simpler, which may decrease the benefit of elimination. For example, when $nf = 12$ (see the table above), to solve the problems, the solver only needs about a thousand backtracks. In this case, the variable elimination will not be able to save much. We notice that when $nf = 9$, the variable elimination approach is slower. There are two possible explanations. The first is that variable elimination changes the topology of the problem, which may affect the effectiveness of the heuristics of the general solver. The second is that we use only 10 problem instances per configuration which may cause some unstable results. We have also manually tried many configurations. The results show very similar trend to the one in Fig. 5.

Remark. Views which are used in several existing CP systems (e.g., [9]) can be thought of as an efficient way to enforce arc consistency on bi-functional constraints. We used our own solver rather than one with views due to the following reason. The percentage of functional constraints in our problem instances is less than 2%. Improving the arc consistency efficiency on them won't affect the overall performance too much.

6   Variable Elimination and Non-binary Constraints

Non-binary constraints such as arithmetic or global constraints are common in CP systems. We discuss how variable elimination of functional constraints can be applied to these constraints.

Non-binary constraints are either extensional (defined explicitly) or intensional (defined implicitly). To substitute a variable in an extensional non-binary constraints, we can define the composition of a non-binary constraint with a binary constraint as a straightforward generalization of the composition operation defined in Section 2.

For intentional constraints, there are usually particular propagators with specific algorithm for the constraint. We sketch below an approach which allows variable elimination to be employed with generic propagators. Assume we have a linear constraint c_1: $ax + by + cz < d$ and a constraint c_{wy} functional on y. To substitute y in c_1, we simply modify c_1 to be $ax + bw + cz < d$ and mark w as a *shadow variable* (w needs special treatment by the propagator, which will be clear later). We call y the *shadowed* variable. Assume we also have c_{uw} functional on w. To eliminate w, c_1 is further changed to $ax + bu + cz < d$. Since w is a shadow variable, we generate a new constraint c_{uy} using c_{uw} and c_{wy} in a standard way as discussed in this paper. Now u becomes the shadow variable while the shadowed variable is still y (variable w is gone). Assume we need to make c_1 arc consistency. First "synchronize the domains" of y and u using c_{uy}, i.e., enforce arc consistency on c_{uy}. (Note that due to elimination, c_{wy} and c_{uw} are no longer involved in constraint solving). Next, we enforce arc consistency on c_1. During the process, since u is a shadow variable, all domain operations are on y instead of u. After making c_1 arc consistent, synchronize the domain of y and u again. (If the domain of u is changed, initiate constraint propagation on constraints involving u.) This approach is rather generic: for any intensional constraints, synchronize the domains of the shadow variables and shadowed variables, apply whatever propagation methods on the shadowed variables (and other non-shadow variables), synchronize the domains of shadow variables and shadowed variables again. In fact, the synchronization of the domains of the shadow and shadowed variables (e.g., u and y above) can be easily implemented using the concept of views [9].

7   Related Work

Bi-functional constraints have been studied in the context of arc consistency (AC) algorithms since Van Hentenryck et al. [11] proposed a worst case optimal AC algorithm with $O(ed)$, which is better than the time complexity ($\mathcal{O}(ed^2)$) of optimal AC algorithms such as AC2001/3.1 [2] for arbitrary binary constraints.

Liu [8] proposed a fast AC algorithm for a special class of *increasing* bi-functional constraints. Affane and Bennaceur [1] introduced a new type of consistency, label-arc consistency, and showed that the bi-functional constraints with limited extensions to other constraints can be (globally) solved, but no detailed analysis of their algorithms is given. In [12], we proposed a variable elimination method to solve *bi-functional* constraints in $\mathcal{O}(ed)$. Functional constraints are not discussed in those works.

David introduced *pivot consistency* for binary functional constraints in [3]. Both pivot consistency and variable substitution help to reduce a CSP into a special form. There are some important differences between pivot consistency and variable substitution. First, the concept of pivot consistency, a special type of directional path consistency, is quite complex. It is defined in terms of a variable ordering, path (of length 2) consistency, and concepts in directed graphs. Variable substitution is a much simpler concept as shown in the paper. For both binary and non-binary CSPs, the concept of variable substitution is intuitive and simple. Next, by the definition of pivot consistency, to make a CSP pivot consistent, there must be a certain functional constraint on each of the *non-root* variables. Variable substitution is more flexible. It can be applied whenever there is a functional constraint in a problem. Finally, to reduce a problem, the variable elimination algorithm takes $\mathcal{O}(ed^2)$ while pivot consistency algorithm takes $\mathcal{O}((n^2 - r^2)d^2)$, where r is the number of *root* variables.

Another related approach is bucket elimination [4]. The idea in common behind bucket elimination and variable substitution is to exclude the impact of a variable on the whole problem. The difference between them lies in the way variable elimination is performed. In each elimination step, substitution does not increase the arity of the constraints while bucket elimination could generate constraints with *higher arity* (possibly exponential space complexity). The former may generate more constraints than the latter, but it will *not* increase the total number of constraints in the problem.

CLP [6] systems often make use of variable substitution and elimination. The classic unification algorithm is a good example. A more complex example is CLP($\mathcal{R}$) [5] which has constraints on finite trees and arithmetic. Variables in arithmetic constraints are substituted out using a parametric normal form which is applied during unification and also when solving arithmetic constraints. Our approach is compatible with such CLP solvers which reduce the constraint store to a normal form using variable substitution. We remark that any CLP language or system which has finite domain constraints or CSP constraints will deal with bi-functional constraints because of unification. Thus, a variable substitution approach will actually be more powerful than just simple finite domain propagation on equations.

8   Conclusion

We have introduced a variable substitution method to reduce a problem with both functional and non-functional constraints. Compared with the previous work on bi-functional and functional constraints, the new method is not only conceptually simple and intuitive but also reflects the fundamental property of functional constraints. Our experiments also show that variable elimination can significantly improve the performance of a general solver in dealing with functional constraints.

For a binary CSP with both functional and non-functional constraints, an algorithm is presented to transform it into a canonical functional form in $\mathcal{O}(ed^2)$. This leads to a substantial simplification of the CSP with respect to the functional constraints. In some cases, as one of our results (Corollary 2) shows, the CSP is already solved. Otherwise, the canonical form can be solved by ignoring the eliminated variables. For example, this means that search only needs to solve a smaller problem than the one before variable substitution (or elimination).

References

1. Affane, M.S., Bennaceur, H.: A Labelling Arc Consistency Method for Functional Constraints. In: Freuder, E.C. (ed.) CP 1996. LNCS, vol. 1118, pp. 16–30. Springer, Heidelberg (1996)
2. Bessiere, C., Regin, J.C., Yap, R.H.C., Zhang, Y.: An Optimal Coarse-grained Arc Consistency Algorithm. Artificial Intelligence 165(2), 165–185 (2005)
3. David, P.: Using Pivot Consistency to Decompose and Solve Functional CSPs. J. of Artificial Intelligence Research 2, 447–474 (1995)
4. Dechter, R.: Bucket elimination: A Unifying Framework for Reasoning. Artificial Intelligence 113, 41–85 (1999)
5. Jaffar, J., Michaylov, S., Stuckey, P.J., Yap, R.H.C.: The CLP($\mathcal{R}$) Language and System. ACM Trans. on Programming Languages and Systems 14(3), 339–395 (1992)
6. Jaffar, J., Maher, M.J.: Constraint Logic Programming. J. of Logic Programming 19/20, 503–581 (1994)
7. Kirousis, L.M.: Fast Parallel Constraint Satisfaction. Artificial Intelligence 64, 147–160 (1993)
8. Liu, B.: Increasing Functional Constraints Need to be Checked Only Once. In: IJCAI 1995, pp. 119–125. Morgan Kaufmann, San Francisco (1995)
9. Schulte, C., Tack, G.: Views and Iterators for Generic Constraint Implementations. In: Hnich, B., Carlsson, M., Fages, F., Rossi, F. (eds.) CSCLP 2005. LNCS, vol. 3978, pp. 118–132. Springer, Heidelberg (2006); In: van Beek, P. (ed.) CP 2005. LNCS, vol. 3709, pp. 817–821. Springer, Heidelberg (2005)
10. Stallman, R.M., Sussman, G.J.: Forward Reasoning and Dependency-directed Backtracking in a System for Computer-aided Circuit Analysis. Artificial Intelligence 9(2), 135–196 (1977)
11. Van Hentenryck, P., Deville, Y., Teng, C.M.: A Generic Arc-consistency Algorithm and its Specializations. Artificial Intelligence 58, 291–321 (1992)
12. Zhang, Y., Yap, R.H.C., Jaffar, J.: Functional Elimination and 0/1/All Constraints. In: AAAI 1999, pp. 275–281. AAAI Press, Menlo Park (1999)

Two WAM Implementations of Action Rules

Bart Demoen[1] and Phuong-Lan Nguyen[2]

[1] Department of Computer Science, K.U.Leuven, Belgium
[2] Institut de Mathématiques Appliquées, UCO, Angers, France

Abstract. Two implementations of Action Rules are presented in the context of a WAM-like Prolog system: one follows a meta-call based approach, the other uses suspended WAM environments on the WAM heap. Both are based on a program transformation that clarifies the semantics of Action Rules. Their implementation is compared experimentally to the TOAM-based implementation of Action Rules in B-Prolog. The suspension based approach is faster at reactivating agents on the instantiation event. The meta-call approach is easier to implement, performs overall very good and much better for synchronous events, and it is more flexible than the suspension based approaches.

1 Introduction

The first publication of an implementation of delayed goals in the context of the WAM is by Carlsson [2]: a delayed goal is represented by a term on the heap and attached to a variable. The term is meta-called later. This method was originally only used for implementing *freeze/2*, and it has evolved into a more generally useful feature using attributed variables, in particular it is used in the implementation of (finite domain) constraint solvers.

In constraint solver programming, a constraint is often specified as a goal that waits to be re-executed every time one of the involved variables changes, e.g., an element of the domain is excluded, or the variable is fixed. It is important that the goal - usually a propagator - can be executed quickly, i.e., that the context switch from the normal execution to the propagator and back is cheap.

If the delayed goal needs to be executed on the instantiation of one variable, the term is meta-called just once. In other cases - e.g., when a domain change is the trigger - the goal possibly needs to be re-executed many times and the meta-call approach meta-calls the same term many times. Implementing this in the WAM is quite well understood and it requires no changes to the basic WAM architecture. However, in the WAM, meta-calling a term involves filling the argument registers, and most often, an environment for the called predicate must be allocated. Both add to the cost of the context switch.

In B-Prolog the cost of the context switch is kept down by exploiting the overall architecture of the TOAM [9,10]. Generally speaking, the TOAM pushes the execution state of predicates on the execution stack (including the information on alternative clauses) and passes arguments to calls on the same stack. Zhou used this mechanism for implementing *freeze/2* in [11]: for a delayed goal (named

M. Garcia de la Banda and E. Pontelli (Eds.): ICLP 2008, LNCS 5366, pp. 621–635, 2008.
© Springer-Verlag Berlin Heidelberg 2008

an agent), the implementation builds a suspension frame on the execution stack, blocks it - i.e., protects it from being popped prematurely - and reuses it every time the agent is reactivated. In this way, the setup of the goal which the meta-call approach performs at every activation, is done only once. However, there are some disadvantages to blocking frames on the execution stack, the most prominent being that other frames can become unreachable while not on the top of the stack and that in the absence of backtracking, the space occupied by these frames cannot be recovered without a garbage collector for the execution stack.

In B-Prolog, suspended goals can be specified by Action Rules: the predecessors of Action Rules were named delay clauses in [11]. Action Rules offer two highly valuable features. First, with their powerful surface syntax, they allow a compact and concise specification of a goal waiting to be re-executed on different conditions. Secondly, Action Rules can be effectively mapped to efficient abstract machine code, at least in the TOAM. Indeed, the constraint solvers of B-Prolog derive their high performance partly from translating constraints to specialized Action Rules predicates [12]. The efficiency of the B-Prolog constraint solvers, as implemented with Action Rules, should be enough motivation to explore the implementation of Action Rules in any Prolog system. However, the perception exists that an efficient Action Rules implementation is reserved to the TOAM as implemented in B-Prolog. The challenge to WAM implementors is therefore clear: design an efficient WAM implementation of Action Rules, while not changing the WAM in a fundamental way.

Two designs for implementing Action Rules in the WAM look attractive: the first uses the meta-call approach to delaying goals and carefully applies a number of optimizations so that the desired performance is obtained. The second design uses suspension frames in the spirit of the TOAM, but in contrast with the B-Prolog approach, the suspension frames are kept on the WAM heap, not on the control stack. Similar optimizations are applied here as well. We have implemented these two approaches in hProlog (see [5] for the origin of hProlog). This allows us to compare these approaches experimentally in a meaningful way with each other, and with B-Prolog. The experience reported here shows that the TOAM does not have an inherent advantage over the WAM for implementing Action Rules.

We first introduce some Action Rules terminology in Section 2. Section 3 explains Action Rules by means of a program transformation to Prolog: such a transformation has not been described before. It is the starting point for an efficient meta-call based implementation of Action Rules. Section 4 describes the basics of how a WAM environment can be kept on the heap and used as a suspension frame for re-entering the same clause more than once. In Section 5 we use suspension frames on the WAM heap for implementing Action Rules, following a variant of the transformation in Section 3. Section 6 describes a number of implementation details. Section 7 contains an empirical evaluation and comparison of our implementations with B-Prolog. Section 8 argues why we prefer the meta-call approach. Section 9 concludes.

We assume working knowledge of Prolog [3], the WAM [1,7], the TOAM [10], and some acquaintance with Action Rules [12] and attributed variables (see for instance the documentation of [8]).

2   Action Rules Terminology

The words *event* and *agent* are overloaded in the original Action Rules terminology of [12]. Therefore, just for the sake of this paper, we will stick to the meanings described hereafter. One rule in Action Rules has the form:

```
Head, Guard, {EventPats} => Body.
```

The *Head* looks like the head of a Prolog clause: instead of full unification, it uses one-way unification, otherwise named matching. The *Guard* is a conjunction of guard goals. It functions like the guard in committed choice languages: once a guard succeeds, execution commits to that rule. [12] refers to the constituents between the {} as *event pattern*: *EventPats* is a comma separated list of such event patterns each of which can lead to reactivation of the agent. The *Body* looks like an ordinary Prolog clause body. We assume that the *Head* has distinct variables as arguments: one can move the head matching to the guard. B-Prolog puts restrictions on which guards are allowed, but such restrictions are not relevant for this paper.

The principal functor of the head is an Action Rules predicate symbol. An Action Rules predicate can be defined by more than one rule, but it cannot be the head of an ordinary Prolog clause at the same time. An *agent* corresponds to a call to an Action Rules predicate: it can be suspended and activated more than once.

3   How Action Rules Work

Informally, the meaning of an Action Rules predicate, is as follows: if *ins(X)* appears as the event pattern of the selected rule, the agent is reactivated when X is instantiated, or, said differently, when the *event* 'X becomes instantiated' occurs; if *event(X,M)* appears as the event pattern, the agent is reactivated every time there is a call *post_event(X,Mess)* and in the reactivated agent, M is replaced by Mess; if *generated* appears in the event pattern, the agent's body is executed immediately when the agent is created. We treat only these three event patterns explicitly in this paper, but extending our approach to other event patterns is straightforward. An agent dies when a rule without event patterns is selected.

This short description is not detailed enough for building a complete implementation of Action Rules, and lacking a formal Action Rules semantics, we have made a specification of the most important aspects of Action Rules by means of a program transformation to Prolog with attributed variables[1]. Our specification does not capture every aspect of Action Rules, let alone the full B-Prolog

---

[1] We use SWI-Prolog [8] syntax, but any variant will do.

behavior, but it makes the essentials of Action Rules easier to understand and it will be clear how to add the other features of the B-Prolog implementation. We start by showing the transformation on an example in Section 3.1. Section 3.2 describes the transformation in general, while Section 3.3 fills out the remaining details about events.

3.1   Transforming Action Rules to Prolog: An Example

Below is an Action Rules predicate *p/2* with three rules:

```
1   p(X,Y), G1, {ins(X), ins(Y), event(X,M)} => B1(X,Y,M).
2   p(X,Y), G2, {ins(Y), generated}          => B2(X,Y).
3   p(X,Y), G3                                => B3(X,Y).
```

in which G and B denote a guard and a body. We transform it to Prolog as follows:

```
4    p(X,Y) :- G1, !,
5               SuspGoal = p_agent(Message,Alive,X,Y),
6               register_events([ins(X), ins(Y), event(X,M)],SuspGoal).

7    p(X,Y) :- G2, !,
8               SuspGoal = p_agent(Message,Alive,X,Y),
9               register_events([ins(Y)],SuspGoal),
10              B2(X,Y).

11   p(X,Y) :- G3,
12              B3(X,Y).


13   p_agent(_,Alive,_,_) :- Alive == dead, !.

14   p_agent(M,_,X,Y) :- G1, !, B1(X,Y,M).
15   p_agent(_,_,X,Y) :- G2, !, B2(X,Y).
16   p_agent(_,Alive,X,Y) :- G3, Alive = dead, B3(X,Y).
```

The transformation generates two Prolog predicates: *p/2* and *p_agent/4*. The three clauses for *p/2* in lines 4..12 correspond to the three rules for *p/2* in lines 1..3. If the rule corresponding to the clause has event patterns, a term SuspGoal is created, and the call to *register_events/2* makes sure that this term is attached to the relevant variables as specified by the event patterns of the rule. The latter happens in lines 6 and 9. If the corresponding rule has no event patterns, or *generated* is one of its event patterns, the body is executed. This happens in lines 10 and 12.

The predicate *p_agent/4* has two extra arguments: the argument *Alive* represents the liveness of the agent; killing an agent is done by unifying this variable with the atom *dead*. The argument *Message* is a placeholder for the message sent in a *post_event(X,Message)* goal and thus corresponds to the second argument in an event pattern of the form *event(X,Message)*.

p_agent/4 is called when an event takes place that reactivates the agent. Its first clause checks the liveness of the agent: if the agent is dead already, then its reactivation just succeeds. The other clauses correspond to the rules of the Action Rules predicate: they check the guard, commit to a clause and execute the corresponding body. If the corresponding rule has no event patterns, the agent is killed, as in line 16. Note that this unifies the second argument of SuspGoal with the atom *dead*.

The two predicates *p/2* and *p_agent/4* correspond to two phases in the life of an agent. *p/2* is executed on the initial call and can register events depending on the event patterns of the selected rule: the agent is created, and then goes to sleep while waiting for events. *p_agent/4* is executed when the agent is reactivated: the event patterns are no longer needed. Reactivation of an agent happens by meta-calling the term, constructed as SuspGoal, as is explained in Section 3.3.

3.2   General Transformation from Action Rules to Prolog

The general transformation of an Action Rules predicate *p/n* is shown. Let

```
p(X1,...,Xn), Guard_i, {EventPats_i} => Body_i.
```

be the ith rule. The transformation generates:

```
% code for p/n
% i-th clause corresponding to i-th rule
p(X1,...,Xn) :- Guard_i, !,
        SuspGoal = p_agent(Message,Alive,X1,...,Xn),
        register_events(EventPats_i,SuspGoal),
        exec_body(EventPats_i,Body_i).


% code for the suspended p_agent/(n+2)
% first clause
p_agent(_,Alive,_,...,_) :- Alive == dead, !.

% (i+1)-th clause corresponding to i-th rule
p_agent(Message,Alive,X1,...,Xn) :- Guard_i, !,
        kill(EventPats_i,Alive),
        Body_i.
```

Note that the arguments to *exec_body/2*, *kill/2* and *register_events/2* are manifest at transformation time, so their calls can be unfolded. We use {} for denoting the absence of event patterns; syntactically, this is not accepted by B-Prolog. The definitions of *exec_body/2* and *kill/2* are:

```
exec_body(EventPats,Body) :-
        ((isin(generated,EventPats) ; EventPats == {}) ->
              Body
        ;
              true
        ).


kill(Es,Alive) :- Es == {} -> Alive = dead ; true.
```

3.3   Registering and Dealing with Events

The event pattern *generated* has no explicit post associated to it. We show the details for the two other event patterns: *ins/1* and *event/2*. Instantiation happens asynchronously, i.e., the Prolog unification routine intercepts the instantiation of a variable which has a goal waiting on its instantiation, and puts the goal in a queue. Goals from this queue are executed as early as possible. *Event/2* events happen by explicitly calling the predicate *post_event/2*.

Registering Events. For every event pattern in its first argument, the predicate *register_events/2* calls *register_event/2*[2]:

```
register_events([],_).
register_events([E|Es],G) :- register_event(E,G), register_events(Es,G).

register_event(ins(X),G) :- attach_goal(X,ins1,G).
register_event(event(X,_),G) :- attach_goal(X,event2,G).
register_event(generated,_).

attach_goal(X,E,G) :-
        (var(X) ->
              (get_attr(X,E,Gs) ->
                     put_attr(X,E,[G|Gs])
              ;
                     put_attr(X,E,[G])
              )
        ;
              true
        ).
```

attach_goal/3 builds a list of all the agents waiting on the same event.

---

[2] According to the B-Prolog manual, the *ins1* goal should be attached to all variables in the term X in *ins(X)*, but this does not affect the benchmarks.

Posting Events and Activating Agents. *Post_event/2* is implemented as:

```
post_event(X,Mes) :- get_attr(X,event2,Gs), !, send_message(Gs,Mes).
post_event(_,_).

send_message([],_).
send_message([G|Gs],Mes) :-
           send_message(Gs,Mes),
           G =.. [Name,_|Args],
           NewG =.. [Name,Mes|Args],
           call(NewG).
```

Posting a Herbrand event (corresponding to *ins/1*) consists in instantiating a variable. If X has an *ins1* attribute, and X is unified with a non-variable T, then *ins1:attr_unify_handler/2* is called with as first argument the *ins1* attribute of X and as second argument T. Remember that the *ins1* attribute is a list of goal terms. The handler is defined as[3]:

```
ins1:attr_unify_handler(Ins1AttrX,_) :- call_reverse_list(Ins1AttrX).

call_reverse_list([]).
call_reverse_list([G|Gs]) :- call_reverse_list(Gs), call(G).
```

Note that *call_reverse_list/1* and *send_message/2* are left-recursive: in this way, we respect the B-Prolog order of reactivating agents.

This concludes the transformation of Action Rules to Prolog: our implementations of Action Rules later on respect the implied semantics. Moreover, our meta-call approach is really an optimized version of the transformation.

4   Suspension Frames on the WAM Heap

We start with an example: below is a declaration and a clause for *foo/3*, one clause for *p/0* and a query with its resulting output.

```
:- suspension(foo/3).        p :-                          ?- p.
foo(X,Y,SuspTerm) :-             foo(X,Y,SuspTerm),            first(X,Y)
        writeln(first(X,Y)),     X = 1,                        next(1,Y)
        yield(SuspTerm),         resume(SuspTerm),             next(1,2)
        writeln(next(X,Y)),      Y = 2,
        leave.                   resume(SuspTerm).
```

The idea is that *yield/1* transfers control back to the caller and returns a description of an execution environment in its argument. The predicate *resume/1* uses this description to resume execution just after the call to *yield/1*. The predicate *leave/0* returns to the caller. With this informal explanation, the output

---

[3] The shown handler deals only with the case of unification of a variable with a non-variable: it can be extended easily to deal with the unification of two suspension variables.

from the query *?- p* can already be understood. A more detailed explanation follows.

The declaration *:- suspension(foo/3).* tells the compiler that the code for the (single) clause for *foo/3* must start with the instruction *alloc_heap*: it acts like the WAM instruction *allocate*, except that it allocates the environment - named a suspension frame - on the heap. No other changes to code generation are needed for *foo/3*. *Yield/1*, *resume/1* and *leave/0* are new built-in predicates.

The goal *yield(SuspTerm)* performs two actions:

– SuspTerm is unified with a *suspension term* with arity four. Its first two arguments are the current environment pointer, i.e., the pointer to the current suspension frame on the heap, and a code pointer that points just after the goal *yield(SuspTerm)*, i.e., the point at which execution can be resumed later; the other two arguments are used for holding a message and for indicating whether the term represents a live agent: this anticipates the use of suspension terms for implementing Action Rules.
– control returns to the caller of *foo/3* without deallocating the suspension frame.

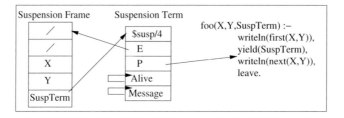

Fig. 1. Just after the execution of yield(SuspTerm)

The situation regarding the suspension frame and the suspension term (both on the heap) is depicted in Figure 1. The frame looks like an ordinary WAM environment, but its E and CP fields are irrelevant while the agent is sleeping, i.e., while no code in *foo/3* is executed.

The goal *resume(SuspTerm)* installs the environment pointer from SuspTerm in the WAM E register, and transfers control to the code pointed at by the code argument in the suspension term. It also fills out appropriately the E and CP fields in the suspension frame, for later use by *leave*. *Resume* can be called more than once with the same SuspTerm.

The goal *leave* returns to the caller of *foo/3* by using the E and CP fields in the current environment, which is in fact a suspension frame; *leave/0* does not deallocate the suspension frame.

The names *yield* and *resume* were chosen because of the obvious connection to coroutining. hProlog was extended with the new built-in predicates especially for our Action Rules experiment.

5 Using Heap Suspension Frames for Implementing Action Rules

This section is similar to Section 3: we start by redoing the example in Section 3.1, now using suspension frames on the heap. We skip Section 3.2 which generalizes the example: it should be clear how to do that. Section 5.2 is the heap suspension frame analogue of Section 3.3.

5.1 The Example

We reuse the example from Section 3.1. The transformation results in the following code for the two predicates *p/2* and *p_agent/3*:

```
15  p(X,Y) :- G1, !,
16             register_events([ins(X), ins(Y), event(X,M)],SuspTerm),
17             p_agent(X,Y,SuspTerm).

18  p(X,Y) :- G2, !,
19             register_events([ins(Y)],SuspTerm),
20             p_agent(X,Y,SuspTerm),
21             B2(X,Y).

22  p(X,Y) :- G3,
23             B3(X,Y).


24  :- suspension(p_agent/3).

25  p_agent(X,Y,SuspTerm) :-
26             yield(SuspTerm),
27             ( G1 -> pickup_message(SuspTerm,M), B1(X,Y,M), leave
28             ;
29               G2 -> B2(X,Y), leave
30             ;
31               G3, kill(SuspTerm), B3(X,Y), leave
32             ).
```

It should be clear how the three clauses in lines 15..23 correspond to the three rules in line 1..3. Also, the three disjunctive branches of *p_agent* in lines 27..31 correspond readily to those rules.

The goal *pickup_message(SuspTerm,M)* unifies variable *M* with the message slot in the suspension term SuspTerm: this slot is set by the predicate *set_message/2* that is explained in Section 5.2. The goal *kill(SuspTerm)* sets the live slot in the suspension term SuspTerm to *dead*: the built-in *resume/1* checks this slot before reactivating an agent. That is why *p_agent* does not check for liveness itself.

5.2 Registering and Dealing with Events

Registering Events. The code is the same as in Section 3.3, but now *attach_goal/3* builds a list of suspension terms.

Posting Events and Activating Agents. We need to redefine a number of predicates so that they take into account the fact that the attributes now contain a list of suspension terms. For the predicates dealing with the *ins1* event, these are:

```
ins1:attr_unify_handler(Ins1AttrX,_)  :- resume_goals(Ins1AttrX).

resume_goals([]).
resume_goals([X|R])  :- resume_goals(R), resume(X).
```

Of the predicates dealing with the event2 event, only *send_message/2* needs adapting - *post_event/2* remains the same:

```
send_message([],_).
send_message([S|Ss],M)  :-
     send_message(Ss,M),
     set_message(S,M),
     resume(S).
```

The idea is that at the reactivation of the agent the message is put in the *message* slot of the suspension term by the new built-in *set_message/2*. It is subsequently picked up in the body of the agent by *pickup_message/2*.

6   Making It Work

There are a few more issues to mention before the evaluation can take place.

The transformations. The transformations from Action Rules to Prolog described in Sections 3 and 5, have served as an explanation vehicle, and as the starting point for our implementations. However, as presented, the generated code still can benefit from some well understood optimizations: inlining, specialization, moving side-effect free code blocks ... Our final implementation applies such techniques. The most drastic change is that the two generated predicates p and p_agent for the suspension based method, are collapsed to one.

The representation of attributed variables. Our two implementations of Action Rules and the one in B-Prolog are based on some form of attributed variables. In B-Prolog those variables have several dedicated slots. We have applied that specialization to hProlog as well: for the purpose of this experiment, we have given hProlog attributed variables nine slots. The first slot is dedicated to the *ins/1* event pattern (used by *attach_goal(_,ins1,_)*) and the second to *event/2* (used by *attach_goal(_,event2,_)*). The seven remaining slots are meant for five different domain changes, a passive attribute and a finite domain: these are not used during the benchmarks, but they are properly initialized.

Low Level Support The predicates *yield/1, resume/1, leave/0* deal with the internals of the abstract machine, so they clearly must be implemented as low level built-ins. We have done the same with *pickup_message/2* and *set_message/2*. On top of that, some more effort was needed to achieve the desired performance:

- the last goal in a suspension predicate is *leave*; just before it, there is often a *call* instruction; a new instruction performs the action of both *leave* and *call*: the reason is mainly tail-call optimization.
- the code *G =.. [Name,_|Args], NewG =.. [Name,Mes|Args], call(NewG)* in Section 3.3 was collapsed to *event_call(Mes,G)*; *event_call/2* is one more new built-in predicate; in this case, a small implementation effort resulted in a large performance gain.
- the code implementing the meta-call moves the arguments of a term to the WAM argument registers; if *p* points just before the first argument of the term, then this code would routinely be written as:

```
for (i = 1; i =< arity; i++) Areg[i] = p[i];
```

However, for performance it is better to unroll this, for instance to:

```
Areg[1] = p[1]; Areg[2] = p[2]; Areg[3] = p[3];
if (arity < 4) get_out_of_here;
Areg[4] = p[4]; Areg[5] = p[5]; Areg[6] = p[6];
...
```

One should experiment to find the good unrolling granularity.
- we have also introduced a new instruction at the abstract machine level, that speeds up the reverse traversal of lists, as was needed in the predicates *call_reverse_list* and *send_message/2* (Sections 3.3 and 5.2).
- the general *attach_goal/3* predicate was specialized for its second argument to two built-ins *attach_ins1/2* and *attach_event2/2*.
- like some other implementations of the WAM, hProlog uses a separate stack for the choice points and the environments. With suspension frames on the heap, the *prev_E* field in an environment can point to the heap: code that maintains the top of environment stack TOS was adapted for this; moreover, the TOS is also pushed on the heap just before the suspension frame.

7   Evaluating the WAM Implementation of Action Rules

For the experiments, we have used B-Prolog 7.1b4.1 (the TOAM Jr. version [13]) and hProlog 2.9. The benchmarks were all run on a 1.8 GHz Pentium 4 CPU, under Debian. Garbage collection was avoided by starting the Prolog systems with enough initial memory. We always show timings relative to B-Prolog. B-Prolog is always at 100, and lower is faster. For the traditional benchmark set (not using Action Rules) hProlog 2.9 is about 10% faster than B-Prolog 7.1b4.1.

7.1   Original Benchmarks

Table 1 shows the results of running the benchmarks that were used in [11] to provide evidence for the qualities of the suspension mechanism in B-Prolog: it seems
only fitting to use the same set here. These benchmarks only use the *ins/1* event
pattern. The benchmarks are versions of the well known naive reverse, nqueens,
sendmoremoney, and permutation sort, all adapted to use delayed goals: these
benchmarks come with the B-Prolog distribution. In order to obtain meaningful
timings, nrev was run on a list of length 500, nqueens computes all solutions for
an 11x11 board, and the sort benchmark was given a list of 19 integers.

Table 1. The benchmark set of [11]

	bprolog	meta-call	suspension	# goals	# react
nrev	100	80	102	1	1
queens	100	88	111	10	4966
send	100	87	89	3	18412
sort	100	85	87	2	72827

Apart from the relative timings, Table 1 shows two characteristics of the
benchmarks. Column *# goals* is the number of agents suspended on each variable,
or equivalently, it is the length of the list built by *attach_goal* (for send, 3 is
actually the maximal length and the average is 1.9). The last column shows the
average number of times an agent is reactivated: the difference between nrev and
the other benchmarks stems from the fact that only nrev is deterministic.

Table 1 shows that our implementation of suspension frames on the heap
performs similar to the B-Prolog suspensions on the execution stack. It also
shows that the meta-call approach performs very well.

The performance of the above benchmarks is not dominated enough by the
operations related to delaying or waking goals. We therefore set up an artificial
experiment that measures the operations in isolation as much as possible. The
intention is to cancel out intrinsic performance differences between B-Prolog and
hProlog as much as possible. This seems the best way to gain more insight in
the relative performance of the operations we are really interested in.

7.2   Artificial Benchmarks for ins/1 and event/2

Table 2 summarizes the measurements on some artificial benchmarks. The B-
Prolog agents have arity 7. Note that this means arity 9 for the term to be
created and meta-called in the *meta-call/event2* entry . The benchmarks were
implemented in B-Prolog with Action Rules, and by using their translation to
our approaches. The columns represent the time needed to

- *freeze*: freezing a variable on a single goal; this measures agent creation.
- *melt*: melting a goal by instantiating a variable with a single goal suspended
  on it; this measures single agent reactivation on the *ins/1* event.

- *conjfreeze*: freezing one variable on 10^6 goals.
- *conjmelt*: melting a conjunction of 10^4 goals by instantiating a variable.
- *event2*: this corresponds to the cost of a goal *post_event(X,M)* when 10^4 agents are waiting on X to receive an *event/2* event.

Table 2. Some artificial benchmarks

	freeze	melt	conjfreeze	conjmelt	event2
bprolog	100	100	100	100	100
meta-call	70	87	56	86	44
suspension	97	57	78	58	101

The frozen goal was always of the form $p(\overline{X})$:- q, $r(\overline{X})$. (with trivial facts for $q/0$ and r/n) so that in the meta-call approach an environment is allocated, and some argument saving/restoring is needed. Otherwise the meta-call approach would have been given an unfair advantage.

Table 2 shows that for both types of events, the meta-call approach is always faster than B-Prolog, and often significantly so. This seems incompatible with the idea that the TOAM has an inherent advantage over the WAM for suspending and reactivating agents. hProlog suspensions on the other hand perform almost equal to B-Prolog for *event/2* events, and hProlog is much faster for instantiation events. This shows that our implementation of suspension frames on the heap is of a decent quality.

hProlog is the first system to implement both a meta-call approach to Action Rules and a suspension frame approach. It is therefore interesting to see that the hProlog suspension approach performs better than the hProlog meta-call approach when goals are melted: this confirms the analysis of [11] experimentally.

8   Discussion

The outcome of the performance experiment does not make the choice between the two WAM approaches for implementing Action Rules easy: on one hand, the suspension based approach reacts faster to instantiation events, but the meta-call approach is much faster on sending messages. The latter is very common in constraint solvers, for all kinds of domain changes. Other considerations besides performance must be taken into account. Here is a short account of what we consider important.

- The memory foot-print is larger for the suspension approach than for the meta-call approach: one needs the suspension term and the suspension frame in the former case, and only the term to be meta-called in the latter case. We have measured total memory consumption[4] on some of the benchmarks of Section 7.1. B-Prolog uses between 15% more and 7% less memory than our suspension based method. The meta-call based method uses systematically 30% less than B-Prolog.

---

[4] The sum of the memory usage in the control stacks plus the heap.

- The suspension approach makes it more difficult to support recursive activation of agents, as for instance in the following rule:

```
p(X,Y), {ins(X), ins(Y)} => foo(X), Y = 2, bla(X,Y).
```

On the query *?- p(X,Y), X = 1.* the goal *Y = 2* reactivates the running agent. Also re-entering an Action Rules body through backtracking (which is not even supported in B-Prolog) is cumbersome and has a performance cost. In the meta-call approach, recursive activation of agents, as well as supporting backtracking into the Action Rules body, comes at no implementation or performance price.
- Clearly, the meta-call approach lends itself better to implementing custom tailored scheduling of agents: the agent is just a term which can be inspected and manipulated with the standard predicates. This is more difficult for suspension frames, whether on the heap or on the control stack.
- A dead agent is semantically garbage, but it can still be in the conjunction of agents attached to a variable: such a dead agent can be garbage collected, and B-Prolog does so. This can be done in both of our approaches. Neither approach seems to offer an advantage over the other on this issue.

Given the performance of the meta-call approach, its flexibility and its zero impact on the rest of the WAM implementation, we have a clear preference for the meta-call approach.

9   Conclusion

The basic suspension frame mechanism goes back to the first description of coroutines in [4]. It has been applied and reinvented many times. Environments on the WAM heap were used by Shen [6] in the DASWAM to implement and-parallelism: code executing with a heap environment can be suspended at any point, and resumed later from the same point once. In the case of Action Rules, execution can be resumed many times from the same suspension point. Those differences are not really important.

We are generally interested in understanding to what extent the TOAM gives a performance advantage over the WAM, and in this particular case for implementing Action Rules. Our results show that the WAM performs similar to the TOAM when a similar technique is used, namely suspension frames. Whether these frames are kept on the heap or on the control stack plays only a minor role, but in the WAM one would prefer the heap because that requires smaller changes to the abstract machine. However, it seems that a rather traditional meta-call approach to implementing Action Rules performs very good and often better. This is good news for WAM implementors, as a few small non-intrusive additions to the WAM suffice to achieve excellent performance. The choice for a meta-call approach to implementing Action Rules is justified further by the ease with which one can cater for recursive activation of agents, agents with a non-deterministic body, and custom build scheduling strategies.

[12] shows that Action Rules form a powerful tool for the constraint solver programmer. The efficient implementation of Action Rules seemed reserved to B-Prolog. This paper shows that also WAM based implementations can take advantage of the expressive power of Action Rules. Hopefully, this will have a positive impact on the future development of constraint solvers in WAM-based Prolog systems.

Acknowledgements. We thank Neng-Fa Zhou for helping us understand Action Rules. This work was partly done while the first author enjoyed the hospitality of the Institut de Mathématiques Appliquées of the Université Catholique de l'Ouest in Angers, France. We also thank Henk Vandecasteele letting us use his hipP compiler.

References

1. Aït-Kaci, H.: The WAM: a (real) tutorial. Technical Report 5, DEC Paris Research Report (1990)
2. Carlsson, M.: Freeze, Indexing, and Other Implementation Issues in the WAM. In: Lassez, J.-L. (ed.) Logic Programming: Proc. of the Fourth International Conference, vol. 1, pp. 40–58. MIT Press, Cambridge (1987)
3. Clocksin, W., Mellish, C.: Programming in Prolog. Springer, Heidelberg (1984)
4. Conway, M.E.: Design of a Separable Transition-Diagram Compiler. Communications of the ACM 6(7), 396–408 (1963)
5. Demoen, B., Nguyen, P.-L.: So many WAM variations, so little time. In: Lloyd, J., Dahl, V., Furbach, U., Kerber, M., Lau, K.-K., Palamidessi, C., Pereira, L.M., Sagiv, Y., Stuckey, P.J. (eds.) CL 2000. LNCS, vol. 1861, pp. 1240–1254. Springer, Heidelberg (2000)
6. Shen, K.: Overview of DASWAM: Exploitation of Dependent And-parallelism. JLP 29(1-3), 245–293 (1996)
7. Warren, D.H.D.: An Abstract Prolog Instruction Set. Technical Report 309, SRI (1983)
8. Wielemaker, J.: SWI-Prolog release 5.4.0 (2004), http://www.swi-prolog.org/
9. Zhou, N.-F.: Global optimizations in a Prolog compiler for the TOAM. Journal of Logic Programming 15(4), 275–294 (1993)
10. Zhou, N.-F.: On the Scheme of Passing Arguments in Stack Frames for Prolog. In: Proceedings of The International Conference on Logic Programming, pp. 159–174. MIT Press, Cambridge (1994)
11. Zhou, N.-F.: A Novel Implementation Method for Delay. In: Joint Internatinal Conference and Symposium on Logic Programming, pp. 97–111. MIT Press, Cambridge (1996)
12. Zhou, N.-F.: Programming Finite-Domain Constraint Propagators in Action Rules. Theory and Practice of Logic Programming (TPLP) 6(5), 483–508 (2006)
13. Zhou, N.-F.: A Register-Free Abstract Prolog Machine with Jumbo Instructions. In: Dahl, V., Niemelä, I. (eds.) ICLP 2007. LNCS, vol. 4670, pp. 455–457. Springer, Heidelberg (2007)

Constraint-Level Advice for Shaving

Radoslaw Szymanek[1] and Christophe Lecoutre[2]

[1] Artificial Intelligence Laboratory, EPFL, Switzerland
radoslaw.szymanek@epfl.ch
[2] CRIL-CNRS UMR 8188, Universite d'Artois, Lens, France
lecoutre@cril.fr

Abstract. This work concentrates on improving the robustness of constraint solvers by increasing the propagation strength of constraint models in a declarative and automatic manner. Our objective is to efficiently identify and remove shavable values during search. A value is shavable if as soon as it is assigned to its associated variable an inconsistency can be detected, making it possible to refute it. We extend previous work on shaving by using different techniques to decide if a given value is an interesting candidate for the shaving process. More precisely, we exploit the semantics of (global) constraints to suggest values, and reuse both the successes and failures of shaving later in search to tune shaving further. We illustrate our approach with two important global constraints, namely alldifferent and sum, and present the results of an experimentation obtained for three problem classes. The experimental results are quite encouraging: we are able to significantly reduce the number of search nodes (even by more than two orders of magnitude), and improve the average execution time by one order of magnitude.

1 Introduction

Constraint Programming (CP) has become one of the dominant approaches to model and solve real-world combinatorial problems [1]. However, while CP has many success stories, it is believed that improving the usability of the technology is a key factor in its future success [2]. This is largely due to the fact that using constraints technology often requires considerable expertise in the use of its tools. In this paper, we aim at improving CP usability by using constraints semantics to augment propagation strength of the constraint model, without excessive computational cost, through means of shaving.

A shavable value is a value which, if assigned to the variable it is associated with followed by constraint propagation, entails an inconsistency. Shaving (introduced in the scheduling context [3,4]) can be defined as the attempt of identifying and removing some shavable values. Shaving, as presented in [5], has two different flavors. The first one assumes that shaving always pays off no matter how many values are tested. Moreover, any shaved value will cause the re-execution of shaving for all variables which may then be susceptible to shaving again. Shaving applied in such a manner makes the problem Singleton Arc Consistent (SAC) [6].

M. Garcia de la Banda and E. Pontelli (Eds.): ICLP 2008, LNCS 5366, pp. 636–650, 2008.
© Springer-Verlag Berlin Heidelberg 2008

In this work, we concentrate on a different flavor of shaving, which tries only some values in the shaving process. By reducing the number of values being evaluated, we hope to reduce the computational load without compromising too much on the quality of pruning. In the ideal case, we would like to achieve SAC by evaluating only values which are not SAC. The work presented in [5] points out the need for good heuristics which choose the values used in shaving. Here, we propose to use (global) constraints to suggest values to be used in the shaving procedure. In this way, we can utilize the constraint semantics to achieve a higher success ratio of shaving and an improved performance of search.

Our motivation is that any additional cost-effective propagation obtained without explicit user involvement will improve the quality of CP based approaches especially when the user is not fully aware of the intricate relationship between model and search. Although being different, this can be related (in terms of objectives) to recent works about constraint acquisition [7,8]. Indeed, learning so-called implied constraints is just another means to improve the propagation capabilities of a constraint solver, without any expertise requirement on the users.

Interestingly, the work presented in [9] also proposes some form of constraint guided shaving. It is mainly implemented for global cardinality constraint (GCC) and as a result of successful shaving attempts, implied constraints in the shape of Among are added to the model. GCC is a generalization of alldifferent. Therefore, this approach is also concerned with alldifferent. In the context of alldifferent, this technique concentrates on values which, if successfully shaved, create Hall intervals which can lead to strengthening alldifferent propagation. This approach evaluates multiple values, therefore it is more costly in terms of finding values and shaving effort. Unfortunately, there is little experimental results to support the claim that shaving done in such a manner actually provides efficiency gains. In addition, in case of GCC while shaving, cheaper/weaker propagator of GCC is employed to reduce the cost of shaving as all values for cardinality variables are tried to be shaved.

We concentrate on proposing shaving in such a manner so tweaking the level of consistency strength is not required to recover costs, as well as we propose a complete framework where the effects of past multiple shaving attempts across multiple constraints are combined to improve future shaving attempts.

The remainder of this paper is organized as follows. After some preliminaries in Section 2, Section 3 presents the shaving framework. An illustration of how constraints can be used to propose values for shaving is presented in Section 4. Section 5 presents a detailed empirical evaluation. We conclude in Section 6.

2   Preliminaries

A Constraint Network (CN) P is a pair $(\mathscr{X}, \mathscr{C})$ where $\mathscr{X}$ is a finite set of n variables and $\mathscr{C}$ a finite set of e constraints. Each variable $X \in \mathscr{X}$ has an associated domain, denoted $dom(X)$, that contains the set of values allowed for X. Each constraint $C \in \mathscr{C}$ involves an ordered subset of variables of $\mathscr{X}$ and has an associated relation[1], denoted $rel(C)$, which is the set of tuples allowed for this subset of variables. This subset of variables is the *scope* of C and is denoted $scp(C)$. The *arity* of a constraint is the number of variables in its scope. A *binary* constraint has arity 2.

A solution to a CN is an assignment of a value to each variable such that all the constraints are satisfied. A CN is said to be *satisfiable* iff it admits at least one solution. The Constraint Satisfaction Problem (CSP) is the NP-hard task of determining whether a given CN is satisfiable or not. A CSP instance is defined by a CN which is solved either by finding a solution or by proving unsatisfiability.

Usually, the domains of the variables of a given CN are reduced by removing inconsistent values, i.e. values that cannot occur in any solution. In particular, it is possible to filter domains by considering some properties of constraint networks. These properties are called domain-filtering consistencies [10,11]. By exploiting consistencies, the problem can be simplified (and even, sometimes solved) while preserving solutions.

Given a consistency ϕ, a CN P is said to be ϕ-consistent iff the property ϕ holds on P. Enforcing a domain-filtering consistency ϕ on a CN means taking into account inconsistent values (removing them from domains) identified by ϕ in order to make the CN ϕ-consistent. The new obtained CN, denoted by $\phi(P)$, is called the ϕ-closure[2] of P. If there exists a variable with an empty domain in $\phi(P)$ then P is clearly unsatisfiable, denoted by $\phi(P) = \bot$.

A pair (X, a) with $X \in \mathscr{X}$ and $a \in dom(X)$ will be called a *value* (of P). The set of values of P that can be built from a constraint C is $values(C) = \{(X, a) \mid X \in scp(C) \wedge a \in dom(X)\}$. $P|_{X=a}$ denotes the CN obtained from P after removing all values but a from $dom(X)$. Shaving can then be defined as the attempt of identifying and removing some shavable values.

Definition 1. *Let P be a CN, and ϕ be a consistency. A value (X, a) of P is ϕ-shavable iff $\phi(P|_{X=a}) = \bot$.*

An attempt to shave value a from the domain of variable X is then performed in the following manner. First, variable X is assigned the value a. Second, the consistency ϕ is enforced. If in the process of reaching the consistency fix-point, one domain becomes empty, then it clearly indicates that assigning a to X does not lead to any solution. Therefore, it is possible to remove a from the domain of X. On the other hand, if assigning a to X does not entail a domain wipe-out, then the effects of constraint propagation (while enforcing ϕ) as well as the assignment of a to X must be retracted. The shaving attempt has failed. Sometimes, when the context is clear or unimportant, we will omit ϕ to simply refer to shavable values.

The most studied and employed consistency is generalized arc consistency (GAC), simply called arc consistency (AC) when constraints are binary. For a

---

[1] The introduction of $rel(C)$ does not prevent us from exploiting intensional representation of constraints.
[2] We assume here that $\phi(P)$ is unique. This is the case for usual consistencies [12].

formal definition, see e.g. [12]. Notice that a GAC-shavable value is a value that is not singleton arc consistent (SAC).

Definition 2. *Let P be a CN. A value (X, a) of P is singleton arc-consistent (SAC) iff $GAC(P|_{X=a}) \neq \bot$.*

Consider a CN composed of three variables X_1, X_2, X_3 such that $dom(X_1) = \{1,3\}$, $dom(X_2) = \{1,2\}$, and $dom(X_3) = \{2,5\}$, and two constraints C_1 : $alldifferent(X_1, X_2, X_3)$ and $C_2 : X_3 = X_1 + X_2$. The first constraint imposes that all variables must be assigned different values, whereas the second one imposes that X_3 is equal to the sum of X_1 and X_2. If value $(X_1, 1)$ is tested for shaving then alldifferent and sum constraints will together discover inconsistency (when enforcing GAC) leading to the removal of 1 from $dom(X_1)$. This successful shaving attempt will cause further domain reductions making $dom(X_2) = \{2\}$ and $dom(X_3) = \{5\}$. On the other hand, if value $(X_1, 3)$ had been tested for shaving, no inconsistency would have been detected. In other words, $(X_1, 1)$ is shavable, whereas $(X_1, 3)$ is not.

Enforcing SAC on a given CN involves removing any value that is not single-ton arc-consistent, i.e. any shavable value. This is a systematic approach which requires to consider each value in turn. Even if there exists some sophisticated approaches [13,14,15] to enforce SAC, this may be very time consuming. Main-taining such a consistency during search seems quite counter-productive. This is the reason why some limited forms of SAC have been devised such as bound SAC and existential SAC [16]. In this paper, contrary to previous works, we exploit the semantics of constraints to guide the shaving process.

3   Framework for Constraint-Guided Shaving

In this section, we introduce the principles of constraint-guided shaving, before introducing a general algorithm and discussing some extensions.

3.1   Principles

Backtracking search is commonly employed for solving CSP instances. It corre-sponds to a depth-first search in order to instantiate variables and a backtracking mechanism when dead-ends occur.

With binary branching, at each step of the search, a pair (X, a) is selected where X is an unassigned variable and a a value in $dom(X)$, and two cases are considered: the assignment $X = a$ and the refutation $X \neq a$. Classically, we start by assigning variables before refuting values. We then explore a binary tree where left children correspond to variable assignments and right children to value refutations.

The motivations for the choice of binary branching (an alternative is d-way branching) are numerous. First, binary branching is commonly used in industry solvers. Second, there is a number of research work (e.g. [17]) which advocates the use of a binary branching scheme. Roughly speaking, binary branching is more general as it does not prohibit switching to a different variable after exploring only one variable-value pair.

With shaving, at each node, we not only enforce a given consistency ϕ as usual to prune some portions of the search space[3], but also make some attempts to discover shavable values. This work incorporates a number of simple principles or techniques to increase the success ratio of shaving as well as the impact of shaved values on further pruning. The worst case scenario for shaving is trying many different values and not being able to shave them. This incurs only cost and does not give any benefit to the search. Besides, shaving in order to be efficient must at least shave some values from variable domains. However, please keep in mind that reducing the domains of the variables through shaving does not necessarily improve the overall search efficiency. The shaved values could have been removed with much smaller effort deeper in a search tree (even if it may be repeated several times).

In order to control the shaving overhead and to increase the effects of shaved values, we propose to exploit the semantics of constraints. More precisely, each constraint is asked to select one value to be used in shaving. Each constraint should aim at proposing one value which, if shaved, has the highest impact on the immediate pruning strength of the constraint. Moreover, we hope that increasing the pruning capabilities of the guiding constraints will in turn increase the propagation of the other constraints.

Another principle that we adopt, to limit shaving overhead, is the restriction of constraint advice for shaving only in search nodes which correspond to left children. The argument for this restriction is quite simple: the equality constraint (a variable assignment) added to reach the left child is usually much tighter than the negation of this constraint (a value refutation) added to reach the right child. Therefore, the difference between the root and the left child will most likely be larger than the difference between the root and the right one. We speculate that the left child has more chances to create new shaving capabilities than the child on the right.

Finally, the last technique to improve the success ratio of shaving is the use of a set (called *recentlyUnshaved* in the algorithm below) which records all values for which shaving attempts have recently failed. If a constraint proposes the value (X, a) which belongs to this set then (X, a) is skipped, but it is also removed from the set. Therefore, if the value is proposed again later in the search then it may be tried again.

3.2   Algorithm

The pseudo-code for binary search with shaving is depicted in Algorithm 1. This is an algorithm with two embedded recursive calls. In this paper, we use the terms *search node*, *decision*, *wrong decision*, and *backtrack* as defined in [19]. This algorithm takes four parameters: P, *leftChild*, *recentlyShaved*,

---

[3] For example, MAC [18] is the backtracking search algorithm that maintains (generalized) arc consistency at each step of search. So, we have $\phi = (G)AC$.

Algorithm 1. ϕ-SHAVINGSEARCH

Input:
  P - the constraint network $(\mathscr{X}, \mathscr{C})$,
  $leftChild$ - the Boolean specifying if P corresponds to a left child
Input/Output:
  $recentlyShaved$ - the set of values that were recently shaved,
  $recentlyUnshaved$ - the set of values that recently failed to be shaved
Output   :
  true/false to specify if a solution to P was found

1 $P \leftarrow \phi(P)$
2 **if** $P = \bot$ **then**
3 | **return** false

4 **if** $\forall X \in \mathscr{X}, |dom(X)| = 1$ **then**
5 | **return** true

6 $locallyShaved \leftarrow \emptyset$
7 **if** $leftChild = true$ **then**
8 | **foreach** constraint C in $\mathscr{C}$ **do**
9 | | $(X, a) \leftarrow C.getValueForShavingAttempt()$
10 | | **if** $(X, a) \in recentlyUnshaved$ **then**
11 | | | $recentlyUnshaved \leftarrow recentlyUnshaved \setminus \{(X, a)\}$
12 | | **else**
13 | | | **if** $\phi(P|_{X=a}) = \bot$ **then**
14 | | | | $P \leftarrow \phi(P|_{X \neq a})$
15 | | | | **if** $P = \bot$ **then**
16 | | | | | $recentlyShaved \leftarrow recentlyShaved \cup locallyShaved$
17 | | | | | **return** false
18 | | | | **else**
19 | | | | | $locallyShaved \leftarrow locallyShaved \cup \{(X, a)\}$
20 | | | **else**
21 | | | | $recentlyUnshaved \leftarrow recentlyUnshaved \cup \{(X, a)\}$

22 **else**
23 | **foreach** $(X, a) \in recentlyShaved$ **do**
24 | | **if** $\phi(P|_{X=a}) = \bot$ **then**
25 | | | $P \leftarrow \phi(P|_{X \neq a})$
26 | | | **if** $P = \bot$ **then**
27 | | | | **return** false
28 | | **else**
29 | | | $recentlyShaved \leftarrow recentlyShaved \setminus \{(X, a)\}$
30 | | | $recentlyUnshaved \leftarrow recentlyUnshaved \cup \{(X, a)\}$

31 $(X, a) \leftarrow selectVariableValue()$
32 **if** $\phi\text{-}ShavingSearch(P|_{X=a},\ true,\ locallyShaved,\ recentlyUnshaved)$ **then**
33 | **return** true

34 **if** $\phi\text{-}ShavingSearch(P|_{X \neq a},\ false,\ locallyShaved,\ recentlyUnshaved)$ **then**
35 | **return** true

36 $recentlyShaved \leftarrow recentlyShaved \cup locallyShaved$
37 **return** false

recentlyUnshaved that denote respectively the given constraint network, a Boolean value specifying if the current search node is a left child (i.e. reached after assigning a variable), the set of values which were recently successfully shaved, and the set of values which were recently attempted to be shaved without any success. The two first parameters are handled in the input mode whereas the parameters *recentlyShaved* and *recentlyUnshaved* are handled in the input/output mode. This algorithm returns true if there is a solution to the given constraint network.

Initially, the consistency ϕ is enforced (see line 1). If a failure is detected (see line 2), *false* is returned since no solution can be found. Otherwise, if all domains of variables are singleton (see line 4), it means that a solution has been found. Notice that we suppose here that ϕ is a consistency that is at least as strong as backward checking, i.e. (at least) allows to detect any unsatisfied constraint involving variables which have all a singleton domain. This is quite a reasonable assumption.

If P corresponds to a constraint network reached on a left child (see lines 7 to 21), then we ask each constraint to propose one value for shaving attempt (line 9), and take it into account except if we recently failed to shave it (lines 10 and 11). If adding constraint $X = a$ and propagating (using consistency ϕ) makes the problem inconsistent, then we can shave value a from the domain of X and propagate this deletion. If this shaving makes the problem inconsistent (lines 14 and 15), then the *recentlyShaved* set is updated and search is forced to backtrack. If shaving value (X, a) does not entail inconsistency then we can continue search and update the *locallyShaved* set (line 19). Finally, if the shaving attempt was unsuccessful then the *recentlyUnshaved* set is updated (line 21).

If P corresponds to a constraint network reached on a right child (see lines 22 to 30), we simply check for shaving all values in *recentlyShaved*. Indeed, if shaving guided by constraints is always performed after variable assignments, one can note that the results of these shaving attempts may influence shaving done in the remaining parts of the search (e.g. siblings). This is the reason why we use the *recentlyShaved* set to perform shaving in right children. Each value (X, a) from this set is then attempted to be shaved. If (X, a) is shavable and removing it causes inconsistency then the search is forced to backtrack. On the other hand, if the shaving attempt was unsuccessful, then both *recentlyShaved* and *recentlyUnshaved* are updated (lines 29 and 30).

Here, we speculate that both children are similar enough to actually make it useful to use shavable values from left child when entering the child on the right. Moreover, if a value was successfully shaved in both children then this value is added to the set of shavable values of the root node (effectively, by not executing line 29 in the right child and executing line 36 upon exiting the parent of the right child). Therefore, the values which were successfully shaved deep in the left subtree will be tried in the right subtree. We restrict shaving speculation to only right children, as upon entering the left child the shavable list does not contain a value which could be used for speculation. The left child does not have a sibling which was executed earlier and all values which were successfully shaved by the parent node of the left child are still shaved.

To finish the description of the algorithm, we have to consider the recursive calls. Lines 31 to 35 allows to select a variable and a value for branching (using variable and value ordering heuristics) and to proceed to the left and right children. Before backtracking from the current node (line 37) the set *recentlyShaved* is updated (line 36) by adding to it all values which were successfully shaved in this search node.

3.3   Extensions

Guiding constraints Even if the algorithm is presented in such a way that any constraint participates to shaving, it may be more realistic to consider that only a subset of the constraints of the network are solicited for shaving attempts. For example, we may only consider (global) constraints whose semantics renders easy or natural such an exploitation. We discuss this aspect in the next section.

Quick Shaving It is rather easy to further incorporate the quick shaving technique proposed in [5]. In order to simplify the presentation of this incorporation to Algorithm 1, we use a global Boolean variable $leftChildWrongDecision$ which is set to true only when the left child was a wrong decision. To achieve this, we only need to insert the following instructions between lines 2 and 3:

> **if** $leftChild = true$ **then**
> $\quad$ $LeftChildWrongDecision \leftarrow true$

When the left child led to a dead end immediately then the search proceeds to the following instructions (inserted between lines 33 and 34) which implement Quick shaving:

> **if** $leftChildWrongDecision$ **then**
> $\quad$ $locallyShaved \leftarrow locallyShaved \cup \{(X, a)\}$
> $\quad$ $recentlyUnshaved \leftarrow recentlyUnshaved \setminus \{(X, a)\}$
> $\quad$ $leftChildWrongDecision \leftarrow false$

In short, Quick shaving adds a value which led to a wrong decision to the *recentlyShaved* set just before the search exits the parent node of the wrong decision.

4   Constraint Guidance

We now discuss about constraint guidance for shaving. We concentrate on global constraints such as *sum* and *alldifferent* since they are commonly used in many problem classes.

We first need to introduce pruning events (see for example [20]) which can be specifically treated to speed up constraint propagation. The *bound* event occurs if the minimal or maximal value from the variable domain is removed. The *ground* event occurs if all but one value are removed from the domain. If the domain of a variable shrinks in another way then it qualifies as event *any*. It is often the case that the design of the constraint propagation algorithms makes it impossible to infer any additional domain pruning in case of occurrence of the event *any*. Therefore, we adapted our suggestion mechanisms within constraints to prefer/suggest values which cause a *bound* or *ground* event if a value is successfully shaved. This preference increases the chance of additional inferences based on just shaved values.

4.1   Alldifferent

Our example uses the *permutation* constraint to demonstrate how the internal data structures maintained by this global constraint can be used to propose values for shaving. A *permutation* constraint is applicable when the numbers of variables and values are equal and we wish to ensure that each variable takes a different value. Therefore, the *permutation* constraint can be regarded as a special case of the *alldifferent* constraint [21]. A filtering algorithm for *permutation* can be readily derived from the filtering algorithm for *alldifferent*. The *alldifferent* constraint maintains an internal data structure called the value graph to achieve generalized arc consistency (GAC) [21]. The value graph is a bipartite graph in which the edges link variables to values in their current domain. An example of the value graph is presented in Figure 1. This value graph can be efficiently reused to identify values that can be assigned to a small number of variables. In our example, thanks to the value graph an important observation can be made. We can observe that all variables can be assigned at least three different values, however value 1 can be assigned to only two variables. Based on this knowledge, we can choose variable X_1 and value 1 or variable X_2 and value 1 for shaving, hoping that the chances of successful shave will increase.

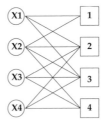

Fig. 1. An example of a value graph

The suggestion mechanism of the *alldifferent* constraint considers all variables within a constraint scope which have a domain consisting of two elements, as well as all values which are in the domain of only two variables. For any entity ε (either a variable or a value) such that $|dom(\varepsilon)| = 2$, it computes the following metric m, where $m = min(|dom(el_1)|, |dom(el_2)|)$, where $dom(\varepsilon) = \{el_1, el_2\}$. We abuse a notation here by using $dom(a)$ to specify the set of variables which can be assigned to value a. The variable or value which has the highest value for metric m is chosen to participate in the proposed variable-value pair for shaving. For example as presented in Figure 1, 1 is the entity with the highest value for metric m (trivially satisfied as there is only one variable/value with the domain equal 2). Therefore value 1 is retained. $dom(1)$ contains two variables $\{X_1, X_2\}$. The variable X_2 with larger domain is chosen for shaving. Therefore, for the given example, the value $(X_2, 1)$ is proposed for shaving. If there are multiple candidates among variables and values then the constraint chooses a value which produces a *ground* or *bound* event when successfully shaved. If there is no variable/value with domain consisting of two elements then alldifferent will not propose any value for shaving. In the process of selection, the preferred value is the one which, if shaved, greatly enhances the immediate propagation of the proposing constraint.

4.2   Sum

The implementation of the *sum* constraint in most constraint systems is rather simple. First, a propagator based on *bound* events is used as it provides decent propagation at low cost. It takes lower and upper bounds for all variables and checks for each bound value if there exists an assignment to other variables which satisfies the constraint. If such an assignment does not exist then the bound is tightened. This is the approach implemented in the solver used in the experiments.

The guiding function within the *sum* constraint analyzes the domains of the variables in its scope and comes up with a value within a domain of a variable which, if removed, causes the maximum amount of pruning in the other variables. The likely candidates are the domains like $\{1, 10..20\}$ (resp. $\{1..10, 20\}$), where there is a large gap between the smallest (resp. the largest) element in the domain and the one which follows (resp. precedes). In this example, removing element 1 (20) from the domain will significantly tighten the bounds of a variable, probably causing some domain reductions in other variables.

Sum constraint computes for every variable X within constraint scope the following metrics, d_{min} and d_{max}. Given $dom(X) = \{v_1, v_2, ..., v_{l-1}, v_l\}$ then $d_{min} = v_2 - v_1$ and $d_{max} = v_l - v_{l-1}$. The variable X_i, for which we have $m = max(d_{min}(X_i), d_{max}(X_i))$ maximized and greater than 1, is chosen for shaving. If $d_{min}(x_i)$ is greater than $d_{max}(x_i)$ then the value (X_i, v_1) is proposed for shaving, otherwise it is value (X_i, v_l).

5   Experimental Results

In order to demonstrate the practical interest of the approach introduced in this paper, we have conducted an experimentation using different shaving approaches. We have used four metrics to compare the different approaches. They respectively correspond to the number of search nodes (# Nodes), the number of values tested for shaving (# Tests), the success shaving ratio which corresponds to the percentage of values which were shaved, and the execution time (CPU) given in seconds. For all metrics, except for the shaving ratio, we computed both average and median values (denoted by Avg and Med).

All experiments were performed on laptop with Intel Core Duo 2.0 GHz processor and 1GB of RAM running Linux Kubuntu 6.10. We have used in experiments the Java-based JaCoP solver version 2.3, which is available for free for non-commercial purposes [22]. We have considered three problem classes, namely Quasigroup Completion Problems (QCP), Nontransitive Dice Problems (NTD), and Magic Squares Problems (MSP). The different approaches are:

- NoShaving: JaCoP alone,
- QShaving: JaCoP embedding the quick shaving technique,
- GShaving: JaCoP embedding our constraint-guided shaving technique,
- GQShaving: JaCoP embedding both the quick shaving and the constraint-guided shaving techniques.

We will show that in all problem classes, we can obtain a reduction in the number of search nodes. This reduction in all problem classes translates to a time reduction. We will show that different shaving approaches complement each other.

5.1   Nontransitive Dice Problems

NTD(d,s) represents a problem involving dices. Here, d denotes the number of dice and s denotes the number of faces on each die. All faces are assumed to be different, so there is no possibility of a draw when two dice are rolled. In short, the solution to this problem assigns to each face of each die a unique value. Moreover, we are looking for an assignment of dice faces, such that for each die we can pick up another die and reach the maximum probability of winning with the first chosen die. The optimal solution for NTD(3,6) with the winning probability 21/36 is presented in Figure 2. The arrows represent the winning relation (e.g. the die on the left is winning over the die in the middle). The optimization (maximization of the minimal winning probability) is achieved by restarts with stepwise increase of the maximal probability. As soon as for a given probability no solution exists, the previous solution is proved to be optimal. By arranging experiments in such a way, we ensure that each search solves the same series of sub-problems and each search finds and proves the optimal solution.

The model of this problem is not trivial since it contains dual viewpoints, symmetry breaking constraints, and global constraints such as *sum* and *alldifferent*. In the process of experimentation with different search heuristics, we

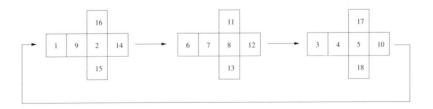

Fig. 2. NTD(3, 6) and one of the optimal solutions

Table 1. Experimental results for Nontransitive Dice Problem

		# Nodes		# Tests		Shaving	CPU [s]	
Approach	#Solved	Avg	Med	Avg	Med	Ratio	Avg	Med
NoShaving	22	$9,935,361$	$92,915$	0	0	−	667	8.57
GShaving	26	$1,191,156$	$7,650$	$54,302$	440	49	104	3.50
QShaving	26	$583,125$	$5,932$	$105,578$	$1,117$	43	70	3.02
GQShaving	26	$217,398$	$4,381$	$51,706$	$1,072$	43	32	3.11

found the best one for JaCoP alone. This heuristic orders the face variables by taking them one by one from each die. The face variables taken from each die are ordered in the fashion which maximizes constraint propagation. In addition, this heuristic uses middle value ordering which starts with values from the middle of the domain.

Table 1 presents results for 26 problem instances, namely NTD(3, {4, 5, 6, 7, 8, 9, 10}), NTD(4, {4, 5, 6, 7, 8, 9, 10}), NTD(5, {4, 5, 6, 7, 8}), NTD(6, {4, 5, 6, 7}), and NTD(7, {4, 5, 6}). JaCoP alone (NoShaving) was not able to solve 4 problems with a generous backtrack limit of 10 millions backtracks. Both shaving techniques run alone (QShaving and GShaving) already obtain substantial time gains when solving the same problem set. However, it is when both shaving techniques are combined that a 20 times reduction of average execution time is obtained. These experimental results clearly show that we are able to improve the pruning strength of the constraint model by using shaving techniques.

5.2   Quasigroup Completion Problems

A quasigroup is a set Q with a binary operation $\star : Q \times Q \rightarrow Q$, such that for all a and b in Q there exist unique elements in Q such that $a \star x = b$ and $y \star a = b$. The cardinality of the set, $n = |Q|$, is called the order of the quasigroup. A quasigroup can be viewed as an $n \times n$ multiplication table defining a Latin square, which must be filled with unique integers on each row and column. The Quasigroup Completion Problem (QCP) is the problem of completing a partially filled Latin square. We will concentrate on one of many possible constraint models which uses *alldifferent* global constraint to ensure uniqueness of elements across columns and rows. In our work, we use a generalized arc consistency (GAC) version of the *alldifferent* constraint. One of the best variable orderings, given the fact that the model consists only of global constraints, is based on the minimal domain size. We have used as value ordering heuristic the one which chooses the minimal value from the current domain. The QCP problems were generated using Carla Gomes generator. We have generated 3000 problems for QCP of order 25 at difficulty phase transition for sat balanced QCP. The generator can produce unsat instances for this type of QCP problems therefore we retained only the sat instances which gave the total number of instances equal to 1214.

Table 2 presents experimental results for this problem class. JaCoP alone (NoShaving) had a 10 times increased search node limit yet it still could not solve 9% of the problems for which more than 1000 seconds on average were

Table 2. Experimental results for QCP of order 25

Approach	#Solved	# Nodes		# Tests		Shaving	CPU [s]	
		Avg	Med	Avg	Med	Ratio	Avg	Med
NoShaving	1, 103	437, 321	123, 070	0	0	–	264.59	74.44
QShaving	1189	212, 372	47, 236	88, 931	19, 238	32	167.90	38.33
GShaving	1, 214	12, 972	3, 113	92, 737	22, 280	18	92.86	24.20
GQShaving	1, 214	12, 681	3, 051	94, 006	22, 520	18	61.49	17.23

not sufficient to solve them. We were initially running experiments without any node limit. Unfortunately, we were not able to get results for some instances even within days therefore we had to revert to a node limit and present approximate results (i.e. results given for NoShaving and QShaving must be considered as lower bounds of real values). QShaving was given the same node limit as NoShaving. All remaining shaving approaches were given only one tenth of search nodes limit given to the heuristic without shaving.

The guided shaving (GShaving, GQShaving) compares favorably against No-Shaving and QShaving. First, it solves all the problems in a significant smaller numbers of search nodes even if we count shaving attempts as search nodes. Assuming that unsolved instances are solved at the node limit we can still see significant reduction in median time. We run QShaving with a node limit equal to NoShaving method, because if given the same node limit as other shaving approaches it would not be able to solve 25% of the problems. QShaving takes on average more than 16 times more nodes and 80% more time when compared to GShaving results. Moreover, QShaving still despite 10-fold increase of node limit can not solve 2% of problems making it also less robust than GShaving. It is interesting to see that guided shaving significantly improves the quality of quick shaving since all problems are solved. On the other hand, quick shaving changes the distribution of shaving attempts (there are more of them in the lower parts of the search tree) as well as makes shaving attempts more compatible with constraint consistency mechanisms (reuse of previous work is more likely, the consistency function of alldifferent is highly incremental), resulting in further reduction of time even if all other metrics are similar.

5.3   MagicSquares Problems

An order n magic square is a $n \times n$ matrix containing the numbers 1 to n^2, with each row, column and the main diagonals summing up to the same number. The constraint model of this problem consists of one alldifferent constraint and $2n + 2$ sum constraints. Therefore, the guiding for this problem class is mostly performed by sum constraints.

Table 3 presents experimental results for this problem class. We have used the variable ordering heuristic that selects the smallest domain first and the value ordering heuristic which starts with the values from the middle of the domain. The difficulty of the problems increases very fast. Therefore, only instances with small n (n starting at 4) were solved. For this problem class, we can observe a

Table 3. Experimental results for MagicSquares Problems

Approach	#Solved	# Nodes		# Tests		Shaving Ratio	CPU [s]	
		Avg	Med	Avg	Med		Avg	Med
NoShaving	6	321, 112	9, 052	0	0	−	43.43	3.06
QShaving	6	56, 751	8, 182	8, 496	920	40	10.12	3.09
GShaving	6	18, 443	5, 047	8, 936	2, 258	56	6.55	3.70
GQShaving	6	14, 338	4, 765	9, 903	2, 667	53	5.69	2.83

reduction in terms of the average number of search nodes as well as the average execution time. Clearly, guided shaving allows again to improve the search robustness: it is about one order of magnitude faster than the classical search algorithm (NoShaving) and two times faster than quick shaving (QShaving).

6   Conclusions

We have presented a shaving framework, which uses advice from (global) constraints. The underlying principle of constraint-guided shaving is to ask each constraint suggesting one value which is more likely to be shaved as well as cause more propagation when shaved. We have discussed how it can be implemented for two important global constraints, namely *alldifferent* and *sum*. Interestingly enough, we have also shown that the past successes and failures can be exploited to improve shaving performance.

Constraints provide reliable guidance which always allows pruning some portions of the search space while, most of the time, giving significant reduction of execution time (one order of magnitude). Indeed, the practical results that we have obtained on different series of problems show that using constraints for guiding shaving increases dramatically the robustness and the efficiency of the search algorithm, not only in terms of search nodes but also in terms of cpu time. We have also shown that our approach is complementary to Quick shaving.

References

1. Wallace, M.: Practical applications of constraint programming. Journal of Constraints 1, 139–168 (1996)
2. Puget, J.: The next challenge for CP: Ease of use. In: Wallace, M. (ed.) CP 2004. LNCS, vol. 3258, pp. 5–8. Springer, Heidelberg (2004)
3. Carlier, J., Pinson, E.: Adjustments of heads and tails for the job-shop problem. European Journal of Operational Research 78, 146–161 (1994)
4. Martin, P., Shmoys, D.: A new approach to computing optimal schedules for the job-shop scheduling problem. In: Cunningham, W.H., Queyranne, M., McCormick, S.T. (eds.) IPCO 1996. LNCS, vol. 1084, pp. 389–403. Springer, Heidelberg (1996)
5. Lhomme, O.: Quick shaving. In: Proceedings of AAAI 2005, pp. 411–415 (2005)
6. Debruyne, R., Bessiere, C.: Some practical filtering techniques for the constraint satisfaction problem. In: Proceedings of IJCAI 1997, pp. 412–417 (1997)

7. Hnich, B., Richardson, J., Flener, P.: Towards automatic generation and evaluation of implied constraints. Technical Report 2003-014, Uppsala Universitet (2003)
8. Bessiere, C., Coletta, R., Petit, T.: Learning implied global constraints. In: Proceedings of IJCAI 2007, pp. 50–55 (2007)
9. Regin, J.: Combination of among and cardinality constraints. In: Barták, R., Milano, M. (eds.) CPAIOR 2005. LNCS, vol. 3524, pp. 288–303. Springer, Heidelberg (2005)
10. Debruyne, R., Bessiere, C.: Domain filtering consistencies. Journal of Artificial Intelligence Research 14, 205–230 (2001)
11. Bessiere, C., Stergiou, K., Walsh, T.: Domain filtering consistencies for non-binary constraints. Artificial Intelligence (to appear, 2008)
12. Bessiere, C.: Constraint propagation. In: Handbook of Constraint Programming. Elsevier, Amsterdam (2006)
13. Bartak, R., Erben, R.: A new algorithm for singleton arc consistency. In: Proceedings of FLAIRS 2004 (2004)
14. Bessiere, C., Debruyne, R.: Optimal and suboptimal singleton arc consistency algorithms. Proceedings of IJCAI 2005, 54–59 (2005)
15. Lecoutre, C., Cardon, S.: A greedy approach to establish singleton arc consistency. In: Proceedings of IJCAI 2005, pp. 199–204 (2005)
16. Lecoutre, C., Prosser, P.: Maintaining singleton arc consistency. In: Proceedings of CPAI 2006 workshop held with CP 2006, pp. 47–61 (2006)
17. Hwang, J., Mitchell, D.: 2-way vs d-way branching for CSP. In: van Beek, P. (ed.) CP 2005. LNCS, vol. 3709, pp. 343–357. Springer, Heidelberg (2005)
18. Sabin, D., Freuder, E.: Contradicting conventional wisdom in constraint satisfaction. In: Proceedings of CP 1994, pp. 10–20 (1994)
19. Bessiere, C., Zanuttini, B., Fernandez, C.: Measuring search trees. In: Proceedings of ECAI 2004 workshop on Modelling and Solving Problems with Constraints, pp. 31–40 (2004)
20. Schulte, C., Carlsson, M.: Finite domain constraint programming systems. In: Handbook of Constraint Programming, pp. 495–526. Elsevier, Amsterdam (2006)
21. Regin, J.: A filtering algorithm for constraints of difference in CSPs. In: Proceedings of AAAI 1994, pp. 362–367 (1994)
22. Kuchcinski, K.: Constraints-driven scheduling and resource assignment. ACM Transactions on Design Automation of Electronic Systems 8, 355–383 (2003)

A High-Level Implementation of Non-deterministic, Unrestricted, Independent And-Parallelism[*]

Amadeo Casas[1], Manuel Carro[2], and Manuel V. Hermenegildo[1,2]

[1] Depts. of Comp. Science and Electr. and Comp. Eng., Univ. of New Mexico, USA
[2] School of Comp. Science, Univ. Politécnica de Madrid, Spain and IMDEA-Software
amadeo@cs.unm.edu, mcarro@fi.upm.es,
herme@fi.upm.es, herme@cs.unm.edu

Abstract. The growing popularity of multicore architectures has renewed interest in language-based approaches to the exploitation of parallelism. Logic programming has proved an interesting framework to this end, and there are parallel implementations which have achieved significant speedups, but at the cost of a quite sophisticated low-level machinery. This machinery has been found challenging to code and, specially, to maintain and expand. In this paper, we follow a different approach which adopts a higher level view by raising some of the core components of the implementation to the level of the source language. We briefly present an implementation model for independent and-parallelism which fully supports non-determinism through backtracking and provides flexible solutions for some of the main problems found in previous and-parallel implementations. Our proposal is able to optimize the execution for the case of deterministic programs and to exploit *unrestricted* and-parallelism, which allows exposing more parallelism among clause literals than fork-join-based proposals. We present performance results for an implementation, including data for benchmarks where and-parallelism is exploited in non-deterministic programs.

Keywords: And-Parallelism, High-level Implementation, Prolog.

1 Introduction

New multicore technology is challenging developers to create applications that take full advantage of the power provided by these processors. The path of single-core microprocessors following Moore's Law has reached a point where very high levels of power (and, as a result, heat dissipation) are required to raise clock speeds. Multicore systems seem to be the main architectural solution path taken

---

[*] This work was funded in part by EU FP6 FET project IST-15905 *MOBIUS*, FP7 grant 215483 *S-Cube*, Spanish MEC project TIN2005-09207-C03 *MERIT-COMVERS*, ITEA2/PROFIT FIT-340005-2007-14 *ES_PASS*, and by Madrid Regional Government project S-0505/TIC/0407 *PROMESAS*. M. Hermenegildo and A. Casas were also funded in part by the Prince of Asturias Chair in IST at UNM.

M. Garcia de la Banda and E. Pontelli (Eds.): ICLP 2008, LNCS 5366, pp. 651–666, 2008.

by manufacturers for offering potential increases in performance without running into these problems. However, applications that are not *parallelized*, will show little or no improvement in performance as new generations with more processors are developed. Thus, much effort is currently being put and progress being made towards alleviating the hard task of producing parallel programs. This includes the design of new languages that provide better support for the exploitation of parallelism, libraries that offer improved support for parallel execution, and parallelizing compilers, capable of helping in the parallelization process.

In particular, declarative languages (and logic programming languages among them), have been traditionally considered an interesting target for exploiting parallelism. Their high-level nature allows a coding style closer to the problem which preserves more of the original parallelism. Their separation between control and the declarative meaning, together with relatively simple semantics, makes logic programming a formally simpler framework which, however, allows studying and addressing most of the challenges present in the parallelization of imperative languages [12].

There are two main forms of parallelism in logic programming [10,9]. *Or-parallelism* (Aurora [19] and MUSE [2]) refers to the execution of different branches in parallel, while *And-parallelism* executes simultaneously some goals in the resolvent. The latter can be exploited independently of whether there is implicit search or not. Two main forms of and-parallelism have been studied. Independent and-parallelism (IAP) arises between two goals when the execution of one of them does not influence the execution of the other. For pure goals a sufficient (and a-priori) condition for this is the absence of variable sharing at run-time among these goals. "Dependent" and-parallelism (DAP) is found when the literals executed in parallel share variables at run-time, and they compete to bind them. In this paper we will focus on independent and-parallelism.

Systems like &-Prolog [14], DDAS [25] and others have exploited and-parallelism, while certain combinations of both and- and or-parallelism have been exploited by e.g. &ACE [23], AKL [17], and Andorra-I [24]. Many of these systems adopted similar implementation ideas. This often included a parallelizing compiler to automatically transform the original program into a semantically-equivalent parallel version of it and a run-time system to exploit the potential increase in performance provided by the uncovered parallelism. These systems have been shown very effective at exploiting parallelism efficiently and obtaining significant speedups [14,22]. However, most of them are based on quite complex, low-level machinery (which included an extension of the WAM instructions, and new data structures and stack frames in the stack set of each agent), which makes implementation and maintenance inherently hard.

In [8], we proposed a high-level implementation that raised some of the main components of the implementation to the source level, and was able to exploit the flexibility provided by unrestricted and-parallelism (i.e., not limited to fork-join operations). However, [8] provided a solution which is only valid for the parallel execution of goals which have exactly one solution each, thus avoiding some of the hardest implementation problems. While it can be argued that a large part of application execution is indeed single-solution, on one hand this cannot always be determined a priori, and on the other there are also cases of parallelism among non-deterministic goals, and thus a system must offer a complete implementation, capable of coping with parallel non-deterministic goals, in order to be realistic. Other recent related work includes [20] which proposes a set of high-level multithreading primitives. This work (as, e.g., also [6]) focuses more on providing a flexible multithreading interface, rather than on performance.

In this paper, we present a high-level implementation that is able to exploit unrestricted IAP over non-deterministic parallel goals, while maintaining the optimizations of previous solutions for non-failing deterministic parallel goals. Our proposal provides solutions for the trapped-goal and garbage-slot problems, and is able to cancel the execution of a parallel goal when needed.

2   Decomposing And-Parallelism

Independent and-parallelism has traditionally been expressed using the (restricted, i.e., fork-join) `&/2` operator as the lowest-level construct to express parallelism between goals. However, our intention is to support *unrestricted* and-parallelism, which has been shown capable of exploiting more of the parallelism intrinsic in programs [7]. To this end, we will use more flexible primitives [5]:

- `G &> H` schedules the goal `G` for parallel execution and continues with the code after `G &> H`. `H` is a *handler* which contains (or *points to*) the state of `G`, and will be used for communicating the executing state between agents.
- `H <&` waits for the goal associated with `H` to finish. After `H <&` succeeds, all the bindings that `G` could possibly generate are ready. Note also that, assuming goal independence between `G` and the calls performed while `G` was being executed, no binding conflicts will arise.

With the previous definitions, the `&/2`[1] operator can be expressed as:

$$A \ \& \ B \ :- \ A \ \&> \ H, \ \text{call}(B), \ H \ <\&. \tag{1}$$

The particular order of literals is for performance, since when running the common tail-recursive case `p:-q&p`, `p` should spawn parallel `q`'s with no delay. [13]

Also, note that `&>/2` and `<&/1` are not intended to replace `&/2` at the language level, due to its expressiveness and conciseness, in case no extra parallelism can be exploited with them (i.e., we leave the door open to more optimized implementations of `&/2` than what the definition above suggests). The `&>/2` and `<&/1` primitives are not dependent on any particular architecture, and were in fact first implemented in a distributed-memory setting [5]. However, as the implementation we propose now addresses shared-memory multiprocessors, the bindings made by `G` while executing will be immediately visible, and goal independence makes it possible to work out a solution with the no-slowdown property.

`G &> H` ideally takes a negligible amount of time to execute, although the precise moment in which `G` actually starts depends on the availability of resources

---

[1] The meta-call is expanded at compile-time to avoid extra overhead in the execution.

(primarily, free agents or processors). On the other hand, H <& suspends until the associated goal finitely fails or returns an answer. Actual backtracking is performed at H <&, and the memory reserved by the handler is released when G &> H is reached on backtracking. If G &> H is reached on backtracking but H <& was not reached on forward execution, this means that some of the goals between these two points has failed without a solution, and the execution of goal G (whatever its state) is to be cancelled. Section 3 explains further the design and implementation of these operators.

3   Shared-Memory Implementation

Our shared-memory implementation for unrestricted IAP is based on the *multi-sequential, marker model* introduced by &-Prolog and adopted by many and-parallel systems, both for IAP [14,23] and DAP [25]. It has some general similarities with that model, such as the concept of agent, which corresponds to a thread associated to a particular stack set, mostly a Warren Abstract Machine [26,1], and the ring of stack sets which interconnects all the agents. For simplicity, each thread will be always associated to the same stack set.

However, there exist significant differences between our proposal and the &-Prolog run-time model, which we will present in the following sections.

3.1   Goal Stacks vs. Goal Lists

In our model, each agent is extended with a goal list, implemented as a doubly-linked list in C, whose functionality is similar to that of the goal stack in the &-Prolog run-time model. The goal list entries store pointers to those goals which have been prepared for parallel execution, and thus agents that are idle can search for parallel goals to execute by consulting the goal lists of the rest of the agents. A list is used instead of the traditional stack due to the greater flexibility needed in order to deal with the *unrestricted* nature of the &>/2 and <&/1 operators (instead of, or in addition to &/2): goals can be joined in any order —not necessarily the inverse to the order in which they were published— and, in the case of goal cancellation, arbitrary goal entries inside the list may have to be removed. For instance, the conjunction $(g_1\&g_2\&\ldots\&g_n)$ can be executed as

$$(g_1\&>H_1, g_2\&>H_2, \ldots, g_n, \ldots, H_2<\&, H_1<\&)$$

as per Equation (1), but in fact any order for the joins would be equally correct.

3.2   Parcall Frames vs. Handlers

Parcall frames in the &-Prolog run-time model are additional (environment) stack frames used for the coordination and synchronization of the parallel execution. In &-Prolog a parcall frame is created as soon as a parallel call is made, and it has a slot for each of the literals $g_1, g_2 \ldots g_n$ in the parallel call $g_1\&g_2\&\ldots\&g_n$, in order to keep track of the execution of each of these goals.

In most WAM implementations the handling of environments is relatively brittle and introducing different elements in the environment stack complicates things. As an alternative to parcall stack frames, our proposal makes use of heap structures, created by and accessible from source-level code that we call *handlers*, as already mentioned in Section 2.[2] Each handler is associated to a particular parallel goal and is used to synchronize the publishing agent and the agent which picks up the goal. Handlers store information such as, e.g., pointers to the parallel goal and its location in the goal list (to remove it from there in case the goal is not taken by any other agent), a field to mark the goal as deterministic or not, the state of the execution, and pointers to both the publishing and the executing agents to release their execution when so needed.

3.3   Markers vs. (Prolog) Choice Points

Markers are used in the &-Prolog run-time model to set boundaries between different sections in the stack, each of them corresponding to the *segment* of execution of a parallel goal. This separation of segments in the stack is used to provide a solution to the *trapped goal* problem [15]. Markers are also used in &-Prolog to implement storage recovery mechanisms during backtracking of parallel goals, in order to solve the *garbage slot* problem [15].

Our proposal to avoid the use of new stack frames to implement markers is the creation of normal choice points, and in a simple way by creating alternatives (through predicates with more than one clause) directly in the source-level code of the scheduler (see Section 3.4). This is done whenever a parallel goal is to be executed (see Figure 1(e)). In addition to that, pointers to the choice points that mark the beginning and end of the goal execution will be stored in the handler associated to that goal, in order to delimit the segment of execution and make them accessible during backwards execution. This is also done in part at the source level. Section 3.4 provides further explanation of how backwards execution over parallel goals is performed using these choice points.

3.4   Implementation

Figure 1 presents a sketch of our high-level implementation of the scheduler for unrestricted IAP. The implementation divides the responsibilities between different layers. The user-level parallelism primitives &>/2 and <&/1 (and thus &/2) are at the top of the Prolog level. The algorithms for goal publishing, goal searching, and forward and backwards execution are implemented in Prolog, with some support from low-level primitives designed to provide, e.g., locking, untrailing, and management of segments of executions. Primitives related to forward execution of parallel goals were already presented in [8].

In our implementation, agents are created with a small stack (which can grow on demand) and they wait for some work to be available. They do not continuously search for new tasks to be performed, in order to avoid active waiting.[3] Several high-level primitives are provided for the creation of a particular number

---

[2] A related approach (but combined with the choice-point stack) was used in ACE [23].
[3] We took this decision because it gave slightly better speedups in our experiments and it is in general good usage of a multiuser system.

```
Goal &> Handler :-
    add_goal(Goal,nondet,Handler),
    undo(cancellation(Handler)),
    release_some_suspended_thread.
```

(a) Non-deterministic goal publishing.

```
Handler <& :-
    enter_mutex_self,
    (
        goal_available(Handler) ->
        exit_mutex_self,
        retrieve_goal(Handler,Goal),
        call(Goal)
    ;
        check_if_finished_or_failed(Handler)
    ).
Handler <& :-
    add_goal(Handler),
    release_some_suspended_thread,
    fail.
```

(b) Goal join and speculation.

```
check_if_finished_or_failed(Handler) :-
    (
        goal_finished(Handler) ->
        exit_mutex_self,
        sending_event(Handler)
    ;
        (
            goal_failed(Handler) ->
            exit_mutex_self,
            fail
        ;
            suspend,
            check_if_finished_or_failed(Handler)
        )
    ).
```

(c) Checking status of goal execution.

```
sending_event(_).
sending_event(Handler) :-
    enter_mutex_self,
    enter_mutex_remote(Handler),
    set_goal_tobacktrack(Handler),
    add_event(Handler),
    release_remote(Handler),
    exit_mutex_remote(Handler),
    check_if_finished_or_failed(Handler).
```

(d) Sending event to executing agent.

```
call_handler(Handler) :-
    retrieve_goal(Handler,Goal),
    save_init_execution(Handler),
    call(Goal),
    save_end_execution(Handler),
    enter_mutex(Handler),
    set_goal_finished(Handler),
    release(Handler),
    exit_mutex(Handler).
call_handler(Handler) :-
    enter_mutex(Handler),
    set_goal_failed(Handler),
    release(Handler),
    metacut_garbage_slots(Handler),
    exit_mutex(Handler),
    fail.
```

(e) High-level markers definition.

```
agent :-
    enter_mutex_self,
    work,
    agent.
agent :- agent.

work :-
    (
        read_event(Handler) ->
        (
            more_solutions(Handler) ->
            move_execution_top(Handler)
        ;
            move_pointers_down(Handler)
        ),
        exit_mutex_self,
        fail
    ;
        (
            find_goal(H) ->
            exit_mutex_self,
            call_handler(H)
        ;
            suspend,
            work
        )
    ).
```

(f) Agent code.

Fig. 1. High-level solution for unrestricted IAP

of agents. When an agent is created, it executes the code shown in Figure 1(f), and during normal execution it will start working on the execution of some goal, or will sleep because there is no task to perform. An agent searches for parallel goals by using a work-stealing scheduling algorithm based on those in [11,14].

Figure 1(a) presents the code for &>/2, which publishes a goal for parallel execution. A pointer to the parallel goal is added to the goal list,and a signal is sent to one of the agents that are currently waiting for some task to do. This agent will resume its execution, pick up the goal, and execute it. In addition, when

&>/2 is reached in backwards execution, the memory reserved by the handler is released. Also, if the goal was taken by another agent and the goal execution was not finished yet, `cancellation/1` (which raises a per-agent flag which is periodically polled by every agent) asks the executing agent to abort the execution of the goal. This increases the overall performance of the system by avoiding unnecessary work, as we will show in Section 4. Moreover, in order to be able to execute this operation in the presence of cuts in the code of the clause, it is invoked via the `undo/1` predicate.

Figure 1(b) presents the implementation of `<&/1`. First, the publishing agent needs to check whether the goal was picked up by some other agent or not. If it was not taken then the publishing agent will remove it from the goal list and execute it locally (using `call/1`), and then it will continue executing scheduler code. If the goal was taken by some other agent then its status will be checked (i.e., to know whether the goal execution has already finished or failed) as shown in Figure 1(c). If the goal execution fails then the parallel goal will be added to the goal list of the publishing agent, so it can be reexecuted by some other agent. This is a form of speculative execution, since the reexecution of that literal may not be needed for the actual computation. However, it increases the actual parallelism in the system. It should be noted that the goal execution will be canceled if the corresponding `&>/2` is reached on backtracking.

If the goal execution succeeds and `<&/1` is reached on backtracking, then backwards execution needs to be performed. If the goal was not taken by some other agent then backwards execution is trivially performed. If it was picked up by some other agent then the publishing agent sends a signal to the executing agent with a request for a new solution for that goal. The executing agent will serve the signal as soon as it is able. In order to enable this communication, each agent has an *event queue* from which the agent pops events consisting of pointers to handlers associated to the goals to be backtracked over. The primitives which perform this communication are `add_event/1`, which pushes a new pointer to a handler in the event queue of the agent which executed the associated goal, and `read_event/1`, which either removes the item in the event queue to perform backwards execution over the parallel goal associated to it, or fails if the event queue is empty. Figure 1(d) presents the source code to push the corresponding event to the executing agent, releasing its execution if it was suspended.

When an agent pops an event (Figure 1(f)), backwards execution over a parallel goal needs to be performed. If the segment of execution is at the top of its stack, then the agent will invoke `fail/0` and a new solution will be obtained. However, it might be the case that the segment of execution of the parallel goal is *trapped*, i.e., it is currently not at the top of the stack. In this case, there are two possible scenarios. If the goal is known not to have additional solutions,[4] then the segment where the goal lies does not need to be expanded and the pointers to the top of the segment in the handler are simply made to point to the beginning of the segment. The trail section corresponding to that segment

---

[4] For example, because it did not push any choice point or because it has been marked as deterministic during compilation, or by the user [4,16].

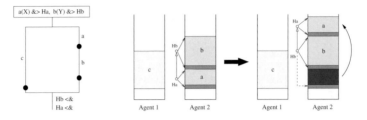

Fig. 2. Copying trapped goal onto the top of the stack

is used to undo the bindings. After this, the stack and trail pointers are restored to their previous values —i.e., they point to the top of the corresponding stacks.

If there may be more solutions for that goal, then a mechanism is needed to untrap its segment of execution. Several solutions have been proposed to solve this problem. A first approach consists of avoiding it altogether by carefully selecting goals to be executed so that they cannot cause trapped goals (which would dramatically reduce the amount of exploited parallelism). Another solution is to create a new, independent stack set for every goal taken, which would probably be memory-inefficient or impose an extra overhead in memory management. Our proposal is a variant of the solution adopted by several parallel systems (e.g., &-Prolog, ACE, DASWAM, . . .), which essentially try to continue the goal execution on top of the stack. However, in our case, and for simplicity, when a trapped goal is to be backtracked over, its execution segment is *copied* on top of the stack, where it can expand freely. The garbage slot created is marked as such, and can be recovered when everything between this garbage slot and the top of the stack turns into garbage (or on backtracking). Most implementations of garbage collectors do not recover dead choice points, and thus the garbage collection algorithm needs to be changed to work with parallel execution and cross-agent pointers. Improved garbage collectors could use the pointers to boundaries of every live segment stored in the handlers.

Figure 1(e) shows how the limits of the segment of execution of the parallel goal are stored in the handler, so their values can be accessed in backwards execution, via the save_init_execution/1 and save_end_execution/1 primitives, which actually have similar behavior to that of the input markers and end markers in the &-Prolog model. Note that the choice point created by the predicate call_handler/1 is in fact the input marker of the parallel execution, but again defined in the source language. Finally, when the goal execution fails, the metacut_garbage_slots/1 primitive will pop from the stack those discarded segments of the stack that are right underneath the segment of execution.

Figure 2 shows an example of this solution for the trapped goal and garbage slot problems. We assume that variables X, Y, and Z are independent. When the literals a/1 and b/1 are taken and executed by the second agent, the pointers that define the actual segment of execution of both literals are stored in the corresponding handler. Thus, when Ha <& is reached in backtracking, the segment of execution

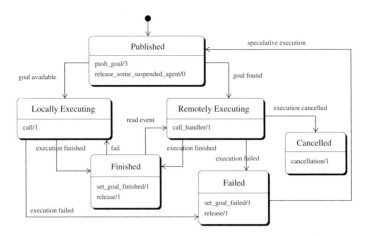

Fig. 3. State diagram of a parallel goal

of literal a/1 is trapped, and it is copied on top of the stack in order to have enough space to expand and obtain a new solution for the goal a/1. The handler associated to the literal b/1 will in addition mark the garbage slot left by the literal a/1, which will be freed when the execution of the literal b/1 fails.

Figure 3 presents a diagram which shows the different states in which a parallel goal can be according to the code in Figure 1. First, a goal is published to be executed in parallel by adding a pointer to it in the goal list and releasing the execution of an agent that is currently idle. When performing the goal join, if the goal is still available it will be executed locally. If the goal was picked up by some other agent, it will be executed remotely. A goal execution can be cancelled if the outcome of the execution is not needed for the actual computation. If the goal execution is not cancelled and succeeds, it may be backtracked over with the communication between agents performed via pushing and popping events. If it fails, the goal will be published again for parallel execution.

4   Performance Evaluation

We will now present some performance results obtained with our implementation for a selection of both deterministic and non-deterministic benchmarks (see Table 1), parallelized with unrestricted independent and-parallelism. Our proposal has been implemented on the Ciao multiparadigm system [3]. All the benchmarks were automatically parallelized [21,7] using CiaoPP [16] and starting from their sequential code. The performance results were obtained by averaging ten runs on a state-of-the-art multiprocessor, a Sun Fire T2000 with 8 cores (4 threads each) and 8 Gb of memory running in 32-bit compatibility mode.

Table 2 presents the speedups obtained for some deterministic benchmarks parallelized using unrestricted IAP. The speedups were obtained with respect to the execution time of the sequential version of the benchmarks. Thus, the

Table 1. Benchmarks executed with unrestricted IAP

AIAKL	Simplified *AKL* abstract inter-preter.	**MMatrix**	Matrix multip. (50×50).
Ann	Annotator for and-parallelism.	**Numbers**	Obtains a number from a list of others.
Boyer	Simplified version of *Boyer-Moore* theorem prover.	**Palindrome**	Generates a palindrome of 2^{14} elements.
Chat-80	Question parser of *Chat-80*.	**Progeom**	Constructs a perfect differ-ence set of order n.
Deriv	Symbolic derivation.		
FFT	Fast Fourier Transform.	**Queens**	The *n-queens* problem.
Fibonacci	Doubly recursive *Fibonacci*.	**QueensT**	Solves the *n-queens* prob-lem T times.
Hamming	Calculates *Hamming* num-bers.		
		QuickSort	Sorts a 10,000 element list.
Hanoi	Solves *Hanoi* puzzle.	**Takeuchi**	Computes *Takeuchi*.

columns tagged *1* measure the *slowdown* coming from executing a parallel pro-gram in a single processor. Rows tagged with the '**&!**' symbol measure the exe-cution of the benchmarks with some optimizations for the case of deterministic parallel goals, on our previous, determinism-only model and implementation [8]. Rows tagged with the '**&**' symbol measure the speedups obtained with all the mechanisms required by the implementation presented in Section 3. The differ-ence in speedups between both parallel versions is of little significance in most cases, and only in very few cases (for example, `Boyer` and `Fibonacci`) the differ-ence is relevant. Note that determinism can either be annotated by hand or, in many cases, automatically detected [4,16]. In any case, reasonably good speedups are obtained, despite the fact that the proposal suffers from the overhead added by the source-level coded scheduler etc., but which, in return, offers other advan-tages such as significantly reduced development (and maintenance) time, more flexibility, simpler and faster experimentation, etc.

Table 3 presents the speedups obtained for some non-deterministic bench-marks. Some of them do not obtain any speedup when executed in parallel due to the very fine granularity of the parallel goals and the high-level nature of our implementation. However, super-linear speedups can be achieved in other benchmarks (e.g., Chat-80), thanks to the implementation of goal cancellation.

A fact that limits the system performance is the expansion of the agent stack sets when running out of space. Stack sets are initially created small and they dynamically grow as needed. This fits the behavior of a naive user who lets the system run and adjust itself; a more seasoned user could create the stack sets with a size which appropriate for a particular application. Due to the work-stealing strategy adopted and the shared-memory nature of our implementation, there may be cross-agent pointers. The approach we have taken to ensure a correct stack set expansion is to suspend the execution of all the agents. The stack set which is short on space is then expanded, the pointers pointing to that stack set (from any agent) are updated, and the execution of the agents finally resumes.[5]

---

[5] We acknowledge that a smarter algorithm could be implemented, but this topic is out of the scope of this paper and a subject for further work.

Table 2. Speedups obtained for deterministic unrestricted IAP benchmarks

Benchmark	Op.	Number of agents								
		Seq.	1	2	3	4	5	6	7	8
AIAKL	&!	1.00	0.99	1.82	1.82	1.82	1.83	1.83	1.83	1.82
	&	1.00	0.93	1.70	1.71	1.72	1.74	1.75	1.72	1.72
Ann	&!	1.00	0.96	1.84	2.72	3.56	4.38	5.16	5.88	6.64
	&	1.00	0.96	1.85	2.72	3.57	4.35	5.14	5.87	6.61
Boyer	&!	1.00	0.92	1.76	2.58	3.16	3.39	4.01	4.31	4.55
	&	1.00	0.90	1.21	1.83	2.06	2.26	2.30	2.39	2.56
Deriv	&!	1.00	0.83	1.59	2.38	3.07	3.78	4.49	4.98	5.49
	&	1.00	0.84	1.60	2.34	2.99	3.73	4.43	4.56	4.85
FFT	&!	1.00	0.98	1.73	2.06	2.67	2.78	2.95	2.96	3.11
	&	1.00	0.98	1.72	1.97	2.65	2.67	2.75	2.93	2.97
Fibonacci	&!	1.00	0.98	1.91	2.84	3.73	4.62	5.51	6.41	7.35
	&	1.00	0.98	1.58	2.04	2.53	3.28	4.06	4.61	5.46
Hamming	&!	1.00	0.92	1.04	1.43	1.65	1.65	1.65	1.65	1.65
	&	1.00	0.92	1.02	1.41	1.63	1.62	1.62	1.62	1.62
Hanoi	&!	1.00	0.95	1.76	2.47	3.09	3.39	3.65	3.87	4.10
	&	1.00	0.96	1.77	1.91	2.84	3.13	3.54	3.76	4.02
HanoiDL	&!	1.00	0.73	1.44	2.08	2.77	3.37	4.04	4.58	5.19
	&	1.00	0.74	1.43	1.89	1.87	2.73	3.07	3.59	3.87
MMatrix	&!	1.00	0.77	1.51	2.31	3.02	3.76	4.52	5.21	5.72
	&	1.00	0.77	1.48	2.16	2.88	3.51	4.05	4.57	4.96
Palindrome	&!	1.00	0.95	1.77	2.36	2.95	3.33	3.62	3.94	4.15
	&	1.00	0.96	1.78	2.14	2.56	3.11	3.30	3.74	3.90
QuickSort	&!	1.00	0.97	1.74	2.26	2.91	3.16	3.39	3.49	3.54
	&	1.00	0.97	1.71	2.17	2.43	2.60	2.93	3.06	3.19
QuickSortDL	&!	1.00	0.95	1.69	2.30	2.81	3.10	3.25	3.47	3.60
	&	1.00	0.95	1.68	2.14	2.39	2.56	2.92	2.94	3.19
Takeuchi	&!	1.00	0.86	1.17	2.24	2.97	3.29	3.75	4.28	5.69
	&	1.00	0.86	0.89	1.69	2.23	3.00	3.34	3.36	4.29

Table 3. Speedups obtained for non-deterministic unrestricted IAP benchmarks

Benchmark	Number of agents								
	Seq.	1	2	3	4	5	6	7	8
Chat-80	1.00	2.31	4.49	5.42	6.91	9.79	9.95	11.10	17.29
Numbers	1.00	1.84	1.79	1.79	1.79	1.79	1.79	1.78	1.78
Progeom	1.00	0.99	0.96	0.97	0.98	0.98	0.98	0.98	0.98
Queens	1.00	0.99	0.94	0.94	0.94	0.94	0.94	0.94	0.94
QueensT	1.00	0.99	1.90	2.41	3.18	4.71	4.61	4.58	4.57

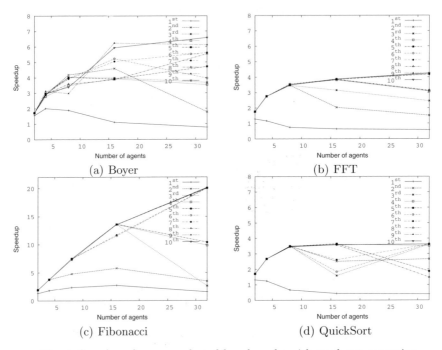

Fig. 4. Speedups for some selected benchmarks with stack set expansion

Table 4. Behavior of **Queens(8)** with different numbers of agents

			Benchmark										
		Queens, 2 agents				Queens, 4 agents				Queens, 8 agents			
		No		Gr		No		Gr		No		Gr	
		1	N	1	N	1	N	1	N	1	N	1	N
G &> H		11,810	171,858	9	290	11,810	171,858	9	290	11,810	171,858	9	290
Taken	$\overline{x}$	6,649	97,798	9	290	6,860	99,373	9	290	6,476	96,056	9	290
	σ	9.35	45.04	0.00	0.00	16.15	65.02	0.00	0.00	13.49	59.04	0.00	0.00
LBack	$\overline{x}$	858	14,319	0.00	0.00	618	10,905	0.00	0.00	755	12,786	0.00	0.00
	σ	1.03	1.25	0.00	0.00	14.93	99.89	0.00	0.00	5.79	23.59	0.00	0.00
RBack Top	$\overline{x}$	1,838	29,725	2	234	2,345	38,420	2	234	2,208	36,261	2	234
	σ	0.46	2.14	0.00	0.00	15.14	98.66	0.00	0.00	6.34	26.53	0.00	0.00
Tp	$\overline{x}$	0	0	0	0	0	0	0	0	0	0	0	0
	σ	0.00	0.00	0.00	0.00	0.00	0.00	0.00	0.00	0.00	0.00	0.00	0.00

That scheme indeed affects the performance of the execution. Figure 4 presents the speedups obtained by executing ten times some selected benchmarks with 2, 4, 8, 16 and 32 agents. By joining together the points corresponding to the n-th execution with a given number of processors, we can construct a profile of how the speedup evolves as the system executes several times the same program. The first executions suffer from stack expansions but, after some runs, the stack set of each agent reaches an appropriate size, the number of expansions diminishes, and thus the performance results stabilize. Note also that, for the case of more

Table 5. Behavior of **Progeom(5)** with different numbers of agents

			Benchmark										
			Progeom, 2 agents				Progeom, 4 agents				Progeom, 8 agents			
			No		Gr		No		Gr		No		Gr	
			1	N	1	N	1	N	1	N	1	N	1	N
G &> H			215	154,260	1	60	215	154,260	1	60	215	154,260	1	60
Taken		$\bar{x}$	100	72,375	0	1	91	65,643	0	1	55	75,113	0	1
		σ	1.85	248.69	0.00	0.80	1.36	414.68	0.00	0.70	3.49	192.25	0.00	0.78
LBack		$\bar{x}$	1	738	0	29	3	2,131	0	29	9	364	0	29
		σ	0.46	52.03	0.00	0.80	1.10	83.78	0.00	0.70	0.80	26.82	0.00	0.78
RBack	Top	$\bar{x}$	10	6,530	0	1	8	5,131	0	1	2	6,907	0	1
		σ	0.57	52.08	0.00	0.80	1.10	84.26	0.00	0.70	0.80	27.02	0.00	0.78
	Tp	$\bar{x}$	0	0	0	0	0	0	0	0	0	0	0	0
		σ	0.00	0.00	0.00	0.00	0.00	0.00	0.00	0.00	0.00	0.00	0.00	0.00

Table 6. Behavior of **Fibonacci(25)** with different numbers of agents

			Benchmark										
			Fibonacci, 2 agents				Fibonacci, 4 agents				Fibonacci, 8 agents			
			No		Gr		No		Gr		No		Gr	
			1	N	1	N	1	N	1	N	1	N	1	N
G &> H			121,392	121,392	1,596	1,596	121,392	121,392	1,596	1,596	121,392	121,392	1,596	1,596
Taken		$\bar{x}$	1	1	1	1	5	5	5	5	37	37	31	31
		σ	0.00	0.00	0.00	0.00	0.00	0.00	0.00	0.00	3.97	3.97	2.39	2.39
LBack		$\bar{x}$	121,391	121,391	1,595	1,595	121,387	121,387	1,591	1,591	121,355	121,355	1,565	1,565
		σ	0.00	0.00	0.00	0.00	0.00	0.00	0.00	0.00	3.97	3.97	2.39	2.39
RBack	Top	$\bar{x}$	1	1	1	1	5	5	5	5	18	18	16	16
		σ	0.00	0.00	0.00	0.00	0.00	0.00	0.00	0.00	2.40	2.40	0.98	0.98
	Tp	$\bar{x}$	0	0	0	0	0	0	0	0	19	19	15	15
		σ	0.00	0.00	0.00	0.00	0.00	0.00	0.00	0.00	2.86	2.86	1.68	1.68

than 8 agents, the limitations in the hardware of the multiprocessor machine[6] used also affect the actual performance of the execution.

Tables 4 to 6 present data from the execution of some of the non-deterministic, and-parallel benchmarks. They present data from executions with 2, 4, and 8 agents, using or not granularity control [18] (resp., Gr and No), and in cases where only one solution (1) or all solutions (N) are requested. The first row in the table (G &> H) contains the number of parallel goals. The second row (*Taken*) presents the number of parallel goals picked up by some other agent ($\bar{x}$ stands for the average and σ for the standard deviation in ten runs). The third row (*LBack*) represents the number of times that backtracking over parallel goals took place locally because the goal was not picked up by some other agent.[7] The fourth row (*RBack*) shows the number of times a parallel goal was backtracked over remotely. *Top* and *Tp* count, respectively, how many times remote backtracking was performed at the top of the stack and on a trapped goal. A conclusion from these results is that, while the amount of remote backtracking is quite high, the number of trapped goals is low. Therefore the overhead of copying trapped

---

[6] Mainly, the availability of a reduced number of integer units and a single FP unit. In our experiments, completely independent computations do not show linear speedup from 8 processors onwards.

[7] The backtracking measured for **Fibonacci** in Table 6 corresponds to the stack unwinding performed when failing after the execution is finished.

segments to the top of the stack should not be very high in comparison with the rest of the execution.

We expect to see a similar behavior in most non-deterministic parallel programs where parallel goals are of fine granularity or very likely to fail: these two behaviors make the piling up of segments corresponding to the execution of loosely related parallel goals in the same stack relatively uncommon, which indeed reduces the chances to suffer from trapped goal and garbage slot problems.

5   Conclusions

We have presented a high-level implementation of unrestricted, independent and-parallelism that can execute both deterministic and non-deterministic programs in parallel. The approach helps taming the implementation complexity of previous solutions by raising many of the main implementation components to the source level. This makes the system easier to code, maintain, and expand. Our evaluation of actual parallel executions shows that quite useful speedups can be obtained with the approach, including for benchmarks which perform backtracking over non-deterministic parallel goals In several cases, super-linear speedups were obtained thanks to the backtracking model implemented.

We believe that the results obtainable with this approach will improve further as the speed of the source language continues to increase. Recent compilation technology and implementation advances provide hope that it will eventually be possible to recover most of the efficiency lost due to expressing the parallel machinery using the high-level language. In the meantime, performance can also be improved by, once the components of the system are stabilized, selectively lowering again the implementation of those flagged as bottlenecks, if the benefits surpass the added complexity and reduced flexibility. Performance can also be improved, e.g., by exploiting the fact that smarter schedulers are, in principle, easier to write than with other approaches.

References

1. Ait-Kaci, H.: Warren's Abstract Machine, A Tutorial Reconstruction. MIT Press, Cambridge (1991)
2. Ali, K.A.M., Karlsson, R.: The Muse Or-Parallel Prolog Model and its Performance. In: 1990 North American Conference on Logic Programming, pp. 757–776. MIT Press, Cambridge (1990)
3. Bueno, F., Cabeza, D., Carro, M., Hermenegildo, M., López-García, P., Puebla, G. (eds.): The Ciao System. Ref. Manual (v1.13). Technical report, C. S. School, UPM (2006), http://www.ciaohome.org
4. Bueno, F., López-García, P., Puebla, G., Hermenegildo, M.: A Tutorial on Program Development and Optimization using the Ciao Preprocessor. Technical Report CLIP2/06, Technical University of Madrid (UPM), Facultad de Informática, 28660 Boadilla del Monte, Madrid, Spain (January 2006)
5. Cabeza, D., Hermenegildo, M.: Implementing Distributed Concurrent Constraint Execution in the CIAO System. In: Proc. of the AGP 1996 Joint Conference on Declarative Programming, pp. 67–78 (July 1996)

6. Carro, M., Hermenegildo, M.: Concurrency in Prolog Using Threads and a Shared Database. In: 1999 International Conference on Logic Programming, pp. 320–334. MIT Press, Cambridge (November 1999)
7. Casas, A., Carro, M., Hermenegildo, M.: Annotation Algorithms for Unrestricted Independent And-Parallelism in Logic Programs. In: King, A. (ed.) LOPSTR 2007. LNCS, vol. 4915, pp. 138–153. Springer, Heidelberg (2008)
8. Casas, A., Carro, M., Hermenegildo, M.: Towards a High-Level Implementation of Execution Primitives for Non-restricted, Independent And-parallelism. In: Hudak, P., Warren, D.S. (eds.) PADL 2008. LNCS, vol. 4902, pp. 230–247. Springer, Heidelberg (2008)
9. Conery, J.S.: The And/Or Process Model for Parallel Interpretation of Logic Programs. Ph.D thesis, The University of California At Irvine, Technical Report 204 (1983)
10. Gupta, G., Pontelli, E., Ali, K., Carlsson, M., Hermenegildo, M.: Parallel Execution of Prolog Programs: a Survey. ACM Transactions on Programming Languages and Systems 23(4), 472–602 (2001)
11. Hermenegildo, M.: An Abstract Machine for Restricted AND-parallel Execution of Logic Programs. In: Shapiro, E. (ed.) ICLP 1986. LNCS, vol. 225, pp. 25–40. Springer, Heidelberg (1986)
12. Hermenegildo, M.: Parallelizing Irregular and Pointer-Based Computations Automatically: Perspectives from Logic and Constraint Programming. Parallel Computing 26(13–14), 1685–1708 (2000)
13. Hermenegildo, M., Carro, M.: Relating Data–Parallelism and (And–) Parallelism in Logic Programs. The Computer Languages Journal 22(2/3), 143–163 (1996)
14. Hermenegildo, M., Greene, K.: The &-Prolog System: Exploiting Independent And-Parallelism. New Generation Computing 9(3,4), 233–257 (1991)
15. Hermenegildo, M., Nasr, R.I.: Efficient Management of Backtracking in AND-parallelism. In: Shapiro, E. (ed.) ICLP 1986. LNCS, vol. 225, pp. 40–55. Springer, Heidelberg (1986)
16. Hermenegildo, M., Puebla, G., Bueno, F., López García, P.: Integrated Program Debugging, Verification, and Optimization Using Abstract Interpretation (and The Ciao System Preprocessor). Science of Computer Programming 58(1–2), 115–140 (2005)
17. Janson, S.: AKL. A Multiparadigm Programming Language. Ph.D thesis, Uppsala University (1994)
18. López-García, P., Hermenegildo, M., Debray, S.K.: A Methodology for Granularity Based Control of Parallelism in Logic Programs. J. of Symbolic Computation, Special Issue on Parallel Symbolic Computation 21, 715–734 (1996)
19. Lusk, E., Butler, R., Disz, T., Olson, R., Stevens, R., Warren, D.H.D., Calderwood, A., Szeredi, P., Brand, P., Carlsson, M., Ciepielewski, A., Hausman, B., Haridi, S.: The Aurora Or-parallel Prolog System. New Generation Computing 7(2/3), 243–271 (1988)
20. Moura, P., Crocker, P., Nunes, P.: High-level multi-threading programming in logtalk. In: Warren, D.S., Hudak, P. (eds.) PADL 2008. LNCS, vol. 4902, pp. 265–281. Springer, Heidelberg (2008)
21. Muthukumar, K., Bueno, F., García de la Banda, M., Hermenegildo, M.: Automatic Compile-time Parallelization of Logic Programs for Restricted, Goal-level, Independent And-parallelism. Journal of Logic Programming 38(2), 165–218 (1999)

22. Pontelli, E., Gupta, G.: Efficient Backtracking in And-Parallel Implementations of Non-Deterministic Languages. In: Lai, T. (ed.) Proc. of the International Conference on Parallel Processing, pp. 338–345. IEEE Computer Society, Los Alamitos (1998)
23. Pontelli, E., Gupta, G., Hermenegildo, M.: &ACE: A High-Performance Parallel Prolog System. In: International Parallel Processing Symposium, pp. 564–572. IEEE Computer Society Technical Committee on Parallel Processing, IEEE Computer Society (April 1995)
24. de Morais Santos-Costa, V.M.: Compile-Time Analysis for the Parallel Execution of Logic Programs in Andorra-I. Ph.D thesis, University of Bristol (August. 1993)
25. Shen, K.: Overview of DASWAM: Exploitation of Dependent And-parallelism. Journal of Logic Programming 29(1–3), 245–293 (1996)
26. Warren, D.H.D.: An Abstract Prolog Instruction Set. TR 309, SRI International (1983)

Inference with Logic Programs with Annotated Disjunctions under the Well Founded Semantics

Fabrizio Riguzzi

ENDIF, Università di Ferrara, Via Saragat, 1, 44100 Ferrara, Italy
`fabrizio.riguzzi@unife.it`

Abstract. Logic Programs with Annotated Disjunctions (LPADs) allow to express probabilistic information in logic programming. The semantics of an LPAD is given in terms of well founded models of the normal logic programs obtained by selecting one disjunct from each ground LPAD clause. The paper presents SLGAD resolution that computes the (conditional) probability of a ground query from an LPAD and is based on SLG resolution for normal logic programs. SLGAD is evaluated on classical benchmarks for well founded semantics inference algorithms, namely the stalemate game and the ancestor relation. SLGAD is compared with Cilog2 and SLDNFAD, an algorithm based on SLDNF, on the programs that are modularly acyclic. The results show that SLGAD deals correctly with cyclic programs and, even if it is more expensive than SLDNFAD on problems where SLDNFAD succeeds, is faster than Cilog2 when the query is true in an exponential number of instances.

Topics: Probabilistic Logic Programming, Well Founded Semantics, Logic Programs with Annotated Disjunctions, SLG resolution.

1 Introduction

The combination of logic and probability is a long standing problem in philosophy and artificial intelligence. Recently, the work on this topic has thrived leading to the proposal of novel languages that combine relational and statistical aspects. Each of these languages has a different semantics that makes it suitable for different domains.

When we are reasoning about actions and effects and we have causal independence among different causes for the same effect, Logic Programs with Annotated Disjunctions (LPADs) [1] seem particularly suitable. They extend logic programs by allowing program clauses to be disjunctive and by annotating each atom in the head with a probability. A clause can be causally interpreted in the following way: the truth of the body causes the truth of one of the atoms in the head non-deterministically chosen on the basis of the annotations. The semantics of LPADs is given in terms of the well founded model of the normal logic programs obtained by selecting one head for each disjunctive clause.

[2] showed that acyclic LPADs can be converted to Independent Choice Logic (ICL) [3] programs. Thus inference can be performed by using the Cilog2

M. Garcia de la Banda and E. Pontelli (Eds.): ICLP 2008, LNCS 5366, pp. 667–671, 2008.

system [4]. An algorithm for performing inference directly with LPADs was proposed in [5]. The algorithm, that will be called SLDNFAD in the following, is an extension of SLDNF derivation and uses Binary Decision Diagrams. Both Cilog2 and SLDNFAD are complete and correct for programs for which the Clark's completion semantics and the well founded semantics coincide, as for acyclic and modularly acyclic programs [6], but can go into a loop for cyclic programs.

In this paper we present the SLGAD top-down procedure for performing inference with possibly (modularly) cyclic LPADs. SLGAD is based on the SLG procedure [7] for normal logic programs and extends it in a minimal way.

SLGAD is evaluated on classical benchmarks for well founded semantics inference algorithms, namely the stalemate game and the ancestor relation. In both cases, extensional databases encoding linear, cyclic or tree-shaped relations are considered. SLGAD is compared with Cilog2 and SLDNFAD on the modularly acyclic programs. The results show that SLGAD is able to deal with cyclic programs and, while being more expensive than SLDNFAD on problems where SLDNFAD succeeds, is faster than Cilog2 when the query is true in an exponential number of instances.

2   Preliminaries

A Logic Program with Annotated Disjunctions [1] T consists of a finite set of formulas of the form $(H_1 : \alpha_1) \vee (H_2 : \alpha_2) \vee \ldots \vee (H_n : \alpha_n) : -B_1, B_2, \ldots B_m$ called *annotated disjunctive clauses*. In such a clause the H_i are logical atoms, the B_i are logical literals and the α_i are real numbers in the interval $[0,1]$ such that $\sum_{i=1}^{n} \alpha_i \leq 1$. The head of LPAD clauses implicitly contains an extra atom *null* that does not appear in the body of any clause and whose annotation is $1 - \sum_{i=1}^{n} \alpha_i$.

In order to define the semantics of a non-ground T, we must generate the grounding T' of T. By choosing a head atom for each ground clause of an LPAD we get a normal logic program called an *instance* of the LPAD. A probability distribution is defined over the space of instances by assuming independence among the choices made for each clause.

A *choice* κ is a set of triples (C, θ, i) where $C \in T$, θ is a substitution that grounds C and $i \in \{1, \ldots, |head(C)|\}$. (C, θ, i) means that, for ground clause $C\theta$, the head $H_i : \alpha_i$ was chosen. A choice κ is *consistent* if $(C, \theta, i) \in \kappa, (C, \theta, j) \in \kappa \Rightarrow i = j$, i.e. only one head is selected for a ground clause. A consistent choice is a *selection* σ if for each clause $C\theta$ in the grounding T' of T there is a triple (C, θ, i) in σ. We denote the set of all selections of a program T by $\mathcal{S}_T$. A consistent choice κ identifies a normal logic program $T_\kappa = \{(H_i(C) : -body(C))\theta | (C, \theta, i) \in \kappa\}$ that is called a *sub-instance* of T. If σ is a selection, T_σ is called an *instance*.

The *probability of a consistent choice* κ is the product of the probabilities of the individual choices made, i.e. $P_\kappa = \prod_{(C, \theta, i) \in \kappa} \alpha_i(C)$. The *probability of instance* T_σ is P_σ. The semantics of the instances of an LPAD is given by the well founded semantics (WFS). Given a normal program T, we call $WFM(T)$ its *well founded partial model.* For each instance T_σ, we require that $WFM(T_\sigma)$ is two-valued, since we want to model uncertainty solely by means of disjunctions. We call *sound* such a program.

The probability of a formula χ is given by the sum of the probabilities of the instances where the formula is true according to the WFS: $P_T(\chi) = \sum_{T_\sigma \models_{WFS} \chi} P_\sigma$.

3   SLGAD Resolution Algorithm

In this section we present *Linear resolution with Selection function for General logic programs with Annotated Disjunctions* (SLGAD) that extends SLG resolution [8,7] for dealing with LPADs.

SLG uses X-clauses to represent resolvents with delayed literals: an *X-clause* X is a clause of the form $A : -D|B$ where A is an atom, D is a sequence of ground negative literals and (possibly unground) atoms and B is a sequence of literals. Literals in D are called *delayed literals*. If B is empty, an X-clause is called an *X-answer* clause. An ordinary program clause is seen as a X-clause with an empty set of delayed literals.

SLG is based on the operation of SLG resolution and SLG factoring on X-clauses. In particular, SLG resolution is performed between an X-clause $A : -|A$ and a program clause or between an X-clause and an X-answer.

In SLGAD, X-clauses are replaced by XD-clauses: an *XD-clause* G is a quadruple (X, C, θ, i) where X is an X-clause, C is a clause of T, θ is a substitution for the variables of C and $i \in \{1, \ldots, |head(C)|\}$. Let X be $A : -D|B$: if B is empty, the XD-clause is called an *XD-answer* clause. With XD-clauses we keep track not only of the current resolvent but also of the clauses and head that originated it.

In SLGAD, SLG resolution between an X-clause $A : -|A$ and a program clause is replaced by SLGAD goal resolution and SLG resolution between an X-clause and an X-answer is replaced by SLGAD answer resolution. SLG factoring is replaced by SLGAD factoring.

We report here the definition for SLGAD goal resolution. Let A be a subgoal and let C be a clause of T such that A is unifiable with an atom H_i in the head of C. Let C' be a variant of C with variables renamed so that A and C' have no variables in common. We say that A is *SLGAD goal resolvable* with C and the XD-clause $((A : -|body(C'))\theta, C', \theta, i)$ is the *SLGAD goal resolvent* of A with C on head H_i, where θ is the most general unifier of A and H_i'.

SLGAD answer resolution and SLGAD factoring differ from SLG answer resolution and SLG factoring because they produce an XD-clause that contains the clause and head index of the starting XD-clause while the substitution is updated. We refer to [9] for the details of these operators.

With respect to SLG, SLGAD keeps an extra global variable that is a choice κ to record all the clauses used in the SLGAD derivation together with the head selected. This extra global variable is updated by ADD_CLAUSE that is the only procedure of SLGAD not present in SLG. ADD_CLAUSE is called when an answer for a subgoal has been found and generates different derivation branches for different choices of atoms in the head of the ground clause $C\theta$ that contains the answer in the head. ADD_CLAUSE first checks whether the clause $C\theta$ already appears in the current choice κ with a head index different from i: if so, it fails the derivation. Otherwise, it non-deterministically selects a head index j from $\{1, \ldots, |head(C)|\}$: if $j = i$ this means that the subgoal in the head is derivable in the sub-instance represented by κ, so the calling procedure can add the answer to the table. If $j \neq i$, then the table is not altered. In backtracking, all elements of $\{1, \ldots, |head(C)|\}$ are selected. Since an answer ia added to the table only when an XD-clause is reduced to an answer and eventually all XD-clauses for successful derivations will reduce to answers, it is sufficient to consider the available choices only at this point.

With this approach, SLGAD is able to exploit all the techniques used by SLG to avoid loops: the delaying of literals, the use of a global stack of subgoals, the recording of the "depth" of each subgoal and the tracking, for each subgoal A, of the deepest subgoal in the stack that may depend on A positively or negatively. For the full details of the algorithm, we refer the reader to [9].

SLGAD is sound and complete with respect to the LPAD semantics and the proof is is based on the theorem of partial correctness of SLG [8,10]: SLG is sound and complete given an arbitrary but fixed computation rule when it does not flounder.

4   Experiments

We tested SLGAD on some synthetic problems that were used as benchmarks for SLG [7,11]: win, ranc and lanc. win is an implementation of the stalemate game and contains the clause $win(X) : 0.8 : -move(X, Y), \neg win(Y)$. ranc and lanc model the ancestor relation with right and left recursion respectively. Various definitions of move are considered: a linear and acyclic relation, containing the tuples $(1, 2), \ldots, (N - 1, N)$, a linear and cyclic relation, containing the tuples $(1, 2), \ldots, (N - 1, N), (N, 1)$, and a tree relation, that represents a complete binary tree of height N, containing $2^{N+1}+1$ tuples. For win, all the move relations are used, while for ranc and lanc only the linear ones.

SLDAG was compared with Cilog2 and SLDNFAD. Cilog2 [4] computes probabilities by identifying consistent choices on which the query is true, then it makes them mutually incompatible with an iterative algorithm. SLDNFAD [5] extends SLDNF in order to store choices and computes the probability with an algorithm based on Binary Decision Diagrams. For SLGAD and SLDNFAD we used the implementations in Yap Prolog available in the cplint suite[1]. SLGAD code is based on the SLG system. For Cilog2 we ported the code available on the web to Yap.

The computation time of the queries win(1) and ancestor(1,N) were recorded as a function of N for win, ranc and lanc respectively. win has an exponential number of instances where the query is true and the experimental results show the combinatorial explosion. On the ancestor datasets, the proof tree has only

---

[1] http://www.ing.unife.it/software/cplint/

one branch with a number of nodes proportional to N. However, the execution time of SLGAD increases roughly as $O(N \log N)$ because each derivation step requires a lookup and an insert in the table $\mathcal{T}$ that take logarithmic time.

Cilog2 and SLDNFAD are applied only to the problems that are modularly acyclic and right recursive, i.e. **win** with linear and tree **move** and **ranc** with linear **move**, because on the other problems they would go into a loop. In **win** all the algorithms show the combinatorial explosion, with SLGAD performing better than Cilog2 and worse than SLDNFAD. On **ranc** with linear **move**, SLGAD takes longer than Cilog2 and SLDNFAD: the execution times for $N = 20,000$ are 4726.8, 8.3 and 1165.4 seconds respectively. Thus the added complexity of avoiding cycles has a computational cost. However, this cost is unavoidable when we are not sure whether the program under analysis is (modularly) acyclic or not.

Acknowledgments. This work has been partially supported by the FIRB project TOCAI.IT: *Tecnologie orientate alla conoscenza per aggregazioni di imprese in Internet.*

References

1. Vennekens, J., Verbaeten, S., Bruynooghe, M.: Logic programs with annotated disjunctions. In: Demoen, B., Lifschitz, V. (eds.) ICLP 2004. LNCS, vol. 3132, pp. 431–445. Springer, Heidelberg (2004)
2. Vennekens, J., Verbaeten, S.: Logic programs with annotated disjunctions. Technical Report CW386, K. U. Leuven (2003),
   http://www.cs.kuleuven.ac.be/~joost/techrep.ps
3. Poole, D.: The Independent Choice Logic for modelling multiple agents under uncertainty. Artif. Intell. 94(1-2), 7–56 (1997)
4. Poole, D.: Abducing through negation as failure: stable models within the independent choice logic. J. Log. Program. 44(1-3), 5–35 (2000)
5. Riguzzi, F.: A top down interpreter for LPAD and CP–logic. In: Basili, R., Pazienza, M.T. (eds.) AI*IA 2007. LNCS (LNAI), vol. 4733, pp. 109–120. Springer, Heidelberg (2007)
6. Ross, K.A.: Modular acyclicity and tail recursion in logic programs. In: Symposium on Principles of Database Systems, pp. 92–101. ACM Press, New York (1991)
7. Chen, W., Swift, T., Warren, D.S.: Efficient top-down computation of queries under the well-founded semantics. J. Log. Program. 24(3), 161–199 (1995)
8. Chen, W., Warren, D.S.: Query evaluation under the well founded semantics. In: Symposium on Principles of Database Systems, pp. 168–179. ACM Press, New York (1993)
9. Riguzzi, F.: The SLGAD procedure for inference opn logic programs with annotated disjunctions. Technical Report CS-2008-01, University of Ferrara (2008),
   http://www.unife.it/dipartimento/ingegneria/informazione/informatica/
   rapporti-tecnici-1/cs-2008-01.pdf/view
10. Chen, W., Warren, D.: Towards effective evaluation of general logic programs. Technical report, State University of New York, Stony Brook (1993)
11. Castro, L.F., Swift, T., Warren, D.S.: Suspending and resuming computations in engines for SLG evaluation. In: Krishnamurthi, S., Ramakrishnan, C.R. (eds.) PADL 2002. LNCS, vol. 2257, pp. 332–350. Springer, Heidelberg (2002)

Safe Formulas in the General Theory of Stable Models (Preliminary Report)

Joohyung Lee[1], Vladimir Lifschitz[2], and Ravi Palla[1]

[1] School of Computing and Informatics, Arizona State University, USA
[2] Department of Computer Sciences, University of Texas at Austin, USA
{joolee,Ravi.Palla}@asu.edu, vl@cs.utexas.edu

Abstract. Safe first-order formulas generalize the concept of a safe rule, which plays an important role in the design of answer set solvers. We show that any safe sentence is equivalent, in a certain sense, to the result of its grounding—to the variable-free sentence obtained from it by replacing all quantifiers with multiple conjunctions and disjunctions. It follows that a safe sentence and the result of its grounding have the same stable models, and that stable models of a safe sentence can be characterized by a formula of a simple syntactic form.

1 Introduction

The definition of a stable model proposed in [1] is more general than the original definition from [2]: it applies to models of arbitrary first-order sentences. Logic programs referred to in the 1988 definition are identified in this theory with first-order formulas of a special form. For instance, the rule

$$p(x) \leftarrow not \ q(x) \qquad (1)$$

is treated as alternative notation for the sentence

$$\forall x (\neg q(x) \rightarrow p(x)). \qquad (2)$$

In this example, stable models are the interpretations of the unary predicate constants p and q (in the sense of first-order logic) that make p identically true and q identically false.

This general definition of a stable model involves a syntactic transformation of formulas, which is similar to the circumscription operator [3]—it turns a first-order sentence into a stronger second-order sentence. There is an important difference, however, between stable models and models of circumscription. Two sentences may be equivalent (that is, have the same models), but have different *stable* models. For instance, formula (2) is equivalent to

$$\forall x (\neg p(x) \rightarrow q(x)),$$

but the stable models of these two formulas are not the same. The equivalent transformations of formulas that preserve their stable models are studied in [4].

M. Garcia de la Banda and E. Pontelli (Eds.): ICLP 2008, LNCS 5366, pp. 672–676, 2008.
© Springer-Verlag Berlin Heidelberg 2008

They are represented there by a subsystem of classical logic called **SQHT**$^=$ ("static quantified logic of here-and-there with equality"). This deductive system includes all axioms and inference rules of intuitionistic logic with equality, the decidable equality axiom

$$x = y \lor x \neq y \tag{3}$$

and two other axiom schemas, but it does not include the general law of the excluded middle $F \lor \neg F$.

In [5], the new approach to stable models is used to define the semantics of an answer set programming language with choice rules and counting, called RASPL-1. The meaning of a RASPL-1 program is defined in terms of the stable models of a first-order sentence associated with the program, which is called its "FOL-representation." For instance, the FOL-representation of the RASPL-1 rule

$$p \leftarrow \{x : q(x)\} \, 1 \tag{4}$$

is the formula

$$\neg \exists xy (q(x) \land q(y) \land x \neq y) \rightarrow p. \tag{5}$$

In this note, we continue one line of research from [5], the study of safe sentences and their stable models. The definition of a safe sentence, reproduced in the next section, is related to some ideas of [6].[1] It extends the familiar concept of a safe rule, which plays an important role in the design of answer set solvers [7, Section 2.1]. For instance, rule (1) is not safe, and for this reason it is not allowed in the input of any of the existing systems for computing stable models. Rule (4) is safe, and we expect that it will be accepted by a future implementation of RASPL-1.

According to Proposition 1 below, stable models of a safe sentence (without function symbols) have what can be called the "small predicate property": the relation represented by any of its predicate constants can hold for a tuple of arguments only if each member of the tuple is represented by an object constant. We show, furthermore, that any safe sentence is equivalent, in a certain sense, to the result of its grounding—to the variable-free sentence obtained from it by replacing all quantifiers with multiple conjunctions and disjunctions (Proposition 2). We derive from these two facts that a safe sentence and the result of its grounding have the same stable models (Proposition 3). This theorem leads us to the conclusion that stable models of a safe sentence can be characterized by a sentence of a simple syntactic structure—not just first-order, but universal and, moreover, "almost variable-free" (Proposition 4).

---

[1] Topor and Sonenberg [6] defined the notion of "allowed" formulas, similar to the notion of safe formulas, in a much more limited setting of stratified deductive databases. (That paper was written before the invention of the stable model semantics.) The definitions are not equivalent to each other. For example, $\exists x (\neg p(x) \rightarrow q)$ is safe but not allowed; $\exists x (\neg p(x) \rightarrow q(x))$ is allowed but not safe.

2   Review: Safe Sentences

We consider first-order formulas that may contain object constants and equality but no function constants of arity > 0. $\neg F$ is shorthand for $F \rightarrow \bot$, $F \leftrightarrow G$ is shorthand for $(F \rightarrow G) \wedge (G \rightarrow F)$, and $\top$ is shorthand for $\bot \rightarrow \bot$. A *sentence* is a formula without free variables.

Recall that a traditional rule—an implication of the form

$$(L_1 \wedge \cdots \wedge L_n) \rightarrow A, \tag{6}$$

not containing equality, where $L_1, \ldots, L_n$ are literals and A is an atom—is considered safe if every variable occurring in it occurs in one of the positive literals in the antecedent. The definition of a safe formula from [5], reproduced below, generalizes this condition to arbitrary sentences in prenex form. The assumption that the formula is in prenex form is not a significant limitation in the general theory of stable models, because all steps involved in the standard process of converting a formula to prenex form are equivalent transformations in $\mathbf{SQHT^{=}}$ [8].

To every quantifier-free formula F we assign a set $\mathrm{RV}(F)$ of its *restricted variables* as follows:

- For an atomic formula F,
    - if F is an equality between two variables then $\mathrm{RV}(F) = \emptyset$;
    - otherwise, $\mathrm{RV}(F)$ is the set of all variables occurring in F;
- $\mathrm{RV}(\bot) = \emptyset$;
- $\mathrm{RV}(F \wedge G) = \mathrm{RV}(F) \cup \mathrm{RV}(G)$;
- $\mathrm{RV}(F \vee G) = \mathrm{RV}(F) \cap \mathrm{RV}(G)$;
- $\mathrm{RV}(F \rightarrow G) = \emptyset$.

It is clear, for instance, that a variable is restricted in the antecedent of (6) iff it occurs in one of the positive literals among $L_1, \ldots, L_n$.

Consider a sentence F in prenex form: $Q_1 x_1 \cdots Q_n x_n M$ (each Q_i is $\forall$ or $\exists$; $x_1, \ldots, x_n$ are distinct variables; the matrix M is quantifier-free). We say that F is *safe* if every occurrence of each of the variables x_i in M is contained in a subformula $G \rightarrow H$ that satisfies two conditions:

(a) the subformula is positive in M if Q_i is $\forall$, and negative in M if Q_i is $\exists$;
(b) x_i is restricted in G.

3   Properties of Safe Sentences

We assume that the reader is familiar with the definition of the stable model operator SM from [1]. Proposition 1 below shows that all stable models of a safe sentence have the small predicate property: the relation represented by any of its predicate constants p_i can hold for a tuple of arguments only if each member of the tuple is represented by an object constant occurring in F. To make this idea precise, we will use the following notation: for any finite set $\mathbf{c}$ of object constants, $in_{\mathbf{c}}(x_1, \ldots, x_m)$ stands for the formula

$$\bigwedge_{1\leq j\leq m} \bigvee_{c\in\mathbf{c}} x_j = c.$$

The small predicate property can be expressed by the conjunction of the sentences

$$\forall\mathbf{x}(p_i(\mathbf{x}) \rightarrow in_{\mathbf{c}}(\mathbf{x}))$$

for all predicate constants p_i occurring in F, where $\mathbf{x}$ is a list of distinct variables. We will denote this sentence by $SPP_{\mathbf{c}}$. By $c(F)$ we denote the set of all object constants occurring in F.

Proposition 1. *For any safe sentence F, SM$[F]$ entails $SPP_{c(F)}$.*

Corollary 1. *For any safe sentence F that does not contain object constants, SM$[F]$ entails the formulas $\forall\mathbf{x}\neg p_i(\mathbf{x})$ for all predicate constants p_i of arity > 0.*

Indeed, $SPP_\emptyset$ is equivalent to the conjunction of all these formulas.

The process of grounding replaces quantifiers by multiple conjunctions and disjunctions. To make this idea precise, we define, for any sentence F in prenex form and any nonempty finite set $\mathbf{c}$ of object constants, the variable-free formula $\text{Ground}_{\mathbf{c}}[F]$ as follows. If F is quantifier-free then $\text{Ground}_{\mathbf{c}}[F] = F$. Otherwise,

$$\text{Ground}_{\mathbf{c}}[\forall x F(x)] = \bigwedge_{c\in\mathbf{c}} \text{Ground}_{\mathbf{c}}[F(c)],$$

$$\text{Ground}_{\mathbf{c}}[\exists x F(x)] = \bigvee_{c\in\mathbf{c}} \text{Ground}_{\mathbf{c}}[F(c)].$$

As in [4], by $\mathbf{INT}^=$ we denote intuitionistic predicate logic with equality, and DE stands for the decidable equality axiom (3). The importance of the logical system $\mathbf{INT}^= + $ DE is determined by the fact that it is a part of $\mathbf{SQHT}^=$, so that the provability of a sentence $F \leftrightarrow G$ in this system implies that SM$[F]$ is equivalent to SM$[G]$.

Proposition 2. *For any safe sentence F and any nonempty finite set $\mathbf{c}$ of object constants containing $c(F)$, the equivalence*

$$\text{Ground}_{\mathbf{c}}[F] \leftrightarrow F$$

is derivable from $SPP_{\mathbf{c}}$ in $\mathbf{INT}^= + $ DE.

Using Proposition 2 we can prove that the variable-free formula obtained by grounding a safe sentence F has the same stable models as F:

Proposition 3. *For any safe sentence F and any nonempty finite set $\mathbf{c}$ of object constants containing $c(F)$, SM$[\text{Ground}_{\mathbf{c}}[F]]$ is equivalent to SM$[F]$.*

In general, the second-order definition of a stable model cannot be expressed in first-order logic. The following theorem shows, however, that in the case of a safe sentence, stable models can be characterized by a very simple first-order formula, almost variable-free:

Proposition 4. *For every safe sentence F there exists a variable-free formula G such that SM$[F]$ is equivalent to $G \wedge SPP_{c(F)}$.*

4   Conclusion

In this paper we investigated properties of stable models of safe formulas in a semantically general situation, not limited to Herbrand models, and established a few positive results. We saw, in particular, that grounding a safe sentence preserves its stable models even in this general case, and that the stable models of a safe sentence can be characterized in first-order logic. We hope that these theorems will help us in future work on non-Herbrand answer set programming.

Acknowledgements

We are grateful to Paolo Ferraris and the anonymous referees for useful comments on the draft of this paper. The first and the third author were partially supported by the National Science Foundation under Grant IIS-0839821. The second author was partially supported by the National Science Foundation under Grant IIS-0712113.

References

1. Ferraris, P., Lee, J., Lifschitz, V.: A new perspective on stable models. In: Proceedings of International Joint Conference on Artificial Intelligence (IJCAI), pp. 372–379 (2007)
2. Gelfond, M., Lifschitz, V.: The stable model semantics for logic programming. In: Kowalski, R., Bowen, K. (eds.) Proceedings of International Logic Programming Conference and Symposium, pp. 1070–1080. MIT Press, Cambridge (1988)
3. McCarthy, J.: Circumscription—a form of non-monotonic reasoning. Artificial Intelligence 13, 27–39, 171–172 (1980)
4. Lifschitz, V., Pearce, D., Valverde, A.: A characterization of strong equivalence for logic programs with variables. In: Baral, C., Brewka, G., Schlipf, J. (eds.) LPNMR 2007. LNCS, vol. 4483. Springer, Heidelberg (2007)
5. Lee, J., Lifschitz, V., Palla, R.: A reductive semantics for counting and choice in answer set programming. In: Proceedings of the AAAI Conference on Artificial Intelligence, AAAI (to appear, 2008)
6. Topor, R.W., Sonenberg, E.A.: On domain independent databases. In: Minker, J. (ed.) Foundations of Deductive Databases and Logic Programming, pp. 217–240. Morgan Kaufmann, San Mateo (1988)
7. Leone, N., Faber, W., Pfeifer, G., Eiter, T., Gottlob, G., Perri, S., Scarcello, F.: The DLV system for knowledge representation and reasoning. ACM Transactions on Computational Logic 7, 499–562 (2006)
8. Lee, J., Palla, R.: Yet another proof of the strong equivalence between propositional theories and logic programs. In: Working Notes of the Workshop on Correspondence and Equivalence for Nonmonotonic Theories (2007)

Non-determinism and Probabilities in Timed Concurrent Constraint Programming*

Jorge A. Pérez[1] and Camilo Rueda[2,3]

[1] Dept. of Computer Science, University of Bologna, Italy
[2] Dept. of Science and Engineering of Computing, Universidad Javeriana - Cali, Colombia
[3] IRCAM, Paris, France

Abstract. A timed concurrent constraint process calculus with probabilistic and non-deterministic choices is proposed. We outline the rationale of an operational semantics for the calculus. The semantics ensures consistent interactions between both kinds of choices and is indispensable for the definition of logic-based verification capabilities over system specifications.

Motivation. *Concurrent constraint programming* (CCP) [1] is a model for concurrency in which systems are described by *constraints*, pieces of partial information that might include explicit quantitative parameters (such as, e.g., $x \leq 42$). Processes interact in a shared *store*; they either add new constraints or synchronize on the already available information. Notably, processes in CCP can be seen, at the same time, as computing agents and logic formulas. This not only constitutes a rather elegant approach for verification; it is fair to say that CCP provides a unified framework for system analysis.

In CCP, however, we find that properly taking into account some phenomena is cumbersome. Particularly challenging is the case of *uncertain behavior*. In areas such as, e.g., computer music [2] and systems biology [3], the uncertainty underlying interactions goes way beyond what can be modeled using partial information only. Crucially, many systems featuring uncertain behavior can be described *probabilistically*. In fact, probability distributions provide intuitive specifications of alternative behaviors and ease the integration of statistic and empirical data into models.

We are interested in the analysis of *reactive systems*. As such, we restrict ourselves to the realm of *timed* CCP. More precisely, we aim at a timed CCP approach for systems featuring *both* probabilistic and non-deterministic behavior. Probabilistic behavior in CCP might both enhance the accuracy of specifications (since, e.g., more empirical information could be considered) and give more significance to verification (as provable properties would involve explicit quantitative information). As for non-determinism, it allows to define compositional models and to abstract away from unimportant details. Also, it is fundamental to faithfully represent the interactions of a system with its environment. Sometimes in literature non-determinism has been represented using probabilistic choices. We do not endorse such an approach: replacing non-deterministic choices with probabilistic ones entails making strong assumptions on interactions and/or

* Research partially supported by the COLCIENCIAS project REACT (No. 1251-330-18902) and by the INRIA Équipe Associée FORCES.

M. Garcia de la Banda and E. Pontelli (Eds.): ICLP 2008, LNCS 5366, pp. 677–681, 2008.

conditions that are usually very hard or impossible to predict. Rather, we prefer the idea of specifying *probabilistic systems* within *non-deterministic environments*. As a compelling example of this idea, consider the analysis of security protocols as in [4]. There, the reactive system (the protocol) can be well described probabilistically, whereas the changing environment (the protocol users) is non-deterministic, as the frequency of the interactions is inherently unpredictable. Similar scenarios arise in very different areas such as interactive music improvisation [2].

Here we propose pntcc, a probabilistic, non-deterministic extension of tcc [5]. To the best of our knowledge, pntcc is the first timed CCP calculus featuring both kinds of choices. The semantic treatment associated with the interaction of non-determinism and probabilities is more complex than the required by each kind of choice in isolation. pntcc is endowed with an operational semantics based on a *probabilistic automaton* [6]: it separates the choices made probabilistically by the *process* from those made non-deterministically under the influence of a *scheduler*. As a result, the *observable behavior* of a system given by the semantics —what the environment perceives from its execution— is purely probabilistic; non-determinism is regarded as unobservable.

The observable behavior sets the ground for performing model checking processes. In fact, the rationale given by the language and the support provided by the semantics make it possible a natural relation between pntcc and the probabilistic logic PCTL [7]. The relation is based on the fact that the observable behavior of a process can be interpreted as the discrete time Markov chain (DTMC) defining satisfaction in PCTL. Since formulas in PCTL explicitly include a time bound and a probability, model checking for timed CCP process specifications with quantitative information becomes possible.

This approach to process verification is what distinguishes our proposal from similar CCP calculi with explicit time (e.g. [8]), which rely on proof systems. We are not aware of other explicitly timed CCP calculi with quantitative parameters in both models and properties, and with the possibility of model-checking procedures. Moreover, since we advocate a rationale in which verification is an orthogonal concern, we can safely rely on the developed field of probabilistic model checking for this.

All in all, by relying on well-established techniques from logic and concurrency theory, we provide the initial foundations for a timed CCP-based *framework* for the analysis of reactive systems.

Related Work. In [9], CCP and tcc are extended with *stochastic choices* rather than with probabilistic ones. The untimed CCP language in [10] replaces non-deterministic choices with probabilistic ones; hence, the associated semantics could be seen as a particular case of ours. In [11] it is shown how to extract model checking structures directly from tcc programs. A similar approach is used in sCCP [12], a stochastic CCP language in which discrete and continuous time can be treated only *implicitly*. (In contrast, pntcc features explicit discrete time.) Model-checking in sCCP relies on an encoding into the input language of a probabilistic model checker. Our approach for model checking has to be different —more involved— than those in [11] and [12]: because of non-determinism, we need an additional semantic support to be able to derive a DTMC, and in turn, to perform a model checking process.

The Language and Its Semantics. Here we describe the syntax and operational semantics for pntcc. We begin by introducing some notions of (timed) CCP-based calculi.

A *constraint system* formalizes the interdependencies between constraints. It is given by a pair (Σ, Δ) where Σ is a signature of function and predicate symbols, and Δ is a decidable theory over Σ. Given a constraint system (Σ, Δ), let $\mathcal{L}$ be its underlying first-order language, with variables $x, y, \ldots$, and the set of logic symbols $\neg, \wedge, \vee, \Rightarrow, \exists, \forall,$ true and false. The set of *constraints* (with elements $c, d, \ldots$) are formulas over $\mathcal{L}$. We say that c *entails* d in Δ, written $c \models d$, iff $c \Rightarrow d$ is true in all models of Δ. The relation $\models$ is assumed to be decidable.

Time is assumed to be divided into *units*. In a given time unit, a process P gets an input (a constraint) c from the environment, it executes with this input as the initial *store* and when it reaches its resting point it *outputs* the resulting store d to the environment. The resting point determines a residual process Q to be executed in the next time unit. Information is not automatically transferred from one time unit to another.

Syntax. Processes in pntcc are built from constraints some underlying constraint system by the following syntax:

$$P, Q ::= \text{ skip } \Big| \text{ tell}(c) \ \Big| \ \sum_{i \in I} \text{when } c_i \text{ do } P_i \ \Big| \ \bigoplus_{i \in I} \text{when } c_i \text{ do } (P_i, a_i) \ \Big| \ P \parallel Q \ \Big| \ \text{local } x \text{ in } P$$
$$\Big| \ \text{next } (P) \ \Big| \ \text{unless } c \text{ next } (P) \ \Big| \ !P$$

The upper line describes untimed CCP processes, whose action takes place during a single time unit. skip does nothing. tell(c) adds constraint c to the current store, thus making it available to other processes. In CCP, a *positive ask* when c do P checks if the current store is strong enough to entail the guard c; if so, it behaves like P. In pntcc, given a finite set of indices I, process $\sum_{i \in I}$ when c_i do P_i generalizes positive asks as a *non-deterministic choice*: a process P_j ($j \in I$) whose guard c_j is entailed from the current store is scheduled for execution; the chosen process precludes the others. Process $P \parallel Q$ describes the concurrent operation of P and Q, possibly "communicating" via the common store. Hiding on a variable x is enforced by process local x in P: it behaves like P, except that all the information on the x produced by P can only be seen by P and the information on x produced by other processes cannot be seen by P. In the *probabilistic choice* $\bigoplus_{i \in I}$ when c_i do (P_i, a_i), I is a finite set of indices, and for every $a_i \in \mathbb{R}^{(0,1]}$, $\sum_{i \in I} a_i = 1$. Each a_i represents the probability of scheduling process P_i for execution. The collection of all a_i thus represents a probability distribution. The guards that can be entailed from the current store determine a subset of *enabled processes*, which are used to determine an eventual normalization of the a_is. In the current time unit, the summation probabilistically chooses one of the enabled process according to the distribution defined by the (possibly normalized) a_is. The chosen alternative, if any, precludes the others. If no choice is possible then the summation is precluded. We sometimes use "$\oplus$" to denote binary probabilistic sums.

Constructs in the lower line allow processes to have effect along the time units. next (P) schedules P for execution in the next time unit; it is thus a one-unit delay. Process unless c next (P) is similar: P will be activated only if c cannot be inferred from the current store. It behaves like a (weak) time-out, waiting one time unit for a piece of information c to be present and if it is not, triggering activity in the next time unit. The *replication* operator ! represents infinite behavior: $!P$ represents $P \parallel$ next $(P) \parallel$ next$^2 P \parallel \ldots$, i.e. unboundedly many copies of P but one at a time.

Probabilistic Eventuality. By exploiting the encoding of recursion in [8], pntcc allows to define a parametric form of *probabilistic eventuality*. This operator may come in handy to express the influence the passage of time has on the eventual execution of a process. It integrates the partial information on process occurrence as probability distributions:

$$\text{STAR}_f(P, r) \stackrel{\text{def}}{=} (P, r) \oplus (\text{next STAR}_f(P, f(r)), 1 - r).$$

We assume $\text{STAR}_f(P, r)$ is defined over a sufficiently large (yet finite) subset of the reals in $(0, 1]$. It depends on two parameters, r and f. The first stands for the current probability of executing P: the closer to 1 r is, the greater the probability of executing P will be. Conversely, $1 - r$ denotes the probability of *delaying* P's execution. Function f governs the execution of P by modifying r in each recursive call.

Semantics. An informal description of an operational semantics for pntcc follows. We consider *configurations* of the form $\langle P, c \rangle$, where P is a process and c is a constraint representing a store.

The semantics considers two transition relations: one *internal* —meant to be hidden to the environment—, and an *observable* one that serves as an "interface" between the process and its environment. *Internal transitions* describe activity *within a time unit*, considering both non-deterministic and probabilistic behavior. Similarly to [13], internal transitions are defined over a *probabilistic automaton* [6]. Roughly, a probabilistic automaton differs from an ordinary one only in the transition relation, which allows non-deterministic choices to take place before performing the probabilistic choice that determines the state to be reached. In our case, the states of the automaton correspond to configurations. Every sequence of internal transitions is influenced by a particular *scheduler*, which solves the non-deterministic choices. By confining non-determinism to internal computations we obtain that only probabilistic behavior can be observed along time. An *observable transition* defines the smallest account of *observable behavior*. It assumes a sequence of internal transitions leading to a state where no further computation is possible (*quiescence*). It is denoted by $P \xRightarrow{\langle c, d, a \rangle}_{S_j} R$, with the following intuitive meaning: in one time unit, under the influence of scheduler S_j, configuration $\langle P, c \rangle$ can evolve to configuration $\langle R, d \rangle$ with probability a. The explicit reference to the scheduler becomes relevant when one considers that what can be observed from a process execution might differ depending on the particular scheduler.

Observable Behavior for Verification. We conclude by sketching the relation between pntcc processes and the temporal logic PCTL [7]. We claim that the observable behavior of a pntcc process corresponds to the discrete time Markov chain upon which satisfaction in PCTL is defined.

Informally speaking, PCTL allows to reason about properties such as "after a request, a task will be accomplished within 5 minutes with a probability of at least 95%". Such statements, so-called *soft deadlines*, explicitly define both a probability and a time bound. Unlike *hard* deadlines, soft deadlines are meant to characterize systems in which a failure does not imply catastrophic consequences. For space reasons, we omit details of PCTL syntax and semantics; see [7] for an in-depth description.

Formulas in PCTL are interpreted over models that are discrete time Markov chains (DTMCs). A DTMC is composed of a finite set of states, a transition probability function, and a labeling function assigning atomic propositions to states. In a DTMC each transition is considered to require one time unit. To go from the observable behavior of a process to the DTMC underlying satisfaction in PCTL, all that is required is to give structure to the derivatives that can be observed from a process execution along time. The set of such derivatives, called *alternatives*, gives a one-step account of all the possibilities for observable behavior. They allow to articulate the notion of *observable sequences*, the description of one of the possible computations starting in a given configuration, along the time units.

The observable sequences originating in a given process represent the confinement of non-deterministic behavior to the scheduler used over internal evolutions. This rôle of schedulers allows to interpret the observable behavior of a process as a DTMC. Indeed, given a process P, it is not difficult to think of a correspondence between *states* and all the possible configurations reachable from $\langle P, \texttt{true} \rangle$ through observable sequences. The *transitions* of the DTMC can be obtained from the alternatives of each derivative of P. Notice that, in this setting, an observable sequence would then correspond to a particular path of the DTMC. Finally, we can assume a *labeling function* that relates states with the store of the given configuration.

References

1. Saraswat, V.: Concurrent Constraint Programming. The MIT Press, Cambridge (1993)
2. Rueda, C., Assayag, G., Dubnov, S.: A Concurrent Constraints Factor Oracle Model for Music Improvisation. In: CLEI 2006 (2006)
3. Gutiérrez, J., Pérez, J.A., Rueda, C., Valencia, F.D.: Timed concurrent constraint programming for analysing biological systems. Electr. Notes Theor. Comput. Sci. 171(2), 117–137 (2007)
4. Palamidessi, C.: Probabilistic and nondeterministic aspects of anonymity. Electr. Notes Theor. Comput. Sci. 155, 33–42 (2006)
5. Saraswat, V.A., Jagadeesan, R., Gupta, V.: Foundations of timed concurrent constraint programming. In: LICS, pp. 71–80. IEEE Computer Society, Los Alamitos (1994)
6. Segala, R.: Modeling and Verification of Randomized Distributed Real-Time Systems. PhD thesis, MIT (1995)
7. Hansson, H., Jonsson, B.: A logic for reasoning about time and reliability. Formal Asp. Comput. 6(5), 512–535 (1994)
8. Nielsen, M., Palamidessi, C., Valencia, F.D.: Temporal concurrent constraint programming: Denotation, logic and applications. Nord. J. Comput. 9(1), 145–188 (2002)
9. Gupta, V., Jagadeesan, R., Saraswat, V.A.: Probabilistic concurrent constraint programming. In: Mazurkiewicz, A., Winkowski, J. (eds.) CONCUR 1997. LNCS, vol. 1243, pp. 243–257. Springer, Heidelberg (1997)
10. Pierro, A.D., Wiklicky, H.: An operational semantics for probabilistic concurrent constraint programming. In: ICCL, pp. 174–183 (1998)
11. Falaschi, M., Policriti, A., Villanueva, A.: Modeling concurrent systems specified in a temporal concurrent constraint language-i. Electr. Notes Theor. Comput. Sci. 48 (2001)
12. Bortolussi, L.: Constraint-based approaches to stochastic dynamics of biological systems. PhD thesis, University of Udine (2007)
13. Herescu, O.M., Palamidessi, C.: Probabilistic asynchronous pi-calculus. In: Tiuryn, J. (ed.) FOSSACS 2000. LNCS, vol. 1784, pp. 146–160. Springer, Heidelberg (2000)

Stochastic Behavior and Explicit Discrete Time in Concurrent Constraint Programming[*]

Jesús Aranda[1,2], Jorge A. Pérez[3], Camilo Rueda[4,5], and Frank D. Valencia[6]

[1] INRIA Futurs and LIX, Ecole Polytechnique, France
[2] Escuela de Ingeniería de Sistemas y Computación, Universidad del Valle, Colombia
[3] Dept. of Computer Science, University of Bologna, Italy
[4] Dept. of Science and Engineering of Computing, Universidad Javeriana - Cali, Colombia
[5] IRCAM, Paris, France
[6] CNRS and LIX, Ecole Polytechnique, France

Abstract. We address the inclusion of stochastic information into an *explicitly timed* concurrent constraint process language. An operational semantics is proposed as a preliminary result. Our approach finds applications in biology, among other areas.

Motivation. The study of *quantitative information* within languages for concurrency has recently gained a lot of momentum. In many applications, quantitative information becomes crucial when refining models with empirical data, and is of the essence for verification purposes. Two main models of quantitative information can be singled out from the vast literature on the subject. Given a computation that can perform different, competing actions, a *probabilistic* model provides a probability distribution over such actions. In contrast, a *stochastic* model relates each action to a random variable which determines its *duration*: given a set of competing actions, the fastest action (i.e. the one with the shortest duration) is executed. Consequently, notions not considered in a probabilistic model (e.g. speed) are fundamental in a stochastic setting. Not surprisingly, areas in which time is essential (e.g. systems biology, performance modeling) have found in languages featuring stochastic information adequate frameworks for analysis.

Concurrent constraint programming (CCP) [1] is a declarative model for concurrency with strong ties to logic. In CCP, systems are described by pieces of partial information called *constraints*. Processes interact in a shared *store*; they either add new constraints or synchronize on the already available information. Timed concurrent constraint programming (tcc) [2] is a declarative framework for reactive systems. In tcc, time is explicitly represented as discrete time units in which computation takes place; tcc provides constructs to control process execution along such units. In the light of stochastic models for quantitative information, the explicit time in tcc poses a legitimate question, that of determining to what extent the notions of stochastic duration and

---

[*] Research partially supported by the COLCIENCIAS project REACT (No. 1251-330-18902) and the INRIA Équipe Associée FORCES. The work of Jesús Aranda has been supported by COLCIENCIAS (Instituto Colombiano para el Desarrollo de la Ciencia y la Tecnología "Francisco José de Caldas"), INRIA Futurs and ÉGIDE (Centre français pour l'accueil et les échanges internationaux).

M. Garcia de la Banda and E. Pontelli (Eds.): ICLP 2008, LNCS 5366, pp. 682–686, 2008.

of discrete time unit can be harmoniously conciliated within a CCP-based framework. The question is relevant because it can give clues on clean semantic foundations for quantitative information in CCP, which in turn, should contribute to the development of more effective reasoning techniques over reactive systems in many emerging applications. In this paper, we outline preliminary results on an operational semantics for a tcc language with explicit stochastic durations.

More into details, the proposed semantics aims at an explicit account of stochastically derived events using the description power of timed CCP calculi. This is a feature that in other CCP calculi (e.g. [3]) is handled at best implicitly. We define stochastic events in terms of the time units provided by the calculus: this provides great flexibility for modeling and, as mentioned before, it allows for a clean semantics. Most importantly, by considering stochastic information and adhering to explicit discrete time, it is possible to reason about processes using *quantitative* logics (both discrete and continuous), while retaining the simplicity of calculi such as ntcc [4] for deriving *qualitative* reasoning techniques (such as denotational semantics and proof systems). We consider existing qualitative reasoning techniques have a great potential for guiding/complementing the use of (usually costly) quantitative ones. Such an approach for applying qualitative techniques has shown to be useful in the biological context [5].

This work is part of a larger research programme aimed at developing robust CCP-based techniques for analyzing complex applications and systems in computer music, security and biology. As such, it is our objective to formalize stochastic information in tcc in such a way that resulting languages and techniques (i) remain generic enough so to fit well in the target applications, and (ii) be amenable to efficient implementations, in the form of e.g. simulators and model-checkers.

Description. We consider a variant of tcc in which certain processes are annotated with a function λ, which represents the stochastic information in the language (see below). Annotated processes are tell, when and unless. With a slight abuse of notation, in tell and unless processes λ also stands for the constant value 1. We annotate unless as we see it as a counterpart of when processes. A careful definition of unless in the stochastic context, however, is yet to be completely determined. We do not discard that different applications (e.g. biological systems and computer music) need different unless definitions.

$$P, Q ::= \mathsf{tell}_\lambda(c) \mid \mathsf{when}\, c\, \mathsf{do}\, (P, \lambda) \mid P \parallel Q \mid \mathsf{local}\, x\, \mathsf{in}\, P \mid !P \mid iP \mid \mathsf{unless}_\lambda\, c\, \mathsf{next}\, (P)$$

Operational Semantics. We use the same notion of discrete time as in ntcc and tcc. We assume that there are discrete time units of uniform size, each of them having its own constraint store. At each time unit, some stimuli are received from the environment; the process then executes with such stimuli as input. At the end of the time unit, some output is produced in the form of responses to the environment, and a residual process to be executed in the next time unit is scheduled. Information does not automatically transfer from one time unit to the following.

The operational semantics, given in Table 1, is defined over process-store configurations. We use γ, γ' to range over configurations, and assume a structural congruence relation $\equiv$ to identify processes with minor syntactic differences. The rules of the semantics carry both a *probability value* (denoted p) and a global *rate value* (denoted r).

Table 1. Operational semantics: internal transition rules

$$\text{IMMTELL} \quad \frac{}{\langle \text{tell}_1(d), c\rangle \longrightarrow_{1,\max} \langle \text{skip}, c \wedge d\rangle} \qquad \text{IMMREP} \quad \frac{\langle P, c\rangle \longrightarrow_{1,\max} \langle P', c'\rangle}{\langle !\, P, c\rangle \longrightarrow_{1,\max} \langle P \parallel i!\, P, c'\rangle}$$

$$\text{IMMUNLESS} \quad \frac{}{\langle \text{unless}_1 \ c \ \text{next}\ (P), d\rangle \longrightarrow_{1,\max} \langle \text{skip}, d\rangle} \ \text{if}\ d \models c \quad \text{IMMINT} \quad \frac{\langle P, c\rangle \longrightarrow_{1,\max} \langle P', c'\rangle}{\langle P \parallel Q, c\rangle \longrightarrow_{1,\max} \langle P' \parallel Q, c'\rangle}$$

$$\text{STOTELL} \quad \frac{}{\langle \text{tell}_\lambda(d), c\rangle \longrightarrow_{1,\lambda(c)} \langle \delta^m(\text{tell}(d)), c\rangle} \ \text{with}\ m = \Delta(1, \lambda(c))$$

$$\text{STOCHOICE} \quad \frac{}{\langle \sum_{i \in I} \text{when}\ c_i\ \text{do}\ (P_i, \lambda_i), c\rangle \longrightarrow_{p,r} \langle \delta^m(P_j), c\rangle} \ \text{if}\ c \models c_j$$
$$\text{with}\ r = \sum_{i \in \{j\ |\ c \models c_j\}} \lambda_i(c); \ p = \lambda_j(c)/r; \ m = \Delta(p, r).$$

$$\text{STOINT} \quad \frac{\langle P, c\rangle \longrightarrow_{p_1,r_1} \langle P', c\rangle \quad \langle Q, c\rangle \longrightarrow_{p_2,r_2} \langle Q', c\rangle}{\langle P \parallel Q, c\rangle \longrightarrow_{p',r'} \langle P' \parallel Q', c\rangle} \ \text{with}\ p' = p_1 \times p_2; \ r' = r_1 + r_2.$$

$$\text{STOUNLESS} \quad \frac{}{\langle \text{unless}_\lambda\ c\ \text{next}\ (P), d\rangle \longrightarrow_{p,r} \langle \delta^m(\text{unless}\ c\ \text{next}\ (P)), d\rangle} \ \text{with}\ m = \Delta(p, r).$$

$$\text{STOREP} \quad \frac{\langle P, c\rangle \longrightarrow_{p,r} \langle \delta^m(P), c'\rangle}{\langle !\, P, c\rangle \longrightarrow_{p,r} \langle \delta^m(P) \parallel i!\, P, c'\rangle} \qquad \text{NEXT} \quad \frac{\langle P, c\rangle \longrightarrow_{p,r} \langle P', c\rangle}{\langle P \parallel iQ, c\rangle \longrightarrow_{p,r} \langle P' \parallel iQ, c\rangle}$$

$$\text{LOCAL} \quad \frac{\langle P, c \wedge \exists_x d\rangle \longrightarrow_{p,r} \langle P', c'\rangle}{\langle (\text{local}\ x, c)P, d\rangle \longrightarrow_{p,r} \langle (\text{local}\ x, c)P', d \wedge \exists_x c'\rangle} \qquad \text{STRCONG} \quad \frac{\gamma_1 \longrightarrow_{p,\ r} \gamma_2}{\gamma'_1 \longrightarrow_{p,\ r} \gamma'_2} \ \text{if}\ \gamma_i \equiv \gamma'_i \ (i \in \{1, 2\})$$

They decree two kinds of process execution, *immediate* (probability value equal to 1 and rate value max), and *stochastic*. In this sense, processes can be either immediate or stochastic. The idea of the semantics is to schedule immediate processes first, and then move to stochastic processes, whose execution involves a certain duration.

Rules for immediate execution resemble analogous rules in tcc and ntcc. The rule IMMTELL adds a constraint to the store as soon as possible. The rule IMMREP specifies that process $!P$ produces a copy P at the current time unit and then persists in the next time unit. There is no risk of infinite behavior within a time unit. In the Rule IMMUNLESS, process P is precluded if c is entailed by the current store d. The rule IMMINT allows for compositional extension.

Rules for stochastic executions consider the aforementioned function λ. Using the current store as parameter, λ describes how the global rate of the whole process varies. We use $\delta^m(P)$ to denote a *delay process* P with duration m: P will be executed at the m-th time unit from the current one. Given probability and rate values for a process, function Δ determines its duration. The duration can be thus seen as an exponentially distributed random variable that depends on a probability and a rate.

The rule STOTELL defines stochastic tell actions. The rule STOCHOICE defines a choice over a number of guarded processes. Only those *enabled* processes, i.e., those whose guards entail from the current store, are considered. The rule STOINT defines the simultaneous occurrence of stochastic actions. As usual, the probability value is calculated assuming independence of the actions. Notice that the current store is not affected by stochastic actions; their influence is only noticeable in the following time units. The rules STOUNLESS and STOREP define unless and stochastic replicated actions, resp. The rule NEXT extends stochastic actions to next processes. In the rule LOCAL, local in P behaves like P, except that all the information on x produced by P

can only be seen by P and the information on x produced by other processes cannot be seen by P. Notation $(\text{local } x, c) \, P$ expresses that c is the local information produced by process local x in P. The rule STRCONG is self-explanatory.

These rules define behavior within a time unit; internal behavior takes place until reaching a configuration where no further computation is possible (*quiescence*). We need to define the *residual process* to be executed in the following time unit. We start by conjecturing that each quiescent configuration γ has a "standard" form:

$$\gamma \equiv \langle \prod_{j \in J} .P_j \parallel \prod_{k \in K} \text{unless } c_k \text{ next } (Q_k) \parallel \prod_{i \in I} \delta^{m_i}(P_i), d \rangle.$$

In the following definition we use A to denote the set of delayed processes in a quiescent configuration.

Definition 1 (Future function). *Given a quiescent configuration γ, its residual process is given by function F:*

$$F(\gamma) = \prod_{j \in J} P_j \parallel \prod_{k \in K} Q_k \parallel F'(A)$$

where function F' is defined as

$$F'(\delta^{m_1}(P_1) \parallel \ldots \parallel \delta^{m_n}(P_n)) = G(\delta^{m_1}(P_1)) \parallel \ldots \parallel G(\delta^{m_n}(P_n))$$

and where G is defined as

$$G(\delta^m(P)) = \begin{cases} \delta^{m-1}(P) & \text{if } m > 1 \\ P & \text{if } m = 1. \end{cases}$$

Unlike other languages like the stochastic π-calculus [6] or sCCP [3], it is worth noticing that in our semantics stochastic actions can evolve simultaneously; there is no a predefined order for execution. This way, for instance, $\text{tell}_{\lambda_1}(c_1) \parallel \text{tell}_{\lambda_2}(c_2)$ evolves into $\delta^{m_1}(\text{tell}(c_1)) \parallel \delta^{m_2}(\text{tell}(c_2))$ and in the next unit time, the configuration is $\delta^{m_1-1}(\text{tell}(c_1)) \parallel \delta^{m_2-1}(\text{tell}(c_2))$ (assuming $m_1, m_2 > 0$). This allows to naturally represent the evolution of different components in parallel.

Discussion. Since variables in tcc are logic (i.e. they can be defined at most once in each time unit), a potential source of inconsistencies is the simultaneous execution of several stochastic actions involving the same variables. This could represent a limitation in modeling. Consider for instance the kind of systems in which it is required to deal with quantities of elements of a certain type (as in biological reactions). In such systems, variables could be part of several actions, which would represent the changes over the elements in consideration. An inconsistency caused by two actions simultaneously altering the value of the same variable is clearly an undesirable feature. Therefore, there is the need for enhancing the semantics with a mechanism that imposes some kind of order over those actions related with potential inconsistencies. This would also presuppose modifications over rules calculating duration of stochastic actions, as concurrent actions would be simulated in a specific order. The formal definition of such a consistency mechanism is part of ongoing work.

Applications in Biology. We think that our language and semantics have applications in the biological domain. This is supported by the fact that CCP-based calculi have shown to be convenient for modelling, simulating and verifying several kinds of biological systems [7,8,3]. In [3], stochastic concurrent constraint programming (sCCP) is used to model biochemical reactions and gene regulatory networks. Functional rates in sCCP give considerable flexibility to formulate reactions. However, sCCP does not include an explicit notion of time and does not exploit the logic nature of CCP for verification. Also, sCCP lacks a means of expressing absence of information, which has proven most useful in the biological context [8]. The explicitly timed ccp language ntcc [4] provides both a proof system and a means of representing absence of information. In fact, ntcc was used in [7,8] to model different biological systems using two kinds of partial information: *behavioral* (e.g. the unknown relative speeds on which a system evolves) and *quantitative* (e.g. the set of possible values that a variable can take). It must be noticed that ntcc does not allow for stochastic or probabilistic information.

Based on the above, we think that the extension to tcc here proposed could serve several purposes in the biological context. The most immediate use is the definition of enhanced models of systems already modeled in ntcc (the Sodium-Potassium pump, regulation and mutation processes in genetic regulatory networks). Also, although it is not evident that every sCCP process can be translated into our language (the tell operator in sCCP has continuation), we are confident we can model most of the biological systems described in [3]. We also plan to analyse the model in [9], which describes the cycle of Rho GTP-binding proteins in the context of phagocytosis.

References

1. Saraswat, V.: Concurrent Constraint Programming. The MIT Press, Cambridge (1993)
2. Saraswat, V.A., Jagadeesan, R., Gupta, V.: Foundations of timed concurrent constraint programming. In: LICS, pp. 71–80. IEEE Computer Society, Los Alamitos (1994)
3. Bortolussi, L.: Constraint-based approaches to stochastic dynamics of biological systems. PhD thesis, University of Udine (2007)
4. Nielsen, M., Palamidessi, C., Valencia, F.D.: Temporal concurrent constraint programming: Denotation, logic and applications. Nord. J. Comput. 9(1), 145–188 (2002)
5. Fages, F., Soliman, S.: Formal cell biology in biocham. In: Bernardo, M., Degano, P., Zavattaro, G. (eds.) SFM 2008. LNCS, vol. 5016, pp. 54–80. Springer, Heidelberg (2008)
6. Priami, C.: Stochastic pi-calculus. Comput. J. 38(7), 578–589 (1995)
7. Gutiérrez, J., Pérez, J.A., Rueda, C., Valencia, F.D.: Timed concurrent constraint programming for analysing biological systems. Electr. Notes Theor. Comput. Sci. 171(2), 117–137 (2007)
8. Arbeláez, A., Gutiérrez, J., Pérez, J.A.: Timed Concurrent Constraint Programming in Systems Biology. Newsletter of the ALP 19(4) (2006)
9. Cardelli, L., Gardner, P., Kahramanogullari, O.: A process model of rho gtp-binding proteins in the context of phagocytosis. Electr. Notes Theor. Comput. Sci. 194(3), 87–102 (2008)

TopLog: ILP Using a Logic Program Declarative Bias

Stephen H. Muggleton, José C. A. Santos, and Alireza Tamaddoni-Nezhad

Department of Computing, Imperial College, London
{shm,jcs06,atn}@doc.ic.ac.uk

Abstract. This paper introduces a new Inductive Logic Programming (ILP) framework called Top Directed Hypothesis Derivation (TDHD). In this framework each hypothesised clause must be derivable from a given logic program called top theory ($\top$). The top theory can be viewed as a declarative bias which defines the hypothesis space. This replaces the metalogical mode statements which are used in many ILP systems. Firstly we present a theoretical framework for TDHD and show that standard SLD derivation can be used to efficiently derive hypotheses from $\top$. Secondly, we present a prototype implementation of TDHD within a new ILP system called TopLog. Thirdly, we show that the accuracy and efficiency of TopLog, on several benchmark datasets, is competitive with a state of the art ILP system like Aleph.

1 Introduction

In this paper we introduce a new approach to providing declarative bias called Top-Directed Hypothesis Derivation (TDHD). The approach extends the use of the $\bot$ clause in Mode-Directed Inverse Entailment (MDIE) [1]. In Inverse Entailment $\bot$ is constructed for a single, arbitrarily chosen training example. Refinement graph search is then constrained by the requirement that all hypothesised clauses considered must subsume $\bot$. In TDHD we further restrict the search associated with each training example by requiring that each hypothesised clause must also be entailed by a given logic program, $\top$.

The $\top$ theory can be viewed as a form of first-order declarative bias which defines the hypothesis space, since each hypothesised clause must be derivable from $\top$. The use of the $\top$ theory in TopLog is also comparable to grammar-based declarative biases [2]. However, compared with a grammar-based declarative bias, $\top$ has all the expressive power of a logic program, and can be efficiently reasoned with using standard logic programming techniques.

The SPECTRE system [3] employs an approach related to the use of $\top$. SPECTRE also relies on an overly general logic program as a starting point. However, unlike the TopLog system described in this paper, SPECTRE proceeds by successively unfolding clauses in the initial theory. TDHD is also related to Explanation-Based Generalisation (EBG) [4]. However, like SPECTRE, EBG does not make the key MDHD distinction between the $\top$ theory and background knowledge. Moreover, EBG is viewed as a form of deductive learning, while the clauses generated by TDHD represent inductive hypotheses.

M. Garcia de la Banda and E. Pontelli (Eds.): ICLP 2008, LNCS 5366, pp. 687–692, 2008.
© Springer-Verlag Berlin Heidelberg 2008

2   Theoretical Framework

MDIE was introduced in [1] as the basis for Progol. The input to an MDIE system is the vector $S_{MDIE} = \langle M, B, E \rangle$ where M is a set of mode statements, B is a logic program representing the background knowledge and E is set of examples. M can be viewed as a set of metalogical statements used to define the hypothesis language $\mathcal{L}_M$. The aim of the system is to find consistent hypothesised clauses H such that for each clause $h \in H$ there is at least one positive example $e \in E$ such that $B, h \models e$.

The input to an TDHD system is the vector $S_{TDHD} = \langle NT, \top, B, E \rangle$ where NT is a set of "non-terminal" predicate symbols, $\top$ is a logic program representing the declarative bias over the hypothesis space, B is a logic program representing the background knowledge and E is a set of examples.

The following three conditions hold for clauses in $\top$: (a) each clause in $\top$ must contain at least one occurrence of an element of NT while clauses in B and E must not contain any occurrences of elements of NT, (b) any predicate appearing in the head of some clause in $\top$ must not occur in the body of any clause in B and (c) the head of the first clause in $\top$ is the target predicate and the head predicates for other clauses in $\top$ must be in NT.

The aim of a TDHD system is to find a set of consistent hypothesised clauses H, containing no occurrence of NT, such that for each clause $h \in H$ there is at least one positive example $e \in E$ such that the following two conditions hold: (1) $\top \models h$ and (2) $B, h \models e$.

Theorem 1. *Given $S_{TDHD} = \langle NT, \top, B, E \rangle$ assumptions (1) and (2) hold only if for each positive example $e \in E$ there exists an SLD refutation R of $\neg e$ from $\top, B$, such that R can be re-ordered to give $R' = D_h R_e$ where D_h is an SLD derivation of a hypothesis h for which (1) and (2) hold.*

According to Theorem 1, implicit hypotheses can be extracted from the refutations of a positive example $e \in E$. Let us now consider a simple example.

Example 1. Let $S_{TDHD} = \langle NT, \top, B, E \rangle$ where NT, B , e and $\top$ are as follows:

$$NT = \{\$body\}$$
$$B = b_1 = \text{pet(lassy)} \leftarrow \qquad \top = \begin{cases} \top_1 : \text{nice}(X) \leftarrow \$body(X) \\ \top_2 : \$body(X) \leftarrow \text{pet}(X) \\ \top_3 : \$body(X) \leftarrow \text{friend}(X) \end{cases}$$
$$e = \text{nice(lassy)} \leftarrow$$

Given the linear refutation $R = \langle \neg e, \top_1, \top_2, b_1 \rangle$, we now construct the re-ordered refutation $R' = D_h R_e$ where $D_h = \langle \top_1, \top_2 \rangle$ derives the clause $h = \text{nice(X)} \leftarrow \text{pet(X)}$ for which (1) and (2) hold.

3   System Description

TopLog is a prototype ILP system developed by the authors to implement the TDHD described in section 2. It is fully implemented in Prolog and is ensured to run at least in YAP, SWI and Sicstus Prolog. It is publicly available at http://www.doc.ic.ac.uk/~jcs06 and may be freely used for academic purposes.

3.1 From Mode Declarations to $\top$ Theory

As the user of TopLog may not be familiar with specifying a search bias in the form of a logic program, TopLog has a module to build a general $\top$ theory automatically from user specified mode declarations. In this way input compatibility is ensured with existing ILP systems. Below is a simplified example of user specified mode declarations and the automatically constructed $\top$ theory.

$$\text{modeh(mammal(+animal)).} \qquad \top = \begin{cases} \top_1 : \text{mammal}(X) \leftarrow \$\text{body}(X). \\ \top_2 : \$\text{body}(X) \leftarrow .\%emptybody \\ \top_3 : \$\text{body}(X) \leftarrow \text{has\_milk}(X),\$\text{body}(X). \\ \top_4 : \$\text{body}(X) \leftarrow \text{has\_eggs}(X),\$\text{body}(X). \end{cases}$$

$$\text{modeb(has\_milk(+animal)).}$$
$$\text{modeb(has\_eggs(+animal)).}$$

Fig. 1. Mode declarations and a $\top$ theory automatically constructed from it

The above illustrated $\top$ theory is extremely simplified. The actual implementation has stricter control rules like: variables may only bind with others of the same type, a newly added literal must have its input variables already bound.

It is worth pointing out that the user could directly write a $\top$ theory specific for the problem, potentially restricting the search better than the generic $\top$ theory built automatically from the mode declarations.

3.2 TopLog Learning Algorithm

The TopLog learning algorithm consists of three major steps: 1) hypotheses derivation for each positive example, 2) coverage computation for all unique hypotheses, H, derived in previous step, 3) construct the final theory, T, as the subset of H that maximizes a given score function (e.g. compression).

Hypotheses derivation. Contrary to MDIE ILP systems, there is no construction of the bottom clause but rather an example guided generalization, deriving all hypotheses that entail a given example w.r.t. the background knowledge, B.

This procedure consists of two steps. Firstly an example is proved from B and the $\top$ theory. That is, the $\top$ theory is executed having the example matching the head of its start clause (i.e. $\top_1$). This execution yields a proof consisting of a sequence of clauses from the $\top$ theory and B. For instance, using the $\top$ theory from figure 1 and $B = b_1 = \text{has\_milk(dog)}$ to derive refutations for example $e = \text{mammal(dog)}$, the following two refutations would be yielded: $r_1 = \langle \neg e, \top_1, \top_2 \rangle$ and $r_2 = \langle \neg e, \top_1, \top_3, b_1, \top_2 \rangle$. Secondly, Theorem 1 is applied to r_1 and r_2 deriving, respectively, the clauses $h_1 = mammal(X)$ from $\langle \top_1, \top_2 \rangle$ and $h_2 = mammal(X) \leftarrow has\_milk(X)$ from $\langle \top_1, \top_3, \top_2 \rangle$.

Coverage computation. Each $h \in H$ is individually tested with all the examples (positives and negatives) to compute its coverage (i.e. the examples it entails). Positive examples used to derive h are not tested for entailment as it is guaranteed by the hypothesis derivation procedure that h entails them.

Constructing the final theory. The final theory to be constructed, T, is a subset H' of H that maximizes a given score function (e.g. compression, coverage, accuracy). Each $h \in H$ has associated the set of examples from which it was derived, Eg_h, and the set of examples which it entails, Ec_h.

The compression score function (the default) evaluates T as the weighted sum of the examples it covers (positive examples have weights > 0 and negative examples < 0) minus number of literals in T. This is the minimum description length principle and is analogous to Progol's and Aleph's compression measure. T is constructed using a greedy approach where at each step the hypothesis, if any, that maximizes current T' score is added to the next round.

Efficient cross-validation. Prior to N fold cross-validation (CV) all possible hypotheses are derived and their coverage is computed on all examples. This is the most time consuming step. Then, examples are randomly assigned a fold and N theories are built each using a distinct combination of $N - 1$ folds as training and one fold as testing.

Hypotheses generated exclusively from examples in the test set are not eligible for the theory construction step. Also, the merit of a hypothesis is evaluated only taking into account the hypothesis coverage on examples belonging to the training folds. At the end of cross-validation, N fold average training and test accuracies and standard deviations are reported.

It is not possible to do efficient cross-validation with Aleph or Progol as no relationship exists between hypotheses and the examples that generated it.

4   Experimental Evaluation

Materials & Methods. We used four datasets: mutagenesis [5], carcinogenesis [6], alzheimers-amine [7] and DSSTox [8] as they are well known to the ILP community. TopLog was compared with the state of the art MDIE ILP system Aleph [9]. Both were executed on YAP Prolog 5.1.3. The experiments were performed on a Core 2 Duo @ 2.13 GHz with 2Gb RAM.

Aleph and TopLog were executed with similar settings to ensure a fair test. Clause length=4 (in DSSTox=10), noise=100%, evaluation function= compression and search nodes per example=1000. Aleph was called both with *induce* and *induce_max* settings. In *induce* (the default), after finding a compressive clause for an example, it retracts all positive examples covered by that clause while *induce_max*, as TopLog, does not.

Results. In the table below, time is the CPU seconds the ILP systems took to build a model in the training data and for ten folds (CV column). We distinguish between the two to highlight the benefits of TopLog's efficient cross validation. The accuracy column has the average (over the ten folds) percentage of correct predictions made by the ILP models with the respective standard deviation.

In the *induce_max* setting TopLog is clearly faster than Aleph. In the *induce* setting the speed advantage for training is dataset dependent but considering only CV then TopLog is again clearly faster. Although this may seem a side

Table 1. Accuracy and time comparison between Aleph and TopLog

	Aleph with induce			Aleph with induce_max			TopLog		
		Times			Times			Times	
Dataset	CV Accuracy	Train	CV	CV Accuracy	Train	CV	CV Accuracy	Train	CV
Mutagenesis	77.2%±9.2%	0.4s	4s	68.6%±11.4%	2s	17s	70.2%±11.9%	0.4s	0.5s
Carcinogenesis	60.9%±8.2%	6s	54s	65.1%±8.6%	29s	245s	64.8%±6.9%	7.0s	7.4s
Alzheimers	67.2%±5.0%	5s	40s	72.6%±6.2%	18s	156s	70.4%±5.6%	17s	16s
DSSTox	70.5%±6.5%	30s	253s	71.3%±3.4%	82s	684s	71.7%±5.6%	3.4s	3.6s

point, built-in efficient CV is important both to tune parameters and to properly assess model accuracy. The accuracies are identical with none being statistically significantly different at $\rho = 0.01$ level.

5   Conclusions and Future Work

The key innovation of the TDHD framework is the introduction of a first order $\top$ theory. We prove that SLD derivation can be used to efficiently derive hypotheses from $\top$. A new general ILP system, TopLog, is described implementing TDHD. An empirical comparison demonstrates the new approach is competitive, both in predictive accuracy and speed, with a state of the art system like Aleph.

Parallelization. Since building the hypotheses set is example independent, it is straightforward to parallelize TopLog main algorithm by dividing the examples through all available cpus.

Sample hypotheses space. If the $\top$ theory represents a Stochastic Logic Program [10] rather than a regular logic program (as it is now), it would be possible to elegantly bias the hypotheses search space.

Acknowledgments. We thank James Cussens for illuminating discussions on the TDHD framework and Vítor Santos Costa for his prompt help with YAP. The first author thanks the Royal Academy of Engineering and Microsoft for funding his present 5 year Research Chair. The second author thanks Wellcome Trust for his Ph.D. scholarship. The third author was supported by the BBSRC grant BB/C519670/1.

References

1. Muggleton, S.H.: Inverse entailment and Progol. NGC 13, 245–286 (1995)
2. Cohen, W.: Grammatically biased learning: Learning logic programs using an explicit antecedent description language. Artificial Intelligence 68, 303–366 (1994)
3. Boström, H., Idestam-Almquist, P.: Specialisation of logic programs by pruning SLD-trees. In: Proceedings of the 4th ILP Workshop (ILP 1994), Bonn, pp. 31–48 (1994)

4. Kedar-Cabelli, S.T., McCarty, L.T.: Explanation-based generalization as resolution theorem proving. In: Langley, P. (ed.) Proceedings of the 4th Int. Workshop on Machine Learning, Los Altos, pp. 383–389. Morgan Kaufmann, San Francisco (1987)

5. Srinivasan, A., Muggleton, S., King, R., Sternberg, M.: Mutagenesis: ILP experiments in a non-determinate biological domain. In: Wrobel, S. (ed.) Proceedings of the 4th ILP Workshop, ILP 1994, GMD-Studien Nr 237 (1994)

6. Srinivasan, A., King, R.D., Muggleton, S.H., Sternberg, M.: Carcinogenesis predictions using ILP. In: Džeroski, S., Lavrač, N. (eds.) ILP 1997. LNCS (LNAI), vol. 1297, pp. 273–287. Springer, Heidelberg (1997)

7. King, R.D., Srinivasan, A., Sternberg, M.J.E.: Relating chemical activity to structure: an examination of ILP successes. New Gen. Comp. 13, 411–433 (1995)

8. Richard, A.M., Williams, C.R.: Distributed structure-searchable toxicity DSSTox public database network: A proposal. Mutation Research 499, 27–52 (2000)

9. Srinivasan, A.: The Aleph Manual. University of Oxford (2007)

10. Muggleton, S.: Stochastic logic programs. In: De Raedt, L. (ed.) Proceedings of the 5th International Workshop on ILP, Katholieke Universiteit Leuven (1995)

Towards Typed Prolog

Tom Schrijvers[1,*], Vítor Santos Costa[2], Jan Wielemaker[3], and Bart Demoen[1]

[1] Department of Computer Science, K.U.Leuven, Belgium
[2] CRACS & FCUP, Universidade do Porto, Portugal
[3] HCS, University of Amsterdam, The Netherlands

Abstract. Prolog is traditionally not statically typed. Since the benefits of static typing are huge, it was decided to grow a portable type system inside two widely used open source Prolog systems: SWI-Prolog and Yap. This requires close cooperation and agreement between the two systems. The type system is Hindley-Milner. The main characteristics of the introduction of types in SWI and Yap are that typing is not mandatory, that typed and untyped code can be mixed, and that the type checker can insert dynamic type checks at the boundaries between typed and untyped code. The basic decisions and the current status of the *Typed Prolog* project are described, as well as the remaining tasks and problems to be solved.

1 Introduction

We resolutely choose for the most established type system, that of Hindley and Milner [1]. It is in wide-spread use in functional programming languages and has already been proposed various times for logic programming. The first and seminal proposal in the context of LP is by Mycroft and O'Keefe [2], and the most notable typed Prolog variants are Gödel [3], Mercury [4], Ciao [5] and Visual Prolog [6]. However, traditional Prolog systems have not followed that trend towards types, and many Prolog programmers continue to use an untyped Prolog, because switching to a new language is usually not an option. Our approach intends to remedy this by addressing the following critical issues:

- Our type system is presented as an add-on (a library) for *currently used Prolog systems*, SWI and YAP, rather than being part of yet another LP language. This means that programmers just need to learn the type system and can stay within their familiar programming language.
- The type system is *optional* with granularity the predicate. This allows users to gradually migrate their existing untyped code, to interface with untyped legacy code (e.g. libraries) and to hold on to Prolog idioms and built-ins for which Hindley-Milner typing is not straightforward.

---

* Tom Schrijvers is a post-doctoral researcher of the Fund for Scientific Research - Flanders.

M. Garcia de la Banda and E. Pontelli (Eds.): ICLP 2008, LNCS 5366, pp. 693–697, 2008.
© Springer-Verlag Berlin Heidelberg 2008

- Particular care goes to *interfacing typed with untyped code*. Our approach can introduce a runtime[1] type check at program points on the border between typed to untyped code. In this way, bugs in untyped code are caught at the boundary and do not propagate into the typed code, i.e. the user knows where to put the blame.

In its current incarnation, our system only type checks predicate clauses with respect to programmer-supplied type signatures. In the future, we intend also to automatically infer signatures to simplify the programmer's job.

2   The Hindley-Milner Type System

In order to support the Hindley-Milner type system, we follow standard practice, with a syntax that is nearly identical to the Mercury syntax. *Types* are represented by terms e.g. `boolean`, `list(integer)`, ... Types can also be or contain variables; those are named type variables and polymorphic types respectively, e.g. T and `list(T)`.

A *type definition* introduces a new type, a so-called *algebraic data type*. It is of the form `:- type t(X̄) ---> f₁(τ̄₁) ; ...; fₙ(τ̄ₙ).`, which defines a new polymorphic type `t(X̄)`. The type variables $\bar{X}$ must be mutually distinct. The $\bar{\tau}_i$ are arbitrary types whose type variables are a subset of $\bar{X}$. Also, the function symbols f_i/a_i must be mutually distinct, but they may appear in other type definitions.

A *type signature* is of the form `:- pred p(τ̄)` and declares a type τ_i for every argument of predicate p. If a predicate's signature contains a type variable, we call the predicate polymorphic.

A fully *typed program*, i.e., there is a signature for each predicate, is well-typed iff each clause is well-typed.

A clause is well-typed if we can find a consistent typing of all variables in the clause such that the head and body of the clause respect the supplied type signatures. The arguments of the head must have the same type (up to variable renaming) as the corresponding predicate's signature. The types of the arguments in body calls must be instances of the corresponding predicates' signatures. We refer the reader to [2] for a formal treatment and for concrete examples to later sections.

While this works fine for fully typed programs that do not use the typical Prolog built-in constructs, some care is needed for programs calling built-ins or containing a mix of typed and untyped code. Sections 3 and 4 deal with these issues.

3   Support for Prolog Features

Arithmetic Expressions. Prolog-style arithmetic does not fit well in the Hindley-Milner type system. The problem is that variable X in `Y is X + 1` can be a

---

[1] In contrast with the compile time checking of typed code.

number, or a full-fledged arithmetic expression. Hence, numbers are a subtype of arithmetic expressions. Unfortunately, it is an old result that subtyping in Prolog can go wrong [7]!

In the current implementation, variables in arithmetic expressions can be of a numeric type only. We are considering to relax this by overloading the expression argument types to be *either* arithmetic expression *or* numeric types.

Built-ins. Some Prolog built-ins cannot be given a sensible Hindley-Milner type, such as `arg/3`[2], which extracts an argument of a term. In general, the type of the argument depends on the index number, which may not be statically known.

Nevertheless, for many Prolog built-ins there is a straightforward signature. Some of the built-ins our system supports are:

```
:- pred var(T).      :- pred ground(T).     :- pred write(T).
:- pred (T == T).    :- pred (T @< T).

:- pred compare(cmp,T,T).               :- pred reverse(list(T),list(T)).
:- type cmp ---> (<) ; (=) ; (>).   :- type list(T) ---> [] ; [T|list(T)].
```

Meta-Predicates. Meta-predicates take goals as arguments. They are supported through the higher-order type `pred`. For instance, the types of some well-known built-in meta-predicates are:

```
:- pred \+(pred).    :- pred once(pred).    :- pred setof(T,pred,list(T)).
```

It may seem problematic in a goal like `setof(X,Goal,List)` to figure out the type of `X`. This is not so: the necessary information is usually provided by an earlier goal, e.g. `Goal = between(1,10,X)`. The former forces the type of `Goal` to be `pred`. Hence, from the latter it follows that `X` has type `integer`, assuming the signature `:- pred between(integer,integer,integer)`.

The meta-predicate support is generalized to higher-order predicates with closures as arguments, i.e. goals missing one or more arguments. For instance, the well-known `maplist/3` predicate has the signature:

```
:- pred maplist(pred(X,Y),list(X),list(Y)).
```

Atoms. For lack of the conventional strings, many Prolog programmers resort to using atoms instead. In order to support this convention, our type system offers the `atom` type containing all atoms. Hence, the ISO-Prolog built-in `atom_concat/3` has signature

```
:- pred atom_concat(atom,atom,atom).
```

Note that a true `string` type would offer a cleaner solution.

---

[2] Its type-friendly counterpart are typed (record) field selectors.

4   Interfacing Typed and Untyped Code

One of the most distinguishing properties of our type system is its support for interfacing typed with untyped code.

Untyped to Typed. While typed code is statically verified by the type checker, untyped code is not. Hence, any call from untyped code (or the Prolog toplevel) to typed code can go wrong, if the provided arguments are not of the required types. If left unchecked, such an ill-typed call may manifest itself elsewhere far away in the code and greatly complicate the debugging process.

By default, we prevent this scenario by performing a runtime type check on any call from untyped to typed code (by means of a simple program transformation). If the call is ill-typed, it is caught before the actual call is executed. Then, the programmer knows the untyped code leading up to the call is to blame.

Typed to Untyped. Also in the inverse situation, when calling untyped code from typed code, we want to catch type violations early on in order to blame the untyped code. In order to do so, the programmer has to supply a type annotation for the call to untyped code. This allows to statically verify whether the surrounding typed code is consistent with this annotation. On top of that, a runtime check whether the untyped code satisfies the type annotation is inserted. The check is performed right after the call returns: any logical variables improperly bound by the call are detected in this way.

As an example, consider the following predicate from Santos Costa's red-black tree library:

```
:- pred list_to_rbtree(list(pair(K,V)),rbtree(K,V)).

list_to_rbtree(List, T) :-
        sort(List,Sorted) :: sort(list(pair(K,V)),list(pair(K,V))),
        ord_list_to_rbtree(Sorted, T).
```

Assume the `sort/2` predicate is untyped, whereas the other predicates are typed. The programmer has annotated the call (after `::`) with the missing type information `sort(list(pair(K,V)),list(pair(K,V)))`. Based on the annotation, the type checker assumes that the arguments `List` and `Sorted` both have the type `list(pair(K,V))`. Moreover, a runtime type check is inserted right after the call, to check whether the two arguments actually have this type.

The programmer can optionally declare that the runtime check need not be performed.

Untyped Terms. The programmer is forced to make a single one-off decision for a predicate: either she provides a signature and the predicate is typed, or she does not and the predicate is untyped. The former choice is the most desirable, but may require pervasive changes to the code as all terms handled by the predicate must be typeable, and hence be made to respect the Hindley-Milner data type conventions.

We provide the programmer a way out of this dilemma with the universal type **any**, which covers all possible terms. Now the programmer only provides precise types for the terms she wants, and defers the job for the others by typing them with **any**. For the subsequent gradual and localized instruction of more precise types, terms of type **any** can be coerced to other types, and vice versa.

5   Conclusion

The Typed Prolog project is based on the belief that it is better to gradually introduce types in an existing language than to start from scratch with a new language. People tend not to migrate to another system just because of types, hence our decision to introduce types into Yap and SWI, two widely used Prolog systems, and in such a way that users can gradually adapt to the use of types.

We aim at making this process as pleasant as possible, with special support for Prolog language features and for interfacing typed with untyped code, and while not forcing the Prolog programmer to give up essential functionality.

The Typed Prolog project started in the spring of 2008 and now consists of about 1,000 lines of code. It is no surprise that there are still many issues to tackle: error messages, handling floats and rationals, complete integration with the module system, dealing with large sets of facts, adaptation of the runtime checks to delayed execution, general support for constraint solvers, ...

The simultaneous introduction of the same type system into SWI and Yap is another clear sign of the commitment of their development teams to unify their functionality. Library **type_check** will be available in their next release. Most other Prolog systems could include our library with little effort, in particular Ciao Prolog, because its overall design principles are compatible with ours.

Acknowledgements. The authors are grateful to Roberto Bagnara, Fred Mesnard and Ulrich Neumerkel for there helpful comments.

References

1. Milner, R.: A theory of type polymorphism in programming. Journal of Computer System Sciences 17, 348–375 (1978)
2. Mycroft, A., O'Keefe, R.A.: A polymorphic type system for prolog. Artif. Intell. 23(3), 295–307 (1984)
3. Hill, P.M., Lloyd, J.W.: The Gödel Programming Language. MIT Press, Cambridge (1994)
4. Somogyi, Z., Henderson, F., Conway, T.: The execution algorithm of mercury: an efficient purely declarative logic programming language. Journal of Logic Programming 29, 17–64 (1996)
5. Pietrzak, P., Correas, J., Puebla, G., Hermenegildo, M.: A Practical Type Analysis for Verification of Modular Prolog Programs. In: ACM SIGPLAN 2008 Workshop on Partial Evaluation and Program Manipulation (PEPM 2008), pp. 61–70. ACM Press, New York (2008)
6. Prolog Development Center (Visual Prolog), http://www.visual-prolog.com
7. Hill, P.M., Topor, R.: A semantics for Typed Logic Programs. In: Pfenning, M. (ed.) Types in Logic Programming, pp. 1–62. MIT Press, Cambridge (1992)

Environment Reuse in the WAM

Bart Demoen[1] and Phuong-Lan Nguyen[2]

[1] Department of Computer Science, K.U.Leuven, Belgium
[2] Institut de Mathématiques Appliquées, UCO, Angers, France
bmd@cs.kuleuven.be, nguyen@ima.uco.fr

Abstract. The TOAM reuses eagerly allocated stack frames, while the WAM avoids to allocate environments. This is investigated by using the tak/4 benchmark as an inital case study for better understanding what one can expect from environment reuse for deterministic predicates in the WAM. Additionally, artificial programs are used to amplify the findings. The experiment compares the impact of reusing an environment versus avoiding to create it: the latter seems a superior technique.

1   Introduction

We assume familiarity with Prolog [1], the WAM [2,3] and the TOAM [4]. Acquaintance with the B-Prolog implementation of the TOAM and with hProlog [5] can also help.

The TOAM and the WAM treat stack frames/environments differently: the TOAM allocates eagerly a stack frame for a predicate, and reuses it when possible. The WAM avoids to allocate an environment for a predicate call, e.g., in case the selected clause is a fact, but possible needs to allocate many environments for the same predicate. This difference stems from different design choices in the two abstract machines and their compilers: the TOAM compiles a predicate at a time, and passes arguments through the stack. The WAM compiles clauses at a time[1], and passes the arguments through a fixed set of argument registers. One can argue endlessly about which is better. We take here a different approach: we investigate to what extent the WAM can benefit from environment reuse, and how effective the environment avoidance optimization, which is in fact known in classical compiler literature as a leaf procedure optimization, compared to environment reuse. We start by using tak/4 as a case study in Section 2. The experiment indicates that the WAM approach can be improved in principle by adopting an environment reuse schema as in the TOAM, at least for tak/4. Section 3 discusses the dynamics of tak/4 and provides a more general insight in the experimental data. Section 4 uses artificial benchmarks for showing the relative merit of environment reuse versus environment avoidance. Section 5 concludes.

The experiments were done on a 1.8 GHz Pentium 4 with Linux (hProlog 2.7 and B-Prolog 7.1b3.2) and on an Intel Mac (hProlog 2.7 and B-Prolog 7.0). The versions of B-Prolog use the TOAM Jr. [6]. Timings are always in milliseconds.

---

[1] Except for the glue code for indexing.

M. Garcia de la Banda and E. Pontelli (Eds.): ICLP 2008, LNCS 5366, pp. 698–702, 2008.
© Springer-Verlag Berlin Heidelberg 2008

2   Tak/4 and Its Abstract Machine Code

Below is the source code for tak/4.

```
tak(X,Y,Z,A):-
        (X =< Y ->
            Z = A
        ;
            X1 is X - 1, tak(X1,Y,Z,A1),
            Y1 is Y - 1, tak(Y1,Z,X,A2),
            Z1 is Z - 1, tak(Z1,X,Y,A3),
            tak(A1,A2,A3,A)
        ).
```

The original tak/4 code uses two clauses, but the hProlog compiler and the B-Prolog compiler effectively transform them to the version above with if-then-else. The code generated by B-Prolog and hProlog can be obtained by using 'bpc'/1 and *print_code/1* respectively. A more high level description of the code follows:

```
B-Prolog                                  hProlog
========                                  =======
@tak:                                     @tak:
     allocate_det
@afteralloc:
     if (! X =< Y) goto @else                  if (! X =< Y) goto @else
     unify(Z,A)                                unify(Z,A)
     return_det                                proceed
@else:                                    @else:
                                               allocate
                                               move (X,Y,Z,A) to environment
     X1 is X - 1, tak(X1,Y,Z,A1),              X1 is X - 1, tak(X1,Y,Z,A1),
     Y1 is Y - 1, tak(Y1,Z,X,A2),              Y1 is Y - 1, tak(Y1,Z,X,A2),
     Z1 is Z - 1, tak(Z1,X,Y,A3),              Z1 is Z - 1, tak(Z1,X,Y,A3),
     move (A1,A2,A3) to (X,Y,Z)                load (A1,A2,A3,A) from env
     goto @afteralloc                          deallocate
                                               goto @tak
```

B-Prolog has clearly taken the *allocate* out of the tak loop.

hProlog performs slightly less instruction compression than B-Prolog, it executes some extra instructions for dealing with the argument registers, and it never reuses an environment. Still, hProlog is faster by 33% on the Linux machine, and about 9% on the Mac. This was measured by repeating the goal *tak(18,12,6,_)* 100 times: the first two columns of the table in Section 3 show the figures. The next section explains why the WAM approach works so well.

3   The Dynamics of Tak/4

During one run of the query, the then-branch is taken 47.707 times, while the else-branch is taken 15.902 times: that is (close to) 3 times less. So, in total,

B-Prolog allocates 47.707 times an enviroment, while hProlog does the same 3 times less. The factor 3 results from the fact that 3 out of 4 calls in the body are non-tail calls. One can also see this by considering the execution tree for tak/4: each call-node has outgoing degree equal to 4. Its leaves correspond to calls of the form $tak(X,Y,Z,A)$ in which $X \leq Y$, for which the WAM does not allocate an environment. Since the number N of nodes relates to the number I of internal nodes by the simple formula $N - 1 = 4 * I$, the conclusion follows. It is easy to generalize these findings, at least for deterministic programs.

Seemingly, the eager allocation of a stack frame (for deterministic programs) is counterproductive, and it would be a nice experiment to modify B-Prolog to do lazy stack frame allocation, as the WAM does. Since the source code of B-Prolog is not available to us, we have taken the other path: we have modified hProlog to *reuse* its environments, first in the tak/4 benchmark, and later in some artificial benchmarks.

hProlog had already enough instructions to generate code that performs both lazy allocation and environment reuse. The resulting code for tak/4 is:

```
hProlog+reuse
=============
@tak:
        if (! X =< Y) { allocate;
                        move (X,Y,Z,A) to environment;
                        goto @else }
        unify(Z,A)
        proceed
@allocated:
        if (! X =< Y) goto @else
        unify(Z,A)
        deallocate
        proceed
@else:
        X1 is X - 1, tak(X1,Y,Z,A1),
        Y1 is Y - 1, tak(Y1,Z,X,A2),
        Z1 is Z - 1, tak(Z1,X,Y,A3),
        move (A1,A2,A3) to environment slots (X,Y,Z)
        goto @allocated
```

	hProlog	B-Prolog	hProlog +reuse
tak on Linux	315	473	278
tak on Mac	375	412	367

The table above shows the timings for B-Prolog, hProlog and the hProlog version with environment reuse. There is a clear gain in re-using the environment for hProlog, although it depends on the combination of the platform and the gcc version. The above code avoids the allocation of environments and at the same time reuses environments when possible, albeit at the cost of some seemingly duplicate code. Note however that the first $X =< Y$ takes its arguments from the argument registers, while the second takes them from the environment.

It seems clear that the hybrid compilation schema that combines environment avoidance with environment reuse is worth investigating further.

Environment Reuse in the WAM   701

4 Artificial Benchmarks

In order to amplify the potential advantage of environment reuse and environment avoidance, we have constructed a set of benchmarks with a characteristic similar to tak/4, but from which the fluff was removed. We defined predicates $taklike_n$ for $n = 1..10$. As an example, $taklike_5$ is defined as:

```
taklike_5(X) :-
        (X =< 1 -> true                           s .
        ;
          s, s, s, s, s,   % 5 calls to s
          X1 is X - 1, taklike_5(X1)
        ).
```

The execution tree is also shown: the black nodes correspond to calls that can reuse the current environment. The other nodes cannot. For $taklike_n$, the ratio between the calls that can avoid an environment and the calls that can reuse the environment is $n : 1$.

The goal is always of the form $? - taklike_n(5000000)$. The table below shows the timings for hProlog and B-Prolog on two platforms: the upper half on the Linux machine, the seond one on the Mac.

The first (and fifth) row shows the results of running hProlog unaltered on the benchmarks. The second (and sixth) row shows the effect of making hProlog allocate an environment for the s. fact: normally the WAM (and hProlog alike) generates just a *proceed* instruction; in this case, hProlog was made to generate an *allocate, deallocate_proceed* sequence, mimicking an eager allocation. The third (and seventh) row shows the result for hProlog with reuse of the environment for the tail call to *tak_like*.

	1	2	3	4	5	6	7	8	9	10	avi
hProlog	150	250	418	450	478	514	542	586	590	630	53
hProlog+extra env	208	458	542	628	714	798	888	972	1056	1148	104
hProlog+reuse	110	208	374	404	432	462	500	524	558	589	53
B-Prolog	226	492	596	692	792	894	994	1100	1204	1304	119
hProlog	183	199	229	252	369	398	422	454	484	492	34
hProlog+extra env	249	325	496	572	670	739	817	899	980	1058	89
hProlog+reuse	123	147	170	196	317	340	364	397	417	444	35
B-Prolog	254	466	590	704	826	959	1154	1191	1367	1456	133

The table also indicates the average increment between successive values of n. It is interesting to see that the B-Prolog figures are the closest to hProlog+extra env. The hProlog columns further show that

- the relative gain of environment reuse depends on n: the gain is larger with smaller n; this gain goes from 26% to 6.5% (on Linux) and 27% to 9.7% (on Mac); note that those are overestimates of what can be achieved in practical programs, because the artificial benchmarks contain hardly any fluff.

– the relative loss of creating the extra environment is about 27% to 45% (on Linux) and 26% to 53% (on Mac); again, those figures overestimate the relative effect.

When one considers the absolute figures (for Linux), one sees that environment avoidance reduces the runtime by 58 msecs up to 518 msecs. Environment reuse gives an almost constant gain between 30 and 40 msecs.

One can conclude that the WAM optimization of not allocating an environment for a fact, is more effective that the TOAM optimization of reusing the stack frame. Both the absolute and relative figures suggest that. Moreover, as expected, environment avoidance becomes better when there are more goals in the body.

5   Conclusion

Tak/4 lends itself easily to environment reuse in the WAM: such reuse is more difficult if a predicate has more than one clause with an allocate, and if one still wants to compile clauses in isolation, as the WAM does. So we cannot claim that we have ultimate answers and solutions. We observed that environment reuse for tak/4 was quite effective, but depending on the platform-gcc combination. The analysis of the experimental results shows that environment avoidance is a better optimization than environment reuse. Of course, for performance reasons, one would like to have them both. The next step should be an adaptation of the hProlog compiler to exploit the reuse of environments.

Acknowledgements

Bart Demoen thanks Research Foundation-Flanders (FWO-Vlaanderen) for support. Part of this work was performed during a visit to IMA, UCO, Angers.

References

1. Clocksin, W., Mellish, C.: Programming in Prolog. Springer, Heidelberg (1984)
2. Aït-Kaci, H.: The WAM: a (real) tutorial. Technical Report 5, DEC Paris Research Report (1990)
3. Warren, D.H.D.: An Abstract Prolog Instruction Set. Technical Report 309, SRI (1983)
4. Zhou, N.F.: Global optimizations in a Prolog compiler for the TOAM. Journal of Logic Programming 15(4), 275–294 (1993)
5. Demoen, B., Nguyen, P.L.: So many WAM variations, so little time. In: Palamidessi, C., Moniz Pereira, L., Lloyd, J.W., Dahl, V., Furbach, U., Kerber, M., Lau, K.-K., Sagiv, Y., Stuckey, P.J. (eds.) CL 2000. LNCS (LNAI), vol. 1861, pp. 1240–1254. Springer, Heidelberg (2000)
6. Zhou, N.F.: A Register-Free Abstract Prolog Machine with Jumbo Instructions. In: Dahl, V., Niemelä, I. (eds.) ICLP 2007. LNCS, vol. 4670, pp. 455–457. Springer, Heidelberg (2007)

Logic Engines as Interactors

Paul Tarau

Department of Computer Science and Engineering
University of North Texas
tarau@cs.unt.edu

Abstract. We introduce a new programming language construct, *Interactors*, supporting the agent-oriented view that programming is a dialog between simple, self-contained, autonomous building blocks.

We define *Interactors* as an abstraction of answer generation and refinement in *Logic Engines* resulting in expressive language extension and metaprogramming patterns.

Interactors extend language constructs like Ruby, Python and C#'s multiple coroutining block returns through *yield* statements and they can emulate the action of monadic constructs and catamorphisms in functional languages.

The full version of this paper [1] describes source level emulation of Prolog's dynamic database and various built-ins in terms of an *Interactor* API and design patterns for algorithms involving combinatorial generation and infinite answer streams.

Keywords: generalized iterators, logic engines, agent oriented programming language constructs, metaprogramming.

1 Introduction

Agent programming constructs have influenced design patterns at "macro level", ranging from interactive Web services to mixed initiative computer human interaction. *Performatives* in Agent communication languages [2] have made these constructs reflect explicitly the intentionality, as well as the negotiation process involved in agent interactions.

In a logic programming context, the Jinni agent programming language [3,4,5] and the BinProlog system [6] have been centered around logic engine constructs providing an API that supported reentrant instances of the language processor. This has naturally led to a view of logic engines as instances of a generalized family of iterators called *Fluents* [7], that have allowed the separation of the first-order language interpreters from the multi-threading mechanism, while providing a very concise source-level reconstruction of Prolog's built-ins.

Building upon the *Fluents* API described in [7], this paper will focus on bringing interaction-centered, agent oriented constructs from software design frameworks and design patterns to programming language level.

The resulting language constructs, that we shall call *Interactors*, will express control, metaprogramming and interoperation with stateful objects and external

M. Garcia de la Banda and E. Pontelli (Eds.): ICLP 2008, LNCS 5366, pp. 703–707, 2008.

services. They complement pure Horn Clause Prolog with a significant boost in expressiveness, to the point where they allow emulating at source level virtually all Prolog builtins, including dynamic database operations.

As paradigm independent language constructs, *Interactors* are a generalization of *Coroutine Iterators* [8] and *Interruptible Iterators* [9].

2   First Class Logic Engines

Our *Interactor API* is an natural extension of of the *Logic Engine API* introduced in [7]. An *Engine* is simply a language processor reflected through an API that allows its computations to be controlled interactively from another *Engine*, very much the same way a programmer controls Prolog's interactive toplevel loop: launch a new goal, ask for a new answer, interpret it, react to it.

A *Logic Engine* is an *Engine* running a Horn Clause Interpreter with LD-resolution [10] on a given clause database, together with a set of built-in operations. The command

```
new_engine(AnswerPattern,Goal,Interactor)
```

creates a new Horn Clause solver, uniquely identified by `Interactor`, which shares code with the currently running program and is initialized with `Goal` as a starting point. `AnswerPattern` is a term, usually a list of variables occurring in `Goal`, of which answers returned by the engine will be instances.

The `get/2` operation is used to retrieve successive answers generated by an Interactor, on demand.

```
get(Interactor,AnswerInstance)
```

It tries to harvest the answer computed from `Goal`, as an instance of `AnswerPattern`. If an answer is found, it is returned as `the(AnswerInstance)`, otherwise the atom `no` is returned. As in the case of `Maybe` Monad in Haskell, returning distinct functors in the case of success and failure, allows further case analysis in a pure Horn Clause style, without needing Prolog's CUT or if-then-else operation.

Note that bindings are not propagated to the original `Goal` or `AnswerPattern` when `get/2` retrieves an answer, i.e. `AnswerInstance` is obtained by first standardizing apart (renaming) the variables in `Goal` and `AnswerPattern`, and then backtracking over its alternative answers in a separate Prolog interpreter. Therefore, backtracking in the caller interpreter does not interfere with the new Interactor's iteration over answers. Backtracking over the Interactor's creation point, as such, makes it unreachable and therefore subject to garbage collection.

An Interactor is stopped with the `stop/1` operation (that is also called automatically when no more answers can be produced.)

So far, these operations provide a minimal *Coroutine Iterator API*, powerful enough to switch tasks cooperatively between an engine and its client and emulate key Prolog built-ins like `if-then-else` and `findall` [7], as well as higher order operations like *fold* and *best_of* [1].

3 From Fluents to Interactors

We will now describe the extension of the *Fluents* API of [7] that provides a minimal bidirectional communication API between interactors and their clients.

The following operations provide a "mixed-initiative" interaction mechanism, allowing more general data exchanges between an engine and its client.

A Yield/Return Operation

First, like the `yield return` construct of `C#` and the `yield operation` of Ruby and Python, our `return/1` operation

`return(Term)`

will save the state of the engine and transfer control and a result `Term` to its client. The client will receive a copy of `Term` simply by using its `get/1` operation. Similarly to Ruby's `yield`, our `return` operation suspends and returns data from arbitrary computations (possibly involving recursion) rather than from specific language constructs like a `while` or `for` loop.

Note that an Interactor returns control to its client either by calling `return/1` or when a computed answer becomes available. By using a sequence of `return/get` operations, an engine can provide a stream of *intermediate/final results* to its client, without having to backtrack. This mechanism is powerful enough to implement a complete exception handling mechanism (see [7]) simply with

`throw(E):-return(exception(E)).`

When combined with a `catch(Goal,Exception,OnException)`, on the client side, the client can decide, upon reading the exception with `get/1`, if it wants to handle it or to throw it to the next level.

The mechanisms discussed so far are expressive enough, as described in [7], to implement at source level key built-in predicates of Prolog like `if-then-else`, `findall` and `copy_term`.

Interactors and Coroutining. The operations described so far allow an engine to return answers from any point in its computation sequence. The next step is to enable its client to *inject* new goals (executable data) to an arbitrary inner context of an engine. Two new primitives are needed:

`to_engine(Engine,Data)`

used to send a client's data to an Engine, and

`from_engine(Data)`

used by the engine to receive a client's Data.

A typical use case for the *Interactor API* looks as follows:

1. the *client* creates and initializes a new *engine*
2. the client triggers a new computation in the *engine*, parameterized as follows:

(a) the *client* passes some data and a new goal to the *engine* and issues a `get` operation that passes control to it

(b) the *engine* starts a computation from its initial goal or the point where it has been suspended and runs (a copy of) the new goal received from its *client*

(c) the *engine* returns (a copy of) the answer, then suspends and returns control to its *client*

3. the *client* interprets the answer and proceeds with its next computation step
4. the process is fully reentrant and the *client* may repeat it from an arbitrary point in its computation

Using a metacall mechanism like `call/1` (which can also be emulated in terms of engine operations [7]), one can implement a close equivalent of Ruby's `yield` statement as follows:

```
ask_engine(Engine,Goal, Answer):-
   to_engine(Engine,Goal),
   get(Engine,Answer).

engine_yield(Answer):-
   from_engine((Answer:-Goal)),
   call(Goal),
   return(Answer).
```

where `ask_engine` sends a goal (possibly built at runtime) to an engine, which in turn, executes it and returns a result with an `engine_yield` operation.

As the following example shows, this allows the client to use from outside the (infinite) recursive loop of an engine as a form of *updatable persistent state*.

```
sum_loop(S1):-engine_yield(S1=>S2),sum_loop(S2).

inc_test(R1,R2):-
   new_engine(_,sum_loop(0),E),
   ask_engine(E,(S1=>S2:-S2 is S1+2),R1),
   ask_engine(E,(S1=>S2:-S2 is S1+5),R2).

?- inc_test(R1,R2).
R1=the(0 => 2),
R2=the(2 => 7)
```

Note also that after parameters (the increments 2 and 5) are passed to the engine, results dependent on its state (the sums so far 2 and 7) are received back. Moreover, note that an arbitrary goal is injected in the local context of the engine where it is executed, with access to the engine's *state variables* S1 and S2. As engines have separate garbage collectors (or in simple cases as a result of tail recursion), their infinite loops run in constant space, provided that no unbounded size objects are created.

4   Conclusion

Logic Engines encapsulated as Interactors have been used to build on top of pure Prolog (together with the Fluent API described in [7]) a practical Prolog system, including dynamic database operations [1], entirely at source level.

In a broader sense, Interactors can be seen as a starting point for rethinking fundamental programming language constructs like Iterators and Coroutining in terms of language constructs inspired by *performatives* in agent oriented programming. Beyond applications to logic-based language design, we hope that our language constructs will be reusable in the design and implementation of new functional and object oriented languages.

References

1. Tarau, P.: Logic Engines as Interactors (2008), `http://arXiv.org/abs/0808.0556`
2. Mayfield, J., Labrou, Y., Finin, T.W.: Evaluation of KQML as an Agent Communication Language. In: Wooldridge, M., Müller, J.P., Tambe, M. (eds.) ATAL 1996. LNCS, vol. 1037, pp. 347–360. Springer, Heidelberg (1996)
3. Tarau, P.: Orthogonal Language Constructs for Agent Oriented Logic Programming. In: Carro, M., Morales, J.F. (eds.) Proceedings of CICLOPS 2004, Fourth Colloquium on Implementation of Constraint and Logic Programming Systems, Saint-Malo, France (September 2004)
4. Tarau, P.: Agent Oriented Logic Programming Constructs in Jinni 2004. In: Demoen, B., Lifschitz, V. (eds.) ICLP 2004. LNCS, vol. 3132, pp. 477–478. Springer, Heidelberg (2004)
5. Tarau, P.: The Jinni Prolog Compiler: a fast and flexible Prolog-in-Java (2008), `http://www.binnetcorp.com/download/jinnidemo/JinniUserGuide.html`
6. Tarau, P.: BinProlog 11.x Professional Edition: Advanced BinProlog Programming and Extensions Guide. Technical report, BinNet Corp. (2006)
7. Tarau, P.: Fluents: A Refactoring of Prolog for Uniform Reflection and Interoperation with External Objects. In: Palamidessi, C., Moniz Pereira, L., Lloyd, J.W., Dahl, V., Furbach, U., Kerber, M., Lau, K.-K., Sagiv, Y., Stuckey, P.J. (eds.) CL 2000. LNCS, vol. 1861. Springer, Heidelberg (2000)
8. Liskov, B., Atkinson, R.R., Bloom, T., Moss, J.E.B., Schaffert, C., Scheifler, R., Snyder, A.: CLU Reference Manual. LNCS, vol. 114. Springer, Heidelberg (1981)
9. Liu, J., Kimball, A., Myers, A.C.: Interruptible iterators. In: Morrisett, J.G., Jones, S.L.P. (eds.) POPL, pp. 283–294. ACM, New York (2006)
10. Tarau, P., Boyer, M.: Nonstandard Answers of Elementary Logic Programs. In: Jacquet, J. (ed.) Constructing Logic Programs, pp. 279–300. J. Wiley, Chichester (1993)

Global Storing Mechanisms
for Tabled Evaluation

Jorge Costa and Ricardo Rocha*

DCC-FC & CRACS
University of Porto, Portugal
c0607002@alunos.dcc.fc.up.pt, ricroc@dcc.fc.up.pt

Abstract. Arguably, the most successful data structure for tabling is tries. However, while tries are very efficient for variant based tabled evaluation, they are limited in their ability to recognize and represent repeated terms in different tabled calls or/and answers. In this paper, we propose a new design for the table space where tabled terms are stored in a common global trie instead of being spread over several different tries.

1 Introduction

Tabling is an implementation technique where intermediate answers for subgoals are stored and then reused whenever a repeated call appears. The performance of tabled evaluation largely depends on the implementation of the table space – being called very often, fast lookup and insertion capabilities are mandatory. Applications can make millions of different calls, hence compactness is also required. Arguably, the most successful data structure for tabling is *tries* [1].

However, while tries are very efficient for variant based tabled evaluation, they are limited in their ability to recognize and represent repeated terms in different tabled calls or/and answers. In [2], Rao *et al.* proposed a *Dynamic Threaded Sequential Automata* (DTSA) that recognizes reusable subcomputations for subsumption based tabling. In [3], Johnson *et al.* proposed an alternative to DTSA, called *Time-Stamped Trie* (TST), which not only maintains the time efficiency of the DTSA but has better space efficiency.

In this paper, we propose a different approach. We propose a new design for the table space where all terms in a tabled subgoal call or/and answer are stored in a *common global trie* instead of being spread over several different trie data structures. Our approach resembles the *hash-consing* technique [4], as it tries to share data that is structurally equal. An obvious goal is to save memory usage by reducing redundancy in term representation to a minimum. We will focus our discussion on a concrete implementation, the YapTab system [5], but our proposals can be easy generalized and applied to other tabling systems.

---

* This work has been partially supported by the research projects STAMPA (PTDC/EIA/67738/2006) and JEDI (PTDC/ EIA/66924/2006) and by Fundação para a Ciência e Tecnologia.

M. Garcia de la Banda and E. Pontelli (Eds.): ICLP 2008, LNCS 5366, pp. 708–712, 2008.

2   Table Space

A trie is a tree structure where each different path through the trie data units, the *trie nodes*, corresponds to a term. Each root-to-leaf path represents a term described by the tokens labelling the nodes traversed. Two terms with common prefixes will branch off from each other at the first distinguishing token. For example, the tokenized form of the term $p(X, q(Y, X), Z)$ is the stream of 6 tokens: $p/3, VAR_0, q/2, VAR_1, VAR_0, VAR_2$. Variables are represented using the formalism proposed by Bachmair *et al.* [6], where the set of variables in a term is mapped to the sequence of constants $VAR_0, ..., VAR_N$.

Internally, the trie nodes are 4-field data structures. One field stores the node's token, one second field stores a pointer to the node's first child, a third field stores a pointer to the node's parent and a fourth field stores a pointer to the node's next sibling. Each node's outgoing transitions may be determined by following the child pointer to the first child node and, from there, continuing through the list of sibling pointers. A threshold value controls whether to dynamically index the sibling nodes through a hash table. Further, hash collisions are reduced by dynamically expanding the hash tables. YapTab implements tables using two levels of tries - one for subgoal calls, the other for computed answers. More specifically, the table space of YapTab is organized in the following way:

- each tabled predicate has a *table entry* data structure assigned to it, acting as the entry point for the predicate's *subgoal trie*.
- each different subgoal call is represented as a unique path in the subgoal trie, starting at the predicate's table entry and ending in a *subgoal frame* data structure, with the argument terms being stored within the path's nodes.
- the *subgoal frame* data structure acts as an entry point to the *answer trie*.
- each different subgoal answer is represented as a unique path in the *answer trie*. To increase performance, answer trie paths enforce the *substitution factoring* mechanism [1] and hold just the substitution terms for the free variables which exist in the argument terms.
- the subgoal frame has internal pointers to the first and last answer on the trie and the leaf's child pointer of answers are used to point to the next available answer, a feature that enables answer recovery in insertion time order. Answers are loaded by traversing the answer trie nodes bottom-up.

An example for a tabled predicate t/2 is shown in Fig. 1. Initially, the subgoal trie is empty. Then, subgoal t(a(1),X) is called and three trie nodes are inserted: one for the functor a/1, a second for the constant 1 and one last for variable X. The subgoal frame is inserted as a leaf, waiting for the answers. Next, subgoal t(a(2),X) is also called. It shares one common node with t(a(1),X) but, having a/1 a different argument, two new trie nodes and a new subgoal frame are inserted. At the end, the answers for each subgoal are stored in the corresponding answer trie as their values are computed. Note that, for this particular example, the completed answer trie for both subgoal calls is exactly the same.

3   Global Trie

We next describe the YapTab's
new design for the table space.
In this new design, all terms in
a tabled subgoal call or/and answer are now stored in a common global trie (GT) instead of
being spread over several different
trie data structures. The GT data
structure still is a tree structure
where each different path through
the trie nodes corresponds to a
term. However, here a term can
end at any internal trie node and
not necessarily at a leaf trie node.

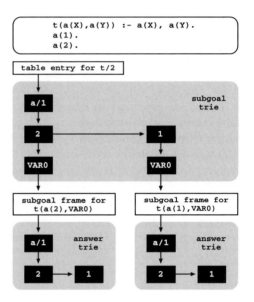

Fig. 1. YapTab's original table organization

The previous subgoal trie and
answer trie data structures are
now represented by a unique level
of trie nodes that point to the corresponding terms in the GT (see
Fig. 2 for details). For the subgoal tries, each node now repre-
sents a different subgoal call where the node's token is the pointer to the
unique path in the GT that represents the argument terms for the subgoal
call. The organization used in the subgoal tries to maintain the list of sibling
nodes and to access the corresponding subgoal frames remains unaltered. For
the answer tries, each node now represents a different subgoal answer where
the node's token is the pointer to the unique path in the GT that represents the substitution terms for the free variables which exist in the argument terms. The organization used in the answer tries to maintain the list of
sibling nodes and to enable answer recovery in insertion time order remains
unaltered. With this organization, answers are now loaded by following the
pointer in the node's token and then by traversing the corresponding GT's nodes
bottom-up.

Figure 2 uses again the example from Fig. 1 to illustrate how the GT's design works. Initially, the subgoal trie and the GT are empty. Then, the first
subgoal t(a(1),X) is called and three nodes are inserted on the GT: one to
represent the functor a/1, another for the constant 1 and a last one for variable X. Next, a node representing the path inserted on the GT is stored in
the subgoal trie (node labeled call1). The token field for the call1 node
is made to point to the leaf node of the GT's inserted path and the child
field is made to point to a new subgoal frame. For the second subgoal call,
t(a(2),X), we start again by inserting the call in the GT and then we store a
node in the subgoal trie (node labeled call2) to represent the path inserted on
the GT.

For each subgoal call we have two answers: the terms a(1) and a(2). However, as these terms are already represented on the GT, we need to store only two nodes, in each answer trie, to represent them (nodes labeled answer1 and answer2). The token field for these answer trie nodes are made to point to the corresponding term representation on the GT. With this example we can see that terms in the GT can end at any internal trie node (and not necessarily at a leaf trie node) and that a common path on the GT can simultaneously represent different subgoal and answer terms.

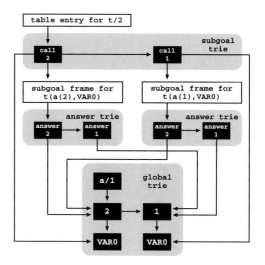

Fig. 2. YapTab's new table organization

4   Preliminary Experimental Results

To evaluate the impact of our proposal, we have defined a tabled predicate t/5 that stores in the table space terms of a certain kind, and then we use a top query goal test/0 that recursively calls t/5 with all combinations of one and two free variables in the arguments. We next show the code example used in the experiments for functor terms of arity 1 (500 terms in total).

```
t(A,B,C,D,E) :- term(A), term(B), term(C), term(D), term(E).

test :- t(A,f(1),f(1),f(1),f(1)), fail.        term(f(1)).
...                                            term(f(2)).
test :- t(A,B,f(1),f(1),f(1)), fail.           ...
...                                            term(f(499)).
test.                                          term(f(500)).
```

The environment for our experiments was an AMD Athlon XP 2800+ with 1 GByte of main memory and running the Linux kernel 2.6.24-19. Table 1 shows the memory usage and the running times to store to the tables (first execution) and to load from the tables (second execution) the complete set of subgoals/answers for YapTab with and without support for the global trie data structure. We tested 5 different programs with functor terms of arity 1 to 5.

The results show that GT support can significantly reduce memory usage proportionally to the depth and redundancy of the terms stored in the GT. On the other hand, the results indicate that this reduction comes at a price in execution time. With GT support, we need to navigate in two tries when checking/inserting a term. Moreover, in some situations, the cost of inserting

Table 1. Memory usage (in KBytes) and store/load times (in milliseconds) for YapTab with and without support for the global trie data structure

Terms	YapTab (a)			YapTab+GT (b)			Ratio (b)/(a)		
	Mem	Store	Load	Mem	Store	Load	Mem	Store	Load
500 f/1	49172	693	242	52811	1029	243	1.07	1.48	1.00
500 f/2	98147	842	314	56725	1298	310	**0.58**	1.54	**0.99**
500 f/3	147122	1098	377	60640	1562	378	**0.41**	1.42	1.00
500 f/4	196097	1258	512	64554	1794	435	**0.33**	1.43	**0.85**
500 f/5	245072	1418	691	68469	2051	619	**0.28**	1.45	**0.90**

a new term in an empty/small trie can be less than the cost of navigating in the GT, even when the term is already stored in the GT. However, our results seem to suggest that this cost also decreases proportionally to the depth and redundancy of the terms stored in the GT. The results obtained for loading terms do not suggest significant differences. However and surprisingly, the GT approach showed to outperform the original YapTab design in some experiments.

5   Conclusions

We have presented a new design for the table space that uses a common global trie to store terms in tabled subgoal calls and answers. Our preliminary experiments showed very significant reductions on memory usage. This is an important result that we plan to apply to real-world applications that pose many subgoal queries with a large number of redundant answers, such as ILP applications.

References

1. Ramakrishnan, I.V., Rao, P., Sagonas, K., Swift, T., Warren, D.S.: Efficient Access Mechanisms for Tabled Logic Programs. Journal of Logic Programming 38(1), 31–54 (1999)
2. Rao, P., Ramakrishnan, C.R., Ramakrishnan, I.V.: A Thread in Time Saves Tabling Time. In: Joint International Conference and Symposium on Logic Programming, pp. 112–126. The MIT Press, Cambridge (1996)
3. Johnson, E., Ramakrishnan, C.R., Ramakrishnan, I.V., Rao, P.: A Space Efficient Engine for Subsumption-Based Tabled Evaluation of Logic Programs. In: Middeldorp, A. (ed.) FLOPS 1999. LNCS, vol. 1722, pp. 284–300. Springer, Heidelberg (1999)
4. Goto, E.: Monocopy and Associative Algorithms in Extended Lisp. Technical Report TR 74-03, University of Tokyo (1974)
5. Rocha, R., Silva, F., Santos Costa, V.: YapTab: A Tabling Engine Designed to Support Parallelism. In: Conference on Tabulation in Parsing and Deduction, pp. 77–87 (2000)
6. Bachmair, L., Chen, T., Ramakrishnan, I.V.: Associative Commutative Discrimination Nets. In: International Joint Conference on Theory and Practice of Software Development. LNCS, vol. 668, pp. 61–74. Springer, Heidelberg (1993)

Thread-Based Competitive Or-Parallelism[*]

Paulo Moura[1,3], Ricardo Rocha[2,3], and Sara C. Madeira[1,4]

[1] Dep. of Computer Science, University of Beira Interior, Portugal
{pmoura, smadeira}@di.ubi.pt
[2] Dep. of Computer Science, University of Porto, Portugal
ricroc@dcc.fc.up.pt
[3] Center for Research in Advanced Computing Systems, INESC–Porto, Portugal
[4] Knowledge Discovery and Bioinformatics Group, INESC–ID, Portugal

Abstract. This paper presents the logic programming concept of *thread-based competitive or-parallelism*, which combines the original idea of competitive or-parallelism with committed-choice nondeterminism and speculative threading. In thread-based competitive or-parallelism, an explicit disjunction of subgoals is interpreted as a set of concurrent alternatives, each running in its own thread. The subgoals compete for providing an answer and the first successful subgoal leads to the termination of the remaining ones. We discuss the implementation of competitive or-parallelism in the context of Logtalk, an object-oriented logic programming language, and present experimental results.

1 Introduction

Or-parallelism is a simple form of parallelism in logic programs, where the bodies of alternative clauses for the same goal are executed concurrently. Or-parallelism is often explored *implicitly*, without input from the programmer to express or manage parallelism. In this paper, we introduce a different, explicit form of or-parallelism, *thread-based competitive or-parallelism*, that combines the original idea of competitive or-parallelism [1] with committed-choice nondeterminism [2] and speculative threading [3]. Committed-choice nondeterminism, also known as *don't-care* nondeterminism, means that once an alternative is taken, the computation is committed to it and cannot backtrack or explore in parallel other alternatives. Committed-choice nondeterminism is useful whenever a single solution is sought among a set of potential alternatives. Speculative threading allows the exploration of different alternatives, which can be interpreted as competing to provide an answer for the original problem. The key idea is that multiple threads can be started without knowing *a priori* which of them, if any, will perform useful work. In competitive or-parallelism, different alternatives are interpreted as competing for providing an answer. The first successful alternative leads to the termination of the remaining ones. From a declarative programming perspective, thread-based competitive or-parallelism allows one to

---

[*] This work has been partially supported by the FCT research projects STAMPA (PTDC/EIA/67738/2006) and MOGGY (PTDC/EIA/70830/2006).

M. Garcia de la Banda and E. Pontelli (Eds.): ICLP 2008, LNCS 5366, pp. 713–717, 2008.

specify alternative procedures to solve a problem without caring about the details of speculative execution and thread handling. Another important key point of thread-based competitive or-parallelism is its simplicity and implementation portability when compared with classical, low-level or-parallelism implementations. The ISO Prolog multi-threading standardization proposal [4] is currently implemented in several systems including SWI-Prolog, Yap and XSB, providing a highly portable solution given the number of operating systems supported by these Prolog systems. In contrast, most or-parallelism systems described in the literature [5] are no longer available, due to the complexity of maintaining and porting their implementations.

Our competitive or-parallelism research is driven by the increasing availability of multi-core personal computing systems. These systems are turning into a viable high-performance, low-cost and standardized alternative to the traditional (and often expensive) parallel architectures. The number of cores per processor is expected to continue to increase, further expanding the areas of application of competitive or-parallelism.

2   Thread-Based Competitive Or-Parallelism

The concept of thread-based competitive or-parallelism is based on the interpretation of an *explicit disjunction of subgoals* as a set of concurrent alternatives, each running in its own thread. Each individual alternative is assumed to implement a different procedure that, depending on the problem specifics, is expected to either fail or succeed with different performance results. For example, one alternative may converge quickly to a solution, other may get trapped into a local, suboptimal solution, while a third may simply diverge. The subgoals are interpreted as competing for providing an answer and the first subgoal to complete leads to the termination of the threads running the remaining subgoals.

Consider, for example, the *water jugs* problem. In this problem, we have several jugs of different capacities and we want to measure a certain amount of water. We may *fill* a jug, *empty* it, or *transfer* its contents to another jug. Assume now that we have implemented several methods to solve this problem, e.g. breadth-first, depth-first, and hill-climbing. In Logtalk, we may then write:

```
solve(Jugs, Moves) :-
    threaded((
       breadth_first::solve(Jugs, Moves)
    ;  depth_first::solve(Jugs, Moves)
    ;  hill_climbing::solve(Jugs, Moves)
    )).
```

The semantics of a competitive or-parallelism call implemented by the Logtalk built-in predicate threaded/1 is simple. Given a disjunction of subgoals, a competitive or-parallelism call blocks until one of the subgoals succeeds, all the subgoals fail, or one of the subgoals generates an exception. All the remaining threads are terminated once one of the subgoals succeeds or throws an exception. The competitive or-parallelism call is deterministic and opaque to cuts; there is no backtracking over completed calls. The competitive or-parallelism call succeeds if and only if one of the subgoals succeeds. When one of the subgoals generates an exception, the competitive or-parallelism call terminates with the same exception.

3   Implementation

In this section, we discuss the Logtalk [6] implementation of competitive or-parallelism, based on the core predicates found on the ISO standardization proposal for Prolog threads [4]. Logtalk is an open source object-oriented logic programming language that can use most Prolog systems as a back-end compiler. Logtalk takes advantage of modern multi-processor and multi-core computers to support high level multi-threading programming, allowing objects to support both synchronous and asynchronous messages without worrying about the details of thread management. Using Prolog core multi-threading predicates to support competitive or-parallelism allows simple and portable implementations to be written. Nevertheless, three major problems must be addressed when implementing or-parallelism systems: (i) multiple binding representation, (ii) work scheduling, and (iii) predicate side-effects.

Multiple Binding Representation. A significant implementation advantage of competitive or-parallelism is that only the first successful subgoal in a disjunction of subgoals can lead to the instantiation of variables in the original call. This greatly simplifies our implementation as the Prolog core support for multi-threading programming can be used straightforward. In particular, we can take advantage of the Prolog thread creation predicate `thread_create/3`. Threads created with this predicate run a *copy* of the goal argument using its own set of data areas (stack, heap, trail, etc). Its implementation is akin to the environment copying approach [7], but much simpler as only the goal is copied. Because it is running a copy, no variable is shared between threads. Thus, the bindings of shared variables occurring within a thread are independent of bindings occurring in other threads. This operational semantics simplifies the problem of multiple binding representation in competitive or-parallelism, which results in a simple implementation with only a small number of lines of Prolog source code.

Work Scheduling. Unrestricted competitive or-parallelism can lead to complex load balancing problems, since the number of running threads may easily exceed the number of available computational units. In our implementation, load balancing is currently delegated to the operating system thread scheduler. This is partially a consequence of our use of the core Prolog multi-threading predicates. However, and although we have postponed working on an advanced, high-level scheduler, we can explicitly control the number of running threads using parametric objects with a parameter for the maximum number of running threads. This is a simple programming solution, used in most of the Logtalk multi-threading programming examples.

Side-Effects and Dynamic Predicates. The subgoals in a competitive or-parallelism call may have side-effects that may clash if not accounted for. Two common examples are input/output operations and asserting and retracting clauses for dynamic predicates. To prevent conflicts, Logtalk and the Prolog compilers implementing the ISO Prolog multi-threading standardization proposal allow predicates to be declared synchronized, thread shared (the default), or thread private. Synchronized predicates are internally protected by a mutex, thus allowing for easy thread synchronization. Thread private dynamic predicates may be used to implement thread local dynamic state. Thread shared dynamic predicates are required by the ISO Prolog multi-threading standardization proposal to follow *logical update semantics*.

4   Experimental Results

In order to validate our implementation, we used competitive or-parallelism (COP) to simultaneously explore depth-first (DF), breadth-first (BF), and hill-climbing (HC) search strategies for the *water jugs* problem. Our experimental setup used Logtalk 2.33.0 with SWI-Prolog 5.6.59 64 bits as the back-end compiler on an Intel-based computer with four cores running Fedora Core 8 64 bits.[1]

Table 1. Measuring from 1 to 14 liters with 5-liter and 9-liter jugs

Liters	DF	HC	BF	COP	Overhead	Steps
1	26.373951	0.020089	**0.007044**	0.011005	0.003961	5
2	26.596118	12.907172	**8.036822**	8.324970	0.288148	11
3	20.522287	**0.000788**	1.412355	0.009158	0.008370	9
4	20.081001	**0.000241**	0.001437	0.002624	0.002383	3
5	**0.000040**	0.000240	0.000484	0.000907	0.000867	2
6	3.020864	0.216004	**0.064097**	0.098883	0.034786	7
7	3.048878	**0.001188**	68.249278	0.008507	0.007319	13
8	2.176739	**0.000598**	0.127328	0.007720	0.007122	7
9	2.096855	**0.000142**	0.000255	0.003799	0.003657	2
10	**0.000067**	0.009916	0.004774	0.001326	0.001295	4
11	**0.346695**	5.139203	0.587316	0.404988	0.058293	9
12	14.647219	**0.002118**	10.987607	0.010785	0.008667	14
13	0.880068	0.019464	**0.014308**	0.029652	0.015344	5
14	0.240348	0.003415	**0.002391**	0.010367	0.007976	4

Table 1 shows the running times, in seconds, when 5-liter and 9-liter jugs were used to measure from 1 to 14 liters of water. It allows us to compare the running times of single-threaded DF, BF, and HC search strategies with the COP multi-threaded call where one thread is used for each individual search strategy. The results show the average of thirty runs. We highlight the fastest method for each measure. The last column shows the number of steps of the solution found by the competitive or-parallelism call. The maximum solution length was set to 14 steps for all strategies.

---

[1] The experiments can be easily reproduced by the reader by running the query `logtalk_load(mtbatch(loader))`, `mtbatch(swi)::run(search, 30)`.

The results show that the use of competitive or-parallelism allows us to quickly find a sequence of steps of acceptable length to solve different configurations of the water jugs problem. Moreover, given that we do not know *a priori* which individual search method will be the fastest for a specific measuring problem, competitive or-parallelism is a better solution than any of the individual search methods. The overhead of the competitive or-parallelism calls is due to the implicit thread and memory management. In particular, the initial thread data area sizes and the amount of memory that must be reclaimed when a thread terminates play a significant role on observed overheads. We are optimizing our implementation in order to minimize the thread management overhead. There is also room for further optimizations on the Prolog implementations of the ISO Prolog multi-threrading standardization proposal. Nevertheless, even with the current implementations, our preliminary experimental results are promising.

5   Conclusions and Future Work

We have presented the logic programming concept of thread-based competitive or-parallelism supported by an implementation in the object-oriented logic programing language Logtalk. This concept is orthogonal to the object-oriented features of Logtalk and can be implemented in plain Prolog and in non-declarative programming languages supporting the necessary threading primitives. Future work will include exploring the role of tabling in competitive or-parallelism calls and implementing a load-balancing mechanism. We also plan to apply competitive or-parallelism to non-trivial problems, seeking real-world experimental results allowing us to improve and expand our current implementation.

References

1. Ertel, W.: Performance Analysis of Competitive Or-Parallel Theorem Proving. Technical report fki-162-91, Technische Universität München (1991)
2. Shapiro, E.: The Family of Concurrent Logic Programming Languages. ACM Computing Surveys 21(3), 413–510 (1989)
3. González, A.: Speculative Threading: Creating New Methods of Thread-Level Parallelization. Technology@Intel Magazine (2005)
4. Moura, P.: ISO/IEC DTR 13211–5:2007 Prolog Multi-threading Support, http://logtalk.org/plstd/threads.pdf
5. Gupta, G., Pontelli, E., Ali, K., Carlsson, M., Hermenegildo, M.V.: Parallel Execution of Prolog Programs: A Survey. ACM Transactions on Programming Languages and Systems 23(4), 472–602 (2001)
6. Moura, P.: Logtalk – Design of an Object-Oriented Logic Programming Language. PhD thesis, Department of Computer Science, University of Beira Interior (2003)
7. Ali, K., Karlsson, R.: The Muse Approach to OR-Parallel Prolog. International Journal of Parallel Programming 19(2), 129–162 (1990)

A Logic Language with Stable Model Semantics for Social Reasoning[*]

Francesco Buccafurri, Gianluca Caminiti, and Rosario Laurendi

DIMET, Università degli Studi Mediterranea di Reggio Calabria
via Graziella, loc. Feo di Vito, 89122 Reggio Calabria, Italy
{bucca,gianluca.caminiti,rosario.laurendi}@unirc.it

Abstract. In this paper we present a new language based on logic programming allowing us to represent some forms of social reasoning. The nice feature of this semantics is that the interdependent individuals' requirements might result in a sort of guessing of agreed conclusions, which autonomously each individual cannot derive, thus capturing the common case of mutual influence of a community in the individuals' reasoning.

1 An Overview of the Language

Assume there are three friends, Alice, Bob and Mary. Each wants to buy a bottle of wine as a present for a dinner. In order to decide how much to spend, each reasons about the price of his/her present relating it with the decisions of the other individuals. A possible situation is the following. Everyone, autonomously, decides to spend the maximum value between the amounts decided by the other two individuals. Assuming that a number of possible wines (with distinct prices) are available, any intuitive *equilibrium* answer to the above requirements is that all the individuals choose the same wine. Such an intended meaning is not captured by a traditional logic program obtained by putting together the requirements of all the individuals (directly encoded into logic rules). Indeed, it is easy to verify that a logic program with aggregates[1,2,3,4] like[1]:

$$r_1 : person(alice) \leftarrow \qquad r_2 : person(bob) \leftarrow \qquad r_3 : person(mary) \leftarrow$$
$$r_4 : wine(merlot, 25) \leftarrow \qquad r_5 : wine(cabernet, 30) \leftarrow$$
$$r_6 : \; spend(alice, X) \leftarrow wine(Z, X), \#\texttt{max}\{Y : spend(T, Y),$$
$$person(T), T \neq alice, wine(K, Y)\} = X$$
$$r_7 : \quad spend(bob, X) \leftarrow wine(Z, X), \#\texttt{max}\{Y : spend(T, Y),$$
$$person(T), T \neq bob, wine(K, Y)\} = X$$
$$r_8 : spend(mary, X) \leftarrow wine(Z, X), \#\texttt{max}\{Y : spend(T, Y),$$
$$person(T), T \neq mary, wine(K, Y)\} = X$$
$$r_9 : \qquad spent \leftarrow spend(X, Y), wine(Z, Y)$$
$$r_{10} : \qquad\qquad \leftarrow not \; spent$$

does not admit stable models (according to the semantics given in [2,3] and [4]). Indeed, the symmetrical requirements represented by rules r_6, r_7, r_8 are not able to support each

---

[*] This is an abridged version of the report "A Logic Language to Reason in a Social Modality", *TR Lab. Ing. Inf. 08/01*. The reader may download it in order to find all the technical issues not included here for space limitations (http://www.ai.unirc.it/tr0801.pdf).

[1] We are using here the syntax of [2,3].

M. Garcia de la Banda and E. Pontelli (Eds.): ICLP 2008, LNCS 5366, pp. 718–723, 2008.
© Springer-Verlag Berlin Heidelberg 2008

other, due to the minimality satisfied by stable model semantics. As a consequence the program is not able to produce decisions about the amount to spend, and, then, the integrity constraint r_{10} is not satisfied.

The purpose of this paper is to introduce a language with *social features* allowing us to represent the reasoning of each individual as a distinct logic program, possibly embedding rules that encode the dependency of an individual's conclusion on the conclusions of other individuals (as it typically happens in a community), also by inferring quantities obtained as aggregates computed over the community of individuals. We call this language *Logic Programming with Social Assumptions* ($\mathcal{LP}^{\mathcal{SA}}$, for short). Due to space limitations, we present the language only by example. The reader may find all the technical features in the full report (http://www.ai.unirc.it/tr0801.pdf). Therein, the formal semantics of our language, that extends stable model semantics to social collections of programs can be found. Moreover, we give a polynomial translation to stable model semantics showing that the semantics of a $\mathcal{LP}^{\mathcal{SA}}$ collection can be computed by determining the stable models of a logic program with aggregates.

Let us come back to the informal presentation of our language. Observe that the above situation can be encoded into $\mathcal{LP}^{\mathcal{SA}}$, by writing three programs (labelled with **Alice**, **Bob**, and **Mary**, resp.) each consisting of the following rules:

$$
\begin{aligned}
&r_1 : wine(merlot, 25) \leftarrow && r_2 : wine(cabernet, 30) \leftarrow \\
&r_3 : && spend(X) \leftarrow wine(Z, X), \#\texttt{Smax}\{Y : spend(T, Y), wine(K, Y)\} = X \\
&r_4 : && spent \leftarrow spend(X), wine(Z, X) \\
&r_5 : && \leftarrow not\ spent
\end{aligned}
$$

We thus obtain a collection of programs (each associated with an individual of the community), each allowing the direct encoding of the interdependent individual's requirements. #Smax is a *social aggregate operator*, where the adjective *social* means that its action involves only individuals different from the one where it is used. In particular, considering the program **Alice**, the informal meaning of the term $\#\texttt{Smax}\{Y : spend(T, Y), wine(K, Y))\} = X$ appearing in rule r_3 (that, accordingly is said *social rule*) is that the variable X (representing how much Alice would like to spend) is equal to the maximum between the amounts spent by Bob and Mary (i.e., the social aggregate is *computed* over all the other individuals). The nice feature of $\mathcal{LP}^{\mathcal{SA}}$ programs is that under their semantics the interdependent individuals' requirements result in a sort of guessing of agreed conclusions, that autonomously each individual cannot derive. The stability condition that in traditional programs (with negation) selects those models that can be re-generated by assuming false all external atoms, here operates by assuming true social conditions and by guaranteeing that this assumption allows us to re-generate the intended model. For example, according to the semantics of $\mathcal{LP}^{\mathcal{SA}}$ programs, the $\mathcal{LP}^{\mathcal{SA}}$ collection described above has two intended models, one including (beside the list of available wines) the atoms $spend_{Alice}(30)$, $spend_{Bob}(30)$, $spend_{Mary}(30)$, the other (beside the list of available wines) the atoms $spend_{Alice}(25)$, $spend_{Bob}(25)$, $spend_{Mary}(25)$. Indeed, any other instantiation of the predicate $spend$ cannot allow to derive itself through the rules r_3 of the three individuals. We observe that the above intended models reflect just the intuitive semantics we expect under a *social perspective*, where a given behavior of a community even though supported by the community itself is unfounded if interpreted as the behavior of a single individual.

As another example of mutual influence of a community in the individuals' reasoning, consider the case of the formation of voting coalitions (like the election of the president of a committee). Typically a single individual does not decide autonomously to vote a given candidate, but it might happen that this decision depends on the decisions of other people. Even the formation of a coalition of two electors (say Frank and Brenda) in favor of a candidate (say John) fails when encoded in logic programming (under stable model semantics) by the following program:

$$r_1 : vote(frank, john) \leftarrow vote(brenda, john)$$
$$r_2 : vote(brenda, john) \leftarrow vote(frank, john)$$

since no model for the program different from $\emptyset$ is stable. Again, a $\mathcal{LP}^{\mathcal{SA}}$ collection of two simple programs (labelled with **Frank** and **Brenda**, resp.):

Frank – $r_1 : vote(john) \leftarrow [\textbf{Brenda}]\{vote(john)\}$
Brenda – $r_2 : vote(john) \leftarrow [\textbf{Frank}]\{vote(john)\}$

has two intended models, that are $\emptyset$ and $\{vote_{Frank}(john), vote_{Brenda}(john)\}$, representing all the possible behaviors of the community. The term $[\textbf{Brenda}]\{vote(john)\}$ (as well as the term $[\textbf{Frank}]\{vote(john)\}$) is a *social condition* (with intuitive meaning of the syntax) applied to an individual different from that where it is used. We highlight that our semantics is not in contrast with the prevalent literature in logic programming affirming that the minimality requirement (and thus the absence of unfoundness) must be satisfied by any plausible semantics for logic programs. Indeed, whenever our programs do not include social rules, the semantics of the collection is the trivial combination of the stable models of each program, thus preserving the minimality in the standard (non-social) case (in the trivial case of a singleton social-rule-free $\mathcal{LP}^{\mathcal{SA}}$ collection our semantics coincides with stable model semantics).

In order to prevent a wrong interpretation of our semantics, we highlight that a standard logic rule, like $a \leftarrow b$ in a social program P cannot be viewed as a particular case of a social rule $a \leftarrow [P]\{b\}$ (i.e. a social rule with a *self-reference*). Indeed the semantics operates differently on those predicates that are included in the body of social rules, relaxing only for them the minimality condition given by stable model semantics. In particular the semantics enables a "guessing" mechanism that allows us to apply a sort of circumscription over all predicates (as traditional Stable Model Semantics) but those appearing in the body of social rules, where the minimality is relaxed, in such a way that those models that are mutually supported by the community are generated. In words, social rules enable derivation through "mutual influence", thus reflecting the behavior of a community supported by the community itself even though unfounded if interpreted as the behavior of a single individual. Thus, it is not correct (according to our semantics) to view a standard logic rule as a particular case of a social logic rule, i.e., a social rule with self-reference. Technically, self-reference is forbidden, since semantically self-influence is meaningless. A related approach is [5], introducing the notion of *equilibrium* for *contexts*, i.e. knowledge bases linked by *bridge rules* (similar to social conditions, but allowing self-reference). An equilibrium is a set of elements (from each context) supported by the context they belong and by some other context trough applicable bridge rules. The closest work to this proposal is [6], wherein a language ($SOLP$ - Social Logic Programming) for representing social requirements has been proposed. In $SOLP$, a program is a collection of logic programs, but the semantics is different from that here presented, since in [6] it allows a more liberal guessing of unfounded conclusions, even not related to social rules. From this point of view, $SOLP$ inherits such a feature from a previous language describing compromises between logic programs [7]. Indeed, $SOLP$ incorporates the possibility for an individual to specify *tolerance rules*, that are rules expressing a *desire*, instead of a *requirement*, and bases its semantics on a fixpoint-based semantics instead of stable model semantics. As a consequence, unlike $\mathcal{LP}^{SA}$, the semantics of a singleton social-rule-free $SOLP$ collection does not coincide with stable model semantics (thus it is not true, as it is for $\mathcal{LP}^{SA}$, that $SOLP$ extends stable model semantics with features enabled by social constructs). The other main difference between the language here presented and $SOLP$ is due to the presence in $\mathcal{LP}^{SA}$ of social aggregate operators, that provide the language with the capability of representing in a natural way a number of social-like situations, where costs, distances, numerousness, and other measures related to the community are used to influence the behavior of each individual (consider for example problems of coalition formation in electronic markets – an example of this setting is included below). It is worth noting that, even though it might appear that our aggregates have a *non-stratified* behaviour (in the sense of the definition given in [8,9] – even though, formally, this definition is not applicable to our language), we show that no semantic complications arise from non-stratification (i.e. aggregates involved into recursion) since our semantics is defined on the basis of stable models of traditional logic programs with no aggregates. A more complete contextualization of our work in the literature can be found in the full report. Finally, we give an example showing how social aggregates and social conditions can be used for naturally representing an interesting real-world application.

Coalition Formation. Consider a market with n vendors and m customers. Each vendor sells items in lots of different sizes in such a way that the bigger is a lot, the bigger is the discount. Each customer requires a number of items and specifies the maximum price per item. Let I be the total number of items (of the same type) requested by all the customers and A be the maximum amount they offer for the items. Customers cooperate by forming coalitions for the same item in such a way that one vendor is chosen that sells (i) a number $k \geq I$ of items at the minimum price p w.r.t. other vendors provided that (ii) $p \leq A$. Finally, (iii) *unfair* combinations of customer bids, that is combinations such that a customer sets a maximum unit price that is two times lower than the price set by another one, are forbidden. This scenario is represented by $n + m$ $\mathcal{LP}^{SA}$ programs. The following rules encode a vendor (for instance vendor #1):

$$r_1 : vendor\_name(1) \leftarrow \qquad r_2 : lot(a, 10, 100) \leftarrow \qquad r_3 : lot(a, 100, 900) \leftarrow$$

The j-th program (representing vendor #j) $(1 \leq j \leq n)$ contains a fact $vendor\_name(j)$, identifying the vendor. Vendor #1 sells a lot of 10 items a at 100\$ (rule r_2) and a lot of 100 at 900\$, (rule r_3). Likewise, the other vendors can specify different amounts and prices for items to be sold. A typical customer bid for a is modelled as follows:

$r_4 : bid(a, 36, 4) \leftarrow$
$r_5 : \quad in(a, V) \leftarrow bid(a, J, C), *(J, C, T), \#\texttt{Ssum}\{X : in(a, V), bid(a, X, \_)\} = N,$
$\qquad + (N, J, I), [1,]\{vendor\_name(V), lot(a, K, M)\}, K >= I,$
$\qquad \#\texttt{Smin}\{P : lot(a, K, P)\} = M, M <= A, +(T, B, A),$
$\qquad \#\texttt{Ssum}\{Y : in(a, V), bid(a, X, F), *(X, F, Y)\} = B$
$r_6 : \leftarrow in(a, V1), in(a, V2), V1 <> V2$
$r_7 : \leftarrow in(a, V), bid(a, J, C), [1,]\{in(a, V), bid(a, I, G)\}, *(2, G, H), C >= H$

The predicate $bid(X, Y, Z)$ (rule r_4) means that the customer wants to buy Y items of kind X, each at a price not greater than Z. The coalition formation mechanism is encoded by the rule r_5. First, let us explain the meaning of the variables used. J (resp. N) is the number of items requested by the customer (resp. by all the other customers) and T (resp. B) is the total maximum amount of money offered by him (resp. by them). Both N and B are computed by social aggregate operators computing sums over the customers. Finally, I (the total number of items a requested by all the customers) and A (the maximum amount of money the customers offer for I items) are computed as $J + N$ and $T + B$, resp. Now, we can explain the meaning of rule r_5. The customer will join the coalition buying item a from vendor #V (represented by $in(a, V)$) if he sells a lot having *admissible* size K (i.e., $K \geq I$, see requir.(i)) and such that the corresponding price M both is not greater than A (see requir. (ii)) and is minimum among the prices of lots (of admissible size) offered by other vendors. Note that the social condition $[1,]\{vendor\_name(V), lot(a, K, M)\}$ occurs in r_5. Indeed, besides specifying requirements on single individuals (as shown in the voting example), social conditions may be of the form $[l, h]\{Conj\}$ requiring groups (with cardinality bounds l and h) of individuals to satisfy the conjunction $Conj^2$. In detail, the social condition occurring in r_5 requires that at least one individual[3] satisfies the above conjunction in curly brackets. M is computed by the social aggregate operator #$\texttt{Smin}$. Moreover, if different vendors offer lots (of admissible size) of the same item at the same minimum price, then the customer chooses only one of them (rule r_6). Finally, in rule r_7, the social condition $[1,]\{in(a, V), bid(a, I, G)\}$ is used to drop unfair combinations of bids (requir. (iii)).

References

1. Son, T.C., Pontelli, E.: A Constructive Semantic Characterization of Aggregates in Answer Set Programming. TPLP 7(3), 355–375 (2007)
2. Faber, W., Leone, N., Pfeifer, G.: Recursive Aggregates in Disjunctive Logic Programs: Semantics and Complexity. In: Alferes, J.J., Leite, J. (eds.) JELIA 2004. LNCS, vol. 3229, pp. 200–212. Springer, Heidelberg (2004)
3. Calimeri, F., Faber, W., Leone, N., Perri, S.: Declarative and Computational Properties of Logic Programs with Aggregates. In: Kaelbling, L.P., Saffiotti, A. (eds.) IJCAI, pp. 406–411. Professional Book Center (2005)
4. Ferraris, P., Lifschitz, V.: Weight Constraints as Nested Expressions. TPLP 5(1-2) (2005)
5. Brewka, G., Eiter, T.: Equilibria in Heterogeneous Nonmonotonic Multi-Context Systems. In: AAAI, pp. 385–390. AAAI Press, Menlo Park (2007)

---

2 Social conditions can also be nested in order to declare requirements over sub-groups of individuals, if a super-group satisfying a social condition exists.

3 Since $l = 1$ and h is assumed by default as the total number of individuals in the community.

6. Buccafurri, F., Caminiti, G.: Logic Programming with Social Features. TPLP (to appear)
7. Buccafurri, F., Gottlob, G.: Multiagent Compromises, Joint Fixpoints, and Stable Models. In: Kakas, A.C., Sadri, F. (eds.) Computational Logic: Logic Programming and Beyond. LNCS, vol. 2407. Springer, Heidelberg (2002)
8. Dell'Armi, T., Faber, W., Ielpa, G., Leone, N., Pfeifer, G.: Aggregate Functions in Disjunctive Logic Programming: Semantics, Complexity, and Implementation in DLV. In: IJCAI 2003, Proc. of the 18th Int. Joint Conf. on Artificial Intelligence, pp. 847–852 (2003)
9. Faber, W., Pfeifer, G., Leone, N., Dell'Armi, T., Ielpa, G.: Design and Implementation of Aggregate Functions in the DLV System. CoRR abs/0802.3137 (2008)

ASPVɪᴢ: Declarative Visualisation and Animation Using Answer Set Programming

Owen Cliffe, Marina De Vos, Martin Brain, and Julian Padget

Department of Computer Science,
University of Bath,
United Kingdom
{occ,mdv,mjb,jap}@cs.bath.ac.uk

Abstract. Answer set programming provides a powerful platform for model-based reasoning problems. The answer sets are solutions, but for many non-trivial problems post-processing is often necessary for human readability. In this paper we describe a method and a tool for visualising answer sets in which we exploit answer set programming itself to define how visualisations are constructed. An exciting potential application of our method is to assist in the debugging of answer set programs that, as a consequence of their declarative nature, are not amenable to traditional approaches: visual rendering of answer sets offers a way to help programmers spot false and missing solutions.

1 Introduction

Answer Set Programming (ASP) is a methodology for solving NP and NP-complete problems by representing the problem as a logic program under answer set semantics, such that the answer sets correspond to the solutions of the problem. Although the answer sets represent the solutions of the problem encoded by the program, they only consist of sets of atoms that are true (rendering the missing ones false). To understand these answer sets, one must interpret them in the context of the problem domain, which for simple cases can be done relatively easily (by inspection) but, for any non-trivial problem/domain answer set size is typically large and some post-processing is needed. In addition, post-processing often plays an important role in verifying and debugging answer set programs. There is a large body of literature relating to ASP, for in-depth coverage including commonly used syntax see [1].

In this paper, we introduce ASPVɪᴢ, a tool that enables end-users and ASP programmers to visualise answer sets using the declarative nature of ASP itself to produce graphical representations of solutions. Visualisation of a given domain is achieved by the construction of a small answer set program that defines how elements of the problem solution should be displayed.

2 Declarative Visualisation with ASP

ASPVɪᴢ: is a Java program that constructs two-dimensional images from the answer sets of a given program. The tool takes an answer set program Π, representing

M. Garcia de la Banda and E. Pontelli (Eds.): ICLP 2008, LNCS 5366, pp. 724–728, 2008.

a given problem and a *visualisation program* Π_v which elaborates on the conclusions drawn by the program Π concluding the necessary literals to render a graphic. Visualisation programs conclude atoms in the language $\mathcal{L}_{viz}$, whereof the atoms have the following types: (i) Those defining scene-control properties, such as the display extents, scene-wide transformations and animation orderings (see below), (ii) Those defining colours, brushes (line and fill properties), sprites (2D bitmapped graphics) and text properties which may be referenced in drawing atoms; e.g. the atoms: `brush(thick). brush_color(thick,rgb(0,0,0)). brush_width(thick,3).` define a black line brush called `thick` which is three units thick, (iii) Primitive drawing atoms that relate to the rendering of graphical artifacts including lines, (filled) polygons, ellipses, curves, sprites, and text. Each of these predicates includes the relevant points (as terms) to position the corresponding artifact and drawing properties (brush, font, colour) required to render it; e.g. the atom `draw_line(thick,` `p(0,0),p(1,4))` would draw a line connecting the points $(0,0)$ and $(1,4)$ using the defined brush `thick`.

ASPVIZ supports two visualisation modes: one frame, or multiple frames, per answer set. In the first case a visualisation program Π_v is constructed such that it contains no negative-order cycles and is *stratified* below Π (i.e. Π_v is deterministic w.r.t. Π). The program $\Pi_v + \Pi$ is solved to give zero or more answer sets, each corresponding to an answer set of the original program Π extended with visualisation atoms in $\mathcal{L}_{viz}$ concluded by Π_v. For each of these answer sets ASPVIZ extracts the atoms in $\mathcal{L}_{viz}$ and produces a graphic using a Java-native graphics toolkit (SWT) as follows: (i) Canvas extents and transformation are set using the defined properties—or default values where none are specified, (ii) Native objects (in SWT) are constructed corresponding to the defined colours, brushes, fonts and sprites, (iii) Each of the graphical primitives is rendered using the corresponding native drawing functions to produce a graphic. A full description of language used, detailed examples and software are available from `http://www.cs.bath.ac.uk/~occ/aspviz/`.

In addition to rendering answer sets of a program individually, the same approach may be used to create animations and multi-framed image visualisations based on individual answer sets. In this case the negative cycle restriction on Π_v is relaxed yielding a program which may itself have multiple answer sets (a typical example might be a program which extracts each step of a plan as a frame). For each answer set of Π a corresponding ground program Π_i is produced consisting of the atoms of that answer set. $\Pi_v + \Pi_i$ is then solved yielding zero or more answer sets, each consisting of a partial rendering of the original answer set of Π. These frames are rendered as before. In order to produce animations, frames must be ordered: this is achieved by the inclusion of a unique atom `frame(T)` in the conclusions of Π_v, where `T` is a term. Animations are produced by parsing all produced answer sets of $\Pi_v + \Pi_i$ and then ordering the sets by the value of `T`. The value of `T` is typically an integer and may be determined directly from some value in Π (e.g. the largest time step value in the case of of a planning problem), or may be derived from aggregates or weight values (where supported by the underlying ASP system) over atoms in a solution of Π.

Π:

```
position(1 .. 9).    value(1 .. 9).

% all initial cell positions are final positions
state(X,Y,N):-initial(X,Y.N).

% select at most one value for each cell
1 { state(X,Y,NU) : value(NU) } 1:- position(X;Y),value(NU) .

% no  numbers may appear twice on the same row or column
:- state(XA,Y,N), state(XB,Y,N), XA !=
XB,position(XA;XB;Y),value(N). :- state(X,YA,N), state(X,YB,N), YA
!= YB,position(YA;YB,X),value(N).

% no  numbers may appear twice in the same sub-square
sameSubSquare(NA,NB) :- A = (NA - 1) / 3, B = (NB - 1) / 3, A =
B,value(N;NA;NB) . :- state(XA,YA,N), state(XB,YB,N),
sameSubSquare(XA,XB), sameSubSquare(YA,YB),
    XA != XB, YA != YB,position(XA;XB;YA;YB),value(N).
```

Π_v:

```
% Define brushes and text styles
brush(light). brush_color(light,rgb(5,5,5)). brush_width(light,1).
brush(dark). brush_color(dark,black). brush_width(dark,2).
font(inferred). font_size(inferred,12). font(initial).
font_style(initial,bold). font_size(initial,12).

% Draw grid (use hard lines to separate sub-squares)
draw_rect(light,p((X-1)*30,(Y-1)*30),30,30) :- position(X;Y).
draw_rect(dark,p((X-1)*30,(Y-1)*30),90,90) :- position(X;Y),
    ((X-1) mod 3)==0, ((Y-1) mod 3)== 0.

% draw cells (initial and then inferred) using different fonts
draw_text(initial,c,c,p((PX - 1) * 30+15,(PY - 1) *30+15),V) :-
    initial(PX,PY,V), position(PX;PY;V).
draw_text(inferred,c,c,p((PX - 1) * 30 + 15,(PY - 1) *30 + 15),V)
:-
    state(PX,PY,V), not initial(PX,PY,V),position(PX;PY;V).
```

Fig. 1. Sudoku puzzle solver Π and its visualisation program Π_v

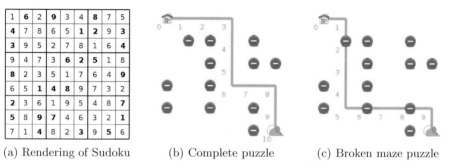

(a) Rendering of Sudoku   (b) Complete puzzle   (c) Broken maze puzzle

Fig. 2. Example output

Example 1 – Simple two dimensional rendering: Consider the program Π given in Figure 1 which produces solutions to Sudoku puzzles consisting of a 9×9 grid containing some initial numbers between 1 and 9 which must be filled such that no number appears twice in any row, column or 3×3 square of the puzzle. The program takes a problem description consisting of a set of atoms describing the initial grid square entries of the form initial(X,Y,N) and computes values for each cell of the form state(X,Y,N). The program Π_v in Figure 1 shows the visualisation program for the Sudoku puzzle, rendering a grid with sub-squares highlighted in a darker brush, and displaying inferred and initial (in bold) cells. Passing both the Sudoku program and its visualisation program to ASPVIZ results in the image in Figure 2(a).

Example 2 – Animated graphics: In some domains, it helps to see an animation of how a result is achieved. In this example Π solves a planning problem in which a mouse must navigate through a maze, avoiding obstacles on its way. Each answer set of Π represents a valid path through the maze. A visualisation program Π_v is constructed such that when it is combined with an answer set of Π (encoded as Π_i), the program $\Pi_v + \Pi_i$ produces multiple answer sets. Each of these answer sets encodes a single frame corresponding to a the movements of the mouse up to a given step of the underlying plan. The frames are ordered using `frame(X)` atoms which are defined using the time point that the frame represents (in the example time is encoded as an integer). These frames may be stepped through within the ASPVIZ tool. Figures 2(b) and 3 show the final state and sequential visualisations of a single solution to the maze puzzle respectively.

Debugging: Debugging is a major challenge in answer set programming—an overview of current work in this area can be found in [2,3]. A typical problem is that a syntactically correct program does not yield the desired answer sets. Current work focusses on adding debugging information to the program or inspecting the structure of the program by generating a support graph for selected parts of the program. Unfortunately, deciding which part is important and inspecting the vast amount of information coming from the program is a very challenging task. A detailed discussion is provided in [3].

Using a graphical representation tool like ASPVIZ one tackles the problem from a different angle. By visualising the outcomes of the program it immediately becomes easier for a designer to understand the nature of a given problem by representing the (faulty) answer sets inside the problem domain, offering a completely different perspective.

We appreciate that this approach to debugging will not always be successful, because only some programs have a natural graphical representation. In cases where it is applicable however, we believe that the approach can make problems easier to spot by showing visually the cases in which the code is not working.

Take for example the maze problem above. On one occasion we obtained the following answer set when encoding the scene above:

```
{move(0,e) move(5,e) move(6,e) move(7,e) move(8,e) move(1,n) move(2,n)
move(3,n) move(4,n) move(9,n) p(0,psn(0,0)) p(1,psn(1,0)) p(2,psn(1,1))
p(3,psn(1,2)) p(4,psn(1,3)) p(5,psn(1,4)) p(6,psn(2,4)) p(7,psn(3,4))
p(8,psn(4,4)) p(9,psn(5,4)) p(10,psn(5,5)) blocked(psn(1,1))
blocked(psn(2,1)) blocked(psn(4,1)) blocked(psn(2,2)) blocked(psn(4,2))
blocked(psn(5,2)) blocked(psn(0,3)) blocked(psn(2,3)) blocked(psn(0,4))
blocked(psn(2,4)) blocked(psn(4,4)) blocked(psn(4,5))}.
```

Is this a correct solution to the problem? The answer can be found in Figure 2(c).

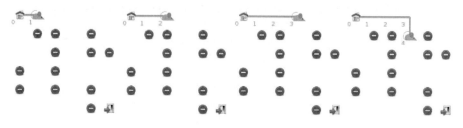

Fig. 3. Frame renderings for maze puzzle

3   Related and Future Work

As far as we know, very little has been published on general tools visualising answer sets. There are a few domain-specific tools, like A-circuit [4], a tool designed to reason about digital circuits. Declarative and constraint-based graphical systems are not new, for instance SWI-Prolog includes its own graphics system [5] and [6,7] address the problem of a user-interface layer using constraint-solvers and visualising the internal state of programs, respectively. Our approach differs in that we focus on re-using the underlying features of the language used to describe the problem itself (ASP), making visualisation more natural for programmers.

ASPViz is still in a very early development state and is limited to the rendering of two-dimensional graphics with Cartesian coordinates; by changing the underlying rendering mechanism the same approach may be trivially extended to render three dimensional scenes or produce input for other graphical systems such as automatic graph layout tools like Graphviz. It is also our intention to incorporate the tool into a broader ASP development environment.

References

1. Baral, C.: Knowledge Representation, Reasoning and Declarative Problem Solving, 1st edn. Cambridge University Press, Cambridge (2003)
2. Brain, M., Gebser, M., Pührer, J., Schaub, T., Tompits, H., Woltran, S.: Debugging ASP programs by means of ASP. In: Baral, C., Brewka, G., Schlipf, J. (eds.) LPNMR 2007. LNCS, vol. 4483, pp. 31–43. Springer, Heidelberg (2007)
3. Brain, M., De Vos, M.: Answer set programming – a domain in need of explanation. In: Exact 2008: International Workshop on Explanation-aware Computing (2008)
4. Balduccini, M., Gelfond, M., Nogueira, M.: A-prolog as a tool for declarative programming. In: Proceedings of the 12th International Conference on Software Engineering and Knowledge Engineering (SEKE 2000), pp. 63–72 (2000)
5. XPCE the SWI-Prolog native GUI library:
   http://www.swi-prolog.org/packages/xpce/
6. Szekely, P., Myers, B.: A user interface toolkit based on graphical objects and constraints. SIGPLAN Not. 23(11), pp. 36–45 (1988)
7. Carro, M., Hermenegildo, M.: Tools for constraint visualisation: The VI-FID/TRIFID tool. In: Deransart, P., Małuszyński, J. (eds.) DiSCiPl 1999. LNCS, vol. 1870, pp. 253–272. Springer, Heidelberg (2000)

Removing Redundancy from Answer Set Programs*

Tomi Janhunen

Department of Information and Computer Science
Helsinki University of Technology TKK
P.O.Box 5400, FI-02015, TKK, Finland
Tomi.Janhunen@tkk.fi

Abstract. In answer set programming, ground programs are used as intermediate representations of logic programs for which answer sets are computed. It is typical that such programs contain many redundant rules—increasing the length of the program unnecessarily. In this article, we address redundancy of rules in answer set programs, and in particular, in program modules that are used as components of programs. To this end, we provide an exact semantical characterization of redundancy and present a translation-based method for detecting redundant rules. A prototype implementation, the *modular optimizer* (MODOPT), has been developed in the context of the SMODELS system. In the experimental part, we study the effects of modular optimization on lengths and run times of programs.

1 Introduction

A typical system for *answer set programming* (ASP) is based on an architecture where a front-end of the system, often called a *grounder*, is responsible for *instantiating* variables and *pre-evaluating* certain expressions appearing in the logic program provided by the user. The outcome is a ground (effectively propositional) logic program which is then forwarded to the answer set *solver* for the actual computation of answer sets. It is common that the ground program involves a number of redundant rules, e.g., in the forms of *tautological*, *subsumed*, and *inactive* rules, which could be safely omitted without affecting answer sets. Such rules are partly due to the grounder which is unable to judge their applicability in advance. The original (non-ground) program may also contain sources of redundancy such as *symmetries* etc. Imagine, for instance, a simple rule "nogood $\leftarrow$ edge(x, y), red(x), red(y). " as part of a graph coloring condition. By substituting constants a and b for x and y, respectively, and vice versa we obtain a pair of ground rules each of which is likely to be redundant given the other. Last, but not least, the programmer may also write needless rules—even unintentionally.

The goal of this research is to develop methods for detecting redundant rules from answer set programs after grounding. Ground programs with millions of rules are becoming increasingly frequent because the demands of applications are interminable. To deal with program instances of this scale, we resort to the theory of modular ASP [1] as well as existing tools for the automated (de)composition of ground logic programs such

* This research is affiliated with the project "*Methods for Constructing and Solving Large Constraint Models*" funded by the Academy of Finland (research grant #122399).

M. Garcia de la Banda and E. Pontelli (Eds.): ICLP 2008, LNCS 5366, pp. 729–733, 2008.

as MODLIST and LPCAT in the ASPTOOLS collection.[1] A brief account of logic program modules and the stable model semantics is provided in Section 2.

On the other hand, the translation-based verification method [2] and its generalization for logic program modules [3] can be used to check whether a particular rule r in a ground logic program P is redundant, i.e., whether P and $P \setminus \{r\}$ have exactly the same answer sets. However, these methods do not exploit the fact that P and $P \setminus \{r\}$ differ only by r and they can be further optimized for the purpose of redundancy checking. In Section 3, we present a model-theoretic characterization of redundant rules and an improved method for detecting such rules. The idea is to translate a set of rules R and a rule $r \in R$ into two *redundancy-checking* programs $\mathrm{Tr}_{\mathrm{RC1}}(R \setminus \{r\}, r)$ and $\mathrm{Tr}_{\mathrm{RC2}}(R, r)$ so that r is redundant in R iff these translations have no stable models. Thus existing answer set solvers can be used to decide the redundancy of individual rules.

In Section 4, we describe the first implementation of the method, the *modular optimizer* for stable semantics (MODOPT), which performs redundancy checks on a rule-by-rule basis. For the sake of efficiency, subsequent checks use approximations of stable models based on *propagation* and *look-ahead* [4]. We use a number of benchmark programs to evaluate the effects of such a procedure. Section 5 concludes the paper.

2   Logic Program Modules in Brief

For the sake of simplicity, we concentrate on *normal logic programs*, or just *normal programs* for short, which form a common syntactic fragment of logic programs supported by answer set solvers. *Normal rules* are expressions of the form "$a \leftarrow b_1, \ldots, b_n, {\sim}c_1, \ldots, {\sim}c_m$." where ${\sim}$ denotes *default negation*. The idea is that the *head* a can be inferred if the *body* of the rule is satisfied, i.e., each b_i is inferable but none of c_j's. Since the order of literals is irrelevant, we also write $a \leftarrow B, {\sim}C$ for the rule using abbreviations B and C for the sets $\{b_1, \ldots, b_n\}$ and $\{c_1, \ldots, c_m\}$ involved.

We assume a Gaifman-Shapiro style module architecture for normal programs [1]. A program module Π is a quadruple $\langle R, I, O, H \rangle$ where R is a finite set of normal rules, and I, O, and H are pairwise disjoint *signatures* for *input*, *output*, and *hidden* atoms, respectively. It is essential that the head $a \in O \cup H$ for each rule $a \leftarrow B, {\sim}C$ of R. The atoms in $I \cup O$ are *visible* and hence accessible by other modules whereas the atoms in H formalize some auxiliary concepts of Π. The *stable model semantics* [5] is generalized for an arbitrary module $\Pi = \langle R, I, O, H \rangle$ as follows. The *reduct* of R with respect to an interpretation $M \subseteq I \cup O \cup H$ and I, denoted by $R^{M,I}$, contains $a \leftarrow (B \setminus I)$ iff there is a rule $a \leftarrow B, {\sim}C \in R$ such that $B \cap I \subseteq M$ and $C \cap M = \emptyset$.

Definition 1 ([1]). *An interpretation $M \subseteq I \cup O \cup H$ is a stable model of a module $\Pi = \langle R, I, O, H \rangle$, denoted by $M \in \mathrm{SM}(\Pi)$, iff $M \setminus I$ is the least model $\mathrm{LM}(R^{M,I})$.*

The *join* $\Pi_1 \sqcup \Pi_2$ is defined as $\langle R_1 \cup R_2, (I_1 \setminus O_2) \cup (I_2 \setminus O_1), O_1 \cup O_2, H_1 \cup H_2 \rangle$ if modules $\Pi_1 = \langle R_1, I_1, O_1, H_1 \rangle$ and $\Pi_2 = \langle R_2, I_2, O_2, H_2 \rangle$ respect each other's hidden atoms and no two atoms $a_1 \in O_1$ and $a_2 \in O_2$ become *positively* interdependent. By the *module theorem* from [1], we have $\mathrm{SM}(\Pi_1 \sqcup \Pi_2) = \mathrm{SM}(\Pi_1) \bowtie \mathrm{SM}(\Pi_2)$ where $\bowtie$ combines any *compatible* pair of interpretations $M_1 \in \mathrm{SM}(\Pi_1)$ and $M_2 \in \mathrm{SM}(\Pi_2)$.

---

[1] Currently available at http://www.tcs.hut.fi/Software/asptools/

3   Translation-Based Method for Redundancy Checking

Given Definition 1, any non-empty set of rules $R' \subseteq R$ is *redundant* in a module $\Pi = \langle R, I, O, H \rangle$ iff $\mathrm{SM}(\Pi) = \mathrm{SM}(\Pi_{R'})$ where $\Pi_{R'} = \langle R \setminus R', I, O, H \rangle$. Likewise, a rule r in a module Π is deemed redundant iff $R' = \{r\}$ is redundant in Π. As observed for *defaults* in [6], the members of a redundant set R' need not be redundant.

Example 1. Consider a module $\Pi = \langle R, \emptyset, \{a, b, c, d, e, f\}, \emptyset \rangle$ where $R = R_1 \cup R_2$ for

$R_1 = \{\, a \leftarrow {\sim}b, {\sim}d, {\sim}e, {\sim}f.\ \ b \leftarrow {\sim}c, {\sim}d, {\sim}e, {\sim}f.\ \ c \leftarrow {\sim}a, {\sim}d, {\sim}e, {\sim}f.\,\}$ and
$R_2 = \{\, d \leftarrow {\sim}e, {\sim}a, {\sim}b, {\sim}c.\ \ e \leftarrow {\sim}f, {\sim}a, {\sim}b, {\sim}c.\ \ f \leftarrow {\sim}d, {\sim}a, {\sim}b, {\sim}c.\,\}.$

By the symmetries present in Π, we have $\mathrm{SM}(\Pi) = \emptyset$ but $\mathrm{SM}(\Pi_{\{r\}}) \neq \emptyset$ for any $r \in R_1 \cup R_2$. But R_1 and R_2 are redundant in Π as $\mathrm{SM}(\Pi_{R_1}) = \mathrm{SM}(\Pi_{R_2}) = \emptyset$.   ∎

Theorem 1. *A set R' is redundant in a normal program module $\Pi = \langle R, I, O, H \rangle$ iff (i) $\forall M \in \mathrm{SM}(\Pi_{R'})$, $M \models R'$; and (ii) $\forall M \in \mathrm{SM}(\Pi)$, $\mathrm{LM}((R \setminus R')^{M,I}) \models R'^{M,I}$.*

Theorem 1 nicely encompasses two aspects of R' being redundant in a module Π. Firstly, any stable model M obtained without rules in R' must also satisfy R'. But this is not enough: the other rules of R must be able to compensate for R' in the construction of the least model $\mathrm{LM}(R^{M,I})$ in the context of each $M \in \mathrm{SM}(\Pi)$. For example, the first two rules of $R^* = \{a_1 \leftarrow a_2.\ a_2 \leftarrow a_3.\ a_1 \leftarrow a_3.\,\}$ compensate for the last in $\Pi^* = \langle R^*, \{a_3\}, \{a_1, a_2\}, \emptyset \rangle$. To develop a method for checking the redundancy of individual rules, we apply Theorem 1 to $R' = \{r\}$. Moreover, due to **coNP**-completeness, we concentrate on finding *counter-examples* to the conditions (i) and (ii) of Theorem 1.

Definition 2. *For a normal program module $\Pi = \langle R, I, O, H \rangle$ and a rule $r \in R$, define $\mathrm{Tr}_{\mathrm{RC1}}(\Pi, r) = \langle (R \setminus \{r\}) \cup \mathrm{Tr}_{\mathrm{F}}(r), I, O, H \cup \{b, f\} \rangle$ where b and f are new atoms and $\mathrm{Tr}_{\mathrm{F}}(a \leftarrow B, {\sim}C) = \{b \leftarrow B, {\sim}C.\ f \leftarrow {\sim}b, {\sim}f.\ f \leftarrow a, {\sim}f.\,\}.$*

The idea of the translation $\mathrm{Tr}_{\mathrm{RC1}}(\Pi, r)$ is that the rules of $R \setminus \{r\}$ capture a stable model M of $\Pi_{\{r\}}$ and, on top of that, the rules of $\mathrm{Tr}_{\mathrm{F}}(r)$ check that $M \not\models r$. To evaluate the second condition for $R' = \{r\}$, we capture the projection of the least model $\mathrm{LM}((R \setminus \{r\})^{M,I})$ on the *strongly connected component* $S(r) \subseteq O \cup H$ of the *positive dependency graph* of Π related to the head of r (see, e.g., [1] for details).

Definition 3. *For a normal program module $\Pi = \langle R, I, O, H \rangle$ and a rule $r \in R$, define $\mathrm{Tr}_{\mathrm{RC2}}(\Pi, r) = \langle R \cup \mathrm{Tr}_{\mathrm{NC}}(R, r, S(r)), I, O, H \cup S(r)^{\bullet} \cup \{b, f\} \rangle$ where $S(r)^{\bullet} \cup \{b, f\}$ is a set of new atoms based on $S(r)$ but renamed as $S(r)^{\bullet} = \{a^{\bullet} \mid a \in S(r)\}$.*
The part $\mathrm{Tr}_{\mathrm{NC}}(R, r, S(r))$ includes a rule $a^{\bullet} \leftarrow (B \cap S(r))^{\bullet} \cup (B \setminus S(r)), {\sim}C$ for each $a \leftarrow B, {\sim}C \in R \setminus \{r\}$ with $a \in S(r)$; and for $r = a \leftarrow B, {\sim}C$ itself, the set of rules $\{b \leftarrow (B \cap S(r))^{\bullet} \cup (B \setminus S(r)), {\sim}C.\ f \leftarrow {\sim}b, {\sim}f.\ f \leftarrow a^{\bullet}, {\sim}f.\,\}.$

For $r = a_1 \leftarrow a_3$ and Π^* given above, we have $S(r) = \{a_1\}$ so that $\mathrm{Tr}_{\mathrm{RC2}}(\Pi^*, r)$ has a set of rules $R^* \cup \{a_1^{\bullet} \leftarrow a_2.\ b \leftarrow a_3.\ f \leftarrow {\sim}b, {\sim}f.\ f \leftarrow a_1^{\bullet}, {\sim}f.\,\}$. As indicated by Theorem 2 below, the resulting method is correct and complete for individual rules but, for the sake of efficiency, incomplete approximations are employed in Section 4.

Theorem 2. *A rule $r \in R$ is redundant in a normal program module $\Pi = \langle R, I, O, H \rangle$ iff $\mathrm{SM}(\mathrm{Tr}_{\mathrm{RC1}}(\Pi, r)) = \emptyset$ and $\mathrm{SM}(\mathrm{Tr}_{\mathrm{RC2}}(\Pi, r)) = \emptyset$.*

Benchmark	Optimization				Solving (before/after)				
(satisfiable (s), or unsatisfiable (u))	$\|R\|$	$\|R'\|$	$\frac{\|R'\|}{\|R\|}$ (%)	t (s)	SMODELS 2.32 (s)	(s)	CLASP 1.0.5 (s)	(s)	$\equiv$ (s)
ephp-8 (u)	10 854	0	0	201	0.50	**0.49**	0.38	**0.35**	2.1
- non-modular	10 854	10 650	98	1 868	0.50	**0.01**	0.38	**0.00**	0.62
factoring-30 (s)	9 391	4	0	314	**2.7**	3.3	**4.0**	5.0	92
- non-modular	9 391	5 727	61	2 073	**2.7**	9.1	4.0	**3.0**	63
factoring-30 (u)	9 391	4	0	308	20	**20**	16	**16**	70
- non-modular	9 391	5 646	60	2 119	**20**	22	16	**10**	49
gryzzles-5 (s)	3 760	980	26	124	499	**357**	**0.066**	0.078	49
gryzzles-48 (s)	4 412	1 172	27	166	10 487	**9 937**	**0.14**	0.17	480
queens-15 (s)	11 050	5 180	47	1 430	0.35	**0.18**	0.040	**0.031**	0.97
qeq-12 (u)	11 277	3 608	32	420	357	**238**	70	**70**	163
qeq-13 (u)	14 381	4 628	32	732	2 278	**1 462**	563	**533**	1 281
schur-4-44 (s)	13 068	4 312	33	1 260	**38**	63	**0.27**	0.348	19
schur-4-45 (u)	13 635	4 498	33	1 334	**581**	598	8.1	**7.6**	19
15-puzzle-19 (s)	21 017	2 736	13	380	16	**12**	**0.53**	0.66	4.2
15-puzzle-20 (u)	22 076	2 880	13	400	0.14	**0.12**	0.055	**0.051**	0.37

4 Experiments

We have generalized the method from Section 3 for SMODELS programs [4]. A translator called REDR implements the respective translations $\text{Tr}_{\text{RC1}}(\cdot)$ and $\text{Tr}_{\text{RC2}}(\cdot)$ for SMODELS program modules. The *modular optimization* of an entire SMODELS program Π is coordinated by script MODOPT, distributed in the ASPTOOLS collection, which (i) splits Π into components $\Pi_1, \ldots, \Pi_n$ using MODLIST, (ii) checks every module Π_i and each rule of Π_i in turn for being redundant (using REDR and SMODELS) and hence removable, and (iii) links a complete program Π' out of the resulting set of optimized modules $\Pi'_1, \ldots, \Pi'_n$ using LPCAT. The implementation is incomplete for two reasons. First, redundancy of rules is inherently context-dependent and hence certain redundant rules might not be detected in a modular approach. Second, due to the **coNP**-completeness of redundancy checking, only consistency checks based on the *propagation* and *look-ahead* functions of the SMODELS engine [4] are performed.

To make experiments, we used a hardware with an Intel Core2 6320 1.86GHz CPU and 2GB of main memory. We took a number of benchmarks from the literature and the ASPARAGUS[2] collection; see the table above. For each instance, we report the number of rules, the number of rules found redundant, the respective *compression rate*, and optimization time in the first four columns. The results indicate substantial portions of redundant rules in ground programs in practise. Since MODOPT removed practically no rules from *ephp-8* and *factoring-30*, we also tried out *non-modular* optimization.

The second block provides average times, reported over 10 runs with random shuffling, to compute at most one stable model. In view of running times, the savings obtained are not so clear-cut and also negative effects are occasionally perceived. Finally, the last column reports the time needed to double-check the weak/ordinary equivalence of the original and optimized programs using LPEQ (v. 1.21) [2] and CLASP.

---

[2] Consult http://asparagus.cs.uni-potsdam.de/ for details.

5 Discussion and Conclusions

Few comments on related work follow. Eiter et al. [7] address the simplification of logic programs under *strong* and *uniform* equivalence. For normal programs, transformations TAUT, RED$^-$, NONMIN, CONTRA, and S-IMP preserve strong as well as *weak/ordinary* equivalence—a special case of *modular equivalence* $\equiv_m$ [1]. Since each of these transformations removes exactly one rule $r \in R$, they are all covered by Theorem 1 by setting $R' = \{r\}$. E.g., a *tautological* rule $a \leftarrow B, \sim C$ with $a \in B$ is always satisfied in the sense of Theorem 1 which enables far more profound simplifications. E.g., the last two rules of $\Pi = \langle \{a \leftarrow \sim b. \ b \leftarrow \sim a. \ c \leftarrow b, \sim c. \ \}, \emptyset, \{a, b, c\}, \emptyset \rangle$ are redundant and removable in the given order which is impossible under strong and uniform equivalence. As shown in [8], certain redundant rules can enable a more efficient splitting of the search space. The removal of such redundant rules is not desirable and we suggest to protect computationally relevant rules using approximations. Indeed, MODOPT leaves the redundant rules of the *pigeonhole* benchmark *ephp-8* [8] intact but they get removed under non-modular optimization in the presence of all other rules.

In conclusion, we address the redundancy of rules in answer set programs, and more precisely, in a modular setting where programs are built of components pertaining to a particular module interface. In contrast to syntactic criteria, a semantic characterization of redundancy is developed and a translation-based method for redundancy checking is proposed. The implementation enables redundancy checking using any SMODELS-compatible solver for computations. The current implementation is still a prototype and the time spent on optimization can be further improved. Nevertheless, as demonstrated by the experiments, it is already sufficient for studying the degree of redundancy in SMODELS programs as well as the effects of removing redundant rules on the performance of solvers. From a programmer's point of view, it can also be very informative to inspect which rules are removed in order to improve the original encoding.

References

1. Oikarinen, E., Janhunen, T.: Modular equivalence for normal logic programs. In: Proceedings of ECAI 2006, Riva del Garda, Italy, pp. 412–416. IOS Press, Amsterdam (2006)
2. Janhunen, T., Oikarinen, E.: Automated verification of weak equivalence within the SMODELS system. Theory and Practice of Logic Programming 7(6), 697–744 (2007)
3. Oikarinen, E., Janhunen, T.: A translation-based approach to the verification of modular equivalence. Journal of Logic and Computation (to appear, 2008); A preliminary version appears in Proceedings of ASP 2007, pp. 255–269 (2007)
4. Simons, P., Niemelä, I., Soininen, T.: Extending and implementing the stable model semantics. Artificial Intelligence 138(1-2), 181–234 (2002)
5. Gelfond, M., Lifschitz, V.: The stable model semantics for logic programming. In: Proceedings of ICLP 1988, Seattle, Washington, USA, pp. 1070–1080. MIT Press, Cambridge (1988)
6. Liberatore, P.: Redundancy in logic III: Non-monotonic reasoning. Artificial Intelligence 172(11), 1317–1359 (2008)
7. Eiter, T., Fink, M., Tompits, H., Woltran, S.: Simplifying logic programs under uniform and strong equivalence. In: Lifschitz, V., Niemelä, I. (eds.) LPNMR 2004. LNCS, vol. 2923, pp. 87–99. Springer, Heidelberg (2003)
8. Järvisalo, M., Oikarinen, E.: Extended ASP tableaux and rule redundancy in normal logic programs. In: Dahl, V., Niemelä, I. (eds.) ICLP 2007. LNCS, vol. 4670, pp. 134–148. Springer, Heidelberg (2007)

ASPARTIX: Implementing Argumentation Frameworks Using Answer-Set Programming*

Uwe Egly, Sarah Alice Gaggl, and Stefan Woltran

Institut für Informationssysteme, Technische Universität Wien,
Favoritenstraße 9–11, A–1040 Vienna, Austria

Abstract. The system ASPARTIX is a tool for computing acceptable extensions for a broad range of formalizations of Dung's argumentation framework and generalizations thereof. ASPARTIX relies on a fixed disjunctive datalog program which takes an instance of an argumentation framework as input, and uses the answer-set solver DLV for computing the type of extension specified by the user.

1 Motivation

The area of argumentation (see [1] for an excellent summary) has become one of the central issues in Artificial Intelligence (AI) within the last decade, providing a formal treatment for reasoning problems arising in a number of interesting applications fields, including Multi-Agent Systems and Law Research. In a nutshell, argumentation frameworks formalize statements together with a relation denoting rebuttals between them, such that the semantics gives an abstract handle to solve the inherent conflicts between statements by selecting admissible subsets of them. The reasoning underlying such argumentation frameworks turned out to be a very general principle capturing many other important formalisms from the areas of AI and Knowledge Representation (KR).

The increasing interest in argumentation led to numerous proposals for formalizations of argumentation. These approaches differ in many aspects. First, there are several ways how "admissibility" of a subset of statements can be defined; second, the notion of rebuttal has different meanings (or even additional relationships between statements are taken into account); finally, statements are augmented with priorities, such that the semantics yields those admissible sets which contain statements of higher priority.

Argumentation problems are in general intractable, thus developing dedicated algorithms for the different reasoning problems is non-trivial. Instead, a more promising approach is to use a reduction method, where the given problem is translated into another language, for which sophisticated systems already exist.

The system we present in this paper follows this approach and provides solutions for reasoning problems in different types of argumentation frameworks (AFs) by means of computing the answer sets of a datalog program. To be more specific, the system is capable to compute the most important types of extensions (i.e., admissible, preferred, stable, complete, and grounded) in Dung's original AF [2], the preference-based AF [3], the value-based AF [4], and the bipolar AF [5]. Hence our system can be used to

---

* This work was partially supported by the Austrian Science Fund (FWF) under project P20704.

M. Garcia de la Banda and E. Pontelli (Eds.): ICLP 2008, LNCS 5366, pp. 734–738, 2008.

compare different argumentation semantics in a profound and novel way, and thus can be used by researchers to compare the different semantics on concrete examples within a uniform setting. Our approach is to use a *fixed* logic program which is capable of computing the different forms of extension from a given framework which is given as input. Hence, the burden of efficient computation is delegated to systems which evaluates this logic program. Due to this simple architecture, our system is easily extendible and suitable for rapid prototyping.

To the best of our knowledge, so far no system is available which supports such a broad range of different semantics, although nowadays a number of implementations exists[1], including Dungine [6] a Java reasoner capable of reasoning with grounded and preferred extensions; an epistemic and practical reasoner which also supports preferred credulous semantics for practical arguments (see [7]); PARMENIDES, a system for e-democracy based on value-based AFs [8]; and CASAPI, a Prolog implementation that combines abstract and assumption-based argumentation [9].

The work which is closest related to ours is by Nieves *et al.* [10] who also suggest to use answer-set programming for computing extensions of argumentation frameworks. The most important difference is that in their work the program has to be re-computed for each new instance, while our system relies on a *single fixed* interpreter program which just requires the actual instance as an input database. Although there is no advantage of the interpreter approach from a theoretical point of view (as long as the reductions are polynomial-time computable), there are several practical ones. The interpreter is easier to understand, easier to debug, and easier to extend. We believe that our approach thus is more reliable and easier extendible to further formalisms. An evaluation of the practical efficiency of the approach is subject of ongoing work.

Our system makes use of the prominent answer-set solver DLV [11]. All necessary programs to run ASPARTIX and some illustrating examples are available at `http://www.kr.tuwien.ac.at/research/systems/argumentation/`

2   Background and System Specifics

The declarative programming paradigm of *Answer Set Programming* (ASP) [11,12] under the stable-models semantics [13] is nowadays recognized as well suited for modeling and solving problems which involve common sense reasoning, and has been fruitfully applied to a range of applications including data integration, configuration, or diagnosis using advanced ASP solvers [14] such as Smodels, DLV, GnT, Cmodels, Clasp, or ASSAT. The basic idea of ASP is to encode solutions to a problem into the intended models of a logic program, in a way such that the solutions are described in terms of rules and constraints instead of specifying a concrete algorithm which singles out the solutions. The problem encoding is then given to an ASP solver, which computes some or multiple answer set(s) of the program together with the input. The solutions of the problem can then be easily read off from the answer sets.

We will use ASP to compute several kinds of extensions in different argumentation frameworks. An *argumentation framework* AF is a pair (A, R) where A is a set of arguments and $R \subseteq A \times A$. The pair $(a, b) \in R$ means that a attacks b. A set $S \subseteq A$

---

[1] See also http://www.csc.liv.ac.uk/~azwyner/software.html for an overview.

of arguments attacks b, if b is attacked by some $a \in S$. An argument $a \in A$ is *defended* by $S \subseteq A$ iff for each $b \in A$, it holds that, if $(b, a) \in R$, then b is attacked by S. A set $S \subseteq A$ is said to be *conflict-free (in AF)*, if there are no $a, b \in S$, such that $(a, b) \in R$. A conflict-free set $S \subseteq A$ is *admissible* (for AF), iff each $a \in S$ is defended by S. A *preferred extension* of AF is a maximal (w.r.t. set inclusion) admissible set of AF.

As an example of a generalization, we give the definitions for value-based argumentation frameworks (VAFs). VAFs are given by tuples $(A, R, V, val, valpref)$, where A and R are as for a standard argumentation framework, V is a non-empty set of values, val assigns to each $a \in A$ an element of V, and $valpref \subseteq V \times V$ is a preference relation (transitive, irreflexive and asymmetric). An argument $a \in A$ attacks or *defeats* an argument $b \in A$ iff both $(a, b) \in R$ and $(val(b), val(a)) \notin valpref$. Using this new notion of an attack provides the definitions of conflict-free sets, and admissible and preferred extensions for VAFs in the same way as for the basic framework.

Computing extensions of argumentation frameworks is quite straight forward within the ASP paradigm. First we guess candidates for extensions (i.e., subsets of arguments) and then rule out via constraints those candidates which do not match the particular requirements of the extension (for instance, constraints can easily eliminate those candidates which are not conflict-free). Typical language extensions in ASP are helpful for different problems. For instance, a suitable use of disjunction in rule heads allow us to formalize how to compute preferred extensions (which are known to be computationally more involved).

The architecture of the system ASPARTIX is as follows: We have a single ASP program which provides all necessary rules to compute extensions of the different argumentation formalisms. The task of the user is just to set up the input database which contains (i) the instance of the argumentation frameworks (ii) the type of extension ASPARTIX should compute. Then, invoking DLV with this input facts together with the ASPARTIX-program provides answer sets which are in a one-to-one correspondence with the specified extensions of the given framework. Technical details of the encoding are provided in a companion paper [15].

3   Applying ASPARTIX

The example we will consider to demonstrate our system is adapted from [16] and describes the case "Popov v. Hayashi" as decided by the honorable Kevin McCarthy in 2002. The case concerned the possession of the baseball which Barry Bonds hit for his record breaking 73rd home run in the 2001 season. When the ball was struck into the crowd, Popov caught it in the upper part of the webbing of his baseball glove. But Popov was not given the chance to complete his catch since, as it entered his glove, he was tackled and thrown to the ground by others trying to secure the ball, which became dislodged from his glove. Hayashi (himself innocent of the attack on Popov), then picked up the ball and put it in his pocket, so securing possession.

After the examination of all testimonies and videotapes neither Popov nor Hayashi were able to establish possession to the baseball. But McCarthy had to make a decision which is fair to both parties. Therefore he considered the following arguments on which he also assigned different values:

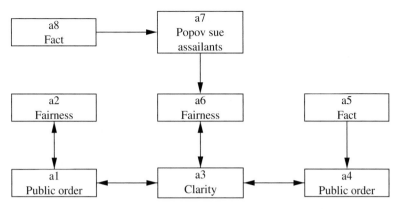

Fig. 1. Value-based Argument Graph for Popov v. Hayashi

1. Where interruption of completing the catch so establishing possession was illegal; decide for Popov; to prevent assault being rewarded; promoting the value of public order.
2. Where it has not been shown that Hayashi did not have possession and did nothing wrong; do not decide for Popov; which would punish Hayashi; demoting the value of fairness.
3. Where Hayashi had unequivocal control of the baseball; decide for Hayashi; to provide a bright line; promoting clarity of law.
4. Where interruption of completing the catch so establishing possession was illegal; do not insist on unequivocal control; which would reward assault; demoting the value of public order.
5. Since Hayashi was not an assailant, finding for Hayashi would not reward assault.
6. Where it has not been shown that Popov did not have possession and did nothing wrong; do not decide for Hayashi; which would punish Popov; demoting the value of fairness.
7. Where interruption of completing the catch so establishing possession was illegal; Popov should sue the assailants of the assault; which would not punish Popov; promoting the value of fairness.
8. Since assailants cannot be identified, suing those responsible for the assault is not a viable action.

Figure 1 shows arguments 1–8 from above together with the attack relation inbetween them (see [16] for details). The input file input.dl for this example (formulated as a simple framework without values) would contain the following facts:

```
prefex. arg(a1). arg(a2). ... arg(a8).
attacks(a1,a2). attacks(a1,a3). attacks(a2,a1). attacks(a3,a1).
attacks(a3,a4). attacks(a3,a6). attacks(a4,a3). attacks(a5,a4).
attacks(a6,a3). attacks(a7,a6). attacks(a8,a7).
```

The fact prefex specifies that the *preferred* extensions should be computed. Executing ASPARTIX thus consists of one call to DLV using input.dl and our program aspartix.dl, using filter options of DLV as follows:

```
./DLV input.dl aspartix.dl -filter=in,input_error
```

which produces the following output representing the preferred extensions

{in(a2),in(a3),in(a5),in(a8)}, {in(a2),in(a5),in(a6),in(a8)},
{in(a1),in(a5),in(a6),in(a8)}.

Hence, one still does not get a clear answer unless the framework is accordingly extended to a VAF. We add the following facts to our input file.

val(a1,public_order). val(a2,fairness). val(a3,clarity).
val(a4,public_order). val(a5,fact). val(a6,fairness).
val(a7,popov_sue_assailants). val(a8,fact).
vaf. valpref(fairness,public_order). valpref(fairness,clarity).
valpref(fairness,fact). valpref(fairness,popov_sue_assailants).

Here, predicate vaf tells ASPARTIX that the input is a VAF, predicate val specifies the values of the arguments, and predicate valpref defines a value ranking.

If we now invoke ASPARTIX as above with the now extended input file we receive as output a single answer set representing the preferred extension of the specified VAF, {a2,a5,a6,a8}. Since the result is that both a2 and a6 are contained in the preferred extension, McCarthy can decide neither for Popov nor for Hayashi. Therefore, he decided that the ball should be sold and the proceeds divided between the two.

References

1. Bench-Capon, T.J.M., Dunne, P.E.: Argumentation in artificial intelligence. Artif. Intell. 171, 619–641 (2007)
2. Dung, P.M.: On the acceptability of arguments and its fundamental role in nonmonotonic reasoning, logic programming and n-person games. Artif. Intell. 77, 321–358 (1995)
3. Amgoud, L., Cayrol, C.: A reasoning model based on the production of acceptable arguments. Ann. Math. Artif. Intell. 34, 197–215 (2002)
4. Bench-Capon, T.J.M.: Persuasion in practical argument using value-based argumentation frameworks. J. Log. Comput. 13, 429–448 (2003)
5. Amgoud, L., Cayrol, C., Lagasquie, M.C., Livet, P.: On bipolarity in argumentation frameworks. International Journal of Intelligent Systems 23, 1–32 (2008)
6. South, M., Vreeswijk, G., Fox, J.: Dungine: A java dung reasoner. In: Proceedings of COMMA 2008, pp. 360–368 (2008)
7. Visser, W.: (2008), http://www.wietskevisser.nl/research/epr/
8. Cartwright, D., Atkinson, K.: Political engagement through tools for argumentation. In: Proceedings of COMMA 2008, pp. 116–127 (2008)
9. Gaertner, D., Toni, F.: (2008), http://www.doc.ic.ac.uk/~dg00/casapi.html
10. Nieves, J.C., Osorio, M., Cortés, U.: Preferred extensions as stable models. Theory and Practice of Logic Programming 8, 527–543 (2008)
11. Leone, N., Pfeifer, G., Faber, W., Eiter, T., Gottlob, G., Perri, S., Scarcello, F.: The dlv system for knowledge representation and reasoning. ACM ToCL 7, 499–562 (2006)
12. Niemelä, I.: Logic programming with stable model semantics as a constraint programming paradigm. Ann. Math. Artif. Intell. 25, 241–273 (1999)
13. Gelfond, M., Lifschitz, V.: Classical negation in logic programs and disjunctive databases. New Generation Comput 9, 365–386 (1991)
14. Gebser, M., Liu, L., Namasivayam, G., Neumann, A., Schaub, T., Truszczyński, M.: The first answer set programming system competition. In: Baral, C., Brewka, G., Schlipf, J. (eds.) LPNMR 2007. LNCS, vol. 4483, pp. 3–17. Springer, Heidelberg (2007)
15. Egly, U., Gaggl, S.A., Woltran, S.: Answer-set programming encodings for argumentation frameworks. Technical Report DBAI-TR-2008-62, Technische Universität Wien (2008)
16. Wyner, A., Bench-Capon, T.J.M., Atkinson, K.: Arguments, values and baseballs: Representation of Popov v. Hayashi. In: Proceedings of JURIX 2007, pp. 151–160 (2007)

An Implementation of Extended P-Log Using XASP

Han The Anh, Carroline D.P. Kencana Ramli, and Carlos Viegas Damásio

CENTRIA, Departamento de Informática, Faculdade de Ciências e Tecnologia, Universidade
Nova de Lisboa, 2829-516 Caparica, Portugal
{h.anh,c.kencana}@fct.unl.pt, cd@di.fct.unl.pt

Abstract. We propose a new approach for implementing P-log using XASP, the
interface of XSB with Smodels. By using the tabling mechanism of XSB, our system is most of the times faster than P-log. In addition, our implementation has query
features not supported by P-log, as well as new set operations for domain definition.

1 Introduction

P-log is a declarative language based on a logic formalism for probabilistic reasoning
and action [1]. P-log uses Answer Set Programming (ASP) as its logical foundation
and causal Bayesian Networks as its probabilistic foundation. Although ASP has been
proven to be a useful paradigm for solving varieties of combinatorial problems, its non-
relevance property [2] makes the P-log system sometimes computationally redundant.
We explore a new approach for implementing P-log using XASP, the interface of XSB
with Smodels [3] - an answer set solver. With XASP, the relevance of the system is
maintained [4].

The paper is organized as follows. The next section provides a description of the
syntax and semantics of the system. Section 3 outlines the implementation, and Section
4 provides some results of benchmarks comparing P-log(ASP) and P-log(XSB) [1]. The
paper finishes with conclusions and directions for future work.

2 Extended P-Log

In this section, the syntax and semantics of extended P-log programs are defined, which
are compatible with the ones of the original P-log system [1]. The extended syntax has
constructs for declaring new sorts by union or intersection of other sorts. This syntactic
sugar enables a more declarative representation of many practical problems. In addition,
by using XASP, the logical part can use arbitrary XSB prolog code, thus, allowing for
the representation of more complex problems that are more difficult or even impossible
to express in the original P-log language. In general, a P-log program Π consists of
a sorted signature, declarations, a regular part, a set of random selection rules, a probabilistic information part, and a set of observations and actions [1]. In our extended
version, a union sort is represented by $c = union(c_1, ..., c_n)$ and an intersection sort
by $c = intersection(c_1, ..., c_n)$, where $c_i, 1 \leq i \leq n$ are declared sorts.

---

[1] We denote the original P-log implementation based on [1] by P-log(ASP) and our implementation by P-log(XSB).

M. Garcia de la Banda and E. Pontelli (Eds.): ICLP 2008, LNCS 5366, pp. 739–743, 2008.
© Springer-Verlag Berlin Heidelberg 2008

The semantics is given by an adapted program transformation from the original P-log program into a XASP program. It is defined in two stages. First, a mapping of the logical part of Π into its XASP counterpart $\tau(\Pi)$ is defined. The answer sets of $\tau(\Pi)$ will play the role of possible worlds of Π. Next the probabilistic part of $\tau(\Pi)$ will be used to define a measure over the possible worlds, and the probability of formulas. This part of the semantics is the same as in [1].

The logical part of a P-log program Π is translated into a XASP program $\tau(\Pi)$ in the following way:

1. **Sort declaration:**
   - for every sort declaration $c = \{x_1, .., x_n\}$ of Π, $\tau(\Pi)$ contains $c(x_i)$ for each $1 \le i \le n$.
   - for every sort declaration $c = \{L..U\}$ of Π, $\tau(\Pi)$ contains $c(i)$ where $L \le i \le U$, with integers $L \le U$.
   - for every sort declaration $c = \{h(L..U)\}$ of Π, $\tau(\Pi)$ contains $c(h(i))$ where $L \le i \le U$, with integers $L \le U$.
   - for every sort declaration $c = union(c_1, ..., c_n)$, $\tau(\Pi)$ contains the rules $c(X) : - c_i(X)$ for each $1 \le i \le n$.
   - for every sort declaration $c = intersection(c_1, ..., c_n)$, $\tau(\Pi)$ contains the rules $c(X) : - c_1(X), \ldots, c_n(X)$.

2. **Regular part:** For each attribute term $a(\bar{t})$, $\tau(\Pi)$ contains the rules:
   - $false : - a(\bar{t}, Y1),\ a(\bar{t}, Y2),\ Y1\backslash = Y2.$
     which is to guarantee that in each answer set $a(\bar{t})$ has at most one value.
   - $a(\bar{t}, y) : - do(a(\bar{t}, y)).$
     which is to guarantee that the atoms which are made true by a deliberate action are indeed true.

3. **Random selection:**
   - For attribute a, $\tau(\Pi)$ contains the rule: $intervene(a(\bar{t})) : - do(a(\bar{t}, Y)).$
   - Each random selection rule
     $random(RndName, a(\bar{t}), DynRange) : - B.$
     is translated into:
     - $a(\bar{t}, Y) : - tnot(intervene(a(\bar{t}))),\ tnot(neg\_a(\bar{t}, Y)),\ B.$
     - $neg\_a(\bar{t}, Y) : - tnot(intervene(a(\bar{t}))),\ tnot(a(\bar{t}, Y)),\ B.$
     - $atLeastOne(\bar{t}) : - a(\bar{t}, Y).$
     - $false : - tnot(atLeastOne(\bar{t})).$
     - $pd(RndName,\ a(\bar{t}, Y)) : - tnot(intervene(a(\bar{t}))),\ DynRange,\ B.$
     - if dynamic range $DynRange$ is not $full$, $\tau(\Pi)$ contains
       $false : - a(\bar{t}, Y),\ tnot(DynRange),\ B,\ tnot(intervene(a(\bar{t}))).$

4. **Observation and action:** $\tau(\Pi)$ contains actions and observations of Π.

5. For each literal l, $\tau(\Pi)$ contains the rule: $false : - obs(l),\ tnot(l).$

In the transformation the XSB default table negation operator $tnot/1$ is used. The rule with *false* in the head denotes an integrity constraint. In the transformation of the random selection part the predicate pd/3 is to define default probabilities. Notice that our semantics is equivalent to the semantics defined in [1] for the original P-log syntax. In fact, we reformulated the transformation from the original paper to adapt it to the XASP syntax. The rationale for the transformation can be found in [1].

3   Implementation of Extended P-Log System

Our system is comprised of two main modules: transformation and probabilistic information processing. The first module transforms the original P-log(XSB) code into an appropriate form for further computation by the second module. Both modules were developed on top of XSB Prolog [3].

The tabling mechanism [5] used by XSB not only provides significant decrease in time complexity of logic program evaluation, but also allows for extending Well-Founded Semantics (WFS) of XSB to other non-monotonic semantics. An example of this is the XASP interface which extends WFS with Smodels to compute stable models [6]. In XASP, only the relevant part to the query of the program is sent to Smodels for evaluation [2]. This allows us to maintain the relevance property for queries over programs, something that ASP does not comply to [4].

The transformation module maps the original P-log(XSB) program into a XASP program using five transformation steps described in Section 2. This program is then used as the input of the probabilistic processing module which will compute all the stable models with necessary information for dealing with the query. Only predicates for random attributes and probabilistic information, which have been coded by predicates pd/2 as the default probability and pa/3 as the assigned probability are kept in each stable model (extra explanation about pa/3 is provided in the next section).

Having obtained stable models with necessary information the system is ready to answer queries about probabilistic information coded inside the program. Besides queries in form of ASP formulas, our system was extended to be able to answer queries in the form of Prolog predicates which can be defined in a variety of ways. The code for defining the predicate can be included in the original P-log(XSB) program, in a separated XSB prolog program or even asserted into the system. The implementation of this new feature can be done easily with XASP, using the query as a filter for ruling out unsatisfied stable models.

4   Examples and System Evaluation

We describe some benchmark problems used to compare the performance of our implementation in XASP with the one of P-log(ASP). The first example is Dice problem taken from [1]. There are 2 dice, d1 and d2, belonging to Mike and John, respectively. Each dice has scores from 1 through 6, and will be rolled once. The dice owned by Mike is biased to 6 with probability $1/4$. This scenario can be coded with the following P-log(XSB) program Π_{dice}

```
1. score ={1..6}.
2. dice ={d1,d2}. owns(d1,mike). owns(d2,john).
3. roll : dice --> score.
4. random(r(D), roll(D), full) :- true.
5. pa(r(D), roll(D,6), d(1,4)) :- owns(D,mike).
```

Notice that the reserved predicate pa/3 represents assigned probability, e.g. line 5 expresses that if owns(D,mike) holds then the probability of rolling a 6 with dice D is $1/4$. The probabilistic information part of a P-log program consists of pa-rules, i.e.

the rules for defining assigned probability of attributes. Also notice that the probabilistic information part is kept unchanged through the transformation. For better understanding of the transformation described in Section 2, we provide here the resulting transformed program $\tau(\Pi_{dice})$ of Π_{dice}:

```
1. score(1). score(2). score(3). score(4). score(5). score(6).
2. dice(d1). dice(d2). owns(d1,mike). owns(d2,john).
3. false :- score(X),score(Y),dice(D),roll(D,X),roll(D,Y),X \= Y.
4. roll(D,X) :- dice(D), score(X), do(roll(D,X)).
5. intervene(roll(D)) :- dice(D), score(X), do(roll(D,X)).
6. roll(D,X) :- dice(D), score(X),
               tnot(intervene(roll(D))), tnot(neg_roll(D,X)).
7. neg_roll(D,X) :- dice(D), score(X),
               tnot(intervene(roll(D))), tnot(roll(D,X)).
8. atLeastOne(D) :- dice(D), score(X), roll(D,X).
9. false :- dice(D), tnot(atLeastOne(D)).
10.pd(r(D),roll(D,X)):-dice(D),score(X),tnot(intervene(roll(D,X))).
11.pa(r(D),roll(D,6),d(1,4)) :- owns(D,mike).
```

Lines 1-2 are the transformation of sorts declaration. Lines 3-4 are the resulting code of the transformation for the attribute `roll` (regular part). Lines 5-10 are the result of the transformation for the random selection part in line 4 of the original program Π_{dice}. Line 11 is the probabilistic information part that is kept unchanged from the original program (line 5 of Π_{dice}).

The second example is the Card problem taken from [7]. Suppose that there is one deck of cards, divided into spades, hearts, diamonds, and clubs. Each suit contains numbers and pictures. Numbers are from 1 to 10 and pictures are jack, queen and king. The corresponding P-log(XSB) program is as follows:

```
1. heart   = {h(1..10), h(jack), h(queen), h(king)}.
   spade   = {s(1..10), s(jack), s(queen), s(king)}.
   diamond = {d(1..10), d(jack), d(queen), d(king)}.
   club    = {c(1..10), c(jack), c(queen), c(king)}.
2. cards   = union(heart,spade,diamond,club).
3. number  = {1..5}.
4. draw : number --> cards.
5. random(r(N),draw(N),full):- true.
6. sameValue(X,Y) :- X =.. [_|V], Y =.. [_|V].
```

Declaration of attributes is defined in lines 1 – 4. Line 5 shows the fact that the distribution of each attribute $draw_i$ is random. In this example, the same card cannot be drawn twice. Line 6 captures the existence of a pair with the same value. Notice that in this example we use the built-in predicate of XSB (=..)/2 that is not supported by ASP. In general, the ability of using any XSB prolog code enables our system to be able to model more complicated problems. To model, for example, the rule for `sameValue/2` in line 6, in P-log(ASP) we must use a number of rules for grounding that rule.

We have tested our system using these two examples [2], with several instances, and for the first query our system is about 1.5 to 2 times slower than P-log(ASP). But from

---

[2] The examples, benchmarks and implementation are available at http://plog.xasp. googlepages.com/home

the second time on, P-log(XSB) is much faster, namely, from 8 to 150 times if the first time is not taken into account and from 3 to 5 times otherwise. Therefore, the more probabilistic information we need to extract from the knowledge base in the program, the more useful our system is. P-log(XSB) is more stable but both systems did not provide the answers to all cases. Although our system managed to compute the list of all stable models for problem $Cards\langle 5, 12 \rangle$, i.e. the Card problem with 5 drawn cards and 12 cards on the desk, it did not provide the answer in the period of 60 minutes (timeout) since the list of stable models was big (95040 stable models) and each with a large number of predicates (70); no answer was obtained with P-log(ASP).

5   Conclusions and Future Work

We have described our approach for reimplementing P-log in XASP. By comparing to P-log(ASP) using some benchmark problems, we have shown that although our system is slower than P-log(ASP) for the first query, in general, it is faster than P-log(ASP), namely, about 3 to 5 times for subsequent queries. In addition, we have extended P-log(ASP) with new features, first of all, to query the system with more expressive queries that are not supported by P-log(ASP). Furthermore, some set operations for domain definition equipped in our system are useful for representing practical problems.

However, the approach to probabilistic reasoning by deriving all possible worlds has to deal with a huge number of stable models. In any cases, we have to compute the unnormalized probability for each stable model. Since the computation can be done in parallel, the performance of the system would very much benefit from multicore CPU computers by using multi-threading, which is very efficient in XSB, from version 3.0 [3]. This approach will be explored in our next version. In the next version we also want to compare our system with another implementation of P-log developed by Gelfold and his students [8].

References

1. Baral, C., Gelfond, M., Rushton, N.: Probabilistic reasoning with answer sets. In: Lifschitz, V., Niemelä, I. (eds.) LPNMR 2004. LNCS, vol. 2923, pp. 21–33. Springer, Heidelberg (2003)
2. Castro, L., Swift, T., Warren, D.S.: Xasp: Answer set programming with xsb and smodels, http://xsb.sourceforge.net/packages/xasp.pdf
3. The xsb system version 3.0 volume 2: Libraries, interfaces and packages (2006)
4. Urgen Dix, J.: A classification theory of semantics of normal logic programs. Fundamenta Informaticae 22, 257–288 (1995)
5. Swift, T.: Tabling for non-monotonic programming. Annals of Mathematics and Artificial Intelligence 25(3-4), 201–240 (1999)
6. Niemelä, I., Simons, P.: Smodels - an implementation of the stable model and well-founded semantics for normal lp. In: Fuhrbach, U., Dix, J., Nerode, A. (eds.) LPNMR 1997. LNCS, vol. 1265, pp. 421–430. Springer, Heidelberg (1997)
7. Michael Shackleford, A.S.A.: Problem 62 solution - probabilities in poker (Last accessed June 10 2008), http://mathproblems.info/prob62s.htm
8. Gelfond, M., Rushton, N., Zhu, W.: Combining logical and probabilistic reasoning. In: AAAI Spring Symposium (2006)

Compiling and Executing Declarative Modeling Languages to Gecode

Raffaele Cipriano, Agostino Dovier, and Jacopo Mauro

Dipartimento di Matematica e Informatica
Università di Udine, via delle Scienze 208, 33100, Udine, Italy
(cipriano,dovier)@dimi.uniud.it

Abstract. We developed a compiler from SICStus Prolog CLP(FD) to Gecode and a compiler from MiniZinc to Gecode. We compared the running times of the executions of (standard) codes directly in the three languages and of the compiled codes for some classical problems. Performances of the compiled codes in Gecode improve those in the original languages and are comparable with running time of native Gecode code. This is a first step towards the definition of a unified declarative modeling tool for combinatorial problems.

1 Introduction

In the past decades a lot of techniques and solvers have been developed to cope with combinatorial problems (e.g., branch and bound/cut/price, constraint programming, local search) and several modeling languages have been proposed to easily model problems and interact with the solvers. In fact, it would be desirable to have both user-friendly modeling languages, that allows to define problems in an easy and flexible way, and efficient solvers, that cleverly explore the search space.

CLP(FD), Gecode, MiniZinc are recent modeling platforms, with different characteristics: Gecode has excellent performances, but is not as user-friendly as declarative approaches, like CLP(FD) or MiniZinc. We present a compiler from SICStus Prolog CLP(FD) to Gecode and a compiler from MiniZinc to Gecode. We have chosen a set of benchmarks, and compare their running times in the original paradigms (SICStus, MiniZinc, and Gecode) and in their Gecode translation. We also compare our results with the translation of MiniZinc into Gecode offered by MiniZinc developers.

The results are rather encouraging. Native code executions are typically faster in Gecode than in SICStus and MiniZinc. However, in all cases, compilation (and then execution) in Gecode improves the performance of the native execution, and, moreover, these times are comparable with running time of native Gecode code. This way, the user can model problems at high level keeping all the advantages of this programming style, without loosing efficiency w.r.t. C++ encoding. Moreover, our encoding of MiniZinc in Gecode outperforms the one presented in [1].

2 The Languages Used

We briefly introduce the languages CLP(FD) and MiniZinc, and the Gecode platform.

M. Garcia de la Banda and E. Pontelli (Eds.): ICLP 2008, LNCS 5366, pp. 744–748, 2008.

$CLP(\mathcal{D})$ is a declarative programming paradigm, first presented in 1986 (e.g., [2]). Combinatorial problems are usually encoded using constraints over *finite domains* ($\mathcal{D} = FD$), currently supported by all CLP systems based on Prolog. We focused on the library `clpfd` of SICStus Prolog [3], but what we have done can be repeated for the other CLP(FD) systems (e.g., ECLiPSe, GNU-Prolog, B-Prolog). We focus on the classical *constraint+generate* programming style. We report the fragment of the N-Queens problem where diagonal constraints are set.

```
1. safe( _,_,[]).
2. safe(X,D,[Q|Queens]) :-
3.    X + D #\= Q,  Q + D #\= X,  D1 is D + 1, safe(X,D1,Queens).
```

MiniZinc is a high-level modeling language developed by the NICTA research group [4]. It allows to express most CP problems easily, supporting sets, arrays, user defined predicates, some automatic coercions, and so on. But it is also low-level enough to be easily mapped onto existing solvers. FlatZinc [5] is a low-level solver-input language. The NICTA group provides a compiler from MiniZinc to FlatZinc that supports global constraints. The NICTA team also provide a solver that reads and executes a FlatZinc model. We report the diagonal constraints of the MiniZinc N-Queens model.

```
4. constraint
5.    forall (i in 1..n, j in i+1..n) (
6.      q[i] + i != q[j] + j /\ q[i] - i != q[j] - j; );
```

Gecode is an environment for developing constraint-based systems and applications [1]. It is implemented in C++ and offers competitive performance w.r.t. both runtime and memory usage. It implements a lot of data structures, constraints definitions and search strategies, allowing also the user to define his own ones. It is C++ like, and, thus, programmer should take care of several low-level details (there exists, however, a FlatZinc frontend). We report the extract of the N-Queens problem encoded in Gecode regarding diagonal constraints.

```
7. for (int i = 0; i<n; i++){
8.   for (int j = i+1; j<n; j++) {
9.     post(this, q[i]+i!=q[j]+j); post(this, q[i]-i!=q[j]-j);}}
```

3   Translation

The translation from SICStus and MiniZinc programs to Gecode is carried out in two stages: first we translate the high-level code into an intermediate language (CNT, defined ad-hoc) that lists explicitly all the constraints. Then we generate C++ code from CNT, using static analysis to improve the second part of the compilation.

CNT. The language CNT is used for listing the constraints and specifying some searching parameters and the output variables. It is very similar to FlatZinc, and in the next future we intend to use only FlatZinc instead of CNT. The complete CNT grammar is defined in the file `parser.y` [6]. An example of CNT code is the following:

```
10. domain [_1, _2, _3, _4], 1, 4;
11. all_different [_1, _2, _3, _4];
```

```
12. ((_1+1)!=_2); ((_2+1)!=_1); ((_1+2)!=_3); ((_3+2)!=_1);
13. ((_1+3)!=_4); ((_4+3)!=_1); ((_2+1)!=_3); ((_3+1)!=_2);
14. ((_2+2)!=_4); ((_4+2)!=_2); ((_3+1)!=_4); ((_4+1)!=_3);
```

CLP(FD) to CNT. For translating SICStus to CNT, we automatically create a new SICStus program where constraints definition is replaced by a printing stage. The execution of the modified SICStus code prints all the constraints in the CNT form, and thus generates CNT code. For instance, the code 15–18 is converted into code 19–22:

```
15. test(X,N):-           19. test(X,N) :-
16.   length(X,N),         20.   length(X,N),
17.   domain(X,1,N),       21.   format("domain ~q,~q,~q;\n",[X,1,N]),
18.   all_different(X).    22.   format("all_different ~q;\n",[X]).
```

Some problems arise when there is a unification. In fact, in some programs the logic variables are known to be FD-variables only at runtime and therefore every time in the program there is a unification we have to add some equality constraints. We developed some particular cases to cope with this and other minor technical problems.

For instance, the execution of the modified version of the SICStus N-Queens code with $N = 4$ generates the CNT code 10–14.

MiniZinc (FlatZinc) into CNT. We took advantage of the existing compiler from MiniZinc to FlatZinc [4] and thus focused on the translation from FlatZinc to CNT. Being these two languages rather similar in spirit, the translation is straightforward. For example, the FlatZinc constraints 23–25 can be defined into CNT code 26–28:

```
23. array[0 .. 2] of var 0 .. 2: v;
24. constraint int_eq(v[0], 0);
25. constraint all_different([v[0],v[1],v[2]]);
26. domain [_0,_1,_2], 0, 2;
27. (_0 == 0);
28. all_different [_0,_1,_2];
```

In principle, starting from MiniZinc one can exploit the existing "for" to obtain a more compact CNT code. Since we pass through FlatZinc, however, this information is lost. Prolog does not have "for" loops, and one could infer some of them through program analysis, but this is, in general, an undecidable problem. One solution (reasonable only from MiniZinc) could be to enrich CNT (or, better, FLatZinc) with a construct that keeps the "for" cycles information.

CNT into Gecode. We have developed a compiler from CNT to C++/Gecode. Before the compilation we perform some simplifying transformation on the CNT code (e.g., precomputation of numerical expressions). Moreover, using static analysis, the compiler groups the constraints that can be defined within a `for` cycle to reduce the size of the final C++ program. This can lead to a dramatic reduction of time needed by Gecode for the compilation of the .cc file with its libraries. For instance, the Gecode file obtained by the instance 100-Queens with this optimization is compiled with the Gecode libraries in 5.8s, while the code obtained by "flat" CNT requires 13 hours and 40 minutes.

The translation is performed using the following tools: for SICStus to CNT: SICStus; FlatZinc to CNT: gcc, Bison and Flex; for CNT to Gecode we used Haskell tools.

4 Experimental Results

We considered instances of four well-known problems, i.e. N-Queens, Sudoku, Golomb Rulers, and Knapsack. Sudoku 16x16 instances are taken from www.live-sudoku.com/play-online/geant, and 25x25 ones are taken from www.eleves.ens.fr/home/frisch/sudoku.html; N-Queens instances range from $N = 100$ to $N = 115$; Golomb Rulers instances have order from 6 to 13, with two different lengths (the biggest satisfiable and the shorter unsatisfiable) for each order; knapsack instances are the same used in [7].

We modeled each problem in SICStus Prolog, MiniZinc, and Gecode. When available, we used the modeling offered by languages libraries. We also considered their translation with the tools described in the paper. All codes and instances, together with all the running times, are available at [6].

There are two kinds of compile times: time of the compilation from high level code to Gecode C++ file and time needed by Gecode for internal compilation and libraries linking. With the proposed automatic detection of "for" loops both of them are rather low (the order of some seconds). Of course, for some small instances this time cannot be ignored w.r.t. execution time, but it becomes negligible for difficult instances.

There is a wide variety of results, that it still has to be investigated. However, the following general considerations can be done.

Native Gecode code is always the fastest, save for some 25x25 Sudoku instances.

Gecode models obtained compiling SICStus prolog models often speeds-up SICStus native, save for some instances of N-Queens. Moreover it has, in average, comparable times with Gecode native code. Let us observe, however, that it solves all the Sudoku instances, while native Gecode does not.

Gecode models obtained compiling SICStus and MiniZinc have substantially the same behavior, while in average they outperforms the MiniZinc to FlatZinc models obtained by the tools provided by NICTA and Gecode team, which are the standard ways to run MiniZinc (FlatZinc) models. Precisely, for Sudoku, N-Queens and Golomb rulers the Gecode encoding obtained from Minizinc with our tool is faster than the ones obtained with NICTA tools of various order of magnitude, while it is slightly slower in the case of Knapsack.

We think that the performances of the Gecode models obtained by our translations are better than the NICTA and Gecode ones because of our precomputations and static analysis (see section 3), that simplify domains and constraints, w.r.t the execution of the flatzinc models. However, the utility provided by NICTA research group and the one of the Gecode Team directly execute the flatzinc files, without returning any intermediate encoding, so we can't perform an exhaustive comparison of the encodings.

5 Conclusion and Future Work

Our compiler from SICStus and MiniZinc to Gecode, although in its preliminary version, shows that Constraint Programming can be done at high level using well-known languages and then executed in new paradigms since running times are comparable w.r.t. those of this latter paradigm. This allows to benefit from both the flexibility of high-level modeling languages and the efficiency of the new low-level solvers.

We would like to improve the static analysis of the generated code to further speed-up the overall process (compilation+execution) and to extend its compiling mechanism (up to now limited to CSP). We also would like to discard the use of CNT and write a front-end from CLP(FD) to FlatZinc to take advantage of FlatZinc solvers, and to port our tools to the Gecode 2.1.1.

The present work is part of a more general project of developing a programming tool for combinatorial problems, made of three main parts: the *modeling part*, where the user will define in a high-level style the problem to solve and the algorithm to use (e.g., constraint programming search, eventually interleaved with local search, heuristics or meta-heuristics phases); the *translating part*, where the model and the meta-algorithm defined will be automatically compiled into the solver languages, e.g. Gecode; and the *solving part*, where the overall compiled program will be run and the various solvers will interact in the way specified, to find the solution of the problem modeled.

We are planning to test the tool on different families of problems including those we have already cope with: a hospital rostering (timetable) problem [8], the protein structure prediction problem [9], and planning problems [10].

Acknowledgements. The work is partially supported by MUR FIRB RBNE03B8KK.

References

1. Team, G.: Gecode: Generic Constraint Development Environment,
   http://www.gecode.org
2. Jaffar, J., Maher, M.J.: Constraint Logic Programming: A survey. Journal of Logic Programming (19/20), 503–581 (1994)
3. Carlsson, M., Ottosson, G., Carlson, B.: An Open-Ended Finite Domain Constraint Solver, 191–206
4. Nethercote, N., Stuckey, P.J., Becket, R., Brand, S., Duck, G.J., Tack, G.: Minizinc: Towards a Standard CP Modelling Language. In: Bessière, C. (ed.) CP 2007. LNCS, vol. 4741, pp. 529–543. Springer, Heidelberg (2007)
5. Nethercote, N.: Specification of FlatZinc,
   http://www.g12.cs.mu.oz.au/minizinc/flatzinc-spec.pdf
6. Cipriano, R., Dovier, A., Jacopo, M.: Tools for Compiling SICStus and Minizinc in Gecode,
   http://www.dimi.uniud.it/dovier/MISIGE/
7. Dovier, A., Formisano, A., Pontelli, E.: A Comparison of CLP(FD) and ASP Solutions to NP-Complete Problems. In: Gabbrielli, M., Gupta, G. (eds.) ICLP 2005. LNCS, vol. 3668, pp. 67–82. Springer, Heidelberg (2005)
8. Cipriano, R., Di Gaspero, L., Dovier, A.: Hybrid Approaches for Rostering: a Case Study in The Integration of Constraint Programming and Local Search. In: Almeida, F., Blesa Aguilera, M.J., Blum, C., Moreno Vega, J.M., Pérez Pérez, M., Roli, A., Sampels, M. (eds.) HM 2006. LNCS, vol. 4030, pp. 110–123. Springer, Heidelberg (2006)
9. Cipriano, R., Dal Palù, A., Dovier, A.: A Hybrid Approach Mixing Local Search and Constraint Programming Applied to the Protein Structure Prediction Problem. In: WCB 2008, Paris (2008)
10. Dovier, A., Formisano, A., Pontelli, E.: Multivalued Action Languages with Constraints in CLP(FD). In: Dahl, V., Niemelä, I. (eds.) ICLP 2007. LNCS, vol. 4670, pp. 255–270. Springer, Heidelberg (2007)

Telecommunications Feature Subscription as a Partial Order Constraint Problem

Michael Codish[1], Vitaly Lagoon[2], and Peter J. Stuckey[2,3,4]

[1] Department of Computer Science, Ben-Gurion University, Israel
[2] Department of Computer Science and Software Engineering
The University of Melbourne, Australia
[3] National ICT Australia, Victoria Laboratory
[4] IMDEA Software, UPM, Spain
mcodish@cs.bgu.ac.il, {lagoon,pjs}@cs.mu.oz.au

Abstract. This paper describes the application of a partial order constraint solver to a telecommunications feature subscription configuration problem. Partial order constraints are encoded to propositional logic and solved using a state-of-the-art Boolean satisfaction solver. The encoding is based on a symbol-based approach: symbols are viewed as variables which take integer values and are interpreted as indices in the order. Experimental evaluation indicates that partial order constraints are a viable alternative to previous solutions which apply constraint programming techniques and integer linear programming.

1 Introduction

Modern telecommunications providers enable a customer to subscribe to services selected from a catalog of features. The configuration of a feature subscription is often personalized based on preferences provided by the customer and constraints imposed by the provider to prevent undesirable feature interactions at run-time. When the subscription requested by a user is inconsistent, one problem is to find an optimal relaxation which is consistent.

In recent research, described in [1], the authors formalize the telecommunications feature subscription configuration problem and prove that the complexity of finding an optimal relaxation is NP-hard. That paper compares three techniques to address the problem using: constraint programming, SAT encoding, and integer linear programming. The authors conclude that the constraint programming approach is able to scale well compared to the other approaches.

This paper reexamines the encoding of telecommunications feature subscription configuration problem to SAT. Our approach to the encoding leads to a scalable solution which is considerably faster than the three techniques reported in [1]. Our approach is based on an encoding of partial order constraints into propositional logic and using the same implementation described in [2]. Partial order constraints are just like usual propositional formulae except that propositions involve also statements about a partial order on a finite set of symbols.

The encoding considered in [1] is atom-based. It models an atom of the form $(f > g)$ (which may be interpreted as f is after g) as a propositional variable.

M. Garcia de la Banda and E. Pontelli (Eds.): ICLP 2008, LNCS 5366, pp. 749–753, 2008.
© Springer-Verlag Berlin Heidelberg 2008

Then, propositional statements are added to encode the axioms of partial orders which the atoms are subject to. For a partial order constraint on n symbols, such encodings typically introduce $O(n^2)$ propositional variables and involve $O(n^3)$ propositional connectives to express the axioms. In contrast, the proposal in [2] takes a symbol-based approach modeling the symbols in a partial order constraint as integer values (in binary representation). For n symbols this requires $k = \lceil \log_2 n \rceil$ propositional variables for each symbol. The integer value of a symbol reflects its index in a total order extending the partial order. Constraints of the form $(f > g)$ are then straightforward to encode in k-bit arithmetic and involve $O(\log n)$ connectives each.

2   Problem Statement

This section presents the formal statement of the telecommunications feature subscription configuration problem and is taken (with slight modification) from [1].

Let F denote a finite set of features. For $f_i, f_j \in F$ a *precedence constraint* $(f_i > f_j)$ indicates that f_i is after f_j. An *exclusion constraint* $(f_i \diamond f_j)$ between f_i and f_j indicates that f_i and f_j cannot appear together in a sequence of features, and is equivalent to the pair $(f_i > f_j)$, $(f_j > f_i)$. A *catalog* is a pair $\langle F, P \rangle$ with F a set of features and P a set of precedence constraints on F. A *feature subscription* S of a catalog $\langle F_c, P_c \rangle$ is a tuple $\langle F, C, U, W_F, W_U \rangle$ where $F \subseteq F_c$ is the set of features selected from F_c, C is the projection of P_c on F, U is a set of user defined precedence constraints on F, and $W_F : F \to \mathcal{N}$ and $W_U : U \to \mathcal{N}$ are maps which assign weights to features and user precedence constraints. The value of S is defined by $Value(S) = \Sigma_{f \in F} W_F(f) + \Sigma_{p \in U} W_U(p)$. The weight associated with a feature or a precedence constraint signifies its importance for the user.

A feature subscription $\langle F, C, U, W_F, W_U \rangle$ is *consistent* iff the directed graph $\langle F, C \cup U \rangle$ is acyclic. Checking for consistency is straightforward using topological sort as described in [1]. If a feature subscription is inconsistent then the task is to relax it and to generate a consistent one with maximum value. A *relaxation* of a feature subscription $S = \langle F, C, U, W_F, W_U \rangle$ is a consistent subscription $S' = \langle F', C', U', W_{F'}, W_{U'} \rangle$ such that $F' \subseteq F$, C' is the projection of C on F', U' is a subset of the projection of U on F', $W_{F'}$ is the restriction of W_F to F', and $W_{U'}$ is the restriction of W_U to U'. We say that S' is an optimal relaxation of S if there does not exist another relaxation S'' of S such that $Value(S'') > Value(S')$. In [1], the authors prove that finding an optimal relaxation of a feature subscription is NP-hard. This is the problem addressed in this paper.

3   Partial Order Constraints

Partial order constraints were introduced in [2]. Informally, a partial order constraint is just like a formula in propositional logic except that statements may involve propositional variables as well as atoms of the form $(f > g)$ where f and g are symbols.[1]

---

[1] For brevity of presentation, we omit here atoms of the form $(f=g)$ considered in [2].

The semantics of a partial order constraint is a set of solutions. A solution is an assignment of truth values to propositional variables and atoms which is required to satisfy both parts of the formula: the "propositional part" and the "partial order part". Namely, if φ is a partial order constraint and μ a truth assignment, then μ is a solution for φ if: it satisfies φ when viewing the atoms as propositional variables, μ does not map an atom of the form $(f > f)$ to true, and if μ maps both $(f > g)$ and $(g > h)$ to true then μ also maps $(f > h)$ to true.

We are concerned with the question of satisfiability of partial order constraints: given a partial order constraint φ does it have a solution? Similarly to the general SAT problem, the satisfiability of partial order constraints is NP-complete, and the reduction from SAT is straightforward.

The following definition from [2] introduces the integer-based interpretation of partial order constraints. Let φ be a partial order constraint on propositional variables $\mathcal{B}$ and symbols $\mathcal{F}$ and let $|\mathcal{F}| = n$. An integer *assignment* for φ is a mapping μ which maps propositional variables from $\mathcal{B}$ to truth values $\{0, 1\}$ and symbols from $\mathcal{F}$ to values from $\{0, \ldots, n-1\}$. We say that μ is an integer *solution* of φ if it makes φ true under the standard interpretation of $>$ on the non-negative integers. In [2], the authors prove that a partial order constraint is satisfiable if and only if it has an integer solution.

To check the satisfiability of partial order constraints we apply an encoding to propositional logic. A partial order constraint φ on a set of propositional variables $\mathcal{B}$ and symbols $\mathcal{F}$ is encoded by a propositional formula φ' such that each solution of φ corresponds to a model of φ' and in particular such that φ is satisfiable if and only if φ' is. The idea is to construct the encoding in terms of the integer-based interpretation of partial order constraints. We view the n symbols in $\mathcal{F}$ as integer variables taking finite domain values from the set $\{0, \ldots, n-1\}$. Each symbol is thus modeled using $k = \lceil \log_2 n \rceil$ propositional variables which encode the binary representation of its value. Constraints of the form $(f > g)$ on $\mathcal{F}$ are interpreted as constraints on integers and it is straightforward to encode them in k-bit arithmetic.

The experiments described in [2] apply a partial order constraint solver written in SWI-Prolog [3] which interfaces the MiniSat solver [4] for solving SAT instances as described in [5]. This paper makes use of the same constraint solver.

4   The Encoding

Let $S = \langle F, C, U, W_F, W_U \rangle$ be a subscription of a catalog $\langle F_c, P_c \rangle$. We seek an optimal relaxation $S' = \langle F', C', U', W_{F'}, W_{U'} \rangle$. With each feature $f \in F$ we associate a propositional variable b_f indicating if f is included in F'. With each constraint $p \in C$ (and $p \in U$) we associate a propositional variable b_p to indicate if p is in C' (or in U').

For each constraint $p = (f > g)$ in C, f and g occur in the relaxation F' iff p occurs in the relaxation C'. Hence we introduce the propositional constraint

$$b_f \wedge b_g \leftrightarrow b_p \tag{1}$$

For each constraint $p = (f > g)$ in U, p may occur in the relaxation U' if f and g occur in F'. Hence we introduce the propositional constraint

$$b_f \wedge b_g \leftarrow b_p \qquad (2)$$

For each constraint $p = (f > g)$ in $C \cup U$, if p occurs in the relaxation (C' or U') then the corresponding partial order constraint must hold

$$b_p \rightarrow (f > g) \qquad (3)$$

Solving the partial order constraint obtained as the conjunction of the above equations (1), (2), and (3) assigns truth values to the propositional variables b_f and b_p indicating a consistent relaxation. To obtain an optimal relaxation we need an additional step. Let φ be the encoding of the above constraints (1) – (3) to a propositional formula.

With each of the propositional variables b_f and b_p, which indicate if feature f and constraint p are selected to appear in the relaxation, we associate a (integer value) weight w_f and w_p. To simplify presentation, consider the multiset $Bits$ of propositional variables which contains w_f occurrences of b_f for each $f \in F$ and w_p occurrences of b_p for each $p \in U$. Let ψ be the propositional formula which specifies that the sum of these $Bits$ is the binary number with digits $Sum = \{s_1, \ldots, s_k\}$.

The Prolog interface to MiniSat described in [5] offers the functionality `maximize(Vector,Cnf)` which seeks a satisfying assignment for the conjunctive normal form `Cnf` which maximizes the binary number `Vector`. If `Cnf` is unsatisfiable this call fails. This functionality is implemented by successively determining the bits in the `Vector`. This involves a call to the underlying SAT solver for each bit. If the `Vector` represents the sum of n bits then this involves $\log n$ calls to the SAT solver.

For the telecommunications feature subscription configuration problem, this functionality is applied taking the conjunctive normal form of $\varphi \wedge \psi$ (`Cnf`) and the sum bits $Sum = \{s_1, \ldots, s_k\}$ (`Vector`). In the actual encoding, the formula representing the Sum is constructed by summing the pseudo Boolean formula $b_f * w_f$ and $b_p * w_p$ and not as described above.

5   Experimental Results

The experimentation is based on a collection of random catalogs and feature subscriptions obtained following the guidelines described in [1].

Table 1 describes the experiments for random catalogs with 50 features and 250 (750) precedence constraints (involving $\{<, >\}$). Each row labeled by $\langle f, p \rangle$ specifies a random subscription with f features and p user precedence constraints with weights selected between 1 and 4. Times are measured in seconds. The column marked `pocsp` corresponds to our Prolog implementation of partial order constraints built on top of MiniSat (average times over 10 random instances[2]). The columns marked `pwmsat`, `cplex` and `cp` are the times taken from Tables 2 and 3 of

---

[2] The precise instances used may be found at http://www.cs.bgu.ac.il/ mcodish/ Papers/Pages/feature_subscription.html

Table 1. Timings (sec) for two catalog sizes

$\langle f, p \rangle$	catalog $\langle 50, 250, \{<, >\} \rangle$				catalog $\langle 50, 750, \{<, >\} \rangle$			
	pocsp	pwmsat	cplex	cp	pocsp	pwmsat	cplex	cp
$\langle 30, 20 \rangle$	0.18	6.40	1.02	0.65	0.44	5.03	18.46	2.38
$\langle 35, 35 \rangle$	0.47	23.95	22.76	7.43	2.30	18.28	126.35	12.88
$\langle 40, 40 \rangle$	1.08	282.76	247.14	67.80	6.37	92.11	514.27	42.27
$\langle 45, 90 \rangle$	39.36	12638.25	7690.90	1115.51	105.51	2443.23	3780.54	188.83
$\langle 50, 4 \rangle$	0.39	195.72	1010.38	413.61	1.00	319.53	3162.08	342.49

[1] for their: SAT encoding[3], ILP solver and CP solver. Note that the random instances for pocsp are most likely different than those applied in [1]. The machines are also different. Theirs is a PC Pentium 4 (CPU 1.8 GHz and 768 MB of RAM). Ours is a PC Pentium 4 (CPU 2.4 GHz and 512 MB of RAM). Ours is running SWI Prolog under Linux, kernel 2.6.11-6. With no intention to compare the two machines, the timings are clear enough.

6   Conclusions

Our encoding indicates the clear benefit in choosing the right tool for the problem at hand: Once stating the feature subscription configuration problem as one of partial order constraints, the solution is straightforward. Our results indicate that the application of partial order constraints to the telecommunications feature subscription configuration problem provides a viable alternative to other solution techniques. The partial order approach improves upon the previous SAT approach by avoiding the $O(n^3)$ encoding of partial order, and over the other approaches because of the nogood learning capabilities of SAT.

References

1. Lesaint, D., Mehta, D., O'Sullivan, B., Quesada, L.O., Wilson, N.: Solving a telecommunications feature subscription configuration problem. In: Stuckey, P.J. (ed.) CP 2008. LNCS, vol. 5202, pp. 67–81. Springer, Heidelberg (2008)
2. Codish, M., Lagoon, V., Stuckey, P.J.: Solving partial order constraints for LPO termination. Journal on Satisfiability, Boolean Modeling and Computation 5, 193–215 (2008), An earlier version appears In: Pfenning, F. (ed.) RTA 2006. LNCS, vol. 4098, pp. 4–18. Springer, Heidelberg (2006)
3. Wielemaker, J.: An overview of the SWI-Prolog programming environment. In: Mesnard, F., Serebenik, A. (eds.) Proceedings of the 13th International Workshop on Logic Programming Environments. CW 371, KU Leuven, December 2003, pp. 1–16 (2003)
4. Eén, N., Sörensson, N.: An extensible SAT-solver. In: Giunchiglia, E., Tacchella, A. (eds.) SAT 2003. LNCS, vol. 2919, pp. 502–518. Springer, Heidelberg (2004)
5. Codish, M., Lagoon, V., Stuckey, P.J.: Logic programming with satisfiability. TPLP 8(1), 121–128 (2008)

---

[3] The authors of [1] use the SAT4J solver - http://www.sat4j.org/

A Constraint Logic Programming Approach to Automated Testing

Hakim Belhaouari and Frédéric Peschanski

Laboratoire d'Informatique de Paris 6
UPMC Paris Universitas
104 avenue du President Kennedy
75016 Paris, France
{hakim.belhaouari,frederic.peschanski}@lip6.fr

Abstract. In this paper we present a new constraint solver for the automated generation of test cases from specifications. The specification language is inspired by the contract-oriented programming extended with a finite state machines. Beyond the generation of correct argument values for method calls, we generate full test scenarios thanks to the symbolic animation of the specifications. We propose a flexible CSP architecture that can operate not only on integer or bounded domains but also on arbitrary types. An original notion of type builder is used to establish the link between the type semantics and the CSP framework. We illustrate this with a string builder that can automatically generate string instances depending on combinations of constraints.

1 Introduction

Testing is the most popular approach to software validation. However in most non-trivial software a systematic and exhaustive testing approach is impossible due to their large input domain. The *model-based testing* (MBT) approach is to generate test cases from specifications [1,2]. We aim to completely automate the testing process. The objectives are (1) to determine the test requirements by analyzing the specifications, (2) to generate test cases accordingly, (3) to extract an oracle, and (4) to perform test on actual implementations.

We focus in this paper on the automation of test-case generation from design by contract specifications [3]. First-order logic assertions are used to express the contracts. We exploit the finite state machine descriptions to extract test scenarios automatically from the speficiations. The generation of values for method parameters that are correct with respect to the specification corresponds to a constraint-satisfaction problem (CSP) [4]. Initially the variable domain is defined by its type, and the CSP reduces the range according to the various constraints represented by each atomic term extracted from the contract.

Interestingly, the CSP architecture we propose does not restrict the constraint language to finite-domain and predefined types. An original notion of *type builder* permits extending the testing framework in a flexible way. We describe in this paper a sophisticated String builder that can automatically generate string

M. Garcia de la Banda and E. Pontelli (Eds.): ICLP 2008, LNCS 5366, pp. 754–758, 2008.
© Springer-Verlag Berlin Heidelberg 2008

instances depending on combinations of constraints based on string sizes and substrings.

2   Automated Testing: Contract Animation

Many automated testing tools analyze methods in isolation, without inspecting deeply inside the contract and the context of the method calls [5,6]. Our tool animates the specifications in order to extract a test scenario that integrates the context of method calls. The scenario is extracted from the finite state machines included in a contract. Thus, the animation reduces to choosing a sequence of automaton's possible transitions. A transition informs both about the called method and the properties' values in the current state. And it also allows to define the future state of the contract.

Figure 1 gives an example of a bank account service specified in pseudo-language. An account has two properties: the balance and the *IBAN* (international standard for identifying bank accounts across countries)[1]. It is possible to credit or to withdraw money from an account. The last part of the specification is the automaton that governs availability of methods.

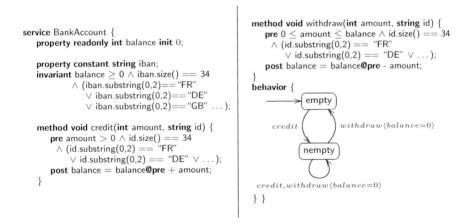

Fig. 1. A bank account contract

In order to animate the contract, the tool analyzes the semantics attached to a transition. This allows to define the notion of *prerequisite condition*. It results from the conjunction of the constraints represented by the precondition, the postcondition, the invariant and the guard of the current transition. Finally, the tool generates an oracle as the conjunction between the postcondition, the invariant and the guard of the current transition.

---

[1] Due to lack of place we consider only constraints on the country code located at the begining of the IBAN.

As an illustration, consider the expressions of type integer: amount and balance. When the status of the bank account is just initialized, the only transition available is a call to the credit functionality. The generated prerequisite condition is the following expression: $(balance \geq 0) \wedge (amount > 0) \wedge (balance@post = balance + amount)$. The notation balance@post represents the value of the balance property in the future state. From the prerequisite condition, the underlying CSP solver can determine value for each variables. Now the state machine informs us about existence of three possibles transitions: (1) continue to credit the account, (2) withdraw some part and (3) withdraw all money from the account. The semantics can distinguish the two last cases with the guard of the transition. In the first case the guard allows the transition only when the balance is empty, while the second case remains in the same state if the balance is not empty. The tool then continues its exploration of the state machine and ultimately generates a complete scenario.

3   Test Data Generation

In this section, we describe the generation of valid arguments for the method calls of test scenarios. This relies on a flexible CSP architecture, which we illustrate with the support of advanced string constraints.

3.1   The CSP Architecture

Our CSP architecture is composed of a rewriting system, a constraint converter, a solving environment and the CSP algorithm itself. The last part is similar to a classical CSP solver with some extensions described below.

A major feature of this architecture is the automated conversion of logical assertions into constraints directly understood by the CSP solver. At first the rewriting system simplifies the input expressions and translates them to disjunctive normal forms (DNF). The DNF induces several clauses, each one represents a classical constraint (equality, inequality, linear equation, ...).

Interestingly, the conversion of an atomic term into a CSP variable uses a delegation technique that leverages extensibility. The conversion delegates a specific object called a *type builder*. The responsibility of a type builder is to "know" the semantics of the type that it implements. The root interface of type builders declares a unique method that returns a CSP variable for a given atomic term (variable, method call and so on). The environment registers all the associated type builders for each variable/property.

We illustrate the conversion algorithm on the bank account example of figure 1. From the precondition of the credit functionality we can extract two constraints: amount>0 and id.size()==34. Both constraints are binary constraints with constant values. The first one has the form of a X_gt_C constraint (where X denotes a variable, and C a constant) constraint and the second one corresponds to a X_eq_C constraint. At this point, the converter uses the int builder in order to get a CSP variable corresponding to the amount variable. It also asks the builder associated to the id variable a reference to the CSP variable of the expression id.size() (cf. string builder). Finally, the CSP solver solves all CSP variables.

Currently we provide builders for primitives types: boolean, integer, real, string and generic (homogeneous) arrays. The two last examples emphasis the support of complex types with (potentially) unbounded domains. An example of a builder for a complex type is described in the next section.

3.2   Case Study: The String Builder

Commonly the size of strings are limited only by the available amount of allocatable memory. This means that the number of instances of a given string constraint is potentially infinite. The string builder is modeled as a pair $\langle regexp, len \rangle$, where $regexp$ is a regular expression, len is the length represented as an integer variable. The main difference with [7] is the extension of substrings.

The variable returned by the string builder depends on the input expression. The size method returns the len integer variable. Any modification of the integer's domain by a constraint produces a regular expression that affects the length of the $regexp$. The substring method is more involved, it creates a pair $\langle regexp_s, len_s \rangle$ with two regexps constraining the location in the parent string. The three finite-state automata (the two padding regexp and the substring regexp) are then merged with the parent regexp.

When the CSP solver instantiates a string variable, it generates a word from the obtained regular expressions. For example, the regexp of 2(e) is extracted from the invariant of the bank account: iban.size() == 34 ∧ iban.substring(0,2) =="FR". The first constraint imposes a precise length for the main string, the corresponding automaton generated by the analysis is shown on Figure 2(a). The second constraint assumes the existence of a substring and this one is affected to a constant as illustrated in figure 2(c). In order to apply the latter automaton onto the parent automaton, we need to consider the automaton from the position zero to the beginning of the substring in the main string represented in Figure 2(b). Figure 2(d) gives the padding automaton that takes into consideration the length of the main regexp. Finally the product of these automata is illustrated in figure 2(e). This is used regular expression for generating some IBAN.

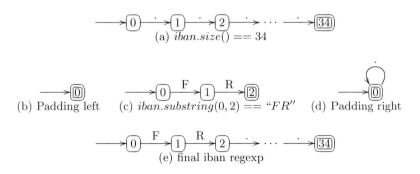

(a) $iban.size() == 34$

(b) Padding left   (c) $iban.substring(0, 2) ==$ "FR"   (d) Padding right

(e) final iban regexp

Fig. 2. Illustration of different regexp

4   Related Works

The tool *Jartege* [6] aims at generating random test cases. An interesting aspect of this tool is to take into account the detection of errors resulting from sequence calls of different methods (test scenarios). We adopt a similar approach but add the CSP-based solving of constraints for method calls arguments.

The tool Korat [5], based on the JML-JUnit approach, supports a form of exhaustive testing for isolated methods. It calls the method with each possible values of the domain of parameters. In our approach the test is not exhaustive but constrained by the CSP, and thus applied to many more practical situations. It also applies to non-trivial domains such as string constraints.

Most of these tools [2,6,8] are designed exclusively to use finite domain values (generally of predefined types). The model of type builders we propose allows to apply our approach on more constrained kinds and, moreover, makes the tool extensible.

The String builder described in this paper is similar to the string solver of [7]. An important improvement is the support of substrings.

Acknowledgment

The authors would like to thank Nicolas Stefanovitch for his help and stimulating arguments.

References

1. Myers, G.J.: Art of Software Testing. John Wiley & Sons, Inc., New York (1979)
2. Utting, M., Legeard, B.: Practical Model-Based Testing: A Tools Approach, 1st edn. Morgan Kaufmann, San Francisco (2006)
3. Meyer, B.: Object-Oriented Software Construction, 2nd edn. Prentice-Hall, Englewood Cliffs (1997)
4. Kumar, V.: Algorithms for constraint-satisfaction problems: A survey. AI Magazine 13, 32–44 (1992)
5. Boyapati, C., Khurshid, S., Marinov, D.: Korat: Automated testing based on java predicates (2002)
6. Oriat, C.: Jartege: A tool for random generation of unit tests for java classes. In: Reussner, R., Mayer, J., Stafford, J.A., Overhage, S., Becker, S., Schroeder, P.J. (eds.) QoSA 2005 and SOQUA 2005. LNCS, vol. 3712, pp. 242–256. Springer, Heidelberg (2005)
7. Golden, K., Pang, W.: Constraint reasoning over strings. In: Rossi, F. (ed.) CP 2003. LNCS, vol. 2833, pp. 377–391. Springer, Heidelberg (2003)
8. Ambert, F., Bouquet, F., Legeard, B., Peureux, F.: Automated boundary-value test generation from specifications - method and tools. In: ICSTEST 2003, Cologne, Allemagne, pp. 52–68 (2003)

Turing-Complete Subclasses of CHR

Jon Sneyers

K.U. Leuven, Belgium
jon.sneyers@cs.kuleuven.be

Abstract. Interesting subclasses of CHR are still Turing-complete: CHR with only one kind of rule, with only one rule, and propositional refined CHR. This is shown by programming a simulator of Turing machines (or Minsky machines) within those subclasses. Single-headed CHR without host language and propositional abstract CHR are not Turing-complete.

1 Introduction

As a stand-alone programming language, CHR is Turing-complete [1]. In this paper we demonstrate that several subclasses of CHR are also Turing-complete. Section 2 shows that CHR with only one kind of rules (simplification, propagation, or simpagation) is still Turing-complete. Then, in Section 3, we see that multiple rules are not needed — one single rule suffices. Finally, Section 4 deals with single-headed CHR and propositional CHR (only zero-arity constraints).

Some very restricted subclasses of CHR turn out to be not Turing-complete. Propositional CHR is not Turing-complete under the abstract semantics, so allowing constraints to have (even only non-compound) arguments does add computational power. Single-headed CHR without host language is not Turing-complete either, so computational power is gained by the availability of either multi-headed rules or a host language. Finally, the added execution control of a more instantiated operational semantics (e.g. the refined semantics [2] or the priority semantics [3]) also adds computational power in the sense that propositional CHR becomes Turing-complete under a more instantiated semantics.

Because of space constraints, we need to assume that the reader is familiar with CHR [4], Turing machines [5], and Minsky machines [6]. Unless otherwise mentioned, we assume that the abstract operational semantics ω_t is used.

2 Only One Kind of Rules

The **TMSIM** program of Listing 1 (adapted from [1]) contains only simpagation rules. It can easily be modified to consist only of simplification rules: the kept part of the simpagation rules can be removed and reinserted in the body.

It is also possible to simulate Turing machines in CHR with only propagation rules. Since there is no way to destructively update the constraints, we add a time-stamp argument to all constraints that are updated. By carefully making sure that all the non-modified tape cells and adjacency constraints are copied

M. Garcia de la Banda and E. Pontelli (Eds.): ICLP 2008, LNCS 5366, pp. 759–763, 2008.
© Springer-Verlag Berlin Heidelberg 2008

Listing 1. TMSIM: Turing machine simulator

```
r1 @ delta(Q,S,P,T,left), adj(L,C) \ state(Q), cell(C,S), head(C)
     <=> state(P), cell(C,T), head(L).
r2 @ delta(Q,S,P,T,right), adj(C,R) \ state(Q), cell(C,S), head(C)
     <=> state(P), cell(C,T), head(R).
r3 @ delta(Q,S,P,T,left) \ left(C), state(Q), cell(C,S), head(C)
     <=> cell(L,b), left(L), adj(L,C), state(P), cell(C,T), head(L).
r4 @ delta(Q,S,P,T,right) \ right(C), state(Q), cell(C,S), head(C)
     <=> cell(R,b), adj(C,R), right(R), state(P), cell(C,T), head(R).
```

Listing 2. TMSIM-2R: Turing machine simulator in two rules

```
% left(C) <=> adj(L,L), adj(L,C), cell(L,b).
% right(C) <=> adj(R,R), adj(C,R), cell(R,b).

r13 @ delta(Q,S,P,T,left), state(Q), head(C) \ adj(L,C), adj(C,R), cell(C,S)
   <=> adj(L,C2), adj(C2,R), adj(C,C), cell(C,b), cell(C2,T), state(P), head(L).
r24 @ delta(Q,S,P,T,right), state(Q), head(C) \ adj(L,C), adj(C,R), cell(C,S)
   <=> adj(L,C2), adj(C2,R), adj(C,C), cell(C,b), cell(C2,T), state(P), head(R).
```

from one time-stamp to the next, and the modified cell (and modified adjacency constraints in case of a tape extension) is not copied, the correct behavior can be obtained without destructive updates. Since the entire tape is copied at every step, the space used by such a propagation-rule-only program is $O(TS)$ when simulating a T-time, S-space Turing machine. This is considerably less efficient than the $O(S)$ space usage of the TMSIM program.

3   Only One Rule

Now let us see how many rules are really needed. In Listing 1, we have two rules for each direction of tape movement (**left** and **right**): one for the normal case and one for the case in which the tape representation needs to be extended. Using a slightly different tape representation, these two cases can be merged.

The idea is as follows. The tape is still represented using adjacency constraints adj/2, but instead of marking the tape ends with left/1 and right/1, we put an extra blank cell with a loop to itself at both ends, as shown in Fig. 1.

When moving to the right (the case for moving to the left is symmetric), we create a new cell and add two adj/2 constraints as shown in Fig. 2(a). We overwrite the current cell symbol with the blank symbol b and remove the incoming and outgoing adj/2 constraints. Finally we add a looping adj/2 constraint at the current cell. In the normal case (Fig. 2(a)) the net result is that the current cell becomes isolated and a tape 'bypass' is created. When we are at the tape end, the net result is that the tape has been extended with one cell, and we remain at the (new) tape end (see Fig. 2(b)). In listing 2 the resulting CHR program TMSIM-2R is shown; it has only two rules. The two rules that are commented out show how to change the old tape representation to the new form, but we assume that the query is already in the correct form.

Fig. 1. Tape representation for TMSIM-2R

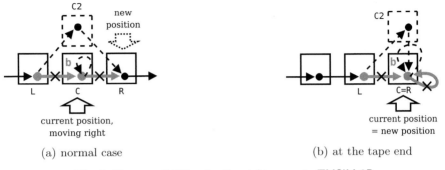

(a) normal case

(b) at the tape end

Fig. 2. Two possibilities for the right move in TMSIM-2R

Now can we further reduce this program? Certainly! It is easy to see that there is a lot of symmetry between the two rules in TMSIM-2R. We can change the tape representation again to take advantage of this symmetry and merge the rules. Instead of using adj(A,B) to represent that cell A is to the left of cell B, we now use the following redundant representation: adj(A,B,left), adj(B,A,right). So adj(A,B,X) means that cell A is to the X of cell B. By replacing every adj/2 constraint in the two-rule program TMSIM-2R by the corresponding two adj/3 constraints, and by connecting the third argument of the adj/3 with the last argument of the delta/5 constraint, both rules in TMSIM-2R become a variable renaming of each other, so only one of them is needed. Listing 3 shows the resulting CHR program TMSIM-1R.

4   Only Single-Headed Rules and Propositional CHR

The program TMSIM-1R consists of only one rule, but that rule has 8 head constraints. All rules with more than two heads can be reduced to several rules with only two heads by explicitly constructing partial joins. However, as we shall see shortly, single-headed rules only do not suffice.

All of the above programs are CHR programs without host language: no host language predicates are used in rule guards or bodies, and constraint arguments are only constants and variables. An arbitrary number of fresh variables can be created if the body of a rule contains variables that do not occur in the head, but all variables are syntactically different objects and they cannot be bound to each other or to constants (as in Prolog). CHR with only single-headed rules can be shown to be Turing-complete if some form of host language arithmetic is allowed [7]. Host language arithmetic can be done directly using integers, or successor term notation can be used, so an argument of the form s(s(s(...s(zero)...))), with n times s, indicates the number n. In both cases however, a nontrivial host language data type is needed — respectively integers

Listing 3. TMSIM-1R: Turing machine simulator in one rule

```
% adj(A,B) <=> adj(A,B,left), adj(B,A,right).

r1234 @ delta(Q,S,P,T,D), state(Q), head(C) \ adj(A,C,D), adj(C,B,D),
                          cell(C,S), adj(C,A,E), adj(B,C,E)
  <=> adj(A,C2,D), adj(C2,B,D), adj(C,C,D), cell(C,b), cell(C2,T),
      adj(C2,A,E), adj(B,C2,E), adj(C,C,E), state(P), head(A).
```

and complex terms. Alternatively, constraint chains can be used to represent numbers, but then either multi-headed rules are needed, or a form of assignment (for example Prolog unification).

Without a host language, CHR with only single headed rules is a very weak formalism — it is not more powerful than propositional CHR, i.e. CHR with only zero-arity constraints:

Lemma. *Single-headed CHR without host language can be reduced to propositional CHR without host language.*

Proof (sketch). Assume there are k distinct constants used in the program and queries. For every CHR constraint c/n, we make "flattened" versions of it, one for every possible combination of arguments. Since variables cannot be bound and since in single-headed rules there can only be matching between the arguments of a single constraint, it does not matter what the variables are, but only which ones are the same. Hence, there are less than $(k + n)^n$ different combinations of arguments for a constraint of arity n. We can replace the body CHR constraints by their flattened version, and duplicate the rule for every matching flattened version of the head. The resulting program is propositional. □

We have the following negative result for propositional CHR-only:

Theorem. *Propositional CHR (without host language) is not Turing-complete.*

Proof (sketch). Propositional CHR programs can easily be encoded as place-transition Petri nets [8], which are not Turing-complete [9]. □

The above lemma and theorem can be combined in the obvious way:

Corollary. *Single-headed CHR without host language is not Turing-complete.*

Somewhat surprisingly, the above theorem only holds when the full abstract semantics ω_t is considered. If the refined operational semantics ω_r [2] is used, the result no longer holds. The reason is that the ω_r semantics allows checking for the *absence* of a constraint, which is not possible in the ω_t semantics. Consider the following encoding of Minsky machines in propositional refined CHR:

$$\llbracket p_i \; : \; \text{succ}(r_1) \rrbracket = \qquad\qquad p_i \; \texttt{<=>} \; \texttt{a}, \; p_{i+1}.$$
$$\llbracket p_i \; : \; \text{succ}(r_2) \rrbracket = \qquad\qquad p_i \; \texttt{<=>} \; \texttt{b}, \; p_{i+1}.$$
$$\llbracket p_i \; : \; \text{decjump}(r_1,p_j) \rrbracket = \qquad p_i, \; \texttt{a} \; \texttt{<=>} \; p_{i+1}.$$
$$\qquad\qquad\qquad\qquad\qquad\qquad\qquad p_i \; \texttt{<=>} \; p_j.$$
$$\llbracket p_i \; : \; \text{decjump}(r_2,p_j) \rrbracket = \qquad p_i, \; \texttt{b} \; \texttt{<=>} \; p_{i+1}.$$
$$\qquad\qquad\qquad\qquad\qquad\qquad\qquad p_i \; \texttt{<=>} \; p_j.$$

It crucially depends on the refined semantics. The value of register r_1 is represented by the multiplicity of the constraint a, and the value of r_2 by the multiplicity of b. Under the abstract semantics this program breaks down because the second rule for decjump instructions can be fired even if the corresponding register does not have the value zero — this cannot happen in the refined semantics because of the rule order. Thus, propositional CHR is not Turing-complete in the abstract semantics, but it is Turing-complete in the refined semantics. In the priority semantics ω_p [3], propositional CHR is also Turing-complete: it suffices to assign a higher priority to the first rule for decjump than to the second rule. We conjecture that *single-headed* CHR without host language remains not Turing-complete even under the ω_r semantics.

5   Future Work

These surprising results indicate the need for further and deeper investigation of the connection between language features, operational semantics, termination and confluence, and computability and expressivity.

Acknowledgments. I thank Thom Frühwirth, Leslie De Koninck, and Bart Demoen for the discussions that lead to some of the ideas presented here. This research was funded by a Ph.D. grant of the Institute for the Promotion of Innovation through Science and Technology in Flanders (IWT-Vlaanderen).

References

1. Sneyers, J., Schrijvers, T., Demoen, B.: The computational power and complexity of Constraint Handling Rules. In: ACM TOPLAS (to appear, 2008)
2. Duck, G.J., Stuckey, P.J., García de la Banda, M., Holzbaur, C.: The refined operational semantics of Constraint Handling Rules. In: Demoen, B., Lifschitz, V. (eds.) ICLP 2004. LNCS, vol. 3132, pp. 90–104. Springer, Heidelberg (2004)
3. De Koninck, L., Schrijvers, T., Demoen, B.: User-definable rule priorities for CHR. In: Leuschel, M., Podelski, A. (eds.) 9th International Conference on Principles and Practice of Declarative Programming, Wrocław, Poland, pp. 25–36. ACM Press, New York (2007)
4. Frühwirth, T.: Constraint Handling Rules. Cambridge University Press, Cambridge (2009)
5. Turing, A.M.: On computable numbers, with an application to the Entscheidungsproblem. Proc. London Mathematical Society 2(42), 230–265 (1936)
6. Minsky, M.L.: Computation: finite and infinite machines. Prentice-Hall, Englewood Cliffs (1967)
7. Di Giusto, C., Gabbrielli, M., Meo, M.C.: Expressiveness of multiple heads in CHR. CoRR abs/0804.3351 (2008)
8. Betz, H.: Relating coloured Petri nets to Constraint Handling Rules. In: Djelloul, K., Duck, G.J., Sulzmann, M. (eds.) 4th Workshop on Constraint Handling Rules, Porto, Portugal, pp. 33–47 (2007)
9. Jantzen, M., Valk, R.: Formal properties of place/transition nets. In: Brauer, W. (ed.) Net Theory and Applications. LNCS, vol. 84. Springer, Heidelberg (1980)

A Soft Approach to Multi-objective Optimization[*]

Stefano Bistarelli[1,2], Fabio Gadducci[3], Javier Larrosa[4], and Emma Rollon[4]

[1] Department of Science, University "G. d'Annunzio" of Chieti-Pescara, Italy
[2] Institute of Informatics and Telematics (IIT), CNR Pisa, Italy
[3] Department of Informatics, University of Pisa, Polo "G. Marconi" (La Spezia), Italy
[4] Department of Software, Technical University of Catalonia, Barcelona, Spain

Abstract. Many combinatorial optimization problems require the assignment of a set of variables in such a way that an objective function is optimized. Often, the objective function involves different criteria, and it may happen that the requirements are in conflict: assignments that are good wrt. one objective may behave badly wrt. another. An optimal solution wrt. all criteria may not exist, and either the efficient frontier (the set of best incomparable solutions, all equally relevant in the absence of further information) or an approximation has to be looked after. The paper shows how the soft constraints formalism based on semirings, so far exploited for finding approximations, can embed also the computation of the efficient frontier in multi-objective optimization problems. The main result is the proof that the efficient frontier of a multi-objective problem can be obtained as the best level of consistency distilled from a suitable soft constraint problem.

1 Introduction

Many real world problems involve multiple measures of performance, or objectives, that should be optimized simultaneously: see e.g. [1] and the references therein. In such a situation a unique, perfect solution may not exist, while a set of solutions can be found that should be considered equivalent in the absence of information concerning the relevance of each objective wrt. the others. Hence, two solutions are equivalent if one of them is better than the other for some criteria, but worse for others; while one solution dominates the other if the former is better than the latter for all criteria.

The set of best solutions is the set of efficient (*pareto-optimal*) solutions. The task in a multi-objective problem is to compute the set of costs associated to efficient solutions (the *efficient frontier*) and, possibly, one efficient solution for any of its elements.

The main goal of the paper is to prove that the computation of the efficient frontier of multi-objective optimization problems can be modeled using soft CSP. More precisely, our main contribution is to show, given a (possibly partially ordered) semiring $\mathcal{K}$, how to compute a new semiring $\mathcal{L}(\mathcal{K})$ such that its elements corresponds to sets of elements of the original semiring; and such that the set of optimal costs of the original problem.

When applied to the multi-objective context, our work is summarized as follows: consider a problem where $\mathcal{K}_1 \ldots \mathcal{K}_p$ are the semirings associated to each objective. If we use their cartesian product $\mathcal{K}_C = \mathcal{K}_1 \times \ldots \times \mathcal{K}_p$ to model the multi-objective problem, the solution corresponds to the lowest vector dominating the efficient frontier; if we use $\mathcal{L}(\mathcal{K}_C)$ to model the problem, the solution coincides with the efficient frontier.

---

[*] Research partially supported by the EU IST-2004-16004 SENSORIA.

M. Garcia de la Banda and E. Pontelli (Eds.): ICLP 2008, LNCS 5366, pp. 764–768, 2008.
© Springer-Verlag Berlin Heidelberg 2008

2   On Semiring-Based Frameworks

Semirings provide an algebraic framework for the specification of a general class of combinatorial optimization problems. Outcomes associated to variable instantiations are modeled as elements of a set A, equipped with a *sum* and a *product* operator. These operators are used for combining constraints: the intuition is that the sum operator induces a partial order $a \leq b$, meaning that b is a better outcome than a; whilst the product operator denotes the aggregation of outcomes coming from different soft constraints.

More in detail, a (commutative) semiring is a tuple $\mathcal{K} = \langle A, +, \times, \mathbf{0}, \mathbf{1} \rangle$ such that A is a set, $\mathbf{1}, \mathbf{0} \in A$, and $+, \times : A \times A \to A$ are binary operators making the triples $\langle A, +, \mathbf{0} \rangle$ and $\langle A, \times, \mathbf{1} \rangle$ commutative monoids, satisfying distributiveness ($\forall a, b, c \in A.a \times (b + c) = (a \times b) + (a \times c)$) and absorptiveness wrt. $\times$ ($\forall a \in A.a \times \mathbf{0} = \mathbf{0}$). A semiring is *tropical* [2] if the sum operator $+$ is idempotent ($\forall a \in A.a + a = a$); it is *absorptive* if it satisfies absorptiveness wrt. $+$ ($\forall a \in A.a + \mathbf{1} = \mathbf{1}$).

Let $\mathcal{K} = \langle A, +, \times, \mathbf{0}, \mathbf{1} \rangle$ be a tropical semiring. Then, the relation $\langle A, \leq \rangle$ such that $\forall a, b \in A.a \leq b$ iff $a + b = b$ is a partial order. Moreover, if $\mathcal{K}$ is absorptive, then $\mathbf{1}$ is the top element of the partial order. If additionally $\mathcal{K}$ is absorptive and *idempotent* (that is, the product operator $\times$ is idempotent: $\forall a \in A.a \times a = a$), then the partial order is actually a *lattice*, since $a \times b$ corresponds to the greatest lower bound of a and b.

2.1   Soft Constraints Based on Semirings

Let $\mathcal{K} = \langle A, +, \times, \mathbf{0}, \mathbf{1} \rangle$ be an absorptive semiring; let V be a set of variables; and let D be a finite domain of interpretation for V. Then, a *constraint* $(V \to D) \to A$ is a function associating a value in A to each assignment $\eta : V \to D$ of the variables.[1]

Note that even if a constraint involves all the variables in V, it must depend on the assignment of a finite subset of them. For instance, a binary constraint $c_{x,y}$ over variables x, y is a function $c_{x,y} : (V \to D) \to A$ which depends only on the assignment of variables $\{x, y\} \subseteq V$. This subset is the *support* of the constraint [3] and correspond to the classical notion of scope of a constraint. Most often, whenever V is ordered, an assignment (over a support of cardinality k) is concisely presented by a tuple in D^k.

The *combination* operator $\otimes : \mathcal{C} \times \mathcal{C} \to \mathcal{C}$ is defined as $(c_1 \otimes c_2)\eta = c_1\eta \times c_2\eta$. Thus, combining two constraints means building a new constraint whose support involves all the variables of the original ones (i.e., $supp(c_1 \otimes c_2) \subseteq supp(c_1) \cup supp(c_2)$), and which associates to each tuple for such variables a semiring element, obtained by multiplying the elements associated by the original constraints to the appropriate subtuples.

Let $c \in \mathcal{C}$ be a constraint and $v \in V$ a variable. The *projection* of c over $V - \{v\}$ (denoted $c \Downarrow_{(V - \{v\})}$), is the constraint c' such that $c'\eta = \sum_{d \in D} c\eta[v := d]$. The projection operator is inductively extended to a set of variables $I \subseteq V$ by $c \Downarrow_{(V-I)} = c \Downarrow_{(V - \{v\})} \Downarrow_{(V - \{I - \{v\}\})}$. Informally, projecting eliminates variables from the support.

A *soft constraint satisfaction problem* is a pair $\langle C, con \rangle$, where C is a set of constraints over variables $con \subseteq V$. The set con is the set of variables of interest for the constraint set C, which may concern also variables not in con. The *solution* of a soft CSP $P = \langle C, con \rangle$ is the constraint $Sol(P) = (\bigotimes C) \Downarrow_{con}$.

---

[1] Alternatively, a constraint is a pair $\langle sc, def \rangle$: sc is the scope of a constraint, and def the function associating a value in A to each assignment of the variables in con.

The solution of a soft CSP plays the role of the objective function in optimization problems. Indeed, efficient solutions are referred to as *abstract solutions* in the soft CSP literature. The best approximation may be neatly characterized by so-called *best level*.

Proposition 1. *Let $P = \langle C, con \rangle$ be a soft CSP, and let $blevel(P) = (\bigotimes C) \Downarrow_\emptyset$ be denoted as the best level of consistency of P. Then, $\sup_\eta \{Sol(P)(\eta)\} = blevel(P)$.*

The soft CSP framework may accomodate several soft constraint frameworks. For instance, the semiring $\mathcal{K}_{CSP} = \langle \{false, true\}, \vee, \wedge, false, true \rangle$ allows for recasting Classical CSPs; the semiring $\mathcal{K}_{WCSP} = \langle \mathcal{R}, min, +, \infty, 0 \rangle$ for Weighted CSPs.

When the set A is totally ordered, as the examples above, $blevel(P)$ is the optimum of P, and thus, it uniquely characterizes the efficient frontier $\mathcal{E}(P) = \{Sol(P)(\eta) \mid \forall \eta'.Sol(P)(\eta) \not\geq Sol(P)(\eta')\}$). That does not hold for partially ordered semirings, as those naturally arising in multi-objective optimization, obtained as the cartesian product of a family $\mathcal{K}_1, \ldots, \mathcal{K}_p$ of semirings, each one associated to an objective function.

Proposition 2. *Let $\{K_i = \langle A_i, +_i, \times_i, \mathbf{0}_i, \mathbf{1}_i \rangle\}_{1 \leq i \leq p}$ be semirings. Then, the tuple $\mathcal{K}_C = \langle A_1 \times \ldots \times A_p, \overline{+}, \overline{\times}, \langle \mathbf{0}_1, \ldots, \mathbf{0}_p \rangle, \langle \mathbf{1}_1, \ldots, \mathbf{1}_p \rangle \rangle$ is a semiring: its set of elements is the cartesian product of A_is, and the operators are defined componentwise.*
    Moreover, if each K_i is tropical (absorptive, idempotent), then so is K_C.

Proposition 1 tells us that the best level of consistency of a problem P over semiring $\mathcal{K}_C$ is the lowest vector dominating the efficient frontier $\mathcal{E}(P)$. In other words, calculating $blevel(P)$ gets only an approximation of $\mathcal{E}(P)$. Our solution is to consider basically the same problem, and choosing an alternative semiring wrt. $\mathcal{K}_C$ for solving it.

3   Semirings Based on Powersets

This section states the main theorem of the paper: for each soft CSP P over a semiring $\mathcal{K}$, a new semiring $\mathcal{L}(\mathcal{K})$ and a semiring morphism $l : \mathcal{K} \to \mathcal{L}(\mathcal{K})$ can be devised such that the best level of consistency for the problem $l(P)$ coincides with the efficient frontier of P. For the sake of readability, we fix a semiring $\mathcal{K} = \langle A, +, \times, \mathbf{0}, \mathbf{1} \rangle$.

Definition 1 (downward closure). *Let $\mathcal{K}$ be tropical. Then, for a set $S \subseteq A$ we let ΔS denote its downward closure, i.e., the set $\{a \in A \mid \exists s \in S.a \leq_{\mathcal{K}} s\}$.*

A set S is *downward closed* if $S = \Delta S$ (and any downward closure is so, since $\Delta(\Delta S) = \Delta S$), and we denote by $\mathcal{L}(A)$ the family of downward closed subsets of A.

Proposition 3. *Let $\mathcal{K}$ be absorptive. Then, the tuple $\mathcal{L}(\mathcal{K}) = \langle \mathcal{L}(A), \cup, \times, \{\mathbf{0}\}, A \rangle$ is an absorptive semiring: its elements are the (not empty) downward-closed subsets of A, $S \cup T$ is set (of subsets) union, and $S \times T = \Delta(\{s \times t \mid s \in S, t \in T\})$.*

Note that the absorptiveness of $\mathcal{K}$ plays a pivotal role, since it means that $A = \Delta\{\mathbf{1}\}$. The ordering states that $\Delta S \leq_{\mathcal{L}(\mathcal{K})} \Delta T$ iff for each $s \in S$ there exists $t \in T$ such that $s \leq_{\mathcal{K}} t$. Our construction of $\mathcal{L}(\mathcal{K})$ is thus reminiscent of the *partial correctness* (or *Hoare*) power-domain, a well-known tool in denotational semantics.

Theorem 1. *Let* $P = \langle C, con \rangle$ *be a soft CSP over semiring* $\mathcal{K}$*; and let* $\mathcal{L}(P) = \langle C_l, con \rangle$ *be the soft CSP over semiring* $\mathcal{L}(\mathcal{K})$ *such that* $C_l = \{l \circ c \mid c \in C\}$ *(thus,* $l \circ c(\eta) = \{c(\eta)\}$ *for any assignment* $\eta : V \to D$*). Then,* $\Delta(\mathcal{E}(P)) = blevel(\mathcal{L}(P))$.

The closure $\Delta(\mathcal{E}(P))$ is necessary, since the sets in $\mathcal{L}(\mathcal{K})$ are downward-closed. However, note that each constraint of a soft CSP P is defined over a finite set of functions $V \to D$, since it is finitely supported and D is finite. Thus, the efficient frontier $\mathcal{E}(P)$ is a finite set: such a remark could be exploited to improve on the previous presentation, describing a downward-closed set S by the family of its *irreducible* elements, i.e., the set I_S such that for no pair s_1, s_2 the element s_1 dominates s_2, and $\Delta(I_S) = S$.

Proposition 4. *Let* $\mathcal{K}$ *be absorptive. If* $\mathcal{K}$ *is idempotent, then also* $\mathcal{L}(\mathcal{K})$ *is so.*

The result above ensures that the local consistency techniques [4] applied for the soft CSPs over an idempotent semiring $\mathcal{K}$ can still be applied for problems over $\mathcal{L}(\mathcal{K})$.

4 Recasting Multi-criteria CSP

A *multi-criteria* CSP (MC-CSP) is a soft CSP problem composed by a family of p soft CSPs. Each criterion can be defined over the semiring $\mathcal{K}_{CSP}$. Then, a MC-CSP problem is defined over semiring $\mathcal{L}(\mathcal{K}_{CSP_1} \times \ldots \times \mathcal{K}_{CSP_p})$.

Consider a problem with two variables $\{x, y\}$, two values in each domain $\{a, b\}$, and two criteria to be satisfied. For the first criteria, the assignments $(x = a, y = a)$, $(x = b, y = a)$, and $(x = a, y = b)$ are forbidden. For the second criteria, the assignments $(x = b, y = a)$, $(x = a, y = b)$, and $(x = b, y = b)$ are forbidden. Let $\mathcal{K}_{2-CSP} = \langle \{f, t\} \times \{f, t\}, \bar{\vee}, \bar{\wedge}, \langle f, f \rangle, \langle t, t \rangle \rangle$ be the cartesian product of two semirings $\mathcal{K}_{CSP}$ (one for each criterion), where f and t are short-hands for $false$ and $true$, respectively. $\bar{\vee}$ is the pairwise $\vee$ and $\bar{\wedge}$ is the pairwise $\wedge$. Then, the problem is represented as a soft CSP $P = \langle \mathcal{C}, \mathcal{X} \rangle$ over $\mathcal{K}_{2-CSP}$, where $\mathcal{C} = \{C_x, C_y, C_{xy}\}$ is defined as $C_x(a) = C_x(b) = C_y(a) = C_y(b) = \langle t, t \rangle$, $C_{xy}(a, a) = \langle f, t \rangle$, $C_{xy}(b, a) = \langle f, f \rangle$, $C_{xy}(a, b) = \langle f, f \rangle$, and $C_{xy}(b, b) = \langle t, f \rangle$.

The solution of P is the constraint $Sol(P)$ with support $\{x, y\}$ given by $C_x \bar{\wedge} C_y \bar{\wedge} C_{xy}$. Since the variables of the problem are the same as the ones in the support of the constraints, there is no need to project any variable out. Moreover, since for all η, $C_x(\eta) = C_y(\eta) = \langle t, t \rangle$ and $\langle t, t \rangle$ is the unit element with respect $\bar{\wedge}$, $Sol(P) = C_{xy}$. The best level of consistency of P is $blevel(P) = \bar{\vee}_\eta \{Sol(P)(\eta)\} = \langle t, t \rangle$.

However, we want to obtain as the best level of consistency the set of semiring values representing the efficient frontier $\mathcal{E}(P) = \{\langle f, t \rangle, \langle t, f \rangle\}$. To that end, we map the problem P to a new one, by changing the semiring $\mathcal{K}_{2-CSP}$ using the partial correctness transformation on finite representations. By applying the mapping, we obtain a problem $\mathcal{L}(P) = \langle \mathcal{C}', \mathcal{X} \rangle$ over semiring $\mathcal{L}(\mathcal{K}_{2-CSP})$, with the following constraint definition $C_x(a) = C_x(b) = C_y(a) = C_y(b) = \{\langle t, t \rangle\}$, $C_{xy}(a, a) = \{\langle f, t \rangle\}$, $C_{xy}(b, a) = \{\langle f, f \rangle\}$, $C_{xy}(a, b) = \{\langle f, f \rangle\}$, $C_{xy}(b, b) = \{\langle t, f \rangle\}$.

The solution of $\mathcal{L}(P)$ is the same as for P. However, its best level of consistency is $blevel(\mathcal{L}(P)) = \{\langle 0, 1 \rangle, \langle 1, 0 \rangle\}$, which is the efficient frontier of P. The corresponding pareto-optimal solutions are $(x = a, y = a)$ and $(x = b, y = b)$.

5   Conclusions, Related Works and Further Developments

Problems involving the optimization of more than one objective are ubiquitous in real world domains. They are probably the most relevant optimization problems with a partially ordered objective function. So far, nobody studied how to use the soft CSP framework to model multi-objective problems. The only attempt is [5], where the least upper bound is the used notion of solution, which is a relaxed one regarding pareto-optimality.

Our paper addresses exactly this issue. For the first time, we distill a semiring able to define problems such that their best level of consistency is the efficient frontier of a multi-objective problem. This formalization is important for two main reasons: we gain some understanding of the nature of multi-objective optimization problems; and we inherit some theoretical result from the soft CSP framework.

We are aware of few papers addressing the handling of preferences with structures that are reminiscent of downward closures. Among others, we cite the work on *preference queries* [6], where a *winnow* operator is introduced. The winnow operator selects from a given relation the set of most preferred tuples, according to a given preference relation. In the same context of relational databases a similar *Skyline* operator is investigated in [7]. The Skyline operator filters out a set of interesting points from a potentially large set of data points, where a point is interesting if it is not dominated by any other point. Moreover, Pareto preference constructors are defined in [8] in the framework of the so-called *Best-Matches-Only (BMO) query model*. In the paper, the author investigates how complex preference queries can be decomposed into simpler ones.

We are currently investigating the semiring $\mathcal{S}(\mathcal{K})$ of *saturated* closures, i.e., whose elements are both downward- and upward-closed sets. We are in general looking for suitable constructions resulting in a *division* semiring, if $\mathcal{K}$ is so. This would allow for the application of local consistency algorithm to a larger family of case studies [9].

References

1. Ehrgott, M., Gandibleux, X.: Multiple Criteria Optimization. State of the Art. Annotated Bibliographic Surveys. Kluwer, Dordrecht (2002)
2. Pin, J.E.: Tropical semirings. In: Idempotency, pp. 50–69. Cambridge University Press, Cambridge (1998)
3. Bistarelli, S., Montanari, U., Rossi, F.: Soft concurrent constraint programming. ACM Transactions in Compututational Logic 7(3), 563–589 (2006)
4. Bistarelli, S., Montanari, U., Rossi, F.: Semiring-based constraint solving and optimization. Journal of ACM 44(2), 201–236 (1997)
5. Bistarelli, S., Montanari, U., Rossi, F.: Soft constraint logic programming and generalized shortest path problems. Journal of Heuristics 8(1), 25–41 (2002)
6. Chomicki, J.: Semantic optimization techniques for preference queries. Information Systems 32(5), 670–684 (2007)
7. Börzsönyi, S., Kossmann, D., Stocker, K.: The skyline operator. In: Proc. ICDE 2001, pp. 421–430. IEEE Computer Society, Los Alamitos (2001)
8. Kießling, W.: Foundations of preferences in database systems. In: Proc. VLDB 2002, pp. 311–322. Morgan Kaufmann, San Francisco (2003)
9. Bistarelli, S., Gadducci, F.: Enhancing constraints manipulation in semiring-based formalisms. In: Brewka, G., Coradeschi, S., Perini, A., Traverso, P. (eds.) Proc. ECAI 2006, pp. 63–67. IOS Press, Amsterdam (2006)

A Multi-theory Logic Language
for the World Wide Web

Giulio Piancastelli and Andrea Omicini

ALMA MATER STUDIORUM—Università di Bologna
via Venezia 52, 47037 Cesena, FC, Italy

Abstract. Despite the recent formalization of the Web in terms of
Representational State Transfer (REST) architectural style and
Resource-Oriented Architecture (ROA), current tools for Web programming generally misunderstand its design. Based on REST/ROA insights,
we claim that logic languages are suited for promoting the Web architecture and principles. The mapping of REST/ROA abstractions onto
elements of Contextual Logic Programming also permits runtime modification of resource behavior. In this paper we present Web Logic Programming as a Prolog-based language for the Web embedding REST/ROA
principles, meant to be the basis of an application framework for rapid
prototyping.

1 Introduction

In the latest years, substantial achievements have been obtained in the understanding of the Web architectural principles and design criteria, in terms of
the Representational State Transfer (REST) architectural style for distributed
hypermedia systems [1], and of a set of Web application guidelines and best
practices called Resource-Oriented Architecture (ROA) [2]. The *resource* is the
main REST/ROA data abstraction, defined as any conceptual target of a hy-
pertext reference identified by a unique name. Communication among resources,
and between the client- and server-side of a Web application, occurs through a
uniform interface by transferring a *representation* of a resource current state.

When confronted with REST/ROA insights, research on logic programming
and the Web shows significant shortcomings. API libraries such as PiLLoW [3]
only allow interfacing logic technologies with the Web instead of promoting a
deeper integration. Internet agents [4] lay the agent-oriented paradigm over the
resource-oriented Web architecture, without treating the relationship between
the two abstractions. *Logic pages* in systems such as LogicWeb [5] are conceptually narrower than resources, in the sense that they could be viewed as resources
with only one representation, and can be only exploited on the client side.

In this paper, we first show how to map Web concepts onto elements of Contextual Logic Programming (CtxLP) [6] according to REST/ROA; then, based
on that mapping, and on the programming model introduced in [7], we present
Web Logic Programming as a Prolog-based logic language specific to the Web,
intended to work as the fundamental brick of a logic framework for prototyping
Web applications while promoting REST/ROA principles and constraints.

M. Garcia de la Banda and E. Pontelli (Eds.): ICLP 2008, LNCS 5366, pp. 769–773, 2008.

2   Resources and Contexts

The properties of Web resources can be immediately identified: a name defined by the URI standard; data representing their state; and behavior, used e.g. to manage interaction with other resources. According to ROA, a resource and its URI ought to have an intuitive correspondence: identifiers should be descriptive, and have a definite structure varying in predictable ways [2]. This *addressability* property is accompanied by the *connectedness* property, that is the quality of resources to be linked to each other in meaningful ways.

When resource names are designed following ROA guidelines, they feature an interesting property on their own: any path can be interpreted as including a set of resource names. More precisely, we say that resource names such as `http://example.com/sales/2004/Q4` *encompass* the names of other resources and at last the name of the resource representing the domain at the URI root:

```
http://example.com/sales/2004
http://example.com/sales
http://example.com
```

This naming structure suggests that each resource lives in an information *context* composed by the resources associated with the names *encompassed* by that resource name. Since more than one name can identify the same resource, the context of a resource is associated with its name. Thus, a resource may live in different contexts at the same time, and feature different behaviors according to the context where the interaction with other elements of the system takes place.

The properties of Web resources can be easily mapped onto elements of logic languages such as Prolog: each resource R uses the atom containing the resource URI as its $N(R)$ name, and clauses in a logic theory $T(R)$ as its data (facts) and behavior (rules). For operations that may involve not only a single isolated resource, we introduce the context $C(R)$ as the locus of computation associated with each resource. Following ROA guidelines on URIs, we define a resource context as the composition of the theories associated with the resources linked to names encompassed by the name of that resource, including the resource itself. Given a resource R with a name $N(R)$ so that $N(R) \subseteq N(R_1) \subseteq \ldots \subseteq N(R_n)$, where the inclusion operator follows the encompassment semantics previously defined, then the associated context $C(R)$ is generated by the composition $T(R) \cdot T(R_1) \cdot \ldots \cdot T(R_n)$, where the theories $T(R_i)$ could be imagined as occupying the slots of a stack structure, with $T(R)$ at the top and $T(R_n)$ at the bottom.

Alongside resources with a URI, we have identified four *implicit* resources corresponding to recurring concepts in Web development: *(i)* the session resource R_S (identified by the atom `session`) representing an interaction session with the application; *(ii)* the `user` resource R_U; *(iii)* the `application` resource R_A containing knowledge that can be applied to every resource in the application; *(iv)* the `environment` resource R_E entailing the Web server where the application has been deployed. They are *implicit* because they are attached, in the presented order, to the bottom of the context of any resource even if their names are not encompassed by the name of that resource.

3   Web Logic Programming

Web Logic Programming (WebLP) is a language to program Web resources and their interaction in ROA-based systems. To define the WebLP computation model, maintaining compatibility with REST constraints, we need to analyze the Web computation model: it revolves around transactions in HTTP, a protocol aimed at transferring *representations* of a resource state. Each transaction starts with a *request*, containing the method information (i.e. how the receiver has to process the request) and the scope information (i.e. the data where the receiver should operate the method) [2]. Computations occur on the receiving side, where the target resource performs the operation indicated by the method. The result is a *response* carrying an optional representation of the target resource.

Adopting a logic programming view of the Web computation model, each HTTP request is translated to represent a deduction: the scope information is used to indicate the target theory, and the method information is mapped onto a logic goal (e.g. `get/3`). The computation takes place in the context associated with the target resource; then, the information resulting from goal solution is translated to a suitable representation and sent back in the HTTP response.

To invoke a computation represented by a goal G on a resource R, we adopt the syntax `N(R):G`, ultimately meaning $C(R) \vdash G$. Let $C(R)$ be the composition of n theories, the query G is asked in turn to each theory, by exploiting context navigation to locate the unifying predicate. The goal fails if no solution is found in any theory, or succeeds when it is solved using the knowledge base of a theory $T(R_i)$. When the goal G is replaced by the subgoals of the matching rule in $T(R_i)$, the computation proceeds from $C(R_i)$ instead of the original context.

As a code sketch example, imagine a bookshelf sharing application: the shelf of the `jdoe` user is represented by the S resource, identified by the URI `http://example.com/jdoe/shelf`; each book is filed under category subjects, e.g. the resource B for biology books lives at `/jdoe/shelf/biology`. When B receives a GET request, a predicate to pick the list of biology books is invoked:

```
pick_biology_books(B) :-
    parent_id(Shelf), pick_books(B, category(biology), Shelf).
```

where `parent_id/1` is a predefined predicate returning the identifier of the parent resource. The `pick_books/3` predicate is defined neither in B nor in S, since it has a wider scope. As shown in Fig. 1, the theories in $C(B)$ are traversed down to the `/` resource, where a definition for `pick_books/3` is found:

```
pick_books(B, category(C), Shelf) :-
    findall(Book, Shelf : book(Book), Books), filter(Books, C, B).
```

Definitions for predicates invoked by `pick_books/3` are then searched beginning from the current context rather than $C(B)$ where the computation started.

3.1   Dynamic Context Composition

The fixed structure of resource identifiers in the Web architecture simplifies computations in that no need for a dynamic context augmentation is envisioned.

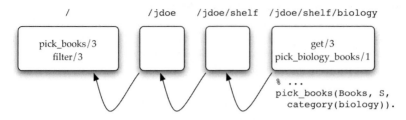

Fig. 1. The `/jdoe/shelf/biology` resource responds to a HTTP GET request by eventually invoking the `pick_biology_books/1` predicate, which in turn calls `pick_books/3`; the context is traversed until a proper definition for it is found in the `/` resource

However, a computation may involve a group of different resources, e.g. in filtering distinct sets of search results. We may express the invocation of a computation on a composition of contexts by the syntax `[N(R1), ..., N(Rn)]:G`. The semantics of this computation roughly corresponds to the *union* operator in Modular Logic Programming [8]: the goal G succeeds as soon as it is solved on at least one context, or it fails when no solution is found in any context. When the goal is replaced by the subgoals of the matching rule in a theory of $C(R_i)$, the computation proceeds from the context union rather than from $C(R_i)$.

3.2 Dynamic Resource Behavior

Another dynamic aspect of a resource comes from the ability to express behavioral rules as first-class abstractions in a logic programming language: on one hand, it is thus possible to exploit well-known stateful mechanisms to change the knowledge base associated with a resource; on the other hand, the HTTP protocol itself allows changing a resource by means of the PUT method, wherein the content should be considered as a modified version of the target resource that has to replace (or be merged with) the original version residing on the server.

As a code sketch example, imagine a reading wish list in a bookshelf sharing application. When a book is added, the resource representing the wish list could check local libraries for book availability, and possibly borrow it on user's behalf; if no book is found, the resource could check online bookstores, reporting prices to the user for future purchase. This behavior may be codified by the rules:

```
check(Book) :- library(L), available(Book, L), borrow(Book, L), !.
check(Book) :- bookstore(S), available(S, Book, Price),
               report_to_user(S, Book, Price).
```

When an online bookstore (e.g. Amazon) offers discounts, the wish list resource should react to the insertion of new books so as to check that store first instead of libraries, directly placing an order if the possibly discounted price is inferior to a certain threshold. This behavior may be represented by the following rule:

```
check(Book) :- available(amazon, Book, Price),
               threshold(T), Price < T, order(amazon, Book), !.
```

The Web application could change the behavior of wish lists by sending HTTP PUT requests that modify the computational representation of those resources by carrying the new clause of the `check/1` predicate. The application could restore the old behavior at the end of the discount period by sending other PUT requests with the previous `check/1` rules.

3.3 Operational Semantics

The semantics is heavily indebted with CtxLP: however, WebLP does not feature rules for context augmentation; its *Explicit Up* rule describes a shortcut to invoke a goal derivation on the immediate ancestor of a resource by means of the `parent` identifier; and it adds a *Context Composition* rule exploiting the *union* operator from Modular Logic Programming. More details are provided in [9].

4 Conclusions and Future Work

WebLP tries to follow the principles and capture the abstractions of the Web as described by REST/ROA: it maps *resources* to logic theories, and maintains the *addressability* property by using URIs to identify theories and label queries; it respects the *uniform interface* by using deductions to access and exchange information; and it embraces the *connectedness* property by binding resources along a single URI path in the notion of *context*. Future work will be devoted to the construction of a logic programming Web framework based on WebLP.

References

1. Fielding, R.T.: Architectural Styles and the Design of Network-based Software Architectures. PhD thesis, University of California, Irvine (2000)
2. Richardson, L., Ruby, S.: RESTful Web Services. O'Reilly, Sebastopol (2007)
3. Cabeza, D., Hermenegildo, M.: Distributed WWW Programming using (Ciao–) Prolog and the PiLLoW Library. Theory and Practice of Logic Programming 1(3), 251–282 (2001)
4. Denti, E., Natali, A., Omicini, A.: Merging Logic Programming into Web-based Technology: A Coordination-based Approach. In: 2nd International Workshop on Logic Programming Tools for Internet Applications, Leuven (B), July 1997, pp. 117–128 (1997)
5. Loke, S.W.: Adding Logic Programming Behaviour to the World Wide Web. PhD thesis, University of Melbourne, Australia (1998)
6. Monteiro, L., Porto, A.: A Language for Contextual Logic Programming. In: Logic Programming Languages: Constraints, Functions, and Objects. MIT Press, Cambridge (1993)
7. Piancastelli, G., Omicini, A.: A Logic Programming model for Web resources. In: 4th International Conference on Web Information Systems and Technologies (WEBIST 2008), Funchal, Madeira (P), May 2008, pp. 158–164 (2008)
8. Brogi, A., Mancarella, P., Pedreschi, D., Turini, F.: Modular Logic Programming. ACM Trans. on Programming Languages and Systems 16(3), 1361–1398 (1994)
9. Piancastelli, G., Omicini, A.: A multi-theory logic programming language for the World Wide Web. Technical Report 2515, Alma Mater Studiorum—Università di Bologna (August 2008), http://amsacta.cib.unibo.it/archive/00002515/

A Case Study in Engineering SQL Constraint Database Systems (Extended Abstract)

Sebastien Siva[1], James J. Lu[1], and Hantao Zhang[2]

[1] Mathematics and Computer Science, Emory University, Atlanta, GA 30322-1950, USA
[2] Computer Science, University of Iowa, Iowa City, IA 52240, USA

1 Introduction

Practical contexts for constraint satisfaction problems (CSP) often involve large relational databases. The recent proposal by Cadoli and Mancini, CONSQL, shows that a simple extension to SQL provides a viable basis for modeling CSP [1]. This enables the transparent integration of CSP solvers with databases using SQL — the most widely known and popular database language, and opens the possibility for making the power of CSP technology accessible to SQL knowledgeable users.

To realize this potential, substantial engineering efforts, each with the goal of delivering increasingly sophisticated tools will be required. To that end, this extended abstract describes a case study in the design and implementation of a SQL constraint data engine (SCDE). SCDE manages the internal representation and solving of constraints through a combination of ordinary SQL and a complete, high-performance satisfiability (SAT) solver, SATO.[1] This design complements the simulator described in [1] for CONSQL, which exploits an incomplete constraint solver JLocal. Motivations for the orthogonal design are as follows. First, many CSPs over relational databases involve finite domains and can be represented and solved within the SAT paradigm. Second, significant advances have occurred in the last decade in (DPLL-based) complete SAT solvers, including systems that allow the process of partial model generation to be intertwined with problem-specific literal selections strategies [10]. Third, the completeness property and the ability to enumerate solutions provides opportunities for interesting post-processing of CSP solutions inside the database engine.

Lessons from our work to date include 1) techniques for representing SQL constraints as a combination of database relations and parse trees, and for modularizing constraint compilation; 2) an understanding of several important constraint patterns and associated algorithms for compilation to SAT clauses; 3) experience from applying the SCDE to two case-studies bring into sharper focus important enhancements that will be necessary to improve the usability of the SCDE. Due to space constraint, we briefly mention related work here but without detailed comparisons.

Related Work. Early efforts to implement CSP techniques in database systems include *deductive* and *constraint databases* that reuse important ideas from *logic* and *constraint logic programming* [3,5,6,9]. While conceptually elegant, these techniques required knowledge outside the scope of traditional relational database users and programmers. Recent work on translating high-level specification languages to SAT include CModels

---

[1] Version 4.2, http://www.cs.uiowa.edu/~hzhang/sato/

M. Garcia de la Banda and E. Pontelli (Eds.): ICLP 2008, LNCS 5366, pp. 774–778, 2008.

[4] and NP-Spec [2]. Their source languages are logic-based, datalog-like rules. To our knowledge, the current work is the first attempt at compiling SQL to SAT.

2 The SCDE System

The SCDE accepts problems in forms similar to CONSQL [1]. Some modifications and extensions have been made to the syntax to facilitate the interactive development, incremental editing and debugging of a problem specifications in either the commandline, an input file, or the GUI. The key concept of CONSQL, the non-deterministic GUESS operator that declares a relation to have an arbitrary extension, is adapted in the SCDE. Given a guess relation Q, a set of constraints, written in ordinary SQL syntax over both existing and other guess relations, specifies conditions that any valid extension of Q must satisfy. The COMPUTE <Q> command directs SCDE to solve for an extension of <Q> consistent with the currently applicable SQL constraints.

Consider the 1997-98 ACC Basketball Scheduling problem (ACCBP) [7].[2] The basic problem is to create a double round-robin schedule for the men's basketball teams of the, at that time, 9 ACC schools. We assume relations team(id:int,name:string) and slot(id:int,date:date). The schema of the guess relation is

```
schedule(slot:ref slot.id,home:ref team.id,away:ref team.id).
```

Below are three simple examples.

```
-- C1: no team can play twice in the same slot.
  CONSTRAINT C1 CHECK (NOT EXISTS
      (SELECT * FROM schedule s1, schedule s2
      WHERE diff(s1,s2) AND s1.slot = s2.slot AND
            (s1.home = s2.home OR s1.away = s2.away OR
            s1.home = s2.away OR s1.away = s2.home)))
-- C2: each team plays every other team, once home, once away
  CONSTRAINT C2 CHECK (NOT EXISTS
      (SELECT * FROM teams t1, teams t2
      WHERE t1.id <> t2.id AND
            1 <> (SELECT COUNT(*) FROM schedule
            WHERE home = t1.id AND away = t2.id)))
-- C3: UNC and Duke must play each other in the final slot
  CONSTRAINT C3 CHECK (EXISTS
      (SELECT * FROM schedule s, teams t1, teams t2
      WHERE s.slot = 17 AND s.home = t1.id AND s.away = t2.id
        AND t1.name = 'Duke' AND t2.name = 'UNC'))
```

Components of the SCDE system architecture include various modules for user and application interfaces. The system kernel contains algorithms for parsing and constructing problem representations, encoding problems as SAT instances, decoding solutions produced by SATO, and analyzing problems for possible optimizations. Relational database support is provided by Sqlite,[3] compiled as part of the SCDE executable.

---

[2] The ACC is a conference of universities along the east coast of the U.S.

[3] Version 3.6.1, http://www.sqlite.org/

2.1   Problem Representation

Given a constraint problem with guess tabe Q, SCDE maintains a variable mapping relation, vbmap, whose schema is the same as Q but with an additional integer attribute, vbid. These unique integer identifiers are used to construct clauses according to the DIMACS syntax for SAT solvers: positive and negative literals are represented as positive and negative integers, respectively.

For each guess relation, auxiliary relations are maintained for managing the original text of each constraint and a set of computed solutions. Methods associated with the parse tree representation of constraints, for extracting and modifying the sub-structures have been implemented. An example, is $nest(C, n)$ that returns, for the given constraint C, the set of queries nested at depth n (with respect to the keyword SELECT).

2.2   Constraint Compilation

Compiling SQL constraints into SAT is very different from traditional piecemeal, syntax-directed compiling of programming languages. Moreover, the "virtual machines" of SQL and SAT have very little resemblance. Indeed, compared to other work on translating high-level specification languages possessing stricter structures (e.g., disjunctive logic and answer set programming [4], NP-Spec [2]), the main difficulty in our work is that a SQL constraint may be of an arbitrary structure. We approach the problem by modularizing compilation around constraint patterns: a separate translation is provided for each possible outer structure of constraints. The advantage of this organization is extensibility; useful new patterns may be incorporated easily when they emerge. In addition, the set of patterns can serve as a useful "programming guide" to assist SQL users learning to write constraints.

From experience applying SCDE, we have identified the three important constraint patterns shown below. (Remarks: Q is the guess relation and does not appear in any sub-query of conditions <c> and <d>; each Bi is a base relation; e evaluates to an integer and @ is a comparison (e.g., <).)

```
* Not-Exist-m Constraint (NEMC):
     CHECK (NOT EXISTS
        (SELECT * FROM Q q1,...,Q qm, B1,...,Bk WHERE <c>))
* Count Constraint (CC):
     CHECK (NOT EXISTS
        (SELECT * FROM B1,...,Bk
         WHERE <c> AND e @ (SELECT count(*) FROM Q WHERE <d>)))
* Exist-m Constraint (EMC):
     CHECK (EXISTS
        (SELECT * FROM Q q1,...,Q qm, B1,...,Bk WHERE <c>))
```

Although there exist other useful patterns currently unsupported, all constraints of the ACCBP may be written naturally as instances of these three. An inspection of the boolean constraints in the examples of [1] shows that they fall into these patterns as well. In addition, all constraints for a recently completed case study to group incoming students at the Emory Oxford campus are easily written as instances of CC. We briefly comment on the algorithms for compiling the three constraint patterns but omit their details.

An NEMC states no more than m - 1 copies of the Q may satisfy <c>. Given a join of the m copies of Q that satisfies <c>, this implies that at least one of the copies must be false. The corresponding clause may be obtained by querying the vbid associated each copy of Q, and forming a negative clause over all the ids. Constraint C1 in Section 2 is an instance of NEMC.

The most frequent uses of EMC contains a single copy of the guess table. That is, m = 1. Compilation is similar to NEMC, but an interesting duality exists. While the result of nest(C, 0) of a given NEMC C, read first by row and second by column, is a CNF of negative clauses, it is a DNF of positive conjunctions in an EMC. Constraint C3 in Section 2 is an instance of EMC.

CC often produces an explosive growth in the size of the clauses. Given a tuple of the outer query that satisfies <c>, suppose T is the set of tuples returned from the query obtained from the inner sub-query by replacing count(*) with vbid. When the comparison operator @ is <, the constraint may be expressed equivalently as $\binom{|T|}{e}$ negative clauses, each of size e. When the comparison is >, the constraint is equivalent to $\binom{|T|}{|T|-e}$ positive clauses, each of size $|T| - e$. To represent these potentially large clause sets, we rely on SATO's non-standard feature to succinctly represent count constraints: Given a clause C in DIMACS format v1 ... vk, the expression C @ e indicates that the number of literals true in C must satisfy @ e. Similar feature is supported by most modern solvers. Using this extended notation for CC, finding a model that satisfies the required number of literals is passed to and handled within the solver. Constraint C2 in Section 2 is an instance of CC.

3   A Case Study Application

For the ACCBP, we succeeded in computing a solution that satisfies various "generic" constraints including 1) each team plays every other team, once home, once away, 2) each team is idle twice, 3) no 3 consecutive away or home games, and 4) rematches occur exactly 9 games from the original match-up. When specialized constraints are added, other constraints became more difficult to satisfy and had to be relaxed. In particular, tuning the value for the spacing between a match-up and its rematch turns out to be key in the solvability and the runtime for many problem instances. The next table summarizes the computing time for several tested instances. Problem **P** has the additional requirement that each team must play four weekends at home, four weekends away and one weekend idle.

	generic	P(4)	P(5)	P(6)	all(4)	all(5)	all(9)
# clauses	179937	173052	174060	174996	175181	176189	182093
compile time	5s	4s	5s	5s	8s	7s	7s
solve time	0s	3s	177s	820s	403s	577s	NA
solution found	yes	yes	yes	no	yes	no	NA

The number in parenthesis indicates the minimum spacing required between a match and its rematch. Problem **all** contains all the constraints of the original problem [7]. The failure to produce an answer for **all(9)** is not surprising given that the same problem also failed to produce a solution (after two days) using procedural programming and SATO

[11]. To succeed with SATO, the three-phase approach described by Nemhauser and Trick [7] was necessary. The number of clauses reported is written over 1458 variables. It is substantially lower than the true count of actual clauses, however, as many of the clauses are written using the extended notation described earlier.

4   Discussion and Conclusion

The case studies show that storing CSPs in a database, compiling and post-processing add a modest but predictable overhead to the performance of SAT solvers. Our experience using the SCDE is that it takes time (about 2 weeks in our case) to become acquainted with writing SQL constraints, but once we are familiar with certain recurrent patterns, translating the English constraints into SQL is straightforward. Relative to our user experience, perhaps the most important benefit of the SCDE is the ease of modifying constraints, both as SQL statements and as data in base relations.

Our experience also highlights several missing features that would help to further improve usability. An example is the ability to trace the effects of a single constraint including the number of vbmap tuples that it satisfies, the number and size of clauses that it generates, and so on. Another example is the ability for incremental and separate compilation of constraints. Modification, addition and removal of constraints should only locally affect the clause set, and recomputation of the entire set should be avoided.

Acknowledgement. This research was supported in part by the University Research Committee of Emory University.

References

1. Cadoli, M., Mancini, T.: Combining Relational Algebra, SQL, Constraint Modelling, and Local Search. Theory Pract. Log. Program. 7(1-2), 37–65 (2007)
2. Cadoli, M., Schaerf, A.: Compiling Problem Specification into SAT. Artificial Intelligence 162(1-2), 89–120 (2005)
3. Chimenti, D., Gamboa, R., Krishnamurthy, R., Naqvi, S., Tsur, S., Zaniolo, C.: The LDL System Prototype. IEEE Transactions on Knowledge and Data Engineering (1990)
4. Giunchiglia, E., Lierler, Y., Maratea, M.: Answer Set Programming based on Propositional Satisfiability. J. of Automated Reasoning 36(4), 345–377 (2006)
5. Jaffar, J., Maher, M.J.: Constraint Logic Programming: A survey. Journal of Logic Programming 19/20, 503–581 (1994)
6. Kanellakis, P.C., Goldin, D.Q.: Constraint Programming and Database Query Languages. In: Hagiya, M., Mitchell, J.C. (eds.) TACS 1994. LNCS, vol. 789, pp. 96–120. Springer, Heidelberg (1994)
7. Nemhauser, G., Trick, M.: Scheduling a Major College Basketball Conference. Operation Research 46(1) (1998)
8. Siva, S.: Ph.D. Thesis (in progress)
9. Zaniolo, C.: Deductive Databases - Theory meets Practice. In: Bancilhon, F., Tsichritzis, D.C., Thanos, C. (eds.) EDBT 1990. LNCS, vol. 416, pp. 1–15. Springer, Heidelberg (1990)
10. Zhang, H.: The Satbox Library (2006),
    http://www.cs.uiowa.edu/~hzhang/satbox/
11. Zhang, H.: Generating College Conference Basketball Schedules by a SAT Solver. In: Proceedings of the Fifth International Symposium on the Theory and Applications of Satisfiability Testing, pp. 281–291 (2002)

Policy-Driven Negotiations and Explanations: Exploiting Logic-Programming for Trust Management, Privacy & Security

Piero A. Bonatti[1,*], Juri L. De Coi[2], Daniel Olmedilla[2], and Luigi Sauro[1]

[1] Università di Napoli Federico II
[2] L3S Research Center & University of Hannover

Abstract. Traditional protection mechanisms rely on the characterization of requesters by identity. This is adequate in a closed system with a known set of users but it is not feasible in open environments such as the Web, where parties may get in touch without being previously known to each other. In such cases policy-driven negotiation protocols have emerged as a possible solution to enforce security on future web applications. Along with this setting, we illustrate PROTUNE a system for specifying and cooperatively enforcing security and privacy policies (as well as other kinds of policies). PROTUNE relies on logic programming for representing policies and for reasoning with and about them.

1 Introduction

Open distributed environments such as the World Wide Web offer easy sharing of information, but provide few options for the protection of sensitive information and other sensitive resources. Even though latest developments such as the Web 2.0 have demonstrated that many users are willing to participate and therefore share information publicly, recent experiences with Facebook's "beacon" service[1] and Virgin's use of Flickr pictures[2] have also shown that users are not willing to accept every possible use (or abuse) of their data. Therefore, protection of services and sensitive data may determine the success or failure of a new service.

Policies with well-defined meaning and their exchange between parties during transactions allow for the dynamic enforcement of security and privacy. However, such a policy-aware web would equally fail if administrators and users do not understand such policies (their own and the ones from other parties they are interacting with), nor are they well informed about the process of enforcing them. Furthermore, in case a negotiation fails, receiving a simple "Transaction failed" is not satisfactory for a common user as it does not provide any clue about what has gone wrong.

---

[*] In alphabetical order.
[1] http://www.washingtonpost.com/wp-dyn/content/article/2007/11/29/
AR2007112902503.html?hpid=topnews
[2] http://www.smh.com.au/news/technology/virgin-sued-for-using-teens-
photo/2007/09/21/1189881735928.html

M. Garcia de la Banda and E. Pontelli (Eds.): ICLP 2008, LNCS 5366, pp. 779–784, 2008.

In this paper, we present the PRovisional TrUst NEgotiation framework PRO-
TUNE [1] which aims at combining distributed trust management policies with
provisional-style business rules and access-control related actions. PROTUNE's
rule language extends two previous languages: PAPL [2] and PEERTRUST [3],
that supports distributed credentials and a flexible policy protection mechanism.

PROTUNE provides a framework with:

- a trust management language supporting (possibly user-defined) actions
- an extensible declarative metalanguage for driving decisions about information disclosure
- a parameterized negotiation procedure, that gives a semantics to the metalanguage and provably satisfies some desirable properties for all possible
  metapolicies
- general ontology-based techniques for smoothly integrating language
  extensions
- advanced policy explanations in order to answer why, why-not, how-to, and
  what-if queries [4]

Policies are basically sets of Horn rules (enhanced with some syntactic sugar) on
which the system has to perform several kinds of symbolic manipulations such
as deduction, abduction, and filtering (as described in Section 4).

We made use of both a tabled logic programming engine (XSB) and a Prolog
compiled on Java bytecode. These two technologies have complementary advantages. Tabling significantly enhances performance in many cases, by factorizing
common subproofs; moreover, tabling makes it possible to process recursive policies without worrying about termination. A direct implementation of the same
features with procedural programming paradigms would raise implementation,
debugging, and maintenance costs enough to prevent the adoption of similar
enhancements. Java-based Prologs, on the other hand, facilitate deployment
and on-the-fly code download by means of technologies that nowadays are in-
stalled on every computer (and well integrated with the security facilities of their
browsers).

The following sections describe more in detail some of these features and how
logic programming plays a crucial role in their definition and/or implementation.

2   Policy Specification

The PROTUNE rule language [1] is based on normal logic program rules "$A \leftarrow
L_1, \ldots, L_n$" where A is a standard logical atom (called the *head* of the rule)
and $L_1, \ldots, L_n$ (the *body* of the rule) are literals, that is, L_i equals either B_i
or $\neg B_i$, for some logical atom B_i. In addition, PROTUNE is enhanced with a
FLORA-like object oriented syntax that, however, is only an abbreviation for
standard first-order syntax. One can express by $X.\texttt{attr} : v$ the fact that X has an
attribute $\texttt{attr}$ with value v. Actually, $X.\texttt{attr} : v$ abbreviates the standard atom
$\texttt{attr}(X, v)$. This representation allows multi-valued attributes. This attribute
semantics is compatible with semantic web standards such as RDF and OWL
(in particular $X.\texttt{attr} : v$ corresponds to an RDF triple).

A *policy* is a set of rules, such that negation is applied neither to *provisional predicates* (defined below), nor to any predicate occurring in a rule head. This restriction ensures that policies are *monotonic* in the sense of [2], that is, as more credentials are released and more actions executed, the set of permissions does not decrease. Moreover, the restriction on negation makes policies *stratified programs*; therefore negation as failure has a clear, PTIME computable semantics that can be equivalently formulated as the perfect model semantics, the well-founded semantics or the stable model semantics [5].

The vocabulary of predicates occurring in the rules is partitioned into the following categories.

- *Decision Predicates*: Currently supported are `allow/1`, which is queried for access control decisions, and `sign/1`, which is used to issue statements signed by the principal owning the policy.
- *Logical Predicates*: Comprise abbreviation and state-query predicates as described in [6]
- *Constraint Predicates*:Comprise the usual equality and disequality predicates
- *Provisional Predicates*: May be made true by executing associated actions that may modify the current state like e.g. `sentCredential/1`, `logged/2`, `sentDeclaration/1`.

3   Metapolicies

Metapolicies consist of rules similar to object-level rules. They allow to inspect terms, check groundness, call an object-level goal G against the current state (using a predicate $holds(G)$), etc. In addition, a set of reserved attributes associated to predicates, literals and rules (e.g., whether a policy is public or sensitive) is used to drive the negotiator's decisions. For example, if p is a predicate, then p.`sensitivity` : `private` means that the extension of the predicate is private and should not be disclosed. An assertion p.`type` : `provisional` declares p to be a provisional predicate; then p can be attached to the corresponding action α by asserting p.`action` :α. If the action is to be executed locally, then we assert p.`actor` : `self`, otherwise assert p.`actor` : `peer`.

As pointed out before, metarules and metaattributes may be used to attach provisional predicates to the corresponding actions. The language for local actions should be flexible and powerful, to facilitate the integration of trust management in the surrounding environment. Script languages are good candidates; multiple action languages may coexist in the same policy.

As an example, the predicate `logged` (which stores a message in a file) can be associated to its action by a simple metafact or an ontology definition:

`logged`(Msg, $File$).`action`:$'$`echo`$' + Msg + '>' + File$.
`logged`(Msg, $File$).`ontology`:$<$ www.L3S.de/policyFramework#Logged $>$.

The exit status of the action determines whether the corresponding provisional atom is asserted.

4   Negotiations, Policy Reasoning and Filtering

In open distributed environments like the World Wide Web parties may make connections and interact without being previously known to each other. Therefore, before any meaningful interaction starts, a certain level of trust must be established from scratch. Generally, trust is established through exchange of information between the two parties. Since neither party is known to the other, this trust establishment process should be bi-directional: both parties may have sensitive information that they are reluctant to disclose until the other party has proved to be trustworthy at a certain level. This process is called trust negotiation and, if every party defines its access control and release policies to control outsiders' access to their sensitive resources, can be automated.

Therefore, during a negotiation both a requester (client) and a server exchange their policies and information with the goal of performing a transaction. The use of set of horn rules for policies together with ontologies provide the advantage of well-defined semantics and machine interoperability, hence allowing for automated negotiations. When a set of policy rules is disclosed by a server in response to a client's request, the client—roughly speaking—works back from the request (goal) looking for the provisional predicates such as credentials and declarations in its portfolio that match the conditions listed in the rules' bodies. In logical terms, the selected credentials and declarations (represented as logical atoms) plus the policy rules should entail the goal: this is called an *abduction problem*. After receiving credential and declarations from a client, a server checks whether its policy is fulfilled by trying to prove the goal using its own rules and the new atoms received from the client, as in a standard *deduction problem*. When a client enforces a privacy policy and issues a counter-request, the roles of the two peers are inverted: the client plays the role of the server and viceversa.

However, policies (or parts thereof) may be sensitive as well, and therefore they should not be exchanged unless there exists enough level of trust on the other party. PROTUNE provides a filtering mechanism [1] which taking into account specified metapolicies (e.g., sensitivity, actor and execution) as well as the information received from the other party may partially hide the "filtered" policy to be sent to the other party.

5   Explanations

The frameworks for protecting security and privacy can be effective only if common users—with no training in computer science or logic—increase their awareness and control over the policy applied by the systems they interact with. Towards this end, PROTUNE introduces a mechanism for answering *why, why-not, how-to*, and *what-if* queries on rule-based policies [4], using simple generic explanation strategies based on the intended meaning of a few core predicates with a special role in negotiations. PROTUNE is *lightweight* and *scalable*. The only extra workload needed during the framework instantiation phase to support explanations consists in writing literal verbalization patterns. Moreover, the extra computational burden on the server can be limited to adding a few more rules to the filtered policies (the literal verbalization rules) because the explanations can be independently produced on the clients. Despite its simplicity, our explanation mechanism supports most of the advanced features of second generation explanation systems. Moreover, it adopts a novel *tabled explanation structure*, that simultaneously shows local and global (intra-proof and inter-proof) information, thereby facilitating navigation. To focus answers in the trust negotiation domain, suitable heuristics are introduced in order to remove the irrelevant parts of the derivations. There are several novel aspects in such an approach:

- We adopt a *tabled explanation structure* as opposed to more traditional approaches based on single proof trees. The tabled approach makes it possible to describe infinite failures (which is essential for *why not* queries).
- Our explanations show the outcome of different possible proof attempts and let users see both local and global proof details at the same time. Such combination of intra-proof and inter-proof information is expected to facilitate navigation across the explanation structures.
- We introduce suitable heuristics for focussing explanations by removing irrelevant parts of the proof attempts. Anyway, we provide a second level of explanations where all the missing details can be recovered, if desired.
- Our heuristics are *generic*, i.e. domain independent. This means that they require no manual configuration.

6   Implementation: The Protune Framework

In PROTUNE policies are basically sets of Horn rules (enhanced with some syntactic sugar) on which the system has to perform several kinds of symbolic manipulations such as deduction, abduction, and filtering. All these forms of reasoning can be implemented with suitable metainterpreters; logic programming languages are perfect for these purposes. Features such as tabling (when available) lead to significant performance improvements with no extra implementation costs—this would not be conceivable with any other programming paradigms. Moreover, we make extensive use of a logic programming language compiled onto Java bytecode as part of a strategy for simplifying the deployment of our user agents, that can be even downloaded dynamically as applets. The rest of the framework and extensible interfaces are provided in Java in order to improve portability. A live demo of PROTUNE in a Web scenario is publicly available[3] as well as a screencast[4]. For a demo of the explanation facility and extensive documentation see `http://people.na.infn.it/rewerse/`

---

[3] `http://policy.l3s.uni-hannover.de/`
[4] `http://www.viddler.com/olmedilla/videos/1/`. Recommended in full screen.

References

1. Bonatti, P.A., Olmedilla, D.: Driving and monitoring provisional trust negotiation with metapolicies. In: IEEE POLICY, Stockholm, Sweden (2005)
2. Seamons, K., Winslett, M., Yu, T., Smith, B., Child, E., Jacobsen, J., Mills, H., Yu, L.: Requirements for Policy Languages for Trust Negotiation. In: IEEE POLICY, Monterey, CA (2002)
3. Gavriloaie, R., Nejdl, W., Olmedilla, D., Seamons, K.E., Winslett, M.: No registration needed: How to use declarative policies and negotiation to access sensitive resources on the semantic web. In: Bussler, C.J., Davies, J., Fensel, D., Studer, R. (eds.) ESWS 2004. LNCS, vol. 3053. Springer, Heidelberg (2004)
4. Bonatti, P.A., Olmedilla, D., Peer, J.: Advanced policy explanations on the web. In: 17th European Conference on Artificial Intelligence (ECAI 2006), Riva del Garda, Italy (2006)
5. Baral, C.: Knowledge representation, reasoning and declarative problem solving. Cambridge University Press, Cambridge (2003)
6. Bonatti, P., Samarati, P.: Regulating Service Access and Information Release on the Web. In: ACM Conference on Computer and Communications Security, Athens (2000)

An Algorithm for Sophisticated Code Matching
in Logic Programs

Wim Vanhoof and François Degrave

University of Namur
Faculty of Computer Science
Rue Grandgagnage 21
B-5000 Namur, Belgium

Abstract. In this work in progress, we develop a program analysis capable of efficiently detecting duplicated functionality within a logic program or a set of logic programs. Our main motivation is to provide an analysis that allows to automatically spot those locations in a program where a transformation could be applied that removes the duplication from the source code.

1   Introduction

Automatically identifying duplicated functionality within the source code of a given program or a set of programs can be of interest for a number of different reasons. One major application is in program refactoring where one applies program transformations – so-called *refactorings* – to improve the design and hence the maintainability of the source code *after* it has been written [1,2]. Although different classes of refactorings exist, removing duplication from the source code is recognised as one of the main incentives to perform refactoring [1].

Duplication can be present in different forms and can be due to different causes. For example, when working on a substantially large code base, one might be tempted to rapidly re-implement a frequently needed procedure rather than searching through the source code to check whether and how this procedure was already implemented before. More importantly, new functionality is often introduced by copy/pasting an existing part of the source code adapting it to the new needs. While the latter does not lead to multiple occurrences of exactly the same procedure, it does create procedures whose source code is similar in structure and whose core functionality is often identical. Let us consider the somewhat contrived example depicted in Figure 1. The predicate getBest/2 represented on the left takes as first argument a list of grades (numerical values between 0 and 20), and computes in its second argument the median value of the "best" grades among them. The predicate first computes the mean value of *all* the grades (variable M), then it takes the maximum of this value and 12 (variable WM) and it filters from the list of grades those being greater than WM. Next, it computes the median value from the resulting list (by sorting and taking the element in the middle of the resulting list). The predicate getBestAdj/2 on

M. Garcia de la Banda and E. Pontelli (Eds.): ICLP 2008, LNCS 5366, pp. 785–789, 2008.

```
getBest(Grades,Best):-                getBestAdj(Grades,Best):-
  sum(Grades,S)₁,                       adjust(Grades,AGrades)₁,
  length(Grades,N)₂,                    sum(AGrades,S)₂,
  M is S / N₃,                          length(AGrades,N)₃,
  max(M, 12, WM)₄,                      M is S / N₄,
  filter(Grades,WM,BGrades)₅,           filter(AGrades,M,BGrades)₅,
  sort(BGrades,Sorted)₆,                sort(BGrades,Sorted)₆,
  length(Sorted,SN)₇,                   length(Sorted,SN)₇,
  Pos is SN div 2₈,                     Pos is SN div 2₈,
  nth1(Pos,Sorted,Best)₉.               nth1(Pos,Sorted,Best)₉.
```

Fig. 1. An example of copy/paste programming

the right is a variant of the former predicate as it might have been obtained by copy/paste programming. It largely performs the same operations, except that initial grades are in some way adjusted before being processed (this is what adjust is meant to do) and the computed mean is used *as is* to filter grades. One way of refactoring the above code is to extract each functionality shared by both definitions into a new predicate, a so-called predicate extraction [2]. For the example above this would mean introducing a predicate that computes the mean value of a list of grades and a predicate that filters a grade list according to a given value and returns the median value of the filtered list.

Another interesting refactoring, studied in [3], is the *generalisation* of two predicate definitions by extracting those code parts that are *not* shared by the definitions. Consider the following example, taken from [3]:

```
rev_all(K,L):- K = []₁, L = []₂.
rev_all(K,L):- K = [X|Xs],₃ L = [Y|Ys]₄, reverse(X,Y)₅, rev_all(Xs,Ys)₆.

add_and_square(A,B):- A = []₁, B = []₂.
add_and_square(A,B):- A = [X|Xs]₃, B = [Y|Ys]₄, N is X+X₅, Y is N*N₆,
                      add_and_square(Xs,Ys)₇.
```

The definitions above implement two different relations: rev_all can be used to reverse all the elements of an input list (a list of lists), while add_and_square transforms each element x of an input list into $4x^2$. Although different, both definitions have a common core which consists of traversing a list and transforming each of its elements. As such, both definitions can be generalised into a single new definition – namely the well-known map/3 predicate – and calls to rev_all and add_and_square can be replaced by calls to map with the higher-order argument instantiated to, respectively, reverse and a lambda expression of the form lambda(X,Y) :- N=X+X,Y=N*N.

The aim of the current work is to devise a program analysis that can automatically find those spots in a program where functionality is duplicated in the sense outlined above. The work is a natural follow-up to [3] where we define a set of sufficient conditions under which each of the abovely illustrated refactorings can be applied. While [3] provide a theoretical framework for the study of refactoring opportunities based on the presence of duplicated code in logic programs, it fails to provide a viable and efficient algorithm for *computing* those parts of the source code that represent duplicated functionality.

2   Efficiently Computing Code Matches

Identifying parts of the source code that contain duplicated functionality clearly is an undecidable problem that nevertheless can be approximated by program analysis. The basic idea in this work, as it was in [3], is to use a very simple syntactic criterion to identify duplication, namely we consider two goals as implementing the same relation if one is a renaming of the other. The following definition introduces the notion of a code mapping identifying, between two given conjunctions, parts that are equal modulo renaming and that represent as such a *match* between two (sub)conjunctions. For a conjunction $C = B_1, \ldots, B_n$ and a set of natural numbers S, $C_{|S}$ denotes the conjunction obtained by restricting C to the atoms B_i with $i \in S$.

Definition 1. *Let $C = B_1, \ldots, B_n$ and $C' = B'_1, \ldots, B'_m$ be two conjunctions. A code mapping from C to C' is an injective and monotonically increasing partial function $\mu : \mathbb{N} \to \mathbb{N}$ such that[1] $C_{|dom(\mu)} \approx C'_{|img(\mu)}$. A code mapping μ is called a basic block mapping iff it represents a mapping between sets of consecutive literals in both conjunctions.*

When reconsidering the clauses for the `getBest/2` and `getBestAdj/2` predicates from before, one can easily see that the mapping $\mu = \{(1,2),(2,3),(3,4)\}$ is a basic block mapping between these clauses whereas the mapping $\mu' = \{(1,2),(2,3),(3,4),(5,5),(6,6),(7,7),(8,8),(9,9)\}$ is a code mapping but no basic block mapping as $4 \notin dom(\mu)$. Likewise, for the definitions of `rev_all` and `add_and_square` one can observe the basic block mapping $\{(1,1),(2,2)\}$ and code mapping $\{(3,3),(4,4),(6,7)\}$.[2] Note that a code mapping can always be decomposed into a set of basic block mappings. The decomposition is *maximal* if no two basic block mappings can be re-joined into a basic block mapping.

Searching for duplicated functionality now boils down to computing all code mappings that exist between predicate definitions. Computing a "maximal" or "longest" code mapping between two conjunctions is related to the problem of finding the longest common subsequence (LCS) of two input strings, see e.g. [4]. There are, however, some important complications that make adapting an LCS algorithm not straightforward:

1. Contrary to the problem of computing the longest common subsequence of two input strings, which can be done in a time $O(nm)$ (with n and m being the lengths of the two input strings), the search process involved in computing a good match between two source code fragments has an exponential flavour to it. The additional complexity stems from the fact that renamings

---

[1] We use $\approx$ to denote the fact that two conjunctions are equal modulo a renaming.
[2] When comparing recursive predicates, we assume that the predicate symbol of a recursive call is consistently renamed to some predefined symbol such as `res_call`.

need to be taken into account. Indeed, when searching for a longest code mapping, the combination of two code mappings μ_1 and μ_2 does not necessarily result in a valid code mapping since the renamings associated to μ_1 and μ_2 may be incompatible – that is, it may be impossible to compose them into a new single renaming. However, it may be possible to combine a submapping of μ_1 (or μ_2) with μ_2 (respectively μ_1) into a longer code mapping. Consequently, at any point during the search, *all* potential code mappings must be explored, rather than retaining and extending only a current longest one, as is the case in most LCS algorithms.

2. In source code matching for refactoring, other characteristics than the sheer size of the code mapping play a role in determining a "best" match between two conjunctions. These characteristics include the size of the individual basic block mappings the code mapping is composed of and the number of *gaps* – subconjunctions that do *not* take part in the code mapping. Moreover, the precise characteristics of the "best" match may depend on the particular refactoring one wishes to achieve. For predicate extraction, one is typically interested in large basic block mappings whereas for predicate generalisation, the size of the individual basic block mappings is less important than the number and the position of the gaps.

Our algorithm comprises two phases. First, all basic block mappings are computed. Then in a second phase, the previously computed basic block mappings are combined to construct larger code mappings. The algorithm is developed around two parameters, that allow to steer the search process. A first parameter, B_{min} denotes the minimal desired size of each basic block mapping in the maximal decomposition of the code mappings under construction. Likewise, the second parameter G_{max} denotes the maximal number of *gaps* one desires to have in the maximal decomposition of the code mappings under construction.

The first phase of this algorithm has a worst-case complexity $O(nm)$ with n and m the length of the conjunctions being matched. It basically constructs a set of basic block mappings that contain, for each pair of atoms B_i and B'_j *all* basic block mappings extending to the right of (i,j). This set of mappings can be computed in a bottom-up way and the operations involved are basically unification and composition of renamings. The hard part of the algorithm is its second phase, which is basically exponential in the number of basic block mappings computed during the first phase. However, this exponential behaviour is exposed in rare cases only. In fact, the execution time of the second phase grows in function of the most complicated code mapping that can be constructed between the conjunctions (typically involving multiple overlapping and interfearing basic block mappings). In most common cases (no match or a match comprising a few non-interfearing basic block mappings, as in the examples given in the introduction) the second phase is only linear in the number of basic block mappings found during the first phase!

3   Discussion

In this work, which is a report on work in progress, we develop an efficient algorithm for finding duplicated functionality in a logic program. A substantial amount of work has been done on the subject, most notably in the context of imperative languages. Known techniques are based on parametrised string matching [5] or can include more involved analysis on a graph representation of a program [6,7]. Most of these latter works, including the more recent [8], however concentrate on finding behavioural differences between programs that are known to be strongly related, which makes them more suited for applications such as plagiarism detection rather than for program refactoring.

The algorithm is being implemented, and first test results are promising. One key element that made the approach feasible was to limit the notion of a code mapping to a monotonically increasing function. This means that the algorithm will not detect duplication if atoms are permuted within a conjunction. We believe this is justified, as for most logic languages either the order within a conjunction is relevant, or conjunctions can be reordered accorded to some predefined scheme [9].

Acknowledgements

The authors would like to thank Alexander Serebrenik for interesting discussions on the subject. We also thank anonymous referees for their feedback that helped to improve this abstract.

References

1. Fowler, M., Beck, K., Brant, J., Opdyke, W., Roberts, D.: Refactoring: Improving the Design of Existing Code. Objet Technology Series. Addison-Wesley, Reading (1999)
2. Serebrenik, A., Schrijvers, T., Demoen, B.: Improving Prolog programs: Refactoring for Prolog. Theory and Practice of Logic Programming 8(2), 201–215 (2008)
3. Vanhoof, W.: Searching semantically equivalent code fragments in logic programs. In: Etalle, S. (ed.) LOPSTR 2004. LNCS, vol. 3573, pp. 1–18. Springer, Heidelberg (2005)
4. Bergroth, L., Hakonen, H., Raita, T.: A survey of longest common subsequence algorithms. In: String Processing and Information Retrieval, pp. 39–48. IEEE, Los Alamitos (2000)
5. Schleimer, S., Wilkerson, D., Aiken, A.: Winnowing: Local algorithms for document fingerprinting. In: Proceedings of the 2003 ACM SIGMOD international conference on Management of Data, San Diego, CA (2003)
6. Horwitz, S.: Identifying the semantic and textual differences between two versions of a program. ACM SIGPLAN Notices 25(6), 234–245 (1990)
7. Yang, W.: Identifying syntactic differences between two programs. Software Practice and Experience 21(7), 739–755 (1991)
8. Winstead, J., Evans, D.: Towards differential program analysis. In: Proceedings of the 2003 Workshop on Dynamic Analysis (2003)
9. Degrave, F., Vanhoof, W.: Towards a normal form for Mercury programs. In: King, A. (ed.) LOPSTR 2007. LNCS, vol. 4915, pp. 43–58. Springer, Heidelberg (2008)

Trace Analysis for Predicting the Effectiveness of Partial Evaluation[⋆]

Germán Vidal

Technical University of Valencia, Spain
gvidal@dsic.upv.es

1 Introduction

The main goal of *partial evaluation* [1] is program specialization. Essentially, given a program and *part* of its input data—the so called *static* data—a partial evaluator returns a new, residual program which is specialized for the given data. An appropriate *residual* program for executing the remaining computations—those that depend on the so called *dynamic* data—is thus the output of the partial evaluator. Despite the fact that the main goal of partial evaluation is improving program efficiency (i.e., producing faster programs), there are very few approaches devoted to formally analyze the effects of partial evaluation, either *a priori* (prediction) or *a posteriori*. Recent approaches (e.g., [2,3]) have considered *experimental* frameworks for estimating the best *division* (roughly speaking, a classification of program parameters into static or dynamic), so that the optimal choice is followed when specializing the source program.

Here, we introduce an alternative, *symbolic* approach for predicting the potential effects of partial evaluation (which is, in principle, computationally less expensive). Basically, we first generate a finite representation that safely describes all possible *call traces* (i.e., sequences of predicate calls) for a given program. Then, we analyze how this finite representation would change by a particular partial evaluation. By comparing the original and the transformed representations, one may in some cases predict the effects of running the partial evaluator. A more detailed description of our approach can be found in [4].

2 Trace Analysis for Logic Programs

We consider a fixed domain of predicate symbols Π. We assume that Π do not contain occurrences of the same predicate name with different arities. Furthermore, we consider a fixed computation rule for call traces, namely Prolog's leftmost computation rule, which we denote by $\mathcal{R}_{left}$. We label SLD resolution steps with the predicate symbol of the selected atom, i.e., we write $Q_0 \overset{p_0}{\leadsto} Q_1 \overset{p_1}{\leadsto} \ldots$ with $pred(\mathcal{R}_{left}(Q_i)) = p_i \in \Pi$, $i \geq 0$, where $pred(A)$ returns the predicate symbol of atom A.

[⋆] This work is partially supported by the EU (FEDER) and the Spanish Ministry MEC/MICINN under grants TIN2005-09207-C03-02, TIN2008-06622-C03-02, and *Acción Integrada* HA2006-0008.

M. Garcia de la Banda and E. Pontelli (Eds.): ICLP 2008, LNCS 5366, pp. 790–794, 2008.

Definition 1 (call trace). *Let P be a program and Q_0 a query. We say that $\tau = p_0\, p_1 \ldots p_{n-1} \in \Pi^*$, $n \geq 1$, is a call trace for Q_0 with P iff there exists a successful SLD derivation $Q_0 \overset{p_0}{\leadsto} Q_1 \overset{p_1}{\leadsto} \ldots \overset{p_{n-1}}{\leadsto} Q_n$.*

The first step of our trace analysis consists in producing a *context-free grammar* (CFG) associated to the considered program. A CFG is a tuple $G = \langle \Sigma, N, R, S \rangle$, where Σ and N are two disjoint sets of *terminals* and *non-terminals*, respectively, $S \in N$ is the *start* symbol, and R is a set of rules. In the following, given a predicate symbol $p \in \Pi$, we denote by $\overline{p} \notin \Pi$ a fresh symbol representing the non-terminal associated to p. Furthermore, we let $\overline{pred}(A) = \overline{p}$ if $A = p(t_1, \ldots, t_n)$. Also, we let $\overline{\Pi}$ denote the set $\{\overline{p} \mid p \in \Pi\}$ of non-terminals associated to predicate symbols. In contrast, we directly use predicate symbols from Π as terminals. We let START be a fresh symbol not in $\Pi \cup \overline{\Pi}$ which we use as a generic start symbol for CFGs.

Definition 2 (trace CFG, CFG_q^P). *Let P be a program and $q \in \Pi$ a predicate symbol. The associated trace CFG is $\mathrm{CFG}_q^P = \langle \Pi, \overline{\Pi} \cup \{\mathrm{START}\}, R, \mathrm{START} \rangle$, where*

$$R = \{\mathrm{START} \to \overline{q}\}$$
$$\cup\ \{\overline{pred}(A_0) \to pred(A_0)\overline{pred}(B_1) \ldots \overline{pred}(B_n) \mid A_0 \leftarrow B_1, \ldots, B_n \in P, n \geq 0\}$$

Roughly speaking, the trace CFG associated to a logic program mimics the execution of the original program by replacing queries (sequences of atoms) by sequences of non-terminals and by producing a terminal with the predicate symbol of the selected atom at each SLD-resolution step.

Example 1. Consider the following program P which defines a procedure for multiplying all elements of a list by a given value:[1]

$(c_1) \quad mlist([\,], I, [\,])$.
$(c_2) \quad mlist([X|R], I, L) \leftarrow ml(X, R, I, L)$.

$(c_3) \quad ml(X, R, I, [XI|RI]) \leftarrow mult(X, I, XI),\ mlist(R, I, RI)$.

$(c_4) \quad mult(0, Y, 0)$. $\quad (c_5)\quad mult(s(X), Y, Z) \leftarrow mult(X, Y, Z1),\ add(Z1, Y, Z)$.
$(c_6) \quad add(X, 0, X)$. $\quad (c_7)\quad add(X, s(Y), s(Z)) \leftarrow add(X, Y, Z)$.

where natural numbers are built from 0 and $s(\cdot)$. The associated trace CFG is $\mathrm{CFG}_{mlist}^P = \langle \{mlist, ml, mult, add\}, \{\mathrm{START}, \mathrm{MLIST}, \mathrm{ML}, \mathrm{MULT}, \mathrm{ADD}\}, R, \mathrm{START} \rangle$, where the set of rules R is as follows:

START $\to$ MLIST	ML $\to$ *ml* MULT MLIST	
MLIST $\to$ *mlist*	MULT $\to$ *mult*	ADD $\to$ *add*
MLIST $\to$ *mlist* ML	MULT $\to$ *mult* MULT ADD	ADD $\to$ *add* ADD

In [4], we prove that CFG_q^P is indeed a correct approximation of the call traces for P w.r.t. the leftmost computation rule $\mathcal{R}_{left}$.

---

[1] In the examples, we write non-terminals associated to predicates using capital letters.

Unfortunately, trace CFGs do not always allow us to produce a simple and compact representation of the call traces of a program (e.g., when the associated language is not regular). To overcome this drawback, we use the transformation from [5] to approximate a trace CFG with a *strongly regular* grammar (SRG). The relevance of SRGs is that they can be mapped to equivalent finite-state automata using an efficient algorithm. Moreover, the transformation of [5] guarantees that the result remains readable and mainly preserves the structure of the original CFG, which is particularly useful in our context.

A grammar is *left-linear* if every rule has either the form $(A \rightarrow t)$ or $(A \rightarrow tB)$, where t is a finite sequence of terminals and A, B are non-terminals.

Definition 3 (trace SRG, SRG_q^P). *Let P be a program and $q \in \Pi$ a predicate symbol. The associated trace SRG, SRG_q^P, is obtained from CFG_q^P as follows. First, we compute the sets of mutually recursive non-terminals of CFG_q^P. Then, for each set M of mutually recursive non-terminals such that their rules are not all left-linear w.r.t. the non-terminals of M (i.e., considering non-terminals from $(\overline{\Pi} \setminus M)$ as terminals), we apply a grammar transformation as follows:*

1. *For each non-terminal $A \in M$, we introduce a fresh non-terminal A' and add the rule $A' \rightarrow \epsilon$ to the grammar (we denote by ϵ the empty sequence).*
2. *For each non-terminal $A \in M$ and each rule $A \rightarrow t_0 B_1 t_1 B_2 t_2 \ldots B_m t_m$ of CFG_q^P with $m \geq 0$, $B_1, \ldots, B_m \in M$, $t_0, \ldots, t_m \in (\Pi \cup (\overline{\Pi} \setminus M))^*$, we replace this rule by the following set of rules:*

$$A \rightarrow t_0 B_1 \qquad B_1' \rightarrow t_1 B_1 \qquad \ldots \qquad B_{m-1}' \rightarrow t_{m-1} B_m \qquad B_m' \rightarrow t_m A'$$

(Note that this set reduces to $A \rightarrow t_0 A'$ when $m = 0$.)

We let $\mathrm{SRG}_q^P = \langle \Pi, \overline{\Pi} \cup N \cup \mathrm{START}, R', \mathrm{START} \rangle$, where R' are the rules obtained as described above and N are the fresh non-terminals added during this process.

Example 2. Consider the CFG_q^P of Example 1. The sets of mutually recursive non-terminals are $\{\{\mathrm{MLIST, ML}\}, \{\mathrm{MULT}\}, \{\mathrm{ADD}\}\}$. Here, the rules for both MLIST and ML are left-linear w.r.t. $\{\mathrm{MLIST, ML}\}$. The rules for ADD are clearly left-linear too. However, the second rule of MULT is not left-linear because, even if ADD is treated as a terminal, it appears *to the right* of the non-terminal MULT. Therefore, in SRG_{mlist}^P we replace the original rules for MULT by the following ones:

$$\{\mathrm{MULT}' \rightarrow \epsilon, \quad \mathrm{MULT} \rightarrow mult \ \mathrm{MULT}', \quad \mathrm{MULT} \rightarrow mult \ \mathrm{MULT}, \quad \mathrm{MULT}' \rightarrow \mathrm{ADD} \ \mathrm{MULT}'\}$$

Once we have an SRG that safely approximates the call traces of a program, there are several possibilities for representing the language generated by this SRG in a compact and intuitive way. Here, we consider the generation of a *finite-state automaton* (FA) that accepts the language generated by the SRG; an alternative approach that produces *regular expressions* can be found in [4].

A finite-state automaton (FA) is specified by a tuple $\langle Q, \Sigma, \delta, s_0, F \rangle$, where Q is a set of states, Σ is an input alphabet, $\delta \subseteq Q \times \Sigma \times Q$ is a set of transitions, $s_0 \in Q$ is the start state and $F \subseteq Q$ is a set of final states. For constructing a

$s_0 = $ START, $s_1 = $ MLIST, $s_2 = \epsilon$, $s_3 = $ ML, $s_4 = $ MULT MLIST, $s_5 = $ MULT$'$ MLIST, $s_6 = $ ADD MULT$'$ MLIST

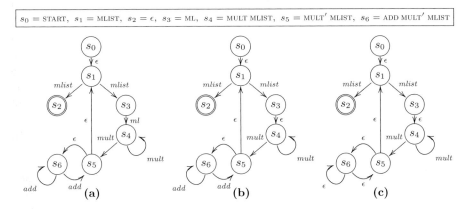

Fig. 1. Transformation of trace FAs

finite automaton $FA(G)$ from an SRG G, called *trace FA*, we follow the classical approach: there is a start state associated to the start symbol of the SRG; for each reduction $w \rightarrow w'$ with a rule $A \rightarrow t\, B$ of the SRG, we have a transition (s, α, s') in the FA, where states s, s' are associated with the sequence of non-terminals in w, w' and character α is set to the sequence t in the applied rule.

Example 3. Consider the SRG SRG^P_{mlist} of Example 2. The associated FA is shown in Fig. 1 (a), where the final state s_2 is denoted with a double circle.

3   Towards Predicting the Speedup of Partial Evaluation

The trace analysis gives us the *context* where every predicate call appears. Now, we informally describe two transformations (a more formal definition can be found in [4]) that modify the computed traces to account for the potential effects of a partial evaluation. By analyzing the traces before/after partial evaluation, one can extract useful conclusions on its effectiveness.

The first transformation is used to eliminate *intermediate* predicates. Basically, for every state with exactly one input transition and one output transition, we replace the label of the output transition by ϵ (i.e., we delete calls to predicates which are called from a single program point). Consider the trace FA of the program of Ex. 1 which is shown in Fig. 1 (a). After the elimination of intermediate states (the case of s_3), we get the trace FA shown in Fig. 1 (b).

Our second transformation is parameterized by the output of a *binding-time analysis* (BTA), which annotates each predicate with either unfold or memo, where unfold means that the predicate can be *safely* unfolded (i.e., without entering an infinite loop), and memo means that it should be specialized (i.e., a residual predicate is produced). Basically, our second transformation replaces the labels of unfoldable predicates with ϵ. Consider, e.g., that the output of a BTA annotates *mlist*, *ml*, and *mult* as memo and *add* as unfold—this is the case when the second argument of the initial call to *mlist* is static. We then get the trace FA of Fig. 1 (c). Here, we achieve a significant improvement since, in every iteration for *mlist*, we save the (recursive) evaluation of the calls to *add*.

Clearly, we could eliminate those states whose transitions are all labeled with ϵ. However, we think that keeping the structure of the original trace FA may help the user—and automated analysis tools—to formally compare the original and transformed trace FAs.

4 Discussion

The closest approach to our trace analysis is that of [6], though we offer a different trade-off between analysis cost and accuracy. Basically, they generate trace *terms* abstracting computation trees independently of a computation rule, while we generate sequences of predicate calls for a specific computation rule; also, they do not include a technique for enumerating the (possibly infinite) set of trace terms of a program, while this is a key ingredient of our approach (though one could also apply the transformation from [5] to the CFG associated to the trace terms of [6] to obtain a finite representation). A deeper comparison with the approach of [6] is an interesting topic for further research.

A proof-of-concept implementation of our technique, called PEPE, is publicly available from `http://german.dsic.upv.es/pepe.html`. Our approach can be seen as a first step for the development of automated techniques and tools for predicting the potential speedup of partial evaluation, thus it opens a number of interesting lines for further research.

Acknowledgments. We would like to thank Elvira Albert, Sergio Antoy, Manuel Hermenegildo, Michael Leuschel, Claudio Ochoa, and Germán Puebla for many interesting discussions on the topic of this paper.

References

1. Jones, N.D., Gomard, C.K., Sestoft, P.: Partial Evaluation and Automatic Program Generation. Prentice-Hall, Englewood Cliffs (1993)
2. Craig, S.-J., Leuschel, M.: Self-tuning resource aware specialisation for Prolog. In: Barahona, P., Felty, A.P. (eds.) PPDP, pp. 23–34. ACM, New York (2005)
3. Ochoa, C., Puebla, G.: Poly-controlled partial evaluation in practice. In: Rama-lingam, G., Visser, E. (eds.) PEPM, pp. 164–173. ACM, New York (2007)
4. Vidal, G.: Predicting the Speedup of Partial Evaluation. Technical report, DSIC, UPV (2008), `http://www.dsic.upv.es/~gvidal/german/papers.html`
5. Mohri, M., Nederhof, M.-J.: Regular Approximation of Context-Free Grammars through Transformation, ch. 9, pp. 153–163. Kluwer Academic Publishers, The Netherlands (2001)
6. Gallagher, J.P., Lafave, L.: Regular approximation of computation paths in logic and functional languages. In: Danvy, O., Glück, R., Thiemann, P. (eds.) Dagstuhl Seminar 1996. LNCS, vol. 1110, pp. 115–136. Springer, Heidelberg (1996)

A Sketch of a Complete Scheme for Tabled Execution Based on Program Transformation

Pablo Chico de Guzmán[1], Manuel Carro[1], and Manuel V. Hermenegildo[1,2]

[1] School of Computer Science, Univ. Politécnica de Madrid, Spain
[2] IMDEA Software, Spain
pchico@clip.dia.fi.upm.es, {mcarro,herme}@fi.upm.es

Abstract. Tabled evaluation has proved to be an effective method to improve several aspects of goal-oriented query evaluation, including termination and complexity. "Native" implementations of tabled evaluation offer good performance, but also require significant implementation effort, affecting compiler and abstract machine. Alternatively, program transformation-based implementations, such as the original *continuation call* (`CCall`) technique, offer lower implementation burden at some efficiency cost. A limitation of the original `CCall` proposal is that it limits the interleaving of tabled and non-tabled predicates and thus cannot be used for arbitrary programs. In this work we present an extension of the `CCall` technique that allows the execution of arbitrary tabled programs, as well as some performance results. Our approach offers a useful trade-off that can be competitive with state-of-the-art implementations, while keeping implementation effort relatively low.

Keywords: Tabled logic programming, Continuation-call tabling, Implementation, Performance, Program transformation.

1 Introduction

Tabling [1,2,3] is a strategy for executing logic programs which *remembers* already processed calls and their answers to overcome several limitations of SLD resolution: non-termination due to repeated subgoals can sometimes be avoided (tabling ensures termination of bounded term-size programs) and some cases of recomputation can also be automatically optimized. The first occurrence (the *generator*) of a call to a predicate marked as *tabled* and subsequent calls which are identical up to variable renaming (the *consumers*) are recognized. The generator applies resolution using program clauses to derive answers for the goal. Conceptually, consumers *suspend* their current execution path and take on a different branch; this can be repeated several times. When some alternative branch eventually succeeds the answer generated for the initial query is inserted in a table associated with the original goal. This makes it possible to reactivate suspended calls and to continue execution at the point where they were stopped.

Implementing tabling is a complex task. In *suspension-based tabling* (e.g., XSB [4] and CHAT [5], among others) the execution state of suspended tabled subgoals is preserved to avoid unnecessary recomputations, but they usually require deep changes to the underlying implementation. *Linear tabling* schemes (as

M. Garcia de la Banda and E. Pontelli (Eds.): ICLP 2008, LNCS 5366, pp. 795–800, 2008.
© Springer-Verlag Berlin Heidelberg 2008

exemplified by B-Prolog [6,7] and the DRA scheme [8]) does not require suspension and resumption of sub-computations, and then, they can usually be implemented on top of existing sequential engines with relatively simple modifications. However, their efficiency is affected by subgoal recomputation.

2   The Continuation Call Technique

The CCall approach to tabling [9,10] is a suspension-based mechanism which requires much simpler modifications to the Prolog implementation or compiler than other suspension-based techniques. A number of low-level optimizations to existing implementations of the CCall approach were proposed in [11] and it was shown that performance could be competitive with other implementations.

The CCall technique implements tabling by a combination of program transformation and side effects in the form of insertions into and retrievals from a table which relates calls, answers, and the continuation code to be executed after consumers read answers from the table. Consumer suspension and resumption is performed by operations which are visible at Prolog level.

Roughly speaking, the original CCall approach calls tabled predicates through the slgcall primitive, which receives a goal and analyzes if it is a generator or a consumer call. When it is a consumer, suspension has to be performed by saving the current environment and program counter in order to resume execution later on. The body goals after the tabled call are associated with a new predicate symbol, which takes the role of the program counter at that particular place. The bindings performed before the tabled call make up the environment of the consumer. Consequently, slgcall takes the name of the auxiliary predicate and a list of bindings as arguments, in order to be able to perform resumption at Prolog level. Answers are inserted in the table by answer/2 primitive, which is added at the end of each clause of the original tabled predicate.

The original transformation is not general because the environments are only correctly saved when tabled calls are themselves in the body of a tabled predicate (except for the first one). If there are non-tabled, SLD predicates between the generator and some consumer, the code after that consumer is not associated with any predicate symbol, and it is not considered for tabled execution (see [12] for more details and examples). Tabling *all* predicates between generators and consumers works around this problem, but it can seriously impact efficiency.

3   A Complete Tabling Translation for General Programs

We have extended the translation to work around the issue presented in the previous section by bringing into the scene a new kind of predicates – *bridge predicates*. Predicate B is a bridge if for some tabled predicate T, T depends on B (i.e., B is called in the subtree rooted at T) and B depends on T. Figure 1, which uses a sugared Prolog-like language,[1] shows the rules for the new translation.

---

[1] Functional syntax is implicitly assumed where needed. The 'o' operator is a general append function which can either join (linear) structures or concatenates atoms.

```
tr((:- table P/N),
   (P(X1..Xn) :- !,slg(P(X1..Xn))))).
tr((H :- B),LC) :- !,
   table(H),
   H_tr =.. ['slg_' o H, H, Id],
   End = answer(Id, H),
   tr_B(H_tr, B, Id, [], End, LC).
tr((H :- B), (H :- B o LC)) :- !,
   bridge(H),
   H_tr =.. [H o '_bridge', H, Id, Cont],
   End = (arg(3, Cont, H), call(Cont)),
   tr_Body(H_tr, B, Id, Cont, End, LC).
tr(C, C).

tr_Body([], [], _, _, [], []).
tr_Body(H, B, Id, CCPrev, End,
        (H :- B_tr o RestB_tr)) :-
   following(B, Pref, Pred, Suff),
   getLBinds(Pref, Suff, LBinds),
   up_Body(Pred, End, Id, Pref, LBinds,
           CCPrev, Cont, B_tr),
   tr_Body(Cont, Suff, Id, CCPrev, End, RestB_tr).
```

```
following(B, Pref, Pred, Suff) :-
   member(B, Pred),
   (table(Pred); bridge(Pred)), !,
   B = Pref o Pred o Suff.

up_Body([], End, _Id, Pref, _LBinds,
        _CCPrev, [], Pref o End).
up_Body(Pred, _End, Id, Pref, LBinds,
        CCPrev, Cont, Pref o slgcall(Cont)) :-
   table(Pred),
   getNameCont(NameCont),
   Cont = NameCont(Id, LBinds, Pred, CCPrev).
up_Body(Pred, _End, Id, Pref, LBinds,
        CCPrev, Cont, Pref o Bridge_call) :-
   bridge(Pred),
   getNameCont(NameCont),
   Cont = NameCont(Id, LBinds, Pred, CCPrev),
   Bridge_call =.. [Pred o '_bridge', Cont].
```

Fig. 1. The Prolog code of the translation rules

The `tr/2` predicate takes a clause to be translated and returns the list of clauses resulting from the translation. Its last clause ensures that predicates which are non-tabled and non-bridge are not transformed. The first one generates the interface with the rest of the code for each tabled predicate. The second and third cases translate clauses of tabled and bridge predicates, respectively.[2] They generate the new head of the clause, `H_tr`, and the code which has to be appended at the end of the body, `End`, before calling `tr_Body/6` with these arguments. The original clauses are maintained in case bridge predicates are called outside a tabled call.

`tr_Body/6` generates, in its last argument, the translation of the body of a clause by taking care, in each iteration, of the code until the next tabled or bridge call, or until the end the clause, and appending the translation of the rest of the clause to this partial translation.

`following/4` splits a clause body in three parts: a prefix, until the first time a tabled or bridge call appears, the tabled or bridge call itself, and a suffix from this call until the end of the clause. `getLBinds/3` obtains the list of variables which have to be saved to recover the environment of the consumer.

The `up_Body/8` predicate completes the body prefix until the next tabled or bridge call. Its first sixth arguments are inputs, the seventh one is the head of the continuation for the suffix of the body, and the last argument is the new translation for the prefix. The first clause takes care of the base case, when there are no calls to bridge or tabled predicates left, the second clause generates code for a call to a tabled predicate,

```
:- table t/1.
t(A):-
    p(B), A is B + 1.
t(0).
p(B):- t(B), B < 1.
```

Fig. 2. A program which needs bridge predicates

---

[2] Predicates `table/1` and `bridge/1` check if their argument corresponds to a tabled or bridge predicate, respectively.

```
t(A) :- slg(t(A)).                      p(B) :- t(B), B < 1.
slg_t(t(A), Id) :-                      p_bridge(Id, Cont) :-
  p_bridge(Id,                            slgcall(
          slg_t0(Id,[A],p(B),[])).          p_bridge0(Id,[],t(B),Cont)).
slg_t0(Id, [A], p(B), []) :-            p_bridge0(Id, [], t(B), Cont) :-
  A is B + 1,                             B < 1,
  answer(Id, t(A)).                       arg(3, Cont, p(B)),
slg_t(t(0),Id) :- answer(Id, t(0)).       call(Cont).
```

Fig. 3. The program in Figure 3 after being transformed for tabled execution

and the last one does the same with a bridge predicate. `getNameCont/1` generates a unique name for the continuation.

An example of a tabled program which needs our extended translation is presented in the figure right above this paragraph (and, at more length, in [12]). If the query ?- `t(A)`. is issued, `t(B)` is called in a consumer position inside `p/1`. This simple combination would incorrectly be dealt by [9]. However, the translation proposed in Figure 1 generates the code in Figure 3, which transforms `p/1` so that the information necessary to resume `t/1` is available where needed, at the cost of some duplicated code and an extra argument when `p/1` is called from inside a tabled execution.

4   Performance Evaluation

We have implemented the proposed technique as an extension of the Ciao system [13] with the efficiency improvements presented in [11] and the new translation for general programs explained in this poster.

Table 1 aims at determining how the proposed implementation of tabling compares with state-of-the-art systems —namely, the available versions of XSB, YapTab, and B-Prolog at the time of writing. We provide the raw time (in milliseconds) taken to execute several tabling benchmarks. Measurements have been made with Ciao-1.13, using the standard, unoptimized bytecode-based compilation, and with the `CCall` extensions loaded, as well as in XSB 3.0.1, YapTab 5.1.1, and B-Prolog 7.0. All the executions were performed using local scheduling and disabling garbage collection; in the end this did not impact execution times very much. We used `gcc` 4.1.1 to compile all the systems (except B-Prolog, which is available as a binary), and we executed them on a machine with Fedora Core Linux, kernel 2.6.9, and an Intel Xeon *Deschutes* processor.

While the performance of `CCall` is clearly affected by the fragment of the execution performed at Prolog level, its efficiency is in general not too far away from than XSB's, whose abstract machine is about half the speed of Ciao's for SLD execution. The relationship with B-Prolog is not so clear, as it features a fast abstract machine, but its tabling implementation sometimes suffers from recomputation. Last, Yap, which has a fast abstract machine which implements SLG resolution, easily beats the rest of the systems. We plan to improve the performance of our implementation by making the `CCall` primitives closer to

Table 1. Comparing Ciao+`CCall` with XSB, YapTab, and B-Prolog

Prog.	Ciao+CCall	XSB	YapTab	BProl.	Prog.	Ciao+CCall	XSB	YapTab	BProl.
path	517.92	231.4	151.12	206.26	kalah	23.152	19.187	13.156	28.333
tcl	96.93	59.91	39.16	51.60	gabriel	23.500	19.633	12.384	40.753
tcr	315.44	106.91	90.13	96.21	disj	18.095	15.762	9.2131	29.095
tcn	485.77	123.21	85.87	117.70	cs_o	34.176	27.644	18.169	85.719
sgm	3151.8	1733.1	1110.1	1474.0	cs_r	66.699	55.087	34.873	170.25
atr2	689.86	602.03	262.44	320.07	peep	68.757	58.161	37.124	150.14
pg	15.240	13.435	8.5482	36.448					

the abstract machine. More details about the execution times and a comparison of the `CCall` time execution complexity with CHAT can be found in [12].

Acknowledgments. This work was funded in part by EU FP6 FET project IST-15905 *MOBIUS*, FP7 grant 215483 *S-Cube*, Spanish MEC project TIN2005-09207-C03 *MERIT-COMVERS*, ITEA2/PROFIT FIT-340005-2007-14 *ES_PASS*, and by Madrid Regional Government project S-0505/TIC/0407 *PROMESAS*. M. Hermenegildo was also funded in part by the Prince of Asturias Chair in IST at UNM. Pablo Chico de Guzmán was also funded by a UPM doctoral grant.

References

1. Tamaki, H., Sato, M.: OLD resolution with tabulation. In: Shapiro, E. (ed.) ICLP 1986. LNCS, vol. 225, pp. 84–98. Springer, Heidelberg (1986)
2. Warren, D.: Memoing for logic programs. Communications of the ACM 35(3), 93–111 (1992)
3. Chen, W., Warren, D.S.: Tabled Evaluation with Delaying for General Logic Programs. Journal of the ACM 43(1), 20–74 (1996)
4. Sagonas, K., Swift, T.: An Abstract Machine for Tabled Execution of Fixed-Order Stratified Logic Programs. ACM Transactions on Programming Languages and Systems 20(3), 586–634 (1998)
5. Demoen, B., Sagonas, K.F.: Chat: The copy-hybrid approach to tabling. In: Practical Applications of Declarative Languages, pp. 106–121 (1999)
6. Zhou, N.F., Shen, Y.D., Yuan, L.Y., You, J.H.: Implementation of a linear tabling mechanism. Journal of Functional and Logic Programming 2001(10) (October 2001)
7. Zhou, N.F., Sato, T., Shen, Y.D.: Linear Tabling Strategies and Optimizations. Theory and Practice of Logic Programming 8(1), 81–109 (2008)
8. Guo, H.F., Gupta, G.: A Simple Scheme for Implementing Tabled Logic Programming Systems Based on Dynamic Reordering of Alternatives. In: Codognet, P. (ed.) ICLP 2001. LNCS, vol. 2237, pp. 181–196. Springer, Heidelberg (2001)
9. Ramesh, R., Chen, W.: A Portable Method for Integrating SLG Resolution into Prolog Systems. In: Bruynooghe, M. (ed.) International Symposium on Logic Programming, pp. 618–632. MIT Press, Cambridge (1994)
10. Rocha, R., Silva, C., Lopes, R.: On Applying Program Transformation to Implement Suspension-Based Tabling in Prolog. In: Dahl, V., Niemelä, I. (eds.) ICLP 2007. LNCS, vol. 4670, pp. 444–445. Springer, Heidelberg (2007)

11. de Guzmán, P.C., Carro, M., Hermenegildo, M., Silva, C., Rocha, R.: An Improved Continuation Call-Based Implementation of Tabling. In: Warren, D., Hudak, P. (eds.) PADL 2008. LNCS, vol. 4902, pp. 198–213. Springer, Heidelberg (2008)
12. de Guzmán, P.C., Carro, M., Hermenegildo, M.V.: Bridge Program Transformation for the CCall Tabling Scheme. Technical Report CLIP6/2008.0, Technical University of Madrid (UPM), Computer Science School, UPM (September 2008)
13. Bueno, F., Cabeza, D., Carro, M., Hermenegildo, M., López-García, P. (eds.): The Ciao System. Ref. Manual (v1.13). Technical report, C.S. School (UPM) (2006), http://www.ciaohome.org

Probabilistic and Concurrent Models for Security

Romain Beauxis

INRIA Futurs and LIX, École Polytechnique

1 Introduction

Recent research in security and protocol verification has shown an important need for probabilistic formal concurrent models. Indeed, the use of probabilities in formal models allows to define and check quantitative properties which are usefull for a lot of applications, such as probabilistic anonymity, failures or information leakage. Several recent research showed very interesting situations for these properties [1]. Research on probabilistic models is also a topic of interest from the mathematical point of view. Topics include relations between probability and non-determinism, expressivity, processus equivalence and denotational semantics. Research domains for these topics include probabilistic process algebras, concurrent constraint programming and domain theory. Interesting references can be found in [2,3].

2 Background of My Research Topic

A particular language for security and communication is the Concurrent Constraint Programming (CCP). In this language, each process is equiped with a constraint store which is used for adding new constraints and testing if a given constraint can be entailed by the current store. This a very interesting framework for defining and analysing security properties in terms of logical constraints. In particular, it can be used to check reachability properties against a given program. A denotational semantics have been defined for the CCP that allows to represent a program in this language as an input/output function on the constraints [4]. This semantics has also been proved fully abstract, meaning that it carries as much informations as the original process. Using this semantics, mathematic tools and properties can then be used to reason about the programs of the language and their properties.

Probabilistic extensions for the CCP have been proposed in the litterature [5,6]. However, in [5] the denotational semantics of the programs can be argued to be not so natural, leading to complicated probability distributions, such as fractal distributions, whereas in [6], the constraint system is limited to finite spaces.

M. Garcia de la Banda and E. Pontelli (Eds.): ICLP 2008, LNCS 5366, pp. 801–802, 2008.
© Springer-Verlag Berlin Heidelberg 2008

3   Goals and Achievements of My Research

I am interested in extending the CCP to a probabilistic language which would fix the limitations explained above. In particular, I want to extends the original CCP with a operational and denotational semantics which would be as similar as possible to the original semantics. I am looking for an application of the research results in the topic of valuations and probabilistic power domain [3]. The probabilistic power domain is a very good model for denotational semantics since it takes into account much of the issues that need to be adressed, in particular the fix point properties needed to define the semantics.

Before defining a probabilistic CCP, I have studied the possibility to assume that all valuations on the constraints can be decomposed into an infinite countable sum of elementary valuations. This allows to define an operational semantics on the probabilistic language on the elementary valuations and then extends this by linearity. I have proved that under some conditions, a valuation could be decomposed that way. This has lead to the definition of finitely branching algebraic lattices (FBL). Any valuation on such a lattice is then a simple valuation, and the similary for the pointwise limit of a directed sequence of bounded valuations.

Using this result, I have defined a language which extends the original CCP by adding a probabilistic non-guarded choice operator. The usual definitions are then lifted from the constrainst system to a vector cone space of simple valuations. I have then defined a denotational semantics for this language, which is the lifted original denotational semantics. As for the original CCP, this semantics have been proved to be fully abstract.

I plan on applying this language to several probabilistic problems, including the dinning cryptographers and the crows routing protocol. I would also like to implement the language in an automated tool, and prove some expressivity result.

References

1. Chatzikokolakis, K., Palamidessi, C., Panangaden, P.: Anonymity protocols as noisy channels. Inf. Comput. 206(2-4), 378–401 (2008)
2. Pradalier, S., Palamidessi, C.: Expressiveness of probabilistic pi. Electr. Notes Theor. Comput. Sci. 164(3), 119–136 (2006)
3. Jones, C.: Probabilistic non-determinism. PhD thesis, University of Edinburgh (1990)
4. Saraswat, V.A., Rinard, M., Panangaden, P.: Semantic foundations of concurrent constraint programming. In: Conference Record of the Eighteenth Annual ACM Symposium on Principles of Programming Languages, ACM SIGACT-SIGPLAN, Orlando, Florida, pp. 333–352. ACM Press, New York (1991) Preliminary report
5. Gupta, V., Jagadeesan, R., Saraswat, V.: Probabilistic concurrent constraint programming. In: Mazurkiewicz, A., Winkowski, J. (eds.) CONCUR 1997. LNCS, vol. 1243, pp. 243–257. Springer, Heidelberg (1997)
6. Pierro, A.D., Wiklicky, H.: A Banach space based semantics for probabilistic concurrent constraint programming (1998)

On the Hybridization of Constraint Programming and Local Search Techniques: Models and Software Tools

Raffaele Cipriano

Dipartimento di Matematica e Informatica
Università di Udine, via delle Scienze 208, 33100, Udine, Italy
`raffaele.cipriano@dimi.uniud.it`

1 Problem Description and State of the Art

Resource management problems are generally modeled as Constraint Satisfaction / Optimization Problems (CSPs or COPs). The solution methods for CSPs and COPs can be split into: *complete methods*, which systematically explore the whole solution space; *incomplete methods*, which rely on heuristics and focus on interesting areas of the solution space. Our focus is manly in Constrain Programming (CP) and Local Search (LS) techniques. *CP languages* are usually based on complete methods that analyze the search space alternating constraint propagation phases and variable assignment phases. Their main advantage is *flexibility*. *LS methods*, instead, rely on the definition of "proximity" and explore only specific areas of the search space. Their main advantage is *efficiency*.

We know two main approaches for combining CP and LS [1,2]: *1) a systematic-search algorithm based on CP can be improved by inserting LS at some point* of the search procedure; *2) a LS algorithm can benefit of the support of CP*. In [3] CP and LS are combined more freely and in [4] they are embedded in a programming language.

There are several languages commonly used for modeling CSPs and COPs. $CLP(\mathcal{D})$ is a declarative programming paradigm, first presented in 1986 (e.g., [5]), where combinatorial problems are usually encoded using constraints over *finite domains* (namely, $\mathcal{D} = FD$). The library `clpfd` of SICStus Prolog (`www.sics.se/sicstus`) is the state of the art $CLP(FD)$ implementation. *MiniZinc* (`www.g12.cs.mu.oz.au/minizinc`) is a high-level modeling language: it allows to express most CP problems easily, but it is also low-level enough to be easily mapped onto existing solvers. *Gecode* is an environment for developing constraint-based applications (`www.gecode.org`); its language style is C++ like (low-level), but it offers very competitive performances. *EasyLocal++* (`tabu.diegm.uniud.it/EasyLocal++`) is a C++ object-oriented framework that allows to easily design, implement and test LS algorithms.

2 Research Summary

The first goal is to *study and apply the hybridization* of CP and LS on several problems, interfacing different tools, to obtain flexible and efficient hybrid methods. This is the starting point to define a *meta-modeling language* (MiniZinc like) that allows the user to easily model CSPs and COPs and define algorithms that combines cleverly constraint propagation phases, neighborhood exploration and other procedures. This meta-modeling language will be part of a *programming framework* made of three parts: the

M. Garcia de la Banda and E. Pontelli (Eds.): ICLP 2008, LNCS 5366, pp. 803–804, 2008.

modeling part, where the user defines in a high-level style the problem to solve and the algorithm to use (e.g., CP search, eventually interleaved with LS); the *translating part*, where the model and the meta-algorithm are automatically compiled into the solver languages (e.g., Gecode and EasyLocal++); the *solving part*, where the overall compiled program runs and the various solvers interacts, to find the solution. As a side effect, this programming framework represents a *new way to run declarative models*: the user can encode the problems with well-known declarative languages (e.g., Prolog), and then make use of new low-level implementations (e.g., Gecode) for efficient executions.

We applied hybrid CP-LS techniques to a real hospital rostering problem [6] and to the protein structure prediction problem [7]. In [6] LS improve solutions obtained by a first CP phase: hybrid approach leads to better results w.r.t. the single use of CP or LS. In [7] we alternate CSP solving phases to LS phases, using a CP model to explore the neighborhood of a LS move: even without developing particular strategies, the solutions of hybrid method improve those of the pure CP approach.

Moreover we developed two compilers: from SICStus Prolog CLP(FD) to Gecode and from MiniZinc to Gecode. In [8] we compared the running times of the executions of codes directly written in the three languages and of the compiled codes for some classical problems, showing that performances of the compiled codes to Gecode improve those in the original languages and are comparable with running time of native Gecode code. This work ensures the feasibility of our three-phases programming tool.

Now we are going to follow two main research lines. *Hybridization*: we want to improve the hybrid algorithms already developed, refining the integration of the two paradigms and trying new hybrid ideas; we also want to test the algorithms on other interesting problems. *Software tools*: we want to extend the functionalities of our Prolog-Gecode and MiniZinc-Gecode compilers, and develop the modeling-translating-solving framework; we are going to define a meta-modeling language for this framework (e.g., starting from MiniZinc) and interfacing the tools in a consistent and homogenous way.

References

1. Focacci, F., Laburthe, F., Lodi, A.: Local Search and Constraint Programming. Handbook of Metaheuristics, 369–403 (2003)
2. Jussien, N., Lhomme, O.: Local search with constraint propagation and conflict-based heuristic. Artificial Intelligence 139(1), 21–45 (2002)
3. Monfroy, E., Frédéric, S., Lambert, T.: On hybridization of local search and constraint propagation. In: Demoen, B., Lifschitz, V. (eds.) ICLP 2004. LNCS, vol. 3132, pp. 299–313. Springer, Heidelberg (2004)
4. Hentenryck, P., Michel, L.: Constraint-Based Local Search. MIT Press, Cambridge (2005)
5. Jaffar, J., Maher, M.J.: Constraint Logic Programming: A Survey. Journal of Logic Programming 19/20, 503–581 (1994)
6. Cipriano, R., Di Gaspero, L., Dovier, A.: Hybrid Approaches for Rostering: A Case Study in the Integration of Constraint Programming and Local Search. In: Blesa Aguilera, M.J., Blum, C., Roli, A., Sampels, M. (eds.) HM 2006. LNCS, vol. 4030, pp. 110–123. Springer, Heidelberg (2006)
7. Cipriano, R., Dal Palù, A., Dovier, A.: A hybrid approach mixing local search and constraint programming applied to the protein structure prediction problem. In: WCB 2008, Paris (2008)
8. Cipriano, R., Dovier, A., Mauro, J.: Compiling and executing declarative modeling languages in gecode. In: Andrea, F. (ed.) Proceedings of CILC 2008, Perugia (2008)

Development of an Automatic Testing Environment for Mercury

François Degrave

Faculty of Computer Science, University of Namur, Belgium

1 Introduction and Problem Description

Testing refers to the activity of running a software component with respect to a well-chosen set of inputs and comparing the outputs that are produced with the expected results in order to find errors. To make testing less repetitive and quicker, a so-called test automation framework can be used to automatically execute a (previously written) test suite[1] without user intervention. An automatic tool runs the software component that is being tested once for each test input, compares the actual result with the expected result and reports those test cases that failed during the test; a well-known example of such a tool being JUnit for Java [1]. However, the construction of test suites remains a mostly manual and thus time-consuming activity [2]. The need of adequacy criteria [3,4] renders the construction of (large) test suites complex and error-prone [5]. The objective of this work is to develop an analysis that automatically creates a set of test inputs that satisfies a particular coverage criterion for a given program written in Mercury.

The problem of test input generation lends itself very well to automation and some research effort has been devoted to automate the generation of test inputs for unit testing. Most of the efforts have concentrated on generating test inputs for programs written in imperative programming languages using simple data like integer and floating point values, e.g. [6]. Recent approaches handle object-oriented programming and some more complex data structures, e.g. [7].

2 Goal of the Research

Obviously, developing an automatic test input generator for Mercury is a challenging research topic. Firstly, the control flow of a logic program component is less obvious than it is in an algorithmic language. This makes porting the existing notions and analysis techniques for imperative/object-oriented languages non-straightforward. Secondly, Mercury uses a symbolic data representation for all but the simplest data. The fact that *all* complex data is represented in a uniform and symbolic way makes it easier to handle by well-known analysis techniques like abstract interpretation and symbolic execution. Therefore it is

---

[1] In testing terminology, a *test suite* for a software component refers to a collection of individual test cases whereas a *test case* refers to the combination of a single test input and the expected result.

M. Garcia de la Banda and E. Pontelli (Eds.): ICLP 2008, LNCS 5366, pp. 805–806, 2008.

actually easier to obtain more coverage for Mercury with a single analysis than it is the case in conventional languages where the diversity and complexity of dynamic data structures make program analysis notoriously difficult.

3 Current Status of the Research and Open Issues

We have currently developed a basic analysis, loosely based on [6] and reported in [8] and [9], for a subset of Mercury. We have defined the notion of a control-flow graph for a Mercury program and how one could derive a set of execution paths from such a graph. Moreover we have shown how an execution path can be translated into a corresponding set of constraints, the solutions of which are the input values such that when the predicate is called with respect to those values, its execution will follow the derivation represented by the given path. In order to solve the constraints, we have written a custom constraints solver in CHR.

In order to prove the feasability of the method, we implemented a prototype in Mercury and tested it with different small-size programs with satisfying results. However, our approach computes a finite set of execution paths and the associated test inputs but makes no effort whatsoever to guarantee a certain degree of coverage. This is an important topic for further research, in particular since one usually wants to focus the test cases generation to so called *interesting* paths – paths that are likely to be followed during a real-life use of the program. Moreover, in order to limit the generation of "useless" paths, one could possibly integrate the constraint solving phase with the execution path generation.

Other topics for further work include exploiting the Mercury module system to perform test case generation in a modular way, and incorporating I/O in the generated test cases.

References

1. Hunt, A., Thomas, D.: Pragmatic unit testing in java with junit. Pragmatic Bookshelf (2003)
2. Artho, C., et al.: Combining test case generation and runtime verification. Theoretical Computer Science 336(2-3) (2005)
3. Zhu, H., Hall, P., May, J.: Software unit test coverage and adequacy. ACM Computing Surveys 29(4) (1997)
4. Weyuker, E.J.: Axiomatizing software test data adequacy. IEEE Trans. Softw. Eng. 12(12), 1128–1138 (1986)
5. Li, K., Wu, M.: Effective software test automation, Sybex (2004)
6. Sy, N., Deville, Y.: Automatic test data generation for programs with integer and float variables. In: 16th IEEE International Conference on Automated Software Engineering (ASE 2001) (2001)
7. Visser, W., Pasareanu, C.S., Khurshid, S.: Test input generation with java pathfinder. SIGSOFT Softw. Eng. Notes 29(4), 97–107 (2004)
8. Degrave, F., Vanhoof, W.: A control flow graph for Mercury. In: Proceedings of CICLOPS 2007 (2007)
9. Degrave, F., Schrijvers, T., Vanhoof, W.: Automatic generation of test inputs for Mercury. In: LOPSTR 2008. LNCS. Springer, Heidelberg (2009)

Resolving CSP with Naming Games

Giorgio Gosti

Univ. degli Studi di Perugia, Dept. of Mathematics and Computer Science
giorgio.gosti@dipmat.unipg.it

1   The DCSP and the Naming Game Background

In constraint satisfaction problems (CSP) we consider N variables $x_1, x_2, \ldots x_N$, their definition domains $D_1, D_2, \ldots, D_N$ and a set of constraints on the values of these variables; solving the CSP means finding a particular value for the variables that satisfies the constraints. In the distributed CSP (DCSP) as defined by Makoto Yokoo [1], the variables of the CSP are distributed among the agents. These agents are able to communicate between themselves and know all the constraint predicates relevant to their variable. The agents through interaction find the appropriate values to solve the CSP.

The naming game describes a set of problems in which a number N of agents bootstrap a commonly agreed name for an object. Each naming game is defined by an interaction protocol/algorithm. An important aspect of the naming game is the hierarchy-free agent architecture. For other references on the naming game see the work of Steels [3] and Baronchelli et al. [2].

2   Research Summary

In the naming game, the agents want to agree on the name given to an object. This can be represented as a DCSP, where the name proposed by each agent is the assignment of the variable controlled by the agent, and an equality constraint connects all the variables. On the other hand, we can generalize the naming game to solve DCSPs.

We attribute an agent to each variable of the CSP (see [1]). Each agent $i = 1, ..N$ names his own variable x_i. in respect of the *variable domain* D_i. We restrict the constraints to binary relation xRy. We define two agents' neighbors if their variables are connected by a constraint. The agents have a *list*, which is a continuously updated subset of the *variable domain*. The elements of this *list* are the possible assignments of the variable proposed by the agent.

At each successive turn $t = 1, 2, \ldots$ an agent is randomly extracted to cover the role of the speaker and he communicates, one by one, with all his neighbors his variable assignment preference. The speaker assignment, the elements on the hearer neighbors *list*, and the relation xRy determine the communication outcome. At the end of the turn the hearers communicate to the speaker the success, or the failure of the communication, thus the communication outcome establishes the agents list update. At each successive turn the system evolves

M. Garcia de la Banda and E. Pontelli (Eds.): ICLP 2008, LNCS 5366, pp. 807–808, 2008.

through interaction between the agents in a global equilibrium state. In the equilibrium state all the agents have only one element for their variable and this element must satisfy the relation xRy with the element chosen by the neighboring agents. We call this the state of global consensus. Once in this state the interactions are always successful and the system will not change any more. We call the turn at which the system finds global consensus *convergence turn* t_{conv}.

This research is currently at the very beginning. We have tested the algorithm previously described in the following classical CSP problems: graph coloring and n-queens puzzle. We plotted the graph of the convergence turn t_{conv} scaling with the number N of the CSP variables, each point was measured by ten runs of the CSP naming game. We considered three types of graph for the graph coloring: the path graph, the cycle graph, and the completely connected graph.

In the study of the path graph and the cycle graph we have restricted ourselves to the $2 - chromatic$ cases, all the path graphs and only the even number of nodes cycle graphs. Thus imposed the agent variable domain to two colors. In this context the t_{conv} of the path graph and the cycle graph exhibit a power law behavior $t_{conv} \propto N^{3.0}$. The cycle graph exhibits a faster convergence.

The graph coloring in the case of a completely connected graph always needs N colors: in this case we find that the time of convergence is $t_{conv} \propto N^{1.3}$.

In the case of the N-queens puzzle with N variables, we see the scaling proportion $t_{conv} \propto N^{4.2}$ for the time convergence.

We expect the following achievements from our research: the first, an improved algorithm that can perform better on different kinds of problems; the second, development of a dynamic representation of negotiation in human behavior as a real world DCSP problem. Moreover our aim is to develop a probabilistic approach to analytically describe the evolution of the system and its equilibrium. In the study of this method we are trying to fully exploit the power of distributed calculation. To do this we generalize the naming game algorithm, letting the CSP solution emerge, rather than being the conclusion of a imperative sequence of statements. This is achieved through the union of new topics addressed in statistical physics (the naming game), and the general frame posed by artificial intelligence.

References

1. Yokoo, M., Durfee, E.H., Ishida, T., Kuwabara, K.: Distributed Constraint Satisfaction for Formalizing Distributed Problem Solving. In: 12th International Conference on Distributed Computing Systems (ICDCS 1992), pp. 614–621 (1992)
2. Baronchelli, A., Felici, M., Caglioti, E., Loreto, V., Steels, L.: Sharp transition Toward Shared Vocabularies in Multi-Agent Systems. Journal of Statistical Mechanics, P06014 (2006)
3. Steels, L.: Self-Organizing Vocabularies. In: Langton, C., Shimohara, K. (eds.) Artificial Life V: Proceeding of the Fifth International Workshop on the Synthesis and Simulation of Living Systems, pp. 179–184 (1997)
4. Nowak, M.A., Plotkin, J.B., Krakauer, J.D.: The evolutionary language game. Journal of Theoretical Biology 200, 147 (1999)

Biosequence Analysis in PRISM

Ole Torp Lassen

Research group PLIS: Programming, Logic and Intelligent Systems
Department of Communication, Business and Information Technologies
Roskilde University, P.O.Box 260, DK-4000 Roskilde, Denmark
otl@ruc.dk

In this work, we consider probabilistic models that can infer biological information solely from biological sequences such as DNA. Traditionally, computational models for biological sequence analysis have been implemented in a wide variety of procedural and object oriented programming languages [1]. Models implemented using stochastic logic programming (SLP [2,3,4]) instead, may draw upon the benefits of increased expressive power, conciseness and compositionality. It does, however, pose a big challenge to design efficient SLP models.

We are currently experimenting with the optimization of a simple model for gene finders written in PRISM [4]. This model plays the role of a canonical model, supposed to hold the best knowledge available about genes, non genes and their respective distributions in DNA. We assume that the canonical model is not computationally practical per se.

As a scheme of preprocessing, we propose to divide the sequence to be analyzed into shorter subsequences that can be analyzed individually by distinct components of the canonical model. We achieve this through decomposition of the canonical model M^{canon} into three distinct components:

    $C1$, a canonical model for distribution of genes and non genes in DNA,

    $C2$, a canonical model for genes and

    $C3$, a canonical model for non genes.

We then define a partitioning model M^{chop} consisting of components:

    $C1$

    $A2$, a simplified generalization of $C2$

    $A3$, a simplified generalization of $C3$.

Given a DNA sequence S, canonical model M^{canon}, and partitioning model M^{chop}, the approximating algorithm can be defined as follows:

1. Apply M^{chop} to S to get the most likely approximate partitioning of S into subsequences, $(s_1, t_1), \ldots, (s_n, t_n)$, where t_i is the supposed type of subsequence s_i ,(i.e.: gene or non gene).
2. For each approximate subsequence (s_i, t_i), apply the canonical component corresponding to t_i, (i.e.: $C1$ or $C2$), to get an ordered list of most likely canonical subsequence explanations, $E^{sub} = \{(t_1, e_1), \ldots, (t_n, e_n)\}$.
3. Apply $C1$ to E^{sub} to combine subsequence explanations into an approximated most likely explanation of the entire sequence S.

An experimental setup of models was implemented using stochastic context free grammars (SCFGs) to allow for sufficient expressive power. In this setup,

M. Garcia de la Banda and E. Pontelli (Eds.): ICLP 2008, LNCS 5366, pp. 809–810, 2008.

explanations can be represented by their corresponding parse trees. For the purpose of evaluation, a good approximation of the canonical analysis of a sequence S is a parse tree similar or equal to the one produced by the canonical model. Assuming that similar parse trees have similar canonical probabilities, a way to avoid explicit comparison of parse trees is to compare their respective probabilities instead. This is not possible for any realistic S because of the assumed complexity of the canonical model. Instead we have been experimenting with an evaluation scheme that compares the probability of a sampled parse of a sequence S with the probability of the best approximating parse of that sequence. This scheme of evaluation by sampling assumes:

i) that randomly sampling the canonical distribution produces sequences with high probability canonical explanations with high frequency, only occasionally producing an atypically sequence and

ii) that high probability in the canonical model indicates high quality and vice versa and thus that similar explanations have similar probabilities

Experimental results suggest, however, that assumption *i)* is not satisfied by the canonical model that we have been experimenting with. In fact, when sampled, it very rarely produces a sequence with a better canonical explanation than the one provided by the approximating algorithm. Because we have so far refrained from specifying the distribution of the model, the PRISM system defaults to symmetric distributions and this likely blurs the distinction between typical and atypical sequences. While assumption *i)* clearly depends on the proper specification of the canonical distribution, one way to repair the experimental distribution is to restrict the outcomes to sequences with good canonical explanations.

Despite the difficulties of evaluation, the compositional approach to probabilistic modeling described here offers an alternative way of implementing well-known bioinformatical models in a concise and flexible declarative framework while keeping complexity in check. It also has the potential of providing a rigorous generic framework for combining separately developed models and specialized modules. Finally, the framework may generalize to a wide spectrum of applications, both in bioinformatics and beyond.

References

1. Durbin, R., Eddy, S., Krogh, A., Mitchison, G.: Biological Sequence Analysis. Cambridge University Press, Cambridge (1998)
2. Cussens, J.: Loglinear models for first-order probabilistic reasoning. In: Laskey, K.B., Prade, H. (eds.), pp. 126–133. Morgan Kaufmann, San Francisco (1999)
3. Muggleton, S.: Learning from positive data. In: Muggleton, S. (ed.) ILP 1996. LNCS, vol. 1314, pp. 358–376. Springer, Heidelberg (1997)
4. Sato, T., Kameya, Y.: Parameter learning of logic programs for symbolic-statistical modeling. J. Artif. Intell. Res (JAIR) 15, 391–454 (2001)

Bi-dimensional Domains for the Non-overlapping Rectangles Constraint

Fabio Parisini

DEIS, University of Bologna
V.le Risorgimento 2, 40136, Bologna, Italy

Given a set of rectangles and a bi-dimensional container, the non-overlapping rectangles constraint aims to obtain consistency such that all the rectangles can be placed without intersection inside the box. So, the $nonOverlapping([R_1, \ldots, R_n], Box)$ holds iff all rectangles are placed inside the Box and no two rectangles R_i and R_j overlap.

The n dimensional version of this constraint, called *diffn* [1], has been used in many applications. In the context of two dimensions, it has an obviously prominent role in various flavors of placement problems (such as 2-dim packing and cutting problems) and scheduling problems to model resource constraints [2].

Many propagation algorithms have been proposed in the literature for the bi-dimensional version of the constraint: to handle its decomposition (pairwise non-overlapping constraints), constructive disjunction or the cardinality operator can be used [3]; the most effective algorithm so far is the specialization of the general sweep pruning technique [4].

Much effort has been recently spent on optimal rectangle packing problem, which is strictly related to the non-overlapping rectangles constraint. Korf [5] exploited relaxations inherited from the bin-packing area and, more recently, a meta-CSP approach has been proposed [6]. Much interest has arisen for techniques using global constraints [7], such as the *cumulative* and the *sweep* constraint, in conjunction with interval-based heuristics to solve the problem.

The traditional way of modeling the non-overlapping rectangles constraint involves the definition of a pair of variables per rectangle, standing for the coordinates of the left-bottom corner of the rectangle itself. However, in this way, the non-overlapping rectangles constraint is expressed through a disjunction of inequality constraints, which cannot perform propagation even when one of the rectangles' position is fixed. Instead, using a bi-dimensional representation of domains, it would be possible to store more precise information about occupied/free surface patches.

Following this idea, I have identified two main issues to face in my research activity:

- The choice of the data structure to be used to represent bi-dimensional domains, which has to be simple to mantain during search.
- The exploitation of the data structure to implement efficient and effective propagation algorithms on its top; the new available information can be used to perform innovative reasoning about rectangles which have already been placed and sum of areas globally available for rectangles still to be placed.

As for the first issue, the *region quad-tree* [8] seems to suite best to the need of representing rectangular domains; in the current constraint implementation a single quad-tree

M. Garcia de la Banda and E. Pontelli (Eds.): ICLP 2008, LNCS 5366, pp. 811–812, 2008.
© Springer-Verlag Berlin Heidelberg 2008

is used for storing all rectangles domains by labeling its nodes with different "colors", representing free or occupied surfaces patches.

Whenever any rectangle placement decision is taken, the quad-tree data structure is updated, i.e. the relevant surface patches are set as occupied. As a consequence, addressing the second issue, ad hoc routines are triggered to check if the remaining area is wide and tall enough to host uninstantiated rectangles.

In addition to that, the whole area remainder is exploited to perform global propagation. Using a graph structure which is similar to the one defined for the global cardinality constraint [9], together with its filtering algorithm, a connection is created between rectangles still to be placed, corresponding to GCC variables, and the available surface patches, corresponding to GCC domain values.

The constraint implementation is being tested on a set of rectangle packing instances, in *SICStus Prolog*, and its perfomances are compared to the *sweep* algorithm [4]. The first results show that the pruning algorithms included into our implementation of the non-overlapping rectangles constraint are effective; a higher number of backtracks is requested to the competitor [4]. In spite of that the algorithm which employs the non-overlapping rectangles constraint needs more time per backtrack, and more total time to solve the problem instances. Preliminary results show that search strategies tailored on the data structure could lead to important performance improvements, so the development of such strategies is one of the main directions in which the research work is heading to.

In general, we can say that the current implementation is still prototipal; we aim to improve its efficiency by defining smart search strategies and combining the copious sub-routines which compose the filtering algorithm in a more clever way. The fact that the number of backtracks is less than the one of the sweep algorithm is a good starting point; the integration of external constraints and related propagation algorithms, such as the *sweep* and *cumulative* constraint, could lead to even better resuts.

References

1. Beldiceanu, N., Contejean, E.: Introducing global constraints in CHIP. Mathl. Comput. Modelling 20(12), 97–123 (1994)
2. Aggoun, A., Beldiceanu, N.: Extending CHIP in order to solve complex scheduling and placement problems. Mathl. Comput. Modelling 17(7), 57–73 (1993)
3. Hentenryck, P.V., Saraswat, V., Deville, Y.: Design, implementation and evaluation of the constraint language cc(fd). Constraints: Basic and Trends 910 (1995)
4. Beldiceanu, N., Carlsson, M.: Sweep as a generic pruning technique applied to the non-overlapping rectangles constraint. In: Walsh, T. (ed.) CP 2001. LNCS, vol. 2239, pp. 377–391. Springer, Heidelberg (2001)
5. Korf, R.E.: Optimal rectangle packing: New results. In: ICAPS 2004, pp. 142–149 (2004)
6. Moffitt, M.D., Pollack, M.E.: Optimal rectangle packing: A meta-csp approach. In: ICAPS 2006, pp. 93–102 (2006)
7. Simonis, H., Sullivan, B.O.: Using global constraints for rectangle packing. In: CP-AIOR (2008)
8. Samet, H.: The design and analisys of Spatial Data Structures. Addison-Wesley, Reading (1989)
9. Regin, J.: Global constraints and filtering algorithms. In: Milano, M. (ed.) Constraint and Integer Programming. Kluwer Academic Publisher, Dordrecht (2004)

Extracting and Reasoning about Web Data

Giovanni Pirrotta

Graduate School in Mathematics, CS curriculum. Univ. of Messina
Sal. Sperone 31. S. Agata di Messina, I-98166 Italy
gpirrotta@unime.it

1 Introduction and Problem Description

The Web contains an enormous quantity of information, virtually supporting all types of reasoning and decision-making. Unfortunately, most of the times automated access to Web data and tracking updates turns out to be hard. Several technological, standardization and research efforts are now under way to make, among other things, *Web data* easily accessed and properly manipulated by machines. Indeed, for several years now, the W3C consortium has released useful recommendations on RDF(s)[1] and OWL[2], which are used to assign semantic to Web data. In particular, making existing Web data available to machine *consumption* can be a challenging task. Obviously, it is impossible to re-write the whole Web using advanced semantic Web languages; hence, various new technologies are currently being proposed for translating existing Web data, into RDF document, as GRDDL[3]. In this manner, it is now possible to transform plain-HTML Web pages into RDF documents, and then apply inferential engines to deduce new knowledge.

2 Goal of the Research

The goal of the research is to test the latest technologies, also finding new strategies, to extract information from "dirty" Web pages, link them other RDF-data, implies new knowledge and distribute them to the user.

3 Current Status of the Research

A framework for scraping data from a large community Web site, the *Rete Civica Milano*[4] has been developed. This instance of data extraction is challenging because that Web site is large (almost 400 forums, some of them active since 1994), diverse, and run on top of a legacy platform that does not support any form of, so to put it, *data parceling an dispatching* akin to RSS feeds. In the current version, important posts appearing on flat Web pages are routinely extracted and stored it in a RDBMS. The data is then mapped with the D2RQ framework[5] and transformed into a SIOC ontology[6] that allows, to some extent, to express information while preserving the meaning of concepts typical of online community sites. A SPARQL[7] endpoint, provided by a JOSEKI server[8], does the

M. Garcia de la Banda and E. Pontelli (Eds.): ICLP 2008, LNCS 5366, pp. 813–814, 2008.
© Springer-Verlag Berlin Heidelberg 2008

invocation that makes data available for various forms of selection and delivery. At that point, the frameworks are intended to offer different services to user; for instance, we could define rules to make explicit relationship among users or classify users by number of posts.

4   Open Issues and Expected Achievements

In order to obtain new knowledge our pilot application needs to combine non-monotonic rules with RDF data. In this context, the latest developments of dl-program[9], an extension of Answer Set Programming toward an interface to Description Logic, and dlvhex[10], a prototype application for computing the models of so-called HEX-program, could be useful for our target. As mentioned in SPARQL example present in [11], we could consider, for example, a simple agreement relationship between two users participating in an on-line thread can be formulated in HEX-program as follows:

```
agreesWith(A2, A1):-  triple(P1, "rdf:type", "sioc:Post"),
                      triple(P2, "rdf:type", "sioc:Post"),
                      triple(P1, "sioc:has_creator", A1),
                      triple(P2, "sioc:has_creator", A2),
                      triple(P1, "sioc:has_reply", P2),
                      triple(P2, "sioc:content", C),
                      &strstr[C,"I agree"].
```

We could add the produced statements in our KB and use these new facts to state acquaintance of users on community. The framework development follows this direction, towards an implementation of a module to manage definition rules in order to make new knowledge and offer new services to users.

References

1. RDF Schema, http://www.w3.org/TR/rdf-schema/
2. OWL Web Ontology Language Guide, http://www.w3.org/TR/owl-guide/
3. Gleaning Resource Descr. from Dialects of Lang., http://www.w3.org/TR/grddl/
4. Milano, R.C.: http://www.retecivica.milano.it/
5. The D2RQ Platform, http://www4.wiwiss.fu-berlin.de/bizer/d2rq/
6. SIOC Core Ontology Specification, http://www.w3.org/Submission/sioc-spec/
7. SPARQL Query Language for RDF, http://www.w3.org/TR/rdf-sparql-query/
8. Joseki - A SPARQL Server for Jena, http://www.joseki.org/
9. Either, E., Lukasiewicz, T., Schindlauer, R., Tompits, H.: Combining Answer Set Programming with Description Logics for the Semantic Web. In: KR, pp. 141–151 (2004)
10. Eiter, T., Ianni, G., Schindlauer, R., Tompits, H.: dlvhex: A System for Integrating Multiple Semantics in an Answer-Set Programming Framework. In: WLP, pp. 206–210 (2006)
11. Baroglio, C., Bonatti, P.A., Maluszynski, J., Marchiori, M., Polleres, A., Schaffert, S. (eds.): Reasoning Web. LNCS, vol. 5224, pp. 190–192. Springer, Heidelberg (2008)

Managing Quality of Service with Soft Constraints

Francesco Santini[1,2]

[1] IMT - Scuola di Studi Avanzati, Lucca, Italy
f.santini@imtlucca.it
[2] Istituto di Informatica e Telematica (CNR), Pisa, Italy
francesco.santini@iit.cnr.it

The term *Quality of Service* (QoS) is "something" by which a user of the service (in a very large meaning) will judge how good the service is. In this research project we mainly focus our attention to three areas related with QoS: *i)* Networks, *ii)* Web Services and *iii)* Trust Management (TM).

We would like to provide expressive means in order to model and solve these frameworks with the help of *Soft Constraints* [1], benefiting from *Artificial Intelligence* background to tackle this kind of optimization problems. Soft constraints will represent the needs of the parties on the traded resources and the consistency value of the store represents a feedback on the current agreement. Using soft constraints gives to the service provider and the clients more flexibility in expressing their requests w.r.t. crisp constraints, and therefore there are more chances to reach a shared agreement. Moreover, the cost model is very adaptable to the specific problem, since it is parametric with the chosen semiring.

In the work so far, we suggested a formal model to represent and solve the multicast routing problem in multicast networks with QoS requirements (e.g. bandwidth and delay) [2,3]. In this model we describe how to represent a network configuration in its corresponding and-or graph, mapping network nodes to and-or graph nodes and links to graph connectors. Afterwards, we propose the *Soft Constraint Logic Programming* (SCLP) [4] framework as a convenient declarative programming environment in which to specify and solve such problem. In particular, we show how to represent an and-or graph as an SCLP program, and how the semantics of such a program computes the best tree in the corresponding weighted and-or graph. This best tree can be used to shape the optimized multicast tree that ensures QoS requirements on the corresponding network. Qos features can be represented with c-semirings algebraic structures.

We suggested the new concept of *multitrust* [5,6]: multitrust extends the usual trust relationship from couples of individuals to one trustor and multiple trustees in a correlated way. The correlation can be expressed in terms of time (i.e. at the same time), modalities (i.e. with the same behavior) or collaboration among the trustees. Some everyday examples can be found when downloading a file from multiple sources in peer-to-peer networks, or, in general, when a task must/can be accomplished with the help of many individuals acting together and a trust

M. Garcia de la Banda and E. Pontelli (Eds.): ICLP 2008, LNCS 5366, pp. 815–817, 2008.
© Springer-Verlag Berlin Heidelberg 2008

feedback must be found for the whole process. We propose SCLP as a mean to quickly represent and evaluate trust propagation for this scenario.

Moreover, we extended the *Datalog* language (we call it $Datalog^W$) in order to deal with weights on ground facts and to consequently compute a feedback result for the goal satisfaction [7,8]. The weights are chosen from a proper c-semiring. As a second step, we use $Datalog^W$ as the basis to give a uniform semantics to declarative RT^W (TM) language family, in order to represent trust levels based on c-semirings. In this way it is possible to manage a score corresponding to a preference or cost associated to the revealed credentials, instead of a plain "yes or no" authorization result. The approach is rather generic and could be applied to other trust management languages based on Datalog.

We extended the *Soft Concurrent Constraint* (SCC) language to allow the non-monotonic evolution of the constraint store [9]. The novelty mainly consists in the possibility of removing soft constraints from the store and to consequently deal with open and reactive systems. To accomplish this, we will introduce some new operations (e.g. a *retract(c)*, where c is the constraint to remove). We present this framework as a possible solution to the management of resources (e.g. web services and network resource allocation) that need a given Quality of Service, which for us is related to all the possible non-functional character-istics associated to the resource, e.g. availability, interoperability and execution time. Our intention is also to further extend the SCC language in order to join together the expressive capabilities of soft constraints and timing mechanisms [10]. Mechanisms as timeout and interrupt can be very useful to force the release of the resources dedicated to a client, or to alert the client if new resources are available.

References

1. Bistarelli, S.: Semirings for Soft Constraint Solving and Programming. LNCS, vol. 2962. Springer, Heidelberg (2004)
2. Bistarelli, S., Montanari, U., Rossi, F., Santini, F.: Modelling multicast QoS routing by using best-tree search in and-or graphs and soft constraint logic programming. ENTCS 190(3), 111–127 (2007)
3. Bistarelli, S., Santini, F.: A formal and practical framework for constraint-based routing. In: ICN (best paper award), pp. 162–167. IEEE Computer Society, Los Alamitos (2008)
4. Bistarelli, S., Rossi, F.: Semiring-based constraint logic programming: syntax and semantics. ACM Trans. Program. Lang. Syst. 23(1), 1–29 (2001)
5. Bistarelli, S., Santini, F.: Propagating multitrust within trust networks. In: Symposium on Applied Computing, pp. 1990–1994. ACM, New York (2008)
6. Bistarelli, S., Santini, F.: SCLP for trust propagation in small-world networks. In: Fages, F., Rossi, F., Soliman, S. (eds.) CSCLP 2007. LNCS(LNAI), vol. 5129, pp. 32–46. Springer, Heidelberg (2008)
7. Bistarelli, S., Martinelli, F., Santini, F.: Weighted datalog and levels of trust. In: ARES, pp. 1128–1134. IEEE Computer Society, Los Alamitos (2008)

8. Bistarelli, S., Martinelli, F., Santini, F.: A semantic foundation for trust management languages with weights: An application to the RT family. In: Rong, C., Jaatun, M.G., Sandnes, F.E., Yang, L.T., Ma, J. (eds.) ATC 2008. LNCS, vol. 5060, pp. 481–495. Springer, Heidelberg (2008)
9. Bistarelli, S., Santini, F.: A nonmonotonic soft concurrent constraint language for SLA negotiation. In: VODCA 2008, ENTCS (to appear, 2008)
10. Bistarelli, S., Gabbrielli, M., Meo, M.C., Santini, F.: Timed soft concurrent constraint programs. In: Lea, D., Zavattaro, G. (eds.) COORDINATION 2008. LNCS, vol. 5052, pp. 50–66. Springer, Heidelberg (2008)

TopLog: ILP Using a Logic Program Declarative Bias

José Carlos Almeida Santos

Department of Computing, Imperial College, London
jcs06@doc.ic.ac.uk

1 Introduction, Background and Problem Description

Although Inductive Logic Programming can have other usages such as program synthesis, it is normally used as a logic based supervised machine learning algorithm. The usual setting for its application is, **given:** 1) a set of background knowledge facts B, 2) a set of examples E, **find:** a set of hypotheses H, such that $B, H \models E$. H, the induced model, is a set of Horn rules thus being easily comprehensible by a human.

Inductive Logic Programming has had several successful practical applications specially in the biology domain (e.g. [1], [2]). However, a major practical problem for widespread use is its lack of efficiency. Current ILP systems (e.g. [3], [4]) take too long to build models for many interesting real world datasets.

The main reason for the significant amount of computational time required is the size of the hypotheses search space. For any non trivial dataset, the hypotheses search space is well beyond what can be searched, even incompletely and with heuristics, in a reasonable time.

2 Research Goals and Literature Overview

Our Ph.D. thesis contribution proposes to alleviate this problem in two ways. Firstly, we change the way the hypotheses search space is defined. In current ILP systems the hypotheses search space is defined through mode declarations, specifying the literals that may appear in the body of any valid hypothesis. This mode declarations are meta-logical and it is purpose is to list the predicates allowed in an hypothesis.

In our setting, the mode declarations are replaced by first-order logic $\top$ theory. The $\top$ theory can be viewed as a form of first-order declarative bias which defines the hypothesis space, since each hypothesized clause must be derivable from $\top$. The use of the $\top$ theory in TopLog is also comparable to grammar-based declarative biases [5]. However, compared with a grammar-based declarative bias, $\top$ has all the expressive power of a logic program, and can be efficiently reasoned with using standard logic programming techniques.

The SPECTRE system [6] employs an approach related to the use of $\top$. SPECTRE also relies on an overly general logic program as a starting point. However, unlike the TopLog system described in this paper, SPECTRE proceeds by successively unfolding clauses in the initial theory. TDHD is also related to

M. Garcia de la Banda and E. Pontelli (Eds.): ICLP 2008, LNCS 5366, pp. 818–819, 2008.

Explanation-Based Generalization (EBG) [7]. However, like SPECTRE, EBG does not make the key MDHD distinction between the ⊤ theory and background knowledge. Moreover, EBG is viewed as a form of deductive learning, while the clauses generated by TDHD represent inductive hypotheses.

Having the hypothesis space defined through a first-order logic ⊤ theory allows for an elegant and more specific way of defining the hypotheses search space. This, just by itself, helps decrease the hypotheses search space because the format of an hypothesis can now be more precisely described.

The second way in which we alleviate the hypotheses search space problem is to upgrade the ⊤ theory definition from a logic program to a Stochastic Logic Program (SLP)[8]. Having the ⊤ theory as a Stochastic Logic Program allows for a stochastic derivation of hypotheses thus providing a natural way for sampling the hypotheses search space. Furthermore, this setting makes it possible to dynamically change the sampling bias by updating the SLP probabilities.

3   Preliminary Results and Expectations

We have created a prototype ILP system, TopLog, which already allows the hypotheses search space to be described through a logic program. Upgrading this to an SLP will be implemented in the near future.

We have submitted a short paper to ICLP which describes in detail the preliminary results of TopLog and compares them with an existing state of the art ILP system like Aleph. The results are promising showing that TopLog is competitive with Aleph in terms of predictive accuracy (no statistical significant difference) and in some datasets is already faster.

By the end of the Ph.D. I expect to have a robust ILP system proving the advantages of having a first order ⊤ theory represented by a SLP. I expect to provide a theoretical analysis together with empirical evidence resulting from applying TopLog to several new problems.

References

1. Srinivasan, A., King, R.D., Muggleton, S.H., Sternberg, M.: Carcinogenesis predictions using ILP. In: Džeroski, S., Lavrač, N. (eds.) ILP 1997. LNCS (LNAI), vol. 1297, pp. 273–287. Springer, Heidelberg (1997)
2. King, R.D., Srinivasan, A., Sternberg, M.J.E.: Relating chemical activity to structure: an examination of ILP successes. New Gen. Comp. 13, 411–433 (1995)
3. Muggleton, S.H.: Inverse entailment and Progol. NGC 13, 245–286 (1995)
4. Srinivasan, A.: The Aleph Manual. University of Oxford (2007)
5. Cohen, W.: Grammatically biased learning: Learning logic programs using an explicit antecedent description language. Artificial Intelligence 68, 303–366 (1994)
6. Boström, H., Idestam-Almquist, P.: Specialisation of logic programs by pruning SLD-trees. In: Proc. Fourth ILP Workshop (ILP 1994), Bonn, pp. 31–48 (1994)
7. Kedar-Cabelli, S.T., McCarty, L.T.: Explanation-based generalization as resolution theorem proving. In: Langley, P. (ed.) Proc. of the Fourth Int. Workshop on Machine Learning, Los Altos, pp. 383–389. Morgan Kaufmann, San Francisco (1987)
8. Muggleton, S.: Stochastic logic programs. In: De Raedt, L. (ed.) Proceedings of the 5th International Workshop on Inductive Logic Programming, Department of Computer Science, Katholieke, Universiteit Leuven (1995)

Generalising Constraint Solving over Finite Domains

Markus Triska

Technische Universität Wien
markus.triska@tuwien.ac.at
http://www.logic.at/prolog/

1 Introduction

Finite domain constraint solvers are typically applied to problems with only quite small values. This is the case in many tasks for which constraint-based approaches are well suited. A well-known benchmark library for constraints, CSPLib ([1]), consists almost exclusively of such examples.

On the other hand, the need for arbitrary precision integer arithmetic is widely recognised, and many common Prolog systems provide transparent built-in support for arbitrarily large integers.

It thus seems natural to enhance a constraint solver over finite domains with the ability to reason over arbitrarily large integers. SICStus Prolog ([2]) already goes in that direction, using the symbolic constants **inf** and **sup** to denote default domain limits, but internally, they still correspond to quite small integers: The system yields a *representation errors* when these limits are exceeded.

2 Background and Applications

The issue of inherent limits in finite domain constraint solvers has so far not been given much attention. A notable exception is [3], where Apt and Zoeteweij remark for one of their examples: "the cost of using arbitrary length integers is roughly a factor four". However, they did not implement a complete constraint solver with large integers, but tested the impact of bignums only on a specialised hand-coded example.

While support for arbitrarily large values has long been taken for granted in solvers over rational numbers, such as Holzbaur's CLP(Q) implementation ([4]), it is new in the context of constraint solvers over finite domains.

Quite a number of theoretically and practically relevant tasks require integer variables with large ranges. Software verification is an important example ([5]): To verify a property for *all* integers, so-called "small-domain" properties can sometimes be used to reduce the problem to finite bounds. For example, in [6], it is shown that when we have m satisfiable linear constraints over n integer variables with unrestricted domains, then a solution can also be found if all domains are restricted to the range $[0, n(ma)^{2m+1}]$, where a is the maximum of the absolute values of all coefficients. Clearly, this upper bound can be quite

M. Garcia de la Banda and E. Pontelli (Eds.): ICLP 2008, LNCS 5366, pp. 820–821, 2008.
© Springer-Verlag Berlin Heidelberg 2008

large even for very modest tasks that arise in the area of software verification. Recently, these bounds could be refined ([7]), but they are typically still well beyond the current abilities of existing CLP(FD) solvers, and in general require a constraint solver with arbitrarily large domains.

Other examples include non-linear problems that are beyond the abilities of common CLP(Q) solvers. For example, consider the so-called "7-11 problem" ([8]), which already surpasses the limits of the finite domain constraint solver of SICStus Prolog on 32-bit systems.

Finally, a generalised finite domain constraint solver can be openly advertised as a more declarative alternative for built-in integer arithmetic, yielding more general programs that are often also easier to understand.

3   Research Goals and Open Issues

Major goals of this research include the design and implementation of a constraint solver with arbitrarily large domains, an investigation of its theoretical properties such as termination and correctness, a comparison with existing solvers via benchmarks of practical relevance, and an evaluation of new application opportunities which are beyond the scope of current solvers.

The current version of the solver is available as `library(clpfd)` in SWI-Prolog ([9]) since version 5.6.40.

In the future, in addition to more extensive testing of the solver, portions of the solver should ideally be generated from a declarative description of the implemented relations to ensure correctness of constraint propagation.

Once correctness is ensured, efficiency is of great importance. The current implementation is written in Prolog, and lags behind other solvers in efficiency.

References

1. Gent, I.P., Walsh, T.: CSPLib: A Benchmark Library for Constraints. In: Proceedings of the 5th Int. Conf. PPCP (1999)
2. Carlsson, M., Ottosson, G., Carlson, B.: An Open-Ended Finite Domain Constraint Solver. In: Hartel, P.H., Kuchen, H. (eds.) PLILP 1997. LNCS, vol. 1292. Springer, Heidelberg (1997)
3. Apt, K.R., Zoeteweij, P.: An Analysis of Arithmetic Constraints on Integer Intervals. Constraints 4 (2007)
4. Holzbaur, C.: OFAI CLP(Q,R) Manual. TR (1995)
5. Bordeaux, L., Hamadi, Y., Vardi, M.Y.: An Analysis of Slow Convergence in Interval Propagation. In: Bessière, C. (ed.) CP 2007. LNCS, vol. 4741, pp. 790–797. Springer, Heidelberg (2007)
6. Papadimitriou, C.: On the complexity of integer programming. Journal of the ACM 28(4) (1981)
7. Seshia, S.A., Bryant, R.A.: Deciding quantifier-free Presburger formulas using parametrized solution bounds. Logical Methods in Computers Science 1(2) (2005)
8. Pritchard, P., Gries, D.: The Seven-Eleven Problem. TR (1983)
9. Wielemaker, J.: An Overview of the SWI-Prolog Programming Environment. In: Proceedings of the 13th International Workshop on LP Environments (2003)

Detection of Security Vulnerabilities Using Guided Model Checking

Aliaksei Tsitovich

University of Lugano, Switzerland
aliaksei.tsitovich@lu.unisi.ch

1 Introduction

Software security problems are good candidates for application of verification techniques. Usually it is not a complex task to represent certain security-related property in a particular verification framework. For instance in any software model checking environment (MC)[1] it is possible to state buffer overflow detection as a reachability problem. The approach works in theory and in practice, but has a major scalability drawback: the state-space, which represents all possible behaviors of the system, might grow exponentially in the size of the product of a model and a property. From the other side MC has an important advantage - a counter-example is produced automatically when the bug is found.

In contrast, several static analysis techniques [2,3] use abstract interpretation [4] to address security problems. They attempt to represent the nature of the vulnerability in the values from some abstract domain and to calculate such an abstract value for each location of the program. Carefully selected abstract domains allow both scalable computation and fairly precise results [2]. The algorithm is sound (no bugs are missed) but, 1) abstraction leads to detection of false bugs (so called false positives) and 2) no counter-example can be produced. Reported comparisons of tools, based on abstract interpretation, state that they are inapplicable in a wide industrial practice because of the unacceptably high number of false positives [5].

Dealing with program's loops is Achilles heel of the most existing static analysis techniques. In order to reason about programs with (possibly infinite) loops one has to unwind all loop iterations or to build an approximation of a program. The first variant is a direct way to countless refinements and/or the state explosion, the second one leads to false positives or even to the loss of soundness (if under-approximation of the loop is used). In this research I particularly tackle loops as a main source of both scalability and precision problems. I want to explore how the existing techniques can be combined in a way that minimizes the effect of their drawbacks in analysis of the program loops.

2 Goals and Achieved Results

The goal of my research is the development of automated methods to detect security vulnerabilities in a large-scale software. I would like to come up with a problem-driven algorithm, which combines model checking and abstract interpretation in application to the reachability analysis. I see a following possible way to achieve the goal:

M. Garcia de la Banda and E. Pontelli (Eds.): ICLP 2008, LNCS 5366, pp. 822–823, 2008.
© Springer-Verlag Berlin Heidelberg 2008

1. Develop an algorithm, which creates an over-approximated model of a program by summarization of the code fragments with a possibly infinite behaviors, i.e., loops.
2. Build reachability analysis using MC algorithms to verify "loop-less" models. In particular bounded model checking (BMC) [6] is a promising candidate because: 1) it targets bug detection but not a bug-absence proof; 2) it removes loops, the main limitation of BMC.
3. Develop a strategy to refine the summarized program.

The first part of the work, dedicated to loop summarization, has been accomplished and presented in [7]. The summarization algorithm was implemented in a tool called LOOPFROG[1]. It targets verification of ANSI-C programs for string-related properties, e.g. buffer overflows. In [7] each loop is summarized with a help of localized abstract domain tailored to the verified property. Abstract domain suggests invariant candidates which are checked to be inductive invariants of a given loop. Repeating this procedure in a bottom-up manner gives an algorithm to over-approximate every loop instance by its *summary*. A summary is a combination of loop's variants (i.e. nondeterministically assigned variables) and discovered invariants. At the end of this *summarization* one obtains an over-approximated *loop-less* model of the program. The important property of this model is that any path in it is finite and, thus, is easily analyzable by BMC.

There are still a lot of ideas to explore such as abstract domains incremental strengthening, abstract counter-examples analysis, effective abstract transformers computation or incremental BMC. Finally, I want to obtain "a guided model-checker" - algorithm that delivers property-tailored and incremental abstraction/refinement scheme, which is applicable to a large-scale software.

References

1. Edmund, M., Clarke, J., Grumberg, O., Peled, D.A.: Model checking. MIT Press, Cambridge (1999)
2. Ganapathy, V., Jha, S., Chandler, D., Melski, D., Vitek, D.: Buffer overrun detection using linear programming and static analysis. In: Proceedings of CCS 2003, pp. 345–354. ACM, New York (2003)
3. Evans, D., Larochelle, D.: Improving security using extensible lightweight static analysis. IEEE Software 19, 42–51 (2002)
4. Cousot, P., Cousot, R.: Abstract interpretation: A unified lattice model for static analysis of programs by construction or approximation of fixpoints. In: POPL, pp. 238–252 (1977)
5. Zitser, M., Lippmann, R., Leek, T.: Testing static analysis tools using exploitable buffer overflows from open source code. In: SIGSOFT FSE, pp. 97–106 (2004)
6. Biere, A., Cimatti, A., Clarke, E.M., Strichman, O., Zhu, Y.: Bounded model checking. Advances in Computers 58, 118–149 (2003)
7. Kroening, D., Sharygina, N., Tonetta, S., Tsitovich, A., Wintersteiger, C.M.: Loop summarization using abstract transformers. In: Cha, S(S.), Choi, J.-Y., Kim, M., Lee, I., Viswanathan, M. (eds.) ATVA 2008. LNCS, vol. 5311. Springer, Heidelberg (to appear, 2008)

---

[1] Loopfrog binaries, benchmarks results and examples are available at http://www.verify.inf.unisi.ch/loopfrog

Author Index

Printing: Mercedes-Druck, Berlin
Binding: Stein+Lehmann, Berlin